THE PAPERS OF
THOMAS JEFFERSON

BARBARA B. OBERG
GENERAL EDITOR

THE PAPERS OF
Thomas Jefferson

Volume 36
1 December 1801 to 3 March 1802

BARBARA B. OBERG, EDITOR

JAMES P. McCLURE AND ELAINE WEBER PASCU,
SENIOR ASSOCIATE EDITORS

MARTHA J. KING, ASSOCIATE EDITOR

TOM DOWNEY AND AMY SPECKART,
ASSISTANT EDITORS

LINDA MONACO, EDITORIAL ASSISTANT

JOHN E. LITTLE, RESEARCH ASSOCIATE

PRINCETON AND OXFORD
PRINCETON UNIVERSITY PRESS

2009

ISBN 978-0-691-137742

Library of Congress Number: 50-7486

This book has been composed in Monticello

Princeton University Press books are printed on
acid-free paper and meet the guidelines for permanence
and durability of the Committee on Production
Guidelines for Book Longevity of the
Council on Library Resources

Printed in the United States of America

SUPPORTERS

THIS EDITION was made possible by an initial grant of $200,000 from The New York Times Company to Princeton University. Contributions from many foundations and individuals have sustained the endeavor since then. Among these are the Ford Foundation, the Lyn and Norman Lear Foundation, the Lucius N. Littauer Foundation, the Charlotte Palmer Phillips Foundation, the L. J. Skaggs and Mary C. Skaggs Foundation, the John Ben Snow Memorial Trust, Time, Inc., Robert C. Baron, B. Batmanghelidj, David K. E. Bruce, and James Russell Wiggins. In recent years generous ongoing support has come from The New York Times Company Foundation, the Dyson Foundation, the Barkley Fund (through the National Trust for the Humanities), the Florence Gould Foundation, the Andrew W. Mellon Foundation, the Pew Charitable Trusts, and the Packard Humanities Institute (through Founding Fathers Papers, Inc.). Benefactions from a greatly expanded roster of dedicated individuals have underwritten this volume and those still to come: Sara and James Adler, Helen and Peter Bing, Diane and John Cooke, Judy and Carl Ferenbach III, Mary-Love and William Harman, Frederick P. and Mary Buford Hitz, Governor Thomas H. Kean, Ruth and Sidney Lapidus, Lisa and Willem Mesdag, Tim and Lisa Robertson, Ann and Andrew C. Rose, Sara Lee and Axel Schupf, the Sulzberger family through the Hillandale Foundation, Richard W. Thaler, Tad and Sue Thompson, The Wendt Family Charitable Foundation, and Susan and John O. Wynne. For their vision and extraordinary efforts to provide for the future of this edition, we owe special thanks to John S. Dyson, Governor Kean, H. L. Lenfest and the Lenfest Foundation, Rebecca Rimel and the Pew Charitable Trusts, and Jack Rosenthal. In partnership with these individuals and foundations, the National Historical Publications and Records Commission and the National Endowment for the Humanities have been crucial to the editing and publication of *The Papers of Thomas Jefferson*. For their unprecedented generous support we are also indebted to the Princeton History Department and Christopher L. Eisgruber, provost of the university.

FOREWORD

THE PERIOD covered by this volume brings to a conclusion Thomas Jefferson's first year as president of the United States. The political and administrative landscape had altered dramatically for him in December, when members of the House of Representatives and Senate began arriving in Washington for the opening of the first session of the Seventh Congress; by 7 December quorums had gathered and, in the absence of the vice president, Abraham Baldwin presided over the Senate. In the early months of the administration, Jefferson's responsibility had been to form a cabinet, sort out questions of patronage, and set priorities for the government. Now, he faced the challenge of communicating his goals to the Congress and persuading and leading legislators to accept and adopt his vision.

Once Congress convened, Jefferson did not leave the nation's capital, even for a brief visit to Monticello. He welcomed Congress on 8 December, not by appearing before them in person but, breaking with the practice of George Washington and John Adams, by transmitting his first communication to them as a written text. His secretary, Meriwether Lewis, brought the copies of his message up to the legislators on Capitol Hill. Jefferson said that he adopted this procedure out of "regard to the convenience of the legislature." He had no love of public speaking, and, in any case, many Republicans scoffed at the idea of the American president and Congress following the British practice of a speech from the throne and a formal reply by Parliament. It was simply too reminiscent of monarchical ritual. Lewis delivered two copies, and the message was read aloud in both houses. By the afternoon of that day, "this important document" had appeared in Samuel Harrison Smith's *National Intelligencer*, and the newspaper could not keep up with the demand for copies.

Jefferson's communication to the new Congress was optimistic in tone and led off with the announcement of good news. As he had learned shortly before they convened, articles restoring peace between England and France had been exchanged in October and commerce was once again open between them. He called the peace "glorious for us," and rejoiced privately that Republicans could now proceed unobstructed toward their goal of "lightening the burthens of our constituents, and fortifying the principles of free government." The message highlighted other positive facts: the results of the recently completed census indicated a geometric increase in the population, which would lead to an increase in the revenue that could, with a "sensible" and "salutary" reduction in expenditures, allow the

removal of all internal taxes; the military establishment could be reduced and the standing army done away with; five frigates had already been laid up, and two others would be as soon as they received
necessary repairs; and a spirit of "peace & friendship" prevailed with
Indian neighbors. For the Republicans, these words could bring only
contentment and rejoicing.

The peace in Europe did not, in fact, guarantee peace for the
United States as the nation moved into the second year of Jefferson's
administration. The volume opens with celebratory comments on the
first American victory in the Barbary War—the defeat of a Tripolitan
corsair by the schooner *Enterprize*—but, Jefferson emphasized, this
was a defensive, not an aggressive action, one taken to protect American commerce. By late December, the secretary of the navy wrote
that as it was probable new orders would be sent to the Mediterranean fleet, it should be done right away. About seven weeks later
Jefferson complied, directing a circular letter that asked officers of
the navy to "subdue, seize, and make prize" of vessels and goods belonging to the bey of Tripoli.

The administration also still had a number of concrete matters to
deal with relating to Indian treaties and rights. The government's
language was couched in formulaic expressions of friendship and
protection of Indian lands and trading rights, but all communications
had the needs of the states and the federal union at their core. U.S.
commissioners had begun a series of talks with representatives of the
Cherokee, Chickasaw, Choctaw, and Creek nations, for example, to
obtain rights of way to roads and to resolve contested boundaries. In
the winter of 1801-2, a delegation of Native Americans led by Little
Turtle of the Miamis and his son-in-law and interpreter, William
Wells, came to Washington. The group visited the President's House
on New Year's Day and, over the next few days, held a series of
conferences with Secretary of War Henry Dearborn and Jefferson,
who had met Little Turtle in Philadelphia in 1798. Both general expressions of greeting and friendship and lists of specific requests
were exchanged between the two parties in formal, highly ritualized
addresses. Jefferson, speaking in abstract, gracious terms, observed
that it was good for friends to meet in person, open their minds to
each other, and "renew the chain of affection."

In February another Indian deputation arrived in the city. It was led
by the Shawnee chief Black Hoof. On this, his first journey to meet
with senior representatives of the American government, he was accompanied by seven Shawnees and five Delawares. Black Hoof and
Little Turtle both lacked the full support of their tribes in their ex-

pectations for assimilation with white society, culture, and economic organization. Black Hoof's words demonstrated serious complaints about the "sad situation" of the tribes and the "bad people" whom the U.S. government employed to implement its policies. It is likely that Jefferson delivered his reply directly, possibly using his words of friendship to introduce Dearborn and the more specific answers to the delegation's requests. Jefferson also took the opportunity of their visit to arrange for Dr. Edward Gantt to vaccinate some of the younger members of the tribe, for which Black Hoof offered thanks.

Another, and very different, delegation arrived in the capital to call on Jefferson. On New Year's Day, he stood at the doorway of the President's House to receive an unusual gift, "a token of the esteem" that was "produced by the personal labor of *Freeborn Farmers*, with the voluntary and cheerful aid of their wives and daughters." This "free-will offering," a "Mammoth Cheese" from the inhabitants of Cheshire, Massachusetts, weighed 1,235 pounds. Jefferson was apparently surprised when the cheese arrived at his doorstep, but he was able to convert his written thanks, penned when he learned a day or two earlier that it would be arriving, into a short speech of gratitude for the Cheshire committee. Along with this gigantic wheel of cheese, John Leland, the clergyman who had transformed the Cheshire Baptist community into a Republican bastion, also brought an address from the Cheshire Baptists expressing their thoughts on the importance of religious liberty to the nation much as the Baptists of Danbury, Connecticut, had done. In fact, although the Danbury Baptists had drafted their well-known address to Jefferson in October, the communication from Danbury was apparently not transmitted from New England to the capital until Leland brought it together with the cheese from Cheshire. Jefferson replied to the addresses from both groups of Baptists on 1 January.

Jefferson's residence in the nation's capital coincided with a thriving print culture in the early American republic. Washington witnessed an expanding market for newspapers, books, and pamphlets, in which Jefferson took an active part. He continued to build his own collection of books, and he subscribed to Richard Dinmore's circulating library at "the first door west of the President's Square." Philadelphia printer William Duane opened the Apollo Press and Aurora Book Store at the corner of Pennsylvania Avenue and Sixth Street, N.W., from which Jefferson purchased books, dinner invitations, red ink, and two Wedgwood ink stands. He also continued to buy from Nicolas Gouin Dufief in Philadelphia, an important source for hard-to-find works. In February, Jefferson wrote Dufief that he would be "very glad" to receive the Foulis Press edition of the *Odyssey* to go with his *Iliad*, also published by that firm, which was known for its elegant editions of the classics. Sometimes Jefferson required books from his library at Monticello. To oblige a "gentleman" in Washington, he asked Thomas Mann Randolph to wrap and send on to him a discourse by Jean Le Rond d'Alembert and a treatise on chess. He gave precise directions to his son-in-law on which cabinets in the "book room" housed these titles. Jefferson was also involved with the nation's library, having received congressional authorization in January to name a librarian to look after the books and maps acquired for the Congress. Jefferson appointed John Beckley, clerk of the House of Representatives, to be the librarian.

Jefferson's message to Congress had recommended two specific matters "to the contemplation of Congress," referring to legislators, as he had to the whole country in his First Inaugural Address, as "fellow citizens." The first matter was a "revisal of the laws on the subject of naturalization." He was emphatic in his statement that the nation should not "refuse to the unhappy fugitives from distress, that hospitality which the savages of the wilderness extended to our fathers arriving in this land." Jefferson had been wrestling with defining the rights of citizens since the mid-1770s, and this eloquent plea, in the aftermath of the Sedition and Alien Friends Acts of 1798 that had so distressed the Jeffersonian Republicans, explicitly addressed the Federalists' lengthy residency requirements for citizenship. His longtime French friend, Pierre Samuel Du Pont de Nemours, praised Jefferson's suggested revisions as a practical strategy, one which would work to the benefit of the nation, "where all useful works are lacking capital and labor and the land lacks buyers."

More challenging to the Congress was the directive to take a close look at the judiciary system, "especially that portion of it recently erected." Although the president provided few details on what he envisioned, the political context to the Judiciary Act of 1801, one of the final pieces of legislation proposed by the Adams administration and one that Jefferson considered an outrage, would have been common knowledge in the capital and to Federalists and Republicans in other parts of the country. On 6 January, Senator John Breckinridge of Kentucky introduced a resolution calling for repeal of the act. Jefferson worried, as he wrote to his daughter Martha two weeks later, that repeal might fail because of the absence of two Republican senators. His anxieties were not unfounded. Because of absences and one Republican defection, the bill made it through its second reading only because Vice President Burr broke a tie vote in favor of the Republicans. At its third reading, however, Jefferson received a severe blow when his vice president joined Federalists to send the bill to a select committee for study, rather than allowing its passage. The arrival of one more Republican senator a few days later permitted the measure to go back to the floor, where it passed by one vote. On 3 March, the final day of Jefferson's first year as president, the House approved it by a wide margin. With this issue resolved, Jefferson hoped the Congress could "press forward the other important matters."

Burr's failure to arrive in Washington until the middle of January and his break with the Republicans on such an important issue as the Judiciary Act were indications of a deeper rift growing between Jefferson and his vice president and within the Republican Party over Burr's place with them. DeWitt Clinton, leader of a rival political group to Burr in New York, reported in detail to Jefferson in early December that a small faction existed in that state "for the aggrandisement of an individual." James Cheetham, a New York newspaper publisher and outspoken critic of Burr, forwarded his opinions on Burr's conduct in the election of 1800, when Burr sought to raise "himself to an eminence to which he was not Destined by the voice of the union." Gathering his information from interviews with Burr himself, Cheetham found this faction "more and more alarming."

Encomiums from all parts of the country continued to reach President Jefferson, praising him for such things as being "full of wisdom, reason, enlightenment, and a heavenly moral philosophy" and his "steady & uniform wish to promote the general good & Interest of mankind." Simon Harris of New Hampshire wrote that he was "so Rejoised that I dont know what to do with my self I have cald my yongest son about four Months old Thomas Jefferson to keep your Name in mem'ry when your are not." Tempering the accolades, however, were two warnings of threats on his life, both from New York, dispatched to him in February. Signing himself "A Federalist Democrat," one anonymous correspondent reported that he had joined a party of Jacobins—that is, radicals who sought to overturn the government—whom he knew to be Federalists. Pretending to be one of them, the writer won their trust, and they asked him to go to Washington "& then assasanate you the first Opurtunity." A second unknown person, "A—X," with an allusion to Shakespeare's *Henry VIII*, warned Jefferson that "a dreadful plot" was forming against him and cautioned him about what might happen in "the last of April." Jefferson apparently did not comment on these threats, but endorsed the letters and noted them in his epistolary record as relating to "assassination."

Bridging divides between factions, individuals, or political parties was a job well suited to Jefferson's abilities and personality. Just as he had enjoyed the stimulating dinner gatherings at the Governor's Palace in Williamsburg when William Fauquier was lieutenant governor in the early 1760s, and just as he had gathered his own groups of French philosophes for excellent wines and lively talk around his table in Paris in the late 1780s, he now strove to re-create these opportunities in the nation's capital. Jefferson was the consummate designer of social occasions at the President's House, and shortly after senators and representatives began arriving in town for the opening of Congress, he set out to entertain them. The invitations to these events were formal, sometimes written out by Meriwether Lewis, and, beginning in late January, in an elegant printed form. Often only a few, and rarely more than a dozen, guests gathered at a round table, where Jefferson, known as a gracious host, provided an outstanding repast, fine wines, and, above all, the environment of an amiable exchange of ideas. Federalist Oliver Wolcott, after an occasion in late December 1801, reported a "Very Philosophic conversation in which I took an active part."

Jefferson's dinners were not only a demonstration of his superb powers as a host, but a representation of his style of political and presidential leadership. He used these opportunities to bring together members of Congress, heads of departments, and occasionally members of the Supreme Court; if individuals knew each other socially, perhaps they could better understand one another politically. An intriguing example is that on 8 January 1802, the very day on which he spoke for an hour against repeal of the Judiciary Act, Federalist senator Gouverneur Morris enjoyed tea at the President's House. He found Jefferson "civil, but with evident marks of constraint." Several Republicans were there as well (Anne Cary Morris, ed., *The Diary and Letters of Gouverneur Morris*, 2 vols. [New York, 1888-9], 2:417).

Important too was Jefferson's belief that being with people, "feeding our sociable principles," was crucial to the contentment of all human beings. Having learned from his own unhappy experiences during the years following his resignation as secretary of state, he urged his younger daughter, Mary Jefferson Eppes, to mix with the world and avoid "an antisocial & misanthropic state of mind" that would only have an "ill effect" on her. Her father was giving sound advice for her good health, of course, but he was also writing from his own personal hunger for the companionship of his daughters and their families, who were hesitant to leave their homes in Virginia and be with him in Washington. He almost rebuked them for their "reluctance" to visit him. When he described his daily schedule to Christopher Ellery, the newly arrived senator from Rhode Island, he sounded eager for company: he would receive visits any time in the forenoon, go out for exercise at noon, be engaged with guests until candlelight, after which his friends would again "find him entirely disengaged."

Socializing did not overcome all roadblocks to getting his proposals accepted by the Congress. The Republicans had a large majority in the House of Representatives, but their margin in the Senate remained slim. In January, Jefferson confided to John Wayles Eppes that "our friends have not yet learned to draw well together," and he feared that a small section of them would join with the Federalists to defeat what the greater section of the party desired. A month later, though, he felt more optimistic and informed his other son-in-law that he now thought the important points sketched out in his message to Congress would prevail as the majority was beginning to draw together, even though there were "some wayward freaks which now & then disturb the operations." Leading Congress in a way that would sustain Republican momentum was the challenge.

ACKNOWLEDGMENTS

MANY individuals have given the Editors the benefit of their aid in the preparation of this volume, and we offer them our thanks. Those who helped us use manuscript collections, answered research queries, assisted with translations, or advised in other ways are Harold James, William C. Jordan, Robert A. Kaster, Angel G. Loureiro, Francisco Prado-Vilar, Princeton University; in the libraries at Princeton, Karin A. Trainer, University Librarian, and Elizabeth Z. Bennett, Colleen M. Burlingham, Stephen Ferguson, Daniel J. Linke, Deborah T. Paparone, AnnaLee Pauls, Ben Primer, and Don C. Skemer; Timothy Connelly of the NHPRC; James H. Hutson, Barbara Bair, and the staff at the Manuscript Division of the Library of Congress, especially Lia Apodaca, Jennifer Brathovde, Jeffrey Flannery, Joseph Jackson, Patrick Kerwin, and Bruce Kirby; Peter Drummey and the library staff of the Massachusetts Historical Society, especially Nancy Heywood for providing digital scans; Robert C. Ritchie, Olga Tsapina, and others at the Huntington Library; Lucia C. Stanton and William L. Beiswanger of the Thomas Jefferson Foundation at Monticello; Michael Plunkett, Regina Rush, and the staff of Special Collections at the University of Virginia Library; Susan A. Riggs, Swem Library, the College of William and Mary; Rebecca Dobyns, William C. Luebke, and Brent Tarter, Library of Virginia; Dennis Northcott and the staff of the Missouri Historical Society; Martin Levitt, Roy Goodman, Charles B. Greifenstein, and Earl E. Spamer of the American Philosophical Society; Thomas N. Baker of SUNY Potsdam; Selby Kiffer of Sotheby's; the staff of the New York Public Library; the Gilder Lehrman Institute of American History and Jean W. Ashton and Edward O'Reilly of the New-York Historical Society; Laura Uhlman of the Free Library of Philadelphia; Margaret Freeland of the Gunn Memorial Historical Museum; Wayne Hammond of Chapin Library at Williams College; Pat Medert of the Ross County Historical Society; Charles M. Harris of the Papers of William Thornton, and our fellow editors at the Thomas Jefferson Retirement Series at Monticello, the Adams Papers at the Massachusetts Historical Society, the Papers of George Washington and the Papers of James Madison at the University of Virginia, the Papers of James Monroe at the University of Mary Washington, and the Papers of Benjamin Franklin at Yale University. For assistance with illustrations we are indebted to Alfred L. Bush of Princeton, Bonnie Coles and Barbara Moore of the

ACKNOWLEDGMENTS

Library of Congress, Jamieson Bunn of the Metropolitan Museum of Art, Leanda Gahegan and Stephanie Ogeneski of the National Anthropological Archives at the Smithsonian Institution, Patricia L. Nietfeld of the National Museum of the American Indian, and Rosemary L. Cullen of Brown University. For IT support with our database and Web site, we are grateful to Josh Allen and Jason Bush. Brian Solomon has contributed to the project in myriad ways, including, most recently, the display proofreading of our legacy volumes for *The Papers of Thomas Jefferson Digital Edition*, University of Virginia Press, Rotunda, 2009. We thank Alice Calaprice for careful reading and Jan Lilly for her unparalleled mastery of what a Jefferson volume must be. We thank those at Princeton University Press who never fail to give these volumes the benefit of their expertise: Chuck Creesy, Daphne Ireland, Dimitri Karetnikov, Neil Litt, Elizabeth Litz, Clara Platter, Linny Schenck, and Brigitta van Rheinberg.

Bland Whitley joined the Jefferson editorial project shortly before this volume went to press. We welcome him and look forward to his appearance on the title page of Volume 37 as an assistant editor.

EDITORIAL METHOD AND APPARATUS

1. RENDERING THE TEXT

Julian P. Boyd eloquently set forth a comprehensive editorial policy in Volume 1 of *The Papers of Thomas Jefferson*. Adopting what he described as a "middle course" for rendering eighteenth-century handwritten materials into print, Boyd set the standards for modern historical editing. His successors, Charles T. Cullen and John Catanzariti, reaffirmed Boyd's high standards. At the same time, they made changes in textual policy and editorial apparatus as they deemed appropriate. For Boyd's policy and subsequent modifications to it, readers are encouraged to consult Vol. 1: xxix-xxxviii; Vol. 22: vii-xi; and Vol. 24: vii-viii.

The revised, more literal textual method, which appeared for the first time in Volume 30, adheres to the following guidelines: Abbreviations will be retained as written. Where the meaning is sufficiently unclear to require editorial intervention, the expansion will be given in the explanatory annotation. Capitalization will follow the usage of the writer. Because the line between uppercase and lowercase letters can be a very fine and fluctuating one, when it is impossible to make an absolute determination of the author's intention, we will adopt modern usage. Jefferson rarely began his sentences with an uppercase letter, and we conform to his usage. Punctuation will be retained as written and double marks of punctuation, such as a period followed by a dash, will be allowed to stand. Misspellings or so-called slips of the pen will be allowed to stand or will be recorded in a subjoined textual note.

English translations or translation summaries will be supplied for foreign-language documents. In some instances, when documents are lengthy and not especially pertinent to Jefferson's concerns or if our edition's typography cannot adequately represent the script of a language, we will provide only a summary in English. In most cases we will print in full the text in its original language and also provide a full English translation. If a contemporary translation that Jefferson made or would have used is extant, we may print it in lieu of a modern translation. Our own translations are designed to provide a basic readable English text for the modern user rather than to preserve all aspects of the original diction and language.

2. *TEXTUAL DEVICES*

The following devices are employed throughout the work to clarify the presentation of the text.

[. . .]	Text missing and not conjecturable.
[ ]	Number or part of a number missing or illegible.
[roman]	Conjectural reading for missing or illegible matter. A question mark follows when the reading is doubtful.
[*italic*]	Editorial comment inserted in the text.
<*italic*>	Matter deleted in the MS but restored in our text.

3. *DESCRIPTIVE SYMBOLS*

The following symbols are employed throughout the work to describe the various kinds of manuscript originals. When a series of versions is recorded, the first to be recorded is the version used for the printed text.

Dft	draft (usually a composition or rough draft; later drafts, when identifiable as such, are designated "2d Dft," &c.)
Dupl	duplicate
MS	manuscript (arbitrarily applied to most documents other than letters)
N	note, notes (memoranda, fragments, &c.)
PoC	polygraph copy
PrC	press copy
RC	recipient's copy
SC	stylograph copy
Tripl	triplicate

All manuscripts of the above types are assumed to be in the hand of the author of the document to which the descriptive symbol pertains. If not, that *fact is stated*. On the other hand, the following types of manuscripts are assumed *not* to be in the hand of the author, and exceptions will be noted:

FC	file copy (applied to all contemporary copies retained by the author or his agents)
Lb	letterbook (ordinarily used with FC and Tr to denote texts copied into bound volumes)

Tr   transcript (applied to all contemporary and later copies except file copies; period of transcription, unless clear by implication, will be given when known)

4. LOCATION SYMBOLS

The locations of documents printed in this edition from originals in private hands and from printed sources are recorded in self-explanatory form in the descriptive note following each document. The locations of documents printed from originals held by public and private institutions in the United States are recorded by means of the symbols used in the National Union Catalog in the Library of Congress; an explanation of how these symbols are formed is given in Vol. 1:xl. The symbols DLC and MHi by themselves stand for the collections of Jefferson Papers proper in these repositories; when texts are drawn from other collections held by these two institutions, the names of those collections will be added. Location symbols for documents held by institutions outside the United States are given in a subjoined list.

CSmH	The Huntington Library, San Marino, California
CU-BANC	University of California, Berkeley, Bancroft Library
CtHi	Connecticut Historical Society, Hartford
CtY	Yale University, New Haven, Connecticut
DLC	Library of Congress
DeGH	Hagley Museum and Library, Greenville, Delaware
FMU	University of Miami, Coral Gables, Florida
ICHi	Chicago Historical Society
LNT	Tulane University, New Orleans
MBCo	Countway Library of Medicine, Boston
MCLong	Longfellow House, Longfellow National Historic Site, Cambridge, Massachusetts
MH	Harvard University, Cambridge, Massachusetts
MHi	Massachusetts Historical Society, Boston
MWA	American Antiquarian Society, Worcester, Massachusetts
MWiW-C	Williams College, Chapin Library, Williamstown, Massachusetts
MdAA	Hall of Records Commission, Annapolis, Maryland
MoSHi	Missouri Historical Society, St. Louis
MsJS	Jackson State College, Mississippi
NHi	New-York Historical Society, New York City

NN	New York Public Library
NNMus	Museum of the City of New York
NNPM	Pierpont Morgan Library, New York City
NcD-MC	Duke University, Medical Center, Durham
NjP	Princeton University
O	Ohio State Library, Columbus
OChHi	Ross County Historical Society, Chillicothe, Ohio
PHi	Historical Society of Pennsylvania, Philadelphia
PP	Free Library of Philadelphia, Pennsylvania
PPAmP	American Philosophical Society, Philadelphia
PWacD	David Library of the American Revolution, Washington Crossing, Pennsylvania
TxU	University of Texas, Austin
Vi	Virginia State Library, Richmond
ViHi	Virginia Historical Society, Richmond
ViU	University of Virginia, Charlottesville
ViW	College of William and Mary, Williamsburg, Virginia
WHi	State Historical Society of Wisconsin, Madison

The following symbol represents a repository located outside of the United States:

AHN	Archivo Histórico Nacional, Madrid

5. NATIONAL ARCHIVES DESIGNATIONS

The National Archives, recognized by the location symbol DNA, with identifications of series (preceded by record group number) as follows:

RG 26	Records of the United States Coast Guard	
	LDC	Lighthouse Deeds and Contracts
RG 28	Records of the Post Office Department	
	LPG	Letters Sent by the Postmaster General
RG 42	Records of the Office of Public Buildings and Public Parks of the National Capital	
	DCLB	District of Columbia Letterbook
	LR	Letters Received
	PC	Proceedings of the Board of Commissioners of the District of Columbia
RG 45	Naval Records Collection of the Office of Naval Records and Library	
	LSO	Letters Sent to Officers

	LSP	Letters Sent to the President
	MLR	Misc. Letters Received
RG 46	Records of the United States Senate	
	EPEN	Executive Proceedings, Executive Nominations
	EPFR	Executive Proceedings, Foreign Relations
	EPIR	Executive Proceedings, Indian Relations
	LPPM	Legislative Proceedings, President's Messages
	LPPMRSL	Legislative Proceedings, Petitions, Memorials, Resolutions of State Legislatures
RG 59	General Records of the Department of State	
	CD	Consular Dispatches
	LAR	Letters of Application and Recommendation
	LOAG	Letters from and Opinions of Attorneys General
	MCL	Misc. Commissions and Lists
	MLR	Misc. Letters Received
	MPTPC	Misc. Permanent and Temporary Presidential Commissions
	NL	Notes from Legations
	PTCC	Permanent and Temporary Consular Commissions
RG 75	Records of the Bureau of Indian Affairs	
	LSIA	Letters Sent by the Secretary of War Relating to Indian Affairs
RG 107	Records of the Office of the Secretary of War	
	LSP	Letters Sent to the President
	MLS	Misc. Letters Sent
	RLRMS	Register of Letters Received, Main Series
RG 233	Records of the United States House of Representatives	
	PMRSL	Petitions, Memorials, Resolutions of State Legislatures
	PM	President's Messages
	RCSH	Reports and Commissions Submitted to the House

RG 360   Records of the Continental Congress
          PCC   Papers of the Continental Congress

6. OTHER SYMBOLS AND ABBREVIATIONS

The following symbols and abbreviations are commonly employed in the annotation throughout the work.

Second Series   The topical series to be published as part of this edition, comprising those materials which are best suited to a topical rather than a chronological arrangement (see Vol. 1: xv-xvi)

TJ   Thomas Jefferson

TJ Editorial Files   Photoduplicates and other editorial materials in the office of The Papers of Thomas Jefferson, Princeton University Library

TJ Papers   Jefferson Papers (applied to a collection of manuscripts when the precise location of an undated, misdated, or otherwise problematic document must be furnished, and always preceded by the symbol for the institutional repository; thus "DLC: TJ Papers, 4:628-9" represents a document in the Library of Congress, Jefferson Papers, volume 4, pages 628 and 629. Citations to volumes and folio numbers of the Jefferson Papers at the Library of Congress refer to the collection as it was arranged at the time the first microfilm edition was made in 1944-45. Access to the microfilm edition of the collection as it was rearranged under the Library's Presidential Papers Program is provided by the Index to the Thomas Jefferson Papers [Washington, D.C., 1976])

RG   Record Group (used in designating the location of documents in the National Archives)

SJL   Jefferson's "Summary Journal of Letters" written and received for the period 11 Nov. 1783 to 25 June 1826 (in DLC: TJ Papers). This register, kept in Jefferson's hand, has been checked against the TJ Editorial Files. It is to be assumed that all outgoing letters are recorded in SJL unless there is a note to the contrary. When the date of receipt of an incoming letter is recorded in SJL, it is incorporated in the notes. Information and discrepancies revealed in SJL but not found in the letter itself are also noted. Missing letters recorded in SJL are, where possible, accounted for in the notes to documents mentioning them or in related documents. A more detailed discussion of this register and its use in this edition appears in Vol. 6: vii-x

SJPL   "Summary Journal of Public Letters," an incomplete list of letters and documents written by TJ from 16 Apr. 1784 to 31 Dec. 1793, with brief summaries, in an amanuensis's hand. This is supplemented by six pages in TJ's hand, compiled at a later date, listing private and confidential memorandums and notes as well as official reports and communications by and to him as Secretary of State, 11 Oct. 1789 to 31 Dec. 1793 (in DLC: TJ Papers, Epistolary Record, 514-59 and 209-11, respectively; see Vol. 22: ix-x). Since nearly all documents in the amanuensis's list are registered in SJL, while few in TJ's list are so recorded, it is to be assumed that all references to SJPL are to the list in TJ's hand unless there is a statement to the contrary

V   Ecu

ƒ   Florin

£   Pound sterling or livre, depending upon context (in doubtful cases, a clarifying note will be given)

s   Shilling or sou (also expressed as /)

d   Penny or denier

₶   Livre Tournois

℗   Per (occasionally used for pro, pre)

7. SHORT TITLES

The following list includes short titles of works cited frequently in this edition. Since it is impossible to anticipate all the works to be cited in abbreviated form, the list is revised from volume to volume.

ANB   John A. Garraty and Mark C. Carnes, eds., *American National Biography*, New York and Oxford, 1999, 24 vols.

Annals   *Annals of the Congress of the United States: The Debates and Proceedings in the Congress of the United States . . . Compiled from Authentic Materials*, Washington, D.C., Gales & Seaton, 1834-56, 42 vols. All editions are undependable and pagination varies from one printing to another. The first two volumes of the set cited here have "Compiled . . . by Joseph Gales, Senior" on the title page and bear the caption "Gales & Seatons History" on verso and "of Debates in Congress" on recto pages. The remaining volumes bear the caption "History of Congress" on both recto and verso pages. Those using the first two volumes with the latter caption will need to employ the date of the debate or the indexes of debates and speakers.

APS   American Philosophical Society

ASP   *American State Papers: Documents, Legislative and Executive, of the Congress of the United States*, Washington, D.C., 1832-61, 38 vols.

Bear, *Family Letters*   Edwin M. Betts and James A. Bear, Jr., eds., *Family Letters of Thomas Jefferson*, Columbia, Mo., 1966

Bedini, *Statesman of Science*   Silvio A. Bedini, *Thomas Jefferson: Statesman of Science*, New York, 1990

Betts, *Farm Book*   Edwin M. Betts, ed., *Thomas Jefferson's Farm Book*, Princeton, 1953

Betts, *Garden Book*   Edwin M. Betts, ed., *Thomas Jefferson's Garden Book, 1766-1824*, Philadelphia, 1944

Biog. Dir. Cong.   *Biographical Directory of the United States Congress, 1774-1989*, Washington, D.C., 1989

Brigham, *American Newspapers*   Clarence S. Brigham, *History and Bibliography of American Newspapers, 1690-1820*, Worcester, Mass., 1947, 2 vols.

Brown, "Frontier Politics"   Jeffrey Paul Brown, "Frontier Politics: The Evolution of a Political Society in Ohio, 1788-1814," Ph.D. diss., University of Illinois, 1979

Bryan, *National Capital*   Wilhelmus B. Bryan, *A History of the National Capital from Its Foundation through the Period of the Adoption of the Organic Act*, New York, 1914-16, 2 vols.

Bush, *Life Portraits*   Alfred L. Bush, *The Life Portraits of Thomas Jefferson*, rev. ed., Charlottesville, 1987

Carter, *Little Turtle*   Harvey Lewis Carter, *The Life and Times of Little Turtle: First Sagamore of the Wabash*, Urbana, Ill., 1987

Cayton, *Frontier Republic*   Andrew R. L. Cayton, *The Frontier Republic: Ideology and Politics in the Ohio Country, 1780-1825*, Kent, Ohio, 1986

Cooke, *Coxe*   Jacob E. Cooke, *Tench Coxe and the Early Republic*, Chapel Hill, 1978

Crackel, *Mr. Jefferson's Army*   Theodore J. Crackel, *Mr. Jefferson's Army: Political and Social Reform of the Military Establishment, 1801-1809*, New York, 1987

Cranch, *Reports*   William Cranch, *Reports of Cases Argued and Adjudged in the Supreme Court of the United States, 1801-1815*, Washington, D.C., 1804-17, 9 vols.

Cunningham, *Jeffersonian Republicans in Power*   Noble E. Cunningham, Jr., *The Jeffersonian Republicans in Power, Party Operations, 1801-1809*, Chapel Hill, 1963

Cunningham, *Process of Government*   Noble E. Cunningham, Jr., *The Process of Government under Jefferson*, Princeton, 1978

CVSP   William P. Palmer and others, eds., *Calendar of Virginia State Papers . . . Preserved in the Capitol at Richmond*, Richmond, 1875-93, 11 vols.

DAB   Allen Johnson and Dumas Malone, eds., *Dictionary of American Biography*, New York, 1928-36, 20 vols.

Dexter, *Yale*   Franklin Bowditch Dexter, *Biographical Sketches of the Graduates of Yale College with Annals of the College History*, New York, 1885-1912, 6 vols.

DHSC   Maeva Marcus and others, eds., *The Documentary History of the Supreme Court of the United States, 1789-1800*, New York, 1985-2007, 8 vols.

Dictionnaire   *Dictionnaire de biographie française*, Paris, 1933-   , 19 vols.

DNB   H. C. G. Matthew and Brian Harrison, eds., *Oxford Dictionary of National Biography, In Association with The British Academy, From the Earliest Times to the Year 2000*, Oxford, 2004, 60 vols.

Dowd, "Thinking and Believing"   Gregory E. Dowd, "Thinking and Believing: Nativism and Unity in the Ages of Pontiac and Tecumseh," *American Indian Quarterly*, 16 (1992)

Downes, *Frontier Ohio*   Randolph Chandler Downes, *Frontier Ohio, 1788-1803*, Columbus, 1935

DSB   Charles C. Gillispie, ed., *Dictionary of Scientific Biography*, New York, 1970-80, 16 vols.

DVB   John T. Kneebone and others, eds., *Dictionary of Virginia Biography*, Richmond, 1998-   , 3 vols.

EG   Dickinson W. Adams and Ruth W. Lester, eds., *Jefferson's Extracts from the Gospels*, Princeton, 1983, *The Papers of Thomas Jefferson*, Second Series

Evans   Charles Evans, Clifford K. Shipton, and Roger P. Bristol, comps., *American Bibliography: A Chronological Dictionary of All Books, Pamphlets and Periodical Publications Printed in the United States of America from . . . 1639 . . . to . . . 1820*, Chicago and Worcester, Mass., 1903-59, 14 vols.

Fitzpatrick, *Writings*   John C. Fitzpatrick, ed., *The Writings of George Washington*, Washington, D.C., 1931-44, 39 vols.

Ford   Paul Leicester Ford, ed., *The Writings of Thomas Jefferson*, Letterpress Edition, New York, 1892-99, 10 vols.

Foster, *Hawkins*   Thomas Foster, ed., *The Collected Works of Benjamin Hawkins, 1796-1810*, Tuscaloosa, Ala., 2003

Gallatin, *Papers*   Carl E. Prince and Helene E. Fineman, eds., *The Papers of Albert Gallatin*, microfilm edition in 46 reels,

Philadelphia, 1969, and Supplement, Barbara B. Oberg, ed., reels 47-51, Wilmington, Del., 1985

Harris, *Thornton*   C. M. Harris, ed., *Papers of William Thornton: Volume One, 1781-1802*, Charlottesville, 1995

HAW   Henry A. Washington, ed., *The Writings of Thomas Jefferson*, New York, 1853-54, 9 vols.

Heitman, *Dictionary*   Francis B. Heitman, comp., *Historical Register and Dictionary of the United States Army*, Washington, D.C., 1903, 2 vols.

Heitman, *Register*   Francis B. Heitman, *Historical Register of Officers of the Continental Army during the War of the Revolution, April, 1775, to December, 1793*, new ed., Washington, D.C., 1914

JCC   Worthington C. Ford and others, eds., *Journals of the Continental Congress, 1774-1789*, Washington, D.C., 1904-37, 34 vols.

JEP   *Journal of the Executive Proceedings of the Senate of the United States . . . to the Termination of the Nineteenth Congress*, Washington, D.C., 1828, 3 vols.

JHD   *Journal of the House of Delegates of the Commonwealth of Virginia* (cited by session and date of publication)

JHR   *Journal of the House of Representatives of the United States*, Washington, D.C., 1826, 9 vols.

JS   *Journal of the Senate of the United States*, Washington, D.C., 1820-21, 5 vols.

King, *Life*   Charles R. King, ed., *The Life and Correspondence of Rufus King: Comprising His Letters, Private and Official, His Public Documents and His Speeches*, New York, 1894-1900, 6 vols.

Kline, *Burr*   Mary-Jo Kline, ed., *Political Correspondence and Public Papers of Aaron Burr*, Princeton, 1983, 2 vols.

L & B   Andrew A. Lipscomb and Albert E. Bergh, eds., *The Writings of Thomas Jefferson*, Washington, D.C., 1903-04, 20 vols.

LCB   Douglas L. Wilson, ed., *Jefferson's Literary Commonplace Book*, Princeton, 1989, *The Papers of Thomas Jefferson*, Second Series

Leonard, *General Assembly*   Cynthia Miller Leonard, comp., *The General Assembly of Virginia, July 30, 1619-January 11, 1978: A Bicentennial Register of Members*, Richmond, 1978

List of Alumni   *A Provisional List of Alumni, Grammar School Students, Members of the Faculty, and Members of the Board of Visitors of the College of William and Mary in Virginia, from 1693 to 1888*, Richmond, 1941

List of Patents   *A List of Patents granted by the United States from April 10, 1790, to December 31, 1836*, Washington, D.C., 1872

Madison, *Papers*   William T. Hutchinson, Robert A. Rutland, J. C. A. Stagg, and others, eds., *The Papers of James Madison*, Chicago and Charlottesville, 1962-   , 31 vols.
   Sec. of State Ser., 1986-   , 8 vols.
   Pres. Ser., 1984-   , 6 vols.

Malone, *Jefferson*   Dumas Malone, *Jefferson and His Time*, Boston, 1948-81, 6 vols.

Marshall, *Papers*   Herbert A. Johnson, Charles T. Cullen, Charles F. Hobson, and others, eds., *The Papers of John Marshall*, Chapel Hill, 1974-2006, 12 vols.

MB   James A. Bear, Jr., and Lucia C. Stanton, eds., *Jefferson's Memorandum Books: Accounts, with Legal Records and Miscellany, 1767-1826*, Princeton, 1997, *The Papers of Thomas Jefferson*, Second Series

Miller, *Alexandria Artisans*   T. Michael Miller, comp., *Artisans and Merchants of Alexandria, Virginia, 1780-1820*, Bowie, Md., 1991-92, 2 vols.

Miller, *Treaties*   Hunter Miller, ed., *Treaties and Other International Acts of the United States of America*, Washington, D.C., 1931-48, 8 vols.

NDBW   Dudley W. Knox, ed., *Naval Documents Related to the United States Wars with the Barbary Powers*, Washington, D.C., 1939-44, 6 vols. and *Register of Officer Personnel and Ships' Data, 1801-1807*, Washington, D.C., 1945

NDQW   Dudley W. Knox, ed., *Naval Documents Related to the Quasi-War between the United States and France, Naval Operations*, Washington, D.C., 1935-38, 7 vols. (cited by years)

Notes, ed. Peden   Thomas Jefferson, *Notes on the State of Virginia*, ed. William Peden, Chapel Hill, 1955

OED   J. A. Simpson and E. S. C. Weiner, eds., *The Oxford English Dictionary*, Oxford, 1989, 20 vols.

Pa. Arch.   Samuel Hazard and others, eds., *Pennsylvania Archives. Selected and Arranged from Original Documents in the Office of the Secretary of the Commonwealth*, Harrisburg, 1852-1935, 119 vols.

Papenfuse, *Maryland Legislature*   Edward C. Papenfuse, Alan F. Day, David W. Jordan, and Gregory A. Stiverson, eds., *A Biographical Dictionary of the Maryland Legislature, 1635-1789*, Baltimore, 1979-85, 2 vols.

Parry, *Consolidated Treaty Series*   Clive Parry, ed., *The Consolidated Treaty Series*, Dobbs Ferry, N.Y., 1969-81, 231 vols.

Peale, *Papers*   Lillian B. Miller and others, eds., *The Selected Papers of Charles Willson Peale and His Family*, New Haven, 1983-2000, 5 vols. in 6

PMHB   *Pennsylvania Magazine of History and Biography*, 1877-

Prince, *Federalists*   Carl E. Prince, *The Federalists and the Origins of the U.S. Civil Service*, New York, 1977

PW   Wilbur S. Howell, ed., *Jefferson's Parliamentary Writings*, Princeton, 1988, *The Papers of Thomas Jefferson*, Second Series

RCHS   *Records of the Columbia Historical Society*, 1895-1989

Robinson, *Philadelphia Directory for 1802*   James Robinson, *The Philadelphia Directory, City and County Register, for 1802*, Philadelphia, 1801

Rowe, *McKean*   G. S. Rowe, *Thomas McKean, The Shaping of an American Republicanism*, Boulder, Colo., 1978

RS   J. Jefferson Looney and others, eds., *The Papers of Thomas Jefferson: Retirement Series*, Princeton, 2004-   , 5 vols.

Saricks, *Du Pont*   Ambrose Saricks, *Pierre Samuel Du Pont de Nemours*, Lawrence, Kans., 1965

Sears, *Thomas Worthington*   Alfred Byron Sears, *Thomas Worthington, Father of Ohio Statehood*, Columbus, 1998

Shaw-Shoemaker   Ralph R. Shaw and Richard H. Shoemaker, comps., *American Bibliography: A Preliminary Checklist for 1801-1819*, New York, 1958-63, 22 vols.

Shepherd, *Statutes*   Samuel Shepherd, ed., *The Statutes at Large of Virginia, from October Session 1792, to December Session 1806 . . . ,* Richmond, 1835-36, 3 vols.

Smith, *St. Clair Papers*   William Henry Smith, ed., *The St. Clair Papers, The Life and Public Services of Arthur St. Clair*, Cincinnati, 1882, 2 vols.

Sowerby   E. Millicent Sowerby, comp., *Catalogue of the Library of Thomas Jefferson*, Washington, D.C., 1952-59, 5 vols.

Stafford, *Baltimore Directory*   Cornelius William Stafford, *The Baltimore Directory, for 1802*, Baltimore, 1802

Stafford, *Philadelphia Directory*   Cornelius William Stafford, *The Philadelphia Directory*, Philadelphia, 1797-1801 (cited by year)

Stanton, *Free Some Day*   Lucia Stanton, *Free Some Day: The African-American Families of Monticello*, Charlottesville, 2000

Stein, *Worlds*   Susan R. Stein, *The Worlds of Thomas Jefferson at Monticello*, New York, 1993

Sturtevant, *Handbook*   William C. Sturtevant, gen. ed., *Handbook of North American Indians*, Washington, 1978- , 14 vols.

Syrett, *Hamilton*   Harold C. Syrett and others, eds., *The Papers of Alexander Hamilton*, New York, 1961-87, 27 vols.

Terr. Papers   Clarence E. Carter and John Porter Bloom, eds., *The Territorial Papers of the United States*, Washington, D.C., 1934-75, 28 vols.

TJR   Thomas Jefferson Randolph, ed., *Memoir, Correspondence, and Miscellanies, from the Papers of Thomas Jefferson*, Charlottesville, 1829, 4 vols.

Tulard, *Dictionnaire Napoléon*   Jean Tulard, *Dictionnaire Napoléon*, Paris, 1987

U.S. Statutes at Large   Richard Peters, ed., *The Public Statutes at Large of the United States . . . 1789 to March 3, 1845*, Boston, 1855-56, 8 vols.

VMHB   *Virginia Magazine of History and Biography*, 1893-

Volney, *View*   C. F. C. Volney, *A View of the Soil and Climate of the United States of America*, trans. Charles Brockden Brown, Philadelphia, 1804; repr. 1968

Washington, *Papers*   W. W. Abbot, Dorothy Twohig, Philander D. Chase, Theodore J. Crackel, and others, eds., *The Papers of George Washington*, Charlottesville, 1983- , 52 vols.

    Confed. Ser., 1992-97, 6 vols.

    Pres. Ser., 1987- , 14 vols.

    Ret. Ser., 1998-99, 4 vols.

    Rev. War Ser., 1985- , 18 vols.

White, *Genealogical Abstracts*   Virgil D. White, *Genealogical Abstracts of Revolutionary War Pension Files*, Waynesboro, Tenn., 1990-92, 4 vols.

WMQ   *William and Mary Quarterly*, 1892-

CONTENTS

·⟨§ 1801 §⟩·

CONTENTS

CONTENTS

CONTENTS

CONTENTS

·◦❳ 1 8 0 2 ❲◦·

CONTENTS

CONTENTS

CONTENTS

CONTENTS

CONTENTS

CONTENTS

[xli]

CONTENTS

CONTENTS

APPENDICES

ILLUSTRATIONS

Following page 406

MAP OF WASHINGTON

This map is from *The Traveller's Directory, or A Pocket Companion: Shewing the Course of the Main Road from Philadelphia to New York, and from Philadelphia to Washington,* a book of road maps published by Mathew Carey in Philadelphia in 1802. Early in 1801, Carey commissioned Joshua J. Moore and Thomas W. Jones to survey the route from Philadelphia to New York and from Philadelphia to Washington at a dollar a mile. By mid-July 1802, Carey advertised for sale the "just published" directory at two dollars a copy. The *Traveller's Directory* is an octavo-sized book containing 52 pages of narrative description and 23 maps by four different engravers. Map 23, the depiction of "Washington City" engraved by John Draper, measures $4\frac{1}{8}$ by 6 inches. Moore and Jones requested and received inclusion on the title page as authors. Moore, a native of Cambridgeshire, England, who became a citizen of the United States in 1799, later became chief clerk of the United States Land Office (Joseph J. Felcone, *New Jersey Books, 1801-1860* [Princeton, 1996], 388-92; *Philadelphia Gazette,* 15 July 1802).

In his preface, Carey admitted that the 1802 *Traveller's Directory* was "not pretended to be absolutely perfect." The map of Washington, a combination of reality and conjecture, documents the building development in the nascent capital city. The book described a city of "upwards of seven hundred and seventy houses, many of which are built in a superior style, dispersed in various parts" (p. 51). The map is the first to depict the open "Mall" west of the Capitol. It shows streets that had been surveyed but not yet built and a projected canal running along the Mall and crossing Tiber Creek in front of the Capitol before diverting to reconnect with the Eastern Branch (the Anacostia River). The cartographers took artistic license in showing formal plantings of trees around the President's House and along the Mall. The map allots space for a "University" west of the President's House (John W. Reps, *Washington on View: The Nation's Capital since 1790* [Chapel Hill, 1991], 51, 60, 61; Daniel Carroll to TJ, 28 Mch. 1802).
Courtesy of Princeton University Library.

MERIWETHER LEWIS

This engraving, the work of the French émigré artist Charles Balthazar Julien Févret de Saint-Mémin, depicts Lewis as he looked when he was Jefferson's secretary. Details of the image, such as Lewis's features and the style of his coat, have led scholars to conclude that he probably sat for this portrait in May 1802, when he visited Philadelphia while Jefferson made a brief trip home to Monticello. Lewis was 27 years old at that time. References in the diary of the Philadelphia attorney and Democratic political operative Mahlon Dickerson place Lewis in the city from at least 13 May to the 24th of that month. Lewis and Dickerson were acquainted, and the fact that Dickerson had Saint-Mémin take his profile on 18 May suggests that Lewis may have done the same sometime during his visit to Philadelphia. To create his portraits, Saint-Mémin used a device called a physiognotrace to record the features of the subject's profile. The artist filled in the details of the portrait by hand, using chalk or crayon. That life-size drawing then became the basis for a small engraving on a copper plate. As indicated by William Barton's letter of 20 Feb. 1802 in this volume, the cost of a Saint-Mémin profile was considered "very moderate." This portrait of Lewis is typical of the prints that Saint-Mémin, a self-taught engraver, produced: a round image, $2\frac{1}{4}$ inches in diameter, with a plain background. The Valentine Museum in Richmond owns a photograph, from the late nineteenth or early twentieth century, of Saint-Mémin's drawing of Lewis from which he made the engraving. Saint-Mémin did another profile of Lewis, as well as a full-length portrait in watercolor, after Lewis's return from his journey to the Pacific (Donald Jackson, ed., *Letters of the Lewis and Clark Expedition with Related Documents, 1783-1854*, 2d ed. [Urbana, Ill., 1978], 677-9; Ellen G. Miles, *Saint-Mémin and the Neoclassical Profile Portrait in America* [Washington, D.C., 1994], 338-9; Ellen G. Miles, "Saint-Mémin's Portraits of American Indians, 1804-1807," *American Art Journal*, 20 [1988], 3, 26-7, 33n; Stein, *Worlds*, 201-2; Jane Turner, ed., *The Dictionary of Art*, 34 vols. [New York, 1996], 27:567; MB, 2:1071-3).

Courtesy of the Library of Congress.

PRINTED DINNER INVITATION

In a 4 Feb. 1802 letter to his wife, Congressman Samuel L. Mitchill enclosed a printed dinner invitation received from Jefferson, explaining that the president "has lately got a printed Card of invitation, to save the Trouble of writing so much every Day." These printed billets contained blank spaces, so that only the name of the guest and date of the dinner needed to be written by hand. Jefferson could send as many as several dozen of these invitations per week while Congress was in session. The example shown here is printed on the bottom half of a sheet measuring $8\frac{1}{4}$ by 10 inches, with the address and text in the blank spaces inserted by Meriwether Lewis. The top half of the paper, not shown here, had no printing and was folded over to serve as an address sheet. Dated 1 Feb. 1802, it is addressed to Dwight Foster, a Federalist senator from Massachusetts, who was asked to dine with Jefferson the "day after tomorrow." In 1802 and 1803, Jefferson ordered invitations from *Aurora* publisher William Duane, who had opened a stationery and printing shop in Washington, D.C., in 1801. On 3 Feb. 1802, the president bought a ream of "printed letters" from Duane for $22. His account with Duane from 1802 to 1803 records additional orders. On 20 Dec. 1802, Duane sold Jefferson another ream of invitations for $20. The following spring, on 6 May 1803, Jefferson purchased "600 Invitations" for $15 (Samuel L. Mitchill to Catharine Mitchill, 4 Feb. 1802, RC in NNMus: Samuel Latham Mitchill Papers; Invoice from William Duane, [3 Feb. 1802]; Statement of Account with William Duane, 4 Jan. 1802 to 7 July 1803, in CSmH; MB, 2:1064n; Vol. 34:72, 74n).

Dinners at the President's House were a celebrated feature of Jefferson's presidency. Smaller, less formal, and more frequent than the weekly levees favored by Washington and Adams, they were seen by Jefferson as an ostensibly nonpolitical way to "cultivate personal intercourse" with members of Congress, both Federalist and Republican, "that we may know one another and have opportunities of little explanations of circumstances, which, not understood might produce jealousies & suspicions injurious to the public interest." Despite their informal tone, these gatherings were nevertheless an important political and social aspect of Washington society during Jefferson's administration. They may also have been Jefferson's only occasion for contact with Senator Foster. The printed invitation shown here and another dated 31 Dec. 1802 are the only extant communications between the two men found by the Editors (TJ to David R. Williams, 31 Jan. 1806; TJ to Foster, 31 Dec. 1802). For the significance of Jefferson's dinners, see Merry Ellen Scofield, "The Fatigues of His Table: The Politics of Presidential Dining during the Jefferson Administration," *Journal of the Early Republic*, 26 (2006), 449-69, and Charles T. Cullen, "Jefferson's White House Dinner Guests," *White House History*, 17 (2006), 24-43.

Courtesy of the American Philosophical Society.

MEMORANDUMS EXCHANGED BY JEFFERSON AND GALLATIN

As he sometimes used whatever scrap of paper was at hand to communicate with his department heads, the president wrote this undated query to his secretary of the Treasury on the recto of an address sheet, without canceling the original address. Jefferson's question regarded the 14 Feb. 1802 letter he had received from Andrew Ellicott, a Jefferson correspondent since 1791 when Ellicott served as surveyor of the Federal District. The president wanted Ellicott, who had recently become secretary of the Pennsylvania Land Office, to serve as surveyor general of the United States. Ellicott proposed terms for his acceptance of the office, including the right to reside at the seat of government in Washington. It is not clear whether Gallatin saw Ellicott's letter or an extract of it. The Treasury secretary, writing his reply directly below Jefferson's query, informed the president that by law the office of surveyor general was "permanently fixed" in the Northwest Territory. According to his endorsement on the verso of the sheet, Jefferson received Gallatin's response on 24 Feb. That same day the president wrote Ellicott, who, subsequently, declined the president's offer (Vol. 19:68-71; Vol. 35:423-4; TJ to Ellicott, 29 Jan., 24 Feb. 1802; Ellicott to TJ, 14 Feb., 10 Mch. 1802).

Courtesy of the Library of Congress

ALBERT GALLATIN

James Sharples probably made this pastel portrait of Gallatin in Philadelphia about 1796 or 1797, the period in which Sharples drew portraits of a number of well-known Americans and visitors to the United States, including Jefferson, James Madison, Dolley Madison, John Adams, and Alexander Hamilton. Gallatin was a member of Congress in that period. This picture measures $9\frac{3}{8}$ inches by $7\frac{3}{8}$ inches in size. Another pastel portrait of Gallatin that became part of a collection in Bristol, England, may be a copy that Ellen Sharples, James Sharples's wife, made in 1804 after the artistic couple returned to Britain (Katharine McCook Knox, *The Sharples: Their Portraits of*

ILLUSTRATIONS

George Washington and his Contemporaries [New Haven, 1930], 12-13, 16, 95, 99, 118; Vol. 28:xxxvii-xxxviii, 336 [illus.]; Vol. 29:xxxviii, xl, 318 [illus.]).

Courtesy of the Metropolitan Museum of Art, New York.

LITTLE TURTLE

Late in May 1800, before he stepped down as secretary of war, James McHenry wrote a letter to the Miami Indian leader Little Turtle, urging him to remain on good terms with the United States. In that letter, which was given wide circulation by newspapers, McHenry referred to a portrait of Little Turtle. "It would have given me pleasure," McHenry wrote, "had it been proper, to have taken home your picture, which I have preserved in my office." McHenry conceded, however, that the picture "must remain to my successor." The portrait, which was destroyed when the British burned Washington in August 1814, was painted by Gilbert Stuart. The lithograph illustrated here may be a representation of that picture. A date of 1797 is often assigned to the likeness, but it was in the early part of 1798 that Little Turtle resided in Philadelphia for several weeks. During that stay, Little Turtle attended social functions, conferred with the Comte de Volney, and almost certainly met Jefferson. He also exchanged gifts with Tadeusz Kosciuszko—the Indian giving Kosciuszko a tomahawk, Kosciuszko returning the gesture by giving his new friend (and fellow celebrity) pistols, a cloak, and, spontaneously, a pair of reading spectacles. The portrait by Stuart may have been commissioned by the government, which would account for McHenry's considering it, in the spring of 1800, a possession of the War Department. It may have been hanging in the department's offices in Washington in January 1802, when Little Turtle met with Jefferson and Secretary of War Henry Dearborn. Some sources ascribe the lithograph, which is illustrated here from a glass negative in the Smithsonian Institution, to Charles Balthazar Julien Févret de Saint-Mémin (Salem, Mass., *Impartial Register*, 7 July 1800; *Georgia Gazette*, 24 July 1800; Harvey Lewis Carter, *The Life and Times of Little Turtle: First Sagamore of the Wabash* [Urbana, Ill., 1987], 3, 5, fig. 4; Julian Ursin Niemcewicz, *Under Their Vine and Fig Tree: Travels through America in 1797-1799, 1805, with some Further Account of Life in New Jersey*, trans. and ed. Metchie J. E. Budka [Elizabeth, N.J., 1965], 44-5, 305n; B. B. Thatcher, *Indian Biography: or, An Historical Account of those Individuals Who Have Been Distinguished among the North American Natives as Orators, Warriors, Statesmen, and Other Remarkable Characters*, 2 vols. [New York, 1832], 2:269; Anthony F. C. Wallace, *Jefferson and the Indians: The Tragic Fate of the First Americans* [Cambridge, Mass., 1999], 118; Conference with Little Turtle, 4 Jan. 1802, in this volume).

Courtesy of the National Anthropological Archives, National Museum of Natural History, Smithsonian Institution.

BLACK HOOF

This undated portrait of the Shawnee chief and orator Black Hoof is from Thomas L. McKenney and James Hall, *History of the Indian Tribes of North America, with Biographical Sketches and Anecdotes of the Principal Chiefs.*

Embellished with One Hundred and Twenty Portraits, from the Indian Gallery in the Department of War, at Washington, 3 vols. [Philadelphia, 1838-44]. McKenney directed the federal government's Indian trade system from 1816 to 1822 and was superintendent of Indian affairs from 1824 until 1830. He collected books, manuscripts, and artifacts relating to Native Americans and assembled a portrait gallery. McKenney decided to publish the portraits along with information about Native American tribes, a project that he continued after he left the office of Indian affairs. He tried with limited success to enlist others, including Albert Gallatin, John Quincy Adams, and Jared Sparks, to do much of the research and writing, and the work languished until McKenney persuaded James Hall, a magazine editor, to write most of the text. The volumes of the *History of the Indian Tribes* had large pages to accommodate lithographs $17\frac{1}{2}$ inches by 14 inches in size, the dimensions of many of the original portraits. Each plate was colored by hand (Herman J. Viola, *Thomas L. McKenney: Architect of America's Early Indian Policy: 1816-1830* [Chicago, 1974], 251-80; John T. Flanagan, *James Hall: Literary Pioneer of the Ohio Valley* [Minneapolis, Minn., 1941], 96-8; ANB, s.v. "Hall, James" and "McKenney, Thomas Loraine").

Black Hoof, who was called Catahecassa in the McKenney and Hall *History*, and a delegation of Shawnees and Delawares met with Jefferson in Washington in February 1802. The artist who painted the original of this likeness is not known. The original oil paintings of many of the portraits reproduced in McKenney's volumes were made by Charles Bird King when Indian delegations visited Washington in the 1820s. During that decade, James Otto Lewis, who worked in the Great Lakes region, also painted portraits that became part of McKenney's collection. However, McKenney indicated in the 1830s that this portrait of Black Hoof had been painted a number of years earlier, which implies that the picture existed before King and Lewis began painting for McKenney's gallery. Because some of the lithographs were made from duplicates of the oil portraits, this print could be a direct copy of a portrait from life or a copy of a copy. A fire at the Smithsonian Institution in 1865 destroyed most of the original portraits of the collection assembled by McKenney (Viola, *McKenney*, 246-7, 262, 278; Francis Flavin, "The Adventurer-Artists of the Nineteenth Century and the Image of the American Indian," *Indiana Magazine of History*, 98 [2002], 17-19; James D. Horan, *The McKenney-Hall Portrait Gallery of American Indians* [New York, 1972], 64-5, 108, 158; ANB, s.v. "King, Charles Bird"; Conference with Black Hoof, at 5 Feb. 1802).

Courtesy of Princeton University Libraries.

"ODE TO THE MAMMOTH CHEESE"

The presentation of the Mammoth Cheese at the President's House on 1 January 1802 remains one of the best remembered events of Jefferson's presidency. Reports on the cheese's journey from Cheshire, Massachusetts, to Washington were staple features in newspapers across the country during the second half of 1801, as were the myriad poems, satires, and parodies that the cheese inspired. Federalist newspapers in particular delighted in mocking the cheese, condemning the 1,235-pound mass of curd as a ludicrous example of democratic excess ushered in by Jefferson's election. The

Washington Federalist derisively described the Mammoth Cheese as "one large and indivisible mass of *Patriotism!*" Jefferson, on the other hand, considered it an "ebullition of the passion of republicanism" (John C. Harriman, ed., "'Most Excellent—far fam'd and far fetch'd Cheese': An Anthology of Jeffersonian Era Poetry," *American Magazine and Historical Chronicle*, 2 [1986-87], 1-26; *Washington Federalist*, 5 Jan. 1802; TJ to Thomas Mann Randolph, 1 Jan. 1802; see also Presentation of the "Mammoth Cheese," printed at 30 Dec. 1801).

Although most of the prose inspired by the Mammoth Cheese flowed from Federalist pens, the "Ode to the Mammoth Cheese" printed here was composed by a Republican. The work is attributed to Thomas Kennedy, a Scottish immigrant and merchant residing in Williamsport, Maryland, who later became a prominent state legislator. The earliest known appearance of the "Ode" was in the 10 Mch. 1802 edition of *Bartgis's Republican Gazette*, published in Fredericktown, Maryland, which, like the broadside shown in this volume, appeared anonymously. Kennedy later included this work in a collection of poetry, simply entitled *Poems by Thomas Kennedy*, which was published in Washington, D.C., by Daniel Rapine in 1816. The following year, Kennedy published a collection of patriotic songs. This printed broadside of Kennedy's "Ode" measures $16\frac{1}{2}$ by $13\frac{1}{3}$ inches. Its date and place of publication are unknown (Thomas J. C. Williams, *A History of Washington County, Maryland, From the Earliest Settlements to the Present Time*, 2 vols. [Hagerstown, Md., 1906; reprint Baltimore, 1968], 1:168-73, 222; Thomas Kennedy, *Songs of Love and Liberty* [Washington, D.C., 1817]; Kennedy to TJ, 26 Aug. 1803).

Courtesy of the John Hay Library, Brown University.

Volume 36

1 December 1801 to 3 March 1802

JEFFERSON CHRONOLOGY
1743 · 1826

1743	Born at Shadwell, 13 Apr. (New Style).
1760	Entered the College of William and Mary.
1762	"quitted college."
1762-1767	Self-education and preparation for law.
1769-1774	Albemarle delegate to House of Burgesses.
1772	Married Martha Wayles Skelton, 1 Jan.
1775-1776	In Continental Congress.
1776	Drafted Declaration of Independence.
1776-1779	In Virginia House of Delegates.
1779	Submitted Bill for Establishing Religious Freedom.
1779-1781	Governor of Virginia.
1782	His wife died, 6 Sep.
1783-1784	In Continental Congress.
1784-1789	In France as Minister Plenipotentiary to negotiate commercial treaties and as Minister Plenipotentiary resident at Versailles.
1790-1793	Secretary of State of the United States.
1797-1801	Vice President of the United States.
1801-1809	President of the United States.
1814-1826	Established the University of Virginia.
1826	Died at Monticello, 4 July.

VOLUME 36
1 December 1801 to 3 March 1802

7 Dec.	First session of Seventh Congress opens.
8 Dec.	Sends first annual message to Congress.
10 Dec.	James Cheetham reports on Republican factions in New York.
21 Dec.	Announces final ratification of the Convention of 1800.
1 Jan. 1802	Receives Mammoth Cheese at the President's House as gift from the citizens of Cheshire, Massachusetts.
1 Jan.	Replies to Danbury Baptist Association, describing the "wall of separation" between church and state in America.
1 Jan.	Reelected president of the American Philosophical Society.
6 Jan.	Presents list of interim appointments to the Senate.
7 Jan.	Replies to address by Little Turtle of the Miami Indians.
8 Jan.	Rufus King signs convention with Great Britain on settlement of British debt claims.
29 Jan.	Appoints John Beckley librarian of Congress.
30 Jan.	Denniston & Cheetham send account of Aaron Burr's role in suppressing John Wood's history of the Adams administration.
3 Feb.	Bill to repeal Judiciary Act of 1801 passes Senate.
10 Feb.	Replies to address by Black Hoof of the Shawnee Indians.
13 Feb.	Arthur St. Clair writes to defend himself against charges of misconduct as governor of Northwest Territory.
17 Feb.	French General Victoire Emmanuel Leclerc declares blockade of Saint-Domingue.
18 Feb.	Authorizes navy commanders to capture Tripolitan vessels.
2 Mch.	Settles account with Edward Gantt for medical services rendered to President's House staff.
3 Mch.	Bill to repeal Judiciary Act of 1801 passes the House.

THE PAPERS OF
THOMAS JEFFERSON

·《═══════》·

To Andrew Sterett

Sir   Washington Dec. 1. 1801.

The Secretary of the Navy, the regular organ for the present communication, being absent from the seat of government for causes which may detain him for some time, I do myself the pleasure without further delay of expressing to you on behalf of your country, the high satisfaction inspired by your conduct in the late engagement with the Tripolitan cruiser captured by you. too long, for the honour of nations, have those barbarians been suffered to trample on the sacred faith of treaties, on the rights & laws of human nature. you have shewn to your countrymen that that enemy cannot meet bravery & skill united. in proving to them that our past condescensions were from a love of peace, not a dread of them, you have deserved well of your country; and have merited the high esteem & consideration of which I have now the pleasure of assuring you

Th: Jefferson

PrC (DLC); in ink at foot of text: "Lieutt. Sterett."

A scion of a prominent family of Baltimore merchants and Federalists, Andrew Sterett (1778-1807) received a lieutenant's commission in the U.S. Navy in March 1798. After seeing extensive service on board the frigates *Constellation* and *President*, Sterett was given command of the schooner *Enterprize* in October 1800. On 1 Aug. 1801, Sterett's vessel defeated the corsair *Tripoli* after a three-hour battle near Malta in the Mediterranean, the first American victory in the Barbary War. Sterett and the *Enterprize* returned to Baltimore in November 1801, then sailed for the Mediterranean again in early 1802. He remained in the navy until 1805, when he resigned after a dispute over rank. He died in Peru shortly thereafter while on a merchant voyage to Latin America (ANB; Vol. 35:588-9).

SECRETARY OF THE NAVY Robert Smith was ABSENT from Washington to contend with illness afflicting his family in Baltimore, which had already claimed the life of his eldest son (Vol. 35:723).

From Joseph Yznardi, Sr.

Exmo. Señor   Philadelphia 1st Disbre. de 1801

Muy Señor mio, y de mi Respecto

Permitame V.E qe por la Ultima ves, le moleste lleno de Sentimientos; y represente mi desgracia pues no tan Solamente, he venido á este Pais, para Sufrir persecusiones de sus Naturales, sino es de mi paisanos

El Cavallero de Irujo á cuyo favor tengo dicho, y hecho lo qe V.E mismo save, y lo qe el tienpo declará, despues de Aver sido Reelecto, me ha reconpensado en perseguir mis pasos, en los terminos qe el General Smith Informará á V.E, y aunqe nada temo pues los Honbres de Providad sienpre Aclaran su Conducta

funda sus quexas en qe yo he procurado desvaler sus Autoridades, de lo qe Apelo á V.E qe save el Honor con qe he prosedido, en Uso de la Mission, puesta á mi Cuidado, guardando el decoro devido, como Oficial publico de este Govo, a sus Cavesas, sino es Mirando como Debo, el Interes de mi Patria, y digno Monarca Siendo el Organo por donde se Aclararon las dificultades qe pendian

Recuerdo á V.E estas Circumstancias, para qe en todo tienpo sea Constante qe jamas he propuesto ablado, ni representado Cosa Alguna con Caracter publico Español, sino es como un Mediador Honrrado, y Proconsul con Claridad, y buen deseo, sin qe jamas pueda resultar Cargo contra mi como Intruso en el Real encargo, pues si es me hiciere Algun Cargo en la Corte, me veré obligado á provar contra lo qe pueda Sospecharce de mi Confiado en la Rectitud de V.E conoserá mi Justicia, pues si el Ministro qe me autorisó no Existe, no es mi Culpa

Se Abla del Consulado de Cadiz V.E tubo la vondad de darmelo, y como Dueño puede quitarmelo, si lo tubiece á bien, quando no sea por defecto mio baxo el Supuesto qe me buelbo á España como ofresí por mi Ultima, y Repito qe liquidados los puntos pendientes daré Aviso puntual, pues pienso retirarme Cansado de las persecusiones de este Mundo, quiero trabajar para el otro, con los prinsipios filosoficos qe fundo en el Borrador qe Continuo Suplicando á V.E perdone el Arrojo de Manifestarcelos como basis de mi Corto talento

assy mismo con veneración, y Respecto no se Olvide librarme de Pleyto de Isrrael por ser Justo como el qe se finalisen los pagos de mis quentas, no dudando qe Sienpre Confesaré, y defenderé con fortalesa, lo Amable de su prudencia, y fondos de su Saviduria,

y pediré á Dios le Conserve en ella para el bien de su Nacion
Exmo. Señor BLM de V.E su mas Obte. Servr

JOSEF YZNARDY

EDITORS' TRANSLATION

MOST EXCELLENT SIR   Philadelphia 1 Dec. 1801
My most illustrious sir, and with my respect.

Full of sorrow, allow me to bother Your Excellency for the last time, and to set before you my misfortune, for not only have I come to this country to endure persecutions from its inhabitants but from my fellow countrymen as well.

The Chevalier Irujo—on whose behalf I have said and done what Your Excellency himself knows, and what time will show—after having been reappointed, has paid me back by persecuting me in ways of which General Smith will inform Your Excellency, and though I fear nothing, men of honor always explain their conduct.

He bases his complaints on the notion that I have tried to undermine his authority, for which reason I appeal to Your Excellency who knows the honorable way in which I have proceeded in the mission that was entrusted to me, maintaining the respect I owe as a public official of this government to its leaders, as well as looking after, as I should, the interest of my country and its worthy monarch, which was the entity through which the difficulties that were pending were cleared up.

I remind Your Excellency of all these events so that it will always be evident that I have never propounded, advised, or represented anything as a Spanish public figure, but rather as an honorable mediator, and a proconsul with frankness and good will, and there could never be a charge against me as an interloper in the royal post. And if I am accused in the royal court, I will be obliged to give evidence against what might be imputed to me, confident in the rectitude of Your Excellency, who will recognize that I am in the right, for if the minister who confirmed me is no longer there, it is no fault of mine.

There is talk about the consulate of Cadiz that Your Excellency had the generosity to give me, and as its master can take it away from me should you see fit, so long as it is not because of any shortcomings, under the assumption that I will return to Spain as I promised in my last letter; and I repeat that once the pending matters are resolved, I will give a timely notice; for I am planning on retiring, as I am tired of the persecutions of this world, and I want to strive for the next, with the philosophical principles that I state in my rough notes; I continue to beg Your Excellency to pardon the boldness of my using them as a basis for my shortcomings.

Likewise with veneration and respect, do not forget to protect me from the lawsuit of Israel, for the sake of justice as the one who settles the payments to my debts, never doubting that I will always proclaim and defend with conviction the kindness of your prudence, and the profundity of your wisdom, and I will ask God that He give you long life for the good of your country.

Most excellent sir, your obedient servant kisses Your Excellency's hand.

JOSEF YZNARDY

[5]

RC (DLC); at foot of text: "Exmo. Sor. Dn. Thomas Jefferson."

LA MISSION, PUESTA Á MI CUIDADO: after the recall of Carlos Martínez Irujo as Spanish minister to the United States and before his reinstatement to that position, the Spanish government authorized Yznardi to act as a channel of communication between the United States and Spain (Vol. 32:396-7; Vol. 33:269n, 457, 483-6; Vol. 35:393n).

SI EL MINISTRO QE ME AUTORISÓ NO

EXISTE: late in 1800, Pedro Cevallos Guerra replaced Mariano Luis de Urquijo as minister of state of Spain (Vol. 33:293-5, 351, 483-6).

PLEYTO DE ISRRAEL: Yznardi continued to hope that TJ and Levi Lincoln would reverse their decision that the United States should not defend him in a suit filed by shipmaster Joseph Israel over actions by Yznardi when he was acting consul at Cadiz (Vol. 32:397n; Vol. 33:557-8, 604; Vol. 34:165, 166, 167n).

ENCLOSURE

Statement of Principles

La Magnifisencia de las Obras, la Magnanimidad del Corason, adorno de las Costumbres, Lusimiento del Ingenio, puresa de Animo, y liveralidad Consertada, Son, fueron, y serán mis principios, como Dones de Naturalesa, para desearme un Honbre Amado, Estimado, y venerado de mis Parientes, y amigos, y si posible fuera, de los Enemigos pero teniendo la fragilidad de ser Ingenuo, y declarado, y Franco en Sentimientos, ni venserme á Adular, distante de Conquistas la Amistad, la pierdo, Culpando mi enteresa pero no mi Consiencia, porqe esta Clama por la Verdad Constante, Moral el mas Sierto

Se qe con la Ingeniudad del Declarado, se Irritan los disimulados con fuego vengante ardiendo la Mina secreta qe sienpre esconden, para una Ocasion y no devo Olvidar, qe de los Amigos enojados, resultan los peores Enemigos porque Inpuestos de las Confiansas asen Uso de ellas, y cada uno abla como Siente, y Siente como desea

Mucho Inporta no llegar á ronpimiento, porqe siempre resulta la Reputasion Lastimada, y me Consta qe qualesquiera vale para Enemigo, y pocos para amigos; qe pocos pueden Aser bien; y los mas aser mal

No deve Usarse del balor porqe paresca bueno, ni por figurada Ipocrecía aserse Apagado, Corto y Miserable, en tolerar las Ofensas, y al Contrario deven repelerse, con Corage en lo Justo quando se defiende el Honor, pues como dise el Filosofo tacito; si á penas con buenos Artes se puede Conservar la Estimacion si la perdemos qe Subsedería

No Ignoro qe si la Virtud no fuese Emulada, ella Misma se Olvidaría, y Aunqe la enbidia es Espina qe punsa la Estimacion; creo qe distante de Consumirla, la Conserva porqe la Gloria de ser Emulado, la Insita á proseder Mejor porqe á Ninguno sele Estima quando el se desestime, siendo Asertado no descaeser porqe la Enbidia persigue con Mayor fuersa á el qe enpiesa á Caer, en Cuyo caso el Generoso deve Calebrar lo enbidien, porqe se despierta, y tanbien qe le emulen, porqe le Insitan á Velar sus prosedimientos

El titulo de Valeroso lo Merese, el qe no deja benserce de Afectos de Pasiones, libertandose de las enfermedades del Animo qe persigue la Imaginasion y si se quiere Conoser deve buscarce en si Mismo, y no en los demas, y con estos Sentimientos es Nesesario presencia de Espiritu, y Animo en los Negocios para no Caer en temor, pues del se Sigue la Irresolusion siendo for-

soso Sobstaner grandesa en el Corason para Obedeser á la Nessecidad, como
para Venserla Sierto qe el fin es el qe las Califica quando son buenas

El Animo generoso no deve desanimarce por Orrores de Peligros ni as-
peras dificultades, porqe Ninguna Cosa buena, y Magna acava sin valor, y
perseverancia, pues el qe reconoce es vensido, es perdido, y assy el Sufrir con
valor, esperar con pasiencia, y Constansia sin dejar de la Mano el Mejor Con-
pañero qe es el tienpo (pues el Savio Felipe Segundo Comunmte desia, yo, y
el tienpo contra dos) es lo Mejor

Enbuelto el Honbre, y Confundido con temores se Espone á Ruinar porqe
cada uno es artifice de su Fortuna, ó su perdida, y esperarla del ofendido, u
del Acaso es Error, y Creer qe está determinado ú prescripto, es Enigma,
pues aunqe el bulgo dice tanto es Uno quanto tiene, yo digo que tanto es uno
quanto Save, porqe Honbre sin Conosimientos, es el Mundo a obscuro y por
lo tanto qe Siencia, Consejo, fuersas, ojos y Manos, son las qe Conservan el
Honor á tienpo

Las mas veses los Honbres se engañan de Modos tan disfrasados y des-
conosidos, qe tememos lo qe no devemos, por prudencía, acusando la Constansia por temeraria, y otras veses sin savernos resolver, en tanto llega el
Peligro, y asi ni todo se deve temer, ni todo dejar de Conciderar, porqe entre
la prudencía, y fortalesa acabó, grandes Cosas el valor, y por lo tanto diria lo
qe el gran Capitan quando le Aconsejaron qe bolviese atras, y dijo; Yo estoy
determinado á ganar Antes un paso para mi Sepultara qe bolver atras,
Saviendo bivir cien Años, porqe el Valor no le Corona el Caso, sino es la
fatiga con Virtud, y perseverancia en el Obrar

todo enpiesa por principios, y nada puede terminar sin ellos, Acontesan
Casos qe por lo General no se esperan, y por lo tanto el Alma grande no deve
Abatirse quando los Aldabones de sus Potencias no las tocan á Separarse.

EDITORS' TRANSLATION

Brilliance in works, nobility of the heart, adornment of morals, luminosity
of talent, purity of spirit, and concerted generosity are, were, and will be my
principles, as natural gifts, for I want to be a man loved, esteemed, and ven-
erated by my family, friends, and if possible by my enemies. However, having
the weakness of being naive, honest, and forthright in my feelings, immune
to adulation and aloof to seduction, I lose friendship, blaming my integrity
but not my conscience, because the latter clamors for unwavering truth and
morality that is the most certain.

I know that those who dissemble are irritated with a vengeful fire by the
sincerity of the honest, lighting the fuse of the secret explosive charge that
they always conceal for an opportune moment; and I should not forget that
from angry friends are born the worst enemies, because when they are
confided in they take advantage of what they know, and each speaks as he
feels, and feels as he wishes.

It very important not to break up a friendship, because one's reputation is
always smeared, and I am absolutely certain that anyone can be an enemy, and
a few can be friends; that a few can do good, and the majority does evil.

One should not act courageously because it looks good, nor should one
pretend to be discouraged, fearful, and miserable when suffering wrongdo-
ings. On the contrary, one should resist with the courage that is just when

defending honor, because as the Silent Philosopher said, if it is scarcely possible to preserve respect with talent, imagine what would happen if we were to lose it.

I am aware that if virtue were not emulated, it would be forgotten, and though envy is a thorn that stabs at respect, I believe that far from getting rid of virtue, one should keep it because the glory of being emulated incites virtue to act better, as no one is respected when he does not respect himself; being right does not ruin anyone, because envy persecutes with more force he who begins to falter, in which case the generous man should rejoice that he is envied, because it inspires him, and also that he be emulated, because it incites him to watch over his actions.

The title of courageous is merited by him who does not allow himself be defeated by the affects of passion, freeing himself of the maladies of the spirit that persecute the imagination, and if one seeks to know himself he should search inside himself and not in others, and with these sentiments it is important to have presence of mind and courage in dealings in order not to become afraid, since indecision results from that, making it necessary to sustain greatness of the heart in order both to obey necessity and to overcome it, truly it is the outcome that distinguishes them when they are good.

A generous soul should not be discouraged by the fear of dangers nor by severe difficulties, because nothing good and great can be accomplished without courage and perseverance, for he who admits to fear is defeated, is lost, and thus suffering with valor, waiting in patience, and with determination without letting go of the best companion, of which time is the best (for as the wise Felipe II often said, "me and time against two").

When man is surrounded with and confused by fear, he exposes himself to ruin, because each one is the author of his own good fortune or its loss, and expecting it from the offended or leaving it to chance is a mistake, and to believe that it is fixed or predetermined is a mystery; for although common folks say that one is worth what one has, I say that one is worth what one knows, because a man without knowledge is like a darkened world, and it is science, good counsel, strength, eyes, and hands that preserve honor in good time.

Sometimes men fool themselves in concealed and unknown ways, fearing what ought not be feared out of prudence, accusing perseverance of being rash, and other times being incapable when in danger; and so not everything should be feared, and not everything should be left without being considered, because great things have been accomplished with prudence and strength; and therefore I would say what El Gran Capitán, when they advised him to retreat, said: "I am determined to win, and I would rather go to my grave than retreat thinking I could live a hundred years, for valor is not attained by chance, but rather by virtue of hard work and perseverance in actions."

Everything starts with principles and nothing can be accomplished without them, things that are generally not expected happen, and therefore a great soul should not be disheartened when its strength is not examined.

MS (DLC); in Yznardi's hand; endorsed by TJ as received 11 Dec. and so recorded in SJL.

EL FILOSOFO TACITO: Secundus, an Athenian of the second century, took a vow of silence after a ruse that he concocted to demonstrate that no woman was virtuous drove his mother to commit suicide. After he gave written answers to a set of interrogatories from the Roman Emperor Hadrian—including such queries as "What is the Universe?"—he became known as the Silent Philosopher. Naming kings and heroes who had all possessed very special talents and gifts, Secundus warned Hadrian: "If Fortune took away from these men the distinctions that were peculiarly their own, how much more likely is she to take them away from you?" (Ben Edwin Perry, *Secundus the Silent Philosopher* [Ithaca, N.Y., 1964], 1-10, 69,

71, 77, 79; Anthony K. Cassell, "*Il Corbaccio* and the Secundus Tradition," *Comparative Literature*, 25 [1973], 355-60).

From 1556 until his death in 1598, FELIPE (Philip) II was king of Spain (Germán Bleiberg, ed., *Diccionario de Historia de España*, 2d ed., 3 vols. [1968-69], 2:16-24).

EL GRAN CAPITAN: Gonzalo Fernández de Córdoba, a famed Spanish general of the late fifteenth and early sixteenth centuries. He is credited with the development of a new model of warfare that replaced Medieval tactics (same, 2:51-2).

To James Currie

DEAR SIR   Washington Dec. 2. 1801.

In my last notes in the case between mr Ross & myself, I mentioned that I would apply to messrs. Lewis & Eppes for information of the credit given at a sale in Elk island, on which the rate of converting money into tobacco in a particular instance depended. I have received their answers, neither of them recollecting what credit was given on particular bonds: they suppose also that mr Ross, or perhaps mr Wickam may be in possession of the particular bonds in question which would shew for themselves. having no additional evidence therefore on this point, I would wish the final decision of the arbitration not to be delayed longer in expectation of it   Accept assurances of my friendly esteem & respect   TH: JEFFERSON

PrC (MHi); at foot of text: "Doctr Currie"; endorsed by TJ in ink on verso.

See TJ to Nicholas LEWIS, 16 Oct., Lewis to TJ, 30 Oct., and TJ to Currie, 19 Oct.

To Thomas Leiper

DEAR SIR   Washington Dec. 2. 1801.

Your favor of Nov. is recieved. my crop of tobacco of the last year's growth was sold in April. that lately severed will be small; the crop of tobacco this year being generally short. mine will not be half a one. I fear too the quality will be indifferent; at least that was the expectation when I was at home in September. in that case I always sell in Richmond where they are less[1] anxious about quality. should it turn out better than was expected, you shall have the offer of it. I congratulate you on the return of peace. it removes out of our way the only rock of which I had any apprehension. I hope we have now a prospect of leisure & opportunity to pay our debts & reduce our taxes. accept assurances of my esteem & respect.

TH: JEFFERSON

PrC (MHi); foot of text: "Mr Lieper"; endorsed by TJ in ink on verso.

YOUR FAVOR: Leiper to TJ, [before 21] Nov.

[1] Canceled: "attentive to."

To George Jefferson

DEAR SIR   Washington Dec. 3. 1801.

In the month of August,[1] mr Barnes shipped from hence by the Schooner William, James Collett master, of Alexandria three cases, small, containing some composition ornaments. I believe the three cases were put into one outer one. they were marked TI. No. 1. 2. 3. and I am not quite certain they were put into one. they were addressed to you. they have never got to Monticello, nor do I recollect that you have ever noted the reciept of them. under these circumstances I take the liberty of asking you to make enquiry for them, if you have the means. possibly the Captain may have dropped them at Norfolk. we know that they were actually put on board his vessel at Alexandria. I note & approve what you did as to Stewart. he is the best workman in America, but the most eccentric one: quite manageable were I at home, but doubtful as I am not. accept assurances of my constant & affectionate esteem.   TH: JEFFERSON

PrC (MHi); at foot of text: "Mr. George Jefferson"; endorsed by TJ in ink on verso.

For the shipment of the COMPOSITION ORNAMENTS to Gibson & Jefferson, see

TJ to John Barnes, 7 Aug., and Barnes to TJ, 24 Aug. 1801.

WHAT YOU DID AS TO STEWART: see George Jefferson to TJ, 16 Nov.

[1] Interlined in place of "September."

To James Madison

[ca. 3 Dec. 1801]

This claim is totally without foundation. M. de Rayneval wrote to me on the subject last spring and I wrote him an answer which I can communicate to mr Madison.   TH:J

[10]

MS (DNA: RG 59, NL); in TJ's hand; undated; written on a slip of paper attached to Louis André Pichon to James Madison, 3 Dec. 1801 (Madison, *Papers, Sec. of State Ser.*, 2:293).

Joseph Mathias Gérard de RAYNEVAL had written to TJ from France in August 1799 and followed up in January 1801 to press a claim for land granted to his deceased brother, Conrad Alexandre Gérard, by the Wabash Company. In conversation with Pierre Samuel Du Pont de Nemours, who in 1799 had acted as Rayneval's intermediary, and in a letter to Rayneval in March 1801, TJ explained that Virginia had voided the claims of the Wabash Company before the land came under Congress's control. Pichon's letter of 3 Dec. to Madison from Georgetown stated that Talleyrand, the French minister of foreign affairs, had instructed him to inquire if Rayneval's claim could be presented to Congress with the president's recommendation (same, 2:293-4; Vol. 31:175-6; Vol. 32:384-5; Vol. 33:373-4).

To Craven Peyton

DEAR SIR   Washington Dec. 3. 1801.

Your favor of Nov. 6. was recieved in due time. a press of business has prevented my answering sooner. I am willing to recieve William Davenport as the assignee of your lease of Shadwell. on considering the parts of the lands of the Hendersons which fall to me, I observe that it would be desireable for me to have all their shares in the three parcels on the river, but most especially in the middle one to have John's, Bennet's & Nancy's. the two latter I suppose are under age. perhaps you could get this little piece of John's for a trifle, or all his shares in those three parcels, which would all be acceptable to me. his part of the back tract would be of the least value to me because the farthest from me. however if he will sell the whole reasonably, I would wish you to engage it, but still in your own name. could you send me a list of the ages of the children under 21. so that I may see when chances will arise of getting their parts? accept my best wishes & respects   TH: JEFFERSON

PrC (ViU); at foot of text: "Mr. Craven Peyton"; endorsed by TJ in ink on verso.

For the CHILDREN of Elizabeth Lewis and Bennett Henderson, see Declaration of Trust with Craven Peyton, [25 Sep. 1801]. Henderson's widow and their five youngest children moved to Shelby County, Kentucky, in November 1801 (Boynton Merrill, Jr., *Jefferson's Nephews: A Frontier Tragedy* [Princeton, 1976], 64-5).

From Andrew Sterett

SIR,   Baltimore, December 3, 1801.

I do myself the honor to acknowledge the receipt of your excellency's letter of the first instant.

It has been my greatest ambition to discharge my duty as an officer of the American navy, at all times, with promptness and fidelity; and to have received my country's and your excellency's approbation of the late conquest over a faithless and barbarian enemy, achieved[1] by the valour and good conduct of the officers and crew I had the honor to command, is a reward which I estimate beyond my merits; but of which I shall ever cherish a greatful recollection, particularly for the very flattering manner in which your excellency has been pleased to convey it.

I have the honor to be with profound respect your excellency's obliged humble servant,

ANDREW STERETT,
Lieut. and commander of the United States
Schooner Enterprize.

Printed in the *Federal Gazette & Baltimore Daily Advertiser*, 12 Dec. 1801. Recorded in SJL as received 4 Dec.

The Baltimore newspaper printed both this letter and TJ's communication of the 1st and introduced them with the following comment: "The editors were politely favored with the following letters several days since; but they overcame their impatience to lay before the public the meed of merit to a brave officer, until it should be published by the proper department. It has not yet appeared, and they can repress their feelings no longer, to withhold it."

[1] *Federal Gazette*: "achived."

From Abishai Thomas

Navy office Decr. 3rd 1801

Agreeably to the instruction of the President A Thomas had the honor to Submit the enclosed *Statement to the Secretary of State, who approved of the information it contains being communicated to Mr. Pichon.

[*In TJ's hand:*]
*of French prizes carried into Mass. New Hamp. Connecticut & Rhode island.

RC (DLC); with TJ's note written in margin; address on verso partially torn away: "[Pr]esident"; endorsed by TJ as received from the Navy Department on 3 Dec. and "French captures" and so recorded in SJL. Enclosure not found.

Memorial from the District of Columbia Commissioners

Commissioners Office
4th December 1801.

The Memorial of the Commissioners appointed by virtue of an Act of Congress, entituled "an act for establishing the temporary and permanent Seat of the Government of the United-States"

Respectfully sheweth—

That on the twenty eighth of January last, the Commissioners addressed to the late President of the United-States a Representation stating such facts respecting the Business committed to their charge as appeared necessary for the Information of the Government; which Representation was by him transmitted to Congress, and by their order referred to a Committee; but no measures having taken place in consequence thereof, either by the Executive or Legislature, your Memorialists deem it expedient to recapitulate the most important facts then stated; and to add such other facts and observations as may tend to enable the President to judge of the Measures proper to be pursued by him, and to aid the Legislature in their Deliberations, should the subject be submitted to their consideration.—The act of Congress authorising the President to locate a District for the permanent Seat of the Government of the United-States, the actual location of that District; the grant of Lands for a federal City; the power given by the President to the Commissioners to sell that part of the Land so granted, which was placed at his disposal; the sale of six thousand lots to Morris and Greenleaf, by agreement dated twenty third December, one thousand seven hundred and ninety three; the modification of that agreement by another entered into in April one thousand seven hundred and ninety four; the failure of those gentlemen to fulfil their Contracts, and the various measures pursued to obtain money to carry on the public Buildings, are recited in the above mentioned Representation; and copies of the Legislative Acts, Deeds, and other writings therein referred to, are annexed, and the whole printed for the use of the Members of Congress.—The Property belonging to the public is therein stated to consist of twenty four million, six hundred and fifty five thousand, seven hundred and thirty five square feet of Ground in the City of Washington, equal to four thousand six hundred and eighty two lots of five thousand two hundred and sixty five square feet, each, exclusive of lots which bind on navigable water; these form fronts to the extent of two thousand and forty three feet, and on them are four wharves in an useful state. Of the first mentioned lots three thousand, one hundred and seventy eight lie north-east of Massachusetts Avenue, the remainder, being fifteen hundred and four, are situated south-west of that Avenue; also, an Island, containing free Stone in Aquia Creek in the State of Virginia.—The above property your memorialists consider as worthy of public attention—its value may be estimated by the prices at which lots have heretofore been sold, the cost of the wharves and the price of the Island.

Lots on the south-west side of Massachusetts Avenue sold by the Commissioners since passing the guarantee Bill in one thousand seven hundred and ninety six, average three hundred and forty three Dollars per lot—those on the north-east side of that Avenue, sold by the Commissioners and proprietors average one hundred and five Dollars per lot—Lots binding on navigable water sold within the same period, average twelve Dollars and seventy one cents the foot front—the Island cost six thousand Dollars, and the wharves three thousand two hundred and twenty one Dollars and eighty eight cents; the whole amounting, at the rate lots have heretofore been sold, with the original cost of the Island and Wharves, to eight hundred and eighty four thousand eight hundred and nineteen Dollars, eighty eight cents.—The lots sold by the Commissioners since the date of the above-mentioned representation, exclusive of a square sold to the United-States for the site of Marine Barracks, average four hundred and seventy Dollars, & seventy one cents per lot.

To elucidate more fully the real value of City property, they have endeavored to ascertain the prices at which proprietors have sold lots within the last eighteen Months, and so far as they have obtained Information, their Sales average 579\frac{15}{100}$ for cash, & on short credit, & 921\frac{37}{100}$ on a credit of 4, 5 & 6 years per lot, and their ground Rents are from one to three Dollars per foot front.—

Your Memorialists readily admit, that the public Property remaining for sale, is not on an average equal in value to that which has been sold—yet, as great abatement was, in many Instances, made in the price of lots, in consideration of building Contracts, and as inducements to purchase in the City, have much encreased, they conceive those on hand may, in the course of a few years, be disposed of, at least, to as great advantage as those already sold; but if the Law authorising a Loan for the use of the City of Washington should be carried strictly into effect, your memorialists are apprehensive that this property must be in a great degree sacrificed. It is known that two hundred thousand Dollars have been borrowed of the State of Maryland under the sanction of that Law, and that the City property abovementioned is to be sold under the direction of the President of the United-States, for the re-payment of that Sum;—An arrear of Interest to the amount of nine thousand Dollars is now due thereon, the accruing Interest of twelve thousand Dollars per annum payable quarteryearly, and the principal which is payable by annual Instalments of forty thousand Dollars after the year 1803, are Sums which your Memorialists conceive, cannot be raised without frequent Sales for ready money; a measure which they consider as highly injurious, if carried to the extent necessary to answer those objects, and which they have in no instance attempted; although the difficulties they have experienced in collecting Debts, convince them that Sales on credit cannot be relied on for the punctual payment of the abovementioned Interest and Instalments: They therefore, with great deference, suggest the propriety of the Government's paying the Money borrowed, and reserving the property pledged for it's repayment, to be sold as advantageous offers may occur—a policy which dictated the guarantee in 1796, and which has been fully justified by the Sales made since that period.

By pursuing a contrary policy, the property pledged will be greatly diminished by the payment of Interest only, while much larger Sums than are necessary to discharge both principal and Interest, will probably lie dead in the Treasury. Your Memorialists also beg leave to state, that the Sum of fifty thousand Dollars, in United-States six per cent stock, has been borrowed from the State of Maryland, to be repaid on the first of November 1802, secured by the Bond of the Commissioners, and real and personal Security given by private persons:—the only fund applicable to the payment of this Sum at the disposal of the President or the Commissioners, is, the Debts contracted for City lots purchased previous to passing the guarantee Law; this Fund is indeed much more than sufficient, could those Debts be called in, to accomplish which, your Memorialists have never ceased their exertions—they are now pursuing a measure not before attempted; a ready money Sale, in which if they fail to sell the property, for as much as is due thereon to the public—The same policy would dictate to the Government to pay this Sum of fifty thousand Dollars likewise, the last mentioned Debts, to a much greater amount, being ultimately secure.

The Commissioners have only received fifty three thousand, two hundred and eighty one Dollars and eighty one cents from the Sales of property pledged by virtue of the guarantee Law—They have paid in conformity to that Law, the Sum of twenty nine thousand, six hundred and eighty seven Dollars and ninety two cents, to the original proprietors, for property appropriated to public use, and forty two thousand Dollars Interest, which has accrued on money borrowed under the sanction of the same Law. Thus, the Sum of eighteen thousand, four hundred and six Dollars and eleven cents, derived from the funds applicable to the payment of Debts contracted on the personal security of the Commissioners, has been applied to the purposes of the guarantee, and thereby the necessity of selling at depreciated rates, the property pledged to Congress, has been avoided.

Your Memorialists would also observe that the Debts due, and to become due to the City fund, and which were considered as good, were stated in the last Representation to the President, at one hundred and forty four thousand, one hundred and twenty Dollars and eighty cents. Since which forty six thousand and eighty one Dollars & ninety nine cents, have been received; but it may be observed that the Sum of eighty thousand Dollars, which by the agreement of April 1794 was to rest on the Bond of Morris, Greenleaf and Nicholson, is not included in that description, although your Memorialists are advised by their Counsel, that certain Squares in the City of Washington, containing one thousand lots, are liable to the payment of that Sum; the same being designated by an agreement of 9th July 1794, as the lots, the payment for which was to rest on the said Bond; and this point is now depending for decision in the Court of Chancery of the State of Maryland.

To shew the progress and the present state of Buildings in the City, your Memorialists have had the number of dwelling Houses taken, and find by an accurate Report, that on the fifteenth of May 1800 there were one hundred and nine of brick, and two hundred and sixty three of wood—and on the fifteenth of the last month there was an addition of eighty four of brick and one hundred and fifty one of wood, besides seventy nine of brick, and thirty five of wood in an unfinished state, total amount, seven hundred and thirty five—Their particular situations will appear from the schedule which accompanies this Memorial.

The above statement of facts and observations, are, with sentiments of the highest respect, submitted to the consideration of the President of the United-States.

WILLIAM THORNTON
ALEX WHITE
TRISTRAM DALTON

RC (DLC); in William Brent's hand, signed by Thornton, White, and Dalton; at head of text: "To the President of the United States." FC (DNA: RG 42, PC). Tr (DNA: RG 233, PM, 7th Cong., 1st sess.); entirely in Meriwether Lewis's hand. Enclosure: "An Enumeration [of the] Houses in the City of Washington, made November 1801" (Tr in DNA: RG 233, PM, 7th Cong., 1st sess.; certified by Thomas Munroe as a "Copy of the Original filed in the Commissioners Office"; endorsed by House clerk). Enclosed in District of Columbia Commissioners to TJ, Commissioners' Office, 4 Dec., which states, "We have the honor of addressing to you a Memorial stating such facts as appear to us requisite for your Information, in addition to those stated in a Representation made to your Predecessor during the last Session of Congress;— which Representation with the Documents accompanying it, being on the files of Congress, and in the Hands of the President and members of the Legislature, we supposed a general reference thereto

sufficient" (RC in DLC, in William Brent's hand and signed by Thornton, White, and Dalton, addressed "President of the United States," endorsed by TJ as received 5 Dec. and so recorded in SJL; FC in DNA: RG 42, DCLB). Trs transmitted to Congress with TJ's message of 11 Jan. 1802 and printed in ASP, *Miscellaneous*, 1:254-7.

John Adams transmitted the 28 Jan. 1800 REPRESENTATION by the commissioners to the House of Representatives on 30 Jan., and the House referred it to a committee the same day (JHR, 3:780). For a printed copy of the letter and its ANNEXED documents, including agreements between the commission and the company of Morris and Greenleaf, see ASP, *Miscellaneous*, 1:219-31.

For the GUARANTEE BILL from 1796, see District of Columbia Commissioners to TJ, 17 Aug. The commission's letter to Adams of 28 Jan. includes a short history of the bill and its relationship to the $200,000 loan by the state of Maryland.

From the Georgia Legislature

Georgia. In the House of Representatives,
SIR,   Friday the 4th. December 1801.

The Legislature of Georgia, reposing high confidence in the Executive of the Union, congratulates the President, on his elevation to the chief Magistracy.—They felicitate themselves, that an office of the first dignity in the Federal Republic, bearing the greatest responsibility, and embracing in its detail, various and complicated relations, on the judicious determination of which, essentially depends the prosperity of the Commonwealth; has been committed to the charge of *him*, in whose justice, integrity and patriotism, the Legislature of Georgia do confide—We have equal confidence in the Legislature of the Union. State rights, State sovereignty, as recognized by the Constitution, when respected by the General Government, will form the Ligament binding each political Fraction to the aggregate, by the indissoluble ties of reciprocal interest—Then Georgia, receiving justice for the past, and wishing no security for the future, will harmonize with the Legislature of the Union, and throw her feeble weight into the Federal scale.

Under an administration which has the public good for its end, and the Constitution for its rule, under the Federal Legislature, when the talents and virtues of the Republic are concentrated; we look forward to that ultimatum of political perfectability, from which we hope never to retrograde.

Receive Sir, this testimony of the Legislature's confidence, together with our wishes, that your private walks may be as eminently happy, as your public life has been conspicuously virtuous.

The foregoing address being read, was unanimously agreed to.

DAVID MERIWETHER Speaker

Teste

HINES HOLT Clk

In Senate, the 5th. December, 1801.
Read & concurred

JOHN JONES President
of the Senate pro tempore

Teste

WILL ROBERTSON Secy

RC (DLC); in a clerk's hand, signed by all including their offices; at head of text: "To Thomas Jefferson, President of the United States"; endorsed by TJ as received 1 Jan. 1802 and so recorded in SJL.

David Meriwether (1755-1822), a native of Albemarle County, Virginia, settled in Wilkes County, Georgia, in 1785. A legislator and brigadier general of the state militia, he was chosen speaker of the Georgia House of Representatives in 1797. He served in Congress from 1802 to 1807, and played an active role in negotiations with the Creeks and Cherokees from 1802 until his death (*Biog. Dir. Cong.*; E. Merton Coulter, "David Meriwether of Virginia and Georgia," *Georgia Historical Quarterly*, 54 [1970], 320-38). John Jones represented Montgomery County in the state senate (*Journal of the Senate of the State of Georgia, for the Year 1801* [Louisville, Ga., 1802], 8, 34).

From George Jefferson

DEAR SIR,   Richmond 4th. Decr. 1801

Not having heard from our friend in Petersburg upon the subject of the Tobacco, I wrote him on the *19th* of last month desiring that he would *immediately* make the purchase, as I expected it would be wanted in a few days. yet I have not yet heard from him! I have written him again to night repeating my request, and write this to you lest you should be as much surprised at my silence, as I am at his.

I am Dear Sir Your Very humble servt.   GEO JEFFERSON

RC (MHi); at foot of text: "Thomas Jefferson esqr."; endorsed by TJ as received 8 Dec. and so recorded in SJL.

TJ was purchasing tobacco in PETERSBURG to pay his debt to David Ross. For the terms of the settlement of TJ's dispute with Ross, see Vol. 31:209-10n.

To George Latimer

SIR   Washington Dec. 4. 1801.

Your favor of Nov. 28. came to hand the night before last, and I thank you for the attentions to the boxes by the ship Pensylvania. the letter you inclosed mentions the contents to be two figures in plaister & one in marble and refers me to a letter I am to recieve from Baltimore for some explanations which it will be necessary for me to recieve before I can direct what is to be done with the boxes. in the mean time I inclose you the bill of lading, and pray you to permit the boxes to remain at the customhouse till I shall hear further on the subject.   Accept assurances of my esteem & respect

TH: JEFFERSON

PrC (MHi); at foot of text: "Mr. Latimer"; endorsed by TJ in ink on verso. Enclosure not found.

LETTER YOU INCLOSED: Arnold Oelrichs to TJ, 14 Sep. The letter TJ was to receive from Baltimore merchant James Zwisler has not been found (Stafford, *Baltimore Directory, for 1802*, 117).

To John Monroe

DEAR SIR   Washington Dec. 4. 1801.

Your favor of Nov. 26. came to hand the night before last. it would have given me great pleasure to have furnished you the accomodation therein mentioned, but my situation disables me compleatly. the outfit for this office has already cost me 10,000. D. besides that the current expences have [been] to be furnished over & above this. the consequence is that after having laid all my private resources under requisition, I have still great outstanding demands which I shall be long working through by the help of expedients from hand to mouth, very oppressive to my spirits.

The event of peace is glorious for us. it removes the only rock ahead which had threatened us with danger. we shall now be at leisure to pursue plans for the amelioration of our affairs, for paying our debts & lightening taxes. we have reason to hope the legislature

[19]

now convening will, in both it's branches, be disposed to cooperate with us in these views. Accept my best wishes for your health & happiness & assurances of my respect   TH: JEFFERSON

PrC (MHi); blurred; at foot of text: "John Monroe esq."; endorsed by TJ in ink on verso.

Monroe's FAVOR of 26 Nov. requested a loan of $1,500 from TJ to open a tavern at the Warm Springs in Bath County, Virginia.

To Thomas Mann Randolph

DEAR SIR   Washington Dec. 4. 1801.

A gentleman here has occasion for a particular purpose to consult the Preliminary discourse written by Dalembert to the antient encyclopedia, which was in fact a developement of Bacon's Arbor scientiae. it is in one of the volumes (the 1st. I believe) of the Melanges de literature in 5. vols. 12. mo. which you will find in the press on the right side of the cherry sash door in my cabinet. I must trouble you to get it from Monticello whenever convenient, & to send it on by post well wrapped in stout paper. I will pray you at the same time to send me Philidor on chess, which you will find in the book room, 2d. press on the left from the door of entrance: to be wrapped in strong paper also. I wrote on the 27th. to my dear Martha. I recieved about that time a letter from mr Eppes. their little one had borne the journey well, tho' it was still under the height of it's whooping cough. Maria's health had suffered sensibly. she had had a rising in her breast which broke the first day after applying the root she had before used. the letter was dated Nov. 21. from Eppington where they expected to remain a fortnight.

I send you a pamphlet giving an account of a water-proof cloth now used in England, which will probably be of value. I have a surtout coat of it, which I have had no opportunity of trying but by dipping it. I inclose you also a specimen of coarse paper, one half of which is water proof, the other not. you recieved the news of peace by the last post probably. in a letter by that post to mr Dinsmore I gave him an account of the tragical end of James Hemmings.   I have been expecting mr Craven to Alexandria, who was to have brought a box of books for me. if he is not come & is still coming, that would be a better opportunity than the post for sending the two books above written for. hoping to hear on Tuesday how the children are this day, I conclude with my tender love to my dear Martha & affectionate esteem to yourself.   TH: JEFFERSON

RC (DLC); at foot of text: "T M Randolph"; endorsed by Randolph. PrC (CSmH); endorsed by TJ in ink on verso. Enclosure: *Analytical Hints Relative to the Process of Ackermann, Suardy, & Co's. Manufactories for Waterproof Cloths, and Wearing Apparel*, advertising the patented waterproofing process developed by James Douglass of Cuper's Bridge in Lambeth (London, [1801]), 15, 24. The enclosure of coarse paper, which demonstrated the water-proofing technique, has not been found, but the enclosed pamphlet indicated that the "invention" was not "confined to cloth," but extended to paper, which would be for sale in August 1801 (same, 21-3).

For TJ's evaluation of Francis BACON'S works as "the first germs of so many branches of science" or ARBOR SCIENTIAE, see Sowerby, Nos. 4915-16.

MELANGES DE LITERATURE: Jean Le Rond d'Alembert's *Mélange de Littérature, d'Historie, et de Philosophie*. TJ owned the edition printed in Amsterdam in 1764 (see Sowerby, No. 4925).

François André Danican, known as PHILIDOR, wrote *L'Analyze des Echecs*, a treatise on CHESS (see Sowerby, No. 1173).

I HAVE A SURTOUT COAT OF IT: for TJ's purchase of the waterproof overcoat, see Statement of Account with Thomas Carpenter, printed at 21 Dec.

The letter from John Wayles EPPES of 21 Nov., recorded in SJL as received from Eppington a week later, has not been found. According to SJL, TJ wrote James DINSMORE on 28 Nov., but the letter is now missing. TRAGICAL END OF JAMES HEMMINGS: for TJ's inquiry into the suicide of Hemings, see Vol. 35:542-3, 569-70.

From Christopher Smith

SIR   Louisa December 4th. 1801

Your favour of 20th. Sept. last was duly received, and its contents attended to immediately on the recpt. of it, I had a search made for the fellow, and could he have been found would have sent him to Mr. Lilly. have since heard he returned to your manager in a few days after he eloped. I wish you to beleive that it is my desire, as well for my own interest as from motives of safety to us all, that my Slaves be kept in proper subjection—

When the money becomes due for the hire, it will be convenient for me to receive it in Richmond, my freind Mr. David Bullock will (on your informing him where to apply) receive the money and deliver your [specialty]

I am respectfully your mo: Obt.   CHRISTOR. SMITH

RC (MHi); endorsed by TJ as received 11 Dec. and so recorded in SJL.

TJ hired slaves from Christopher Smith of Louisa County, Virginia, between 1801 and 1803 or 1804 (MB, 2:1037, 1134).

YOUR FAVOUR: TJ's communication to

Smith, recorded in SJL as a letter of 21 Sep., is missing.

MY SLAVES: on 12 Apr. 1801, TJ recorded in his personal financial memoranda that he gave bonds to Smith for the hire of seven male slaves for £142 ($473.33), payable on 1 Jan. 1802. TJ also recorded the slaves' names (MB, 2:1037, 1062).

To Caspar Wistar

Washington Dec. 4. 1801.

I have the pleasure to inclose for communication to the society observations made on a lunar eclipse at the Observatory of Philadelphia on the 21st of Sep. last by messrs. Patterson & Ellicot. Also some extracts from a letter I recieved from mr Dunbar of the Natchez with Meteorological observations for the year 1800. made there by him, and remarks on the soil, climate & productions of the country.

I recieved some time since a letter from mr Peale, giving an account of his labours and successes towards obtaining a compleat collection of the bones of one of the unknown animals, whose size has attracted so much attention. although the intermixture of other matters showed that this letter was intended as a private one to myself, yet considering that science will wish to know that it is to mr Peale they will be indebted for the collection & possession of these precious remains, I should have communicated so much of the letter as related to that subject, had I not imagined mr Peale might be induced, after his labours shall be compleated, to give a detailed relation of them.

Accept assurances of my great esteem & high consideration.

TH: JEFFERSON

PrC (DLC); faint; at foot of text: "Doctr. Wistar." Enclosures: (1) Robert Patterson and Andrew Ellicott, "Observations made on a Lunar Eclipse at the Observatory in the City of Philadelphia on the 21st, of September 1801," enclosed in Ellicott to TJ, 10 Oct. 1801. (2) William Dunbar, "Monthly Recapitulation" of weather observations at Natchez in 1800 and supplementary remarks, enclosed in Dunbar to TJ, 22 Aug. 1801.

LETTER FROM MR PEALE: Charles Willson Peale to TJ, 11 Oct. 1801.

To Joseph Bloomfield

SIR   Washington Dec. 5. 1801.

I have duly recieved your favor of Nov. 10. and shall be happy in every practicable occasion of proving to you how much I respect whatever comes from you. your position has already probably proved to you that while the real business of conducting the affairs of our constituents is plain & easy, that of deciding *by whom* they shall be conducted is most painful & perplexing. it is the case of one loaf and ten men wanting bread: and we have not the gift of multiplying them. you will percieve, on the contrary, in a few days, that I propose the contrary operation, to reduce public offices fully one half. when so many are to be dropped, it will be difficult for new to find admission.

but I am in hopes that public offices being reduced to so small a number, will no longer hold up the prospect of being a resource for those who find themselves under difficulties, but that they will at once turn themselves for relief, to those private pursuits which derive it from services rendered to others. our duty is not to impede those pursuits by heavy taxes, and useless officers to consume their earnings.

I sincerely congratulate you on the return of peace. it removes the only danger we had to fear. we can now proceed, without risk, in demolishing useless structures of expence, lightening the burthens of our constituents, and fortifying the principles of free government. I hope we have time and quiet enough before us to bring back the government to what it was originally intended to be. Accept assurances of my high respect & consideration.   Th: Jefferson

PrC (DLC); at foot of text: "Governor Bloomfield."

In his FAVOR of 10 Nov., Bloomfield recommended Stephen Sayre for office.

From Sylvanus Bourne

Sir.

Consular Office of the U States
Amsterdam Decr. 5h 1801

I herewith transmit you these successive numbers to this date of the Leyden Gazette: It is difficult at this moment to add much to the contents of the public papers relative to the position of Europe which will ere long receive a more correct & decided modification by the Congress destined to meet at Amiens: we can only Collect from the tenor of many Official documents which have lately emanated from the Govts on each side of the Channell that a good understanding appears to exist between England & France on the great points of the modification alluded to & as we know not of any Power disposed or Capable of Counteracting their views in this regard—it is probable All matters will soon be definitively arranged & that with the Century will commence a new & important epoch in the political existence of Europe

I fondly Entertain the hope that the establishment of peace in this part of the World will among its many pleasing consequences produce that of assuaging the spirit of party & discord which seems to have made such untoward progress in our Country & that a reciprocal desire of reconciliation nourished by a wise administration of the Govt. may tend to ensure to the American people all the blessings which can flow from a well regulated Society, Combined with the natural advantages we enjoy—

I still *anxiously* wait to know the fate of my official situation & prospects as I have had many heavy misfortunes to struggle with in life & on what may be done in this regard will the future w[elfare] of an increasing family very *materially* depend—

I have the honor to be with the greatest respect Yr Ob Sev

S BOURNE

PS. I wait for a translation in french of the late adopted Constitution of this Country to transmit it to you—which as far as I am able to comprehend it, seems essentially defective in not having duly preserved that independence & seperation of the great powers of Govt Legislative Executive Judicial which in the U States are thought to be necessary to the preservation of liberty—

RC (DNA: RG 59, CD); at head of text: "The President of the U States"; endorsed by TJ as received 19 Feb. 1802 and so recorded in SJL. Enclosures not found.

FATE OF MY OFFICIAL SITUATION: for Bourne's concern about the future support of consular establishments, especially in Amsterdam, see Vol. 32:133 and Vol. 35:401-2.

For the LATE ADOPTED CONSTITUTION of the Batavian Republic, see Vol. 35:296, 297n.

From Henry Dearborn

SIR,   War Department 5th. December, 1801.

I take the liberty of suggesting, for your consideration, the propriety of proposing to Congress that provision be made for designating the boundary line between the United States, and the adjacent British possessions, in such manner as may prevent any disputes in future, from the out-let of Lake Ontario to Lake Superior, if not further. There are many valuable islands in the lakes and rivers, some of which are already inhabited, which are claimed on each side: it is to be presumed that the sooner the line is ascertained, the more easily all disputes will be settled.

From Mr. Tracy's report, and from information obtained from other sources, it appears that many disputes now exist, respecting titles to lands, at and about Detroit; as well between the United States and individuals, as between many of the Citizens, and also, between Citizens of the United States and subjects of Great Britain. Will it not be necessary for Congress to authorise the appointment of some board or tribunal for hearing and deciding these disputes?

May it not also be proper to remind Congress of the necessity of taking some measures for enabling this department to complete the issues of Land-warrants to the Officers and Soldiers of the late Army, or their Representatives, which has been prevented by the loss of papers, by fire, in autumn last?

All which is respectfully submitted.   H. DEARBORN

RC (DLC); in a clerk's hand, signed by Dearborn; at foot of text: "The President of the United States"; endorsed by TJ as received from the War Department on 7 Dec. and so recorded in SJL with notation "British boundary. Military lands"; also endorsed by TJ: "line with British possessions. lands for souldiers." FC (Lb in DNA: RG 107, LSP); in a clerk's hand. Tr (DNA: RG 233, PM, 7th Cong., 1st sess.); in Meriwether Lewis's hand, one word interlined by TJ to correct a copying error by Lewis; omits third and fourth paragraphs; endorsed by a clerk. Tr (DNA: RG 46, LPPM, 7th Cong., 1st sess.); in Lewis's hand; omits third and fourth paragraphs; endorsed by a clerk. Trs enclosed in TJ to the Sen-

ate and the House of Representatives, 2 Feb. 1802.

MR. TRACY'S REPORT: in 1800, Uriah Tracy received an appointment to examine army posts and the government's Indian trading stores in the Northwest Territory, on the Mississippi River, and on the frontiers of Tennessee and Georgia. Tracy fulfilled part of the mandate, inspecting the posts at Pittsburgh, Presque Isle, Niagara, Detroit, and Michilimackinac from June to November 1800 (Alexandria *Times; and District of Columbia Daily Advertiser*, 6 May 1802).

For the FIRE in the War Department offices in November 1800, see Vol. 32:435-6n.

From John Glendy

SIR   Baltimore Decbr. 5th. 1801.

I should deem myself lost to the best Emotions of the human heart, did I not seize with Avidity this flattering Opportunity of Addressing You, (thro' the medium of a dignified Citizen Genl. S. Smith) and acknowledging the debt of gratitude I owe You—Debt, beyond expression to calculate—Gratitude, too ardent to be concealed.

But I shall forbear to wound your refined Sensibility, either by venting the overflowings of a thankful heart, or yielding a Just tribute of praise to unexampled Merit.

Your kind and benevolent Recommendation, has raised me very high indeed, in the scale of public estimation, and given to an obscure Individual, personal, moral, and political consequence in this City. Here am I, exhibiting a trial of skill in sound Divinity, pure Rhetoric, and natural Elocution.—It is true, I carried wh. me my Cloak and parchments; but they shall not be left behind like Paul's at Troas—I wear my Cloak indeed, but neither to cover the defects of the Mind, or conceal the black traits of an ill heart—And tho' my parchments have no claim to the impress of Infallibility, yet I trust, they are not wholly devoid of some Sentiment & expression "point blank to the heart."

Shall I render thanksgiving to Heaven, and congratulate You Sir, on the general peace of Europe? Humanity bids me rejoice, while my heart bleeds for my devoted Country—Ah poor Erin! ill-fated Hibernia! much I fear thy chains are rivetted forever—Yet my Soul triumps in the persuasion, that it will have direct tendency to tranquillize your Administration. Party-spirit begins already to hide its hateful Head; whilst Aristocracy blushes as ashamed of the light.

Let them now felicitate each other on the issue of Billy Pitt's struggle for true Religion, social Order, and good Government.

You will have the goodness to pardon my boldness and Intrusion, in calling off for a fleeting instant your Attention from the momentous concerns of a Mighty Empire, over which, the smiling Providence of beneficent Heaven hath raised you to Rule in Wisdom & Equity.

That you may long live the darling of the People, the father of your Country, the firm friend, and resistless Advocate of civil and Religious Liberty, is not only the devout wish of my heart, but a primary Object in my Morning and evening sacrifice to the great God.

Believe me Sir with lively Gratitude and cordial Esteem, yours truly   JOHN GLENDY

N.B. I hope for the pleasure of seeing You on my return home.

RC (DLC); above postscript: "Thos. Jefferson Esquire"; endorsed by TJ as received 7 Dec. and so recorded in SJL.

John Glendy (1755-1832) was a Presbyterian clergyman. His "strikingly bold and beautiful" preaching style was very popular. One observer later remembered a Glendy sermon as "a perfect torrent of Irish eloquence." In September 1801, TJ called Glendy's pulpit oratory "unrivalled" and pronounced him "the most eloquent preacher of the living clergy." Glendy was "without exception the best preacher I ever heard," TJ later asserted to Thomas McKean. Born in the north of Ireland, Glendy attended the University of Glasgow, received ordination in the Presbyterian Church, and became a pastor in his native city of Londonderry. An enthusiast of the French Revolution and a partisan in the resistance to British rule in Ireland, Glendy was arrested for his role in the Irish insurgency of 1798, tried, and, like several other outspoken Presbyterian ministers, forced to emigrate. He arrived in Norfolk, Virginia, in 1799, and became

the minister of two congregations in Augusta County. In 1803, he moved to Baltimore to be the pastor of a newly formed congregation, the Second Presbyterian Church. He declined appointments as chaplain of the U.S. House of Representatives in December 1805 and the Senate in December 1816. He later received a doctor of divinity degree from the University of Maryland (William B. Sprague, *Annals of the American Pulpit or, Commemorative Notices of Distinguished American Clergymen of Various Denominations*, 6 vols. [New York, 1857-69], 4:229-37; Michael Durey, *Transatlantic Radicals and the Early American Republic* [Lawrence, Kans., 1997], 96, 138, 332n; David A. Wilson, *United Irishmen, United States: Immigrant Radicals in the Early Republic* [Ithaca, N.Y., 1998], 119-20; JHR, 5:188, 198; JS, 6:34, 50; Vol. 35:350-1; TJ to Thomas McKean, 3 Mch. 1805).

TRIAL OF SKILL: with TJ's encouragement, Glendy had gone to Baltimore in October 1801 in hope of succeeding Patrick Allison as minister of the city's

Presbyterian congregation. Other preachers who wanted the position included Washington McKnight, Archibald Alexander, and James Inglis, who proved to be the successful applicant (Sprague, *American Pulpit*, 4:231; Terry D. Bilhartz, *Urban Religion and the Second Great Awakening: Church and Society in Early National Baltimore* [Rutherford, N.J., 1986], 39-40; Vol. 35:350-1, 406-7, 426).

In the Bible, the apostle Paul asked Timothy to bring him items he had left at TROAS: a cloak, some books, and, in particular, his parchments (2 Tim. 4:13).

POINT BLANK TO THE HEART: in Laurence Sterne's comic novel *Tristram Shandy*, the vicar Yorick declares that he would "rather direct five words point blank to the heart" than communicate by means of a long, intellectual sermon (Laurence Sterne, *The Life and Opinions of Tristram Shandy, Gentleman: The Text*, ed. Melvyn New and Joan New, 3 vols. [Gainesville, Fla., 1978-84], 1:377).

ILL-FATED HIBERNIA: despite indications from William Pitt that the British government would allow some concessions to the Irish in return for the union of Ireland with Britain in January 1801, King George III refused to drop any restrictions on the primarily Catholic population of Ireland. With peace between Britain and France, the prospect of a French-backed Irish rebellion faded (John D. Grainger, *The Amiens Truce: Britain and Bonaparte, 1801-1803* [Rochester, N.Y., 2004], 20, 23-4).

To Gideon Granger

Dec. 5. 1801

Th: Jefferson presents his compliments to mr Granger and incloses him a letter from mr Lyon a printer of this city, a young man of bold republicanism in the worst of times, of good character, son of the persecuted Matthew Lyon. tho' of real genius, he has not succeeded in his newspapers, owing to his making them vehicles of other kinds of information, rather than of news, which is not within the general object in taking newspapers. in handing his character to mr Granger, Th:J. means to act only as a witness to enable him to judge among the candidates for his favor, which Th:J. wishes not to influence. he has written a line to mr Lyon asking him to name to him the tory printer who shares the public patronage. he is inclined to believe that an error. health & respect.

PrC (DLC): endorsed by TJ in ink on verso. Enclosure: Lyon to TJ, 2 Dec. 1801 (recorded in SJL as received 4 Dec. but not found).

From James Hall

SIR   Iredell County, N. Carolina, Decr. 5th. 1801

Permit me the honour of presenting to your Excellency a copy of a brief history of the Mississippi Territory, which I have lately published. The appendix will apologize for the brevity of the work.

It is not sent for any supposed degree of merit which it displays; but as my worthy friend, the Comptroller of the United States, informed me, that the history of the territory is but little known, even at the seat of government, I flatter myself that the transient view given in the work may afford to your Excellency some gratification.

Should the business of your very important station admit, your observations, as a naturalist, on my theory of hail would be highly desirable.

Permit me further to observe, that in Summer 1800, with the assistance of a coarse mechanic, I constructed, in a very crude manner, an instrument on astronomic principles, which promises to serve as a solar & lunar dial, and also as a solar compass, without the magnetic needle.

It has lien in Salisbury since Septr. 1800, together with a letter, containing a description of the instrument, addressed to your Excellency, as President of the American Philosophical Society. I have been strangely unfortunate in conveying it to Philadelphia. This I do not now expect before next Summer.

I would not have mentioned this matter, had I not been lately informed, that one of my pupils, to whom alone I developed the principles on which the instrument is constructed, has employed a finished workman to make another of the same kind.

I know not that the young man has any undue designs on the subject; but should the instrument be of any real advantage, which I think it may, if constructed with accuracy, it is hoped that government will admit of nothing, to the prejudice of the inventor.

Confiding therefore in your excellency, as a friend to science & the rights of men, should any undue measures be attempted, I will promise myself your patronage & influence as far as they may be necessary.

I am, Sir, your Excellency's most obedient and very humble servant,

JAS HALL.

RC (DLC); addressed: "His Excellency, Thomas Jefferson, President of the United States City of Washington"; endorsed by TJ as received 21 Dec. and so recorded in SJL. Enclosure: James Hall, *A Brief History of the Mississippi Territory, to Which is Prefixed, a Summary View of the Country Between the Settlements on Cumberland-River, & the Territory* (Salisbury, N.C., 1801); Sowerby, No. 4047.

Presbyterian minister James Hall

(1744-1826) was born in Pennsylvania. His family moved to North Carolina during his childhood. He studied under John Witherspoon at the College of New Jersey in Princeton, graduated in 1774, obtained a license to preach, and was ordained in 1778. He served congregations in North Carolina but also completed a number of missions. One of those journeys, under the auspices of the Presbyterian General Assembly, took him and two companions to the Mississippi Territory for several months in 1800-1801. Hall taught school and supported various educational institutions. For much of his career he was active in the Synod of the Carolinas and the Presbyterian General Assembly (Richard A. Harrison, *Princetonians, 1769-1775: A Biographical Dictionary* [Princeton, 1980], 386-91; DAB).

Hall explained in the APPENDIX to his work on the Mississippi Territory that his intention to write a longer book was curtailed when "the weight and diversity of my professional business obliged me to bring it into narrow bounds" (Hall, *Brief History of the Mississippi Territory*, 67).

COMPTROLLER: John Steele.

Hall's THEORY OF HAIL conjectured that hailstones formed when whirlwinds drew water vapor high into the air, where water droplets froze and increased in mass as they collected more ice on their fall to earth. He wrote an essay on the subject that Philadelphia clergyman Ashbel Green, a member of the American Philosophical Society, presented to the society in October 1794. Hall also outlined the idea in a footnote on pages 64-7 of his *Brief History of the Mississippi Territory*. Hall had an interest in natural philosophy, and in 1798, when the APS devoted attention to a mysterious stone wall uncovered in North Carolina, correspondence between Hall and Dr. James Woodhouse was one of the pieces of information the society received on the subject (APS, *Proceedings*, 22, pt. 3 [1884], 168, 225, 271; Vol. 31:317, 318n, 353n).

In a meeting on 16 July 1802, the APS received Hall's description and model of the astronomical INSTRUMENT. The de-vice had five dials, one of which was a SOLAR COMPASS for marking a course or running a line using the sun rather than a magnetic compass. The other dials related to positions and cycles of the sun, moon, and stars. In the early 1790s, Hall had sent a diagram of an early version of the instrument to Samuel Stanhope Smith at Princeton, who passed the information along to David Rittenhouse, and it was at Rittenhouse's suggestion that Hall incorporated a solar compass in the device. Hall confessed that the prototype he built of the mechanism was somewhat crude, having been constructed not by an instrument-maker but by Hall's combination of his own labor with that of a blacksmith, a wheelwright, and one of Hall's students. Hall's LETTER to TJ of 22 Sep. 1800, which described the instrument's development and included instructions for its use, is not recorded in SJL or endorsed by TJ. Hall may have conveyed both the letter and the model directly to the APS in Philadelphia in 1802. Fearful that someone might steal his ideas, Hall hoped that he might secure "the Copy-Right" to the instrument. After reviewing the device and its description, an APS committee reported that although the device showed "ingenuity," Hall's description of it did not merit publication in the society's *Transactions* (Hall to TJ, 22 Sep. 1800, RC in PPAmP, addressed: "The President of the American Philosophical Society Philadelphia" and "Care of the Honble John Steele," endorsed for the APS; APS, *Proceedings*, 22, pt. 3 [1884], 326, 328).

To James Lyon

Dec. 5. 1801

Th: Jefferson presents his compliments to mr Lyon and informs him that he has inclosed his letter to mr Granger, with such a statement of facts as may inform, without constraining, his judgment, which must be left entirely free in the disposal of the business of his department. Th:J. would thank mr Lyon for the name of the tory printer to whom he alludes as sharing the public patronage, & from what office he recieves it; being persuaded there must be a want of information somewhere on the subject.

PrC (DLC); endorsed by TJ in ink on verso.

LETTER TO MR GRANGER: see TJ to Granger, 5 Dec.

To Isaac Story

SIR   Washington Dec. 5. 1801.

Your favor of Oct. 27. was recieved some time since, and read with pleasure. it is not for me to pronounce on the hypothesis you present of a transmigration of souls from one body to another in certain cases. the laws of nature have witheld from us the means of physical knowlege of the country of spirits and revelation has, for reasons unknown to us, chosen to leave us in the dark as we were. when I was young I was fond of the speculations which seemed to promise some insight into that hidden country, but observing at length that they left me in the same ignorance in which they had found me, I have for very many years ceased to read or to think concerning them, and have reposed my head on that pillow of ignorance which a benevolent creator has made so soft for us, knowing how much we should be forced to use it. I have thought it better, by nourishing the good passions, & controuling the bad, to merit an inheritance in a state of being of which I can know so little, and to trust for the future to him who has been so good for the past. I percieve too that these speculations have with you been only the amusement of leisure hours; while your labours have been devoted to the education of your children, making them good members of society, to the instructing men in their duties, and performing the other offices of a large parish. I am happy in your approbation of the principles I avowed on entering on the government. ingenious minds, availing themselves of the imperfection of language, have tortured the expressions out of their plain meaning in order to infer departures from them in practice. if revealed language has not been able to guard itself against misinterpretations, I could not expect it. But if an 'administration quadrating with the obvious import of my language can conciliate the affections of my opposers' I will merit that conciliation. I pray you to accept assurances of my respect & best wishes   TH: JEFFERSON

PrC (DLC); at foot of text: "The revd. Isaac Story. Marblehead."

Story's letter of 27 Oct. enclosed a transcript of his essay, "The Metempsychosis doctrine, in a limited sense, defended," which presented his theory on the TRANSMIGRATION OF SOULS.

From "Philanthrophos"

MAY IT PLEASE YOUR EXCELLENCY
SIRE   [on or before 6 Dec. 1801]

I am so Happy, so exceedingly Rejoiced to hear, that your Excellency encourages the Publishing the "glad tidings of Glory to God in the highest, on Earth Peace, Goodwill to Men;" the Gospell of Righteousness, Peace & Joy in the Holy Ghost";—that I cannot easily resist the impulse that prompts me to send herewith—two small publications, which I hope will not unprofitably entertain your Excellency, some liesure half hour:—

Your Excellency will percieve; by the small detached one (in Reply to a *detached* Publication by Mr. Paine, his first part) that I am a sincere Friend to the Christian Religion, it's consolations & supports in various very trying Circumstances, and near prospect of Death, have been powerfully felt by thousands; and Gratitude binds me—in particular—to speak well of, & to recomend to the happy experience of my truly Beloved Bretheren of Mankind—what I clearly apprehend to be from the Great First Cause, and Donor of all Good, to whom I am so unspeakably indebted;—

That Your Excellency may long be a Blessing to Your Beloved Country, enjoying all possible hapiness here, & hapiness unmixed hereafter;—is the Cordial wish & prayer of

Your Exellency's most Respectfull most Obedient & very humble Servt.   PHILANTHROPHOS

P.S. No other Man on Earth knows that I have written the above}
3.3.3.

RC (DLC); undated; endorsed by TJ as received 6 Dec. and so recorded in SJL. Enclosures not found, but see below.

REPLY TO A DETACHED PUBLICATION BY MR. PAINE: this may refer to *A Reply to the False Reasoning in the "Age of Reason,"* a pamphlet published by "A Layman" in Philadelphia in 1796 and attributed to Philadelphia attorney and Quaker Miers Fisher. An unsigned note by the author on TJ's copy states: "In this first & small Essay, Brevity was consulted. Would the Infidells admitt of Scripture proof, it would probably have been three times the size; consistent with said Brevity. A plain & familiar Stile was also chosen, that it might be more generally usefull to those for whose perusall it was chiefly intended; The Author had not seen the 2d part of T. Paine's 'Age of Reason' when he wrote this—but that 2d part is fully answered,—and in a more Masterly manner by the Bp. of Landaff" (Sowerby, No. 1654; PMHB, 4:427-8). The reply by the Bishop of Llandaff referred to is Richard Watson's *An Apology for the Bible, in a Series of Letters, Addressed to Thomas Paine, Author of a Book Entitled, The Age of Reason, Part the Second, Being an Investigation of True and of Fabulous Theology* (Philadelphia, 1796; Sowerby, No. 1652; Vol. 32:190-1, 193n).

Bill to Establish a Government for the Territory of Columbia

I. DRAFT BILL, [BEFORE 7 DEC. 1801]

II. FROM JOHN THOMSON MASON, [7 DEC. 1801]

E D I T O R I A L   N O T E

The Residence Act of 1790 gave Congress until 1800, when the government moved to the Federal City, to decide what form its exclusive jurisdiction over the seat of the federal government, as enumerated in the U.S. Constitution, would take, or if the right would be exercised at all. In his 22 Nov. 1800 address to Congress, President Adams reminded the legislators "to consider whether the local powers over the district of Columbia" vested in them by the Constitution should be "immediately exercised." The Federalists in Congress decided in the affirmative. On 23 Jan. 1801, Henry Lee of Virginia introduced an encompassing bill for the "government of the District of Columbia," printed in the *National Intelligencer* on 30 Jan. It called for a bicameral legislature and a governor appointed by the president with the consent of the Senate. Voting by free, white male citizens was limited to those who were "seized of an estate for life," owned 10 acres of land within the district, or had a lot with a house built on it. Electors chosen by the voters would appoint the members of the district's senate. Fearing that there would not be enough time for the passage of Lee's plan or that it would be defeated, his colleagues, in the end, backed a more limited Senate bill. Approved 27 Feb. 1801, the "Act concerning the District of Columbia," later known as the Organic Act, divided the Federal District into Alexandria and Washington counties and set up a court system for both, to which the president appointed officers, including U.S. judges, a marshal and attorney, and justices of the peace (U.S. Statutes at Large, 1:130; 2:103-8; JS, 3:106-7; JHR, 3:771; JEP, 1:387-90; Kenneth R. Bowling and Donald R. Kennon, eds., *Establishing Congress: The Removal to Washingon, D.C., and the Election of 1800* [Athens, Ohio, 2005], ix-x, 39-55). For an analysis of Lee's bill and Federalist support for the congressional assumption of jurisdiction over the District of Columbia, see William C. diGiacomantonio, "'To Make Hay while the Sun Shines': D.C. Governance as an Episode in the Revolution of 1800," in same. For Republican arguments against assuming jurisdiction, see *Annals*, 10:868-9, 991-2, 996-7.

It is not clear when Jefferson began to draw up his own bill to establish a government for the Territory of Columbia, but before 7 Dec. he gave John Thomson Mason, U.S. attorney for the District of Columbia, a version of it to review and copy. On that day, Mason notified TJ that he had completed the task, making "some few alterations," which TJ evidently agreed with because they were incorporated into the bill (see Document II). Mason probably delivered the draft of the bill in his hand to a committee appointed by the House of Representatives on 8 Dec. "to inquire whether any, and, if any, what, alterations or amendments may be necessary in the existing Government and laws of the District of Columbia." Richard Sprigg, Jr., of Maryland

and Richard Brent of Virginia headed the seven-member committee. On 26 Jan. 1802, Sprigg presented a bill "for establishing the Government of the Territory of Columbia." Consisting of 15 sections, the bill closely followed TJ's draft, with many sections taken verbatim. The bill was published by the House of Representatives and appeared in the *National Intelligencer* on 5 Feb. On the same day Sprigg introduced the bill, however, the House received a memorial from the inhabitants of Alexandria concerning a "plan of government for the District of Columbia." They protested "that any scheme of a subordinate legislature and executive, by which the whole district shall be united under one and the same government, will be found inconvenient, disagreeable, injurious and expensive." The memorialists argued that the "diversity of the views and employments of the citizens of Georgetown, Washington and Alexandria, is so great, that no subordinate legislature can be expected to give general satisfaction; hence would arise much schism." When the House debated the bill on 29 Mch., Joseph H. Nicholson argued against it, noting that the expense of the proposed government "would prove very oppressive" and that the people of the district were "very generally averse to it." On that day the House voted to postpone consideration of the bill until the next session (JHR, 4:7, 70; *Annals*, 11:463, 1095-6; *A Bill, For establishing the Government of the Territory of Columbia* [Washington, D.C., 1802; Shaw-Shoemaker, No. 3222]; *Memorial and Remonstrance of Sundry Inhabitants of the County and Town of Alexandria, in the District of Columbia. 26th January, 1802* [Washington, D.C., 1802; Shaw-Shoemaker, No. 3333], 3-4).

Anxious that Congress would not pass the territorial bill for the District of Columbia, Mason in mid-March thought about introducing legislation confined to the city of Washington. Late in the session, Congress passed an act incorporating Washington, with a mayor appointed by the president and a 12-member council, divided into two chambers, "elected annually, by ballot, in a general ticket, by the free white male inhabitants of full age" who had resided in the city for 12 months and had paid taxes. TJ signed the legislation on 3 May 1802. On that day he also signed a bill that further defined the 1801 act concerning the District of Columbia, giving the circuit courts in Washington and Alexandria counties the power to proceed in common law and chancery causes and to grant licenses for businesses; appropriating funds to build a jail; empowering Georgetown to tax its residents for paving streets and other improvements; and authorizing the president to form, and appoint officers for, a militia in Washington and Alexandria counties (U.S. Statutes at Large, 2:193-7; Bryan, *National Capital,* 445-6; Mason to TJ, 14 Mch. 1802).

On 10 Feb. 1803, Virginia congressman Philip R. Thompson introduced another bill for "establishing the Government of the Territory of Columbia." While the measure still included several sections from TJ's draft bill, there were significant changes. The legislature included not one but two chambers, a senate and house of representatives, and the position of governor was eliminated, with the executive power instead "vested in the President of the United States." Eligibility requirements were added for candidates for office. The bill also included a section which restrained the legislature of the territory of Columbia "from passing any law for building a bridge or bridges over the Potomac river, or the Eastern branch, or from doing any other act or thing, which may in any way obstruct, impede, or injure the navigation of the said rivers." In the same section, the legislature was "restrained from passing any law to raise money from one county to make or repair roads, highways or bridges, in any other county but that from which such money" was levied. Instead of passing this bill, Congress, in February 1804, amended and extended the May 1802 act for the incorporation and governance of the city of Washington (JHR, 4:332; *A Bill For establishing the Government of the Territory of Columbia* [Washington, D.C., 1803; Shaw-Shoemaker, No. 5219]; U.S. Statutes at Large, 2:254-5).

I. Draft Bill

[before 7 Dec. 1801]

Be it enacted by the Senate & H. of R. of the US. in Congress assembled that The government of the territory of Columbia, (with a reservation of the Constitutional authority of Congress over the same) shall be exercised[1] in manner following

The powers of legislation shall be vested in a H. of representatives[2] to be chosen annually by the freemen citizens[3] of the sd territory in the separate counties or other divisions[4] into which they are or shall be laid off[5] each county or other division electing a number of representatives proportioned to the number of it's freemen,[6] according to a ratio to be established by the legislature from time to time. for which purpose a census of the freemen shall be taken in every bissextile year at least. and whensoever by an increase or decrease of the number of freemen the number of representatives shall exceed 75. or fall below 25. the existing ratio shall be altered by the legislature[7] so as to bring it within those limits.

Every free white male citizen[8] of the US. of full age residing within the territory and paying a tax to the same, or being a member of it's militia, shall be a freeman of the territory & after a year's residence in his town or division next preceding an election of represent shall be capable of electing or being elected a representative for the same.[9]

The H. of R. shall chuse it's own Speaker & other officers, and shall by law prescribe the time, places & manner of holding elections. it shall meet on the 1st[10] day of July, or if that be Sunday then on the next day[11] in every year after that of 1802,[12] and at other times on it's own adjmt or the call of it's Governor or of the Presidt. of the US. it shall be the judge of the qualification of it's own members, & a Majority shall constitute a Quorum to do business; but a small number may adjourn from day to day & may be authorized to compel the attendance of absent members in such manner & under such penalties as it may have provided. it may determine the rules of it's own proceedings, punish it's members for disorderly behavior, & with the concurrence of two thirds, expel a member. it shall keep a journal of it's proceedings, & from time to time publish the same; & the Yeas & Nays of the members on any question, shall, at the desire of one fifth of those present, be entered on the journal.

No compensation shall be allowed for their services until it shall have been[13] enacted into a law by one legislature, and repassed by a second legislature after the intervention of an election, which compensation so allowed[14] shall be payable out of the Treasury of the territory. they shall in all cases, except Treason, felony & breach of the peace, be privileged from arrest during their attendance at the session of their house, & in going to & returning from the same; & for any speech or debate therein,[15] they shall not be questioned in any other place. no representative shall during the time for which he was elected be appointed to any civil office:[16] and no person holding any office under the US. or the territory shall be a member of the sd house during his continuance in office.

Every bill shall, before it becomes a law, have passed the H. of R. at two several sessions, one month at least intervening between them, and at three several readings on three several days each: unless in the opinion of two thirds of the house the case be urgent; in which case the bill may be introduced at any time after the day of it's first passage, and proceed on to it's second passage. every bill, or resolution (excepting decisions on elections, or votes which respect the members or officers of the house & no others)[17] shall also, before it become a law or take effect be presented to the President of the US. if he approve, sign & return it within 10 days[18] it shall become a law; but if not, it shall not be a law. and in all cases & at all times the legislature of the US. shall have a power to repeal by law, but not to modify any law passed by the legislature of the territory.

The legislature of the territory shall have power[19] to pass all laws which the freemen of the territory might themselves pass of natural right & which are not restrained[20] from it by this act, nor from the states of the union by the constitution of the US.

The privilege of the writ of Hab. corp. shall not be suspended, unless when in cases of rebellion or invasion the public safety may require it. no bill of attainder or ex post facto law shall be passed. no money shall be drawn from the treasury but in consequence of appropriations made by law: and a regular statement & account of the reciepts & expenditures of all public money, shall be published from time to time.

The Executive power shall be vested in a Governor of the territory to be[21] nominated, & by & with the advice & consent of the Senate of the US. appointed & commissioned by the President of the US. or in case of his temporary inability, by a Lieutenant Governor to be nominated, appointed & commissioned in like manner & for each special occasion.

No person, except a freeman of the sd territory, who is now a citizen of the US. or shall be a natural born citizen,[22] and who shall have attained the age of 30. years shall be capable of[23] the office of governor or Lieutenant governor.

The Governor shall at stated times recieve for his services a compensation from the treasury of the territory[24] which shall[25] be fixed by the legislature at their first & second session in every bissextile[26] year, and shall be changed at no other time, and he shall not receive, while in office, any other emolument from the territory, or from the US. or any of them.

Before he enter on the execution of his office, he shall[27] solemnly swear or affirm that he will support the constn of the US. & faithfully execute the office of Governor of the territory of Columbia.

He shall be commander in chief of the militia of the sd territory, shall have power to grant reprieves & pardons for offences against the territory, and shall appoint & commission all officers of the territory, whose appointments are not herein otherwise provided for, and which shall be established by law. but the legislature may by law vest the appointment of any such[28] officers as they think proper, in other persons, themselves excepted.

He shall from time to time give to the H. of R. information of the state of the territory, & recommend to their consideration such measures as he shall judge necessary & expedient: he may on extraordinary occasions convene the H. of R. & shall take care that the laws be faithfully executed.

The judicial power shall be vested in such courts[29] as the legislature may from time to time ordain & establish.[30]

The judge or judges of the supreme court shall be nominated, & by & with the advice & consent of the Senate of the US. shall be appointed & commissioned by the President of the US. shall hold the sd office during[31] life, unless removed by the President of the US. on the application of two successive legislatures between which an election shall have intervened.[32] they shall at stated times recieve from the treasury of the territory[33] a compensation for service which shall not be diminished during the sd term.

No[34] person shall be held to answer for a capital or otherwise infamous crime, unless on a presentment or indictmt of a grand jury, except in the militia when in actual service in time of war or public danger; nor shall any person be subject for the same offence to be twice put in jeopardy of life or limb; nor shall be compelled in any criminal case to be witness against himself, nor be deprived of life, liberty or property without due process of law; nor shall private property be taken for public use without just compensation.

In all criminal prosecutions, the accused shall enjoy the right to a speedy & public trial, by an impartial jury of the vicinage, and to be informed of the nature & cause of the accusation; to be confronted with the witnesses against him; to have compulsory process for obtaining witnesses in his favor & to have the assistance of counsel for his defence.

In suits at common law, where the value in controversy shall exceed 20. Dollars, the right of trial by jury shall be preserved.[35]

Excessive bail shall not be required, nor excessive fines imposed nor cruel & unusual punishment inflicted.

No law shall be made respecting an establishment of Religion, or prohibiting the free exercise thereof; or abridging the freedom of speech, or of the press, otherwise than by a liability to private action for falsehood in point of facts;[36] or abridging[37] the right of the people peaceably to assemble, & to petition for a redress of grievances. nor shall the right of the people to keep & bear arms be infringed; nor shall a souldier, in time of peace be quartered in any house without the consent of the owner, nor in time of war, but in a manner to be prescribed by law.   The right of the people to be secure in their persons, houses, papers & effects, against unreasonable searches & seizures, shall not be violated, & no warrants shall issue, but upon probable cause, supported by oath or affirmation, & particularly describing the place to be searched, & the persons or things to be seized.

And for carrying this government into effect, be it further enacted that the Marshal of[38] the sd territory by himself or his deputies shall cause to be assembled on the 1st. Monday in January next at the usual place of holding the court of their respective counties all the free white male inhabitants of 21 years of age, citizens of the US. who shall have resided one whole year then last past in the sd territory, then & there to chuse 15. representatives for their county, qualified as themselves,[39] and to make return thereof to the Presidt. of the US. which sd representatives shall on the 30th. day after their election meet at such place in the city of Washington as the President of the US. shall direct, then & there to hold their first session: one calendar month after the end of which first session, they shall meet at the same place, or any other to which they shall have adjourned to hold their 2d. session: ten days after the end of which 2d. session the present government of the said territory, & all offices & authorities exercised under it shall cease; and so much of all acts of Congress as authorized the organization or appointments now existing shall stand repealed: and that the sd legislature shall make provision for taking a census of the persons qualified as freemen by this act, and for the election of a new house [of re]presentatives according to the same to be assembled on or before the 1st day of October next, at which time [the office of those] first chosen shall cease; & that the[40] governor first to be appointed shall recieve until the first bissextile year a compensation of 2500. D. to be paid out of monies which shall be provided for that purpose by the legislature, after which time his salary shall be regulated by law as herein before provided.

Dft (DLC: TJ Papers, 232:42012-13); torn; entirely in TJ's hand, with a wide margin for revisions; undated, but see Document II; at head of text: "An act for establishing the Government of the territory of Columbia"; endorsed by TJ: "[Columbia]."

NUMBER OF REPRESENTATIVES: in the bill brought before the House on 26 Jan., blanks were substituted for TJ's figures of "75" and "25." EVERY BISSEXTILE YEAR: see Document II. BEING A MEMBER OF IT'S MILITIA: the House bill did not include this means to qualify to vote. The House bill also left blanks where TJ specified the 1ST DAY OF JULY and the year 1802 (*A Bill, For establishing the Government of the Territory of Columbia* [Washington, D.C., 1802], 1-2).

APPOINTED TO ANY CIVIL OFFICE: the 26 Jan. House bill followed TJ's language against holding any other government office while serving as a legislator, but excepted "that of justice of the peace or in the militia" (same, 3).

IT SHALL NOT BE A LAW: the House bill gave the territorial legislature the power to reconsider and override the president's decision. According to the bill, "if after such reconsideration, two thirds of the House shall agree to pass the bill, it shall

become a law." The names of the persons voting for and against the bill were to be "entered on their journal" (same, 4).

In the House bill the JUDICIAL POWER was vested "in the present existing court, a court of chancery, and such other inferior courts as the legislature may from time to time ordain and establish." The House bill included TJ's process by which the JUDGE OR JUDGES OF THE SUPREME COURT could be removed. Instead of compensation through the territorial treasury, the House bill called for payment through the "treasury of the United States" (same, 6-7).

CARRYING THIS GOVERNMENT INTO EFFECT: here the 26 Jan. bill departed from TJ's text. A section on taxation was added, including a clause "That the country parts of the said territory shall not be taxed for buildings, improvements or accommodations in any town or city," nor should one town be taxed for improvements in another, except for accommodations for the territorial government. The House bill also called for dividing the territory into three electoral divisions, the two divisions east of the Potomac River to elect seven representatives each and the third division consisting of the territory west of the Potomac to elect eleven representatives. While TJ specified that TEN DAYS AFTER THE END of the second legislative session the PRESENT GOVERNMENT of the territory should cease, the House bill left the number of days blank and excepted the "judges of the present existing court." SHALL STAND REPEALED: here the House bill added "save only that the corporations and charters, existing under the laws of Virginia and Maryland, shall remain in force, but subject to such alterations as the legislature of the territory shall at any time make by law" (same, 8-10).

[1] Word interlined in place of "administered."

[2] TJ here interlined and canceled "*consisting of persons* freemen."

[3] TJ first wrote "to be chosen by the freemen" before altering the passage to read as above.

[4] TJ first wrote "separate towns or counties" before altering the phrase to read as above, and later in the sentence he changed "each town or county" to "each county or other division."

[5] Remainder of paragraph interlined and inserted in margin in place of "and according to the numbers of freemen in each as nearly as fractions will permit," with which TJ originally concluded the paragraph.

[6] TJ first wrote "electing one member for every hundred freemen it contains" before altering the passage to read as above.

[7] TJ here canceled "of the US."

[8] TJ first wrote "Every male person."

[9] Paragraph interlined in place of "Every person capable of electing shall be capable of being elected."

[10] Ordinal written over a dash.

[11] Preceding eight words interlined.

[12] Preceding three words and year interlined.

[13] TJ interlined the passage that follows, from "enacted" through "election," in place of "voted by a majority of the freemen assembling on legal call, & in the form of a law prepared & passed by the legislature and presented under their authority to the freemen."

[14] Preceding two words interlined.

[15] Word interlined in place of "in either house."

[16] TJ here canceled before the colon: "which shall have been created by the legislature, or the emoluments whereof shall have been increased during such time."

[17] Sentence to this point interlined in place of "nor shall it it"; TJ first wrote "(except in cases of adjournment & of decisions on elections)" before altering that text to read as above.

[18] TJ first wrote "he shall sign it; but if not" before altering the passage to read as above.

[19] TJ here canceled "to do every act of."

[20] Remainder of paragraph interlined in place of "by the constitution of the US. or by this act."

[21] TJ here canceled "named & commissioned by the President of the US."

[22] TJ first began the paragraph "No person, except a natural born citizen" before altering the passage to read as above.

[23] Preceding two words interlined in place of "appointable to."

[24] Preceding six words interlined.

[25] TJ here canceled "neither be increased nor diminished during his continuance in office, or during the space of years from his entrance into be determined."

[26] Word interlined in place of "leap."

[27] TJ here canceled "take the."

[28] Preceding two words interlined in place of "such inferior."

[29] TJ first wrote "in one supreme court and in such inferior courts" before altering it to read as above.

[30] TJ here continued "the *judge or judges* both of the supreme & inferior courts shall hold their offices during the term of years, and" before making minor alterations and then canceling the passage.

[31] TJ interlined the remainder of the sentence in place of "the term of four years."

[32] Within his interlineation TJ here canceled "and voting by a majority of two thirds of the members present."

[33] Preceding six words interlined.

[34] TJ began this paragraph "*The trial of all.*"

[35] TJ here canceled "& no fact, tried by a jury, shall be otherwise re-examined,

than according to the rules of the common law." He wrote the remainder of the document's text in the margins.

[36] TJ first wrote "a liability for false facts" before altering the passage to read as above.

[37] Word interlined.

[38] Two words interlined in place of "sheriffs of Washington & Alexandria counties in."

[39] Two words interlined in place of "in like manner."

[40] TJ here canceled "[census] so taken shall [. . .]."

II. From John Thomson Mason

DEAR SIR   Monday morning [7 Dec. 1801]

In the copy I have prepared some few alterations are made which I beg leave to submit to you before it goes out of my hands

Instead of Bissextile read "every fourth year" if it stands bissextile will it not be confined to what is commonly called Leap year? if so it would involve us in difficulty as to the commencement of the election for Governor &c. Cowels Interpreter thus defines it "Bissextile   Bissextiles vulgarly called leap year, because the sixth day before the Calends of March is twice reckoned viz on the 24th & 25th of February: so that the Bissextile year hath one day more than other years, and happens every fourth year."

In the 4th clause including the preamble but excluding the title read after the word quallification "and due election" without this addition I do not see that any authority is given them to judge of the due election of their own members, which I presume it was intended they should have.

at the end of the 4th clause limitting executive powers add "And the Lieutenant Governor in case one be appointed shall before he enters upon the execution of his office solemnly swear or affirm in like manner" Unless this be added there is no provision for placing him under the obligation of an Oath of Office

I think as the Executive of the U.S. appoints the Governor the U.S. ought to pay him. I think Congress would consent to do so. I wish you would think of this

I am so unwell today that I have been compelled to take Medicine and cannot go to the Capitol this morning, but I shall be able I believe and will certainly be there in the morning of tomorrow

With great respect yours   J. T. MASON

RC (DLC); partially dated; endorsed by TJ as received 7 Dec. and so recorded in SJL.

TJ had two editions of John Cowell's

INTERPRETER, a law dictionary, one edited by Thomas Manley and published in London in 1672, the other edited by White Kennett and published there in 1708 (see Sowerby, Nos. 1812, 1813).

The bill presented to the House on 26 Jan. incorporated Mason's language and "bissextile" does not appear in it (*A Bill, For establishing the Government for the Territory of Columbia* [Washington, D.C., 1802], 2).

DUE ELECTION: the third section of the bill for the Territory of Columbia included the passage that elected members of the House of Representatives would be the "judge of the qualifications and due election of its own members." The House bill included a passage on the oath of office for the LIEUTENANT GOVERNOR with the wording recommended by Mason. U.S. OUGHT TO PAY HIM: in the 26 Jan. bill, the governor received his salary from the U.S. Treasury (same, 5-6).

From Tench Coxe

[before 7 Dec. 1801]

British private Vessels.

The important and curious document, in this inclosure, appears to be well adapted to the use of the government of the U.S. It exhibits the whole of the private British Shipping owned in Great Britain, proper, & Ireland, exclusively of the Colonies, in August 1801. also their actual employment or situation. There are 124 pages at about 80 on a page giving 9920 Vessels. They are supposed to average more than 200 Tons, which will give about two Millions of Tons of actual shipping, defended by a navy as in the last 15 pages, and expenditures, from 14 to 18 millions Sterling ℔ Annum.

The opportunities of Commerce may be collected by a clerkship that should digest, columnwise, all in the different trades aggregately, and perhaps it might be worth the money.

There can be no doubt, that Great Britain will struggle hard to maintain herself in the trades, which have employed this vast body of shipping: and no hint more important is given by this Document than the inducements she has to maintain her navigation system. Her duties must give her much of the carriage from this country of our own produce. A British Ship has lately been taken up in Philada. to carry our cotton to England by a friend of mine, who owns ten vessels of the U.S. The sole reason is the British duty on Cotton in our ships of about 75 pence Sterling, I think, ℔ 100 ℔s. A vessel, *in peace*, laden with pot & pearl ashes, bees wax, pig iron, indigo, and tobacco as far as one half or two thirds could carry cotton in and on her at that rate ℔ 100 ℔s.

The conflicts with foreigners in consequence of a navigation system, the possible effects of our navigation system on some articles of our produce, the necessity for navy, which a great Tonne.[1] produces, the discontents of the merchants, if navigation shall not be

encouraged, the discontents of some of the states under such circumstances, the injuries to our navigation & insults to our flag, if we
should have no navy, and many other relative circumstances demand
consideration in adopting our line of conduct. Are we to pursue
additions to our present System,—or are we to repeal it and adopt a
navigation system uniform, consistent & de novo—or are we to
decline a navigation system by the repeal of all regulations of that
nature, only leaving our present system, merely, in operation? These
are Momentous objects for our government in all its parts.

MS (DNA: RG 59, LAR); undated; in Tench Coxe's hand; endorsed by TJ as received 7 Dec. and "Tench Coxe Anon" and so recorded in SJL. Enclosure not found.

[1] That is, "tonnage."

Henry Dearborn's Plan for Reorganizing the Army

[7 Dec. 1801]

Proposed Military Peace Establishment.

List of Posts and the Force proposed for each.

Names of Posts	In what State, &ca.	No. of Comps of Artillery	No of Comps of Infantry
Michilimackinac	North Western Territory	1	1
Detroit	Dit to	1	4
Niagara	New York	1	1
Fort Wayne	North Western Territory		1
Pittsburgh & Cincinnati	Pennsylvania & N.W. Terry.		1
St. Vincennes	Indiana Territory		1
Fort Massac	near the mouth of the Ohio		1
Southwest Point, &ca.	Tennessee	1	2
Chickasaw Bluffs	On the Mississippi	1	
Fort Adams	On Ditto—near the Spanish Boundary	1	4
Fort	On the Mobile river, near the Spanish Boundary }		1
Fort Green, Fort Wilkinson & (say) Cumberland Island }	Georgia	1	3
Fort Moultrie, &ca. & Fort Johnston	South Carolina & North Carolina	2	
Forts Norfolk, &ca. & Fort McHenry	Virginia & Maryland	2	

Fort Mifflin & the Arsenal	near Philadelphia, Pennsylva.	2	
Fort Jay & Westpoint	New York	2	
Fort Wolcott & Fort Trumbull	Rhode Island & Connecticut	2	
Fort Independence, and Magazine at Springfield	Massachusetts	2	
Fort Constitution and Fort	New Hampshire & District of Maine	1	
Total.		20	20

Twenty Companies of Artillery, and
Twenty Companies of Infantry.

Organization of the proposed Military Peace Establishment.
One Regiment of Artillery, to consist of

    1 Colonel,
    1 Lieutenant Colonel,
    4 Majors,
    4 Teachers of Music,

and 20 Companies, each to consist of

    1 Captain,
    1 First Lieutenant,
    1 Second Lieutenant,
    2 Cadets,
    4 Sergeants,
    4 Corporals,
    4 Musicians,
    8 Artificers and
   56 Privates.

Total—Artillery—Non-Commissioned Officers, Musicians, Artificers and Privates—(exclusive of Cadets.)—1,524.

Two Regiments of Infantry, to consist of, each,

    1 Colonel,
    1 Lieutenant Colonel,
    1 Major,
    1 Adjutant,
    1 Quarter Master,
    1 Sergeant Major,
    1 Quarter Master Sergeant,
    2 Teachers of Music,

and 10 Companies, each to consist of

    1 Captain,

1 First Lieutenant,
1 Second Lieutenant,
1 Ensign,
4 Sergeants,
4 Corporals,
4 Musicians, and
64 Privates.

Total—Infantry—Non Commissioned Officers, Musicians
and privates   1,528
Total Artillery   (as above)   1,524
                                                              3,052

Total Artillery and Infantry, exclusive of Commissioned Officers and Cadets, Three Thousand and fifty two.

Commissioned Officers and Cadets, One hundred & ninety two.

Total—Artillery and Infantry—Three Thousand, two hundred and forty four.

Adjutants and Quarter Masters to be taken from the line.

In addition to the foregoing, a Corps of Engineers, organized as follows, is proposed, viz;

1 principal Engineer, with the rank, pay & emoluments of a Major;
2 Assistant Engineers, with the rank, pay & emoluments of Captains;
2 other Assistants, with the rank, pay & emoluments of First Lieutenants;
2 other Assistants, with the rank, pay & emoluments of Second Lieutenants;
10 Cadets, with the pay of 16 Dollars ℔ month & two Rations ℔ Day.

The Corps to be so organized by law as to admit of the promotion of the principal Engineer to the rank, pay & emoluments of a Lieutenant-Colonel, and thence to those of a Colonel; and of the promotion of the several Assistants and Cadets to the several grades before mentioned: which promotions should be made by the President of the United States, with a view to particular merit, and without regard to original rank. Those with the rank of Field-Officers to be called Engineers, and the other Officers Assistant Engineers. The Corps, in time of peace to be restricted to, at most, 1 Colonel, 1 Lieutenant Colonel, 2 Majors, 4 Captains, 4 First Lieutenants, 4 Second Lieutenants & 4 Cadets.

This Corps to be stationed generally at the Military Academy at Westpoint, subject to the orders of the President of the United States.

The principal Engineer, and, in his absence, the next in rank, to have the superintendance of the Military School, under the direction of the President of the United States.

The foregoing plans contemplate the appointments of Surgeons and Mates to Posts, and not to Regiments; and the appointments of Paymasters to Districts and not to particular Corps. There should be a Surgeon or Mate to each post, and the pay-districts may be six—the Paymasters to be stationed as follows. viz:

One at Detroit—to pay the troops at that post, at Niagara, at Michilimackinac and Fort Wayne—and to have an Assistant to reside at Michilimackinac.

One at Fort Adams—to pay the troops on the Mississippi & Mobile, and to have an Assistant to reside on the Ohio.

One at Savannah—to pay the troops in Georgia and South Carolina.

One at Fort McHenry, near Baltimore—to pay the troops at that post, at Norfolk and at Philadelphia.

One at New York—to pay the troops at that place, at Westpoint, in Connecticut & Rhode Island.

One at Boston—to pay the troops in Massachusetts, including the District of Maine, and in New Hampshire.

The Troops in Tennessee may be paid by the Agent of the War Department resident in that state, and those in North-Carolina, by an Assistant stationed there.

The Paymaster of the Army to be authorised to appoint, with the Consent of the President of the United States, the several Paymasters and Assistants, taking sufficient security for their faithful performance of their duties. The Paymasters & their Assistants to have charge of, and account for all Clothing delivered to the troops within their respective districts.

At each post, one of the Officers should do the duty of Assistant Military Agent, as a substitute for an Assistant of the Quarter Master General's Department; for which service he should be allowed, say, from eight to twelve Dollars ℔ month extra, according to the number of troops at each post.

The whole of the troops to be mustered and inspected, at least once in every year, and more frequently when practicable, by the Commanding Field-Officers of the respective Pay Districts, for which service and the extra expences attending the performance of it, those Officers should receive a reasonable compensation; it should also be their duty to examine all muster and pay-rolls made by other Officers in their absence, and report any errors which may be discovered to the Paymaster of the Army. All musters & inspections, not made as above, should be made by the Commanding Officers of the respective posts, and when not made by a Field-Officer, the pay-rolls certified by such commanding Officer, should be also certified by the Surgeon or Surgeon's Mate at the Post.

From the dispersed situation of the troops, and the various and distant directions in which their supplies are necessarily to be conveyed, a Quarter Master General can be of but little use, compared with the duties which such an Officer is expected to perform, with an Army in the field: it is therefore proposed to substitute, say, three Military Agents, whose duty it shall be to receive and forward all military stores and other articles, not only for the troops in their respective Departments, but also, all goods, annuities, &ca. for the Indians, and to account annually with the Department of War, for all property which may pass through their hands, and for all monies which they shall expend.—One of these Agents should reside either at New York, Albany or Schenectady; one at Philadelphia, and one at Savannah in Georgia: the pay of each of them to be equal to the pay and emoluments, say, of a Major in the Army, and bonds should be given for their faithful performance of their duties.

It will be proper to make the Officers, who may be appointed Assistant Military Agents at Pittsburgh and Niagara, a greater additional compensation for the duties which they will have to perform as such, than is above recommended to be made to the like officers at the posts generally.

The establishment, proposed above, contemplates the appointment of one General Officer, with one or two Aids de Camp, and one detail Officer, who may be designated as Adjutant & Inspector of the Army: the Aids de Camp to be taken from the line of Captains or Subalterns, and the Adjutant & Inspector from the line of Field-Officers.

The General and the Adjutant & Inspector should reside at such central position, as would best enable them to communicate with the Government and the different posts. The General should be allowed such pay ₩ month, as will be sufficient, without any other such emoluments as rations, forage, quarter master's stores, &ca. &ca. except Stationary—by which means all disputes in settling his accounts would be avoided.

The Adjutant and Inspector should receive   dollars ₩ month, in addition to his pay and emoluments in the line, and no other emoluments, except Stationary.

The Aid de Camp should be allowed   dollars ₩ month, in addition to his pay in the line.

The Paymaster of the Army should reside at or near the seat of Government, and should have a certain monthly pay, without any emoluments.

It may be advisable to allow the General, the Pay-master, and the Adjutant and Inspector to frank their public letters.

MS (DLC); in a clerk's hand; undated; endorsed by TJ as received from the War Department on 7 Dec. and "Military establishmt."

Dearborn sent a copy of the first element of this document, the table containing the LIST OF POSTS with the number of companies allocated to each garrison, to the House of Representatives on 23 Dec. 1801. That version of the table was titled "Estimate of all the Posts and Stations where Garrisons will be expedient, and of the number of men required for each garrison." A note at the foot of the table stated that each of the 20 companies of infantry and 20 companies of artillery would consist of 76 men, not counting commissioned officers and cadets (MS in DNA: RG 233, RCSH, 7th Cong., 1st sess., in a clerk's hand, signed by Dearborn; ASP, *Military Affairs*, 1:156). At some point TJ received another copy of the table. That version, titled "A proposed Military, Peace establishment," designated the company at Massac to be artillery rather than infantry, and showed all three companies at Southwest Point to be infantry. According to that table, each company would have 72 rank and file (MS in DLC: TJ Papers, 119:20553; in a clerk's hand).

Also on 23 Dec., Dearborn transmitted to the House of Representatives "A General Return of the Army of the United States" in tabular form, prepared by the army's inspector, Major Thomas H. Cushing. The return showed the numbers of officers and enlisted men of each rank, and the numbers called for by the existing organization of the army. According to that report, which was dated 19 Dec., the army consisted of 4,051 officers and men, some 1,384 less than the authorized number of 5,438. The return included two troops of dismounted cavalry, two regiments of artillerists and engineers, and four regiments of infantry (DNA: RG 233, RCSH, 7th Cong., 1st sess.; ASP, *Military Affairs*, 1:155). In TJ's papers there is a "Disposition proposed for the Artillerists and Engineers, 1801," showing the locations of 32 companies making up two regiments of artillerists and engineers. TJ also received an undated "Return of the present Military Establishment of the United States complete," which was probably from 1801 since it is in the same handwriting as the "Disposition," and, like the return that Dearborn sent to the House in December, accounted for two troops of cavalry, two regiments of artillery, and four regiments of infantry. The undated return, which reported the potential size of the army rather than numbers of men actually in service, showed an aggregate number of 5,598 officers and enlisted men (DLC: TJ Papers, 119:20554, 20558; in a clerk's hand).

Jonathan Williams called on Dearborn early in December 1801 and found the secretary of war "fully occupied" with the plan for the organization of the army's "Peace Establishment." Dearborn shared the details of the proposal with Williams but asked him to keep the plan secret. TJ broached the subject of a reduction of the size of the army in his annual message, and on 22 Dec. the House of Representatives passed a resolution asking the secretary of war for "a statement of the present Military establishment; together with an estimate of all the posts and stations where garrisons will be expedient, and of the number of men requisite for each garrison." Dearborn's transmittal of the "Estimate of all the Posts" and the "General Return of the Army" to the House on 23 Dec. was in response to that resolution. The promptness of his response, and the similarity of the resolution's specifications to documents he already had on hand, imply that he and TJ had been expecting the resolution. The House received the documents on 24 Dec., and on the 30th passed a resolution declaring that it was "expedient to reduce the Military establishment of the United States." Dearborn privately conveyed the army reorganization plan to Congressman Joseph B. Varnum, who was on the committee. Reporting for the committee on 11 Jan. 1802, Varnum introduced a bill founded on Dearborn's prospectus. The "Act fixing the military peace establishment of the United States" became law on 16 Mch. (Crackel, *Mr. Jefferson's Army*, 40-3; JHR, 4:24, 26, 28-9, 45; Dearborn to the speaker of the House, 23 Dec. 1801, in DNA: RG 233, RCSH, 7th Cong., 1st sess.; U.S. Statutes at Large, 2:132-7).

The act of 16 Mch. followed the plan printed above with regard to the size and organization of the army, calling for one REGIMENT OF ARTILLERY and two infantry regiments of the sizes indicated by Dearborn's proposal. The act omitted any provision for TEACHERS OF MUSIC in the artillery regiment and called for that regi-ment to have an adjutant. There would be no quartermaster general, regimental quartermasters, or quartermaster sergeants. The statute authorized the president to establish a CORPS OF ENGINEERS with officers and cadets of the ranks listed in Dearborn's plan. The army would have two SURGEONS and 25 surgeons' mates, "to be attached to garrisons or posts, and not to corps." Seven PAYMASTERS and two assistant paymasters, under a PAYMASTER OF THE ARMY, would be appointed from the ranks of the army's commissioned officers and "attached to such districts as the President of the United States shall direct." Mirroring Dearborn's proposal, the law called for THREE MILITARY AGENTS along with assistant agents at the posts. Under the act, the army would have ONE GENERAL OFFICER, a brigadier, supported by an aide-de-camp and another officer acting as both adjutant and inspector. Those two officers of the general's staff were to have the ranks indicated by the secretary's plan (U.S. Statutes at Large, 2:133, 137).

From Albert Gallatin

DEAR SIR   Decem. 7th. 1801

I have not been at the office these three days, having found that I would be less interrupted here than there in finishing & correcting statements &a. — Mr. Jones writes me that you had requested by your Secretary to be furnished this forenoon with copies of the papers preparing to be submitted to Congress.

Exclusively of five distinct reports on tonnage, exports, and importations which by sundry resolutions are to be laid before Congress during the session, and which (all the returns not being yet received,) cannot be transmitted till sometime in January, there are three reports intended to be made at the commencement of the session vizt. 1st Estimate of appropriations for next year including summary statement of expenditures of last year—This after having received sundry corrections & alterations is now in the hand of the Register, by whom it must be signed, and who has promised it for Wednesday. To have it transcribed in full would delay its transmission at least two days. It is in fact a mere form, and the alterations I have made are only in the arrangement and not in the sums. For that estimate is always compiled from those sent by the other Departments. I think that if it is sent to you, before it goes to Congress, it will answer every end—

2d. Receipts & Expenditures of 1800—This is printed, one table excepted, which is now printing. I write to the Register to send you a copy—This is only an abstract from the register's books, and as it relates to last year—I only transmit it without any alteration from the usual form. The Register has promised it for Thursday

3d. My own report under the law of 1800—In this I have been obliged to do so much of the clerks work & correct so many details, that the tables in relation to it are not yet transcribed. This report with all its tables, is intended of course, to be submitted to you before it is transmitted to Congress. And that will not be before Monday next. For the report of the Commissr. of the revenue was not transmitted till Saturday and I could not prepare that part which relates to the internal revenues without it. He had indeed offered to make his report earlier; but I wanted it as complete as possible, and by waiting till Saturday we obtained the actual returns from Kentucky, which, before, we had only an estimate—I must add that as the two other reports go this week [and] I do not wish them to be blended with [my report] I had concluded all along not to transmit this last till the second week of the session—

With sincere respect Your most obt. Servt

ALBERT GALLATIN

RC (DLC); torn at seal; addressed: "The President of the United States"; endorsed by TJ as received from the Treasury Department on 7 Dec. and "documents for Congress" and so recorded in SJL.

On 14 Dec., the House of Representatives received the ESTIMATE OF APPROPRIATIONS for 1802 and the SUMMARY STATEMENT OF EXPENDITURES for 1 Oct. 1800 to 30 Sep. 1801 from the Treasury Department and referred it to the Committee of Ways and Means the same day. Joseph Nourse, the REGISTER of the Treasury, signed the documents on Saturday, 11 Dec. (MS in DNA: RG 233, RCSH, 7th Cong., 1st sess.). Gallatin wrote the transmittal letter to the speaker of the House the next day (RC in same; in a clerk's hand, signed by Gallatin). The documents, printed by an order of the House, became a 91-page

pamphlet entitled *Letter and Report from the Secretary of the Treasury, Accompanied with Estimates of the Sums Necessary to be Appropriated for the Service of the Year One Thousand Eight Hundred and Two; Also, A Statement of the Receipts and Expenditures at the Treasury of the United States, for One Year, Preceding the first day of October, one thousand eight hundred and one* (Washington, D.C., 1801; see Shaw-Shoemaker, No. 1493). Gallatin recommended appropriations of $564,235 for the civil list; $283,564.26 for miscellaneous expenses, including $93,000 for military pensions and almost $45,000 for lighthouses "and other establishments for the security of navigation"; $132,116.67 for intercourse with foreign nations; $1,366,840.68 for the War Department, including $60,750 for Indian affairs; and $1,101,390.57 for the Navy; for a total appropriation of $3,448,147.18 (same, 5-7).

SEND YOU A COPY: on 8 Dec., Nourse wrote TJ from the Register's Office, indicating that at Gallatin's suggestion he was sending a copy of the receipts and expenditures for 1800 (RC in DLC; in a clerk's hand, signed by Nourse; at foot of text: "The President of the United States"; endorsed by TJ as received from the Treasury Department on 8 Dec. and "Receipts & Expenditures" and so recorded in SJL). In that letter, Nourse may have enclosed a copy of his letter to Gallatin of the same date, transmitting the same account to the Treasury secretary and explaining that "The tables in relation to the Imports & Tonnage, and of the internal revenues for the year 1800

are in a course of preparation. Only a sufficient number for the immediate use of the Legislature have been prepared in the present form, the residuary copies with the tables will be transmitted as early as possible" (Tr in same; in a clerk's hand, signed by Nourse; at head of text: "Copy"). This document, presented to the House of Representatives on 9 Dec., and the transmittal letters from the Treasury secretary and Nourse have not been found (JHR, 4:12).

MY OWN REPORT: see Gallatin to TJ, 13 Dec.

COMMISSR. OF THE REVENUE: William Miller.

From Horatio Gates

DEAR SIR   New York 7th. Decemr. 1801:—

To relieve your[1] mind from the Fatigue of National Affairs, which must necessarily oppress it; I send you the inclosed from the pen of my ingenious friend, & relation, John Garnet; I take this Liberty, knowing how much you wish to be early acquainted with all Discoveries tending to Enlighten Mankind.—perhaps it may be the means of bringing two Men of Science to an intimate acquaintance;—Mr: Garnet has a Farm, about a Mile West of Brunswick, in Jersey; where he is indulging his passion for Agriculture, and his rage for Science; His means are happily more than adequate to all his pursuits; so if you should hereafter add one to your Scientific acquaintance, you will not increase your Number of Official Expectants—Go on as you have begun, and United America will bless the hour when they placed Power in your Hands—Mrs: Gates presents you her Compliments. I trust you will always believe me your Sincere Friend, and Obedient Servant,   HORATIO GATES.

RC (DLC); at foot of text: "His Excellency Thomas Jefferson"; endorsed by TJ. Recorded in SJL as received 10 Dec. Enclosure: probably John Garnett, *A Plain and Concise Projection for Clearing the Lunar Distances from the Effects of Parallax and Refraction* (New Brunswick, N.J., 1801; see Sowerby, No. 3778).

FRIEND, & RELATION: Gates in 1798

had introduced John Garnett as his cousin (Vol. 30:110-11). HIS RAGE FOR SCIENCE: on 1 May 1801, the American Philosophical Society acknowledged receiving a paper from Garnett, with the same title as the enclosure listed above. It became part of a longer work, which was also published in New Brunswick in 1801, entitled *Clarke's Seaman's Desiderata: or, Concise, Practical Rules for Computing the Apparent Time at Sea, the Latitude from Double Solar Altitudes, and the Longitude from the Lunar Observations . . . With Additions and Corrections by J.G.* (Sowerby, No. 3807). Garnett was elected a member of APS on 16 July 1802. For many years, he edited the annual *Nautical Almanac and Astronom-* *ical Ephemeris* and presented papers to the APS (APS, *Proceedings*, 22, pt. 3 [1884], 311, 326, 376, 378, 400, 402, 412-13; Sowerby, No. 3810).

[1] MS: "you."

From George Jefferson

DEAR SIR   Richmond 7th. Decr. 1801

In reply to your favor of the 3d. I have to inform you that the 3 boxes of composition ornaments from Alexandria were received some time since, though not until some weeks after they were shipped—they are still here, as only one boat I believe has gone to Milton since their arrival, and that could not take them. there are likewise some sash-weights & cords, which came from Philadelphia; & also a small box and some bar-iron which Stewart brought round.

I am Dear Sir Your Very humble servt.   GEO. JEFFERSON

RC (MHi); at foot of text: "Thos. Jefferson esqr."; endorsed by TJ as received 11 Dec. and so recorded in SJL.

From the Senate

Congress of the United States, In Senate, December the 7th 1801,

Ordered, that the Secretary wait upon the President of the United States, and acquaint him, that a quorum of the Senate is assembled, and that in the absence of the Vice President, they have elected the Honorable

President of the Senate pro tempore. Attest,

SAM: A. OTIS Secretary

MS (DLC); in clerk's hand, signed by Otis; endorsed by TJ as received 7 Dec. and "Pres. pro tem."

The Senate elected Abraham Baldwin PRESIDENT OF THE SENATE PRO TEMPORE on 7 Dec. On that day a joint committee from the Senate and House of Representatives notified TJ that quorums of the two houses had assembled. Senator Joseph Anderson and Congressman Samuel Smith reported back to their respective bodies that they had waited on the president (JS, 3:155-6; JHR, 4:5-6).

Annual Message to Congress

I. TO THE SPEAKER OF THE HOUSE OF REPRESENTATIVES AND
THE PRESIDENT OF THE SENATE, 8 DEC. 1801

II. FIRST ANNUAL MESSAGE TO CONGRESS, 8 DEC. 1801

III. NOTE FOR THE NATIONAL INTELLIGENCER,
CA. 8 DEC. 1801

EDITORIAL NOTE

On Monday, 7 Dec. 1801, the opening day of the first regular session of the Seventh Congress, a joint committee consisting of Joseph Anderson and James Jackson of the Senate and Samuel Smith, Roger Griswold, and Thomas T. Davis of the House of Representatives called on the president to report that both houses were "ready to receive any communications." Jefferson had already decided that his first annual message would take the form of written comments rather than a speech, and he had devoted time to the preparation of the message during November, developing the text over several drafting stages and consulting the members of his cabinet. He was ready, then, on 7 Dec. to tell the lawmakers "that he would make a communication" the following day, "by message." On Tuesday the 8th, the president's secretary, Meriwether Lewis, went to the Capitol and gave each house of Congress a copy of the finished message, a letter of transmittal from Jefferson to the presiding officer of the chamber, and a compilation of documents to supplement the annual message (JHR, 4:5-11; JS, 3:156-60; Drafting the Annual Message to Congress, at 12 Nov. 1801, Vol. 35:611-52).

Fifteen months later, when Jefferson needed to find a replacement for Lewis as secretary, the president gave the impression that the position did not involve much paperwork. The amount of writing required was "not considerable," Jefferson declared, "because I write my own letters & copy them in a press." Tallying the secretary's "chief business," the president did mention "messages to Congress," but he referred to that duty in conjunction with others such as running errands or going to speak with legislators or government officials "where it cannot so well be done in writing." One might infer from Jefferson's description that the secretary's involvement with messages to Congress consisted only of carrying the papers to the House and Senate (TJ to Lewis Harvie, 28 Feb. 1803; TJ to William A. Burwell, 26 Mch. 1804; see also Cunningham, *Process of Government*, 36-8).

In fact, Lewis must have spent a "considerable" amount of time at a desk making the two presentation copies of the 1801 annual message before taking them to the Capitol on 8 Dec. The letters of transmittal to the speaker of the House and the president of the Senate were in Lewis's hand, signed and dated by the president (Document I). In all likelihood Lewis wrote out the letters from a version in Jefferson's hand that showed the secretary where to insert the name of each house of Congress. Faithfully following that text, Lewis did not use capital letters at the beginning of two sentences, and matched the chief magistrate's spelling of "embarrasment." Like the letters of transmittal, the copies of the annual message that the House and Senate received were neatly written out by Lewis, signed and dated by Jefferson (Document 11). Again, the secretary worked from a copy in the president's hand. For the message, Lewis's source was the fair copy that Jefferson had in near-final shape by 27 Nov., the day he referred it to Levi Lincoln for comments. Lewis's copying followed changes that Jefferson made to that final version of the draft sometime after the attorney general had read it, including the removal of a section on the Sedition Act (Vol. 35:616-17, 647-8, 650n).

Lewis's involvement in the final preparation of the annual message makes clear that when Jefferson later wrote that the clerical demands on his secretary were not great, he did not mean that the secretary never acted as a clerk. In addition to copying the final version of the message, Lewis copied a report on postage on newspapers, a topic that arose late in the process of drafting the message. Some other lists and extracts of documents made during his time as Jefferson's secretary are also in his handwriting. Lewis was something of a confidential assistant to the president, as when he coded a list of the army's officers to show their abilities and political inclinations. Jefferson may have had that aspect of Lewis's role in mind when he characterized the secretary's job as "more in the nature of that of an aid de camp than a mere secretary" (Donald Jackson, *Thomas Jefferson & the Stony Mountains: Exploring the West from Monticello* [Urbana, Ill., 1981], 120-1, 157n; Vol. 34:629-30; Vol. 35:649-50n; TJ to Harvie, 28 Feb. 1803, and to Burwell, 26 Mch. 1804).

Jefferson carefully reviewed Lewis's transcription of the message, as shown by corrections in Jefferson's hand on the copies that Lewis delivered to the House and Senate (see notes to Document 11 below). Jefferson made more corrections to the copy received by the Senate (DNA: RG 46) than to the one received by the House of Representatives (DNA: RG 233), which may indicate that the one in the Senate's records was Lewis's first effort. That supposition is reinforced by the erasure of topic headings from the margin of the copy received by the Senate. Throughout the drafting process, Jefferson framed the message as a series of sections with named subject headings, from "Peace" through "Naturalisation" (see Vol. 35:620, 641-8). Initially Lewis included the subject headings as they appeared in Jefferson's fair copy, placing nine of the headings, from "Peace," "Indians," and "Tripoli" through "Appropriations" and "Army," in the margin of what became the Senate's version of the message. In the course of Lewis's copying Jefferson decided to abandon the section titles, or perhaps he never meant them to be part of the finished message, for Lewis stopped putting the headings in the margin, leaving out the ones from "Navy" through "Naturalisation." He erased but did not entirely obliterate the nine that he had already written (see notes to Document 11 below). Lewis never put any of the marginal headings on the copy of the message that went to the House of Representatives.

One change to the text by Jefferson provides indirect evidence that he allowed Samuel Harrison Smith to copy the message before it went to Congress on 8 Dec. In his fair copy, Jefferson indicated that information about expenses for navy yards "shall be" supplied. Lewis followed that phrasing when he transcribed the message for the House and the Senate. Jefferson made a late change to all three manuscripts, marking out "shall be" and substituting "is now" (see Document 11, note 34, below). He apparently made those alterations after Smith had already copied the document, for the text that Smith published in his newspaper, and separately as a *Message and Communication from the President*, reads "shall be" rather than "is now" (*National Intelligencer*, 9 Dec. 1801; *Message and Communication from the President of the United States to the Senate and House of Representatives; Delivered on the Commencement of the First Session of the Seventh Congress, The 8th of December, 1801* [Washington, 1801], 12; Shaw-Shoemaker, No. 1509).

On 8 Dec., after Lewis delivered the papers, Jefferson's letter of transmittal and the annual message were read aloud in both houses of Congress. The Senate also commenced the reading of all the supplementary documents, a task that carried over to 9 Dec. (see notes to Document II for the additional papers that accompanied the message). The House of Representatives on 8 Dec. committed the message to the Committee of the Whole in reference to "the state of the Union," and the Senate took a similar step on the 16th. Each house also determined that the message and the additional papers, which were extensive, should be printed. In the House of Representatives, clerks assigned a number to each document or group of documents in the supplementary papers, in the sequence in which the topics appeared in Jefferson's message. When Smith printed the annual message and the additional papers by order of the House as a *Message and Communication from the President*, he followed that system of organization. In that printing, which ran to more than a hundred pages, each document had its own page numbering, probably to facilitate typesetting (JHR, 4:7-11; JS, 3:156-61, 162).

Smith's *National Intelligencer* issued the printed text of the message, without the additional papers, by the afternoon of 8 Dec. and included it in the regular edition of the newspaper on the 9th. On Monday the 14th, the newspaper had this to report about demand for the annual message:

> So great was the demand for this important document, on the evening of its appearance, that the greatest efforts of the Press were unequal to it, and we were reluctantly obliged to stop its sale two hours before midnight, from a respect to the superior claims of distant subscribers. To the honor of the Post Master, he kept the mail open until 12 o'clock, which was seven hours later than the usual time of closing. The demand did not cease here. Gaining strength from a more general perusal of the Message, it continued for three days during which we issued several successive editions.

Smith printed the first of the supplementary documents, a report on the Creek Indians by Benjamin Hawkins, in the *Intelligencer* on 18 Dec. He managed to find space for the second item of the supplementary materials, a lengthy collection of information about relations with the Barbary Coast states, in two issues early in January. Other news always demanded space in the columns of the *Intelligencer*, particularly after the newspaper received permission from the Senate in January to report that body's debates. If Smith intended to print all of the supplementary documents in the *Intelligencer* soon after TJ sent the annual message to Congress, he was not able to do so (*National Intelligencer*, 4, 6, 8 Jan. 1802).

Jefferson failed to notice a few errors when he reviewed Lewis's copying work. As a result, some slips of the pen in the version Lewis made for the House of Representatives were incorporated into the text as Smith published it. In the first sentence of the message as Jefferson wrote it, and as Lewis transcribed it in the Senate's copy, Jefferson called Congress "the great council of our nation." In the copy for the House of Representatives, however, and subsequently in the published and widely disseminated version, "our" nation became simply "the" nation. While Jefferson, naming the various forms of internal taxes, used the singular form of the word "excise," Lewis inadvertently multiplied that source of revenue, writing "excises." A slip in the second paragraph changed the clause "they are becoming more and more sensible" into "they are become more and more sensible." In his fair copy, Jefferson made a cautionary comment about government consuming "the whole residue of what it was instituted to guard." Lewis copied the passage correctly for the Senate version, but omitted the word "whole" from the one for the House, draining some of the impact from Jefferson's wording. Lewis wrote that a standing army was not "considered"—rather than Jefferson's word, "concieved"—to be "needful or safe." He also changed "guarding from the exercise of force" to "guarding against the exercise of force," and made other minor errors. In the copy for the Senate as well as the one for the House, Lewis read Jefferson's "forts" as "posts" (see notes 8, 13, 16, 19, 20, 27, 29, 31, 32, and 38 to Document ii).

The manuscript the Senate received had other copying errors. Most significantly, where Jefferson in the fair copy (and Lewis, correctly, in the version for the House) had said that the bey of Tripoli "had already declared war in form," Lewis omitted the last two words of the sentence in the copy for the Senate. According to that version of the message, the bey had simply "declared war." In the first paragraph, the Senate's document said that neutral commerce had been "affected" rather than "afflicted" by war in Europe. Lewis also made a few other, less significant mistakes in the copy for the Senate (notes 5, 6, 9, 11, 14, and 24; js, 3:157-60). The Senate version, however, did not gain the broad circulation of the House version. The widely distributed text of the message, reprinted by many newspapers after Smith's initial publication, included the transcription anomalies from the text as the House received it. When a bilingual edition appeared in France, printing the message in English and French on facing pages, the English text was the one that originated with Smith and included Lewis's accidental alterations (*Discourse of Thomas Jefferson, President Of the United-States, for the Opening of the Session. Discours de Thomas Jefferson, Président des États-Unis pour l'ouverture de la derniere session du Congrès* [*Traduction Littérale*] [Paris, 1802]).

Although the message received scrutiny from Jefferson's political enemies, none of Lewis's copying errors came to anything. From December 1801 to April 1802, the pseudonymous "Lucius Crassus" attacked the message, and the program of government it spelled out, in a series of 18 essays in a Federalist newspaper, the *New-York Evening Post*. The articles were reprinted as a pamphlet, *The Examination of the President's Message, at the Opening of Congress December 7, 1801*, which included the text of the annual message as an appendix (New York, 1802; Shaw-Shoemaker, No. 2363). Almost certainly Alexander Hamilton wrote or dictated the "Lucius Crassus" pieces.

Yet despite Hamilton's insistence that the Constitution was in jeopardy, the essays had very little effect. In the final installment, published by the *Evening Post* on 8 Apr. 1802, "Lucius Crassus" did give attention to a passage that Lewis had unknowingly altered, the one concerning the absorption by government of "the residue" of labor's production. Hamilton, unaware that "whole" had been omitted from the president's message at that spot, actually focused attention on that word. The issue he was interested in, however, was "whether it is the *whole* of the earnings of labor, which government is instituted to guard, or only the *residue* after deducting what is *necessary to enable it* to fulfil the duty of protection" (Syrett, *Hamilton*, 25:444-53, 454, 489, 501, 590; *American Historical Review*, 84 [1979], 254; WMQ, 3d ser., 50 [1993], 461).

Various newspapers published the annual message from those copies distributed so energetically by Smith's print shop beginning on 8 Dec. As printed in several newspapers, the text included a footnote ostensibly written by the editor of the *National Intelligencer*. That note was actually written by Jefferson (Document III). Keyed to a passage in the annual message that referred to "an anxious solicitude for the difficulties under which our carrying trade will soon be placed," the footnote called attention to what were called "countervailing duties," extra import charges that Great Britain imposed on goods carried in American ships. Jefferson had expected a strong reaction to the British policy when it went into effect in 1798, but at that moment the deterioration of relations with France quickly overwhelmed other topics in American public opinion. The footnote in the *National Intelligencer* was a means of bringing notice back to the topic of Britain's countervailing duties. The note, as Jefferson wrote it and Smith published it, promised that the *Intelligencer* would provide more information on the subject. Smith did follow up on 23 Dec., and at least one other newspaper, the *Independent Chronicle* of Boston, reprinted that commentary (New York *American Citizen and General Advertiser*, 12 Dec. 1801; Newark, N.J., *Centinel of Freedom*, 12 Dec.; *New-York Gazette and General Advertiser*, 14 Dec.; *Albany Centinel*, 18 Dec.; *Salem Impartial Register*, 21 Dec.; *Otsego Herald: or, Western Advertiser*, 31 Dec.; *Independent Chronicle*, 7 Jan. 1802).

Debates in the House of Representatives stimulated more discussion of the issue. On 14 Dec. 1801, another Smith—Samuel Smith, who had retained his seat in Congress while acting as secretary of the navy ad hoc during the spring and early summer—introduced a resolution in the House of Representatives for the removal of what were called discriminating duties, U.S. imposts that favored American ships and could be seen to have instigated Britain's countervailing duties. It was the first legislative item prompted by the annual message to come before the House. Smith argued that insurance costs on British shipments during that country's war with France had kept American shipping competitive. Peace between the hostile powers meant an end to the high insurance premiums on British shipping, so the countervailing duties would make it uneconomical to ship goods to Britain in American vessels. Federalists, especially Roger Griswold, argued that the nation's commerce would suffer more from a repeal of the discriminating duties, which had been intended to protect a developing American mercantile trade, than from the effects of Britain's countervailing charges. Congress made no change to the discriminating duties in that session, and Jefferson brought the countervailing and discriminatory duties up again in his 1802 annual message. His use of the planted footnote and, no doubt, his contact with Samuel Smith and other allies in Congress were elements of what he called his "winter campaign" of getting legislation through Congress (*Annals*, 11:325, 329-33; New York *American Citizen and General Advertiser*, 9 Jan. 1802; *New-York Evening Post*, 2 Feb. 1802; *New-York Herald*, 3 Feb. 1802; Cunningham, *Process of Government*, 220; TJ to Benjamin Rush, 20 Dec. 1801).

I. To the Speaker of
the House of Representatives and
the President of the Senate

SIR   Dec. 8. 1801.

The circumstances under which we find ourselves at this place rendering inconvenient the mode heretofore practised, of making, by personal Address, the first communications, between the legislative and Executive branches, I have adopted that by Message, as used on all subsequent occasions through the session. in doing this, I have had principal regard to the convenience of the legislature, to the economy of their time, to their relief from the embarrasment of immediate answers, on subjects not yet fully before them, and to the benefits thence resulting to the public affairs. trusting that a procedure, founded in these motives, will meet their approbation, I beg leave through you, Sir, to communicate the inclosed message, with the documents accompanying it, to the honorable the House of Representatives, and pray you to accept, for yourself and them, the homage of my high respect and consideration.   TH: JEFFERSON

RC (DNA: RG 233, PM, 7th Cong., 1st sess.); in Meriwether Lewis's hand except date, signature, and inside address; signed and dated by TJ; in TJ's hand at foot of text: "The honble The Speaker of the H. of Representatives"; endorsed by a clerk. RC (DNA: RG 46, LPPM, 7th Cong., 1st sess.); in Lewis's hand except date, signature, and inside address; signed and dated by TJ; in TJ's hand at foot of text: "The honble The President of the Senate"; endorsed by a clerk. FC (DLC); entirely in TJ's hand; probably used as copy text for the RCs;

in the final sentence after "the honorable the," TJ wrote both "Senate" and "H. of R.," one above the other, enclosing the chambers' names in braces. Enclosure: Document II.

THROUGH YOU, SIR: the House of Representatives elected Nathaniel Macon its speaker on 7 Dec. As vice president, Aaron Burr was president of the Senate, but on 8 Dec., when the Senate received TJ's annual message, Abraham Baldwin presided in Burr's absence (JHR, 4:5; JS, 3:155-7).

II. First Annual Message to Congress

Fellow citizens of the Senate & House of Representatives.

It is a circumstance of sincere gratification to me,[1] that on meeting the great council of the[2] nation, I am able to announce to them, on grounds of reasonable certainty,[3] that the wars and troubles, which have for so many years afflicted our sister-nations, have at length come to an end; and that the communications of peace and commerce are once more opening among them. whilst we devoutly return thanks to the beneficent being who has been pleased to breathe into them the spirit of conciliation and forgiveness, we are bound, with peculiar gratitude, to be thankful to him that our own peace has been preserved through so perilous a season, and ourselves permitted quietly to cultivate the earth, and to practise and improve[4] those arts which tend to increase our comforts. the assurances indeed of friendly disposition recieved from all the powers, with whom we have principal relations, had inspired a confidence that our peace with them would not have been disturbed. but a cessation of the[5] irregularities which had afflicted[6] the commerce of neutral nations, and of the irritations and injuries produced by them, cannot but add to this confidence; and strengthens at the same time, the hope that wrongs committed on unoffending friends, under a pressure of circumstances, will now be reviewed with candor, and will be considered as founding just claims of retribution for the past, and new assurance for the future.

Among our Indian neighbors also a spirit of peace & friendship generally prevails;[7] and I am happy to inform you that the continued efforts to introduce among them the implements and the practice of husbandry and of the houshold arts have not been without success: that they are become[8] more and more sensible of the superiority of this dependance, for clothing and subsistence, over the precarious resources of hunting and fishing: and already we are able to announce that, instead of that constant diminution of numbers[9] produced by their wars and their wants, some of them begin to experience an increase of population.

To this state of general peace with which we have been blessed, one only exception exists.[10] Tripoli, the least considerable of the Barbary states, had come forward with demands unfounded either in right or in compact, and had permitted itself to denounce war, on our failure to comply before a given day. the style of the demand admitted but one answer. I sent a small squadron of frigates into the Mediterranean, with assurances to that power of our sincere desire to remain in peace; but with orders to protect our commerce against the threatened attack. the measure was seasonable and salutary. the Bey had already declared war in form.[11] his cruisers were out. two had arrived at Gibralter.[12] our commerce in the Mediterranean was blockaded; and that of the Atlantic in peril. the arrival of our squadron dispelled the danger. one of the Tripolitan cruisers having fallen in with, and engaged the small schooner Enterprize, commanded by Lieut. Sterritt, which had gone out[13] as a tender to our larger vessels, was captured, after a heavy slaughter of her men, without the loss of a single one on our part. the bravery exhibited by our citizens on that element will, I trust, be a testimony to the world, that it is not a[14] want of that virtue which makes us seek their peace; but a conscientious desire to direct the energies of our nation to the multiplication of the human race, and not to its destruction. unauthorised by the constitution, without the sanction of Congress, to go beyond the line of defence, the vessel being disabled from committing further hostilities, was liberated with it's crew. the legislature will doubtless consider whether, by authorising measures of offence also, they will place our force on an equal footing with that of it's adversaries. I communicate all material information on this subject, that in the exercise of the important function, confided by the constitution to the legislature exclusively, their judgment may form itself on a knolege and consideration of every circumstance of weight.

I wish I could say that our situation with all the other Barbary states was entirely satisfactory.[15] discovering that some delays had taken place in the performance of certain articles stipulated by us, I thought it my duty, by immediate measures for fulfilling them, to vindicate to ourselves the right of considering the effect of departure from stipulation on their side. from the papers which will be laid before you, you will be enabled to judge whether our treaties are regarded by them as fixing at all the measure of their demands, or as guarding, against[16] the exercise of force, our vessels within their power: and to consider how far it will be safe and expedient to leave our affairs with them in their present posture.

I lay before you the result of the census lately taken of our inhabitants,[17] to a conformity with which we are now to reduce the ensuing ratio of representation and taxation. you will percieve that the increase of numbers during the last ten years, proceeding in geometrical ratio, promises a duplication in little more than twenty two years. we contemplate this rapid growth, and the prospect it holds up to us, not with a view to the injuries it may enable us to do to others in some future day, but to the settlement of the extensive country still remaining vacant within our limits, to the multiplication of men, susceptible of happiness, educated in the love of order, habituated to self-government, and valuing it's blessings above all price.

Other circumstances,[18] combined with the increase of numbers, have produced an augmentation of revenue arising from consumption in a ratio far beyond that of population alone: and tho the changes in foreign relations, now taking place so desireably for the whole world, may for a season affect this branch of revenue, yet weighing all probabilities of expence, as well as of income, there is reasonable ground of confidence that we may now safely dispense with all the internal taxes, comprehending excises,[19] stamps, auctions, licenses, carriages and refined sugars: to which the postage on newspapers may be added to facilitate the progress of information: and that the remaining sources of revenue will be sufficient to provide for the support of government, to pay the interest of the public debts, and to discharge the principals in[20] shorter periods than the laws, or the general expectation had contemplated. war indeed[21] and untoward events may change this prospect of things, and call for expences which the impost could not meet. but sound principles will not justify our taxing the industry of our fellow citizens to accumulate treasure for wars to happen we know not when, and which might not perhaps happen but from the temptations offered by that treasure.

These views however of reducing our burthens,[22] are formed on the expectation that a sensible, and at the same time a salutary reduction may take place in our habitual expenditures. for this purpose those of the civil government, the army and navy, will need revisal. when we consider that this government is charged with the external and mutual relations only of these states, that the states themselves have principal care of our persons, our property, and our reputation, constituting the great field of human concerns, we may well doubt whether our organisation is not too complicated, too expensive; whether offices and officers have not been multiplied unnecessarily, and some times injuriously[23] to the service they were meant to promote. I will cause to be laid before you an essay towards a statement, of those who, under public employment of various kinds, draw money from the treasury, or from our citizens. time has not permitted a perfect enumeration, the ramifications of office being too multiplied and remote to be compleatly traced in a first trial. among those who are dependant on Executive discretion, I have begun the reduction of what was deemed unnecessary. the expences of diplomatic agency have been considerably diminished. the Inspectors of internal revenue, who were found to obstruct the accountability of the institution, have been discontinued. several agencies, created by Executive authority, on salaries fixed by that also, have been suppressed, and should suggest the expediency of regulating that power by law, so as to subject it's exercises to legislative inspection and sanction. other reformations of the same kind will be pursued with that caution which is requisite, in removing useless things, not to injure what is retained. but the great mass of public offices is established by law, and therefore by law alone can be abolished. should the legislature think it expedient to pass this roll in review, and to[24] try all it's parts by the test of public utility, they may[25] be assured of every aid and light which Executive information can yield. considering the general tendency to multiply offices and dependancies, and to increase[26] expence to the ultimate term of burthen which the citizen can bear, it behoves us to avail ourselves of every occasion, which presents itself, for taking off the surcharge; that it never may be seen here that, after leaving to labour the smallest portion of it's earnings on which it can subsist, government shall itself consume the residue[27] of what it was instituted to guard.

In our care too of the public contributions entrusted to our direction,[28] it would be prudent to multiply barriers against their dissipation, by appropriating specific sums to every specific purpose susceptible of definition; by disallowing all applications of money varying from the appropriation in object, or transcending it in amount; by reducing the undefined field of contingencies, and thereby circumscribing discretionary powers over money; and by bringing back to a single department all accountabilities for money, where the examinations may be prompt, efficacious, and uniform.

An account of the reciepts and expenditures of the last year, as prepared by the Secretary of the Treasury, will as usual be laid before you. the success which has attended the late sales of the public lands shews that, with attention, they may be made an important source of reciept. among the payments, those made in discharge of the principal and interest of the national debt, will shew that the public faith has been exactly maintained. to these will be added an estimate of appropriations necessary for the ensuing year. this last will of course be effected[29] by such modifications of the system of expence as you shall think proper to adopt.

A statement has been formed by the Secretary at war,[30] on mature consideration of all the posts[31] and stations where garrisons will be expedient, and of the number of men requisite for each garrison. the whole amount is considerably short of the present military establishment. for the surplus no particular use can be pointed out. for defence against invasion, their number is as nothing. nor is it considered[32] needful or safe that a standing army should be kept up, in time of peace, for that purpose. uncertain as we must ever be of the particular point in our circumference where an enemy may chuse to invade us, the only force which can be ready at every point, and competent to oppose them, is the body of neighboring citizens, as formed into a militia. on these, collected from the parts most convenient, in numbers proportioned to the invading force, it is best to rely, not only to meet the first attack, but, if it threatens to be permanent, to maintain the defence until regulars may be engaged to relieve them. these considerations render it important that we should, at every session, continue to amend the defects, which from time to time shew themselves, in the laws for regulating the militia, until they are sufficiently perfect: nor should we now, or at any time, separate until we can say we have done every thing, for the militia, which we could do, were an enemy at our door.

The provision of military stores on hand will be laid before you, that you may judge of the additions still requisite.

With respect to the extent to which our naval preparations should be carried some difference of opinion may be expected to appear: but just attention to the circumstances of every part of the Union will doubtless reconcile all. a small force will probably continue to be wanted, for actual service, in the Mediterranean. what ever annual sum beyond that you may think proper to appropriate to naval preparations, would perhaps be better employed in providing those articles which may be kept without waste or consumption, and be in readiness when any exigence calls them into use. Progress has been made, as will appear by papers now communicated, in providing materials for seventy-four-gun ships as directed[33] by law.

How far the authority given by the legislature for procuring and establishing sites for naval purposes, has been perfectly understood and pursued in the execution, admits of some doubt. a statement of the expences already incurred on that subject is now[34] laid before you. I have in certain cases, suspended or slackened these expenditures, that the legislature might determine whether so many yards are necessary as have been contemplated. the works at this place are among those permitted to go on: and five of the seven frigates directed to be laid up, have been brought and laid up, here, where, besides the safety of their position, they are under the eye of the executive administration, as well as of it's agents, and where yourselves also will be guided by your own view, in the legislative provisions respecting them, which may from time to time be necessary.

they are preserved in such condition, as well the vessels as whatever belongs to them, as to be at all times ready for sea on a short warning. two others are yet to be laid up, so soon as they shall have recieved the repairs requisite to put them also into sound condition. as a superintending officer will be necessary at each yard, his duties and emoluments,[35] hitherto fixed by the Executive, will be a more proper subject for legislation. a communication will also be made of our progress in the execution of the law respecting the vessels directed to be sold.

The fortifications of our harbours, more or less advanced, present considerations of great difficulty. while some of them are on a scale sufficiently proportioned to the advantages of their position, to the efficacy of their protection, and the importance of the points within it, others are so extensive, will cost so much in their first erection, so much in their maintenance, and require such a force to garrison them, as to make it questionable what is best now to be done. a statement of those commenced, or projected, of the expences already incurred, and estimates of their future cost as far as can be foreseen, shall be laid before you, that you may be enabled to judge whether any alteration is necessary in the laws respecting this subject.

Agriculture,[36] manufactures, commerce and navigation, the four pillars of our prosperity, are then most thriving when left most free to individual enterprize. protection from casual embarrasments however may sometimes be seasonably interposed. if in the course of your observations or enquiries, they should appear to need any aid, within the limits of our constitutional powers, your sense of their importance is a sufficient assurance they will occupy your attention. we cannot indeed[37] but all feel an anxious solicitude for the difficulties under which our carrying trade will soon be placed. how far it can be relieved, otherwise than by time, is a subject of[38] important consideration.

The judiciary system of the United States, and especially that portion of it recently erected, will of course present itself to the contemplation of Congress. and that they may be able to judge of the proportion which the institution bears to the business it has to perform, I have caused to be procured from the several states, and now lay before Congress, an exact statement of all the causes decided since the first establishment of the courts, and of those which were depending when additional courts and judges were brought in to their aid.

And while on the Judiciary organisation, it will be worthy your consideration whether the protection of the inestimable institution of juries has been extended to all the cases involving the security of our persons and property. their impartial selection also being essential to their value, we ought further to consider whether that is sufficiently secured in those states where they are named by a marshal depending on Executive will, or designated by the court, or by officers dependant on them.

I cannot omit recommending a revisal of the laws on the subject of naturalization. considering the ordinary chances of human life, a denial of citizenship, under a residence of fourteen years, is a denial to a great proportion of those who ask it; and controuls a policy pursued, from their first settlement, by many of these states, and still believed of consequence to their prosperity. and shall we refuse to the unhappy fugitives from distress, that hospitality which the savages of the wilderness extended to our fathers arriving in this land? shall oppressed humanity find no asylum on this globe? the constitution indeed has wisely provided that, for admission to certain offices of important trust, a residence shall be required, sufficient to develope character and design. but might not the general character and capabilities of a citizen be safely communicated to every one manifesting a bonâ fide purpose of embarking his life and fortunes permanently with us? with restrictions perhaps to guard against the fraudulent usurpation of our flag; an abuse which brings so much embarrasment and loss on the genuine citizen, and so much danger to the nation of being involved in war, that no endeavor should be spared to detect and suppress it.

These, fellow citizens, are the matters, respecting the state of the nation, which I have thought of importance to be submitted to your consideration at this time. some others of less moment, or not yet ready for communication, will be the subject of separate messages. I am happy in this opportunity of committing the arduous affairs of our government to the collected wisdom of the Union. nothing shall be wanting on my part to inform, as far as in my power, the legislative judgment; nor to carry that judgment into faithful execution. the prudence and temperance of your discussions will promote, within your own walls, that conciliation which so much befriends rational conclusion: and by it's example, will encourage among our constitutents that progress of opinion which is tending to unite them in object and in will. that all should be satisfied with any one order of things is not to be expected: but I indulge the pleasing persuasion that the great body of our citizens will cordially concur in honest and disinterested efforts, which have for their object to preserve the general and state governments in their constitutional form and equilibrium; to maintain peace abroad, and order and obedience to the laws at home, to establish principles and practices of administration favorable to the security of liberty and property, and to reduce expences to what is necessary for the useful purposes of government.   TH: JEFFERSON

Dec. 8. 1801.

MS (DNA: RG 233, PM, 7th Cong., 1st sess.); in Meriwether Lewis's hand with emendations by TJ; signed and dated by TJ; endorsed by a clerk: "Communication from the President of the United States to both Houses of Congress. Accompanying a letter to the Speaker of the House of Representatives dated 8th. December, 1801." MS (DNA: RG 46, LPPM, 7th Cong., 1st sess.); in Lewis's hand with emendations by TJ; partially erased section headings in margin (see notes below); signed and dated by TJ; endorsed by a clerk: "Message." Enclosed in Document I.

The papers that supplemented the message, identified here by number, as in the House records and the printed *Message and Communication*, were:

No. 1. "A sketch of the present state of the objects under the charge of the principal agent for Indian affairs, south of the Ohio," an overview by Benjamin Hawkins of the government and economy of the Creek Indians, with a paragraph on expenditures for the Creek agency (Tr in DNA: RG 233, PM, 11 p., in a clerk's hand, with notation at foot, "to be continued"; Tr in DNA: RG 46, LPPM, in a clerk's hand; printed copy in same); ASP, *Indian Affairs*, 1:646-8. Enclosed in Hawkins to TJ, 1 Mch. 1801; at that time Hawkins expected to augment and amend the report after he visited the Creeks' Upper Towns (see Vol. 33:109-10).

No. 2. Papers relating to Tripoli and the Barbary States, consisting of extracts or full copies of the following: James Madison to William Eaton, 20 May 1801; Madison to Richard O'Brien, 21 May 1801; Madison to James Leander Cathcart, 21 May 1801; TJ to Yusuf Qaramanli, pasha and bey of Tripoli, 21 May 1801; "Form of a letter which Commodore Dale was directed to write to the Dey of Algiers and the Bey of Tunis," [May 1801];

Madison, circular letter to U.S. ministers Rufus King, David Humphreys, William Loughton Smith, and William Vans Murray, 21 May 1801; Madison, circular letter to U.S. consuls around the Mediterranean, 21 May 1801; Cathcart to the secretary of state, 18 Apr. 1800; same to same, 12 May 1800; Cathcart to Charles Lee, 18 Oct. 1800 (labeled Cathcart to secretary of state, 18 Oct. 1801, in ASP and *Message and Communication*); Cathcart to secretary of state, 27 May 1800; Yusuf Qaramanli to president of the U.S., 25 May 1800; O'Brien to William Bainbridge, 9 Oct. 1800; O'Brien to secretary of state, 22 Oct. 1800; Cathcart to secretary of state, 4 Jan. 1801; O'Brien to secretary of state, 27 Jan. 1801; O'Brien to William Loughton Smith, 7 Feb. 1801; Cathcart to secretary of state, 16 May 1801; Eaton to secretary of state, 8 Dec. 1800; declaration by Cathcart, 29 Oct. 1800; Nicholas C. Nissen and Pedro Ortiz de Zugasti, statement recounting an audience Cathcart had with Yusuf, 13 Nov. 1801 (Trs and PrCs in DNA: RG 233, PM, 72 p., in various hands; Trs and PrCs in DNA: RG 46, EPFR, in various hands); ASP, *Foreign Relations*, 2:347-57. See Madison, *Papers, Sec. of State Ser.*, 1:199-201, 209-15.

No. 3. Returns of the census of 1800; see Madison to TJ, 8 Dec., and enclosures listed there.

No. 4. "Expenditures on account of Materials for building Six 74 Gun Ships, to the 1st of October 1801," 2 Dec. 1801, showing $268,187 spent on timber, $46,645 for cannons, $116,913 for copper, and $26,666 for two additional ship frames for a total of $458,411 (MS in DNA: RG 233, PM, in Abishai Thomas's hand and signed by him; MS in DNA: RG 46, LPPM, in Thomas's hand and signed by him); ASP, *Naval Affairs*, 1:79. For the six 74-gun ships authorized by Congress in 1799, see also Robert Smith's

Remarks on the Draft Message, Vol. 35:638-41.

No. 5. "Expenditures on account of Navy Yards Docks and Wharves to 1st October 1801," 2 Dec. 1801, indicating a total of $240,906 spent on purchase of property and improvements at six navy yards (MS in DNA: RG 233, PM, in Thomas's hand and signed by him; MS in DNA: RG 46, LPPM, in Thomas's hand and signed by him); ASP, *Naval Affairs*, 1:79-80. TJ had received a version of this statement from Robert Smith in November; see Vol. 35:641n.

No. 6. "Statement of the Sales of public Vessels and stores, payable into the Treasury," 8 Dec. 1801, listing the sales of 15 vessels sold at various ports for a total of $275,767.73 (MS in DNA: RG 233, PM, in Thomas's hand, signed by Smith; MS in DNA: RG 46, LPPM, in Thomas's hand, signed by Smith); ASP, *Naval Affairs*, 1:80.

No. 7. "Statement of monies applied for the defence of certain Ports and Harbors in the United States," 16 Nov. 1801, tallying $578,387.41 in expenditures on fortifications at 18 locations from 1794 to 16 Nov. 1801, with a notation that additional "large expenditures" had been made through the Treasury Department (MS in DNA: RG 46, LPPM, in hand of William Simmons, accountant for the War Department, and signed by him; MS in DNA: RG 233, PM, in a clerk's hand, lacking signature, date, or notation); printed in ASP, *Military Affairs*, 1:153.

No. 8. Statements of the numbers of suits instituted in circuit courts of the United States, 1790 to 15 June 1801, with a table for each judicial district showing numbers of common law suits, chancery suits, criminal prosecutions, and admiralty cases, plus the total of cases of all types, the number of cases that had been disposed of, discontinued, or dismissed, and the number of cases still pending. A "Recapitulation" omitted the classification of the figures by types of cases, giving only the total number of cases instituted in each district and the number of them still pending. According to that summary table, 8,276 cases had been instituted and 1,539 were still active (MS in DNA: RG 233, PM, 36p., in a clerk's hand; MS in DNA: RG 46, LPPM, in a clerk's hand). TJ made a tally of circuit court cases during November. Only for the districts of Vermont and Kentucky did the figures available to him in November match the totals of the "Recapitulation" accompanying the statements of December (see Notes on Circuit Court Cases, 12 Nov. 1801). For the submission of updated information to Congress in February 1802, see Madison to TJ, 25 Feb., and TJ to the Senate and the House of Representatives, 26 Feb.

Albert Gallatin had the list of people in PUBLIC EMPLOYMENT OF VARIOUS KINDS ready in February; see Gallatin to TJ, 12 Feb. 1802, and TJ to the Senate and the House of Representatives, 16 Feb.

For the ACCOUNT of the previous year's receipts and expenditures and the ESTIMATE OF APPROPRIATIONS for the next year, which were not transmitted to Congress with the annual message, see Gallatin to TJ, 7 Dec. 1801.

Henry Dearborn sent the statement of GARRISONS to the House of Representatives on 23 Dec.; see Dearborn's Plan for Reorganizing the Army, [7 Dec. 1801].

TJ transmitted the information on PROVISION OF MILITARY STORES to the House and Senate with his separate message of 2 Feb. 1802.

ANXIOUS SOLICITUDE FOR THE DIFFICULTIES: see Document III below.

Regarding FRAUDULENT USURPATION of the flag that might compromise the American neutrality, see Vol. 35:620, 621n.

[1] Erased in margin of MS in RG 46: "Peace." Lewis omitted the sectional headings from MS in RG 233. For the headings, see TJ's fair copy of the message (Vol. 35:641-50).

[2] Fair copy and MS in RG 46: "our."

[3] Word repeated by Lewis in MS in RG 46 and canceled, probably by TJ.

[4] Word repeated by Lewis in MS in RG 46 and canceled, probably by TJ.

[5] Word lacking in MS in RG 46.

[6] MS in RG 46: "affected."

[7] Erased in margin of MS in RG 46: "Indians."

[8] Fair copy and MS in RG 46: "becoming."

[9] MS in RG 46: "their numbers."

[10] Erased in margin of MS in RG 46: "Tripoli."

[11] Preceding two words lacking in MS in RG 46.

[12] Fair copy: "Gibraltar." MS in RG 46: "Gibralter" corrected to "Gibraltar."

[13] Word lacking in fair copy and MS in RG 46.

[14] MS in RG 46: "the."

[15] Erased in margin of MS in RG 46: "Algiers. Tunis."

[16] Fair copy and MS in RG 46: "from."

[17] Erased in margin of MS in RG 46: "Census."

[18] Erased in margin of MS in RG 46: "Finances."

[19] Fair copy and MS in RG 46: "excise."

[20] Fair copy and MS in RG 46: "within."

[21] Fair copy and MS in RG 46 have a comma after this word.

[22] Erased in margin of MS in RG 46: "Economies."

[23] Corrected, probably by TJ, from "injuriouly."

[24] Word lacking in MS in RG 46.

[25] In MS in RG 46, Lewis omitted this word and TJ interlined it.

[26] In MS in RG 46, TJ interlined this word to correct a misspelling.

[27] Fair copy and MS in RG 46: "the whole residue."

[28] Erased in margin of MS in RG 46: "Appropriations."

[29] Fair copy and MS in RG 46: "affected."

[30] Erased in margin of MS in RG 46: "Army."

[31] Fair copy: "forts." MS in RG 46: "posts."

[32] Fair copy and MS in RG 46: "concieved."

[33] In MS in RG 46, this word is in TJ's hand, written over an erasure.

[34] In MS, fair copy, and MS in RG 46, TJ interlined the preceding two words in place of "shall be."

[35] MS: "emolumoluments." Fair copy and MS in RG 46: "emoluments."

[36] Comma, omitted in MS, supplied from fair copy and MS in RG 46.

[37] Preceding word interlined by TJ to correct an omission by Lewis. The correction was not required in MS in RG 46.

[38] Fair copy: "for." MS in RG 46: "of."

III. Note for the *National Intelligencer*

[ca. 8 Dec. 1801]

—an anxious solicitude for the * difficulties under which &c

*Note. The Editor is not very certain to what this refers: but conjectures it is principally to the countervailing act passed by the British parliament in 1797. under the 15th. article of the British treaty: the 11th. section of which act lays additional duties of 10. percent on the amount of former duties on all articles except tobacco, & of 1/6 sterl. on every hundred weight of that, carried to Great Britain in *American bottoms*. this act was communicated to Congress, by the then President, by a message of Feb. 2. 1798. and was printed in the Aurora; perhaps in some, but certainly very few, other papers. the passions of the day wished[1] it to be kept out of sight, & especially in that part of the Union to which it was to be most ruinous, where it is probably little known to this day. the circumstances of the war have prevented it's effect[2] from being felt; but the case will be changed on the return of peace. it will in certain cases make a difference of 8. or 10. Dollars a ton in favor of shipping goods in a British rather than an American bottom. the act shall be given at length in an ensuing paper.

MS (DLC: TJ Papers, 110: unnumbered, following 18835); undated; entirely in TJ's hand; endorsed by Samuel Harrison Smith: "Th. Jefferson Note to Message 1801-1802." Printed in the *National Intelligencer*, 9 Dec. 1801, as a footnote to TJ's annual message, keyed to the text of the message as indicated in the first line above.

By the 15th ARTICLE of the Jay TREATY, the United States and Great Britain "agreed, that no other or higher Duties shall be paid by the Ships or Merchandize of the one Party in the Ports of the other, than such as are paid by the like vessels or Merchandize of all other Nations." However, the article also stated that "the British Government reserves to itself the right of imposing on American Vessels entering into the British Ports in Europe a Tonnage Duty, equal to that which shall be payable by British Vessels in the Ports of America: And also such Duty as may be adequate to countervail the difference of Duty now payable on the importation of European and Asiatic Goods when imported into the United States in British or in American Vessels." John Adams's MESSAGE to Congress of 2 Feb. 1798 transmitted two acts of Parliament, one of which, dated 4 July 1797, concerned the implementation of the Jay Treaty. The 4 July act placed additional duties on American goods carried to

British ports in American ships. In February 1798, TJ expected a swelling of outrage as merchants and shippers, especially in the northeastern United States, saw what the British policy would do to American commerce. However, despite efforts by Benjamin Franklin Bache's *Aurora* to call attention to the topic, the PASSIONS OF THE DAY intervened in the form of the XYZ affair, which during March and April 1798 focused public attention on relations with France (Miller, *Treaties*, 2:257; ASP, *Foreign Relations*, 2:103-15; Philadelphia *Aurora*, 28 Feb. 1798; Vol. 30:93-4, 112, 124, 125-6, 128, 165-6).

IN AN ENSUING PAPER: Samuel Harrison Smith needed several days to obtain a copy of the 4 July 1797 act of Parliament. Smith found the legislation too long to print in full, but he gave the topic two and a half columns of the *National Intelligencer* on 23 Dec. 1801, quoting extracts from the act and commenting on it. The article concluded by suggesting that U.S. discriminatory duties, which had given the British justification for their countervailing duties, should be revoked. Some newspapers did print the entire act of Parliament (*National Intelligencer*, 21, 23 Dec. 1801; *New-York Evening Post*, 27, 28 Jan. 1802; *New-York Herald*, 30 Jan. 1802).

[1] *National Intelligencer*: "induced."
[2] *National Intelligencer*: "effects."

Henry Dearborn's Statement on Indian Trading Houses

The Secretary of War has the honor of submitting, for the consideration of the President of the United States, the following statement and observations on the subject of the establishment of

Trading Houses with the Indians, from a careful examination of which it appears

That Congress in March 1795, appropriated 50,000 Dollars, and in April, 1796, the additional sum of 150,000 Dollars, to be applied, under the direction of the President of the United States, to the purpose of carrying on trade with the Indian Nations; and that, in consequence, one trading house was opened on the frontiers of Georgia, and another on the boundary between the State of Tennessee and the Cherokee Nation: that for these objects the sum of 90,000 Dlls. only has yet been drawn from the Treasury, and that the business of thse two houses has been so managed, as, from the best information to be obtained, not only to save the original stock from diminution, but even to encrease it, about 3 or 4 pr. cent.

As far as the system has been carried into operation, it appears to have had a very salutary effect on the minds of the Indians, and there can be little doubt remaining but that a much more extensive distribution of the fund, among the several Indian Nations, would be attended with all the good effects that were originally contemplated by the Government, and might be made without any diminution of the fund.

The several Nations of Indians appear extremely desirous of participating in the advantages, which result from their being enabled to procure supplies, made under the immediate direction of the Government, from a confidence that they will be fairly and honestly dealt with, and that they will not so frequently be subjected to the inconveniencies of travelling a great distance to an uncertain Market, and of being imposed on in their dealings.

The intercourse which grows out of such establishments, has a powerful tendency towards strengthening and confirming the friendship of the Indians to the people and Government of the United States, and towards attaching them more and more from the influence of neighboring Governments.

All which is respectfully submitted.   (signed) H. DEARBORN

War Department
  Dec: 8. 1801.

Tr (DNA: RG 46, LPPM, 7th Cong., 1st sess.); in a clerk's hand; endorsed by a Senate clerk. Tr (DNA: RG 233, PM, 7th Cong., 1st sess.); in a clerk's hand; endorsed by a House clerk. FC (Lb in DNA: RG 107, LSP); in a clerk's hand; in margin at head of text: "The President of the United States." Recorded in SJL as received from the War Department on 8 Dec. with notation "Indian trade." Transmitted to Congress with TJ's message of 27 Jan. 1802 and printed in ASP, *Indian Affairs*, 1:654-5.

For the financial STATEMENT that William Irvine prepared concerning the trading "factories" at Tellico and on the Georgia frontier, see TJ's communication to Congress of 27 Jan. 1802.

The act of CONGRESS of 3 Mch. 1795 appropriated $50,000 for goods to be used in trade with Indians during that year. The act of 18 Apr. 1796 authorized the president to establish trading houses, appropriating $150,000 plus up to $8,000 annually to pay the trading stores' agents and clerks (U.S. Statutes at Large, 1:443, 452-3).

To Albert Gallatin

DEAR SIR   Dec. 8. 1801.

The object of my message to the offices yesterday, was in general for such documents as were to accompany the message. those mentioned in your letter of yesterday I knew were to go afterwards, & had made the expressions future. but I did not know whether the list of offices of every kind might not be ready. however I shall express that in the future also.

Your's affectionately   TH: JEFFERSON

RC (NHi: Gallatin Papers); addressed: "The Secretary of the Treasury." Not recorded in SJL.

LIST OF OFFICES: the "Roll of the Officers, Civil, Military, and Naval, of the United States," which Gallatin did not send to TJ until February 1802 (Gallatin to TJ, 12 Feb. 1802).

From George Jefferson

DEAR SIR   Richmond 8th. Decr. 1801

Our friend in Petersburg has at length made a purchase of 14 Hhds Tobo. weighing 15,308 @ 28/. = £214.6.3. he has omitted to charge commission, which we calculate in paying him. he assigns as the reason for his not having sooner made the purchase, that he could not get it for less than 30/. and was satisfied that it would soon be lower. I suspect the fact is he did not like to acknowledge his error in not having made the purchase immediately on his receiving the order; when *such a parcel* might have been bought even lower than 28/.

I am Dear Sir Your Very humbl. servt.   GEO. JEFFERSON

RC (MHi); at foot of text: "Thos. Jefferson esqr."; endorsed by TJ as received 12 Dec. and so recorded in SJL.

From Matthew Lawler

SIR   Philada. Decem. 8th. 1801.

Publick Opinion has been a long time that a Change would take place in the Custom House of this District. I have held back any Application for the Collectorship expecting there would be numerous persons that would take more pains than I should and some of which perhaps personally acquainted, with the heads of the departments, but being more strongley urged by some of my Frinds, and Acquaintances lately, has induced me to make this Application if it meets Your Approbation it will be confiring a favour which will be verry exceptable and if given to any other person I shall consider it as done being more conducive to the Publick Good and more strongly to cement the Republican interest in this District

I am sir Your Moast Obt: MATW. LAWLER

RC (DNA: RG 59, LAR); at head of text: "Thomas Jefferson, President of the U.N. States"; endorsed by TJ as received 11 Dec. and so recorded in SJL; also endorsed by TJ: "for office in the Customs."

Matthew Lawler (b. ca. 1757) served as captain of several privateers sent out by Philadelphia merchants during the Revolution. In 1785 he was master of the ship *Fame* and engaged in the tobacco trade with France and in October 1789 returned from a prosperous seven-month voyage to India. Lawler was among the first elected to serve as director of the Bank of Pennsylvania in 1793 and was later chosen a director of the Philadelphia Bank. He was also active in local and state politics, having been elected mayor of Philadelphia by the Select and Common Councils in October 1801 and reelected the following three years. He served as a presidential elector in 1804. In the fissure that developed

among Philadelphia Republicans, Lawler allied himself with William Duane and Congressman Michael Leib against moderate Republicans Thomas McKean and Alexander J. Dallas. After McKean won the fiercely contested gubernatorial election of 1805, he instituted suits for libel against Lawler, Leib, Thomas Leiper, and Duane. Still allied with Leiper and Duane in 1819, Lawler chaired a meeting to encourage protection of domestic manufactures through protective tariffs (*Pa. Arch.*, 9th ser., 3:1774, 2066-7; PMHB, 17 [1893], 462-75; 79 [1955], 28-9, 35-40, 62n; *Pennsylvania Packet*, 17 Oct. 1785; Philadelphia *Independent Gazetteer*, 16 Oct. 1789; *Federal Gazette, and Philadelphia Evening Post*, 15 June 1793; *Philadelphia Gazette*, 28 Sep. 1796; *Gazette of the United States*, 27 Oct. 1801; Philadelphia *Aurora*, 8 Sep. 1804, 6 Nov. 1805; *Carlisle Republican*, 7 Sep. 1819; Vol. 9:390-3).

From James Lyon

SIR,   Washington City Dec 8 1801

I should not fail to wait on you personally to tender my grateful acknowledgement for the favor done me with the Post Master Gen.

was I not convinced that you must be at the present time, crowded with visitors, and business of a more important nature.

I enclose a copy of a piece of Work done for the Registers office (I believe) by Way & Groff, within two weeks past. They are now employed from the office of the Treasurer. In the summer of the year 1800, when I was urged by several of the most worthy republicans of Georgetown and this City to establish a Press here, Arrangements were made with a Printer of Alexandria to join in the enterprize, and dependence was placed upon him for materials till the period fixed for our commencement had expired, when he declined, leaving me disagreeably situated: I applied to Way & Groff to strike a few Numbers of "The Cabinet." They were then idle, and to bar every objection of a pecuniary nature, I offered them money in advance for all the work I wanted: after deliberation they said they could not print for me;—that the work was in favor of democracy, and they could not disoblige their friend by interfering with it: they added, that they had such compensation from the public as to enable them to be idle a few weeks—When they were applied to, to print the 1st number of the National Magazine they were so engaged preparing to print the public accounts &c—

Many of the Clerks have the given out of Small jobs of printing, and they follow their prejudices—

Perhaps it might not be improper for the Heads and the Officers of the departments to Appoint their Printers, or at least to designate them to their Clerks, who have printing to give out.

Mr. Israel Smith Rep. from Vermont has given me a letter from Judge Elias Buell, of Burlington Co. V.t. Mr. Buell is apprehensive that the Collector of the port of South Hero will be dismissed on account of his having been, (ever since he deserted the republican cause, for he was once a partner of the Democratic printer Haswell in Bennington, V.t.) a violent Tory,—his habitual overbairing superciliousness, particularly to republicans,—while the tories have enjoyed his partiality,—and the general expectation of such an event. Mr. Buell is desirous of the appointment, and has deceived himself so far as to suppose that I could have it in my power to assist him in his application. Mr. Israel Smith has written to Mr. Gallattin in his favor, and is now disposed to serve him in this respect by personal application. Persecution by the tories has been the reward of his democratic writings and exertions for ten years past—He has been a uniform Patriot,—and done much good, is a man of talents and great legal knowledge—

I must take the liberty of troubling you within a few days, on the subject of my father's application for remuneration, for his damage by the Sedition Law, to beg your advice

With Grateful Respect Yours &c   J LYON

RC (DLC); addressed: "Thos. Jefferson, Esqr"; endorsed by TJ as received 11 Dec. and so recorded in SJL. Enclosure not identified.

FAVOR DONE ME: TJ to Gideon Granger, 5 Dec.

WAY & GROFF: Washington printers with an establishment at North E Street near the Post Office. They printed the Senate journal for the Sixth Congress, second session, and Seventh Congress, first session. In 1802, brothers Andrew and George Way continued with the printing of the Senate journal for the sec-

ond session of the Seventh Congress, but William Duane and Son received the government contract the following year (Shaw-Shoemaker, Nos., 202, 1486, 3285, 7510; Bryan, National Capital, 517).

COLLECTOR OF THE PORT OF SOUTH HERO: David Russell (Vol. 35:36-7).

ISRAEL SMITH wrote to Albert Gallatin, 31 Sep. 1801, recommending Elias Buell as "a man of Industry and unquestionable Integrity and competant and well Qualified for the office he seeks" (Gallatin, Papers, 5:811).

From James Madison

SIR,   Department of State 8 Decr. 1801

I have the honor to transmit herewith two copies of the second census (except for the State of Tennessee, which is not yet received) and to notice the following deviations from the law under which it was taken, affecting the uniformity of some of the returns.

The return for the counties of Dutchess, Ulster & Orange in the District of New York was not recd. at this office until the 21st. of Septr. last.

The return for a portion of Baltimore County in the District of Maryland was not recd. until the 19th. ult.

The return for the western District of Virginia was not recd. in its present form until the 20th. of Octr. last.

The Marshal for the District of South Carolina did not take the Oath prescribed by law until three days after the date of his return.

In the return for the Indiana Territory, the population of some of its settlements is grouped together instead of being divided into classes.

It is proper that I should add, that I have no reason to suppose that the above irregularities have happened from culpable neglect in the Marshals themselves.

I have added to these copies an aggregate Schedule of the returns from each District and Territory.

With perfect respect I remain Your most Obedient servant

JAMES MADISON

RC (DNA: RG 46, LPPM, 7th Cong., 1st sess.), in a clerk's hand, complimentary close and signature in Madison's hand; printed with Enclosure No. 1 as the No. 3 set of documents in *Message and Communication from the President of the United States to the Senate and House of Representatives* (Washington, D.C., [1801]). Enclosures: (1) "Enumeration of persons in the Several Districts of the United States," a table showing the number of free white males, free white females, slaves, and "all other free persons except Indians not taxed" in each of 12 census categories in each district, for a total of 5,172,312 people, 875,626 of whom were slaves; omitting Tennessee but including additional returns from Baltimore County, Maryland, and a portion of New York State (MS in DNA: RG 46, LPPM; undated; in a clerk's hand; endorsed by a Senate clerk). (2) Census returns for New Hampshire, Massachusetts, the District of Maine, Connecticut, Vermont, Rhode Island, New York, New Jersery, the eastern and western districts of Pennsylvania, Delaware, Maryland, the eastern and western districts of Virginia, North Carolina, South Carolina, Georgia, Kentucky, Northwest Territory, Indiana Territory, Mississippi Territory (MSS in DNA: RG 46, LPPM; in various hands). All printed in *Return of the Whole Number of Persons within the Several Districts of the United States* (Washington, D.C., 1801; see Shaw-Shoemaker, No. 1559).

For the CENSUS, see TJ's Calculation of Population Increase, Vol. 35:532n.

RETURN FOR A PORTION OF BALTIMORE COUNTY: in an undated petition to TJ, census enumerator Thomas Bailey of Baltimore County explained why he failed to submit returns for his division of the Maryland census in the time allotted by law. In July 1800, he applied to the U.S. marshal for Maryland, Jacob Graybell, for an appointment as a census assistant. Graybell died before making the appointment, however, and another four weeks elapsed before the new marshal,

David Hopkins, succeeded to the office. The delay caused Bailey to begin his enumeration late in the year, when the days were shorter and the roads "almost impassable." His efforts to complete his assignment "caused the Death of a valuable Horse," while "fatigue and exposure to wet and cold" brought on a "fit of Sickness" that confined Bailey to his house for two months. These circumstances, the complicated instructions regarding the completion of returns, and "difficulties unforeseen and almost innumerable" all conspired to prevent Bailey from submitting his returns on time. As a result, the U.S. district court for Maryland, during its November 1801 term, indicted Bailey for failing to make a timely return. Before the indictment, however, Bailey stated that he had submitted a "full and complete" return to the new marshal, Reuben Etting, and requested that TJ grant a nolle prosequi to stay all further proceedings against him (RC in DNA: RG 59, MLR; at head of text: "To his Excellency Thomas Jefferson President of The United States of America").

Andrew Moore, marshal of the WESTERN DISTRICT OF VIRGINIA, submitted a return to Madison on 13 Oct. 1801 (MS in DNA: RG 46, LPPM, 7th Cong., 1st sess.; in a clerk's hand; endorsed by a Senate clerk).

MARSHAL FOR THE DISTRICT OF SOUTH CAROLINA: Charles B. Cochran submitted a return for his state on 24 July 1801 ("Schedule of the whole number of Persons in the District of South Carolina," printed in *Return of the Whole Number of Persons*).

In his RETURN FOR THE INDIANA TERRITORY of 4 July 1801, Secretary John Gibson grouped together enumerations totaling 766 people for settlements at "Machilamakanac," boatmen from Canada, Prairie du Chien on the Mississippi, Green Bay on Lake Michigan, and Opee on the Illinois River ("Schedule of the whole number of Persons in the Territory of Indiana," printed in *Return of the Whole Number of Persons*).

To Bishop James Madison

DEAR SIR   Washington Dec. 8. 1801.

Doctr. Logan of Philadelphia brought on his son here, to place him at the college of Georgetown during his own stay with Congress. but that College is on such a footing that I advised him to send him on to William & Mary, where I could prevail on you to take him under your special patronage. understanding that you sometimes take students to board with you, he is most [peculiarly] anxious that his son could have that benefit. if he could he thinks he would let him remain there to compleat his education. otherwise his anxiety for his morals will induce him probably, according to his first plan, to leave him there only during his own stay here. in that case I would ask you to set him a going in some branch of science, within the measure of that period, whether natural philosophy, or some branch of the mathematics, or both, you will be the best judge. he is tolerably well master of the languages, to wit Greek, Latin, & French. your attentions to him will confer a favor on me. accept assurances of my constant esteem & respect.   TH: JEFFERSON

P. S. should he not get a place with you, will you be so good as to interest yourself in procuring a good boarding house for him?

PrC (DLC); faint; endorsed by TJ in ink on verso as a letter to Bishop James Madison.

George LOGAN and his 18-year-old SON Albanus traveled to Washington where the senior Logan took his seat in the Senate, filling the position vacated by John Peter Muhlenberg (Frederick B. Tolles, *George Logan of Philadelphia* [New York, 1953], 52, 222, 224; Vol. 33:28-9).

COLLEGE OF GEORGETOWN: the Roman Catholic college in Washington had experienced a number of difficulties since its founding in 1792, including poor funding, frequent faculty and presidential turnover, and competition from a rival Baltimore institution. In 1798 its third president resigned after accusations of amassing large debts and giving a French character to the college. He was succeeded the following year by a president who enforced strict adherence to student regulations (*College of George-Town, [Potomack] in the State of Maryland, United States of America* [Georgetown, 1798; Evans, No. 48455]; Robert Emmett Curran, *The Bicentennial History of Georgetown University: From Academy to University, 1789-1889,* Vol. 1 [Washington, D.C., 1993], 31-56).

From James Monroe

DEAR SIR   Richmond Decr. 8. 1801.

I shod. have answer'd yours of the 24. ulto. as soon as I recd. it, had I not perceived it was yr. wish that our communication on the subject of it, shod. form no part of my publick letter to the legislature.[1] Being at the time engaged in writing that letter I delayed an answer till it was finished. It is not possible to entertain a doubt of the propriety of any part of yr. letter, the last paragh. excepted: nor am I satisfied that there is the slightest objection to that or any part of it. Still I suggest a doubt as to a possible effect it may have. You hint the propriety of leaving the power of designating the place to the ch: magistrate in concert with the President of the US. May not this excite jealousy and suspicion with some holding slaves. The idea perhaps did not occur, and perhaps is undeserving attention. You will think of it, and if you think it has any weight modify it otherwise. Inclining to think it does not I retain the letter, presuming if you think it does you have the means in a copy of correcting it. The term "him" might be changed into "it" without altering the import, & wod. be grateful to the council, in which you have friends. I will not send the communication in till I hear from you, provided it be, in time to avoid censure, which I presume will give you full time to answer me. I write in great haste, there being several gentn. with me. Sincerely I am yr. fnd. & servt   JAS. MONROE

[*In TJ's hand:*]
last page. line 9. 10. § 'him, and executed with the aid of the Federal executive? these' and insert 'them. they'

RC (DLC); notation by TJ at foot of text; endorsed by TJ as received 12 Dec. and so recorded in SJL.

For Monroe's LETTER TO THE LEGIS-LATURE, see Monroe to TJ, 21 Dec.

LAST PAGE. LINE 9. 10.: TJ's notation recorded changes he marked on his press copy of the letter he had written to Monroe on 24 Nov. in response to a request from the Virginia General Assembly. TJ thought he was altering his retained copy of that letter to match changes that Monroe would make to the original. However, Monroe changed only two words before transmitting the letter to the legislature; see note 2 to TJ to Monroe, 24 Nov. (second letter), and Monroe to TJ, 21 Dec.

[1] MS: "legisture."

General Statement of Account with John Barnes

Thomas Jefferson Esqr. In General a/c with John Barnes—

1801.

Novr 5th:	To Appt Balce ℔ a/c renderd		3051.46.
Decr 4th	To Amot: of Househd: ℔ a/c		1031.83.
"	To do private do		573.43.
" 9th	To M Lewis, Note of 7th. Octr a 60 days due and paid at B of C.	}	2000
			$6656.72

Novr 7	By Treasury Warrt:		2000.
Decr. 3d	By M Lewis Note of 9 Novr a 60 days for discounted at B.C.	}	1000.
7th.	By Treasury Warrt.		2000.
	By Appt. Balce due, this a/c		1656.72.
			$6656.72.

" 9	To Appt. Balce due this a/c brot: down		$1656.72.

EE: Geo: Town this
9th. Decr: 1801.
JOHN BARNES

MS (ViU); entirely in Barnes's hand; arranged by Barnes in two columns with the credit column beginning at 7 Nov. to the right of the debit column; endorsed by Barnes as accounts of 4 and 9 Dec., with the balance of $1,656.72.

LEWIS'S NOTE OF 7TH. OCTR: in a note dated Washington, 7 Oct., Meriwether Lewis promised in 60 days "to pay to the order of John Barnes Two Thousand dollars (negociable at the Bank of Columbia) for value received" (MS in MHi; in Lewis's hand and signed by him; signature later canceled with diagonal strokes; endorsed by Barnes: "paid 9th Decr. JB—and Debited for in last Genl a/c"; signature by Barnes on verso, later canceled; endorsed by a clerk).

LEWIS NOTE OF 9 NOVR.: in a note dated Georgetown, 11 Nov., Lewis promised to pay $1,000 in 60 days to the order of Barnes negotiable at the Bank of Columbia (MS in same; in Lewis's hand and signed by him; signature later canceled with diagonal strokes; endorsed by Barnes: "taken up 9th Inst. & Entd. 81—NB. This Note was Credited @ 9th Novr instead of the 11 Novr ℔ a/c"; signature by Barnes on verso, later canceled; endorsed by a clerk).

Barnes also prepared a "Rough Sketch, Presidents a/c, 4th. Decr 1801 with John Barnes," recording the balance in Barnes's favor brought forward on 5 Nov. of $3,051.46 from which was deducted on 7 Nov. a Treasury warrant of $2,000, being TJ's compensation, for a sum of $1,051.46 in Barnes's favor; with debits on 4 Dec. of $249.56 for purchases from Barnes's store and $782.27 for cash and orders on TJ's household account for the sum of $1,031.83—which Barnes incorrectly rendered as $1,032.83, with the subsequent totals being off by $1—to which was added $573.43 from TJ's private account for Barnes's total of $2,657.72; Barnes then crediting TJ's account with $1,000 by Lewis's note of 9 Nov.; Barnes indicating that when Lewis's note of 9 [i.e. 7] Oct. for $2,000 became due on 9 Dec. and his November note for $1,000 became due 9 Jan., TJ's total debits would be increased by $3,000, for a sum of $4,657.72 in Barnes's favor; with credits for TJ's compensation of $2,000 due on 8 Dec. and 8 Jan. to reduce the total sum in Barnes's favor to $657.72, that is, $656.72 (MS in ViU; 1 p.; entirely in Barnes's hand and initialed by him as "Exclusive of expenditures from & after the present 4th. Decr 1801," with a closing note that the 4 Dec. account was "not yet fairly drawn out, but closed in JB' Ledger").

Memorandum from John Barnes

[9 Dec. 1801]

Memdm. from this statemt. if Correct—
Exclusive of the within Ballance $1656.72.
M Lewis Note of the 9th: Novr.— } for 1000.
a 60 days become payble: 10 Jany

2656.72.

To meet which, the Compensation } for 2000
due 4th. Jany. recevable 7th Jany

leaves still a balce of $ 656.72.

of course J.B. have placed $1800 Mr S. to your debit for the present—and in the Course of the present Mo must Venture on another discount at B. of C.—ML: for another $2000

If you have any considerable payment—could not the person payable to a., be induced to drawn on me at 30—or 60 days—sight which is Usualy done—would aid your paymts. considerably—

MS (ViU); entirely in Barnes's hand; undated.

THIS STATEMENT: see preceding document.

MR S: William Short (see statement of TJ's general account with John Barnes, 31 Dec. 1801, in Appendix IV).

For TJ's use of Short's funds, see Vol. 31:502-3, Vol. 32:86-7, 156-7, 565; Vol. 34:235, 375; TJ to Short, 19 Apr. 1802.

From William P. Gardner

SIR, Philadelphia 9th. decr. 1801

I have received a letter from my friend Mr. Campbell and have to render you my Acknowledgements for the Honor you have done me in bestowing your Approbation upon my Conduct.

It is almost unnecessary for me to declare, at this time, that in my political Conduct, as the Main Spring of my Actions, I have ever had the Welfare of our Country in View.

I was introduced by my Friend Mr. Israel to Colo. Burr, a day or two before he left Philadelphia: I am happy to say that he received me with mark'd Attention and Politeness. He was so kind as to assure me that my Conduct had his entire Approbation—and of the interest which he took in my Welfare. I took the Liberty of referring him to you—for the particulars which I have stated relative to myself.

That I have Enemies among the Federalists at the City of Washington, and those of the most bitter kind, is what I cannot doubt, and it was for that Reason that I particularly cautioned Mr. Gallatin on that Score. As they can never forget, so I am confident they never will forgive me for the Spirited Conduct which I have ever shewn towards them, and for this last Act of mine on quitting the Treasury Department; But Sir, permit me to observe to you, that I will not presume to solicit any Appointment whatever under the Government untill I produce such Recommendations, as will, I trust, be deem'd highly honorable to me and perfectly satisfactory to you. I propose going to Lancaster Tomorrow and immediately on my Return shall proceed to the City of Washington. Be pleasd to excuse me for the Trouble which I have given you on this Business. Accept Sir, the Assurance of my highest Respect and Esteem. WM. P. GARDNER

RC (DNA: RG 59, LAR); at foot of text: "His Excellency Thomas Jefferson President of the United States"; endorsed by TJ as received 12 Dec. and so recorded in SJL.

MY FRIEND MR. CAMPBELL: see Anthony Campbell to TJ, 12 Oct. 1801 (Vol. 35:437-41).

MY POLITICAL CONDUCT: see Gardner to TJ, 20 Nov. At that time Gardner had not yet met the vice president, but he had a letter of introduction to him from Israel ISRAEL. Gardner enclosed it in his letter to TJ of 20 Nov. He also enclosed his letter to GALLATIN of 21 June (Vol. 35:704-5n).

From John Vaughan

D Sir.   Philad: Decr: 9. 1801

I have to apologize for the manner in which I sent down the last Small Pox matter for Dr Gantt I must have lost two days, in retaining it in order to have acompanied it with a letter

A Second Edition of Aikin is published here, with an important appendix; I shall have the pleasure of sending you a Copy as soon as I can get it from the publisher, who is getting it bound. I enclose the advertisement, with the information, That the letter of Yours alluded to, is the one to Dr Waterhouse, which was found in an English publication—The fear that you might see the Advert: & should for one moment conceive that I had permitted your letter to me, to be made use of, has induced me to trouble you with the present—Vaccination is beginning to spread fast here—Several Practitioners have commenced.

I remain with respect Your obedient Servant   Jn Vaughan

RC (DLC); at head of text: "His Excellency Thomas Jefferson"; endorsed by TJ as received 11 Dec. and so recorded in SJL. Enclosure not found, but see below.

SMALL POX MATTER FOR DR GANTT: see Vaughan to TJ, 19 Nov.

SECOND EDITION OF AIKIN: Charles R. Aikin's *Jennerian Discovery; or, A concise view of all the most important facts which have hitherto appeared concerning the Vaccine or Cow-Pock* was, with a slightly expanded title, the Philadelphia edition of his work that had already been published in London and Charlestown, Massachusetts. The APPENDIX was Edward Jenner's history of smallpox vaccine, published in London under the title, *On The Origin of the Vaccine Inoculation* (Philadelphia, 1801; Shaw-Shoemaker, No. 25). See also Vol. 34:277n; Vol. 35:430, 490-1.

An ADVERTISEMENT of 8 Dec. for the "just published" *Jennerian Discovery* appeared in the Philadelphia newspaper *Poulson's American Daily Advertiser*, with the announcement that prefixed to the book were "the recommendations of Doctors RUSH and COX, And a letter from Mr. JEFFERSON." Vaughan was quick to reassure TJ that the LETTER OF YOURS ALLUDED TO was TJ to Benjamin Waterhouse, 25 Dec. 1800, which appeared in John Coakley Lettsom's *Observations on the Cow-Pock*, published in London in 1801, and not TJ's letter to Vaughan of 5 Nov., which TJ had declined to have published (Vol. 35:424-5, 698-9, 709-10, 722-3).

DeWitt Clinton's Statement on a Political Faction in New York

[before 10 Dec. 1801]

A statement of interests in N.Y. by Dewitt Clinton[1] to mr Cheetham.

It is presumed that no serious evil can result from the designs of the little faction which has existed for a short time previous to the Presidential election, & which is governed by no principle but is solely devoted to the aggrandisement of an individual. it possesses neither talents, property virtue or any of the attributes of general confidence. it's strength is founded on the secrecy of it's plans, the arts & rapid movements of it's leader, & the prevelent opinion that he has in a great degree regulated the appointments in the genl. govmt for his state. the most influential of his adherents have derived their consequence from this latter source.

How far the contagion has spread cannot be ascertained, as the subjects of it dare not expose it. the following have been suspected of being under an undue bias in the respective counties hereafter mentioned, to wit.

Suffolk.	none	Washington	none
Queens	do.	Clinton.	do.
Kings	do.	Essex	do.
Richmond	do.	Saratoga. qu. as to mr Comstock, bror in law of Govr. Fenner of R. Isld.	
New York. you know.			
Westchester. none of any consequence.		Schoharie. qu. as to Geo. Tiffany & brother	
Dutchess. the same.		Montgomery. none.	
Rockland none		Oneida do.	
Orange. George Gardiner & Peter Townsend.		Otsego. qu. as to some individuals.	
Ulster. none of any consequence.		Herkemer. none.	
Columbia. the Van Ness's		Ontario. qu. as to Oliver Phelps	
Green none		Steuben. none	
Delaware do.		Tioga none.	
Albany do.		Cayuga qu. as to Joseph Israel Smith &c	
Renslaer do.		Onondago none	
		Chenango do.	

so far as Hamilton's weight will go, the federal party will not join him. some however of minor consquence will. and these combined with the renegadoes of the Republican party will form as curious a compound as history ever recorded.   the following representatives may be relied on.

Smith. Mitchell. V. Cortlandt. Elmendorf. Thomas. Bailey.

Two measures will effectually destroy these unprincipled intrigues.

1. An uniform mode of chusing electors.

2. A designation in the electoral balots of the office voted for.

MS (Profiles in History, Beverly Hills, California, 1998); entirely in TJ's hand; undated, but see the next document.

INDIVIDUAL: Aaron Burr.

In 1800, Adam COMSTOCK, a Rhode Island native who moved to New York after the Revolution, represented Saratoga County in the New York Assembly from 1792 to 1804 and in the state senate from 1806 to 1809 (Kline, *Burr*, 1:374n). George TIFFANY and his younger brother Isaac Hall Tiffany were graduates of Dartmouth College, in the classes of 1786 and 1793, respectively. They both studied law before moving to Schoharie County (George T. Chapman, *Sketches of the Alumni of Dartmouth College* [Cambridge, Mass., 1867], 43, 71).

George Gardner (GARDINER) was a prominent Republican in Newburgh, Orange County, New York. Peter TOWNSEND, of Chester, arranged for Burr's election to the state assembly by placing his name on the assembly ticket in Orange County (Kline, *Burr*, 1:421, 429, 2:842-3). VAN NESS'S: Peter Van Ness, first judge of the Columbia County Court of Common Pleas, and his eldest son John Peter served as Republican electors in 1800. John and his younger brother William P. Van Ness attended Columbia

College and became attorneys. They were lifelong friends and political allies of Burr. In 1801, John P. Van Ness took a seat in Congress, which he forfeited in 1803, after TJ appointed him a major of militia for the District of Columbia (Alfred F. Young, *The Democratic Republicans of New York: The Origins, 1763-1797* [Chapel Hill, 1967], 251n; *Biog. Dir. Cong.*; Kline, *Burr*, 1:584; 2:612-13).

OLIVER PHELPS, the Massachusetts land speculator who, along with Nathanial Gorham, gained title to three million acres in western New York, moved to Ontario County in 1796 (Young, *Democratic Republicans of New York*, 232-3; Kline, *Burr*, 1:44-5, 341). A former Dutchess County resident, ISRAEL SMITH settled at Cayuga in 1800. He was the brother of Mary Smith Swartwout, wife of U.S. marshal John Swartwout, and the nephew of Burr's political ally Melancton Smith (Kline, *Burr*, 2:785).

MAY BE RELIED ON: John Smith, Samuel L. Mitchill, Philip Van Cortlandt, Lucas C. Elmendorf, David Thomas, and Theodorus Bailey all represented New York in the Seventh Congress (*Biog. Dir. Cong.*).

[1] TJ perhaps added remainder of sentence at a later sitting.

From James Cheetham

TO THE PRESIDENT.   [10 Dec. 1801]

I Called on Mr. Madison yesterday but he was too indisposed to be seen. I Shall Return to New york by the Mail in the morning. And lest I should not have an opertunity of Seeing Mr. Madison During my stay, I have Committed to writing what I had to say to him

Concerning the subject on which I had the honor of speaking with you the other night.

If you have taken a copy of the note written by Mr. Clinton I Shall be much obliged to you for the original when convenient. I board at Mr. Stelle's. But if not Convenient while I stay you will be pleased to transmit it to me at New york.

RC (DLC); undated, but see enclosure; in Cheetham's hand; endorsed by TJ as received 10 Dec. and so recorded in SJL.

For the COPY OF THE NOTE, see the preceding document.

ENCLOSURE

James Cheetham's Statement on a Political Faction in New York City

I became *personally*[1] acquainted with Mr. Burr at the Election of the City and County of New York, for members of the State Legislature, in april 1800. The part I took in that Election, attracted the attention of Mr. Burr, whose well laid plans Did not a little Contribute to its success. This acquaintance, thus formed, Continued to increase, untill my attachment, as I Supposed, to the Constitution of the Commonwealth, and my exertions in Conjunction with those of my fellow Citizens to bring about the present Change in our affairs, obtained for me much of the Confidence, and, I have reason to believe, of the esteem of Mr. Burr. Few events occurred in the union, from our State Election in 1800, untill some months after the 4th March 1801, however Secret, with which I was not made acquainted by Mr. Burr. During this time, though I was not Ignorant of the suspicions entertained of Mr. Burr's views by many of our best informed and most honest Citizens, I perceived nothing in the general tenor of his Conduct that manifested intentions incompatible with the liberty of the Country, or the wishes of its Citizens. The first event which gave me occasion to question the Justice of Mr. Burr's views was the Presidential Election. In the general conduct of Mr. Burr in that Election, I Saw much to regret. It is not necessary to Say a word Respecting the wishes of the people on the Choice of the Chief-magistrate—they were too evident to be misunderstood by the sound and faithful politician. But the intention of Mr. Burr to Set aside those wishes, by raising himself to an eminence to which he was not Destined by the voice of the union, was too palpably manifested to me—not by words, but by actions less ambiguous—to admit of a Doubt. If it be asked upon what foundation these bold assertions are made? I answer, upon interviews which I had with Mr. Burr every Day During that pending and important Crisis, together with a Combination of Circumstances which left no Doubt in my mind of his intentions

In the State of New-york, the appointment of Mr. Lespinard to the important function of Elector was, there Can be no Doubt, a result of the exclusive arrangement of Mr. Burr. Mr. Lespinard is a Citizen of much influence in the Sixth ward, the most Republican one in the City and County of New-york. He is a Republican; and his attachment to the Cause Cannot, perhaps, otherwise be Doubted, than as he is Connected with, and wholly Devoted to, the views of Mr. Burr, which I, with many other persons, think hostile to it. This entire Devotion, from the very warm friendship which mutually Subsisted at the time between Mr. Lespinard and Mr. Burr, could not have been unknown to the latter. And Mr. Burr, being a member of the Legislature at the time the Electors were chosen, procured, there is every reason to believe, the appointment of Mr. Lespinard to accomplish personal and of Course private views.

Much mischief was apprehended by a few of our well meaning and Discerning citizens from the blind attachment of Mr. Lespinard to Mr. Burr. Among this Class of Citizens, Mr. De Witt Clinton Stood in the foremost rank. This citizen, Suspecting some foul play, took the liberty to question Mr. Lespinard, previous to the meeting of the Electors, Respecting the persons for whom he himself was elected to vote. Mr. Clinton hinted at a Report which prevailed in the best informed political Circles, that *Some* of the electors meant to *Drop* Mr. Jefferson: but that all of them intended to vote for Mr. Burr. This was in the presence of many of the electors who were Dining, if I mistake not, at Mr. Edward Livingston's. They all, however, promptly Declared their Determination to vote for the two Candidates, except Mr. Lespinard who remained Silent! This Statement was related to me by Mr. De Witt Clinton, and there Can be no Doubt of its being Correct.

This Silence, however, was of use. Justly apprehending mischievous effects from the Connection between Mr. Lespinard and Mr. Burr; and anticipating, from the undue attachment of the former to the latter, a contravention of the wishes of the Country in the election of the President, Mr. De Witt Clinton attended the meeting of the electors; but previously Suggested to Dr. Ledyard, one of the electors, a friend of Mr. Clinton and of liberty, to propose to the electors to Shew to each other their ballots anterior to their being Deposited in the ballot Box. This was accordingly proposed and readily assented to by every one of the electors but Mr. Lespinard, who hesitated. But finding his Colleagues So unanimous and pertinaceous in their Determination, he at length agreed to the proposition

During the Contest in the house of Representatives Mr. Lespinard, however, asserted, that if he had known the two Candidates would have had an equal number of votes he would have Dropped Mr. Jefferson.

In this manner Mr. Burr's views were Defeated in the state of New-york.

Afterwards Mr. Burr went himself to Rhode-Island to electioneer, as was generally Supposed, in behalf of himself. On his Return he Dispatched Col. Willet to Rhode Island to Complete what he had begun. This gentleman is a partizan of Mr. Burr. With the result of both these expeditions the President is Doubtless acquainted.

At the Seat of Government of S. Carolina Mr. Burr had a *Secret* agent, Mr. Timothy Greene, now an Attorney in New-york, for Several weeks. Mr. Greene wrote to Mr. Burr by every Post untill the S. Carolina votes were given. Mr. Greene's letters were Directed to Mr. John Swartwout, a warm partizan, and a Confidential friend of Mr. Burr, to avoid Suspicion, and were by him conveyed to Mr. Burr. Mr. Burr often mentioned to me the letters he recieved from Mr. Greene, but never permitted me to see their Contents.

It is not necessary for me to Depict the Conduct of Mr. Burr from the giving of the electoral votes in S. Carolina untill the happy termination of the Contest in the house of Representatives. The President Cannot be unacquainted with it.

In May last I entered into partnership with Mr. David Denniston who was before that time the Sole proprietor of the American Citizen. Mr. Denniston is nearly related by blood to Governor Clinton. This paper Mr. Burr wished to suppress. What his *real* motives were for wishing to Suppress it, we are left to Conjecture, but his *avowed* one was its lak of ability. Mr. Burr heard that I was about to enter into partnership with Mr. Denniston, and to take upon myself the Editorship of the paper. He accordingly Sent for me. Advised me to commence a *new paper* myself, and to have nothing to Do with Mr. Denniston; assuring me that Mr. Denniston's paper might be easily suppressed, and offering to obtain for me one thousand Subscribers. He added that now (meaning now he was vice President of the united States) he wished to have a paper under his patronage. The offer was Declined, and I entered into partnership with Mr. Denniston.

Still, however, our intimacy Continued; Mr. Denniston and myself Concluding that it might be well to Develope the plans of Mr. Burr that we might be prepared for every Contingency that might arise. Nor Did Mr. Burr long Conceal what he thought prudent to unfold, and he unfolded Sufficient to Demonstrate his views. Early in May he began to express his Dislike of the administration. He Said that much was expected from the administration of Mr. Jefferson, but little had been Done. No Removals had been made but Such as he had pointed out and almost Demanded. And that, had it not been for his importuning the President untill he was himself both tired and Disgusted, not a Single Removal would have been made in the State of New-york. This language was propagated with great freedom in the City by his runners, Mr. Mathew L. Davis, and David Gelston, now Collector of the Port. The office Conferred upon Mr. Gelston, has, however, Silenced him. The usual intimacy and correspondence, nevertheless, is Still kept up between Mr. Burr and himself, and he is as much Devoted to him as ever. But he is now, *externally*, mute. It is not so, however, with Mr. Davis. He is exceedingly Clamorous and loquacious. And he is so very intimate with Mr. Burr, and so well known to be at his command; and, withal, so perfectly Destitute of an independent mind, that, whatever Sentiments he utters against the present administration, and he expresses many, they are generally suspected of coming originally from Mr. Burr, and I believe very Justly. Mr. Swartwout, Mr. William P. Van Ness, and Mr. Timothy Greene, of New york, are also agents of Mr. Burr and entirely Devoted to him. Indeed Mr. Swartwout and Mr. Gelston are given to understand by Mr. Burr, and I *know* them to be of opinion, that they owe their offices to him.

These Sentiments of Dislike of the present administration, Mr. Burr expressed in Copious Streams to every person who visited him, and with whom he Could Converse with any Degree of Confidence; but to none, perhaps more than to myself. For, as I have before observed, I was Desirous of fathoming the intriguing and inexplicable man as far as I Could without

Dishonoring myself by a palpable affectation of entering into his views, or of being guilty of a Dereliction of my own Sentiments. He was Solicitous, not indeed in Definite words, but in a manner Sufficiently clear to be understood, for us to Commence an open but mild opposition to the administration. But this we Did not nor will not Do, unless, indeed, we Should find, in the *acts* of the administration, an unequivocal and Systematic Design, as in the one which preceded the present, to violate the Constitution, which is by no means expected in the acts of him who now fills the Presidential Chair. But when Mr. Barnes was appointed District Judge of Rhode Island, Mr. Burr was outrageous. In a Conversation which I had with him on the Subject of the appointment, he laid hold, in great warmth, of two letters which lay upon his table, and Said that one was from Governor Fenner of Rhode Island, and the other from one of the most influential Characters in that State, in both of which great indignation, he Said, was expressed at the appointment, and that the writers added, that Such was the Dissatisfaction of the Citizens of that State on account of the appointment, as well as the general tenor of the President's Conduct, that were he to be elected at that moment he would not have a Single vote in the State. Mr. Burr added that he wondered that the Republican papers Did not notice these things. He enquired whether any thing was Said in them on the Subject. And among others, he mentioned the Albany Register, the Aurora, the Boston Chronicle, the Richmond Examiner, and the Baltimore American?

Immediately after the appointment of Mr. Barnes, Mr. Linn was appointed to the office of Supervisor for the District of New Jersey. This appointment was loudly and openly reprobated by Mr. Davis and the rest of the faction, but particularly by those whose names are above mentioned. They Said it was in vain any longer to Conceal the facts Concerning this appointment and a few others Connected with it. They Stated that the election of Mr. Jefferson was the result of a Compromise which they Said was of the following nature. That Mr. Linn was known in Congress to be a *trimmer*. That on the vote for the appropriation to Carry into effect the British Treaty, Mr. Theodorus Bailey of New-york abandoned the Republicans. That consequently no reliance Could be placed on the promise of these two Gentlemen to give their votes for Mr. Jefferson. It was therefore, expected by the Republicans that after voting three or four times in the house, they would become alarmed, Join the federalists, and vote for Mr. Burr. Mr. Edward Livingston, they Still Say, was also Suspected, but from what Cause I know not, as he has always Signalized himself as an inflexible Republican. To prevent these three Gentlemen's voting with the federalists, and thereby Defeating the election of Mr. Jefferson, they have liberally Disseminated the story that the Confidential friends of Mr. Jefferson informed them, in a *Caucus* that was held for the purpose, that if they would Continue to vote for Mr. Jefferson, Mr. Linn Should be appointed to the office he now holds; that Mr. Livingston should be made District attorney of New-york, and that Mr. Bailey Should be appointed Naval officer in the Custom-house of New-york. The appointment of the two former is a confirmation, they say, of the Compromise which they boldly assert took place. Mr. Bailey has not been appointed according to promise, they add, because Mr. Davis was so powerfully recommended by Mr. Burr and his friends for the Same office, and Mr. Jefferson was thrown into Such a Dilemma thereby, that, rather than arouse the indignation of Mr. Burr and his friends by the appointment of Mr. Bailey, he Chose to Keep Mr. Rogers in office, and has thus been guilty of a breach of faith toward Mr. Bailey. That this Story Came originally from Mr. Burr to these persons I am Convinced. Since, independent of what these unprincipled men Say even in the public Streets on this Subject, Mr. Burr mentioned it to me as a fact in the early part of last august, from which time I have not Spoken with him on any Subject.

Thus far I have Spoken of the means employed by Mr. Burr and his panders. The end is obvious. It is to bring the present administration into Disrepute, and thereby to place Mr. Burr in the Presidential Chair—a thing Devoutly to be Deprecated.

This little faction, which appears to be rapidly increasing in the city of New-york, becomes more and more alarming, and more and more audacious every Day. It is, however, happily Confined to the *City* of New York, with very few exceptions. Such as those pointed out in the note of Mr. De Witt Clinton. The means of averting the menaced Storm are in the hands of the federal Legislature, and with which the executive is well acquainted.

My Duty to freedom and the Constitution has induced me to pen this brief Statement, and to Submit it to your excellency's Consideration. Extraordinary enterprises, whose Known objects are Dishonorable and unjust, Call for Commensurate means of Counteraction. And I am Sensible that nothing but the nature of the Case Could warrant my penning the Contents of this paper. If it Should happen, however, to be of Service to the general Cause, I have my reward.

You are at liberty to make Such use of this paper as in your wisdom you may Deem meet.

Accept my Sincere friendship

JAMES CHEETHAM
Washington December 10. 1801

MS (DLC); at head of text: "Some account of the plans and views of aggrandizement of a faction in the City of New York, Respectfully Submitted to the Consideration of the President of the United States"; at foot of text: "To his Excellency Thomas Jefferson President of the United States"; endorsed by TJ as received 10 Dec. and so recorded in SJL.

Anthony Lispenard (LESPINARD), Isaac LEDYARD, and Marinus Willett (WILLET) all corresponded with TJ on 7 Sep. 1801, providing Matthew L. Davis—Burr's choice for naval officer at the port of New York—with references when Davis visited Monticello seeking the appointment.

SECRET AGENT: after graduating from Brown in 1786, Timothy Green studied law with Levi Lincoln. He moved to New York in 1793 or 1794 (Kline, *Burr*, 1:188-9). For the correspondence on the vote of

electors in South Carolina, see same, 1:470. In March 1801, TJ appointed JOHN SWARTWOUT U.S. marshal for New York (Vol. 33:12n, 330-1, 675).

For Cheetham's PARTNERSHIP with David Denniston at the *American Citizen and General Advertiser*, see Denniston & Cheetham to TJ, 1 June.

TJ heeded the recommendation by Rhode Island senator Theodore Foster and named David Leonard BARNES U.S. district judge for Rhode Island on 30 Apr. 1801. Arthur FENNER wrote TJ that the appointment was "unexpected" and that many other candidates had applied to him for the office. Fenner also communicated these views to Foster (Vol. 34:66, 121, 131-2, 145-6). Levi Lincoln reported on the controversy surrounding the appointment in his letter to TJ of 15 June.

Solomon Southwick, associated with the ALBANY REGISTER, was a prominent Jeffersonian Republican in New York

(Vol. 33:573n). BOSTON CHRONICLE: that is, the *Independent Chronicle*, the leading Jeffersonian-Republican newspaper in New England (Vol. 30:25-6, 228n). For TJ's subscription to the Richmond EXAMINER, see Vol. 33:602-3. TJ also subscribed to the Baltimore AMERICAN (MB, 2:1070).

Burr favored the appointment of William Rossell as supervisor of the revenue in New Jersey, instead of James LINN (Vol. 34:6n). For TJ's consideration of appointments for THEODORUS BAILEY and Davis, see Vol. 34:127-8, 158-9.

[1] Word interlined.

From the District of Columbia Commissioners

SIR   Commissioners Office 10th. December 1801

Since we had the honor of addressing to you our memorial relative to the affairs of the City, we wrote to Mr. L'Enfant, and received his answer, copies of which we take the liberty of enclosing to you, with the memorial to which his letter refers—We send the Original, not knowing whether Mr. L'Enfant has before transmitted a Duplicate to the President, and we request this may be returned after perusal, a copy of which we shall send if not already received, or if desired—We are &c

WM. THORNTON
A. WHITE

FC (DNA: RG 42, DCLB); in a clerk's hand; at foot of text: "President of the United States." Enclosures: (1) Commissioners to Pierre Charles L'Enfant, 5 Dec., informing him that their recent memorial to TJ included a statement of accounts, "which necessarily brings into consideration the Claim you have on the Public for the Services rendered in planing this City," and noting that while the board refuses to reconsider a former offer of 500 guineas in compensation, it does "acknowledge the principal & Interest due to you as also the Lot purchased by you, for which a Title will be given on Demand" (Dft in DLC; FC in DNA: RG 42, DCLB). (2) L'Enfant to commissioners, 8 Dec., encouraging them to remember his claim for compensation in their communications with the president and Congress and noting: "I avail of the opportunity you now gave me, persuading my self that you will not in this Instance dissappoint anew the expectation which you encouraged by a former offer of your aid to the adjustment of the affair" (RC in DNA: RG 42, LR). Enclosed memorial not identified, but see L'Enfant to TJ, 3 Nov. 1801.

OUR MEMORIAL: Memorial from the District of Columbia Commissioners, 4 Dec.

From James Madison

Thursday night. [10 Dec. 1801]

J. M. havg received notice this afternoon of the oppy. by a packet, has hastily written to Mr. King. The President will please to read it & return it as soon as possible, that if approved, it may be got into the mail tonight, witht. which the opportunity will be lost.

RC (DLC); partially dated; endorsed by TJ as received from the State Department on 10 Dec. and so recorded in SJL with notation "lre. to King on countervailg act." Enclosure: Madison to Rufus King, 10 Dec. 1801, stating that peace between Great Britain and France will bring a "shock" to the American carrying trade because Britain's countervailing duties "must inevitably banish American vessels from all share in the direct trade with any part of the British Dominions, as fast as British vessels can enter into competition"; that three "remedies" suggest themselves; first, the United States might impose "*light duties* on foreign vessels," which would probably be considered an indirect violation of the Jay Treaty; second, the U.S. might repeal its own discriminating duties while calling on Britain to repeal its countervailing duties, which would take time and could complicate relations with other nations;

and last, because Britain's countervailing duties are calculated at rates that actually give an advantage "infinitely greater in favour" of Britain rather than bringing equality between Britain and the United States as anticipated by the treaty, the third solution would be "an immediate amendment of the British Act, adjusting the countervailing duties to a real equality with those of the U. States"; while it is not known what course Congress may choose, it is "the wish of the President that no time may be lost in stating to the British Government the light in which their countervailing Act is received here, and in endeavouring to obtain an accommodation of it to some rule that will produce a real equality to the navigation of the two countries, as intended by the parties, instead of that ruinous inequality to the navigation of one of them which must result from the rule adopted" (Madison, *Papers, Sec. of State Ser.*, 2:299-301).

From the War Department,
with Jefferson's Reply

From a recurrence to the Deeds registered in the Office of the Department of War, in relation to a purchase made by the United States, of a quantity of Iron Ore contained in a certain tract of Land situate in the State of Virginia, the following facts appear—That on the 7th. day of May 1800 Henry Lee and Anne his wife, for the consideration of Twenty four thousand dollars, executed to the President of the United States, a Deed, conveying to the United States all right and title to the Iron Ore, contained in a certain tract of land situate in the County of Berkley in the Commonwealth of Virginia, adjoining the river Potomack, near to the Keep Triste Furnace, in quantity about

sixteen hundred acres, to the use and benefit of the United States forever (excepting so much of said Ore as had been sold and conveyed
by the sd. Henry Lee, unto John Potts, William Wilson & George
North by his deed duly executed and recorded) Also all the right of
the said Henry Lee, to dig Ore in any part thereof and to remove the
same; Provided that the Earth shall be leveled at the expense of the
United States after the Ore shall have been removed—Also the free
and absolute use of Roads thro' the said Land, and wharves on the
river for the purpose of moving said Ore. Moreover all the annual
rent reserved to be paid forever to the said Henry Lee, his heirs and
assigns by the said John Potts, William Wilson and George North,
their heirs and assigns, issuing out of said tract of Land and every
part thereof. Also one half-Acre of land adjoining the said river to be
selected for the use of the United States aforesaid by their Agent duly
authorised by the Secretary of War under the direction of the President of the United States.—

It further appears that on the same 7th. day of May 1800, James
Mc.Henry Secretary of War, and Benjamin Stoddert Secretary of the
Navy on behalf of the United States for the consideration of Forty
two thousand dollars did purchase (for the use and benefit of the
United States) of John Potts, William Wilson and George North,
severally mentioned in the above described deed executed by sd
Henry Lee and Anne his wife, all that part of the real estate which
they the sd. Potts, Wilson and North purchased from said Henry Lee
on the river Potomack, in the County of Berkley and Commonwealth
of Virginia, containing about two hundred and thirty Acres, including the Keep Triste Furnace, Mill, Saw Mill, Houses and improvements of every kind with the whole right of the water of Elk branch
by which the sd. Furnace and Mills are worked, and also the right of
digging Ore, which they hold under the said Henry Lee from *Freinds
Ore bank*. The said United States being subject to pay the rent received for General Lee.

[*Reply by TJ*:]
I think it would be proper that the statement of the titles should be
either made or sanctioned by the Attorney General, & copies of the
deeds be annexed that then any circumstances which might enable
the legislature to judge whether they had better keep or sell these
mines, should come to me in the form of a report from the Secretary
at war, the whole of which I should lay before Congress. duplicate
copies to be furnished for that purpose   TH: JEFFERSON
                                                 Dec. 10. 1801.

RC (DLC); in a clerk's hand, reply by TJ at foot of text; endorsed by TJ: "Department War. Ore-banks."

In 1788, HENRY LEE acquired title to Friend's Orebank, an iron-bearing stretch of the bank of the Potomac River, and the KEEP TRISTE blast furnace, which was downriver from the ore bank and about two miles from Harpers Ferry. He sold the furnace site to a partnership that included John Potts, Jr., William Wilson, and an ironmaster, George North. Lee also leased them the rights to some of the deposits from the ore bank, and they produced iron at Keep Triste during the 1790s. By the latter part of that decade, Lee, who had invested heavily in speculative land purchases, experienced severe financial difficulties and began to sell many of his holdings for whatever price he could obtain. He would later go bankrupt. In the spring of 1800, Secretary of War James McHenry and Secretary of the Navy Benjamin Stoddert advocated that the United States should acquire a supply of iron ore close to Harpers Ferry and create a "National Foundry" there for the casting of cannons and shot. Early in May 1800, shortly before McHenry left the War Department, he and Stoddert made their case to John Adams, who deemed the project necessary for "the public interest, and service" and authorized McHenry "to execute this business as soon as possible." The United States government never utilized the Keep Triste furnace and never mined Friend's Orebank, although other users did draw ore from the five-mile-long deposit (McHenry to the secretary of war, 29 May 1800, incorporating Adams to McHenry, 5 May 1800, in Lb between 23 and 28 Dec. 1801 in DNA: RG 107, MLS; William D. Theriault, "Friend's Orebank and Keep Triste Furnace," *West Virginia History*, 48 [1989], 43-60; Michael A. Palmer, *Stoddert's War: Naval Operations during the Quasi-War with France, 1798-1801* [Columbia, S. C., 1987], 33-5; Merritt Roe Smith, *Harpers Ferry Armory and the New Technology: The Challenge of Change* [Ithaca, N.Y., 1977], 36-40; Charles Royster, *Light-Horse Harry Lee and the Legacy of the American Revolution* [New York, 1981], 15, 102-3, 172-6; Charles Varle, *Topographical Description of the Counties of Frederick, Berkeley & Jefferson, Situated in the State of Virginia* [Winchester, Va., 1810], 27).

ATTORNEY GENERAL: in a letter to Dearborn of 25 Jan. 1802, Levi Lincoln summarized the government's agreements with Lee and with Potts, Wilson, and North, the conveyance of the deeds, and the possibility that the United States had become responsible for the payment of mortgages on the ore bank property. TJ transmitted Lincoln's statement to CONGRESS on 2 Feb. 1802 with other papers relating to the War Department (ASP, *Military Affairs*, 1:159; *National Intelligencer*, 15 Feb. 1802).

From "An American"

SIR—   Charleston South Carolina Dec 11. 1801

According to the 46 Section of the Collection Law approved 2nd March 1799. *the Wearing Apparel and other personal Baggage*, and the tools or implements of a mechanecal trade only, shall be free from duty; that is to say of persons who arrive in the United States; *notwithstanding* which the Collector of this port obliges, such persons to pay Duty on their Books &c which they bring for their own use; indeed he has gone so far as to oblige them to pay on *old Books & Furniture*—Again the 57th Section of said Act obliges the Capt. of a vessel who does not make out & deliver a perfect Manifest in the first instance, to make a post Entry or addition thereto & allows a fee of 2 Dollars to the office therefor; but the Collector of this Port, obliges every person who makes an imperfect *Entry* of Any Goods imported in any vessel, & afterwards has occasion to make an addition thereto, pay 2 Dollars for each & every such addition which appears to me to be a very great imposition & contrary to Law—

The boarding officer who receives the manifests & certifies the Copies thereof is a very ignorant illiterate person; he also has the business of granting protections to American Seamen intirely entrusted to him except in very particular c[ases], & whenever he thinks proper refus[es to] receive the oath prescribed by Law, in consequence of which native born American Seamen have been prevented by him from procuring Protections & been exposed to the risk of being impressed on board British ships of War there to remain perhaps for life—These facts have come within my own personal knowledge, & may be proved to your satisfaction provided you may think proper to investigate them, & indeed I am convinced from my frequently having occasion to transact Business at this office & several other circumstances that this Government would promote the Interest [of] The Union greatly by appointing a proper person to examine the manner of transacting the Business of all the different Departments of this Office *in detail*, as I have good reason to believe the Collector is unacquainted with the common principles of Accounting & is unable to *execute* any one single difficult branch of the business although he may pretend to understand the theory thereof, the consequence is that his safety & dependence rests on the experience of 2 or 3 particular Clerks who have acquired a knowledge of his Accounts &c by Study & application in hopes of receiving a compensation therefor, which he has promised him for 3 years past & which he still withholds, notwithstanding the expences of living have increased nearly 50 pr Cent in that time, the consequence is that he holds these Clerks on very precarious ground, & should they leave him it would be utterly impossible to procure others who could qualify themselves to prepare examine transmit the Collectors Quarterly Accounts within the time prescribed by Law, This I Know from undoubted authority—he allows his accounting Clerks only 800 Dollars pr Annum, while Clerks in the Banks of this City receive 1400 Dollars pr Annum—while their Business is quite simple, compared with the complicated system of a Custom House

I have made this communication in hopes of your taking the matter into your most serious consideration; at the same time relying on your keeping the whole of it a perfect secret from said Collector which no doubt your own wisdom will dictate as well as not to suffer this Letter to go out of your own hands—as in that case he might perhaps receive a hint of its contents, which policy dictates should be prevented—

With sentiments of consideration I remain Your most obed Servt

AN AMERICAN

RC (DNA: RG 59, LAR, 10:0781-5); torn; at foot of text: "Thomas Jefferson Esqr"; endorsed by TJ as received 25 Dec. and so recorded in SJL with notation "T."

TJ received two other letters from an unidentified critic or critics of James Simons, the customs collector at Charleston. The first, signed "An Observer & Friend to Justice," was dated 23 Nov. 1801. The second, from "A. B.," was dated 2 Jan. 1802.

According to the 46th SECTION OF THE COLLECTION LAW of 1799, personal baggage included items intended for the use of the person or family only and were "not directly or indirectly imported for any other person, or persons, or intended for sale." Section 57 of the act stipulated that the master of a vessel could be charged $500 if the manifest did not agree with the cargo. If the collector's office decided the discrepancy was due to an "accident or mistake," the fine did not apply, but the captain was required to MAKE A POST ENTRY or addition to the manifest of the omitted items. Section 2 of the 1799 "Act to establish the compensations of the officers employed in the collection of the duties on imports and tonnage" allowed a fee of $2 "for every post entry" (U.S. Statutes at Large, 1:661-2, 671, 704, 706).

From Benjamin Hawkins

Fort Adams 11th. december 1801

We expect to commence our conference with the Choctaws tomorrow, they have met us today and informed us they would be then ready. From present appearances we shall obtain permission to open the road towards Nashville. As soon as our commission terminates here I shall go to Tookaubatche on the Creek agency about 500 miles, General Pickens will accompany me on his way home, and General Wilkinson will attend to his military duties untill the best period for convening the Creeks, which will be sometime the last of april, I believe it not practicable to do it sooner. On this subject the Commissioners will write to the Secretary of War.

Governor Claiborne has been well received at Natchez and his deportment such as to entitle him to the confidence of the well disposed in his government; among whom I find some very estimable characters. The inhabitants are in a state of uncertainty about the rights to their lands, altho they do not admit that they are so, or that a right derived from the officers of Spain during the exercise of their temporary government can be made void. The placing the acquisition of rights to Lands on a sure footing would tend greatly to the peace and prosperity of the Territory and the sooner this is done the better by the adjustment of the conflicting claims between Georgia and the United States and establishing a mode of granting out the Vacant land.

I shall send you by the first safe conveyance a map of the river Tennessee, with the notes and courses taken by me as I descended that river, I have it now complete within one day.

With the sincerest wishes for your present and future welfare I have the honour to be My dear Sir your obedient Servant

BENJAMIN HAWKINS

RC (DLC); at foot of text: "Mr. Jefferson President of the United States"; endorsed by TJ as received 12 Feb. and so recorded in SJL.

Hawkins, James Wilkinson, and Andrew Pickens met with the CHOCTAWS at Fort Adams on the Mississippi River, 12-18 Dec. The commissioners wanted permission for a ROAD between Mississippi Territory and Tennessee. The Chickasaw Indians had already agreed to allow the roadway through their lands, and by a treaty signed on 17 Dec., Choctaw leaders agreed to the opening of "a convenient and durable wagon way." In addition, a boundary line agreed to by the Choctaws and British authorities before the American Revolution was to be newly marked as

the border between the Choctaws' country and Mississippi Territory. At the conclusion of the talks at Fort Adams, the commissioners gave the Choctaws goods valued at $2,000 and the promise of three sets of blacksmith's tools. TJ submitted the Choctaw treaty to the Senate on 10 Mch. 1802 (ASP, *Indian Affairs*, 1:648-9, 658-63).

The commissioners wrote a brief letter to the SECRETARY OF WAR on 21 Dec. 1801 to report that since the Creek chiefs were unavailable for a conference during the winter, Wilkinson, Hawkins, and Pickens had determined to open their negotiation with that tribe in the spring, at the beginning of May (Foster, *Hawkins*, 412).

To the Senate

GENTLEMEN OF THE SENATE

Early in the last month I recieved the ratification, by the first Consul of France, of the Convention between the US. and that nation. his ratification not being pure and simple, in the ordinary form, I have thought it my duty, in order to avoid all misconception, to ask a second advice and consent of the Senate, before I give it the last sanction by proclaiming it to be a law of the land.   TH: JEFFERSON

Dec. 11. 1801.

RC (DNA: RG 46, EPFR); endorsed by a Senate clerk. PrC (DLC).

Meriwether Lewis delivered this message on the 11th. The Senate referred

Bonaparte's RATIFICATION of the Convention of 1800 to a committee composed of George Logan of Pennsylvania, James Jackson of Georgia, and Uriah Tracy of Connecticut (JEP, 1:397; JS, 3:155).

To the Senate

GENTLEMEN OF THE SENATE

I nominate Jonathan Williams of Pensylvania, major, to be Inspector of fortifications.

Joseph Willcox of (Killingsworth in) Connecticut to be Marshal for the district of Connecticut in the place of Philip B. Bradley resigned.   TH: JEFFERSON

Dec. 11. 1801.

PrC (DLC).

The Senate approved the nomination of JONATHAN WILLIAMS on 14 Dec. and immediately informed TJ (Senate to TJ, 14 Dec. 1801, RC in DLC, attested by Samuel A. Otis, endorsed by TJ as received 17 Dec., also endorsed by TJ: "approbn of Williams"; JEP, 1:397). The Senate did not consent to the nomination of JOSEPH WILLCOX until 21 Dec. and TJ signed a commission for him the same day (FC in Lb in DNA: RG 59, MPTPC; JEP, 1:399).

For the resignation of PHILIP B. BRADLEY, see Bradley to TJ, 19 Nov. 1801.

From Jean Chas

MONSIEUR LE PRESIDENT.   paris 12 decembre 1801.

j'ai reçu La Lettre que vous m'aves fait L'honneur de m'ecrire. je suis sensible aux marques honorables de votre estime. c'est avec une noble fierté que je me crois digne de votre bienveillance et de votre protection.

daignés, monsieur Le president, accepter un exemplaire du tableau historique et politique des operations civiles, et militaires de bonaparte premier consul de La republique francoise; ce n'est point un vain eloge que j'ai entrepris, et j'ecris pour tous Les siecles, et pour tous Les peuples. j'ai proclamé ces veritables principes qui doivent regir Les societés politiques, et ces verites saintes de La morale sur Les quelles reposent La prosperité des etats, et Le bonheur des nations.

je travaille a une nouvelle edition de L'histoire politique et philosophique de La revolution de L'amerique septentrionale. j'entrerai dans de nouveaux details. cet ouvrage merite de paroitre sous vos auspices, jespere avec confiance, monsieur Le president que vous daignerés en accepter La dedicace.

depuis Longtems je desire de visiter Les heureuses contrées que vous habités, qu'il seroit heureux et honorable pour moi de presenter mes hommages a ce chef d'une grande nation qui honore sa patrie et son siecle par ses vertus et son genie. mais je suis pauvre, je vis dans La retraite et L'obscurité, je cultive Loin du tumulte et des passions des hommes Les sciences et Les Lettres.

daignés, monsieur Le president, accepter avec bonté Lhommage de ma sincère admiration, et de mon profond respect   J CHAS

E D I T O R S'   T R A N S L A T I O N

MISTER PRESIDENT   Paris, 12 December 1801
I received the letter which you honored me to write. I am moved by the honorable tokens of your esteem. It is with a noble pride that I consider myself worthy of your kindness and your protection.

Kindly accept, Mister President, a copy of the historical and political tableau of the civil and military operations of Bonaparte, first consul of the French Republic. It is not empty praise that I have undertaken, and I write for all posterity and all peoples. I have proclaimed those true principles that must rule political societies, and those holy truths of morality on which rest the prosperity of states and the happiness of nations.

I am working on a new edition of the political and philosophical history of the North American Revolution. I shall go into new details. This work deserves to appear under your auspices; I hope, Mister President, that you will kindly accept its dedication.

For a long time, I have desired to visit those fortunate lands in which you live. How fortunate and honorable it would be for me to present my homage to that chief of a great nation who honors his fatherland and his century through his virtues and his genius. But I am poor, I live in retirement and obscurity, I cultivate the sciences and literature far from the tumult and the passions of men.

Mister President, pray accept with kindness the offering of my sincere admiration and profound respect.   J CHAS

RC (DLC); alongside signature: "rue du bout du monde n 184"; endorsed by TJ as received 25 Feb. 1802 and so recorded in SJL. Enclosure: Jean Chas, *Tableau historique et politique des opérations militaires et civiles de Bonaparte, premier consul de la République Française* (Paris, 1801); Sowerby, No. 237.

LA LETTRE: TJ to Chas, 3 Sep. 1801. L'HISTOIRE POLITIQUE ET PHILOSOPHIQUE: for Chas's book on the American Revolution, see Vol. 33:515-17. Apparently he did not publish a new edition (Sowerby, No. 485).

From James Currie

DEAR SIR   Richmond Decr. 12th 1801

  on receipt of your former letter I waited on Mr Wickham & the Other gentlemen who are joined with him, in the arbitration between yourself & Mr Ross who waited for the information to be received from Messrs Lewis & Eppes in regard to the time when the bonds were payable, your last of the 2d Inst. informs me they cannot give the information required. I have called on Mr Ross as likewise Mr Wickham to Enquire concerning the time of paymt of the Bonds above mentioned as yet have not got the information as neither have the Bonds in possession, after the U.S. District Court now sitting is over shall have some further Enquiry about the Bonds & a final decision which as soon as received shall be transmitted, to you, & in regard to the papers & accounts mentd. in your letter of Octr. 19th I have recd. them all back from Mr Ross immediately tho I neglected to mention the circumstance before now. they shall likewise be taken care of & transmitted in due time, with constant & sincere wishes for your health & happiness

  I am Dr Sir with the most Respectfull Esteem & Regard—your very Hble Serv   JAMES CURRIE

RC (MHi); endorsed by TJ as received 17 Dec. and so recorded in SJL.   FORMER LETTER: TJ to Currie, 19 Oct.

From John Dickinson

MY DEAR FRIEND,   Wilmington the 12th of the 12th Month 1801—

  Thy late Communications to Congress are so important to the wellfare of our Country, and such Demonstrations of thy Love to thy Fellow Citizens, that I feel it as a Duty to give thee my hearty Thanks, for thy strenuous Exertions to realize the public Blessings contemplated by thy Policy.

  I hope and trust, that a system will be now established, plainly shewing, how all the Ends of Government may be obtained in the best Manner, and the operation of the Principles contributing to those Ends, be most effectually secured against future Violations. Thus may a Monument be erected by the united Efforts of Wisdom and Virtue, that, when thy Head can no longer form Plans for promoting the Interests of Humanity, and thy Heart can beat no more with patriotic sensations, with a Duration outlasting all structures of

Metals and of Marbles, shall point out to succeeding Ages the Ways that lead to true Honor and national Felicity.

With fervent Prayers for thy Happiness in public and in private Life I am thy most affectionate Friend   JOHN DICKINSON

RC (DLC); at foot of text: "The President"; endorsed by TJ as received 17 Dec. and so recorded in SJL. Dft (PHi).

From James Dinsmore

SIR   Monticello Dec. 12th 1801

your favour of Nov. 28th with its inclosures is recieved. Mr Wanschaw has done plaistering & is now engaged in Mixing up Stuff for the dineing room; I am rather afraid I will not have it ready for plaistering by the 1st of March. I will do my endeavour. I do not remember that we ever fixed on the Size of the architrave to go round the Sky light. the joist is 10 in. deep. Mr Moran has quit Some time ago. Mr Wash. requested me to Mention that he would be glad to have the balance Settled which he Says is five Dollar. if it is right & you request it I Can advance him that Much—Mr Perry says he will get the timber hauled in Imediately, for roof of the offices, we will have to get more plank Sawed. I think it would also be best to have what flooring plank is wanted got now the Course of the winter; you will please to Mention if we Must Include the Hall in the Bill—

I Congratulate you Sir on the Conclusion of peace, between Frans & Great Briatain, &, hope it will ease you of a great Maney Embarrassments in the administration of our Government.   with Respect I am Sir your Hbl svt.

Nails made from the 16th Nov to the 15 Dec Inclusive—

	~~lbs.~~		
XXX.	60		
XVI.	34	Amt. nails sold in same time	£ 9.12.5
X.	151.5		
VI.	109.5	Cash rd	5.19.6
IV.	50.5		
	[. . .]		

FC (ViU: Monticello); in Dinsmore's hand; bottom of sheet trimmed; on same sheet as letters of 1 Jan., 23 Jan., and 12 Feb. 1802. Recorded in SJL as received 16 Dec.

YOUR FAVOUR: TJ's letter of 28 Nov. is recorded in SJL but has not been found.

The brothers Reuben and John PERRY both worked as carpenters at Monticello in 1801, but John Perry probably had the

TIMBER HAULED. TJ later noted that John Perry knew "nearly all the plank I have ever bought for my house, & the prices of it" (MB, 2:1000, 1022-3, 1063; Jack McLaughlin, *Jefferson and Monti-*

cello: The Biography of a Builder [New York, 1988], 294).

For Dinsmore's supervision of the nailery orders and accounts, see TJ to Dinsmore, 22 June 1801.

To Christopher Ellery

Dec. 12. 1801.

Th: Jefferson presents his compliments to mr Ellery. he is glad to recieve visits either of business or society at any hour of the forenoon. he generally goes out for exercise at noon. and is then engaged with company till candle-light, after which his friends will again find him entirely disengaged. he takes the liberty of mentioning this to mr Ellery, lest doubts on his part might deprive Th:J. of the pleasure of his visits which he shall be glad to recieve as often as convenient.

RC (MCLong); addressed: "The honble Mr. Ellery."

Christopher Ellery had taken his seat as the newly elected U.S. senator from Rhode Island on 7 Dec. (JS, 3:155).

From Lewis Littlepage

SIR,   Washington 12th. of Decbr. 1801.

An affair of a very singular nature having once taken place between the Austrian Ministry and myself, I send for your perusal the enclosed printed letter, which I beg may be returned to me. You will please to observe that the question is one of *Public Right*, as Austria had nothing to do with my military conduct in Poland. Suwarow had settled my affairs with the Empress, and the battles of Warsaw, Villna, Povonski, and Prague, did not regard Austria. With the highest respect I have the honor to be,

Sir, your most obedient humble Servant—

LEWIS LITTLEPAGE.

RC (DLC); at foot of text: "T. Jefferson President of the United States." Enclosure: Littlepage's printed letter to Baron Thugut (see below).

In 1795, Littlepage went to Vienna but was soon ordered to leave the AUSTRIAN Empire. The Austrians mistakenly thought, according to Littlepage, that he

was an enemy of Russia. He suspected also that the Austrians distrusted him because he was on friendly terms with Lafayette. Earlier, Littlepage had served under the Russian general Alexander Suvorov (SUWAROW) in a military campaign against the Ottoman Empire. Littlepage attempted to persuade the EMPRESS Catherine of Russia that his service to

[99]

King Stanislas of Poland had not constituted support of Polish nationalism or opposition to Russia. He answered his eviction from Austria—to no avail—in a letter addressed to Baron Thugut, who directed the Austrian chancellery's foreign affairs. Littlepage had the letter printed, but did not give it wide circulation (Curtis Carroll Davis, *The King's Chevalier: A Biography of Lewis Littlepage* [Indianapolis, 1961], 194-6, 330-2, 336-42; Nell Holladay Boand, *Lewis Littlepage* [Richmond, 1970], 214, 222-7, 285; Karl A. Roider, Jr., *Baron Thugut and Austria's Response to the French Revolution* [Princeton, 1987], 113).

From Elijah Paine

SIR   Williamstown, Vermont, Decr. 12th. 1801

In addressing you upon the subject of this letter I am sensible I transgress the practice established in the Government of the United States; and I beg you to accept as an apology, my want of acquaintance with the Secretary of State—

I have been led to believe there will be several applications for the Office of Marshall in this State, & that those applications will originate from an opinion among the political friends of the present Marshall that he is an improper person to hold the office—

Should you think it proper to alter the appointment in consequence of the representations which may be made to you upon the subject, I know of no one who would discharge the duties of the office with better abilities & to more general acceptance than Mr. Reuben Atwater—He is about thirty five years of age, worked to the law, & is a person of strict integrity & of an amiable disposition—

I hope you will do me the justice to believe that this recommendation is not owing to a disposition on my part in the smallest degree to embarrass your Administration—Mr Atwater is a Brother-in-law of General Bradley now of the Senate, & of the same politics, & he married a Daughter of General Lamb—

I am with great respect Your Obedt Servt.   ELIJAH PAINE

RC (DNA: RG 59, LAR); at foot of text: "The President of the United States"; endorsed by TJ as received 2 Jan. 1802 and so recorded in SJL; also endorsed by TJ: "Reuben Atwater to be marshal of Vermont vice Willard."

Elijah Paine (1757-1842), a Revolutionary War veteran and jurist from Brooklyn, Connecticut, graduated from Harvard College in 1781 and practiced law in Massachusetts before settling in Willamstown and Northfield, Vermont.

There he pursued agricultural and manufacturing interests, including owning a mill and textile factory. He served from 1787 to 1790 in the lower house of Vermont's legislature and as probate judge and state supreme court justice, prior to becoming a United States senator for Vermont from 1795 until his resignation in September 1801. He subsequently returned to Williamstown and became a federal judge for the district of Vermont, serving until his death (DAB; *Biog. Dir. Cong.*).

TJ received the names of John Willard, Isaac Clarke, and James Witherill as possible replacements for Jabez G. Fitch, who held the OFFICE of marshal for the district of Vermont and was criticized for his behavior toward Republican printer Matthew Lyon. Willard received the nomination in early January 1802 (JEP, 1:403; Vol. 33:111, 113, 533, 666, 668, 673).

REUBEN ATWATER of Connecticut be-

came secretary and eventually governor of the Michigan Territory. His older sister, Merab, was the first wife of Stephen Row BRADLEY, who was elected in Paine's place upon his resignation from the Senate. Atwater married Sarah, the daughter of General John LAMB (*Biog. Dir. Cong.;* Francis Atwater, comp., *Atwater History and Genealogy* [Meriden, Conn., 1901], 125, 153, 155, 156).

From Albert Gallatin

DEAR SIR   Sunday morning [13 Dec. 1801]

I send the statements which are to accompany the report, (one excepted which is not yet transcribed, but a rough & incorrect draught of which I enclose in this letter)

The object of the report is to show the probable revenues & expenditures on an average of eight years 1802-1809

The permanent revenues are stated to be impost, int. revenues, lands, & postage, (besides incidental vizt fines &a.)

Impost As the duties on importation have varied from year to year, no deduction can be drawn of the probable amount of impost, from A view only of the annual receipts in the Treasury.

It is therefore necessary to recur to the actual annual consumption of imported articles & to calculate *at the present rate of duties* the revenue which would have accrued on that consumption, in any given year the result of which is wanted.

For that purpose the tables A to H. have been compiled, which show both the quantities paying duty, and the average rate of duty paid by those articles (ad valorem, spirits, wines, & teas) which according to their quality, pay different duties.

The Statement K relates to the proportion of american & foreign tonnage employed in foreign trade, from which has been calculated the extra-duty paid by foreign vessels, by supposing that—As the total amount of tonnage employed in foreign trade, is, to the amount of foreign tonnage employed in do. So is the total amount of goods imported to the amount imported in foreign vessels & paying the extra duty.

The Statement I is intended to show the amount of tonnage duties, & to enable to calculate the expences of collection and the duties retained on drawbacks.

From those Statements is formed the table L showing the annual impost revenue of 1790-1792 & 1793-1798 respectively; calculated, not at the then existing, but at the present rate of duties; and to which as connected with the report, I request your attention as the preceding documents are only the materials out of which this is formed. It gives a result of 6,160,000 dollars for that revenue in 1790-1792, to which adding 50 per cent, for increase of population from that period to that of 1802-1809, (the revenue of which is the required object) gives 9,240,000 dollars for what I call the Minimum of the average revenue of 1802-1809—The same table gives a result of 8,350,000 dollars for the revenue of 1793-1798, to which, adding 30 & $\frac{1}{2}$ per cent for increase of population, gives 10,900,000 for what I call the maximum— and instead of assuming the medium, I mean to assume only 9,500,000

Internal—Statement *M* requires no explanation—So far I have written & left yesterday with you the rought draught of report.

Lands— The documents to be communicated are 1st estimate of quantity of lands for sale vizt about nine millions of acres as pr. Statement N (with which is connected a general map of our lands which is to accompany the report & which is also sent to you by the bearer) and 2d. Statement *O* of sales which have already taken place; from which in the report, O will be deduced a probable revenue of 350,000 dollars

Postage & incidental, (exclusively of dividends on Bank Stock) will be estimated at 50,000 dollars.

Total permanent revenue—impost.	9,500,000
internal	600,000
lands	350,000
postage	50,000
	10,500,000

The estimate of appropriation is 3,500,000 dollars; but on account of several temporary objects therein included the permanent expence will be stated at something less.

The residue applicable to payment of debt would be 7 millions. But as the demands for Dutch debt exceed that sum, it will be stated as expedient that a sum of 7,300,000 should be appropriated annually and a table, being the rough one enclosed will show the effect produced on the debt in eight years by that payment. (The statements P & R in relation to the actual state of public debt, you will easily understand. That P. shows that we have paid in 1801— Dolrs. 2,275,317.$\frac{30}{100}$ of the principal of the debt).

The report neither will, nor can, go any further. Our friends must draw the result[1] which is this—

Revenue, (including internal)	10,500,000
deduct internal	600,000
recommended	9,900,000
Expences other than debt	3,500,000
reductions recommended	1,000,000
Expences as requested	2,500,000
Annuity for public debt as requested	7,300,000
	9,800,000

leaving 100,000 dollars surplus—All we want, therefore is 1st— reductions to the amt. of one million—2d—repeal of internal taxes— The Stamps, Direct tax, arrearages of internal revenue, proceeds of bank shares & excess of specie over what is wanted in Treasury, are intended to meet the demands under British & French treaty.

Please to send back the enclosed, with the other papers—Any time to day will do—.

Respectfully Your obedt. Servt   ALBERT GALL[ATIN]

RC (DLC); partially dated; torn at seal; addressed: "The President of the United States"; endorsed by TJ as received from the Treasury Department on 13 Dec. and so recorded in SJL with notation "Finance"; also endorsed by TJ: "redemption of debt." Enclosures: Statements A through I, K through P, R, and S, subsequently attached to Gallatin's report of 18 Dec. (MSS in RG 233, RCSH, 7th Cong., 1st sess.; in the hands of different clerks, with emendations by Gallatin on several documents, including statement M, where he noted: "d. The last quarter from Massachussets an estimate"; statements A through I, K, and P signed by Joseph Nourse, register of the Treasury, on 12 Dec., statements O and R signed by Nourse on 11 Dec. 1801, with each statement endorsed by a House clerk). Printed in ASP, *Finance*, 1:707-17.

ACCOMPANY THE REPORT: Gallatin had evidently sent a partial draft of his report on the state of finances to TJ on 12 Dec. Gallatin signed the completed report on 18 Dec., and transmitted it with

letters of the same date to Speaker of the House Nathaniel Macon and to Abraham Baldwin, president pro tempore of the Senate. The report and statements were laid before both branches of Congress on 21 Dec. (Gallatin, *Papers*, 6:208-9; JS, 3:163; JHR, 4:21). The House of Representatives had the documents published as *Letter From the Secretary of the Treasury, Accompanying a Report, and Sundry Statements Prepared in Pursuance of the Act Supplementary to the Act, Intituled "An Act to Establish the Treasury Department"* (see Shaw-Shoemaker, No. 1496). The publication, however, did not include the accompanying tables. For both the report and statements, see ASP, *Finance*, 1:701-17.

In TABLE L and in Gallatin's report, the revenue for 1790 to 1792 is stated as $6,163,000, a discrepancy of $3,000 from what he wrote above. After calculating for the increase of population, Gallatin gave $9,250,000 as the MINIMUM OF THE AVERAGE REVENUE between 1802 and 1809. He kept his medium figure of projected revenue from imposts at $9,500,000 (*Letter from the Secretary of the Treasury, Accompanying a Report,* 6-7; ASP, *Finance,* 1:702, 713). STATE-MENT M included the income from internal revenues for 1800. Gallatin transmitted a more detailed account of these revenues when he submitted the statements for 1800 prepared by William Miller, commissioner of the revenue, to the House of Representatives on 21 Dec. (same, 1:718-23; JHR, 4:22).

Gallatin described the GENERAL MAP of the nine million acres of public lands as "including the Virginia reservation, and the grants to the Ohio company, and to John C. Symmes, which has been compiled from the survey of the Indian boundary line, and from the draughts returned to the Treasury Department." Considering the sale of public lands as a valuable source of revenue, Gallatin encouraged Congress "to provide against the progress of intrusion on the public lands, and especially to devise some efficient and prompt mode of giving quiet possession to every person purchasing under the law." In his 18 Dec. report to Congress, Gallatin increased the estimated income from the sale of public lands to an average of $400,000, instead of the $350,000 noted above. In his comments to TJ in November, Gallatin had estimat-ed proceeds from land sales at $250,000. He also increased the estimated figure for internal taxes to $650,000 in the TOTAL PERMANENT REVENUE. The grand total, therefore, increased by $100,000 to $10,600,000 (ASP, *Finance,* 1:703; Vol. 35:632).

ROUGH ONE ENCLOSED: Table S, entitled "Statement exhibiting the amount of the principal of the Public Debt, which may be discharged in the eight years, 1802-1809, by applying an annual sum of 7,300,000 dollars to the payment of the principal and interest." Being a projection, the statement was not signed by Nourse. WE HAVE PAID: Statement P actually indicated that the public debt had been reduced from $80,161,207.60 on 1 Jan. 1801 to $77,881,890.29 on 1 Jan. 1802, for a total of $2,279,317.31. Statement R consisted of a table of the annual payment of principal and interest to Holland. With the payment of $7,300,000 annually for eight years, to 1 Jan. 1810, Gallatin reported, the public debt would be reduced to $45,592,739.59 and all of the Dutch debt would be paid (ASP, *Finance,* 1:704-5, 716-17).

[1] Word interlined in place of "consequence."

To James Monroe

DEAR SIR   Washington Dec. 13. 1801.

I recieved last night your favor of the 8th. and I readily embrace both ideas of amendment suggested by you. I will pray you therefore in the last page of the letter, lines 9. & 10. to strike out the words 'him, and executed with the aid of the Federal executive? these' and insert 'them. they' or rather turn 'him' into 'them' by prefixing a t, and putting a loop to the i, thus e. and turn 'these' into they by writing a *y* on the *se.* and obliterate the intermediate words with the pen. indeed the word *these* was first written *they,* so that it may be restored by scratching with the point of a knife.

In cleansing the Post office, Davies must be removed. pray recommend to me one or more good characters. the place is profitable, and worthy the acceptance of gentlemen of respectable standing in society; and to such I would wish give offices, because they would add respect & strength to the administration, & besides pecuniary security, give us their character as a pledge of fidelity. perhaps some member of your council would be proper. but of this judge yourself on view of all circumstances saying nothing about it. health & affectionate esteem.   TH: JEFFERSON

RC (DLC: Monroe Papers); addressed: "Governor Monroe Richmond"; franked; postmarked Washington, 14 Dec.; endorsed by Monroe. PrC (DLC); endorsed by TJ in ink on verso.

For the alterations to the LAST PAGE of TJ's letter of 24 Nov., see Monroe's letter of 8 Dec.

DAVIES: Augustine Davis, postmaster and Federalist newspaper publisher of Richmond (Vol. 31:180-1n).

From James Ray

SIR,   Annapolis 13th. December 1801.—

Relying on the high character You have for Justice I flatter Myself You will permit a Foreigner to apply to You for redress—where He thinks himself aggrieved.—

I hold on Acct. my Wife a Mortgage in The City, on Square So. of Square 744. Two Instalments have been paid to The Commissioners, the third is due from the Person who bought the Property, altho' I lent him the Money. This Person, of the Name of Peircy, in Jany. last, absconded from the City, & Carried off in the Night, Property of mine, to the Amount of thirty thousand Dollars—& for being his Security I was put in Confinement, which has hitherto prevented me from liquidating the Instalment due to The Commissioners.—

Last Week, I received a Letter from My Friend Dr. Thornton, in reply to a request I had made him, begging the Commissioners would not Sell the Property immediately, but wait till January, when I expected to be able to pay them, wherein He tells me, He had proposed to the Board to let me Select the Lots already paid for, or to Wait a little longer, both which requests they had refused. Under these Circumstances, I take leave to apply to You, hoping You will have the goodness to direct The Commissioners to delay Selling the Property, 'till I can pay the Instalment, or that at all Events they may not sacrifice the whole of it.—

You will, I am persuaded, Sir, excuse this intrusion on Your time & Attention from a Stranger, who has the honor to be with great respect,

Your Most Obedt. & Most hble Servt   JAMS RAY.

RC (DNA: RG 42, LR); at foot of text: "The President of the United States"; endorsed by TJ as received 14 Dec. and so recorded in SJL.

James Ray was an English merchant who had lived in India and New York (Harris, *Thornton*, 1:506n; Allen C. Clark, *Greenleaf and Law in the Federal City* [Washington, D.C., 1901], 145, 274).

Ray and James Piercy (PEIRCY) invested in the construction of a sugar refinery on the southern half of square 744 in Washington in 1797-98. Piercy indebted himself heavily to Thomas Law, Ray, and others in order to purchase the land from Law and to cover other costs. The sugar house closed by 1801 (Bryan, *National Capital*, 1:292, 304-5n, 434; Clark, *Greenleaf and Law*, 245, 274).

According to minutes of the meeting of the District of Columbia commissioners, the board put up for sale individual lots in the square south of square 744 on 10, 14, and 18 Dec. At a meeting on the day after the final sale, commissioner William THORNTON characterized as "particularly oppressive" the sale of the WHOLE property for delinquency of payment, rather than single lots, given that two-thirds of the purchase money had been paid. He contended that "some of the many Creditors of the original purchaser, Mr. Piercy," might yet be able to "discharge the Debt" on the remainder. The commissioners executed a deed to six lots on the square for a December bidder on 18 Feb. 1802 (DNA: RG 42, PC).

To Mary Jefferson Eppes

MY DEAR MARIA   Washington Dec. 14. 1801.

I recieved in due time yours & mr Eppes's letters of Nov. 6. and his of Nov. 26. this last informed me you would stay at Eppington 2. or 3. weeks. having had occasion to write during that time to mr F. Eppes, without knowing at the moment that you were there, you would of course know I was well. this with the unceasing press of business has prevented my writing to you. presuming this will still find you at Eppington, I direct it to Colesville. mr Eppes's letter having informed me that little Francis was still in the height of his whooping cough, & that you had had a sore breast, I am very anxious to hear from you. the family at Edgehill have got out of all danger. Ellen & Cornelia have been in the most imminent danger. I hear of no death at Monticello except old Tom Shackleford. my stonemasons have done scarcely anything there.   Congress is just setting in on business. we have a very commanding majority in the house of Representatives, and a safe majority in the Senate. I believe therefore all things will go on smoothly, except a little ill-temper to be expected from the minority, who are bitterly mortified.—I hope there is a letter on the road informing me how you all are. I percieve that it will be merely accidental when I can steal a moment to write to you. however that is of no consequence; my health being always so firm as to leave you without doubt on that subject, but it is not so with yourself & little one. I shall not be easy therefore if either yourself or mr Eppes do not once a week or fortnight write the three words 'all are well.' that you may be so now, & so continue is the subject of my perpetual anxiety, as my affections are constantly brooding over you. heaven bless you my dear daughter. present me affectionately to mr Eppes & my friends at Eppington if you are there.

P.S. after signing my name, I was called to recieve Doctr. Walker who delivers me a letter from mr Eppes informing me of your state on the 7th. inst. which is not calculated to remove all anxiety.

RC (DLC); signature clipped; addressed: "Mrs. Maria Eppes at Eppington near Colesville"; franked and postmarked. Address sheet later covered with calculations; drawings of figures; a rectangular marker with the initials of Mary and John Wayles Eppes and 13 Oct. 1797, the date of their marriage, perpendicular to a smaller semicircular marker with the initials of Francis Eppes and his birth date, 20 Sep. 1801; a notation "F.E. born Dec. 31}Died Jan. 19," for the first child, a daughter, who died shortly after birth; and various other notations in an unidentified hand.

HIS OF NOV. 26: John Wayles Eppes to TJ, 26 Nov., has not been found and is not recorded in SJL, but a letter of 21 Nov., also not found, is recorded in SJL as received 28 Nov.

TOM SHACKLEFORD, a gardener who was a slave at Monticello, frequently made purchases and transmitted funds on TJ's behalf. In his financial records, TJ recorded payments to him for travel expenses and, in November 1800, payment for hops (MB, 2:1030, 1585).

To Albert Gallatin

TH:J. TO MR GALLATIN   Dec. 14. 1801.

Before your papers of to-day came, I had read the report & inclosed it with a word of answer. I have gone through those last sent, rapidly as the time required. your former explanations had already prepared me for them. they are entirely satisfactory. I believe I should have taken ranker ground, by assuming a higher amount of impost to proceed on. but your's is safest and answers all our purposes.   health & affection.

RC (NHi: Gallatin Papers); addressed: "The Secretary of the Treasury." Not recorded in SJL.

PAPERS OF TO-DAY: Gallatin sent TJ a list of 19 warrants, Nos. 162 to 180, issued between 7 and 12 Dec., which TJ endorsed as received on this date but did

not record in SJL. Warrant No. 162, dated 7 Dec., for $2,000, was issued to John Barnes, an installment on TJ's salary as president. Warrants were also issued for the payment of Congress (MS in DLC: TJ Papers, 118:20408; in a clerk's hand; endorsed by Gallatin: "Warrants issued on Treasurer Week end. 14th

Decer. 1801"; with notation in Gallatin's hand: "The President will be pleased to excuse this rough draught as made out by the clerk—I had not time to transcribe & arrange it.—A.G."; endorsed by TJ as received from the Treasury Department on 14 Dec. and "Warrants"). No other papers sent by the Treasury Department have been identified.

TJ's WORD OF ANSWER has not been found. THOSE LAST SENT: TJ apparently refers to the statements that Gallatin sent him on 13 Dec. The Treasury secretary had previously provided TJ with EXPLA-

NATIONS during the preparation of the president's annual message to Congress (Vol. 35:622-4, 626-36).

A week earlier, the Treasury Department had sent TJ a list of six warrants, Nos. 156 to 161, issued between 30 Nov. and 5 Dec., totaling $77,753.28, and including No. 159, for $70,000, for payment of the Dutch debt (MS in DLC: TJ Papers, 118:20368; in a clerk's hand, with initials "A.G." and the total in Gallatin's hand; endorsed by TJ as received from the Treasury Department on 7 Dec.).

From William Judd

SIR   Farmington in Connecticut Decr. 14th 1801

I was born and Educated in the State of Connecticut, I have served my Country as an Officer in the Late revolutionary Warr, I am by profession an attorney and Counsellor at Law, I have seen the whole of the late revolution & the strugles of my Country for Independance, have Never withdrawn my Aid

The best part of my life is past, I was born July 10th 1743, I Love my Country its Constitution & Government—& because I differ in Politics & am an Advocate for the equal rights of Man, I can have expectations from my Native State, I still possess my Powers of mind unimpared, and Should gratefully Accept any Appointment under the General Government, that is honourable, & that will ensure a competency to ease down the Evening of Life

a professional imployment would best Accord with my Wishes— Habituated to command have the Vanity to beleive I might beneficially Administer some Government in the Gift of the President if any are Vacant, or fill a place in the Judiciary—This Communication from a Stranger may possebly be considered rude by some but that frankness which becomes a Republican I presume will not be considered as disrespectfull by the President of these States; for republican Integrety scorns Adulation—I hope and beleive I shall be pardoned while I feel & express, the frankness of A Soldier and the dignety of A Citizen, determined to be free dutifull and Obedient—My Person my Character & Talents are fully known to my friend Mr. Granger Post Master General, Ephraim Kirby Esqr. Supervisor of Connecticut and to all the Republican Citizens of Connecticut—I fear no

Scrutiny If the president in his goodness should in any degree favour my Wishes Any communication to the Post Master General will I fancy reach me without delay—

I have the honour to be with high Consideration Your Excellencys most Obedt. & very humble Servant WILLIAM JUDD

RC (DNA: RG 59, LAR); at head of text: "His Excellency Thos. Jefferson Esqr. President of the American States"; endorsed by TJ as received 24 Dec. and so recorded in SJL; also endorsed by TJ: "office."

During the Revolutionary War, William Judd (1743-1804) served as a major in the Connecticut militia, then as a captain in the Continental army. A graduate of Yale and former state legislator, he was described by Gideon Granger as a steadfast Republican and a "respectable but not a great Lawyer," who lost his life's savings speculating in Georgia land. He was among the "respectable republicans in Connecticut" recommended to TJ by John C. Ogden, and he also signed the 11 June 1801 letter to Levi Lincoln that urged the removal of Federalists from office in the state. TJ appointed Judd a commissioner of bankruptcy for Connecticut in December 1802 (Heitman, *Register*, 326; Dexter, *Yale*, 3:25-7; TJ to Ephraim Kirby, 10 Dec. 1802; Judd to Gideon Granger, 5 Jan. 1804, in DNA: RG 59, LAR; Vol. 31:74n; Vol. 34:344n).

From George Meade

At Sea, near St. Croix, Monday
Morning, December 14th. 1801.

DEAR SIR

The health of Mrs. Meade, & my Dr. Daughter Charlotte (who was married last Octor was a Twelve Month to a Mr. Wm. Hustler) obliged me to leave home, on Saturday 31st. Octobr, & our Capes 3d. Novr,—we had a most disagreable Passage to Barbados, where we arrived after a Passage of 24 days from the Capes. we spoke a Liverpool Ship, as we came out, who told us she had a Short Passage (our Capt. was so Stupid, he[1] did not enquire when she Saild) & that there was no News when he Saild; You will therefore naturally Conclude, I was much Surprised the day before we landed to be Informd, by a Sloop of War, to Windward, of Barbados, that they had an Account of a general Peace. on my geting a shore, my first object was to enquire for the English Papers, not one was to be procured for love or Money. my next enquirey was for the Barbados Paper, that Containd the out lines of Peace. the Stupid Printer only Publichd a number Sufficient for his Customers, & tho' I offered a Dollar for one, neither Money or the assistance of my friend could procure the Paper— my desire & wish was to forwd. it to you. the disapointment has however provd of the less Consequence, because no oppy has offerd for my Country, but the Vessell that I came out in—she proceeded for

Port Republick, where she was to lay 30 days for her Cargo. I left Barbados (where Mrs Meade & my Dr Daughter who is very ill, remain) this day week, at 10 O'Clock at night. I arrd. the next Afternoon at 4 o'Clock at Martinique. I came down in the British October Packet & am now Proceeding[2] there are two every Month that comes out. one goes to all the Islands down to Tortola, & then Sails for Falmouth—the other only Stops a few hours at Barbados then to Martinique, where the General & Admiral resides—& after Stoping one night goes down to Jamaica. the Novr. Packet came down to Martinique Thursday 10th Inst. & thro' the Interest of my Nephew General Maitland I procured 32[3] Papers. which I forwd. you by this Conveyance some have 3 or 4 Papers fastend together[4]—knowing how uncertain it is to receive news from England during our long winters. & besides that our careless Capts. very often come without News Papers. the British are to give up every thing taken, except Trinidad in the West Indies & the Island of Sylong in the East Indies[5] & it is said, are to hold the Island of Tobago (in the West Indies) till the French Government Pay them Two Millions Sterling, owd them for feeding the French Prisoners[6]—

Pray are our Laws so weak, I was told by a Gent. & two British officers that some of our People, on board the Frigates had behavd Infamously in the West Indies Yet the Capts. could not punish them, if true, it is high time, different laws should be Passed, without Subordination there is an end to all authority.

I hope you & Congress will take care that we are not brought to trouble by having a Consul General & Consuls at St. Dominigo they ought (in my humble opinion) all to be orderd home & you should give that Clever fellow Mr Lair a better office. I wish you to think of me too—I shall leave Barbados for Philada. by the 1st April, if you write me under Cover to my son Richd W. Meade of Philada. I shall have the honor of hearing from You.—I would wish to be Collector at Philada. I will forwd. you such Proof as will Convince You & the Senate that G. Latimer ought to be removd. my Son would Act for me till I get home.[7]

RC (MHi); in Meade's hand; endorsed by TJ as a letter from Meade received 10 Jan. 1802 and so recorded in SJL.

CHARLOTTE Meade married Englishman WILLIAM HUSTLER in October 1800. She died at Barbados on Christmas Day, 1801 (R. W. Meade, "George Meade, A Patriot of the Revolutionary Era," *Records of the American Catholic Historical Society of Philadelphia*, 3 [1888-91], 218).

MY NEPHEW: Frederick Maitland, the British quartermaster general in the West Indies (same, 206; DNB).

MR LAIR: Tobias Lear, the U.S. general commercial agent for Saint-Domingue.

¹ MS: "the."
² Ampersand and preceding three words interlined.
³ Number interlined in place of "26."
⁴ Preceding eight words and numbers interlined.
⁵ Preceding eight words and ampersand interlined.

⁶ Meade here inserted "I am now on my last sheet-Thro' a mistake this Side was overlookd."
⁷ Final two sentences written perpendicularly in right margin.

From J. P. G. Muhlenberg

Philadelphia Decr. 14th. 1801.

The President will—I hope, pardon the Liberty I take of addressing a line to Him, on a subject relating merely to myself—I have been honord with the appointment of Supervisor in this State—my intention was, to execute the duties of the Office, faithfully, & diligently, and to enable me to do this, I disengagd my self from all other business whatever, & the short time I have been in Office—owing to my removal from the Country to the City, has involvd me in expences, far superior to the emoluments I have receivd—From The Presidents Message, I am led to believe, that all the Offices attendant in the system of Internal Revenue will be abolishd—I confess that the idea of supporting Government without this mode of Taxation gives me pleasure—I never was a friend to it, but gave it all the opposition in my power, until the Law had passd, when I concievd it my duty to acquiesce.—

From the Opportunity I have had, while in Office to examine the Accounts, I find the outstanding Debts, to be very considerable, & that probably, time will be requird before matters can be finally arrang'd—to do this I presume some Officer must be continued, or a new one appointed—

I now beg leave to mention To the President, That the Office I now hold, is the only one I have ever held, except those conferrd on me by the People, & I have never held a lucrative one—my wish heretofore was—to end my days, on my lands in the Western Territory, but I am allmost too far advanc'd in Life to emigrate to that Country, & should wish—if possible to remain with my Friends & Connexions—If therefore the Office I now hold is abolish'd—I beg leave to sollicit The President for some Post in which I can be usefull, either in the Custom house, or elsewhere—It is true, great exertions are making to prevail on me, to enter the list against our present Governor—The friendship I have for Him forbids it—and as the sollicitations derive their Origin chiefly from our former Political Opponents, Principle shall—and ever will, prevent me from acceding to the measure.

I have the honor to be with the highest Respect, Your Most Obedt Servt   P. MUHLENBERG

RC (DNA: RG 59, LAR); at foot of text: "The President of The United States"; TJ's endorsement partially clipped. Recorded in SJL as received 16 Dec.

For the politics surrounding Muhlenberg's APPOINTMENT as SUPERVISOR of the revenue for Pennsylvania, see Sanford W. Higginbotham, *The Keystone in*

the Democratic Arch: Pennsylvania Politics 1800-1816 (Harrisburg, 1952), 32-4, and Vol. 33:28-9.

LANDS IN THE WESTERN TERRITORY: in 1797, Muhlenberg traveled west to survey his military bounty lands along the Scioto River, but then returned to his family home in Montgomery County, Pennsylvania (ANB).

From François Soulés

SIR/   Paris, Rue projetée No. 798, December the 14th 1801.

I have long wished for an opportunity of expressing to you my sentiments upon your nomination to the presidency of Congress, and now mr. Livingston offers me one. The United-states cou'd not certainly have made a better choice, and I hope that those little dissentions which have for sometimes agitated the sons of liberty, will soon, by your wisdom, be quieted. I always look with the greatest anxiety for the prosperity of that new republick, the history of which I wrote with your assistance, and I see with pleasure the daily encrease of its population, whilst at the same time it preserves its primitive freedom. Our revolution has been very different from yours: America has had the wisdom to name to the first places of the state those true patriots who had exposed their fortunes and their lives to assert her rights; but france has ungratefully sacrificed those bold and enterprising men who had the courage to oppose the despotism of several ages and a numerous standing army. They all fell victims upon the scaffold or were discarded by intrigue, so that, a few excepted, we see now at the head of affairs a set of new men entirely unknown in 1789—The french, I believe, are too hot-headed and too vain ever to be free. They have not the patience to discute cooly any question, and they are too fond of a military coat or feather, and I need not tell you that when soldiers enjoy too great a regard, they become the murderers of liberty. since thirteen years our wiseacres are making constitutions, and they have finished by leaving us without any: for the government we now live under, is neither republican nor monarchichal. It is absolutely military or despotic. The first consul has all the attributions of the King of England without the same check upon his power, for the senators, Tribuns and members of the legislative body have not the weight of the houses of peers and commons; they cou'd not prevent a stretch of power, and indeed so light are they in the constitutional scale, that a company of grenadeers might frighten them with their whiskers. The clergy is less than nothing; the judiciary power has but little influence, so that france is entirely under the government of one man. It is true that man conducts himself with mildness and that we lay under great obligations to him, since he prevented the dismemberment of the empire, and even extended its limits, since he put to flight a new terror which already began to spread her bloody claws upon the french; but then where will it end? Suppose that man shou'd happen to die, the generals, like in the roman empire, will contend amongst themselves for the government of the state; and Jealousy perhaps will raise contestations among them even before the death of Bonaparte. I tremble for the safety of my country, and since I cannot be now of any service, I really wish I cou'd spend the remainder of my days in America. But will not your Excellency laugh at my talkativeness or throw aside this letter as tedious? no, either I am greatly mistaken or mr. Jefferson is still glad to hear from his ancient acquaintances, from those who first cherished the seeds of liberty, who were admitted to his little committee dinners, and whom he seemed pleased to entertain. Tho' I have rendered great services, I am nothing in this new government. But I must comfort myself: it is the fate of mr. Lafayette and many others. I have often applied to be sent to America, because I shou'd have been extremely happy to be near you, but intrigue has always supplanted me. I beg leave to subscribe myself most respectfully your excellency's most obedient and most humble servant,

F: SOULÉS

RC (MoSHi: Jefferson Papers); addressed: "His Excellency Thomas Jefferson, president of the United-states of America"; endorsed by TJ as received 27 Feb. 1802 but recorded in SJL under 26 Feb.

LONG WISHED FOR AN OPPORTUNITY: Soulés (or Soulès) was a French writer, historian, and translator who had developed his skill in the English language during several years' residence in Britain. In 1786-87, TJ provided Soulés with detailed information and comments for a revision of the author's *Histoire des troubles de l'Amérique Anglaise*, a history of the American Revolution first published in London in 1785. A revised edition was printed in Paris in 1787. TJ praised the work and purchased copies in France for friends in the United States. Soulés consulted TJ again in 1789 in the preparation of a "pocket-book" guide to the British Parliament (*Biographie universelle, ancienne et moderne*, new ed., 45 vols. [Paris, 1843-65], 39:677-8; J. C. F. Hoefer,

Nouvelle biographie générale depuis les temps les plus reculés jusqu'a nos jours, 46 vols. [Paris, 1855-66], 44:233-4; Vol. 10:166, 201, 352-3, 363-83; Vol. 11:43, 56, 110, 666; Vol. 12:42, 130, 588; Vol. 14:684, 691; Sowerby, No. 484).

Robert R. LIVINGSTON had arrived in Paris and had begun to send dispatches to Washington; see Livingston to TJ, 26 Dec. 1801.

DISCUTE, meaning to discuss or debate, was obsolete in English before the nineteenth century (OED, 4:761). The French form of the verb, *discuter*, has survived.

From Antoine Félix Wuibert

SIR!

Upper-Dublin Township, Montgomery-County, State of Pennsylvania—14th of Xber 1801

Forever Rememberfull of Your Excellency's past favors, When you was Ambassador at the Court of Versailles, on account of my Prisemoney; I do Dare to Loock for again to, & now Beg very humbly for that Same your Kindness & Justice: for, as I have always heard, "it is Better to Recur to God, than to his Saints". my present hard Case, Sir, is thus—

By an original Deed Herewith inclosed, Congress of the United-States did grant me 405. acres of Land as my allowance in the military-lands, for my past Services. I have paid my taxes for it in the Same year; &, in the Course of few months afterwards, my Said land has been Seized & Executed By the Sheriff as it appears By a Letter which I have newly received from one George Taylor-Junior, Broker In Philadelphia & agent of one John Matthews Surveyor in the Western-territories, who is the Very Same Surveyor of my Land, as it appears By the Deed not only of my Land which he has Surveyed, But also his receipt which he gave me of my taxes. Expecting to See again Mr. John Matthews in Philadelphia last month, I did Call at his lodging in 3d. Street were he was not yet arrived, there I Left my Direction with the only View of paying my taxes, for I do never Shrink from Doing Right.

By what fatality my Land has been Sold By the Sheriff of that Country, I will not Say: However, I Do very much doubt of the Contents of the Letter; for when Congress intends to favor or Reward any of his Servants one may Depend upon their Kind Justice. But If I must Lose my Land in Such way, then I will Strike with all Due Submission! & Lay Down this land along with my old Dead-prise-money at the foot of the holy-Cross—

My unfortunate Case Being thus Stated, the only Comforting hope, Sir, Left to me, is to most humbly Intreat your Excellency's

Kind intercession for the preservation of my Land, an object too Dear to your Servant, Since it may make up Some of my Losses during the revolutionary war of this Country, & help along the poor Remains of my Shattered frame: Were I more hearty, I would immediately Set off for the Western-territories, Where I am totally unknown, & Where I do not Know one Single individual, to Whom I Could *Safely* apply in any Way—

I Pray God will please to Keep your Excellency's health in the hapiest State & grant you the most pleasing & prosperous Government—

I am with the most profound Respect Sir Your Excellency's The most Gratefull & the most obedient Servant   WUIBERT

Colonel of Engineers at fort Washington . . . 1776. Commander of the Volunteers on board of the pauvre Bonhomme Richard 1779. Governor-general for Congress, at fort Texel in holland 1779. & Engineer of the Western department 1782-3.

RC (DLC); at foot of first page: "His Exellency Mr. Thos. Jefferson, Esqr. President of the United States of America"; ellipses in original; endorsed by TJ as received 21 Dec. and so recorded in SJL. Enclosures not found.

A native of France, Antoine Félix Wuibert served as a lieutenant colonel of engineers in the Continental army during the American Revolution, during which time he suffered multiple imprisonments and saw action as a volunteer aboard John Paul Jones's frigate *Bonhomme Richard*. After the war, he went to Saint-Domingue, where in the mid-1780s he sought and received TJ's assistance in recovering prize money due him from the French government. TJ recorded in SJL that Wuibert wrote him twice in 1807, on 12 July and 16 Aug., in an apparent attempt to secure a military appointment, but neither letter has been found (Washington, *Papers, Rev. War Ser.*, 5:149n; same, *Confed. Ser.*, 3:360-2; Vol. 9:78-9, 294, 303, 378, 548, 563-4; Vol. 10:501-2; Vol. 11:39-40).

MILITARY-LANDS: in 1796, Congress ordered the survey of a tract of land east of the Scioto River in the Northwest Territory, which would be reserved for holders of land warrants received for military service. Priority for locating warrants in the tract would be determined by lots. Delays prevented the act from being implemented until 1800 (U.S. Statutes at Large, 1:490-1, 724; 2:7, 14-16; Downes, *Frontier Ohio*, 83-5; Payson Jackson Treat, *The National Land System, 1785-1820* [New York, 1910], 238-41).

GEORGE TAYLOR, Jr., a broker in Chestnut Street, was the former chief clerk and translator at the State Department. He was also the Philadelphia AGENT for surveyors John Mathews (MATTHEWS) and Ebenezer Buckingham, who offered themselves as agents for holders of U.S. military land warrants to survey and sell land in the western military tract, and to pay the taxes on them as well (Stafford, *Philadelphia Directory, for 1798*, 139; Stafford, *Philadelphia Directory, for 1801*, 89; Robinson, *Philadelphia Directory for 1802*, 239; *Philadelphia Gazette*, 26 July 1799, 4 May 1801; Vol. 17:358n; Vol. 23:291-2; Vol. 27:635-6; Vol. 30:129).

From Jacob Crowninshield

Sir   Salem 15th December 1801.

Being always anxious to support the honor and fair fame of the Republican cause, to the utmost efforts of my feeble abilities, may I beg permission to lay before the President and Father of our Nation, some facts relative to the Office of Collector of the Revenue for the Port of Salem and to make a few observations on the appointmt of another Officer should a vacancy happen,—at a time almost as early as when "the People" of our beloved Country burst open the doors of honor and confidence, too long shut and barr'd against the real Republicans, and placed at the Helm the man and the patriot of their first and best choice at this period the Republicans in this District cast their eyes on a proper person to fill the Office of Collector of this Port, provided the President should deem it necessary to make a vacancy therein, and I may say with great truth, that John Gibaut, a native of this town, was designated as a suitable man, in preference to any other, and representations and recommendations to this effect were intended to be made to Government, but too timid and over-cautious, few men among us on the Republican side would venture to make the necessary and proper statements, to you, on the subject, because nearly all our rich men, being highly federal and vindictive, should they come to a knowledge of the transaction, would have it in their power to oppress them, and we have had too many instances to know that having the disposition and the power, those persons have seldom ceased to exercise both, and to pursue, with persevereing obstinacy, these innocent victims of their federalism. however by the earnest solicitations of my own family, and some few select friends, I was induced to address myself to a Gentleman in Boston whom you had recently appointed to an important station, and who now fills it with honor and credit to the Nation and himself, in consequence of which some applications were made to other Officers of Government, but as about this time, you retired from Washington to your family seat at Monticello I fear whether any representation ever reached you on the subject. things have remained in this state untill very lately rumour has announced that William Lee of Marblehead, was making very great interest for the place, indeed as it comes immediately from Mr. Lee no doubt is entertained of its truth,—I assure you Sir that this information has greatly alarmed the Republicans in this neighbourhood generally, and *particularly those in Salem* for however Mr. Lee's best friends may be partial towards him, and it is admitted that he has one or two, who are high in the esteem of the Citizens, in particular a Gentleman whom the Republicans hope, next year, to place at the head of the Government of Massachusetts, yet it might be demonstrated, that these friends have not well considered the consequences and impolicy of the measure they have recommended.—

It is a very delicate subject to write about, and it is more delicate to impeach the judgement of those we regard, especially when we have to warn of danger in a quarter where none, at first, was apprehended, but having the public good in view and wishing to support your Administration and knowing in whose hands I shall deposit these remarks, I hesitate not to inform you that I have good authority to state, that the person from Marblehead is on several accounts an improper man to fill the Collectorship of Salem, in the first place from commercial and other speculations, in which he was very unfortunate (and which I sincerely regret) his circumstances are considered so far involved as to make it hazardous to be intrusted with large sums of the public money, in the next place his political character is doubtful, to say the best of it, "during *the contest of opinion through which we have past*," he has trimed to the federal breeze, and by the party which then governed was claimed as a *federalist*, and so far was he from being considered as a Republican, that he never was counted upon in our Elections, either for his own vote or his influence among others. these are facts Sir, which you may depend upon I would not dare to misstate to you. in the third place there is not any thing of the kind which would more disappoint the real republicans of Salem than the appointment of this person to the Collectorship here, many of the *federalists* would rejoice at it for *several reasons*, and by the majority of all it would be considered as a reflection upon the fair character of our town that it could not present to the President, a Citizen from its own bosom worthy of his choice, that in consequence of this deficiency, the President had been obliged to resort to another Town, and where indeed he had unfortunately selected another, who could not have the confidence and approbation of the great body of those who love and revere the first Magistrate, and whose interests and feelings, he would never willingly injure, being well convinced and assured of this, I have, after due reflection, ventured to address you on the subject, sincerely wishing that you should know the undisguised situation of our hopes and our fears.—

I must now beg leave to state the character political and private of the person whom the Republicans here would wish might have the place, if the President contemplates making any change therein. Mr. Gibaut is a Republican in word and in deed, undisguised and without hesitation. he has always expressed himself and acted as such, in the perilous seasons of federal power, in times when the finger of scorn pointed to the Republican, and said, "this is a Jacobin, come let us kill him and his inheritance shall be ours," in times such as these, which we have all seen, Mr. Gibaut with about twenty others in this town boldly stem'd the torrent, which then seemed as it were to threaten every thing dear to us, and thanks be to Heaven, we have had the pleasure to find that their exertions have not a little contributed to the success of the Republican cause in this neighbourhood, it was a link of the great chain of efforts throughout this extensive Continent which have been finally crowned with glorious success.—

I am certain that I may with great confidence recommend Mr. Gibaut to your favour, as a man of very handsome abilities, as the scholar and the gentleman, as the man of information, the Merchant of practical knowledge, the correct Accountant, and the persevereing advocate of Republican principles and measures, as the warm supporter of your Administration, and the open and declared opponent of anti-republican tendencies.—with respect to his private & moral character, it is perfectly good. he supports an aged father who intirely depends upon him, he *stand's high in the esteem of his fellow Citizens* and particularly so among his friends and near acquaintance. after he left the University of Cambridge, where he graduated at an early age, about 15 years ago, he went to Sea, and the second voyage was intrusted with the charge of a large Indiaman & a valuable Cargo, the last voyage he performed, he fell sick, and his health is now indifferent, so much so, that he finds himself unable to undertake another voyage.—perhaps I am partial in my opinion of him, but I really think he is fit and able to fill the Office refered to, or even another of more importance, his private affairs are in a good situation, he is not in debt & he possesses a small unencumbered estate, I mention these minute things, that you should be correctly informed of every thing relative to the candidate I have taken the liberty to recommend to your notice in preference to the other from Marblehead with respect to whom I ought to have explained, that I do not mean to be understood as wishing to injure his private character as the good neighbour or honest man, however I can not but feel surprized that he should solicit the *Salem* appointment, where if he succeeded, his residence must be quite unpleasant to himself, and certainly very unpopular among the Citizens. I assure you Sir from my heart that you had better let the present incumbent remain in office some time longer rather than appoint any other, who would not have the confidence of the

Republicans of this district, for these subordinate appointmts being filled with Citizens on the *real* Republican side of the question, will have great influence with the Public, and from them a solid weight will be felt in the political scale. whereas if by any reason whatever, it should unfortunately happen, that an opposite appointment should be made the injury to our cause would be almost incalculable in a political point of view. but I trust these observations are unnecessary, and I must claim your forgiveness for obtruding them into this already too lengthy communication

Most sincerely wishing you all imaginable happiness, I remain with sentiments of the highest esteem and respectful attachment Your Obedt and humble servt   JACOB CROWNINSHIELD

PS. the present possessor, Mr. Hiller, has acquired about 40,000 Dolls of the public money by his Office. he has held it upwards of 12 years and being *rich*, it can do him no injury to give it to another who is more deserving, he is a *decided federalist*, was recommended to his place by Mr. *Goodhue*, the former Senator from this District. to this moment he employs an abusive federal Gazette in this town, which is continually and *systematically* engaged in the work of slander and defamation against your Administration.—The Naval Officer of this port, Mr. Pickman is a federalist but *a worthy man*, being prudent in his conduct, I should be very sorry to see him removed.—the US. revenue collected in the Salem Custom house is very considerable. the East India trade is our most important branch. there has been at one time 30 vessels of all sizes employed, from this town, in Commerce on the other side of the Cape of Good Hope. at this time I beleive there may be about 20 ships in that trade, they are much larger than those formerly employed & their Cargoes are much more valuable. our Merchants generally speaking are rich but most unfortunately of federal principles with the exception of a few, indeed there are only 3 or 4 Commercial houses that are really republican & among these I am proud to mention the name of George Crowninshield & Sons, which consists of a whole family, firmly devoted to the support of your Administration and the Republican cause

I am most respectfully and with great sincerity your well wisher & Obedt servt   JACOB CROWNINSHIELD

RC (DNA: RG 59, LAR); addressed: "Honble. Thomas Jefferson Esqre. President of the United States Washington"; endorsed by TJ as received 24 Dec. and so recorded in SJL; also endorsed by TJ: "Hiller, collector of Salem to be removed Lee not to be appointed John Gibaut recommended."

Mariner and merchant Jacob Crowninshield (1770-1808) was a member of one of Salem's most prominent mercantile families, whose members were also avid Republicans. He captained trading voyages to the West Indies, East Indies, and India before devoting himself to commercial interests and politics in the late 1790s. Elected to the Massachusetts Senate in 1801, he defeated Timothy Pickering for a seat in Congress the following year. Arriving in Washington, Crowninshield's talent and ability were soon recognized by the Republicans. TJ offered him the secretaryship of the navy in 1805, but Crowninshield reluctantly declined. Suffering from chronically poor health, he died in Washington (DAB; William T. Whitney, Jr., "The Crowninshields of Salem, 1800-1808, A Study in the Politics of Commercial Growth," *Essex Institute Historical Collections*, 94 [1958], 1-36, 79-118).

JOHN GIBAUT, a Harvard graduate and mariner from Salem, was the son of Edward Gibaut and Sarah Crowninshield. He did not receive the Salem collectorship, but Crowninshield's recommendation led to his appointment as collector at Gloucester in 1802. He retained the position until his death in 1805 (JEP, 1:432; *Essex Institute Historical Collections*, 71 [1935], 142-3; 94 [1958], 20-1; Gallatin to TJ, 9 Aug. 1802; TJ to Gallatin, 14 Aug. 1802).

A GENTLEMAN IN BOSTON: possibly Boston attorney George Blake, the recently appointed U.S. attorney for Massachusetts (Kline, *Burr*, 1:443n; Vol. 33:677). For the interest of William R.

LEE in the Salem collectorship, see Lee to TJ, 28 Sep. 1801. A GENTLEMAN WHOM THE REPUBLICANS HOPE: James Sullivan (Vol. 35:686-7).

HIS INHERITANCE SHALL BE OURS: the quoted passage is a paraphrase of Mark 12:7.

Joseph HILLER had served as collector for the district of Salem and Beverly since 1789 and was considered an influential member of the Essex Junto (JEP, 1:9; Prince, *Federalists*, 31-3).

Benjamin GOODHUE represented Massachusetts in the U.S. House of Representatives from 1789 to 1796 and in the Senate from 1796 to 1800 (*Biog. Dir. Cong.*).

ABUSIVE FEDERAL GAZETTE: the *Salem Gazette*. In 1800, the Crowninshields helped establish the Salem *Impartial Register* as a counter to the vehemently pro-Federalist *Gazette* (*Essex Institute Historical Collections*, 94 [1958], 8-9; Brigham, *American Newspapers*, 1:400; Jeffrey L. Pasley, "*The Tyranny of Printers*": *Newspaper Politics in the Early Republic* [Charlottesville, 2001], 210-11).

William PICKMAN, a prominent Federalist and former state legislator, was appointed naval officer at Salem in 1789 (JEP, 1:9; Prince, *Federalists*, 33).

Established by family patriarch George Crowninshield, the firm of GEORGE CROWNINSHIELD & SONS included Jacob and his four brothers and was a leading participant in the East India trade (David L. Ferguson, *Cleopatra's Barge: The Crowninshield Story* [Boston, 1976], 27; *Essex Institute Historical Collections*, 94 [1958], 2, 13-14).

From Albert Gallatin

DEAR SIR   Tuesday Morning [15 Dec. 1801]

The enclosed requires but little comment. Why Mr Beckley did not divide the printing between Mr Duane & Mr Smith I do not know; but I am sure that most of our friends are so chagrined at it, that they speak of altering the rules of the house, so as to have the printer appointed by the House & not by the clerk. Mr Smith came here before the fate of the election was ascertained & at a risk. He was promised by myself & others every reasonable arrangement. But this cannot be construed into an exclusive monopoly. He has already the printing of the laws & of every department, and the Congress business might have been divided.

I wish however that Mr D.'s application for purchase of his stationary might be communicated to the several heads of Departments; &, if you think it proper, the letter being transmitted by you may be better attended to. We may in the Treasury purchase a part, but cannot pay until Congress shall have made an appropriation; ours being exhausted.

No Letters which required immediate answers having been received these three days, I have delayed acting on them until I had got rid of the report to Congress. This is the reason of your not receiving any these two days.

With sincere respect & affection Your obedt. Servt.

ALBERT GALLATIN

RC (DLC); partially dated; at foot of text: "The President of the United States"; endorsed by TJ as received 15 Dec. and so recorded in SJL with notation "Duane." Enclosure: William Duane to Gallatin, Washington, 13 Dec. 1801, noting his disappointment at failing to obtain the printing of the journals of the House of Representatives as he had been given reason to hope by Nathaniel Macon; encouraged to keep the *Aurora* at Philadelphia, even though it afforded him a bare maintenance, and noting the service it provided to the public, Duane thought it "not unreasonable to expect the preference of printing for Congress," and many influential members of Congress questioned why he had not received it; having incurred thousands of dollars of debt in setting up his printing establishment and acquiring "a stock of Stationery, adequate to any demand of Congress," Duane hoped, by soliciting Gallatin's friendship "and that of the gentlemen of the administration," to acquire advance orders and payments for stationery from the public offices before he left for Philadelphia on 20 Dec.; the proceeds would enable him to pay debts, which were coming due, and thus preserve his credit (Gallatin, *Papers*, 6:176; Cunningham, *Jeffersonian Republicans in Power*, 268-9).

One explanation for Beckley's failure to DIVIDE THE PRINTING of the House of Representatives is that he had learned that Duane had kept him from becoming clerk of the Senate. In September 1801, Samuel A. Otis reported on "pretty good authority" that Republicans planned to elect Beckley clerk in his place. Although Beckley and Duane were friends, Duane reportedly met with Otis shortly before Congress convened and proposed that if Otis would give the Senate printing contract to him, he would assure Otis of keeping his office, in spite of the Republican plan to oust him (Edmund Berkeley and Dorothy Smith Berkeley, *John Beckley: Zealous Partisan in a Nation Divided* [Philadelphia, 1973], 229, 231; Gerard W. Gawalt, ed., *Justifying Jefferson: The Political Writings of John James Beckley* [Washington, D.C., 1995], 245; Beckley to TJ, 27 Oct.). Duane received the printing contracts for the journal of the Senate for the Eighth and Ninth Congresses but not for the Seventh (Shaw-Shoemaker, Nos. 1486, 3285, 7510, 9535, 11586, 13935).

THEY SPEAK OF ALTERING THE RULES: on 17 Dec., John Randolph informed the House that he had learned it would take 20 days to get a report printed for the Committee of Ways and Means, thus impeding their work. He, therefore, moved that a committee "be appointed to devise a plan for expediting the printing work of the House." The committee, chaired by Randolph, reported the next day with two recommendations. First, the committee thought it expedient to give the heads of the departments the responsibility for printing "all such documents, reports, and statements, as are directed by law to be annually laid before the House." Second, they asked that a printer be appointed who would provide the "faithful and prompt execution of all business confided to him by order of the House." The House accepted the first recommendation, but not the second. Randolph, Joseph H. Nicholson, and Samuel Smith argued for the appointment of a printer by the House, while Roger Griswold, Thomas Lowndes, and William Eustis argued against it. Griswold "could see no reason for altering the mode in which the printing business was now and had ever been done; it now lies with the Clerk, who is empowered to employ as many persons as he pleases or deems expedient" (JHR, 4:20; Annals, 11:335-7; Biog. Dir. Cong.).

PURCHASE OF HIS STATIONARY: the Treasury Department had earlier ordered supplies from Duane, including paper for stamps, for which Duane requested a $3,000 advance in September (Gallatin, Papers, 5:299, 727). For the debts acquired by Duane in setting up his printing office and bookselling business in Washington, which led to his dire financial condition, see Duane to TJ, 10 May 1801.

From Abishai Thomas

SIR   Navy Office 15th Decemr. 1801

John Thompson Mason Esquire having applied for an official copy of the instructions to the commanders of armed Vessels in the Service of the United States of the 10th July 1798, as being necessary to be exhibited as testimony in a trial now pending in the Supreme Court in relation to the French Schooner Peggy

I have the honor to transmit the copy herewith, and in the absence of the Secretary of the Navy to submit to your approbation the propriety of furnishing the same to Mr. Mason—

With the utmost consideration & respect, I have the honor to be Sir yr. mo. obt Ser   AB. THOMAS

RC (DLC); at foot of text: "President U.S."; endorsed by TJ as received from the Navy Department on 16 Dec. FC (Lb in DNA: RG 45, LSP). Enclosure not found, but see below.

In accordance with acts of Congress passed 28 May, 28 June, and 9 July 1798, John Adams and Benjamin Stoddert issued INSTRUCTIONS TO THE COMMANDERS OF ARMED VESSELS on 10 July, authorizing them to capture "any armed French Vessel" found "within the Jurisdictional Limits of the United States, or elsewhere on the high seas," and to recapture any U.S. vessels taken by the French. Such captures were to be carried into U.S. ports "in Order that Proceedings may be had concerning such Capture or Recapture in due Form of Law, and as to right shall appertain" (NDQW, Feb. 1797-Oct. 1798, 187).

THE FRENCH SCHOONER PEGGY was captured by the U.S. frigate Trumbull off Saint-Domingue in April 1800, after being forced aground near Port-au-

Prince. The vessel was taken to New London, where the U.S. District Court of Connecticut declared that the *Peggy* was not a lawful prize since it was not taken on the high seas and was armed for defensive purposes only. The federal circuit court at Hartford reversed the decision, however, and on 23 Sep. 1800 the court ordered the vessel and its cargo sold and the proceeds divided evenly between the captors and the United States. On 2 Oct. 1800, the ship's master, Joseph Buisson, filed a writ of error with the U.S. Supreme Court, appealing the circuit court's decision. The Supreme Court heard arguments during its December 1801 term, with John Thomson Mason representing Buisson. Delivering the opinion of the court on 21 Dec., Chief Justice John Marshall declared that the *Peggy* ought to be restored under the terms of the Convention of 1800 because it had not been "definitively condemned" before the treaty went into effect (Cranch, *Reports*, 1:103-10; Syrett, *Hamilton*, 25:429-31; Marshall, *Papers*, 6:99-102).

From Thomas Bruff

SIR,   George Town Decr 16th 1801. At Mr. Semmes's
A person unworthy your attention has taken upon him, to address a few lines to you, in consequence of a promise last winter to make and present to you, a machine for perpetual time. As you had not time properly to investigate the plan, I considerd your sentiments as rather unfavourable, but you gave me every assurance of patronage that I could wish, provided I brought the machine into operation. I should not have taken the liberty to address you, had not unforeseen events, prevented the fulfilment of my promise. I beg you will excuse the detail of my misfortunes, as I cannot expect you, as a stranger to my character, to consider the bare assertion of misfortunes, as a proper apology. I mentiond to you, that I had concieved a plan for a spoon manufacturing machine, which previous to my interview with you, I had engaged to George Riggs of this place, silversmith, for which he was to give one thousand dollars, which sum would have put me in a situation to work on the time piece. Notwithstanding a fair bargain before evidence, he refused it when done, after causing me a great deal of expence and labour to bring to perfection, and I had to sue him for the money. I had it tried here and at Philadelphia, by different silversmiths, in the presence of a number of gentlemen; and have by me certificates to shew, that the product is more than 60 to one faster than with the hammer, and same number of hands. I then sold one for Charles Town S. Carolina, but the purchaser hearing of my dispute with Riggs, followd his example, and by the two, I have missd 1300 dollars, which in my circumstances, has been seveerly felt. I was calld from this scene of disappointment, to my

family 9 in number, out of which 5 were taken dangerously ill, 3 of whom died, and the expence aded to other losses, and being kept all the summer from my business, has brought me into such difficulties, that I am obliged to travel all the winter for support. My companion in life was one of those who were ill, her constitution is broken by the disease, she has every symptom of an approaching decline, and I am seriously apprehensive, that my absence at this time will soon effect, our final seperation. You will readily percieve, that amidst these difficulties, having on me the care of a helpless family, whose wants calld aloud for my exertion, I could not with a human heart, set down to such a piece of business as the machine, with the degree of composure necessary for so nice a performance. The only experiment I have had it in my power to try, has proved beyond all controversy, in my opinion, the efficacy of the plan; and permit me to repeat, that the first time I have it in my power to undertake it, free from other anxieties, it will be seen, that I was not prepossessd in favour of my own production. I have laid out, in improvements and patents, all the money I ever had, and there is no encouragement either publick or private, for the most useful inventions, and he that does most to lessen the enormous price of labour, unless he has the means of providing a capital, is like to be the poorest man. I now stand in need of publick patronage, and if I can find in the house, any gentlemen of the members, who are friends to genious, and can make any intrust among them, I mean to apply. Nature has designd me for inventing, such things are almost as easy to me, as to eat or sleep; and if I could live by it; I would devote my life in that way, to the service of my country. Many useful things I have thought of, but for want of means to bear me out, I have let them pass. Exclusive of the machine I am most anxious about, I have brought to perfection the patent tooth instruments, and others; a coffee mill, that grinds a pound in 4 & $\frac{1}{2}$ minutes; the spoon machine, that produces from a flat bar, a spoon, ready for the punch, in 12 seconds: fixings for bed steads, to superceed the necessity of screwing them and lacing the sacking: I have modeld here, a machine for treading wheat, cheap and simple, avoiding the fault of those lately patented, such as leaving in the straw, from 60, to 100 bushels of a thousand, and cuting off the heads where the straw is unsound. I have pland a grist mill; to be set up like a coffee mill, and turnd by hand; and a sider mill, that is to be workd the same way, to grind, to press, to seperate the pummice, and conduct the liquor to the cask, all by the turn of one hand. These are not all, but sufficient to shew, that nature has formd me for such employment, and I hope you will say, I ought to have assistance. Hopeing my promise, respecting the time piece, will be considerd as my apology for calling your attention to the subject, I remain with all sentiments of respect.

Your Huml. Servt.   THOS. BRUFF.

RC (DLC); addressed: "Thos. Jefferson. Esquire. President of the United States"; franked and postmarked; endorsed by TJ as received 16 Dec. and so recorded in SJL.

Thomas Bruff (c. 1772-1816), dentist and inventor, received six patents over his lifetime. He advertised his services as a dentist at "Mr. Semmes's" in Georgetown in 1799 and moved to the city of Washington in 1802. Described by TJ in 1812 as a "mighty good, and very ingenious man," TJ employed Bruff several times as his personal dentist (Georgetown *Centinel of Liberty*, 29 Nov. 1799; *Washing-*

ton Federalist, 1 Dec. 1802; *Daily National Intelligencer*, 13 Apr. 1816; *List of Patents*, 25, 61, 68, 126; MB, 2:1093, 1144, 1235; Vol. 32:513; TJ to Madison, 6 June 1812).

Bruff met TJ the previous WINTER to discuss the development of a perpetual motion machine. In September 1801, Bruff acquired a patent for his silver SPOON MANUFACTURING MACHINE. The 8 Dec. issue of the *Federal Gazette & Baltimore Daily Advertiser* published CERTIFICATES of trials of the machine in Georgetown and Philadelphia (Vol. 32:512-3; *List of Patents*, 25).

From Henry Dearborn

SIR   War Department Decmr. 16th 1801

Will it not be necessary to intimate to Congress the necessaty of some provision for making the proposed establishment of a Magazine & Armoury in South Carolina, and also for making some improvements at Harpers ferry.

I am Sir with the highest respect Your Huml. Servt.

H. DEARBORN

RC (DLC); at head of text: "To the President of the United States"; endorsed by TJ as received 17 Dec. from the War Department regarding "Magazine in S. Carola" and so recorded in SJL.

TJ brought the subjects of this letter to the attention of CONGRESS in his message of 2 Feb. 1802.

From Tadeusz Kosciuszko

SIR   25. Frimaire Paris [i.e. 16 Dec. 1801]

I suppose Mr Dawson wrote to your Excellency a lettere by my desire, in whiche I had recomendet somes Officers my Countrymen, of talents, Character, Probity, and who in severales Campagnes distinguished themself by bravery. To this time i have no enswer. I beg you would do me that honor, and wether my Countrymen can expect to bi employed in your Army.

my respect and frindship   T: Kosciuszko

RC (PP: Historical Manuscripts Collection, Rare Book Department); English date supplied; endorsed by TJ as a letter of 15 Dec. received 27 Feb. 1802 and so recorded in SJL.

If John DAWSON wrote to TJ about Kosciuszko's recommendation of Polish military officers, TJ may not have received the letter. No correspondence of the sort has been found. TJ's reply to Kosciuszko on 2 Apr. 1802 acknowledged the letter printed above, but revealed nothing about any communication from Dawson.

On 1 Nov. 1801, TJ authorized Jonathan Smith, the cashier of the Bank of Pennsylvania in Philadelphia, to receive Kosciuszko's stock dividends: "Know all men by these presents that I Thomas Jefferson of Virginia, Attorney in fact for General Thaddeus Kosciuzko with authority to substitute others of every denomination & power, do hereby appoint Jonathan Smith of Philadelphia a substitute for the sd Thaddeus Kosciuszko, for the special purpose and with full power to recieve from time to time and at all times as they shall become due from the bank of Pensylvania all dividends to which he the said Thaddeus may be entitled as a holder of shares of the stock in the said bank, and to give valid reciepts & discharges for the same as fully as I myself might do. In testimony whereof I have hereto set my hand & seal this 1st. day of November 1801" (PrC in MHi, entirely in TJ's hand, including at foot of text, in anticipation of signatures of witnesses, "Attest"; TJ to Smith and Smith to TJ, both 20 July 1802).

From Bishop James Madison

DEAR SIR   Decr. 16th. 1801, Wmsburg.

I recd. your Favr. by the Son of Dr Logan; & tho' I cannot take him into my Family, at present, yet I will, with great Satisfaction, make a Point of having him established in a Manner which cannot fail of being agreable. I will also superintend his Education with Zeal; & I trust, with that Success which will neither disappoint the Solicitude of a Parent, nor be unworthy of your Recommendation. Nothing shall be wanting on my Part; & if the young Gentleman should discover Talents for Improvement, & the requisite Disposition, I am assured his Friends will have no Reason to regret his having become a Student of this Place.

I cannot refrain from expressing the real Pleasure which I have felt in the Perusal of your Message to Congress. You have brought Government back to it's original & proper objects; and every[1] Friend to the union must rejoice at the Prospect, which is now before them, of experiencing the Blessings which such a Government is capable of dispersing, when virtuously & wisely administered. I hope Congress will second your Views with Ardour;—and then, we shall have, at least, one Example of a Govt. which will be faithful to the Purposes of it's Institution —

With the sincerest Regard & Esteem, I am Dr Sir, Yr. Friend & Sert.   J MADISON

RC (DLC); endorsed by TJ as received 21 Dec. but recorded in SJL at 22 Dec.

YOUR FAVR.: TJ to Bishop James Madison, 8 Dec.

SUPERINTEND HIS EDUCATION:

Albanus Logan enrolled in the College of William and Mary and graduated in the same class as Bishop Madison's son John in 1803 (*List of Alumni*, 26).

[1] Madison here canceled "real."

From Pierre Samuel Du Pont de Nemours

MONSIEUR LE PRÉSIDENT   New York 17 Xbre 1801.

Votre Message est, comme toutes vos pensées et tous vos écrits, plein de sagesse, de raison, de lumieres, et d'une morale celeste. — Mais, quoique je respecte votre Nation, je crains que vous ne soyiez trop fort pour Elle.

Vous la félicitez de la Paix. — Cette bénédiction du Ciel parait à tous les habitans de vos Ports une calamité publique.

Vous la félicitez de ce que les Sauvages se civilisent un peu; et de ce que, au lieu de déperir, les progrès de quelques unes de leurs Tribus dans l'Agriculture augmentent leur Population. — Les habitans de vos campagnes regardent, à très grand tort il est vrai, les Sauvages et les Arbres comme des ennemis naturels qu'il faut exterminer par le fer, par le feu, par le *Brandy* pour occuper leur territoire.

Ils se regardent, eux et leur Postérité comme des héritiers collatéraux de tous les beaux domaines que Dieu a créés depuis la Cumberland et l'Ohio jusqu'au grand Océan, soidisant pacifique.

Et quelle est, même en Europe ou dans les Etats unis, la branche cadette d'une Famille qui se réjouisse bien sincerement de la multiplication des enfans de la branche ainée dont elle ambitionne la Succession?

Vous lui donnez à pressentir que, en améliorant l'ordre judiciaire, on pourra faire une grande économie des *deniers publics*; vous auriez pu ajouter, *et particuliers*: car plus il y a de Juges, plus il nait de procès qui sont les plus lourds des impôts pour les Familles.

Et presque tous ceux de vos jeunes gens qui ont été au College, avec assez d'esprit pour ne vouloir pas être Prêtres, et trop-peu de fortune ou de patience pour les longues études qu'exige l'etat de

Medecin, lequel d'ailleurs n'a, ni ne mérite en Amérique la considération dont il devrait jouir, veulent être *Lawyers* ou Juges, quelquefois l'un et l'autre en même tems, plaidans devant un Tribunal, allant
prononcer dans l'autre: ce qui a beaucoup d'inconvéniens joints à
quelque ridicule.

Quant aux Prêtres, vous avez beau ne leur dire mot et protéger leur
liberté, vous êtes Philosophe; partant, il n'y en a pas un dans le monde,
ni d'aucune Secte, qui ne soit votre Ennemi.

Ainsi vous faites, vous proposez, vous vantez avec justice, des biens
très réels, qui déplaisent et déplairont *seulement* à vos Agriculteurs, à
vos Commerçans, et à vos gens de lettres.

Que peut, contre tous ces Citoyens là, le Suffrage d'un Etranger
comme moi, et d'une douzaine peut-être d'autres Penseurs dispersés
dans ce Pays?

Vous trouverez donc des épines sous vos roses, vos olives, et vos
lauriers.

Cependant persévérez. Car Socrate, et Caton, et Confucius, et Marc
Aurele, et mon Saint Ami Mr. Turgot, avec qui vous avez de grands[1]
rapports, auraient persévéré à votre place.

D'abord, pour un homme tel que vous, il ne s'agit pas de savoir ce
qu'on dira; mais de voir juste, et de faire le bien.—Et puis, si votre
Peuple ne vous entend guere, il est doux et nullement disposé à trou-
bler le Gouvernement. vous avez encore quarante mois à rêgner, et
beaucoup de vraisemblance d'etre réélu. Car autre chose est de se voir
universellement applaudir dans les sociétés de *parleurs*, ou de réussir
aux Elections. Il y a dans les Etats unis plus qu'ailleurs un bon sens
silencieux, un esprit de justice froide, qui lorsqu'il est question d'emettre un *vote* couvre les bavardages de ceux qui font les habiles.

Et parmi ces derniers même une hypocrisie nécessaire ne leur per-
met point de montrer le fond de leur cœur.—On n'ôserait pas s'elever
ouvertement contre la Paix.—On n'ôserait pas dire tout haut à son
voisin, ni peut-étre méme à sa Femme, que ce serait bien fait de tuer
les Sauvages.

La pudeur et le tems sont donc pour vous. La diminution des Impôts, espece d'argument à la portée de tout le monde est pour vous.
La suppression des Impôts vexatoires, pour lesquels il fût si triste
d'employer la force militaire, qui ne les a pas rendu plus aimables, est
entierement pour vous.

Si vous êtes réelu une fois, comme je n'en doute point, vous le serez
toute la vie. Washington l'aurait êté, s'il ne se fût pas démis. Et malgré votre impôsante concurrence Mr Adams lui même l'eut peut-être
êté, s'il avait eu un peu plus de tête, et si Mr Hamilton ne l'eut pas

trainé dans la boue.—Le changement n'a point de charme pour les Américains. Il en aura moins encore à votre égard, où l'on ne trouverait pas même un prétexte plausible pour le justifier.

Vous êtes robuste et sobre. vous devez vivre autant que Franklin.— C'est plus qu'il n'en faut pour créer, avec les enfans qui n'ont que dix ans aujourd'hui, une génération nouvelle qui n'aura reçu aucune mauvaise influence de la guerre ni du gaspillage.

Par l'effet même de votre Gouvernement, et peut-être par l'instruction que vous leur ferez donner, ces enfans là vaudront mieux que leurs Peres.

Vous serez aidé dans leur éducation par tout ce qu'il y aura d'hommes estimables et éclairés en Europe, qui d'ici à dix ans se remettront avec ardeur à cultiver les sciences morales et politiques, prècisement parceque leurs Gouvernemens ne le voudront point. Car les Européens, qui ne savent pas réellement braver l'autorité, aiment cependant à la contredire. Ils ont un demi courage, en paroles et en écrits, qui vous sera un très bon instrument. Et le petit nombre de ceux dont le courage est vraiment élevé viendront vivre sous vos loix comme j'ai fait, parceque d'ici à un siecle ou deux il n'y a point de liberté à esperer dans aucune partie de l'Europe, et que la Paix même sans la liberté n'a que des plaisirs froids et plats.—le fils de ma jeunesse s'est appellé *Victor*. J'ai nommé celui de ma raison *Eleuthère Irénée*. Il y en aura d'autres que lui.

Ce *pacifique ami de la Liberté* espere en faisant de la Poudre qu'elle ne servira point à la guerre, mais aux exercices préservateurs de la guerre auxquels la milice et la jeunesse doivent se livrer, au Commerce du Pays, à la chasse, à l'ouverture des montagnes et des canaux, aux travaux publics.

Je n'ai pas voulu vous écrire à son sujet pendant que vous étiez occupé à souder avec Galatin les plaies de vos finances, et à préparer pour le Congrès vos travaux politiques, vos propositions.—A présent que tout cela est en marche, et ne vous coutera pas plus vis-à-vis des Représentans et du Sénat de la nation qu'une correspondance ordinaire, je vous rendrai compte de nos idées et du point où nous en sommes. ce sera l'objet d'une autre Lettre.

Béni soyez vous de songer à faciliter la naturalisation dans un Pays où tous les travaux utiles manquent de capitaux et de bras, et les terres d'acheteurs.

Vous dites à cet égard une chose charmante aux hommes qui refuseraient à leurs contemporains ce que les déserts et les Sauvages ne refuserent point à leurs Peres.

J'aime aussi votre jolie remarque sur la tentation d'accumuler des

Trésors qui conduiraient à d'autres Tentations funestes, et qui pour-
raient enfanter la guerre en s'y préparant.

Et l'invitation encore de songer aux moyens de multiplier les
hommes, non à ceux de les détruire.

Avec ces maximes là vous enchanterez la moitié du genre humain,
et ensuite l'autre.

Il est impossible qu'un Philosophe, homme d'Etat, ne soit pas un
grand Ecrivain. car il exprime nécessairement avec clarté les vérités
dont l'éclat le frappe, et avec sensibilité celles qui interessent la nation
qu'il gouverne, et comme vous dites *les Soeurs nations*.

Salut et respect. DU PONT (DE NEMOURS).

Madame Du Pont partage tous mes sentimens sur vous et vos
ouvrages. Dites quelque chose pour moi à Mr. Madison.

EDITORS' TRANSLATION

MISTER PRESIDENT New York, 17 Dec. 1801
Your message is, like all your thoughts and all your writings, full of wis-
dom, reason, enlightenment, and a heavenly moral philosophy. But, although
I respect your nation, I fear that you may be too powerful for it.

You congratulate it on the peace. That heavenly blessing seems to all the
inhabitants of your ports like a public calamity.

You congratulate it on the fact that the savages are becoming a little civilized; and that, instead of wasting away, the progress of some of their tribes
in agriculture is increasing their population. The inhabitants of your coun-
tryside—very wrongly, it is true—look upon savages and trees as natural enemies that must be exterminated by fire, sword, and *brandy* in order to
occupy their territory.

They look upon themselves, themselves and their posterity, as collateral
heirs of all the beautiful domains that God created, from the Cumberland and
the Ohio, as far as the great ocean, so-called "Pacific."

And where is there, in Europe or the United States, the junior branch of a
family that very sincerely rejoices at the multiplication of the children of the
elder branch whose inheritance it covets?

You give a hint that, by improving the judicial order, it will make a great
economy of the *public monies*; you could have added *also of the private*: for
the more judges there are, the more lawsuits are born, which are the heavi-
est of taxes for families.

And almost all those of your young men who have been to college, with
enough wit not to want to be priests, and too little fortune or patience for
the long studies demanded by the medical profession—which moreover
does not have or rate in America the respect it ought to enjoy—want to be
lawyers or judges, sometimes both at once, pleading before one tribunal,
going to rule in the other: which has many drawbacks combined with some
ridiculousness.

As for the priests, in vain you say nothing to them and protect their freedom, you are a philosopher; hence there is not a single one in the world, of whatever sect, who is not your enemy.

Thus you do, you propose, you justly praise very real good things, which displease and will displease *merely* your farmers, your merchants, and your literary folk.

Against all those citizens, what can the support of a foreigner like me, and perhaps a dozen other thinkers scattered throughout this country, what can we do?

Thus you will find thorns under your roses, your olives, and your laurels.

Nonetheless, persevere. For Socrates, and Cato, and Confucius, and Marcus Aurelius, and my saintly friend Mr. Turgot, with whom you have much in common, would have persevered in your place.

In the first place, for a man like you, it is not a question of what people will say, but of seeing precisely and of doing good. And then, if your people barely understand you, they are gentle and in no way disposed to upset the government. You still have forty months to reign, and a great likelihood of being re-elected. For it is a different thing to see oneself universally applauded in the *babbling* societies, and to succeed in the elections. There is in the United States, more than elsewhere, a silent good sense, a spirit of cool justice, which, when it is a question of placing a *vote*, covers over the chattering of those would-be clever ones.

And even among those latter, a necessary hypocrisy prevents them from revealing the bottom of their heart. They would not dare stand up openly against the peace. They would not dare say aloud to their neighbor, or perhaps even to their wife, that it would be a good thing to kill the savages.

Hence modesty and time are for you. The lowering of taxes, a kind of argument within reach of everyone, is for you. The suppression of the nuisance taxes, for which it was so sad to employ military force, which did not make them more agreeable, is entirely for you.

If you are re-elected one time, which I do not doubt, you will be for all your life. Washington would have been, if he had not resigned. And despite your impressive competition, Mr. Adams might have been, if he had had a little better judgment, and if Mr. Hamilton had not dragged him through the mud. Change has no charm for Americans. It will have even less with respect to you, in whom they could not find even a plausible pretext to justify it.

You are sturdy and sober. You will live as long as Franklin. That is more than enough time to create, with the children who are only ten years old now, a new generation that will have received no bad influence from war or profligacy.

By the very effects of your government, and perhaps by the education you will furnish them, those children will be worth more than their forefathers.

You will be aided in their education by all the worthy and enlightened men in Europe, who ten years from now will apply themselves again with zeal to cultivate the moral and political sciences, precisely because their governments will not desire it. For Europeans, who do not really know how to stand up to authority, nevertheless love to contradict it. They have a half-courage, in words and writings, which will be a good instrument for you. And the small number of those who have truly high courage will come to live under your laws as I did, because one or two centuries hence there will be no freedom to hope for in any part of Europe, and peace without freedom has only cold and insipid pleasures. The son of my youth was named *Victor*. I have named the one of my maturity *Eleuthère Irénée*. There will be others besides him.

This *peaceful friend of freedom* hopes while making powder that it will not serve for war, but for the exercises that prevent war to which the militia and youth should address themselves, to the country's commerce, hunting, the opening up of mountains and canals to public works.

I did not wish to write to you about him while you were occupied with Gallatin in knitting the wounds of your finances and in preparing for the Congress your political tasks, your proposals. Now that all that is under way, and will not cost you more with respect to the House of Representatives and the nation's Senate than an ordinary relationship, I will give you an account of our ideas and where we are with respect to them. That will be the subject of another letter.

May you be blessed for planning to facilitate naturalization in a country where all useful works are lacking capital and labor, and the land lacks buyers.

In that respect you say a charming thing to the men who would refuse to their contemporaries what the deserts and the savages did not refuse to their forefathers.

I also like your pretty remark about the temptation of accumulating treasures that would lead to other fatal temptations, and which could give birth to war by preparing for it.

And again, the invitation to think about the means of multiplying men, not about the ways of destroying them.

With those maxims you will charm half of the human race, and later, the other half.

It is impossible for a philosopher, a statesman, not to be a great writer. For he necessarily expresses with clarity the truths whose radiance strikes him, and with sensitivity those that affect the nation he governs, and as you say, *the sister nations*.

All hail and respect,   Du Pont (de Nemours)

Madame Du Pont shares all my feelings about you and your accomplishments. Give my greetings to Mr. Madison.

RC (DLC); at head of text: "Son Excellence Thomas Jefferson"; endorsed by TJ as received 21 Dec. and so recorded in SJL.

votre message: TJ's annual message, 8 Dec. 1801.

When Anne Robert Jacques turgot served as controller general of French government finances from 1774 to 1776, Du Pont was his secretary and assistant. Turgot, many of whose ideas of political economy corresponded with those of the physiocrats, was a great influence on Du Pont. After Turgot's death in 1781, Du Pont composed a biographical memoir of his mentor and friend. Later, Du Pont published several volumes of Turgot's works (Saricks, *Du Pont*, 39-40, 43, 44, 46, 61-70, 74-5, 305, 314-16; Vol. 12:213; Vol. 14:40).

si triste d'employer la force militaire: a reference to the government's use of military force against the whiskey tax resisters in 1794.

eleuthère irénée: Du Pont's

younger son's name came from the Greek words for liberty and peace, which accounts for Du Pont's reference to his son as a peaceful friend of liberty. Turgot, who was Éleuthère Irénée's godfather, had suggested the name (Saricks, *Du Pont,* 56).

[1] Preceding two words interlined in place of "beaucoup de" (many).

From Hugh Holmes

DEAR SIR   Winchester Decemr. 17h. 1801

I hope to be excused for the liberty I have taken of recommending to Your Attention a friend of the Present Administration, upon the Assurance that whatever May be the result of your Judgement it will be satisfactory as well to this friend as myself.   As a Virginian I have been proud to hear that no case from our State exists of personal and but few applications through the Medium of friends, for offices within the disposal of the executive nor is it a circumstance less to be appreciated by republicans, that no partiality like that of the preceding administration has been shewn by you to the citizens of your Native State in appointments to office; I trust the republican spirit (especially in the southern States) is Moved by Motives superior to those of emolument of office; but it is believed they are not less worthy of appointments, whose sentiments are not directed by Interest but conviction—

My friend Captn. Samuel Croudson being informed that a Vacancy (perhaps a New appointment) was to take place of Consul or Commercial agent at New Orleans intimated to My brother and Myself a desire to become a candidate for such appointment—knowing his capacity and Personal integrity, We did not hesitate to second his wishes—It is possible that a private as well as political friendship for this Young gentleman Might lead My Pen to a description of Character fitted for a Station superior to that now sought, but I am certain that the reflection of being accessory to an appointment unfit led to its Object, thereby throwing the responsibility on yourself will be a sufficient gaurrantee from your republican friends, of their faithfull representations—I can with safety State that I have known Captn. Croudson from a child, that he has been educated in the Mercantile business by his father, who I believe as an accomptant is second to but very few in the United States, whose integrity is unquestionable & his retirement from business honorable—Captn. Croudsons intercourse with the Merchants of Philadelphia, Baltimore and Alexandria will No doubt secure their testimony of his honor and capacity in the Mercantile line. unacquainted myself with the whole duties of a consul or commercial agent it May be presumption to say, that he is as worthy of the appointment as any other Man but of this Sir be assured, he is too inflexible in patriotism, to be Warped by avarice from that line of conduct which will secure to his Country the friendship of the Government to which he May be sent; and if I am Not Mistaken, this is Not among the least worthy qualifications of a consul, since the Interests of a Country have sometimes been put at hazard by secret or corrupt infringements of the prohibatory Laws respecting commerce permit Me Sir to refer you to My brother Mr. David Holmes of Congress for further information as to Capn. Croudson and to add that although information on the subject of appointments May be acceptable to the executive, I too much regard your situation in Public life (especially at this busy Moment) to require any answer or to consider your silence as any want of respect to

Your friend & humble Serv.   HH HOLMES

RC (DNA: RG 59, LAR); addressed: "Thomas Jefferson esqr. President of the United States Washington City"; endorsed by TJ as received 21 Dec. and so recorded in SJL; also endorsed by TJ: "Samuel Croudson to be Consul."

Hugh Holmes (1768-1825), a lawyer and judge born in York, Pennsylvania, moved with his family to Frederick County, Virginia, and later settled in Winchester, where he was mayor in 1795. He served as a state senator from 1795 to 1799, as an elector in the election of 1800, and represented Frederick County in the House of Delegates from 1802 to 1806, serving as its speaker from 1803 to 1805, when he was elected judge to Virginia's General Court. An acquaintance of TJ's, he corresponded with him about agricul-

tural and textile manufacturing matters and, in 1818, was one of the Rockfish Gap commissioners who worked with TJ on early plans for the University of Virginia. His brother, David Holmes, served as a United States congressman from Virginia for the Fifth through Tenth Congresses (Betts, *Farm Book,* 518; J. E. Norris, *History of the Lower Shenandoah Valley Counties of Frederick, Berkeley, Jefferson and Clarke* [Chicago, 1890], 573; CVSP, 8:275; 9:190, 436; VMHB, 8 [1900], 125; Leonard, *General Assembly,* xv, 202, 206, 210, 214, 227, 231, 235, 239; Providence *Patriot,* 9 Feb. 1825; *Biog. Dir. Cong.*; MB, 2:1290, 1352).

In a recess appointment in 1807, TJ named SAMUEL CROUDSON as naval officer for the port of New Orleans (JEP, 2:56-7). See Vol. 35:27-8.

From David Walker

Union Tavern 17th. Decr. 1801.

It gives me regret that I cannot have the pleasure of delivering the inclosed in person—I have this moment received it, and as I shall depart from the City in a few hours, I do my self the pleasure to forward it—

With great respect yrs &c.   DAVID WALKER

RC (MHi); endorsed by TJ as received 17 Dec. and so recorded in SJL with notation "Washn." Enclosure not found.

UNION TAVERN: a Georgetown tavern that boarded some members of Congress and was kept by Charles McLaughlin until 1807 (Bryan, *National Capital*, 1:520; MB, 2:1011).

From John Devereux DeLacy

SIR   Decr. the 18th 1801

Having shortly after I did myself the honour of writing to you last set out on a tour through the Creek or Muscogee nation of Indians I take the liberty of transmitting to you, Sir; an account of that Country together with the remarks that my short stay has enabled me to make some of which I flatter myself will not be unacceptable to you—

The Land around Pensacola are extremely poor being a light barren sandy soil, but esculent and medicinal herbs grow there in abundance as they do through all this Country especially the Sassaparilla, Snake root, Ginseng, Angelica, Golden Rod, Palma Christi or Castor oil nut &c &c—which are all extremely valuable. Pensacola is going to decay fast, the few people moving away and the buildings going to ruin, there is no more than the bare site of the old forts and fortifications to be seen tho the spaniards make a shew of preserving them by keeping Centinels &c on duty at them. Pensacola can be of no use to any power whatsoever either american or european except as a means to throw away or expend monies by sinecure officers & Commanders. Since the arrival of Genl. Bowles in the Indian nation they imposed a tax on the Inhabitants around and a pretty smart one, for the stockading the town which was before entirely open they have done most part of it but a good deal remains as yet undone for want of funds and public spirit. The soil around Pensacola is so very poor as not to be able to support its inhabitants. The nearest settlements to it on the N. N.W. & W. sides are Mobile distant about 30 leagues where is the strongest fort in the Country, but the place swampy low subject to be overflown and is very unhealthy above that is the american post of no use under heaven but to have military there to keep up a dust with the inhabitants and Wy[1] of them across the Lakes Mauripias and Ponche-train is New Orleans from whence the other places (Pena & Mobe) draw their supplies—on the E. & N.E. lye the Indian Towns being the nearest settlements to Pensacola, and about 250 or 300 miles from it.—In Pensacola is one Mercantile house that has become immensely rich by the Indian trade namely the House of Panton Leslie & Co. Panton Resided in Pensacola, Leslie in London and Forbes the other Partner in New Providence all scotchmen some of whom had Retired from america to St. Augustine at the commencement of the american War, Panton who remained at St. augustine began to trade with the Indians under the British sanction while the British remained there, and managed his matters so well that the House of Panton Leslie & Co was established in consequence of a demand made by the Creek or Muscogee Nation who not understanding the treaties made between european powers to relate in any manner to them but being at once alarmed and surprized at the loss of that trade to which they had been so long accustomed declared at once that an English Merchant must be left to trade with them or that they would instantly declare war against the Spaniards, this being made known to the spanish Govermt, they prudently agreed to it, and received Panton Leslie & Co as British merchts. residt. in C. Mys. dominions and they established themselves at St. Augustine, but afterwards finding that St. Augustine was not a good situation they removed to St. Marks on the appalachee as being within their territory and had houses immediately built by their own People Here it was the House of Panton Leslie & Co forgetting their obligations to the Indians and seeing the door open for a monopoly eagerly grasped at it and by their intrigues with the Spanish goverment effected it, of all the Indian trade, they first procured a guard to be stationed at St. Marks to prevent smugglers as they said to trade, and also procured the supplying of all the Spanish Posts settlements and Colonies in this quarter. And thus was the trade secured to them on all sides except against the americans whose traders occasionally entred the nation to trade and were protected by the Indians therein thus they were placed and under british patronage and sanction and possessing all the passions prejudices and resentments of Englishmen against the americans, and also incensed at the intrusion of the american traders into the nation they chimed with the spanish policy of the day and in conjunction with the late Alexander McGilveray who beyond a doubt privately held a Cols. Commission in the Spanish service and Recd. two thousand Dollars a year and had also a partial interest in the House of Panton & Co. easily excited the Indians to the Commission of Hostilities against the frontiers of Georgia, the Georgians themselves having given a pretext for it by killing some of the Hunters and plundering their Camps, but which would not have brought on the war but for the intrigues and[2] influence of Panton & McGilvarey and the influence of Govr. ONeal, at the time Comdt. at Pensacola for all the Indians wished or wanted was satisfaction for their losses Panton supply'd them in Conjunction with the Spanish Government with arms and ammunition, And openly purchased their plunder be it what it would that offered. and thus had he three motives for urging on the War. 1st. gratifying his resentments 2nd. the immense profit the plunder of Negroes & horses afforded him. And 3d. the Consequential consumption of his goods. Mr Bowles then growing into favour with the Indians opposed this war with all his might tho when declared he acted in it and in consequence of that spirited opposition has commenced the antipathy between Genl. Bowles and that house of Panton & Co which has so long convulsed this Indian world and which if I mistake not bids fair to establish the Indian independence in spite of the Spanish intrigues and oppressions which I most devoutly wish they may do, but of this subject I shall speak more at large hereafter. McGilvary tho holding a commission also in the american service played on both sides but especially with the Spanish side which was the cause of his overthrow altogether[3]—

About 12 miles from Pensacola on the Path to the Indian Nation is a very fine bed of Iron Ore apparently very rich close to a small stream and within three miles of the Bay—and about four miles from thence is a saw mill seat, one of the finest I ever saw it is cut out of the solid rock which is a kind of soft Grey grit. the place for the sleepers and other timbers being cut of the rock—and the mill race about 80 feet long is cut in like manner through the rock. the mill was burned down by the british on their giving up pensacola so that nothing remains but a part of the dam and this seat which will long continue a monument of their industry, there is a saw mill erected close to the old seat Just now finished by the spaniards but it is on a most injudicious plan and is one among the many spanish follies to be met with in this Country—from thence to the River Scanby is about 30 miles, no change in the soil, adjoining scanby is a rich valuable swamp—Scanby a River that I do not see laid down by any of our Geographers is a beautiful River and navigable for a considerable distance near the upper Crossing place. there is a Creek that empties into it from a small lake distant about half a league on the N.E side of the River which increases its beauty very considerably on the N.E side is a white man of the name of Miller settled, but a very little diff't from[4] an Indian and who has a large family of young half indians, all of whom are kind Courteous and hospitable, this and the saw mill are the only inhabited places between Pensacola and the Indian towns a distance not less than 250 miles as I have before stated—The Country in general is a good deal broken but in no where does it rise into mountains, about 150 miles from Pensacola are some hills of a loose reddish grit stone but nothing like ore. There is a great abundance of the white or mast pine and of the pitch pine—some of the swamps abound with Cedar & Cypress. the soil you may therefore Judge is generally very sandy and light the whole way to the Indian town and but very badly watered. there is nothing remarkable or worth mentioning but a littling gurgling rill, that meanders through a large hollow, and all at once sinks with a hollow noise, and rises again below at some distance pursuing its course in a thousand little merry vagaries, the Road leading immediately over this little natural Bridge.

Within 20 miles or there abouts the traveller from Pensacola to the Cowetas sees the first indian houses being farms and settlements made by the principal Indians or others of them which display an astonishing degree of taste and industry in the arrangment and management of their farms more by far than a great many of the American or Spanish planters—at those plantations they raise and feed large Stocks of Horses Cattle Hogs Poultry &c &c together with Corn, other grains, Potatoes and vegetables of all kinds, and this spirit of industry and neatness I have observed among them throughout insomuch that I belive whatever an Indian does or intends doing that he will do neat and well they having a personal vanity that not only prompts but stimulates them to excel rather than emulate their competitors. from the first houses that I saw untill I Reached the River Chatahooche at the Coweta town those pretty plantations presented themselves alternately, for their share of admiration, and here I can not help saying that I met with a most disagreeable disappointment for I expected the Indians had Patterned after Col. Hawkins's and therefore enquired for it anxiously, but Judge Sir my mortification on being shewn a wretched hovel as the House of Col Hawkins while he lived at the Cowetas from whence he has moved. there is a negro wench stays in the House to take Care of it. But I must assert that it is the meanest and shabbiest building I saw in the whole place, devoid of taste and decency and must from its every mark & appearance have been always so—I turned away from it with indignation and Regret and Pursued my rout to the Chatahoochee passing several other neat little houses, there I crossed this beautiful River to a Mr Marshals a wealthy and Respectable trader indeed one of the first in this nation, being an honest industrious man in the strictest sense of the word. about three miles above the Coweta town or Mr Marshals House (which is an handsome one for this Country) are the falls of the River Chatahoochee, these I may say are picturesque & handsome without any thing of the sublime or beautiful being attached to them, the river for some distance running with considerable velocity down a kind of broken rugged channel untill it meets with a ledge of Rocks over which it precipitates itself about 12 or 13 feet perpendicular, tho' at its Jut-off the water is a little broken by Rocks—

At the foot of the falls is one of the best shad Striped Bass and herring fisheries in America, and from whence all the Indians draw their stock of summer provisions and a plentiful supply it affords them, as they dry salt smoke and put them up in great earthen Jars or pots—

The attempt of Col Hawkins to wrest this fishery from them and apply it to his own particular use and profit has been one of the principal[5] causes of his extreme unpopularity and of that invincible dislike the indians have all for him, and it certainly was sufficient of itself to give them a dislike to him for it was a most unjustifiable act of his to endeavour to speculate on those poor Creatures and wrest from them that never failing supply which they and their ancestors had for ages long past enjoyed uninterruptedly, and when they refused giving it up to him, that he should threaten them with the vengeance of the U.S. if they hesitated about giving it up to him at once, I pitied the poor Creatures from my soul when they told me the story with a pathos peculiar to themselves, and told them that the U.S. was too Just Magnanimous and equitable to sanction a proceeding of the kind and the present president to great and good to pass it by unnoticed did he but know of it. they said that they had several times wished and endeavoured to send him a talk but could find no safe hand (about all Col Hawkins) conduct and indeed I beleive the poor Creatures have reason to complain for from what I have heard his policy and conduct have been extremely wrong not to give it an harsher name, insomuch that I who came to this Country with the violent prejudices in his favour from every thing I had heard, Judging him to be at once the philanthrophist the legislator and the man of feeling and humanity, but I now almost execrate his name and wish for the sake of those poor Creatures, and the honour of the U.S. and his own that he had been Recalled 5 Years ago—It is not my province to detail the many improper acts with the commission of which he is charged by almost every person here, nor is it my wish to enter into a paper war with him on the subject, my intention being but barely to communicate to you as Thomas Jefferson Esqr. and not as President of the U.S. the true and undisguised state of things in so remote a part of the world as this, where as the Indians say no white man ever travels but those who come to trade, and those they say are all Hawkins's Creatures, which I know to be a fact for in public those men have asserted him to be a character which in private and in confidence they have in a few minutes after denied to me and painted him in Colours black indeed and which on my objecting to them as improper they stated him to be so vindictive that he would immediately stop their trade and order them out of the Country if they were to do otherwise than as (he) Col Hawkins wished—therefore they were obliged to be cautious in what they said before any persons that might Retail it, such Sir is the General character of the Agent of the U.S. in this Country which I am extremely sorry for as it tends to alienate the affections of this people from the U.S. a Matter that by all means should be avoided but he seems to be an object of universal abhorrence with this people at present, I have never seen Col Hawkins therefore have no private pique resentment nor passion to gratify in the giving of this statement, nor am I impelled by any other motive than that of conveying to you information that may enable you to Judge impartially of the situation of things and not have fallacious self interested statements altogether to depend upon—from the Falls I proceeded down the River to its Junction with the Flint River or there abouts, but here Sir I am convinced that my pen is not adequate to giving you a competent Idea of the beauty of this River, its banks are bold majestic and sublime, and the scenery inexpressibly beautiful, they being in general of a solid Rock near 50 and from that to 30 feet in height at the lowest there is a pleasing but rather terrific Idea excited in veiwing them as you glide along its silver or rather Transparent current, the Nodding summit crowned with a rich growth of trees and luxurious Herbage And the sides clothed with a beutiful kind of Moss together with the moss rose and small Ivy the moss especially in abundance giving the sides an hoary appearance insomuch that the traveller is Ready to exclaim that old father time must have made this his earliest residence, and again the River laving the base of the Rock which is generally a kind of soft Granite which the water rolling by for a sucession of ages has eaten away so as to make it exhibit the appearance of the segment of an Arch, from the extreme prominence of which hanging over the River the banks rise in a perpendicular boldly to the summit, and thus the banks present themselves on either side alternately all the way down the River. I have gone under one of those prominences that I have spoken of and which are in general uniform for shelter from a heavy shower of rain & have been both myself Boat and little Crew completely sheltered from it—About 160 miles from the falls in the N.E Bank is one of the greatest natural curiosities that I have seen. in a beautiful reach of the River where the Bank appears uncommonly beautiful and bold under the Archified prominence at the base that I have spoken of, a beautiful row of little Pillars each in regular order and supporting its architrave present themselves to veiw, on these Architraves the whole stupenduous mass appears to rest and be supported altogether. It bearing an exact but miniature resemblance to those heavy Columns or Pillars and Cloisters that stood in such formally formidable array at the fronts of the Convents or religious houses in France Spain and Italy, its appearance is indeed inexpressibly beautiful and Pleasing—

At the falls is a most beautiful and rich pipe Clay, so much so that they use it to plaister and white wash their houses, with no other addition to its natural state than that of Water to give it the necessary temperament, and it answers those purposes extremely well; but it will not answer for a manufactory of Pipes or earthen ware from the immense quantities of Nitre with which it is impregnated and which of course renders it unfit to stand the fire—

on this River are seventeen of the principal Towns in the nation and its banks are inhabited and cultivated on either side all the way. The River is navigable from its mouth to the falls for large Batteax at all seasons of the year tho there are some few Islands and a good many apparent shallows, but at either Bank there is a channel with water enough for any flat bottomed boat in any season—the distance being somewhat more than 300 miles and above the falls it is navigable with Canoes near an hundred more. Some distance from the Cowetas (about 30 miles) on the River there is an inexhaustible mine of salt Petre and little below that is a valuable native Allum, there are rich mines of Iron, Copper tin & lead both on this River and on Flint River—but the Indians are cautious of shewing them—at the Junction of the River Chatahoochee with the Flint River it assumes a most beautiful appearance and they uniting their streams glide down a southerly course towards the sea with uncommon beauty and majesty which the aweful sublimity of the banks contributes to heighten very considerably—The distance from the falls to the Junction of the Flint River is about 220 or 30 miles, there are inexhaustible quantities of the Red & yellow ochres and of a Clay that would make a porcelain superior to the dresden and which I have been informed has been adjudged by English Artists who have essayed it to be equal to any in the world for the earthen ware manufacture—

The Flint River is nearly as large as the Chatahoochee but does not possess its beauty and is extremely Rapid and broken, it is navigable for 30 Miles from its mouth to the House of a Mr James Burgess a Gentleman who would command Respect any where, but I shall have occasion to say more about him immediately—There are on the Flint River, Ten towns all of whom are improving their Lands fast as are all the Indians in the Nation. I have passed the Ochclocknee and several other Rivers but as they are not navigable I shall pass them over by saying that there are some large towns situate on them and that this nation is thickly inhabited—now—

It is said and asserted as a fact that there is a gold mine in this Country to which I can give no Credit for the famous Mississippi bubbles having had such strong asseverations to support them, where nothing of the kind is to be seen nor found that I pay no attention to reports of that kind especially as the soil and face of the country appear to give the lie direct to every thing of that sort, neither bearing the semblance of a neighbourhood with the precious metals—or Golden ore beds—It is said however that an Indian took a small quantity of the ore to the Spaniards at Augustine who having essayed it begged of the Indians to bring him a larger quantity and that he would pay him well for it—which coming to the ears of the Head men[6] of the Nation they assembled in general Council and decreed the death of any person that should ever attempt to shew discover or open the mine or take carry or give any of the ores to any white persons whatsoever but especially to the Spaniards whose inordinate thirst for it they considered as the source of all the evils inflicted on them and the many oppressions exercised by the Spaniards in this Country heretofore. they therefore concluding that its being generally known to be in their Country would be a certain means of involving them in continual wars if not risk the loss of their Country and independence have wisely resolved to shut it up for ever if any such thing there be—

I must here make mention more particularly of Mr James Burgess whom I have before mentioned. A truly Respectable worthy honest sensible old Gentleman, his house is for this Country an Elegant one, and he really lives in a genteel hospitable and pleasing stile the only white man in the Nation who does so, he is now within a year or two of his 70th. year and appears perfectly sound hearty athletic and vigorous, a proof of his vigour I saw in his wifes arms and a number of little ones around him he told me that he had forty in all, and in my opinion he bids fair to equal if not surpass King Priam in the number of his Children, The old Gentleman will now set out a hunting and will I am told kill a deer before any of the Indians. He has been in this Country 52 Years and speak their language of Course extremely well and has a good knowledge of their Laws and Customs the Indians are extremely fond of him insomuch that his honesty and veracity has become proverbial among them, so much so that from the different accounts of all the Indians I was strongly prepossessed in his favour for

I am convinced that he merits the character they have given of him and much more for I am convinced that he is a man of the strictest integrity and most inviolate truth and veracity—It is much to be regretted that the U.S. have lost the benefit of his services as a deputy agent which he has been and it appears that had his advice and opinion to Mr Seagrove first and to Mr Hawkins since been followed there never would have been any difficulties here in this nation—for Mr Burgess besides his influence and the love all the Indians have for him & Respect is a⁷ man wealthy and independent and therefore did not serve from lucrative motives, but from a Respect to the U.S. and a desire to establish harmony and Good will between them and this nation, but after Mr Hawkins's being in office some time the old man threw up and said that did the U.S. know Mr Hawkins Conduct they would not sanction nor could he Justify to his own feelings the continuing in office under when he considered his measures as wrong and wilfully so, Indeed he with many others dwelled largely on Col Hawkins ministry here and universally condemn him they tell very strange stories of which should the one third be true he must be a bad man, of that I do not take upon me to Judge, but this I will say that the Indians and all appear so unanimously averse to him that his immediate removal and the sending somebody else would be the most politic step that can be taken, two other private speculations that he attempted one on the ockmulgee and the other somewhere else the name I forget added to the one before mentioned together with the application or distribution of a sum of monies intended by the U.S. as an annual present appears to be the cheif grounds of their complaint, they say that the presents that are at any time given are given to five Indians whom he keeps in pay and that those are not head men nor even head warriors, And that no other persons see or know any thing of those presents, That he arrogated to himself by pompous peice in News papers that he had instructed them to build houses and make fences whereas they say that All his houses are the most miserable in the nation and that for time immemorial their Cornfeilds have had fences around them therefore that those puffs in the papers were to gloss his conduct in this country and make him be thought popular there—these sir are the Indian sentiments and with Respect to the Houses I acknowledge the Justness of the remark, and with Respect to the fences I agree that I have seen numbers much older and better than than that put up by Mr Hawkins—But there is one part of his conduct on which I must say that I think he has erred namely the interfering at all for the Spaniards—this nation being at war with them, a war that was most undoubtedly began by the Spaniards nor

was there in my opinion the shadow of a pretext for when they commenced Hostilities, therefore as it was the act of the Spaniards in the
first instance, and as the people unequivocally declared that they
would not war with the U.S. nor that they did by no means intend
such a thing, Mr Hawkins was certainly to blame to take so active a
part at least untill there was some appearrance of an hostile intention
towards the U.S. in their parts and the offering a reward for the as-
sassinating of their favorite Genl. Bowles was another wrong step
and an unpardonable thing (if it was, so,) which it is asserted by the
Indians as a fact that he did the sum of one thousand Dollars and has
also been a Step towards his present unpopularity and drew on him
the order by proclamation from Mr Bowles to withdraw from this nation, for Genl. Bowles was Hardly landed when he was attacked by
Col Hawkins in that treacherous way, a way that the Government of
the U.S. is to Just and magnanimous to sanction. There is one incident which from its humour I cant. pass over in silence. And is
known here as the Keynard Farce, I shall give it as I had it from an
Indian who was by—and I beleive with Col Hawkins—Col Hawkins
hearing that Genl. Bowles was to be on a visit somewhere near Keynards collected all the white traders and some Cusseta Indians and
set out for Keynards and travelled night and day that he might get
there time enough as he said to catch Mr Bowles and tie him or put
him to death, it seems it was asserted to a certainty that Mr Bowles
had gone to St. Marks and would not be at the meeting there. But Mr
Bowles had arrived previous to Mr Hawkins which Hawkins hearing
he refused going to the square or place of Meeting to see Genl.
Bowles who had sent for him to come that matters might be talked
over before the Indians and debated between them, but Mr Hawkins
refused going on which Mr Bowles sent him word that he would
come to the House and see him on which Mr Hawkins mounted his
horse the Indian said in great confusion and apparent perplexity and
Rode away night and day nor did he stop untill he got to Fort Wilkinson leaving his party behind to meet their fate. shortly after Mr
Bowles came (the Indian said) when Barnet Col Haws. deputy went
to see him that Mr Barnet appearred so frightened that tho he had
taken off his hat he was not able to hold it in his hands without letting it fall nor could Genl Bowles who repeatedly assured him that he
did not mean to hurt him nor would any harm happen to him, restore
him to his self confidence and presence of mind, this farce has also
abated the Indian Respect for Col Hawkins & Mr Barnet very much,
I beleive I have given you the principal heads of the business as it
happened incidentally tho' I am told that it has been a good deal

perverted in the representation by them in the U.S. If you should be disposed to learn the particulars of the difft. charges made against Mr Hawkins here old Mr Burgess would at once at your Request inform you fully. as to the American traders here you can get nothing from them but what will be dictated by Col Hawkins whom the Indians say is too much under the influence of the House of Panton & Co and the neighbouring Spanish Governors to be their freind or uncontaminated by their practises, however it is my most decided opinion that from the universal dislike to him amounting almost to an abhorrence that his life depends on his immediate removal, and of course a war between this country and the U.S a fear of and Respect for the US. having been hitherto it appears to me the only thing that preserved him. I must here state that I am heartily rejoiced at the good understanding existing between the people on the frontiers and this nation at present, And I must also say that I have been most agreeably disappointed in my opinion of this people having been led to beleive them savage Barbarous inhospitable and inhuman whereas the contrary is the case. I have found them uniformly courteous hospitable kind civil and obliging fond of white men and strangers (if they were not Col Hawkins freind) they have made rapid strides towards civilization both in their manners and Customs as well as in agriculture. they are very anxious to have Cotton Ginns & Saw mills erected among them but they would not permit Col Hawkins to put them up by any means much as they want them, for I have been told that he offered it but they refused having any thing to do with him Indeed their progression in Civilization is astonishing.—I never saw a people possessed of more parental filial & fraternal affection in my life there are so fond of each other as to extend it to the remotest relationship they can possibly trace, nor can I help quarrelling with those persons who give them a difft. or extremely barbarous Character they being the direct opposite, nor can any thing be more prase worthy than the modest respectful behaviour of the young men and warriors in presence of the head men and older Warriors as well as of all the Children in their families to their parents and when abroad to those older or superior to themselves in society for they have ranks and degrees in society here as well as in america England or elswhere their Government in its present state partaking of an Aristocracy tho formerly a Monarchy—I would here mention many of their Laws which bear a wonderful similitude to the Mosaic Law in almost every one of their old Customs but as it would swell this letter to an uncommon bulk already grown too lengthy I shall reserve in a small collection for some other time to be transmitted to you Sir—

Having spoken of the present Spanish War I will enter into a short history of this Country and a detail of facts relative to it which I have collected here and which I beleive are not generally known—

In the Century before last[8] when the spaniards had the peaceable possession of this Country it was highly improved and the population very great insomuch that were handsome towns and large villages within every ten or fifteen miles of each other and the Country around highly improved and cultivated with plantations farms vin'-yards orchards and fine Gardens spread all over the face of the Country, the remains of all which are very evident this day, as the site of all the old towns and villages can still be easily traced and known and wherever there has wood grown on them it is immediat'ly known for a late or Recent growth and the famous Andalusian yellow, Red green and black plumb, some grapes and many other spanish Fruits. towards the latter end of the Century the aborigines (the present Muscogees) beginning to feel the severeties of Spanish oppressions and Bigotry but were loth or afraid to complain or openly oppose them untill at last the fanaticism and intemperate zeal of the Spanish Friars and monks with which the Country at that time abounded together with their extreme avarice excited them to the commission of many and innumerable cruelties upon the unfortunate Aborigines (the people who now possess the Country) for the love of good mother Church and the Honour of God and Christianity The discontent which rankled in the bosoms of the natives excited by the oppressions and cruelties of the Spanish Governors and clergy was at last blown into a flame that ended in the extirpation and expulsion of the spaniards and their allies from this Country. by the following incident in or about the close of the Century before last the year 1700 The friars or monks having hold of a boy the son of one of the natives or aborigines kept him close housed, and was (whether from pious motives or what other) drilling most cruelly and unmercifully to suit his purposes, when the father passing by hearing cries was alarmed and on looking closely he perceived they proceeded from his son and saw the miserably pitiable situation to which he was reduced, he thereupon drew out his knife and flying to the rescue of his son buried his knife in the bosom of the friar and then like the great Tell urged his country men to arouse and assert their liberty and independence, for when he killed the friar he took his heart out and carried it in his hand to the square where the Head man and warriors immediately assembled and there by an animated and spirited speech he aroused his country men from the lethargy into which they had fallen and prevailed on them by recounting what had passed and the many wrongs and oppressions they had laboured under to take up arms in defence of their native rights liberties and independence and not lay them down untill they expelled or extirpated those unwelcome invaders. The whole nation in whose bosoms black brooding discontent had long rankled now fired by the decision spirit and firmness of the one town immediately took arms to a man and declared war against spain on the 17th. of Feby 1701, and an universal massacre of all the Monks and friars they could lay their hands on immediately followed—And on the 25th. of March the first action between them and the spanish army was fought opposite to the ockmulgee town on the Flint River where they defeated the spaniards who lost 800 men in the action, (the place is now known by the name of Bloody run) and immediately retreated to the forks of the Flint River & the Chatahoochee where they were met by a cheif called the Cherokee Leegha (or Cherokeekiller) who defeated them also with a very great loss on the spanish side—the Spaniards then Retreated across the ockolocknee to St. Lucea the Capital at that time of this Country, being at that time a large populous and flourishing town situate on the top of a steep hill of the form of an horse shoe and walled in all round with a Citadell ditch Fosse Counter Fosse Ramparts &c &c, and being so completely fortified was considered as impregnable; into this town the remains of the Spanish army retreated, all except the Governor who retired to the present Fort St. Marks distant from St Lucea about 18 miles taking with him 1400 men, The Indians then seized and took all the spanish towns and settlements throughout the Country and put all they found in them to the sword and also cut off and put to the sword the aborigines that had entred into an alliance with the spaniards and fought for the spaniards against them—having taken and destroyed all the spanish ouposts towns and settlements as also all those belonging to the indians that waged war against them they proceeded to invest St. Lucea the Capital. here they were Joined by a British Captain named Edwards together with his Company consisting of 57 men and also got a complete supply of British muskets with locks to them in which they had a considerable advantage over the spaniards who fought that whole war with matchlocks, they thus provided proceeded to St. Lucea and formed the seige of it, and attempted 3 several times to take it by storm, in which they lost numbers of men, but in the 4th. attempt to storm it they carried it, after the seige had continued twenty days and in spite of the exertions of the British they put every soul to the sword and rased and levelled the town, so that the site of it only Remains together with the Cannon, most of which have lost their arms or have been split or otherwise broken by the Indians lying on the ground most of them overgrown with grass and weeds, some few of them there are that if cleansed from the Rust might be again serviceable the Church Bells also lye in the same way as does all the other things of that nature, not touched nor meddled with by the Indians, all of whom still veiw the place with Horror as the seat of Spanish oppressions and Cruelties

The spaniards it was said had during the seige built a kind of subterranean vault in which they buried the treasure of the town, one of the poor Indians in alliance with the Spaniards being privy to the burying the treasure and afterwards taken by the Muscogeons offered to discover where the treasure was hid if they would spare his life which they refused doing preferring that the treasure should remain buried in oblivion to eternity as the source of every evil than be again brought to light, the Indian poor fellow to induce a beleif in his veracity described the place in which the treasure had been deposited which only hastened his end as the cheifs feared that he would make it so well known as to be easily discovered which they did not all wish in them days—

After the sacking of St. Lucea they proceeded to the attack of Fort St. Marks whither the Governor had Retired with the 1400 men, the Governor had previously sent of by sea most of the principal inhabitants, but the fort being extremely small he was obliged to entrench the greater number of his men without the walls where the Indians attacked them and killed 1100 and odd men, and were proceeding to storm the Fort but the Governor surrendered the next day by Capitulation to the British officer and was together with the Garrison marched across to Charlestown, and this was the whole of the Spaniards found in the Country that were saved from the General Massacre, the whole of the Appalachias the tribe from whom this Country took its name, together with the Yamasees, Collossees Tigetas and a small tribe whose name I could not learn these unfortunate Indians that took the part of the Spaniards were wholly extirpated, the Resentment of the Creeks or Muscogeons being such that having heard a few years ago that some few of them had escaped and were living on some of the small Quays or Islands they pursued them to put them to death but found that they were misinformed—

Pensacola was also burned down and the few inhabitants and soliders obliged to fly to the extreme point of Rose Island where they continued untill the Peace of 1762 when the Territory that legally and equitably belonged to the Spaniards was Ceded to the British, and thus did this nation after a struggle of 38 Years in which they lost numbers of men, establish their independence and free themselves from Monkish Cruelties and Bigottry, and the oppress avarice of Spanish Governors and their long train of concommittant evils, And they are all so feelingly alive to all that at this day that they say a war with the Spaniards is a natural and hereditary war that it had been the war of their fathers and ancestors, and that it having been entailed on them by their Ancestors it is a necessary duty incumbent on them to perform, the making war agst. the Spaniards when ever they shall afford them a reasonable pretext (which the Spaniards have more than done in the present war) and an Indian at this day after he has used the bitterest language and invective in Reviling and abusing any person they are at enmity with, will to wind up and give the finishing stroke to all if they have a real bad opinion of the person tell him that he is as bad as a spanish Christian—

All over the lower parts of this Country where it was usurped by the Spaniards (as it certainly was an usurpation) there are Cannons Church bills and other monuments of Spanish[9] usurpation. There are two very fine large Bells at this moment lying in a little run of Water that notwithstanding their prodigious size were carried thither (near 8 miles by the Indians) and there thrown in derision by the Indians and there they lye perfectly sound—The Muscogeons being at time and long previous to it governed by a King, with the assistance of a Council, and this was one reason why they extirpated the tribes that Joined the Spaniards, they being all subjects to the King of Muscogee and taking up arms agst. him were considered and treated as Rebels by the others—The power of the King tho very great insomuch that he could order any member turned out of the Council or order the death of any man for a Crime meriting death yet he durst not confine nor imprison any person not for a single moment, He had his officers of state &c &c and drew his Regal revenue from the first fruits of the Earth from the spoils of the enemy, from the labour and industry of the people and from the Fisherie which has been so unpropitious to Col Hawkins for all persons who fished there were obliged to give the King a certain proportion of what they caught. The last King died shortly after the War I have mentioned, at which time the Government asssumed the shape of an aristocracy and has continued so since, or it rather answers the Arrangments of the Great Alfred of the Government of the towns by Head boroughs and the whole by the Grand Council of the Nation, at present with a director General which makes it a mixed Government which I beleive they are likely to continue. The old Queen died but a few years back, and has left but one or two female Children, the male line being quite extinct.

she untill her death exercised occasionally her regal authority. being attended constantly by officers assigned her who collected and levied the customary tribute as it became due to her and enforced a due obedience to her orders

Having mentioned the first fruits I cannot help remarking the great similarity there is between their feast of the Bursk or thanksgiving or offering of their first fruits, when their Corn begins to Ripen to the Mosaic offering of the first fruits—next their purification of the women their punishments with Respect to Crimes, and the sanctuary for all those offenders that get into the square or temple at the Bursk who are all forgiven except those guilty of Murder by lying in wait or in the first degree, their customs or laws about Marriage and the raising up Children by the nearest of Kin to the deceased Kinsman or Woman, about which custom I can not help relating a fact that took place lately, a spaniard called Spanish Jack having taken an Indian Wife she very ill naturedly took it into her head to die and did so—Jack was of course confined to the House, (she being buried therein under the bed) and a life of Celibacy for the accustomed term of four months for the men (for it is longer with the women—) Jack tired of his lonely recluse situation and dumb House mate or companion, and afraid of the vengeance of the Indians who did not like him as a Spaniard was afraid to stir out, he therefore agreed as they asked him to endeavour to raise up to his deceased wife with the nearest of Kin to her. The Indians scrupulously exact in every thing that relates to that Law after enquiries and Researches found that the deceased wifes Grandmother was the nearest of Kin to her that was at that time single and unmarried, they therefore brot. her to Mr Jack, who bedded with her for that night to take him out of his widowhood and set of with himself next day out of the Country, this I am well assured as a fact and has happened precisely as I have stated it—there is a family here also called the wind family who have many exclusive priveleges that no other family has and which resemble those of the Jewish Levites considerably—there are also many old Indian Mounts or Mounds in this Country about which there are many vague traditions which are not worth detailing they are not fortified like those on the other side of the Mississippi but look some what like those high places thrown up for the Worship of the sun—there are hardly any other curiosities in the Country or any thing else worth mentioning that I have seen—

And here I must once more say in Justice to the Muscogee Indian Character that I have been most agreeably disappointed in them, for instead of finding them a savage barbarous people they, are on the contrary extreme kind courteous liberal hospitable generous and humane, and far advanced in Civilization. much more so in every respect than Many americans I have seen I do assure You Sir—

Convinced that some acct. of Genl. Bowles the great Indian favourite by one who has seen and conversed with him; and whose opinions are formed without prejudice or passion of any kind or if any, a prepossession against him founded on general report; will not be unacceptable to you, I take the liberty of sending you the following on which you may depend as it is faithfully drawn as much so as my Judgment would enable me to do so—

William Augustus Bowles Director General of the Muscogee Nation was born in Fredk. town Maryland his father was Clerk of the Court &c &c there previous to the Revolution, and his mother Brothers & Sisters do all live in that neighbourhood still, he entred as an Ensegn in the 7th. Regt. British Infantry at the Commencement of the Revolutionary War then aged about 14 or 15. Being stationed at Pensacola, he in the attack on french Village now Mobile wherein the British were defeated in their attempt to storm the fort, got into the fort with 5 or 6 Indians, and was knocked down with a Club'd musket and left for dead. the British had retreated but the Indians who had become attached to him took him out of the fort in that situation, and took care of him untill he got well and from the marks of invincible intrepidity he shewed in the attack the Indian who saved him adobted him into his family, which is the origin of the Generals attachment to the indians (the tyger family) one of the strongest families among the Indians. He returned to pensacola and served there during the seige with great Gallantry and after the surrender of that place, served at N. York Long Island and other parts of the U.S. with increasing military Reputation, but as soon as the war was ended he returned to the Indians again by permission at his own Request they being endeared to him by saving his life and many other acts of kindness, and there he continued going through the regular grades of Warrorship &c untill he attained by his conduct the Rank of Head man, and was in 1791 Elected Director General of the Nation—(or rather Emperor[10]) in which title he since his Return from his spanish Captivity has been Recognised and approved of by the Unanimous voice of the Nation in General Council assembled without a dissenting voice

Genl. Bowles is about 5 feet 10 or 11 inches in height, of an elegant athletic form, insomuch that a statuary might well Copy from him; few men Combine in their form more grace simmetry activity and vigour than he does, and must at the age of 24 or 25 have been beautiful as an adonis he is now 40 odd, In his Manners he is easy graceful polite affable and pleasing perfectly the polished Gentleman and Courtier—speaks the English with an accurate purity that few can reach, speaks the Spanish and French Languages as also the Creek tounge not only well but fluently and plays the flute and violin initimably well and the Clarionet and bass violin Tolerabley and is an amateur in painting of which he is so passionately fond as to make it injurious to his health, Historical paintings is his fort and what he is fondest of—He has read a great deal and digested it well, Astronomy and the Mathematics he is a tolerably good proficient. He told me that it was reading Newtons principles of astronomy when a little Boy that gave him such a passion for reading, and has acquired a perfect acquaintance with the Modern Writers both philosophic and Physical, He is beyond a question invincibly brave and coolly intrepid, is open Hearted Candid extremely humane and Generous to a fault—previous to my seeing him I expected to meet with a man harsh savage and ferocious in his manners and appearance but how great was my surprise to meet instead thereof such a man as I have above faithfully delineated and described from my observation of his manners & Character for some days that I stayed with him. The Spaniards are objects of his Resentment for three reasons first from the National resentment and prejudices which he has imbibed secondly from the treacherous way in which they took and kept him prisoner for a length of time and after failing in an attempt to poison him sent him round the world to Manilla the Phillippine Islans & Lima where he was near exciting a general insurrection taking the Country from them and overturning their Government—from them on her way back to spain he made his escape through the connivance of the Officers of a french frigate who were Brother Masons of his, but previous to his leaving the spanish vessel the Crew were about to mutiny and give him the command of the vessel and confine their own officers which being discovered induced the Captn. to put him on board the french frigate from whence he escaped[11]—he refused the title of a Spanish Count & the sum of $200,000. offered him as a bribe if he would change sides and espouse their interest which endears him very much to the nation—

His darling passion and in which he appears an Enthusiast is the benefitting of this people establishing their independence on pure principles and Civilizing them. he is framing a Constitution or rather has framed it on principles drawn from Montesqieu and Plutarch two authors that he appears to have almost by Rote—He has promised me to transmit a Copy to you for your advice and approbation as a

Gentleman a Philanthrophist and the Particular freind and patron of the Red People and for your opinion[12] on it, He is extremely solicitous for keeping peace between the Indians and the U.S. about which he has Issued very Positive orders which I have seen and has by that means opened a free intercourse and caused a good understanding between the Frontier People and the Indians at present, but he hates and detests Col Hawkins & I indeed do not wonder at it. He has opened the Trade to this Country for the americans declaring it free every where to them in spite of the Spaniards—The Spaniards have offered a reward of $10,000 to any person that would assassinate him and Col Hawkins has made use of all his influence to get it done. the Commission of which act would eternally blacken the characters of those who would be in any wise instrumental to it—and would be doing the world a disservice and this nation an irreparable injury for if he lives but five years longer they will be a polite and completely civilised people He being about establishing schools among them for which purpose he seeks for old invalid soldiers in preference to Bigotted missionaries in which I think him perfectly right—The whole Nation is now anxious for the Constitution and a Code of Laws and Government of their own similar to the whites all which he is preparing to give them, (and in which it is devoutly to be wished that may succeed and that he had some assistance in it as he is in many things and opinions extremely excentrac) and which the nation is now fully fitted and prepared to receive. But they tell him it must be such as will suit a Brave and free people that have had their liberties and independence transmitted to them from their ancestors unblimneshed and unsullied in spite of Spanish oppressions and intrigues and that they mean to transmit it to their Children in the same state, they say that the Great Spirit or maker of the world gave them the Land they are now on for an Inheritance, and that they neither will give up this nor seek for a other, they are certainly a brave hardy honest race and it would be cruel to attempt to dispossess them or usurp their Country. Genl. Bowles is extremely anxious for a peace or a suspension of hostitilies with the Spaniards that he might introduce Commerce & agriculture and get them to follow it with the greater energy and do away that necessity for their dependance in any wise on hunting, and that passion they have for a petty warfare occasionally, tho peace now appears the general bent of their wishes especially, a good understanding with the U.S. It would be but good policy in the Spaniards to make peace or agree to a suspension of Hostilities for they have neither forces sufficient to withstand the Indians in this part of the world nor officers that can be matched with Genl. Bowles who is certainly a great military Character which his taking the strong fort of St. Marks from them in such a short time and with so few Indians proves, in fact I think him one of those great Genius's that an age does not produce more than one or two such. so much have I been pleased with him and those Indians & so well convinced of their Generally peaceable intentions towards the U.S. tho I strongly suspect that Genl. Bowles is strongly supported by England—

With every Respect I have the honour to subscribe myself Sir Your truly Obedt Hbl Servant   JOHN DEVX DELACY

RC (DLC); at foot of text: "Thos. Jefferson Esqr. Monticello"; endorsed by TJ as received 10 Mch. 1802 and so recorded in SJL.

HONOUR OF WRITING TO YOU LAST: DeLacy to TJ, 3 Nov. 1801.

SINCE THE ARRIVAL OF GENL. BOWLES: that is, since 1799, when William Augustus Bowles, who had been arrested by the Spanish in 1792 but escaped, returned to the region (Vol. 32:52n).

DeLacy allied himself with Bowles against the firm of PANTON, Leslie & Company, which had the favor of Spanish authorities and controlled much of the commerce with the Creek Indians. The island of NEW PROVIDENCE in the Bahamas was a mercantile center for the trade with Native Americans along the southern frontier of the U.S. As governor of the Bahamas from 1787 to 1796, the earl of Dunmore, the former British governor of Virginia, encouraged Bowles and New Providence merchants who were eager to take over the Panton, Leslie market (J. Leitch Wright, Jr., *William Augustus Bowles: Director General of the Creek Nation* [Athens, Ga., 1967], 20-8; DNB; Vol. 35:559n).

C. MYS. DOMINIONS: that is, territory of "His Catholic Majesty," the king of Spain.

San Marcos, or in English ST. MARKS, was on a river of the same name in West Florida off Apalachee Bay, which is part of the Gulf of Mexico (John H. Hann, *Apalachee: The Land between the Rivers* [Gainesville, Fla., 1988], 34; Wright, *Bowles*, 129; Mark F. Boyd, Hale G. Smith, and John W. Griffin, *Here They Once Stood: The Tragic End of the Apalachee Missions* [Gainesville, Fla., 1951], 101).

THE LATE ALEXANDER MCGILVERAY: in the 1780s and early 1790s, Alexander McGillivray, who died in 1793, had been Bowles's rival for influence with the Creeks and in the competition over the region's trade. McGillivray cooperated with the Spanish and the Panton, Leslie firm, and accompanied a Creek delegation to New York for negotiations with the United States in 1790 (Wright, *Bowles*, 25-6, 29-30, 33-4; John Walton Caughey, *McGillivray of the Creeks* [Norman, Okla., 1938], 35-8, 47-51, 53, 205, 298-300; Vol. 33:62, 64n, 177n).

GOVR. ONEAL: the Spanish governor at Pensacola from 1781 to 1792 was Arturo O'Neill (Caughey, *McGillivray*, 61n).

The river that DeLacy called the SCANBY was the Escambia, which empties into an arm of the bay at Pensacola (John H. Hann, *The Native American World Beyond Apalachee: West Florida and the Chattahoochee Valley* [Gainesville, Fla., 2006], 2, 88; Judith A. Bense, ed., *Presidio Santa María de Galve: A Struggle for Survival in Colonial Spanish Pensacola* [Gainesville, Fla., 2003], 4).

John MILLER lived some miles inland from Pensacola (Foster, *Hawkins*, 36j; Florette Henri, *The Southern Indians and Benjamin Hawkins, 1796-1816* [Norman, Okla., 1986], 330n).

THE COWETAS: Coweta was a prominent Lower Creek town located, during this period, on the Chattahoochee River. A nearby town called Coweta Tallahassee was for a time Benjamin Hawkins's residence as U.S. agent to the Creeks. In the eighteenth century, the French used a variant of the name Coweta to mean all of the Lower Creeks (Robbie Ethridge, *Creek Country: The Creek Indians and Their World* [Chapel Hill, 2003], 12, 29, 55, 59, 68, 94, 105, 170; Sturtevant, *Handbook*, 14:384, 391).

NEGRO WENCH: Hawkins owned more than 70 slaves when he died in 1816 (Henri, *Southern Indians*, 317; Ethridge, *Creek Country*, 66).

MR MARSHALS: Thomas Marshall was a trader living in the Coweta vicinity (Foster, *Hawkins*, 55s, 51, 267-8).

JAMES BURGESS: in 1797, Hawkins appointed James Burges to be one of the assistant agents and interpreters in the Indian agency south of the Ohio River (same, 68, 101, 174).

The predecessor to Hawkins as agent to the southern Indians was James SEA-GROVE of Georgia (Henri, *Southern Indians*, 58, 94; Donald Jackson and Dorothy Twohig, eds., *The Diaries of George Washington*, 6 vols. [Charlottesville, 1976-79], 6:143-4n; Vol. 27:463n, 584-5n, 818).

PUFFS IN THE PAPERS: extracts of letters by Hawkins and others calling attention to the steps being taken by the Creeks under his influence to fence their fields, use plows, raise livestock, and make cloth received circulation in American newspapers. One such report in the spring of 1801 contrasted Hawkins's efforts to instill "good order" with Bowles's supposed leadership of "infamous banditties" (Litchfield, Conn., *Monitor*, 6 Feb. 1799; *Alexandria Advertiser*, 30 May 1801).

Hawkins had not posted a REWARD for the assassination of Bowles. Spanish officials did offer a reward, of $4,500. Earlier in 1801, Henry Dearborn asked Hawkins to counteract Bowles's activities as much as possible and to try to apprehend him if he came within the limits of the United States. In 1803, Hawkins prevailed on the Upper Creeks to capture Bowles (Wright, *Bowles*, 125, 162-7; Merritt B. Pound, *Benjamin Hawkins—Indian Agent* [Athens, Ga., 1951], 193).

KEYNARD: Caleb Swan, who traveled into the Creeks' territory in 1790, described Jack (John) Kinnard as an influential half-Scots, half-Indian "despot"

who lived and traded among the Lower Creeks and Seminoles. According to Swan, Kinnard, who owned large herds of cattle and horses as well as black and Indian slaves, had gotten his start "by plunder and freebooting" during the American Revolution (Henry R. Schoolcraft, ed., *Information Respecting the History, Condition and Prospects of the Indian Tribes of the United States*, 6 vols. [Philadelphia, 1851-57], 5:254, 260-1; John Walton Caughey, *McGillivray of the Creeks* [Norman, Okla., 1938], 54-5, 355, 357; Foster, *Hawkins*, 44j; Kathryn E. Holland Braund, *Deerskins & Duffels: The Creek Indian Trade with Anglo-America, 1685-1815* [Lincoln, Neb., 1993], 174, 182).

In the same part of the Chattahoochee Valley as Coweta was CUSSETA, an important Lower Creek town somewhat less influential than Coweta (Ethridge, *Creek Country*, 29, 55, 61, 170; Sturtevant, *Handbook*, 14:384, 391).

FORT WILKINSON, a U.S. army post on the Georgia frontier, was not the same as Cantonment Wilkinsonville on the Ohio River (Crackel, *Mr. Jefferson's Army*, 100; Vol. 34:81-7; Henry Dearborn's Plan for Reorganizing the Army, at 7 Dec.).

Timothy Barnard—not BARNET—began working under Hawkins in March 1797 as an assistant agent and interpreter (Foster, *Hawkins*, 96-8, 101; Vol. 32:50).

EXTIRPATION AND EXPULSION OF THE SPANIARDS: beginning about 1701, Lower Creeks who favored trade connections with English merchants attacked Spanish missions and military posts located among the Apalachee Indians. The conflict was part of a larger contest between the British and Spanish empires, and troops from South Carolina joined the Creeks in some of their campaigns against the Spanish provinces. If, as DeLacy asserted, Chislacaliche, who was known to the English as Cherokeeleechee or CHEROKEEKILLER, fought the Spanish in the early part of the 18th century, he changed his allegiance within a few years. By the 1710s that chief, who was probably of the Uchise group of Lower Creeks, was prominently pro-Spanish. By ST. LUCEA,

DeLacy apparently meant San Luis, in the vicinity of the present Tallahassee, Florida, where a Spanish blockhouse and a key mission were located. Accounts of the war do not support all of the facts related by DeLacy. The Creeks and English from South Carolina did drive the Spanish, who were commanded by Manuel Solano, a deputy governor, from San Luis in 1704, when the Spanish effectively withdrew from the Apalachee province. The South Carolinians enslaved many of the mission Indians, and the war dealt a heavy blow to the Franciscan missions in the region (David H. Corkran, *The Creek Frontier, 1540-1783* [Norman, Okla., 1967], 52-6, 66-7; Hann, *Apalachee*, 2, 34, 60-1, 123, 150, 203-5, 264-83, 288, 325-6; Steven C. Hahn, *The Invention of the Creek Nation, 1670-1763* [Lincoln, Neb., 2004], 59-65, 84-5, 90, 94, 109, 115, 118, 178, 235; Boyd, Smith, and Griffin, *Here They Once Stood*, 33-95, 99; John R. Swanton, *Early History of the Creek Indians and their Neighbors* [Washington, D.C., 1922], 120-4; Verner W. Crane, *The Southern Frontier, 1670-1732* [Durham, N.C., 1928], 9, 34, 79-80, 134, 247, 255; Sturtevant, *Handbook*, 4:485; 14:391).

Before 1715, the YAMASEES were allied with the English and participated in the slave trade that preyed on Spanish-affiliated tribes to capture Indian slaves for South Carolina. The Yamasees turned on the English in 1715, beginning a regional war that also brought Creeks and Catawbas into the fight against South Carolina. The Native Americans drove back the Carolina frontier but were unable to destroy the colony, which began a series of reprisal campaigns that stretched through the 1720s. The Yamasees took refuge near St. Augustine and other Spanish missions and forts, but the tribe was almost destroyed by the South Carolinians' counteroffensive. Later in the century most of the surviving Yamasees migrated to Mexico and Cuba under Spanish protection (Sturtevant, *Handbook*, 4:5, 8-9, 140; 14:245, 251-2).

KING OF MUSCOGEE: the Creek confederacy was not a centralized monarchy. Towns, councils, and clans all had degrees of political power. Some towns did have greater influence than others, and Europeans tended to call a principal chief of an important town, or of the confederation, a "king." Beginning in the late 1790s, Benjamin Hawkins pressed for centralization and more unified action through the confederation's council. The Muskogee people formed the core of the Creek confederation (Duane Champagne, *Social Order and Political Change: Constitutional Governments Among the Cherokee, the Choctaw, the Chickasaw, and the Creek* [Stanford, Calif., 1992], 30-1, 33, 37, 42, 64-5, 72, 85, 113-15; Sturtevant, *Handbook*, 14:384-5).

Late in 1799, Bowles issued a proclamation declaring himself the DIRECTOR GENERAL of a polity he called Muskogee or the Creek Nation. His followers included some Creeks, but also people of a variety of origins, including other Indians, whites, and runaway slaves. Contrary to DeLacy's depiction, Bowles's Creek Nation and the Creek confederacy were not synonymous (Wright, *Bowles*, 143-8, 182n; New York *Daily Advertiser*, 7 Feb. 1800; Vol. 32:52n).

The busk, or green corn ceremony, was the Creeks' annual ritual of purification and renewal that lasted four to eight days and culminated in a FEAST (Sturtevant, *Handbook*, 14:387; Joel W. Martin, *Sacred Revolt: The Muskogees' Struggle for a New World* [Boston, 1991], 34-42).

WIND FAMILY: within the Creeks' social and kinship system, the Wind clan had certain prerogatives (Sturtevant, *Handbook*, 14:382, 383, 384-5; Ethridge, *Creek Country*, 110).

Bowles was from Frederick, MARYLAND, as DeLacy stated. In 1777, Bowles went to the British-occupied city of Philadelphia and enlisted briefly, at the age of 14, as a common soldier in a British regiment. He soon obtained a commission as ensign, not in the British Army but in a regiment of Maryland Loyalists. After serving in New Jersey and New York, the unit went to Pensacola, where by some transgression Bowles lost his commission. He then went to live with the Creeks and first established his ties to them. When the British recruited Native American auxiliaries to fight against the Spanish in 1780, Bowles returned to Pensacola. He was involved in the attempt to take Mobile, but was not LEFT FOR DEAD there. He was one of the last attackers to withdraw, but joined the retreat of survivers from that failed assault. Restored to his commission in the Maryland Loyalist regiment, he spent the last part of the Revolutionary War in Long Island, where he took the stage as an actor in theatrical productions put on by British and Loyalist officers. At the war's close Bowles went to the Bahamas, where he allied himself with merchants interested in supplanting Panton, Leslie & Company along the U.S.-Spanish frontier. Under those auspices Bowles returned to that region and began to challenge McGillivray for influence with the Creeks (Wright, *Bowles*, 7-28).

TYGER FAMILY: the Tiger or Panther clan was associated with war and military leadership. The Wind clan, by contrast, was of a set of clans associated with peace and civil leadership (Sturtevant, *Handbook*, 14:382-3; Martin, *Sacred Revolt*, 49-50; Hahn, *Invention of the Creek Nation*, 21-22).

Bowles talked with several people about the CONSTITUTION he said he intended to write for his nation-state, which had no fixed boundaries, but he did not complete the frame of government (Wright, *Bowles*, 148-9).

TAKING THE STRONG FORT OF ST. MARKS: in the spring of 1800, Bowles with an armed force of several hundred men, primarily Creeks and Seminoles, forced the surrender of the isolated outpost at St. Marks, where 88 Spanish soldiers defended a stone fort. A little over a month later, Spanish ships came up the river and began a bombardment. Bowles and his followers withdrew, allowing the Spanish to reclaim the fort (same, 127-32; David Hart White, *Vicente Folch, Governor in Spanish Florida, 1787-1811* [Washington, D.C., 1981], 53-4).

[1] That is, "westerly" or "westwardly."
[2] MS: "and and."
[3] DeLacy interlined this sentence.
[4] Preceding two words interlined in place of "better than."
[5] MS: "pricipal."
[6] MS: "me."
[7] Word supplied by Editors.
[8] DeLacy first wrote "last Century" before altering the phrase to read as above. He went through the same steps at the spot where "Century before last" appears later in the same paragraph.
[9] Canceled: "ostentation &c."
[10] Word interlined in place of "King."
[11] Remainder of paragraph interlined.
[12] Word interlined in place of "advice."

To Peter Lyons

DEAR SIR   Washington Dec. 18. 1801.

I yesterday recieved your favor of the 10th. covering the Voucher I had asked. I have this morning written to mr Eppes, the acting exr of mr Wayles (for I have never meddled since 1773.) who is in possession of all his papers, that you had noticed a balance due to you on the face of your account of which I inclosed you a copy. whether mr Wayles had any counter-claims I know not. mr Eppes will examine into it & do what is right: and if he meets with any difficulty, I shall be with him in the spring, somewhere on a settlement with mr Skelton's representatives, when all mr Wayles's books & papers will be with us, and will then see to the examination of it. Accept my assurances of sincere & respectful esteem.   TH: JEFFERSON

PrC (DLC); at foot of text: "Peter Lyons esq."; endorsed by TJ in ink on verso.

YOUR FAVOR OF THE 10TH.: recorded in SJL as received 17 Dec. from Studley, Virginia, but not found.

I HAVE THIS MORNING WRITTEN TO MR EPPES: TJ to Francis Eppes, 18 Dec., recorded in SJL, has not been found. John Wayles, TJ's father-in-law, died in 1773 (Vol. 1:96n).

From Nathaniel Macon

SIR   Washington 18 Decr. 1801

I this morning received the enclosed. Mr. Blount is the half brother of the late Wm. Blount, and of Col. Thomas Blount. He is I beleive a man of respectability.—I have never heard any thing against him— He went from Carolina to Tennessee when a young man, & has lived there ever since

I am Sir with highest respect yr. most obt. sert.

NATHL MACON

RC (MHi); endorsed by TJ as received 18 Dec. and so recorded in SJL. Enclosure: Willie Blount to TJ, 14 Nov. 1801.

From William Short

DEAR SIR   Paris Decr. 18th. 1801

I recieved some days ago the letter which you did me the favor to write me by Chanor. Livingston. I have not written any since those you there acknowlege (except one by Mr Victor Dupont, of the 18th. of Octob.) I have been fearing for some time, as the commissions mentioned in your letter of March 17th., had not been heard of during the summer, that you might perhaps have been considering me as guilty of neglect—but I see by your last that you had not sent them as you intended. There can be of course no need for my repeating again, what I hope you will be always assured of, the pleasure I shall have in executing any commissions you may have occasion for here & charge me with.

In your letter of March 17th. by Mr Dawson also, you were so good as to say that as soon after your return from Monticello (whither you were then going) as the first press of business would permit, you would resume the subject of my affairs & give me a statement in continuation of the last of April 1800. But I apprehended at the time, what is confirmed by your favor of Octob. 3. just recieved, that it would be impossible for you at present to find a moment for such details; & it is really more than I can expect or desire under the constant pressure of public affairs. It has been indeed for some time past a source of more uneasiness to me than I can express, that my affairs should unavoidably break in on the few moments which those of the public allow you for your own. I can assure you that I do not lose sight a moment of the means of making some permanent arrangement so as to relieve you from the trouble to which your kindness has hitherto exposed you. I had hoped that by means of the agency of Mr Barnes this end might have been in some degree attained, at least as to the business of my public funds, & therefore entered into correspondence with him; but the experience of the last year does not allow me to count on that source for information. I ask the favor of you to run over the letter which I here take the liberty of inclosing for him open. You will see from it that his last letter to me was that of March by Mr Dawson, at which time the small sums he had recieved for me in Octob. 1800. & Jany. 1801. were still on hand & that he has now allowed the conveyance by Chanor. Livingston to pass without breaking his long silence; so that I am yet ignorant how those sums have been disposed of, & of course know nothing of those he has been since recieving. Such a long silence would at any rate have been contrary to the most common kind of mercantile proceeding; but in the present case it is additionally mortifying, as Mr Barnes has been during this interval frequently recieving letters from me shewing my desire to hear from him & to which he has not given one word of answer. I hope there is no expression in my letter to Mr Barnes which can be disagreeable to him, but if you should think so, I beg the favor of you to suppress it altogether. I will thank you in that case to be so good as to give him the directions as to the kind of funds to be purchased, which I there desire him to ask of you, if you should approve of them. When Mr Barnes shall have once recieved your directions how to proceed as to any monies of mine which may come to his hands, it seems to me he might avoid giving you any further trouble on this head. And I see then only two articles remaining to trouble you, the Canal shares & Indian camp—As to the first I suppose they lay dormant at present & as to the second (Indian camp) as the only thing to be done is to endeavour to tenant it out, perhaps your steward or agent at Monticello might be employed (with an allowance proportioned to the business) so as to relieve you; & this would be really a great relief to me. I asked the favor of you formerly to endeavor to place tenants on this tract, but I suppose you will have found difficulty—I was agreeably surprized to find from the acct. you were so good as to send me on a former occasion that the few tenants who were there, paid more regularly than I had expected their small rents. I should have been very glad if others of the same kind could have been found to have covered the land; but as you do not mention any progress in the plan you were so good as to communicate to me as to the leases, I take it for granted it will have been found too difficult to realize & I regret it sincerely; as lands well tenanted form the estate I like best.

I observe by your last favor also of Octob. 3. the state of the affair of the 9 M dollars. I hope it will be ere long struck off the list altogether. I never could concieve why the late administration did[1] insist on compounding it with their suit with E.R. For if he should gain his suit would there be any justice in Government making use of this to wrong me? They know how that matter stood—that I never recieved a shilling, & that this non-reception was the act of Government, that is to say of their Sec. of State. I had concieved that when you were so good as to treat of this subject for me with the late administration, you had viewed it in the same light, & I had hoped that the official documents in the Secy. of State's office would have sufficed to have shewn the validity of my title. I do not know the particulars of the suit of E.R, but only in general that it is for sums unaccounted for— nor do I understand how he gets such delays. All such things are difficult of course to judge of at this distance & with so little information as we have here. I observe that Messrs. Pendleton & Lyons paid a part which was transferred to the Government. Suppose then E.R. should gain his suit I do not understand how that would operate— Would Government keep this sum & take back the 8. M dollars also vested for this affair? Would it not have been possible to have applied the money recieved from Pendleton & Lyons to my use & to have given the Government credit for that amount? so as that I should have substracted[2] the amount from the 8 M dollars vested. If that had been practicable it would have been securing at least so much, in whatever way the suit with E.R. may be determined. After all I suppose it indifferent, because I cannot concieve that Government will not do me justice whatever may be the event of their suit with E.R.

You are so good as to inform me in your last of what you did as to the packet containing my vouchers. It is a considerable relief to me to know that it is arrived safe to the hands of government. On reflexion it will be as well perhaps when these accounts come to be settled to pass over in silence my letter to the Sec. of State of June 1795.—It alone can produce any difficulty as to my salary being continued until the reciept of my letters of recall—That is the proper & natural term for the salary of a foreign minister ceasing—The difficulty if there be any, arising from my letter of June 95, is of my own making—And as no one is held to do himself wrong, I invoke of course the abolition of that letter, that the things may be left to take their natural course. I am at ease now that the vouchers are safe, & I have no objection to their remaining in their present state, until I can be present myself to put the finishing hand to them—This mode has in my eyes the advantage also of avoiding you trouble, which I very much desire.

I have now to return you my thanks for the details into which you are so good as to enter in your last on another subject. You are the only person to judge of the principles you there state, & your mind being made up as to the matter would suffice to prevent my combating them. Besides if the experience of what has passed in the relations of the U.S. with some foreign countries during the late war has not sufficed to shew that there are other kinds of knowlege at least as necessary in their foreign agents as those mentioned, nothing that I could say would have that effect. As a public matter therefore I will never trouble you on it—And as respecting me personally I should never have quitted the silence which I had observed with you on it from the time of its being foreseen here that you would be called to the Presidential chair, if newspapers & letters from America had not arrived stating positively that you had named me to this mission. After that, I had no hesitation to express to you my sentiments on the subject, & they have not changed. Had you thought my services necessary on this ticklish ground & chosen to call them to the aid of your administration, it would have been certainly honorable for me, & moreover peculiarly gratifying to my personal feelings on account of past circumstances, & the relation in which I stood with you in the eyes of the public. But as you have concieved that the public interests would be better served here by another, I should be certainly the last person in the world to have expected or desired that my nomination should have taken place. If I know myself at all it is the public good which is my first wish.

I should apprehend from your last letter that some of mine must have conveyed ideas which I did not intend, as to the connecting ourselves with the politics of Europe. My sentiments on that head have been uniform & pronounced, as will appear from what took place at different times in the course of my negotiation in Spain, & are conformable to what you state to be those of our country. As to the means of securing neutral rights, you will observe that in stating the late crisis in the North I mentioned it as the production of chance, & that so far as it regarded the two principal powers was merely a matter of circumstance—the mission which I mentioned was to be only a mission of observation & I expressly excluded any idea of co-operation by measures of force. It appeared to me that it was by a course of judicious observation on the ground that it could be best ascertained whether there be not some other means of hastening the event we desire. If it be already ascertained however in the mind of Government that this can be more surely effected by ourselves alone so soon no body can doubt that it will be preferable, as it is always best, both in public & private affairs, to do by ourselves alone whatever we can do without the aid of others.

At the request of Mde. de Chastellux who is still in Spain, I have seen here a friend of hers, the wife of a relation of her husband & sister to the person who desires to be Consul of the U.S. at Smyrna. Mde. de Chastellux concieved that I could be of use to her on this occasion. I have told the lady that I believed it a rule of our Government to prefer American citizens; but that if she would give me a note on the subject I would transmit it to America—She has sent me that which I now inclose—I have of course not flattered her with the idea that my recommendation would have any weight—All that I intend hereby is merely that it should be known to Government that this gentleman desires the place; & if perchance they should be in want of such a person they will of course take information as to his merits from those who may have connexions with that port.

Only one year of the *Connaissance des tems* has been published since the last I sent you. I will forward it by the first conveyance. In the mean time I have the honor to be with sentiments of perfect respect, Dear Sir, your most obedient & most humble servant

W: SHORT

RC (PHi); at foot of first page: "Thomas Jefferson President of the U.S."; endorsed by TJ as received 19 Mch. 1802 and so recorded in SJL. FC (DLC: Short Papers); a summary in Short's epistolary record; Short added a notation that the letter went on a ship that left Bordeaux for New York early in February 1802. Enclosure: Short to John Barnes, 15 Dec., concerning Short's financial affairs (FC in same; a summary in Short's epistolary record).

Robert R. LIVINGSTON carried TJ's letter to Short of 3 Oct.

TJ's letter to Short of 13 Apr. 1800 included a STATEMENT of Short's financial affairs (Vol. 31:500-18).

INDIAN CAMP was the name of the property in Albemarle County that Short bought from William Champe Carter in 1795 (Vol. 28:332-4).

ACCT. YOU WERE SO GOOD AS TO SEND ME: the statement of account TJ sent in April 1800. At that time TJ also sent a form he intended to use for tenants' LEASES on the Indian Camp land (Vol. 31:514, 518).

AFFAIR OF THE 9 м DOLLARS: see Short to TJ, 9 June, and TJ to Short, 3 Oct., for the continuing issue of Short's salary claim against the State Department. Resolution of that problem had come to depend on the outcome of the government's lawsuit against Edmund Randolph (E.R.). During the Adams administration, TJ spoke and corresponded with Timothy Pickering and Oliver Wolcott about resolving the issue. The matter was further complicated by payments Edmund PENDLETON and Peter LYONS made to Randolph for a private debt (Vol. 29:574; Vol. 30:35-6, 298-9, 317; Vol. 31:62-3, 464, 497-9, 504-5, 574).

For Short's JUNE 1795 letter to the secretary of state, see Short to TJ, 9 June 1801.

LATE CRISIS IN THE NORTH: in his letter of 19 Apr., Short suggested that the formation of the league of armed neutrality by Russia, Denmark, Sweden, and Prussia pointed to the need for a U.S. envoy in Denmark (Vol. 33:616).

The Marquise de CHASTELLUX, widow of the Marquis de Chastellux who had traveled extensively in the United States in the early 1780s, served in the household of the Duchesse d'Orléans as a lady-in-waiting (Howard C. Rice, ed. and trans., *Travels in North America in the Years 1780, 1781 and 1782 by the Marquis de Chastellux*, 2 vols. [Chapel Hill, 1963], 1:23; Vol. 28:344n, 463-4). In May 1802, TJ appointed William Stewart of Philadelphia to be the consul at SMYRNA, Turkey (Madison, *Papers, Sec. of State Ser.*, 3:185; Deborah Stewart to TJ, 10 Apr. 1802).

[1] Word interlined in place of "should."
[2] Word interlined in place of "recieved."

To James Taylor, Jr.

SIR   Washington Dec. 18. 1801.

I ought a this time to have remitted you 700. Dollars for the 4th. & 5th. pipes of Madeira but it will not be in my power under three weeks from this time when it shall certainly be remitted. I am uneasy at this failure, but thought it might at any rate lessen the inconvenience to you to apprize you of it, and assure you of what might be depended on. Accept my best wishes & respects.

TH: JEFFERSON

RC (Mary Cabell Sheppard, Winston-Salem, North Carolina, 1955); addressed: "Mr. James Taylor Norfolk"; franked and postmarked; endorsed by Taylor. PrC (MHi); endorsed by TJ in ink on verso.

TJ ordered the PIPES of Brazil quality Madeira wine with payment in 90 days in a letter to Taylor of 28 Aug. The wine arrived in Washington in late September (Vol. 35:348, 588).

From David Austin

RESPECTED SIR.   Washington Decr. 19th A.D. 1801—

Will you have the goodness to look over a communication of 28th ulto & seriously to weigh its contents.—

Stretch the line of my general intimations upon the opening face of things, on Capitol Hill: & believe me Sir, that what you may now, dimly, discern is but the rising breath of a mighty storm.

Your Excell'y will ee'r all is over, be as anxious to find water with which to quench this enkindling, & flaming fire, as you have had opportunity to discern me willing to lend my aid, in preserving an equipoise in favor of this tottering Ship; which "the winds & waves" have, & will again mightily assail.—

With all due esteem   DAVID AUSTIN

RC (DNA: RG 59, LAR); at foot of text: "Th: Jefferson"; endorsed by TJ as received 19 Dec. and so recorded in SJL.

Austin's COMMUNICATION of 28 Nov. requested a place in the secretary of state's office.

From William Cranch

SIR,   City of Washington Decr. 19th. 1801

In consequence of a note at the bottom of a petition to you in behalf of Charles Houseman, I have the honour to state, that he was indicted at June term last for stealing plank, and Carpenter's tools from three several persons. It appear'd in evidence that the articles were found in his possession, but were of little value. He was found guilty on each indictment, and sentenced to be burnt in the hand, whip'd a certain number of stripes, and to pay four fold the value of the articles stolen. The corporal part of his punishment was inflicted, and he was thereupon discharged from the custody of the Marshall by order of the Court, who were inform'd that it was not in his power to pay the fine. A Capias was afterwards issued, as I believe, to compel him to pay the fine and costs, upon which he was arrested and not being able to satisfy them, he has remain'd in custody ever since. I do not recollect whether any evidence was offer'd as to his character, at the trial, or any other circumstances, except his inability to discharge the fine & Costs, which would entitle his case to peculiar regard from the Executive; but I hope I shall not be deem'd officious in saying that there seems to be no probability that the United States, or the district of Columbia, will be benefited by his further imprisonment.

I have the honour, to be, Sir, with great respect, your obedt. servt.

W. CRANCH

RC (DLC); at head of text: "To the President of the United States"; endorsed by TJ as received 26 Dec. and so recorded in SJL with a brace connecting it with John Thomson Mason's letter of 26 Dec. (see below) and the notation "Houseman's case"; also endorsed by TJ: "Charles Houseman's case."

William Cranch (1769-1855), a Harvard graduate and nephew of Abigail Adams, came to Washington from Massachusetts in 1794. In February 1801, John Adams nominated him to the U.S. Circuit Court for the District of Columbia, a nomination approved by the Senate on 3 Mch., the day before TJ took office. Despite the midnight appointment, TJ nominated Cranch to be chief judge of the circuit in 1806 and he went on to serve on the court for more than 50 years. He also acted as recorder for the U.S. Supreme Court from 1801 to 1815 (ANB; JEP, 1:387, 389; 2:21, 22).

A PETITION to TJ on behalf of

CHARLES HOUSEMAN has not been found, nor has any record of TJ issuing a pardon in his favor.

On 26 Dec., John Thomson Mason, as the U.S. attorney for the District of Columbia, also wrote TJ regarding Houseman's case. Mason concurred with Cranch in the details of the case, adding the observation that Houseman was unable to pay the demand against him, "for I believe he is not worth one shilling" (RC in DLC; endorsed by TJ as received 26 Dec. and so recorded in SJL; also endorsed by TJ: "Charles Houseman's case").

To John Dickinson

DEAR SIR   Washington Dec. 19. 1801.

The approbation of my antient friends, is, above all things, the most grateful to my heart. they know for what objects we relinquished the delights of domestic society, of tranquility & of science, & committed ourselves to the ocean of revolution, to wear out the only life god has given us here[1] in scenes, the benefits of which will accrue only to those who follow us. surely we had in view to obtain the theory & practice of good government. and how any, who seemed so ardent in this pursuit, could so shamelessly have apostatised, and supposed we meant only to put our government into other hands, but not other forms, is indeed wonderful. the lesson we have had will probably be useful to the people at large, by shewing to them how capable they are of being made the instruments of their own bondage. a little more prudence & moderation in those who had mounted themselves on their fears, and it would have been long & difficult to unhorse them. their madness has done in three years what reason alone acting against them would not have effected in many; and the more as they might have gone on forming new entrenchments for themselves from year to year. my great anxiety at present is to avail ourselves of our ascendency to establish good principles, and good practices; to fortify republicanism behind as many barriers as possible; that the outworks may give time to rally & save the citadel should that be again in danger. on their part they have retired into the Judiciary as a strong hold. there the remains of federalism are to be preserved & fed from the treasury, and from that battery all the works of republicanism are to be beaten down & erased. by a fraudulent use of the constitution which has made judges irremoveable, they have multiplied useless judges merely[2] to strengthen their phalanx.

You will perhaps have been alarmed, as some have been, at the proposition to abolish the *whole* of the internal taxes. but it is perfectly safe. they are under a million of dollars, and we can economise the government two or three millions a year. the impost alone gives us 10. or 11. millions annually, increasing at a compound ratio of $6\frac{2}{3}$ per cent per ann. & consequently doubling in 10. years. but leaving that increase for contingencies, the present amount will support the government, pay the interest of the public debt, and discharge the principal in 15. years. if the increase proceeds, and no contingencies demand it, it will pay off the principal in a shorter time. exactly one half of the public debt, to wit, 37. millions of dollars are owned in the US. that capital then will be set afloat to be employed in rescuing our commerce from the hands of foreigners, or in agriculture, canals, bridges, or other useful enterprizes. by suppressing at once the whole internal taxes we abolish three fourths of the offices now existing & spread over the land.[3]   seeing the interest you take in the public affairs, I have indulged myself in observations flowing from a sincere & ardent desire of seeing our affairs put into an honest & advantageous train. accept assurances of my constant & affectionate esteem & high respect.   TH: JEFFERSON

RC (PHi); torn, with several words supplied from PrC; addressed: "John Dickinson esq. Wilmington. Del."; franked; postmarked 20 or 21 Dec.; endorsed by Dickinson. PrC (DLC). Recorded in SJL. as a letter of 20 Dec.

[1] Word interlined.
[2] Word written over partially erased "and."
[3] Sentence interlined.

From the District of Columbia Commissioners

SIR,   Commissioners Office, 19th. December 1801

Agreeably to the information given in our memorial of the 4th. Instant we have held a sale of Lots for ready money which we kept open ten days—It has produced by actual sales $4234, and by payments made by Debtors to prevent their property from being sold $7613, making together $11,847—yet our expenditures have been such as to leave at this time no more than $5,880 in our hands—. During the sale we pursued our general policy of not selling any property for less than the sum due on it to the public thinking it improper to change that system till it should be known what measures Government will take with respect to it; although (besides the interest due to the State of Maryland) the Commissioners note for $5000 discounted at the Bank of Columbia will become due 22/25th January next, and we estimate the Sums due for Operations on the roads and buildings, expenses of the Commissioners Office, and other contingencies to the end of the year at $1870, demands to which our present means are very inadequate.—

We are with sentiments of the highest respect Sir, Yr mo Ob Servts

WILLIAM THORNTON
ALEX WHITE
TRISTRAM DALTON

RC (DLC); in Thomas Munroe's hand, signed by Thornton, White, and Dalton; at foot of text: "President of the United States"; endorsed by TJ as received 20 Dec. and so recorded in SJL. FC (DNA: RG 42, DCLB); with statement of account at foot of text. Tr (DNA: RG 233, PM, 7th Cong., 1st sess.); in Meriwether Lewis's hand; in TJ's hand on verso: "President of the United States" and the names of the commissioners. Transmitted to Congress with TJ's message of 11 Jan. 1802.

From Benjamin Henfrey

SIR   Baltimore Decr. 19th 1801

I might have had the honor of addressing you thro the medium of a member of Congress but encouraged by the general tenor of your Conduct which I have now had an opportunity of viewing for the last Ten Years and seeing that it is your steady & uniform wish to promote the general good & Interest of mankind.

I under these impressions venture to submit some Ideas for your consideration when at leisure which I have long thought if put in practice would be attended with great and lasting advantages to the Citizens of the United States—

Considering every moment of your time as precious to your country I shall in the most concise manner I am capable of lay before you the outlines of the plan alluded to the liberty I take in doing which I humbly hope that you will pardon should my plan not be so fortunate as meet your approbation—

Query 1st. Might it not answer an invaluable purpose if one or more men possessing a general knowledge of the different branches of Science as noted below were employed by Government to be constantly travelling thro the united States—

Viz: 1st. A general knowledge how to discover mines of every description of Minerals

2d How to assay the Ores and make proper reports to the owners of the land together with an opinion if the Mine could be worked to advantage the person should also be able to construct Furnaces and give directions how to smelt the Ores—

3d. To attend to the discovery of Marles & Limestone and to point out their use in Agriculture—

4th. To Attend to the discovery of Pit Coal & Iron & to shew the use of Boring Rods in the discovery of Coal & Water—

5—The person employed should have a general knowledge of all kind of Machinery so as to be able to confirm what he found perfect and to give advice where he saw any Errors

6th He should have some knowledge of Inland Navigation and should note where Canals of Communication may be cut in future to advantage—

7th He should know how to construct the new mode of Making Roads that is now partially in use in England on which one horse will draw about Ten Tons which would make a great saving in a variety of cases &c &c

Should this plan be so fortunate as meet your Approbation I beg leave to offer my services for the first years trial and I humbly trust that the long practice I have had say upwards of 20 Years in England and 10 in America may enable me to give satisfaction both to your Excellency and the public—

Having travelled much already thro this extensive Continent, I might note many instances where I have been serviceable in this way also some Service that I rendered this Government with several Indian Nations that I was amongst and also some valuable discoveries that I have made in the Mineral Kingdom but I am fearfull to occupy too much of your valuable time—

I have so far been unfortunate in the connections I have made otherwise I should have succeeded in working a very valuable Copper Mine in Lancaster County—A description of which may be found in the pamphlet that I have taken the liberty to enclose.

By the company not fulfilling their engagements with me I sunk a considerable sum & they are still 1200 Dollars in my debt but as the property is mine I calculate on reviving the work as I know it to be a mine of great value. I am now opening a Mine of Fossil Coal which I discovered last winter this Mine is $8\frac{1}{2}$ miles from Baltimore but I have lately made a discovery of the same Species of Coal within one

Mile of Town which will if Opened become of great consequence to the citizens in general as wood is a rising Article here—

Permit me now sir in a few words to inform you of a discovery that I have lately made in making experiments upon this new Coal. It is a mode of making the Vapour inflammable and of Obtaining a lively flame without Smoak at the Extremity of a long tube which leads me to hope that this discovery will be peculiarly adapted to illuminate Light Houses and will I conceive make a very considerable saving—

Should I be so fortunate as to receive your commands to come to the seat of Government I shall bring a small Apparatus with me and shall solicit the Honor of being permitted to know your Opinion on the probable utility of this discovery as there are various other purposes that it may be applied to—Being a Stranger to your Excellency it is proper that I should inform you that I can bring forward such testimonies from Men of Character as will I trust be Satisfactory if I am permitted to have the honor of waiting upon you.

In the humble hope of which I remain with the greatest Veneration and respect—

Sir Your Obedt & most Humble Servt—

BENJAMIN HENFREY

RC (DLC); at head of text: "His Excellency Thomas Jefferson"; endorsed by TJ as received 21 Dec. and so recorded in SJL. Enclosure: Benjamin Henfrey, *A Plan With Proposals for Forming a Company to Work Mines in the United States; and to Smelt and Refine the Ores Whether of Copper, Lead, Tin, Silver, or Gold* (Philadelphia, 1797); Sowerby, No. 3776.

An English-born mineralogist and entrepreneur, Benjamin Henfrey (d. ca. 1818) had arrived in America by 1791, when he began advertising his assaying services in the Philadelphia press. He subsequently undertook a series of unsuccessful mining schemes, including copper in Pennsylvania, coal in Maryland, gypsum in western Virginia, and drilling salt wells in North Carolina. In 1807, Henfrey wrote TJ from western Virginia to report finding a "Very considerable bank of Sulphur Ore," to which TJ replied with interest and a request for more information. Like Henfrey's earlier schemes, however, nothing apparently came of his sulfur discovery. He reportedly died in poverty some years later in Bellefonte, Pennsylvania (Philadelphia *General Advertiser*, 23 Nov. 1791; Baltimore *Federal Gazette*, 26 Aug. 1801; Richmond *Enquirer*, 30 Sep. 1806; Raleigh *Star*, 1 June 1809; *Baltimore Patriot*, 15 July, 8 Aug. 1828; Henfrey to TJ, 1 Dec. 1807; TJ to Henfrey, 3 Jan. 1808).

The SERVICE that Henfrey RENDERED THIS GOVERNMENT included efforts to secure the return of Americans taken prisoner by Indians (*Baltimore Patriot*, 8 Aug. 1828).

Henfrey spent several years during the 1790s promoting the Gap COPPER MINE IN LANCASTER COUNTY, Pennsylvania, including the publication of the enclosed PAMPHLET (see above). In 1799, the Navy Department offered Henfrey and John Ross of Philadelphia a $10,000 advance for copper bolts, spikes, nails, and sheets, provided said materials were fabricated from copper from the Gap mine or other domestic copper mines, and that the order be filled by November 1800 (NDQW, Apr.-July 1799, 194).

Henfrey's DISCOVERY of a means to

manufacture gas from coal closely resembled the "thermolampe" developed by French engineer Philippe Lebon. In April 1802, Henfrey received a patent for developing a "cheap mode of obtaining light from fuel." That same year, he gave public demonstrations of his "thermo-lamp" system in Baltimore, Richmond, and Washington that attracted considerable attention (including a visit by TJ), but few investors. He also submitted a proposal to the secretary of the Treasury for supplying lighthouses with gas produced by his thermo-lamp, which likewise came to naught (Christopher J. Castaneda, *Invisible Fuel, Manufactured and Natural Gas in America, 1800-2000* [New York, 1999], 5, 13; *List of Patents*, 27; Baltimore *Republican or, Anti-Democrat*, 18 Feb. 1802; Norfolk *Commercial Register*, 25 Aug. 1802; *Philadelphia Gazette & Daily Advertiser*, 28 Dec. 1802; MB, 2:1071; *Daily National Intelligencer*, 30 Nov. 1816; Henfrey to TJ, 1 Dec. 1807).

From Robert Patterson

SIR Philadelphia Decr. 19th. 1801

The art of secret writing, or, as it is usually termed, *writing in cypher*, has occasionally engaged the attention both of the states-man & philosopher for many ages; and yet I believe it will be acknowledged, by all who are acquainted with the present state of this art, that it is still far short of perfection. A *perfect* cypher, as it appears to me, should possess the following properties.—

1. It should be equally adapted to all languages.

2. It should be easily learned & retained in memory.

3. It should be written and read with facility & dispatch.

4. (Which is the most essential property) it should be absolutely inscrutable to all unacquainted with the particular key or secret for decyphering.

I shall not enter into a tedious detail of the various systems of secret writing that have been, or are still in use,[1] or point out their several defects; but shall immediately proceed to lay before you a system which, I flatter myself, will be found to possess the above requisites, in as great a degree as can reasonably be desired. For 1st. it is equally applicable to all alphabetical languages. 2d) it may be learned by any person of moderate capacity in ten minutes; so that he shall be as expert in the use of it, as one who may have practised it for many years. 3d) it may be written and read with nearly the same facility and dispatch as common writing. & 4thly it will be absolutely impossible, even for one perfectly acquainted with the general system, ever to desypher the writing of another without his key.

In this system, there is no substitution of one letter or character for another; but every word is to be written at large, in its proper alphabetical characters, as in common writing: only that there need be no use of capitals, pointing, nor spaces between words; since any piece of writing may be easily read without these distinctions.

The method is simply this—Let the writer rule on his paper as many pencil-lines as will be sufficient to contain the whole writing— Then, instead of placing the letters one *after* the other, as in common writing, let them be placed one *under* the other, in the Chinese manner; namely, the first letter at the beginning of the first line, the second letter at the beginning of the second line, and so on, writing column after column, from left to right, till the whole is written.

This writing is then to be distributed into sections of not more than nine lines in each section, and these are to be numbered 1. 2. 3 &c 1. 2. 3 &c (from top to bottom).[2] The whole is then to be transcribed, section after section, taking the lines of each section in any order at pleasure, inserting at the beginning of each line respectively any number of arbitrary or insignificant letters, not exceeding nine; & also filling up the vacant spaces at the end of the lines with like letters.

Now the Key or secret for decyphering will consist in knowing— the *number* of lines in each section, the *order* in which these are transcribed, and the *number* of insignificant letters at the beginning of each line—All which may be briefly, and intelligibly expressed in figures, thus—

5 8
7 1
3 3
4 9   The first rank of figures expressing the number and
    order of the lines in each section, and the 2d rank, the
8 3   number of arbitrary letters at the beginning of each
1 4   respective line
6 2
2 0

For example, let the following sentence be written in cypher according to the above key

"Buonaparte has at last given peace to Europe! France is now at peace with all the world. Four treaties have been concluded with the chief Consul within three weeks, to wit, with Portugal, Britain, Russia, and Turkey. A copy of the latter, which was signed at Paris on Friday, we received last night, in the French Journals to the nineteenth. The news was announced, at the Theatres on the sixteenth, and next day by the firing of cannon, and other demonstrations of joy."

First Draft.

1 b i n l e i h t s h e e e n a e e a r
2 u v c l s t i h i e d c f i n s x n a
3 o e e t h h n p a l a e r n n o t n t
4 n n i h a t t o a a t i e e o n d o i
5 a p s e v h h r n t p v n t u t a n o
6 p e n w e e r t d t a e c e n h y a n
7 a a o o b c e u t e r d h e c e b n s
8 r c w r e h e g u r i l j n e s y d o
1 t e a l e i w a r w s a o t d i t o f
2 e t t d n e e l k h o s u h a x h t j
3 h o p f c f e b e i n t r t t t e h o
4 a e e o o c k r y c f n n h t e f e y
5 s u a u n o s i a h r i a e h e i r
6 a r c r c n t t c w i g l n e n r d
7 t o e t l s o a o a d h s e t t i e
8 l p w r u u w i p s a t t w h h n m
1 a e i e d l i n y s y i o s e a g o
2 s f t a e w t r o i w n t w a n o n
3 t r h t d i w u f g e t h a t d f s
4 g a a i w t i s t n r h e s r n c t

Transcribed in cypher-

w s a t a i s p a p s e v h h r n t p v n t u t a n o
e a a o o b c e u t e r d h e c e b n s b v a t d e p d n o
c h n o e e t h h n p a l a e r n n o t n t u t i o h
n e m e y e e s a n n i h a t t o a a t i e e o n d o i
r t l r c w r e h e g u r i l j n e s y d o t h d s e a r
s e e o b i n l e i h t s h e e e n a e e a r t a n r m
a r p e n w e e r t d t a e c e n h y a n o a b i
u v c l s t i h i e d c f i n s x n a h o n y l e n r f
s d t r o d i e s u a u n o s i a h r i a e h e i r p
s t o e t l s o a o a d h s e t t i e u a h r d c i u y
f t s h o p t³ c f e b e i n t r t t t e h o r e o y p u
p o r t e r e p i a e e o o c k r y c f n n h t e f e y o
t l r l p w r u u w i p s a t t w h h n m e n t
e r r e t e a l e i w a r w s a o t d i t o f n g e
w h a r c r c n t t c w i g l n e n r d h f o w s h
e t t d n e e l k h o s u h a x h t j o r u i y i
s a u t r h t d i w u f g e t h a t d f s l t m
a d t r o d i i e g a a i w t i s t n r h e s r n c t
n o n o a e i e d l i n y s y i o s e a g o d l l m n
s f t a e w t r o i w n t w a n o n s y o u r c h

It will be proper that the supplementary letters, used at the beginning and end of the lines, should be nearly in the same relative proportion to each other in which they occur in the cypher itself, so that no clue may be afforded for distinguishing between them and the significant letters[4]—

The easiest way of reading the cypher will be, after numbering the lines according to the key, and cancelling the arbitrary letters at the beginning of the lines, to cut them apart, and with a bit of wafer, or the like, stick them on another piece of paper, one under the other, in the same order in which they were first written: for then it may be read downwards, with the utmost facility—

On calculating the number of changes, and combinations, of which the above cypher is susceptible, even supposing that neither the number of lines in a section, nor the number of arbitrary letters at the beginning of the lines, should ever exceed nine, it will be found to amount to upwards of *ninety millions of millions**, nearly equal to the number of seconds in three millions of years—! Hence I presume the utter impossibility of decyphering will be readily acknowledged—

I shall conclude this paper with a specimen of secret writing, which I may safely defy the united ingenuity of the whole human race to decypher, to the end of time—but which, however, by the help of the key, consisting of not more than eighteen figures, might be read, with the utmost ease, in less than fifteen minutes—

bonirnrsewehaipohiluoeettiseesnhiestctfhuesraeas
opiacdasthtaleeletubegtneinnfdecwebssssuifemsetnb
tfcabaenniaepatwethaharhefeisnueisutvaesdihfrsrniboi
kinrrgdvsconhsnheleltentngtsctlhshlbdpetguaistnjvtrscm
odneteitieedrebanirnnrhooifehtelstieisefcretcnuspecenr
bohsutirrsesolototamfyiysdhthiuhtloealobusiotntykjeetu
asesntdmeoatsbehracststnetmomrnosewdaneymnamcreseedoym
edneesemithfrtteaeaeeebttcfhdustslurisvucysiucremystvam
cohasefbsiesashtieadiiocftpricdnarswunhreshegitht
edaapthutheeaapueyeenlhhiemhniasaoaksienoimetesfsesaapnore
eevrslyedclnarcssndeetnreeensattciunngrrechhogaeecmrsreshy
nesvomethenetovrnnrrgeouhoeilamaitsgterewtnrttdmreiisrth
gbrhsearysuwebdrethetorpsgnspwcttebcnfgaiernuecfrnssamrnpsie
oeolgelsujntlncretpehdebtgvvotermrtndnehhitensfimoeheootanp
psgfinhsataatoptwiugtedegiocteodftlnditrsogedttnwfsenrs
neaguatnadaedtlradhsvedspvlhyahdrrenachntcsvtsbtingfad
lonmnhxtednywsnfedtaysirrarersmngnnmbotititslrrrriswmyst

* Equal to the sum of all the changes on any number of quantities not exceeding nine, multiplied by the ninth power of nine.

haebyhcstfhudnoeiltttnjtutnasdoggolrraahtouoanipstormno
oxoxiesnotnouahegropdeooptthcraehovugaienoauaadwot
zinmeerrolthoimeapcolhhomuwcomnhhvelremabeipcnimrahor
wshhurrierdeirssaohdatbtueihtleeeataieafgretdyotebuledsnnreer
gunnaaerceqtilnmeafeshtaedaaedyetsilmsrhineatmplmlxeerhh
raoitalonhmarirenraatpuvttrlpnoliaootnpvasttnonobprsnob
trihsseoiorpvnssntorropawvoraaenelepthaeeidbnehssoemrri
pvlneuofseegtgshleenireefoyneenixooibsrreedmeaaftsmaaree
reertcohauunaweithnteilnolprfadhtnyutohesniierddmerei
stddiehvsnaeoctaooedcagnerrtriimstgpsrcuaadnesthhlapiorpi
esttdrctahtsueaoleoehacmpsoeeelgsimrlsnwfhdeisahtintvoumiu
lneabmopohtdfctrtteisahanzmssheeihsmbuenuoiilniprimci
motedtrhenponauearessrysoinsroaithhsooyghhlttablmnsrry
inaaopteecmocwtikeeeiehimoeisildgdnstynjuoapserriotimit
perervraadteotiswtdtaattrnsftieetcuhadettranryynlf
axnyeflneiemaheohsnfnebgiopltrdgteestwtcasshassm
trsnomiieeinierwlnhrehrtuhmdhosknsreferucehdtotooguaa
inafpeeshshiuteontnsstwsttofeltgtunneoteabltueitoovsepr
smrnpnesdshediuqcetteosiupectahfmestdrsiwhffipcrsny
noiiueoeohfchehharisdogtadwyibstrecrvswonhihedtssrces
whfaairdegtvmhtmumttaecmsvsdtrodieshvuanoftsnfperre
ophrcvstoitrctueloecfitnoleanaesaueeofetetrnetyofssyst
supeinnuonsnnletheqisltfeanoinaetnlihwlcpiporterepiybst

I shall take the liberty of presenting this through the hands of Mr. Daniel T. Patterson, a young gentleman of the navy, who has for some time, I trust not unprofitably, been engaged, under my care, in the study of navigation, and other parts of practical mathematics.

I am, Sir, with the greatest respect and esteem, Your most obedient Servant
RT. PATTERSON

RC (DLC); address clipped; addressed: "Thomas Jefferson Esqre President of the American Philosophical Society City of Washington [. . .]vd. by [. . .]nl. T. Patterson"; endorsed by TJ as received 25 Dec. and so recorded in SJL; also endorsed by TJ: "Cyphers."

LET THE FOLLOWING SENTENCE BE WRITTEN IN CYPHER: to demonstrate the process of encipherment, Patterson used the opening lines of a piece that originated in the *True Briton*, a British publication, in October 1801 (Walpole, N.H., *Farmers' Museum, or Literary Gazette*, 22 Dec.).

France and TURKEY—the Ottoman Empire—signed articles of peace in Paris on 9 Oct. (Parry, *Consolidated Treaty Series*, 56:227-30).

SPECIMEN OF SECRET WRITING: by applying the statistical technique of maximum likelihood analysis to letter sequences, Lawren Smithline of the Center for Communications Research unscrambled the passage that Patterson considered to be indecipherable (Lawren M. Smithline, "A Cipher to Thomas Jefferson," *American Scientist*, 97 [2009], 142-9). The passage consists of the opening lines of the published version of the Declaration of Independence, beginning "in congress july fourth one thousand seven hundred and seventy six" and ending "let facts be submitted to a candid world." Patterson made several errors in the encipherment as he transposed the text, such as writing the wrong letter, repeating a letter, or placing a letter on the wrong line. The key that Patterson used to encrypt the text, according to Smithline's decipherment, was

1 3
3 4
5 7
6 5
2 2
7 8
4 9

(presented in the form Patterson used for another key in the letter above). The figures in the left column indicate the order in which the lines of each seven-line section of the passage would be rearranged (1, 3, 5, 6, 2, 7, 4), and the right column shows the number of random letters added to the beginning of each line. Patterson obviously believed that a passage enciphered using his system could never be read without the key, basing his defiance of the UNITED INGENUITY OF THE WHOLE HUMAN RACE on his calcula-

tion of the chances of guessing the key. The Editors have found no evidence that TJ attempted to decipher the passage.

In addition to his classes at the University of Pennsylvania, Patterson taught "practical mathematics," arithmetic, and bookkeeping. Daniel Todd Patterson, the YOUNG GENTLEMAN OF THE NAVY, was not related to him. Daniel, who was 15 years old in December 1801, was a son of John Patterson—and, therefore, a brother of the William Patterson whom TJ appointed commercial agent for L'Orient. Daniel joined the navy at the age of 13 and received a midshipman's warrant in August 1800. He remained a naval officer until his death in 1839 (Edward Potts Cheyney, *History of the University of Pennsylvania, 1740-1940* [Philadelphia, 1940], 134; ANB, 17:134; Vol. 35:664).

[1] Preceding eight words interlined.
[2] Words in parentheses interlined. Closing parenthesis and period supplied by Editors.
[3] Thus in MS, but this letter should be "f."
[4] Patterson first wrote "between the arbitrary and significant letters" before altering the passage to read as above.

From Richard Williams

SIR   Baltimore Decr the 19th. 1801
   please to Except of A few fresh Cod-Fish; this day taken alive from on board the Smack Lewis of Newbury port Commanded by
   Yr Obedt & Hle Sevt.   RICHD. WILLIAMS

PS as this Smack is intended to Suply this place & the City of Washington Information may be had from Mr Enoch Bayley, Markett Space No. 38. Enquire of Genrl. Dearborn Secretary at War for Particulars & place   RW

RC (DLC); endorsed by TJ as received 21 Dec. and so recorded in SJL.

Richard Williams was a drayman at Lexington Street, Baltimore. Williams and a co-proprietor of a "fishing smack" advertised a subscription to raise $2,000 for building another smack to bring fish to market (Stafford, *Baltimore Directory, for 1802*, 113; *Baltimore Republican or, Anti-Democrat*, 27 Mch. 1802).

ENOCH BAYLEY was an innkeeper at 38 Market space, Baltimore (Stafford, *Baltimore Directory, for 1802*, 11).

To Horatio Gates

DEAR GENERAL   Washington Dec. 20. 1801.

I have duly recieved your favor of the 7th. inclosing the work of your mathematical friend mr Garnet. I should once have been better able to estimate it's merit and accuracy than I am now. many years of constant application to matters of a very different kind have lessened my familiarity with mathematical operations. the paper however sufficiently proves that your friend is an adept in this line, and much better able to decide on the strictness of a solution than I am. with such a mind, enamoured with science, and at leisure to pursue it, his situation is enviable.

I am made happy by the expressions of approbation in your's of the 7th. altho' I should have been more so had they been dated a week later. I cannot however apprehend they would have been less strong. I suppose the line we are pursuing is so obviously advantageous to the public, that our friends cannot be divided on that. accordingly it is not the real business of the government which presents any difficulty or doubt of division, it is only on the question by whom shall the public be served? here are so many wants, so many affections, & passions engaged, so varying in their interests & objects, that no one can be conciliated without revolting others. in this, as in all other cases of difficulty, we must do what is right, confident that in the end it will have the best issue, and be the best way of solving perplexities. I have great hopes that the proceedings of this session of Congress will reconcile all the disinterested & unprejudiced part of our country; all in short who are not in opposition to us because their objects are foreign to our country or constitution.—I pray you to present my best respects to mrs Gates, & to accept yourself assurances of my affectionate esteem & high consideration.   TH: JEFFERSON

PrC (DLC); at foot of text: "Majr. Genl. Gates."

To Levi Lincoln

Dec. 20. 1801.

Th: Jefferson asks the favor of the Attorney general to prepare a proclamation agreeable to the inclosed advice of Senate. he understands the Judges have some cases awaiting this determination. it would be well therefore if they could be certified of the ultimate sanction of the treaty either by the proclamation itself, or by a communication of the advice of Senate on Monday.

RC (Privately owned, on deposit MWA). Not recorded in SJL. Enclosure not found.

On 18 Dec., George Logan reported to the SENATE on behalf of the committee to which France's ratification of the Convention of 1800 had been referred. On the

19th, which was a Saturday, the Senate voted 22 to 4 to consider the convention "as fully ratified" (JEP, 1:398-9).

CASES AWAITING THIS DETERMINATION: see Abishai Thomas to TJ, 15 Dec., for the case of the schooner *Peggy* that was before the Supreme Court.

From James Monroe

DEAR SIR   Richmond Decr 20. 1801

Dr. Barraud who will present you this is a very respectable citizen & able physician of Norfolk. Having been intrusted with the care of the marine hospital at that port, he thinks it incumbent on him to make some communications relative to it to the Executive of the UStates, for which purpose he makes a visit to the seat of govt. you will I am well persuaded find his communication very deserving of attention. with great

respect & esteem I am Dear Sir sincerely yours

JAS. MONROE

RC (NHi: Gallatin Papers); endorsed by TJ as received 24 Dec. and so recorded in SJL; also endorsed by TJ: "by Dr. Barraud, Marine hospital refd to Secy. of Treasury Th:J."

To Benjamin Rush

DEAR SIR   Washington Dec. 20. 1801.

I have recieved your favor of Nov. 27. with your introductory lectures which I have read with the pleasure & edification I do every thing from you. I am happy to see that vaccination is introduced & likely to be kept up in Philadelphia. but I shall not think it exhibits all it's utility until experience shall have hit upon some mark or rule by which the popular eye may distinguish genuine from spurious virus. it was with this view that I wished to discover whether *time* could not be made the standard, and supposed, from the little experience I had, that matter, taken at 8. times 24. hours from the time of insertion, would always be in the proper state. as far as I went I found

[177]

it so. but I shall be happy to learn what the immense field of experience in Philadelphia will teach us on that subject.

Our winter campaign has opened with more good humor than I expected. by sending a message, instead of making a speech at the opening of the session, I have prevented the bloody conflicts to which the making an answer would have commited them. they consequently were able to set in to real business at once, without losing 10. or 12. days in combating an answer. hitherto there has been no disagreeable altercations. the suppression of useless offices, and lopping off the parasitical plant engrafted at the last session of the judiciary body will probably produce some. bitter men are not pleased with the suppression of taxes. not daring to condemn the measure, they attack the motive; & too disingenuous to ascribe it to the honest one of freeing our citizens from unnecessary burthens, & unnecessary systems of officers they ascribe it to a desire of popularity. but every honest man will suppose honest acts to flow from honest principles; & the rogues may rail without interruption.

My health has been always so uniformly firm, that I have for some years dreaded nothing so much as the living too long. I think however that a flaw has appeared which ensures me against that, without cutting short any of the period during which I could expect to remain capable of being useful. it will probably give me as many years as I wish, and without pain or debility. should this be the case, my most anxious prayers[1] will have been fulfilled by heaven. I have said as much to no mortal breathing, and my florid health is calculated to keep my friends as well as foes quiet as they should be. Accept assurances of my constant esteem & high respect.   TH: JEFFERSON

RC (NcD-MC: Trent Collection); at foot of first page: "Doctr. Rush." PrC (DLC).

On 12 Mch. 1802, Rush asked for details about the FLAW in TJ's health. TJ did not answer for almost a year, then revealed that the problem, which he first encountered in 1801, was a persistent diarrhea "after having dined moderately on fish which had never affected me before" (TJ to Rush, 28 Feb. 1803).

[1] Word interlined in place of heavily canceled "[wishes]."

From George Baron

SIR   West Point State of New York Dec 21st. 1801

I humbly solicit your perusal of a hint concerning the dissemination of scientific knowledge in the United States.

Many institutions have been formed in this country for the instruction of youth in the Mathematical Sciences and it is much to be lamented that these institutions have not produced the desired effect. Some Mathematicians and philosophers in Europe finding that notwithstanding the various Seminaries of scientific instruction in the United States the Elementary principles of these sciences still remain almost unknown; have concluded the genius of the American people much inferior to that of Europeans. Four years experience in teaching these sciences in the United States, however, fully demonstrates to me the falsity of that rash opinion. The want of abilities in the teachers and professors is a cause that certainly does exist and naturally accounts for the slow progress of scientific knowledge. To remedy this evil is no easy task as the people are not sensible of the impositions of the teachers to whom they entrust the instruction of their children, and many of the teachers are not themselves aware of the ill effects their want of ability produces. The ignorance of schoolmasters has fixed a kind of stigma on that useful and honourable profession and we seldom hear of a young man studying with the intention of becoming a schoolmaster. A certain course of study is thought absolutely necessary in every other profession but very little attention is paid to the instruction of a teacher. An unsuccessful person in any other line of life generally has recourse to turning schoolmaster, and it is no uncommon thing for such a one who can only cast accounts, to consider himself as a mathematician. The columns of our newspapers abound with the advertisements of such teachers of Mathematics and many a young man pays for learning what he conceives to be Mathematics, when in reality he has not been taught one mathematical principle. The mathematical Sciences are of vast importance to civilized man and without them we might perhaps have been yet in the savage state. Philosophers demonstrate the good effects of these Sciences on the minds of young people and contend that the dissemination of science is the best way of fortifying the liberties of a free people. Surely then the Legislature of the country will no longer overlook these sciences. They have already enacted Laws to prevent impositions of all kinds, the education of youth excepted. The wisdom of the Legislature will no doubt find out means to promote the progress of science and to defend the citizens against the impositions of teachers.

Convinced sir of your paternal regard for the prosperity and improvement of the Citizens of these states, and conceiving some Legislative Act highly necessary at this time, to regulate and accelerate the progress of Scientific knowledge; I have addressed you as the friend and protector of these Sciences. Should your opinion agree with mine on this Subject I shall be happy in laying before you a sketch of a simple plan for disseminating Scientific knowledge in the United States; but if not I most humbly crave your pardon for the liberty I have taken

I am with profound respect Your Excellency's most humb. Servt.

GEO. BARON

RC (DLC); addressed: "His Excellency Thos. Jefferson President of the United States of America Washington City"; franked; postmarked Peekskill, 25 Dec.; endorsed by TJ as received 30 Dec. and so recorded in SJL.

George Baron (1769-1812), an English native and mathematics teacher, emigrated with his wife and family to the United States in 1797 and served as the tutor for the children of Benjamin Vaughan in Hallowell, District of Maine, prior to moving to New York City, where he conducted a private academy. In April 1801, Secretary of War Henry Dearborn offered him a job as a mathematics instructor at the military academy then forming at West Point. Baron initially turned down the offer in hopes of getting higher compensation but later accepted the 6 June 1801 post, with the president's "especial trust and confidence" in his skills and integrity, and became "Teacher of the Arts and Sciences to the Artillerists and Engineers." During a short-lived and stormy tenure at West Point, Baron, a civilian, received Dearborn's support but clashed with both the military administration, which had been appointed under Federalist leadership, and with insubordinate students. A court of inquiry held over the last two weeks of January 1802 explored charges against Baron for fomenting mutiny, accusing

officers of theft, attempting the murder of his wife and children, and cohabiting with a prostitute. Baron asked Aaron Burr to appeal to TJ on his behalf but on 6 Feb. 1802, TJ declined to comment on the matter and chose not to intervene. Baron was dismissed on 11 Feb. 1802 "for his conduct as a man, and as a public officer." He returned to New York City, where he was a member of the Clintonian Theistical Society and editor-in-chief, from 1804 to 1806, of the *Mathematical Correspondent*, the first U.S. periodical devoted exclusively to mathematics (Emma Huntington Nason, *Old Hallowell on the Kennebec* [Augusta, Me., 1909], 89; New York *Daily Advertiser*, 24 Apr. 1799; *New-York Herald*, 25 Sep., 6 Oct. 1802; New York *Commercial Advertiser*, 18 June 1812; Henry Dearborn to George Baron, 11 Apr., 27 May, 6 June, 30 Oct., 2 Dec. 1801, 13 Jan., 11 Feb. 1802 in DNA: RG 107, MLS; Kline, *Burr*, 2:674; Theodore J. Crackel, *West Point: A Bicentennial History* [Lawrence, Kans., 2002], 304; Thomas N. Baker, "Trouble at West Point: The Stormy Tenure of George Baron, Teacher of Mathematics," unpublished paper presented at the Bicentennial Celebration of Mathematics Journals in America symposium, American Philosophical Society, 30 Apr. 2004; Vol. 34:87; TJ to Aaron Burr, 6 Feb. 1802).

Statement of Account with Thomas Carpenter

Thomas Jefferson Esq.

1801	To Thomas Carpenter	Dr:
October 1st.		
	To Making a Surtout Coat & materials	$ 4.50
	2⅞ yds Superfine Cloth @ 48/9	18.68
	22 Steele Buttons and a Velvet Collar	3.60
20	To a Superfine blue Coat, Silk Sleeve Lynings Steele Buttons and a Velvet Collar	23.75
	New Silk Sleeve Lynings to a Coat	2—
Novr 9	To Making Breeches and materials—5 pockets and pearl Buttons	4.12
	To Making a Water proof surtout—Silk Sleeve Lynings—steele Buttons & Velvet Collar— with apron	10.—
Decr 21	Putting an Apron to a Surtout Coat	1.25
	½ yd blue Cloth	3.25
	Putting a Collar to a Coat	1.75
	Facing an under Waist & new Flannel Sleeves	2.—
		74.90
November 30th—	For the Servants—	
	Making 5 Coats and materials with plated Buttons as before @ 34/3	22.80
	Making 5 Waistcoats & materials— plated Buttons 18/—	12.—
	Making 5 pr pantaloons & Do.—Strings & Do. 16/6	11.—
	9½ Yds Silver Lace @ 7/6	9.50
	3½ Yds Crimson Cloth @ 40/	18.67
		73.97
		$ 148.87

MS (ViU: Edgehill-Randolph Papers); in Carpenter's hand, with figures in italics added by TJ; checkmarks, not shown above, probably added by TJ during a review of the account in John Barnes's office; at foot of statement TJ ordered: "Mr. Barnes will be pleased to pay the above Th. Jefferson Jan. 15. 1802"; receipt acknowledging payment in full on 16 Jan. in Barnes's hand, signed by Carpenter; endorsed by Barnes; endorsed by TJ.

According to his financial memoranda, TJ ordered payment by John Barnes to CARPENTER, a Washington tailor, "for his bill 148.87" on 15 Jan. 1802 (MB, 2:1063). A previous account with Carpenter is printed at 1 July 1801.

From Albert Gallatin, with Jefferson's Reply

DEAR SIR   Treasury Department Decer. 21st 1801

Did you read the long report in A. M'Clene's case, which I had sent to you & which you returned?

It appears to me that the whole amounts to this—that the Bargemen have repeatedly been employed in levelling the wharf of the Collector—but, that it does not appear, that they were ever so employed to the detriment of the public business—If so, it should seem that there is not sufficient cause of removal; but that he should be advised not to employ the boatmen hereafter at any time in any occupation but relative to the revenue. If you approve, I will prepare an official report & transmit it to you.

With sincere respect Your obedt. Servt.   ALBERT GALLATIN

I enclose a private letter from Dallas—He like the other Philadelphians are more particularly averse to Maj. Jackson than to any other of the custom officers—

[*Reply by TJ*:]
Mclane's conduct appears to me not to have been honourable; but yet not criminal enough to call for removal.   TH:J.

I retain the paper respecting Ebenezer Thompson.

RC (NHi: Gallatin Papers); addressed: "The President"; with TJ's reply subjoined. Enclosures: (1) Alexander J. Dallas to Gallatin, 16 Dec. 1801, contending that a complaint brought against George Latimer as customs collector was groundless; Dallas derides "a certain arrangement in the Excise department" and responds negatively to reports that customs officer William McPherson "is to be turned out" but Major William Jackson is to be retained; lastly, Dallas requests that Wilson Cary Nicholas, Joseph H. Nicholson, or John Randolph provide him "with a hint of what is designed in relation to the Judiciary Department" (RC in same; Gallatin, *Papers*, 6:205). (2) Probably "Weekly list of Warrants issued on the Treasurer by the Sec. of the Treasy. for the week ending 19th Decer. 1801," reporting 17 warrants, Nos. 181 to 197, including 6 warrants to loan commissioners for the payment of interest and principal on the public debt, totaling $657,600, and one of $50,000 for the military establishment, with a total of $719,692.14 for all warrants (MS in DLC; entirely in Gallatin's hand).

The LONG REPORT has not been found. M'CLENE'S CASE: for the accusations brought against Allen McLane, the collector at Wilmington, Delaware, and the appointment of George Read, Jr., and James Tilton to investigate the case, see Gallatin to TJ, 23 May. According to one charge, McLane had employed BARGEMEN "in menial services for himself, to the detriment of the public service" (same). I WILL PREPARE AN OFFICIAL REPORT: on 2 Jan. 1802, Gallatin wrote McLane that the president had "examined the evidence given in relation to certain charges exhibited against" him by

Benjamin Reynolds and approved the opinion formed by the Treasury Department that there were "no grounds for a removal." Gallatin enclosed an extract of the Department's report, dated 1 Jan. 1802, with TJ's signature of approval. In the report Gallatin concluded that McLane was a "vigilent and active officer" and that the barges under his direction were "employed with more benefit to the public than has generally been the case" (Gallatin, *Papers*, 6:410).

For an earlier letter from Philadelphia recommending the replacement of William JACKSON, the surveyor of customs, but not William McPherson, the naval officer, see Enclosure No. 3, listed at Gallatin to TJ, 17 Aug.

To Levi Lincoln

DEAR SIR   Washington Dec. 21. 1801.

Observing that the usage has been to insert the treaty at full length in the proclamation, on a conference with the Secretary of state, we have concluded it safest to follow the usage, and further to insert Buonaparte's ratification & the subsequent advice of Senate verbatim. this being merely mechanical will be done by the clerks in the office of state; but in the mean time I must ask of you the advice of Senate of which I did not retain a copy. I will return it to you immediately, that you may shew it to the court, as well as inform them that I have directed a proclamation to be prepared for promulgating it, if any cause should be in danger of being put off for want of it. as it will take time to copy the treaty into the proclamation, I do not expect it can be done before the court will have risen to day. health & affectionate esteem.   TH: JEFFERSON

RC (MHi: Lincoln Collection). Not recorded in SJL.

IN THE PROCLAMATION: see Proclamation on Ratification of the Convention with France, 21 Dec., below.

Resolution of the Mississippi Territory General Assembly

House of Representatives of the Mississippi Territory December 21st. 1801—

This assembly having understood that a copy of a malicios and Libellous Pamphlet published in Boston in the state of Massachusetts: and purporting to be "An account of the public and private life of Winthrop Sargent" was in circulation in this Territory: and in which publication many of the citizens thereof had been greatly calumniated and in particular our Delegate to Congress Narsworthy Hunter Esqr.: thought it their duty to take some public notice thereof: with this view every exertion has been made to get possession of the said Pamphlet in order that such Calumniations might be repelled and exposed: But having hitherto failed of success in such exertions: This assembly for the present deem it their duty to adopt the following Resolutions—

Therefore unanimously Resolved by the Legislative Council and House of Representatives of the Mississippi Territory, that a great majority of the citizens of this Territory are much attached to the United States, and equally so to a free Government: that they will never be reconciled to oppression; or confide in the man who oppresses them hence arose their great desire for a Legislative assembly of their own: and the removal of Winthrop Sargent their late Governor—

2nd. Resolved that Narsworthy Hunter Esqr: the delegate from this Territory to Congress has uniformly displayed great Patriotism and fidelity in public employments and much integrity and Probity in private life: and therefore it is that he is Justly esteem by a great majority of his fellow Citizens—

3rd. Resolved that the supersedeing of Winthrop Sergent in the office of Governor of this Territory was essential to the welfare thereof: and that the thanks of this assembly be returned for the same to the President of the United States—

4th. Resolved: that our present Governor possesses the confidence and esteem of this Legislature and that from his Political and private character we fully expect that his administration will be Conducive to the happiness and welfare of this Country—

5th. Resolved that the speaker of this House be and he is hereby requested to transmit one Copy of these resolves to Thomas Jefferson President of the United States—

6th. Resolved that another Copy be also forwarded to Narsworthy Hunter Esqr. our delegate to Congress with a request that he will have them published in the public papers in the City of Washington—

H. HUNTER Speaker of the
House of Representativs
JOHN ELLIS President
of the Council

MS (DLC); in a clerk's hand, signed by Hunter and Ellis; attested by Edwin L. Harris as clerk of the Mississippi Territory House of Representatives; endorsed by TJ as received 24 Feb. 1802 and so recorded in SJL.

Henry Hunter was elected to the new

House of Representatives of Mississippi Territory in 1800 and became its first speaker. He had been one of the territorial residents opposed to Winthrop Sargent, the first governor. Hunter, who during his career was also a county sheriff and a militia officer, sat in the legislature until 1807. Like Hunter, John Ellis first took up residence in the region when it was governed by Spanish authority. Ellis was not part of the opposition to Sargent, and in December 1800, Ellis signed a memorial to Congress supporting Sargent through an unsuccessful attempt to postpone the creation of a territorial assembly. Before that memorial reached Congress, John Adams named, and the U.S. Senate approved, Ellis as a member of the first legislative council for the territory. In a structure adopted from that of the Northwest Territory, the council formed the upper chamber of the general assembly, and the members of the first council made Ellis their president. Later he was elected to the territorial House of Representatives, serving for a time as its speaker (Dunbar Rowland, ed., *Encyclopedia of Mississippi History*, 2 vols. [Madison, Wis., 1907], 1:684, 909, 914; 2:76-8; *Terr. Papers*, 5:109-14; U.S. Statutes at Large, 1:51-3; JEP, 1:363-4).

PAMPHLET: *Papers, in Relation to the Official Conduct of Governour Sargent*, published at Boston on 1 Aug. 1801; see also William C. C. Claiborne to TJ, 27 Nov.

On a trip to Philadelphia early in 1800, NARSWORTHY HUNTER represented the faction in Mississippi Territory that opposed Sargent. On that visit, Hunter supplied information to William Claiborne, who was then a member of Congress prominent in the investigation of Sargent's governorship. In 1801, Narsworthy Hunter was elected the first delegate to Congress from Mississippi Territory. As a delegate, he could participate in debates in the U.S. House of Representatives, but had no vote. On 8 Dec. 1801, he presented his credentials, which the House accepted on the 21st of that month. However, Hunter, a native of Virginia, died in Washington early in his term as delegate, on 11 Mch. 1802. According to SJL, he wrote a letter to TJ of 18 Feb. 1802 that has not been found (*Papers, in Relation to the Official Conduct of Governour Sargent*, 6-10; JHR, 4:7, 21-2; Rowland, *Encyclopedia of Mississippi History*, 1:909; *Biog. Dir. Cong.*).

From James Monroe

DEAR SIR   Richmond Decr 21. 1801.

Our communication will be laid before the assembly to morrow with its doors closed. The objection which I suggested applied to a delegation of any confidence or trust over the subject, from the legislature to our Executive, not to the agency of the federal Executive in the affair. In the latter view I saw no objection to the clause, for what was proposed in that respect was precisely what the legislature sought. The modification so as to comprize the council was material. In other respects it stands perhaps as well as it possibly can.

Your late communication to the Congress, has plac'd yr. admn. on such ground, with the republican party, as to leave it in yr. power to act with respect to removals from office, as you may judge expedient; by which I mean that if you are disposed in any case, where the merit of the party interests you, to indulge feelings of benevolence towards

[185]

him or them, yr. so doing will excite no uneasiness among the republicans. It may also be said that it has produc'd such an effect among the people generally, as to put it in yr. power, especially if the taxes named be repeald without the danger of future recurrence to them, to remove whomever you may think, of the dependants of the late admn., are entitled to that mark of attention. The impression is a strong one and likely to be durable, if ground be not lost in any other quarter. It will always be recollected that from the chiefs, who sinned knowingly, we have nothing to hope, and that if it were justifiable to pass by those who were really criminal, it is impossible to reconcile them to the existing state of things—

You ask me to mention some person for the p. office in this city, & seem to look to the council from wh. to make the selection. There are you know five members in it, republican any of whom are competent to the trust. Perhaps any of them wod. accept it but I do not know that either wod. I think them all honest men and very deserving of confidence. Dr. Foushee or Genl. Guerrant wod. perhaps be best recd. by the publick as successors to the present officer. They are the oldest men and I am persuaded the appointment of either, wod. be more acceptable to the other members, than of either of the others. I do not think the first named wod. accept it; it is probable the latter, who is in more contracted circumstances wod.; tho' I have spoken to no one on the subject. Out of that body, in Richmond, I think Mr. Hylton, & Major Dunscomb, wod. be most deserving of attention, the latter of whom voted for the alpabetical envoy, but abandoned him as soon as he found he was deceived. Of the latter correct information may be had of several of our reps. in Congress; it is certain that he injur'd himself by the error referr'd to. Any further information in my power to give you I will with pleasure. yr. friend & servant

JAS. MONROE

The present incumbent is very attentive & accomodating, and is I think an inoffensive being.

RC (DLC); endorsed by TJ as received 25 Dec. and so recorded in SJL.

OUR COMMUNICATION: TJ to Monroe, 24 Nov. 1801 (second letter). On 7 Dec., in his message on the opening of the legislative session, Monroe stated that in "a future and early communication" he would send the General Assembly his correspondence with TJ pursuant to the assembly's resolution of 31 Dec. 1800, the intent of which was to find a location outside the limits of Virginia "whither persons obnoxious to the laws or dangerous to the peace of society" could be transported. On 22 Dec. 1801, Monroe sent the speaker of the House of Delegates, Larkin Smith, his correspondence with TJ on the subject. In a cover letter dated 21 Dec., Monroe said that TJ "has stated fully and ably the objections which occur to such an establishment within the limits of the United States. He also presents to view all the other places on this continent, and elsewhere, which furnish alternatives, with the advantages and disadvantages attending each." It was up to the assembly, Monroe indicated, "to explain more fully the description of persons who are to be thus transported, and the place to which it is disposed to give the preference." After receiving the papers from the governor, the House of Delegates ordered the gallery and lobby cleared of spectators, went into a closed-door session, and referred the matter to a select committee of 25 members (JHD, Dec. 1801-Feb. 1802, 3, 35; *Annals*, 9th Cong., appen., 998; *National Intelligencer*, 28 Dec. 1801; Monroe to TJ, 15 June 1801, first letter).

ALPABETICAL ENVOY: John Marshall, who was one of the American envoys to France during the XYZ affair. In 1798, he won a seat in Congress representing Henrico County, Virginia (Vol. 30:524, 525n).

PRESENT INCUMBENT: Augustine Davis.

Proclamation on Ratification of the Convention with France

Whereas a Convention for terminating certain differences, which had arisen between the United States of America and the French Republic, was concluded and signed by the Plenipotentiaries of the two nations, duly and respectively authorised for that purpose, and was duly ratified and confirmed by the President of the United States, with the advice and consent of the Senate, which convention so ratified is in the form following:

[*Text omitted.*][1]

And whereas the said Convention was on the other part ratified and confirmed by the first Consul of France in the form of which the following is a translation from the French language, to wit:

Bonaparte, First Consul, in the name of the French People—The consuls of the Republic, having seen and examined the Convention concluded, agreed to, and signed at Paris, the 8th Vendemiaire, 9th year of the French republic, (30th September 1800) by the citizens Joseph Bonaparte, Fleurieu and Rœderer, counsellors of state, in virtue of the full powers which have been given to them to this effect, with Messieurs Ellsworth, Davie, and Murray, ministers plenipotentiary of the United States, equally furnished with full powers, the tenor of which convention follows: [Here follows a copy of the convention in the French language.]

Approves the above convention in all and each of the articles which are therein contained; declares that it is accepted, ratified and confirmed, and promises that it shall be inviolably observed.

[187]

The government of the United States having added in its ratification, that the Convention should be in force for the space of eight years, and having omitted the second article, the government of the French republic consents to accept, ratify & confirm the above convention, with the addition importing that the convention shall be in force for the space of eight years, and with the retrenchment of the second article: Provided that by this retrenchment the two states renounce the respective pretensions, which are the object of the said article.

In Faith whereof these presents are given. Signed, countersigned & sealed with the great seal of the Republic, at Paris the twelfth thermidor, ninth year of the Republic (31st July 1801.)

(Signed) BONAPARTE.
The Minister of Exterior Relations,
(Signed) Ch. Mau. Talleyrand
By the First Consul,
The Secretary of State.
(Signed) Hugues B. Maret.

Which ratifications were duly exchanged at Paris on the 31st day of July in the present year, and having been so exchanged were again submitted to the Senate of the United States, who on the 19th day of the present month resolved that they considered the said Convention as fully ratified, and returned the same to the President for the usual promulgation. Now therefore to the end that the said Convention may be observed and performed with good faith on the part of the United States, I have caused the premises to be made public, and I do hereby enjoin and require all persons bearing office, civil or military, within the United States, and all others, citizens or inhabitants thereof, or being within the same, faithfully to observe and fulfil the said Convention and every clause and article thereof.

In Testimony whereof I have caused the seal of the United States to be affixed to these Presents, and signed the same with my hand.

Done at the City of Washington, the twenty-first day of December in the year of our Lord one thousand eight hundred and one, and of the sovereignty and independence of the United States the twenty-sixth.   TH: JEFFERSON.

Printed in *National Intelligencer*, 23 Dec. 1801; at head of text: "By the President of the United States of America. A Proclamation"; at foot of text: "By the President, James Madison, Secretary of State"; includes earlier presidential proclamation with text of the convention, not printed above (see note 1); the first bracketed notation about omission of text is supplied; the second bracketed notation, about omission of the French text of the convention, is from the *Intelligencer*.

[1] TJ's proclamation included here John Adams's proclamation of 18 Feb. 1801,

which announced the Senate's original ratification of the convention and incorporated the full text of the convention in English.

From John Vaughan

Dr SIR.   Philad: Decr 21. 1801

I have the pleasure of sending you a Philadelphia Edition of Aikin, with an appendix, containing some important Documents from Letsom &c—I have also sent a short abstract of some leading points in Dr Husson's work on this subject printed this year at Paris—He was one of the Paris Medical Committee of the Vaccination Hospital— Not knowing whether you have time to look at all the Philada newspapers, I have added from them a letter of D Coxe's & the Certificate of Dr Farquhar of its success in Jama. I have sent a Book to M Dunbar with some of the Virus—When you write to him, it would possibly be rendering a great service to him & to humanity to send him Some of the Virus—least what I have sent should not prove sufficient. The Society was much gratified by the paper you forwarded from him, which is highly interesting & we shall be happy to receive[1] the further one promised.—D Coxe & several other Physicians are now going on with Vaccination, very satisfactorily

I remain with respect D sir Your obt Serv   JN VAUGHAN

RC (DLC); endorsed by TJ as received 24 Dec. and so recorded in SJL. Enclosures: see below.

PHILADELPHIA EDITION OF AIKIN: see Vaughan to TJ, 9 Dec.

HUSSON'S WORK: the *Philadelphia Gazette* on 16 Dec. printed a summary of Henri-Marie Husson's *Recherches historiques et médicales sur la vaccine,* recently published in Paris (Elinor Meynell, "French Reactions to Jenner's Discovery of Smallpox Vaccination: The

Primary Sources," *Social History of Medicine,* 8 [1995], 300; *Dictionnaire,* 18:94).

On 17 Dec., the *Philadelphia Gazette* and *Poulson's American Daily Advertiser* published a LETTER by John Redman Coxe, addressed to the public, on the "efficacy" of cowpox in the prevention of smallpox, and the *Philadelphia Gazette* printed a letter to Coxe from George FARQUHAR of Jamaica on 21 Dec.

[1] MS: "recive."

From Charles Douglas and Susan Douglas

St. Asaph Street Alexandria

S<small>IR</small>   22 December 1801.

Permit us, with our most respectful Compliments, to invite you to favor us with your company to dinner on Christmas Day—a bed attending your convenience.

We are Sir Your most Affectionte. Servants

C<small>H</small>: & S<small>US</small>: D<small>OUGLAS</small>

We have hopes of the company of Messrs. Randolph and Giles.

RC (DLC); in Charles Douglas's hand; endorsed by TJ as received 23 Dec. and so recorded in SJL.

Susan Douglas (b. ca. 1759), daughter of Brett Randolph and Mary Scott, married Charles Douglas in England in 1783, and the couple had five children. Susan's father and TJ's mother, Jane

Randolph Jefferson, were cousins (Jonathan Daniels, *The Randolphs of Virginia* [Garden City, N.Y., 1972], x, xiv-xvii; vmhb, 19 [1911], 398-400].

The other guests expected were probably John <small>RANDOLPH</small> of Roanoke, a first cousin of Susan's, and William Branch <small>GILES</small>, both U.S. representatives for Virginia.

To the Senate

G<small>ENTLEMEN OF THE</small> S<small>ENATE</small>.

The states of Georgia and Tennissee being peculiarly interested in our carrying into execution the two acts passed by Congress on the 19th. of February 1799. (chap. 115.) and 13th. of May 1800. (chap. 62.) commissioners were appointed early in summer, and other measures taken for the purpose. the objects of these laws requiring meetings with the Cherokees, Chickasaws, Choctaws and Creeks, the inclosed instructions were prepared for the proceedings with the three first nations. our applications to the Cherokees failed altogether. those to the Chickasaws produced the treaty now laid before you for your advice & consent, whereby we obtained permission to open a road of communication with the Missisipi territory; the Commissioners are probably at this time in conference with the Choctaws. further information having been wanting, when these instructions were formed, to enable us to prepare those respecting the Creeks, the Commissioners were directed to proceed with the others. we have now reason to believe the conferences with the Creeks cannot take place till the Spring.

[190]

The journals and letters of the Commissioners relating to the subject of the treaty now inclosed, accompany it.   TH: JEFFERSON
Dec. 22. 1801.

RC (DNA: RG 46, EPIR, 7th Cong., 1st sess.); with "chap. 115." and "chap. 62." struck out, not by TJ, and those references do not appear in the letter as printed in ASP, *Indian Affairs*, 1:648. PrC (DLC). Recorded in SJL with notation "Chickasaw treaty." Enclosures: (1) Treaty "of reciprocal advantages and mutual convenience" between the United States and the Chickasaws, signed at Chickasaw Bluffs, 24 Oct. 1801, by U.S. commissioners James Wilkinson, Benjamin Hawkins, and Andrew Pickens and by 17 Chickasaw leaders; the Chickasaws agreeing to allow the running of a road from the Mero District of Tennessee to the Natchez settlements through their land, and the commissioners agreeing to give the Chickasaw representatives goods to the value of $700 as compensation for "the expense and inconvenience" of holding the negotiation (ASP, *Indian Affairs*, 1:648-9; also printed in U.S. Statutes at Large, 7:65-6). (2) Henry Dearborn to William R. Davie, Wilkinson, and Hawkins, 24 June 1801, instructions for holding talks with the Cherokees, Chickasaws, and Choctaws (Tr in DNA: RG 46, EPIR; in a clerk's hand; certified by John Newman, chief clerk of the War Department, 17 Dec. 1801, as a true copy from the department's records; endorsed by a Senate clerk). (3) Dearborn to Davie, Wilkinson, and Hawkins, 3 July, providing additional instructions asking the commissioners not to attempt any negotiation with the Cherokees over land, advising the commissioners also that the Cherokees might be reluctant to discuss the opening of a road (Tr in same; in a clerk's hand; with an appended note that Pickens had been substituted as a commissioner for Davie; certified by Newman, 17 Dec.; endorsed by a Senate clerk). (4) Dearborn to Wilkinson, Hawkins, and Pickens, 17 July, instructions for negotiations with the Creeks (Tr in same; in a clerk's hand; endorsed by a clerk). (5) Wilkinson, Hawkins, and Pickens to Dearborn, Chickasaw Bluffs, 25 Oct. 1801, reporting on their talks

with the Chickasaws since the commissioners arrived at Chickasaw Bluffs on 18 Oct. (RC in same; in a clerk's hand; signed by Wilkinson, Hawkins, and Pickens; endorsed by a Senate clerk). (6) Minutes of a conference between the commissioners and the Chickasaws, held at Chickasaw Bluffs, 21-24 Oct. (MS in same; in a clerk's hand; signed by Wilkinson, Hawkins, and Pickens; endorsed by a Senate clerk). (7) "Invoice of goods delivered the Chickasaw nation agreeably to treaty the 24th October 1801," listing items including gunpowder, lead, gunflints, rifles, axes, hoes, knives, clothing, cloth, whiskey, and tobacco with a total value of $696.21, Hawkins noting the addition of one gun for $6 to bring the total to $702.21 (MS in same; in a clerk's hand; signed by Wilkinson, Hawkins, and Pickens; one additional item and new total in Hawkins's hand; endorsed by a Senate clerk). (8) Wilkinson to Dearborn, 27 Oct. 1801, from Chickasaw Bluffs, reporting orders given for eight companies of infantry to go to Tennessee for opening the road from that end; if the Choctaws also agree to the road, as he expects, he will order six companies to begin work at the Natchez end of the route; and he will see that the course of the road is surveyed (RC in same; in a clerk's hand, with complimentary closing and signature by Wilkinson; endorsed by a Senate clerk). Enclosures printed in ASP, *Indian Affairs*, 1:649-53.

At the outset of TJ's presidency, a senator and a congressman from GEORGIA and the two senators from Tennessee asked that the government move forward with the acquisition of lands claimed by Indian tribes along those states' frontiers. TWO ACTS: the legislators from Georgia, Abraham Baldwin and Benjamin Taliaferro, had directed TJ's attention to an act of 19 Feb. 1799 that appropriated funds for a treaty to resolve Georgia's claim to the Tallassee district, which by a treaty of 1790 had gone to the

Creek Indians. The Tennessee senators, Joseph Anderson and William Cocke, were interested in obtaining more lands from the Cherokees, and referred to legislation of 13 May 1800 that appropriated funds to hold a treaty with Indians south of the Ohio River. On 17 May, TJ and the cabinet determined that negotiations should be held with the Cherokees, the Chickasaws, the Choctaws, and the Creeks to obtain particular tracts of land and rights-of-way for roads (Vol. 33:69-70, 174-8; Vol. 34:129-31).

ADVICE & CONSENT: Meriwether Lewis delivered the message, with the treaty and accompanying papers, to the Senate on 23 Dec. The Senate took up the treaty in executive session on 29-30 Dec., and after a series of postponements voted on the matter on 29 Apr. 1802. On that day, a motion to strike a clause in the treaty that called on the president "to assist the Chickasaws to preserve entire all their rights against the encroachments of unjust neighbors, of which he shall be the judge," failed. The Senate then unanimously approved the treaty as submitted. On 4 May 1802, TJ issued a proclamation stating that "Whereas a Treaty between the United States of America and the Chickasaw nation of Indians, was concluded and signed by the commissioners of both nations fully and respectively authorized for that purpose on the twenty-fourth day of October 1801, and was duly ratified and confirmed by the President of the United States, with the advice and consent of the Senate, on the first day of May ensuing, which treaty is in the words following, to wit," followed by the full text of the treaty, followed by "Now Therefore, To the end that the said treaty may be observed with good faith on the part of the United States, I have caused the premises to be made public, and I do hereby enjoin and require all persons bearing office, civil or military, within the United States, and all others, citizens or inhabitants therof, or being within the same, faithfully to observe and fulfil the said treaty and every clause and article thereof. In Testimony Whereof, I have caused the seal of the United States to be affixed to these presents, and signed the same with my hand" (*National Intelligencer*, 12 May 1802; JEP, 1:399-400, 405, 410, 423-4).

WE HAVE NOW REASON TO BELIEVE: in letters to the secretary of war on 6 Sep. and 14 Nov., Hawkins pointed out the difficulty of convening the Creeks for talks during their winter hunting season, which usually extended from October through February. Wilkinson, who did not favor postponing talks with the Creeks, referred to the subject in his 27 Oct. letter to Dearborn listed as Enclosure No. 8 above. Hawkins's letter to TJ of 11 Dec., which also discussed the delay, did not reach TJ until February (Foster, *Hawkins*, 385-6, 396).

To the Senate and the House of Representatives

GENTLEMEN OF THE SENATE AND OF THE HOUSE OF REPRESENTATIVES.

I now inclose sundry documents supplementary to those communicated to you with my message at the commencement of the session. two others, of considerable importance, the one relating to our transactions with the Barbary powers, the other presenting a view of the offices of the government, shall be communicated as soon as they can be compleated.

TH: JEFFERSON
Dec. 22. 1801.

RC (DNA: RG 233, PM, 7th Cong., 1st sess.); endorsed by a House clerk, including: "Such documents as relate to the transactions of the United States with the Barbary powers, referred to the Committee appointed to prepare and bring in a bill or bills further and more effectually to protect the Commerce of the United States against the Barbary powers" and "The other document, Containing a Schedule of the whole number of persons within the district of Tennessee, referred to the Committee of the whole House on the bill for the apportionment of Representatives among the Several States, according to the Second enumeration." PrC (DLC). RC (DNA: RG 46, LPPM, 7th Cong., 1st sess.). Recorded in SJL with notation "documents." Enclosures: (1) William Eaton to secretary of state, Tunis, 28 June 1801 (RC in DNA: RG 233, PM, endorsed by a House clerk as "No. 1"; PrC in DNA: RG 46, EPFR). (2) Hammuda Pasha, bey of Tunis, to president of the U.S., 15 Apr. 1801 (Tr in DNA: RG 233, PM; PrC in DNA: RG 46, EPFR; printed in Vol. 33:591-2). (3) TJ to Hammuda Pasha, 9 Sep. 1801 (Tr in DNA: RG 233, PM; PrC in DNA: RG 46, EPFR; printed in Vol. 35:240-1). (4) Extract, secretary of the navy to Richard Dale, 20 May 1801 (Tr in DNA: RG 233, PM, misdated 30 May 1801; Tr in DNA: RG 46, EPFR). (5) Extracts of Dale to secretary of the navy, 2, 19 July, 18 Aug. 1801, copy of Andrew Sterett to Dale, 6 Aug., extract of Dale to secretary of the navy, 4 Oct. (Tr in DNA: RG 233, PM, endorsed by a House clerk as "No. 2"; Tr in DNA: RG 46, EPFR, endorsed by a Senate clerk). (6) David Humphreys to secretary of state, 20 Oct. 1801 (Tr in DNA: RG 233, PM, endorsed by a House clerk as "No. 3"; PrC in DNA: RG 46, EPFR). (7) Census schedule "of the whole number of persons in the District of Tennessee," giving totals, by census categories, for counties and towns in the Mero, Hamilton, and Washington dis-

tricts for a total population of 105,602 (Tr in DNA: RG 46, LPPM, in a clerk's hand, including signature of Robert Hays, marshal of the district of Tennessee; endorsed by a Senate clerk). Message and Enclosures Nos. 1-6 printed in ASP, *Foreign Relations*, 2:358-61.

Meriwether Lewis delivered the above message and the accompanying DOCUMENTS to the House of Representatives on 22 Dec. The House then referred the papers to two committees that had been created during consideration of TJ's annual message. The papers pertaining to relations with the Barbary states went to a committee consisting of William Eustis of Massachusetts, Samuel Smith of Maryland, Samuel W. Dana of Connecticut, Samuel L. Mitchill of New York, and William Jones of Pennsylvania. That panel was formed on 15 Dec. to bring in a bill to fulfill a resolution "that the President be authorized, by law, further and more effectually to protect the commerce of the United States against the Barbary Powers." The census schedule for Tennessee went to a committee consisting of John P. Van Ness of New York, Manasseh Cutler of Massachusetts, and Joseph Stanton, Jr., of Rhode Island. They had been appointed on the 16th to draft legislation following up on a resolution that representation in the House should be in the ratio of one representative for every 33,000 people. The Senate received its copy of the transmittal and the documents from Lewis on 23 Dec. After hearing the papers read, the Senate ordered them "to lie for consideration" (JHR, 4:18, 19, 24; JS, 163-4).

TWO OTHERS: see Gallatin to TJ, 29 Jan. 1802, for the preparation of statements of expenditures pertaining to TRANSACTIONS WITH THE BARBARY POWERS. See 16 Feb. 1802 for TJ's transmittal of those papers and the roll of OFFICES OF THE GOVERNMENT to Congress.

From Lewis Littlepage

SIR,   City of Washington—23d. Decembr. 1801.

The state of my health deprives me of the pleasure I had promised to myself in seeing you this evening. Tomorrow I shall set out for Virginia and entreat you to have the condescention to take charge of the enclosed paper, until you hear further from me.—Should any letters to me arrive under your address, either by the indescretion of persons with whom I am little acquainted, or by my directions to a very few friends, both here and in Europe, I hope you will have the goodness to address them to me under cover to the Reverend James Stevenson, Fredericksburg, Virginia.

I have the honor to be with the highest respect, and permit me to add every sentiment of personal esteem and attachment

Sir, your most obedient humble Servant

LEWIS LITTLEPAGE.

RC (DLC); at foot of text: "Thos. Jefferson—President of the United States"; endorsed by TJ as received 23 Dec. and so recorded in SJL; also endorsed by TJ: "June 18. 1802. the sealed paper deposited with me & herein referred to was sent to mr Littlepage by post in compliance with his letter of June 16." Enclosure not found.

JAMES STEVENSON was married to Littlepage's half-sister, Frances Littlepage Stevenson (Nell Holladay Boand, *Lewis Littlepage*, [Richmond, 1970], 287; WMQ, 1st ser., 9 [1901], 239).

To Lewis Littlepage

TH: JEFFERSON TO MR LITTLEPAGE   Dec. 23. 1801.

The paper inclosed in your letter is safely recieved and shall be disposed of as you desire; that is to say kept safely. I should have been happy to have seen you this evening, and am sorry for the cause which prevents it. should I not have that pleasure before your departure, I wish you a pleasant journey, assuring you of my esteem & respect.

RC (ViHi); addressed: "Mr. Littlepage." Not recorded in SJL.

To the Senate and
the House of Representatives

GENTLEMEN OF THE SENATE & OF
THE HOUSE OF REPRESENTATIVES

Another return of the Census of the State of Maryland is just recieved from the Marshal of that state, which he desires may be substituted as more correct than the one first returned by him and
communicated by me to Congress. this new return with his letter is
now laid before you.   TH: JEFFERSON
                                                       Dec. 23. 1801.

RC (DNA: RG 233, PM, 7th Cong., 1st sess.); endorsed by a House clerk. PrC (DLC). RC (DNA: RG 46, LPPM, 7th Cong., 1st sess.); endorsed by a Senate clerk. Recorded in SJL with notation "Census of Maryland." Enclosures: (1) Reuben Etting to Madison, 21 Dec. 1801, Baltimore, enclosing a revised return he made out after a letter from John Archer, which alerted him to errors in the return for Harford County, led him to review all the returns on which the earlier return for the state had been based; explaining that he had little time to work with the assistants' returns before he had to submit the original return for the state (Tr in DNA: RG 233, PM, in a clerk's hand, endorsed by a House clerk; Tr in DNA: RG 46, LPPM; Madison, *Papers, Sec. of State Ser.*, 2:329-30). (2) "Schedule of the whole Number of Persons in the District of Maryland," 21 Dec. 1801 (Tr in DNA: RG 233, PM, endorsed by a House clerk; a note in DNA: RG 46, LPPM, by a Senate clerk states that the Senate's copy of the return was delivered to "Smith the printer"). (3) "Abstract of the Whole Number of Persons in the District of Maryland," 21 Dec. 1801 (Tr in DNA: RG 233, PM, endorsed by a House clerk). Message and enclosures printed as *Message from the President of the United States, Communicating a Letter from the Marshal of the State of Maryland, and a Return of the Census of that State* (Washington, 1801), printed by order of the House of Representatives (Shaw-Shoemaker, No. 1510), and in the *Return of the Whole Number of Persons* (Shaw-Shoemaker, No. 1559, cited at Madison to TJ, 8 Dec.).

The House of Representatives received the above message and the accompanying papers from Meriwether Lewis on 23 Dec. and referred the documents to the committee composed of John P. Van Ness and others who were considering the apportionment of representation (see TJ to the Senate and the House of Representatives, 22 Dec.). The Senate also received the documents from Lewis on the 23d. After the papers were read, the Senate ordered that they "lie for consideration" (JHR, 4:19, 25; JS, 3:163-4).

From Albert Gallatin

DEAR SIR   Dec. 24. 1801

I enclose Mr Gerry's letter—There was, in my opinion, but one
way in which he might have saved his brother, and that was to have

at once paid the deficiency for which he is, at all events, ultimately responsible as security.

I had seen the attack as to over drawing Heth, & had ascribed it to himself. His vanity is such that he cannot believe that it was his own fault in not making his return in the manner prescribed by regulations of the Treasury. And I found that he had talked so much on the subject that it was well known in Richmond. The fact of the weekly returns being in my possession, & of the data stated in the paragraph are precisely his own statement as contained in his letter to me on the subject, which, as it remains unanswered, until the business shall have been closed, has never been in the possession of any clerk.— Yet I may be mistaken & it may have been written by a clerk—I would not be misunderstood that Heth wrote the piece or wished it written—but only that the information was derived from him.

I am informed that the list of officers of revenue & salaries cannot be extracted under 12 days—they have already been at least 12 days at it.[1] Shall we wait that time or give the other officers by themselves?

With sincere respect & affection Your obedient Servant

ALBERT GALLATIN

The words which in my understanding of the idioms would with most precision have conveyed the meaning of the words *bien entendu* are "it being understood however"—The word "*however,*" is in that case a better translation of "*bien*" than "*well*" would be.—

RC (DLC); endorsed by TJ as received from the Treasury Department on 24 Dec. and so recorded in SJL; also endorsed by TJ: "Gerry," "Heth," "officers," and "bien entendu." Enclosure not found.

HIS BROTHER: Samuel R. Gerry, customs collector at Marblehead, was the younger brother of Elbridge Gerry. In August 1801, Gallatin wrote the Marblehead collector "a very pressing letter" about his delinquent accounts. In November, the Treasury secretary ordered Benjamin Lincoln, customs collector at Boston, to head an investigation into the state of the records at the custom house at Marblehead. Gallatin had recently received the results of that inquiry and he sent the report to John Steele so that the account could be compared with the last quarterly figures received from Marblehead. Gallatin noted: "If I understand this rightly, he has applied the public money to his private use. Who are his securities?" Elbridge Gerry, serving as security for his brother, owed the government nearly $6,800 in 1810 (George A. Billias, *Elbridge Gerry: Founding Father and Republican Statesman* [New York, 1976], 5, 305-6; Gallatin, *Papers*, 6:299; Vol. 35:108, 109n, 587n).

ATTACK AS TO OVER DRAWING HETH: on 14 Dec., the *Washington Federalist* printed a letter addressed to William Heth, collector at Petersburg, signed by "A Virginian." The anonymous author had heard from Norfolk and Richmond that on 29 Oct., the Treasury Department drew on the Petersburg collector for $12,000 more than his weekly returns to the Treasury indicated that he had in hand. He asked Heth what would induce the secretary of the Treasury "by *overdrawing*, to embarrass a public officer, and to bring the character and the credit of the government, in its most tender and vital part, into hazard and disrepute?" and further queried: "Are our fiscal affairs under the guidance of the present *wise* and *frugal* administration forced from an inadequacy of funds to resort to such measures to prop the sinking credit of the nation." The Petersburg collector should not have to protect the Treasury secretary from charges of misconduct or inability to discharge his duties. Heth's letter to the Treasury secretary ON THE SUBJECT of the overdraft has not been found. On 22 Dec., Heth assured Gallatin that he was not author of the anonymous letter, as he was accused of by "some base, underhanded, & malignant wretch" at Petersburg. Months earlier, Virginia Republicans expressed surprise that Heth had not been removed from office. In 1801, Heth's fees and commission exceeded $8,000 (Gallatin, *Papers*, 5:251; 6:294-5; ASP, *Miscellaneous*, 1:274).

IDIOMS: Gallatin commented on a letter dated 23 Dec. from Washington and signed "Observator" that was printed in the *Washington Federalist* on 24 Dec. The writer questioned the translation of BIEN ENTENDU as "Provided that," rather than "understanding," in the president's 21 Dec. Proclamation on Ratification of the Convention with France, noting that the translation "grossly mistated" Bonaparte's ratification. "Observator" claimed "that the expunging of the second article of the convention was in effect a renunciation of all claims, on the subject matter of it. The First Consul in his ratification expresses that to be his understanding of the procedure." Other newspapers commended the *Washington Federalist* for detecting "a very material error" in the translation (*Poulson's American Daily Advertiser*, 29 Dec.; *New-York Evening Post*, 30 Dec.; *Massachusetts Spy, or Worcester Gazette*, 6 Jan. 1802). The president discussed Bonaparte's proviso in letters to Peter Carr and Stevens Thomson Mason on 25 and 28 Oct., respectively.

[1] Preceding nine words and figure interlined.

From George Hadfield

SIR   City of Washington Decr 24th, 1801

I have received a letter from my Sister Cosway wherein she desires me to deliver the enclosed—

I have at the same time recieved some papers which I sent for in consequence of hearing from Capt. Tingey, some months ago, that plans of English Dock Yards would be of use in the public works of that nature in this City.—I immeately wrote to England on the subject, and have in consequence received plans of all the principal Dock Yards there, it appears by letters that they were procured with much difficulty and some hazard—I have the honor to leave them for your perusal, and hope they will be thought useful—

I am Sir, with all respect Yr. Obt. Servant

GEO. HADFIELD.

RC (DLC); at foot of text: "The President of the United States"; endorsed by TJ as received 24 Dec. and so recorded in SJL. Enclosures: Maria Cosway to TJ, 20 July 1801. Other enclosures not found.

The six major ENGLISH DOCK YARDS were Deptford, Portsmouth, Woolwich, Chatham, Plymouth, and Harwich, which was replaced by Sheerness (Philip Mac-Dougall, *Royal Dockyards* [North Pomfret, Vt., 1982], 7-9).

PUBLIC WORKS OF THAT NATURE IN THIS CITY: see Thomas Tingey to TJ, 28 June 1802.

From Josiah Hook

Collector's Office
SIR   Castine Decem 24 1801

I do myself the honor to acknowledge the receipt of my commissions from your Exelency.

I feel the weight of obligation which your good opinion has laid on me, and desire you to accept of my most hearty and sincere thanks for the trust and confidence that you have seen fit to place in me—

It shall be my greatest study to fulfil the duty of my office with fidelity and correctness, and in such a manner as I hope will meet the approbation of your Exelency.—

Sir I have the honor to be with consideration your obedient humble servent   JOSIAH HOOK

RC (MHi); at foot of text: "Thomas Jefferson Esquire"; endorsed by TJ as received 22 Jan. and so recorded in SJL.

TJ appointed Josiah Hook (d. 1827) inspector and collector at Penobscot in Maine on 14 Nov., after his first choice, Benjamin Jarvis, declined the appointment. Hook had been recommended to TJ by Henry Dearborn, who described Hook as a young man of unblemished character and "a sound Republican." He retained the Penobscot collectorship until his death (*Essex Register*, 9 Apr. 1827; Vol. 33:673, 677; Dearborn to TJ, 1 Sep. 1801).

From Kennebec County, Maine, Constitutional Republicans

SIR,   Augusta, December 24. 1801

We do not approve of formal addresses to our rulers generally, but we consider that under peculiar circumstances, it may render such an act in the Citizens, justifiable & proper—As a considerable difference of political opinion yet continues in some parts of our Country, & as this State has not publically expressed their full confidence in the present Administration of the general[1] government, we deem it proper though at this late period, to tender you our congratulations on your[2] appointment to the first & most important office in the federal government, & in so doing, we do not offer you that adulation which characterizes unprincipled sychophants: & which we are sure must wound your feelings, & our consciences: but we are sincere in our belief, that your talents, integrity & patriotism have merited the confidence which the Citizens of America have manifested to you—

We esteem your inaugural address as containing the genuine principles of republicanism, such principles being the basis of Administration, must add dignity to the government, & increase the happiness of the Citizens—

Permit us Sir, to assure you, that your administration thus far, has our cordial approbation—and that with pleasure & confidence we anticipate the propriety of your future conduct—

Your appointment of men, as heads of the Departments, & your constitutional advisers, merits the approbation of all those who are attached to our system of government—From the union & exercise of so much personal virtue, & political wisdom, in the first & other important officers of the government, we are encouraged to hope that harmony, & uninimity of political opinion will more generally prevail through the Nation—

We esteem the Constitution as the grand palladium, & sheet anchor of our national rights—Not to enumerate its various checks & balances, to regulate the different branches of the government; nor the numerous priviledges garranteed to the people as deduceable from it, we view the right of citizens to candidly watch & examine the doings of those whom they appoint to the high offices of government. But that their remarks on governmental measures should be temperate and judicious is the natural dictate of true patriotism—

It is with peculiar pleasure, that we observe, public economy forms one of the characteristic traits of the present administration. As from the local situation of the country, & the general habits & enterprize of the inhabitants, agriculture & commerce must form the principal sources of individual wealth & of revinue to the United States; so a provident care of the financial intrests of the Nation, should be manifested by all, more especially in its rulers. We conceive that the reduction of national expences which has already been made, presages the enlargement of public confidence and the relief of indigent citizens—

The late inteligence of a general European peace is a subject, which must interest the feelings of every friend to humanity. Rejoicing in an event so auspicious to the welfare of Mankind, we cannot refrain congratulating you, & our common country, that the slaughter of the human species is once more staid—May the benign influences of peace long continue where it is established, & may those countries which have been so often encrimsoned with human gore, never become again the theatre of War.

With ardent supplications to the supreme arbiter of the universe, that he will continue your life, health & usefulness for a long time, & that every blessing may be extended to your family we subscribe ourselves respectfully, your fellow citizens   NATHAN WESTON

DUDLEY B HOBART

JOSHUA WINGATE

RC (DLC); in Hobart's hand and signed by him and the two others; at head of text: "An Address to the President of the United States, from the Constitutional Republicans of the County of Kennebec, in the District of Maine, who have appointed the undersigned a Committee to transmit the same—To Thomas Jefferson Esquire President of the United States"; endorsed by TJ as received 7 Jan. 1802 and so recorded in SJL.

Captain Nathan Weston settled in Hallowell, District of Maine, where he built a store and potash manufactory on the Kennebec River and ran a sloop in the coasting business between Hallowell and Boston. He represented Augusta in the General Court in 1799 and 1801, became a selectman in 1803, and later became a member of the state senate and executive council. Dudley B. Hobart, a selectman and assessor of the town of Gardiner who was married to Henry Dearborn's daugh-

ter Sophia, became collector at Bath from 1805 to 1806. He was succeeded in this position by his brother-in-law Joshua Wingate, Jr., also a son-in-law of Henry Dearborn, who served as his father-in-law's chief clerk in the War Department before returning to Maine. Joshua Wingate, Sr., settled in Hallowell in 1794 where he was a merchant and postmaster who died at the age of 97 in 1844 (James W. North, *The History of Augusta* [Augusta, Me., 1870], 501-2; J. W. Hanson, *History of Gardiner, Pittston and West Gardiner* [Gardiner, Me., 1852], 199, 309; William H. Smith, "Gen. Henry Dearborn. A Genealogical Sketch," *Maine Historical and Genealogical Recorder*, 3 [1886], 3, 6-7; Emma Huntington Nason, *Old Hallowell on the Kennebec* [Augusta, Me., 1909], 32, 130-1; JEP, 2:20).

[1] MS: "genera."
[2] MS: "you."

From John Stuart Kerr

SIR,   Manila 24th. Decr. 1801

I have the honour to enclose for your Excelly. a Letter from a Gentln. who remits for the Philosofical Society a box of Marine Curiostys, wch. I wish safe to hand & worthy your Excellys. approban.

This Gentleman has resided at Manila and the Provinces of this Island, thirty years, and in all his Occupations and Employments, always dedicated his Studys in Naturalena, amongst his ivestigationes in different places of this Archipeligo, particular observationes for more than twenty Years, touching the flux and reflux of the Sea round the Philipines and an object little known before this, altho many Navigators affirms that the Tides throughout the Archipeligo Oriental is irregular, haveing the contrary a constante order, altho difft. to that of Europe. he has compared his Observationes with all the informationes that he could obtain of the pacific Ocean: and no doubt that his discoverys touching these objects so interesting deserves the Attention & Applause of the Learned and Studious when they are Published,

and beg to have the honour to be Your Excellys. most Obt. Humbe. Servt.

JOHN STUART KERR

RC (DLC); at head of text: "His Excelly. Thoms. Jefferson Esqr."; endorsed by TJ as received 22 Nov. 1802 and so recorded in SJL. Enclosure: José García Armenteros to TJ, 22 Dec. 1801, recorded in SJL as received from Manila on 22 Nov. 1802, but not found.

John Stuart Kerr of Philadelphia was appointed U.S. consul at Manila on 8 Jan. 1801 (JEP, 1:366).

LETTER FROM A GENTLN.: José García Armenteros, secretary of the Manila branch of the Royal Philippine Company and a noted amateur naturalist (Andrew David and others, eds., *The Malaspina Expedition, 1789-1794, Journal of the Voyage by Alejandro Malaspina*, 2 vols. [London, 2001-3], 2:280, 299; María Lourdes Diaz-Trechuelo Spínola, *La Real Compañia de Filipinas* [Seville, 1965], 261).

The letters from Kerr and Armenteros were forwarded to TJ from Philadelphia by Robert Bridges, whose letter of 19 Nov. 1802 is recorded in SJL as received 22 Nov., but has not been found. On 23 Nov. 1802, TJ requested that Bridges deliver the box of shells from Armenteros to Caspar Wistar at the American Philosophical Society (PrC in DLC; at foot of text: "Mr. Robert Bridges"; endorsed by TJ in ink on verso). The same day, TJ wrote Wistar, informing him to expect the shells and forwarding the letters from Bridges and Armenteros (PrC in DLC; at foot of text: "Doctr. Wistar"; endorsed by TJ in ink on verso). The society acknowledged the donation of shells at their 3 Dec. 1802 meeting (APS, *Proceedings*, 22, pt. 3 [1884], 329; APS, *Transactions*, 6 [1809], xix).

From James Madison

Dec. 24. [1801]

J. Madison's respectful compliments to the President

It appears that the Secy. of State, the Secy. of the Treasury, & the Attorney General were appd. Commissrs. to settle with Georgia, by their names, but with their official titles annexed. On the resignation of Col. Pickering, Mr. Marshal was appd. *in his room*, No resignation of his Commission for the Georgia business being referred to or implied. It seems to have been understood, that altho' these public officers were appd. as private individuals, these commissions ceased with their Official characters, and consequently the three commissions are at present vacant.

RC (DLC); partially dated; endorsed by TJ as a letter of 24 Dec. 1801, received from the State Department on the same day, and so recorded in SJL with notation "Georgia Commrs."; also endorsed by TJ: "Commrs. for settlg. dispute with Georgia."

COMMISSION FOR THE GEORGIA BUSINESS: authorized by an act passed in April 1798 and amended in May 1800, President John Adams appointed secretaries of state Timothy Pickering and John Marshall, secretary of the Treasury Oliver Wolcott, and former Pennsylvania congressman Samuel Sitgreaves (not attorney general Charles Lee) to serve as United States commissioners to settle with Georgia commissioners the conflicting claims in the Yazoo lands (U.S. Statutes at Large, 1:549-50; 2:69-70; JEP, 1:331, 356, 400; Vol. 33:678). For the nominations to succeed these commissioners, see TJ to the Senate, 5 Jan. 1802.

From Overton Carr

DR SIR,   Decbr 25th 1801.

The Bearer will deliver to your Steward, a Bacon Ham, which has been cured Seven years, & which I request the favour of you to accept as a present. Dean Swift observes, that a present should consist of something, of no great value, and which cannot be purchased with money. If his definition be correct, of which I have no doubt, this Ham comes perfectly within it; for although Bacon Hams may be had in abundance, yet one that is Seven years old, & Sound, I think it will be difficult to find: my only solicitude is, that it may be[1] worth your acceptance, in that case, I shall lament, that I have not a dozen of the same kind, as the Deans definition would not be departed from. I wish you many happy returns of the Season, & am Dr Sir with great respect, & esteem, yr friend & obliged Hm Servt

OVERTON CARR

RC (ViU: Carr-Cary Papers); endorsed by TJ as received 25 Dec. and so recorded in SJL.

Overton Carr (b. 1752), the brother of TJ's brother-in-law, Dabney Carr, settled in Georgetown and was an original proprietor of land in the Federal District. He owned a 358-acre plantation in the Hopyard tract, which he conveyed in trust for the district in 1791 and later sold (Bryan, *National Capital*, 1:135, 321; RCHS, 57-59 [1957-59], 146; Edson I. Carr, *The Carr* *Family Records* [Rockton, Ill., 1894]; Vol. 6:167).

PRESENT SHOULD CONSIST: a paraphrase of a remark that Jonathan Swift attributed to his longtime friend Esther Johnson ("Stella") in a tribute written at the time of her death ("On the Death of Mrs. Johnson," printed in Herbert Davis and others, eds., *The Prose Works of Jonathan Swift*, 16 vols. [Oxford, 1939-74], 5:233).

[1] Word supplied by Editors.

To James Currie

DEAR SIR   Washington Dec. 25. 1801.

I inclose you a publication of Aiken's on the Cowpox, as also some pieces from the newspapers. you will see Dr. Coxe's experiments of the variolous after the vaccine inoculation. the matter for the latter was from me, & consequently proves that we kept the disease in it's genuine form at Monticello, as well as that the matter I sent you was genuine. but as you deferred using it, it probably became effete, as it quickly does. the inoculation here is kept up from the same matter. health & best wishes.   TH: JEFFERSON

PrC (DLC); at foot of text: "Dr. Currie." Enclosure: Charles R. Aiken, *Jennerian Discovery* (see John Vaughan to TJ, 9 Dec.). For other enclosures, see Vaughan to TJ, 21 Dec. Probably enclosed in TJ to Currie, 14 Jan. 1802 (see Benjamin Waterhouse to TJ, 11 Jan. 1802).

To Benjamin Waterhouse

DEAR SIR   Washington Dec. 25. 1801.

I am indebted to you for several favors unacknoleged. I have waited till I could inform you that some variolous after vaccine inoculations had proved that I had preserved the matter of the cow pox in it's genuine form. Dr. Coxe of Philadelphia has ascertained this, having recieved his vaccine matter from hence. to this is added your information that the matter I sent you produced the genuine disease: and consequently those in Virginia who recieved the matter from me are now in security. knowing how little capable the people in general are of judging between genuine & spurious matter from their appearance, or that of the sore, I endeavored in the course of my inoculations at home to find some other criterion for their guide. with this view I was very attentive to discover whether there be not *a point of time* counted from the vaccination, when the matter is genuine in all cases. I thought the 8. times 24 hours furnished such a point; I governed myself by it, and it has been followed here successfully by Dr. Gant. but your experience, so much greater, can inform us whether this rule is a sure one: or whether any other point of time would be still more certain. to the eye of experience this is not necessary: but for popular use it would be all-important: for otherwise the disease degenerates as soon as it gets into their hands, and may

[203]

produce a fatal security. I think some popular criterion necessary to crown this valuable discovery. Accept assurances of my great esteem & respect.   TH: JEFFERSON

RC (MBCo); at foot of text: "Dr. Benjamin Waterhouse." PrC (DLC). Enclosed in TJ to Waterhouse, 14 Jan. 1802 (see James Currie to TJ, 8 Jan. 1802).

SEVERAL FAVORS UNACKNOLEGED: Waterhouse to TJ, 1 Oct. and 16 Nov. The latter reported on cowpox sent from Monticello.

Memorandum to Albert Gallatin, with Gallatin's Reply

[on or before 26 Dec. 1801]

The Secretary of State has sent me the list of officers named during the recess of Senate, and now to be nominated to them, among these are

Josiah Hook	*Inspector* for Penobscot as well as Collector
Jonas Clark	Inspector for Kennebunk
M. E. Chisman	Inspector for Hampton as well as Collector.
Thos. Worthington	Inspector of N.W. district
John Oakley.	Inspector as well as Collector of George town
Wm. Chribbs	Inspector of Massac as well as Collector.
Danl. Marsh	Inspector of Perth Amboy as well as Collector

are not these among the offices of Inspectors which were abolished, & consequently not necessary to be renominated?   TH:J.

[Reply by Gallatin:]

Thomas Worthington is the only Inspector of internal revenue, and he was thus appointed, with an intention that he should be made Supervisor. But as his commission of Inspector will continue till the end of the Session, it will be best to delay his nomination until we know what Congress mean to do with the system of internal taxation—The others must be nominated, as they have nothing to do with the int. revenues   A. G.

MS (DLC: TJ Papers, 119:20479); undated; addressed by TJ: "Mr. Gallatin"; with Gallatin's reply subjoined; endorsed by TJ as received from the Treasury Department on 26 Dec. and "Inspectors." Not recorded in SJL.

Worthington's COMMISSION OF INSPECTOR was issued in September 1801. The Senate approved his appointment as supervisor on 29 Apr. 1802 (JEP, 1:422-3; Vol. 33:677; Vol. 35:227, 230n).

From Albert Gallatin

DEAR SIR   Decer. 26th 1801

No letter directed to me is opened by the Clerks, unless they are endorsed with the words "Custom house," which designates the species of letters called *public*, meaning thereby the weekly or monthly returns—

All the persons nominated as inspectors are, Thomas Worthington excepted, officers of the external revenues appointed in relation to certificates for spirits, teas & wines. *His* nomination should be suspended.

I enclose another letter from Mr Gerry. His brother's case is so strong & so public, that I do not know how a removal can be avoided. We cannot remove any man for delinquency if we pass over this one. But, if you please, we may converse with Mr Lincoln & perhaps Dr. Eustis before you decide.   With sincere respect

    Your obedt Servt   ALBERT GALLATIN

RC (DLC); at foot of text: "The President of the United States"; endorsed by TJ as received from the Treasury Department on 26 Dec. and "Inspectors Gerry's case" and so recorded in SJL. Enclosure not found.

OPENED BY THE CLERKS: for Gal-latin's contention that the information in the letter to William Heth published in the *Washington Federalist* did not come from the Treasury Department, see Gallatin to TJ, 24 Dec. PERSONS NOMINATED AS INSPECTORS: see the preceding document.

From Albert Gallatin

DEAR SIR   Decer. 26th 1801

Is it not necessary that you should communicate to Congress the "Order" abolishing the offices of inspectors & erecting the Country North of the Ohio into a separate district? and suggest the necessity of providing by law for the compensation of the Supervisor of that district?

The law authorized the erection of new districts, but has made no provision for the compensation of new Supervisors. Thomas Worthington has, on that account, received only a commission of Inspector—But as Inspector he cannot appoint collectors in case of vacancies & this impedes the operation of the law—Respectfully submitted by   ALBERT GALLATIN

RC (DLC); addressed: "The President"; endorsed by TJ as received from the Treasury Department on 28 Dec. and "Inspectors N.W. district" and so recorded in SJL.

ABOLISHING THE OFFICES OF INSPEC-

TORS: see the Executive Order on Revenue Districts, printed at 29 July. For a discussion of the legislation authorizing the ERECTION OF NEW DISTRICTS, see Gallatin's Report on Collection of Internal Revenues, printed at 28 July.

From Robert R. Livingston

DEAR SIR   Paris 26th. decr 1801

I sent my letters to the secretary some days ago by the way of Havre. I am in hopes that the ship that takes them may not yet have sailed. as I wish to congratulate you on your being elected a member of the national institute tho not without opposition. Ct Rumfort who has just left this was warmly supported.

It gives me pleasure to find the number of friends that you have among the literary & leading characters here tho philosophy is very much out of fashion at present.

For politicks I refer you to my letters to the Secretary since this goes thro' the post Office. What I there mention as a well founded conjecture relative to Luissania you may consider as confirmed tho the minister has not yet thought it proper to be explicit in his replies to my enquiries on that subject. I have so much information & from such different quarters that I have no doubt that all is arranged. The govt. has been offered to Genl. Massena & refused by him. Genl Bernadotte is now marked out for it. The possession of Luissania is a favorite object under an idea that french manufactures may pass thro' that channel into our western territory. They know little of the navigation of the Missisipi & that so far from forwarding the sale of their manufactures they will only afford another market for British goods, which will be sent down the Ohio in spite of all their vigilance. It is a fact that these have been sent by that channel from Philadelphia even to New Orleans in preference to sending them by sea during the war. The only true mode of creating a market for French fabricks in America (which consists in creating American capitals in France by the payment of their debts) is as yet neglected, & I fear will continue to be so for some time.

The minister of exterior relations is gone to Lyons to meet the deputies of the Cisalpine republic. It is still problematical whether the first consul will go, tho this was the original intention & he was certainly expected there. On this subject I can not enlarge tho it contains some interesting details because the departure of the post will not afford me leasure to put this in cypher.

We have had continued rains ever since my arrival which have swolen all the rivers in France & Italy & Germany in so much that the destruction of the winter crops & the consequent scarcity of bread is apprehended for the ensuing season—The price of flower is already very high & increasing. It seems that large exportations were made under permits that were carryed far beyond their original intention

I have the honor to be with the most respectful attatchment & esteem Dear Sir Your Most Obt hum: Servt

ROBT R LIVINGSTON

P.S. *12000[1] of the men sent to st domingo are destined for louisiaana in case tousaint make no opposition some secret discontent here both among the army & people*
The Secretary of States Cypher

RC (DLC); body of postscript written in code by Thomas Sumter, Jr. (see below for the code used); text in italics is TJ's interlinear decipherment of the coded passage, with his corrections of coding anomalies; spaces within deciphered words have been eliminated, but misspellings resulting from the coding process have not been corrected; the "P.S." and the line below the coded passage are in Livingston's hand; endorsed by TJ as received 5 Mch. 1802 and so recorded in SJL.

Livingston landed at L'Orient on 12 Nov., traveled through Nantes, and arrived in Paris on the evening of 3 Dec. He wrote LETTERS TO THE SECRETARY of state on 10 and 12 Dec., after he had presented his credentials to the French government (Madison, *Papers, Sec. of State Ser.*, 2:237-8, 265-6, 302-5, 309-10).

MEMBER OF THE NATIONAL INSTITUTE: see National Institute of France to TJ, [26 Dec.]. Count Rumford (RUMFORT) was elected a foreign associate of the institute in August 1802 (Amable Charles, Comte de Franqueville, *Le Premier Siècle de l'Institut de France, 25 Octobre 1795-25 Octobre 1895*, 2 vols. [Paris, 1895-96], 2:58).

The CONJECTURE in Livingston's dispatches to Madison was that Louisiana had definitely been ceded to France, reportedly in exchange for the return of the Spanish portion of the island of Saint-Domingue to Spanish control. To Talleyrand, the French MINISTER of foreign affairs, Livingston voiced concerns about the Louisiana retrocession, and suggested that Spain and France should consider ceding the Floridas to the U.S. Talleyrand acknowledged only that Louisiana "had been a subject of conversation." No decision "had been concluded or even resolved on" about it, he told Livingston (Madison, *Papers, Sec. of State Ser.*, 2:304).

Jean Baptiste BERNADOTTE oversaw preparations for the expeditionary force to Saint-Domingue. In January 1802, Madison believed that Bernadotte would have the command of the endeavor, which continued to be Livingston's presumption late in February. However, Victoire Emmanuel Leclerc received the command of the expedition and Bernadotte stayed in France (same, 373, 374n, 493; Tulard, *Dictionnaire Napoléon*, 200-1; Vol. 35:398n).

The council of the CISALPINE REPUBLIC met at Lyons in January to promulgate a new constitution. On 31 Dec., Livingston reported to Madison that Talleyrand's absence in Lyons "puts a stop to all public business" (Madison, *Papers, Sec. of State Ser.*, 2:311, 359).

SECRETARY OF STATES CYPHER: the code Livingston used is printed in Ralph E. Weber, *United States Diplomatic Codes and Ciphers, 1775-1938* (Chicago, 1979), 467-77, designated WE027. The code, which was similar to others TJ had used, assigned numbers to stand for words and groups of letters. A coded passage consisted of a series of numbers. In the code used for Livingston's postscript above, "an" was the number 1, "people" was number 537, and the word "case" was coded by writing 1160 for "c" and 1658 for "ase." Such a code could only be used if the sender and the receiver had the same code list. Rufus King used a different code, but one based on the same model, for his confidential communications as minister to Great Britain. A copy of the code used by Livingston is in TJ's papers at ViU, on a printed form that could accommodate up to 1,700 words or groups of letters. Code lists of that size, and the use of printed forms to facilitate their construction, had been initiated by Livingston himself in the early 1780s, when he was secretary of foreign affairs under the Articles of Confederation. Livingston used this particular code throughout his tenure as minister to France (MS in ViU, on a form with printed numbers in columns, words and parts of words having been written alongside the appropriate numbers in an unidentified hand, undated, untitled, endorsed by Jacob Wagner: "Mr. Livingston's cypher," labeled by ViU as Code B5; Tr in DLC: Peter Force Papers, 1857, which Weber used as his source; Weber, *Diplomatic Codes*, 153-4, 177; Edmund C. Burnett, "Ciphers of the Revolutionary Period," *American Historical Review*, 22 [1917], 332; Ralph E. Weber, *Masked Dispatches: Cryptograms and Cryptology in American History, 1775-1900* [Washington, D.C., 1992], 65-8).

[1] As coded, and in TJ's decipherment, the figure is "12 1000."

From the National Institute of France

à Paris le 5 Nivose an 10 de la République.

MONSIEUR,   [i.e. 26 Dec. 1801]

L'Institut national des Sciences et des arts, dans Sa Séance générale de ce Jour, vient de vous élire *associé-étranger*, pour la classe des Sciences morales et politiques.

Persuadés que vous apprendrez avec plaisir votre nomination, nous nous hâtons de vous l'annoncer.

Veuillez, Monsieur, agréer le sincére hommage de notre estime la plus haute.   VINCENT Président
VILLAR, Secrétaire
LA PORTE DU THEIL

EDITORS' TRANSLATION

SIR,   Paris, 5 Nivose Year 10 of the Republic
The National Institute of Sciences and Arts, in its general meeting of this day, proceeded to elect you a foreign associate, for the Class of Moral and Political Sciences.

Persuaded that you will learn of your nomination with pleasure, we make haste to announce it to you.

Please accept, Sir, the sincere respect of our highest esteem.

VINCENT, President
VILLAR, Secretary
LA PORTE DU THEIL

RC (DLC); on printed letterhead of Institut National des Sciences et des Arts; English date supplied; in a clerk's hand, signed by the officers; below dateline: "Le Président et les Secrétaires de l'Institut national des Sciences et des arts, à Monsieur Jefferson, Président du Congrés des Etats-unis" ("the president and secretaries of the National Institute of Sciences and Arts, to Monsieur Jefferson, president of the Congress of the United States"); endorsed by TJ as received 31 July 1802 and so recorded in SJL. RC (MHi); also on the institute's letterhead stationery, in a clerk's hand, signed by the three officers, with La Porte du Theil also identified as a secretary; endorsed by TJ. RC (same); letterhead stationery, clerk's hand, signed by the three officers. RC (same); letterhead stationery, clerk's hand, signed by the three officers.

François André Vincent (1747-1816), a painter and academic; Noël Gabriel Luc de Villar (1748-1826), who had held several offices, including a seat in the Council of Five Hundred, and had been a bishop in the government-controlled religious establishment of revolutionary France; and scholar, translator, and archivist François Jean Gabriel de La Porte du Theil (1742-1815) had all been members of the National Institute since its beginnings in 1795. Authorized by the French constitution of that year and soon thereafter established by law, the institute was intended to consolidate the activities of separate learned academies that had originated in the seventeenth century. The institute originally had three classes, for physical sciences and mathematics, moral and political sciences, and literature and fine arts, with subdivisions in each class. Volney, Pierre Samuel Du Pont de Nemours, and Talleyrand were among the original members of the moral and political sciences category, which had not had an academy prior to the revolution (Amable Charles, Comte de Franqueville, *Le Premier Siècle de l'Institut de France, 25 Octobre 1795-25 Octobre 1895*, 2 vols. [Paris, 1895-96], 1:102, 103, 105-6, 450-1; Joseph C. Kiger, ed., *International Encyclopedia of Learned Societies and Academies* [Westport, Conn., 1993], 123-4, 139; *Biographie universelle, ancienne et moderne*, new ed., 45 vols. [Paris, 1843-65], 34:146-7; 43:557-8; Tulard, *Dictionnaire Napoléon*, 29, 932, 1724-5).

ASSOCIÉ-ÉTRANGER: beginning in 1796, the institute began to elect nonresident associates, including Crèvecoeur and André Michaux, but the people selected for that category were natives of France or French colonies. The meeting of 26 Dec. 1801 marked the first elections to the category *associé étranger*, and TJ was the first American chosen for the honor. Elected on that day as the institute's first foreign associates were Sir Joseph Banks, to the class of physical sciences and mathematics; TJ, to the class of moral and political sciences; and Franz Joseph Haydn, for the class of literature and fine arts. According to a rule adopted the previous month, upon his election a foreign associate was to receive an institute medal engraved with his name. As the organization of the National Institute changed, TJ was placed in the class of history and *littérature ancienne* in 1803 and in the Académie des Inscriptions et Belles-Lettres in 1816 (Franqueville, *Premier Siècle*, 2:55-6, 127-8, 141-2; Léon Aucoc, comp., *L'Institut de France. Lois, statuts et règlements concernant les anciennes académies et l'Institut, de 1635 à 1889. Tableau des fondations* [Paris, 1889], 61-2; Bedini, *Statesman of Science*, 495).

TJ wrote replies to the above letter on 3 and 14 Nov. 1802.

From Albert Gallatin

I enclose the general outlines of the list of public officers. The paper which wraps up the others is the general sketch of the whole under its proper heads.

The three Schedules B. C. D are the sketches of the returns which should be filled by the three departments of State, War & Navy—The Schedule A. which relates to the civil department, being very long to transcribe & to be filled by myself, is not enclosed—The deputy post masters must be returned with their emoluments for the last year which can be ascertained—say 1800, by the Postmaster general— The revenue officers with all their details will be furnished by the Treasury Department. As almost all the officers under the heads of Military & Naval Establishments are salary officers, those two departments can furnish the lists within half the time which will be necessary to complete the general return of the officers of the external revenues. These & the clerks are the most difficult or at least lengthy to ascertain—The last, (the clerks) for all the departments will be furnished by the Treasury department more correctly than by the respective Departments to which they belong.

The classification is made in relation to the manner in which they are paid, &, with a few irregularities arising from that manner of classing the officers, will make on the whole as methodical arrangement as we can form for this year

I have not the returns of the State department nor that of the War do. That of the Navy I also enclose in order that by comparing it with Schedule D you may see in what it is deficient[1] vizt.

1st. It includes the salaries of Secretary, Accountant & Clerks which the Treasury will return under the head of civil department

2d. it does not include the officers of the navy

3d. it does not include those of the marines

4th. it does not designate the names of the navy agents, superintendents & store keepers

5th. it does not state the rate of commission of the navy agents, but only, on estimate, the supposed gross amount of the same for one year

6th. it does not, I believe, include the names & offices of all the agents yet employed. In this, however, I may be mistaken—

Perhaps,[2] it would be well, in relation to every class of officers to include the officers abolished by you (inspectors of int. revenues— superintendents for building vessels &a) written in red ink & to be printed in italics, so as to show at one glance what has already been done. Please to let me know your opinion, as, in transcribing the returns to be furnished by the T.D. I would direct the clerks accordingly.[3]

If you approve of the general distribution, I think it will be best to give the outlines of it to each department. they are taken, with a few alterations in the arrangement, principally from the annual estimates. It is probable that Captain Lewis might improve that of the War department from his knowledge of the agents, unknown to law, employed in various capacities & many of whom I am confident I have omitted.

The whole may certainly be prepared this week, & the revenue officers will not be completed before the middle of the ensuing one—

The whole when done will form a formidable list; but I had no idea that it would be so complex & difficult completely to obtain—

I will try to day to complete the *three column* list of expenses & proposed savings.

The business of Doct. Barraud will come of course in the report on the hospitals which will be prepared in the course of about ten days. It cannot be done sooner, as the whole of it with all the details can only be prepared by myself, & of course must be done only at leisure hours.

This will complete every official document from the Treasury Dept. intended for Congress; but I am afraid the investigation in the public expenditure will give the four departments more work than the whole of their current business put together.[4]

With perfect respect & sincere affection Your obedt. Servt.

ALBERT GALLATIN

RC (DLC); with one cancellation and other markings inserted in pencil, perhaps by TJ, indicating text to be omitted in Tr (see notes below); addressed: "The President of the United States"; endorsed by TJ as received from the Treasury Department on 27 Dec. and "list of officers" and so recorded in SJL. Tr (DLC: Madison Papers); in Meriwether Lewis's hand; partial text only (see notes below). Tr enclosed in TJ to Madison, 29 Dec. Enclosure: perhaps "Estimate of Compensations to Clerks &c. in the Navy department, Navy Agents, Superintendants & Clerks of Navy yards & Storekeepers, for the year 1802," Navy Department, 14 Dec. 1801, listing four clerical positions in the secretary's office

and eight in the accountant's office plus a messenger in each for a total compensation of $12,960; commissions to unnamed navy agents in seven cities and Georgia, ranging from $500 in Charleston to $2,500 in Boston, New York, Philadelphia, and Norfolk, for a total of $13,000; salaries of $1,200 for superintendents of navy yards at Charlestown, Massachusetts, and Washington, D.C., and $600 for clerks and storekeepers at Portsmouth, New Hampshire, Boston, New York City, Philadelphia, Norfolk, and Washington for a total of $6,000; for a grand total of $31,960 (MS in DLC; in a clerk's hand, signed by Robert Smith; endorsed by TJ: "Departmt. Navy"; endorsed by a clerk; endorsed in another hand: "Duplicate"). Other enclosure printed, in part, below.

TJ evidently agreed with Gallatin's proposal to highlight by printing IN ITALICS the names of those officers dismissed when their positions were abolished. For instance, the finished list includes William Loughton Smith, at the court of Portugal, with other U.S. ministers, but in italics with the notice "vacated," making it clear that the salary and expenses of $11,250 would be saved, along with an additional savings of $1,350 for a secretary. The same information is evident in the elimination of the office of inspector under internal revenues (ASP, *Miscellaneous*, 1:280-7, 306-7). William Duane printed the list by the 16 Feb. 1802 order of the Senate as *Message from the President of United States, Transmitting a Roll of the Persons Having Office or Employment under the United States* (Washington, D.C., 1802).

On 24 Dec., TJ sent Gallatin the 20 Dec. letter he received from Monroe, recommending Philip BARRAUD. Monroe also wrote the Treasury secretary directly on 20 Dec., introducing the Norfolk physician, who wished to confer with Gallatin on the marine hospital at the port. Barraud had written the Treasury secretary in September in an effort to retain his position. Gallatin submitted his REPORT ON THE HOSPITALS to the president on 16 Feb. 1802 (Gallatin, *Papers*, 5:744, 6:253).

INVESTIGATION IN THE PUBLIC EXPENDITURE: on 14 Dec., the House of Representatives passed a resolution calling for the establishment of a committee

"to inquire and report whether moneys drawn from the Treasury have been faithfully applied to the objects for which they were appropriated, and whether the same have been regularly accounted for; and to report, likewise whether any further arrangements are necessary to promote economy, enforce adherence to legislative restrictions, and secure the accountability of persons entrusted with the public money." Joseph H. Nicholson headed the committee of seven appointed to carry out the resolution. The investigation was prompted by Gallatin, who advocated reforms to assure greater accountability in the distribution of public funds. TJ referred to several of Gallatin's recommendations in his first annual message to Congress, including the need for specific appropriations to circumscribe discretionary spending. On 19 Jan. 1802, Gallatin sent Nicholson a letter addressing the "objects of enquiry for your committee." The questions posed by the Treasury secretary formed the statement submitted by Nicholson to the committee on 21 Jan., which the panel approved and sent to Gallatin as the questions they wished answered (JHR, 4:17, 60; ASP, *Finance*, 1:754-5; Gallatin, *Papers*, 6:505; Documents VIII and X in Drafting the Annual Message to Congress, printed at 12 Nov. 1801).

[1] Tr lacks remainder of paragraph, that is, the statements numbered one through six.

[2] Word canceled in RC, probably by TJ. Tr lacks the word.

[3] Tr lacks preceding sentence.

[4] Tr lacks two preceding paragraphs.

ENCLOSURE

Outline of Government Offices

General Sketch of officers of Government
First class— Paid out of monies which have come in the Treasury
Second class— Collectors of public monies paid out of collection money
First Class—
    I. Civil department—*paid by Treasury*, as pr Schedule A
        1– President & Vice President
        2– Legislature

    3– Judiciary
    4– Departments at seat of Government
    5– Territories
    6– General establishments
II. Intercourse with foreign nations—*heretofore paid by Depart. of State*
    as pr Schedule *B*
    1– Public ministers
    2– Barbary Consuls
    3– Other Consuls
    4 & 5— British treaty
    6– Agents for seamen
III. Military establisht.—*paid by War department* Schedule *C*
    1– Army
      1. General Staff
      2. Artillery
      3. Infantry
      4. Quarter master
    2– Ordnance
      1. Armouries
      2. Military stores
    3 Indian department
IV. Naval estabt.—*paid by Navy department* Schedule *D*
    1. Navy
      1. Commd. officers & warrant do. attached to vessels in service
            Do.   do to do. in ordinary
            Do.   retained but not in actual service
    2– Navy agents
    3– Superintendents navy yards & build. ships
    4– Marines
Second Class
  I. External revenues—   settled at Treasury
    1. Collectors
    2. Naval officers
    3. Surveyors
    4. Inspectors
    5. Guagers, measurers, weighers
    6. Revenue cutters & barges
  II. Internal revenues—   settled at Treasury
    1. Supervisors
    2. Inspectors–3 yet subsisting
    3. Collectors
    4. Auxiliary, including venders of stamps
III. Direct tax—*temporary*—   settled at Treasury
    1. Assessment
      1. Commissioners
      2. Assessors
      3. Surveyors
    2. Collection
    Supervisors & Inspectors as for int. taxes but addit. commission
    Collectors

IV. Lands —   settled at Treasury
    1. Registers
    2. Receivers
V. Postage —   settled at Post office general
    Deputy post masters

The Secretary of the Treasury will furnish the whole of the Second class—
Postage excepted, and the *Civil department* of first class

The IId Item of First Class vizt. Int. with for. nations to be furnished by
Secy. of State

The IIId do of Do   vizt. Military establisht.—by Secy. of War

The IVth do of Do   vizt. Naval do.   by Secy. of Navy

The Vth Item of Second class viz Deputy Post masters by Post master
General

Note Contractors for provisions, clothing, cannon & small arms, military &
naval stores, (timber for ships included) carrying the mail might make
a third general class—

Heads of Departments & their clerks included in "Civil departmt." & will be
returned by Secy. of Treasury.

MS (DLC: TJ Papers, 119:20490); undated; in Gallatin's hand; on recto and verso of one sheet, followed by Schedules B, C, and D, each on a separate sheet (MS in same, TJ Papers, 119:20490.a-20492, not printed, but see below). Tr (DNA: RG 59, MLR); in Meriwether Lewis's hand; with Schedules B, C, and D subjoined; endorsed by Lewis: "Roll of Governmental officers." Tr enclosed in TJ to Madison, 29 Dec. 1801.

On SCHEDULE B (see above), Gallatin requested information from the State Department on the salaries and residences of U.S. ministers and their secretaries and on other appointments as noted above. BRITISH TREATY: under No. 4 of the schedule or outline, Gallatin indicated that he wanted the names and salaries of all those appointed under Article 6 of the Jay Treaty; under No. 5, the names and salaries of those commissioners, secretary, and agents in London appointed under Article 7 of the treaty.

SCHEDULE C: Gallatin requested the names and salary of "each individual" in the ARMY, including the general staff, the two artillery regiments, the four infantry regiments, the two troops of "dismounted dragoons," and those agents, deputies, and clerks under the quartermaster's department. Under ORDNANCE, Gallatin requested the names, compensation, and residence of those employed at the armories and military stores, including "Store keepers at sund. places." INDIAN DEPARTMENT: Gallatin requested information on "Agents to promote civilization" and "Trading agents" and added: "*Query* whether any other." Gallatin added a fourth section entitled "All other agents not known to law," where he included superintendents of fortifications, engineers, and "Agents as E. Stevens at New York."

SCHEDULE D: Gallatin requested the names, salary (including extra rations and forage), and vessel (or residence when on shore) of all those employed by the navy, including captains, lieutenants, midshipmen, surgeons, chaplains, pursers, cooks, coopers, stewards, gunners, and others. The rate of commission was to be provided for all navy agents. SUPERINTENDENTS NAVY YARDS: Gallatin completed this section by noting he wanted information on store keepers and clerks at the navy yards and "2. All other agents in relation to building vessels, timber, military stores, arms not known to law."

From Albert Gallatin

DEAR SIR   Decer. 27th 1801

The late Doctor Jackson of Philadelphia had formerly supplied the army with medicines. The business was very suddenly taken from him, on account solely of his politics, not by Mr Hamilton as his widow believes, but by Tench Francis purv. of supplies & by order of Mr McHenry—He had on hand, & received immediately after a large quantity of medicines imported for that sole purpose, a great part of which remained, to my knowledge, unsold for a great while & on which he was eventually a considerable loser. When, on his death-bed, he requested Mr Dallas to write to me & to remind me of the circumstance. I promised, and he received my answer the day before he expired, that I would use my endeavours to have him or rather his widow[1] restored. I cannot tell whether I have been mistaken, but the only time I had touched the subject to General Dearborn, which was before the Doctor's sickness, I thought he was not inclined to change the persons who now supply & whose name I have forgotten. On that account I concluded to wait the arrival of the members of Congress, as I knew that nothing could be more gratifying to the majority of the Pennsylvania delegation & to many other of our republican friends in Congress, than to see Mrs Jackson, who in partnership with a respectable man of the name of Betton, pursues the same business, obtaining the same kind of contract which her husband had formerly had. I have lately received a letter from her which I enclose; and, if not improper, I request the favour of your good offices for her with Gen. Dearborne & Mr Robt. Smith. I would not ask a thing, which it is true will be considered by me as in some degree a personal favour, was it not perfectly consistent with the general rule you have adopted in the appointments which depend immediately on yourself, and had not the political & private character of Doctr. Jackson deserved an interference in favor of his family.

The paper from Charleston is enclosed; it is impossible to act on anonymous information; but it may serve as a caution & induce to keep a stricter eye on the officer.

Enclosed also you will find a memorandum on the subject of the Supervisor of N. West district, which had escaped my attention till this day.

My refusing to interfere with Bank elections will, I hope, meet with your approbation.

With respect & affection Your obedt. Servt.

ALBERT GALLATIN

RC (DLC); at foot of text: "The President of the United States"; endorsed by TJ as received from the Treasury Department on 28 Dec. and "mrs Jackson Simmonds bank elections" and so recorded in SJL; also endorsed by TJ: "N.W. district." Enclosures: (1) Susanna Kemper Jackson to Gallatin, Philadelphia, 20 Dec. 1801, wishing the Treasury secretary, as a friend, to advise her on an application to General Dearborn, entreating the secretary of war to procure medical supplies for the military establishment from the house of Jackson & Betton and thus help her recoup the loss her late husband sustained when, under the former administration, he "purchased a large quantity of articles for the use of the Army he had been accustomed to supply," but then was deprived of the business by Alexander Hamilton (Gallatin, *Papers*, 6:252). (2) Probably "An American" to TJ, 11 Dec. 1801. (3) Probably Gallatin to TJ, 26 Dec. (second letter).

On 30 Sep., Alexander J. Dallas informed Gallatin of the death of Dr. David JACKSON. He observed that Susanna Jackson, his widow, was forming a partnership with Dr. Samuel Betton, a druggist of excellent character and "considerable capital." According to Dallas, the arrangement was indispensable to the maintenance of the Jackson family. At the behest of Jackson, Dallas also reminded Gallatin of his promise to do everything possible to restore the government contract for medical supplies to the family (Gallatin, *Papers*, 5:809; *Philadelphia Gazette*, 9 May 1801; *Poulson's American Daily Advertiser*, 19 Nov. 1801).

BANK ELECTIONS: on 22 Dec., Matthew L. Davis wrote Gallatin, urging the Treasury secretary to use his influence—as Davis was certain his predecessors had done—in the election of directors for the New York City branch of the Bank of the United States. Observing that the bank was "conducted by the most violent Monarchists in this City," Davis singled out Robert Lenox for removal and noted that while Gallatin lacked the direct power to remove Lenox and make a new appointment, he could do it indirectly. "How far you may consider an interference proper, is a question entirely for your decision," Davis commented. "If, however, you should think it proper," he continued, "you will do the institution no injury, & highly gratify the Republicans in this place" (Gallatin, *Papers*, 6:293).

[1] Preceding four words interlined.

To Adam Lindsay

SIR   Washington Dec. 27. 1801.

I was in hopes to have recieved from you before this some white backs. I should have sent for them, but understood you would chuse to deliver them here. I am ready to take all you kill at the price paid by Gadsden in Alexandria; or if you will twice a week bring or send me half a dozen pair at the same price, I will pay you two dollars additional each time for bringing or sending them; or if that is not convenient, I will send for them twice a week, on fixed days, half a dozen pair at a time. if you have any on hand the bearer will bring them. Accept my best wishes.   TH: JEFFERSON

PrC (DLC); at foot of text: "Mr. Lindsay"; endorsed by TJ in ink on verso.

In the 1790s, Adam Lindsay, an acquaintance based in Norfolk, had provided TJ with an annual supply of myrtle wax candles and an occasional procurement of Hughes crab cider. He later resided in the easternmost section of Washington where he started a mulberry grove and became interested in domestic silkworm cultivation. Lindsay was a member of the Board of Common Council of Washington, an elected director of the Commercial Company of Washington in 1808, and was active in the building of the Anacostia or Eastern Branch Bridge in 1819 (MB, 2:816, 867, 873, 896; RCHS, 4 [1901], 215-6; 28 [1926], 24; 33-34 [1932], 278; Vol. 22:148, 376, 425).

WHITE BACKS: a local name for canvas-back ducks (OED; MB, 2:1088).

From Caesar A. Rodney

HONORED & DEAR SIR,   Wilmington Decr. 27th. 1801

Whilst I most sincerely congratulate you on the happy prospects, which the wisdom & virtue of your administration have placed before us, & which I flatter myself will be realized in the fullest extent, there is at present a local subject, as it relates to this State of the first importance. In its consequences it may however affect the Union generally & therfore it may have been incorrect to consider it as entirely local. The government are interested in the issue, & ought to have a controling power over our conduct with respect to it. Not a single step should be taken in the path, which we may conceive proper, without their approbation, least the glorious cause in which "we are all embarked" should be in any degree compromitted by the measures which we may think it right to pursue.

Since the termination of our late election I have constantly corresponded with the Secretary of State & have communicated to him from time to time all the information I could collect on the subject of controverting it. By the last mail I gave him a pretty correct veiw of the present posture of affairs. This was contained in a letter to himself & one enclosed unsealed for the purpose of his perusal directed to my friend Mr. Giles as the leveling member in the house of Representatives, in which I fully & confidentially entered into the detail of the business

With the contents of these you may perhaps be acquainted, & I hope from them you will be enabled to judge what course we ought to steer so as to produce the happiest effects.

The line of conduct we have thus far pursued begins to be sensibly felt by our Opponents. The moderate but firm front we present to them is productive of much good. Those who were yesterday the warmest advocates for destroying the voice of the people are now changing their sentiments. It is remarkable & every days experience justifies the observation, that your men of timid minds are always the first to fan the fire of contention and the last to aid in extinguishing the blaze which they themselves have kindled. They generally retire & leave to others the labor & danger of the day. This has been emphatically the case on this occasion. The men of real nerve discountenanced the attempt as impolitic & unjust whilst those who intended to face no danger urged with great zeal the propriety of the measure. I love peace as much as any man, I love moderation & every prudent conciliatory measure which can be adopted consistent with principle. I wish to return to those of a different sentiment good for evil & on all occasions to give "equal & exact justice to all men of whatever state or persuasion religious or political." Those principles will wear well & stand the severest test of time. Such conduct will form so striking a contrast to theirs as to make those blush who are not insensible.

But there are great occasions, on which you are compelled to call on virtues of a different kind. When moderation & acquiescence like all other passions carried to an extreme become criminal. Such I believe is the present moment here which demands the prudence of a Fabius combined with the firmness of a Regulus. Let the advice of government be what it may, it should be inveloped in secrecy. On their own account if we are permitted to proceed, to extremities should imperious circumstances force it upon us, but which I little fear if they discover us prepared for any & every event. We do not wish any aid from Administr. nor that they should be committed in the business. We are sufficiently strong within our selves. The spirit which began & accomplished the late revolution has just been resuscitated & if but a single spark only remained it would burst into a flame that would politically destroy all the enemies of our independence.

On the other hand if we must submit to their usurpation, This should be unknown or it would immediately ensure the act. Whereas by preserving it a secret displaying a firm temper they will desert.

I would yield without a murmur almost, to their setting aside the election of our candidate, *without cause*, provided they give us a new election, or if there was just grounds I would even go so far as to bear the conduct they talk of pursuing, but to overturn the voice of the people & in the same act, place an Usurpur over them without any earthly cause, but that of a domineering spirit of party is what I cannot bring my[1] mind to submit to unless wiser heads should be of that opinion, & to whose better judgment I should bow with respect. Rely upon it nothing but fear will controul those most anxious to set aside the election.

Since your election to the dignified office you fill with such cordial satisfaction to the country, the clouds which suspended over our heads darkened our political horizon have been dispelled, the mist yet remaining will be gradually dispersed by the rays of light & truth, & we shall then enjoy a pure serene Republican Skye. The affairs of Delaware will I trust be as prudently conducted as not to throw a shade over the scene but will rather tend to brighten it, by fixing in the chair of our State a Chief Magistrate of correct sentiment & adding one more to the constellation of Republican Governors.[2]

Your message to Congress at the opening of the Session, has had a wonderful operation here. You know my Dr. Sir, that the friends have been generally with us in this County, except a few old hands, even those now to a man profess themselves converted & say they will support us hereafter. It answers the most sanguine expectations of all our friends, & we consider it of so much importance that we are about publishing in pamphlets three thousand copies thereof to be distributed among the people in the three counties.

The people of this State will be so much pleased with the idea of having two representatives, that this of itself will at least produce in my opinion an entire change in Kent County. One political topic much harped on by Mr. Bayard when here, is that Virginia & the other large States[3] wish to swallow up the powers of the small ones, that in fact the real struggle now existing is between the little & big States. A single circumstance therefore of this kind will have a greater effect on the minds of our citizens generally than a volume of evidence such as he relys on.

Permit me to mention the case of our Loan Officer J. Stockton who has been unfortunate & indeed unexpectedly so in his mercantile transactions. His sureties I understand are good & I should apprehend it would have an unfavourable effect to remove him on account of his present embarrasments. Some of the Republicans have requested me to mention this. With great esteem & respect I remain

Yours most Sincerely   C. A. RODNEY

RC (DLC); endorsed by TJ as received 30 Dec. and so recorded in SJL.

Rodney wrote to SECRETARY OF STATE James Madison on 25 Dec., and enclosed a letter to Madison of 20 Dec. on the subject of the controverted Delaware gubernatorial election and the resignation of the state chancellor. Rodney also enclosed to Madison a letter to William Branch GILES (not found) and a copy of a 23 Jan. 1798 act to prevent aliens from voting at elections (Madison, *Papers, Sec. of State Ser.*, 2:327, 339).

EQUAL & EXACT JUSTICE: from TJ's First Inaugural Address, Vol. 33:150.

SETTING ASIDE THE ELECTION OF OUR CANDIDATE: Federalists contested Republican David Hall's narrow victory, especially among the Irish Republicans of New Castle County, by invoking the 1798 act that prohibited aliens from voting in state elections. Hall's opponents hoped to seat Nathaniel Mitchell as governor instead (John A. Munroe, *Federalist Delaware, 1775-1815* [New Brunswick, N.J., 1954], 210; Dr. John Vaughan to TJ, 10 Oct. 1801).

YOUR MESSAGE TO CONGRESS: in 1802, Wilmington printers Bonsal and Niles published a 16-page pamphlet of TJ's first annual message to Congress (Rosaria Gibbons, "A Check-list of Delaware Imprints from 1801 through 1815" [M.S. thesis, Catholic University of America, 1956], 36).

IDEA OF HAVING TWO REPRESENTATIVES: Congress debated an apportionment bill on 18 Dec., including the effect on large and small states of raising the ratio of representation from one member for every 30,000 people, as originally provided in the Constitution, to one for every 33,000. Based on Delaware's population computed from the 1800 federal census, the state was entitled to at least one representative, but with a large unrepresented fraction, some citizens thought it should merit an additional member of Congress. From 4 to 6 Jan., James A. Bayard engaged in further debate in Congress over the apportionment

issue, particularly in relation to Delaware and Virginia. The bill became law on 14 Jan. keeping a ratio of one representative to every 33,000 citizens, thereby leaving Delaware with only one representative (*Annals*, 11:337-42, 365-75, 377-404; U.S. Statutes at Large, 1:253; 2:128; Vol. 23:370-7).

OUR LOAN OFFICER: John Stockton of New Castle County was appointed commissioner of loans for Delaware in 1795. According to Delaware resident Thomas Mendenhall writing in December 1801, a John Stockton had "failed, in Business, trading under the firm of Stockton & Craigh" (JEP, 1:189; Gallatin, *Papers*, 4:714; 6:134; J. Thomas Scharf, *The History of Delaware, 1609-1888*, 2 vols. [Philadelphia, 1888], 1:267).

[1] MS: "my my."
[2] Canceled: "who will support your measures."
[3] Canceled: "will."

To Oliver Wolcott, Jr.

Sunday Dec. 27. 1801.

Th: Jefferson requests the favor of Mr. Wolcott's company to dinner the day after tomorrow at half after three oclock.—

RC (CtHi); in Meriwether Lewis's hand; at foot of text in Wolcott's hand: "Answered—Mr Wolcott presents his respectful Compts. to the Pr. of the U.S. and will have the honour to dine with him tomorrow agreably to invitation. Monday

Decr. 28. 1801"; with addition by Wolcott perpendicular to text at a later sitting: "Dined with Mr. Jefferson in Company with Mr. Grainger solely—Very Philosophic conversation in which I took an active part. OW."

From William Adamson

ESTEEMED FRIEND   Philadelphia the 28th. of Decem: 1801.

Since I had the pleasure of seeing thee at Washington City, I have visitted my friend Henry Jackson, & spent a week with him at Carlisle, in this state;—I strongly recommended him to make choice of the Federal City as a place of residence, rather than the place he now lives at, where his family are not happy; & pointed out to him Scott's House wch. thou mention'd to me:—he has agree'd to go &

view it, and I wish he may purchase it, as certainly both he & his family wd. be happier there than they can possibly be amongst a set of inveterate aristocratic Hornets, with which they are now surrounded!—in this case I thought it unnecessary to send thee a Copy of Rufus Kings Letr. to him, consenting to his coming out to this Country, by wch. he was liberated from the Dungeons of an Irish Bastile, where he, with many other virtuous & respectable characters were detain'd, some for *many months*, & others for *years*, at the instance of Rufus King, as Minister from the United States at the British Court, in consequence of which, most of those worthy men, still remain immured in the cells of Irish, English, & Scotch prisons, to the amount of a considerable number:—to my friend Jackson *alone* he condescended to grant his *plenipotentiary Licence* to cross the Atlantic, & breathe the air of a free Country; & that, after he suffer'd near two years imprisonment!—this document is worth thy perusal, & he has promised me that he wd. present thee with it when he visits the City, in the original: by which thou will see that it was *principle* alone, not crime, that was persecuted[1] both by the British Ministry & American Minister in Britain. & that the latter enter'd into collusion with the former in order to oppress the advocates of liberty in Ireland, & suppress the sacred flame wch. that virtuous band kindled & fan'd throughout that oppress'd & ill fated nation: and who, with a noble generosity becoming patriots, risk'd their own personal safety, extensive property (for many of them were very wealthy,) & in fine their all on earth, in order to secure for their Country that best boon of Heaven, *celestial* Liberty, at whose shrine many thousands of my brave & virtuous countrymen have been immolated by the Iron-hand of Lawless power: and many hundreds are now pining in Dungeons, or coerced on board of ships of war, & forced to *fight against principles* the most sacred to them! And ah! America, didst thou participate in this scene of iniquitous oppression, even in a remote degree, after the fond & flattering sympathies thou so pathetically express'd towards an oppress'd people in the day of thine adversity, when thou wast sore afflicted, & invited their aid & sympathy?—pardon I pray thee, worthy friend, a digression which natures feelings, true as the magnetic power, forces on me, when I contemplate my Country's wrongs, and causes my heart to vibrate towards her as the needle to the poles.—But thanks to that providence wch. presides over the destinies of Man, there is still hope left for the oppress'd patriot of every nation, whilst this free & happy country offers him an asylum, & he may look with happy expectation to America as his adopted home:—how must his prospects brighten at the consideration that there is still left to the lover of freedom, of virtue & benignity, even one portion of the Globe possess'd of a free constitution, & *that* at present administer'd by it's best friends?—in such a happy predicament it may well be call'd 'the worlds best hope' indeed.—Here the industrious manufacturer over loaded with taxes, saddled upon him by the profligacy & voluptuous extravagance of a corrupt government, may find relief from his burdens, & enjoy the fruits of his labor in quiet! so that I have not a doubt but that America will become a manufacturing Country much sooner than was generally expected, or than the British Agents & adherents here are willing to admit:—The chief objection is the extra price of manuel labor, but this will be found futile when put in competition with the enormous taxes of Britain, wch. now take from the manufacturer at least 1/2 of the product of his industry, & wch. cannot be lessen'd, if they must not be increased, even on a peace establishment!—The Cotton manufacture particularly, must soon find it's way into this Country, where the raw material is raised in the highest perfection, & must be always lower than in Europe, where it cannot be raised; besides that the perfection to wch. machinery is brought in that business, supercedes in a considerable degree, the necessity of much manuel aid in the first processes, & so far puts the American Manufactures on a footing with those of the Countries where labor can be had the cheapest.—Then the consideration is, what part of the united states would be most eligible for the establishment of such an undertaking?—my own opinion is that the City of Washington wd. be as eligible as any other place, from the facility of conveying goods to distant markets from thence, as well as it's central situation; it's vicinity to a plentiful supply of fuel, & the certainty that it's growing population & consequence will excite abundance of the necessaries of life to flow into it's market from the surrounding Country: with other considerations, amongst wch. the convenience of Water for machinery and other purposes, is not the smallest!—I am led to these reflections from a wish I have to invite out to this Country a particular friend of mine who resides in Dublin, & who has acquired some property in the Cotton business, & is conversant in the Linen also; but who abominates the Tyrannical Government under wch. he lives, & pants for the enjoyment of a happier system—such Men, with their property, their talents & their industry, must be an advantage to this Country to fix their abode in it, & I doubt not will be countenanced by the present enlighten'd & Philantropic administration; but before I undertake to recommend such a step to my friend (wch. if he shd.

adopt, I am sure wd. be follow'd by many others,) I feel desirous of being informd by persons better acquainted with the local circumstances of this Country than myself, as to the probable success of such an undertaking, & shd. be much obliged to thee for the communication of thy sentiments hereon, & any information thou canst render me on the subject.—To one matter more I crave thy indulgent attention—There are a Lady & Gentleman of my acquaintance now in this Country, who quitted Ireland a few months ago on account of the troubles there; & not finding themselves possess'd of a competency to support them here, they design to open a female boarding school; for which the Lady's talents & accomplishments are well calculated, having received the most liberal education that the best female seminaries in Dublin could afford, & besides her literary acquirements, being a perfect mistress of music.—she has been educated according to the most improved modern system, wch. besides the sphere of female tuition formerly in use, embraces a knowledge of Geography, with the use of the Globes & Maps: History, Chronology, Belles-Letters, Drawing &c:—her husband is an excellent Pensman, Arithmetician &c.—Such a couple could not fail to become useful to themselves & the public, if properly encouraged—the Lady inclines much to settle in Washington City, but being an entire stranger to the Southward, she is loth to undertake it without the sanction of some person of respectability, who wd. recommend her to public notice—I feel the more freedom in communicating this case to thee, as my solicitation on the behalf of my frd: Robinson late of Dublin College, & thy consequent recommendation of him to thy friends in Virginia, some two years ago, resulted in the happiest consequences to him, and the most satisfactory to that generous people.—Thy advice & sanction on the present occasion, might be productive of still more beneficial effects!!—I cannot allow myself to conclude without imploring Heaven to increase thy happiness, as thou art endeavouring to increase that of others; & especially for thy benevolent recommendation to the humane consideration of Congress, of the case of Unfortunate emigrants who seek an asylum from political persecution in this favor'd Land, & are denied a birth right or inheritance in it!—I trust that the wisdom of that body will induce it also to consider the case of those Aliens who had nearly compleated the residence required by the Law (as it stood when they arrived,) for being enfranchized, but were not exempted from the operation of the 14 years act.—I am with much consideration & regard

 Thy respectful friend   WM ADAMSON

RC (DLC); at head of text: "Thomas Jefferson Esqr:"; endorsed by TJ as received 2 Jan. 1802 and so recorded in SJL.

PLEASURE OF SEEING THEE: the date of Adamson's meeting with TJ in Washington is not known. He last wrote TJ on 29 June 1801.

For the emigration of United Irish exile HENRY JACKSON, see Vol. 35:93. Arriving at Norfolk in December 1799, Jackson brought considerable financial assets garnered from the sale of his Dublin iron business. He eventually settled in Baltimore, where he died in 1817 (King, *Life*, 2:645-7; New York *Mercantile Advertiser*, 21 Dec. 1799; Washington, Pa., *Herald of Liberty*, 3 Feb. 1800; *Daily National Intelligencer*, 9 July 1817).

SCOTT'S HOUSE: possibly the home of former District of Columbia commissioner Gustavus Scott, who died in December 1800 (Vol. 32:377).

RUFUS KINGS LETR.: King's letter to Jackson, dated 28 Aug. 1799, was written in response to Jackson's request for permission to leave Ireland for America. In the aftermath of the failed Irish rebellion, King had pressed British authorities not

to exile the rebellion's imprisoned leaders to the United States. While the letter granted Jackson permission to emigrate, it also underscored King's hostility toward Irish state prisoners, as well as Irish immigrants in general, most of whom he considered "indigent and illiterate, who, entertaining an attachment to freedom, are unable easily to appreciate those salutary restraints, without which it degenerates into anarchy" (King, *Life*, 2:645-7). Adamson later sent TJ a copy of the letter (see Adamson to TJ, 30 Jan. 1803). The letter became a prominent campaign tool during the 1807 state elections in New York, appearing in Clintonian newspapers to galvanize Irish support against the Federalist ticket led by King (David A. Wilson, *United Irishmen, United States: Immigrant Radicals in the Early Republic* [Ithaca, N.Y., 1998], 64-6; Robert Ernst, *Rufus King, American Federalist* [Chapel Hill, 1968], 261-4, 303-4).

For TJ's recommendation on behalf of the United Irish refugee Thomas ROBINSON LATE OF DUBLIN COLLEGE, see Vol. 31:381-2.

[1] MS: "perecuted."

From James Jackson

SIR,   Washington, December 28h, 1801.

A circumstance has occurred, which I deem it proper you should be informed of—General Bradley, of Vermont, left this City yesterday Morning, having received the alarming intelligence of the near approach of Mrs Bradleys death, and her last request to see him before the event took place—   He has assured me that he will return, the moment propriety will admit of it—and that should he receive the melancholy account of her dissolution prior to his leaving New York on his road home, he will stay there, for a day or two, as well to indulge his grief, as to give directions for his Family, and immedeately after return—I should have given you this information personally yesterday, but found you were gone to Church in the Morning, and supposed you to be engaged with company in the evening—Mr Bradley wishes any consequential nominations withheld—if you think proper so to do—until his return—if I might presume to express my opinion, it would be similar—for we are again nearly tied in the Senate, with certain Members who are in some cases deemed doubtful—but with whom Mr B—s acquaintance and Friendship occasions confidence, and perhaps influence.

I am Sir with due respect and consideration, Your most Obedt Servt
JAS JACKSON

I am led to believe that no objection would be made to any nomination on the Georgia business

RC (DLC); above postscript: "The President of the United States"; endorsed by TJ as received 28 Dec. and so recorded in SJL.

NEAR APPROACH OF MRS BRADLEYS DEATH: Thankful Taylor Bradley, the second wife of Vermont senator Stephen Row Bradley, died on 10 Jan. 1802 at the age of 34, in Westminster, Vermont (ANB, s.v. "Stephen Row Bradley"; *Rutland Herald*, 25 Jan. 1802).

YOU WERE GONE TO CHURCH: when the federal government moved to Washington, TJ began attending Sunday worship services at Christ Church, an Episcopalian parish founded in Washington in 1795 that met in a converted tobacco house at what is now New Jersey Avenue and D Street. In 1807, the Christ Church congregation moved to G Street to a newly constructed building designed by Benjamin Henry Latrobe, which had a pew reserved for the president. TJ was an admirer and supporter of its pastor, Reverend Andrew McCormick. He also chose to attend services held in the House of Representatives on occasion (Margaret Bayard Smith, *The First Forty Years of Washington Society*, ed. Gaillard Hunt [New York, 1906], 13; "James H. Hutson Responds," WMQ, 3d ser., 56 [1999], 823; MB, 2:1130, 1154, 1214, 1216).

From John F. Mercer

DEAR SIR
Annapolis Dec. 28th. 1801.

Mr. William Polk of Somerset County in this state will have the honor of presenting you this—he is anxious to be made known to you & I feel gratified by introducing him as one of the distinguish'd supporters' of an Revolution in this State; He has since invariably maintaind his original principles & standing almost alone in the lower District of the Eastern Shore, nothing but his rank in society & his personal qualities perhaps ensur'd his safety,—they scarcely procurd him tolerance till the late change offerd him a seat in the Senate of this State:, I feel also another gratification in repeating the expression of the respectful attachment with which

I am Dr Sir yr Ob hble Sv.
JOHN F. MERCER

RC (DLC); endorsed by TJ as received 1 Jan. 1802 and so recorded in SJL.

An attorney from Somerset County, WILLIAM POLK was elected to Maryland's senate to represent the Eastern Shore in 1801, although he did not attend. He became chief justice of a Maryland judicial district in 1802 (Papenfuse, *Maryland* *Legislature*, 2:654-5; Paul Baker Touart, *Somerset: An Architectural History* [Annapolis, Md., 1990], 230).

From David Stone

Senate Chamber 28th December 1801

Enclosed are two applications for office which I take the Liberty to lay before you, and to add of Mr. David Ker one of the applicants that he is originally from Ireland, has been in the United States many years, was after his arrival for a considerable time employed as a Minister of the Gospel and Teacher of a Grammar School—on the first establishment of the University of North Carolina he was engaged by the Trustees to superintend that Institution and to Teach the Latin and Greek Languages. He has since turned his attention to the Law and in the year 1796, I believe, obtained a License and entered upon the practise in the neighborhood of Fayette Ville—since which time I have known little more of him than is contained in the enclosed Letter to me. Upon his examination for admittance to the Bar he was thought to acquit himself very well; He has at all times since my acquaintance with him shewn himself firmly republican, has a wife with a large family of Children and is poor.

Of the other Applicant Mr. Davis that he has been in the practise of the Law since the year 1790 or '91 has some Talents and I believe Honesty but I fear wants application, whether Republican or not I know not but suppose from his connections he has not been uniformly republican.

If a preference is not already determined on between Mr. Bloodworth and Mr. Potts and it should be in my power to make that determination more satisfactory it will give me pleasure to have stated That tho Mr. Potts stands equally fair with Mr. Bloodworth for Honesty and Firmness as a republican, and probably before him as a Clerk—several circumstances in the History of Mr. Potts have recurred to my recollection that convince me he is in point of understanding far inferior to Mr Bloodworth. The Honorable Testimony which the State of North Carolina has on several occasions borne in favor of the latter Gentleman & the respectable standing he at present maintains there may also weigh something. Mr. Gallatin is personally acquainted with Mr. Bloodworth and doubtless judges from his own knowlege; but a recollection of the warmth and zeal with which his Election into the Senate of the United States was opposed by the present Comptroller prepares me to expect an opposition from the Treasury.

I have the Honor to be with the most profound Respect Your Humble Servant   DAVID STONE

RC (NHi: Gallatin Papers); endorsed by TJ as received 28 Dec. and so recorded in SJL with notation "Ker D. Bloodworth. Potts. Davis"; also endorsed by TJ: "David Ker to be judge of Missi territory vice Tilton. Bloodworth, Potts, Davis. Collector for Wilmington." Enclosures: (1) David Ker to TJ, 3 Oct. 1801. (2) David Ker to Stone, Natchez, 3 Oct. 1801, in which Ker offers to distribute "republican information" in Mississippi in order to counteract the continuing influence of the "partizans of the late administration" and to temper the zealous Republicans in the territory, who lack "information & moderation"; Ker also seeks an appointment as judge or secretary of the territory, despite concerns that immigrants in America "have some impediments in the way to public appointments," and asks that Stone convey his letter of application to the president (RC in DNA: RG 59, LAR; endorsed by TJ: "Ker David to be judge of Missisipi vice Tilton abandoned"). (3) George Davis to Stone, Wilmington, undated, apologizing for addressing Stone "after an omission so long and so inexcusable" and expressing his desire to obtain the Wilmington collectorship (RC in NHi: Gallatin Papers; endorsed by TJ: "Davis George to mr Stone to be Collector of Wilmington"). Enclosed in TJ to Gallatin, 29 Dec.

David Stone (1770-1818) graduated first in his class at Princeton before returning to North Carolina to study law under William R. Davie. During the 1790s, he served in the state legislature and on the state supreme court before being elected to Congress in 1799. Nominally elected as a Federalist, Stone demonstrated his political independence by generally supporting the Republicans, including voting for TJ on all 36 House ballots during the election crisis of February 1801. The Republican-dominated legislature of North Carolina elected Stone to replace Timothy Bloodworth in the U.S. Senate in 1801, where he served until 1807. After two terms as governor of North Carolina, Stone returned to the Senate in 1813, but he resigned the following year due to his lack of support for the War of 1812 and retired to his plantation in Wake County (ANB; Ruth L. Woodward and Wesley Frank Craven, *Princetonians, 1784-1790: A Biographical Dictionary* [Princeton, 1991], 288-92; *Biog. Dir. Cong.*).

For the candidacy of Timothy BLOODWORTH for the Wilmington collectorship, see Bloodworth to TJ, 6 Oct. 1801, and Gallatin to TJ, [19 Oct. 1801].

MR. POTTS: Joshua Potts, a merchant and former member of the state legislature from Wilmington. TJ appointed him a bankruptcy commissioner for North Carolina in December 1802 (John L. Cheney, Jr., ed., *North Carolina Government, 1585-1979: A Narrative and Statistical History* [Raleigh, 1981], 220; commission for Joshua Potts, 20 Dec. 1802, in DNA: RG 59, MPTPC). On 12 Dec., Nathaniel Macon sent Gallatin two recommendations in favor of Potts from "men of respectability" in the state. Macon determined, as the result of his inquiries, that Potts was "the most suitable person to appoint" to the collectorship. Letters from Raleigh and Fayetteville described Potts as an "upright, Honest, and Benevolent Man," about 50 years old, and a "correct accountant," who in every respect was properly qualified to fill the vacancy, having had experience in the collector's office under former collector James Read. He was also "a true and faithfull Republican at the time when that Cause was almost deserted." Gallatin sent Macon's letter and the recommendations to the president (RC in DNA: RG 59, LAR; endorsed by TJ: "mr. Macon to mr Gallatin Potts to be collector of Wilmington").

John Steele, THE PRESENT COMP-TROLLER, ran unsuccessfully against Bloodworth for election to the U.S. Senate in 1795 (William S. Powell, ed., *Dictionary of North Carolina Biography*, 6 vols. [Chapel Hill, 1979-96], 5:433).

From James Cheetham

SIR   New york Decr. 29th. 1801

The history of the administration of John Adams, late President of the United States, written by John Wood, of this City, will in all probability, be *suppressed*. It was printed and ready for Sale when I returned from Washington. The persons engaged in its suppression are those whose plans I in some Degree unfolded to you During my Stay in Washington. Their motives for suppressing it are not yet *Completely* Developed: but they are sufficiently understood to convince us that they are not the most honorable. The work is Republican; and why *Republicans* should be Solicitious to Suppress it, is enigmatical. One of the avowed reasons is that it Contains remarks Calculated to offend many of the federalists, from which and many other Circumstances it is inferred that to form a *coalition* with them at a Suitable time is in Contemplation. It will be finally Determined *this night* whether the work will be Suppressed or not. The publishers (in whose hands the work is, and who employed Mr. Wood to write it) have acceded to the proposition of the *faction* to give $1100 for its Suppression. If the money be paid to-night according to promise, it will be Consigned to the flames, and Mr. Wood is to write another under the *influence*, it is supposed, of Mr. Burr.

My friends think it would be Desirable to *anticipate* the intended new copy, by an *impartial* History of the administration of Mr. Adams, and by so Doing Defeat the views of the Suppressors of the present one. But there are Several Documents necessary to connect events which Cannot be had but from the Departments of State. There is, perhaps, an intimate connection between the prominent measures of the *latter part* of the administration of General Washington and those of Mr. Adams. Perhaps General Washington began the System upon which Mr. Adams acted and which he matured. It might, in writing the History of the administration of Mr. Adams, be necessary, in order to "Speak of things as they were," and to trace effects to their Causes, to go back to the appointment of John Jay to negotiate the British Treaty, and to the subsequent and perhaps Consequent Denunciation of the *self-created* Societies by General Washington. For this purpose, and in order to "Command a view of the whole ground" the *Secret instructions* of Mr. Jay would be necessary. These are Solicited; and if you should not think it incompatible to give them, they will be recieved with much thankfulness.

It would also be Desirable to know whether Mr. Jay recieved Compensation both as Chief Justice and Envoy During the negotiation? It is supposed that he received pay as Chief Justice *only*, but I Do not remember that this has been accurately ascertained.

An answer to this as early as may be Convenient will be very acceptable.

I am most sincerely, your friend.   JAMES CHEETHAM

RC (DLC); addressed: "To His Excellency Thomas Jefferson President of the United States"; franked; postmarked 30 Dec.; endorsed by TJ as received 2 Jan. 1802 and so recorded in SJL.

For an account of the attempted suppression of John Wood's HISTORY OF THE ADMINISTRATION OF JOHN ADAMS, see Kline, *Burr*, 2:641-8. PLANS I IN SOME DEGREE UNFOLDED TO YOU: see Cheetham to TJ, 10 Dec., and the enclosure on politics in New York. The attempt to suppress Wood's history and personal financial difficulties delayed Burr's departure for Washington and his assumption of duties as vice president. On 26 Dec., William Barlass and Matthias Ward, the PUBLISHERS who had also commissioned the history, agreed to suppress the edition, already printed, for $1,100. The payment, however, did not take place on 29 Dec. and the dispute continued. Cheetham played a major part in the "pamphlet war" that ensued among New York Republicans. The controversy, it is said, "signaled the end of that brief period in which Clintonians and Jeffersonians paid lip service to their alliance" with Burr (Kline, *Burr*, 2:641-5).

Washington nominated John Jay to NEGOTIATE with Great Britain in April 1794. The president criticized "certain" SELF-CREATED SOCIETIES in his 19 Nov. 1794 annual message to Congress, arguing that the democratic societies had encouraged the rebellion against the excise tax in western Pennsylvania. SECRET INSTRUCTIONS OF MR. JAY: when Washington appointed Jay as special envoy to Great Britain, he did not provide the Senate with guidelines for Jay's negotiations. On 17 Apr. 1794, some senators tried, but failed, to pass a motion requesting that the president inform the body "of the whole business with which the proposed Envoy is to be charged." The Senate confirmed Jay's appointment two days later. On 8 June 1795, Washington submitted the Jay Treaty, along with papers relating to the diplomatic mission, including Jay's instructions, to the Senate for ratification. At the same time, the Senate invoked "an injunction of secrecy on the communications" (JHR, 2:233-4; JEP, 1:150-2, 178). While vice president, TJ took extensive notes on the papers relating to Jay's mission from the documents in the Senate files (see Vol. 29:605-31).

From Andrew Ellicott

DEAR SIR   Lancaster December 29th. 1801

I have enclosed a few astronomical observations; they are principally intended to determine by practice, what dependence may be placed in the lunar theory, for the determination of the longitude.—

If I could have found leisure, the observations should have been more numerous, but the duties of my office require so great a proportion of my time, that I have none left for the pursuit of any branch of science, but what I borrow from those hours generally devoted to sleep.—

Being now the only native of the United States left, which time has not spunged away, and who has cultivated practical astronomy for the purpose of rendering it useful to commerce, to the division of territories, and the determination of the relative positions of the different parts of our own country, I feel a desire to keep the subject alive, till succeeded by some American, whose fortune may put it in his power to be more useful, by enabling him to devote his whole time to the improvement of so important a branch of science.

I have the honour to be with due respect your friend and Hbl. Servt.   ANDW; ELLICOTT.

RC (PPAmP); at foot of text: "Thos. Jefferson President of the U.S. and of the A.P.S."; endorsed for the American Philosophical Society. Recorded in SJL as received 6 Jan. 1802. Enclosure: "Astronomical observations made at the Borough of Lancaster in the State of Pennsylvania," containing data of observations made 2 Nov. to 24 Dec. 1801 to find longitude by daily observations measuring distances between the sun and the moon; Ellicott reporting that "in several respects" measurement of "lunar distances" to find longitude seemed to be superior to the generally preferred method, which was based on observations of Jupiter's moons (MS in PPAmP; in Ellicott's hand, unsigned and undated; endorsed for the APS).

TJ transmitted Ellicott's letter and the enclosed OBSERVATIONS to the APS, where the paper was read at a meeting on 15 Jan. 1802. The paper was referred to a committee consisting of Robert Patterson and Benjamin Latrobe, who at the next meeting, on 5 Feb., reported that it was worthy of publication. The observations were not, however, printed in the society's *Transactions*. Instead, the paper appears to have been superseded by another set of observations Ellicott sent in December 1802, this time in a letter to Patterson. Observations in the new paper overlapped with some of the data Ellicott sent with the letter above, and both papers were aimed at testing the theory of using the moon to find longtitude. The new report was read at an APS meeting in January 1803, approved for publication, and included in the sixth volume of the *Transactions* (APS, *Proceedings*, 22, pt. 3 [1884], 320, 330, 333; APS, *Transactions*, 6 [1809], 61-9).

Partly because measurements of the moon's position could be made more frequently, and with a less powerful telescope, than observations of the disappearance and reappearance of Jupiter's moons, Ellicott, Patterson, and TJ concluded that the LUNAR THEORY was the method best suited for determining longitude in the field. In 1803, they instructed Meriwether Lewis and William Clark to collect data using the lunar method during the journey of the Corps of Discovery to the Pacific (Bedini, *Statesman of Science*, 342-9; Richard S. Preston, "The Accuracy of the Astronomical Observations of Lewis and Clark," APS, *Proceedings*, 144 [2000], 168-91; Donald Jackson, *Thomas Jefferson & the Stony Mountains: Exploring the West from Monticello* [Urbana, Ill., 1981], 176).

To Albert Gallatin

Dec. 29. 1801.

I inclose you a letter I recieved yesterday from mr Stone on the subject of the Wilmington collectorship. you will percieve he is in favor of Bloodworth, and counting on a personal opposition from mr Steele, confides another in the judgment you will form on your own knolege of mr Bloodworth. his letter of course must not be seen by mr Steele. if you have an opportunity of seeing mr Franklin, I wish you would ask his opinion, as he is an honest judicious man. does Johnston come from the quarter of Wilmington? I know nothing of him personally, nor how far his opinion would merit confidence.

Is it worth while for me to state to Congress the particular inspectorships put down, while we expect confidently they will put down the whole internal system? Will you prepare a message to them respecting the erection of the N. Western district & compensation for the Supervisor, as you are more familiar with the laws & facts relating to the subject than I am? I suppose the compensation is only to be retrospective. health & esteem.   TH: JEFFERSON

P.S. I approve of your not medling with the bank elections. I will do what I can, delicately, for mrs Jackson.

RC (NHi: Gallatin Papers); addressed: "The Secretary of the Treasury"; endorsed. PrC (DLC). Enclosure: David Stone to TJ, 28 Dec. 1801.

YOUR OWN KNOLEGE OF MR BLOODWORTH: Gallatin and Timothy Bloodworth served together in the Fourth, Fifth, and Sixth Congresses, Gallatin as a representative from Pennsylvania, Bloodworth as senator from North Carolina.

For Gallatin's earlier evaluation of Bloodworth as a candidate for the collectorship, see Gallatin to TJ, [19 Oct. 1801]. Jesse FRANKLIN served as senator and Charles Johnson (JOHNSTON) as a representative from North Carolina in the Seventh Congress. Johnson lived near Edenton, in Chowan County (*Biog. Dir. Cong.*).

BANK ELECTIONS: see Gallatin to TJ, 27 Dec. (second letter).

To James Madison

DEAR SIR   Dec. 29. 1801.

To compleat the roll of governmental officers on the plan inclosed will give the departments some serious trouble: however it is so important to present to the eye of all the constituted authorities, as well as of their constituents, & to keep under their eye, the true extent of the machine of government, that I cannot but recommend to the heads of departments to endeavor to fill up each, their portion of the roll as compleatly as possible and as early too, that it may be presented to the legislature.   health and affectionate respect.

TH: JEFFERSON

P.S. As the Post master general has a part to perform, will you instruct him accordingly? I inclose a spare copy of the papers which you can hand him.

RC (DNA: RG 59, MLR); signature and date clipped, supplied from PrC; at head of text: "Circular"; at foot of text: "The Secretary of State." PrC (DLC). Enclosure: Tr of Gallatin to TJ, 27 Dec., and enclosure.

TJ recorded this letter in SJL as "Departments circular." He undoubtedly sent the same letter, without the postscript, and the enclosures to Henry Dearborn and Robert Smith, but those letters have not been found.

Jacob Wagner sent TJ an undated document entitled "Salaries & Compensation to the Secretary of State, his Clerks, and the officers acting in connection with the Department of State." While the document served as the State Department's answer to Gallatin's request for information, Wagner probably sent it to TJ before the Treasury secretary specified the information he needed for the roll of government officers. Wagner named the six department clerks, with the total allowance for their salaries, information Gallatin clearly indicated the Treasury Department would provide. Wagner also provided the names and salaries of the U.S. ministers and their secretaries,

the U.S. consuls to the Barbary nations, the U.S. agents for managing claims in prize cases, agents for the relief of seamen, and the commissioners appointed under the 7th Article of the Jay Treaty, all information requested by the Treasury secretary. Wagner did not include the names of the scores of unsalaried U.S. consuls, who received fees and "a commission on their lawful disbursements, not exceeding five per cent," information requested by Gallatin and subsequently included in the roll of officers presented to Congress. Wagner also failed to provide information on the commissioners appointed under Article 6 of the Jay Treaty, as Gallatin requested. Perhaps Wagner's list provided information on State Department expenses for 1802, and, therefore, the salaries of the commissioners under Article 6, who had completed their work, were not included (MS in DLC: TJ Papers, 119:20522-3, undated, entirely in Wagner's hand, endorsed by Wagner: "Salaries of the Department of State," endorsed by TJ as received from the State Department in "Dec. 1801" and "Salaries"; Madison, *Papers, Sec. of State Ser.*, 2:350; ASP, *Miscellaneous*, 306-8; Gallatin to TJ, 27 Dec., and enclosure).

To James Madison

SIR   Washington Dec. 29. 1801.

Having no confidence that the office of the private secretary of the President of the US. will ever be a regular & safe deposit for public papers or that due attention will ever be paid on their transmission from one Secretary or President to another, I have, since I have been in office, sent every paper, which I deem meerly public, & coming to my hands, to be deposited in one of the offices of the heads of departments; so that I shall never add a single paper to those now constituting the records of the President's office; nor, should any accident happen to me, will there be any papers in my possession which ought to go into any public office. I make the selection regularly as I go along, retaining in my own possession only my private papers, or such as, relating to public subjects, were meant still to be personally confidential for myself. Mr. Meredith the late treasurer, in obedience to the law which directs the Treasurer's accounts to be transmitted to & remain with the President, having transmitted his accounts, I send them to you to be deposited for safe keeping in the Domestic branch of the office of Secretary of State, which I suppose to be the proper one. Accept assurances of my affectionate esteem & high respect.

Th: Jefferson

RC (DNA: RG 59, MLR); at foot of text: "The Secretary of State." PrC (DLC).

In an undated letter to TJ, Albert Gallatin wrote that the TREASURER'S ACCOUNTS "are by law to be transmitted to the President, & to remain with him" (RC in DLC; endorsed by TJ as received from the Treasury Department on 28 Dec. and "Treasurer's accounts" and so recorded in SJL). Congress received Samuel Meredith's general account of receipts and expenditures, from 1 Oct. 1800 to 30 June 1801, and accounts of receipts and expenditures of the navy and war departments, extending from 1 Oct. 1800 to 30 Sep. 1801, on 11 Dec. (JHR, 4:15; JS, 3:161).

From Julian Ursin Niemcewicz

Sir.   Elizabeth Town N.J. 29 December 1801.

I do myself the pleasure to present you with two Copies of a brief account of the Invention of a Water-proof Manufactory, which has been send to me by the Inventor. As the discovery appears to me very useful, & tending to promot health & lives of men, I thought it would be agreable to you, that you would give it publicity & make use of it for the benefit of our Citizens, particularly husbandmen, Seafaring, & Soldiers. I have the honor to be with great respect.

Sir Your obedient humble Servant   J. U. Niemcewicz

Each half of the two inclosed bloting papers, are water proof as may be seen by springling water on.

RC (DLC); endorsed by TJ as received 2 Jan. 1802 and so recorded in SJL. Enclosures: probably copies of the *Analytical Hints* pamphlet (see TJ to Thomas Mann Randolph, 4 Dec.).

From Edmund O'Finn

THOS. JEFFERSON ESQR:

No. 1. Rue de la Salpetrieres.
Bordeaux 29 Decr. 1801

In the Number of those who unsuccesfully struggled for the Liberty of Ireland, my Name has the Honor of being enroled as a proscribed—& seeing our Hopes deferd, I have fixd here as a merchant in the general line of Comn. business

To my Countrymen, every where,
your Character is well known
as their Friend & Benefactor,
and Citizen of the World.

You will never be deceived in whatever favorable opinion you may entertain of us—

I am happy in the opportunity of forwarding some Papers to your Adress, as it procures me the means of offering my mite of respect and attachment.—

Any Command you may be disposed to send or commit to my Care, I shall receive as a particular Honor.—
EDMD. O'FINN
formerly of Cork

RC (DLC); addressed: "Thos. Jefferson Esqr. President of the United States"; endorsed by TJ as received 22 Feb. 1802 and so recorded in SJL. Enclosures not found.

In 1798, Edmund O'Finn was an agent of the Society of United Irishmen in France, where he met with that country's government to request military assistance for the Irish rebellion. A number of United Irishmen fled to France when the uprising failed (Marianne Elliott, *Partners in Revolution: The United Irishmen and France* [New Haven, 1982], 175-8, 265-9).

From Robert Smith

Navy Dept. Dec. 29. 1801

Under the impression that the President will be obliged to send to the Medn. Squadron *new* orders in consequence of measures, which, there is reason to believe, will be adopted by Congress and that such orders will be conveyed in the Enterprize, it is believed that the proper Officers ought to be ordered immediately to that vessel. For this purpose it is proposed to send the accompanying Letters. Taking into view the places of residence of some of these Officers and accidents that may occur, it is probable that this Tender will not be ready before the 1st. Feby. next.

RC (DLC); endorsed by TJ as received 29 Dec. from the Navy Department and "orders to Enterprize" and so recorded in SJL. Enclosures: see below.

For the NEW ORDERS to U.S. naval commanders and the measures ADOPTED BY CONGRESS regarding hostilities with Tripoli, see TJ's Circular to Naval Commanders, 18 Feb. 1802.

On 29 Dec., Smith sent ORDERS to several navy officers, directing them to repair immediately to Baltimore and report to the commanding officer of the schooner *Enterprize*, including lieutenants John Rush and John Foote, surgeon George Davis, purser Silas Butler, and midshipmen Benjamin Turner, States Rutledge, Daniel Simms, and Joseph Israel (FCs in Lb in DNA: RG 45, LSO).

From John Vaughan

DR SIR   Philad: Decr 29. 1801

By Mr Brun, a friend of Kosiusco's, & who is strongly recommended to me, I have the pleasure of sending, some Specimens of Coins & Medals made in England, they are from Mr Jos: Priestly, & were meant to have been sent to you long since, had not an accident prevented, which it is immaterial now to mention—I have taken the Liberty to annex a list of Certain Societies to which (by an order of some standing) our Transactions were to be sent—The Existence or State of these Societies being unknown—I am desirous of getting some information on the Subject—M De Nemours, to whom I had written relative to those of France, seems very uncertain whether they[1] exist & if they do, under what name—with respect to those of Spain, The minister here refers me to the Consul General, daily expected, who is a man of Letters, & belongs to the Sociedad Bascongada The most ancient in Spain—As to the Italian Societies I am completely in the Dark, & wish as early as you have opportunity, that some light could be thrown upon it; by seizing the first moments of Peace, we shall render the delay, less perceptible, because it will be accounted for by the War—The Truth has been that we never could procure them from Mr. Aitkin, until the present moment—I should not have intruded on the time you must now necessarily devote to Political Objects—Could I have thought of any other Channel from whence I could get correct information.

I remain with the greatest respect Your obt. Servt. & friend

JN VAUGHAN

D Coxe & the other Physicians are progressing with the Vaccine—he wd be happy when opportunity offers to learn, the Result of the use of the Variolous Matter sent for Dr Gantt.—

RC (DLC); at foot of text: "His Excellency Thomas Jefferson Washington." Recorded in SJL as received 9 Jan. 1802.

For BRUN, see Charles Le Brun to TJ, 10 Mch. 1802.

MINISTER: Carlos Martínez de Irujo. On 22 Jan. 1802, Irujo wrote Madison to announce the arrival at Philadelphia of the new Spanish CONSUL GENERAL, Valentín Tadeo Echavarri de Foronda. TJ recognized Foronda's credentials in an exequatur signed on 29 Jan. (FC in Lb, DNA: RG 59, Exequaturs; Madison, *Papers, Sec. of State Ser.*, 2:416; 3:493-4).

The American Philosophical Society elected Foronda to membership in July 1802. Since 1776, he had been a member of the Real SOCIEDAD BASCONGADA de los Amigos del País, which was organized in the Basque region in 1765. The group pursued questions relating to science, technology, agriculture, and commerce. It was the oldest provincial or municipal society of the kind in Spain (APS, *Proceed-*

ings, 22, pt. 3 [1884], 326; Robert S. Smith, "Economists and the Enlightenment in Spain, 1750-1800," *Journal of Political Economy*, 63 [1955], 346-7; J. Ignacio Tellechea Idigoras and others, *Real Sociedad Bascongada de los Amigos del País, Euskalerriaren Adiskideen Elkartea: Edición Conmemorativa del II Centenario de la Muerte del Fundador de la Real Sociedad Bascongada de los Amigos del País, D. Xavier Ma. de Munive e Idiáquez, Conde de Peñaflorida (1729-1785)*, 12 vols. [San Sebastian, Spain, 1985], 1:1-352; 5:93, 96; 12:53).

MR. AITKIN: Philadelphia printer Robert Aitken published the first three volumes of the *Transactions* of the APS. In November 1801, the society gave a committee "discretionary powers" to settle Aitken's accounts (APS, *Proceedings*, 22, pt. 3 [1884], 132, 186, 213, 317; Vol. 26:79).

¹ MS: "the."

ENCLOSURE

List of Learned Societies

In our Library

Transactions orderd for
Royal Academy of Sciences Turin. See below
    Society of Milan—We have of the Transactions of the Patriotick Society of
        Agriculture, Arts & Manufactures Milan 1783 Vol 1 pt. 1. only
    Society of Bologna See below
    Society of Florence—we have nothing of this Society

Academy of Mexico—Mr Irujo thinks there is a University where the Arts
    &c. are taught—but no *Society* so called
Academy of Lyons—M. De nemours thinks there is now a Lycèe
Academy of Rouen
Royal academy of Belles Lettres at Seville—almost expired under this Title
Society for promoting Arts Manufac & Commerce London   ⎫
Society for Idem—Arts & Manufactures—   do.   ⎬ Supposed¹

We have of Turin Memoires
5 Vol old Series from 1759 a 1773 Inclusive
5 Vol. new Series 1784 to 1791 Inclusive
    Also. Memorie dè Matematica e fysica de la Società Italiana

Vol 1	Vol 2 pt 1	Vol 2. pt 2
Verona. 1782	Verona 1784	Vera: 1784

Also Raccolta d'opucoli sulle Scienze e sulle artè Tome 1 Milan 1779
Also. De Bononiensi Scientiarium et artium Instituto atque Academia
Conmentarii

Vol 1	2 in 3 pts	3	4	
1748	1745.6.7	1755	1757	printed Bononice. So far Complete

MS (DLC); in Vaughan's hand, probably written in stages, with his notations added to the list of societies; endorsed by TJ as received 9 Jan. 1802.

Exchanges of information and published transactions between the American Philosophical Society and the scientific group at TURIN began in 1773. The Turin organization began as a private scientific society in 1757, publishing its first volume of papers two years later, and in 1783 became a royal academy with financial support from the monarchy of the Two Sicilies. From its inception, the society at Turin communicated with a wider scientific community, and Joseph Priestley and Benjamin Franklin were among its foreign members. In the 1780s, the new Società Patriotica of MILAN began to exchange publications with the APS. Franklin and Benjamin Rush were made corresponding members of the Milan association. The science academy of the institute at BOLOGNA, which developed from some earlier societies, was founded in 1714. It began to receive support from the Vatican in the 1740s. The academy's publication was *De Bononiensi Scientiarum et Artium Instituto atque Academia Commentarii*. In 1773, Philip Mazzei acted as courier in the initiation of correspondence between the APS and the academies at Bologna and Turin. FLORENCE in the seventeenth century had been the site of one of the most significant societies, the Accademia del Cimento. In the eighteenth century, the Reale Accademia dei Georgofili, which concentrated on economics, agriculture, and some science, began in Florence as a private society and was chartered as an official academy in 1767. The Academia Botanica, a group that began to meet in Florence in 1739 and was devoted to natural history, merged with the Georgofili organization in 1783. The Italian learned societies went through changes during and following the French Revolution. The academies at Milan and Florence did not survive the disruptions in Europe. The institution at Turin was closed from 1792 to 1801. The academy at Bologna became, under French influence, a national institute for a number of years (James E. McClellan III, *Science Reorganized: Scientific Societies in the Eighteenth Century* [New York, 1985], 44-9, 99-104, 127-31, 173, 264, 269, 279, 284-5; Antonio Pace, "The American Philosophical Society and Italy," APS, *Proceedings*, 90 [1946], 389-90, 391, 395, 397, 399, 409, 411-12; APS, *Transactions*, 3 [1793], 355-6, 358).

The university in MEXICO, modeled on the one at Salamanca, Spain, and authorized by royal decree, had been in existence since the middle of the sixteenth century (Agueda María Rodríguez Cruz, *Historia de las Universidades Hispanoamericanas: Periodo Hispanico*, 2 vols. [Bogotá, 1973], 1:249-50).

In France, academies at LYONS and ROUEN had ceased to function in 1793. The association at Lyons had met first as a private learned society, receiving letters patent in 1724, then royal patronage, and finally the status of an academy in the 1750s. The academy developed a library and collections of natural history specimens, came to foster work in practical technology as well as pure science, offered prizes, and sponsored a ballooning experiment in 1783. It published one volume of *Mémoires couronnés* in the 1780s, but apparently did not establish regular communication with the APS. At Rouen, a society devoted to science and the arts began in the 1730s, formed an academy in 1744, and received the patronage of the French crown, but never published its minutes or papers. A plan to form an association of the learned societies of the French provinces, an idea that originated in the Rouen academy in the 1770s, never came to fruition (McClellan, *Science Reorganized*, 98, 112, 134, 183-4, 271-2, 277, 325n).

SEVILLE: the Academia Sevillana de

Buenas Letras had its origins in Sevilla in 1751 and received support from the Spanish crown soon thereafter. The academy suspended its meetings for a time in 1800-1801 due to the yellow fever epidemic in southern Spain. The election of some new members helped reinvigorate the group, but the academy ceased to function in 1808 after France invaded Spain. There was no academy in Spain dedicated to the natural and physical sciences until later in the nineteenth century (Francisco Aguilar Piñal, *La Real Academia Sevillana de Buenas Letras en el Siglo XVIII* [Madrid, 1966], 79-83, 92-9, 176-84; Joseph C. Kiger, ed., *International Encyclopedia of Learned Societies and Academies* [Westport, Conn., 1993], 258, 261-2).

Observing that prizes and premiums awarded at races and horse fairs stimulated the improvement of horse stock, William Shipley believed that innovations in the practical arts should be promoted by similar means. Shipley proposed the formation of the Society for the Encouragement of Arts, Manufactures, and Commerce, which was organized in LONDON in 1754 ([James Theobald], *A Concise Account of the Rise, Progress, and Present State of the Society for the Encouragement of Arts, Manufactures, and Commerce* [London, 1763], 1-12; D. G. C. Allan, "The Society of Arts and Government, 1754-1800: Public Encouragement of Arts, Manufactures, and Commerce in Eighteenth-Century England," *Eighteenth-Century Studies*, 7 [1974], 434-6).

Anton Maria Lorgna, who hoped that there might one day be a single learned society for Italians, established the SOCIETÀ ITALIANA delle Scienze at VERONA in 1782. Franklin was made an honorary member of the society. Both the Società Italiana and its publication, the *Memorie di Matematica e di Fisica*, ceased with Lorgna's death in 1796, although the society was revived in the nineteenth century (McClellan, *Science Reorganized*, 133, 187, 291; Pace, "American Philosophical Society and Italy," 391, 397, 399, 406, 407).

RACCOLTA: the *Raccolta d'Opuscoli sulle Scienze e sulle Arti* was a compilation of articles issued at Milan in 1779.

[1] Vaughan began to write something below this word, perhaps the beginning of "th," but did not complete the action.

From Dr. John Vaughan

ESTEEMED SIR,   Wilmington December 29th. 1801.

It has been suggested to me by a member of Congress, who has seen the specimen volumes of the political writings of Mr. Dickinson, that you would probably accept one of those volumes for the present—on this belief, I have enclosed a copy per mail, which you will please to accept:—permit me to add, the work will be completed & delivered about the first of February; & the editors design to prefix a portrait of the Author, to convey his likeness with his precepts to posterity.

The late fugitive condition of those valuable papers, rendered them useless to the public, & they would eventually have been forgotten in the lumber rooms of political science; but it is to be hoped, their present aggregated form will tend to preserve & disseminate the important doctrines they contain, & contribute to the final establishment of republicanism in our much envied country.

With a sincere devotion to the political happiness of my country, I remain, Dear Sir, with accumulating reverence, your much obliged & devoted humble Servt.   JNO. VAUGHAN

RC (DLC); at foot of text: "Thomas Jefferson Esquire"; endorsed by TJ as received 2 Jan. 1802 and so recorded in SJL. Enclosure: *The Political Writings of John Dickinson, Esquire, Late President of the State of Delaware, and of the Commonwealth of Pennsylvania. In Two Volumes,* printed in Wilmington in 1801 by Bonsal and Niles, with TJ listed among the subscribers included at the end of the second volume (Sowerby, No. 3055).

MEMBER OF CONGRESS: perhaps Pennsylvania senator George Logan. On 15 Apr., TJ paid Logan $5 for Dickinson's works (MB, 2:1070).

From Henry Voigt

SIR   Philada 29th. Decr. 1801

The Citizens of Philadelphia, friends to our Government and your administration, have often expressed a desire of seeing a Medalion struck to commemorate the declaration of Independence and the last triumph of republicanism on the 4th March 1801—, and I know that not only the Citizens of this State but every true Patriot in the Union would be pleased to have those Epochas handed down to posterity.— Happily for all our wishes at this time there was found a German Artist of Superior talents equal to do justice to our ideas.—but it was not enough that America should be free—this German Artist must also Obtain his liberty, before anything could be done.

It was not long after, I heard of his situation, that this was accomplished.—and you will please to recollect that he then endeavored to recommend himself to your notice, by a Specimen of his work, (viz) two Medalions of Block tin, one of Bonaparte, and the other, the present King of Prussia, and you had the goodness to recommend him to the Director of the Mint.—

At that time there were several medalions wanted for the Indian Nations; but, unfortunately, Mr Scot the Engraver to the mint, had contracted for the execution of them. He was however induced at the instance of the Director, to employ Mr. Reish, under him, to do the work, but the compensation that he received was barely sufficient to defray his necessary expences. Having completed those dies he became as destitute as ever I therefore suggested to him the propriety, and proposed to him the plan, of executing the Medalion which we have now jointly the honour of presenting for your inspection. I have supported him while he was employed in sinking the Dies, and he is to have half the profits that may accrue from their sale, which I think will be rapid and extensive, when we consider the exquisite work-manship and the Subject—

These Sir were the motives which induced me to bring forward this Medalion—first to please our friends, and second to retain in the Country such a Valuable acquisition as the Artist. I hope Sir you will pardon us if we have taken too much liberty in representing you on the Medalion, without first having obtained leave. The faults it may have, as to likeness or character, the artist may well be excused for, since he never had the pleasure of seeing the Original.

I beg leave to explain the Allegorical representations on the reverse.—The Goddess Minerva is made to represent Liberty as well as Wisdom (The one not being able to exist without the other), She holds the declaration of Independence, and lays it on a *rock*, representing the Constitution, about which winds the Cornucopia, and discharches its Treasure, under the protection of the implements and insignia of War. The Eagle on his wing, represents the United States, crowning the whole with laurel.

Should the Artist meet with suitable encouragement in this first Essay, he will certainly come forward with additional proofs of his genius in the same line he is an excellent draughtsman himself, and wants no further assistance than the *impression* for this Medal the Director has granted the use of one of the presses when it is not employed about the business of the Mint. but it would be more satisfactory still, if you would add your approbation if it [. . .] be done, consistant with propriety.

[I am] Sir with due respect yr most Obedt Servt

HENRY VOIGT

RC (DLC); torn at seal; addressed: "His Excelleny Thos Jefferson President of the United States"; endorsed by TJ as received 15 Jan. 1802 and so recorded in SJL.

German native Henry Voigt (d. 1814) was a talented Philadelphia watchmaker, mechanic, and inventor, who had also worked at the mint in Saxe Gotha before emigrating to America. Acting upon recommendations by David Rittenhouse and others, George Washington appointed Voigt chief coiner of the United States Mint in 1792, which appointment was confirmed by the Senate in January 1793. While in Philadelphia, TJ made frequent use of Voigt's watch repair services, and later purchased watches for himself and others from Voigt. In 1811-12, Voigt's son, Thomas, made the astronomical clock that resided in TJ's study at Monticello (Washington, *Papers, Pres. Ser.*, 10:261-2; JEP, 1:127; MB, 2:829, 838, 868, 900, 908, 980, 997, 998, 1015, 1192, 1218, 1289; Bedini, *Statesman of Science*, 421-2; *Poulson's American Daily Advertiser*, 9 Feb. 1814; TJ to Voigt, 11 July, 5 Nov. 1806, 6 Jan. 1808; Voigt to TJ, 19 Dec. 1807; RS, 3:83-4).

For background on the GERMAN ARTIST John Reich and the medals he engraved, see Vol. 34:71-5.

RECOMMEND HIM TO THE DIRECTOR: TJ to Elias Boudinot, 23 May 1801.

From Timothy Bourn

Massachusetts, [before 30] Dec. [1801]. Bourn rhetorically asks why his property of $18 to $20 was taken to answer a fine of just $1.66 despite answering a militia warning. He replies that it is because he was opposed to some of his state's laws. At a Fourth of July muster, a verbal warning was left with his wife, but Bourn claims it was against his principles to carry arms to threaten "the hart of our Libarty and To defend thes Tiront Rulors in this State," who were attempting to set themselves up as monarchs. He asserts that the sergeant failed to follow the militia laws and leave a warning in writing, although the sergeant lied and claimed that he had done so. Bourn further states that the militia captain dismissed him before the roll was called, but the company clerk nevertheless considered him absent despite Bourn's insistence that he belatedly answered the call. Bourn is determined not to submit to the arbitrary laws imposed by the rulers of his state, who, along with the under officers who enforce such laws, he condemns for "Brackin the Contitusion." He wishes they were made to resign and never hold office again, while those who have lost office by opposing such measures should be reinstated. He condemns the Massachusetts legislature for enacting "Laws Beyond the Limets of thare power" and calling citizens to militia duty without compensation. They are given nothing and suffer "hongor and thirst Cold and Nacked and Nothing Soficiont to defend ourselves and our Contry With." Legislators have also extended the age requirements, raising the limit to 45 years from 40 years, and Bourn assumes they will raise the limit to 50 "and then Nover to Bee out of the List and Ever to Bee thare Slaves." Legislators tax the people's property to the last value and distress the people as they please. Fishing rights have been usurped by incorporated towns with the consent of the legislature, and America's "free Bornd Sons" now cannot feed their hunger with herring, clams, cockles, and eels because the legislature gave them to incorporated towns. Such fisheries are the common property of the state and the people are now barred from "feeding thare apetite on those fish that god gave us To Improve." Why did Jefferson receive no votes for president from Massachusetts? Because legislators used "intreag" and appointed the electors themselves. Bourn claims they have broken the Constitution and therefore have "No Rite In Congris and Compleetly Brock of From the Eunion." He returns to his assertion that he has been unfairly fined for failing to heed a militia warning, claiming that he belatedly received a verbal warning left with his wife and that no written warning was made. He presented himself, but the clerk fined him anyway for not answering to his name. "Now Shall my efects Bee tackin By Vilont hands," and Bourn feels compelled to acquaint the president and Congress of this and to see if they are willing to take the Constitution "out of the hands of our usorping Rulers." Bourn offers his life in the struggle to regain liberty from tyrants, that God is about to make his righteous judgment known, and that he will follow wherever He goes. Bourn trusts that the president will "Exclame a ganst the Rulors of this State of brackin the Contitusion and aposing on the pepel Tiranackel Laws," and offers his assistance if needed. "Will your honor put forth your hand and Rite us or must the Indevideals Bee A most mesarabel Set of Beeing," he asks and hopes TJ will reply soon. In a postscript, Bourn adds that he has employed the last two summers experimenting with salt manufacturing, and that he can make four times as much salt on one foot of works as any on Cape Cod. He wishes to expand his works and to acquaint Congress with his plan and render the states independent of foreign places for their salt. But, as he has explained, his property has been seized and he has an 80-year-old mother and a wife and four children to care for, "an No other mans help But my Self and a farme." Militia officers used intreague, fraud, and lies and carried off the milk cow he procured to "Sattisfie my Smol Infunts appetits." If the president will help him, Bourn will never forget his gratitude. But if TJ is inclined to let him suffer, then he need not trouble himself further about Bourn. Within six months, "those Tironts Will Beset me and may Tare me as it Ware from Lim to Lim," but it will be said of Bourn that he died striving to defend his right and liberty and those of his country. "I think I may Luse my Life But I dont think To Bee Cold a Coward."

RC (MHi); 4 p.; addressed: "his Excelency Thomas Jefferson Washington City"; franked; postmarked "Falmouth" but canceled; endorsed by TJ as received 30 Dec. and "Massach:" and so recorded in SJL.

To William Eustis

Wednesday Dec. 30. 1801.

Th: Jefferson requests the favor of The Honble Doctr. Eustis's company to dinner the day after tomorrow at half after three oclock—

RC (facsimile in *Washington Post*, 8 Oct. 1961); in Meriwether Lewis's hand.

William Eustis (1753-1825), a native of Cambridge, Massachusetts, and a graduate of Harvard College, was a surgeon during the Revolutionary War. Eustis held a seat in the lower house of the Massachusetts legislature from 1788 to 1794, and he served from 1801 to 1805 in the U.S. House of Representatives, where he was known as a moderate Republican. TJ consulted Eustis in Washington about chronic diarrhea, for which Eustis recommended English physician Thomas Sydenham's remedy of riding "a trotting horse." During Madison's administration, Eustis was secretary of war from 1809 until his resignation in 1812. Thereafter he was minister to the United Nether lands, a congressman again, and governor of his native state from 1823 until his death. Eustis married Caroline Langdon of Portsmouth, New Hampshire, in 1810 (ANB; Vol. 32:349n; TJ to Henry Fry, 17 June 1804).

From William Henry Harrison

SIR   Vincennes 30th. Decr. 1801.

A few days ago I received the petition herewith enclosed from Kaskaskias with a request from the Subscribers that I would forward it to you with such remarks as I thought necessary to make. Altho' the present alarm of these citizens is not without foundation—I can hardly suppose it probable that the Delaware Nation generally have any disposition to make war upon us—I have been at great pains to explain to the chiefs of that and every other Tribe within my reach, the circumstances which led to the execution of one of their war-riors—and as far as I can judge from the answers of the chiefs my ex-planations have been satisfactory—I am however persuaded that an establishment of Troops in the vicinity of Kaskaskias and an other on the Illinois river would be found extremely useful—it would proba-bly put an end to the petty depredations which a Banditti composed of outcasts from all the Tribes (who have established themselves on the Illinois river) & the Kickapoos of the Prairie are continually making upon our settlements—In the article of stolen horses these depredations have become very frequent and vexatious—and my re-monstrances to the chiefs have hitherto been attended with no good effect—the establishment of a garrison on the Illinois would be fur-ther beneficial as it would prevent the Spanish Traders from Mo-nopolising the valuable Trade of that River—A trade which is now entirely carried on with goods which have paid no duty to the United States—these goods are in the first Instance brought from Canada in the Package, opened in Louisiania & then smuggled into our Terri-tory—The falsehoods propagated by these, & the British Traders, who have a perfect understanding with each other; is one reason of the contempt with which the American Traders are treated by the In-dians—Indeed so well have the exertions of these people been sec-onded by the Neglect of the United States towards the Indians and the violence and injustice with which they have been treated by some of our citizens, that the American name has become almost univer-sally odious to the Tribes upon this frontier—To remove those im-pressions has been my constant aim since the Indian affairs in this country have been Committed to my management—their Complaints have been attended to, and as far as my power would go, redressed—and I have taken the liberty to assure them that, you Sir, who had al-ways been the friend & defender of their race would do every thing necessary to remove their grievances and promote their comfort and happiness—On the subject of these people my communications to the Secretary of War have been frequent—but I have not yet been honoured with your commands—When I do receive them, give me leave to assure you Sir that they shall be executed with Zeal & fidelity.—Nothing certainly could be more gratifying to me, than to contribute towards the success of your administration by my humble exertions to place upon a better footing the affairs of the Wretched Indians—

With the Most perfect Respect I have the honour to be Sir your Most Hume Sert.   WILLM. HENRY HARRISON

RC (DLC); at foot of text: "Thomas Jefferson President of the United States"; endorsed by TJ as received 12 Feb. 1802 and so recorded in SJL. Enclosure not found.

William Henry Harrison (1773-1841), born into a prominent family of Tidewater Virginia, studied medicine under Benjamin Rush before taking an officer's commission in the infantry. Harrison resigned from the army in 1798 and obtained the position of secretary of the Northwest Territory. The next year the territorial legislature elected him the territory's delegate to Congress. When the Northwest Territory was divided in 1800, John Adams appointed Harrison governor of the newly formed Indiana Territory. The term of the office was three years, but Harrison was renominated and confirmed several times, until he resigned in December 1812 to command American troops in the northwest during the War of 1812. He was elected president of the United States in 1840, but died soon after taking office (ANB; *Terr. Papers*, 7:13-14n; 8:227).

KASKASKIAS: the settlement at Kaskaskia, on the Mississippi River on the western edge of the Indiana Territory, had its origins a century earlier as a village of French traders. Since the American Revolution, the isolated settlement, which had fewer than 500 inhabitants according to the 1800 census, had been the scene of political disruption, friction between French-speaking and English-speaking inhabitants, vulnerability to Indian attacks, and competition over land titles (Clarence Walworth Alvord, *The Illinois Country, 1673-1818* [Urbana, Ill., 1920; repr., 1987], 132, 358-9, 362, 366, 368-9, 372-3, 405, 407; Vol. 18:194-6, 198, 207-15).

ALARM OF THESE CITIZENS: another petition from Kaskaskia in November 1802 referred to the inhabitants there as "exposed to the Unrelenting fury of a Cruel enemy, destitute of Troops for their defence without the most distant prospect of Obtaining assistance from any part of the United States" (*Terr. Papers*, 7:77).

See Notes on Actions for the War Department, 10 Nov. 1801, regarding the EXECUTION of Wapikinamouk, a member of the Delaware tribe convicted of murdering a white man, and for Harrison's efforts to stay on good terms with the tribe's leaders. The murder had occurred near Kaskaskia. A letter from Harrison to Henry Dearborn early in December announced the carrying out of the execution (Harrison to secretary of war, 22 Oct., 3 Dec. 1801, noted in DNA: RG 107, RLRMS).

ESTABLISHMENT OF TROOPS: on 23 Feb. 1802, Dearborn informed Harrison that as a result of the petition from Kaskaskia and the information in Harrison's letter above, a company of soldiers would be posted in the vicinity of the settlement "as early in the spring as circumstances will permit" (*Terr. Papers*, 7:48-9).

The KICKAPOOS OF THE PRAIRIE lived in the watershed of the Sangamon and Illinois Rivers in what is now central Illinois. They were called "of the Prairie" to distinguish them from the other major band of Kickapoo Indians, who lived to the west of the Wabash River and were known as "of the Vermilion" (Sturtevant, *Handbook*, 15:596, 599, 657, 662).

Harrison had written letters touching on Indian affairs TO THE SECRETARY OF WAR on 1 Aug., 1, 26 Sept., 22 Oct., and 3 Dec. (noted in DNA: RG 107, RLRMS).

From Thomas Oben

Dublin, Decembr, the 30th, 1801
N. 49. Marlborough Street.

SIR,

As soon as the intelligence of your election to the Presidentship arrived here, I had the honour to adress you a letter, concerning some pictures of the best Italian masters: for I conceived, that an application of such a nature would be favourably received by a person, high in litterary fame, and considered both as a patron, and a connoisseur of the fine Arts. As I had spent many years in Italy, professing Architecture, & Mathematicks, I wished to ascertain what encouragement such sciences would receive in a city, destined to be the residence of the Government of a great nation; & whether there be reason to think, that posterity will apply to its buildings the high praising sentence "materiam superabat Opus."

Such an idea must naturally occur to every thinking man, before he would undertake so long, and (I may add) so perilous a navigation, as that from Europe thither: particularly considering the many stories, that are circulated in the european ports; tho' they be mere inventions calculated to prevent emigration. To be known to, or rather to seek the patronage & benevolence of a person in high authority, seemed to be a necessary and prudent step; & therefore I took the liberty to address you the above mentioned letter, which for more safety & expedition had been enclosed to his Excellency Rufus King, the american Minister in London, & who afterwards wrote of its having been forwarded.

Not hearing any more about it, I take the liberty to write this second: but would regret to find it were not satisfactory to that person, whose political sentiments have met with so many enthusiastic admirers, among whom there is none more ardent than

Your most obedient & most humble Servant

THOMAS OBEN LL.D.

RC (DLC); endorsed by TJ as received 20 Mch. 1802 and so recorded in SJL.

Oben's previous LETTER was dated 22 Apr. According to SJL, TJ responded neither to that letter nor to the one printed above.

MATERIAM SUPERABAT OPUS: "the workmanship was superior to the material" (Ovid, *Metamorphoses*, 2.5).

Presentation of the "Mammoth Cheese"

I. FROM THE COMMITTEE OF CHESHIRE, MASSACHUSETTS,
[30 DEC. 1801]

II. FROM THE COMMITTEE OF CHESHIRE, MASSACHUSETTS,
[1 JAN. 1802]

III. TO THE COMMITTEE OF CHESHIRE, MASSACHUSETTS,
[1 JAN. 1802]

EDITORIAL NOTE

On New Year's Day, 1802, Jefferson stood in the doorway of the President's House to receive a most unusual gift from the citizens of Cheshire, Massachusetts: an enormous wheel of cheese, measuring more than 4 feet in diameter and weighing an estimated 1,235 pounds. Derisively dubbed the "Mammoth Cheese" by the Federalist press, the giant Cheshire cheese had become a national celebrity by the time it was carted down Pennsylvania Avenue on the final leg of its journey to the president's door. Since its creation during the summer of 1801, newspapers across New England and the mid-Atlantic states had followed the progress of the Mammoth Cheese with either admiration or scorn, depending upon the political sympathies of the paper reporting. Republican editors portrayed the cheese as a sincere and selfless token of affection for the president and an admirable example of republican labor and ingenuity. Federalists ridiculed it as a ludicrous example of democratic excess and Jeffersonian idolatry. They filled their newspapers with poetry, satire, and puns inspired by the cheese, as well as proposals to create a "Mammoth Pye," a mammoth bread, and a mammoth cask of cider in emulation of the Cheshire example. Observing the ferocity of the Federalist outcry, the Pittsfield *Sun* opined that only Samuel Bishop's appointment as the New Haven collector had drawn forth as many "*federal* objections against the *New* Administration" as the gift of the Mammoth Cheese (Stockbridge *Western Star*, 14 Sep. 1801; Pittsfield *Sun*, 16 Nov. 1801; *Washington Federalist*, 31 Dec. 1801, 2 Jan. 1802; *New-York Herald*, 2 Jan. 1802; Newark, N.J., *Centinel of Freedom*, 12 Jan. 1802). For articles about the Mammoth Cheese and its significance, see C. A. Browne, "Elder John Leland and the Mammoth Cheshire Cheese," *Agricultural History*, 18 (1944), 145-53; L. H. Butterfield, "Elder John Leland, Jeffersonian Itinerant," *Proceedings of the American Antiquarian Society*, 62 (1952), 155-242, especially 214-29; John C. Harriman, ed., "'Most Excellent—far fam'd and far fetch'd Cheese': An Anthology of Jeffersonian Era Poetry," *American Magazine and Historical Chronicle*, 2 (1986-87), 1-26; Daniel L. Dreisbach, "Mr. Jefferson, a Mammoth Cheese, and the 'Wall of Separation Between Church and State': A Bicentennial Commemoration," *Journal of Church and State*, 43 (2001), 725-45; and Jeffrey L. Pasley, "The Cheese and the Words: Popular Political Culture and Participatory Democracy in the Early American Republic," in *Beyond the Founders: New Approaches to the Political History of the Early American Republic*, edited by Jeffrey L. Pasley, Andrew W. Robertson, and David Waldstreicher (Chapel Hill, 2004), 31-56.

Whatever their politics, newspapers across the country tracked the journey of the Mammoth Cheese overland from Cheshire to the Hudson River, thence by water to New York and Baltimore, and finally by wagon to the nation's capital. Accompanying the cheese were Darius Brown, the son of Cheshire committee chairman Daniel Brown, and the Reverend John Leland. A Baptist clergyman and ardent foe of established religion, Leland spent more than a decade in Virginia before returning to his native Massachusetts in 1791. Settling at Cheshire, his charismatic leadership helped transform the Baptist community into a zealous Republican bastion in a state otherwise dominated by Federalists (ANB; Browne, "Elder John Leland," 147, 150; Butterfield, "Elder John Leland," 196-202, 214-17).

Details regarding the presentation of the cheese are somewhat unclear. It arrived in Washington on 29 Dec. and was presented to Jefferson at the President's House on 1 Jan. 1802. According to surviving accounts, the presentation was accompanied by an exchange of addresses between Leland and the president. Two versions of the Cheshire committee's address survive. The first, Document I, is an undated contemporary copy of the signed address that was presented to the president. According to historian C. A. Browne, this unsigned copy, as well as Jefferson's reply, were retained by Daniel Brown, then passed down through his descendants and into the possession of William B. Browne (the historian's brother), from whom copies were obtained by the Editors of the Jefferson Papers. The documents are now housed at Chapin Library, Williams College. The missing signed recipient's copy of Document I is probably the letter that Jefferson recorded in SJL as received on 30 Dec. 1801 (Browne, "Elder John Leland," 150n).

The second version, Document II, appeared first in the Baltimore *American* under the dateline 10 Jan. 1802 (no copy of this issue has been found). The text was then reprinted by the *Aurora* (15 Jan.), *New-York Evening Post* (16 Jan.), *American Citizen* (18 Jan.), *National Intelligencer* (20 Jan.), *Gazette of the United States* (20 Jan.), and a host of other newspapers. Both Documents I and II are undated, but the latter is described in newspaper headnotes as being presented with the Mammoth Cheese on 1 Jan. 1802. Besides including the names of the Cheshire committee, Document II is also more partisan in tone and content, with pointed references to monarchy, the "late triumphant return of republicanism," the Alien and Sedition Acts, the provisional army, and revenue stamps. The description of the cheese as a "token" of esteem in Document I is more colorfully rendered as a "peppercorn" in the second version. Document II omits, however, the reference in Document I to the contributions by Cheshire's "wives and daughters" in making the cheese, an omission all the more curious since the earliest newspaper accounts of the cheese attributed its origin to the women of Leland's congregation. Accounting for the differences between the two versions is problematic, since it is not known how or where the *American* acquired its source text. Since the signed copy was presented to Jefferson, perhaps Leland supplied the *American* with a copy written from memory, or perhaps a representative from the newspaper was on hand to record the address as delivered by Leland. Given the impromptu nature of the presentation ceremony, Leland may have altered the address to better suit himself and the public nature of the occasion (Butterfield, "Elder John Leland," 219-20; Pasley, "The Cheese and the Words," 47-8).

Jefferson likely penned Document III in reply to Document I, which he received on 30 Dec., thus giving him two days to prepare his response. Some newspapers reported that his reply of 1 Jan. 1802 was made orally. If so, it was a rare instance of public speaking by the president, and one which drew the ire of Federalist editors for dignifying the Mammoth Cheese with an oration while addressing Congress by written message only. His decision to present it verbally, however, appears to have been a last minute one, imposed upon him by the appearance of Leland and the cheese at his very doorstep. According to the 7 Jan. 1802 edition of the *New-York Evening Post*, the situation left Jefferson feeling "some little embarrassment what to do with a Message which had been framed for the occasion, and was to have been sent to meet the Cheese." The president solved his dilemma by converting the message into a speech, "and read it aloud to Parson Leland, ingeniously changing the third person into the second as he went on" (Boston *Mercury and New-England Palladium*, 15 Jan. 1802; *Gazette of the United States*, 20 Jan. 1802; Pasley, "The Cheese and the Words," 35).

Following its reception, the Mammoth Cheese took up residence in the East Room of the President's House, resting on a custom frame prepared by Washington artisan Peter Lenox. In accordance with his practice of refusing gifts while president, Jefferson paid Leland $200 for the cheese. Portions were distributed at Independence Day gatherings in Washington in 1802 and 1803, while another account asserted that a large piece was served with the "Mammoth Loaf" presented to Congress in March 1804. Congressman Samuel L. Mitchill recorded that the cheese was still being served at the President's House as late as New Year's Day, 1805. A section was displayed in Boston in August 1802, and Congressman Richard Stanford reportedly distributed a piece among his North Carolina constituents the following year. Decay also contributed to the diminution of the cheese. By June 1802, reports circulated that "Skippers" (maggots) had invaded it. Visiting the cheese on New Year's Day, 1803, Massachusetts congressman Manasseh Cutler was informed that 60 pounds had been removed due to spoilage. The fate of the final remnants of the Mammoth Cheese is uncertain. Conflicting accounts claim that the last of it was served in 1805, or that it was dumped into the Potomac River (MB, 2:1062, 1069; Baltimore *Republican or, Anti-Democrat*, 14 June 1802; *National Intelligencer and Washington Advertiser*, 7 July 1802, 8 July 1803; *Boston Gazette*, 5 Aug. 1802; Boston *New-England Palladium*, 8 Apr. 1803; *New-Hampshire Sentinel*, 14 Apr. 1804; Samuel L. Mitchill to Catharine Mitchill, 2 Jan. 1805, in NNMus; Butterfield, "Elder John Leland," 227-9; Pasley, "The Cheese and the Words," 35, 36).

Historians of Jefferson have generally portrayed the saga of the Mammoth Cheese as a memorable, yet largely insignificant, episode of his presidency. But his contemporaries, both Federalist and Republican, understood its political implications. Like the Baptists of Danbury, Connecticut (to whom Jefferson also replied on 1 Jan. 1802), the Cheshire Baptists presented themselves as an oppressed minority who saw in Jefferson's election a promising new era of political and religious liberty. Jeffrey L. Pasley posits that the Mammoth Cheese was more than just a "colorful stunt" and should more properly be considered as a "political expression and mobilization of people who would never write a philosophical essay or give an oration" (Pasley, "The Cheese and the Words," 45; Dreisbach, "Mr. Jefferson, a Mammoth Cheese, and the Wall of Separation," 743-5).

I. From the Committee of Cheshire, Massachusetts

SIR   [30 Dec. 1801]

Notwithstanding we live remote from the seat of our national government, & in an extreme part of our own state, yet we humbly claim the right of judging for ourselves.

Our attachment to the National Constitution is indissoluble. We consider it as a discription of those powers which the people have delegated to their Magistrates, to be exercised for definite purposes; and not as a charter of favors granted by a Sovereign to his subjects.

Among its beautiful features,—The right of free suffrage, to correct all abuses—The prohibition of religious tests, to prevent all hierarchy—and the means of amendment which it contains within itself, to remove defects as fast as they are discovered, appear the most prominent.

Such being the sentiments which we entertain, our joy must have been exquisite on your appointment to the first office in the nation.

The trust is great. The task is arduous. But we believe the Supreme Ruler of the Universe, who raises up men to achieve great events, has raised up a *Jefferson* at this critical day, to defend *Republicanism*, and to baffle the arts of *Aristocracy*.

We wish to prove the love we bear to our President not by words alone, but in *deed and in truth*. With this Address we send you a Chees by the hands of Messrs. John Leland and Darius Brown, as a token of the esteem which we bear to our chief Magistrate, and of the sense we entertain[1] of the singular blessings that have been derived from the numerous services you have rendered to mankind in general, and more especially to this favored nation over which you preside. It is not the last stone of the Bastile; nor is it an article of great pecuniary worth; but as a freewill-offering, we hope it will be favorably received.

The Chees was produced by the personal labor of *Freeborn Farmers*, with the voluntary and cheerful aid of their wives and daughters, without the assistance of a single slave. It was originally intended for an elective President of a free people, and with a principal view of casting a mite into the even scale of *Federal Democracy*. We hope it will safely arrive at it's destined place, and that it's quality will prove to be such as may not disappoint the wishes of those who made it.

To that infinite Being who governs the Universe we ardently pray, that your life and health may long be preserved—that your usefulness may be still continued—that your Administration may be no less pleasant to yourself than it is grateful to us and to the nation at large, and that the blessing of generations yet unborn may come upon you.

In behalf of ourselves and our fellow citizens of Cheshire, we render you the tribute of profound respect.

N.B. The chees above mentioned was made July 20. 1801, and on the 20th of August it weighed 1235℔.

FC (MWiW-C); undated; at head of text: "To Thomas Jefferson, President of the United States of America." Recorded in SJL as received 30 Dec. 1801.

[1] MS: "entain."

II. From the Committee of Cheshire, Massachusetts

SIR,   [1 Jan. 1802]

Notwithstanding we live remote from the seat of the national government, and in an extreme part of our own state; yet we humbly claim the right of judging for ourselves.

Our attachment to the national constitution is strong and indissoluble.[1] We consider it a description of those *powers*, which the people have submitted to their magistrates, to be exercised for *definite* purposes, and not a charter of favors, granted by a sovereign to his subjects.—Among its beautiful features, the right of free suffrage, to correct all abuses—The prohibition of religious tests, to prevent all hierarchy—The means of amendment, which it contains within itself, to remove defects as fast as they are discovered, appear the most prominent. But for several years past, our apprehension[2] has been, that the genius of the government was not attended to in sundry cases; and that the administration bordered upon monarchy: Our joy, of course must have been great, on your election to the first office in the nation; having had good evidence, from your announced sentiments and uniform conduct that it would be your strife and glory to turn back the government, to its virgin purity. The trust is great! The task is arduous! But we console ourselves, that the supreme ruler of the universe, who raises up men to achieve[3] great events, has raised up a Jefferson for this critical day, to defend republicanism and baffle all the arts of aristocracy.

Sir, we have attempted to prove our love to our president, not in words alone, but in deeds and truth. With this address, we send you a CHEESE, by the hands of Messrs. John Leland and Darius Brown, as a pepper-corn of the esteem which we bear to our chief magistrate, and as a sacrifice to republicanism. It is not the last stone in the Bastile, nor is it of any great consequence as an article of worth; but as a free-will offering, we hope it will be received. The cheese was not made by his lordship, for his sacred majesty; nor with a view to gain dignified titles or lucrative offices; but by the personal labour of free-born farmers (without a single slave to assist) for an elective president of a free people—with the only view of casting a mite into the scale of democracy.

The late triumphant return of republicanism has more animated the inhabitants of Cheshire, to bear the burthens of government, and treat the characters and persons of those in authority with all due respect, than the long list of alien—sedition—naval, and provisional army laws, ever did.

Sir, we had some thoughts of impressing some significant inscription on the cheese; but we have found such inconveniency in STAMPS on paper, that we chose to send it in a plain republican form.

May God long preserve your life and health, for a blessing to the United States, and the world at large.

Signed by order of all Cheshire,

DANIEL BROWN
HEZEKIAH MASON
JONA. RICHARDSON ⎬ Committee.
JOHN WATERMAN
JOHN WELLS, JUN.

P.S. The cheese was made, July 20, 1801.—Weight 1235 lbs.

Printed in the Philadelphia *Aurora*, 15 Jan. 1802; at head of text: "The Greatest Cheese In America, For The Greatest Man In America."

[1] *Aurora*: "indissoluble."
[2] *Aurora*: "apprehensions."
[3] *Aurora*: "atchieve."

III. To the Committee of Cheshire, Massachusetts

GENTLEMEN   [1 Jan. 1802]

I concur with you in the sentiments expressed in your kind address on behalf of the inhabitants of the town of Cheshire, that the constitution of the United States is a Charter of authorities and duties, not a Charter of rights to it's officers; and that among it's most precious provisions are the right of suffrage, the prohibition of religious tests, and it's means of peaceable amendment. nothing ensures the duration of this fair fabric of government so effectually as the due sense entertained, by the body of our citizens, of the value of these principles, & their care to preserve them.

I recieve, with particular pleasure, the testimony of good will with which your citizens have been pleased to charge you.[1] it presents an extraordinary proof of the skill with which those domestic arts, which contribute so much to our daily comfort, are practised by them, and particularly by that portion of them most interesting to the affections, the cares & the happiness of man.

To myself, this mark of esteem from freeborn farmers, employed personally in the useful labors of life, is peculiarly grateful. having no wish but to preserve to them the fruits of their labour, their sense of this truth will be my highest reward.

I pray you, gentlemen, to make my thanks for their favor acceptable to them, & to be assured yourselves of my high respect and esteem.   TH: JEFFERSON

RC (MWiW-C); undated; at head of text: "To Messrs. Daniel Brown, Hezekiah Mason, Jonathan Richardson, John Waterman and John Wells junr. a committee of the town of Cheshire in Massachusets." PrC (DLC); dated by TJ in ink "Jan. 1. 1802."

[1] PrC: TJ here interlined in ink "for me."

Reply to the Danbury Baptist Association

I. DRAFT REPLY TO THE DANBURY BAPTIST ASSOCIATION
[ON OR BEFORE 31 DEC. 1801]

II. FROM GIDEON GRANGER [31 DEC. 1801]

III. TO LEVI LINCOLN, 1 JAN. 1802

IV. FROM LEVI LINCOLN, 1 JAN. 1802

V. TO THE DANBURY BAPTIST ASSOCIATION, 1 JAN. 1802

EDITORIAL NOTE

On the first day of the new year, Jefferson prepared the final version of his response to an October address from the Danbury Baptist Association, a group of 26 churches in western Connecticut and eastern New York. He had received the address only two days earlier, almost three months after it was written, on the same day that a wheel of cheese from the citizens of Cheshire, Massachusetts, another predominantly Baptist New England town, arrived in Washington. He began to draft his answer to the Baptists right away. John Leland, the itinerant preacher who presented the cheese and the Danbury address on 30 Dec. to the president, had a theological affinity with Nehemiah Dodge of the Danbury Baptist Association and, like Jefferson and Madison, was an advocate for religious freedom in Virginia in the late 1780s. Leland might have been asked to deliver the Danbury Baptists' address in person to Jefferson, which could account for its delay in reaching the federal city (L. H. Butterfield, "Elder John Leland, Jeffersonian Itinerant," *Proceedings of the American Antiquarian Society*, 62 [1952]`, 189, 207; John Leland, *Some Events in the Life of John Leland* [Pittsfield, Mass., 1838], 31, 32; William G. McLoughlin, *New England Dissent, 1630-1833: The Baptists and Separation of Church and State,* 2 vols. [Cambridge, Mass., 1971], 2:930; Hartford *Connecticut Courant*, 8 Feb. 1802; From the Danbury Baptist Association, [after 7 Oct. 1801], in Vol. 35:407-9; Presentation of the "Mammoth Cheese," above).

The convergence of the arrival of Massachusetts citizens bringing the cheese, the address of the Danbury Baptists, and the New Year's Day public reception at the President's House provided an ideal occasion for Jefferson to express his thoughts on the place of religion in American civil society. Jefferson seems to have been writing directly to New Englanders, but also for a national audience. He knew of the appointment by the United States House of Representatives of its first Baptist chaplain and he was keenly aware of the "antient habit" of proclaiming days of thanksgiving in the New England states (Margaret Bayard Smith, *The First Forty Years of Washington Society*, ed. Gaillard Hunt [New York, 1906], 397-8, 400; JHR, 4:13; Robert V. Remini, *The House: The History of the House of Representatives* [New York, 2006], 513).

Jefferson began to prepare his reply, consulted with Republicans Gideon

Granger and Levi Lincoln, who were knowledgeable about the New England constituents, and requested their prompt attention and critique of his draft reply (see Documents II, III, and IV). Both men expeditiously reviewed the president's draft and returned their comments, with Granger recommending no changes and Lincoln advising Jefferson to be more guarded in his discussion of fast days. Heeding that advice, Jefferson removed a sentence from the draft, just as he had taken a passage out of his annual message in response to comments from members of the cabinet (see Document II, note 5, and Vol. 35:616-7, 647-8, 650n). Jefferson also invited William Eustis, a moderate Republican congressman from Massachusetts who could offer insights on the New England political climate, to dine with him on New Year's Day (TJ to William Eustis, 30 Dec. 1801).

Jefferson's surviving papers give no indication that he consulted with other congressmen or cabinet members on crafting his response. Whatever conversations he may have had on the matter including those with Secretary of State Madison, a friend and fellow Virginian with whom Jefferson might very well have discussed the free exercise of religion, have gone unrecorded.

Jefferson's New Year's reply to the Danbury Baptists does not seem to have appeared in the Washington press at all. Its first known publication was on 18 Jan. 1802 in Denniston and Cheetham's New York newspaper, *American Citizen*. The minutes of the Danbury Baptist Association make no mention of the president's reply to their address, and it received little coverage in Connecticut newspapers (Hartford *American Mercury*, 28 Jan. 1802; New London *Bee*, 3 Feb. 1802; *Minutes of the Danbury Baptist Association, Held at Wallingford, October 6 and 7, 1802; Together with Their Circular and Corresponding Letters* [New Haven, 1802]; Shaw-Shoemaker, No. 1812). Yet the letter, with its now-famous phrase of the "wall of separation between church and state," continues to be reprinted, reinterpreted, and debated to this day.

I. Draft Reply to the Danbury Baptist Association

GENTLEMEN [on or before 31 Dec. 1801]

The affectionate sentiments of esteem & approbation which you are so good to express towards me on behalf of the Danbury Baptist association, give me the highest satisfaction, my duties dictate a faithful & zealous pursuit of the interests of my constituents, and in proportion as they are persuaded of my fidelity to those duties, the discharge of them becomes more & more pleasing.

Believing with you that religion is a matter which lies solely between man & his god, that he owes account to none other for his faith or his worship, that the legitimate powers of government reach actions only[1] and not opinions, I contemplate with sovereign reverence that act of the whole American people which declared that *their* legislature should make no law respecting an establishment of religion, or prohibiting the free exercise thereof; thus building a wall of[2] separation between church and state. Congress thus inhibited from acts respecting religion and the Executive authorised only to execute their acts, I have refrained from prescribing even[3] occasional performances of devotion prescribed indeed legally where an Executive is the legal head of a national church,[4] but subject here, as religious exercises only to the voluntary regulations and discipline of each respective sect.[5] Adhering to this expression of the supreme will of the nation in behalf of the rights of conscience[6] I shall see with sincere satisfaction[7] the progress of those sentiments which tend to restore to man all his natural rights, convinced he has no natural right in opposition to his social duties.

I reciprocate your kind prayers for the protection and blessing of the common father and creator of man, and tender you for yourselves and your religious[8] association, assurances of my high respect & esteem.

TH: JEFFERSON

Dft (DLC); at head of text: "To messrs. Nehemiah Dodge, Ephraim Robbins, & Stephen S. Nelson a committee of the Danbury Baptist association in the state of Connecticut"; note in margin written after TJ's receipt of Document IV, TJ also marking a sentence for deletion (see note 5 below); TJ added "Jan. 1. 1802." below his signature.

PERFORMANCES OF DEVOTION: in October 1801, in accordance with their annual practice, the governors of New Hampshire, Massachusetts, and Connecticut issued proclamations for the observance of 26 Nov. as a day of public thanksgiving. Rhode Island appointed no set day, but "left every one to pray on such day, and in such manner, as their consciences should tell them was best." Several religious societies in Newport voluntarily agreed to observe 26 Nov. as a day of thanksgiving (Hudson, N.Y., *Balance, and Columbian Repository*, 26 Nov. 1801; *Boston Gazette*, 26 Nov.; Newport *Rhode-Island Republican*, 12 Dec.).

News of the ratification of the peace treaty with France prompted speculation that TJ would proclaim a national day of thanksgiving (Boston *Columbian Centinel*, 28 Nov. 1801). For an interpretation of the fast day implications of TJ's reply

to the Danbury Baptists, see James Hutson, "'A Wall of Separation': FBI Helps Restore Jefferson's Obliterated Draft," *Library of Congress Information Bulletin*, 57 (1998), 136-9, 163. Other recent studies of TJ's response can be found in the "Forum" on TJ's letter to the Danbury Baptists in wMQ, 3d ser., 56 (1999), 775-824; Daniel L. Dreisbach, *Thomas Jefferson and the Wall of Separation between Church and State* (New York, 2002), especially 9-54, 142-8; Philip Hamburger, *Separation of Church and State* (Cambridge, Mass., 2002), especially 155-80; and Johann N. Neem, "Beyond the Wall: Reinterpreting Jefferson's Danbury Address," *Journal of the Early Republic*, 27 (2007), 139-54.

[1] Word written over partially erased, illegible word.

[2] TJ here canceled "eternal."

[3] TJ here canceled "those."

[4] TJ first wrote "practiced indeed by the Executive of another nation as the legal head of the church" before altering the passage to read as above.

[5] TJ circled the preceding sentence and wrote in the margin: "this paragraph was omitted on the suggestion that it might give uneasiness to some of our republican friends in the eastern states where the

proclamation of thanksgivings &c by their Executive is an antient habit, & is respected."

⁶ Sentence to this point interlined in place of "confining myself therefore to the duties of my station, which are merely temporal, be assured that your religious rights shall never be infringed by any act

of mine and that" and "*Concurring with* adhering to this great act of National legislation in behalf of the rights of conscience."

⁷ Preceding two words interlined in place of "friendly dispositions."

⁸ Preceding two words interlined in place of "the Danbury Baptist."

II. From Gideon Granger

[31 Dec. 1801]

G Granger presents his compliments to The Presidt. and assures him he has carefully & attentively perused the inclosed Address & Answer—The answer will undoubtedly give great Offence to the established Clergy of New England while it will delight the Dissenters as they are called. It is but a declaration of Truths which are in fact felt by a great Majority of New England, & publicly acknowledged by near half of the People of Connecticut; It may however occasion a temporary Spasm among the Established Religionists yet his mind approves of it, because it will "germinate among the People" and in time fix "their political Tenets"—He cannot therefore wish a Sentence changed, or a Sentiment expressed equivocally—A more fortunate time can never be expected.—

RC (DLC); undated; endorsed by TJ as received 31 Dec. and so recorded in SJL. Enclosures: (1) Danbury Baptist Association to TJ, [after 7 Oct. 1801]. (2) Document I.

III. To Levi Lincoln

Tʜ:J. ᴛᴏ ᴍʀ. Lɪɴᴄᴏʟɴ   Jan. 1. 1802.

Averse to recieve addresses, yet unable to prevent them, I have generally endeavored to turn them to some account, by making them the occasion by way of answer, of sowing useful truths & principles among the people, which might germinate and become rooted among their political tenets. the Baptist address now inclosed admits of[1] a condemnation of the alliance between church and state, under the authority of the Constitution. it furnishes an occasion too, which I have long wished to find, of saying why I do not proclaim fastings & thanksgivings, as my predecessors did. the address to be sure does not point at this, and it's introduction is awkward, but I foresee no opportunity of doing it more pertinently. I know it will give great offence to the New England clergy. but the advocate for religious freedom is to expect neither peace nor forgiveness from them. will you be so good as to examine the answer and suggest any alterations which might prevent an ill effect, or promote a good one among *the people*? you understand the temper of those in the North, and can weaken it therefore to their stomachs: it is at present seasoned to the Southern taste only. I would ask the favor of you to return it with the address in the course of the day or evening. health & affection.

PrC (DLC). Enclosures: (1) Danbury Baptist Association to TJ, [after 7 Oct. 1801]. (2) Document I.

[1] TJ here canceled "laying down the principle of."

IV. From Levi Lincoln

Jany 1. 1802—

Sir I have carefully considered the subject you did me the honor of submiting to my attention. The people of the five N England Governments (unless Rhode Island is an exception) have always been in the habit of observing fasts and thanksgivings in "pursuance of proclamations from their respective Executives." This custom is venerable being handed down from our ancestors. The Republicans of those States generally have a respect for it. They regreted very much the late conduct of the legislature of Rhode Island on this subject. I think the religious sentiment expressed in your proposed answer of importance to be communicated, but that it would be best to have it so guarded, as to be incapable of having it construed into an implied censure of the usages of any of the States. Perhaps the following alteration after the words "but subject here" would be sufficient, viz, only to the voluntary regulations & discipline of each respective sect, as mere religious exercises, and to the particular situations, usages & recommendations of the several States, in point of time & local circumstances. with the highest esteem & respect yours

LEVI LINCOLN

RC (DLC); first closing quotation mark supplied; at head of text: "The President of the U States"; endorsed by TJ as received 1 Jan. and so recorded in SJL.

V. To the Danbury Baptist Association

GENTLEMEN   Jan. 1. 1802.

The affectionate sentiments of esteem and approbation which you are so good as to express towards me, on behalf of the Danbury Baptist association, give me the highest satisfaction. my duties dictate a faithful & zealous pursuit of the interests of my constituents, & in proportion as they are persuaded of my fidelity to those duties, the discharge of them becomes more and more pleasing.

Believing with you that religion is a matter which lies solely between Man & his God, that he owes account to none other for his faith or his worship, that the legitimate powers of government reach actions only, & not opinions, I contemplate with sovereign reverence that act of the whole American people which declared that *their* legislature should "make no law respecting an establishment of religion, or prohibiting the free exercise thereof," thus building a wall of separation between Church & State. adhering to this expression of the supreme will of the nation in behalf of the rights of conscience, I shall see with sincere satisfaction the progress of those sentiments which tend to restore to man all his natural rights, convinced he has no natural right in opposition to his social duties.

I reciprocate your kind prayers for the protection & blessing of the common father and creator of man, and tender you for yourselves & your religious association, assurances of my high respect & esteem.

TH: JEFFERSON

PrC (DLC); at head of text: "To messrs. Nehemiah Dodge, Ephraim Robbins, & Stephen S. Nelson, a committee of the Danbury Baptist association in the state of Connecticut."

LEGITIMATE POWERS OF GOVERN-MENT REACH ACTIONS ONLY, & NOT OPINIONS: TJ expressed similar sentiments in his 1779 draft bill for establishing religious freedom, "the opinions of men are not the object of civil government, nor under its jurisdiction" (Vol. 2:545-53).

A Bill for the Relief of Sufferers under Certain Illegal Prosecutions

[1801]

A Bill for the relief of sufferers under certain illegal prosecutions[1]

Whereas the constitution of the US. has provided that 'Congress shall make no law abridging the freedom of speech or of the press,' and that 'the powers not delegated to the US. by the constitution, nor prohibited by it to the States, are reserved to the states respectively or to the people;' and Congress did nevertheless on the 14th. day of July 1798. pass an act intituled 'an act in addition to the act intituled an act for the punishment of certain crimes against the US.' which did 'abridge the freedom of the press,' and did assume the exercise of 'a power not delegated to the US. by the constitution nor prohibited to the states' & consequently 'reserved to them respectively or to the people;' and sundry citizens, under colour of the said act, tho' unauthorised & null by the constitution, suffered prosecutions, fines & imprisonments, in violation of rights never placed under the controul of the General government.[2]

And whereas the Constitution of the US. hath enumerated specially all the cases to which 'the judicial power of the US. shall extend,' and the statutes of the US. have declared how, & what, crimes, shall be punishable in their courts, and certain courts of the US. have nevertheless taken cognisance of cases other than those specially enumerated in the constitution, & have punished citizens for acts not declared criminal or punishable by the statutes of the US. deducing their authority from what they have denominated a *Common law*, binding on all these US. whereby a code of crimes would be imposed, & a system of laws recognised, placing in jeopardy the lives, liberty, property & reputation of the citizens of these US.[3] and deriving no sanction from their will:[4]

Be it therefore enacted by the Senate & H. of R. of the US. of America in Congress assembled, that every person who has suffered prosecution, fine or imprisonment under colour of the said act of Congress commonly called the Sedition act, or for acts not declared criminal or punishable by the statutes of the US[5] shall be authorised to petition the court wherein such prosecution was carried on, or such judgment of fine or imprisonment was rendered, praying for a writ of enquiry into the damages they have[6] sustained by[7] such prosecution fine or imprisonment, whereon a jury shall be empanelled in the usual form, and judgment shall be rendered according to their verdict: and that the party complaining shall be entitled to recieve out of any monies in the treasury of the US. not otherwise appropriated, the amount of the damages which may be so assessed & adjudged to them, with the legal costs of the said suit for redress.

MS (DLC: TJ Papers, 232:42028); entirely in TJ's hand, with a wide margin for revisions; undated, but see below.

It seems likely that TJ drafted the above document sometime during 1801 with the intention of submitting it to the first session of the Seventh Congress, in which Republicans held a majority in both houses. Pinpointing a precise date of composition is problematic. The subject of the Sedition Act and its victims arose early and often during the first year of TJ's presidency, as manifested by the pardons issued to David Brown and James Thomson Callender, the decision to halt the prosecution against William Duane, and the denunciation of the act that TJ removed from his first message to Congress. Any of these events may have inspired TJ to draft the above document, or he may have waited until after Congress convened on 7 Dec. No evidence has been found to indicate that this bill was ever introduced in the House or Senate (Vol. 33:251-2, 309-10; Vol. 34:169-70, 597-8; Vol. 35:125, 543-4, 616-17, 635, 640, 647-8).

¹ Preceding three words inserted in place of "the act of Congress commonly called the Sedition act."

² TJ first wrote "in violation of their rights secured to them by the constitution," then altered it to "in violation of rights never submitted to the General government," and finally altered it to read as above.

³ TJ first wrote "the citizens of these US. tho' not sanctioned by their will: as *delivered* expressed in the constitution, or by their legislative organs:" before altering the remainder of the paragraph to read as above.

⁴ Preceding paragraph written by TJ in left margin.

⁵ Passage interlined from "commonly called" to this point.

⁶ Preceding two words written over an illegible erasure.

⁷ TJ here interlined, then erased, "the defendants under."

From James Dinsmore

SIR   Monticello Jany 1st 1802

Your favor of 17th Dec. is recived & contents noted. the Size of the Pannel is 5 feet 4 in we did not get a fair trial in the Making of it. as well as I remember I Calculated we Could Make one per day, if of pine & put together in the Manner of the one done. but I expect they will have to be put together differently on account of the tonngue & groove giveing way by wetting, so that Some allowance May be Made. I Cannot well say how much as I am not Certain yet what Method of putting them together will have to be Substituted. Mr Wanschaw is latheing the Cellar under the Squre room, next to the one already plaistered. & intends plaistering it he says the frost will not Injure it.—I will be obliged to take down the Studding rond the Sky light of the dineing room & the Counter Ceiling, to get the joist raised. they are Sunk 4 ins

with respect I am Sir   J D.

nails made from the 12th to the 24th Dec Inclusive

℔

X.	285.6	}	Amnt. Sold in Same time £12.	0	7½
XI	70 9				
	356.5	}	Cash recd		0.12

FC (ViU: Monticello); in Dinsmore's hand; at foot of text: "Mr Jefferson"; on same sheet as letters of 12 Dec. 1801, 23 Jan., and 12 Feb. 1802. Recorded in SJL as a letter of 2 Jan. received on the 6th.

YOUR FAVOR: TJ's letter of 17 Dec. 1801, recorded in SJL, has not been found.

MR WANSCHAW: that is, Martin Wanscher.

To John Wayles Eppes

DEAR SIR   Washington Jan. 1. 1802.

I wrote to Maria on the 14th. of Dec. My occupations are now so incessant that I cannot command a moment for my friends. 7. hours of close business in the forepart of the day, and 4. in the evening leave little time for exercise or relaxation.

Congress have not yet done anything, nor passed a vote which has produced a party division. the sending a message, instead of making a speech to be answered, is acknowleged to have had the best effect towards preserving harmony. the real strength of the two parties in the H. of R. is 66. & 37. it would be 69. but that Dawson is absent & Sumpter's place vacant. in the Senate it would be 18. & 14. were all here. but hitherto we have been so nearly equal there, that I have not ventured to send in my nominations, lest they should be able to dismast the administration.—the expedition from France against St. Domingo, of 40,000. men, is probably sailed. until the island is reduced, it is probable our supplies of provision, except to their fleet & army, will be prohibited.

The Mammoth cheese is arrived here, & is to be presented to-day. it is 4. f. $4\frac{1}{2}$ I. in diameter, 15. I. thick, & in August weighed 1230. ℔. it is an ebullition of republicanism in a state where it has been under heavy oppression. that state of things however is rapidly passing away, and there is a speedy prospect of seeing all the New England states come round to their antient principles; always excepting the real Monarchists & the Priests, who never can lose sight of the natural alliance between the crown & mitre.—are you laying off our counties into hundreds or captaincies? there can be no other basis of republican energy. police, justice, elections, musters, schools, and many other essential things can have no other effectual bottom. there is not a single political measure for our state which I have so much at heart. the captain or headborough would be there what the Serjeants are in an army; the finger of execution. I shall be glad to hear what you are doing, and how you do. health & affectionate attachment.

TH: JEFFERSON

P.S. I inclose you a pamphlet giving an account of the waterproof invention for cloths, paper &c. and a piece of waterproof paper, one half only being so. the prices of preparation are so moderate, that if the cloth be not injured it will be of real utility. I have a surtout coat, which I have found entirely effectual against rain.

RC (ViU); at foot of first page: "J. W. Eppes." Enclosures: see enclosure listed at TJ to Thomas Mann Randolph, 4 Dec. 1801.

John DAWSON of Virginia did not take his seat in the House of Representatives until 14 Jan. 1802. Thomas Sumter

(SUMPTER), Sr., of South Carolina resigned his House seat on 15 Dec. 1801 in order to fill the Senate vacancy created by the resignation of Charles Pinckney. Sumter was replaced in the House by Richard Winn, who did not take his seat until 24 Jan. 1803 (JHR, 4:51; *Biog. Dir. Cong.*, 66).

To Thomas Mann Randolph

TH:J. TO TMR.   Washington Jan. 1. 1802.

I inclose you a pamphlet giving some account of the new operation of making cloths &c. waterproof; as also a piece of paper, one half of which is waterproof. I have recieved cloth for a surtout coat, which I find, on wearing it in rain, to answer perfectly. the prices for making cloathes waterproof are so moderate, that if it does not injure the quality of the stuff, it will become extensively useful. — the Mammoth cheese is arrived here and is to be presented this day. it is 4 f $4\frac{1}{2}$ I. diameter, 15. I. thick, and weighed in August 1230. ℔. They were offered 1000. D. in New York for the use of it 12. days as a shew. it is an ebullition of the passion of republicanism in a state where it has been under heavy persecution.

By a letter from Stewart at Monticello, I find his company of boys very much reduced. as I am not able to judge here of the causes of this I must ask the favor of you to ride over and decide who of them may be better employed elsewhere (say with Lilly) and have the rest placed in the nailhouse.

Congress have not yet done any thing, nor passed a vote which has produced a division. the sending a message instead of making a speech to be answered, is acknoleged to have had the best effect towards preserving harmony. the real strength in the H. of R. is 66. against 37. two being absent, both republicans. in the Senate it would be 18. & 14. were all here. but there has hitherto been a tye, so that I have not been able to send in the general list of nominations. — the expedition from France against St. Domingo has probably sailed before now. it is of 40,000. men. till it is reduced we shall probably be allowed only to send provisions to the fleet & army.

The last letter I have recieved from Edgehill is of Dec. 6. however the children were then past all danger. my tenderest love to my dear Martha, and affectionate attachment to yourself.

RC (DLC); endorsed by Randolph. Enclosures: see enclosure listed at TJ to Randolph, 4 Dec. 1801.

The LETTER FROM William STEWART to TJ of 16 Dec., recorded in SJL as received a week later, has not been found.

TJ's reply of 24 Dec., recorded in SJL, is also missing.

LAST LETTER: Randolph's letter to TJ of 6 Dec., recorded in SJL as received from Edgehill on the 9th, has not been found.

From Philip Turner

[. . .]   New York 1st Janry: 1802

Pray let my situation apologies for my troubling your excellency to listen a minute to my wishes, at this blessed period, when you are on the minds of the people (all in all) serving the whole race of mankind, on the general scale of Justice and political happiness, especially our own national concerns &c, and those who realy suffer persecution in consequence of our late exertions, I am a distinguished man in favor of our present glorious administration, have left my native home, domestic happiness, and an extensive practice of Physic and surgery, to get away from the bitter envious, and mischievous Clergy of Connecticut, who I have been publicly abused by, all on Acct. of Electioneering, I have resided in N:York for twelve months past where I would wish to continue and move my family, the medical department of the United States is an expensive one, some experienced gentleman appointed (at the Head) to superintend the practice of physic and surgery and direct its affairs may be of great use, in our late revolution of this country from the first Action of Bunker-Hill, I served to the close, was appointed as Surgn. Genl. of the eastern department by congress as appears by their Journals, if it should be tho't best to appoint, I shall be happy to serve in that charactor or any other where the public may be benefited, it frequently happens here in this City the landing of Sick &c, by our navy which requires constant medical attendance and no one particular appointed for that purpose, if I might be Honrd. by your excellency in an appointment, or requested by letter from either of our secretarys of War or Navy to the discharge of that duty, it will be most gratefully Acknowledged, at a monthly pay or the keeping of a running Acct. of Services and medicine (occasionally) certified to, and settled by our Agent here as Customary—

Your Excellency's most Obedient and very Humble servt,

P: Turner

The Honble. Genl. Bradley Esqr. and the Honble. Gideon Granger Esqr. are both my friends who will do every thing to serve   P:T—

RC (DNA: RG 59, LAR); upper left corner clipped. Recorded in SJL as received 8 Jan. with the notation "to be employed medically."

Philip Turner (1740-1815), a physician and surgeon, was born in Norwich, Connecticut. During the Revolutionary War, Turner attended Connecticut troops until the Continental Congress in 1777 appointed him surgeon general of the military hospital of the eastern department. In 1780, Congress reorganized the army's medical department, abolished Turner's office, and assigned him as hospital physician and surgeon. After he retired from the army in 1781, he sought back pay with interest from the U.S. government. In 1805, Turner wrote to TJ to ask him to assist the claim. An act passed by Congress on 22 Apr. 1808 allowed Turner compensation at a rate determined by his last position with the army. From 1809 until his death, Turner served as an army surgeon in New York City and its harbor (Charles B. Graves, "Dr. Philip Turner of Norwich, Connecticut," *Annals of Medical History*, 10 [1928], 15, 17-23; Washington, *Papers, Rev. War Ser.*, 2:321n; ASP, *Claims*, 1:394; U.S. Senate, *Report of the Committee on the Petition of Philip Turner, Late Surgeon General in the Revolutionary War* [Washington, 1808]; U.S. *Statutes at Large*, 6:73; Turner to TJ, 10 Oct. 1805).

Turner RESIDED at 426 Pearl Street in New York City in 1802 (*Longworth's American Almanac, New-York Register and City-Directory for the Twenty-Seventh Year of American Independence* [New York, 1802], 337).

A letter from Turner to TJ of 26 Mch. 1802, recorded in SJL as received 31 Mch. from New York with the notation "to be in Medical line," has not been found.

From Caspar Wistar

Dear Sir   Philada. Jany. 1—1802.

The fear of intruding upon you at a time when you had not leisure, & the belief that you seldom have leisure now, have prevented me so long from offering you my sincere thanks for your kindness in the appointment of Mr Dobell—I hope & believe that he will merit your confidence, and am certain that he will ever retain a grateful sense of it—Since my last I have been favoured with two notes from you inclosing communications for the Philosophical Society, which were delivered accordingly, & will appear in our Sixth Volume now going to the Press, altho the fifth is not yet published, owing to copper plate work which however is at length done—

Mr. Peale has erected the Skeleton of the Mammoth & commenced an exhibition of it. It resembles greatly the Skeleton of the Elephant, & particularly in some points where the Elephant differs from other Quadrupeds, as in the large size of the lower end of the Ulna, & the figure of some of the bones of the hind foot—The tusks however are very different, they are not only longer but have a particular twist or tendency to a spiral direction, like the horns of some Cows, so that they cannot lay flat on a level surface—this appears to be the case with the tusks found in Siberia represented in one of the volumes of the Abridgement of the Transactions of the Royal Society—Your suggestion that these bones were similar to those found in Siberia was very happy, especially as so few of the American bones at that time had been found—There certainly was another large Animal in both countries, you know we have other teeth as large as those of the Mammoth but constructed differently, having a resemblance in their structure to those of the Elephant, but differing materially in the size of the transverse Septa of enamel, which form the ridges of that Substance upon the grinding surface of the tooth. A figure of this tooth is also to be seen in the plate above mentioned which contains the view of the Spiral tusk from Siberia—A tooth of this kind, & also a Mammoths tooth, & some fragments of bones have been found in digging the canal at Santee in South Carolina. We must endeavour to procure the Skeleton of this Animal, & no man is so likely to be successful as Mr Peale for I believe no other in the U.S would have compleated the Skeleton of the Mammoth—Two great Animals existing formerly in America & Siberia give additional importance to the Sagacious remark of Buffon respecting those animals which are common to both Continents.

Your valuable time is now occupied with so many more important subjects that I ought only to add the assurance of the greatest regard & attachment of your obliged friend   C. WISTAR JUNR.

RC (DLC); endorsed by TJ as a letter from "Caleb" Wistar received 4 Jan. and so recorded in SJL; TJ later corrected the endorsement to "Caspar."

Wistar's last letter was undated, received by TJ on 9 Apr. 1801. In it, Wistar recommended Peter DOBELL, who received an appointment in June as U.S. commercial agent at Le Havre. TJ had written only once, on 4 Dec., since receiving that letter. Wistar's reference to TWO NOTES may have included TJ's letter of 31 Mch. In both that letter and the one of 4 Dec., TJ passed along scientific papers

he had received from others (Vol. 33:511-12, 556-7; TJ to Wistar, 4 Dec.).

Charles Willson PEALE had mounted the SKELETON of the mastodon in Philosophical Hall in Philadelphia and opened the exhibit on 24 Dec. The skeleton stood 11 feet high at the shoulder. Borrowing language from TJ's comments about the mammoth in *Notes on the State of Virginia*, Peale advertised the creature as "the LARGEST of *Terrestial Beings!*" (distinctions between mastodons and the larger mammoths were not yet understood). Peale, who needed to repay a loan from the American Philosophical Society for the expenses of excavating the bones in New York State, charged visitors 50 cents to view the skeleton. That was twice the cost of admission to his regular museum. The excavations by Peale and his son Rembrandt during the summer had yielded enough bones to mount, with the reconstruction of some elements, two skeletons. Rembrandt Peale hoped to exhibit the second one in Europe (*Philadelphia Gazette*, 24 Dec. 1801; Paul Semonin, *American Monster: How the Nation's First Prehistoric Creature Became a Symbol of National Identity* [New York, 2000], 327-30; Charles Coleman Sellers, *Mr. Peale's Museum: Charles Willson Peale and the First Popular Museum of Natural Science and Art* [New York, 1980], 141-7; *Notes*, ed. Peden, 47; Charles Willson Peale to TJ, 11 Oct. 1801).

PARTICULAR TWIST: Wistar may have been referring to a paper given by Dr. John P. Breyne at Danzig in 1728 and subsequently sent to the ROYAL SOCIETY in London. Reporting on some mammoth bones and teeth found in Siberia, Breyne described and illustrated the curvature of the tusks. He also discussed and illustrated a ridged tooth (mentioned by Wistar in the letter above), a skull, and a femur bone. Breyne's report appeared in the Royal Society's *Philosophical Transactions* in the 1730s and subsequently in an abridged version of the publication ("A Letter from John Phil. Breyne, M.D. F.R.S. to Sir Hans Sloane, Bart. Pres. R.S. with Observations, and a Description of some Mammoth's Bones dug up in Siberia, proving them to have belonged to Elephants," *Philosophical Transactions (1683-1775)*, 40 [1737-8], 124-38; John Martyn, ed., *The Philosophical Transactions (From the Year 1732, to the Year 1744) Abridged, and Disposed under General Heads . . . In Two Volumes, viz. Vol. VIII . . . Vol. IX* [London, 1747], 9:87-93).

TJ's SUGGESTION that elephant-like teeth, tusks, and bones found in North America were "of the same kind with those found in Siberia" appeared in *Notes on the State of Virginia* (*Notes*, ed. Peden, 44).

In a paper given before the APS in July 1797 and published in the society's *Transactions*, George Turner mentioned the fossils from SOUTH CAROLINA (APS, *Proceedings*, 22, pt. 3 [1884], 261; APS, *Transactions*, 4 [1799], 511).

One premise advanced by the Comte de BUFFON—one of his "dreams," in TJ's opinion—was that animals native to both the Eastern and the Western Hemispheres were smaller in size in the Western Hemisphere (*Notes*, ed. Peden, 47; Vol. 31:62).

From "A. B."

SIR,   Charleston So Carolina 2 January 1802

I have had frequent occasion to transact Business at the Collectors Office in this Port & for a year or two past the Business of the different departments has been executed entirely by Clerks, many of whom are perfectly ignorant of their Business; the Collector during that time has not been at the office once a fortnight on an average, the consequence of which is a great inconvenience to merchants & must hazard the Interest of the United States in a very material manner—

The cancellation of Export Bonds has been neglected for some time past, & notices therefore have not been sent to the parties in due time; the Clerk who formerly executed this Business has been appointed Deputy Collector in the Room of Mr Webb who has filled that office for several years past, & who was compelled to leave it on account of the Salary allowed by the Collector being insufficient to support him decently (only 800 Dollars pr Annum) & the Business of cancelling exportation Bonds imposed on another Clerk in addition to his former Business in consequence of which he cannot execute all that is required of him; this is consistent with the Collectors system of saddling a few of his best Clerks continually with additional Business while others are idle & inattentive to their duty as well as ignorant *and yet all receive the same Salary.* This certainly is neither just, reasonable, nor consistent with the interest of the United States—I have good reason to believe that this office is worth from 10 to 12 Thousand Dollars pr annum *clear profit* to this Collector who is seldom at his office himself, & who will not allow a Clerk of abilities a decent Salary in consequence several of his best Clerks have left his offices at different times within 3 or 4 years past, & he has supplyed their places with others who have been of no other use than to create disorder Errors & confusion & who have been intrusted with the calculation of Duties & other important Particulars of the Business—I certainly think it would promote the Interest of the United States to appoint a Collector for this Port who is a man of Business himself, & who is a perfect accountant in practice & not in theory, & who will attend *personally* to the Duties of his office, which I am certain is not the case with the present Collector—I understand he has acquired great credit from Government on account of his punctuality to their Instructions but this was not difficult, & he well knew that the existance of *his* office depended on it; the labor & perplexity of *executing* the most important parts of his Business has depended entirely on 2 or 3 of his Clerks who may shortly leave him on account of the low Salary allowed them, It therefore appears to me proper, that the Collector should be allowed *a certain Salary* by Government, & that they should also pay the Clerks, in which case, if the allowance should be liberal there will be an inducement to men of abilities & information to desire & wish to continue as Clerks in the Collectors office.

The principal part of the foregoing remarks have come within my own knowledge, therefore I have thought proper to make this communication in hopes of your duly considering the importance of the subject & making such alterations as may be in your power provided you think proper—

I remain with considerations of the highest respect Your Most Obedt. Sevt—   A B

RC (NHi: Gallatin Papers); at foot of text: "Thomas Jefferson Esqr."; endorsed by TJ as received 15 Jan. and so recorded in SJL. Enclosed in TJ to Gallatin, 16 Jan. 1802.

CANCELLATION OF EXPORT BONDS: when imported goods upon which duties had been paid were exported, certificates or debentures for payment of drawbacks, or a reimbursement of the duties, were issued. At the same time, an export bond, with one or more sureties, equal to double the amount of the drawback, was issued to guarantee that the goods were not "relanded in any port or place within the limits of the United States." The collector canceled the bond when the exporter provided the proofs required by law, signifying that the goods were delivered at a port outside the limits of the United States within a designated period of time, a year for exports to ports in Europe or America and two years for ports in Asia or Africa (U.S. Statutes at Large, 1:680-2, 687-90).

OFFICE IS WORTH: James Simons's total compensation as collector of customs was over $8,000 in fees and commissions in 1800. The total paid for the hire of clerks at Charleston was over $8,600 (ASP, *Miscellaneous*, 1:278). Congress passed legislation in April 1802, limiting the annual income of collectors from fees and commissions, after deducting expenditures incident to the office, to $5,000. Any surplus was to be paid into the U.S. Treasury. The limitation did not extend to income from fines, forfeitures, and penalties (U.S. Statutes at Large, 2:172-3).

From Gideon Granger

Saturday Jan: 2d. 1802

G Granger presents his Complim'ts. to the President and informs him that the mails are made up for Charlotteville evry Sunday at *four* OClock PM. and proceed immediately for Fredericksburg arrive there Tuesday Evning and at Charlotteville on Thursday at *One* OClock PM—under the present Arangement.

RC (DLC); endorsed by TJ as received 2 Jan. and so recorded in SJL; also endorsed by TJ: "mail for Charlvlle."

From George Jefferson

DEAR SIR   Richmond 2d. Janr. 1802

I now inclose your account made up to the end of the year, by which there appears to be a balance in your favor of £19.17.6.

I am Dear Sir Your Very humble servt.   GEO. JEFFERSON

Tobacco 30/.
Wheat 6/—

RC (MHi); at foot of text: "Thos. Jefferson esqr."; endorsed by TJ as received 7 Jan. and so recorded in SJL. Enclosure not found.

To James Oldham

SIR   Washington Jan. 2. 1802.

Your's of the 26th came to hand two days ago. I immediately engaged mr Barnes to remit ten dollars for you to mr Trump.

I shall be glad to hear from you from time to time, informing me of your progress, what work you have prepared, what you have put up and what you are engaged in at the time, as it is interesting to me to know how we advance. accept my best wishes.

                                                            TH: JEFFERSON

RC (PWacD: Feinstone Collection, on deposit PPAmP); addressed: "Mr. James Oldham Monticello near Milton"; franked and postmarked.

James Oldham (d. 1843), a Philadelphia-trained artisan, began his employment as a house joiner at Monticello in April 1801. In 1804, he moved to Richmond, where he continued to receive orders from TJ for doors and sashes. In 1819, TJ encouraged Oldham to work on the construction of the University of Virginia. Oldham later opened a public house in Albemarle County (Richard Charles Cote, "The Architectural Work-men of Thomas Jefferson in Virginia" [Ph.D. diss., Boston University, 1986], 101-5; Vol. 33:265, 377, 603; RS, 3:520n; TJ to Oldham, 1 Jan. 1819).

YOUR'S OF THE 26TH: Oldham's letter to TJ, recorded in SJL as received 29 Dec. from Monticello, has not been found.

At an entry dated 31 Dec. 1801 in his financial memoranda, TJ recorded that Oldham owed $40 in total for payments by John BARNES on TJ's account to Daniel TRUMP in Philadelphia, including the remittance of $10 mentioned by TJ in the letter above (MB, 2:1061).

To Samuel Smith

TH: JEFFERSON TO
GENL. SAML. SMITH   Jan. 2. 1802. Washington.

Can you get me at Baltimore a gross of *good claret* and order it round here, to serve me till I can recieve a supply from Philadelphia, which at this season is quite precarious. health and best wishes.

PrC (DLC); endorsed by TJ in ink on verso.

From James Taylor, Jr.

SIR   Norfolk Jany 2nd. 1802

I have the pleasure to acknowledge the receipt of your favor of the 18 Decr. The remittance which you contemplate making for the wine will be fully in time, but I must request that you will consult your convenience in doing it—

Colonel Newton, who is now confined with a Severe attack of the Gout, has procured for you, 10 Barrels of Cyder which I shall ship as directed by you, by the first conveyance. This Cyder is thought by judges to be good *now*—I presume your Butler is acquainted with the management of it, but I hope you will excuse my recommending the Bottles to be rinsed with old apple Brandy when he bottles it.

I am with great respect Yr: ob: Serv   JAS TAYLOR JR

RC (MHi); endorsed by TJ as received 9 Jan. and so recorded in SJL with notation "18."

From Albert Gallatin

DEAR SIR   Jany. 3d 1802

If you wish to avoid the formality of a message in relation to the Supervisor North West of the Ohio, I may write the enclosed letter to the Chairman of the Committee of Ways and Means. Please to return it, if you approve that mode.

But if you think it better to make the communication by message, you may make one out of the letter, as this contains all the necessary facts.

Respectfully Your most obt. Servt.   ALBERT GALLATIN

RC (DLC); addressed: "The President of the United States"; endorsed by TJ as received from the Treasury Department on 4 Jan. and so recorded in SJL with notation "Inspections. communcn to Congr."; also endorsed by TJ: "Suppression of inspections &c—Notice to Congress." Enclosure: see below.

On 6 Jan., Gallatin wrote John Randolph, CHAIRMAN OF THE COMMITTEE OF WAYS AND MEANS, and enclosed the president's Executive Order on Revenue Districts of 29 July 1801. Gallatin explained why a new revenue district had been erected northwest of the Ohio River, formerly part of the district that included the state of Kentucky. He also noted that the old arrangement was "always incompetent to the complete execution of the revenue laws," and with the great increase in population, it had "become extremely inconvenient in practice." While the laws authorized the president to erect new districts, the act of 11 July 1798 had given Congress the right "to determine whether any, and if any, what compensation shall be allowed" to the supervisor of the new district. "It is of some importance," Gallatin concluded, "that this should be ascertained, as, in the mean while, the duties of supervisor are done by an inspector, who, under existing laws, has no power to fill the vacancies in the offices of collectors" (*Report from the Committee of Ways and Means, Who Were Instructed to Enquire into the Expediency of Repealing the Laws Laying Duties . . . 8th March, 1802* [Washington, D.C., 1802], 17-19; Shaw-Shoemaker, No. 3388). Rather than passing separate legislation, Congress decided to include the salary of $500 for the supervisor and $300 for a clerk for the Northwest District as Section 4 of the "Act to repeal the Internal Taxes" (U.S. Statutes at Large, 2:148, 150; Gallatin to TJ, 12 Apr. 1802).

From David Austin

Alexandria

MAY IT PLEASE YR. EXCELLENCY—   Jan'y 4th. AD. 1802

Being in this place to supply the place of Docr. Muir, gone on the affairs of the Church to Baltimore; I take the liberty of addressing a line from this place.

To a mind filled with all the sensibilities, incident to a tolerable acquaintance with men & things, you must be sensible that *to be obliged* to write to you the things that I have written, must be matter of trial. The President, however, has been pleased to accept these communications, without rebuke.

On the Barbary business I have toutched. The Criterion, founded *in the progress of events*, by me heretofore set down, *certainly speaks in my favor*. It is said Commodore Dale's boat has upset. If it be so, consider it as a comment upon the failure of the Expedition. It has failed: & when the causes of the failure, become to be developed, the discerning & sensible will be apt to say, that the gingerbread stile of your Excelly's Instructions, letters & offerings have been principally operative in murling the mouth of the expedition.—

I, again, say that there is a secret in this business, which the arrangments of the Executive have not toutched; & as things now stand, may be incapable to toutch.

It is still within my power, under God, to afford relief, in this matter.—

The United States will, also, soon have other matters of serious moment to attend to. The present idea of Universal pacification may prove a phantom. If it prove, eventually, a truth, the shaking of the sea, after a tempest, is frequently, more than the storm itself, trying to the Ships upon the waters. Your Ship, Sir, is not yet safely in port. It would require pages, to present the real state of our present national relations, & national dangers.—

I shall not commit myself, without reward, or appointed service; by a development of those means, by which the evils existing, or to come are to be met, & remedied.

Extraordinary as the matter may seem, the Executive cannot be more sure of national safety, than by an intelligent, prompt & persevering Agent at the British Court.

As matters now stand, the Executive cannot count upon European favor in reference to Republican governments. Several of those powers have the means of dashing our prospects at a stroke: And the paralizing of our national strength, affords to foreign policy, inviting arguments in favor of an anticipated, & it may be, combined design.—

I offer my service, to fill the place of Rufus King. The Medium of the British government, in matters of extensive moment, may present a tube, through wh our part may be successfully played. The idea I know may seem extraordinary & novel to a Republican mind: but Sir! it is power that decides national questions, or that parries national strokes.

There may be a design brewing, of whose operation & extent yr. Excellency may not be fully aware.

I submit the matter of employing my talents, again, to the President: being willing to submit myself to any interrogatories the Executive may think proper to place upon paper: reserving, always, to myself the secret of the operation; at least so far as to withhold the power of execution from another than myself.—There are infirmities in the late plan of operation in the Mediterranean, which a Child may be made to understand.—I am taking up Subscriptions, in this City, for a publica: I am about to give to the World: & I would wish, thro' a hopeful prospect with the Executive, to be able to withold things, wh. otherwise; the obligations of truth may oblige me to disclose. Shall be in the City, God willing, tomorrow, & am, with high esteem—   D. AUSTIN.

RC (DLC); addressed: "His Excell'y Thomas Jefferson Prest. U:States Washington"; franked and postmarked; endorsed by TJ as received 5 Jan. and so recorded in SJL with notation "to be M.P. vice Rufus King."

The Reverend James MUIR was a native of Scotland and pastor of the Presbyterian church in Alexandria (James Grant Wilson and John Fiske, eds., *Appletons' Cyclopædia of American Biography*, 6 vols. [New York, 1887-9], 4:456; Miller, *Alexandria Artisans*, 1:350; 2:52-3; *Alexandria Gazette & Daily Advertiser*, 9 Aug. 1820).

On 22 Oct. 1801, a cutter belonging to the U.S. frigate *President*, flagship of Richard DALE's squadron in the Mediter-ranean, UPSET while returning from Gibraltar, resulting in the loss of all but one of the boat's officers and crew (NDBW, 1:607; *Washington Federalist*, 19 Dec. 1801).

In December 1801, Austin began advertising for SUBSCRIPTIONS to a publication of "Two Discourses, Delivered at the Treasury-Office, City of Washington: To Which Will Be Annexed, Three Numbers of A Prophetic Alphabet." The price to subscribers was 50 cents (*Washington Federalist*, 11 Dec. 1801). The subsequent publication, appearing in January 1802, was entitled *The National "Barley Cake," or, The "Rock of Offence" Into A "Glorious Holy Mountain": in Discourses and Letters* (Washington, D.C., 1802).

From Sarah Blackden

New York January the 4th. 1802.

SIR!   No. 260 Pearl Street.

The friendship with which you condescended to honor my late Husband and myself in former years and your favorable reception of him a few months ago, lead me to the liberty of writing you on the subject of the Compensation which we had hoped for from our Country as due to his services and sacrafices in the late War for its Independence.

The public prints have probably 'ere now announced to you the death of Colo. Blackden.—This melancholy and distressing, and at the same time sudden and unexpected event, took place on the Evening of the 22nd. ulto. after a short tho' severe illness, which commenced just at the moment when he intended to have prepaired a renewal of his memorial or Petition to Congress.—As this task now devolves on me as the legal and only representative of my Husband, I have by recommendation of his Honor the Vice President and other Gentlemen of Influence and respectability, determined to undertake it.

To General Bailey, one of the representatives from this State, who in the last Session was kind Enough to bring forward this subject, I shall under the present date transmit my Petition together with such documents as were then Exhibited.—It is my intention to write also to Mr Rutledge and Colo. Talmadge in the lower House and to Mr Baldwin, Mr. Brown & Mr Bradlie of the Senate. but to your Excellency I can address myself with more freedom.   Your Humane feelings, the Knowledge you have had of our situation at the close of the war, and after of our subsequent losses, of the Colonels confinement to the use of Crutches during more than Seven of the last years of his life, of our total deprivation of income in Consequence, and of the reasonableness of our pretentions on the Score of Public relief, all tend to inspire me with Confidence that you will be interested in my behalf and that you will Cause to be done whatever you can consistently with your high Station for procuring me that provision and protection which under all circumstances I shall be found to merit.

I pray your Excellencys Indulgence for this Intrusion and am With Great respect & Consideration Your Excellencys Most Humble & Afflicted Servt.   SARAH BLACKDEN

RC (MHi); at foot of text: "His Excellency Thomas Jefferson Esqr. President of the United States"; endorsed by TJ as received 7 Jan. and so recorded in SJL.

THE DEATH OF COLO. BLACKDEN: Sarah Blackden was the widow of Revolutionary War veteran and light dragoon colonel Samuel Blackden, whose death at the age of 53 was initially reported in the New York press under the name of Blagden. TJ and his daughters first made the acquaintance of the Blackdens in France in 1786 (*New-York Evening Post*, 26 Dec. 1801; New York *American Citizen*, 28 Dec. 1801; Washington, *Papers, Rev. War Ser.*, 9:153; same, *Pres. Ser.*, 2:398; Vol. 10:517; Vol. 11:486; Vol. 28:187-9, 216).

PETITION TO CONGRESS: in December 1800, Samuel Blackden unsuccessfully petitioned Congress for half pay and land compensation legally due to officers of equal rank who had served during the Revolution. Sarah Blackden continued to seek his redress posthumously on 11 Jan. 1802 and again on 12 Dec. 1804 (JHR, 3:739, 743; 4:44; 5:51).

BY RECOMMENDATION OF HIS HONOR THE VICE PRESIDENT: Aaron Burr had previously interceded on Samuel Blackden's behalf in a letter to Albert Gallatin on 8 May 1801, hoping "to bring him to the Recollection of Mr. Jefferson and to solicit his patronage" by expressing Blackden's desire to be placed in Washington even if in an inferior clerkship (Kline, *Burr*, 1:576-7).

Conference with Little Turtle

I. ADDRESS OF LITTLE TURTLE, [4 JAN. 1802]

II. JEFFERSON'S REPLY, 7 JAN. 1802

III. HENRY DEARBORN'S REPLY, 7 JAN. 1802

IV. RESPONSE OF LITTLE TURTLE, [7 JAN. 1802]

EDITORIAL NOTE

In the spring of 1801, the Miami Indian leader Little Turtle expressed an intention to travel from his home on the Wabash River to see the new president of the United States in Washington. Little Turtle's interpreter and son-in-law, William Wells, apparently knew Meriwether Lewis, who had served with the army on the frontier, and Wells informed Lewis of the intended visit. "Our friend the Little Turtle has requested me to inform you," Wells wrote from Fort Wayne in May, "that he wishes to visit his father, the President, this fall, when Congress meets: he wishes to take five other Chiefs with him, and wishes you to obtain the President's permission for that purpose, if you can with propriety: he says he wishes you to answer him on the subject as soon as possible. The Indians are all well disposed towards the United States." Lewis copied part of Wells's letter for Jefferson, who endorsed it: "The little Turtle asks leave to visit us" (MS in DLC, an extract in Lewis's hand, at head of text: "Extract of a letter from Capt. William Wells to M. Lewis, dated Fort Wayne, May the 10th. 1801," endorsed by TJ; Vol. 33:51, 95n, 239).

Little Turtle and Jefferson were almost certainly already acquainted. Little Turtle had visited Philadelphia for several weeks in January and February 1798. While there, he became a linguistic source for Jefferson's acquaintance, the Comte de Volney, who used a printed form furnished by Jefferson to record a word list of the Miami language. Volney conferred with Little Turtle and Wells several times, quizzing them about Native American life and culture as well as vocabulary. Tadeusz Kosciuszko called on Little Turtle, and the Miami was acquainted with Benjamin Rush. It is likely that Jefferson and Little Turtle encountered one another on several occasions in Philadelphia that winter. When Jefferson sent seeds to William Strickland in March 1798, he included some from what he called the "Wabash melon." He informed Strickland that the plant, which he described as producing a fruit similar to pumpkins or squash, was native to "the country of the Miamis at the head of the Wabash & thence to Lake Erie." Little Turtle was the likeliest source of the seeds (Volney, *View*, 356-86; Carter, *Little Turtle*, 5; George W. Corner, ed., *The Autobiography of Benjamin Rush: His "Travels Through Life" together with his* Commonplace Book *for 1789-1813* [Princeton, 1948], 240; Vol. 30:82n, 213).

The primary purpose of Little Turtle's trip to Philadelphia that winter was to call on the president, John Adams. Little Turtle also met George Washington, perhaps more than once. In the fall of 1796, he was one of a group of Native Americans who saw Washington in Philadelphia. There may have been an earlier meeting, since Little Turtle, in treaty negotiations with General Anthony Wayne at Greenville in July 1795, implied that there had been contact between him and Washington. "Here are papers which have been given to me by General Washington, the great chief of the United States," Little Turtle said on that occasion. "He told me they should protect us in the possession of our lands, and that no white person should interrupt us in the enjoyment of our hunting grounds, or be permitted to purchase any of our towns or lands from us" (*Claypoole's American Daily Advertiser*, 1 Jan. 1798; *The Times and Alexandria Advertiser*, 30 Mch. 1798; Carter, *Little Turtle*, 3-5; R. David Edmunds, *The Potawatomis: Keepers of the Fire* [Norman, Okla., 1978], 158-9; ASP, *Indian Affairs*, 1:577).

Little Turtle's journeys to call on successive presidents of the United States reinforced his political position among the Miamis. He was not a hereditary chief, but a former war captain who had been among the most prominent and successful Indian leaders in battles against the U.S. in the Northwest. After Great Britain ceased its involvement with the region's Indians and Wayne defeated the confederated tribes at Fallen Timbers in 1794, Little Turtle was among those who, after initial resistance, agreed to the Greenville treaty. He asserted himself as the chief of the Miamis, and as the spokesman of smaller affiliated tribes, in their dealings with the United States, particularly in regard to the annuity payments called for by the treaty. This made him the Miamis' premier advocate of assimilation, and he promoted the adoption of cultural, agricultural, and economic practices favored by missionaries and the United States government. That position put him at odds with many of his tribe who favored maintaining the group's established ways and resisted transformation of their lifestyle. Wells told Volney that Little Turtle, who on his visit to Philadelphia in 1798 wore a blue suit and trousers "in the American style," would change that garb for native dress when he returned to the Wabash. Traditionalists killed his first milk cow, and he had to be discreet about adopting elements of non-Indian lifestyle. Some hereditary chiefs also resented him for his assumption of a powerful role in diplomacy and civil governance. For these various reasons, Little Turtle was, William Henry Harrison speculated in 1805, at odds with nine tenths of the Miami people. Maintaining his power and influence, and occupying the key position between the tribe and the U.S. government, required constant effort (Rob Mann, "The Silenced Miami: Archaeological and Ethnohistorical Evidence for Miami-British Relations, 1795-1812," *Ethnohistory*, 46 [1999], 399-402, 404-7; Richard White, *The Middle Ground: Indians, Empires, and Republics in the Great Lakes Region, 1650-1815* [Cambridge, 1991], 495-6, 501; Dowd, "Thinking and Believing," 315-16; Volney, *View*, 360-1, 378-9).

With Little Turtle and Wells on the trip to Washington in the winter of 1801-1802 were two Potawatomi chiefs, Five Medals and Topinbee (He Who Sits Quietly), as well as an unidentified Miami and a Wea Indian. The Weas were closely affiliated with the Miamis. The Potawatomis were from what is now northern Indiana and southern Michigan, to the west and north of the Miamis' territory. Many Potawatomi leaders opposed assimilation, hoped to continue a relationship with the British, and wanted nothing to do with the United States, but Five Medals, like Little Turtle, was committed to building a relationship with the U.S., accepting annuities, and adopting the agricultural methods and other changes urged upon them. Five Medals and Topinbee also wanted to curtail the sale of whiskey to Indians (Edmunds, *Potawatomis*, 133, 158-60, 164, 166-7; Sturtevant, *Handbook*, 15:600, 681, 682).

In December 1801, the travelers made their way to Pittsburgh. From there they took mail stages to Philadelphia and Baltimore, and after a stop in Baltimore they went on to Washington. They were among the crowd at the President's House on New Year's morning as callers came by to pay their respects to Jefferson. Sources differ concerning the date of the group's first formal meeting with Jefferson and Henry Dearborn. When the *National Intelligencer*, in February, printed documents associated with the conference, the newspaper gave 2 Jan. as the date of the meeting at which Little Turtle delivered the opening address. In the War Department's record of the conference, however, the date associated with Little Turtle's oration is 4 Jan. (see Document 1). That date might refer only to Wells's certification, not the day on which Little Turtle spoke the address. Yet when Jefferson sent an extract of Little Turtle's talk to Congress later in the month, the copies received by the House and the Senate both gave the 4th as the date of the speech. The address may have been given on the 2d (which was a Saturday) and attested to on the 4th (a Monday), but 4 Jan. is the only date associated with Little Turtle's oration in the government's record of the event (Carlisle, Pa., *Kline's Carlisle Weekly Gazette*, 16 Dec.; New York *Daily Advertiser*, 21 Dec.; *Federal Gazette & Baltimore Daily Advertiser*, 26 Dec. 1801; *National Intelligencer*, 12 Feb. 1802; Samuel L. Mitchill to Catharine Mitchill, 10 Jan. 1802, in NNMus; Enclosure No. 4 listed at TJ to the Senate and the House of Representatives, 27 Jan. 1802).

Conferences with Native American deputations were formal events that had a common structure. At the first gathering, the visitors' primary spokesman made a speech that enumerated the Indians' concerns and requests. After an interval of a few days, the parties reconvened and the government's officers replied to the address. Apparently all the transactions were oral, even if speakers on the part of the U.S. government, unlike their Native American counterparts, composed their parts of the exchange on paper beforehand.

When representatives of the Cherokees visited Washington in the summer of 1801, Jefferson did not meet with them himself. Instead, the speaker for the delegation, The Glass, made an address to Henry Dearborn, who replied a few days later with a statement based on a draft by Jefferson. At that time, Jefferson and Dearborn hoped to discourage Native American deputations from coming to Washington, and keeping the president out of the official proceedings, letting the Cherokee visitors deal directly only with the secretary of war, may have been part of that plan. Some measures were necessary, the president and the secretary of war reasoned, to avoid "frivolous" trips to the capital by Indian chiefs. The experience with The Glass had an unsatisfactory result, however. After Dearborn's meetings with the Cherokee delegation, Jefferson and Dearborn thought they understood the tribe's primary concerns, and they instructed the treaty commissioners who would be meeting with the Cherokees to limit the scope of the negotiations. Not long afterward, however, the Cherokees refused to meet with the commissioners, an action that threatened to jeopardize negotiations with other southern tribes (Vol. 34:505-11; Vol. 35:196-7, 307-8; TJ to the House of Representatives and to Nathaniel Macon, 8 Feb. 1802). Perhaps that outcome would have been no different if the president had participated in the meetings with the Cherokees in Washington. But the experience with The Glass may have influenced Jefferson to take a different approach with Little Turtle in January 1802. Jefferson continued to leave some visiting Native American delegations entirely in Dearborn's hands, but when certain groups came calling, such as Little Turtle's and one headed by the Shawnee Black Hoof a month later, the president took part in the proceedings.

Jefferson's participation in the conference with Little Turtle is not readily apparent from the record in the War Department's Indian affairs letterbook (Documents I-IV below). In the letterbook, Dearborn's reply to Little Turtle's address comes first, and nowhere is it stated that Jefferson was present when Little Turtle spoke or when the delegation received the government's response. However, when Samuel Harrison Smith's *National Intelligencer* printed the proceedings of the conference on 12 Feb., the newspaper's heading stated that the talks were "in the presence of the President of the United States." Moreover, when Five Medals, briefly, and then Little Turtle, at length, made their formal addresses, they spoke directly to a symbolic "Father," which implies that Jefferson was in the room. If he had not been there, the chiefs would have addressed themselves to Dearborn, probably calling him "Brother" (as he addressed them on 7 Jan.). They would have asked him to convey their concerns to the president, and at the conclusion of their addresses Dearborn would have told them that he would inform Jefferson of what they had said. Such was the pattern of Dearborn's exchange with The Glass's delegation in July, when Jefferson was not present (Vol. 34:505-6).

A comment in Jefferson's reply to Little Turtle (Document II) indicates that Dearborn and the Indians conferred sometime after Little Turtle made his address and before the second ceremonial gathering, which was held on the 7th. There is no record of those intermediate discussions, and evidently Jefferson was not involved in them. As reconstructed from the contents of the addresses and the order in which they appear in the *National Intelligencer*, the meeting on the 7th followed this sequence: Jefferson addressed the visitors (Document II), then Dearborn did so (Document III), followed by the brief acknowledgment from Little Turtle that closed the conference (Document IV). Jefferson's comments took a general tone, did not go into details of issues raised by Little Turtle in the earlier meeting, and served to introduce Dearborn's answer to the delegation. Dearborn's address was longer than the president's and discussed more specific matters—Jefferson, while recognizing a need to play a role in the conference, probably did not want to give the impression that visiting Native Americans could expect the president himself to deal with their particular concerns. That Jefferson was present on the 7th, and did not just send his response to the deputation, may be inferred from his epistolary record, where he made the notation "speech" alongside the entry for his address to the group. Additional evidence of his participation comes from Little Turtle's closing remarks (Document IV). In that polite rejoinder, the Miami again addressed himself to "Father," referring also to "your red children," and Little Turtle did not ask Dearborn to convey his sentiments to the president, as he would have done if Jefferson were not present.

We do not know by what means the War Department's clerks received Jefferson's address for entry in the letterbook's record of the conference. Little Turtle's and Five Medals's addresses were evidently taken down in shorthand as they spoke, then written out in the letterbook, but a clerk may simply have copied Jefferson's written text. The version in the letterbook matches Jefferson's text fairly well, except his phrase "the evils which of necessity encompass the life of man" became, ungrammatically, "the evils which of necessity accompanies the life of man"—either a mishearing by a shorthand recorder or a misreading by a clerk making a transcription from the written copy (see notes to Document II). The *National Intelligencer* on 12 Feb. repeated the mistake, which suggests that the record of the conference in the Indian affairs letterbook was the newspaper's source for the texts of the conference's addresses.

Although Little Turtle's address to Jefferson was not solely, or even predominantly, about the evils of liquor among the Indians, the portion of his talk that concerned the "fatal poison" drew particular attention as news of the conference spread (Philadelphia *Poulson's American Daily Advertiser*, 9 Feb. 1802; Salem, Mass., *Salem Register*, 15 Feb.; New Bedford, Mass., *Columbian Courier*, 19 Feb.; Philadelphia *Temple of Reason*, 20 Feb. 1802; Samuel L. Mitchill to Catharine Mitchill, 4 Feb. 1802, in NNMus). Jefferson helped bring notice to that topic when he mentioned "ardent spirits" in a message to Congress later in January and enclosed the relevant portion of the Miami's address (TJ to the Senate and the House of Representatives, 27 Jan.). In addition, in Baltimore in December, Little Turtle, Five Medals, and their companions had attended a yearly meeting of the Society of Friends. A committee of the yearly meeting was investigating the liquor trade's impairment of efforts to bring "the most simple and useful arts of civil life" to the Indians. On 27 Dec., Little Turtle gave a speech at the Quaker meeting that concentrated on the liquor issue. As he spoke and Wells translated, the committee had his words taken down in shorthand, and Little Turtle's Baltimore address became part of a memorial to Congress from the committee asking for the prohibition of, or at least restrictions on, alcohol sales to Indians. On

7 Jan., the same day they had their second formal meeting with Jefferson and Dearborn, the Indian deputation attended Congress to be present in the House of Representatives when Samuel Smith of Maryland introduced the memorial. The House referred the matter to a committee consisting of Smith and four others. In March, Congress approved an act "to regulate trade and intercourse with the Indian tribes" that empowered the president to stop or regulate the selling of liquor to Indians (*Memorial of Evan Thomas, and Others, A Committee Appointed for Indian Affairs, By the Yearly Meeting of the People Called Friends* [Washington, 1802], Shaw-Shoemaker, No. 3334; Alexandria *Times; and District of Columbia Daily Advertiser*, 9 Jan. 1802; New York *Commercial Advertiser*, 13 Jan.; Norwich, Conn., *Courier*, 13 Jan.; *Alexandria Advertiser and Commercial Intelligencer*, 20 Jan.; TJ to the Senate and the House of Representatives, 27 Jan.).

On 11 Jan., while Little Turtle and Wells were still in Washington, they met with William Thornton at Jefferson's request and again served as sources for a Miami-English vocabulary list. Jefferson later gave Thornton's and Volney's word lists, along with other data on Native American languages, to the American Philosophical Society (Carter, *Little Turtle*, 162, 261; *Transactions of the Historical & Literary Committee of the American Philosophical Society*, 1 [1819], xlix). According to a published report that appeared a few months later, Jefferson also talked to Little Turtle about vaccination and had the kinepox vaccine given to him and his traveling companions. However, Little Turtle had received smallpox inoculation on an earlier visit to the seaboard, and the published report may actually refer to Black Hoof (see note to Document I of the Conference with Black Hoof, 5 Feb. 1802). Little Turtle and his colleagues stayed in Washington several days, a much shorter visit than he had made in Philadelphia in 1798. When they prepared for departure, Dearborn arranged for each of the visitors to receive at Pittsburgh a new hat, two shirts, and $25 in goods for their families. Dearborn authorized horses for the last part of the journey, from Cincinnati to Fort Wayne, and allowed the chiefs to keep some of the animals afterward (Dearborn to Wells and to John Wilkins, Jr., 11 Jan., Lb in DNA: RG 75, LSIA).

The president expected "to use every means in his power," Dearborn informed Harrison in February 1802, to bring "the arts of husbandry and domestic manufactories" to Native Americans "with whome we have the means of easy intercourse." Writing after the visit of Black Hoof of the Shawnees, Dearborn called it "a great misfortune" that some of the Miamis' neighbors were jealous of Little Turtle. He "really appears to be a man of extraordinary tallent, and capable of doing much good or harm according as he may be induced to act." In January, Dearborn authorized an individual annuity for Little Turtle of up to $150 in goods each year. Later, after the Miami chief and his colleagues had returned home, Dearborn informed Harrison that "there is reason to believe that the Little Turtle will have considerable influence" with the western Indians (Dearborn to Wells, 11 Jan., to Harrison, 23 Feb., 23 Apr. 1802, in Lb in DNA: RG 75, LSIA; *Terr. Papers*, 7:50, 51).

I. Address of Little Turtle

[4 Jan. 1802]

Father you have heard the observasions of my Brother Chief, Pottawottama. It gives us great pleasure that the Great Spirit who made us both, has permitted us to take you by the hand at the Great Council of the sixteen fires.

Father, we have confidence, in our Interpreter, he is a great advantage both to us and to you, as through him we[1] have the means of communicating with, and perfectly understanding each other.

Father, it has again fell to my lot to make known to you the wish of your children. I was in hopes that my brethren the Great Chiefs would have spoken for themselves, but by their desire I have undertaken to speak for them.

Father, A Treaty was made six years since at Greenville between the President of the United States and your children the Red People.

Father, I with some of my Brethren made certain objections to that Treaty, but finally thought it best it should be signed, and we wish to adhere to it, and hope our white brethren will do so.

My Father, at that Treaty it was understood that the white people would be the fathers friends and protectors of the red People, that they would use their best endeavours to maintain friendship and good understanding[2] between us and the United States, and we believe it has been generally attended to both by the White and Red People.

My Father, and Brothers, by the Treaty it was mentioned that certain reservations should be made for the white people in our Country that the white people should not settle over the line described by the Treaty, that no individual of the white people should be allowed to purchase any land of the Indians, nor any Indians to sell to individuals of the White people, but that when your children were willing to sell any of their lands it should be sold to the United States, which we think a very happy circumstance, because the United States will not allow their Red Brothers to be cheated.

Father some parts of the Treaty has not been so well understood as could be wished one part which was not understood was mentioned to the President of the United States four years since at Philadelphia concerning the lands at Fort St. Vincenes. By the Treaty the United States were to have all the land which had before been ceeded by the Indians to the English or French.

Father, we think some of the white people are settling over the line and we are fearful some of our young men may interrupt the harmony which prevails between the Red and White people, as the white people are considered out of the protection of the United States, when they settle over the line, and as the Chiefs cannot be at all places to watch over their young men.

Father we therefore request that the lines may be run, and persons appointed to explaine those parts of the Treaty of Greenville, which are not perfectly understood. If you do not think proper, father, to appoint persons to meet their Red Brethren at St. Vincenes to explaine those parts of the Treaty not understood by your children the Red people, we wish you would appoint some person to examine all the circumstances and make report to you.

Father we are anxious that those parts of the Treaty of Greenville not well understood, may be explained, that the harmony and friendship which prevails between the white people and your children the Red people may be placed on a lasting foundation.

Father, by the Treaty of Greenville your children were promised a certain quantity of goods and money should be paid them annually, and this they expected would have been done.

Father, when the goods arrive your Children meet with pleasure to receive them; but father we are sorry to mention that the goods do not come in good order, that more or less of our annuities have always been unfit for use and particularly the powder, we believe it is your wish that they should be delivered in good order.

Father, the chiefs, your children knowing the route by which the goods come, are not surprised that they get damaged. We have twice received our annuities by the way of Cincinnati at which times they arrived in good order. Once, they came by Presque Isle to Miami where we went to receive them concerning which complaints were made to Governor St. Clair.

Father, it is my opinion and the opinion of the Pottawottama, Miami, Delaware, Shawaneses, Eel River, Weas, Kickapoos, Peankashaws, and Kaskaskais, that Fort Wayne is the best place for distributing their annuities, and that it would be best for the Chipaways, Ottoways and Wyandots to receive their annuities at Detroit.

Father, your children wish to know your opinion relative to these things. The United States are indebted to us one hundred dollars for the year 1800 we were also promised several horses which we never received. Of the annuity of Five hundred dollars promised to the Eel River Indians only seventy five dollars worth of brass Kettles have been received and we do not know what has become of the remainder of the annuity. Your children expect that the deficiencies of their annuities will be made up to them.

Father, it was mentioned by the Executive that a trading house should be established in our Country for the benefit of the Red people, we wish it might be established at Fort Wayne.

Father a number of reasons might be given to prove that Fort Wayne is the most suitable place, one I think will be sufficient to convince you Fort Wayne is the best place, it is at a distance from the white settlements, and the farther a trading house is established from the white people the better it will be for both.

Father, we are sorry to trouble you so much; but these things are of consquence to us. We are imposed upon by the British traders, who ask very dear for their goods, when we ask them why they demand so much they reply it is owing to the taxes the American Government lay on their goods and that we never shall get them cheaper. We are of opinion that if a trading house was established in our Country this imposition would be remedied.

Father, when your children go to Fort Wayne to receive their annuities they have no house to meet in, the Fort from which the goods are delivered is so small, but two or three can enter at the same time, this looks suspicious to some of our Brethren. We wish father a house may be built at this place for us to meet and hold our Councils in, and receive our annuities from.

Father, I was requested by my children before I left home to ask you to place a Blacksmith at Fort Wayne to repair our different Tools, we cannot have it done now without going to Cincinnati or Detroit.

Father, We wish to reap advantages from cultivating the Earth as you do, and request ploughs and other necessary tools may be put into the hands of the Interpreter at Fort Wayne to be dealt out to any who will receive and make use of them for the purpose intended.

Father, Should this request be granted nothing shall be wanting on the part of your children the Chiefs, to introduce husbandry among their children, if the United States will furnish them with the proper utensils. But Father nothing can be done to advantage unless the great Council of the Sixteen fires now assembled, will prohibit any person from selling any Spiritous Liquors among their Red Brothers.

Father, the introduction of this poison has been prohibited in our camps, but not in our Towns, where many of our Hunters, for this poison, dispose of not only their furs &ca. but frequently of their guns & Blankets and return to their families destitute.

Father, Your children are not wanting in industry, but it is the introduction of this fatal poison, which keeps them poor. Your children have not that command over themselves you have, therefore before any thing can be done to advantage this evil must be remedied.

Father, When our White Brothers come to this land our forefathers were numerous and happy: but since their intercourse with the white people, and owing to the introduction of this fatal poison we have become less numerous and happy.

Father, Your children the Red People have had several friendly talks with the people called Quaokers, in which they have made many friendly proposals relative to the introduction of Husbandry among us; but as yet nothing has been done.

Father, Your children only wish to mention to you things, which are of the greatest importance to them, we wish for a conversation with the Secretary of War to whom we wish to communicate certain things.

FC (Lb in DNA: RG 75, LSIA); in a clerk's hand; at head of text: "Little Turtle"; at foot of text: "I certify the above is a true translation of the Talk made by the Indian Chiefs therein mentioned William Wells Interpreter City of Washington January 4th: 1802"; follows Document III in Lb. Printed in *National Intelligencer*, 12 Feb. 1802, as the first address of the conference following the introduction by Five Medals (see below); at head of text: "Talk held with the Little Turtle, and the Chiefs of the Miamies, Pottawattoma and Weas, in the presence of the President of the United States. January 2, 1802."

Little Turtle (Michikinikwa, Meshikinoquak) was probably born in 1747 or 1752 on the Eel River in what later became the state of Indiana. He rose in prominence as a war leader, perhaps earning a high position by a victory over an American force in 1780. He was the primary leader and strategist, at least of the Miamis and perhaps of all the confederated tribes, when the Indians of the Northwest decisively routed expeditionary forces commanded by Josiah Harmar and Arthur St. Clair in 1790-91. By 1795, he decided that continued resistance to the United States would be useless, and he became an advocate of acculturation and cooperation with the U.S. Although the United States government treated him as the primary chief of the Miamis, he met

strong resistance from members of the tribe who opposed change and accommodation. Along with William Wells, by 1808 he came into conflict with the Shawnee Prophet and Tecumseh, who tapped into the traditionalist strain and tried to mobilize the western tribes against the United States. When Little Turtle died in 1812, he was buried with U.S. military honors. He stood six feet tall and was a persuasive orator. Samuel L. Mitchill described him in 1802 as "a very handsome man; of a colour rather whiter than the common Indians," and Volney also commented on the relative paleness of Little Turtle's complexion. John Adams called him "a remarkable man," and in 1794 a British officer at Detroit called him the "most decent, modest, sensible Indian I ever conversed with." TJ told Mitchill that Little Turtle was "the most intelligent man of his Race" that TJ had ever met (Samuel L. Mitchill to Catharine Mitchill, 13 Jan. 1802, in NNMus; Carter, *Little Turtle*, 4, 43-5; Richard White, *The Middle Ground: Indians, Empires, and Republics in the Great Lakes Region, 1650-1815* [Cambridge, 1991], 467, 495; ANB; DAB; Sturtevant, *Handbook*, 15:684-5, 687; Barbara Alice Mann, "The Greenville Treaty of 1795: Pen-and-Ink Witchcraft in the Struggle for the Old Northwest," in Bruce E. Johansen, ed., *Enduring Legacies: Native American Treaties and Contemporary Controversies* [Westport, Conn., 2004],

170, 175-6; Dowd, "Thinking and Believing," 316, 318-21; Volney, *View*, 361-2).

BROTHER CHIEF: the Potawatomi chief Five Medals, referred to above as POTTA-WOTTAMA, spoke first, saying: "Father, Listen to your children, your children are happy that the Great Spirit has given them permission to speak with you this day. Father, your children have travelled a great distance, and are happy to meet you at the great Council of the sixteen fires. Father, your children have something to communicate which they think of importance, both to your children the Red People and to you, as the Great Spirit made both, your children hope that no accident will happen to destroy the friendship and good understanding, which exists between them and their Brothers the white people. Father, our Brother Chief the Little Turtle will communicate to you our wishes and desires" (Lb in DNA: RG 75, LSIA).

GREAT COUNCIL OF THE SIXTEEN FIRES: Congress, composed of 16 states. For council fires symbolically representing deliberative bodies or the locales where discussions took place, see Francis Jennings and others, eds., *The History and Culture of Iroquois Diplomacy: An Interdisciplinary Guide to the Treaties of the Six Nations and Their League* (Syracuse, N.Y., 1985), 118.

WE HAVE CONFIDENCE, IN OUR INTERPRETER: William Wells, born in Pennsylvania in 1770, was captured in Kentucky by Miami warriors in 1784. Adopted into the tribe, he participated in raids against the frontier and married Little Turtle's daughter. In 1792, after a stay with relatives in Kentucky, he decided to give up his life with the Miamis. He became an interpreter for Rufus Putnam, who was attempting to negotiate a peace with the Indians of the Northwest Territory. Wells then headed a company of scouts for Anthony Wayne's army in 1794, fighting against the Miamis and their allies. He interpreted for the tribe and five other groups at the Greenville negotiations the following year. Reestablishing a relationship with Little Turtle, he was his father-in-law's interpreter on the visits to Philadelphia in 1796 and 1798, and from 1798 to 1800 was interpreter and deputy Indian agent for the U.S. at Fort Wayne (Paul A. Hutton, "William Wells: Frontier Scout and Indian Agent," *Indiana Magazine of History*, 74 [1978], 183-222; ASP, *Indian Affairs*, 1:582).

Anthony Wayne held treaty negotiations at GREENVILLE from mid-June to early August 1795. More than 1,100 Native Americans were present for at least a portion of the talks. Ninety-five leaders, including Little Turtle, signed the treaty directly or through proxies. The treaty specified the course of a "general boundary line" that would follow various rivers and portages from the mouth of the Cuyahoga River on Lake Erie to the Ohio River opposite the mouth of the Kentucky River. Ceding all claim to lands "lying eastwardly and southwardly" of the boundary, the Indians also had to give up, on their side of the line, several parcels of land around forts or settlements or otherwise obligated by the United States (Richard H. Kohn, *Eagle and Sword: The Federalists and the Creation of the Military Establishment in America, 1783-1802* [New York, 1975], 156-7; ASP, *Indian Affairs*, 1:562-83; U.S. Statutes at Large, 7:49-54).

CERTAIN OBJECTIONS: in the protracted talks at Greenville, which involved interaction among the tribes as well as with Wayne, Little Turtle asked for proof that the United States truly had peace as its goal. By the end of the conference, he accepted Wayne's explanations on that subject. Little Turtle objected to the government's reliance on a treaty made at Fort Harmar in 1789, arguing that the concessions made then were not by the tribes that had true claim to the territory in question. He tried to assert the Miamis' sovereignty over much of the land subject to division between the United States and the Indians, but failed to get the course of the boundary line changed or to alter the terms of some of the tracts reserved for U.S. posts. Wayne argued that the Indians had made concessions to the French and the British, and that the European powers had then yielded the region to the United States by the terms of the peace at the end of the American Revolution. Wayne also used the Jay Treaty to bring home the point that the Northwest Territory tribes could expect no support from Great Britain. Little Turtle, to no avail, protested an article in the treaty that required some chiefs to remain at Greenville as hostages until the Indians had released all their captives. Wayne did agree to his request that some traders who had previously dealt with the Miamis be allowed to continue in that trade under the new treaty. In a private meeting after the close of the negotiations, Little Turtle explained to Wayne that he had become "fully convinced that the treaty was wisely and benevolently calculated to promote the mutual interest, and insure the permanent happiness of the Indians," and he had made it "his determined resolution to adhere religiously to its stipulations" (ASP, *Indian Affairs*, 1:567, 569, 570-1, 573-8, 583; Mann, "Greenville Treaty," 183-94).

LANDS AT FORT ST. VINCENES: by the Greenville treaty, the United States gave up claim to Indian lands north of the Ohio River and east of the Mississippi, with certain exceptions. One such exception was the post at Vincennes on the Wabash River, plus an unspecified amount of "lands adjacent, of which the Indian title has been extinguished." In the discussions at Greenville, Little Turtle had protested that the Miamis never gave up possession of "lands on the Wabash." Wayne retorted that the Miamis had allowed the French to have Vincennes, the British received possession from the French, and the British ceded the claim to the United States. In other cases in which land outside the limits of a post was retained by the U.S., the treaty indicated the size and shape of the reserved tract (U.S. Statutes at Large, 7:50-1; ASP, *Indian Affairs*, 1:570, 573).

The annual QUANTITY OF GOODS AND MONEY the tribes were to receive under the Greenville treaty totaled $9,500. Seven tribes had annual allotments of $1,000, while five smaller groups were each to get $500. These annuities were in addition to $20,000 in goods given to the tribes collectively at the time the treaty was signed (U.S. Statutes at Large, 7:51).

The EEL RIVER Indians were generally thought of as a band of the Miamis, but through Little Turtle's efforts at Greenville they were recognized as a separate tribe in the treaty and granted an annuity of $500. The WEAS and the Piankashaws were closely related to the Miamis and were sometimes considered to be part of that tribe. They were generally treated as independent entities, however, and like the Eel River group they received separate annuities under the treaty. At the Greenville negotiations, Little Turtle spoke on behalf of several groups, including the KICKAPOOS, the Kaskaskias, and the Potawatomis (same; ASP, *Indian Affairs*, 1:576, 577; Sturtevant, *Handbook*, 15:681, 682, 686; Dowd, "Thinking and Believing," 315).

The government did establish a TRADING HOUSE at Fort Wayne, and one at Detroit, later in the year after Congress revived and continued in force an expired act that authorized the trading houses (*Terr. Papers*, 7:52, 63; TJ to the Senate and the House of Representatives, 27 Jan. 1802).

INTO THE HANDS OF THE INTERPRETER AT FORT WAYNE: on 1 Jan., Dearborn appointed Wells assistant agent for Indian affairs for Indiana Territory, residing at Fort Wayne. Wells's salary was to be $600 per annum, plus four daily food rations "in kind or in money." Wells owned land at Fort Wayne, where he farmed, raised hogs, had an orchard, and kept slaves that he obtained from his brother in Kentucky (Lb in DNA: RG 75, LSIA; Hutton, "Wells," 203).

RETURN TO THEIR FAMILIES DESTITUTE: in addition to authorizing the president to control the trade of liquor to Indians, Congress in March 1802 prohibited anyone from receiving in "trade or barter" from an Indian any gun, hunting or farming implement, cooking vessel, or article of clothing not made of "skins or furs" (U.S. Statutes at Large, 2:142, 146; Anthony F. C. Wallace, *Jefferson and the Indians: The Tragic Fate of the First Americans* [Cambridge, Mass., 1999], 296-7).

PEOPLE CALLED QUAOKERS: Little Turtle's relationship with religious organizations, including the Society of Friends, dated from his earlier visits to the seat of government. In February 1798, his name appeared at the head of the list of original subscribers to the constitution of the Missionary Society of Philadelphia. In 1804, Quakers established a demonstration farm in the Miamis' territory on the Wabash (*Boston Gazette, and Weekly Republican Journal*, 26 Mch.

1798; Chambersburg *Farmers' Register*, 18 Apr. 1798; Volney, *View*, 357, 375; Dowd, "Thinking and Believing," 316, 317, 318).

[1] MS: "whe."
[2] MS: "undestanding."

II. Jefferson's Reply

BROTHERS & FRIENDS OF THE MIAMIS,
POUTEWATAMIES & WEEAUHS.

I recieve with great satisfaction the visit you have been so kind as to make us at this place, and I thank the great spirit who has conducted you to us in health and safety. it is well that friends should sometimes meet, open their minds mutually, and renew the chain of affection. made by the same great spirit, and living in the same land with our brothers the red men, we consider ourselves as of the same family; we wish to live with them as one people, and to cherish their[1] interests as our own. the evils which of necessity encompass[2] the life of man are sufficiently numerous. why should we add to them by voluntarily[3] distressing & destroying one another? peace, brothers, is better than war. in a long & bloody war, we lose many friends, and gain nothing. let us then live in peace and friendship together, doing to each other all the good we can. the wise and good on both sides desire this, and we must take care that the foolish and wicked among us shall not prevent it. on our part, we shall endeavor in all things to be just & generous towards you, and to aid you in meeting those difficulties which a change of circumstances is bringing on. we shall with great pleasure see your people become disposed to cultivate the earth to raise herds of the useful animals, and to spin and weave, for their food & clothing. these resources are certain: they will never disappoint you. while those of hunting may fail, and expose your women & children to the miseries of hunger & cold. we will with pleasure furnish you with implements for the most necessary arts, and with persons who may instruct you how to make and use them.

I consider it as fortunate that you have made your visit at this time when our wise men from[4] the sixteen states are collected together in council, who being equally disposed to befriend you can strengthen our hands in the good we all wish to render you.

The several matters you opened to us in your speech the other day, and those on which you have since conversed with the Secretary at

war, have been duly considered by us. he will now deliver answers, and you are to consider what he says, as if said by myself, and that what we promise we shall faithfully perform.   TH: JEFFERSON
Jan. 7. 1802.

MS (DLC); entirely in TJ's hand. FC (Lb in DNA: RG 75, LSIA); in a clerk's hand; at head of text: "Brothers and Friends of the Miamis, Pottowattama and Weas"; other significant variations are noted below; follows Document I in Lb; marginal notation by clerk indicating that Dearborn's reply (Document III) should follow this document in sequence. Printed in *National Intelligencer*, 12 Feb. 1802, following Document I; at head of text:

"ANSWER Of the President, delivered January 7, 1802." Recorded in SJL with notation "speech."

[1] Word interlined in place of "your."
[2] FC and *National Intelligencer*: "accompanies."
[3] TJ first wrote "to them voluntarily by" before altering the passage to read as above.
[4] FC and *National Intelligencer*: "for."

III. Henry Dearborn's Reply

BROTHERS,

I am authorised by your father the President of the United States, to assure you that it gives him great pleasure to see you at the great Council fire of the sixteen States, and to have an opportunity of taking by the hand the great and wise men of so many of the Nations of his red Children.

Brothers,

Your Father the President is happy to find that the great Spirit who made all the white and red people has produced in them a desire to be like one people and to live together like brothers in peace and friendship, and your Father the President, most sincerely hopes that the same friendly dispositions will continue and encreace in strength in all parts of the United States, as long as the Great Lakes & Rivers remain.

Brothers,

Your Father the President has fully considered and digested all that you said to him; he was highly pleased with the open and friendly manner in which you communicated to him your sentiments, and the feelings and wishes of his red children, & he has authorised me to give you the following Answer.

Brothers,

When the Treaty between the white people and the red, was made at Greenville it was undoubtedly the intention of both parties, to live together in future as friends and Brothers, and that every part of the

Treaty should be honestly and faithfully complied with on both sides, and you may rest assured, that it is the real wish, and intention of the great Council and your Father the President that every part of the Treaty should be honestly and faithfully complied with on the part of the United States, & they have no doubt but you and our other red brethren feel an equal desire to fullfill every article on your part.

Brothers,

Your Father the President is convinced that by some accedent or neglect the goods which his red Children were entitled to by the Treaty have not all been punctually delivered in good order, and he is willing to make good to his red children all real deficiences, and in future such measures will be taken, as will insure the delivery of whole of the articles in July or the first of August annually in good order at Fort Wayne and Detroit.

Brothers,

What you said to your Father the President respecting the lands at St. Vinsuns on the Wabash has been attended to and proper instructions will be given to your good friend Governor Harrison for having the whole business fairly settled so as to prevent any uneasiness hereafter, and measures will likewise be taken for having the lines run and marked round each of the tracts of land reserved for the use of the United States by the Treaty of Greenville.

Brothers,

Your Father the President, was much pleased with what you said to him respecting strong drink, he rejoices to find that you wish to have no more of that poison introduced among his red children which has done them so much mischief; he will consult with the great Council of the sixteen States, which is now sitting,[1] on the subject of guarding you against this great evil, and also on that of establishing trading houses in your Country sufficient to supply your wants.

Brothers,

Your Father the President will order ploughs and hoes to be furnished at Fort Wayne for supplying his red children in the manner you have requested, and a Black-smith will also be placed there to mend your axes hoes and Guns, it is the wish of your father the President that two or three of his young red children should be selected, and placed with the Black-smith to learn of him how to mend axes hoes and Guns, so that in a few years you may have workmen of your own in your towns. Your Father will likewise give directions for having a convenient building erected at Fort Wayne, in which his red children may be accomodated when they meet to receive their goods.

Brothers,

You are hereby authorised to assure all the red people of the several Nations to which you belong that they may at all times depend on the friendship and fatherly protection, of your father the President, while their conduct continues to be friendly fair and honest towards each other and towards their white brethren, and it is the wish of your Father the President that when you shall be prepared to set out on your journey home that you may be protected by the great Spirit on your way and that you may return in safety to your own fire sides, and find all your families and friends in good health.

Given at the War Office City of Washington 7th: January 1802

H DEARBORN
Secretary of War.

FC (Lb in DNA: RG 75, LSIA); in a clerk's hand; at head of text: "To the great Chief the Little Turtle, and the other great Chiefs now with him from the Miamis, Pottowattama and Weas"; "L.S." within facsimile seal alongside dateline; in Lb this is the first document of the conference, with clerk's heading in margin: "Conference held with the Little Turtle and other Indian Chiefs." Printed in *National Intelligencer*, 12 Feb. 1802, following Document II; at head of text: "ADDRESS of the Secretary of War delivered January 7, 1802."

LANDS AT ST. VINSUNS: on 23 Jan. 1802, Dearborn informed William Henry Harrison that Little Turtle had raised the matter of "that tract on the Wabash, called Vincennes." The Indians, Dearborn wrote, "are uneasy & probably will be more so unless some measures are taken for adjusting the differences relative to the boundaries of that tract." At the president's request, Dearborn asked Har-

rison to confer with Indian leaders, and with those whites who claimed land around Vincennes, about a boundary for the tract. "It will be important that the Chiefs of the Nations interested are satisfied that no more land is inclosed," Dearborn advised, "than what the Treaty will fully & fairly justify." At a conference at Vincennes in August and September 1802, Harrison met considerable resistance from Indians when he pushed for an expansive definition of the intended tract. Recruiting influential leaders, including Little Turtle, to help him make the terms final at Fort Wayne the following June, Harrison succeeded in making the tract that was reserved to the United States at Vincennes some 1,800 square miles in size (*Terr. Papers*, 7:46-7, 63-4n; Robert M. Owens, *Mr. Jefferson's Hammer: William Henry Harrison and the Origins of American Indian Policy* [Norman, Okla., 2007], 62-6, 78-80).

[1] MS: "siting."

IV. Response of Little Turtle

FATHER   [7 Jan. 1802]

I now thank you for what you have said to us, I am also authorised to give you the thanks of my Brother Chiefs.

We have come a great distance to see you in order to make such arrangements with you as would be of service to your red children.

We are happy to find our expectations have been realised, what you have said to us shall be collected in our hearts & taken home and there communicated to your Red Children.

FC (Lb in DNA: RG 75, LSIA); in a clerk's hand; at head of text: "Little Turtle"; follows Document II in Lb. Printed in *National Intelligencer*, 12 Feb. 1802, following Document III; at head of text: "Answer of the Little Turtle, to the Secretary of War."

From Joseph Crockett

SIR   Jessamine County State of Kentucky Janry 4th. 1802

I am sensible of the Multiplicty of business you are Nessarily engaged in; and expect you Scarcely have a moment to Spare, But hope you will indulge me a few minutes until I make my acknowledgements for the late appointment you was pleased to confer on me, I flatter my self my conduct has been Such as will be approved of by the Honorable the Judges—and the people in general—As I have had a recent proof of this, Since I came into Office I have Served upwards of three hundred writs, All ranks of people Seems were Satisfyed and expresses their Obediance to the laws of the United States—

But do rejoice at the prospect of the excise and Stamp laws being repealed,

Their united wishes are that you Sir may live long to See the blessings of a lasting peace and the effects of a well regulated goverment which is by None more Sincerly wished for then your most Obedt and very Hble Servt   JOSEPH CROCKETT

RC (DLC); endorsed by TJ as received 22 Jan. and so recorded in SJL.

LATE APPOINTMENT: Crockett became marshal for the district of Kentucky in June 1801 (Vol. 32:592; Vol. 33:220, 676).

From Louis Desmarets

New-York, thomas street No. 17.

MONSIEUR LE PRÉSIDENT   Ce 4 janvier 1802.

Je suis Né Français, mais par circonstances et par inclination il y a neuf ans que je réside dans les E.U: je n'avais rien quand j'y arrivai, j'y ai toujours veçu dans la médiocrité, et j'y suis aujourd'hui dans la Misère; je me suis marié il y a deux ans avec une femme du pays, voila, avec deux enfans ma seule acquisition, si moralement j'en suis satisfait, d'un autre côté mon fardeau et mes peines en sont augmentées au triple et il ne me reste aujourd'hui pour toute ressource que celle de vous prier, Monsieur le Président de vouloir bien m'accorder votre aide; si j'avois quelque chose, peut-être qu'avec mes foibles talens et ma bonne conduite, je pourrois faire quelque chose, mais sans un Ami généreux et sans argent dans un pays étranger où l'Egoïsme reigne, je ne conçois pas qu'avec de l'honneur on puisse arracher le bandeau de la fortune

j'ai l'honneur d'être avec respect Monsieur le Président Votre très humble Et très obéissant serviteur   LOUIS DESMARETS

EDITORS' TRANSLATION

MISTER PRESIDENT

New York, 17 Thomas Street
this 4 January 1802.

I was born a Frenchman, but because of circumstances and my own inclination, I have been residing in the U.S. for nine years. I had nothing when I arrived, I have always lived in a poor condition and I am presently here in misery. I got married two years ago to a woman of this country, and that is, along with two children, my only acquisition. If morally I am satisfied with that, on the other hand my burden and my troubles have tripled, and today for all resource I have only to beg you, Mister President, to kindly grant me some help. If I had something, perhaps I could do something with my feeble talents and my good conduct, but, without a generous friend and without money in a foreign land where selfishness is king, I cannot imagine that one can honorably tear off the blindfold of fortune.

I have the honor to be with respect, Mister President, your very humble and very obedient servant   LOUIS DESMARETS

RC (DLC); endorsed by TJ as received 9 Jan. and so recorded in SJL.

To Theodore Foster

Jan. 4. 1802.

Th: Jefferson presents his compliments to the honble mr Foster. having now attentively considered the papers on the subject of offices in Rhode island, he will be happy to have a conference with mr Foster the first evening he can spare.

RC (WHi: Howard Green Papers); addressed: "The honble Mr. Theodore Foster." Not recorded in SJL.

From Gideon Granger

Jany. 4th. 1802

G Granger presents his Compliments to the President & takes the liberty to inclose The "Genius of Liberty" it may afford some Amusement in a liesure moment. he presumes it came from the pen of the Revd. Mr. Griswold of New Milford. Connecticut—he also takes the liberty of presenting to the President the following Extract of a Letter recd. from Alexr. Wolcott Esq Collector of Customs at Middletown—

"The removal of old Capt: Hinman would excite universal pity, for tho he is a man of very limited understanding and has been Warm in his devotion to federalism—yet he is universally esteemed in Other respects blameless, and of great benevolence and Integrity. His party zeal has originated in the military principle that being an Officer under Govermt. it is his duty without a very strict Investigation of measures to defend those by whom he is fed. The same principle will now make him as warm a defender of the Republican Administration. In truth so far as he understands the Question he is really a republican—Besides this he served with reputation thro, our revolutionary war, part of the time as Commander of a Ship of Ware of the United States. He is now old and depends for the Support of his family on his pay as Commander of a Revenue Cutter."

G Granger solicits pardon if he has assumd. too much liberty in forwarding this extract. And he takes pleasure in assuring the Presidt: that from Letters recd. last Mail [for] half the Counties in Connecticut he is persuaded [of] the rapid progress of Republican principles in [that] State.

RC (DNA: RG 59, LAR); torn; endorsed by TJ as received 4 Jan. and so recorded in SJL with notation "Capt Hinman"; also endorsed by TJ: "in favr. of Capt. Hinman, of revenue cutter New London." Enclosure: probably a copy of the poem, "Genius of Liberty," which concluded: "GENIUS of LIBERTY! thy dictates fram'd / Our CIVIL FABRIC, far thro' empires fam'd / Built on the Equal Rights of human kind / Here Honest men, not *Knaves* protection find. / The Structure stands, REPUBLICANS' bright boast / The dread of *Kings* and all the *Priv'leg'd* host" (printed in the Hartford *American Mercury*, 7 Jan. 1802).

For other publications by Stanley GRISWOLD, the Republican clergyman from New Milford, see Vol. 33:352-3.

Elisha HINMAN appealed directly to the president in an attempt to maintain his position (see Hinman to TJ, 16 Nov. 1801).

From Benjamin Henfrey

SIR   Baltimore Jany 4th. 1802
    Two Weeks ago I ventured to address a few Ideas for your Consideration on a subject in which I conceive that I could render the Public very essential service
    I now most humbly beg that your Excellency will order your Secretary to inform me what your sentiments are on the plan that I ventured to lay before you and if I have been so unfortunate as to have acted wrong by making the communication immediately to your Excellency, I shall ever esteem it a mark of great condecension & goodness if you will Order that I shall be informed through what department to make my Application—
    I have the honor to be with the highest degree of Veneration & Respect Sir Your Obedt. & most Humble Servt.
                                            BENJAMIN HENFREY

RC (DLC); at head of text: "His Excellency Thomas Jefferson"; endorsed by TJ as received 4 Jan. and so recorded in SJL.

TWO WEEKS AGO: Henfrey to TJ, 19 Dec. 1801.

From John F. Mercer

DEAR SIR   Annapolis Jan. 4th. 1802.
    Mr. Digges the President & Mr. Duckett a Member of the Council proposing to visit the City of Washington I beg leave to introduce them to your notice, if their personal qualifications & general estimation in Maryland have not already made them known to you—they are two main props of the Republican Administration in this State & altho' I am sensible that any addresses of this nature, may too frequently recur, yet I may safely trust to the merits of these Gentlemen for my excuse in this instance without relinquishing any pretensions which can be founded on the affectionate & respectful attachment, with which I am always
    Dr Sir yr Obed hb Serv.   JOHN F: MERCER

RC (DLC); endorsed by TJ as received 7 Jan. and so recorded in SJL with notation "Digges & Ducket."

Francis DIGGES represented Charles County and Allen Bowie DUCKETT represented Prince George's County in the Maryland House of Delegates in the 1790s, and both men served as members of the five-person advisory Governor's Council from 1801 through 1805. TJ appointed Duckett assistant judge of the circuit court for the District of Columbia in 1806 (Edward C. Papenfuse and others, eds., *Archives of Maryland: An His-* *torical List of Public Officials of Maryland*, new ser., 1 [Annapolis, 1990], 20, 21, 198, 237; JEP, 2:25).

From Louis de Tousard

MONSIEUR LE PRÉSIDENT
DES ETATS-UNIS.   Philadelphie ce 4 Janvier 1802.

Dans l'espoir dun acceuil favorable en présentant à Votre Excellence, des objects qui tendent à la Gloire de la Nation dont le Vœu vous a fait son premier Magistrat; à l'utilité du service militaire dont vous êtes le Chef et à l'accroissement des sciences que vous avez encouragées et protégées dans ce Pays; J'ai l'honneur de vous adresser le Mémoire cy inclus; de vous prier de vouloir l'acceuillir avec indulgence et le soumettre aux observations de la Société philosophique de Philadelphie que vous présidez: C'est le fruit de quelqu' expérience depuis trente sept années que je sers dans l'artillerie; ce sont des Extraits de Mémoires présentés et approuvés par l'académie Royale des sciences; des ouvrages de Mr. de Buffon, de plusieurs militaires distingués; et les remarques que j'ai faites durant le cours de mes dernieres Inspections. Si vous daignez le recevoir comme un témoignage de mon Zèle, Je regretterai moins, qu'un service très actif m'ait tenu constamment éloigné du siège du gouvernement et empêché jusqu'à présent d'ofrir à Votre Excellence l'hommage de mon respect. Je m'estimerai heureux, si dans le motif qui l'a dicté, vous daignez y distinguer un sincere désir d'être utile à un pays auquel Je me suis dévoué depuis 1776; dont j'ai arrosé de mon sang l'Indépendance, dans le quel J'ai réuni mes plus cheres espérances, et à la reconnoissance du quel J'ose prétendre même après moi, par le genre de travail dont je m'occupe depuis six ans. C'est un traité élémentaire à l'usage des officiers d'artillerie de Milice et de ligne, dans lequel les uns et les autres trouveront tout ce qui peut être utile dans ce genre de service; Le tout traduit et extrait des meilleurs auteurs de toutes les Nations qui ont le plus perfectionné cette Arme. Je l'avois porté avec moi, au mois d'avril dernier pour vous prier de me permettre de le publier sous vos auspices, aussitôt que les planches, et quelques changemens nécessaires dans l'ordre des matières et dans le style auroient été finis: En votre absence je l'ai móntré au Général Dearborn et au Gl. Smith.

J'aurois à me reprocher comme pere de famille si je ne profitois pas de cette occasion pour intéresser votre Excellence à mon sort futur.

Remarié depuis sept ans à Mlle Anna Maria Geddes, dont la famille vous est connue, J'ai trois filles de mon premier Mariage. À leur Education j'ai sacrifié tout ce que les fréquens changemens de résidence, une famille nombreuse et une multitude de compatriotes dans le malheur, m'ont laissé de libre de ma paye. J'ai fait part de ma Situation au Général Sam. Smith avec priere de vous la communiquer. Quoique dans les Mesures, nécessitées par le bien Général, les Intérêts particuliers soient comptés pour peu; J'ose cepandant faire valoir auprés de votre Excellence les droits qu'un bras perdû pour la liberté me donne à la reconnoissance des Etats Unis; une conduite, j'ose le dire, irréprochable; tout mon temps employé au service auquel je me suis dévoué; et par dessus tout, si l'on mettoit en question mon droit de citoyen Américain, si légitimement acquis le 4 Juillet 1776, votre protection, qu'alors je reclammerois comme français et que vous ne leur avez jamais refusée.

La langue française est tres familière à votre Excellence, et il m'est bien plus aisé de m'exprimer dans ma langue naturelle; c'est pourquoy J'ai pris la liberte de l'employer dans ma lettre et dans le mémoire cy joint, et sur quoy je réclamme votre Indulgence.

J'ai l'honneur d'être avec le plus profond respect De Votre Excellence Le tres humble et tres obeissant Serviteur

Louis Tousard
Lt Col. et Inspect d'artillerie

NB. Obligé de me servir de ma main gauche Je rèclamme votre indulgence pour l'écriture de ma lettre et du Mémoire.

EDITORS' TRANSLATION

MISTER PRESIDENT
OF THE UNITED STATES   Philadelphia, this 4 January 1802.
   In the hope of a favorable reception in presenting to your excellency subjects tending to the glory of the nation whose wish has made you its first magistrate; to the utility of the military service of which you are the chief, and to the increase of the sciences, which you have encouraged and protected in this country; I have the honor to address to you the enclosed memorandum, to pray you to kindly accept it with indulgence, and to submit it to the philosophical society of Philadelphia over which you preside. It is the fruit of some experience in the 37 years that I have been serving in the artillery; these are extracts of memoranda presented to and approved by the Royal Academy of Sciences, works of Mr. de Buffon, of many distinguished military men, and the remarks that I have made during the course of my latest inspections. If you condescend to receive it as a testimony of my zeal, I shall regret less that a very active service has constantly kept me far away from the seat of the government and until now prevented me from offering to your

excellency the tribute of my respect. I shall consider myself fortunate if you deign to distinguish in the motive that dictated therein a sincere desire to be useful to a country to which I have devoted myself since 1776; whose independence I have watered with my blood, in which I have united my dearest hopes, and to whose gratitude I dare lay claim, even after my lifetime, by the kind of work that has occupied me for the last six years. It is an elementary treatise for the use of militia and line officers of artillery, in which both will find everything that can be useful in that kind of service; the whole translated and extracted from the best officers of all the nations that have most perfected that branch. I had carried it with me last April to beg you to allow me to publish it under your auspices as soon as the plates and some necessary changes in the order of the material and in the style would have been finished. In your absence I showed it to General Dearborn and General Smith.

I should have cause to reproach myself as the father of a family if I did not take advantage of this occasion to interest your excellency in my future destiny. Remarried for seven years to Miss Anna Maria Geddes, whose family is known to you, I have three daughters by my first marriage. I have sacrificed for their education everything that frequent changes of residence, a large family, and a multitude of compatriots in misfortune have left me unspent from my pay. I have communicated my situation to General Samuel Smith with a request to apprise you of it. Although in the measures required for the general good private interests count for very little, I nevertheless dare bring up for your excellency's consideration: the rights that an arm lost for liberty give me to the gratitude of the United States; a behavior, I daresay, beyond reproach; all the time employed in the service to which I have been devoted; and, above all, should my right as an American citizen, so legitimately acquired on 4 July 1776, be called in question, your protection, which I would then claim as a Frenchman, knowing that you have never refused it to them.

The French language is very familiar to your excellency, and it is much easier for me to express myself in my native tongue; that is why I have taken the liberty of using it in my letter and in the attached memorandum, and on that score I lay claim to your indulgence.

I have the honor to be, with the deepest respect, your very humble and very obedient servant,   LOUIS TOUSARD
Lt Col. and Inspector of Artillery

N.B. Obliged to use my left hand, I claim your indulgence for the handwriting of my letter and the memorandum.

RC (CSmH); endorsed by TJ as received 7 Jan. and so recorded in SJL. Enclosure: probably a paper by Tousard, in French, on "épreuve de canons" (proof of cannons); presented to the American Philosophical Society at a meeting on 15 Jan., when Justus Erich Bollmann was requested to make a translation; referred to Benjamin Henry Latrobe at an APS meeting in February 1803 (APS, *Proceedings*, 22, pt. 3 [1884], 320, 333).

Anne Louis de Tousard (1749-1817) graduated from the French artillery school in Strasbourg in 1765. He volunteered to serve with the Continental Army during the American Revolution, was an aide-de-camp to Lafayette, and lost his right arm from a battle wound in 1778. Afterward he was with the French army in Saint-Domingue, returning to the United States in 1793. In 1795, he received a commission as an officer of artillery and engineers. He oversaw the construction of fortifications, drew up plans for the curriculum and operation of a military academy, and was appointed inspector of artillery. Tousard resigned from the army in March 1802 and joined the French military expedition to Saint-Domingue. From 1805 to 1816, he held consular positions for France in New Orleans, Philadelphia, and Baltimore. Meriwether Lewis, when classifying the U.S. Army's officers by politics and ability in 1801, put Tousard in the category "professionally the soldier without any political creed" (DAB; ANB; Norman B. Wilkinson, "The Forgotten 'Founder' of West Point," *Military Affairs*, 24 [1960-61], 177-88; Crackel, *Mr. Jefferson's Army*, 201n; list of officers, 24 July 1801, in DLC; Vol. 34:629-30).

Although best known for his work in natural history, the Comte de BUFFON also investigated a variety of scientific, technological, and mathematical subjects. In the 1760s, Buffon was interested in metallurgy and forges, performed experiments in the fabrication of naval cannons, and published the results (DSB, 2:576-7; Jacques Roger, *Buffon: A Life in Natural History*, trans. Sarah Lucille Bonnefoi, ed. L. Pearce Williams [Ithaca, N.Y., 1997], 354-7, 362-3, 393-4).

UN TRAITÉ ÉLÉMENTAIRE: Tousard had begun to compile a treatise on artillery in 1795, in response to a request from George Washington. In 1807, Tousard issued a prospectus seeking sub-

scribers for the publication of the work. Published in the United States in English, the *American Artillerist's Companion* appeared in installments from the fall of 1807 to the spring of 1809. When complete, it consisted of two volumes of text and one volume of plates. Advertisements noted that the material had been "extracted from the best memorials, and most recent publications on this important branch of Military Science." In the preface, Tousard quoted a brief letter from TJ in August 1807, in which TJ agreed to become a subscriber (Louis de Tousard, *American Artillerist's Companion, or Elements of Artillery*, 3 vols. [Philadelphia, 1809; repr. New York, 1969], v, xx; Sowerby, No. 1160; *Poulson's American Daily Advertiser*, 2 Dec. 1807; New York *American Citizen*, 3 Sep. 1807; Tousard to TJ, 1 Aug. 1807; TJ to Tousard, 7 Aug. 1807).

Tousard's second wife, ANNA MARIA GEDDES, who married him in 1795, may have been related to David Geddes. During the Revolutionary War, David Geddes was paymaster of the prisoners from General John Burgoyne's surrendered army. In that capacity Geddes had some contact with TJ in the period 1779-81, when TJ was governor of Virginia. Tousard's first wife, Maria Francisca Regina Joubert St. Martin, who was from Saint-Domingue, died in 1794 (DAB; Washington, *Papers, Rev. War Ser.*, 14:455; Vol. 3:64, 66; Vol. 4:516-17, 698; Vol. 27:689-90).

From William Goforth

MAY IT PLEASE THE PRESIDENT   Jan. 5th. 1802.

I would wish to bring into your immediate view the Government of the Northwestern territory under which the adventures to this remote part of the Empire have Sustained a deprivation of those privileges injoyed by our fellow citizens in the States in the Union.

Secondly to lay before the President the rational views we had in a short time to rise from that depresst State.

Thirdly to shew the means persued by our placemen to prevent our political resurection.

And fourthly to implore Presidential aid to restore us to the precious privilege of a free Elective Republican Government.

First as to our ordinance Government it is a true transcript of our old English Colonial Governments, our Governor is cloathed with all the power of a British Nabob, he has power to convene, prorogue and dissolve our legislature at pleasure, he is unlimitted as to the creation of offices, and I beleive his general rule is to fill all the important leading offices with men of his own political Sentiments, and I beleive he has not Issued a Single commission in the territory, not even excepting the Presideing Judges of the Common Pleas, on any other terms than those which he and the Judges of the Supreme Court in their adopting capacity have by a resolution declared to be dureing his will and pleasure except his own son who holds on the tenure of good behavior, it is easy to conceive that the influence of a Governor thus circumstanced will pervade our Elections, and hence we have seen (notwithstanding he holds in his hands an intire and commanding Branch of the Legislature a majority of his will and pleasure creatures in both houses of the Legislature, and if any man or the friends of any man wished their country to be benifitted by his services either in the Legislative Council or as an agent to Congress, to use the old Colonial dialect it would be prudent for him or them to be on exing[1] good terms with his Excellency

Secondly I was to lay before the President the reasonable views we had to emerge from this deprest State.

The Confederate Congress who gave assistence to the ordinance Government seem to have been conscious that such a Government would not sit well on citizens from the free states and therefore appear to meliorate it by the Solemn and unalterable compact with which they prop it, in the fifth article of which they divide the territory into States and assertain their boundaries and pledge the national faith that when either of these states shall have sixty thousand free inhabitants therein they shall be at liberty to form a perment State constitution and be received into the Union, and indeed the grand pivot on which this business hinges seems not to depend as much on numbers as the general interest of the confederacy, now it certainly must be for the general intrest to save the annuel Stipend paid to our placemen and it must finally be more to the general intrest, provided we mean to preserve our most excellent Republican Government, to have the citizens rared and nutured and matured under a free elective govment, than under a government highly tinctured with Aristocracy and monarchy which will rather fit the citizens for a monarchical than a Republican Government, I now beg leave to lay before you an extract taken from the Secretary of the territorys account of the Census taken last year.

The county of Hamilton laying on the Great Miami in which is Cincinati	14,671
The county of Wayne in which is detroit	3,206
The county of Washington in which is Marietta	5,427
The county of Ross in which is Chilicothe	8,540
The county of Adams on the Ohio opposite Limestone in Kentucky	3,452
The county of Jefferson county adjoining Pennsylvania	8,766
The county of trumble	1,303
If we substract from the Number Total which is 45,365	45,365
the citizens from Wayne county	3,260
the remaining Number will be	42:105

which have migrated to this territory in thirteen years which will average between three and² four thousand pr. year but it should be remembered that the first, 2d. 3d. and 4th. years did not amount to more than three 4 or five hundred a year, Since that time the numbers have been progressing and are not now less than 8,000 pr. year and as the census was taken a year ago I may with propriety place that number to the acct.   8,000

increase by population Since takeing the Census   1,000

and without casting any odium on the gentleman or gentlemen who took the Census an allowance may with Justice be made for the families that were missed oweing to our Scatterd situation in a wilderness, one of our placemen who is averse to going into a state Government told me six families had been missed just in his neigbourhood, I allow every 12th. family to have been missed which would be   3,780

57,145 total 57,145

Thirdly I come now to lay before the President the means persued by our placemen to prevent our political resurrection

The foregoing number of persons in the territory threw our placemen into the horrors Something must be done, a grand caucus was held in the town of Cincinati consisting of placemen expectants and those under their immediate influence, at which I think the very first charactors in the government attended and at which I have reason to beleive it was determined to divide the territory and in order to mask the treason against the majesty of the people petions were pushed about with great assiduity, the President may rely upon it that these petions did not originate with the body of Yeomonry in the country but with the aforesaid charactors of Cincinati, a friend of mine by my request favoured me with a copy of each of the petitions one to the Legislature and the other to Congress I have taken the liberty of incloseing them to the President in the last articles of each of these the President may see their efforts goes to prevent going into a State government and thereby protract their dominion over the citizens. This caucus as I apprehend was held before the meeting of the Legislature and was well understood by the Junto in and out of the Legislature and the bill for divideing the territory was passed before they received the petition to pass it, I have also taken the liberty to inclose the bill which I am informed passed without alteration in the house of Representative haveing orignated with the Legislative Council the perswasive inducements held out to the citizens in order to enduce them to sign said petitions were that if we went into a state government we should lose the forty four hundred dollars paid annually to our placemen, that their lands would be consumed by a Federal tax and that if we went into a division of the territory the towns of Cincinati and Marietta would become the seats of government, by going into a division of the government they expect to reduce our numbers to about 30,000 and to keep us in the State we are untill run upon 60,000 denova, nothing in my opinion can be a higher proof of my first position with respect to the governors powers than carrying a bill through both houses of the Legislature for altering the boundaries of the government in order to keep himself in power without the knowledge instructions or wish of the main body of the citizens

Fourthly I come now to implore Presidential aid in order to restore us to our former privileges which are injoyd by our fellow citizens in the Union, in this we only ask the nation to be Just and maintain inviolate the compact entered into by Congress under the confederation and maintain the National honour and faith and admit us to form a permanent State constitution And admit us into the Union, on it appearing that we have performed our part of the covenant; but if they suffer our government to be divided and thereby reduce our number to about 30,000 and keep us in the State we are until we amount to 60000 souls denova it will be dealing with us with as much duplicity as Laban made use of with Jacob respecting his daughter Rachel.

Permit me to observe to you that one of the members of the Legislature was very strenious for divideing the Government on seeing the petition to Congress, gave it as his opinion that it would not do to send it forward at the *present period* and whether they will send it forward at all I am not warranted to say, perhaps Mr McMillen who was agent from the territory to Congress last year may bring it with him as he is now ingaged by the gentlemen of Cincinati as their particular delagate and on the wages of a member of Congress it is supposed his influence will be equal to the accomplishment of their most Sanguine expectations, If any impediment should arise to government to put it out of their power to perform the covenant of the Confederate Congress, we object not to submit to what may be done by Congress provided we are emancipated from our present antirevolutional government, I have reference to the State of Virginia altering her line of session, with respect to which I am uninformed not having the Virginia code, if we must be divided, government may as well support us as free states, as territories, but if I might be permitted to give my opinion, that as we lean on the general government for protection in case of a war I think we could make out very well if we were excused from paying a federal tax on land or otherwise untill the next takeing the general Census. I shall only add that I beg your forgiveness for the present intrusion and that you would beleive me to be with every species of respect your most obedient Humble servant

WILLIAM GOFORTH.

RC (DLC); at foot of text: "To Thomas Jefferson President the United States"; endorsed by TJ as received 26 Jan. and so recorded in SJL with notation "N.W. territory." Enclosures: (1) Petition to the Council and House of Representatives of the Northwest Territory in the legislative session of 1801, praying for a resolution to land disputes within the Symmes tract; that trustees be appointed to take charge of school and ministerial tracts; that county levy laws be revised, township officers be elected by township residents, and the poll tax on married men be repealed; that the stray laws be amended to require advertisement in public papers; that less public money be spent on the salaries and travel of legislators; that territorial and county taxes be reduced; and that the legislature "not take any measure whatever towards entering into a state government," which action would be "highly prejudicial to our interest and happiness at this time"; the petitioners instead request that the territorial representative to Congress be instructed "to move for a redivision of the Territory," which would result in "material advantages" to the citizens at large (Tr in same; undated and unsigned; entirely in Goforth's hand). (2) Petition from the inhabitants of the Northwest Territory to Congress, praying that the formation of a state government be postponed, citing the large size of the territory, the isolation of its settlements from each other, the expense and inconvenience of rotating the general court between two locations, the lack of progress made in improving the territory overall, and the lack of convenient markets; statehood is being urged by only "a few designing, disconted Ambitious men"; the petitioners are happy to remain under the paternal care of Congress until the territory has developed further and suggest that a new division of the territory be made along the Scioto River, the western boundary of the French grant opposite Little Sandy Creek, or any other line that Congress deems proper (Tr in same; undated and unsigned; entirely in Goforth's hand). Other enclosure not found.

William Goforth came to the Northwest Territory from New York, where he had suffered financial reverses as a result of the Revolutionary War. He settled at Columbia, near Cincinnati in Hamilton County, where he served as a judge of the court of common pleas and justice of the peace. In October 1801, TJ appointed Goforth a commissioner for settling claims regarding the Miami Purchase lands of John Cleves Symmes. A Republican and staunch advocate of statehood, Goforth was elected to the Ohio constitutional convention in November 1802, where he presided briefly as president pro tempore. He would not write TJ again until 1807, when he recommended his son, Aaron, for office (ANB, 9:172-3; Terr. Papers, 3:141-2, 177-8, 295, 405, 413; Goforth to John Adams, 11 Aug. 1791, in MHi: Adams Papers; Downes, Frontier Ohio, 150, 181-3, 240; Sears, Thomas Worthington, 76-7, 94; Cayton, Frontier Republic, 63, 76-7; Vol. 33:671, 677; Goforth to TJ, 9 Oct. 1807).

OUR GOVERNOR: Arthur St. Clair.

HIS OWN SON: Arthur St. Clair, Jr., who was appointed attorney general of the Northwest Territory by his father in 1796 (Terr. Papers, 3:460).

The FIFTH ARTICLE of the Northwest Ordinance of 1787 stated that no less than three nor more than five states would be formed from the Northwest Territory, and fixed BOUNDARIES for the establishment of three future states: a western state bound by the Mississippi River on the west and a line from Vincennes on the Wabash River north to the Canadian border on the east; a middle state bound by the Vincennes line on the west and a line north from the mouth of the Great Miami River on the east; and an eastern state bound by the Great Miami River line on the west and Pennsylvania on the east. Congress reserved the right to alter these lines in the future, as well as to create one or two additional states north of an east-west line drawn from the southernmost point of Lake Michigan. Once each of these states attained a population of 60,000 free inhabitants, it would be RECEIVED INTO THE UNION on an equal footing with the original states. The article also permitted a state to be admitted with less than 60,000 residents, "so far as it can be consistent with the general interest of the Confederacy" (Terr. Papers, 2:48-9).

ANNUEL STIPEND PAID TO OUR PLACEMEN: on 3 Mch. 1801, Congress appropriated $5,500 for the salaries of the governor, secretary, and judges of the Northwest Territory and the contingent expenses of its government (U.S. Statutes at Large, 2:120).

Charles Willing Byrd was appointed SECRETARY of the Northwest Territory in December 1799, replacing William Henry Harrison (JEP, 1:330, 331).

DETERMINED TO DIVIDE THE TERRITORY: the Northwest Territory had been divided by Congress in 1800, when the territory of Indiana was created from most of the land west of the mouth of the Kentucky River. In an effort to maintain their power in the eastern division of the territory, Federalists sought to deflect Republican calls for statehood by recommending a new division of the entire territory, dividing the Ohio country down its center along the Scioto River and extending the eastern boundary of Indiana further west. Such a move would not only delay statehood by halving the population of the Ohio country, but would enhance the influence of the Federalist strongholds of Marietta and Cincinnati while simultaneously dividing Republican strength in the Scioto River valley around Chillicothe. Despite passing a redivision bill in the territorial legislature in December 1801, Federalists would not see the measure enacted in Washington. Rejecting the division act, Congress instead passed the Enabling Act on 30 Apr. 1802, which authorized the inhabitants of the eastern division of the Northwest Territory to meet in November 1802 and form a constitution and state government. The state of Ohio was subsequently admitted to the Union in 1803 (U.S. Statutes at Large, 2:58-9, 173-4; Annals, 11:465-6; Laws of the Territory of the United States, Northwest of the River Ohio: Passed at the First Session of the Second General Assembly, Begun and Holden at Chillicothe, on Monday, the Twenty-Third Day of November, One Thousand Eight Hundred and One [Chillicothe, 1802], 130-2; Brown, "Frontier Politics," 240-3; Cayton, Frontier Republic, 71-8; Downes, Frontier Ohio, 165, 186-200).

DENOVA: that is, de novo; anew (Bryan A. Garner, ed. in chief, Black's Law Dictionary, 8th ed. [St. Paul, Minn., 2004], 467).

In the Book of Genesis, chapter 29,

LABAN promised that JACOB could marry his younger daughter RACHEL after serving him for seven years. At the completion of the term, Laban instead tricked Jacob into marrying his elder daughter, Leah. He then promised Rachel to Jacob again in exchange for an additional seven years of service.

William McMillan (MCMILLEN) served in Congress as the delegate from the Territory Northwest of the River Ohio from 24 Nov. 1800 to 3 Mch. 1801 (*Biog. Dir. Cong.*).

[1] Thus in MS.
[2] MS: "and and."

To Benjamin Henfrey

Washington Jan. 5. 1802.

Th: Jefferson presents his compliments to mr Henfrey, and acknoleges the reciept of his 1st. & 2d. letters proposing that persons should be employed by the general government to explore mines of metal & coal, to assay ores & make proper reports thereof to the owners of the land, to search for marles, limestone, designate canals, roads &c but observes to him that these objects not being among the powers transferred by the States to the General government, nor among the purposes for which the latter is authorized to levy money on the people, the State governments alone are competent to the pursuits proposed.

PrC (DLC); endorsed by TJ in ink on verso.

HIS 1ST. & 2D. LETTERS: Henfrey to TJ, 19 Dec. 1801 and 4 Jan. 1802.

To the Senate

GENTLEMEN OF THE SENATE

The late Secretaries of State and of the Treasury & late Attorney General having been appointed Commissioners under the act entitled 'An act for an amicable settlement of limits with the state of Georgia, and authorising the establishment of a government in the Missisipi territory,' and the act supplementory thereto passed on the 10th. of May 1800. I now nominate, in their stead,
the present Secretary of State, James Madison,
the present Secretary of the Treasury, Albert Gallatin, and
the present Attorney General, Levi Lincoln
    to be Commissioners under the same acts.

TH: JEFFERSON
Jan. 5. 1801 [i.e. 1802].

RC (DNA: RG 46, EPEN); with figure "1," in last digit of year in dateline, overwritten to "2," probably by a Senate clerk; endorsed by a Senate clerk. PrC (DLC); lacks change in dateline.

APPOINTED COMMISSIONERS: for a description of the acts under which the president made the nominations, see Madison to TJ, 24 Dec. 1801. The Senate confirmed the appointments on 6 Jan. and requested that Samuel A. Otis inform the president of their action (JEP, 1:400, 404).

From Samuel R. Demaree

DEAR SIR,   Harrodsburgh (Ky.) Jan. 6th. 1802

Reflecting on the happy situation of America—that her Rulers are not inaccessable tyrants nor bloody despots; but patriots, friends of mankind, and of the unfortunate; examples to the world & patrons of science, I am emboldened to communicate a few of my wishes even to our chief Magistrate, which however defective in form and matter, I hope you will not attribute to any unworthy motive.

For your satisfaction I would just inform you, I am the son of a poor but independent *farmer*; in the dispensations of divine Providence, I am nearly deprived of the use of my right arm which consequently prevents me from engaging in the peacible employment of husbandry, and almost forces me to seek the tempestous road of public life: which I will gladly do if I may be of service to my country.

It must be painful to every patriot, to see the negligence and supineness of the youth here—how ignorance and vice triump over reason and knowledge! Pardon me if I entreat you, if possible, by some method or other to inspire my fellow-youth with application and virtue. I forbear saying anything about our masters lest for want of penetration I might mistake: but I would fain see them more concerned for the advancment of their pupils, and the improvement of science.

I am particularly unfortunate in a way of procuring Books—No peculiar friend of extensive information to whom I might apply for direction in the purchasing of books—there are many branches of the sciences, and different authors have written on the same branch—so expensive that I cannot buy them all, and I know not which branch, and what author thereon, is preferable:—I therefore humbly request you to send me the names of those books which would make the cheapest and most useful *library** for an individual citizen. From your extensive knowledge of books I was induced to apply to you, and

---

* What Authors on rhetoric, Logic, Philosophy, Astronomy &c by name, if you please, viz *Simson's* or *Barrow's* Euclid—S.R.D.

from your goodness as a literary character I hope you will indulge me a little in this request. If you are so good as to take notice of this, I entreat you to add what directions and information you may think proper, and I will cheerfully attend to them: but if I have erred, (as I possibly may) and you should not think it worthy of attention, at least pardon me for intruding upon you thus—my intention I trust is philanthropic

If you should grant my request I will rejoice, if not, I can but bemoan my ignorance and misfortune: yet I hope to remain a sincere patriot and admirer of your conduct hitherto and as long as it shall be worthy, which I hope will be untill you descend with honor to the grave

Yours affectionately,   SAML. R. DEMAREE

RC (DLC); addressed: "Honorable Thomas Jefferson President U.S. Washington (City)"; franked; postmarked 8 Jan. 1802; endorsed by TJ as received 3 Feb. and so recorded in SJL.

Samuel R. Demaree, a teacher and newspaper publisher, carried on an infrequent correspondence with TJ during his presidency and retirement, primarily on topics related to education. In 1805, TJ forwarded Demaree's thoughts on orthography to the American Philosophical Society, whose committee report on the subject was sent to Demaree by the president. Later that same year, Demaree and Samuel Ogilsby commenced publication of the *Informant* in Danville, Kentucky. Although TJ did not reply to the above request for book recommendations, he did respond to another request from Demaree in 1809 by supplying him with an extensive list of titles (Brigham, *American Newspapers*, 1:149; APS, *Proceedings*, 22, pt. 3 [1884], 370, 371; RS, 1:455-7, 575-7, 580-2; Demaree to TJ, 28 Dec. 1804, 28 Aug. 1805; TJ to Demaree, 6 May 1805).

SIMSON'S OR BARROW'S EUCLID: Scottish mathematician Robert Simson published a definitive edition of Euclid's *Elements* in 1756. TJ owned a copy of Simson's work and recommended it to Demaree in 1809. English mathematician and theologian Isaac Barrow published versions of Euclid's works in the late 1650s (DNB; Sowerby, No. 3702; RS, 1:576).

From the District of Columbia Commissioners

SIR,   Commissioners Office 6th. January 1802

William Rhodes having raised a frame for the purpose of a stable within eight feet of the building in which this Office is kept, and little more than twelve feet of the Office of the Clerk of Washington County, and still nearer than either to another brick building, the Commissioners on the 10th. ulto. wrote him the Letter, A. whereupon Mr. Rhodes agreed with a Gentleman for liberty to place the frame on an adjacent Lot, and declared his intention to remove it thither as soon as it should be in a state to remove with ease and safety—We however observed that he was preparing to underpin the frame, where it now stands, and in consequence wrote him the Letter (B); since which, we understand, legal advice has been sought, and an Opinion obtained, that no power exists in us to remedy this evil in a summary way; a principle which leads to important consequences, and which we presume may as well be determined in the present as in any future case; but, although we are of opinion, that such avowed infractions of established rules should be checked, and that this building in particular should be removed or demolished, yet we do not think it prudent to engage in a measure, which may probably end in litigation, without the direction of the President, or the opinion of his Counsel, as to the power of the Commissioners to enforce a compliance with the rules and regulations established by the President respecting the materials & manner of building in the City, and the mode of carrying that power into effect.—That such Opinion may be obtained we enclose an Extract of the Deeds of Trust (C) and a Copy of the rules and regulations established by President Washington in pursuance thereof (D).

It may be proper to observe that the operation of the 1t. & 3d. Articles of those rules has been suspended till the first day of the present month, with this exception, that no wooden building should be placed within twenty four feet of a brick or stone building. This frame being within that distance we presume must be subject to the rules first established—We are

with sentiments of the highest respect, Sir, Yr most Obt Servts.

WILLIAM THORNTON
ALEXR. WHITE
TRISTRAM DALTON

RC (DLC); in Thomas Munroe's hand, signed by Thornton, White, and Dalton; addressed: "President of the United States"; endorsed by TJ as received 6 Jan. and so recorded in SJL. FC (DNA: RG 42, DCLB). Enclosures: (1) District of Columbia commissioners to William Rhodes, Commissioners' Office, 10 Dec. 1801, asking Rhodes to remove the wooden building just erected near the office, "contrary to rules and regulations established for building in the City of Washington" (Tr in DLC; in Munroe's hand; endorsed as letter "A"). (2) Commissioners to William Rhodes, 5 Jan. 1802, reiterating their letter of 10 Dec. in observation of Rhodes's measures to make the building permanent despite his agreement with "Mr. Munroe" to move the building to Munroe's lot (Tr in DLC; in William Brent's hand; endorsed as letter "B"). For other enclosures, see below.

For the DEEDS OF TRUST between proprietors of land in the District of Columbia and trustees of the federal government drawn up in June 1791, see Samuel Burch, comp., *A Digest of the Laws of the Corporation of the City of Washington, to the First of June, 1823* (Washington, D.C., 1823), 330-4; Vol. 34:198-200.

The building REGULATIONS, also es-tablished in 1791, and TJ's approval of the suspension of ARTICLES 1 and 3 until 1 Jan. 1802, are discussed in Vol. 33:154-5.

From Blair McClenachan

SIR,   Philada. Jany. 6th. 1802.

Upon a former occasion I took the liberty of applying for Some place under the Government—and of explaining the personal circumstances that induced the Solicitation.

I trust I do not Seek an improper or an unmerited favour—indeed the purity of your principles, must repel any man, who knows you; from obtruding an improper request.

When I was young and rich, my means were devoted to the independance of America; and now when I am Neither, if my Services and industry in any office could procure me independence I should be happy.

Permit me to mention Sir, That the place now held by Israel Whelen the purveyor of Stores, it is Said, will be Soon vacant—Should it be So, may I presume to Specify, that, as a Situation the duties of Which I trust I Should discharge Without detriment to the people or discredit to Myself.

Pray Sir, accept My unfeigned respect.

BLAIR MCLENACHAN

RC (DNA: RG 59, LAR); in a clerk's hand, signed by McClenachan; endorsed by TJ as received 20 Jan. and so recorded in SJL; also endorsed by TJ: "to be Purveyor of stores."

UPON A FORMER OCCASION: see Blair McClenachan to TJ, 16 May 1801.

WHEN I WAS YOUNG AND RICH: during the American Revolution, McClenachan had been a member of the First Troop of Philadelphia cavalry, an outfitter of privateers, as well as a public creditor for the American war effort. A wealthy trader, banker, and shipowner who maintained a grand country estate at Cliveden for eighteen years, he rivaled Robert Morris as the largest importer in Philadelphia. A failed partnership, numerous business speculations, and the fraudulent transfer of assets to his children changed his fortune and led to the merchant's financial ruin and imprisonment for debt. After service in the state assembly and as a Republican congressman in the House of Representatives from 1797 to 1799, McClenachan continued to look for steady employment and, in 1801, was listed in the *Philadelphia Directory* simply as a "gentleman" who lived at 167 Walnut Street (John H. Campbell, *History of the Friendly Sons of St. Patrick and of the Hibernian Society for the Relief of Emigrants from Ireland* [Philadelphia, 1892], 126; E. James Ferguson and others, eds., *Papers of Robert Morris, 1781-1784*, 9 vols. [Pittsburgh, Pa., 1973-2000], 1:250; Bruce H. Mann, *Republic of Debtors: Bankruptcy in the Age of American Independence* [Cambridge, Mass., 2002],

214; Abraham Ritter, *Philadelphia and Her Merchants* [Philadelphia, 1860], 159-60; PMHB, 88 [1964], 35; Stafford, *Philadelphia Directory, for 1801,* 94).

PURVEYOR OF STORES: the position left vacant by the resignation of Israel Whelen was not filled until November 1803 when TJ nominated Tench Coxe (JEP, 1:453; Blair McClenachan to TJ, 8 July 1803).

From Thomas Newton

DR SIR   Norfolk Jany 6. 1802

Mr. Taylor has inform'd me, that he has forwarded the Cyder, which I hope may get up safe & good, in bottling it will be a good way to rince the bottle with good apple brandy, it not only preserves it, but prevents the bottles in some measure from bursting. a raison thrown into each bottle, assists it much, & makes it sparkle like Champagne; if you bottle small beer, by throwing a teaspoonful of good French brandy in a bottle, it adds much to its taste, & saves the bottles—direct that no more brandy, be left in the bottle than sticks to it by rincing, in which you have the Cyder put.—the whites in St Domingo, escaped a general Masacre, we are inform'd, by a mistake in the day, it was to take place, some going by the old & the others by the new calendar, which caused a discovery in time, Genl Moyse having lost an eye, in an action with the whites, it seems was the cause & he vowed a general extirpation of the whole, on account of it, these are the accts. we had yesterday, by an arrival from that Island.—

May health & many happy years attend you are the wishes of yours respectfully   THOS NEWTON

I have been laid up with the gout near a fortnight & unable to attend my duty in the Senate—

RC (DLC); endorsed by TJ as received 14 Jan. and so recorded in SJL.

By late December 1801, news arrived to the U.S. about the November trial and execution of General MOYSE for conspiracy against Toussaint-Louverture's government in Saint-Domingue. Moyse rallied hatred against whites to gain support for the rebellion that occurred in October 1801 (Savannah *Georgia Gazette*, 24 Dec. 1801; *Philadelphia Gazette*, 31 Dec. 1801; Madison, *Papers, Sec. of State Ser.,* 2:207-8; Thomas O. Ott, *The Haitian Revolution 1789-1804* [Knoxville, 1973], 79, 148-9).

Newton served in the Virginia state SENATE from 1797 to 1805 (Leonard, *General Assembly*, 210-38).

To the Senate: Interim Appointments

EDITORIAL NOTE

Jefferson wrote his son-in-law, John Wayles Eppes, on 1 Jan. 1802 that although Republicans held an 18 to 14 majority in the Senate, through absences "hitherto we have been so nearly equal there, that I have not ventured to send in my nominations, lest they should be able to dismast the administration." Meanwhile, the president was giving thought to the arrangement of the list of more than 120 interim appointments he would place before the Senate. Upon taking office, Jefferson made it clear that he considered the numerous appointments made by Adams after 12 Dec. 1800, when the result of the election was known, as nullities. He characterized them as "midnight appointments" and did not think of them as removals, but as nominations that should never have taken place. While he could not revoke the "life appointments" of judges, Jefferson believed the other "midnight" nominees did not hold their offices "by any title meriting respect." In the early weeks of the administration, he maintained that even Adams's best friends did not "disapprove of this" policy. However, the outrage expressed over the president's appointment of Samuel Bishop to the New Haven collectorship in place of Elizur Goodrich, considered a midnight appointment by Jefferson, made it clear that many Federalists did not accept the argument. Others questioned Jefferson's interim appointments due to resignations, believing that some officeholders were pressured to resign. According to the president, the principles that governed his removals included delinquency of accounts, default, or other "malversations"; the restoration to office of those dismissed by Adams solely for political reasons; to "counterpoise the federalism of the courts" by appointing Republican marshals and district attorneys; and, lastly, to give some participation to Republicans. After perusing a list of interim appointments in chronological order, and developing his own list arranged by states, Jefferson decided to submit the interim appointments arranged according to his principles for appointments and removals. He presented the document to the Senate for approval on 6 Jan. 1802, a month after Congress convened (Malone, *Jefferson*, 4:73-9; Carl E. Prince, "The Passing of the Aristocracy: Jefferson's Removal of the Federalists, 1801-1805," *Journal of American History*, 57 [1970], 563-75; Lucius Junius Brutus, *An Examination of the President's Reply to the New-Haven Remonstrance; with an Appendix, Containing the President's Inaugural Speech, the Remonstrance and Reply; Together with a List of Removals from Office, and New Appointments, Made since the Fourth of March 1801* [New York, 1801]; Vol. 33:413-15, 427-8, 465-6, 668-74; Vol. 34:381-4, 554-7; Document v, below).

In December 1801, Jacob Wagner sent Jefferson a list of the appointments made during the recess of the Senate, for which the State Department had provided temporary commissions, which were valid until the Senate adjourned at the close of the session. The Senate had to approve the nominations before permanent commissions could be issued. The list from the State Department was arranged, for the most part, in chronological order by categories (see Document III). The longest section, consisting primarily of general government and State Department appointments, including judges, marshals, district attorneys, and extending to the appointment of Thomas Tudor Tucker as U.S. treasurer on 30 Nov., was followed by Treasury Department appointments to offices for the collection of internal and external revenues, arranged in a random order, with the final entries appearing after the section on consular appointments. The section on "Consuls & Commercial Agents" was arranged chronologically, except for the appointment of Charles Pinckney to Madrid, his secretary, and the secretary of the French legation, which appeared at the end. Jefferson carefully considered the list he received from the State Department. At most entries he indicated an abbreviated geographic designation of the state or territory, or in the case of consuls and commerical agents, the country of the port of residence. He wrote "Genl." at the names of Albert Gallatin and Robert Smith, cabinet members, and several others, including Gideon Granger, postmaster general.

The president had thoroughly perused the State Department list by the time he wrote Gallatin an undated memorandum inquiring whether Josiah Hook, Thomas Worthington, and five others should remain on the list as inspectors, a position abolished under the Executive Order on Revenue Districts of 29 July 1801 (see Vol. 34:676-7). Jefferson received Gallatin's reply on 26 Dec. The Treasury secretary noted that only Worthington had been appointed inspector of internal revenues. The others were collectors of external revenues at ports and their additional appointment as inspectors had nothing to do with the abolished positions. Jefferson subsequently drew a diagonal line through Worthington's entry in Document III (see note 8) and did not enter his name in the subsequent list he drafted.

Using the marginalia he had entered on the list from the State Department, Jefferson probably drafted his first list of nominations (Document IV), shortly after he received the information from Gallatin. Jefferson brought all of those he had designated as "Genl." to the top of the list. He then arranged the appointments according to states, beginning with New Hampshire and extending down the coast to Georgia, followed by Kentucky, the territories, the District of Columbia, and the commissioners to treat with the Indians.

He closed the list with "Consul appointments uncommissioned," arranged by the country of residence or by the country controlling the port. As Jefferson entered the nominations using his geographical arrangement, he drew a line, in ink, through his abbreviations in the margin of the State Department list and placed a check mark, in pencil, by the entry. After transferring the nominations from the State Department list to his own draft, Jefferson added information, which appears in a darker ink, at the end of the entries, giving the reason for the appointment. At first Jefferson used the information provided by the State Department that indicated whether the position had been filled because of resignation, vacancy, or promotion. He probably relied on that list when he added "promoted" at the appointment of John S. Sherburne of New Hampshire in place of Jeremiah Smith. In subsequent manuscripts, Jefferson noted that Sherburne was appointed in place of Edward St. Loe Livermore, an 18 Feb. nominee of Adams (see Document VI). But Jefferson soon began to provide new information in his short emendations. With the word "dead," he pointed out that Samuel Jasper and Richard Wylly had died in office. The State Department never used "removed" to explain a change; Jefferson used that specific designation 24 times. An entry and cancellation by Jefferson under Northwest Territory indicates that he was consulting his personal list of appointments and removals, which he kept from the beginning to the end of his presidency (see Vol. 33:674-9). The president entered the names of William Goforth and John Reily as commissioners for the John Cleves Symmes land contracts on his personal list at 3 Oct. He interlined the entry on his list of nominations at Northwest Territory and then canceled it when he realized the entry was not included on the State Department list and did not require Senate confirmation. The president may have obtained the information that James Powell was "removed for delinquency" and Samuel McDowell was "removed for misconduct" by consulting his personal list. At several nominations, the State Department noted the position was "vacant" and did not include the name of the person who had been replaced. Jefferson added, in pencil, at 15 entries, the names of people chosen late in the Adams administration who were not recognized by the new administration. Eight of these were consular appointments. In Jefferson's personal list they were designated as midnight appointments. Jefferson emended other State Department entries pertaining to consuls. The State Department noted that William Buchanan was appointed instead of Jacob Lewis, and Jefferson emended the entry to indicate that Buchanan replaced George Stacey and that Lewis was appointed to Calcutta (see Document IV, note 9). Jefferson subsequently placed Stacey with midnight appointments and dropped the reference to Lewis from the entry (see Document VI).

Building on his emendations to Document IV, Jefferson prepared a draft of the nominations as he would present them to the Senate on 6 Jan. (Document VI). The president organized the list according to his rationale for removals and appointments and provided keys to his new arrangement, explaining the categories by which the appointments were organized (see Document V). In preparing the manuscript he gave to the Senate, Jefferson moved only four names from the arrangement in his final draft, three marshals and one district attorney near the close of the document (see Document

VI, note 11). He transferred them from the category of those removed for default to those removed to give some participation to Republicans, who had been systematically excluded, especially in the courts.

Jefferson completed his list of interim nominations as presented to the Senate with the 30 justices of the peace appointed for the District of Columbia. They were not included in the keys Jefferson prepared to explain the arrangement of the nominees. He considered the justices late-term appointments, but he did not arrange them with the other midnight appointments on the list. The appointment of the justices had become controversial, and Jefferson may have recognized that the Senate was likely to consider them apart from the other nominations, which is indeed what occurred.

The problem had its origins on 27 Feb. 1801, when John Adams signed "An Act concerning the District of Columbia," which called for the appointment of various officers, including justices of the peace. According to the legislation, the president was to appoint for a five-year term "such number of discreet persons to be justices of the peace" as he "shall from time to time think expedient." The justices were to take an oath "for the faithful and impartial discharge of the duties of the office," including "all matters, civil and criminal, and in whatever relates to the conservation of the peace" (U.S. Statutes at Large, 2:107). On 2 Mch., Adams submitted the nominations for 23 justices of the peace for Washington County and 19 for Alexandria County. The Senate approved the nominations the next day. During the last day of the administration, the State Department rushed to make out the commissions for these and numerous other appointments. Daniel Brent, a State Department clerk, later testified that after the commissions for the justices of the peace were prepared, he carried them to President Adams for his signature. After they were signed, he carried them back to the secretary's office, where the seal of the United States was affixed to them. He did not believe, however, that the commissions were recorded or delivered (JEP, 1:388, 390; Cranch, *Reports*, 1:143).

Shortly after taking office, Jefferson ordered that the commissions for the justices remaining at the State Department should not be delivered and began compiling his own list of candidates for justices of the peace (see Documents I and II). Jefferson later explained that he believed delivery was essential to give validity to a commission, and until it was delivered the president was entitled to withhold it at his discretion (TJ to George Hay, 2 June 1807, in DLC). By 16 Mch. 1801, the new president was ready to reveal his nominees. Concluding that 15 justices for each county would be sufficient, he ordered two general commissions to be made out. The one for Washington County included 13 justices appointed by Adams and 2 by himself, including the last minute inclusion of Benjamin More instead of John Laird (see Document II). The commission for justices of the peace for Alexandria County included 11 named by Adams and 4 new candidates added by Jefferson. On 18 Mch., the names of the newly appointed justices appeared in the *National Intelligencer*. That same day Chief Justice John Marshall wrote his brother: "to withhold the commission of the Justices is an act of which I entertaind no suspicion. I shoud however have sent out the commissions which had been signd & seald but for the extreme hurry of the time & the absence of Mr. Wagner who had been calld on by the President to act as his private Secretary" (Marshall, *Papers*, 6:90). Of the 18 justices of the peace who were named by Adams but not by Jefferson, 4 later came to the office of the secretary of state requesting their commissions. When they failed to receive a satisfactory response, William Marbury, Dennis Ramsay, Robert T. Hooe, and William Harper brought their case before the December 1801 term of the Supreme Court with Charles Lee, former attorney general, acting as counsel. Madison did not appear before the court to argue why a mandamus should not be issued commanding the delivery of the commissions. Lee argued that the justices of the peace "hold their offices independent of the will of the President. The appointment of such an officer is complete when the President has nominated him to the senate, and the senate have advised and consented, and the President has signed the commission and delivered it to the secretary to be sealed. The President has then done with it; it becomes irrevocable." On 18 Dec., Marshall ruled that at the next term of court arguments would be heard on the issuance of a writ of mandamus (Cranch, *Reports*, 1:151; Madison, *Papers, Sec. of State Ser.*, 2:319-20; Marshall, *Papers*, 6:160-5).

On 26 Jan., the Senate approved all of the interim nominations, except those of justices of the peace for the District of Columbia. After conferring with Francis Peyton, the president, on 5 Apr., sent a message to the Senate revising the list of justices, replacing those who had resigned or declined to qualify with new candidates, three for each county. The Senate approved the appointment of the justices, both those nominees of 5 Apr. and then those of 6 Jan., on 27 Apr., a week before the session ended (JEP, 1:405, 417-18, 422-3, 425; TJ to Francis Peyton, 31 Mch., and Peyton to TJ, 2 Apr. 1802).

I. Tables of Justices of the Peace for the District of Columbia

Justices' Commissions given out.	Commissions not given.				
Washington county					
l 1 William Thornton	-	Daniel Carrol	a	5	Daniel Reintzell
f 2 Thomas Peter.	-	Thomas Sim Lee	k	12	John Mason
n 3 W. H. Dorsey.		John Laird	g	8	Robert Brent
d. 9 Daniel Carrol		Uriah Forest	i	10	Abraham Boyd
b. 4 Thomas Sim Lee		Marshan Warring	o	15	Joseph Sprigg Belt
j 14 John Laird		Benjamin Stoddert	c.	6	Thomas Corcoran
h 11 Thos. Addison	l	John Mason			
		Abraham Boyd	m	13	Thomas Law
		Joseph Sprig Belt			*<John Oakley>*
	-	James Barry	e.	7	Cornelius Cunningham.
		Thomas Addison			
		Tristram Dalton			
		William Marbury			
		John Threlkeld			
	x	Daniel Reintzell			
		Thomas Beall			
	-	Robert Brent			

Alexandria county.					
6 Charles Alexander.	qu.	*<Francis Peyton>*		3	Francis Peyton
<George Gilpin>		William Harper		1.	George Gilpin
9 Jonah Thompson.		Simon Summers		5	Elisha Cullen Dick
11 John Herbert		Robert T. Hooe		7	George Taylor
13 Cuthbert Powell		John Potts		10	Abraham Faw
15 Jacob Houghman.	-	*<William>* Fitzhugh.		12	Alexander Smith.
2. William Fitzhugh.		*<Richard Conway>*		14	Peter Wise junr.
4. Richard Conway				qu.	Thomas Darne.

MS (DNA: RG 59, LAR); undated; entirely in TJ's hand; TJ wrote on verso: "Samuel Hanson of Samuel Notary public"; endorsed by TJ: "Columbia. Justices."

COMMISSIONS GIVEN OUT: an undated memorandum that Jacob Wagner sent the president, probably shortly after TJ took office, includes the names of three justices of the peace in Washington County and six in Alexandria County whose commissions were not in the State Department office and had presumably been delivered. They were for Thornton, Peter, and Dorsey in Washington County and Alexander, Gilpin, Thompson, Herbert, Powell, and Houghman in Alexandria, all of whom appear in the same order in the first column above. TJ included them all in his final list of justices, perhaps because of his belief that commissions became valid upon delivery. Wagner's memorandum also included a column for "Commissions not made out," with the names of five Adams appointees who do not appear on TJ's lists above and were not considered for appointment. They are Richard Forrest, Lewis Deblois, Dennis Ramsay, Jonathan Swift, and Cleon Moore. Others named by Wagner in that column whom TJ did consider were Republicans Cornelius Coningham, George Taylor, and Abraham Faw. TJ added their names to the tables above and they were appointed (see Document II; Vol. 33:173n; 180, 235-6, 452n; Matthew Lyon to TJ, 5 Mch. 1807, and enclosures, in DNA: RG 59, LAR, 10:0702-6). Ramsay sought his commission from the State Department and was one of the plaintiffs in the case of Marbury vs. Madison. Daniel Brent, a State Department clerk, testified in 1803 that "he made out the list of names by which the clerk who filled up the commissions was guided" and that he believed Ramsay's name was omitted by mistake (Cranch, *Reports of Cases*, 1:143).

COMMISSIONS NOT GIVEN: Wagner's list of commissions not in the office and presumably delivered is indicative of the confusion surrounding the commissions for Adams's appointments for the justices of the peace. Daniel Brent later testified that he believed none of them was "ever sent out, or delivered to the persons for whom they were intended; he did not know what became of them." James M. Marshall, brother of John Marshall, recalled that on his way home on 4 Mch. he stopped in the office of the secretary of state for the commissions for Alexandria County. He thought as many as 12 commissions were delivered to him, for which he gave a receipt. Finding that "he could not conveniently carry the whole, he returned several of them, and struck a pen through the names of those, in the receipt, which he returned." He believed he had returned those for William Harper and Robert T. Hooe. Many years later TJ recalled: "among the midnight appointments of mr Adams were commissions to some federal justices of the peace for Alexandria. these were signed and sealed by him, but not delivered. I found them on the table of the Department of State, on my entrance into office, and I forbade their delivery" (Cranch, *Reports of Cases*, 1:143, 146; TJ to William Johnson, 12 June 1823).

A comparison of the tables above with Wagner's memorandum suggests that TJ created his tables by listing in the first column those who had received their commissions, that is, Thornton through Dorsey in Washington County and Alexander through Houghman in Alexandria County. He next listed those Adams appointees for whom commissions were made out but not "given" or delivered, including all of the names in the second column, Carrol through Conway. TJ then moved some names from one column to another and added names to complete the tables as printed above. The first and third columns contain names of those people who received appointments as justices of the peace, except for John Laird and Thomas Law, who were replaced later in the process (see Document II). In the Washington County table, TJ did not cancel names as he moved them to different positions (as with John Mason, for example). In the table for Alexandria County, he struck through names that he transferred to different columns. TJ followed the numerical sequence indicated by figures before the candidates' names for Alexandria County when he made out his final list for the general commission. He omitted the number "8," but in his subsequent list George Taylor precedes Jonah Thompson (see Document II). Similarly, TJ may have been working out the sequence of names for the Washington County commission when he placed numbers and then letters alongside the justices he selected for that county. For considerations that influenced Adams and TJ in the selection of the justices, see David F. Forte, "Marbury's Travail: Federalist Politics and William Marbury's Appointment as Justice of the Peace," in *Catholic University Law Review*, 45 (1995-96), 395-402.

II. Memorandum on Justices of the Peace for the District of Columbia

[on or before 16 Mch. 1801]

reduced the number from about 20. to 15. for each county adding to 11. of those named by mr Adams for Alexandria[1] county, the 4. others marked with an * in the following list, & to 14. of those named by mr Adams for Washington county, 1 other have been added.[2] a commission is consequently made out as follows.

for Washington county	for Alexandria county
Thomas Sim Lee	George Gilpin
Daniel Reintzell	William Fitzhugh
* Thomas Corcoran	Francis Peyton
Daniel Carrol	Richard Conway
Cornelius Cunningham	* Elisha Cullen Dick
Thomas Peter	Charles Alexander
Robert Brent	George Taylor
Thomas Addison	Jonah Thompson
Abraham Boyd	Abraham Faw
Benjamin More[3]	John Herbert
John Mason	* Alexander.Smith
William Thornton	Cuthbert Powell
Benjamin Stoddert[4]	* Peter Wise junr.
William Hammond Dorsey	Jacob Houghman
Joseph Sprigg Belt.	qu * Thomas Darne

MS (DNA: RG 59, MCL); entirely in TJ's hand; undated, but the names for Washington County are in the same order as they appear in the Washington County commission dated 16 Mch.; perhaps prepared in two sittings (see notes below).

In 1803, Levi Lincoln testified that when he came into office as acting secretary of state there were "several commissions for justices of peace for the district made out; but he was furnished with a list of names to be put into a general commission, which was done, and was considered as superseding the particular commissions; and the individuals whose names were contained in this general commis-sion were informed of their being thus appointed." TJ may have given Lincoln the list above to prepare the commission naming the 15 justices of the peace for Washington County. The names in the temporary commission, dated 16 Mch., appear in the same order as above. In the commission, TJ noted: "reposing special Trust and Confidence in your Integrity, Ability, diligence and discretion, I have appointed you jointly and severally and every one of you Justices of the Peace in the County of Washington in the District of Columbia, and to keep and cause to be kept all laws for the good of the peace, and for the preservation of the same, and for the quiet rule and government of the people" and "further to do and perform every act and thing within the said County, which by law, you or either of you may do and perform as Justices of the Peace" (Cranch, *Reports*, 1:145; RCHS, 5 [1902], 265-7). A similar commission naming the 15 for Alexandria County has not been found, but undoubtedly was made out at the same time. On 18 Mch., Samuel H. Smith printed the names of the newly appointed officeholders in the *National Intelligencer*. The names of Benjamin More and Benjamin Stoddert, interlined in place of John Laird and Thomas Law, respectively, appear in the commission, indicating that TJ made the substitutions before it was issued (see notes below). In early 1802, Jacob Wagner recalled that More's name was inserted "on an erasure of the original commission." More's name does not appear in Document I, but perhaps TJ was persuaded to make the substitution by the recommendation he received from Nicholas King and others in early March 1801 (Vol. 33:180). As the document above indicates, TJ did not place an asterisk by More's name and he continued to maintain that he had kept 14 of Adams's nominations in Washington County. Although More appeared on the State Department list of interim appointments (see Document III), the president named Laird, not More, as justice of the peace in his message to the Senate, a mistake he corrected by another message on 5 Apr. (JEP, 1:417-18; Wagner to TJ, 6 Feb.; TJ to Samuel A. Otis, 8 Feb. 1802).

¹ Interlined in place of "Washington." At the same time TJ interlined "Washington" in place of "Alexandria" later in the sentence and overwrote the figures to reflect the changes.

² TJ first wrote "4 others have been added" before altering the passage to read as above.

³ Name interlined by TJ in place of "John Laird."

⁴ Name interlined by TJ in place of "Thomas Law."

III. List of Interim Appointments from the State Department

[on or before 26 Dec. 1801]

List of appointments made by the President of the United States, in the recess of the Senate.

E.P.	Alexander James Dallas, Attorney of the United States for the Eastern District of Pennsa., Vice John W. Kittera.
E.P.	John Smith, Marshal of the same District; vice John Hall
W.P.	James Hamilton, Attorney for the Western District
W.P.	Presley Carr Lane, Marshal for the same District
Verm.	David Fay, Attorney for the Vermont District, in place of A. Marsh.
Verm.	John Willard, Marshal, Vice Jabez G. Fitch.
Col.	George Gilpin, William Fitzhugh, Francis Peyton, Richard Conway, Elisha Cullen Dick, Charles Alexander Jr. George Taylor, Jonah Thompson, Abraham Faw, John Herbert, Alexander Smith, Cuthbert Powell Peter Wise Jr. Jacob Houghman and Thomas Darne } Justices of the Peace for Alexandria County in the District of Columbia.

	Daniel Reintzel, Thomas Corcoran, Thomas Addison, Abraham Boyd, Benjamin Moore[1], John Mason, William Thornton, Benjamin Stoddert, William Hammond Dorsey, Joseph Sprigg Belt, Daniel Carroll, Cornelius Cunningham, Thomas Peter, and Robert Brent	Justices of the Peace for the County of Washington in the District of Columbia.

Col. John Thompson Mason, Attorney for the District of Columbia

Col. Daniel Carroll Brent, Marshal of the same.

Col. William Kilty, of Maryland, Chief Judge of the Circuit Court of the United States for the District of Columbia, Vice Thomas Johnson resigned.

E.Virg. Joseph Scott, Marshall of the Eastern District of Virginia, vice David Meade Randolph.

Col. John Hewitt, Register of Wills for the County of Washington in the District of Columbia.

N.H. Wiliam Gardner, of N Hampshire, Commissr. of Loans for that State Vice John Pierce.

N.Y. Edward Livingston, Attorney of the District of New York, vice Richard Harrison.

N.Y. John Swartwout, Marshal of the same District in place of Aquilla Giles.

Col. Walter Jones Jr. of Columbia District, Attorney for the Potomac District.

Col. William Baker, Marshal of the same District

W.V. John Monroe, Attorney for the Western District of Virginia

W.V. Andrew Moore, Marshal of the same District

R.I. David Leonard Barnes, Judge of the District Court for the District of Rhode Island, *vice Benj. Bourne, appointed a Circuit Judge*

N.C. Henry Potter, of North Carolina, a Judge of the Circuit Court of the US. for the fifth Circuit, *vice John Sitgreaves declined*

Genl. Albert Gallatin, Secretary of the Treasury of the U States, vice Samuel Dexter resigned.

Col. George Gilpin, of Columbia District, Judge of the Orphans Court for the County of Alexandria in the said District

Mis. William C. C. Claiborne, of Tennessee, Governor of the Mississippi Territory[2], *vice W. Sargent, whose term expired*

Mar. Reuben Etting, Marshal of the Maryland District Vice David Hopkins.

R.I. David Howell, Attorney for the District of Rhode Island vice David L Barnes, appointed a Judge.

N.J. George Maxwell, Attorney for the New Jersey District vice Lucius H Stockton resigned.

W.N.Y. Hermanus H. Wendell, of New York State, Marshal of the Albany District.

N.W.T. William McMillan, of the North Western Territory, Attorney for the District of Ohio.

N.W.T. James Findlaye, Marshal of the same District

K.   Joseph Crockette, Marshal for the District of Kentucky—Vice Samuel McDowell—

D.   Joel Lewis, Marshal of the Delaware District, Vice Hamilton whose term expired.

S.C.   Dominic Augustin Hall, of South Carolina, Chief Judge of the Circuit Court of the U.S. for the fifth Circuit *vice Thomas Bee, who declined*

N.H.   John S. Sherbourne, Attorney for the New Hampshire District vice[3] *Jeremiah Smith, appointed a Judge*

Genl.   Robert Smith, Secretary of the Navy of the U States, *vice Benjamin Stoddert resigned.*

Indians[4] James Wilkinson, ⎱ Commrs. of the U.S. to Treat with the
         Benjamin Hawkins and ⎬ Creek, Choctaw, Chickasaw, & Cherokee
         Andrew Pickins   ⎰ Nations of Indians

Maine   Silas Lee, of Massachusetts, Attorney for the District of Maine Vice Daniel Davis, *appointed to a State office.*

Mas.   George Blake Attorney of Massachusetts, Vice Harrison G Otis

N.J.   John Heard of New Jersey, Marshal for that District in place of Thomas Lowry.

G.   William Stephens of Georgia, Judge of the District Court for Georgia District, Vice Joseph Clay resigned

Indians. William R. Davie, of N Carolina, Commissioner to hold a treaty with the Tuscarora nation of Indians.

G.   James Alger, of Georgia, Commissioner of Loans in that State Vice Richard Wylley.

N.Y.   James Nicholson, of New York, Commissioner of Loans for that State, vice Mathew Clarkson.

Genl.   Gideon Granger, Post Master General of the U.S. vice Joseph Habersham resigned.

Genl.   Thomas Tudor Tucker, of South Carolina, Treasurer of the U States vice Saml. Meredith resigned.

N.J.   James Lynn of N Jersey, Supervisor of the U.S. in the District of N Jersey—vice A. Dunham[5]

P.   Peter Muhlenberg, of Pennsa, Supervisor for the district of Pennsa. vice Henry Miller

Con.   Ephraim Kirby of Connecticut Supervisor for that District Vice *J. Chester*

N.Y.   Samuel Osgood of New York Supervisor for the District of New York, *vice N. Fish*

N.H.   Joseph Whipple, of New Hampshire, Collector for the District of Portsmouth Vice Thomas Martin

N.W.T. David Duncan, of North Western Territory, Collector for the District of Michillimakinac

Con.   Alexander Wolcott, of Connecticut, Collector for the District of Middleton vice Chauncy Whittlesey.

Maine	Josiah Hook,[6] of Massachusetts, Collector for the District of Penobscot;[7] also Inspector of the Revenue for the port of Penobscot, vice John Lee.
Maine	Jonas Clark, of Massachusetts, Inspector of the Revenue for the Port of Kennebunk.
Virg	Mount Edward Chisman, of Virginia, Collector for the District of Hampton; also Inspector of the Revenue for the port of Hampton—.
N.W.T.	Thomas Worthington, of the North Western Territory, Inspector of the Revenue for the Survey forming the "North West" District.[8]
G.	Thomas De Mattos Johnson, of Georgia, Collector for the District of Savannah. Vice James Powell
Col.	John Oakley, of Columbia District, Collector for the District of George Town; also Inspector of the Revenue for the said Port, vice James M. Lingan resigned
Virg.	Isaac Smith, of Virginia, Collector for the District of Cherrystone.
	Josiah Hook, of Massachusetts, Inspector of the Revenue for the port of Penobscot.[9]

Consuls & Commercial Agents

[. . .]	Tobias Lear, of Virginia, General Commercial Agent in the Island of St Domingo, *vice E.*[10] Stevens, resigned
[. . .]	William Lee, of Massachusetts, Commercial Agent for the Port of Bordeaux, in France, *vacant*
F.D[11]	Edward Jones, of Columbia District, Commercial Agent in the Island of Guadaloupe, *vacant*
F.	The Sieur de La Motte, a citizen of the French Republic, Vice Commercial Agent, for the Port of Havre De Grace *vacant*
F.D	Thomas Aborn, of Rhode Island, Vice Commercial Agent of the United States for the Port of Cayenne, *vacant*
F.	Peter Dobell, of Pennsa, Commercial Agent for the Port of Havre de Grace, in France, *vacant*
F.	Fulwar Skipwith, of Virginia Commercial Agent for the City of Paris, *vacant*
E.	John J Murray, of New York, Consul of the United States for the Port of Glasgow, in Scotland, *vacant*
F.	James Blake, of Pennsa, Commercial Agent of the United States for the City of Antwerp—*vacant*
S.D.	John E. Caldwell, of Pennsa, Commercial Agent of the United States for the City of St. Domingo,[12] *vice James Blake appointed to Antwerp*
M.	Joseph Pulis, of the Island of Malta, Consul of the United States for the Island of Malta, *vacant.*
E.	George W Erving, of Massachusetts, Consul of the United States for the Port of London, vice S. Williams.
F.D.	William Buchanan, of Maryland, Commercial Agent of the United States for the Isles of France, [and] Bourbon, *vice Jacob Lewis.*

F.	The Sieur Etienne Cathalan the younger, Commercial Agent of [the] United States, for the port of Marseilles, *vacant*
S.D.	Daniel Clark, of New Orleans, Consul of the United States for the Port of New Orleans; *vice E. Jones*
F.	Theodore Peters of Bordeaux in France, Vice Commercial Agent for the Port of Bordeaux, *vacant*
F.	Thomas T. Gantt, of Maryland, Commercial Agent of the US. for the Port of Nantz, in France, *vacant*
F	Francis L Taney, of Maryland, Commercial Agent of the US for the Port of Ostend, *vacant*
A	Jacob Lewis, of Massachusetts, Consul of the United States for the Port of Calcutta, in the Province of Bengal, *vacant*
S	Joseph Yznardi, of Spain, Consul of the U States, at Cadiz *vice Joseph M. Yznardi*
F	William Patterson, of New York, Commercial Agent of the U.S. for the Port of L'Orient in France.
F.	Charles D Coxe, of Pennsa. Commercial Agent for the Port of Dunkirk, in France.
[. . .]	Bartholomew Dandridge, Commercial Agent of the U States for Port Republican, in the Island of St Domingo[13]
A.	Thomas Hewes, of Massachusetts Consul of the U States for the Port of Batavia in the Island of Java *vacant*
Genl.	Charles Pinckney Minister Plenipotentiary of the United States to the Court of Madrid, *vice D. Humphreys*
Genl.	John Graham, of Kentucky, Secretary of the Legation, *vacant*
[Genl.]	Thomas Sumter Jr. Secretary of the Legation to the French Republic, *vacant*

Collectors of the Customs continued

R.I.	Jonathan Russell, of Rhode Island Collector for the District of Bristol. *This gentleman was nominated by Mr. Adams & the appointment concurred in by the Senate: but no commission having been been made out he received a temporary one from President Jefferson*
Con.	Samuel Bishop, of Connecticut, Collector for the District of New Haven, vice E Goodrich.
Indiana	William Chribbs of the Indiana Territory, Inspector of the Revenue for the port of Massac; also Collector for the District of Massac.
N.J.	Daniel Marsh, of New Jersey, Collector for the District of Perth Amboy; also Inspector of the Revenue for the several ports within the District of Perth Amboy, *vice Bell*
N.Y.	David Gelston of New York, Collector for the District of New york, Vice Joshua Sands.
N.C.	Malachi Jones, of N Carolina Surveyor for the Port of Currituck.

MS (DLC: TJ Papers, 119:20524); undated, but on or before 26 Dec. 1801 (see TJ's memorandum to Gallatin, and Gallatin's reply at 26 Dec. 1801); in a clerk's hand, with emendations by Jacob Wagner rendered in italics; with one interlineation by TJ (see note 1, below); abbreviations or words in TJ's hand, in ink, in left margin, usually designating the state where the office was held, except for the designations of the consuls and commercial agents, which he wrote in pencil; as TJ made a new list (see Document IV), he drew a vertical line, in ink, through the designations in the left margin and added a check mark, in pencil, beside each entry; torn; endorsed by TJ as received from the State Department in December 1801 and "Appointments."

A. MARSH: that is, Charles Marsh (JEP, 1:219).

JUSTICES . . . FOR THE COUNTY OF WASHINGTON: Thomas Sim Lee is missing from the list (see Document II).

[1] TJ wrote "John Laird," in pencil, above this name and in subsequent lists Laird's name appears instead of Benjamin More's.

[2] Remainder of entry interlined by Wagner in place of "vice Winthrop Sargeant" in a clerk's hand.

[3] Remainder of entry interlined by Wagner in place of "Edward St. Loe Livermore." In Document IV, TJ restored Livermore.

[4] TJ first wrote and then canceled "Western."

[5] Entry interlined.

[6] Interlined in place of "Benjamin Jarvis."

[7] Remainder of entry interlined in place of "vice John Lee."

[8] TJ drew a diagonal line through this entry after receiving Gallatin's reply to the memorandum printed at 26 Dec. 1801.

[9] Entry canceled (see notes 6-7 above).

[10] Preceding word and initial interlined by Wagner in place of "Doctor."

[11] TJ wrote this and the subsequent designations for consuls and commercial agents in pencil.

[12] Wagner began writing "vacant," then canceled it and interlined the remainder of the entry.

[13] Three diagonal lines are drawn through this entry, but TJ included the entry in his draft (see Document IV).

IV. Draft of Interim Appointments

GENTLMEN OF THE SENATE   [on or after 26 Dec. 1801]

During the late recess of the Senate I have issued commissions for the following persons & offices, which commissions will expire at the end of this present session of the Senate. I therefore nominate the same persons to the same offices for reappointment, to wit

Albert Gallatin of Pensylvania, Secretary of the Treasury of the United States in the room of Samuel Dexter, resigned

Robert Smith of Maryland Secretary of the Navy of the US. vice Benjamin Stoddert, resd.

Thomas Tudor Tucker of South Carolina Treasurer of the US. vice Samuel Meredith. resigned

Gideon Granger of Connecticut Postmaster Genl. of the US. vice Joseph Habersham. resignd.

Charles Pinckney of S. Carolina Minister Plenipy. of the US. to the court of Madrid vice David Humphreys.

John Graham of Kentucky Secretary of the legation to Madrid. vacant

Thomas Sumpter of S. Carolina Secretary of the legation to the French republic. vacant

William Gardner of New Hampshire, Commissioner of loans for N. Hampshire vice John Pierce remd New Hamps.

Joseph Whipple of do. Collector for the district of Portsmouth. vice Thomas Martin. removed

John S. Sherbourne of New Hampshire attorney for the district of New Hampshire vice Jeremiah Smith promoted

Silas Lee of Massachusets Attorney for the district of Maine vice Daniel Davis appointd to a state office Maine.

Josiah Hook of do. Collector for the district of Penobscot & Inspector of the revenue for that port vice John Lee. remvd.

Jonas Clark of Massachusets, Inspector of the revenue for the port of Kennebunk. vacant

George Blake Attorney for the district of Massachusets, vice Harrison G. Otis, nomind. Feb. 18. Massachusets.

David Leonard Barnes of Rhode island judge of that District court vice Benjamin Bourne promoted. R. Island.

David Howell of Rhode island Attorney for the district of Rhode island, vice David L. Barnes promoted

Jonathan Russell of Rhode island, Collector for the district of Bristol in R.I. nominated Mar. 2

Ephraim Kirby of Connecticut, Supervisor for that district vice J. Chester. removd Connecticut

Alexander Wolcott of Connecticut, Collector for the district of Middleton v. Chancey Whittlesey. removd

Samuel[1] Bishop of Connecticut Collector for the district of Newhaven vice Elizur Goodrich of Feb. 18.

David Fay of Vermont Attorney for the district of Vermont vice A. Marsh. removed Vermont

John Willard of Vermont Marshal for the district of Vermont vice Jabez G. Fitch. removed

Edward Livingston of New York Attorney for the district of New York vice Richard Harrison removed New York

John Swartwout of New York Marshal of the district of New York vice Aquilla Giles removed

Hermannus H. Wendell of New York Marshal of the district of Albany. *v. James Dole*

James Nicholson of New York, Commissr. of loans for New York vice Matthew Clarkson resd

Samuel Osgood of New York, Supervisor for the district of New York, vice   Fish removd

David Gelston of New York Collector of the district of New York, vice Joshua Sands. removd

New Jersey George Maxwell of New Jersey Attorney for the district of New Jersey, *v. Fred. Frelinghuysen*[2] vice Lucius H. Stockton resd.

John Heard of New Jersey marshal of the district of New Jersey, vice Thomas Lowry. removd

Daniel Marsh of New Jersey. Collector for the district of Perth Amboy & Inspector of the revenue for the several ports in that district, vice   Bell removed

James Lynn of New Jersey Supervisor for the district of New Jersey vice A. Dunham removd

Pensylva Alexander James Dallas, of Pensva, Attorney for the Eastern district of Pensylvania vice John W. Kittera.

John Smith of Pensylva, Marshal for the Eastern district of Pensylva vice John Hall removed

James Hamilton Attorney for the Western district of Pensylvania. *v. Thos. Duncan*

Presly Carr Lane Marshal for the Western district of Pensylvania. *v. Hugh Barclay*

Peter Muhlenberg of Pensylva, Supervisor for the district of Pensylva, vice Henry Millar removd

Delaware Joel Lewis Marshal of the Delaware district. vice   Hamilton commission expd[3]

Maryland Robert Etting of Maryland. marshal of the district of Maryland, vice David Hopkins removed

Virginia Joseph Scott of Virginia, Marshal of the Eastern district of Virginia vice David M. Randolph. removed

John Monroe of Virginia Attorney for the Western district of Virginia. *v. Saml. Blackburn*

Andrew Moore of Virginia Marshal for the Western district of Virginia. *v. Robt. Grattan*

Mount Edward Chisman of Virginia. Collector & Inspector for the district of Hampton, vice   removd.

Isaac Smith of Virginia Collector for the district of Cherrystone vice Nathanl Wilkins[4] removd

[324]

Henry Potter of North Carolina a judge of the 5th. Circuit court vice N. Carola.
John Sitgreaves declind

Malachi Jones of N. Carolina, Surveyor for the port of Curratuck[5]
vice Saml. Jasper. dead.

Dominic Augustine Hall of S. Carolina Chief judge of the 5th. Circuit S. Carola
court vice Thomas Bee. declined

William Stephens of Georgia judge of the District court of Georgia. Georgia.
vice Joseph Clay. resigned

James Alger of Georgia, Commissioner of loans in Georgia vice
Richard Wylley. dead.

Thomas de Mattos Johnson of Georgia, collector for the district of
Savanna, vice James Powell, removed for delinquency.

Joseph Crocket Marshal of the district of Kentucky, vice Samuel Kentucky.
Mc.Dowell removed for misconduct

William Mc.Millan of the N.W. Territory Attorney for the district of N.W. Territy.
Ohio. vacant.

James Findlaye of the N.W. Territory Marshal of the district of Ohio.
vacant

David Duncan of the N.W. Territory, Collector for the district of
Michillimacinac. vacant

<*William Goforth & John Reily Commissioners for settling titles to
land under Symmes's contracts. vacant.*>[6]

William Chribbs of the Indiana Territory Collector of the district & Indiana.
Inspector of revenue of the port of Massac vacant

William C. C. Claiborne of Tenessee, Governor of the Missisipi terri- Missisipi.
tory. vice Winthrop Sargeant. commission expired

William Kilty of Maryland. Chief judge of the Circuit court of the Columbia.
district of Columbia. vice Thos. Johnson declined

John Thompson Mason of Maryland Attorney for the district of Columbia. *v. Thos Swan*

Daniel Carrol Brent of Virginia Marshal of the district of Columbia.
v. James L. Lingan

Walter Jones junr. of Virginia, Attorney for the district of Potomac.
vacant

William Baker of Maryland Marshal for the district of Potomac.
vacant.

George Gilpin of Virginia, judge of the Orphan's court for the county
of Alexandria in Columbia.

John Hewitt of Maryland, Register of wills for the county of Washington in Columbia.

Thomas Sim Lee, Daniel Reintzell, Thomas Corcoran, Daniel Carrol,

Cornelius Cunningham, Thomas Peter, Robert Brent, Thomas Addison, Abraham Boyd, John Laird, John Mason, William Thornton, Benjamin Stoddert[7] William Hammond Dorsey & Joseph Sprigg Belt, all of Maryland justices of the peace for Washington county in Columbia.

George Gilpin, William Fitzhugh, Francis Peyton, Richard Conway, Elisha Cullen Dick, Charles Alexander, George Taylor, Jonah Thompson, Abraham Faw, John Herbert, Alexander Smith, Cuthbert Powell, Peter Wise junr. Jacob Houghman, Thomas Darne, all of Virginia, justices of the peace for Alexandria county in Columbia.

John Oakley of Maryland, Collector & Inspector of the revenue for the district of George town. v. James M. Lingan resigned

Indians. James Wilkinson Benjamin Hawkins & Andrew Pickens, commissioners to treat with the Cherokees, Chickasaw Choctaws & Creeks.

William R. Davie of N. Carolina Commissioner of the US. for treaty between the state of North Carolina and the Tuscaroras.

Consular appointments uncommissioned

France Fulwar Skipwith. of Virginia. Commercl. agent at Paris in France vice *J. C. Mountfl.*

James Blake of Pensylva do. for Antwerp. vacant

Francis L. Taney of Maryland do. for Ostend. *v John Mitchel*

Charles D. Coxe of Pensylvania. do. at Dunkirk. *v John H. Hooe*

Peter Dobell of Pensylva. do. for Havre *v. John M. Forbes*

the Sieur de la Motte of France Commercial vice-agent for Havre. vacant

William Patterson of New York Commercial agent at Lorient. *v. Turell Tufts*

Thomas T. Gantt of Maryland do. at Nantes[8] v. John Jones Waldo vice P. F. Dobree

William Lee of Massachusets. do. at Bordeaux. *v. Isaac Cox Barnet*

Theodore Peters of France, Commercial vice-agent at Bordeaux. vacant

the Sieur Etienne Cathalan junr. of France. Commercial agent at Marseilles. *v Wm Lee*

Tobias Lear. General Commercial agent in the island of St. Domingo, vice Edwd. Stevens. resigned

Bartholomew Dandridge of Virginia. do. at port republicain St. Domingo. vacant

Edward Jones of Columbia. do. in the island of Guadeloupe. vacant

Thomas Aborne of Rhode island do. at Cayenne. nominated Feb. 21.

William Buchanan of Maryland. do. for the isles of France & Bourbon v. George Stacey[9] v. Jacob Lewis appointed to Calcutta

George W. Erwin of Massachusets. Consul for the port of London in Gr. Britain.[10] vice Saml. Williams removd. — Gr. Britain

John J. Murray of New York do. for the port of Glasgow. vacant

Joseph Yznardi of Spain. Consul for the port of Cadiz in Spain. *v.* *Henry Preble* — Spain

John E. Caldwell of New Jersey. Commercl. agent for the city of St. Domingo.[11] v. James Blake appointed to Antwerp

Daniel Clarke of New Orleans. Consul at New Orleans v. E. Jones removed.

Joseph Pulis of Malta. Consul for the island of Malta. vacant — Malta

Thomas Hewes of Massachusets Consul for the port of Batavia in the isld. of Java. vacant — Asia

Jacob Lewis of Massachusets, Consul for the port of Calcutta in Bengal. vacant

Dft (DLC: TJ Papers, 119:20630-1); undated, but the absence of Thomas Worthington's entry indicates that it was prepared after Gallatin's reply to TJ's memorandum printed at 26 Dec.; entirely in TJ's hand; with words in italics, except for the cancellation in angle brackets (see note 6), added by TJ in pencil; perhaps at a later sitting, TJ added the words and abbreviations at the end of most entries, giving the reason for the open position, in a darker ink and often interlined; in the left margin at each entry, TJ later added, in pencil, a check mark and a symbol, not shown above, to organize his subsequent list; with a key to the symbols written by TJ at foot of text, in pencil too faint to discern wholly, but indicating that an "x" appeared by those appointments due to resignation and an "o" by those due to vacancies.

VICE JEREMIAH SMITH: in the subsequent draft and message to the Senate, TJ dropped Smith's name and noted that John S. Sherburne was appointed instead of "Edw. St. Loe Livermore, nominatd Feb. 18. but not appointed" (see Document VI).

CONSULAR APPOINTMENTS UNCOM-

MISSIONED: TJ learned from Jacob Wagner in an undated memorandum entitled "An additional list of commissions remaining in the Office of the department of State" that commissions for 14 consuls and commercial agents approved by the Senate during the final days of the Adams administration had not been delivered. While the State Department had listed these positions as "vacant," TJ added in pencil (rendered in italics in the document above) the names of several of those being replaced as midnight appointments (see Vol. 33:173n).

VICE P. F. DOBREE: Pierre Frédéric Dobrée, appointed vice consul at Nantes in 1794, died in 1801. President Adams nominated John Jones Waldo as commercial agent at Nantes on 18 Feb. 1801 and the Senate approved the appointment six days later (JEP, 1:381, 385; Henry Preble to TJ, 23 Oct. 1801). As with many of the consular positions, the list from the State Department (Document III) indicated that this position was "vacant" when TJ appointed Thomas T. Gantt.

TJ consistently rendered George W. Erving as GEORGE W. ERWIN, and it is so printed in the Senate journal of executive proceedings (JEP, 1:403).

V. Key to the Arrangement of Interim Nominations

[before 6 Jan. 1802]

the first 17. (ending with Alger) are on resignation, declining or death.

Lewis. marsh. of Del. vice Hamilton who had accepted a state office & it was understood did not wish to be continued

Claiborne. Gov. Missipi. v. Sarjeant. time expired. not renewed because of his unpopularity, & malpractice

the next 21. from Graham to Jacob Lewis inclusive, were vacancies unfilled, or newly occurring.

the next 21. from Sherbourne to Buchanan are midnight appointments.

Skipwith
Cathalan
Yznardi
de la Motte
Gardner
Whipple
}
are restorations to offices they had formerly held, & were removed from for political principles, or to make room for political principles.

Cathalan was appointed by Dr. Franklin during the revolution, & has served us faithfully & zealously ever since. Yznardi was appointed by Genl. Washington among the first consuls, no native asking the place. he has served with great zeal.

de la Motte was an early and good appointment by Genl. Washington

the following are all removals, of which 12. are for default, and 6.[1] to make room for some participation by those who had been systematically excluded.

Jones & Humphreys on particular grounds clear of blame

Randolph. marsh. of Virginia, packing juries & pecuniary
   default

Hall. marsh. Pensylva. packing juries

Mc.Dowell. Marsh. Kentucky for multiplied extortions,
   proved of record

in addition to the delinquency of the first 6. the necessity of providing republican marshls. & attornies as barriers for the citizens against the federalism of the courts, was a sufficient cause of removal.

Marsh. marshal of Vermont ⎱ for malignant severities in
Fitch attorney of   do.   ⎰ their office against the
                             victims of party injustice.

Hopkins marsh. of Maryld pecuniary default.

Lowry. marsh. of Jersey

Harrison atty of N.Y.

Giles Marshl. of N.Y.

Bell collector of Perth Amboy. removed as a revolutionary
   tory.

Dunham Supervisor of N.J. for habitual & beastly
   drunkenness & open debauchery.

Collector of Hampton for pecuniary default.

Wilkins Collector of Cherrystone for do.

Powel Commissioner of loans Georgia for do.

Williams. Consul at London. for never rendering any
   account tho' expressly instructed & great sums thus
   passed through his hands[2]

John Lee. Collector of Penobscot ⎫ removed to
Chester. Supervisor of Connecticut ⎬ make room for
Whittlesey Collector of Middleton Connect. ⎭ participation

Fish. Supervisor of N. York ⎫ removed on the principle
Sands Collector of N. York ⎬ of participation.
Miller Supervisor of Pensylva. ⎭

<Williams. Consul at London.>

Jones. Consul at N. Orleans. Jones was an insignificant federalist.
   Clarke a federalist, but of extreme worth, & omnipotent influence
   at N. Orleans

Humphreys. Min. Plen. at Madrid. Humphreys was withdrawn for
   no particular blame but on a rule established in Genl Washington's time & communicated to Humphreys on his appointment
   that no foreign minister would be continued more than 6. or 7.
   years. he had been absent just 7. years when Genl. Washington
   went out of office.

17. cases of resignation & death.
2. expirations of appointment
21. vacancies unfilled by the former administration
21. midnight appointments
6. restorations to former office
12. removals for default
3. do. of Marshals & attories for others to counterpoise the federalism of the courts
6. removals to give some participation of office to republicans

PrC (DLC: TJ Papers, 120:20748-9); undated; with summary of positions at foot of text letterpressed separately, evidently providing a synopsis of TJ's second key to the arrangement of the nominations (see below).

12 ARE FOR DEFAULT: TJ listed 15 names here, including Thomas LOWRY, Richard Harison (HARRISON), and Aquila GILES. TJ often placed them in other categories, as he did in his second key to appointments described below. In his personal lists of appointments, TJ indicated that Lowry was removed "on general principle" and Harison "on genl. principle of havg. republicn. officers where the court is federal." Giles was "one of the midnight renewals" removed on "mixed grounds," including "money delinquency" (Vol. 33:673, 675, 678). COLLECTOR OF HAMPTON: William Kirby (JEP, 1:216-17). In an undated list of appointments and removals, probably completed in May 1802, TJ named only eight who were removed for "malversation" or misconduct (Vol. 33:668-70). On a separate sheet, TJ listed, by last name only, 17 officers replaced due to resignation, appointment declined, promotion, or death; 2 removed for expiration of term or commission; 21 appointed to fill vacancies or new positions; 21 removed as midnight appointments; and 6 "restorations to former office." TJ designated 12 removals for misconduct; he named Ran-

dolph, Hall, McDowell, Marsh, Fitch, Hopkins, Bell, Dunham, Wilkins, Powell, and Williams and left a blank space for Kirby's name. Lowry, Harison, and Giles appear as a separate category with their positions as "marshal," "Attorney," "Marshal" appearing, respectively, by their names, the only case where this is done. They are followed by the 6 names, as above, designated as "removals to give some participation in government to those who had been systematically excluded." The list concludes with Jones and Humphreys (PrC in DLC: TJ Papers, 120:20750; entirely in TJ's hand). COUNTERPOISE THE FEDERALISM OF THE COURTS: this entry for three marshals and attorneys connects this summary of appointments and removals with the list of the last names of the officers described above in this paragraph rather than the key to the arrangement of the nominations printed above.

It is possible that TJ sent Wilson Cary Nicholas, who appears to have served as the president's contact in the Senate on interim appointments, one or both of the manuscripts as keys to the arrangement of the nominations (TJ to Nicholas, 26 Jan. 1802).

[1] TJ interlined this and the preceding figure "12" over canceled and illegible numbers.
[2] Entry interlined by TJ.

VI. To the Senate

GENTLEMEN OF THE SENATE

During the late recess of the Senate, I have issued commissions for the following persons and offices, which commissions will expire at the end of this present session of the Senate. I therefore nominate the same persons to the same offices for re-appointment. to wit

Albert Gallatin of Pensylvania, Secretary of the Treasury, vice Samuel Dexter resigned.

Robert Smith of Maryland, Secretary of the Navy, vice Benjamin Stoddert resigned.

Thomas Tudor Tucker of South Carolina, treasurer, vice Samuel Meredith resigned.

Gideon Granger of Connecticut, Postmaster Genl. vice Joseph Habersham resigned.

Silas Lee of Massachusets, Attorney for the district of Maine, vice Daniel Davies appointed to a State office.

David Leonard Barnes of Rhode island, judge of that District court, vice Benjamin Bourne promoted.

David Howell of Rhode island, Attorney for the district of Rhode island, vice David L. Barnes promoted.

James Nicholson of New York, Commissioner of loans for New York, vice Matthew Clarkson resigned.

Henry Potter of North Carolina, a judge of the 5th. circuit, vice John Sitgreaves declined.

Dominic Augustine Hall of South Carolina, chief judge of the 5th. circuit, vice Thomas Bee declined.[1]

William Stephens of Georgia, judge of the district court of Georgia, vice Joseph Clay resigned.

William Kilty of Columbia,[2] Chief judge of the Circuit court of the district of Columbia, vice Thos. Johnson declined.

John Oakley of Columbia, Collector & Inspector of the revenue for the district of Georgetown v. Matthew Lingan resigned

Tobias Lear, General Commercial Agent in the island of St. Domingo, vice Edward Stevens resigned.

John E. Caldwell of New Jersey, Commercial agent for the city of St. Domingo, vice Jas. Blake appointd. to Antwerp.[3]

Malachi Jones of N. Carolina, Surveyor of the port of Curratuck, vice Samuel Jasper dead.

James Alger of Georgia, Commissioner of loans in Georgia, vice Richard Wylley dead.

Joel Lewis of Delaware, Marshal of Delaware district vice Robert Hamilton whose term had expired

William C. C. Claiborne of Tennissee, Governor of the Missisipi territory, vice Winthrop Sarjeant whose term had expired.

John Graham of Kentucky, Secretary of the legation to Madrid, on the salary, & in the stead of a private Secretary.

Thomas Sumpter of S. Carolina, Secretary of the legation to Paris,[4] on the salary, & in the stead of a private Secretary.

Jonas Clark of Massachusets, Inspector of the revenue for the port of Kennebunk.

Jonathan Russell of Rhode island, Collector for the district of Bristol.

William Mc.Millan of the North Western territory, Attorney for the district of Ohio.

James Findlaye of the North Western territory, Marshal of the district of Ohio.

David Duncan of the North Western territory, Collector for the district of Michillimackinac.

William Chribbs, of the Indiana territory, Collector of the district, & Inspector of revenue of the port of Massac.

Walter Jones junr. of Columbia, Attorney for the district of Potomac.

William Baker of Columbia[5] Marshal for the district of Potomac.

James Wilkinson, Benjamin Hawkins, & Andrew Pickens, commissioners to treat with the Cherokees, Chickasaws, Choctaws and Creeks.

William Richardson Davie of N. Carolina, a Commissioner to hold a treaty between N. Carolina & the Tuscaroras.

James Blake of Pensylvania, Commercial Agent for Antwerp.

Theodore Peters of France Commercial Vice-agent at Bourdeaux.

Bartholomew Dandridge of Virginia, Commercial Agent at Port-republicain St. Domingo.

Edward Jones of Columbia, Commercial agent in the island of Guadeloupe.

Thomas Aborne of Rhode island Commercial agent at Cayenne.

John J. Murray of New York, Consul for the port of Glasgow in Great Britain.

Joseph Pulis of Malta, Consul for the island of Malta.

Thomas Hewes of Massachusets, Consul for the port of Batavia in the island of Java.

Jacob Lewis of Massachusets, Consul for the port of Calcutta in Bengal.

John S.[6] Sherbourne of N. Hampshire, attorney for the district of New Hampshire, v. Edw. St. Loe Livermore nominatd Feb. 18.[7] but not appointed.

George Blake of Massachusets Attorney for the district of Massachusets, vice Harrison G. Otis, nominated Feb. 18.

Samuel Bishop of Connecticut, Collector for the district of New haven, vice Elizur Goodrich nominated Feb. 18.

Hermannus H. Wendell of N. York, Marshal of the district of Albany, vice Jas. Dole, nominated Feb. 21. but not appointed.

George Maxwell of New Jersey, Attorney for the district of New Jersey, vice Fred. Frelinghuysen, nominatd. Mar. 2. but not appointed.

Alexander James Dallas of Pensylva, Attorney for the Eastern district of Pensylva, vice John W. Kittera, nominated Feb. 18.

James Hamilton of Pensylva, Attorney for the Western district of Pensylva, vice Thos. Duncan, nominatd. Mar. 3. but not appointed.

Presly Carr Lane of Pensylva, Marshal for the Western district of Pensylva, vice Hugh Barclay, nominatd. Mar. 3. but not appointed.

John Monroe of Virginia, Attorney for the Western district of Virginia, vice Saml. Blackburn nominatd. Feb. 21. but not appointed.

Andrew Moore of Virginia, Marshal for the Western district of Virginia, vice Robt. Grattan, nominatd. Feb. 21. but not appointed.

John Thompson Mason, of Columbia, Attorney for the district of Columbia, vice Thomas Swan, nominatd Feb. 28. but not appointed.

Daniel Carrol Brent of Columbia, Marshal of the district of Columbia, vice Jas. L. Lingan nominatd. Feb. 28. but not appointed

George Gilpin of Columbia, judge of the Orphan's court for Alexandria county Columbia, vice John Herbert, nominatd. Mar. 2. but not appointed.

John Hewitt of Columbia, register of wills, for Washington county Columbia, vice John Peter, nominated. Mar. 2. but not appointed.

Francis L. Taney of Maryland, Commercial Agent for Ostend, vice John Mitchel, nominated Feb. 18. but not appointed.

Charles D. Coxe of Pensylvania, Commercial agent for Dunkirk, vice John H. Hooe, nominatd. Feb. 18. but not appointed.

Peter Dobell of Pensylva, Commercial agent at Havre, vice John M. Forbes, nominated Feb. 18. but not appointed.

William Patterson of New York, Commercial agent at Lorient, vice Turell Tufts, nominatd. Feb. 21. but not appointed.

Thomas T. Gantt of Maryland, Commercial agent at Nantes, vice John Jones Waldo, nominated Feb. 18. but not appointed.

William Lee of Massachusets, Commercial Agent at Bordeaux, v. Isaac Cox Barnet, nominated Feb. 18. but not appointed.

William Buchanan of Maryland, Commercl. Agent for the isles of France & Bourbon, v. George Stacy,[8] nominatd. Feb. 18. but not appointed.

Fulwar Skipwith former Consul at Paris, to be Commercl. agent[9] at Paris, vice J. C. Mountflorence, nominatd. Feb. 21. but not appointd.

the Sieur Etienne Cathalan of France, former Consul at Marseilles, Commercl. Agent at Marseilles v. Wm. Lee, nomind Feb. 18. not appointd.

Joseph Yznardi senr. of Spain, former Consul at Cadiz, to be Consul at Cadiz, vice Henry Preble, nominatd. Feb. 18. but not appointed.

the Sieur de la Motte of France, former Vice-Consul at Havre, to be Commercial Vice-agent at Havre.

William Gardner of New Hampshire, former Commr. of loans, to be Commissioner of loans for N. Hampshire v. John Pierce, removed.

Joseph Whipple of New Hampshire, former Collector of the district of Portsmouth, to be Collector of that district, v. Thomas Martin, removed.

Joseph Scott of Virginia, Marshal of the Eastern district of Virginia, vice David M. Randolph removed.

John Smith of Pensylva, Marshal of the Eastern district of Pensylvania, vice John Hall removed.

Joseph Crockett of Kentuckey, Marshal of the district of Kentuckey, vice Saml. Mc.Dowell removed.

David Fay of Vermont, Attorney for the district of Vermont, vice A. Marsh removed.

John Willard of Vermont, Marshal for the district of Vermont, vice Jabez G. Fitch removed.

Daniel Marsh of New Jersey, Collector & Inspector of the revenue in the district of Perth Amboy v. Andrew Bell removed.

James Lynn of New Jersey, Supervisor for the district of New Jersey, vice A. Dunham removed.

Mount Edward Chisman of Virginia, Collector & Inspector for the district of Hampton vice   Kirby removed.

Isaac Smith of Virginia, Collector for the district of Cherrystone, vice Nathaniel Wilkins, removed.

Thomas de Mattos Johnson of Georgia, Collector for the district of Savanna, vice James Powell removed.

George W. Erwin of Massachusets, Consul at London,[10] vice Samuel Williams removed.

Josiah Hook of Massachusets, Collector for the district of Penobscot, & Inspector for that port, vice John Lee removed.

Reuben Etting of Maryland, Marshal of the district of Maryland, vice David Hopkins removed.

John Heard of New Jersey, Marshal of the district of New Jersey, vice Thomas Lowry removed.

Edward Livingston of New York, attorney for the district of New York, vice Richard Harrison removed.

John Swartwout of New York, Marshal of the district of New York, vice Aquilla Giles removed.[11]

Ephraim Kirby of Connecticut, Supervisor for the district of Connecticut vice J. Chester removed.

Alexander Wolcott of Connecticut, Collector for the district of Middleton, vice Chancey Whittlesey removed.

Samuel Osgood of New York, Supervisor for the district of New York, vice Nicholas Fish removed.

David Gelston of New York, Collector of the district of New York, vice Joshua Sands removed.

Peter Muhlenberg of Pensylva, Supervisor of the district of Pensylva, vice Henry Millar removed.

Daniel Clarke of New Orleans, Consul at New Orleans, vice Evan Jones.

Charles Pinckney of S. Carolina, Minister Plenipotentiary at the court of Madrid, vice David Humphreys, recalled on account of long absence from the US.

The nominations which took place on the 2d. of March, of justices of the peace for the district of Columbia having been thought too numerous, a commission issued to fourteen of those then nominated for Washington county, to wit, Thomas Sim Lee, Daniel Reintzell, Daniel Carrol, Cornelius Cuningham, Thomas Peter, Robert Brent, Thomas Addison, Abraham Boyd, John Laird, John Mason, William Thornton, Benjamin Stoddert, William Hammond Dorsey, & Joseph Sprigg Belt, and to one other, to wit Thomas Corcoran to be Justices of the Peace for Washington county;[12] and another commission issued to eleven of those then nominated for Alexandria county, to wit George Gilpin, William Fitzhugh, Francis Peyton, Richard Conway, Charles Alexander, George Taylor, Josiah[13] Thompson, Abraham Faw, John Herbert, Cuthbert Powell, and Jacob Houghman, and to four others, to wit, Elisha Cullen Dick, Alexander Smith, Peter Wise junr. & Thomas Darne, to be Justices

of the peace for Alexandria county, all of whom are now nominated for reappointment to the same offices.[14] TH: JEFFERSON
Jan. 6. 1802.

RC (DNA: RG 46, EPEN, 7th Cong., 1st sess.); with "agd." written by a Senate clerk in the left margin by each entry except the final nominations of justices of the peace for the District of Columbia; in the nomination of the Columbia justices of the peace, a mark, in pencil, appears above the names of Lee, Laird, Stoddert, Dorsey, Fitzhugh, Conway, and Darne, probably inserted by a Senate clerk after receiving TJ's message to the Senate of 5 Apr. PrC (DLC: TJ Papers, 119:20632-5); with two emendations by TJ in ink (see notes 6 and 13). Dft (DLC: TJ Papers, 119:20628-9); entirely in TJ's hand; with variation in placement of four consecutive entries (see note 11 below); emendations added by TJ at a later date (see notes 6, 13 and 14 below). Recorded in SJL with notation "nominations. general list."

Congress had been in session for almost a month when Meriwether Lewis delivered TJ's message on interim nominations to the Senate on 6 Jan. On 7, 12, 18, and 21 Jan., the Senate considered the nominations. On 22 Jan., the Senate postponed until the 26th, a motion to advise and consent to the nomination of James Linn (LYNN), who had received his appointment, the Federalists charged, as a reward for casting his vote for TJ, not Burr, thus keeping the New Jersey delegation in the House of Representatives from supporting the New Yorker for president. On the appointed day, the motion passed the test vote, 16 yeas to 14 nays. The Senate then passed a resolution consenting to the appointment of Linn. After agreeing to the nominations of Ephraim Kirby and Alexander Wolcott, they consented to all of the others except to those OF JUSTICES OF THE PEACE FOR THE DISTRICT OF COLUMBIA. On 5 Apr., TJ informed the Senate of changes in the nominations of the justices of the peace.

He noted that Laird's name had been "inserted by mistake" for that of Benjamin More. He withdrew Laird's name and nominated More, who had already been commissioned and qualified as a justice of the peace. For other changes, see TJ to the Senate, 7 Apr. On 27 Apr., the Senate consented to TJ's new nominations and then to the justices included in the nominations of 6 Jan. (JEP, 1:400-5, 417-18, 422-3; Annals, 11:640; Vol. 33:432).

[1] Entry interlined in Dft.

[2] Dft: word interlined in place of "Maryland."

[3] Entry interlined in Dft.

[4] Dft: "the French republic."

[5] Dft: word written over "Maryland."

[6] Meriwether Lewis later wrote the "S" over a partially erased "H" (see TJ to Samuel A. Otis, 9 Jan. 1802). In PrC and Dft, TJ interlined "S," in ink, in place of "H."

[7] Preceding word and date interlined in Dft.

[8] Preceding name interlined in Dft.

[9] Dft: preceding two words interlined in place of "Consul."

[10] In Dft, TJ here added "in Gr. Britain."

[11] In Dft, TJ placed the preceding four entries between the entries for Willard and Marsh above.

[12] Preceding nine words interlined in Dft.

[13] Name corrected later, perhaps by Meriwether Lewis, to read "Jonah" (see TJ to Samuel A. Otis, 8 Feb. 1802). TJ altered the name in PrC and Dft.

[14] Dft: in the preceding paragraph, TJ later inserted square brackets around Thomas Sim Lee, John Laird, Benjamin Stoddert, William Hammond Dorsey, William Fitzhugh, Richard Conway, and Thomas Darne and interlined above the names "withdrawn Apr. 5. 1802."

To the District of Columbia Commissioners

GENTLEMEN   Washington Jan. 7. 1802.

I have recieved and duly considered your letter of yesterday on the subject of the frame house erected contrary to rule by mr Rhodes, and approve of your opinion that measures should be taken for it's removal. I suppose it will be best for you to apply to mr Mason the Attorney for the district. Accept my respect & best wishes.

TH: JEFFERSON

RC (PWacD: Feinstone Collection, on deposit PPAmP); clipped below signature. PrC (DLC); at foot of text: "The Commissioners of Washington"; endorsed by TJ in ink on verso.

From William Duane

SIR,   Washington, Jan. 7th, 1802

The appearance of the Indian Chiefs in the House of Representatives this morning, has revived in my mind a subject upon which I have long reflected, and concerning which it was my purpose long since to have taken the liberty of addressing you.

A consciousness of the superiority of the Whites, has at all times prevailed among the Indians, and influenced them much more than the generally received notions, that they felt a consciousness of *their* superiority over the Whites.

To remove their prejudices would I respectfully presume be the most effectual mode of rendering them happy, securing their attachment to us, and for ever depriving European nations of their instrumentality.

This I conceive might be affected by provisions for allowing each of the Indian Nations, a Representative in the Congress of the United States, under such limitations and conditions as would give them a due sense of their consequence in the American nation, and the common blessings and advantages which would accrue to them, by their incorporation with a nation so important, and under circumstances perfectly analogous to their own ideas of delegation.

I will not enter into a detail of the form of producing this momentous change. I flatter myself that the difficulties would be trivial, and the expence inconsiderable, compared with the advantages which it would produce to the Indians and to the Union.

[337]

I can only just add, that this subject being mentioned a considerable time since to a Canadian Englishman, he deprecated the idea, and solicited earnestly that it might not be mentioned as it would destroy the British influence for ever, and throw the Fur trade wholly into the States.

I am, Sir, Your faithful and respectful Servt   WM DUANE

RC (DLC); at foot of text: "The President of the United States"; endorsed by TJ as received 7 Jan. and so recorded in SJL.

To George Jefferson

DEAR SIR   Washington. Jan. 7. 1802.

I was in the act of beginning this letter when I recieved your's of the 2d. inst. covering your account, balance in my favor £19.17.6. not having time at this moment even to cast an eye over it, I proceed to my object of inclosing you fifteen hundred dollars, in bank bills, to wit 14. of 100. D. each, 1. of 50. 1. of 20. & 3. of 10. D. each. these, for greater security, I have cut in two, and forward now only one half of each bill. the other half shall follow by another post. they are wrapt in water-proof paper. the intention of this remittance is to enable you to pay for me

	D c.
to Colo. Charles Lilburne Lewis or order of Albemarle	562.50
to mr Joseph Bullock, atty, for Christopher Smith of Louisa, or order	473.33
to a mr Bonduron of Albemarle or order	112.50
	1148.33

I shall inclose these orders on you; but as they have reason to expect the money is lodged in your hands *subject to their order*, be pleased to answer their orders, without waiting the ceremony of recieving mine now inclosed to them. accept assurances of my affectionate esteem.   TH: JEFFERSON

PrC (MHi); at foot of text: "Mr. George Jefferson." Enclosures: see below.

TJ paid CHARLES LILBURNE LEWIS for 225 bushels of corn (MB, 2:1062). BONDURON: that is, Reuben Burnley. For the confusion resulting from the incorrect name, see TJ to William Wardlaw, 30 Jan., and Thomas Mann Randolph to TJ, 6 Feb. 1802.

NOW INCLOSED TO THEM: see TJ to Christopher Smith, immediately below. TJ's letter to Lewis, recorded in SJL at 7 Jan., has not been found.

To Christopher Smith

SIR   Washington. Jan. 7. 1802

I have this day remitted to messrs. Gibson & Jefferson in Richmond a sum of money, of which they are desired to hold four hundred and seventy three dollars thirty three cents subject to your order or to that of mr Bullock as you permitted me. this letter being presented to them will have the effect of an order although they were desired to make paiment without it, should yourself or mr Bullock in the mean time have directed it to be called for. accept my best wishes and respects.

TH: JEFFERSON

PrC (MHi); at foot of text: "Mr. Christopher Smith"; endorsed by TJ in ink on verso.

To James Taylor, Jr.

SIR   Washington Jan. 7. 1802

I have the satisfaction now to inclose you bank bills amounting to 705. dollars, to wit, 7. of one hundred each, and 1 of five, which for greater security I have cut in two and now forward one half of each bill wrapped in water-proof paper, and by another post will send on the remaining halves. the 5. dollar bill is entire. the amount of the two last pipes of wine with the costs according to your letter to mr Barnes, for which this is paiment, was 704.75 to which the inclosed comes within a fraction. accept my respects & best wishes

TH: JEFFERSON

PrC (MHi); at foot of text: "Mr. James Taylor Norfolk."

See TJ to Taylor, 18 Dec. 1801, and MB, 2:1062.

YOUR LETTER TO MR BARNES: at the foot of his letter to John Barnes dated 17 Dec. 1801, Taylor wrote an invoice show- ing that TJ owed Taylor $0.50 from a previous balance, $700 for two pipes of wine and $4.25 for shipping, for a total of $704.75. At the entry for the wine a line is drawn through "16th Sept. 90 days" (RC in MHi; endorsed by Barnes as received 24 Dec.).

To Antoine Félix Wuibert

Washington Jan. 7. 1802.

Th: Jefferson with his compliments to Colo. Weibert, returns him the papers inclosed in his letter, respecting his lands, and has only to advise a compliance with the law by paiment of his tax as proposed by mr Taylor, in order to save the land.

PrC (DLC); endorsed by TJ in ink on verso.

HIS LETTER: Wuibert to TJ, 14 Dec. 1801.

From David Austin

Washington

MAY IT PLEASE YR. EXCELLENCY.   Jan'y 8th. A.D 1801 [i.e. 1802].

A Bill is about to be offered to the House of Representatives by the Senate, in which it is proposed that the nomination of the person to take charge of the books of the Congressional Library, shall be made by the President to the Senate, as is usual in other official appointments. I have several particular friends and acquaintances in the Senate: and should my name be so fortunate as to meet the nomination of the President; I doubt not but the decision of the Senate would prove their readiness to concur in the appointment.—

I am, Sir, with all esteem,   DAVID AUSTIN

RC (DLC); at foot of text: "Th: Jefferson"; endorsed by TJ as received 8 Jan. and "to be librarian" and so recorded in SJL.

A BILL: on 26 Jan., Congress passed "An Act concerning the Library for the use of both Houses of Congress," which directed that all books and maps acquired for the library be placed in the Capitol room previously occupied by the House of Representatives. The act also authorized the president to appoint, without Senate consent, a librarian, who was to receive $2 for each day in attendance (U.S. Statutes at Large, 2:128-9). TJ appointed John Beckley on 29 Jan. (Vol. 33:678).

From James Currie

DR SIR   Richmond Jany. 8th. 1802

On the 5th Inst. I was supplied with the inclosed statement in regard to the former Award between you & Mr Ross & which may now be regarded I presume as final. in regard to the compensation to the arbiters by the parties Mr Ross told me whatever I would do on your account he should offer the same & tho they have said they wishd for nothing—I am of Opinion $100. between the parties $50 each would be a very handsome compensation by yorself & Mr Ross[1] to them for their trouble in the business—20$ I am told is the present common fee for pleading a cause in any of the Superior Courts—perhaps that sum to be offered to each Gentleman may be fully adequate, you'll please direct which appears to you most Expedient & proper—Indisposition has prevented me sending on this paper sooner—I recd inclosed in a favor addressd to me, the Jennerian Discovery &ca. &ca. concomitants & a letter from you to Dr B Waterhouse (of Massachusetts)—Cambridge dated Xmas day[2] which I presume has been a mistake, I have taken the liberty to read the Book & have been deeply gratified in so doing, his Ingenuity & researches into, the history & nature of the disorder—merit highly of mankind in General I now return it not doubting it to be your wish I should do so—& Dr Whouse's letter, with a corrected Copy of the award of the Arbitrators not recollecting whether you returned to me the former One sent you with the Other papers—the papers you mentioned not before having received from me. I called on Mr Ross for & recd them they shall be retained (or delivered to your Order) till your return home whichever you may direct. I am glad this business is ended & it is inconcieveable the numerous & little Obstructions that have impeded its final decision, I have only to add it will always afford me real pleasure to serve you & that I ever am with Unfeigned regard & sincere Esteem

Your most Obedt & Very Hble Servt   JAMES CURRIE

RC (MHi); at foot of text: "Thomas Jefferson Esqr"; endorsed by TJ as received 13 Jan. and so recorded in SJL. Enclosed statement not found.

[1] Preceding four words and ampersand interlined.

[2] Preceding three words interlined.

From Henry Dearborn

SIR   January 8th. 1802

The concurrence of the Senate appears necessary in the appointment of John Taylor Esqr. as Commissioner in the Treaty with the St. Regis Indians.

with respectfull concideration I am Sir Your Hume Sert.

H. DEARBORN

RC (DLC); at foot of text: "The President of the United States"; endorsed by TJ as received from the War Department on 8 Jan. and "John Taylor of N.Y. Commr. to hold treaty between N.Y. & the St. Regis Indians" and so recorded in SJL.

See TJ's message to the Senate of 1 Feb. for his transmittal of the APPOINTMENT. John Tayler was an Albany merchant and politician (Kline, *Burr*, 1:82n).

The reservation at ST. REGIS (Akwesasne) was on the St. Lawrence River, on the far northern edge of New York. Most of the residents of the settlement, which dated from the mid-eighteenth century, were Mohawks. On 26 Nov. 1801, Governor George Clinton of New York wrote Dearborn that the people at St. Regis were ready to cede a tract of land one mile square. The transaction prepared the way for the establishment of a ferry, the income from which was to support a school. Clinton asked that the United States appoint a commissioner to attend the negotiation at Albany (ASP, *Indian Affairs*, 1:655; *Albany Centinel*, 26 Mch., 6 Apr. 1802; Bruce Elliott Johansen and Barbara Alice Mann, eds., *Encyclopedia of the Haudenosaunee (Iroquois Confederacy)* [Wesport, Conn., 2000], 12-13; Sturtevant, *Handbook*, 15:471, 473).

At the same time TJ named Tayler as commissioner for the St. Regis meeting, he also nominated him to be the U.S. commissioner for talks between the Seneca Indians and representatives of the Holland Land Company. Those negotiations were to resolve the boundaries of reservations retained by the Senecas through the 1797 treaty of Big Tree. Paul

Busti, the company's agent, had written to Madison on this subject from Philadelphia on 27 Dec. 1801. The Senate received TJ's message with the nominations on 2 Feb. On the 4th, Tayler's nomination was referred to a committee consisting of Uriah Tracy, Gouverneur Morris, and Abraham Baldwin. In response to queries from that committee, Dearborn wrote Tracy on 9 Feb. to state that "the Treaties alluded to are to be holden at the expense of the parties applying for them," and that he had "no other information respecting the wishes of the Indians" than what had already been conveyed to the Senate. On 15 Feb., after hearing a report from Tracy's committee, the Senate confirmed Tayler's appointment. On that day TJ signed the two commissions. The St. Regis transaction was completed by mid-March. When Dearborn sent Tayler the commission for the Seneca negotiation, he noted that "you will act in some measure in the character of an umpire between the State and the said Indians in any bargains which may be made between the parties, and you will of course pay due attention to the interest of the Indians, and see that all transactions relative to our bargains are explicit and fair." Tayler was to be compensated for his services by the state and the Holland Land Company (JEP, 1:406-7; ASP, *Indian Affairs*, 1:655-6; Dearborn to Tracy, 9 Feb. 1802, in DNA: RG 46, EPIR; Dearborn to Tayler, 17 Mch. 1802, Lb in DNA: RG 75, LSIA; commissions, 15 Feb. 1802, in DNA: RG 59, MPTPC; Tracy to [Madison], 8 Feb. 1802, recorded in DNA: RG 107, RLRMS; Madison, *Papers, Sec. of State Ser.*, 2:343; *Albany Centinel*, 26 Mch. 1802; Vol. 35:695-6).

To George Jefferson

DEAR SIR   Washington Jan. 8. 1802.

I yesterday inclosed you the first halves of bank bills to the amount of fifteen hundred dollars. I now inclose the remaining halves, arranged exactly in the order of those sent yesterday, so that you may have no trouble in tallying them. the 10. D. bills are sent entire. I percieved on reflection on the balance of the account rendered, that

1500. D. would not meet the paiments noted in my letter of yesterday & cover the purchase of the tobo. for mr Ross. I therefore now inclose 350. Doll. more, one set of halves in this letter, the other set to come on by another post. Accept assurances of my affectionate esteem.

TH: JEFFERSON

PrC (MHi); at foot of text: "Mr. George Jefferson."

I THEREFORE NOW INCLOSE: in his financial records, TJ noted that he was sending George Jefferson $350 in bank bills he had just received from John Barnes (MB, 2:1062).

To James Taylor, Jr.

SIR   Washington Jan. 8. 1802.

I yesterday inclosed you the first halves of bank bills amounting to 705. Dollars. I now inclose the remaining halves, arranged exactly in the order of the first so that you may have no trouble in tallying them. these are in paiment for the 4th. & 5th. pipes of wine recieved from you. it will be satisfactory to know the bills have got safe to hand. accept my respects & best wishes.   TH: JEFFERSON

P.S. Colo. Newton has been so kind as to purchase for me some casks of Hughes's crab cyder which I shall be glad to recieve.

PrC (MHi); at foot of text: "Mr. James Taylor. Norfolk"; endorsed by TJ in ink on verso.

From Albert Gallatin

DEAR SIR   Jany. 9th 1802

Will you look at the enclosed letters & remarks of the Comptroller in E. Randolph's case. I think it is best to take no steps in relation to the commissions for testimony abroad. But the conduct of the Court, through the whole of this business has been very extraordinary.

Respectfully Your obt. Servt.   ALBERT GALLATIN

RC (DLC); address clipped: "President [of] the United States"; endorsed by TJ as received from the Treasury Department on 9 Jan. and "E. Randolph's case" and so recorded in SJL. Enclosures not found, but see below.

John Steele, the COMPTROLLER, was in charge of pressing the U.S. suit against Edmund Randolph to recover about $50,000 in expenditures unaccounted for while he was secretary of state. The suit began in U.S. circuit court at Richmond in 1797. Attorneys argued the case in December of the following year, but the court's two judges were divided on some issues and could not render a judgment. A series of continuances then prolonged the suit. After each term of court the U.S. attorney for the district, Thomas Nelson, reported on the case to the secretary of the Treasury or the comptroller. Those letters, or an abridged compilation of them, were probably part of what Gallatin enclosed with the letter above. TJ learned from Nelson's reports that the circuit court's judges had split in 1798 over whether the government was responsible for William Short's claim of back diplomatic salary (see TJ to John Wickham, 29 Jan., and TJ to Short, 19 Apr. 1802). Later in 1802, Gallatin transmitted extracts of Nelson's correspondence to a committee of the House of Representatives that was investigating expenditures (ASP, *Finance*, 1:757, 760-2; Madison, *Papers, Sec. of State Ser.*, 2:240; Henry M. Wagstaff, ed., *The Papers of John Steele*, 2 vols. [Raleigh, N.C., 1924], 1:246-7; Vol. 31:62-3).

In 1800, Justice Samuel Chase, whose circuit included Virginia, had changed the means by which the case could be resolved when he ruled that the 1797 law under which the suit had been filed could not prevent Randolph from having the case decided by a jury. In November 1801, Gallatin passed along to Madison a request from Randolph for copies of some correspondence relating to expenditures during his tenure as secretary of state. In December the suit was argued before a jury for four days, but the jury, after a long deliberation, was unable to reach a verdict. In his most recent communication, dated 28 Dec. 1801, Nelson reported that the court had granted COMMISSIONS for Randolph to obtain depositions in Europe, which the district attorney feared could mean further delay. On 9 Jan. 1802, Gallatin informed Steele that he did not "see that any thing can or ought to be done in relation to the dedimus in E. Randolph's case" (Gallatin, *Papers*, 6:437; ASP, *Finance*, 1:761-2; Madison, *Papers, Sec. of State Ser.*, 2:240).

To George Jefferson

DEAR SIR   Washington Jan. 9. 1802.

On the 7th. inst. I forwarded you the first halves of bank bills to the amount of 1500. D. on the 8th. I forwarded the 2d. halves of the same bills, and the first halves of other bills amounting to 350. D. I now inclose the second half of the same bills for 350. D. arranged in order for tallying as the first. this compleats a remittance of 1850. D. to be applied as desired in my letter of Jan. 7. Accept my best wishes for your health & happiness.   TH: JEFFERSON

PrC (MHi); at foot of text: "Mr. George Jefferson"; endorsed by TJ in ink on verso.

From David Mandeville

SIR,   Philadelphia, January 9th. 1802.

Permit me the honor to present to you through the medium of my worthy friend Doctor Tucker a Calendar for the Nineteenth Century to which I have recently given publicity—should I learn that in your estimation, I have combined usefulness with originality and comliness, I shall be highly gratified, being no less sensible of your capacity to investigate than your ability to judge

I have the honor to be with due respect your very obt. H'ble Servt.

D. Mandeville

RC (ViW); at head of text: "Thomas Jefferson, Esqr."; endorsed by TJ as received 14 Jan. and so recorded in SJL. Enclosure: *Calender for the Nineteenth Century,* published as a broadside in Philadelphia in 1801, being a series of concentric circles engraved by John Draper measuring about four inches in diameter, "shewing the arrangement and the method of finding the Day of the Week or Month in any year from 1800 to 1900, inclusive" (Shaw-Shoemaker, No. 269; *Salem Register,* 21 Jan. 1802; *New-York Evening Post,* 1 Feb. 1802).

The writer was probably David Mandeville, who lived at North Sixth Street in Philadelphia in 1801 and 1802 and worked as an "accomptant" and clerk in the Bank of the United States (Stafford, *Philadelphia Directory, for 1801*, 37; Robinson, *Philadelphia Directory for 1802,* 163).

To Samuel A. Otis

Sir   Jan. 9. 1802.

In the recess of Senate I issued a commission to John S. Sherburne of N. Hampshire to be attorney for that district. I discover that in my list of nominations of the 6th. inst. sent to the Senate, I mistook a letter in copying, and called him John H. Sherburne instead of John S. Sherburne, the name intended. if the Senate has not confirmed that nomination I pray you that my Secretary Capt. Lewis may be permitted to correct the literal error in the original, by converting the H. into an S. which I presume will be perfectly regular, & preferable to encumbering your journals with a formal message. Accept my salutations & best wishes.

Th: Jefferson

RC (DNA: RG 46, EPEN); addressed: "Samuel A. Otis esquire Secretary of the Senate"; endorsed by Otis: "A Letter from the President UStates correcting a mistake in message 6th Instant. Jany 9th 1802." PrC (MoSHi: Jefferson Papers); endorsed by TJ in ink on verso.

For the appointment of JOHN S. SHER-BURNE as U.S. attorney for New Hampshire, see Vol. 34:129, 131n. For the correction of his initial, see Document VI in To the Senate: Interim Appointments, printed at 6 Jan.

To Thomas Mann Randolph

DEAR SIR   Washington Jan. 9. 1802.

My last letter from Edgehill was of the 6th. of Dec. I wrote you on the 1st. inst. the debate on the repeal of the last judiciary law was commenced in the Senate yesterday. it has also been touched on in the other house, where some members, generally sound, will have some qualms on this subject, because they are afraid to distinguish between a fraudulent use of the constitution, and a substantial & honest adherence to it.

Having occasion to inclose to mr Lilly 940. Dollars for debts payable in Albemarle, I have thought his letter would go safer under your cover; and as he cannot read, I will pray you to send for him and deliver the letter & money yourself, counting it to him, for which purpose I have left the letter open. my tender love to my dear Martha & the little ones, and affectionate esteem to yourself.

TH: JEFFERSON

RC (DLC); at foot of text: "Thomas M. Randolph"; endorsed by Randolph. Enclosure: TJ to Gabriel Lilly, 9 Jan. (recorded in SJL but not found).

LAST LETTER FROM EDGEHILL: Randolph's letter of 6 Dec., recorded in SJL as received on the 9th, has not been found.

DEBTS PAYABLE IN ALBEMARLE: TJ requested that Lilly pay $350 to Mr. Simmons for corn; $133.33 to Hancock Allen for the hire of Myntas and Ben and $63.33 to Abraham Johnson for the hire of Joshua, as agreed on 12 Apr. 1801, payable 1 Jan. 1802; and $316.67 and $76.67 to John and Reuben Perry, respectively, carpenters at Monticello (MB: 2:1000, 1023, 1037, 1063).

From Albert Gallatin

DEAR SIR   January 10th 1802

The Commissrs. of the City, without consulting any person on the subject, have offered, to the Legislature of the State of Maryland, six per cent stock in payment of the loan guaranteed by Congress, upon a presumption that that arrangement would be convenient to the U. States. As the first instalment of that loan becomes due only on the 1st Jany. 1804, there was no necessity of bringing the subject at present before Congress, & there was want of policy to state *at present* that the lots pledged for the loan were insufficient for that purpose. At the same time the idea of creating stock instead of paying off that small debt, if it is more eligible for the United States not to sell the lots, is altogether contradictory with our principle of paying the public debt. You will also perceive by the letter of the Comm[rs. to] the legislature of Maryland that they in [fact] charge to you the non-payment of interest [for the?] last year on the loan. Maryland has, however, accepted their offer, & formally laid their resolution to that effect before Congress who have referred the same to the Secretary of the Treasury.

I have thought it was best to write to the Commissioners before I should make a report, and enclose the rough draft of a letter prepared for them.

It is of some importance that the manner in which the subject should be presented to Congress, should be well weighed. Will you be pleased to communicate your ideas on the letter, & on the subject generally, before I take any further steps in the business?

With respect & affection Your obedt. Servt.

ALBERT GALLATIN

RC (DLC); torn; at foot of text: "The President of the United States"; endorsed by TJ as received from the Treasury Department on 11 Jan. and "Commrs. Washington" and so recorded in SJL. Enclosure not found.

On 17 Oct. 1801, the District of Columbia commissioners addressed a memorial to the LEGISLATURE OF THE STATE OF MARYLAND regarding the repayment of $250,000 in loans, which the commissioners had received from Maryland to prepare "the Federal Seat for the reception of the General Government," using public lands in the District of Columbia as the principal collateral. As they were unable to pay the interest promptly and did not see how they would be able to repay the $50,000 loan of 1799, which would become due on 1 Nov. 1802, the commissioners proposed that the Maryland legislature extend an offer to Congress to repay the loans with U.S. stock assigned to Maryland. WANT OF POLICY: in closing, the commissioners warned that if the law for raising the sums necessary to repay the loans was "strictly pursued, the public property must be sold at a very great loss, and the punctual payment of the principal and interest may notwithstanding be found impracticable." CHARGE TO YOU THE NON-PAYMENT OF INTEREST: in the memorial, the commissioners observed that the funds they had raised were insufficient to execute the

works which the president "deemed essential for the accommodation of Congress" and also to pay the interest on the loans (Tr in DLC, in William Brent's hand, including signatures of William Thornton, Alexander White, and Tristram Dalton; FC in DNA: RG 42, DCLB). For the Maryland loans, see the commissioners to TJ, 17 Aug. 1801. For criticism of the 1799 loan, see Vol. 33:508-10. TJ received a copy of a 17 Oct. memorial on 21 Oct. (Vol. 35:372n).

ACCEPTED THEIR OFFER: on 18 Oct. 1801, the commissioners forwarded the memorial to Maryland Governor John F. Mercer, along with a 17 Oct. letter to John Johnson, a state senator who had dealt with the commissioners (FCs in DNA: RG 42, DCLB). The Maryland Senate read the memorial on 6 Nov. and referred it to a committee, headed by Johnson, to consider "whether it would not be adviseable to offer to congress a release of the public property pledged, and other securities given for the payment of the sums loaned to the said commissioners, on congress assigning to the state United States stock, equivalent in value to the stock transferred by the state to the commissioners." The committee reported on 3 Dec. and six days later the Senate passed resolutions that called for the transfer of $250,000 in U.S. stock, bearing an interest of six percent, on or before 4 Mch. 1802, along with the payment of all interest due, after which Maryland would release claims to "any property in virtue of the loans." The House of Delegates concurred and on 31 Dec., the governor was directed to send the Maryland congressmen copies of the resolutions and the memorial of the commissioners, along with instructions to seek implementation of the resolutions (*Votes and Proceedings of the House of Delegates of the State of Maryland, November Session, One Thousand Eight Hundred and One* [Annapolis, 1802], 68; *Votes and Proceedings of the Senate of the State of Maryland, November Session, One Thousand Eight Hundred and One* [Annapolis, 1802], 5, 22, 28, 54; see Shaw-Shoemaker, Nos. 2602-3, respectively).

On 7 Jan. 1802, Maryland congressman Joseph H. Nicholson presented to the House of Representatives the governor's letter, the 17 Oct. memorial of the District of Columbia commissioners, and the resolutions of the Maryland legislature "agreeing to the proposition of the Commissioners." On the same day, the House REFERRED the documents to Gallatin "with instruction to examine the same, and report his opinion" to the House (JHR, 4:35; *Annals*, 11:406).

From John Hughes

SIR   S:C: Columbia 10th Jany 1802

The Idea of a Peace in Europe seems to be here generally believed, as certain, and has been a ground of some Debates in our National Councill—I hope that you will not be off your Guard—by this delusive Expectation—As a Man of Extensive Information, you can be no Stranger to the Views of the fell Agitators concerned in the present bloody Drama—

I do not doubt your Integrity, or Capacity—As a Man you cannot see every where. therefore in your Collection of Information, must have it, in many instances from Others—A Moderate share of political foresight induces me to disregard the protestations of Men blackned with so many Crimes—there is no sincerity in their Professions, inured to Wickedness, they are not to be trusted—As Experience will soon Demonstrate,—It is declared by unquestionable Authority, That a Universal Revolution must ensue, And a New Order of things take Place under divine Direction. Experience of human Goverment has, as yet, produced nothing permanently Safe; you have seen the Risque of loosing all in a few Years, which Virtuos Energy had long laboured to Produce—When the foul Pages of Ancient & Modern History are justly appreciated and Truth is discovered—What a lowring Horrison Astonishes the Daring reformer! As Brissot justly observes, there is something more necessary, than human Effort to Conduct the Enterprise, and Sustain the Adventurer—I know you to be more Manly than to reject the well meant Endeavours of an Individual, however humble his Station—I therefore take the Liberty of reccommendg to your perusal 2 Vols. of the Worlds Doom, I am certain you will agree with me in Opinion, That Richard Brothers has displayed more sanity of Judgement, then the British Administration; who indecently rejected his salutary warning—Your unfortunate Predecessor has in my Opinion, involved us, as a People in National Guilt, by his hostility to France. It remains for you as our Chief to attone, by avoiding an Evil of Such Magnitude—To be frank with you, I advise you to prepare promptly for War with England—It is not in your Power, or the Wisdom of Congress to put it by, the principal purpost of this Letter to you, has been to suggest to your Consideration; the Condition of Prisoners of War—and to induce to attempt a revisal of the laws. to aliviate the Oppressions of those innocent Sufferers—It is against the Goverment, and not the People, that War should operate—the Atrocious Goverment of England has already alienated the Affections of her best Men. At the begining of our Revolution, the Pride, and Ferocity of the british Soldiery was urged to heights, which were only surpressed by threats of retaliation, and favorable resistance—But the Seamen of Britain were generally well disposed to America, especially at the commencement, when their Wages, Ventures &c were paid out of the Sale of the Prizes taken Unfortunately, this just, and truely Politick conduct was lost Sight of in the Progression of the War. Sir I would advise you to pay attention to this Important Subject, Britains Wealth may buy Men. her Arrogance cannot ensure affection, and I trust no cruel Example of hers or any other Nation will ever induce the United States of America to deviate, from the Cause of humanity or from setting so laudable an Example to a barbarous Æra I trust on reflection She will consider the Cause of the Stranger & not, vex, or Oppress him—It has been generally thought in Europe that America was the Common Asylum of those who wished to become Inhabitants—I think that sacred Writ warrants my considering the whole Globe as a common Right of Inheritance. Honest Legislators may easily prevent Foreigners from any Dangerous interference in a Goverment. It is the Monied Agents of dishonest Goverments who are Dangerous to the repose of every People—It is Mammon—the Idol worshiped by Europe and most of America, that wars with the Rights of Man and usurpes the Adoration, alone due to the Father of Mankind   May, he who gives liberally and upbraids not, bestow on you, every thing needfull, to assist you in your Important Station   Is the wish of him who is

yours with Esteem   JOHN HUGHES

RC (DLC); at foot of text: "Thos. Jefferson"; endorsed by TJ as received 29 Jan. and so recorded in SJL.

The World's Doom; or the Cabinet of Fate Unlocked, a two-volume work published anonymously in London in 1795, was a reprint of 20 pamphlets relating to prophecy. It included writings by RICHARD BROTHERS, a former British naval officer turned self-proclaimed prophet, whose millennial claims gained a wide audience during the 1790s (J. F. C. Harrison, *The Second Coming: Popular Millenarianism, 1780-1850* [New Brunswick, N.J., 1979], 57-8, 241; DNB).

To Edward Savage

SIR   Washington Jan. 10. 1802.

Hearing that you have removed to New York and still carry on your business there, I take the liberty of applying to you for some print-frames with their glasses of the sizes mentioned below. my reason for troubling you particularly is that you know the style in which I like the frames to be made, having before made some for me by a model I furnished, and which I greatly prefer to those which are all gilt. when done be pleased to have them packed in a tight box and sent to Richmond to the address of Messrs. Gibson & Jefferson, who will forward them for me to Monticello sending me at the same time your bill which shall be immediately paid. accept my respects & best wishes   TH: JEFFERSON

1. frame to shew $20\frac{3}{4}$ I. height & $14\frac{1}{4}$. breadth within the frame
4.   do.   to shew 18. I. height & 13. I. breadth   do.
2 pair (say 4. frames) for Trumbull's two prints (death of Warren & Montgomery) I have not the measures, but you possess the prints.

PrC (DLC); at foot of text: "Mr. Savage"; endorsed by TJ in ink on verso.

Edward Savage (1761-1817), a native of Princeton, Massachusetts, was an artist and the owner of a museum gallery that he first developed in Philadelphia. In 1801, Savage moved from Philadelphia to New York City, where his museum collection expanded beyond paintings, prints, and sculptures to include natural history specimens and other attractions. A mezzotint of a portrait by Savage of TJ was available for sale in Philadelphia in 1800 (ANB; Vol. 31:xlv; Vol. 34:53n, 90).

For John TRUMBULL'S TWO PRINTS, see Stein, *Worlds*, 164-5; Vol. 16:550n; Vol. 31:374-5, 557-8.

To Joseph Yznardi, Sr.

SIR   Washington Jan. 10. 1802

I recieved in due time your favor of Dec. 1. and have been prevented answering sooner by a constant press of business. I am sorry to learn that an uneasiness has grown up between the Chevalier Yrujo and yourself. as far as is within my own observation I can bear witness in favor of both that I have never heard either say a word to the prejudice of the other. with respect to yourself particularly I can say with truth & pleasure that when you mentioned to me the recall of M. Yrujo, you placed it expressly on the ground of his having differed with a former Secretary of State, and that when I observed to you that I had considered that as a matter which was only personal between him & mr Pickering, and that the latter being out of office now, M. Yrujo would experience no difficulty with the present officer & that on the contrary, his worth & candour being known to us would facilitate affairs between the two governments, you appeared to learn it with great pleasure, expressed yourself amicably & delicately towards him, and said you should take care to make it known to your government: and I observed your conduct on all subsequent occasions to have been in the same spirit.

You have never been so kind as to furnish me a note of the amount of the wines you have sent me. if you will now be so good as to do this either to myself or mr John Barnes of Georgetown he will immediately order paiment for them. I will still ask your attention to the procuring me a pipe of dry Pacharette of first quality and as old as you can get it. Accept my best wishes for your health & happiness & assurance of my esteem & respect. TH: JEFFERSON

RC (AHN: Papeles de Estado, legajo 3891 bis, expediente 1, no. 128); addressed: "Joseph Yznardi esq. Philadelphia"; franked; postmarked 12 Jan.; endorsed by Yznardi as received on 13 Jan. and answered on the 15th. PrC (DLC); endorsed by TJ in ink on verso.

I OBSERVED TO YOU: TJ to Yznardi, 26 Mch. 1801. For their correspondence in that period that touched on Irujo, see Vol. 33:457, 483-6, 549-50.

From David Austin

MAY IT PLEASE YOUR EXCELL'Y Washington Jan'y 11th. AD. 1802.

The Senate have, this day, so far amended the report of the Committee on the Library Bill, as to place the sole power of appointment, in the President.

This was the more agreeable to my wishes, as it will enable the President to exercise that good will towards me, in this matter, of which I have never entertained a doubt, provided a situation had offered, in the judgment of the President, suited to my views & situation.

I cannot but hope that I am correct in my reliance on the President's favor in this instance; & I think it will need no confirmation, when I say, that by the stricktest attention to the duties of the appointment, I shall endeavor to shew that the president could not have been more correct in confering the favor.—

With all due esteem: D: Austin.

RC (DLC); endorsed by TJ as received 11 Jan. and so recorded in SJL.

From Richard Dinmore

Sir   Washington 11 Janry 1802

When the appointment of a Librarian, was brought before the legislature, I solicited my friends for their nomination and support; Encouraged by their partiality, when it was expected that the president of the Senate, and the speaker of the house of representatives would have the appointment, I still persevered in my application; I am this moment informed, that the Senate has passed the Bill, relative to the Library, vesting the appointment of Librarian, solely in you; permit me then Sir to make this application directly to yourself, to which I am induced, not only by the unequal state of my Health, and the want of employment adequate to the maintenance of my Family, but by the belief that I could fill that Station, reputably to the nomination. Conscious of the difficulty with which an unpatronized indivedual ought to attract your attention, permit me to add, that I brought letters from Europe to Drs. Mitchell and Thornton, and that since I have been in this Country, I have received flattering marks of friendship from Genl. Mason, Govr. Mercer, Mr: Richd. Sprigg &c. I remain Sir

With respect Yrs.   R Dinmore

RC (DNA: RG 59, LAR); endorsed by TJ as received 11 Jan. 1802 and so recorded in SJL.

Richard Dinmore (1765-1811) was a native of Norwich, England, who studied medicine and then abandoned the practice to go into mercantile trade and become an author and publisher. He published two political pamphlets in England before emigrating to Washington in 1797, where he operated a school and grocery in Georgetown. In partnership with James Lyon, he was involved in several newspaper and literary publishing ventures including the *National Magazine; or, Cabinet of the United States* and the *Expositor*, which started in Alexandria in 1802 and moved to Washington in 1807. TJ was a subscriber to the circulating library he directed in Washington and also to his *Select and Fugitive Poetry: A Compilation with Notes Biographical and Historical* published in Washington in 1802. TJ received a copy of Dinmore's *A Long Talk, Delivered before the Tammany Society, of Alexandria, District of Columbia, at their First Anniversary Meeting, May 12, 1804.* Dinmore was the father of 16 children, most of whom predeceased him. He died at the age of 46 and received an unusually lengthy obituary in the Washington press (*Centinel of Liberty, and George-Town and Washington Advertiser*, 13 June 1800; *National Intelligencer*, 8 Oct. 1811; MB, 2:1043, 1123, 1227; Shaw-Shoemaker, No. 2148; Sowerby, No. 3312; Vol. 34:405, 603; Vol. 35:487-8).

From Henry Esch

MONSIEUR LE PRÉSIDENT.   New-York 11 Janvr. 1802.

J'ai l'honneur de vous adresser cijoint, une lettre que Monsieur le Professeur Pictet me remit à mon départ de Genève ma ville natale, j'espérois toujours avoir la douce jouissance de vous la présenter & de me mettre par là à même de vous exprimer de bouche combien les qualites si respectables qui vous distinguent, me penètrent d'admiration; mais je vois que mes affaires ne me permettront pas de me rendre a votre résidence. Je pris la liberté de vous envoyer le mois passé par Mr. le Docteur Mitchel, à qui je suis recomandé, un apperçu de la Bibliotèque Britanique dont Mr. Pictet est un des principaux Rédacteurs: je ne sais Monsieur le President si malgré toutes les occupations majeures qui sont votre partage, vous voudrez bien prendre en considération les efforts que font mes compatriotes pour donner plus d'impulsions aux Arts & aux Sciences s'il suffisoit de vous assurer pour vous intéresser à leur intention, qu'ainsi que moi ils vous portent dans leurs coeurs, sans peine je vous en donnerais des preuves convaincantes.

Le pleine persuasion ou je suis de votre amour pour la justice me détermine peut être sans avoir assez murement pesé (étant encore fort jeune) à profiter de cette occasion pour me plaindre à vous de personnes qui étant sous votre autorité me traitent cruellement.

J'arrivois dans ce port-ci le 1er. 8ber. dernier. Trois jours après mon arrivée le 3 dit. je remis à un négotiant de cette ville Mr. J. Dupuis la facture de 19 montres que j'avais dans ma malle, afin que ne connoissant, ni les loix, ni les usages de ce pays, il eut la complaisance de faire l'entrée de ces articles pour moi. Le matin du 3 8ber. à onze heures il se transporta à la Douane & come on exiga que la facture fut traduite de français en anglais, je demandais un permis pour entrer simplement mes hardes en ayant besoin, elle me fut accordée, l'après midi je vais à bord à 4 heures, présente mon permis à l'officier & lui dit Voici un permis pour mes hardes, mais avec elles dans ma malle j'ai deux boëtes contenant des montres, je vais les remettre au Capitaine qui les gardera jusques à ce que je puisse les retirer. Puis ouvrant ma malle je prens les deux boëtes & lorsque je veux les remettre au capitaine, l'officier me les arrache des mains & les lui remets lui même en disant Capitaine gardez cela dans votre cabine: Le surlendemain c'étoit un Lundy, il va de bonneheure porter à la custom house les deux boëtes qu'il mavoit si honnètement arrachées. Depuis ce moment je n'ai pas revu mes montres, aucune justice ne m'a été rendue. Je désirerois donc ardemment Monsieur le Président que vous intimiez à ces Messieurs de ne pas persévérer davantage à être injuste envers moi. Tant plus il tardent à me rendre mes articles tant plus je perds, car oûtre qu'ils déperissent à la Douane, le tems de la vente se passe rapidement. Je trouve par hazard l'occasion de les vendre à présent je serais bien aise d'en profiter.

Excusez Monsieur le President, un jeune home peut être trop osé, qui fait les voeux les plus ardens pour votre prosperité.

Je suis avec estime & considération Votre très obéissant Serviteur

HENRY ESCH

EDITORS' TRANSLATION

MISTER PRESIDENT   New York, 11 Jan. 1802

I have the honor to address to you, attached herewith, a letter that Professor Pictet entrusted to me upon my departure from Geneva, my native city; I always hoped to have the sweet enjoyment of presenting it to you and thereby to put myself in a position to express to you orally how much the respectable qualities that distinguish you fill me with admiration; but I see that my occupations will not allow me to reach your residence. I took the liberty of sending you last month by Doctor Mitchill, to whom I have been recommended, a brief survey of the *Bibliothèque britannique*, of which Mr. Pictet is one of the principal editors. I do not know, Mister President, whether, despite all the major occupations that are your lot, you will be willing to take under consideration the efforts that my compatriots are making to give more impetus to the arts and sciences, or if it would be enough to interest you in their intentions, to assure you that they, like myself, bear you in their hearts. I could give you convincing proof of it without any trouble.

The complete persuasion that I have of your love for justice determines me, perhaps without having given close enough consideration (being still very young), to take advantage of this opportunity to complain to you about people who, being under your authority, are treating me cruelly.

I arrived in this port on the first of last October. Three days after my arrival, the third of that month, I turned over to a merchant of this city, Mr. J. Dupuis, the invoice for 19 watches that I had in my trunk so that, I knowing neither the laws nor the customs of this country, he would have the kindness to bring in those articles for me. The morning of 3 Oct., at 11:00, he betook himself to the custom house, and, since they required that the invoice be translated from French into English, I requested a permit to bring in my clothes, being in need of them; it was granted to me; in the afternoon I go on board at 4:00 o'clock, present my permit to the officer and tell him, "Here is a permit for my clothes, but with them I have in my trunk two boxes containing watches; I am going to turn them over to the captain who will keep them until I can withdraw them." Then, opening my trunk, I take the two boxes, and when I try to hand them over to the captain, the officer snatches them from my hands and he himself hands them over, saying to the captain, "Captain, keep that in your cabin." Two days later it was a Monday, he goes early to the custom house carrying the two boxes that he had so honestly seized from me. Since that moment I have not seen my watches again; no justice has been rendered to me. I would ardently desire, Mister President, that you should suggest to those gentlemen not to persist any more in being unjust to me. The more they delay in giving back to me my property the more I lose, for, besides the fact that they are wasting away in the custom house, the time for their sale is passing by rapidly. I have found by chance the occasion to sell them at present; I should be quite happy to take advantage of it.

Forgive, Mister President, a young man, perhaps too bold, who makes the most ardent wishes for your prosperity.

I am with esteem and respect your very obedient servant,

HENRY ESCH

RC (NHi: Gallatin Papers); at foot of text: "No. 160. Broadway"; endorsed by TJ as received 15 Jan. and so recorded in SJL. Enclosure: Marc Auguste Pictet to TJ, 20 May 1801. Enclosed in TJ to Gallatin, 16 Jan. 1802.

LA BIBLIOTÈQUE BRITANIQUE: see Pictet's 20 May letter to TJ, Vol. 34:152, 154n.

MR. J. DUPUIS: likely James Dupuy (also spelled Dwpuy), a New York merchant who imported goods from Europe and the West Indies. Later in 1802, Dupuy was summoned to France "on immediate business of importance," leaving his affairs in the hands of an agent (*The*

New Trade Directory, for New-York, Anno 1800 [New York, 1799], 108; New York *Daily Advertiser*, 20 Mch. 1798; *New-York Gazette and General Advertiser*, 26 Jan. 1799; New York *American Citizen and General Advertiser*, 8 Oct. 1801; New York *Mercantile Advertiser*, 18 Nov. 1801, 1 Oct. 1802).

CAPITAINE: Esch apparently arrived in New York from Hamburg aboard the *Elizabeth* of Portland, Maine. The ship's master was Peter Dyer (David Gelston to Albert Gallatin, 19 Apr. 1802, in NHi: Gallatin Papers; *New-York Gazette and General Advertiser*, 2 Oct. 1801; *Jenks' Portland Gazette*, 5 Oct. 1801).

From La Rochefoucauld-Liancourt

Liancourt 21 Nivose an 10 [i.e. 11 Jan. 1802]

Le Cit Lequinio nommé par le pr consul son Commissaire des relations exterieures a Newport, me prie de vous l'introduire Monsieur. Sans le Connaitre particulierement, Je suis assuré que Le chois de notre gouvernement vous le fera acueillir avec bonté. Je trouve dans cette recommandation, uné occasion de me rappeller a votre souvenir, et je profiteray toujours avec empressement de Celles qui me donnerons Le Moyen de vous parler de ma reconnoissance et de mon attachement sincere   LA ROCHEFOUCAULD-LIANCOURT

EDITORS' TRANSLATION

Liancourt, 21 Nivose Year 10 [11 Jan. 1802]
Citizen Lequinio, whom the first consul named as his commissioner of foreign relations in Newport, has asked me to introduce him to you. Without knowing him personally, I am confident our government's choice will prompt you to welcome him kindly. I take this opportunity to send you my greetings, and I will always be eager to take advantage of any opportunities that allow me to express to you my gratitude and sincere fidelity.

LA ROCHEFOUCAULD-LIANCOURT

RC (MoSHi: Jefferson Papers); English date supplied; endorsed by TJ as received 2 July 1802 and so recorded in SJL with notation "by Lequinio." Enclosed in Joseph Marie Lequinio de Kerblay to TJ, 20 June 1802.

Joseph Marie LEQUINIO de Kerblay took up his duties as French commissary of commercial relations at Newport, Rhode Island, in June 1802 (Madison, *Papers, Sec. of State Ser.*, 2:494n).

This letter from La Rochefoucauld-Liancourt is the last correspondence between him and TJ recorded in SJL. The French aristocrat had fled France in 1792, returning in 1799. In that period he signed his letters to TJ simply "Liancourt," but after his return to his home country he was restored to privileges as the seventh Duc de La Rochefoucauld (Vol. 29:148-9n; Vol. 31:104).

To the Senate and the House of Representatives

GENTLEMEN OF THE SENATE, & OF
THE HOUSE OF REPRESENTATIVES

I now communicate to you, a memorial of the Commissioners for the City of Washington together with a letter of later date, which, with their memorial of Jan: 28: 1801. will possess the legislature fully of the state of the public interests, & of those of the city of Washington, confided to them. The monies now due, & soon to become due to the State of Maryland, on the loan guarantied by the U.S. call for an early attention. The lots in the city which are chargeable with the paiment of these monies, are deemed not only equal to the indemnification of the public, but to ensure a considerable surplus to the city, to be employed for it's improvement, provided they[1] are offered for sale only in sufficient numbers to meet the existing demand. but the act of 1796 requires that they shall be positively sold in such numbers as shall be necessary for the punctual paiment of the loans. 9000 D. of interest are lately become due; 3000 D. quarter-yearly will continue to become due; and 50,000 D. an additional loan, are[2] reimburseable on the 1st. day of November next. these sums would require sales so far beyond the actual demand of the market, that it is apprehended that the whole property, may be thereby sacrificed, the public security destroyed, & the residuary interest of the city entirely lost. under these circumstances, I have thought it my duty, before I proceed to direct a rigorous execution of the law, to submit the subject to the consideration of the legislature. whether the public interest will be better secured in the end, & that of the city saved by offering sales commensurate only to the demand at market, & advancing from the treasury in the first instance what these may prove deficient, to be replaced by subsequent sales, rests for the determination of the legislature. if indulgence for the funds can be admitted, they will probably form a resource of great & permanent value; and their embarrasments have been produced only by overstrained exertions to provide accomodations for the government of the Union.   TH: JEFFERSON

Jan. 11. 1802.

RC (DNA: RG 233, PM, 7th Cong., 1st sess.); in a clerk's hand, corrected, dated, and signed by TJ; endorsed by House clerk. Dft (DLC); entirely in TJ's hand. Enclosures: (1) Memorial from the District of Columbia Commissioners, 4 Dec. 1801, and enclosure. (2) District of Columbia Commissioners to TJ, 19 Dec. 1801.

On this date, Meriwether Lewis delivered TJ's message to Congress, where it was read in the Senate and referred to Uriah Tracy and the Maryland senators Robert Wright and John E. Howard for a report. The House of Representatives read and referred the message to Joseph H. Nicholson of Maryland, James A. Bayard of Delaware, John Taliaferro of Virginia, Seth Hastings of Massachusetts, and Willis Alston of North Carolina, to

examine and report their opinion (JS, 3:167; JHR, 4:44-45).

For a discussion of THEIR MEMORIAL OF 28 JAN. 1801, see note to the Memorial from the District of Columbia Commissioners, 4 Dec. 1801.

MAY BE THEREBY SACRIFICED: in an act that became law on 1 May 1802, Congress gave the president the right to appropriate money from the U.S. Treasury to repay the Maryland loans if, in his opinion, a sufficient number of lots could not be sold "without an unwarrantable sacrifice of the property" (U.S. Statutes at Large, 2:175-6; John F. Mercer to TJ, 5 June 1802).

[1] Here in Dft TJ canceled "can be sold only."
[2] In Dft TJ first wrote "is" before overwriting it to read "are."

From Isaac Story

MOST RESPECTED SIRE,   Marblehead Jany. 11. 1802.

I view it as an instance of Condescension, that you vouchsafed to answer my letter with your own hand; & the contents were such, as gave pleasure to my heart.

I have a letter by me, which I received from President Washington. They lay side by side as precious deposits.—

I little thought that I should have occasion to address you so soon again.—

Colo. Johonnot of Hampden requested me to write to Mr. Gerry, that he might use his influence with the President, for obtaining the office of Collector & Searcher for the District of Penobscot. In compliance with his request, I wrote to Mr. Gerry on the Subject; & his answer I now enclose.—

All I shall attempt to say of Colo. Johonnot is that he is a capable man; but as Genl. Dearborn could be no Stranger to him, I shall refer you to him for his moral character & qualifications.

And if Genl. Dearborn feels justified in recommending him, it is well, & I am content. But if he will not recommend him, & the office should still continue vacant, I should esteem it a perticular favor, if it might be confered on me.

I am about leaving the ministry; for I have had the care of 3000 Souls & upwards, & the labors have pressed too hard upon me for some time, & I have desired my people to seek after a new Minister, which they mean to do immediatly, so that I can be disengaged at any time.—

And should the appointment devolve upon me, I hope, the public will find a faithful servant. I do not ask for this office, for the sake of the Emoluments of it, for my circumstances are independant: but I ask for it, that I may not be idle, & that I might have an employment, in which I may render service to the Community.

Were it necessary, I might procure a request, signed by many respectable Characters.—

I pray God to take you into his holy keeping & accept the homage of my most profound respects   Isaac Story

N.B. I have wrote to Mr. Madison & Genl. Dearborn on the Subject

RC (DNA: RG 59, LAR); endorsed by TJ as received 21 Jan. and so recorded in SJL; also endorsed by TJ: "to be collector of Penobscot." Enclosure not found.

ANSWER MY LETTER: TJ to Story, 5 Dec. 1801.

In 1795, Story sent George WASHING-TON a brief, undated letter, which enclosed copies of sermons he composed for a national day of thanksgiving proclaimed by the president (DLC: Washington Papers; Evans, No. 29571). Washington replied on 14 Apr. with a brief letter of thanks (Fitzpatrick, Writings, 34:176).

Gabriel JOHONNOT, of Hampden, Maine, was a former Boston merchant and a lieutenant colonel during the Revolutionary War. He was also Story's brother-in-law. Johonnot wrote Story on 22 Nov. 1801, requesting that he ask Elbridge GERRY to use his influence with the president to secure an appointment for Johonnot, preferably the Penobscot collectorship. Johonnot described the behavior of the current collector, John Lee, as "Uniformly inimical to this country, to the Republican interest peculiarly so" (DLC: Madison Papers; Madison, Papers, Sec. of State Ser., 2:386; Washington, *Papers, Rev. War Ser.,* 1:330). Johonnot did not receive the Penobscot appointment, which had already been granted to Josiah Hook (Hook to TJ, 24 Dec. 1801).

Story's letter to James MADISON, also dated 11 Jan. 1802, was largely identical to his letter to TJ printed above, but closed with a reminder that both Story and Madison had attended Princeton together and a wish that the secretary of state might "render service to an old College-friend." It also enclosed Johonnot's letter to Story of 22 Nov. 1801 (Madison, *Papers, Sec. of State Ser.,* 2:385-6).

From James Sullivan

SIR   Boston 11th. January 1802

The very great pleasure which I should enjoy, in paying my respects, in person, to Mr. Jefferson, as President of the United States, it is not probable that I shall have very soon, unless you shall give us the honor of a visit to the northward. My son John Langdon Sullivan, who is in the mercantile line, is making a tour to the seat of government; I have requested some of my friends there, to shew him the way, where he can, for himself, pay his duty to the first national magistrate of his country. And through him, as a proxy peculiarly dear to me, I wish you to receive the homage and best wishes of

Your very humble Servant   JA SULLIVAN

RC (DLC); at foot of text: "The President of the United States"; endorsed by TJ as received 16 Feb. and so recorded in SJL.

Boston merchant JOHN LANGDON SULLIVAN became a noted canal engineer and inventor, receiving a patent for a steam towboat in 1814 (James Grant Wilson and John Fiske, eds., *Appletons' Cyclopædia of American Biography,* 6 vols. [New York, 1887-9], 5:741-2; *List of Patents,* 137).

From Benjamin Waterhouse

SIR   Cambridge Janry 11th. 1802.

The enclosed letter came to my hands two days ago. I return it from an apprehension that it is a mistake. I conjecture that Aikens publication, as also some pieces from the news paper, were sent to some person to whom you wished to communicate information respecting the vaccine inoculation, and that by mistake you directed this letter to me, as no such articles came with it. It gives me however, the pleasing hope, provided I am right in my conjecture, of being soon honored with a letter from you.

I am inoculating almost every day, and with undeviating success.

[359]

We scarcely see any thing like a spurious taint, and when we do the cause is apparent and the remedy certain. The weather is favourable to the practice, for instead of frost & snow, we have showers like spring and the weather continues so warm that we are endanger of a double vegetation, after which "may come a frost, a killing frost!" and nip the hopes of the cultivator.

Altho' this new inoculation prospers, it is not without its opponents among the faculty here, as well as elswhere. Some are loathe to give up their old *freind* the small-pox. They slyly throw stumbling blocks in my way, while others plant themselves like reptiles in the high road of improvement & try to hiss back all that would advance. I mention this not in the tone of complaint, but merely to apprise you of the falshoods & misrepresentations that are floating on the breath of the ignorant, interested, envious & malignant. I have been so attentive in tracing every case that has been brought forward to injure us, & so careful to dissect it before the public that our enemies are rather cautious in their movements, especially as they know the popular opinion is against them. None of the printers in Boston will admit any piece against the practice without the writers name to it. It was early attempted, but the public voice cried out against it. Nay more, the printers of all parties in Boston have not only declined printing such pieces but in several instances sent them to me

The most mischievous idea spread abroad is this,—"the kine-pox will secure you for a *few years only* from the s.pox, after which you are as liable as ever to the disease." It is here, after being beaten from every post, that our enemies have entrenched themselves with an air of defiance.

As the practice now stands on the firm ground of experiment, I mean to continue the history of it in the form of a communication to the next number of the Medical Repository at New-York. In that paper I could wish to make use of the whole, or a part of one of your letters to me, merely to aid the cause by shewing the American people that you think well of the discovery & the practice: unless indeed you would think fit to express your *present* opinion as you have been able to form one from your own knowledge of the business. If this idea accords with your own, I should rejoice at it, but otherwise, I must beg you to excuse the suggestion, while I remain satisfied that it would be improper. I never knew if the letter, which you thought had best be published at Washington, ever has appeared. Col. Varnum used to send me the National Intelligencer, but he has forgotten me this session.

I have just sent the vaccine virus to Dr. Ramsey of Charleston by sea; he writes very earnestly for it. At N. York the worthy Dr. Seaman conducts the business with perfect success by matter I sent him. He says he shall hereafter make it a *point of conscience never to inoculate another person for the small-pox*, unless it be after the vaccine process by way of trial.

Accept the sentiments of esteem & veneration from
                                          BENJN. WATERHOUSE

RC (DLC); endorsed by TJ as received 18 Jan. and so recorded in SJL. Enclosure: TJ to James Currie, 25 Dec. 1801.

A FROST, A KILLING FROST: Shakespeare, *Henry VIII*, 3.2.

The NEXT NUMBER OF THE MEDICAL REPOSITORY, dated 1 Apr. 1802, included an extract of a 26 Sep. 1801 letter from Waterhouse to Samuel L. Mitchill, in which Waterhouse reported the success of vaccination at Monticello. "President Jefferson informs me," wrote Waterhouse, "that the kine-pox has pervaded, or is pervading, his family at Monticello, more than twenty having already gone through the *genuine* disease—at least I presume so from the virus sent him, and the description he has given me of its effects. It is progressing in this quarter with undeviating success, *very few* spurious cases having occurred this season." In the following issue, dated 1 Aug., the

Repository reprinted extracts of TJ's letter to Waterhouse of 25 Dec. 1801 and Waterhouse's reply of 28 Jan. 1802 (*Medical Repository*, 5 [1802], 235-6, 347-8).

In his 17 Sep. 1801 letter to Waterhouse, TJ observed that the doctor's letter to him of 8 June contained "a great deal of useful information" and suggested that it BE PUBLISHED AT WASHINGTON. TJ had forwarded it to Edward Gantt to assist him with his vaccine experiments in the nation's capital.

Physicians David Ramsay (RAMSEY) of South Carolina and Valentine SEAMAN of New York promoted vaccination in Charleston and New York City, respectively (Waterhouse, *A Prospect of Exterminating the Small-Pox, Part II* [Cambridge, Mass., 1802], 35-7; Joseph I. Waring, *A History of Medicine in South Carolina, 1670-1825* [Columbia, S.C., 1964], 294-7; *Medical Repository*, 5 [1802], 236-8).

To Albert Gallatin

DEAR SIR   Washington Jan. 12. 1802.

The proceedings of the Commissioners of Washington with Maryland seem not to be accurately understood. Maryland lent them 250,000 D. of stock at par, on which they lost 15. percent. they proposed therefore that Maryland should leave Congress free to repay in stock. they did not propose, nor ever thought of, shortening the terms of paiment. Maryland agrees to recieve stock on condition it is delivered in March. they did not send this to the Commissioners, or it would have been flatly rejected; but sent it to Congress and leave the Commrs without an answer. as things are we are uncommitted. their proposition should be rejected. not knowing of this answer of

Maryland or that the H. of R. were acting on it, I yesterday sent in a message with a Memorial of the Commissioners supplementary to that of Jan. 28. 1801 & a letter of later date. to understand the ground on which we stand, and on which your report to Congress should be predicated, it will be necessary you should take the trouble of reading these papers, for which purpose I inclose them to you, and will ask an interview whenever you shall be at leisure after your perusal of them, and a return of the papers. you have already had their accounts. I do not believe you will find it necessary to make any further enquiry of them; however if you should it will be better after our interview. health & best wishes.   TH: JEFFERSON

RC (NHi: Gallatin Papers); at foot of text: "The Secretary of the Treasury"; endorsed. PrC (DLC). Enclosures: see TJ to the Senate and the House of Representatives, 11 Jan., and enclosures.

SENT IT TO CONGRESS: the resolutions of the Maryland legislature, forwarded to the state's congressional delegation by Governor John F. Mercer (see Gallatin to TJ, 10 Jan.).

YOU HAVE ALREADY HAD THEIR ACCOUNTS: on 21 Dec., Gallatin sent a statement of the commissioners' receipts and expenditures, and of "the progress made in the public buildings" from 18 Nov. 1800 to 18 Nov. 1801, to the House of Representatives, where they were immediately referred to the Committee of Ways and Means (JHR, 4:23; *Letter from the Secretary of the Treasury, Covering Two Letters from the City Commissioners, with Documents, Exhibiting, I. Receipts and Expenditures by Them, and II. State and Progress of their Business and Funds* [Washington, D.C., 1801]; Shaw-Shoemaker, No. 1499).

From John Gardiner

Pensylvania Avenue
TO HIS EXCELLENCY   (Fourth House NW of the War Office)
THOS. JEFFERSON   12 Januy 1802

Your Excellencys condescending attention to a plan for a Ship Company in this City that I had the honor to submit (but which plan I fear will not soon be put into execution) emboldens me to sollicit your Excellencys favor in my own behalf—

The prospects I had when I left Europe of settling here in the Mercantile Line, have been destroyd by my Shipwreck; I am link'd to this City by having vested the Wreck of my Property in a Building, & by the difficulties of removing a Family to a place of more Trade.—I have been unsuccessfull in applications for personal employment; & the Profits of a small Store, which my Family attend, are inadequate to the Necessities of a Family.—The dreary Veiw before me, *urges*, whilst your Excellencys Character encourages me to sollicit from your Excellency the Office of Librarian to Congress, *or any other employment*—I can only recommend myself by stating that I can give security for the trusts that may be repos'd me—I rest my hopes *solely* on your Excellencys Benevolence—

I have the honor to be With the utmost Respect Your Excellencys obedt. hu Servt.   JOHN GARDINER

RC (DNA: RG 59, LAR); endorsed by TJ as received 12 Jan. and "to be librarian."

PLAN FOR A SHIP COMPANY: see Gardiner to TJ, 1 Nov. 1801.

To the House of Representatives

GENTLEMEN OF THE
HOUSE OF REPRESENTATIVES.

According to the request in your resolution of the 8th. Inst., I now lay before you a letter from the Secretary of State, containing an estimate of the expences necessary for carrying into effect the convention between the United States of America and the French Republic.

TH: JEFFERSON
Jany. 12th. 1802.

PrC (DLC); in Meriwether Lewis's hand, signed and dated by TJ. RC not found, but an endorsement by a House clerk in DNA: RG 233, PM, 7th Cong., 1st sess., indicates that the message and enclosures were referred to the Committee of Ways and Means on 12 Jan. Recorded in SJL with notation "Exp. of French convention." Printed with enclosures in ASP, *Foreign Relations*, 2:365.

The House RESOLUTION of 8 Jan. stated that "the President of the United States be, and he is hereby, requested to cause to be laid before this House an estimate of the expenses which are necessary for the carrying into effect the Convention between the United States of America and the French Republic." The House appointed John Randolph and James A. Bayard to present the resolution to the president (JHR, 4:43).

Meriwether Lewis delivered this message on 12 Jan. After the papers were read, the House committed them to the Committee of Ways and Means. On 12 Mch., Randolph for the committee reported a bill for the appropriation for expenses of CARRYING INTO EFFECT THE CONVENTION. After debate on the 23d, the bill passed on 24 Mch. Following approval by the Senate, the bill became law on 3 Apr. The statute authorized up to $318,000 for claims relating to captured French property and ships, to be spent as directed by the president from funds not appropriated for any other purpose. Language that would have required the funds to be taken first from proceeds of French prizes was struck before the bill passed the House of Representatives (JHR, 4:47, 135, 155-6; U.S. Statutes at Large, 2:148).

I

From James Madison

Department of State,
January 11th 1802.

Sir,

I have the honor to lay before you an estimate of the sum necessary to be appropriated for carrying into effect the Convention between the United States of America and the French Republic of the 30th of Sept. 1801.

I have the honor to be, Sir, your most Obt Sert.   JAMES MADISON

RC (DNA: RG 233, PM, 7th Cong., 1st sess.); in a clerk's hand, signed by Madison; at foot of text: "The President of the United States"; endorsed by a House clerk. Enclosed in the document above. RC (DNA: RG 46, LPPM, 7th Cong., 1st sess.); in a clerk's hand, signed by Madison; at foot of text: "The President of the United States"; endorsed by a Senate clerk. Enclosed in TJ to the Senate, 12 Jan.

II

Estimate of Expenses

[11 Jan. 1802]

Estimate of the expenses necessary for carrying into effect the Convention between the United States of America and the French Republic of the 30th. of Sept. 1801.

For captures made prior to the date of the Treaty on which no final condemnation had then passed, and of which the property was brought into the United States	137 770
For captures made subsequent to the date of the Treaty	70,351
For captures, where the property was not brought into the United States nor any condemnation had	122,156
For cases of capture not at present known and for a possible excess of the indemnities to be paid, above the estimate, say	19,723
Dollars.	350,000

Note—The sum of 2,000 dollars ℔ annum to cover the allowance to an Agent at Paris to perform the Office of soliciting the claims for restitution under the Convention, has been included in the general estimate for the service of the year 1802.

The repairs put upon the Corvette Berceau before her delivery to the French Republic are not included in the above estimate:—they amounted to $32,839 $\frac{54}{100}$.

MS (DNA: RG 233, PM, 7th Cong., 1st sess.); undated; in a clerk's hand; endorsed by a House clerk. PrC (DNA: RG 46, LPPM, 7th Cong., 1st sess.).

From Charles Willson Peale

Dear Sir   Museum Jany. 12th. 1802

The laborious, tho' pleasing task of mounting the Mammoth Skeleton being done, gives me leisure to attend to other Interests of the Museum.

The constant accumulation of articles not only of this but also of other Countries—increasing my imbarrisments to know how to dispose them for exhibition and public utility—these difficulties I expect will be greatly encreased after my Sons have visited Europe, and made the exchanges of subjects of Natural history contemplated.

Things huddled togather as I am now obliged to put them, loose much of their beauty and usefulness, they cannot be seen to advantage for study.

I have long contemplated that by industry such a variety of interresting subjects of Nature might be collected in one view as would enlighten the minds of my country-men, and, demonstrate the importance of diffusing a knowledge of the wonderful and various beauties of Nature, more powerful to humanize the mind, promote harmony, and aid virtue, than any other School yet immagened. That in the end these labours would be crowned in a National Establishment of my Museum. Here I must observe, and it ought never to be forgotten, that the Collection which now constitutes my Museum, is but a part of an Establishment, which in becoming national, should embrace the *exhibition of every article*, by which knowledge, in all its branches, can possibly be communicated.

Mr. Latrobe has made a design for a Building extending from 5th. to 6th. Street, the south side of the State-house Garden, which I mean to offer for the consideration of the Legeslature of this State, now in session, (the substance of which I enclose you) expecting that some grant will be made to erect such a Repository to preserve this Museum.

Before making my application, I wish to know your sentiments on this subject, whither the United States would give an encouragement, and make provision for the establishment of this Museum in the City of Washington.

The income by visitations to a museum *there*, would be far short of what may be had in any of our larger Cities, for many years to come— yet if some funds were provided to make up such deficiences—the donations which would naturely flow in, would amply repay the expence. I need not attempt a detail of the benefits of a well organized Museum—or how it might be conducted to inhance its value to the

Public, your knowledge of the subject is superior to any thing I can suggest, I can only say, for the preservation of Animal subjects, the mode I practice, I have good reasons for beleiving is much superior to those in general use in Europe.

I should not have chosen the time of the Session of Congress to entrude on your precious moments, but that it is of consequence that my application to the state Legislature, should not be delayed—I hope my apology will be accepted.

The Mammoth Skeleton is admired by numbers—and many encomiums are bestowed on my labours of puting it togather.

I long for the favor of your Visit, which will be highly gratifying to your Obliged Friend   C W PEALE

RC (DLC); on printed stationery with a design by Peale, engraved by James Akin, showing a man drawing back a curtain labeled "Nature" to reveal a scene with wildlife, plants, trees, mountains, and a lakeshore, above the caption: "Of grains are Mountains form'd" (also used on printed gift acknowledgments for Peale's museum; see Peale, *Papers*, v. 2, pt. 1:387; Charles Coleman Sellers, *Mr. Peale's Museum: Charles Willson Peale and the First Popular Museum of Natural Science and Art* [New York, 1980], 155); at foot of text: "To Mr. Jefferson"; en-

dorsed by TJ as received 15 Jan. and so recorded in SJL. Dft (Lb in PPAmP: Peale-Sellers Papers).

MAMMOTH SKELETON: for Peale's opening of the mastodon skeleton to public display at Philosophical Hall in Philadelphia on 24 Dec. 1801, see Vol. 35:436n.

The architectural plans that Benjamin H. LATROBE made for a projected new building to house Peale's museum have not been found (Peale, *Papers*, v. 2, pt. 1:389n).

ENCLOSURE

Substance of an Address

[ca. 12 Jan. 1802]

The time is now fully arrived when it has become expedient to decide the fate of the *Museum* to which Pennsylvania has given birth. It has commanded every exertion in my power for 16 years, and meeting with public approbation has certainly arrived to considerable Maturity; but from the uncertain tenure of human life it may not long continue in the same circumstances in which it has progressed, and means must be devised for its durability, perfection and Public utility. It would further be madness to dispise the interest of my family, which now calls for some permanent arrangement. It must either continue private Property or become a Public one; If private, the place where suitable encouragement is given must possess it; if Public, some of the States or the United States, may secure all the advantages of such an Institution, by an inconsiderable appropriation.

To Pennsylvania the *first offerings* are now tendered and the subjoined plan proposed for consideration

1st. either to encourage it as a private establishment (with a proper reference to public utility, as a school for every department of knowledge, without a single exception), of which the Museum now only form a part) and either appropriate the State-house, grant a lottery, or devise other means for the erecting of a suitable Building.   or

2dly. Purchase the Museum in toto & provide for its maintenance and perfection by suitable Regulations and appropriations. And thus lay the foundation of an establishment which the wisdom and policy of all nations have encouraged.

MS (DLC: TJ Papers, 128:22145); in Peale's hand; undated; endorsed by Peale: "The substance of an Address intended to be presented to the Legeslature of Pennsyla. in 1802. by C W Peale."

To the Senate

GENTLEMEN OF THE SENATE.

I now communicate to you a letter from the Secretary of State inclosing an estimate of the expences which appear at present necessary for carrying into effect the Convention between the U.S. of America and the French Republic, which has been prepared at the request of the House of Representatives.   TH: JEFFERSON

Jan. 12. 1802.

RC (DNA: RG 46, LPPM, 7th Cong., 1st sess.); in Meriwether Lewis's hand, signed and dated by TJ; endorsed by a Senate clerk. PrC (DLC). Recorded in SJL with notation "Exp. of French convention." Enclosures: see the enclosures printed at TJ to the House of Representatives, 12 Jan.

The Senate received this message and the enclosures from Meriwether Lewis on the 12th. After the papers were read they were tabled "for consideration." On 24 Mch., the Senate received from the House of Representatives the bill for appropriation of funds to carry out the convention. The following day the Senate referred the bill to a committee. Wilson Cary Nicholas reported for the committee on 26 Mch., offering no amendment to the House version, and the bill passed the Senate on 1 Apr. (JS, 3:168, 195-7, 201).

From Albert Gallatin

DEAR SIR   Jany. 13 1802

From a view of your message, it seems to me that I ought neither to apply to the Commissers. for information, nor give any opinion on the propriety of suspending the sale of the lots; but that my report to the H. of R. should be confined to a short recapitulation of the acts now in force, & to an opinion on the question whether it will be most eligible, in case Congress shall suspend the sale of lots, to reimburse the State of Maryland in specie, or in six per cent stock. On this last subject I have no hesitation, & wish to embrace this opportunity of explicitly giving my opinion in favor of the extinguishment of the public debt. On those grounds, the enclosed rough draft of a report has been prepared, & is now submitted to you.

My own opinion, as to the sale of lots, is that the authority should be discretionary with the President & not obligatory, provided, however, that the amount of what may be conveniently sold, should in the first place be applied to pay the interest on the loans; Congress, of course, directing the deficiency on the interest, & the principal to be paid out of the Treasury.

I heard last night with grief that you had been unwell. I hope to find you to day quite recovered. Take care, I beseech, of your health.

With sincere affection & respect Your obedt. Servt.

ALBERT GALLATIN

RC (DLC); at foot of text: "The President of the United States"; endorsed by TJ as received from the Treasury Department on 13 June and "Washington loans." Interlined in SJL as received on 13 Jan. and relating to "Commrs. Washn." Enclosure not found, but see below.

YOUR MESSAGE: see TJ to the Senate and the House of Representatives, 11 Jan.

MY REPORT: sent by the Treasury secretary to Nathaniel Macon, speaker of the House of Representatives, on 15 Jan., the report was brought before the House four days later. Gallatin recommended that if Congress decided it was unwise to "compel" the sale of city lots in order to repay the debt to Maryland, the U.S. Treasury would have no trouble discharging the debt IN SPECIE, rather than increasing the public debt through the issuance of additional six percent stock as proposed by Maryland. Gallatin concluded that although the resolution of the Maryland legislature "was evidently adopted only with a view of accommodating the United States," he could not recommend the acceptance of the offer (*Letter from the Secretary of the Treasury, Accompanying his Report on a Letter from the Governor of Maryland, and Sundry Documents . . . 19th January, 1802* [Washington, 1802], Shaw-Shoemaker, No. 3320; ASP, *Miscellaneous*, 1:258; JHR, 4:55).

From George Jefferson

DEAR SIR,   Richmond 13th. Janr. 1802

I am to night favor'd with yours of the 9th. covering the remaining halves of the $:350.; the first of which came by last post; and which, with the 1500$: the receipt of which I acknowledged last night, makes $:1850. to your credit.

I am Dear Sir Your Very humble servt.   GEO. JEFFERSON

RC (MHi); at foot of text: "Thos. Jefferson esqr."; endorsed by TJ as received 17 Jan. and so recorded in SJL connected by a brace with George Jefferson's letter of 12 Jan. with notation "1850. D."

I ACKNOWLEDGED LAST NIGHT: on 12 Jan., George Jefferson wrote TJ that he had received his letters of 7 and 8 Jan., enclosing "1500$. in halves, and the last likewise inclosing the first halves of the further sum of $:350" (RC in MHi; at foot of text: "Thos. Jefferson esqr."; endorsed by TJ as received 16 Jan. and so recorded in SJL, where TJ connected it by a brace to the letter printed above).

To John Vaughan and Charles Willson Peale

GENTLEMEN   Washington Jan. 13. 1802.

I have to acknolege the reciept of your favor of the 1st. inst. informing me that the American Philosophical society had again elected me President of the society for the ensuing year. for this mark of their continued favor, I pray you to present them a renewal of my thanks and of my profound respect. I have still to lament that my distance & other occupations leave me nothing but expressions of useless regrets that I have it not in my power to render them the services I would wish.

Accept for yourselves, gentlemen the assurances of my esteem and high consideration.   TH: JEFFERSON

RC (PPAmP); addressed: "Messrs. John Vaughan and Charles W. Peale of the American P.S. Philadelphia"; endorsed for the APS. PrC (DLC).

FAVOR OF THE 1ST. INST.: on 1 Jan., Vaughan and Peale, signing themselves "Judges of Election," sent TJ a one-sentence letter informing him that he had been "duely elected" president of the American Philosophical Society in a

meeting held that day (RC in DLC; in Vaughan's hand, signed by Vaughan and Peale; at foot of text: "Thomas Jefferson President of the United States Washington"; endorsed by TJ as received 4 Jan. and so recorded in SJL).

PRESENT THEM A RENEWAL OF MY THANKS: the APS received TJ's acknowledgment of his election at a meeting on 19 Mch. 1802 (APS, *Proceedings*, 22, pt. 3 [1884], 322).

To James Currie

DEAR SIR   Washington Jan. 14. 1802.

I recieved yesterday your favor of Jan. 8. covering the award of the Arbitrators, and I consent willingly to the paiment to them of 50. Dollars on my part for their trouble, which mr Jefferson will do for me. I write to him to this effect. he had already, at my desire procured as much tobo. as would have discharged the award, had it been corrected as I believed it would. but it will now want about 4000. ℔. to make up the whole, which I desire him to purchase & pay immediately. I am glad to be rid of this business on any terms, and it has been owing to mr Ross that it was not decided 10. years ago.

I thank you for returning Dr. Waterhouse's letter, as it detects the error I had committed. I wrote to you on the same day, and by mistake sent his letter to you & yours to him. but the book was intended for you, as I have another copy. I therefore now return it to you for acceptance. the Cow-pox is rising above all objection, liable however to the risk of spurious infection, which will frequently take place when the matter is taken by an unskilful person. Dr. Gant thinks the matter good as soon as it forms, which is sometimes as early as the 6th day, and that to the end of 8. times 24. hours it is always in a proper state; but that after that, tho' still good in tardy cases, it is bad in early ones.

Accept my respects & best wishes   Th: Jefferson

PrC (MHi); at foot of text: "Doctr. James Currie"; endorsed by TJ in ink on verso. Enclosure: see TJ to Currie, 25 Dec. 1801.

I WRITE TO HIM: see the following document.

To George Jefferson

Dear Sir   Washington Jan. 14. 1802.

I yesterday recieved by post from Doctr. Currie the award of the arbitrators to pay to mr Ross of the tobacco of the upper James river or Appomatox inspections 12,485. ℔. with interest at 5. per cent from Oct. 15. 1790.

I must in the first place ask the favor of you to put 50. D. into the hands of Doctr. Currie for the arbitrators, and then to enlarge the purchase of tobo. for one of the cheapest to be had at Petersburg, for I care not for the quality if it satisfies the award. supposing paiment made by the last of this month, the whole amount will be 19,534. ℔. you already have 15,308. ℔. consequently there is a deficiency of 4,226. ℔. now to be bought. please to have the purchase made payable at 60. days from it's sale, as my funds till then are fully engaged. in the mean time you may deliver to mr Ross what you have, taking a receipt for so much *in part of the sum awarded*. Accept assurances of my affectionate esteem.   Th: Jefferson

PrC (MHi); at foot of text: "Mr. George Jefferson"; endorsed by TJ in ink on verso.

RECIEVED BY POST: James Currie to TJ, 8 Jan. 1802.

From George Jefferson

DEAR SIR,   Richmond 14th Janr. 1802

I have to day received of the Treasurer of the James River Company $.198., being a dividend of 3 ℔ Cent on Mr. Short's 33 shares, the directors having lately determined to make now, and to continue such a dividend half yearly, so long as the tolls will justify it, & likewise enable them to continue improving the bed of the River with about 15 or 20 hands.

By going on in this way they calculate upon compleating the bed of the river in about 2 or 3 years, and then, judging from their last years receipts, they expect to make dividends of about 10 ℔ Cent ℔ annum until they are compelled to make the Canal communicate with tide water.

Of the receipt of this money be pleased to inform Mr. Barnes to whose credit, as usual, we have placed it.

I am Dear Sir, Your Very humble servt.   GEO. JEFFERSON

RC (DLC: William Short Papers); at foot of text: "Thos. Jefferson esqr."; endorsed by TJ as received 18 Jan. and so recorded in SJL.

Robert Pollard served as secretary and TREASURER OF THE JAMES RIVER COMPANY from 1793 to 1823 (Washington, *Papers, Pres. Ser.*, 12:304). COMMUNICATE WITH TIDE WATER: for the canal company plans, see Vol. 31:224-5.

From George Washington McElroy

SIR.   Lancaster 14th. January 1802

I had flattered myself with the hope of paying personally my respects to your Excellency, but extreemly regret indisposition must deprive me of that anticipated honor.

I have taken the freedom, thro the medium of my friend Mr. Duane to lay before you a letter from Governor McKean, Certficates from Le Chevallier d'Yrujo and Don Josef Yznardy, as also the memorial of Sundry Merchants of Philadelphia, suplicating in my behalf the Consular Office at the Canary Islands; which should it please you to grant, the hight of my ambition should be, by attention & regularity to merit your Confidence.

Permit me to assure you, of the Sentimts. of respectful Consideration with which I have the honor to be

Your Excellency's Mo. Obd. huml. Sevt.

GO. WASHN. MCELROY

RC (DNA: RG 59, LAR); at foot of text: "His Excellency Thomas Jefferson Esqr. President of the U.S."; endorsed by TJ as received 27 Jan. and "to be Consul at Teneriffe" and so recorded in SJL. Enclosures: (1) Thomas McKean to TJ, 11 Jan. 1802 (not found, but recorded in SJL as received 27 Jan. with notation "G. W. McElroy to be Consul Teneriffe"). (2) Certificate of Carlos Martínez de Irujo, undated, stating that McElroy would fill the position of U.S. consul at Tenerife "in a manner as useful to his Countrymen as agreeable to the people" among whom he would reside (MS in DNA: RG 59, LAR; in Irujo's hand and signed by him). (3) Certificate of Joseph Yznardi, Sr., 7 Jan. 1802, testifying that McElroy resided with him for 12 months in Cadiz, where he "made considerable progress in the Spanish language," then served an additional 11 months as consular agent at Sanlúcar de Barrameda; McElroy's knowledge of the language and "his acquaintance with the manners and customs of the people and his other necessary qualifications" made him a proper choice for the Canary Islands consulship (MS in same; in a clerk's hand, signed by Yznardi). (4) Memorial of merchants of Philadelphia to TJ, 2 Jan. 1802, stressing the need for a U.S. consul at Tenerife and stating that McElroy's "punctual performance of his duty" would merit the president's confidence in his appointment; McElroy spent three years in Spain and the Canary Islands, and his skills in the Spanish and Portuguese languages can be attested to by Irujo and Josef Ignacio de Viar (MS in same; in a clerk's hand, signed by Chandler Price, Philip Micklin, and 18 others).

In February 1802, TJ appointed George Washington McElroy (d. 1804) consul at Tenerife in place of John Culnan, who had abandoned the place due to poor health (JEP, 1:406, 407; Madison, *Papers, Sec. of State Ser.*, 2:371-2; 8:121-2; commission for George Washington McElroy, 10 Feb. 1802, in Lb in DNA: RG 59, PTCC; Vol. 33:678).

To John Vaughan

DEAR SIR   Washington Jan. 14. 1802.

In answer to your favor of Dec. 29. it is not in my power to inform you as to the existence or title of the several literary societies you therein mention; but we have Consuls in every country of Europe almost, and through them I can transmit packages for any literary institution, leaving to them to superscribe the proper address. if you approve of this, and will send me a list of the packages and institutions about which you are at a loss, I will write letters to the most convenient Consuls, which being returned to you, you can make up the packages to accompany each letter, and be more likely to find a passage by a vessel from Philadelphia than there would be from this place, were they to come here. I shall be happy in being thus good for something to the society. Accept my respects and best wishes.

TH: JEFFERSON

PrC (DLC); at foot of text: "Mr. John Vaughan"; endorsed by TJ in ink on verso.

SOCIETY: the American Philosophical Society.

To Benjamin Waterhouse

DEAR SIR   Washington Jan. 14. 1802.

The inclosed letter was written to you on the day of it's date. I wrote to Dr. Currie of Richmond on the same day. by mistake I put your letter under his address, and probably I put the one for him under cover to you. he has returned the one addressed to you, which discovers to me my mistake. I forward it now to you for the purpose of rectifying it with you. Accept my respects and best wishes

TH: JEFFERSON

PrC (DLC); at foot of text: "Doctr. Waterhouse"; endorsed by TJ in ink on verso. Enclosure: TJ to Waterhouse, 25 Dec. 1801.

To Philip Barraud

Washington Jan. 15. 1802.

Th: Jefferson presents his compliments to Doctr. Barraud and sends him some vaccine virus recently taken here by Doctr. Gantt.

PrC (DLC).

Philip Barraud (1757-1830) was a physician, surgeon, and proprietor of a medicine shop in Norfolk. He first practiced in Williamsburg, where he served as physician to the public hospital for the insane during the late 1790s and was closely acquainted with St. George Tucker and Bishop James Madison. Moving to Norfolk in 1799, he took charge of the marine hospital there, but was replaced by navy surgeon George Balfour in 1801 as a cost-cutting measure put forth by Albert Gallatin. Efforts by Tucker and Bishop Madison on Barraud's behalf, however, helped him regain the Norfolk appointment following Balfour's dismissal in June 1802. Barraud remained with the marine hospital until his death (Wyndham B. Blanton, *Medicine in Virginia in the Eighteenth Century* [Richmond, 1931], 87, 294-5, 343-4, 403; E. M. Barraud, *Barraud: The Story of a Family* [London, 1967], 38-9; Madison, *Papers, Sec. of State Ser.*, 1:88-9; 2:88, 104-5; 8:556, 559; Robert Smith to George Balfour, 21 June 1802, in Lb in DNA: RG 45, LSO; Vol. 29:488-9; Vol. 34:68; Vol. 35:219-21, 268, 358).

From John James Dufour

Firstvineyard Kentuky

TRES HONNORÉ MONSIEUR   ce 15me. Janvier 1802

Vous serez certainement tres étonné qu'un inconnu ose vous adresser une lettre, surtout pour vous prier d'une faveur; Mais la renommée de vos vertus m'enhardi, surtout l'amour et la protection que vous donné a lagriculture a qui il manque dans les Etats Unis Une branche tres consequente, la Culture du Vin.

Il y a passè cinq ans que j'ai quitté les bords du lac de Geneve pour venir dans ce pays tenter la culture de la vigne, et pendant trois ans j'ai voyagé dans les Etat Unis pour etudier le Climat et le terrein et voir par moi même les essais qu'on avoit deja fait, je me suis arreté à la fin en Kentuky ou j'ai planté une vigne sous les auspices d'une Souscription qui promet un succes complet, le bruit duquel a deja atiré cinq familles de vignerons auxquels une quantité dautre doivent suivre. Mais comme cest tous de pauvres gens qui n'ont eu que le moyen de faire leur route et sont incapables ainsi que moi dacquerir les terres qu'ils auroient besoins pour leur établissement, ils font respectueusement présenter une petition au Congres par M. John Brown, pour obtenir en faveur de la Culture de la vigne un plus long credit que la loi de vente n'accorde, pour environ trois Sections de terre sur les bords de l'Ohio ou ils auroient envie de se placer, et c'est pour vous prier d'accorder votre patronnage a cette petition que je prends la liberté de vous écrire; Lannée passe je vous incomodai deja d'une lettre pour le même Sujet mais trop tard pour le Congre[s.] Notre petition est là même que lannée passé, eccepté pour la quanti[té;] jen demandois alors un grand tract parce qu'une grande Colonie setoit formée en Societé pour venir cultiver la vigne et me marquoit de leur acheter des terres, mais a cause de la guerre cette association a été rompue et seulement une petite partie de là Colonie est venue. Il me seroit inutile de vous dire combien la vigne seroit avantageuse pour le pays en General, ny qu'il n'est point douteux de reussir a la faire produire aussi bien que nulle part en Europe, quand elle sera duëment cultivée, car vous étes persuades de ces verites; Si jusque a present les tentatives quon a faites nont pas repondu a leur attente, cest qu'il y a eu peu de vigneronts praticiens qui y ayent travaille, et lorsque cella est arrivé, des circonstances malheureuses ont deranges les travaux, Mais cette fois ci j'ose assurer que la Culture de la vigne a pris son essor, et que l'epoque n'est pas loin que nos ports de mer au lieu de recevoir des vins et des liqueurs en enveront dehors, et le Congres en nous accordant la faveur que nous demandons en abregera le période; C'est sur les bords du Lac de Gèneve que la vigne est cultivée avec le plus de soin et on peut compter sur des milliers de vignerons de ce pays la si on leur facilite les moyens de setablir proche les uns des autres, et c'est a quoi les bords de L'Ohio sont tres propres étant si montueux qu'ils ne sont bons a nule autre culture, eccépte une lisiere de terrein bas imediatement le long de la Riviere, qui fourniront justement assez de prairie pour nourir le betail nécessaire a faire les engrais pour les vignes qui occuperont les Coteaux, et je prévois le tems que l'Ohio disputera le Rhin ou le Rhone, pour la quantité des vignes, et la qualité du vin.

Daignez recevoir les voeux et hommages de notre petite Colonie, et particulierement lassurance du devouement et du respect avec lequel Jai lhonneur detre

Tres honoré Monsieur Votre tres humble et Obeissa[nt] Serviteur
JEAN JAQUES DUFOUR

E D I T O R S '   T R A N S L A T I O N

VERY HONORED SIR
First Vineyard, Kentucky
this 15th January 1802

You will certainly be very surprised that an unknown dares to address you a letter, especially to beg a favor of you; but the fame of your virtues emboldens me, especially the love and protection that you have given to agriculture, which lacks a very important branch in the United States, viticulture.

It has been more than five years since I left the shores of Lake Geneva to come to this country to attempt viticulture, and for three years I traveled in the United States to study the climate and the soil, and to see for myself the attempts that had already been made. I finally ended in Kentucky, where I planted a vineyard, under the auspices of a subscription that promises a complete success, the news of which has already attracted five families of wine growers, a number of others of whom are to follow. But as they are all poor people who had merely enough for their travel, and who are incapable, as I am, to acquire the land they would need to establish themselves, they are respectfully presenting a petition to the Congress through Mr. John Brown in order to obtain in favor of viticulture a longer credit than sales law grants, for about three sections of land on the banks of the Ohio where they desire to settle, and it is to beg you to grant your patronage of this petition that I take the liberty of writing you. Last year I already disturbed you with a letter on the same subject, but it was too late for the Congress. Our petition is the same as last year's except for the quantity: then I requested a large tract because a large group of settlers had formed a corporation to come and cultivate vineyards and chose me to buy land for them, but because of the war that corporation broke up and only a small number of settlers came. It would be useless for me to tell you how much vineyards would be advantageous for the country in general, or that there is no doubt of success in making them as productive as anywhere in Europe when they are properly cultivated, for you are convinced of those truths. If, up until now, the attempts that have been made have not lived up to their expectations, it is because there have been few professional wine growers who have put their hand to it, and when that did happen, unfortunate circumstances have upset their labors. But this time, I dare give assurance that viticulture is expanding rapidly, and that the time is not far off when our seaports, instead of receiving wines and liquors will be sending them abroad, and the Congress, by granting us the favor that we are requesting, will shorten that time; it is on the shores of Lake Geneva that vineyards are cultivated with the greatest care, and one can count on thousands of wine growers from that country if the means of establishing them close to one another are facilitated, and for that the banks of the Ohio are very well suited, being so hilly that they are good for growing nothing else, except for a ribbon of bottom land along the edge of the river which will precisely provide enough pasture to feed the cattle necessary to make the fertilizer for the vines that will cover the hillsides, and I foresee the time when the Ohio will rival the Rhine or the Rhone in quantity of vineyards and quality of wine.

Kindly accept the best wishes and the respects of our small group of settlers and particularly the assurance of the devotion and respect with which I have the honor to be

Very honored Sir, your very humble and obedient servant

JEAN JAQUES DUFOUR

RC (DLC); damaged; addressed: "To his Excellency Thomas Jefferson President of the United States Washington City"; postmarked Lexington, Kentucky, 19 Jan.; franked; endorsed by TJ as received 1 Feb. and so recorded in SJL.

On 15 Feb., Senator JOHN BROWN of Kentucky presented Dufour's petition to the Senate. On 17 Mch., the Senate passed a bill, which the House of Representatives approved on 30 Apr. and TJ signed on 1 May. The act enabled Dufour and his comrades to purchase, for two dollars an acre, without interest, and payable by 1 Jan. 1814, up to four sections of land in the area between the Miami River and "the Indian boundary line." The arrangement allowed Dufour and the vineyard specialists who had joined him from Switzerland to relocate from First Vineyard, on the Kentucky River, to the place in Indiana they named Second Vineyard (U.S. Statutes at Large, 6:47-8; JS, 3:181, 193, 231; JHR, 4:229; Vol. 32:533n).

UNE LETTRE POUR LE MÊME SUJET: Dufour to TJ, 1 Feb. 1801 (Vol. 32:529-33).

From Lewis Geanty

Baltimore, 15 Jan. 1802. He proposes the establishment of a workshop for the fabrication of scientific and mathematical instruments. A former attorney and notary in Saint-Domingue, he was permanent secretary of the royal society of arts and sciences at Cap-Français and a member and presiding officer of the colonial assembly. He fled to the United States as a refugee with his family in 1793. He brought with him a fine collection of instruments for a physics laboratory, some of which he sold to the faculty of the University of Pennsylvania, and, if he is not mistaken, TJ purchased an English and French thermometer from his collection. He hopes to remain in the United States rather than return to Saint-Domingue, which has an inhospitable climate and which he dislikes for other reasons. He has constructed electrical apparatus and is building a set of instruments for a school in Baltimore. He is also interested in teaching a physics course and in writing an elementary treatise on that subject. Hoping that TJ will put him in touch with someone willing to finance the enterprise, he intends to gather superior examples of instruments from Paris and London to use as models. He knows an American clockmaker who has an interest in natural science, and there is now a glassworks in Baltimore with workers who can make flint glass. They could make medicine bottles for sale to help support the instruments factory. He wishes also to publish a periodical that would, in addition to providing information about physics and science, illustrate and promote the apparatus for sale. It will be necessary for him to travel to France and Germany to acquire materials, gather information about procedures, and recruit artisans. Additionally, the establishment of a tinware factory is of importance to the United States, and he could direct such a facility. He has friends in the French government and the National Institute, and he speaks English well enough to carry out his plans.

RC (DLC); 8 p.; in French; at head of text: "Mr Jefferson"; endorsed by TJ as received 22 Jan. and so recorded in SJL.

Lewis (Louis) Geanty had a "Pewter Manufactory" in Baltimore. In 1797 and 1798, he advertised syringes and bidets as his primary stock on hand for sale, declaring that he could make "all sorts of philosophical and chemical apparatus" to custom specifications. Geanty also invested in real estate. In 1803, he was on a prize committee of the Maryland Society for Promoting Useful Knowledge. Médéric Moreau de St. Méry, who like Geanty had

been a lawyer at Cap-Français, referred to Geanty as his "friend and former colleague" and called on him in Baltimore soon after Moreau de St. Méry arrived in the United States in 1794 (*Federal Gazette & Baltimore Daily Advertiser*, 2 July 1796, 9 Aug. 1797, 12 July 1798, 1 Apr. 1800; *Baltimore Patriot*, 11 Nov. 1816; *Maryland Herald and Elizabeth-Town Weekly Advertiser*, 7 Dec. 1803; Kenneth Roberts and Anna M. Roberts, trans. and eds., *Moreau de St. Méry's American Journey [1793-1798]* [Garden City, N.Y., 1947], x, 75, 177-8).

To the Georgia Legislature

GENTLEMEN   Washington Jan. 15. 1802.

The confidence which the Senate and Representatives of the state of Georgia are pleased to repose in my conduct, and their felicitations on my election to the chief magistracy, are testimonies which, coming from the collected councils of the state, encourage continued efforts to deserve them in future, and hold up that reward most valued by me.

State rights, and State-sovereignties, as recognised by the constitution, are an integral and essential part of our great political fabric. they are bound up by a common ligament with those of the National government, and form with it one system, of which the Constitution is the law and the life. a sacred respect to that instrument therefore becomes the first interest and duty of all.

Your reliance on the talents & virtues of our republic, as concentrated in the federal legislature, that the public good will be it's end, & the constitution it's rule, is assuredly well placed; and we need not doubt of that harmony which is to depend on it's justice.

I pray you to accept for yourselves and the Houses over which you preside my grateful thanks for their favorable dispositions, and the homage of my high consideration and respect.

TH: JEFFERSON

RC (George Stevens, Kingston, New Jersey, 1946); at head of text: "To the honorable the President of the Senate, and Speaker of the House of Representatives of Georgia." PrC (DLC).

THEIR FELICITATIONS ON MY ELECTION: Georgia Legislature to TJ, 4 Dec. 1801.

From Simon Harris

State of New Hampshire
Bridgwater January 15th 1802

SIR

your Highness all most forbids me to rite to you though I am ancious to comunicate to you some of the difference of sentiment Republicans & Federals Whigs & Tories takes the houl I never saw you nor is it likely I ever shall yet I feel a Simpethy with you because you have one half of this Little world to throw clubs at you but I perceive they dont hurt you very much I am very sorry to see so much disunion here as here is some are very sorry that your are elected President of the United States and some rejoice, as much as others weep as for my part I am so Rejoised that I dont know what to do with my self I have cald my yongest son about four Months old Thomas Jefferson to keep your Name in mem'y when your are not—I am very glad you have turnd out of offic some of the old tories I wish they might all have the same fate we suffer here by having too many in office for the Maills & post masters I am afraid are none too good we dont get the Republian News papers very corect we feer there is cudling amoung them we can get the federist papers without any trouble the anglo federats—some hot headed fellows say come let us go and impeach the President four we cant Live so for he has dissmisd Duane from trial he is agoin to remove the Contintal stores from Springfield and he is a selling ships of war and we are all on dun mercy on us what shall we do. what shall we do is the cry of some— but the good old Republicans dont fear none of there noise they remain firm and un moved and Sir I will tell you the anglo Federals begin to Look down hill very fast Republian prinsibles gain in a most rapid manner and we are in greate hopes of having a Republican Govenor for the ensuing year in this state I am very much plesd with your message to Congress in taking off stampt papers and News papers postage these things will naturley shake of as a viper from the hand our [. . .]tes are a going to raise the head and flourish [. . .] we hope the secty office will not [. . .]nt a scond time

I have sent on proposells to Mr. Granger how I will carry the Mail from Haverhill in Massachusetts to Haverhill in this State I know not what Mr. Clerk has I have sent proposells Cheaper then I can aford I am tird of these anglos being too much in business in our Quarter of the world. Mr Clerk dont ride him self but hires yong fellows to ride makes others shake the bush and he ketch the bierd.

now Sir I will end my letter hoping your servise to the Nation will end in the same spirit and faith fullness that you have begun may you never srink nor give bak though anglos & rusty [. . .] make a dolefull Noise you have one mark of a good Christian when your are revild you react not again may you ever remain so.

Post Marsters & Mail Carrers ought to be true Republicans this from you sincear friend and humble Servent   SIMON HARRIS
a true Republican

N.B

you will forward the in closed Letter to Mr. Granger your influence in that matter will be of great utility.

RC (DLC); torn at seal; above post-script: "Thomas Jefferson Presd, of the United States"; endorsed by TJ as received 31 Jan. and so recorded in SJL. Enclosure not found.

Simon Harris wrote TJ again in 1805, seeking an appointment in Louisiana (Harris to TJ, 16 Aug. 1805).

For the alleged plan to REMOVE federal arms from SPRINGFIELD, Massachusetts, see Theodore Foster to TJ, 29 Oct. 1801.

On 10 Aug. 1801, Postmaster General Joseph Habersham wrote Ebenezer Clark (CLERK) of Concord, New Hampshire, awarding him a contract for carrying the mail between Haverhill, Massachusetts, and Haverhill, New Hampshire (FC in Lb in DNA: RG 28, LPG).

To David Mandeville

Jan. 15. 1802. Washington.

Th: Jefferson presents his compliments to mr Mandeville and his thanks for his ingenious, compact & useful Calendar, recieved in his letter of the 9th. instant.

PrC (MHi); endorsed by TJ in ink on verso.

From Robert Smith

SIR, Nav Dep 15th Jany 1802

I have the honor to request your signature to the enclosed Warrants—

The persons for whom they are intended have been recommended by Capt. Murray—those stations being vacant on board the Constellation.

I have the honor to be, with the greatest respect, Sir, Your mo ob hb sr. RT SMITH

RC (DLC); in a clerk's hand, signed by Smith; at foot of text: "Honble Th Jefferson Prest U States"; endorsed by TJ as received from the Navy Department on 15 Jan. and "Commissions" and so recorded in SJL. FC (Lb in DNA: RG 45, LSP). Enclosures not found, but see below.

On 16 Jan. 1802, Smith wrote Captain Alexander MURRAY of the frigate *Constellation*, enclosing warrants for William Johnson, gunner; John Hall, boatswain; and William Godby, carpenter (FC in Lb in DNA: RG 45, LSO; NDBW, 2:27).

From Augustus B. Woodward

Jan. 15. 1802.

Mr. William O'Neale of the City of Washington, was originally invited to this place by the late Genl. Washington, for the purpose of exploring quarries for the public works. He has vested very considerable property in the City; but owing to that stagnation of business which has affected the United States generally, and which has particularly retarded the progress of the City, he finds himself now without any active employment. He is solicitous, if the appointment of a librarian should be vested in the President, as he has understood is contemplated, to obtain from him a notice of his pretensions. He is known to be a man of respectability and integrity, and I should presume as well adapted to act in that capacity as any other who may probably apply. AUGUSTUS B. WOODWARD

RC (DNA: RG 59, LAR); at foot of text: "The President of the United States"; endorsed by TJ: "O'Neale Wm. to be librarian."

Augustus B. Woodward (1774-1827), a political writer and jurist born in New York City, was named Elias Brevoort Woodward but later exchanged Elias for Augustus and occasionally used both names. After graduating from Columbia

College, he worked as a Treasury Department clerk in Philadelphia. In 1795, he moved to Rockbridge County, Virginia, where he read law, taught school, and first met TJ. He settled in Georgetown two years later and in 1801, under the pseudonym "Epaminondas," began publishing scientific and political works, including a series advocating home rule for the District of Columbia. He had a lucrative law practice and was a member of the district's first city council. TJ nominated him chief justice of the supreme court of the Michigan Territory in 1805, and the following year Woodward compiled the first code of laws for the Territory (ANB; DAB; RS, 1:165; Vol. 29:151n; Vol. 33:212n; Vol. 35:755).

WILLIAM O'NEALE: in June 1794, George Washington authorized a "Mr. Oneil" of Chester County, Pennsylvania, to open a freestone quarry at Mount Vernon. James Greenleaf employed O'Neale to develop a quarry along the western boundary of the city of Washington and one at Mount Vernon for $60 a month plus expenses and pay for three to six workmen. In addition to agreeing to deliver 500 tons of stone a month out of the public quarry, O'Neale became involved in real estate speculation and by autumn

1799 had opened his own boardinghouse and general store. On 20 Jan. 1801, he witnessed the Treasury building fire and helped rescue the department's public papers. He wrote to Gallatin on 1 July 1801, requesting a position in the office of the commissioner of the revenue or any public office (Bob Arnebeck, *Through a Fiery Trial: Building Washington 1790-1800* [Lanham, Md., 1991], 214, 283, 539, 612-13; Fitzpatrick, *Writings*, 33:400; 34:59; Gallatin, *Papers*, 5:285; *Prologue*, 31 [1999], 28, 34n).

On 14 Jan. 1802, Woodward wrote to the vice president recommending O'Neale for the position of LIBRARIAN (RC in DNA: RG 59, LAR; endorsed by TJ: "Woodward Augustus B. to Colo. Burr. Wm. Oneale to be librarian").

From Joseph Yznardi, Sr.

EXMO. SEÑOR   Philadelphia 15 Eno 802
Muy Señor mio, y de mi mayor Benerasion
Doy Muchas gracias á V.E por el favor con qe me honrra por su apreciable de 10 del Corriente

Mientras Conserve, yo mi buena Opinion con V.E todo lo demas es Menos, Cierto que Sienpre prosedere con los Sentimientos de Honor qe mi Caracter profesa confesando con fortaleza el Candor, y Rectitud del Alma Grande qe Fertilisa los prosedimientos de V.E llenos, de Rectitud, y Justicia

Ningun motibo he dado, al Cavallero de Yrujo, le Meresí la Mayor Amistad, el Mismo la ha desecho, me ha perseguido, con Rigor, pensando encontrairme en Algun descubierto baxo el pretesto de tener orden, le he dado mis Quentas, y Creo está Satisfecho de mi Honrrader, pero en perjuicio de mis Intereses en grado Sumo, pasiencia asta ver quien es la Causa, tendré el gusto de qe Oiga del el engaño qe padesio en Jusgar mal de mi

Estava determinado no formar quen[ta] de los Vinos pero Vista la delicadesa de V.E en Insister qe la presente la Mandare á Mr Barnes Solamente de la Bota de Pedro Ximenes Barril de tinta, y media Bota de Malaga qe ha Recivido el General Smith enbarcada por Mr Kirckpatrick qe lo pondera dandole el Nonbre Lacrima christy de 46 Años, ce de la Cosecha del Año 55, y como los 3 Barriles del año pasado tubo V.E la vondad de Admitir le Suplico no me Obligue á Cobrarlos, y que me permita le remita á mi llegada algunas particularidades de mi Cosecha de quando en quando en reconosimiento de qe le tengo presente

como se presentan pocas Ocasiones para España si antes se Alistaren los Buques de Guerra para el Mediteraneo, y V.E me favorese disiendole al Secretar[eo] de Marina de Orden al Comandante de la Fragata qe esta aquí, me Admita de pasage me disenbarcaré en Gibraltar donde precisamente tocará

V.E perdone esta Confiansa con qe le Molesto, y Mras Ruego á Dios gue su Vida ms. as

Exmo. Señor tiene el Honor de V.L.M á V.E su mas Obediente Servidor   JOSEF YZNARDY

the Sherry & Paxarete ware Order when I mentioned to Y. Ey. & will come one of thees Days wich Mr. C. Price Shall Send them to Mr. Barnees

EDITORS' TRANSLATION

MOST EXCELLENT SIR   Philadelphia 15 Jan. 1802
My most illustrious sir, and with my greatest veneration,
I give thanks to Your Excellency for the favor with which you honor me with your esteemed letter of the 10th of this month.

So long as I am in good standing with Your Excellency, everything else is irrelevant. The fact is I will always conduct myself with the sense of honor that my character avows, admitting with fortitude the candor and rectitude of the great soul that fertilizes the actions of Your Excellency, full of rectitude and justice.

I have not given any reason to the Chevalier Irujo, from whom I deserved the greatest friendship, who himself has rejected that relation. He has persecuted me with severity, thinking he would run across some deficit under the pretext of having been instructed to do so. I have disclosed to him my financial records, and I believe that he is satisfied with my honesty, but this was against my own interest in the extreme. Patience is required until I see who is the cause. I will have the pleasure to hear from him the lies that lead him to think badly of me.

I was determined not to prepare an invoice for the wines, but given that Your Excellency has kindly insisted that I do so, I will send it to Mr. Barnes to cover only the pipe of Pedro Jimenez, the barrel of tent, and the half pipe of Malaga that General Smith received via Mr. Kirkpatrick, who praises it, pronouncing it a 46 year old lacryma christi ("tears of Christ"). I know about the harvest from the year 1755, and given that Your Excellency had the kindness to accept the three barrels last year, I beg you not to force me to charge you for them, and that you allow me after my arrival to send you from time to time some specialties from my own vintage in recognition that I am thinking of you.

Since there are few opportunities for travel to Spain before the warships for the Mediterranean are made ready, I ask Your Excellency to do me the favor of telling the secretary of the navy, and from him the captain of the frigate that is here, to allow me passage, and I will disembark in Gibraltar where that ship will in fact go.

May Your Excellency forgive the liberty with which I bother you, and meanwhile I pray that God preserve your life many years.

Most excellent sir your most obedient servant has the honor to kiss Your Excellency's hand.   JOSEF YZNARDY

RC (DLC); damaged; at foot of text: "Exmo. Sor. Dn. Thomas Jefferson."

KIRCKPATRICK: William Kirkpatrick, originally of Scotland, had vineyards at Malaga, Spain (Vol. 25:309n; Kirkpatrick to TJ, 23 Sep. 1803, in MoSHi:

Jefferson Papers). LOS 3 BARRILES DEL AÑO PASADO: for the Spanish wine that Yznardi ordered for TJ earlier, see Vol. 33:362-3, 441.

LA FRAGATA QE ESTA AQUÍ: the *Constellation* (NDBW, 2:19, 43, 68).

ENCLOSURE

Invoice for Wine, with Jefferson's Notations

Mr. John Barnees Dr. to Josef Yznardy for Wines Sent for His Exy. the President

Bota	one Pipe Pedro Ximenes contening 126 Gallons Duty paid at. 2 Dos ℔ Gallon	252
Barril	one qr Cask Rota tent Wine 30 Gallons at 1.50	45
Media Bota	one Hhd of Malaga Lacrima Christy 45 Years owld Chargd in 100 Dos and 6 ℔ Ct Inshurans	106
	Dolls	403

Philadelphia 15 January 1802
Josef Yznardy

from mr Barnes 2. doz. bottles claret @. 8. D.

MC (DLC); in Yznardi's hand; notations by TJ reproduced in italics.

TJ had received the pipe of PEDRO XIMENES sherry and the quarter cask of the wine called TENT the previous May. The MALAGA wine, a variety called lágrima, arrived in Baltimore on the brig *Isabella* in November 1801. Samuel Smith received the shipment from the firm of Robert Oliver and Brothers, paying $22.29 in freight, duties, drayage, and coopering. TJ reimbursed Smith for those charges and received the lágrima in Washington on 7 Jan. 1802. TJ recorded the container as a 60-gallon "tierce." The actual amount of the Malaga wine, ac-

cording to the receipt for the charges paid by Smith, was 57 gallons. In his financial memoranda under 1 Feb., TJ noted that John Barnes was to remit $403 to Yznardi for the wines (invoice of charges, Baltimore, 25 Nov. 1801, in CSmH, in a clerk's hand, with acknowledgment of receipt of payment by William Courtenous for the Oliver firm and TJ's order on John Barnes, signed by TJ 20 Dec. 1801, for payment to Smith, endorsed by Barnes as paid on 21 Dec.; MB, 2:1060, 1064, 1115; Vol. 33:441n).

According to TJ's financial memoranda, the price of the CLARET was $8 per dozen, for a total of $16 (MB, 2:1115).

To Albert Gallatin

Jan. 16. 1802.

Th: Jefferson incloses to mr Gallatin another anonymous letter from Charleston, doubtless from the same hand.—he asks his attention to so much of the letter of mr Esch as respects the seisure of his watches, and to have done on it whatever is right. the young man is recommended by Professor Pictet.—is the object of the inclosed petition within our competence, or must it go to Congress? if the latter be so good as to return it to me.

RC (NHi: Gallatin Papers); addressed: "The Secretary of the Treasury." PrC (DLC). Enclosures: (1) "A.B." to TJ, 2 Jan. 1802. (2) Henry Esch to TJ, 11 Jan. Other enclosure not identified.

To Kennebec County, Maine, Constitutional Republicans

GENTLEMEN   Washington Jan. 16. 1802

The address you have been pleased to forward me from the Constitutional republicans of the county of Kennebeck has been duly recieved, and with that sincere satisfaction which expressions of so much confidence are calculated to inspire. the difference of political opinion which too much divided us, some time past, is, I hope, yielding to the evidences daily arising that the great bulk of our citizens have, as a common object, the preservation of federal & representative government as organized by the constitution, and the administration of it with the least burthen which their safety, foreign and domestic, will admit. to keep it in it's proper line, the doings of those, whom you appoint to high office should be [watched] with strictness and noted with that candour which speaking in the voice of a friend, is thankfully recieved, and weighed with respect.

The principles of my inaugural address, which you are pleased to notice, were dictated by the sincere convictions of my mind, and shall be faithfully adhered to in the [gestion] of your affairs and I am happy that you view my administration so far with cordial approbation. justice and truth require that I ackoledge how much I am indebted to my coadjutors & constitutional advisors, in whose personal virtues and political wisdom you have expressed a confidence so just, so well merited, and so safe.

The restoration of peace is an universal blessing, for which our interests, as well as our religion, call for our thankfulness.

Accept for yourselves, gentlemen, and those whose sentiments you have been desired to communicate, my sincere thanks for the expressions so personally obliging to me, and the assurances of my respect and high consideration. TH: JEFFERSON

PrC (DLC); faint, with words in brackets supplied from Boston *Independent Chronicle,* 22 Feb. 1802; at head of text: "To Messrs. Nathan Weston, Dudley B. Hobart, & Joshua Wingate, a committee of the Constitutional republicans of the county of Kennebeck in the district of Maine."

ADDRESS YOU HAVE BEEN PLEASED TO FORWARD ME: Kennebec County, Maine, Constitutional Republicans to TJ, 24 Dec. 1801.

To Charles Willson Peale

DEAR SIR   Washington Jan. 16. 1802.

I recieved last night your favor of the 12th. instant. no person on earth can entertain a higher idea than I do of the value of your collection nor give you more credit for the unwearied perseverance & skill with which you have prosecuted it. and I very much wish it could be made public property. but as to the question whether I think that the US. would encourage or provide for the establishment of your Museum here? I must not suffer my partiality to it to excite false expectations in you, which might eventually be disappointed. you know that one of the great questions which has divided political[1] opinion in this country is Whether Congress are authorised by the constitution to apply the public money to any but the purposes specially enumerated in the Constitution? those who hold them to the enumeration, have always denied that Congress have any power to establish a National academy. some who are of this opinion, still wish Congress had power to favor science, and that an amendment should be proposed to the constitution, giving them such power specifically. if there were an union of opinion that Congress already possessed the right, I am persuaded the purchase of your museum would be the first object on which it would be exercised. but I believe the opinion of a want of power to be that of the majority of the legislature.

I have for a considerable time been meditating a plan of a general university for the state of Virginia, on the most extensive & liberal scale that our circumstances would call for & our faculties meet. were this established, I should have made your Museum an object of the

[385]

establishment. but the moment is not arrived for proposing this with a hope of success. I imagine therefore the legislature of your own state furnishes at present the best prospect. I am much pleased at the success which has attended your labors on the Mammoth. I understand you have not the frontal bone. if this be so, I have heard of one in the Western country which I could & would get for you. on this I need your information. I shall certainly pay your labours a visit, but when, heaven knows. Accept my friendly salutations & respect.

TH: JEFFERSON

RC (TxU); at foot of text: "Charles W. Peale." PrC (DLC).

[1] Word written over a partially blotted word, possibly "public."

To Henry Voigt

SIR   Washington Jan. 16. 1802.

I recieved last night only[1] your favor of the 29th. Dec. the specimens of his art which mr Reish had shewed me on a former occasion had convinced me of his talents, and produced my recommendation of him to the mint. I sincerely wish he may meet with the encouragement he deserves, and should expect his eminence would soon engage him with the book sellers. the Declaration of independence is[2] certainly an epoch of our being so remarkable as to merit a medal. but the government has issued no medals in commemoration of events purely, unconnected with military exploit. mr Reish's execution in this instance has certainly great merit. he had been so kind as to send me one through mr Duane. having a few friends to whom I would wish to present them, I will ask the favor of you to apply to him in my name for four, & forward them to me with information of the price which I will immediately have paid to him. Accept for him & yourself my salutations and best wishes.   TH: JEFFERSON

PrC (DLC); at foot of text: "Mr. Henry Voigt"; endorsed by TJ in ink on verso.

[1] Word interlined.
[2] Word interlined in place of "was."

To James Cheetham

SIR   Washington Jan. 17. 1802.

Your favor of Dec. 29. was recieved in due time. although it is all important for public as well as personal considerations, that I should recieve information of every interesting occurrence, yet it is little in my power to entitle myself to it by regular correspondence on my part. in fact it is rare I can answer a private letter at all, being for the most part obliged to leave even my best friends to read their answer in what is done, or not done, in consequence of their letters. this must account for my late answer to your's of the 29th. ult. and for my failures to answer at all on other occasions. the fact of the suppression of a work mentioned by you is curious, and pregnant with considerations. is it impossible to get a single copy of the work? a good history of the period it comprehended will doubtless be valuable. should it be undertaken as you suggest, I should suppose it indispensable in you, rather to visit this place, at your own convenience, for the information you desire as to a particular document, and for such other as the work itself will suggest to you. in the mean time I can assure you that I have compared that document with the extract from it in Callender's history of 1796. pa. 172. to 181. and find the latter, not only substantially, but almost verbally exact. with respect to the compensation to the negociator, I think the printed public accounts shew that he recieved his salary as C.J. and his *actual expences on the mission.* a certain description of persons are so industrious in misconstruing & misrepresenting every word from my pen, that I must pray you, after reading this, to destroy it, that no accident happening to it may furnish matter for new slanders. accept my respects & best wishes.

Th: Jefferson

PrC (DLC); at foot of text: "Mr. James Cheetham." Not recorded in SJL.

THAT DOCUMENT: Secretary of State Edmund Randolph's instructions to John Jay as special envoy to Great Britain, dated 6 May 1794. For TJ's notes on the document, including his verification of the extracts FROM IT IN CALLENDER'S HISTORY, see Vol. 29:606-10, 630n.

C.J.: chief justice. At the time of Jay's nomination as envoy, a resolution was introduced in the Senate "That to permit Judges of the Supreme Court to hold at the same time any other office or employment, emanating from and holden at the pleasure of the Executive, is contrary to the spirit of the Constitution, and, as tending to expose them to the influence of the Executive, is mischievous and impolitic" (JEP, 1:152).

To Martha Jefferson Randolph

Washington Jan. 17. 1802.

This is merely, my dear Martha, to say that all is well. it is very long since I have heard from you, my last letter from Edgehill being of the 6th. of Dec. a letter of Jan. 6. from mr Eppes at Richmond informed me that Maria was entirely reestablished in her health, & her breast quite well. the little boy too was well & healthy.—Dr. Gantt has inoculated six of his Cow pox patients with the small pox, not one of which took it. many have been tried in Philadelphia, & with the same issue. as the matter here came from Monticello, and that at Philadelphia from this place, they establish the genuineness of our inoculations & may place our families & neighbors in perfect security.   Congress have as yet passed but one bill. the repeal of the Judiciary law is rather doubtful in the Senate, by the absence of two republican Senators. great opposition is made to the reduction of the army, the navy, and the taxes. they will be reduced; but some republican votes will fly the way on the occasion. mr Dawson arrived here three or four days ago. present me affectionately to mr Randolph, and the young ones, and be assured yourself of my constant & tenderest love.

TH: JEFFERSON

P.S. in my last week's letter to mr Randolph I inclosed one for mr Lilly with 940. D. in it, which I shall be glad to hear got safe to hand.

RC (NNPM). PrC (CSmH); endorsed by TJ in ink on verso.

For the LAST LETTER FROM EDGE-HILL, see TJ to Thomas Mann Randolph, 1 Jan. 1802. For the 6 Jan. letter from John Wayles EPPES, see TJ's letter to him of 22 Jan.

PASSED BUT ONE BILL: on 14 Jan., TJ signed "An Act for the apportionment of Representatives among the several States, according to the second enumeration," as passed by the House on 6 Jan. and the Senate on the 11th (U.S. Statutes at Large, 2:128; JHR, 4:32-4, 50; JS, 3:167).

On 6 Jan. 1802, the Senate began to consider the REPEAL OF THE JUDICIARY LAW of 1801. On 19 Jan., after extensive debate, the Senate moved to bring in a bill calling for repeal. Three days later, the committee brought in the bill and it passed to a second reading. On 27 Jan., when the bill was in its third reading, Federalist Jonathan Dayton and John Ewing Colhoun, who voted with the Federalists on the issue, argued that instead of passing the repeal bill, it should be referred to a select committee. As president of the Senate, Burr disappointed Republicans by breaking the 15 to 15 tie vote in

favor of sending the bill to a committee dominated by Federalists. Not until Vermont senator Stephen R. Bradley, who had received a leave of absence from the Senate in late December, returned to Washington did Republicans have the votes to get the bill out of committee on 2 Feb. and to pass it by a 16 to 15 vote the next day. The Senate sent the bill to the House, where it was debated until early March (JS, 3:164, 166, 169-73, 176-8; Bruce Ackerman, *The Failure of the Founding Fathers: Jefferson, Marshall, and the Rise of Presidential Democracy* [Cambridge, Mass., 2005], 156, 339n; Kline, *Burr*, 2:653-6; James Jackson to TJ, 28 Dec. 1801; TJ to Monroe and to Thomas Mann Randolph, 3 Feb. 1802). ABSENCE OF TWO REPUBLICAN SENATORS: John Armstrong, the other Republican senator who was not present in January 1802, submitted his resignation on 10 Feb. DeWitt Clinton, appointed by the New York state legislature to fill the vacancy, took his seat in the Senate on 23 Feb. (JS, 3:179, 184).

John DAWSON took his seat in the House of Representatives on 14 Jan. (JHR, 4:51).

MY LAST WEEK'S LETTER: TJ to Thomas Mann Randolph, 9 Jan.

To Hore Browse Trist

DEAR SIR Washington Jan. 17. 1802.

I learn with sincere concern that you have made up your mind to leave us, and go to the Missisipi territory, and that you contemplate this as early as the ensuing spring. altho absent from the neighborhood myself for a time, yet I view all it's losses as my own losses, and am moreover interested in the feelings of our common friends. I am led to notice this subject at present by an incident recently happened in the Missisipi territory, which is the death of mr Steele the Secretary of the territory. the salaries there are small, the judges having only 800. D. a piece. the Secretary's salary is but 750. D. it is not on that ground therefore that I would propose it to you, but on account of it's respectability, being the second office in the territory, and the first when the governor is absent; his duties devolving then on the Secretary. imagining that in this point of view it might render your first establishment there more agreeable, I take the liberty of proposing it to you. should you deem it acceptable, it would be of some importance that you should repair thither as early as you can. but it is not necessary that you should make a winter journey of it. I have not waited your [expected] arrival here, to make this proposition, because I thought it might possibly influence your plan as to that, and induce the saving, to mrs Trist at least, the addition of 250. miles to a journey, otherwise long enough. be so good as to present my most friendly salutations to the ladies of the family, and to accept yourself my respects & best wishes.

TH: JEFFERSON

PrC (DLC); blurred; at foot of text: "Mr. Trist"; endorsed by TJ in ink on verso.

DEATH OF MR STEELE: rumors of the death of John Steele, secretary of the Mississippi Territory since 1798, were false (see TJ to Trist, 9 Feb. 1802). Steele wrote to Kentucky senator John Brown from Natchez on 23 Jan. 1802 that despite ill health and duties preventing him from writing, "the office I have held here, would still be a Convenient thing to me; and altho' I have derived My Political Creed in a great Measure, from the Sentiments and opinions of Mr Jefferson and

Mr Madison I have not flattered myself with the hope of being reappointed to the office of Secretary." Steele's official term as secretary expired on 6 May 1802, but he continued these duties as keeper of public records for 13 months thereafter until his replacement arrived. In October 1803, Steele submitted a petition to Congress for payment of his services as acting governor and as unofficial interim secretary (RC in DNA, RG 59, LAR; endorsed by TJ: "Steele John to J. Brown to be continued Secretary of Missi territory"; *Terr. Papers*, 5:241-61; U.S. Statutes at Large, 6:56-7).

To Pierre Samuel Du Pont de Nemours

DEAR SIR   Washington Jan. 18. 1802.

It is rare I can indulge myself in the luxury of philosophy. your letters give me a few of those delicious moments. placed as you are in a great commercial town, with little opportunity of discovering the dispositions of the country portion of our citizens, I do not wonder at your doubts whether they will generally & sincerely concur in the sentiments and measures developed in my message of the 7th. Jany. but from 40. years of intimate conversation with the agricultural inhabitants of my country, I can pronounce them as different from those of the cities, as the inhabitants of any two nations known. the sentiments of the former can in no degree be inferred from those of the latter. you have spoken a profound truth in these words. 'il y a dans les etats unis un bon sens silencieux, un esprit de justice froide, qui lorsqu'il est question d'emettre un *vote* couvre les bavardages de ceux qui font les habiles.' a plain country farmer has written lately a pamphlet on our public affairs. his testimony of the sense of the country is the best which can be produced of the justness of your observation. his words are 'the tongue of man is not his whole body. so, in this case the noisy part of the community was not all the body politic. during the career of fury and contention (in 1800.) the sedate, grave part of the people were still; hearing all, and judging for themselves, what method to take, when the constitutional time of action should come, the exercise of the right of suffrage.' the majority of the present legislature are in unison with the agricultural part of our citizens: and you will see that there is nothing in the message, to which they do not accord. some things may perhaps be left undone from motives of compromise for a time, and not to alarm by too sudden a reformation: but with a view to be resumed at another time. I am perfectly satisfied the effect of the proceedings of this session of Congress will be to consolidate the great body of well meaning citizens together, whether federal or republican, heretofore called. I do not mean to include royalists or priests. their opposition is immoveable. but they will be vox et preterea nihil: leaders without followers. I am satisfied that within one year from this time were an election to take place between two candidates, merely republican and federal, where no personal opposition existed against either, the federal candidate would not get the vote of a single elector in the US. I must here again appeal to the testimony of my farmer, who says 'the great body of the people are *one* in sentiment. if the federal party, and the republican party, should each of them chuse a convention to frame a constitution

[390]

of government or a code of laws, there would be no radical difference in the results of the two conventions.' this is most true. the body of our people, tho' divided for a short time by an artificial panic, and called by different names, have ever had the same object in view, to wit, the maintenance of a federal, republican government; & have never ceased to be all federalists, all republicans: still excepting the noisy band of royalists inhabiting cities chiefly, & priests both of city & country. when I say that in an election between a republican & federal candidate, free from personal objection, the former would shortly get every vote, I must not be understood as placing myself in that view. it was my destiny to come to the government when it had for several years been committed to a particular political sect, to the absolute and entire exclusion of those who were in sentiment with the body of the nation. I found the country entirely in the enemy's hands. it was necessary to dislodge some of them. out of many thousands of officers in the US. 9. only have been *removed* for *political* principle, & 12. for delinquencies chiefly pecuniary. the whole herd have squealed out, as if all their throats were cut. these acts of justice, few as they have been, have raised great personal objections to me, of which a new character would be clear.   When this government was first established, it was possible to have set it a going on true principles. but the contracted, English, half-lettered ideas of Hamilton destroyed that hope in the bud. we can pay off his debt in 15. years: but we can never get rid of his financial system. it mortifies me to be strengthening principles which I deem radically vicious. but this vice is entailed on us by a first error. in other parts of our government I hope we shall be able by degrees to introduce sound principles and make them habitual. what is practicable must often controul what is pure theory; and the habits of the governed determine in a great degree what is practicable. hence the same original principles, modified in practice according to the different habits of different nations, present governments of very different aspects. the same principles reduced to forms of practice accomodated to our habits, and put into forms accomodated to the habits of the French nation, would present governments[1] very unlike each other. I have no doubt but that a great man, thoroughly knowing the habits of France, might so accomodate to them the principles of free government, as to enable them to live free. but in the hands of those who have not this coup d'oeil, many unsuccesful experiments I fear are yet to be tried before they will settle down in freedom & tranquility. I applaud therefore your determination to remain here, where, tho' for yourself & the adults of your family the dissimilitude of our manners & the difference of tongue will be sources of real unhappiness, yet less so than the horrors & dangers which France would present to you. and as to those of your family still in infancy, they will be formed to the circumstances of the country, and will, I doubt not be happier here[2] than they could have been in Europe under any circumstances. be so good as to make my respectful salutations acceptable to Made. Dupont, and all of your family, and to be assured yourself of my constant and affectionate esteem.

TH: JEFFERSON

RC (DeGH); at foot of first page: "M. Dupont." PrC (DLC).

Du Pont's DOUBTS about the general population's attitudes toward Native Americans appeared in his letter of 17 Dec.

MESSAGE OF THE 7TH. JANY.: TJ's reply to Little Turtle, printed at 4 Jan. in the group of documents relating to Little Turtle's visit to Washington.

YOU HAVE SPOKEN A PROFOUND TRUTH: see Du Pont to TJ, 17 Dec.

The PLAIN COUNTRY FARMER was actually the clergyman John Leland, whose pamphlet, *A Stroke at the Branch. Containing Remarks on Times and Things*, was published at Hartford, Connecticut, in 1801 (Sowerby, No. 3273). THE TONGUE OF MAN . . . THE RIGHT OF SUFFRAGE: this quotation is from page 10 of Leland's work. TJ added the clarificatory "(in 1800.)" and altered the end of the passage. In the pamphlet, a paragraph ends with "time of action should come,"

and the next paragraph opens with: "The successful *Junto* might have triumphed without the least fear, had it not been for three English words; '*right of suffrage*.'"

The expression VOX ET PRETEREA NIHIL (also spelled *vox et praeterea nihil*) comes from Plutarch's *Apophthegmata Laconica*, a collection of sayings by Spartans. The phrase, which means "all voice, and nothing more," was supposed to be the reaction of a man who plucked a nightingale and discovered that there was very little meat on the bird (*Plutarch's Moralia*, trans. Frank Cole Babbitt and others, 16 vols. in 17 [London, 1927-2004], 3:398-9).

THE GREAT BODY OF THE PEOPLE . . . TWO CONVENTIONS: TJ quoted page 24 of Leland's pamphlet, omitting some text within the passage.

[1] Preceding two words interlined in place of "be."
[2] Preceding word interlined.

From Allen McLane

Tunnicliffs Hotel Janary 18th 1802

Sir, when I did my self the honor of paying my respects to you on the 16th Inst, it was my intention to have expressed the high sense, I entertain of your Justice and friendship, in the full opportunity offorded me of defense by the mode of investigation you were pleased to direct into the charges exhibited against me as Collector of the Port of Wilmington—from this duty and pleasure I was precluded by the appearance of Company

Knowing as I do Sir, your Constitutional authority to have removed me at any time without inquiry—that your mere pleasure is the tenure by which I hold my office, I review with the highest degree of Gratitude this distinguished proof of your impartiallity and Kindness, for I am well aware that in no other way could I have had with the least chance, of meeting and disproving the unfounded charges of my envious and illiberal accusers—

I have the consolation of beleiving that the testimony taken on that ocasion, can leave not the shadow of a doubt on the mind of Your Excellency or of any other disinterestd. person, that I had ben guilty of any malconduct in office; but on the Contrary had faithfully and Vigelently executed the duties reposed in me

From your past indulgance and Justice I hope I may be permited to congratulate my self on the prospect of holding my office until some cause of removal may arise, and be assured *Sir*, by the prompt and faithful execution of my various duties, it will at all times be my first wish to merit your approbation—

The unwarrantable liberty, for some time, past practiced by certain newspaper Editors in perverting your intentions, and misrepresenting your conduct towards me for the perpose of answering party Views, permit, me to declare Sir, has bene totally without my privity or consent, and Gives me much pain

Please to accept Sir my sincere respects and best wishes and beleive me with sentiments of the highest consideration

Your most obt. Servt.   A McLane

RC (ViW); at head of text: "To the President of the United States"; endorsed by TJ as received 19 Jan. and so recorded in SJL.

Born in Philadelphia, Allen McLane (1746-1829) married Rebecca Wells of Kent County, Delaware, in 1769 and settled there. McLane served with distinction during the Revolutionary War, and, in 1789, Washington appointed him marshal of Delaware. In the election of 1796, McLane's efforts reportedly led to the Federalist victory in that state. Shortly before he left office, Washington nominated McLane for the more influential and lucrative position of customs collector for the district of Delaware. In 1800, his compensation as collector at Wilmington exceeded $3,000. During the 1820s, McLane received recognition as one of the last surviving officers of the Revolution. He remained collector at Wilmington until his death (DAB, 12:112-13; Washington, *Papers, Rev. War Ser.*, 9:5n; JEP, 1:29, 31, 228; ASP, *Miscellaneous*, 1:261, 272; Prince, *Federalists*, 265; John A. Munroe, *Louis McLane: Federalist and Jacksonian* [New Brunswick, N.J., 1973], 4-31).

For the MODE OF INVESTIGATION and results of the inquiry into McLane's conduct, see Gallatin to TJ, 23 May and 21 Dec. 1801. CERTAIN NEWSPAPER EDITORS: see Gallatin to TJ, 19 Nov.

Notes on a Cabinet Meeting

1802. Jan. 18. prest[1] the 4. Secretaries and Atty Genl. agreed to offer peace to Tripoli on eql terms[2] to continue tribute to Algiers. to send 2. frigates & schooner[3] immediately. if war with Tripoli continues, 2 frigates there constantly & one for relief. 400,000. D. to be appropriated for the whole naval business of the year, including navy yards on which little is to be done, & 500,000 to pay contracts due & becoming due this year.—exn of French treaty to be retained by Exve.

MS (DLC: TJ Papers, 112:19297); entirely in TJ's hand; follows, on same sheet, Notes on a Cabinet Meeting of 11 Nov. 1801.

On his arrival at TRIPOLI with the U.S. frigate *President* in July, Commodore Richard Dale refused the request of Yusuf Qaramanli, the bey, that they negotiate a peace on the spot. Dale insisted, through an intermediary, that Yusuf explain his reasons for declaring war. In reply, the bey expressed dissatisfaction with the first and twelfth articles of the 1796 treaty between the United States and Tripoli, which made Algiers the guarantor of the treaty and the arbiter of disputes between Tripoli and the U.S. In April 1802, instructing James

Leander Cathcart about a possible negotiation with Tripoli, Madison told Cathcart to do away with the articles of the existing treaty that mentioned Algiers. Those sections of the treaty, Madison wrote, had given Algiers "an embarrassing connection" to American relations with Tripoli, and, "by wounding the pride" of the bey, had added "the force of another passion to that of cupidity, in slighting his engagements" (Madison, *Papers, Sec. of State Ser.*, 3:135-8; NDBW, 1:531-2, 552-3; Miller, *Treaties*, 2:364-6).

[1] That is, "present."
[2] Preceding three words interlined.
[3] MS: "shooner."

From James Wilkinson

Mississippi Territory
January 18th. 1802

SIR

presuming that a sample of the Waters of the Mississippi & Arkansaw Rivers, remarkable for their difference to each other & to the Waters of all other Rivers within my Knowledge, may not be unacceptable to you, I avail myself of a conveyance by Doctor Carmichael of the Army, who will have the Honor to deliver this, to send you a Bottle of each, taken from those Rivers in their lowest & least disturbed State—that from the Arkansaw being not full—It may not be uninteresting to remark, that the "Voyageurs" of the Mississippi, who drink constantly of, & prefer, its Water, are never afflicted by the Graval, and that they ascribe curative properties to its external application in cutaneous affections: In the same Box I have deposited a few distinct petrefactions, collected in the State of Tenessee during the late Season

With the most respectful attachment I have the Honor to be. Sir Your Obliged, Obedient, & ready Servant   JA: WILKINSON

RC (DLC); at foot of text: "Thomas Jefferson President of the U.S."; endorsed by TJ as received 11 Mch. and so recorded in SJL.

Dr. John F. CARMICHAEL was a U.S. Army surgeon, the collector of the district of Mississippi, and inspector of the revenue at Loftus's Heights (JEP, 1:333; Heitman, *Dictionary*, 1:283; *Terr. Papers*, 5:551n).

From David Austin

RESPECTED SIR.   Washington Jany 19th. A.D. 1801 [i.e. 1802]

It is painful to me to pierce a man of your natural good dispositions, even with the truth. But who can, with good conscience refrain, when the language of providence is so plain?—

In the matter of a successor to my Hond. father, you refused my counsel: & it called forth more smoke, than you have been able, to this day, to dispel. The more you strove against the fire that arose, the more it burned.

In the matter of Mr. Dawson, you gained no credit; and lost the total honor of that National operation, on a pacific scale which I prayed you to give me commission to produce.

In the matter of the Meditn. expedition, you received not my counsel, & what is the consequence? Are your kind & tender methods, & suppliant petitions to Barbarians trampled under foot? Is your money expended, stolen, or gone?—and is the pride of the navy no more? My dear Sir; if you have any regard to the good of the Nation, to your own prosperity, & to the dignity of your administration, let me pray you, to bring me into your counsels.—

It hath been painful to me to be obliged to say what I have said; and it will be more painful to say what I must be obliged to say, if, forever, you continue unmoved at my intreaty?

I tender you my services, in any such way as may be honorary to yourself: and not degrading to the person of him whose study it shall be to clothe your administration with all the benefits which the wisdom that is in me may inspire: and this may be done, notwithstanding all that hath been, or may be said.—

I am, as ever, Yr. sincere friend, in the truth—   D. AUSTIN

PS. 11. o'Clock—For God's Sake Sir, send me to Great Britain. Our foreign relations are suffering. The cloud of Europe will, before all is over be over your head, if it be not dispelled. Many rejoice at the failure of the expedition against the Barbary powers.

The Nation will sustain, an incalculable loss, if you delay at this moment.

Confer with such Senators, as you judge proper. You cannot, Sir, but believe that *I know something of this matter.*

You seem, Sir, not to enter into the jealousies of the European powers, in respect to this Country as they now open upon a pacific estate.

I would offer myself for examina. on this subject: but I may not disclose the means by which the exploit of general relief is to be performed.—

The longer the matter is delayed, the more deeply will the affairs of the Nation be engulphed.—

RC (DLC); addressed: "His Ex'y Th: Jefferson Pres: U: States City of Washington"; endorsed by TJ as received 20 Jan. 1802 and so recorded in SJL.

MY HOND. FATHER: David Austin, Sr., the former collector at New Haven, who died in 1801.

From William Dunnington

SIR,   January 19th. 1802

Pleas your honour this Comes to Sertify That I never have received the money Due me For being in the Service During Last war I have therefore been trying to Settle it & Has became destitute of money & hope That you will Consider my un hapy State And assist me with a trifle to bear My Expences home as I am now four hundred miles from home & Greatly oblige yours &c.   WILLM. DUNNINGTON

NB Dr. Sir Pleas to do your endevers to Desspatch me as I am been Long from Home & wishes to get back

RC (DLC); addressed: "His Excellency the Precident of the united states Jefferson"; endorsed by TJ as received from Washington on 19 Jan. and so recorded in SJL.

William Dunnington (d. 1834) was a Revolutionary War veteran who served as a private in the Maryland line. In 1824, he received 100 acres under a bounty land warrant and after his death in Caldwell County, Kentucky, his widow continued to apply for additional remuneration (Harry Wright Newman, *Maryland Revolutionary Records* [Baltimore, 1967], 63; White, *Genealogical Abstracts*, 1:1047).

ASSIST ME WITH A TRIFLE: in his financial memoranda for 19 Jan. 1802, TJ recorded an order on John Barnes to give Dunnington $10 in "charity" (MB, 2:1063).

From Robert Smith

Sir: Nav Dep 19th. Jan 1802

I do myself the honor to enclose a List of gentlemen, recommended for Surgeon's Mates in the Navy.

The Chesapeak & Constellation are both in want of officers of this grade—

Mr. Rogers—of this city—has been recommended by judge Kilty— Mr. John A Smith—of Georgetown, by Doct. Worthington & others—Mr. Jos W New, by his father Colo New—& Mr Alexr. Mc.Williams has been appointed for a considerable time past, & acted on board the United States on her last cruise

If you should see fit to nominate these Gentlemen to the Senate, we have employment for them all—

I have the honor to be with great respect, Sir, your mo ob sr

RT SMITH

RC (DLC); in a clerk's hand, signed by Smith; at foot of text: "Th Jefferson Esq Pres U States"; endorsed by TJ as received from the Navy Department on 19 Jan. and "Nominations" and so recorded in SJL. FC (Lb in DNA: RG 45, LSP). Enclosure: an undated, unsigned address to the "Gentlemen of the Senate," nominating William Rogers of Maryland, Alexander McWilliams and John A. Smith of Columbia, and Joseph W. New

of Virginia to be surgeon's mates in the United States Navy (MS in DLC, in same clerk's hand, endorsed by TJ; FC in Lb in DNA: RG 45, LSP).

On 1 Feb., TJ nominated William ROGERS, John A. SMITH, Joseph W. NEW, and Alexander MCWILLIAMS to be surgeon's mates. The Senate approved the nominations on 4 Feb. (JEP, 1:406, 407).

From Jacob Bayley

MAY IT PLEASE YOUR EXCELENCY   Newbury Janry 20th 1802

Please to receive my sincere congratulation on your appointment as President of the United States of America which Ofice requires a man not only of abiley and integrety but a true freind to the rights of man a true Republickcan. without flattery according to my opinion those qualifications are united in our present Choice. may the Place of your Grand predecessor Washington be ever filled with as great Magnitude and Honor as it was when he was President. great[1] has been the opposition against Repulickism in this quarter and eaven now some are bold enough to say you will not hold your office two years. but the major part of the people are in favour of the present administration I hope and have reason to hope the rights of man will be better understood as the Citizens are educated and informed. I think that a general and more equal Education is the strength of a Repulick within it self. I need not eaven say that a well Disapplined Militia is our safty from without what signefys twelve Regements to defend so Extensive a Sea Coast or to raise a Standing Army to enforce the Laws of a Repulick, how inconsistant, if a Repulick has not virtue enough to support it self without the Sword fare well repulickism. as to those that oppose the true rights of man need not be used any otherwise than Moses used the Isrealits when they in his absence made Goldan Gods to return into Egypt before them. but to grind[2] it to powder and make them drink the water into which he strew it. far be it from me that I should consent to return into Egypt again. every meathod has been Taken in this vicinety to force me and mine to consent. Should I quit the first Principles of our Seperation from Briton no. when I have spent a number of years to gain our Independance and all my Intrist, Exposed My Self in Battle, and at home for three months together not sleept secure in my own House and now give up the cause to those who faught against us God forbid. our cause is good, and I belive it will prosper your Excelency will be good enough to Excuse my boldness in writing and recieve[3] the best wishes of your Excelencys most

Obedient Humble Servant

JACOB BAYLEY

RC (DLC); at foot of text: "His Excelency Thomas Jefferson"; endorsed by TJ as received 3 Feb. and so recorded in SJL.

A native of Newbury, Massachusetts, Jacob Bayley (1728-1815) became one of the principal settlers of Newbury, Vermont, in the 1760s. He served as a militia general and Continental army officer during the Revolutionary War, in which he directed an abortive attempt to construct a road from Newbury to Canada for the use of retreating American forces. After the war, he served on the Vermont governor's council and as a justice of the peace for Newbury (John J. Duffy, Samuel B. Hand, and Ralph H. Orth, eds., *The Vermont Encyclopedia* [Hanover, N.H., 2003], 51; Washington, *Papers, Rev. War Ser.*, 1:239; *Pres. Ser.*, 10:31; *Records of the Governor and Council of the State of Vermont*, 8 vols. [Montpelier, 1873-80; reprint, New York, 1973], 3:101, 145, 166, 184, 205; 4:1, 21, 41; *Spooner's Vermont Journal*, 28 Oct. 1796; *Essex Register*, 25 Mch. 1815).

[1] MS: "gleat."
[2] MS: "grin."
[3] MS: "reieve."

From Pierre Samuel Du Pont de Nemours

Monsieur le President   New York 20 Janvier 1802.

Il vous arrive d'Espagne, où ils ne sont pas très communs, quoique ce ne soit pas le premier que vous ait envoyé la cour de Madrid, un Philosophe qui est entièrement de votre Religion et de la mienne.

Je vous demande à l'un et à l'autre quand vous ferez ensemble des oraisons à la très Sainte liberté d'avoir quelque mémoire de

Votre respectueux et Zêlé serviteur

Du Pont (de Nemours)

EDITORS' TRANSLATION

Mister President   New York, 20 January 1802

A philosopher is coming to you from Spain who fully shares your religion and mine. Such people are not very common there, although he is not the first one whom the court of Madrid has sent to you.

I request both of you, when you address prayers together to most Holy Liberty, to keep in mind

Your respectful and zealous servant   Du Pont (de Nemours)

RC (DLC); at head of text: "a Son Excellence Thomas Jefferson President des Etats unis"; endorsed by TJ as received 9 Feb. and so recorded in SJL.

UN PHILOSOPHE: Valentín de Foronda (see John Vaughan to TJ, 29 Dec. 1801).

From George Jefferson

Dear Sir,   Richmond 20th. Janr. 1802

I have to day made payment *in full* to Mr. Ross, conformably to the copy of his receipt annexed. As the balance, after paying him the Tobacco we had, would have been so small, I thought it best to pay the whole at once—and although *such Tobacco* might have been bought for less than 28/. with cash, yet as it could not, on the time you mentioned, and as we had not the Tobacco to offer him, we thought it best to allow the current cash price of Petersburg Tobacco.

I am Dear Sir Your Very humble servt.   Geo. Jefferson

RC (MHi); at foot of text: "Thos. Jefferson esqr."; endorsed by TJ as received 25 Jan. and so recorded in SJL. Receipt not found.

From James Madison

[ca. 20 Jan. 1802]

Wm. Foster jr. was named by Mr. Adams to the Senate who concurred; but no commission ever issued. He was of the State of Massachussets.

RC (DNA: RG 59, LAR, 1809-17); undated; endorsed by TJ: "Foster Wm junr. to be Commercl. Agent Morlaix."

President John Adams on 18 Feb. 1801 nominated William FOSTER, Jr., to be commercial agent at Morlaix and on 24 Feb. the Senate CONCURRED. Foster's commission, however, according to an undated memorandum from the State Department, was among those "remaining in the Office of the department of State" when TJ became president; it was never delivered, and the position remained vacant (JEP, 1:382, 385; Vol. 33:173n). On 20 Jan. 1802, TJ issued a new commission, noting the earlier confirmation of the appointment and expressing his "special Trust and Confidence in the Abilities and Integrity of the said William Foster Jr." TJ entered the nomination on two of his personal lists of removals and appointments under the date 21 Jan. 1802, where he commented that Foster had been "nominated by mr Adams & approved by Senate." A notation by a clerk in the State Department letterbook stated, at the foot of the text, that TJ's commission "never was forwarded." Evidently before that commission could be transmitted to Boston, Madison forwarded TJ a letter from William Foster, Sr., dated 14 Jan. 1802, informing the secretary of state that Adams's nomination of the young Foster was "made late & incompleat." The father's letter also complained that the appointment was "paltry" and of "very little consideration," and he sought Madison's help in obtaining from TJ a better post, in the north or south of France or in Spain, "say Cadiz or Malaga" (RC in DNA: RG 59, LAR; endorsed by TJ as received 25 Jan.; also endorsed by TJ: "Foster Wm junr. to be a consul"; commission in Lb in DNA: RG 59, PTCC; Vol. 33:671, 678). In February 1802, William Eustis informed Madison that he had received a recommendation for Foster for a consulate in France, observing that he was "a young man of talents, integrity and amiable manners, a Republican in principle and qualified for such an office." In 1803, Foster was recommended for the consulate at Nantes (Madison, *Papers, Sec. of State Ser.*, 2:457; 4:275).

From the Mississippi Territory House of Representatives

House of Representatives of the Mississippi Territory.—

SIR,   January 20th. A.D. 1802.—

In the course of a Long, Honorable, and useful Life, your Love for Mankind & their Rights; your Wisdom to discern, firmness to pursue, & solicitude to promote the true interest of the American Nation, have been eminently conspicuous, & while such Virtues & talents have attracted our admiration and Esteem, they could not fail to inspire a respect for, & confidence in your Administration.—

In superintending the affairs of United America & forwarding the Welfare of your numerous constituents we are fully assured, that this Territory will occupy a due proportion of your cares, & on all proper occasions, will receive the fostering support of the General Government.—

No part of the United States, Sir, possesses more Local advantages, than this District & her advancement to prosperity, promises to be speedy & certain;—We acknowledge with gratitude, that under your paternal auspices our prospects for political happiness, have greatly brightened, & we anticipate with fondest expectation, the arrival of a period, when this Territory, mature in age, strong in population, & rich in resources, will add still greater security & consequence to the American Union, & we flatter ourselves, that her present & future Legislators, will remain no Less Zealous & firm in the support of Virtuous Rulers, & Virtuous Measures, than in a strict adherence to Constitutional provisions, & those Republican principles which the patriots of Seventy Six had the Goodness to conceive, the Boldness to avow & the fortitude to maintain.—

We pray Almighty God, to prosper your Administration, & extend to a Life so valuable, the particular patronage of Heaven.

H. HUNTER, Speaker of the
House of Representativ,s.—

RC (DLC); in a clerk's hand, signed by Henry Hunter; at head of text: "Mr. West from the Committee appointed for that purpose, presented the Draft of an Address to His Excellency the President of the United States which being twice Read, was unanimously adopted, as follows:—To wit.—An address from the House of Representatives of the Mississippi Territory, to His Excellency Thomas Jefferson President of the United States"; at foot of text: "Resolved that the above address be transmitted by the Speaker, to His Excellency Governor Claiborne, who is hereby requested to forward the same, to the President of the United States.—Extract from the Journal"; attestation by Edwin L. Harris as clerk of the House; endorsed by TJ as received 19 Mch. and so recorded in SJL. Enclosed in William C. C. Claiborne to TJ, 21 Jan. 1802.

To David Austin

SIR   Washington Jan. 21. 1802.

Having daily to read voluminous letters & documents for the dispatch of the public affairs, your letters have consumed a portion of my time which duty forbids me any longer to devote to them. your talents as a divine I hold in due respect: but of their employment in a political line I must be allowed to judge for myself, bound as I am to select those which I suppose best suited to the public service. of the special communications to you of his will by the supreme being, I can have no evidence, and therefore must ascribe your belief of[1] them to the false perceptions of your mind. it is with real pain that I find myself at length obliged to say in express terms what I had hoped you would have inferred from my silence. Accept of my respects & best wishes. Th: Jefferson

PrC (DLC); at foot of text: "The revd. David Austin."

[1] Preceding three words interlined.

From William C. C. Claiborne

Sir,   Natchez January 21st. 1802—

I have the honor to enclose you, an address from the House of Representatives of the Mississippi Territory, and the pleasure to add, that the Sentiments it contains, are in unison with the feelings of a great majority of the Citizens of this Territory.—

I am persuaded, an opinion generally prevails in this District, that the Liberty, Peace, & safety of our Country, greatly depend upon the preservation of our present National Union, and free Government; and [to] give durability to such important Impressions, will be among the greatest objects of my public cares—

With great Respect & sincere Esteem I am Sir, your most obd: Hble: Servant—   William C. C. Claiborne

RC (DLC); in a clerk's hand, signed by Claiborne; torn; at foot of text: "To His Excellency Thomas Jefferson President U. States"; endorsed by TJ as received 19 Mch. and so recorded in SJL. Enclosure: Mississippi Territory House of Representatives to TJ, 20 Jan.

From Thomas Claxton

Honored Sir   Capitol, January 21, 1802

If, in your judgement, I should appear to be as well qualified to take the charge of the Congressional Library, as any other person who might be willing to accept of that appointment—and if there should be no infringment of the constitution, by my holding the Station which I now possess, as well as the other,—I should be happy to be considered as a candidate for that office—Having the honor of being known by you, Sir, and not wishing to trouble the gentlemen in Congress for a recommendation, I have taken the liberty of making my application in a manner which I suppose is not usual on such occasions—

I have the honor to be, Sir, With the greatest respect Your Hble Svt   THOS CLAXTON

RC (DNA: RG 59, LAR); endorsed by TJ as received 22 Jan. and so recorded in SJL.

STATION WHICH I NOW POSSESS, AS WELL AS THE OTHER: see Vol. 33:153n.

From Josias Wilson King

SIR,   City of Washington, January, 21st. 1802.

Anticipating your approbation of an act passed this day, and which I have inrolled, vesting in you the sole appointment of a Librarian to the congressional library; I beg you Sir, to consider this as my application for the said appointment. Having been a clerk in the office of the House of Representatives of the United States, nearly five years, part of which period, I have been principal clerk in the office, and the entire charge of the books attached to the said office, I trust, will together with the necessary enquiry of my character and ability from the members of the Legislature and Senate be a recommendation in my favor. The compensation allowed by the act cannot be an object to any person but myself, being under the employ of Mr. Beckley, and receiving his sanction for this application, will enable me to discharge the duties of both offices. Your confering this appointment on me Sir, will I trust be a pleasing reflection, that you are giving subsistence to a young man with an infant family. The enclosed is a list of Gentlemen who have expressed an approbation of my capability.

With sentiments of the highest respect, I have the Honor to be, Sir, Your Obedient Servant.   JOSIAS WILSON KING.

RC (DNA: RG 59, LAR); at head of text: "The President of the United States"; endorsed by TJ as received 24 Jan. and "to be librarian" and so recorded in SJL. Enclosure: attestation of King's "suitable character" for the appointment of congressional librarian signed by 30 representatives, mostly Republicans (MS in same; in King's hand, signed by congressmen).

Josias Wilson King, a CLERK IN THE OFFICE OF THE HOUSE OF REPRESENTA-

TIVES hired by Federalist Jonathan Condy in 1797, was retained but demoted under John Beckley, who eventually fired him in December 1805. Beckley, to whom TJ had given the post of librarian of Congress, assigned King, without extra compensation, some of the librarian's duties. In a memorial presented to Congress in 1806, King claimed that Beckley had agreed to divide the library compensation equally with him. King protested that he had not been paid since 1802, when, as assistant librarian, he was appointed "to label, arrange, and take charge of the books" in the library (William Dawson Johnston, *History of the Library of Congress* [Washington, D.C., 1904], 1:35; Edmund Berkeley and Dorothy Smith Berkeley, *John Beckley: Zealous Partisan in a Nation Divided* [Philadelphia, 1973], 239, 241; JHR, 5:280; Vol. 29:374; Beckley to TJ, 21 Jan.).

From Charles Willson Peale

DEAR SIR   Museum Jany. 21st. 1802.

Receive my assurances of obligation for the politeness and punctuality with which you have answered my question.—Altho' I conceived it proper, without any loss of time, to make such applications as might insure the preservation and advancement of the Museum, particularly as at the present moment many of the articles are piled in confusion on each other for want of Room; Yet I have determined that it may not be prudent too hastily to bind myself to this residence without sufficient advantages. With respect to an Application to Congress, your communication has satisfied my mind, that at least from the diversity of opinion, if not from the present nature of the constitution, it would be an unproductive one.

Perhaps it will not be possible for me to obtain any permanent establishment, before such a state of affairs shall arrive as would insure success to the grand plan you have in contemplation for your native State. In the mean time I shall propose to our Legislature a plan by which they may possess themselves of more handsome property at the same time that they without expence advance the Interest of Science. I shall ask nothing more than that they authorize a Lottery, the profits of which shall defray the expences of an Ornamental Building to be erected on the South of the State house garden. This building, to contain my Museum while ever it shall remain in Philadelphia—and as the property of the House and land would be theirs, afterwards to be retained for a Museum, or otherwise as they chuse.

I am highly gratified that my success with the Mammoth excites such general approbation, and shall receive your intended visit with the greatest pleasure.

The whole of the upper part of the Head I am in want of, the deficiency of which I supplied by modelling from the Elephants head. But a Gentleman who lives near the Salt licks on the Ohio, (Doctr Jno. Sellman) visited me the other day, who informed me he was in possession of the Skull, which he promised to send me by the first Conveyance. I wish to know whether that to which you allude can be the same. At any rate your assistance, which may the more certainly and expeditiously procure it for me, will be thankfully acknowledged by your friend   C W PEALE

RC (DLC); on same stationery as Peale's letter of 12 Jan.; at foot of text: "Mr. Jefferson." Dft (Lb in PPAmP: Peale-Sellers Papers).

ANSWERED MY QUESTION: TJ to Peale, 16 Jan. 1802. Peale originally intended to respond to TJ on 20 Jan. On that day Peale drafted a letter in which he stated that his mind was "wavering" about whether to ask the Pennsylvania legislature for a grant for the museum. He doubted that the state would make any large appropriation for that purpose, and he worried that the construction of a building for the museum might oblige him to keep it in Philadelphia "when very probably a better establishment may be had for it" elsewhere, especially with TJ's assistance. "Perhaps it will be best to delay for the present my application to the Legislature of Pennsyl. for any particular grant," Peale wrote, "And only intimate them that I am willing to place my Museum in any situation that can be devised to insure a general & lasting benefit to my Country." Peale struck through his draft of that letter without finishing it, and composed the letter above as a substitute (Dft in Lb in PPAmP: Peale-Sellers Papers; Peale, *Papers*, v. 2, pt. 1:391-2n).

In February, Peale submitted a memorial to the LEGISLATURE of Pennsylvania. He also obtained resolutions of support from the American Philosophical Society and the Philadelphia Common Council. In March, the Pennsylvania Senate and House of Representatives agreed to allow him the use of the east end of the first floor of the State House and the entire second floor of the building (*Philadelphia Gazette*, 19 Feb. 1802; Peale, *Papers*, v. 2, pt. 1:393-401).

The part of a SKULL found in Kentucky several miles from Big Bone Lick proved to be from a large extinct bison rather than a mastodon. Dr. John Sellman, whose name was also sometimes written "Sillman," was a native of Maryland who in 1792 had been appointed a surgeon's mate in the army for service on the frontier. In 1807, he sought to become the register of the land office at Cincinnati (Peale, *Papers*, v. 2, pt. 1:392n, 435n; JEP, 1:117; Sellman to Gabriel Duvall, 4 Oct. 1807, RC in DNA: RG 59, LAR, with note by Duvall, endorsed by TJ; Howard A. Kelly and Walter L. Burrage, *Dictionary of American Medical Biography* [New York, 1928], 1092; Peale to TJ, 10 June 1802).

From Anna Young

RESPECTED SIR   Norwich Jany 21st 1802

This Comes With my Greatest respects To You and To request A Favor of You for thus Intruding on You My Necessity must plead for me and be my Excuse I have Tryed Every method that I could In my reduced Situation or I Should not now presumed To ask your advice I have adviced The best of men and they all tell me that it is right I Should have What I have been Trying for—Which is Seven Years half pay Which By A Voluntary act of Congress, Was Given to the Widows or Orphan Children of Officers or Soldiers that died In Service My Father Col John Durkee Engaged In the Late American War with Great Britain and Served till his Death which was a Short time before the peace took place, Lost his right hand in Monmouth Action *remained* a Cripple till Death—his Widow, my mother after his Death Employed Capt. Benjn Durkee to go on to Congress and Settle his Continental accounts which Done he Petitioned the Assembly of the State of Connecticut as Every State payed there own Officers and Got a Grant but before The Notes Were Issued there Came an Order from John Pierce pay Master Genl. to have it Stopped till he Could have a Matter Rectified as he Said the Said Benjn Durkee had got Some final Settlement Certificates from him by Fraud My Mother Died about that Time and I being In Trouble did not att that time know what the Mistake was And about The Same time I Lost my Husband and Left With three small Children To Support by my Industry as the property my Husband Left me was Chiefly In Continental money and I Trusting that I would be made good Keep it to the amount of 6000 Dollars till it was good for Nothing My Father Left No property but Died in full belief that his family Would be benefited by the half pay that failing I was reduced To great Poverty and Still remain So I then had three Brothers they Went to Sea two of them Were Lost the Other Has not been here this Sixteen Years and I know not Whether he be living or not—I after a While Thought I would try to Inform myself, what was the reason of the paye being stopped I wrote to the Comptroller att Hartford and he wrote me as above by order of John Pierce as above I then Wrote To Govr Trumbull then A Member of Congress for his Advice and he wrote me Word To take out Administration and Send on a man With proper Documents and he thought I should recover It but In my Circumstances I Could not do that I had Some Offer if I Would give one half but my Heart recoiled att the Idea of giving away so much that My father Earned with his Life and I had the Idea and Still have that I ought to have without Expence I then wrote To Genl Washington asking his Advice and he Very politely Answered my Letter and said he should be Willing to advise me if he What method it Was best for me to pursue but as he had never turned his Attention To Business of that kind he did not but referred me to some member of Congress as they would be most likely to know what to advise To there being None but Mr Roger Griswould that I had any knowledge of I wrote To him for his advice and Inclosed General Washingtons to me In his and Desired the favor of him to advise me and To return the Inclosed but have never recieved neither after Waiting sometime and Congress had rose he returned home and I heard nothing from him I Applied To Genl Ebenr. Huntington and he very readily gave me his advice and accordingly I Administered on the Estate[1] of my mother and Got Elisha Hyde Esqr To petition for me and it Was Continued

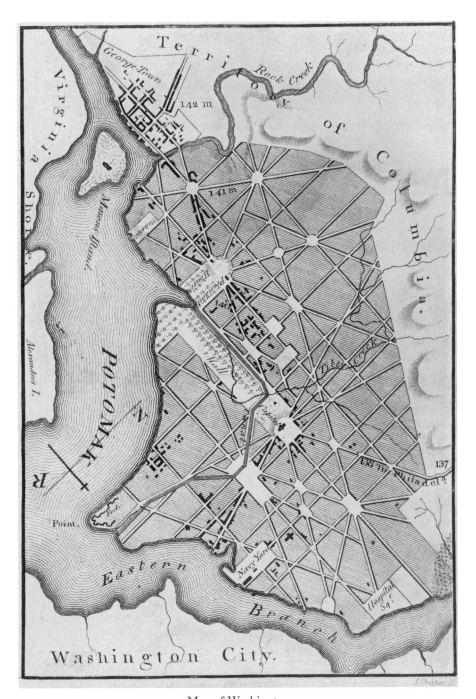

Map of Washington

Meriwether Lewis

Th: Jefferson requests the favour of The Honble Mr Dwight Foster to dine with him the day after tomorrow — at half after three, or at whatever later hour the house may rise.

Monday Feb 1st 1802.

The favour of an answer is asked.

Printed Dinner Invitation

Th⟨J⟩ to mr Gallatin

Are the within terms admissible?

The 1st, 2d & 4th are either in pursuance of, or not inconsistent with the law, excepting only the words "all other documents belonging to the land department," the Surveyor general superintends the Surveying department, & has nothing to do with the sales of the lands, these being under the superintendence of the several registers, who make their reports immediately to the Treasury.

The 3d viz residing at the seat of government is inconsistent with the present laws which contemplate the office of the Surveyor general as permanently fixed in the N.W. territory, & do not require any duties or give any authority in relation to ⟨them⟩ & survey. of the other parts of the U. States. — A copy of the plot of public lands is to be kept open at the Sur. gen. office for public information — he is to transmit plats to the registers of the several land offices & to the Sec'y of the Treasury — The Register shall transmit accounts of sales to the Sur. gen. & to the Sec't of the Treasury — The Sur. gen. receives applications from Registers who want to purchase — On the whole throughout the ⟨...⟩ the Sur. gen. office is considered as the general land office in the Western country, & that of the Sec'y of the Treas'y as its counterpart at the seat of Government. The Sur. gen. is also authorized to let for hire the surveying ⟨...⟩ which can only be done by an officer on the spot. But, in fact his most important duty is the immediate superintendence of the surveyors & surveys which cannot be done at a distance from the scene of action.

29853

A. G.

President of the United States

Memorandums Exchanged by Jefferson and Gallatin

Albert Gallatin

Little Turtle

Black Hoof

ODE

TO THE

MAMMOTH CHEESE,

Prefented to Thomas Jefferfon,

PRESIDENT OF THE UNITED STATES,

BY THE INHABITANTS OF CHESHIRE, MASSACHUSETTS,

JANUARY 1, 1802.

MOST Excellent--far fam'd and far fetch'd CHEESE!
  Superior far in fmell, tafte, weight and fize,
To any ever form'd 'neath foreign fkies,
And highly honour'd--thou wert made to pleafe,
  The man belov'd by all--but ftop a trice,
  Before he's praifed--I too muft have a flice.

II.

Rich too thou art, and pleafant tho' fo large
  As any Millftone--or a North-weft Moon ;
  To meafure thee 'twould take an afternoon--
Few tables can fupport the pond'rous charge,
  Into what cupboard Mammoth canft thou enter,
  And where's the knife can cut clean thro' thy centre.

III.

'Twould take a Gallatin to afcertain
  How many meals for Congrefs--clerks and all
  The fupernumeraries about their Hall,
Thy fpacious limits actually contain :
  What number of WELSH RABBITS, thou wouldft make
  How many thoufand loaves there's caufe to bake.

IV.

For cent'ries paft--in Europe--fometimes here,
  Placemen were faid to fhare the *loaves* and *fifhes*,
  (And where's the man that for a fhare ne'er wifhes)
But now Americans have better cheer,
  And to their worthy fervants 'ftead of thefe,
  They've wifely fubftituted--LOAVES and CHEESE.

V.

Cheefe is the attendant of a New-Year's day,
  Cheefe is the Blithe-meat * when a bairn is born,

    * In Scotland.

Cheefe, may thofe tafte thee ne'er, who tafting fcorn,
Cheefe--ftill proceeding from the milky way,
  Is nature's pureft, plain and fimple food ;
  Cheefe is a lux'ry, when like this 'tis good.

VI.

God blefs the Cheefe--and kindly blefs the makers,
  The givers--generous--good and fweet and fair,
  And the receiver--great beyond compare,
All thofe who fhall be happy as partakers ;
  O ! may no traitor to his country's caufe
  E'er have a bit of thee between his jaws.

VII.

Some folks may fneer, with envy in their fmiles,
  And with low wit at ridicule endeavour,
  Their fenfe and breeding's fhewn by their behaviour,
Well--let them ufe Ariftocratic wiles,
  Do what they can--and fay juft what they pleafe,
  RATS love to nibble at good Chefhire Cheefe.

VIII.

'Tis a good New-Year's Gift I think indeed,
  But the Cheefe-Mafter muft be on his guard,
  And againft *longing women* be prepar'd,
Once they begin to eat--do pray take heed ;
  Once they begin--when they may ftop's unknown,
  Perhaps they will not till the whole is gone.

IX.

To others leaving wealth, and place and pow'r,
  I'll to my home and to my HARRIS hie,
  Our wants are few--thofe induftry fupply ;
All that we want or wifh for in life's hour,
  Heaven ftill will grant us--they are only thefe,
  Poetry--Health--Peace--Virtue--Bread and *Cheefe*.

"Ode to the Mammoth Cheese"

three Sessions then A Comittee appointed and they Say that as the State of Connecticut and the United States have Adjusted their Accounts it must be Determined[2] by Congress Esquire Hyde then told me that he believed he Could get Mr Griswould and Mr Goddard to Undertake it without a fee and Since Told me that he had mentioned it to them but Said that Mr Griswould spoke Very faint as most people of his Calling do Where there No Money in View Mr Goddard Was Willing To do What he Could for which I am much obliged To him but being no more acquainted With him than With you I have Ventured To ask advice of you trusting that you are Willing To assist the Injured and have justice Done to Every Individual I wish to know if there is no way that I can get it without Expence—It is Now Fifteen Years that I have been a Trying To get hold of it and, No one is more Necessitous than I am and if I was not I think it my Just Due My family I Venture To say has done as much to gain Independance as any one according to Their abilities My Father Was I believe if ever there was a true Republican friend To his Country he was one he served also In the old french War spent Life and property in the Late Contest of America I had att one time A Husband A Father two brothers in the Service since I have been Deprived of them all My Life Since the Commencment of the War has been almost one scene of Sorrow Disappointment and poverty—The Husband that I have now is a true republican but an old man and A good Deal Infirm and has brought a large family of Children had a Great Deal of sickness and we are both Too old to do much hard Work our Children are Willing to do what they can for us but are not in a Situation to Do much as Some are Married and families own other Apprentices my Son has four Years Yet to serve and my Daughters have Enough to Do to support themselves and I do not Like this reversing of Nature I had rather Grant Ten favors to a Child than to ask one and if I had my right It Would Enable me To for myself & husband and them too and I hope if in your power you will be kind Enough to Assist me in getting it they Can Certainly say yes or no and not keep me in Suspense any Longer I Cannot help repeating that I Cannot be Willing To give up half of it to any one I think I had rather the Public would have it but I want it myself as it is very Disagreable to me to think and God forbid it should be that after working through so Long as my husband and I have we should become objects of public Charity which I See no avoiding if our health should Decline My Husband knows nothing of my writing to you he would not be willing I write in this way but if he had money to do with No one would be readier to do any thing for another than he would for me but I Lay aside all pride of that kind as it is nothing Criminal to ask for what belongs to us if we know where to ask and I hope you will be able to Inform me and Pardon any thing amiss and impute It to the Weakness of an old Woman that has not much Education and what she has was given her Upwards of forty Years ago if you will be kind Enough to grant me the favor of Your advice I shall take it as a great favor and if a Heart overflowing with Gratitude for it is any Compensation you have a full reward In the mean Time I am with the Greatest respect

Your most Obet Humble Servt. ANNA YOUNG

RC (DLC); at foot of text: "To the Honle. Thomas Jefferson Esqr"; endorsed by TJ as received 1 Feb. and so recorded in SJL; undated note by Henry Dearborn to TJ below inside address: "Sir on application to the Connecticut Gentlemen in Congress, I am informed that no relief can be had in the case of Mrs. Young, that her case is so effectually foreclosed, as to render all further attempts in her favour vain. H. Dearborn."

Anna Young (1753-1839) of Norwich, Connecticut, was the eldest child of John and Martha Wood Durkee. Her first husband, Dr. Dominic Tauzin, died at sea in 1782. She subsequently married Norwich attorney John Young, who died in 1805. Young went to Philadelphia in 1810, then moved to Brooklyn, New York, in 1815. She eventually migrated with her grandchildren to Illinois, where she resided for the remainder of her life. In 1812, Congress finally settled her father's long-standing claim and awarded Anna, as John Durkee's sole surviving heir, his seven years half-pay with interest (Nathaniel B. Curran, "Anna Durkee Tauzin Young, 1753-1839: Connecticut Lady, Illinois Pioneer," *Journal of the Illinois State Historical Society*, 77 [1984], 94-100; ASP, *Claims*, 1:417; U.S. Statutes at Large, 6:110).

A VOLUNTARY ACT OF CONGRESS: on 24 Aug. 1780, the Continental Congress resolved that their resolution of 15 May 1778, granting half-pay for seven years to army officers who served to the end of the

war, was to be extended to the widows of officers who died during their term of service. If the deceased officer had no surviving widow, then the half-pay was to be given to his orphaned children (JCC, 17:773).

JOHN DURKEE was a veteran of the French and Indian War and a leading figure in the settlement of the Wyoming Valley of Pennsylvania, founding the town of Wilkes-Barre. An active patriot, he served as a colonel in the Continental army and saw extensive action before being severely wounded at the battle of Monmouth. He died in 1782 (DAB).

THREE BROTHERS: John, Jr., Phineas, and Isaac Barré Durkee (Curran, "Anna Durkee Tauzin Young," 94-5).

I THEN WROTE TO GENL WASHINGTON: for Young's letter to George Washington of 6 Nov. 1798 and Washington's reply of 20 Nov., see Washington, *Papers, Ret. Ser.*, 3:183-5.

Ebenezer HUNTINGTON was a lieutenant colonel during the Revolutionary War and a brigadier general in the provisional army from 1798 to 1800 (Heitman, *Register*, 310; *Biog. Dir. Cong.*). ELISHA HYDE, a Republican, was mayor of Norwich and a member of the Connecticut legislature (*Norwich Courier*, 22 Dec. 1813; Vol. 34:344n). Roger Griswold and Calvin GODDARD were both congressmen from Connecticut (*Biog. Dir. Cong.*).

[1] MS: "Etate."
[2] MS: "Detemind."

From Joseph Anthony

DEAR FRIEND   Richmond Virginia 1 mo. 22. 1802

It is the indispenceable duty of every enlightened Lawgiver, to have accurate information of the situation, and Circumstances, of the country for whom he is to legislate; & to acquire a perfect knowledge, of the Character, the manners, Habitudes, and inclinations, of its people, before he can expect to be sucessful in laying down those rules which are suitable for their Government, but with this qualification he will be led to decide, not according to his good wishes for mankind; but according to their real condition not according to a perfect state of society, but according to the degree or advancement which they have made toward it: because such laws are more likely to be well received & obeyed and more likely to lead them on at last to happiness such are the reflections which are produced, upon a review of the facts which present themselves in the examination of the History of our Country. We once felt the yoke of oppression ourselves, we saw that freedom was good and we determined to possess it. we asserted our rights, we established our principles and we enforced our demands, in short we were free to make laws for ourselves & to regulate our own concerns in a way that suited us this was perhaps the first oppertunity we had of applyin a remedy for the cure of one of the greatest of our internal defects, that of domestic Slavery; It might have been happier for us if we could have laid the Ax to the root of the tree at this period thou was among the number of those who saw it at the time but thou embraced all that was then fit to be embraced for the most enlightened Philosopher although he may see and lament yet he cannot act, or put in motion more than there is a concurent disposition in his fellows to receive & forward Considering the matter in this way perhaps it is right to conclude that all was done towards it that could be done & that we attained all at that time which was within our power to attain & for it let us claim all the congratulation due to an enlightened & growing people advancing as I trust and am willing to believe to that state of perfection, which earthly beings are qualefied to attain, yet we might have done more by this time than we have. Virtue has not kept pace with knowledge (at least in the bulk of the nation) or we might have approached nearer to such a state than we have, one among the complaints against Great Brittain brought forward as an excuse for withdrawing our affections from our Mother country was that they imposed Slaves upon us contrary to our will it was certainly a good reason for asserting the right of judgeing and acting for ourselves, but how have we acted? we established our right of Self Government but the law of our Strength we made the measure of our justice in as much as we refused to dispence that to men in a station below us which we claimed for ourselves from men (who said they were) above us—Happy Country! its a charming sound charming indeed! and superlatively blessd must be that people who are tenants of a place deserving of the title but might we not have deserved it by this time if we had at the time of obtaining our countries emancepation from the Yoke of foreign oppression laid the foundation upon which to build up an entire free people and gradually to have done away an evil of so great a magnitude as that of domestic Slavery. If we might not have deserved it by this time convinced, I am, that we might at least have had a much better prospect for it. Compare such a situation as might have been ours ere now, with a state of continual uneasiness under oppression on one hand and apprehensions for Safety on the other and let this urge us though late to begin the Work, for delay can only make things worse and put the remedy farther out of our power—as for the work of emancepation itself—it has been begun the natural force of things will impel it forward and it is not in the power of Human contrivance to prevent it—perhaps it goes on as fast as it ought; but a disposition should be cherished to receive it by the white people upon this score it appears to me we are greatly behind hand. for bare emancipation from a particular master is not all, they must have a prospect of other previledges also, a bare discharge from the Yoke and to be like oxen, driven away from their masters crib to roam the barren Heath for food will not do—the laws must relax a little for amendment of their condition they must at least enjoy a prospect of arriveing at some future day to a better destiny, but how is their condition to be amended without risqueing the peace of Society? this is the common enquiry even among those who are willing to admit the equity of their claim the thing is desireable but how is it to be come at—Upon this subject let me hazard a few Suggestions in the first place we say are the Africans to be doomed to perpetual Bondage or are they to be free and we answer without hesitation—they are to be unquestionably free. in the next we enquire what is to become of them must they be driven out like wild beasts to roam in the wilderness without food and without raiment to cover them from the Cold? although perhaps the prime of their days have been spent in labouring for another whose board is now covered with the fruits of his earning & whose body is now warm from the Flocks of his feeding. afflicted christianity recoils at the Idea—Well, must they remain among us and be incorporated with the Whites so as to become a motley multitude of dissonant figures. Pride and deep rooted prejudices, says, no, I forbid it. the only alternative then which is left us, is that a place must be provided to send them to where they may have a Government of their choice and consequently laws of their own makeing—laws of their own makeing because those laws which a people enact for themselves are generally best obeyed—the most respected the best understood and therefore the best adapted to their Capacities and inclinations all these things are necessary to a Well Ordered Society of any people let their condition in other respects be what it may. but what are the first steps towards an establishment of this sort must a country be prepared with Habitations to receive them or must means first be used to prepare the people to go to it. first of all the people must be put in a way of improvement to prepare their minds for embraceing a new Country when one offers & to qualify them for manageing its affairs when they arrive at it. then invitations instead of commands will be sufficient to entice them to leave us but how is this preparation to be brought about so as to put them in a condition for removal my plan would be to enlist them I mean the free ones in the same manner you do Soldiers give them a Bounty &c as you do them let them be officered in the same manner and diciplined which will hold them together and teach them obedience & good Order let stations be provided for them to consist of Land for their cultivation which should be worked under the direction of the officers for publick account the produce of which to come into graneries for the purpose of being again dealt out for their use in pay and Subsistance thus we should get a sort of organized army at command. we should separate the free Blacks and Mulattoes from the Slaves and we should place them where they should be compeled to labour for subsistance and in doing this we should in all likelyhood dry up a source of much mischief not only to the white people but to the remaining Slaves also. Well haveing in this manner drawn all our freed people together and in some sort set up a new society of men whom we have taught to be governed and to earn a subsistance we may then begin to consider them as vergeing towards a better condition as in some sort of preparation to embrace a new country should one present itself as a suitable place to transplant them this transplanting must be carried on by drawing from our first establishments as a skilful farmer would draw apple trees from a nursery a new enlistment must take place from amongst our prepared subjects to people the new colony the Bounty then to be offered must consist of certain enlargement of priviledges and a sufficient space of Land to each as permanent Estate

By this mode of procedure we should have two kinds of establishment one for picking up the freed people & seperateing them from among the Slaves and the other for permanent establishment & self Government but in carrying it on we would instead of Musquets & Bayonets put into their hands "Plowshares and pruning hooks" the implements of peace and husbandry as well as instead of Powder and Shot to do mischief. give them all kinds of prolific seeds to "multiply and replenish the Earth" with; and thus arrayed we shall not be afraid of them because while we are learning War they will be learning peace as the only means of Safety & of bettering their Condition

Perhaps the work might seem a little strange to them at first but if it was begun by some of their known advocates they would be less fearful of engageing and when once established they might appear an inviteing Society for others to come to when the country becomes pretty well drained of those already free others might be sent to the establishment as they become free. it might even be made a condition of their emancepation so in like manner when a Colony was only begun thou would migrate thither of their own accord as naturally as the Waters flow into the sea the thing would become easy as it advanced for the whole country would lend their aid when once the way was pointed out. No force or Compulsion should be practized upon any one more than a man would use in a well ordered family all must be done by perswasion and inducement so as to appear manifestly that their Interest was the object to be improved—they would then come forward willingly

If Congress would place a small sum of money at the present at the disposal of the President of the United States and leave the manner of vesting it to his own judgment and experience there remains not a doubt in my mind but the foundation of a great work might be laid with it that might in time so operate as to be the means of removeing one of the greatest evils with which a nation was ever cursed entirely from our land. the expence of such an undertakeing would be nothing when suitable Lands were provided and thus provided they would be at moderate prices such as they would at any time Command. again if they should be no longer wanted for this establishment, it would be like furnishing a Capitol Stock in trade and might be made to support and extend itself

The last twelve Months of my life have been almost wholly devoted to the examining as far as I was able into this subject and in enquireing after suitable situations for an establishment of the first descrip-

tion which I have mentioned yet in such a research it has appeared
best to say but little as to the main object in question & not to let "my
left hand know what my right hand doeth" the twelve preceding I
taught School gratis furnishing Books &c (a Sunday school it was
called) at which many of different ages from twelve to Thirty Years
attended and received instruction with unwearied attention and diligence. but it so disgusted the people of this Town that they became
loud in their acclaimations against the institution and a discovery of
the meditated insurrection in this neighbourhood happening about
the same time they almost wholly prevented the attendance of my
Scholars. these discouragements so disheartened me and them that
we dropt the School much to their regret. Robert Pleasants of Curels
near this place emancepated a considerable number and being a
noted friend and advocate in their cause he was in a manner looked
up to as their Common Father and they brought all their complaints
before him to get them redressed and as there subsisted an intimacy
between him & myself known[1] to and approved of by them a considerable share of their affections devolved upon me since his death—
The old man had tenanted out many of these families upon a Tract of
Land near him which he left in his Will for their use in manner following. vizt. a School was opened in which the Children of the Tenants were to be instructed and the rents which the parents were
bound to pay was to go to the support of it. now as there are many
free people of those which him & others liberated with their decen-
dants upon the place which he appropreated exclusively to them &
round about its neighbourhood it seems to me a proper begining for
an establishment upon our first description lands adjoining or con-
tiguous might be purchased at a moderate rate which instead of
being injured might be improved in value by cultivation if proper
care was taken of it in that case the United States could not loose but
gain by the bargain. The place I have been describeing seems best
adapted to such an undertakeing because there we find it already
begun—because there we find plenty of neighbouring subjects for a
first essay and because there a considerable advancement might be
made before any thing would appear to be removed out of its place
and lastly because there the Land is of moderate strength—cheap—
plenty of it vacant and not verry difficult to be come at in sufficient
quantities to answer all the purposes of our first institution without
exciting either the fears or the envy of the surrounding Country

 I have no apology to make for this intrusion upon thy time & patience more than what the importance of my subject affords. I know
thou art one of those who are deeply impressed with our unfortunate

situation in relation to slavery not merely as it regards the poor oppressed African but as it regards also the Welfare, nay, the verry existance of order and happiness in some of the States consider what
would have been our situation had thou not been elected president.
Even the suspence which was occasioned by the clashings of party
prejudices made us tremble the consequences which might have ensued to the Southern States were truly awful—thou was the peoples
choice and therefore the proper person at this time to be their President I rejoiced when I heard thou was chosen because the plans
which it appeared thou held & the policy which thou would be likely
thence to pursue appeared most likely to better our condition as a nation. and to rescue us from a track which seemed to me tending to the
reverse. yet it requires the concurence & approbation of the community to carry into effect the advices which thou sees are best for us and
without it thou can do but little

I hope the President will not be displeased at a plain simple suggestion from one of the great family whose name is among its friends
  And Thine   JOSEPH ANTHONY

P.S. As I am desireous of possessing all the light which can be
thrown upon this subject and as I am aware of the strictness necessary in thy situation to avoid exciteing the least mistaken impressions
in the minds of the people of thy sentiments thereon I engage should
thou find freedom to make me any communications, not to impart
them to another person of any description—I may receive instruction
from thee upon this subject that may at some future day be useful as
I am but about 32 years of age—the time may come when I may be
useful. If I cannot do it now   J A

RC (DLC); addressed: "Thomas Jefferson President of the United States City
of Washington"; franked; postmarked 24
Jan.; endorsed by TJ as received 28 Jan.
and so recorded in SJL.

This Joseph Anthony may have been
the Richmond merchant of that name
who was involved in a sale of nailrod by
TJ in 1800 (Vol. 31:361-2, 385, 393).

Quaker merchant ROBERT PLEASANTS
of Curles Neck, Virginia, was an advocate of emancipation and education for
African Americans, both slave and free.
He corresponded with TJ on these topics
in 1796 and 1797 and died in 1801 (Vol.
29:120, 177-8, 287-8).

[1] MS: "know."

From John Beckley

SIR,   Washington, 22d: January 1802.

Beleiving that the Office of Librarian to Congress, is not incompatible with my present Station, and that in some views it may be of public convenience, I beg leave, in this form, to repeat the intimation which my friend Judge Lincoln made to you on my behalf, of my being a Candidate for the appointment. It is hardly probable that any person qualified to discharge the duty, will look to the emolument of the Office, as a sole dependance, and in this view, under the present feelings of œconomy, and the scanty provision for my Clerkship of the House, this appointment *may* afford an additional means of support to my family.

With sincere respect, I am, Sir, Your obedt: hble Servt.

JOHN BECKLEY

RC (DNA: RG 59, LAR); endorsed by TJ as received 22 Jan. and so recorded in SJL; also endorsed by TJ: "to be librarian."

"Reposing Special Trust and Confidence" in his "Diligence and Discretion," TJ appointed Beckley LIBRARIAN TO CONGRESS on 29 Jan. (FC of commission in Lb in DNA: RG 59, MPTPC).

SCANTY PROVISION FOR MY CLERKSHIP: as clerk of the House of Representatives, Beckley received an annual salary of $1,750, plus $2 per day while the House was in session. In April 1802, Congress passed an act fixing Beckley's salary at $2,000 per year, with no per diem allowance (ASP, *Miscellaneous*, 1:302; U.S. Statutes at Large, 1:449; 2:58, 170-1).

From the District of Columbia Commissioners

SIR,   Commissioners Office 22d Jany 1802

The term having expired, during which the first and third articles of the terms and conditions declared by the President of the United States on the 17th. October 1791 for regulating the materials and manner of building and improvements on the Lots in the City, of Washington, have been suspended, we have taken the subject into consideration, and are of opinion that it may be expedient to extend the indulgence last given to the end of the present year, with this difference; that no wooden building covering more than three hundred and twenty square feet, or more than twelve feet high from the sills to the eve's shall be permitted. Houses of that discription will be sufficient for tradesmen or others of small property, for whose encouragement and accommodation alone we should think it advisable to permit wooden buildings of any dimensions to be erected in the City—. We enclose a writing agreeably to former precedents for your signature, should you approve of the measure proposed.—

We are, with sentiments of the highest respect Sir, Yr mo Obt Servts.

WILLIAM THORNTON
ALEXR WHITE
TRISTRAM DALTON

RC (DLC); in Thomas Munroe's hand, signed by Thornton, White, and Dalton; at foot of text: "President of the U.S."; endorsed by TJ as received 22 Jan. and so recorded in SJL. FC (DNA: RG 42, DCLB). Enclosure not found, but see below.

On 23 Jan., TJ approved a one-year ex-

tension of the suspension of certain building regulations for the District of Columbia, which had EXPIRED on 1 Jan. 1802. He also approved the two additional rules on wooden buildings that the commissioners requested in their letter printed above. The *National Intelligencer* printed the proclamation on 29 Jan. (Vol. 33:154-5).

To John Wayles Eppes

DEAR SIR   Washington Jan. 22. 1802

Yours of the 6th. has been duly recieved. but the printer has been slow in making up for me the documents you desired. they are now inclosed. the Census is not yet printed. the bill for the Military establishment, on the scale proposed by the Executive, passed the H. of R. yesterday by about 58. or 60. votes against 12. a proposition to strike out the Brigadier General had a good deal divided both Republicans & Federalists. he was retained by a mixt vote of both parties 54. to 36. our friends have not yet learned to draw well together, and there has been some danger of a small section of them, aided by the feds, carrying a question against the larger section. they have seen however that this practice would end in enabling the feds to carry every thing as they please, by joining whichever section of Republicans they chose; and they will avoid this rock. I fancy we are all agreed on all the other interesting points, & that there will be no difficulty on the navy, or repeal of the taxes. when they come to striking out unnecessary officers from the civil list, there will probably be some differences in detail. there will also be a difference on the militia law, whether there shall be a part of it made select? within 2. or 3. days the other party expect their 2. absent Senators, Ross & Ogden. they will then be 15. and 15. we having two absent, Bradley (whose wife is dying) and another of whom nobody has yet heard at all. in this state of things should one of the friends of the Judiciary repeal be out of his seat a moment, that bill could be called up & negatived.

I am sorry the division into Captaincies has not been proposed. but it is not in my power to sketch it. some gentlemen here, who take an interest in the turnpike established at the head of Patomac, have desired me to mention the cost of that kind of road here. we have made some miles here of as fine gravel road as can be shewn in England. but we had one hill to dig through 20. or 30 feet deep, & 2. others to dig down to that depth & kept no separate account. we suppose that the rounding the bed of the road 18. I. high in the middle, clearing it of stones, & laying on a coat of 14. I. gravel costs 1000. D. a mile. in Massachusetts they have done upwards of 100. miles, which costs them from 700. to 1000. D. a mile, according to the convenience & nature of the stone, which they are obliged to use, for want of gravel, breaking it into small pieces. in our country where labour is so much cheaper than in Massachusetts, (to wit negroes hired by the year) it would certainly cost less than there. a letter from Edgehill yesterday informed me all were well there. I hope Maria & the little one continue so. it will always relieve me to hear it as well as of your own health. accept assurances of my affectionate esteem & attachment

Th: Jefferson

RC (NHi); addressed: "John W. Eppes Richmond." PrC (CSmH); endorsed by TJ in ink on verso. Enclosures not found.

YOURS OF THE 6TH.: a letter from John Wayles Eppes to TJ of 6 Jan. 1802, recorded in SJL as received from Richmond on the 12th, has not been found.

William Duane & Son issued a printing of the complete CENSUS from the Apollo Press at Washington in 1802 (Shaw-Shoemaker, No. 3442).

BILL FOR THE MILITARY ESTABLISHMENT: in the House of Representatives on 20 Jan. James A. Bayard moved unsuccessfully to strike out the appointment of a BRIGADIER GENERAL and an aide-de-camp. The final bill passed in the House by a vote of 77 to 12 on 21 Jan. (National Intelligencer, 22 Jan. 1802; JHR, 4:56, 58-59; Henry Dearborn's Plan for Reorganizing the Army, [7 Dec. 1801]).

ANOTHER OF WHOM NOBODY HAS YET HEARD AT ALL: for John Armstrong, see TJ to Martha Jefferson Randolph, 17 Jan.

INTEREST IN THE TURNPIKE: a joint Maryland-Virginia project to fund and build a 40-mile turnpike from the head of the Potomac to the "nearest western navigation" gained support from citizens who subscribed for $50,000 in shares of $50 each. The general assemblies of both states passed legislation to incorporate a company for establishing the "Allegany Turnpike Road" and named subscription agents, including Charles Simms, William Hartshorne, John Mason, and Francis Deakins in Washington. According to his financial memoranda, TJ subscribed six shares "to the turnpike road on upper waters of Potomac in Virginia" at $50 each on 12 Mch. 1802 (Washington Federalist, 5 Jan. 1801 and 15 Feb. 1802; Shepherd, Statutes, 2:249-54, 387-8; Laws of Maryland Made and Passed at a Session of Assembly, Begun and Held at the City of Annapolis on Monday the Second of November, in the Year of Our Lord One Thousand Eight Hundred and One [Annapolis, 1802], chap. 45; MB, 2:1068).

For his correspondence with Enoch Edwards about the cost of GRAVEL roads, see Vol. 34:530; Vol. 35:115-16, 155.

LETTER FROM EDGEHILL: probably an undated letter from Martha Jefferson Randolph to TJ, not found but recorded in SJL as received from Edgehill on 20 Jan. 1802.

From Agnes Jackson

City of Washington January 22d. 1802

The Petition of Agnes Jackson of the City of Washington humbly sheweth that on the 8th day of November 1800 when the War Office was burnt, notwithstanding the vigorous exertions of the Neighbours and Spectators to check the progress of the fire, her dwelling House was soon enveloped in flames and sunk in ruins. That a few hours previous to the fire she had sustained the greatest loss this world can inflict, namely a tender, affectionate and provident Husband, who lay in the House a cold and lifeless Corpse insensible of the Conflicting passions and dangers that surrounded and rent the hearts of his loving Widow and tender Offspring. And thus when she was bereft of the greatest comfort this World could bestow, and the cup of misery filled to the brim,—deprived of the small remaining Comfort, her House and home, and thrown upon an unthinking World to struggle and support a number of small Children.

Your Petioner therefore implores your Excellency to compassionate her sufferings, and use your influence with the Grand Council of the Nation to make her such compensation for her losses as your Excellency shall in his wisdom and goodness think proper, and your Petitioner as in duty bound will pray &c.

RC (DLC); endorsed by TJ as received from Agnes Jackson on 27 Jan. and so recorded in SJL.

A FIRE in the 2100 block of Pennsylvania Avenue destroyed the War Department building owned by the hatter Joseph Hodgson, as well as an adjoining building belonging to Agnes Jackson's husband. Jonathan Jackson, a master carpenter who owned real estate in Washington and Georgetown, had worked on the government buildings prior to his death just six hours before the fire broke out. Although the cause of the conflagration remained unconfirmed, several newspaper and government reports concluded that it had probably originated in the fireplace of the Jackson house. The widow sold her remaining real estate but was still unable to settle with creditors. In 1813, she petitioned Congress for COMPENSATION for her burned house, claiming that a government officer had used the adjacent house as a public office, but she only received permission to withdraw the claim. Agnes Jackson never acquired compensation for her loss, unlike Joseph Hodgson's widow to whom an act of Congress awarded a $6,000 reimbursement in 1822 (Elaine C. Everly, "The Local Impact of the War Office Fire of 1800," *Washington History*, 12 [2000], 8-10; Elaine C. Everly and Howard H. Wehmann, "The War Office Fire of 1800," *Prologue*, 31 [1999], 22-35; *Gazette of the United States*, 11 Nov. 1800; JHR, 9:190, 199; Vol. 32:435-6n).

From William King

Sir   Washington 22 Jan 1802

permit me for a moment to arrest your attention from those great concerns which daily surround you—to one of small magnitude *Indeed* and which principaly respects my self.

a few days ago a Bill was agreed to by both Houses of Congress respecting a Library, in which I observe the appointment of Librarian devolves on your *Excellency.*—my residence being so convenient to the Capitol has Induced me to offer myself a candidate for that appointment;

not having the Honour of a personal aquaintance with you have requested the secretary of the Navy to interfere who obligingly requested me to make any use of his name on my behalf that was necessary—should you please (Sir) to make an Appointment in my favour nothing shall be wanting on my part to discharge the several dutys of the office with faithfullness. permitt me here sir to observe that altho I have shared with the United States in her revolutionary war greatly to the Injury of my fortune and Health I have never required either profitt, Honour, nor trust, (*this being my first application*). during the first administration I was much engaged in comercial concerns and too much disatisfied with late one to hold any place under it but under the present which is that of my choice I confess I should wish to be employed.

permitt me Sir to repeat that Mr Smith will most cheerfully satisfy every enquiry respecting me. and should responsability be required of me I am prepared on that score also.—I have the Honour to be (Sir)

Your Excellencys obt Hbl Servt   Wm King

RC (DNA: RG 59, LAR); addressed: "His Excellency The President of the United States"; endorsed by TJ as received 23 Jan. and "to be librarian" and so recorded in SJL.

From Hore Browse Trist

My Dear Sir,   Birdwood 22 Jan. 1802

I was honor'd by the present Post with yours of 17 Inst. The warm emotions which were excited on perusal of the friendly contents we can only feel—The sincere concern we have experienced since the first Impression of the necessity of a removal to the Missisipi Territory, has been very painful, & the nearer the prospect approaches of our departing from a neighbourhood where we have met with uniform attention—where the society exists which we would select from the world, & where our best & dearest friends reside, the more poignant are the sensations with which we are wounded—So fully have those causes operated on our feelings, that the duty a Parent owes to his family, that of bettering their future Prospects, could alone have induced to such a determination—

In a removal it will most certainly be my highest Gratification to bear with me some mark of your good opinion—I therefore accept your friendly proposal—your advice & the respectability attached to the Office of Secretary of the Missisipi Territory, are reasons the most ample for my so doing—I shall be able to proceed for that country as soon as I have closed some arrangements I have been making for the purchase of some negroes—I beg leave however to mention the situation of my Family is such—particularly that of *Mrs Trist*—that it will render their removal impracticable untill fall—

Among our most pleasing reflections when distant will be those of your friendship & good wishes, & we shall anxiously desire a continuance of your health & happiness—The Ladies of the family present you their affectionate remembrance & unite with me in sentiments of the highest respect
                                                    HORE BROWSE TRIST

RC (DLC); at foot of text: "Mr Jefferson"; endorsed by TJ as received 27 Jan. and so recorded in SJL.

Having fallen on financial hard times from unpaid loans and his purchase of Birdwood in Albemarle County, Trist decided on the NECESSITY OF A REMOVAL to the Mississippi Territory to reclaim his father's lands and make a new start. BEST & DEAREST FRIENDS: among whom were the families of William Bache and TJ's son-in-law, Thomas Mann Randolph. Trist accepted TJ's FRIENDLY PROPOSAL to become secretary of the territory, unaware that the position was not vacant.

In August 1802, he set out for the territorial capital although his family SITUATION, especially the pregnancy of his wife with their second child, prevented them from joining him until later. In November 1803, Trist was named collector for the district of Mississippi and inspector of revenue for the port of Fort Adams (Jane Flaherty Wells, "Thomas Jefferson's Neighbors: Hore Browse Trist of 'Birdwood' and Dr. William Bache of 'Franklin,'" *Magazine of Albemarle County History*, 47 [1989], 4, 6, 8; Madison, *Papers, Pres. Ser.*, 2:424-5; JEP, 1:454, 455; TJ to Elizabeth House Trist, 20 Mch. 1802).

From Thomas Claxton

HONORED SIR   Capitol, January 23d, 1802

A few days ago, I took the liberty of offering myself as a candidate for the office of Librarian, under certain conditions which I mentioned—At the time I wrote the letter I was much hurried with business, and was perhaps rather short in giving the reasons why I had not furnished myself with recommendations, which I perceive some of the applicants very industriously procuring at this period—I beg leave, therefore, at this time, to assign the real causes for the conduct I pursued—The first was, that where the person making application for an appointment, was so fortunate as to be personally known, it might appear improperly urgent to solicit and obtain the interference of others—Another was, that I believed you were acquainted with the circumstance of my conduct in the station I fill being generally approbated, both by the gentlemen of the Senate & House of Representatives—And I do assure you, Sir, that altho' I have passed six elections since I was first chosen, I have never lost one vote in any of them—One other reason was, that I did not wish to be troublesom— I flatter myself, Sir, the foregoing reasons for the method I took in making my application will shew that my intentions were as respectful as others who may come forward on this occasion—

Had the compensation granted in the law been sufficient to support a person without some other calling, I should not have made the application; but believing that no person can afford to pay that attention, which it seems to me will be requisite, unless he has some other support near the capitol, I took the liberty of offering my services—

I hope, Sir, you will pardon the trouble I have given you, and, if in what I have written there is any thing improper, I sincerely ask you to excuse the error

With Sentiments of the highest Respect I am, Sir Your Hble Svt

THOS CLAXTON

RC (DNA: RG 59, LAR); endorsed by TJ as received 23 Jan. and so recorded in SJL.

A FEW DAYS AGO: Claxton to TJ, 21 Jan.

From James Dinsmore

SIR   Monticello Jan. 23d. 1802

I Had the Honour of writing to you on the 1st Inst Since which nothing material has occurred here. the old Woman Junea is dead the rest of the family all well. Mr Oldham is putting up the Cornice round the South Piazza; & I am still enagaged in the Dineing room. the Composition ornaments; sash weights; Sash Cord & a box of glass Came to hand yesterday. the weights are not of the Size ordered. & will not answer for any of the new frames, (I beleive they will do for the old ones.) I expect you will have to use lead—as they will be of such a length if of Iron that they will not be got in to the boxes—

the floors in the plaistered rooms ought to be washed out: but as Critta is gone there is no person to undertake it. you will Please to signify your Pleasure on this subject—John Perrey is getting Plank for us in the upper edge of Fluvana—

I am sir with Respect

nails made from the 25th Dec. to the 16 Jan

℔

XVI d.	204.3.	⎫	
X.	119.3.	⎬	Amount of nails Sold from
VI.	93.	⎭	the 25th Dec to the 23d Jan
IV.	44		
	460.6.		

£37.12.11.$\frac{1}{2}$

Cash recd.   £1.11   4 $\frac{1}{2}$

FC (ViU: Monticello); in Dinsmore's hand; on same sheet as letters of 12 Dec. 1801, 1 Jan., and 12 Feb. 1802. Recorded in SJL as received 27 Jan.

OLD WOMAN JUNEA IS DEAD: on his list of slaves leased to John H. Craven in 1801, TJ canceled Juno's name and noted "d. 1801." Her name appears on TJ's first roll of slaves at Monticello prepared in 1774 (Betts, *Farm Book*, 5, 60; Vol. 32:164). CRITTA IS GONE: see Mary Jefferson Eppes to TJ, 6 Nov. 1801.

To Lewis Geanty

SIR   Washington Jan. 23. 1802.

I recieved last night your favor of the 15th. sincerely a friend to science, and to the promotion of it as the only means of relieving man from the tyranny of body and mind, I should have been happy to have been instrumental to your plans for this purpose. but my duties to the General government are so numerous, that I have been constrained to leave altogether to the states, or to the individuals of the states, those enterprizes which being local, respect them only. the promotion of science is one of those objects not confided to the general government by the grant of powers to them. it remains therefore to the states, who accordingly, each within themselves, are in the practice of establishing or encouraging scientific institutions. Accept my respect & best wishes.   TH: JEFFERSON

PrC (DLC); at foot of text: "M. Lewis Geanty. Baltimore"; endorsed by TJ in ink on verso.

From William Short

Paris Jan. 23. 1802

I had the honor of addressing you on the 18th. ulto. & did not intend to have troubled you again—It is at the particular request of M. de Liancourt that I take up my pen at present—He has been applied to by the agricultural society of Paris to procure from America the seeds of which the extensive list is here inclosed. He says in his letter to me "Je ne vois que M. Jefferson qui par ses rapports etendus dans toute l'Amerique & son obligeant souvenir pour la France puisse nous rendre ce service, auquel je mets du prix," & begs me therefore to sollicit your aid. But neither he or myself can desire that you should do more than to put this commission into such hands as will be most likely to execute it punctually on seeing that you take an interest in it.—Should there be any other seeds growing within our limits which are omitted here, it is requested that they should be added.—It is desired also that such of them as can be procured should arrive in France by the month of Jany. next. They might be addressed to the Consul at the port where they arrive who would forward them to Paris & give M. de Liancourt notice of it. I beg you to pay on my acct. the expences of this business in America.

As I have taken up my pen I cannot omit mentioning to you that I have not yet heard from Mr Barnes—His silence is so extraordinary & so contrary to mercantile usage, that I do not attempt to explain it—I have nothing to add to what I said in the letter which I took the liberty of inclosing you for him. it is reduced to a certainty that he does not intend to write me, or send me the continuation of his account after having so long witheld it, & after so many of my letters, some of which I know he received, it is perfectly useless that I should write him again. I could add nothing to what I said so long ago & which has remained without effect. When he wrote me in March there was already more delay than there ought to have been in vesting the monies which he had on hand—I know not as yet whether he has since vested it or how he has disposed of the quarterly reciepts he has been since making—It is evident of itself, & I had moreover expressed to him, that the cash should be laid out immediately on being recieved—This would be the only way of repairing the loss of the partial re-imbursements of the 6. p cts. It really gives me pain that Mr Barnes should have so totally neglected the promise he made me, as it obliges me thus to trouble you. As you suppose that he sends me the acct. of his proceedings it is possible that you may have relied on that idea, & not recieved it either. I think it therefore indispensable to make known to you the state of things between him & me.—I beg pardon a thousand times for still troubling you, & hope you will recieve assurances of the perfect respect with which I have the honor to be, dear Sir, your most obedt. & humble servant.   W: SHORT

RC (PHi); at foot of text: "T. Jefferson Prest. of the U.S."; endorsed by TJ as received 4 Apr. and so recorded in SJL. FC (DLC: Short Papers); a summary in Short's epistolary record; a note by Short, "(one page & sent to de le M.)," probably indicates that he sent the letter through Delamotte at Le Havre; an additional note by Short states that the letter went by the *John*, sailing for Baltimore on 12 Feb.; according to the Baltimore *Republican; or, Anti-Democrat* of 5 Apr. 1802, the schooner left Le Havre on 14 Feb. and was at Baltimore by 3 Apr. Enclosure, not found, enclosed in TJ to John Bartram, Jr., 5 Apr. 1802; see also Short to TJ, 3 Apr. 1802.

JE NE VOIS QUE M. JEFFERSON: "I do not see anyone but Mr. Jefferson who would be able to render this service, which I value so much, given his extensive connections throughout America, and his positive memories of France."

From John Cleves Symmes

Washington City. 23rd of January 1802

Pardon me Sir, if in this instance I depart from the prescribed mode of addressing the President on a subject of Territorial concern, through Mr. Maddison the proper organ of State business.   My communication being of a delatory nature against the first Magistrate of the Northwestern Territory, whose prompt removal from office rests solely with the President: it would seem only necessary, Sir, correctly to inform the conscience of the President with regard to the mal-administration of Arthur St. Clair esquire governor of said territory, in order to invite a measure so desirable to thousands of the Inhabitants of the western country, as that of his being dismissed from his government. To incline the President to be propitious in this respect to the wishes of the people—I humbly conceive it my duty, Sir, to sketch out some of the leading features in the public character of governor St. Clair.—A few of which are the following.

By constitution a despot, as well as from long imperious habits of commanding, he has become unsufferably arbitrary.

Like other tyrants, he places his confidence for advice and support, in the weak and the guileful of the citizens, who misguide and disgrace him.

The prosperity of the territory is, and always has been, a secondary consideration with him. literally his will is law; and measures (however eligible, considered either as convenient, honorary, or pecuniary) which do not concentrate their good effects in his family or among his favorites, are altogether inadmissible with him.

He is at war with those who do not approach him with adulation on their tongue.

He hesitates not, to sacrifice the best interests of the territory, when they come in competition with his partial aims.

Though of courtly exterior; his heart, if judged of by the tongue, is illiberal beyond a sample.

Destitute of gratitude, he abhors the government that feeds him:—the public or private hand that relieves him in distress, confers no obligation.

Though a commentator of the sedition law, is seditious himself.

Is he commissioned to guide the citizens confided to his charge, to their true interests? he wantonly misleads them.—to protect? he invades their rights.—to harmonize? he irritates dissension.—to revere a republican form of government? he raises the sneer and sends it round the board.

His pious frauds practised on the public, are not calculated for the meridian of his own altars. —there the presiding deities are of grecian Mythology.

Wanting application to his official duties, which lie neglected from year to year;—fain would he arrogate to himself the superintendency of the judiciary.

Outrageous, if a citizen charged with the murder of an Indian, be acquitted by a jury of the country.—he can calmly look on and see citizens murdered by Indians, without one effort of the executive to bring the murderer to a trial.

Notorious for his military blunders,—if we believe him correct, and could he again command; his talents supersedes the necessity of three major, and six brigadier generals, although the Militia law requires them.

Wiser in his own conceit, than the other two branches of the Legislature, collective and unanimous; he withholds his assent to bills of the most salutary nature.

Under his long administration the people are not, nor have they ever been satisfied, and many detesting him, have fled the territory.

Although in a colonial situation, the people are proud of the right they have, to resort to the general government, as they now do, for relief from his oppressive and undue exercise of the executive power.

Do these imputations need proof?—let fetters, prisons, flames, human-bones and tears bear testimony; while neglected french-rights, imbecility of Magistrates of his appointment, executive deception, unequal tenures in office, his usurped prerogatives, and ill placed patronage, fill the Northwestern territory with murmurs, deep—awful—dangerous; while his distracted government totters to its foundation.

All of which, with sincerity and truth, to the President of the United States, is most respectfully submitted, by his Obedient humble servant. JOHN CLEVES SYMMES.

RC (DLC); at head of text: "To Thomas Jefferson esquire, President of the United States"; endorsed by TJ as received 25 Jan. and so recorded in SJL.

From Mary Jefferson Eppes

Eppington jan. 24th [1802]

It makes me blush to think of the length of time which has elaps'd since I wrote to you last My Dear Papa, deprived for 6 weeks of the use of my hands, I was after recovering them so closely employ'd with work which during that time had greatly accumulated that without intending it it has been postponed 'till now, I have only thought the more of you My Dear Papa, of that I hope you need never be assur'd, that you are of all most dear to my heart & most constantly in my thoughts. with how much regret have I look'd back on the last two months that I was with you, more as I fear it will allways be the case now in your summer visits, to have a crowd,[1] & in the spring I am afraid it not be in my power to go up. it would make me most happy to go to Washington to see you. but I have been so little accustom'd to be in as much[2] company as I should be in there[3] to recieve the civilitys & attentions which as your daughter I should meet with & return, that I am sensible it is best for me to remain where I am. I have not heard from Edgehill since I left it, Mr. Eppes wrote once to my sister when I was unable to do it.   but I must bid you adieu. My dear Papa, could I be as certain of the continuance of your good health as you may now be of mine I should endeavour to be satisfied in not hearing from you oftener, but while you are devoting your days & nights to the business of your country I must feel anxious & fearful that your health will suffer by it. Adieu once more my dear Papa I shall write to you once more from here, my little son is getting much better tho' he still engrosses so much of my time that it is scarcely in my power to do any thing else. he is cutting teeth now which makes him more fretful than usual

Adieu yours with the most tender affection   M EPPES.

RC (MHi); partially dated; endorsed by TJ as a letter of 24 Jan. 1802 received on 31 Jan. and so recorded in SJL.

SINCE I WROTE TO YOU LAST: Mary Jefferson Eppes to TJ, 6 Nov. 1801.

USE OF MY HANDS: while the precise nature of Mary's ailment is not known, it may have been related to breast inflammation. She suffered similar post-partum complications in February 1800 (Bear, *Family Letters*, 217; Vol. 31:377; TJ to Mary Jefferson Eppes, 14 Dec. 1801).

[1] Preceding four words and comma interlined.

[2] Preceding four words interlined.

[3] Preceding six words interlined in place of "that I [. . .] I could [. . .]."

From Richard Brent

Monday Morning [25 Jan. 1802]

Richard Brent presents his compliments to the President of the United States and will if in his power give himself the pleasure of dining with the President on Wednesday next but such is the precarious state of his health that he is at all times unable to say one day in advance with any tolerable certainty whether if an opportunity is offered he will have it in his power to enjoy the company of those whose person he most respects and whose society he most values and he can with truth declare that amid the various privations and inquietudes to which a long indisposition has exposed him nothing has been a more abundant source of uneasiness than a consciousness of that incapacity which it frequently produces on his part to evince by a proper return of civility and respectful attentions the gratitude he feels and the high sense he entertains for the honor done by the attentions (far exceeding any thing he had a right to expect) which the President and others who he highly respects have been pleased to discover towards him   RICHARD BRENT

RC (MHi); partially dated; endorsed by TJ as a letter of 25 Jan. 1802 received on the 26th and so recorded in SJL.

Brent was serving his third term as a representative from Virginia (Vol. 32:460n).

From Ebenezer Elmer

Washington Jany. 25. 1802

The President will be pleased to excuse the freedom I take of recommending Dr. Cozens of this place as a Gentleman of good principles & character, very[1] qualified, in my opinion, to take charge, as Librarian, of the books provided for the use of both Houses of Congress.

I am with very great respect The Presidents Obedt. Humbl Servt.

EBEN. ELMER

RC (DNA: RG 59, LAR); endorsed by TJ as received 26 Jan. and "Doctr. Cozens to be librarian" and so recorded in SJL.

Ebenezer Elmer (1752-1843) of Cumberland County, New Jersey, was a founder of the Society of the Cincinnati and a veteran of both the Revolutionary War and War of 1812. Trained in medicine by his brother Jonathan Elmer, he was active in state and national politics, was first elected to the New Jersey assembly in 1789, and served as its speaker for three separate years. A Republican representative to the Seventh, Eighth, and Ninth Congresses, he was also appointed customs collector of Bridgeton, New Jersey, in 1808, and served as vice president of Burlington College (DAB; *Biog. Dir. Cong.*).

DR. COZENS: William R. Cozens, originally of New Jersey, studied medicine under Jonathan Elmer, was a member of the Philadelphia Medical Society, and received his degree in 1791 from the University of Pennsylvania (Cozens, *An Inaugural Dissertation on the Chemical Properties of Atmospheric Air* [Philadelphia, 1791; Evans, No. 23296]; David Stone to TJ, 26 Jan. 1802).

[1] MS: "every."

From Albert Gallatin

[25 Jan. 1802]

The within is written by the republican Senator & Members of Assembly in Pennsylvania from that County which includes Presquile & Allegheny.

Foster is one of the two only officers of customs who has not rendered his accounts for 1800 & is not removed.   A. G.

RC (DNA: RG 59, LAR); undated; address sheet torn; addressed: "The Presi[dent]"; endorsed by TJ as received from the Treasury Department on 25 Jan. and so recorded in SJL; also endorsed by TJ: "Thos. Forster Collector at the port of Erie. to be removed." Enclosure: John Kelso, John Cochran, and William McArthur to Gallatin, Lancaster, 13 Jan. 1802, requesting, on behalf of the "great bulk" of the inhabitants of western Pennsylvania, that Thomas Forster be removed as collector at the port of Erie (Presque Isle), for being partial to the British and declaring in "Public that he would exert himself to keep down every man that possessed Republican principles"; urging that the office be abolished "because the duties collected will not pay the salary," the writers note that if that is not done they hope for the chance to recommend "a suitable person" (RC in same; in Kelso's hand, signed by all; endorsed by TJ: "Kelso & others to mr Gallatin. to remove Forster Collector of Erie").

William McArthur, a REPUBLICAN state senator, represented Crawford, Erie, Venango, Mercer, and Warren Counties. John Kelso and John Cochran were not members of the Pennsylvania House of Representatives in 1801-02 (*Journal of the Senate of the Commonwealth of Pennsylvania, Which Commenced at Lancaster, on Tuesday, the First Day of December, in the Year of our Lord, One Thousand Eight Hundred and One* [Lancaster, 1801, i.e. 1802], 4; *Journal of the First Session of the Twelfth House of Representatives of the Commonwealth of Pennsylvania* [Lancaster, 1801, i.e. 1802], 3-5).

On 12 Feb. 1802, Thomas Forster (FOSTER) wrote Pennsylvania congressman John A. Hanna, who had informed the collector of Gallatin's complaint about his accounts. Forster noted that he had forwarded his accounts through 30 Sep. 1801 by mail on 6 Nov. and his quarterly report through 31 Dec. 1801 on 14 Jan. He could give no reason why they had not been received. The collector requested that Hanna contact Comptroller John Steele and if the accounts had not yet arrived he would "forward others immediately." He also inquired whether the congressman would "confer an obligation on me by informing Mr. Gallatin of the truth of this business." Hanna transmitted Forster's letter, which included a response to local political charges made against him, to the Treasury secretary. Forster remained collector at Presque Isle during TJ's presidency (*Biog. Dir. Cong.*; Gallatin, *Papers*, 6:692-3; 23:653).

From Benjamin Hichborn

SIR   Boston 25th Januy. 1802—

I intended to have written you a line the moment after my arrival, but find the State of the public mind here, very much in unison with that manifested on the Road & in all the great towns between Washington & Boston, I have waited a few days, in hopes that some occurrence might happen to indicate more precisely what we have to expect—hitherto the general Opinion seems to have rested with inactive Complacency on the state of public affairs, & is rather disposed to receive impressions & follow the impulse which may be given to it, than to lead in any thing—our Friends have been divided for some time, upon the Expediency of moving an Address, but it is now agreed that the attempt ought to be made, let the Issue be as it may— I presume the Motion will be made tomorrow in the house of Representatives, & we have great Confidence in it's Success—we shall in a few days make a similar one in the Senate & are not without hopes of a favorable termination; some benefits we are sure must result from it—the Subject will be bro't into public discussion & our Enemies compelled to unmask—I cannot add a word more by this Eveng Mail, but shall trouble you again in a few days—

I am with esteem yours   BENJN HICHBORN

RC (DLC); endorsed by TJ as received 3 Feb. and so recorded in SJL.

ATTEMPT OUGHT TO BE MADE: according to the Boston *Independent Chronicle*, on 26 Jan., Perez Morton, a Republican in the Massachusetts House of Representatives, sought leave to lay the following motion on the table: "That a committee be raised to prepare and report, an ADDRESS to the President of the United States, expressive of the confidence which this House entertain in his Integrity and Patriotism, and in the Wisdom of the measures of his administration." After debate on the question, leave to bring in the motion was defeated. When Morton asked for a reconsideration of the question, the House voted to consider the motion in a week. Noting that opposition to the motion arose "from the general terms in which it was expressed," on 2 Feb., Morton introduced and read a revised motion: "That a Committee be raised to prepare an Address to the President of the United States,—To announce to him the high-sense this House entertain of his important services in the course of the American revolution, and of the ability and fidelity, with which he sustained the various subordinate duties committed to his trust, under the government of the United States;—To express to him our cordial approbation of those republican principles, which he has avowed to the world shall be made the basis of his Presidential administration;—To thank him for the prompt and seasonable protection he has given to our commerce against the Barbary Powers—and for those measures of retrenchment and oeconomy, which he has begun and recommended, as the best means of supporting the public faith, and lessening the burthens of the people;—To assure him of the confidence, which the House possess, of the disposition of their constituents, to support him in all the measures of his administration which shall tend to cherish the interests of agriculture, commerce, the liberal arts, and our infant manufactures, to secure internal peace and social order, to diffuse equal justice and general information among the citizens, to maintain the public faith, to promote oeconomy in the public ex-

pense, to preserve sacred and entire the constitution of the Federal government in the purity of its principles, the rights of the respective State governments, and the union of the whole, as the ark of their safety;—and to congratulate him on the restoration of peace in Europe." During the ensuing debate, the Federalists noted they were induced to oppose the address and to withhold their "confidence from the President" for several reasons. They disagreed with TJ's decision to withhold Ray Greene's commission as district judge for Rhode Island, with the appointment of Gallatin as Treasury secretary instead of "a native American," with the repair of the *Berceau* "upon which a large sum of money had been expended by his order without legislative authority," and with TJ's recommendations calling for the abolition of internal taxes, which they believed would operate "unequally upon the northern state," and for the revision of the judiciary and naturalization laws. The opposition also expressed a "general repugnance to the principle of addresses." The Republicans answered the charges point by point. On the stand against addresses, the Republicans charged: "having heretofore been in the habit of addressing the Chief Magistrate, as the father of the nation and object of our respect & veneration, it would betray a spirit unworthy of the Legislature of Massachusetts to refuse this customary tribute of respect to Mr. Jefferson, merely because he was not elected by our votes, and that such a conduct would betray a total desertion of those principles of Federalism, of which they had heretofore boasted, and would convince the world that it was not the principle, but the name by which we were governed." At the close of the debate, the House approved a motion, 142 to 92, to postpone consideration of the address until the next session of the legislature (Boston *Independent Chronicle*, 28 Jan., 4 Feb. 1802; Vol. 31:454-5).

Hichborn brought a SIMILAR resolution before the state SENATE on Friday, 5 Feb., calling for the appointment of a committee to prepare an address to the president "congratulating him on his accession to the Chief Magistracy of the Union; declaring our unequivocal approbation of the true system of republican principles, which he has assumed as the basis of his administration; and assuring him of our cordial support in effectuating the great objects of national economy, without which, no people can long retain their morality or freedom." The Senate debated the resolution for two days, before voting 14 to 19 against the address. The editors of the *Independent Chronicle* noted that they had "seldom witnessed in a deliberative assembly, a debate conducted with more candor, intelligence and manly reasoning than was displayed on this occasion by those in favor of the motion." On 11 Feb., the newspaper published the substance of the debate in the Senate, as they had earlier that of the House (Boston *Independent Chronicle*, 4, 8, 11 Feb. 1802).

From Edward C. Nicholls

January 25th. 1802.

Sir!   City of Washington.

With the utmost deference and Respect, I take to myself the Liberty of addressing You by Letter.

My Friends have advis'd me to offer myself, as the Superintendant of the Library about to be established by Act of the Legislature.— Having devoted the greater portion of my Life to Books, it wou'd afford me much Happiness to return to their Society, and become their watchful Guardian.

I am unwilling to occupy your important moments, by presenting recommendatory Testimonials, for your perusal: I pray you to be informed, that I am not unknown to the Honorable Messrs. Maddison, Rt. Smith and Gallatin.—If I shall be so fortunate, as to receive the Appointment, I engage to discharge the duties[1] attached to it, whatever they may be, with care & Fidelity.

I do myself the Honor, to subscribe myself Sir! yr. respectful, and Obt Servant.   Edwd. Nicholls

RC (DNA: RG 59, LAR); at head of text: "The President of the United States"; endorsed by TJ as received 25 Jan. and "to be librarian" and so recorded in SJL.

Born into a prominent Catholic family of Cornwall, England, Edward Church Nicholls immigrated to Maryland after being renounced by his family for his refusal to enter the priesthood. He settled in Prince George's County, where he briefly taught school before being admitted to the Maryland bar. In July 1801, Nicholls was hired as a Treasury Department clerk, but he resigned in May 1802 in order to return to his legal practice. Later that same year, he unsuccessfully applied to TJ for an appointment as a bankruptcy commissioner. After traveling to England in 1803 to secure an inheritance, Nicholls returned to America and settled in Louisiana, where he resumed his legal career and obtained appointments as clerk of the governor's court and as a judge of Attakapas County (*Louisiana Historical Quarterly*, 6 [1923], 5-7; *Terr. Papers*, 9:286, 547, 598; Madison, *Papers, Sec. of State Ser.*, 6:338-9; Gallatin, *Papers*, 5:330; 6:943; William Kilty to TJ, 4 June 1802; Nicholls to TJ, 7 June 1802).

[1] MS: "dutchies."

From William Barnwell

HONOURED SIR   Philadelphia January 26th. 1802

Be pleased to excuse my presumption in addressing you, and to accept of the small compliment of a book, from some parts of which it is hoped, you will find some amusement if not information.

Notwithstanding many disappointments, it affords me much consolation, to live under a goverment; the head of which exhibits the principles of a genuine Republican, neither is the liberality of your sentiments towards my poor fugitive countrymen less agreeable to me who has now been nine years among the number. nor is your Philosophical and Literary turn less admired by one who has passed many years in Physical Pursuits I am Sir

with humble respect   WM. BARNWELL

RC (DLC); endorsed by TJ as received 1 Feb. and so recorded in SJL. Enclosure: William Barnwell, *Physical Investigations & Deductions, From Medical and Surgical Facts. Relative to the Causes, Nature and Remedies of the Diseases of a Warm and Vitiated Atmosphere, From Climate, Local Situation, or Season of the Year. Together with an Historical Introduction to Physianthropy: or the Experimental Philosophy of Human Life: That of Diseases, and Also of Remedies* (Philadelphia, 1802; Sowerby, No. 964).

William Barnwell arrived in Philadelphia from Ireland around 1792, after serving as a physician with the British East India Company. Specializing in the study and treatment of tropical diseases, he was elected to the American Philosophical Society in 1802. Two years later, TJ appointed Barnwell physician of the marine hospital at New Orleans, where he served until his removal in 1812 (APS, *Proceedings*, 22, pt. 3 [1884], 320; Gallatin, *Papers*, 26:53; Caspar Wistar to TJ, 10 Apr. 1802; TJ to Gallatin, 11 Feb. 1804; Gallatin to TJ, 16 Apr. 1804).

A letter of 3 Feb. from TJ to Barnwell is recorded in SJL but has not been found.

To James Madison and Family

Tuesday Jan. 26. 1802.

Th: Jefferson requests the favor of Mr. Mrs. Madison's & family's company to dinner the day after tomorrow at half after three oclock.—

RC (NN: Emmet Collection); in Meriwether Lewis's hand.

To Wilson Cary Nicholas

DEAR SIR   Washington Jan. 26. 1802.

The inclosed paper was put into my hands by mr Madison to fill up some dates, but I have been so engaged as to do little to it; and supposing you will want it to-day I send it as it is. to that list may be added the appointment of Gouvr. Morris to negociate with the court of London, by letter written & signed by Genl. Washington, & Dav. Humphreys to negociate with Lisbon by letter. commissions were not given in form because no ministers had yet been sent here by those courts: but the powers were given them, and half the salary. (as they were not to display a diplomatic rank, half salary was thought sufficient.) but they were compleatly officers on salaries, and no notice given the Senate till afterwards.

The phrase in the constitution is 'to fill up all vacancies that may happen during the recess of the Senate.' this may mean 'vacancies that may happen to be' or 'may happen to fall.' it is certainly susceptible of both constructions, and we took the practice of our predecessors as the commentary established. this was done without deliberation; and we have not before taken an exact view of the precedents. they more than cover our cases. but I think some of them are not justifiable. we propose to take the subject into consideration, and to fix on such a rule of conduct, within the words of the constitution, as may save the government from serious injury, & yet restrain the Executive within limits which might admit mischief.—you will observe the cases of Read & Putnam, where the persons nominated declining to accept, the vacancy remained unfilled & had happened before the recess. it will be said these vacancies did not remain unfilled by the intention of the Executive, who had, by nomination, endeavored to fill them. so in our cases, they were not unfilled by the intention of the successor, but by the omission of the predecessor. Chas. Lee informed me that whenever an office became vacant so short a time before Congress rose, as not to give an opportunity of enquiring for a proper character, they let it lie always till recess. however this discussion is too long for a letter. we must establish a correct & well digested rule of practice, to bind up our successors as well as ourselves. if we find that any of our cases go beyond the limits of such a rule, we must consider what will be the best way of preventing their being considered as authoritative examples. in the mean time I think it would be better to give the subject the go-by for the present, that we may have time to consider and to do what will be best for the general safety. health & respect   TH: JEFFERSON

P.S. when you are done with the inclosed paper I shall be very glad to recieve it again to copy it for deliberation.

RC (LNT: George H. and Katherine M. Davis Collection); addressed: "Wilson C. Nicholas of the Senate." PrC (DLC); in ink at foot of first page: "W. C. Nicholas." Enclosure not found.

SUPPOSING YOU WILL WANT IT TO-DAY: on 26 Jan., the Senate confirmed all of TJ's interim appointments except the justices of the peace for the District of Columbia (JEP, 1:405). On 13 Oct. 1789, President Washington sent instructions and a letter of credence to Gouverneur MORRIS, who was traveling in France, for his negotiations WITH THE COURT OF LONDON. Since Morris was an unofficial envoy, Washington did not seek Senate confirmation of his mission (Washington, *Papers, Pres. Ser.*, 4:179-83; 5:117-9). On 11 Aug. 1790, TJ sent instructions to David HUMPHREYS for his secret mission to Lisbon. Humphreys's allowance was $2,250 per year (same, 6:217-20; Vol. 17:125-7). For the events that led to Humphreys's nomination as minister to Portugal on 18 Feb. 1791, see JEP, 1:74-5. PHRASE IN THE CONSTITUTION: Article 2, Section 2. As secretary of state in 1792, TJ sought Attorney General Edmund Randolph's opinion on the constitutional provisions for recess appoint-

ments. Randolph responded that the "Spirit of the Constitution" was that interim appointments should be limited to cases where a vacancy occurred because an officer had resigned or died while Congress was in recess, or to a position remaining unfilled because an appointee declined the office but did not send notification until Congress had adjourned (see Vol. 24:165-7).

CASES OF READ & PUTNAM: probably the interim appointments of John Read and Rufus Putnam. On 29 Nov. 1797, President Adams sought the Senate's approval of the appointment of Read as agent for the U.S. to settle claims under Article 6 of the Jay Treaty, in place of Charles Hall of Pennsylvania, who had declined the appointment. Adams had appointed Hall on 6 July, four days before Congress recessed. In December 1796, Washington sought Senate approval of Putnam's appointment as surveyor general. The president had first appointed Simeon De Witt on 28 May, but even a month after Congress had adjourned on 1 June, Washington did not know whether De Witt had accepted the offer or not (JEP, 1:212-3, 216-7, 248-50, 252; Fitzpatrick, *Writings*, 35:106).

From Wilson Cary Nicholas

DEAR SIR   Janry. 26th. 1802

I have had the pleasure to receive your notes of this date, with their enclosures the subject was not acted upon to day, nor do I presume it will be for several days. in the mean time I hope to have the pleasure of conversing with you more fully upon the subject, to which your notes refer.

I am Dear Sir with the greatest respect your hum. Servt.

W. C. NICHOLAS

The papers shall be returned, as you request.

RC (DLC); endorsed by TJ. Recorded in SJL as received 26 Jan.

To Joseph H. Nicholson and Rebecca Nicholson

Tuesday Jan. 26. 1802.

Th: Jefferson requests the favor of The Honble. Mr. & Mrs. Nicholson's company to dinner the day after tomorrow at half after three oclock, or at whatever later hour the House may rise.

RC (DLC: Shippen Family Papers); in Meriwether Lewis's hand; addressed: "The Honble Mr. Nicholson"; endorsed.

Rebecca Lloyd, daughter of Edward Lloyd of Annapolis and of "Wye house," near Easton, Maryland, married Joseph H. Nicholson in 1793 (DAB, 13:505).

From David Stone

Dear Sir,   Washington 26th January 1802

At the request of Doctor William R Cozens I use the freedom to lay before you the two Letters enclosed—the one from Doctor Priestly to Doctor Cozens—the other from the Reverend Mr Wiley Master of the Columbian Academy at Georgetown to me. I have had the pleasure of an acquaintance with Doctor Cozens only a few Days but understand he is at present engaged in the practice of Physic, residing at Georgetown, and means shortly to remove to the Capitol Hill.

I am with the highest Respect and Esteem Your Obedient & Humble Servant   DAVID STONE

RC (DNA: RG 59, LAR); endorsed by TJ as received 26 Jan. and "Doctr. Wm. R. Cozens to be librarian" and so recorded in SJL. Enclosures: (1) Joseph Priestley to William R. Cozens, Northumberland, 18 June 1801, expressing his confidence in Cozens's qualifications for office, but refusing "to solicit Mr Jefferson on the subject"; if the president learns of Priestley's "good opinion" of Cozens as a physician and in other respects, then "he may of his own accord be disposed to favour you"; otherwise, Priestley declines to add "unnecessarily" to the burdens already affiliated with TJ's high office. (2) David Wiley to David Stone, Georgetown, 18 Jan. 1802, introducing Cozens as a former neighbor in Northumberland, and now as a neighbor and friend in Georgetown; Cozens wishes to be appointed librarian of Congress and already

has letters of introduction from George Logan, John Mason, Andrew Gregg, and John A. Hanna; Wiley recommends Cozens as "well qualified, and as one whose attention to the business might be depended upon" (RCs in same).

David WILEY, a Princeton graduate and Presbyterian minister, spent several years serving congregations in Pennsylvania before becoming MASTER OF THE COLUMBIAN ACADEMY AT GEORGETOWN around 1801. He later edited the *Agricultural Museum*, the first agricultural periodical in the United States, and served as mayor of Georgetown from 1811 to 1812 (DAB; Ruth L. Woodward and Wesley Frank Craven, *Princetonians, 1784-1790: A Biographical Dictionary* [Princeton, 1991], 313-16).

From Richard Willson

Sir   City of Washington Jany 26. 1802

The appointment of Librarian being about to be made, I am impelled by the deranged state of my finances to solicit the appointment:—and not having the honor of a Personal Acquaintance with your Excellency, I beg leave to refer to Joseph H Nicholson Esqr. of the House of Representatives, and Robert Wright Esqr. of the Senate, for any information requisite on the subject, and relative to my qualifications—

I have the honor to be with sentiments of high respect Your Excellencys Obedt. Hum Servt   RICHARD WILLSON

RC (DNA: RG 59, LAR); endorsed by TJ as received on 27 Jan. and "to be librarian" and so recorded in SJL.

TJ received a 26 Jan. letter from Joseph H. NICHOLSON on the 27th, which he recorded in SJL with the notation "Richd. Wilson to be librarian," but the letter has not been found. Also missing is a letter from Robert WRIGHT to TJ of 27 Jan., recorded in SJL as received the 28th, but without a notation. For Willson's QUALIFICATIONS for a government appointment, see Willson to TJ, 15 Oct. 1801.

From James Currie

DEAR SIR   Richmond Jany. 27th. 1802

I had the honor to receive your last favor in due course of Post with the enclosures—I thank you kindly for your present of Dr Jenners Publication, which when properly appreciated by due regard, to the circumstances he dwells so long & impressively upon cannot fail to prove a blessing of the first grade to the human Species, I this day returned all your papers respecting your matters to D Ross lately submitted for Decision & among them the Oxford PB & Richmond accts together with DR's private acct & that with Keys likewise, I recd from Geo. Jefferson $50 on yr acct & 50$ from D Ross which I tenderd to Mr Wickham (being first in the nomination of the referees) for himself & the Other Gentn. & which after seeing the Other Gentlemen was returned to me, & saying they never did intend to accept of any pecuniary Consideration for their opinion & decision I Urged it as being more agreeable to you than that their time as professional Gentlemen should be employed on your account without some Compensation, they Urged their Original intention in which I was obliged to acquiesce, & accordingly returnd the 50$ to each of the Gentlemen I recd them from I am glad the business is brought to an

End. in magnitude so little, claiming the serious attention of either party, had it could possibly have been adjusted by themselves, so capable in any thing assimilated, to this, when Others should only be Concerned— pardon this digression. if you please the impressions of my mind while I am writing—you will please direct the papers in Mr Jefferson's hands—to remain there or be Sent where you choose them to be. with tenders of my best Services—in any thing wherein I can be usefull to you

I always am with Sentiments of the most respectfull Esteem & regard Dr sir your most Obedt H. Servt.   JAMES CURRIE

RC (MHi); endorsed by TJ as received 31 Jan. and so recorded in SJL.

LAST FAVOR: TJ to Currie, 14 Jan. PB: Petersburg.

To Richard Cutts

Th: Jefferson requests the favour of *The Hon'ble Mr Cutts* to dine with him *the day after tomorrow* at half after three, or at whatever later hour the house may rise.

The favour of an answer is asked.

Wednesday Jan'y 27th 1802

RC (ICHi); printed form, with blanks filled by an unidentified hand reproduced in italics.

Richard Cutts (1771-1845) belonged to a prominent family of merchants and Republicans from Saco, Maine. After graduating from Harvard in 1790, he engaged in commercial pursuits before being elected to the Massachusetts legislature in 1799. Elected to Congress as a Republican in 1801, Cutts served in the House of Representatives until 1813. He served as superintendent general of military supplies from 1813 to 1817, then as second comptroller of the U.S. Treasury from 1817 to 1829. He married Anna Payne,

the younger sister of Dolley Payne Madison, in 1804 (*Biog. Dir. Cong.*; Paul Goodman, *The Democratic-Republicans of Massachusetts: Politics in a Young Republic* [Cambridge, Mass., 1964], 121-2; David B. Mattern and Holly C. Shulman, eds., *The Selected Letters of Dolley Payne Madison* [Charlottesville, 2003], 41).

The above document is one of the earliest surviving examples of the printed invitations that TJ used to invite guests to dine at the President's House. They contained blank spaces in which the name of the guest (or guests) and the date of the dinner could be inserted by hand (see illustration).

From Abraham Du Buc de Marentille

Elizabeth-town New-Jersey
Monsieur le Président,   le 27. Janvier. 1802.

Ce n'est point au président des états-unis de l'amérique que je prends la liberté de m'adresser directement, mais à Monsieur Jefferson comme philosophe, ami des arts et des sciences et de tout ce qui tend au bien de l'humanité. Je ne doute pas, Monsieur le Président, que dans le cours de vos travaux et de vos réflexions une observation intéressante sur la marine ne se soit quelquefois présentée à votre esprit et que vous ne vous soyez dit—Comment se peut-il que les progrès étonnans de l'art naval n'aient encore rien enfanté pour le salut des naufragés. Cette réflexion m'a conduit à des idées qui me paroissent d'une grande importance, et le mémoire ci-joint vous fera voir en deux mots ce que j'ai imaginé. Je prétends sauver, Monsieur le président, les neuf dixièmes des malheureux qui périssent à la mer. Je vous demande très humblement la faveur de votre influence et de votre protection pour le succès de ma demande; et sous vos auspices, Monsieur le président, le monde maritime va voir naître une époque intéressante.

Monsieur Jonathan dayton Sénateur des états-unis a bien voulu se charger de présenter au Congrès ma pétition. il paroit qu'une discussion élevée sur la concession des privilèges lui a fait juger convenable d'en suspendre la présentation. J'ose solliciter de votre bonté, Monsieur le président, de vouloir bien accorder quelque intérêt au succès de ma demande sur un sujet d'une aussi grande importance.

Je suis avec respect, Monsieur le président, Votre très humble et très obéissant serviteur   Du Buc Marentille

EDITORS' TRANSLATION

Elizabeth, New Jersey
Mister President,   27 Jan. 1802

It is not to the president of the United States of America that I take the liberty of addressing myself directly, but to Mr. Jefferson, the philosopher, friend of the arts and sciences and of everything that tends towards the good of humanity. I do not doubt, Mister President, that in the course of your labors and reflections, an interesting observation about the navy has presented itself sometimes to your mind and that you have said to yourself, "How is it possible that the astonishing progress of naval art has not yet given birth to anything for the rescue of the shipwrecked?" That reflection led me to some ideas that seem to me to be of great importance, and the attached memorandum will show you in two words what I have imagined. I claim to save, Mister President, nine-tenths of the unfortunates who perish at sea. I ask you very humbly for the favor of your influence and protection for the success of my request; and under your auspices, Mister President, the maritime world will see the birth of an interesting epoch.

Mr. Jonathan Dayton, United States senator, has been willing to take on the task of presenting my petition to the Congress. It seems that a serious discussion on the concession of privileges has caused him to deem it appropriate to defer its presentation. I dare to solicit your kindness, Mister President, to be willing to grant some interest to the success of my request on a subject of such great importance.

I am respectfully, Mister President, your very humble and very obedient servant   Du Buc Marentille

RC (DLC); endorsed by TJ as received 30 Jan. and so recorded in SJL. Enclosure: Memorial of Du Buc de Marentille to Congress, asking for patents on his inventions of a lifeboat, a life raft, and a distress signal "for the preservation of the lives of those who traverse the seas" (MS in DLC: TJ Papers, 127:22016-17; in Du Buc de Marentille's hand, signed; dated "the .   . november. 1802," but very likely the memorial referred to in the letter above).

Abraham Du Buc de Marentille, according to a later letter to TJ, had been an officer with the French army at the siege of Yorktown. He was probably in the West Indies after that, and lived in the United States beginning in 1792. His petition to Congress in 1802 was based on a supposition that aliens could not obtain patents. After learning that foreigners who had resided in the United States for two years could take out patents, Du Buc de Marentille in December of that year patented an "insubmersible boat." His design called for decking to keep water out of the boat and affixing cork to the craft for bouyancy. That arrangement prepared the boat for use as a lifeboat when the ship carrying it was out at sea; in port the special components could be removed to make the boat suitable for ordinary tasks. Du Buc de Marentille launched a prototype at Elizabeth, New Jersey, in the spring of 1803, subjecting it to a public demonstration in which the boat proved resistant to sinking, swamping, or capsizing. Du Buc de Marentille advertised that he would give free licenses for the use of such a lifeboat to the first three shipowners who placed orders. He apparently re-

ceived no response to that offer, and in July 1803, someone stole his demonstration vessel from a wharf in New York City. That year Du Buc de Marentille also took out patents on a "wreck raft," which was a life raft to be carried on board a ship, and a "sea-sitting chair" designed to keep a person afloat in a sitting position. The lifeboat, the raft, and the chair all employed cork flotation and incorporated weighted levers to keep the craft from upsetting. Beginning in 1807, Du Buc de Marentille drew up plans for the defense of New York harbor, but was not able to get them implemented (Philadelphia *Mail; or, Claypoole's Daily Advertiser*, 5 Oct. 1792; Elizabeth, N.J., *Federal Republican*, 10, 17 May, 6, 13 Sep. 1803; New York *Mercantile Advertiser*, 27 May 1803; M. A. Du Buc Marentille, *All People Wrecked at Sea Saved: Description of the Machines Invented for that Purpose, and for which Patents have been Obtained* [Elizabeth, N.J., 1803]; Madison, *Papers, Sec. of State Ser.*, 3:594-5; *List of Patents*, 30, 32; Mary Weatherspoon Bowden, "Knickerbocker's *History* and the 'Enlightended' Men of New York City," *American Literature*, 47 [1975], 171; Du Buc de Marentille to TJ, 30 July, 22 Sep. 1807).

JONATHAN DAYTON of New Jersey presented Du Buc de Marentille's memorial to the Senate on 10 Feb. 1802. The Senate tabled the memorial and took no further action. In December 1804, Du Buc de Marentille wrote to the speaker of the House of Representatives asking the "patronage of Congress" to assist him in getting one of his lifesaving devices adopted by the navy and on merchant vessels (JS, 3:180; JHR, 5:66, 68).

DISCUSSION ÉLEVÉE SUR LA CONCESSION DES PRIVILÈGES: Dayton may have hesitated because the House of Representatives, after forming a committee to prepare a revised naturalization bill on 15 Dec., had begun to send to that committee any petitions from aliens that related to the "privileges and benefits" of citizens (JHR, 4:18, 49-50, 52, 55).

From Albert Gallatin

DEAR SIR   Jany. 27th 1802

I transmitted to you two days ago, under same cover correspondence in case of E. Randolph, and a letter to the Chairman of the Commee. of Ways & Means in relation to certain appropriations with some papers relative thereto. The last is wanted, and neither has been returned

Respectfully Your obt. Servt.   ALBERT GALLATIN

RC (DLC); at foot of text: "The President of the United States"; endorsed by TJ as received from the Treasury Department on 27 Jan. and so recorded in SJL; also endorsed by TJ: "E. Randolph's papers."

TRANSMITTED TO YOU: TJ recorded two letters from the Treasury Department in SJL on 25 Jan. The one concerning "Indn. trading houses" is noted at TJ to the Senate and the House of Representatives, at this date below. The other, recorded in SJL without a notation, has not been found. Gallatin's letter to John Randolph IN RELATION TO CERTAIN APPROPRIATIONS may have pertained to the bill for "making certain partial appropriations" for 1802, introduced by Randolph on 5 Feb. The appropriations included $60,000 for the pay of the army, an additional $1,400 for the printing of public accounts, and other payments. TJ signed the appropriations act on 23 Feb. (U.S. Statutes at Large, 2:131; JHR, 4:85, 106).

To the Senate and the House of Representatives

GENTLEMEN OF THE SENATE & OF
THE HOUSE OF REPRESENTATIVES

I lay before you the accounts of our Indian trading houses, as rendered up to the 1st. day of January 1801. with a report of the Secretary at War thereon, explaining the effects and the situation of that commerce, and the reasons in favor of it's further extension. but it is believed that the act authorising this trade expired so long ago as the 3d of March 1799. it's revival therefore as well as it's extension, is submitted to the consideration of the legislature.

The act regulating trade and intercourse with the Indian tribes will also expire on the 3d. day of March next. while on the subject of it's continuance, it will be worthy the consideration of the legislature whether the provisions of the law inflicting on Indians, in certain cases, the punishment of death by hanging, might not permit it's commutation into death by military execution; the form of the punishment, in the former way, being peculiarly repugnant to their[1] ideas, and increasing the obstacles to the surrender of the criminal.

These people are becoming very sensible of the baneful effects produced[2] on their morals, their health & existence by the abuse of ardent spirits: and some of them earnestly desire a prohibition of that article from being carried among them. the legislature will consider whether the effectuating that desire would not be in the spirit of benevolence & liberality which they have hitherto practised towards these our neighbors, and which has had so happy an effect towards conciliating their friendship. it has been found too in experience that the same abuse gives frequent rise to incidents tending much to commit our peace with the Indians.

It is now become necessary to run and mark the boundaries between them & us in various parts. the law last mentioned has authorised this to be done; but no existing appropriation meets the expence.

Certain papers explanatory of the grounds of this communication are herewith inclosed.   TH: JEFFERSON
Jan. 27. 1802.

RC (DNA: RG 233, PM, 7th Cong., 1st sess.); in the salutation, TJ interlined "Senate & of the"; for other emendations, see notes 1-2 below. RC (DNA: RG 46, LPPM, 7th Cong., 1st sess.); endorsed by a Senate clerk. PrC (DLC). Enclosures: (1) William Irvine to the secretary of war, 11 Nov. 1801, reporting on trade through the Indian "factories" or trading stores at Tellico and on the Georgia frontier, enclosing a statement of expenditures and receipts for each store to 1 Jan. 1801, showing a net gain of $309.53 for the Tellico factory and a net gain of $15,740.83 for the Georgia factory (Tr in DNA: RG 233, PM, in a clerk's hand; Tr in DNA: RG 46, LPPM, in hand of Joshua Wingate, Jr., chief clerk of the War Department). (2) Henry Dearborn to TJ, 8 Dec. 1801. (3) Extract of John Edgar to the secretary of war, Kaskaskia, 20 Nov. 1801, stating that about 50 Delaware Indians who assembled on the Mississippi River declared that if the Delaware man

convicted of murder should be executed by hanging, "they would kill every white man they met with," and that even "our own Indians" expressed dissatisfaction with "the mode of execution" (Tr in DNA: RG 233, PM, in Wingate's hand and attested by him as a true copy, 26 Jan. 1802, endorsed by a House clerk; Tr in DNA: RG 46, LPPM, misdated 1802, in Wingate's hand and attested by him, endorsed by a Senate clerk); see William Henry Harrison to TJ, 30 Dec. 1801; Edgar, a militia commander in the Kaskaskia area, also stated in his letter, which has not been found, that he had ordered a party of militia to be present at the execution (record in DNA: RG 107, RLRMS; Terr. Papers, 2:626-7). (4) Extract of the address of Little Turtle to TJ, 4 Jan. 1802, consisting of four paragraphs beginning "Father, Should this request be granted nothing shall be wanting" and running through "we have become less numerous and happy" (Tr in

DNA: RG 233, PM, in Wingate's hand and attested by him as a true copy, 26 Jan. 1802, endorsed by a House clerk; Tr in DNA: RG 46, LPPM, in Wingate's hand and attested by him as a true copy, 26 Jan., endorsed by a Senate clerk). Message and enclosures printed in ASP, *Indian Affairs*, 1:653-5.

Meriwether Lewis delivered this message and the accompanying copies of documents to the House of Representatives on Wednesday, 27 Jan., and to the Senate on Thursday, the 28th. The Senate, after the papers were read, ordered them to lie for consideration. The House referred the message and enclosures to a committee formed on 7 Jan. to consider the memorial from Evan Thomas and other members of the Baltimore Yearly Meeting of the Society of Friends that enclosed a speech made at their meeting by Little Turtle (see Editorial Note, Conference with Little Turtle, 4 Jan.). The memorial asked "the attention and interference of Congress to prevent the supply of spiritous liquors to the Indian tribes residing in the Territory of the United States Northwest of the river Ohio, by traders and settlers on the frontiers, and to introduce among the said Indian tribes the most simple and useful arts of civil life." The House committee consisted of Samuel Smith and four others (JHR, 4:34, 72; JS, 3:174).

INDIAN TRADING HOUSES: the "Act for establishing Trading Houses with the Indian Tribes," approved 18 Apr. 1796, was in effect "for the term of two years, and to the end of the next session of Congress thereafter" (U.S. Statutes at Large, 1:452-3). Gallatin wrote a brief communication to TJ on 25 Jan.: "It is suggested that the law authorizing Indian trading houses has expired. If, upon examination it should appear to be so, it will be necessary to lay the subject before Congress. I have taken the liberty to mention this, because under existing laws, the Secretary of the War Department should cause the original stocks, advanced out of the Treasury, to be realized, and repaid in the Treasury. I have the honor to be very respectfully Sir Your most obedt. Servt." (RC in DLC; at foot of text: "The President of the United States"; endorsed by

TJ as received from the Treasury Department on 25 Jan. and "Indian trading houses" and so recorded in SJL). Gallatin's reference to "original stocks" apparently meant the funds used to supply the trading stores with inventories of merchandise. Gallatin evidently gave TJ an "Abstract Statement" of expenditures and receipts of the trading houses as accounted for by John Harris, the military storekeeper at Philadelphia, to 4 June 1801 (MS in DLC: TJ Papers, 119:20528, in a clerk's hand; for Harris, see Vol. 34:69). Gallatin received that statement with a covering letter of 7 Dec. 1801 from Richard Harrison, the auditor. In Harrison's opinion, the brief abstract, "unaccompanied by the semi-annual Statements" that the 1796 law required the trading houses' agents to submit, would not be sufficient for the "regular adjustment" of the accounts. There should be a comprehensive accounting, Harrison stated, "by whoever had the general Superintendance of the Trade." Gallatin passed Harrison's letter along to TJ, probably at the same time he gave TJ the "Abstract Statement" (RC in DLC; at foot of text: "The Secretary of the Treasury"; endorsed by TJ with notation "Indian trade").

In the House of Representatives on 27 Apr. 1802, the committee of Smith and others appointed on 7 Jan. reported a bill for the REVIVAL and continuation of the 1796 act that established the trading houses. The bill became law on 30 Apr. 1802. It made no change to the provisions of the earlier act, but put it back into force until 4 Mch. 1803 (JHR, 4:224; U.S. Statutes at Large, 2:173).

The most recent ACT REGULATING TRADE AND INTERCOURSE with Indian tribes, approved 3 Mch. 1799, had a limit of three years. A bill for a new act with the same title, "An act to regulate trade and intercourse with the Indian tribes, and to preserve peace on the frontiers," originated in the Senate and became law on 30 Mch. 1802. Both the new law and its predecessor gave United States courts jurisdiction in cases of crimes committed against or by Indians. Neither law specified the form that PUNISHMENT OF DEATH should take in capital cases, but an act passed by the First Congress in 1790 stated that the infliction of death for federal crimes should be BY HANGING (U.S. Statutes at Large, 1:119, 743-9; 2:139-46; JS, 3:179, 180, 191).

ABUSE OF ARDENT SPIRITS: the 30 Mch. 1802 act contained a section authorizing the president "to take such measures, from time to time, as to him may appear expedient to prevent or restrain the vending or distributing of spirituous liquors among all or any" Indian tribes (U.S. Statutes at Large, 2:146).

According to the 1799 "Act to regulate trade and intercourse," the BOUNDARIES between Native American tribal lands and U.S. territory formed a continuous line that followed rivers, ridges, and the borders of existing land grants to run from Lake Erie to Spanish Florida. The act of 30 Mch. 1802 repeated the boundary's specifications. Both acts authorized the president to have the line "clearly ascertained and distinctly marked" wherever he thought necessary. Congress included an APPROPRIATION of five thousand dollars for "running certain boundary lines between the Indians and white inhabitants of the United States" in a military appropriations act that became law on 1 May 1802. The marking off of reserved tracts in Indiana Territory and the Northwest Territory would also fall under the appropriation for surveying the Indian boundary (U.S. Statutes at Large, 1:743-4; 2:139-41, 183).

[1] TJ here canceled "feelings."
[2] TJ here canceled "by."

From John Davis

SIR,   Baltimore, Jany 28, 1802.

I receive your polite Letter, dated Monticello, at the moment I am about to usher into the World a pamphlet of my production, which I beg permission to present you with. I shall be pardoned, I hope, for having taken a slice from a corner of the Massachusetts' Cheese, when I observe that it has filled my purse, & enabled me to prosecute my studies more uninterruptedly.—Such productions are apparently trifling, but I think it is recorded of some British Statesman that he thought the ballads of a Country might propagate just or false nations.

I am, Sir, With profound respect, Your most obedient Servant,

JOHN DAVIS

RC (DLC); endorsed by TJ as received 29 Jan. and so recorded in SJL. Enclosure not found, but see below.

YOUR POLITE LETTER: TJ to Davis, 11 Sep. 1801.

PAMPHLET: Davis wrote "The Memoirs of the Mammoth Cheese" in late December 1801 or early January 1802 and offered it for publication to the Baltimore booksellers George Keatinge and Henry Semple Keatinge. The Keatinges purchased the copyright for five dollars on 7 Jan. and a week later began to advertise the item for sale "in the press and speedily will be published." They later claimed that Davis had submitted a variant of the manuscript, entitled "The Adventures of the Mammoth Cheese," to another printer who advertised it for sale from the offices of the Baltimore American and William Pechin on 28 Jan. In a public printed apology, Davis insisted that publishing two histories on the same subject was not unprecedented, that the works' contents were not repetitive, and that Massachusetts inhabitants were eager for publications about their Cheshire cheese (Baltimore *Republican or, Anti-Democrat*, 14, 29 Jan. 1802; Roger P. Bristol, *Maryland Imprints, 1801-1810* [Charlottesville, 1953], 19-20).

BALLADS OF A COUNTRY: an allusion to a remark made by the early eighteenth-century Scottish politician Andrew Fletcher of Saltoun, "if a man were permitted to make all the Ballads, he need not care who should make the Laws of a Nation" (Andrew Fletcher, *An Account of a Conversation concerning a right Regulation of Governments for the Common Good of Mankind. In a Letter to the Marquis of Montrose, the Earls of Rothes, Roxburg, and Hadington, from London the 1st of December, 1703* [Edinburgh, 1704], 10).

From Richard Dinmore

SIR   Washington 28th. Janry. 1801 [i.e. 1802]

Impressed with the profoundest respect, I can but fear, in thus addressing you, the imputation either of impertinence or sycophancy. These considerations would have prevented this reapplication to yourself, had I not been impelled to it, by the actual poverty I experience, and by the certain prospect of want. With this apology for my obtrusion, permit me to state, that when I heard of but few applications, for the office of Librarian to Congress, I ventur'd first, unpatronized, to address a letter to yourself, and afterwards procured an introduction from Genl. Mason, to a letter, which I wrote to Mr. Madison, signifying my wish to be considered as a Candidate for that office. Having taken these steps, my applications, I conceiv'd at an end, and I waited with some confidence, for the result; a confidence which arose from the belief, that the characters of the Candidates, would be investigated, that many of them, were more unfit than myself, for the office, and that others, already held situations, adequate to decent and comfortable maintenance. Well knowing that it is the object of the Administration, rather to diffuse those means, than by heaping Office upon Office, give to the few the shew and parade of Opulence. But Sir when I hear how very numerous the applicants are, and consider how difficult, it will be, to investigate the Characters, and compare the relative fitness of the different Candidates, for the Office, I am apprehensive that in the cloud, I must be forgotten. I have determined therefore to break thro' common forms, and place before you, the motives, which induce me, to solicit the appointment. Unfortunately, nurtured by affection and feeling rather than by judgement, and educated, as that useless being a gentleman, when I arrived at manhood, I found myself possessed, of what might be conceived a Competence, yet, certainly not what I had been taught to expect. Strongly disposed towards a doctrine of Ethics, which would permit no bending to the exigencies of the times, my feeble voice, was opposed to those measures, which my judgement told me, must encrease the miseries of my fellow men. I had to contend with the persecution of the powerful, and the bigotry of the multitude, I sunk in the contest, and quitted my country, in the hope of finding in the United States, those principles acted upon, for which I had contended in England, or at least that I should be tolerated in the possession of them. Your own experience will tell you, how just such expectations were, in a man, who landed, at the close of the year 97. I now Sir find all my external resources dried up, and it is only by the application of the few literary talents I possess, that I can expect, either the comforts or the necessaries of life; but they cannot be exerted to advantage, without a recourse to books, which circumstanced as I am, I cannot command. Hence Sir arises my desire to procure the situation I am now soliciting. I might indeed offer another plea, founded on the irregularity of my Health, and the opinion of my friends, relative to my fitness for the Office; but, unfortunately for me, those, you may be supposed most in the habit of meeting, know little of me, except, perhaps Dr. Gaunt and Mr. Oakley. Should these reasons induce you to enquire into my competency, for the situation in question, I can with full confidence rest my Character, on their knowledge. I remain Sir

   With respect Yours

R. DINMORE

RC (DNA: RG 59, LAR); addressed: "The President of the U. S."; endorsed by TJ as a letter of 28 Jan. 1802 received the same day and "to be librarian" and so recorded in SJL.

TO ADDRESS A LETTER TO YOURSELF: Dinmore to TJ, 11 Jan. 1802.

On 17 Jan. 1802, Stevens Thomson MASON wrote to James Madison describing Dinmore as "very Competent to the office he solicits" but acknowledging that he had "heard of other candidates of equal merits and fitness," including Robert Monroe of Washington (RC in DNA: RG 59, LAR; endorsed by TJ: "S. T. Mason to J. Madison" and "Dinmore Monroe to be librarian"). Mason enclosed Dinmore's letter to Madison of the previous day stating that Dinmore had applied directly to the president but had since been informed that applications should be sent to the secretary of state (RC in DNA: RG 59, LAR, endorsed by TJ: "Dinmore to mr Madison. to be librarian"; Madison, *Papers, Sec. of State Ser.*, 2:406).

DR. GAUNT AND MR. OAKLEY: probably Edward Gantt and John Oakley, both of Georgetown (Vol. 33:290, 670).

To Levi Lincoln

Jan. 28. 1802.

Th: Jefferson incloses the Executive proceedings of Govr Sinclair for the consideration of the Attorney General, with a view to the power exercised by the Governor of laying off counties, establishing courts therein fixing the time and place of holding them, and, as would seem from the proceedings of Oct. 30th. of determining their legislative representation. the Attorney General is desired to give an opinion whether his exercise of these powers be lawful under the acts establishing the Northwestern territory?

PrC (DLC). Enclosure not found, but see below.

Charles Willing Byrd, the secretary of the Northwest Territory, sent copies of the journal of EXECUTIVE PROCEEDINGS to the State Department at half-yearly intervals (*Terr. Papers*, 3:263n; Madison, *Papers, Sec. of State Ser.*, 2:431n). TJ may have enclosed the territory's executive proceedings for the period beginning 1 July 1800. Arthur St. Clair is-

sued proclamations to establish COUN-TIES in July 1800, December 1800, and September 1801. In each case he appointed judges, designated a town where the new county's COURTS would meet, and assigned a quarterly schedule for court terms. In the fall of 1800, he issued writs of election to county sheriffs for a general LEGISLATIVE election and to fill particular vacancies. A writ of election issued in the fall of 1801 was to fill two vacancies (*Terr. Papers*, 3:524-31).

From James Lyon

SIR,   Washington City Jan. 28. 1802

I regret that my dependent state dooms me to submit almost constantly to the solicitation of favors; but I flatter myself that the more public Utility is attached to my pursuits, the favor is granted with the less irksomeness.

When I obtruded upon yourself and some others, a plan for raising the means for setting up the printing business, I fondly hoped to extend it to something great; nor is that hope extinguished; I must however suspend it, till by some means, I can throw myself into the command of a Capital; of one of the means of acquiring it, however, I am almost totally disappointed; for while some printers employ from Eight to twelve workmen on public business and even the *tory* I have before mentioned, from three to five, I cannot obtain enough to employ *my own* evening hours after leaving the public office;—it is true that through your goodness I expect to obtain a little more from the Gen. P. Office, after the expiration of this quarter.

Being thus disappointed I have turned my attention to the book printing business; and an opportunity of furnishing a library like the one projected on the paper accompanying this letter would be highly beneficial; and I have no doubt of the success of the institution under the patronage of your approbation, by confering which you will add a link to the chain of obligations, that binds in the bonds of Gratitude

Your Obedient Servt   J. LYON

RC (DLC); at foot of text: "Thos. Jefferson Esqr"; endorsed by TJ as a letter of 28 Jan. received 27 Jan. and so recorded in SJL. Enclosure not found.

I MUST HOWEVER SUSPEND IT: Lyon suspended his *National Magazine, or Cabinet of the United States* with the 11 Jan. 1802 issue (Vol. 35:487n).

THE TORY: David Russell (Lyon to TJ, 8 Dec.).

In August 1801, Lyon proposed a BOOK PRINTING BUSINESS, the Washington Printing and Bookselling Company, also known as the Franklin Press, for "the purpose of printing and selling books in the city of Washington" (Bryan, *National Capital*, 1:435; Lyon to TJ, 22 Oct. 1801).

Lyon also planned to open a circulating LIBRARY on 1 June 1801 at the "first door west of President's Square" on Pennsylvania Avenue but relinquished its control and direction to Richard Dinmore (*National Intelligencer*, 8 June 1801). A 17 Oct. 1801 advertisement in the front of the first issue of *The National Magazine* included Dinmore's notices to subscribers to his library and his willingness to sell his goods for cash or shares in the Washington Printing and Bookselling Company.

From David Austin

RESPECTED SIR   Washington Jan'y 29th. A.D. 1802.

You was obligingly disposed to say, that tho' you did not subscribe, you would receive a copy of the publica. in hand.—The Boy waits on the President with two copies—The price is fifty Cents each. If the President accepts the two, it will be the more obliging; as I have little other means of living but from the avails of the truth I publish to the world.

If the President could accommodate me to the situation of Librarian, it would be a favor long to be remembered.—

With sentiments of esteem   DAVID AUSTIN

RC (DLC); at foot of text: "Th: Jefferson Pres: U: States"; endorsed by TJ as received 29 Jan. and so recorded in SJL.

COPY OF THE PUBLICATION: David Austin, *The National "Barley Cake," or,* *The "Rock of Offence" Into A "Glorious Holy Mountain": in Discourses and Letters* (Washington, D.C., 1802; Sowerby, No. 1668). TJ paid Austin $1 for the two copies presented to him (MB, 2:1064).

To Andrew Ellicott

DEAR SIR   Washington Jan. 29. 1802.

I recieved, through mr Duane, from you, some copying ink, which I find on trial to be very good. if it be made in a way which would enable one when in the country, to furnish themselves, I would ask the reciept. that kind of ink being to be had only in Philadelphia & other large sea port towns, I have found it difficult to get a supply when I have been at home. I wish we had a good red ink which would keep.

When you were here, we proposed to you the office of Surveyor General of the US. which you thought not acceptable unless the public would pay another clerk. on conversation with mr Gallatin he assures me the necessary clerks are paid by the public, & not by the principal. this obstacle being removed, I renew the proposal to you, and shall be glad if you will accept, as I think it very desireable not only that the public work should be done with accuracy, but that some person should be there who would be fixing the interesting points in geography. I ask one favor of you however, not to mention a tittle of this to any mortal breathing however confidential, until I send you the commission, which shall be shortly after I learn from you that you will accept it. health and best wishes.

TH: JEFFERSON

PrC (DLC); at foot of text: "Mr. Andrew Ellicot"; endorsed by TJ in ink on verso.

RECEIPT: that is, the recipe for making the ink.

For Ellicott's refusal of the position of SURVEYOR GENERAL the previous summer, see Vol. 35:424n.

From Albert Gallatin

Jan 29th 1802

The papers which accompany this contain all the documents & the whole information which I can obtain in this department on the subject of the Barbary powers. The rough draft of the letter to the Secretary of State, & the general sketch marked (AA) exhibit the substance of the whole. As soon as the papers are returned they may be transmitted officially to the Depart. of State, as the letter to the Secretary is the only paper to be transcribed—

Respectfully submitted by   ALBERT GALLATIN

RC (DLC); at foot of text: "The President of the United States"; endorsed by

TJ as received from the Treasury Department on 29 Jan. and "Barbary Powers" and so recorded in SJL at 30 Jan. Enclosures: see TJ to the Senate and the House of Representatives, 16 Feb. 1802, Enclosure No. 2.

From Robert Morris

DEAR SIR [on or before 29 Jan. 1802]

When I had the honor of seeing you, it escaped my recollection to mention the subject contemplated in the enclosed note; mr Fitzsimons told me the blank therein was occasioned by his having forgot at the time of writing it wether he had ten or twelve chairs. This furniture is elegant and well suited for your appartments, perhaps better than any other in America, and it may be had for less than its real value by an appraismt of any Gentn. you may think proper to name for the purpose, excuse this intrusion on behalf of my friend and accept the assurance of the respectfull attachment of Dr Sir

Your obedt & hble servt ROBT MORRIS

RC (MHi); undated; at foot of text: "Thos Jefferson President"; endorsed by TJ as received 29 Jan. and so recorded in SJL. Enclosure: Thomas FitzSimons to Robert Morris, Philadelphia, 18 Jan. 1802, noting that he had an undesignated number of chairs and two sofas, imported from France, which were "better adapted to the Presidents than to a Private House," and consequently he wished Morris to "endeavor to dispose of them"; the furniture was packed, ready to be sent, and "with respect to price—that may be left intirely to be settled after they arrive" in Washington (RC in MHi; at foot of text: "Mr R Morris").

From Benjamin Vaughan

DEAR SIR, Jany: 29, 1802.

Notwithstanding your wish to insulate the continent over which you preside, from the confusions of the other hemisphere, yet while the citizens of America pursue trade & navigation, they must necessarily mix with European nations; & it is seldom safe to remain in troublesome company. Quarrels may even reach the U.S. in their own home; for three of the governments of Europe possess territories in the rear of these states. The Indians also are accessible to the three governments referred to.—To know Europe, then, seems an object which is important even for America.

Without presuming upon current anecdotes or a personal knowledge of European politicians, it will be safer to examine *the temper of European governments* upon the basis of the universal principles of human nature & of public facts.

It shall be admitted that those who are at the head of European affairs, do not in the first instance, propose to enslave their subjects; yet they think a firm government requisite for their subjects; & that recent experience has proved it unsafe even for their masters to seek to improve their condition. Thus the ambition of princes affects to be in league with philanthropy; & thus human happiness is left at the discretion of those, who seldom aim to serve any but themselves.— The aristocracy, equally alarmed at the operation of popular principles, and sensible of their own weakness, confirm these pretensions in their sovereigns; persuaded that princes in their worst shapes are preferable to mobs.—By this means, unlimited power is viewed as the only source from which freedom ought to flow: the people are allowed no voice: & the aristocracy are content to expect from favor what they used to possess from right.

This state of things, but subject to some varieties, is as general, as the impression made by the French revolution.—To what does it lead? I conjecture to a new concert of princes.

The late concert of princes was chiefly directed against the popular government of France, which was considered as a common enemy; but the present government of France will be deemed as a common friend, being held abroad as an usurpation against the people. A new concert of princes may then be made stronger by the *double* weight of France, which is removed from one scale & may be thrown into the other.

It is evident that such a concert may have a two-fold object; for it may be calculated to remove *fear* as to subjects, & to gratify *ambition* as to foreign possessions.

There is no need of expatiating on the delusive hope of subduing the domestic liberties of Europe. Such ideas are too strongly innate in princes, to require the late panic either to originate or to confirm them.

On the other hand, if the new concert shall aim at an incorporation of small states into the greater ones, few difficulties will seem to offer, besides those inherent to the nature of the partition; & for these, there will appear an easy cure, as long as the materials for a division shall be thought capable of being increased *ad libitum*. I refer to the general insight which has now been obtained into the Turkish government & dominions, & to the secret developed by yourself respecting the Barbary powers, as well as to the late informations given respecting various retired parts of Asia & Africa; for the probability of a large stock of territory being thrown into the general hotchpot. Five or six European powers, should they combine for the purpose,[1] seem to have all the parts of the globe at their disposition, worthy of possession, excepting China & the United States.—Sudden submission at *home* & sudden conquest *abroad*, resulting from the signature of a single sheet of paper: what a flattering substitute for domestic rebellions & for foreign wars!

Schemes on the subject of a concert of princes certainly have not been wanting, in past moments, to some of the great movers in European politics; & the present state of Europe in general, & of France in particular, as long as Bonaparte has influence in France, may tend to revive them. The light texture of his constitution, his patronage of emigrants, his late sympathy for Mahomet, his present concordat with the pope, his new nominations to ecclesiastical benefices & charges, his respect for the goddess Fortune, his affection for the policy of great conquerors, the splendor of his military court; these & other circumstances which are not counterbalanced by a single atom of republicanism shewn in any one of his actions or writings or speeches or friendships; I say, these & other circumstances (not forgetting his reported tax on newspapers) shew that Bonaparte, if not checked by a confidence in his strength & in his good luck, may be made to incline to a combination such as I have alluded to.—Without perhaps knowing it, he has in part begun it already, in his treaty with Russia; which provides against the shelter of refractory subjects on either side, in a manner not very reconcileable with sentiments of liberty or even of his own modified constitution.

I have no expectation of the final success of such an enterprize; for even should it prosper in its first openings, empires, of which the dimensions were calculated only by the measure of princely ambition & vanity, would soon be too vast for human management. Security would elicit and develope the vices of thrones & of those who sat upon them. An *avowed* system of despotism would revolt the human mind; & the terrors lest it should succeed, would transcend the terrors resulting from[2] an opposition to it. A sense of human rights in these days would easily be recognized, upon a proportionate occasion; for it is not the theory of these rights which is denied, but the prudence of calling it into practice. Many who are content to leave to their children the care of fighting against slavery, where it is only *prospective*; will rouse up against actual oppression in their own day. Were the temper of private soldiers even what it used to be, the extent & magnitude of the late war has disciplined a large mass of people to balance it. If wars should occur between the ambitious chiefs of the universe, the people on each side must be appealed to for carrying them through. If competition for a throne should arise within the pale of either of the great divisions of the world, the people would again count for something.

It is easy to multiply general arguments: Let us now look to some which are particular.—The sentiments of the German philosopher *Kant*, (for he can scarcely be said to have a regular theoretic system,) however they may be taxed as wanting originality or perspicuity; yet have for a time been followed; & being founded on the doctrines of internal dignity, disinterestedness, a disregard for suffering, and a love of liberty,[3] have prepared a number of determined leaders in case of public struggle on the side of Germany. In England, the *evangelical preachers* (as they are called) who are scarcely yet noticed in books or in polite companies, are making an astonishing progress among the lower & some of the middling people; & though they may *profess* loyalty to *men*, yet they are looking for the speedy coming of Jesus as the overturner of human sovereignty, whenever the Ottoman empire shall terminate; in which convulsion, despised as they now are, they expect to take a deep part on the score of religion, while others cooperate on the score of politics. In France, democracy has been intrigued, rather than driven, out of power; and France has never seen the government of honest men in *natural circumstances*, either on representative or on democratical principles, to know sufficiently the blessing of the one system or the vigor of the other. Various other parts of Europe have felt the power of popular principles, without having carried them into action; the sensation in many is still kept alive; & most of them think that they can do better for liberty than France has done.—Two other sources of discontent only shall be mentioned, of great universality & deep operation, & of which the certainty under the circumstances above predicated, is evidenced in every age of history. The one source must arise from the government of *foreign masters*; a government which occurs in many places already, by virtue of modern & even of recent treaties, & which will occur still more under a treaty of *general* partition and of *undisguised* arbitrary power. The other source of discontent regards restraints imposed upon religious sectaries; which though they may perhaps be removed after a time from some of the old sects, may be extended to new ones; & to none more naturally than to the evangelical sect, of which a profusion of commentators & the declining zeal of established religions have laid the foundations. Many of the old clergy however are still rich enough to be plundered, & are consequently open to clamor; & discontent has been connected so long with some other sects, (as with the catholics and dissenters in Ireland,) that there is a chance of its having become habitual with them.

But supposing these particulars & other corresponding ones to be true, why are they mentioned? Certainly not for the sake of idle dissertation; but because the speculation is not only interesting for the philosopher, but the statesman.—Nothing should take us by surprize, & least of all matters of national importance. Measures of inquiry may silently be instituted; the tendency of treaties may be watched; & the [tempers] of courts receive their explanation. Principles of liberty may be encouraged; which can be done by no pen better than your own. A kind reception may be provided for strangers of merit of all descriptions. When the system above pointed out approaches, should its approach happen in our day, the people & the militia may each be prepared.—In short, arguments need not be multiplied or subdivided. Knowledge can never be superfluous or circumspection blameable in matters of immense importance. An air of suspicion may sometimes be mischievous; but in the present instance, this may easily be avoided.

A little pamphlet will accompany or follow this. It never was published in its present form, & there are reasons why it is wished that it may with care be kept dormant.

With my usual respects, believe me, my dear sir, Your much attached friend & servant.

RC (DLC); endorsed by TJ as a letter from Benjamin Vaughan received 25 Feb. and so recorded in SJL; TJ originally endorsed the letter as from John Vaughan.

Britain, the Austrian Empire, and Russia had joined in opposition to France to form the core of the Second Coalition, the previous CONCERT OF PRINCES. The coalition began in 1798 and collapsed in 1800-1801 as Austria and Russia withdrew from the alliance (Samuel F. Scott and Barry Rothaus, eds., *Historical Dictionary of the French Revolution, 1789-1799*, 2 vols. [Westport, Conn., 1985], 2:882-4; Vol. 32:102n, 296-7n, 372-3n). PATRONAGE OF EMIGRANTS: France's revolutionary governments had confiscated the property and ordered the execution of royalists and others who left the country. Under Bonaparte, a series of steps beginning in 1800 eased those restrictions and made it possible for émigrés to return (Thierry Lentz, *Le Grand Consulat, 1799-1804* [Paris, 1999], 331-4; Owen Connelly, ed., *Historical Dictionary of*

Napoleonic France, 1799-1815 [Westport, Conn., 1985], 168-70).

SYMPATHY FOR MAHOMET: in October 1801, France and the Ottoman Empire agreed to preliminary articles of peace (Parry, *Consolidated Treaty Series*, 56:227-30).

For Bonaparte's CONCORDAT with Pope Pius VII in July 1801 and the restoration of the Catholic Church to France, see Vol. 35:194n. NEW NOMINATIONS TO ECCLESIASTICAL BENEFICES: the concordat allowed Bonaparte to name France's archbishops and bishops (Parry, *Consolidated Treaty Series*, 56:164; Margaret M. O'Dwyer, *The Papacy in the Age of Napoleon and the Restoration: Pius VII, 1800-1823* [Lanham, Md., 1985], 56).

As early as 1800, Bonaparte sought to control NEWSPAPERS in France, suppressing a number of political journals in Paris and keeping the remainder under government supervision (Connelly, *Historical Dictionary of Napoleonic France*, 403; Tulard, *Dictionnaire Napoléon*, 1397-8).

France made a TREATY WITH RUSSIA in

October 1801, affirming peace and declaring an intention to restore diplomatic and commercial relations between the two countries (Parry, *Consolidated Treaty Series*, 56:221-5).

The PAMPHLET has not been identified.

[1] Preceding six words interlined in place of "will."
[2] Preceding two words interlined in place of "attending."
[3] Preceding five words interlined.

From Benjamin Waterhouse

SIR   Cambridge Janry. 29th. 1802

Your letter of the 14th. inst, enclosing one of the 25th. ulto. came duly to hand.

I was struck with the expediency of establishing a popular criterion as to the precise time of taking the matter, and I entirely coincide with you in opinion that it should be fixed on *Eight times twenty four hours*, this being the result of my own observation during the last season. I know that it differs somewhat in different subjects, but in the formation of a general rule it is necessary to impose a limitation. Jenner says "I prefer the 5th. 6th. 7th. 8th. and (if the efflorescence is not far advanced beyond the margin of the pustule the 9th."—But I conceive this is impossible to be discovered with requisite precision on the skin of the african? Mr. Aikin is not a good guide on this subject. His publication was not the result of his *own* experience; nor do I believe that Dr Aikin, his very learned & classical father, had any experience with the disease.

As to the criterion of *limpid* matter, I know it to be fallacious; for in the rising of a vesicle, or blister from any cause, the scarf-skin seperates from the true, and a portion of the *superfluous water* of the blood, & sometimes of the *coaguable lymph* is found under it; and I have known this *limpid* fluid exude from the vaccine pustule, especially after being too much exhausted and irritated in procuring virus. This exudation gives a shining glazy appearance to the thread. I know of no writer, or practitioner who has made this distinction.—

I am glad to find that other physicians are following the lead of Dr. Cox in Philadelphia. I have heretofore been surprized at the fastidious style of some of the fathers in the art in that city.—I have never heard anything respecting Dr. Gantt's progress in the business. I have written to him several times, but never had an answer.

I have been made uneasy at one occurrence. In an unrestrained & perfectly confidential correspondence with my intimate friend Dr. Lettsom, I transmitted him a copy of your first letter to me dated

Decr. 25th. 1801. acknowledging the receipt of my pamphlet &c Altho I did this in the pride of my heart, I meant that he and Jenner only should partake of my satisfaction; but my friend Lettsom printed it in his volume on the cow-pox; and the Editors of a new edition of Aikin's little book just published at Philadelphia have prefixed it to that work. Anti-monarchical as I am, I nevertheless think that a strong line of distinction should always be drawn between the private citizen & the Chief Magistrate of a nation, towards whom I am disposed to say in the language and meaning of that old book which all we New England folks sware by, "YE ARE GODS!"

My friend Lettsom has taken one method to check my inclination of spreading abroad his useful & philanthropic volume. My venerable kinsman Dr. Fothergill used to say, "a man's *conduct* should be his *picture*." Accept the sentiments of profound respect.

BENJAMIN WATERHOUSE

RC (DLC); endorsed by TJ as received 10 Feb. and so recorded in SJL. DECR. 25TH. 1801: actually 25 Dec. 1800 (Vol. 32:355).

To John Wickham

DEAR SIR   Washington Jan. 29. 1802.

There is a suit depending in the court of the US. at Richmond in which the US. are plaintiffs against mr E. Randolph def. for monies recieved by him. he takes credit in his account for an article of 9000. D. as paid to mr Short for a year's salary while Minister Plenipo. for the US. at the court of Madrid, which however was never paid. but mr R. alledges that he was the agent of mr Short, and recieved the money for him, & consequently was answerable to him alone. mr Short, when he was appointed to his first diplomatic place in Europe, sent over to me duplicate powers of attorney to act for him in all cases. one of these is filed in the bank of the US. in Philada, the other is at Monticello among my papers: and he denies ever having appointed any other agent; that he desired mr Randolph to pay the money to me, who had his instructions what to do with it, or stock to the amount of it to be delivered to me also. the inclosed papers will possess you fully of this transaction, and taking for granted that mr Randolph would not be allowed the credit without producing an unequivocal authority as agent or attorney for mr Short, & pretty certain he could not do that, I had left the thing to the course explained in the within papers. a few nights ago, a series of letters from mr Nelson to the treasury passing under my review, I remarked the one from which an extract is now inclosed, whereby it appeared that the two judges had been divided on this question. I suppose therefore it is necessary for me to have it attended to on behalf of mr Short, and for this purpose desire you to appear for him and take care of this particular question, the only part of the subject which interests him. mr Pickering on my first application said he would examine mr Short's letters. he did so, and on that examination became satisfied that mr Short had never made mr R. his agent, and wrote to me the explicit acknolegement inclosed. mr Wolcott & mr Pickering in a joint conversation with me acknoleged the same thing to me and in my presence and at my request agreed that they would order 8000. D. (which with 4000. recd. as you will see, was about the amount of principal and interest at that time) invested in 8. percent stock in the name of one of their clerks in trust for mr Short, which was in part done; and constantly whenever I applied to them, expressing as a cer-tainty that the case could not fail to be decided at the next term, wished me to let the matter be till then. before mr Wolcott went out of office last winter, I spoke to him on the subject; he declared he had never entertained a doubt that the public was answerable to mr Short. his letters do not state this so explicitly, but he has never hes-itated to say it. you will see that I received under the judgment as-signed to me 1200. £ Virginia currency: that a further sum being ready to be paid by mr Pendleton to Gibson & Jefferson, I notified the government of it, and they authorised their agent mr Hopkins to re-cieve it from Gibson & Jefferson. you have herein inclosed a copy of the judgment with an endorsement of the sums paid to Gibson & Jef-ferson, and recieved by me for mr Short: to which must be added for mr Randolph's credit the subsequent paiment, which went into the treasury; and indeed I do not see why it should not be for the public interest to credit him the whole amount of the judgment, mr Pendle-ton having in a letter (which I have) desired mr R. to be discharged to it's whole amount, and 'pledged the whole funds of mr Robinson's estate remaining, as well as the stock, for paiment out of the first money we can recieve by collection, or a sale of the stock when such can be made without a ruinous loss, in which we as trustees could not be justified.' I presume nothing is requisite but to bring this sug-gested agency to the best of evidence, to shew it has no foundation, & that no expression can be produced in any letter of mr Short's to mr R. which is not fairly to be understood as addressing him as Secretary of state. surely his saying that he would consider stock if put into my hands as equivalent to money, could not supercede my power of attorney & convey it to mr R. should you consider any other evidence than what is inclosed, as necessary, be so good as to inform me, & in what form it should come. acting on the defensive it seems to me the proof lies on the other side. I inclose you an order on mr Jefferson for your fee, not knowing what it is. accept assurances of my esteem & respect   TH: JEFFERSON

PrC (DLC: William Short Papers); at foot of first page: "John Wickam esq"; endorsed by TJ in ink on verso. Enclosures: (1) Extract of Thomas Nelson to Treasury Department, 16 Dec. 1798, from the abridgment of Nelson's correspondence reporting progress of the government's suit against Edmund Randolph (see Gallatin to TJ, 9 Jan.); stating that the U.S. circuit court at Richmond held a trial in the suit, but no judgment was returned because the two judges, Supreme Court Associate Justice William Cushing and District Judge Cyrus Griffin, disagreed on some points; on the matter of William Short's salary claim, Cushing believed that Randolph had acted as an officer of the U.S. government, whereas Griffin believed that Short's claim was against Randolph personally, not the government (MS in DLC: Short Papers; in TJ's hand; dated 5 June 1799, but according to the papers transmitted to the House of Representatives and printed in ASP, *Finance*, 1:760-2, TJ made this extract from a letter of 16 Dec. 1798; printed in Vol. 31:465n; probably enclosed in TJ to Short, 19 Apr. 1802). (2) Probably an extract from Timothy Pickering's statement on William

Short's claim for salary, 25 Apr. 1798 (see Vol. 30:299n). (3) Probably a copy, not found, of a Virginia High Court of Chancery decree of 19 Mch. 1795 that entitled Randolph to collect a prerevolutionary debt from the estate of John Robinson with interest; see below and Vol. 29:574. Other enclosures not identified.

TJ's JOINT CONVERSATION with Oliver Wolcott and Timothy Pickering likely took place in February 1799, before TJ left Philadelphia for Monticello on 1 Mch. (Vol. 31:62-3, 69n, 504, 574).

As administrators of the estate of John Robinson, Edmund PENDLETON and Peter Lyons were obliged to pay Randolph for the old debt covered by the 1795 chancery decree. Randolph signed the judgment, £1200 in Virginia currency along with an obligation for more, over to TJ as Short's representative. TJ deposited the money with John HOPKINS, the commissioner of the continental loan office in Richmond, to the credit of the U.S. government (Vol. 30:35, 36; Vol. 31:497-9, 514, 574; Vol. 32:374).

A LETTER (WHICH I HAVE): Pendleton to TJ, 25 Apr. 1798 (Vol. 30:298).

From Isaac Briggs

Sharon, 30th. of the 1st. Month 1802.

Will the President do me the favor to accept the enclosed pamphlet; and the additional one to inform me of the title of Arthur Young's performance, alluded to in a late conversation, so *particularly* as to enable me to procure the book?

With deep impressions of esteem and respect, I am thy friend
                                                      ISAAC BRIGGS

RC (DLC); endorsed by TJ as received 31 Jan. and so recorded in SJL; also endorsed by TJ: "near Montgomy. C.H. Maryld." Enclosure: see below.

The PAMPHLET was perhaps Thomas Moore, *The Great Error of American Agriculture Exposed: and Hints for Improvement Suggested* (Baltimore, 1801; Sowerby, No. 820). Briggs and Moore were brothers-in-law. Both were Quakers who lived near the town of Brookeville in Montgomery County, Maryland, and they shared an interest in the improvement of agriculture (Ella Kent Barnard, "Isaac

Briggs, A.M., F.A.P.S.," *Maryland Historical Magazine*, 7 [1912], 409-10, 416, 418; T. H. S. Boyd, *The History of Montgomery County, Maryland, from its Earliest Settlement in 1650 to 1879* [Clarksburg, Md., 1879; repr. Baltimore, 1968], 90-1, 122; Vol. 32:501-3, 560; Briggs to TJ, 26 Apr. 1802; Moore to TJ, 21 June 1802).

It is not known which of ARTHUR YOUNG's works TJ mentioned to Briggs. TJ included Young's *Rural Œconomy* in an extensive reading list covering a variety of subjects that he drew up for a young man in 1800 (Vol. 32:178).

Charges Against Arthur St. Clair

I. FROM THOMAS WORTHINGTON, 30 JAN. 1802

II. LIST OF CHARGES AGAINST ARTHUR ST. CLAIR, [CA. 30 JAN.-20 FEB. 1802]

III. THOMAS WORTHINGTON'S CHARGES AND EXPLANATIONS, 20 FEB. 1802

EDITORIAL NOTE

A former general in the Continental army and president of the Confederation Congress, Arthur St. Clair had served as governor of the Northwest Territory since its creation by Congress in 1787. With the establishment of a territorial legislature in 1799, St. Clair, a Federalist, found himself repeatedly at odds with the growing Republican presence in the territory, which centered on the town of Chillicothe in the Scioto River Valley. Chief among the governor's critics was Thomas Worthington, a native Virginian who came to the territory in 1798. He quickly became an influential member of the assembly and, along with Nathaniel Massie and Edward Tiffin, one of the territory's leading Republicans. St. Clair's opponents accused him of aristocratic and dictatorial behavior, and especially resented St. Clair's efforts to redivide the territory and thus delay its advancement to statehood. In December 1801, they sent Worthington and Chillicothe legislator Michael Baldwin (a half-brother of Senator Abraham Baldwin of Georgia) to Washington, where they were to lobby Congress against St. Clair's redivision plan and, if possible, to secure statehood (ANB; Cayton, *Frontier Republic*, 68-75; Sears, *Thomas Worthington*, 46-68; William Goforth to TJ, 5 Jan.).

Worthington arrived in Washington on 11 Jan. Soon after, he wrote Massie that "should you be active and decided in making proper charges against the governor I have had assurance from some friends" that St. Clair would be removed from office. In additional letters sent to Massie, Tiffin, and other territorial allies, Worthington requested evidence to support a list of charges that he was compiling against St. Clair to lay before the president. Worthington and Baldwin met with Jefferson on 18 Jan. and "Informed him of the Situation of the Terr'y." Worthington met with Jefferson again on 21 Jan. and dined with him four days later. On 1 Feb., Worthington noted in his diary that he "waited on the president and delivered to the Sec'y of state charges ag't Gov'r St. Clair" (Sears, *Thomas Worthington*, 68, 73-7, 79-81; Brown, "Frontier Politics," 248-9; David Meade Massie, *Nathaniel Massie, A Pioneer of Ohio. A Sketch of his Life and Selections from his Correspondence* [Cincinnati, 1896], 179-82, 188, 192-8; Smith, *St. Clair Papers*, 2:571-5).

Worthington's 30 Jan. letter to Jefferson (Document I) is his earliest extant attempt to lay the case for St. Clair's removal in writing before the president. Since Worthington was in Washington and most of his contact with Jefferson was in person, this probably explains why this letter and most of his other correspondence with the president on this matter were not recorded in SJL or endorsed by Jefferson. Document I reveals that Worthington was still working to strengthen his allegations against the governor, with several charges awaiting evidence from Worthington's allies at home or from State Department files in Washington. Writing Massie on 9 Feb., Worthington summarized the list of the seven charges presented in Document I and urged Massie in particular to forward evidence documenting the taking of illegal fees and removal of judicial appointees by St. Clair (Massie, *Nathaniel Massie*, 194-6).

Document II, Jefferson's draft of the charges against St. Clair, was written sometime after Document I and before Worthington prepared his finalized list of charges and supporting evidence dated 20 Feb. (Document III). Jefferson's version of the charges largely repeats those made in Document I, but in a list format and with the lengthier charges in Document I reduced to briefer, more succinct entries. For instance, allegations made by Worthington under charge 1 in Document I are broken into three distinct charges (charges 1, 2, and 4) by Jefferson in Document II. Similarly, charges 9 and 10 on Jefferson's list are taken from charge 6 in Document I. Charge 11 is unique to Jefferson's list and appears in neither Document I nor Document III. This charge, however, was later crossed out by Jefferson.

Sometime shortly after Jefferson drafted Document II, Meriwether Lewis prepared a fair copy of it, including Jefferson's emendations, which was forwarded to Worthington, who made alterations to the final three charges on the list. He added the phrase "(neglected and thereby)" near the start of charge 9 and replaced the blank and word "years" near the end of the charge with "18 mos." At the end of charge 10, Worthington added "and contempt of militia regulations." Worthington also placed a brace in the left margin next to charge 11 with the words "not inserted" (Tr in OChHi: Territorial and Early Statehood Manuscript Collection).

Lewis's fair copy of Document II, with Worthington's emendations, became the list of 10 charges against St. Clair prepared by Worthington on 20 Feb., to which he added explanations and references to supporting evidence (Document III). Worthington forwarded these documents to the president by way of the secretary of state. In a 26 Feb. 1802 letter to Madison,

Worthington wrote: "I have endeavoured to make such explanations and references as will make the Inclosed charges against Governor St Clair easily understood and supposed it would be best to put these explanations on a seperate paper which will accompany the charges. I have the honour now to return them to you together with such documents in support of the charges as have come to my hands with a request that you will do me the favour to lay them before the president of the US" (RC in same).

After forwarding Document III to the president in late February, Worthington continued to send the secretary of state new evidence received from his territorial allies (Worthington to Madison, 11 Mch. and 5 Apr. 1802, RCs in same). Nathaniel Massie sent his own version of the charges against St. Clair to Madison. Although Massie's list only consisted of five charges, they repeated in similar form and content several of the accusations made by Worthington against St. Clair: that he sought to redivide the territory for political purposes, that he received illegal fees, that he usurped legislative authority regarding the creation of counties, that he was hostile to republican government, and that he exercised undue influence over the judiciary (Madison, *Papers, Sec. of State Ser.*, 2:460-2).

In early March, St. Clair traveled to Washington in order to defend himself in person against the charges made by Worthington and Massie. The governor arrived on 19 Mch. and, shortly thereafter, Worthington recorded that St. Clair had been "furnished with the charges against him" (*Washington Federalist*, 22 Mch. 1802; Massie, *Nathaniel Massie*, 204). A transcript of Document III is in the microfilm edition of St. Clair's papers. Upon his arrival, St. Clair spent the next several weeks preparing his defense and writing supporters for evidence to counter Worthington's allegations. These papers were sent to the secretary of state and subsequently forwarded to Jefferson (Smith, *St. Clair Papers*, 2:581-3; Madison, *Papers, Sec. of State Ser.*, 3:199, 268-9). The emendations in Document II inserted by Jefferson at the end of charges 7 and 8 probably refer to documents received as part of St. Clair's defense and were added at a later sitting.

Jefferson deferred taking action on St. Clair's case until the end of April 1802, when he sent a circular letter to the heads of departments enclosing Worthington's 20 Feb. list of charges, St. Clair's answer to them, and the assorted documentation in support or refutation of them. In the end, St. Clair was allowed to retain his office. Jefferson's cabinet agreed that most of the charges against the governor were not established, while those that were did not carry sufficient weight to justify his removal. In June 1802, Madison informed St. Clair of the president's "particular disapprobation" of the tenure of office granted to his son and the "illegal fees" accepted while in office, and trusted that St. Clair's future conduct in office would "coincide with the benevolent policy of the federal Government" toward the "rights and interests" of the inhabitants of the Northwest Territory (TJ to Heads of Departments, 29 Apr. 1802; Madison, *Papers, Sec. of State Ser.*, 3:332).

I. From Thomas Worthington

Feeling no prejudice towards Governor St. Clair as a man but on the other hand viewing him rather with an eye of pity it is not a pleasing task to me to obliged in defence of what I conceive the just and lawfull rights of myself in common with my fellow citizens of the N.W Territory to remonstrate against his conduct—In doing this Sir no circumstance shall be stated which cannot be substantiated by proper testimony—I will not trouble you with every act of Governor St Clair which has caused discontent but will confine myself to those which have given general dissatisfaction & which have tended in their consequences to produce ferment and confusion in his government—

I am well assured Sir that you will need no arguments to convince you that there is always much difficulty in establishing facts which shall be the grounds on which to found the impeachment of an officer placed in the situation of Governor St Clair yet there may be more than enough to prove that the general tenor of his conduct is such as to show him unworthy of so high and confidential a station in the Government of a free people

The very extensive powers given to the Governor by the ordinance for the government of the Territory will in almost every instance be resorted to as a shield to defend him against complaint But when the whole tenor of his conduct is marked with a design to promote his own pecuniary Interest and gratify his ambitious and tyrannical disposition regardless of the welfare and happiness of the people governed by him I trust sir that a wise and Just government (which I believe that of the united states to be and to which the people of the N.W. Territory look up for protection and a distribution of equal rights & Justice) will not be regardless of their well founded complaints—To prove what has been asserted let facts be stated which cannot be confuted

1st

He has wantonly rejected laws passed by the representatives of for the good of the people & as wantonly usurped the power of erecting new counties contrary to any candid construction of words and when the united voice of two branches of the legislature remonstrated against it—At the commencement of the first session of the Territorial legislature in 1799 sundry petitions were presented to the Governor praying that new counties might be laid out their petitions were sent down to the house of representatives and the petitioners informed by the governor that they must apply to their representatives

as his power to lay out new counties ceased with the commencement of the representative government—Six laws was therefore passed erecting new counties by two branches of the Legislature all of which were (not untill the day he prorogued the assembly nor was his change in opinion known before) rejected—Five other laws were rejected in all eleven at the same session the expense of which to the territory could not be less than $3000 and near one third of the labours of the session were lost—Two of these laws were intended to take away the governors fees on tavern and marriage licences and that he might be reconciled to their passage an appropriation of 500 dollars was made him to this last appropriation law he gave his assent but rejected the two former laws the one regulating marriages and the other taverns The paper marked 1 contains the Journals of this session page 207 the Governors address to the assembly on the last day of the session will be found and will verify the foregoing charge
2nd
He has assumed the power of granting commissions during his pleasure and has done so in all cases one only excepted which is the office of Attorney Genl given by him to his son during good behaviour This will be proved by reffering to the report of the secretary of the Territory in one of the years 1795-1796 or 1797 If not noticed in his report the commission is recorded in his office—
3rd
He has in the appointment of civil officers in the new counties within the territory selected persons who resided without the county and were his favourites to the most lucrative offices contrary to the wishes of the people and when there was characters well qualified to fill such offices resideing within such new laid out counties—
4th
He has created perquisites to his office which are unjust and Illegal—For every tavern licence granted before last session of the assembly he recd. four dollars—For every ferry licence granted before the session of 1799 he recd one guinea he now receives one guinea for every marriage licence by him granted—Fees are recd on militia commissions and are also charged on all the commissions of the civil officers in each newly erected county in proportion as the commission is lucrative—Authentick documents to substantiate the foregoing facts will be produced in a few days—Other fees are taken not here mentioned—
5th
He has attempted to make the Judiciary dependant on his will and when Justices have acted with firmness and Independance in giveing such a construction to an existing statute law as appeared to them

reasonable and right their commissions have been revoked by his proclamation

The late case of Colo Finley is nearly a repetion of the same conduct the paper marked 2 states the circumstances attendant on this transaction

6th

He is an open and avowed enemy to a republican form of government and an advocate for monarchy is also an open & declared enemy to militia regulations which declaration his practice hitherto has confirmed as the militia in the territory are without organization although a good militia law has been enacted for two years past

7th

He has created and endeavoured to attach to himself a party and in conjunction with them has made attemps and in some measure succeeded to destroy the harmony and divide the Interests of the people affecting to promote the local interests of certain places thereby enlisting partizans to support his views—The late effort to alter the bounds of the states in the Territory originated with the Governor and has been supported by his influence in every stage—If a letter wrote by him to Mr Pickering then secretary of state in Decr. 1799 or in the succeeding months of Jany. or February 1800 can be found in the office of the secretary of state it will prove this assertion beyond a doubt for in that letter the very plan which the governor and his party have pursued was pointed out to the secretary of state and it was urged by the Governor that the then administration should procure a division of the population of the territory so as to prevent any part from becomeing an independant state because when they did they would oppose the views of the administration—It will be proper for me to observe that Mr Pickering permitted Mr Harrison then a representative in Congress to read this letter and that Mr Harrison on the same day stated to me the substance thereof and is now willing to support with his deposition what I have stated—The paper marked 3 is the copy of a letter from the Governor to Mr Harrison & points out the same plan but in a different shape here Territorial divisions are contemplated as the necessary consequence of state divisions or might be preparatory thereto—

In a few days I shall receive documents to support in the most positive manner the 4th & 6th charges Should it be required many other facts can be stated equally disagreeable to the people and to which they have patienty so far been obliged to submit

I have the honour to be with great Respect

Sir Your Obt Sr   T. WORTHINGTON

RC (OChHi: Territorial and Early Statehood Manuscript Collection); torn; at foot of text: "The president of the United States." Enclosures: (1) Address by Arthur St. Clair to the General Assembly of the Northwest Territory, 19 Dec. 1799 (see below). (2) Probably a copy of the *Scioto Gazette*, 2 Jan. 1802, which reprinted a number of documents relating to the 26 Dec. 1801 confrontation at St. Clair's lodgings in Chillicothe and the ensuing conflict between St. Clair and Samuel Finley (see below). (3) St. Clair to William Henry Harrison, dated 17 Feb. 1800 from Cincinnati, expressing St. Clair's thoughts on dividing the Northwest Territory, since the "vast extent of it" makes it almost impossible to govern; he suggests a division into three districts by revising the boundaries specified in the Northwest Ordinance of 1787 and making the Scioto River the boundary between the eastern and middle districts instead of the Great Miami River; such a division would most likely make Marietta the seat of the eastern district and Cincinnati that of the middle district; a division of the territory into just two districts, St. Clair warns, "must ruin Cincinnati" (printed in *Letter From Arthur St. Clair, Governor of the North-western Territory, on the Subject of a Division of the said Territory; and the Petition of George Tevebaugh and Others, Inhabitants of Knox County, in the North-western Territory. Read the 14th March 1800. Ordered to lie on the Table. Printed by order of the House of Representatives of the United States* [Philadelphia, 1800], 3-6).

A farmer, surveyor, and land speculator from Virginia, Thomas Worthington (1773-1827) moved with his family to Chillicothe in the Northwest Territory in 1798. He soon after became an influential member of the territorial assembly and a leading critic of Governor Arthur St. Clair. In December 1801, opponents of the territorial regime sent Worthington to Washington, where he led the successful campaign to secure statehood for Ohio. A Republican and supporter of TJ's administration, he represented Ohio in the U.S. Senate from 1803 to 1807, and again from 1810 to 1814, then served as Ohio's governor from 1814 to 1818 (ANB; *Biog. Dir. Cong.*).

St. Clair's ADDRESS TO THE ASSEMBLY on 19 Dec. 1799 was delivered at the close of its first session and presented a lengthy defense of his decision to veto several acts of the legislature, deeming them to be either unwise, unnecessary, or, in the establishment of new counties, to be "the proper business of the executive" (*Journal of the House of Representatives, of the Territory of the United States, North-west of the River Ohio. At the First Session of the General Assembly, A.D. 1799* [Cincinnati, 1800], 207-11).

LATE CASE OF COLO FINLEY: on the evening of 26 Dec. 1801, a confrontation occurred at St. Clair's lodgings in Chillicothe among the governor's opponents and supporters. Deeming the incident a riot, St. Clair summoned Samuel Finley, a justice of the peace, and demanded that he bind four persons involved in the affair for appearance at the next court of quarter sessions. After collecting depositions from eyewitnesses, however, Finley stated that he found no evidence of riotous behavior and refused to comply with the governor's demands. St. Clair denounced Finley in a message to the territorial assembly on 29 Dec. and submitted copies of the letters exchanged between them the previous day. The address to the assembly and its related letters were reprinted in the 2 Jan. 1802 edition of the *Scioto Gazette*, as well as a 1 Jan. 1802 letter to the editor by Finley defending his actions. The dispute ended with Finley's resignation from office (Sears, *Thomas Worthington*, 68-71; Cayton, *Frontier Republic*, 74; Smith, *St. Clair Papers*, 2:555-7; *Scioto Gazette*, 9 Jan. 1802).

A GOOD MILITIA LAW HAS BEEN ENACTED: on 13 Dec. 1799, the territorial legislature passed "An Act Establishing and Regulating the Militia," which reorganized the territorial militia and repealed all previous laws on the subject. In doing so, however, all commissions previously granted were vacated, which resulted in "an entire derangement of the militia." To remedy the situation, the assembly passed a supplementary act on 8 Dec. 1800, which directed the governor to commission at least as many officers as necessary to command one regiment in each county, who would then meet the following June at their respective court houses to organize their county militias (*Laws of the Territory of the United States, North-West of the River Ohio; Passed at the First Session of the General Assembly, Begun and Held at Cincinnati, on Monday, the Sixteenth Day of September, A.D. One Thousand, Seven Hundred and Ninety Nine* [Cincinnati, 1800], 121-51; *Laws of the Territory of the United States, North-West of the River Ohio; Passed at the Second Session of the First General Assembly, Begun and Holden at Chillicothe, on Monday, the Third Day of November, One Thousand Eight Hundred* [Chillicothe, 1801], 67-8).

II. List of Charges Against Arthur St. Clair

[ca. 30 Jan.-20 Feb. 1802]

Charges exhibited to the President of the US.[1] against the Honourable Arthur Saint Clair, as Governor of the territory of the US. North West of the river Ohio.

1. He has usurped legislative powers, by the erection of counties and location of the seats of justice by[2] proclamation, on his own[3] sole authority.

2. He has misused the power of negativing legislative acts, by putting his negative on laws[4] useful and necessary for the territory.

3. He has refused to perform the duties of his office but on the paiment of arbitrary fees not established by any lawful authority.

4. He has[5] negatived an act of the legislature abolishing those fees, and passed[6] their act giving him 500. D. meant[7] as a compensation for that abolition;[8] thereby holding both the fees and the compensation.

5. He has attempted to effect the dismemberment of the territory, & to destroy[9] it's constitutional boundaries, in order to prevent it's advancement to those rights of self-government to which it's numbers would entitle it.[10]

6. He has granted commissions generally[11] during pleasure; but that of Attorney-general to his own son during good behavior.

7. He has endeavored arbitrarily to influence and controul the proceedings of the judiciary, and has revoked or effected[12] a surrender of the commissions of those who have refused to bend to his will. *acknold. pa. 22. revoked 3. commns. & pa. 34.*

8. He has appointed persons residing out of a county to offices the duties of which[13] were to be habitually performed within them. *acknold. pa. 20. in the case of Robb his son in law, made Recorder of Clermont tho' living in Hamilton. executd. by depy.*

9. He has[14] obstructed the organisation and disciplining of a militia

for the defence of the territory[15] by witholding the appointment of officers   years[16] after a law had[17] passed establishing them.

10. He has avowed his hostility to the form & substance of republican government.[18]

11. He is in the habit of indulging himself in arbitrary and rude conduct towards those who have to transact business, with him, or under him.[19]

MS (DLC: TJ Papers, 124:21414); undated; entirely in TJ's hand with words in italics added by him at a later date. Tr (OChHi: Territorial and Early Statehood Manuscript Collection); in Meriwether Lewis's hand, with emendations in Thomas Worthington's hand (see notes 14, 16, 18-19 below); lacks TJ's later emendations.

St. Clair appointed Samuel ROBB a justice of the peace and justice of the court of common pleas for Hamilton County on 26 Nov. 1800. Two weeks later, on 9 Dec., Robb was also appointed RECORDER of neighboring CLERMONT County (*Terr. Papers*, 3:526-7).

[1] Preceding five words and abbreviation interlined.
[2] Word written over partially erased "of his."
[3] Word interlined.
[4] TJ here canceled "the most."
[5] Word interlined.
[6] TJ first wrote "passing" before altering the word to read as above.
[7] Word interlined.

[8] Remainder of sentence interlined.
[9] TJ first wrote "He has endeavored to dismember the territory, & destroy" before altering the passage to read as above.
[10] TJ first wrote "to which their numbers would entitle them" before altering the passage to read as above.
[11] TJ first wrote "granted all commissions" before altering the text to read as above.
[12] TJ first wrote "and revoked or forced" before altering the text to read as above.
[13] TJ first wrote "to perform offices which."
[14] In Tr, Worthington here interlined "(neglected and thereby)."
[15] Preceding six words interlined.
[16] In Tr, Worthington inserted "18 mos" in the space and canceled "years."
[17] Word interlined.
[18] In Tr, Worthington here added "and contempt of militia regulations."
[19] Charge canceled by TJ at a later date. In Tr, Worthington inserted a brace next to the charge in the left margin with the words "not inserted."

III. Thomas Worthington's Charges and Explanations

Charges exhibited to the President of the United States against Arthur St Clair Esquire as Governor of the Territory of the United States North West of the River Ohio
1. He has usurped legislative powers by the erection of courts and location of seats of justice by proclamation on his own sole authority
2. He has misused the power of negativing legislative Acts by putting his negative on laws useful and necessary for the Territory

3. He has refused to perform the duties of his office but on the payment of arbitary fees not established by any lawful authority

4. He has negatived acts of the legislature abolishing those fees and passed their act giveing him 500 Dollars meant as a compensation for that abolition thereby holding both the fees and the compensation

5. He has attempted to effect the dismemberment of the Territory and to destroy its constitutional boundaries in order to prevent its advancement to those rights of self government to which its numbers would entitle it

6. He has granted commissions generally during pleasure but that of Attorney general to his own son during good behaviour

7. He has endeavoured arbitarily to influence and controul the proceedings of the judiciary and has revoked and effected a surrender of the commissions of those who have refused to bend to his will

8. He has appointed persons resideing out of a county to offices the duties of which were to be habitually performed within them.

9. He has (neglected and thereby) obstructed the organization and diciplining of a militia for the defence of the territory by withholding the appointment of officers 18 months after a law had passed establishing them

10. He has avowed his hostility to the form and substance of republican government and his contempt of Militia Regulations

T. WORTHINGTON
City of Washington
February 20th 1802

Explanation of and references to documents in support of the foregoing charges.

1.   The paper marked No 1 contains three proclamations of the Govenor erecting the counties of Clermont, Fairfield and Belmont

2.   Eleven laws were rejected at one session Viz 6 erecting new counties 1 regulating marriages 1 regulating taverns 1 createing the office of County surveyor 1 to ascertain the number of souls in the eastern division or state in the territory and 1 establishing Manchester as the seat of justice for the county of Adams. See the journals of that session marked A page 207 the Governors communication to the house of representatives on this subject. At the last session of the assembly he rejected a second time an act regulateing marriages see the journals of that session marked B page 177.

3.   Fees on marriage Ferry & Tavern licences have been demanded and received. It is true there is or was a law in the territorial statute book said to be adopted from the pennsylvania code directing the

payment of 4 dollars to the Governor for each tavern licence but let it be remembered that the governor was a principle in the enacting or adopting this law giveing fees to himself in the other cases fees have been taken without the color or sanction of a law. The paper marked No 2 exhibits full proof of the foregoing charge. Other fees have been taken as shall be made appear hereafter

4.   No official communication was made on the part of the Assembly to the Governor expressive of their real intention in giveing him this sum; A general understanding was believed to exist on this subject. A reliance on the candour and Integrity of the Governor induced the assembly to act open and unguarded. See the journals marked A page 211 the governors acceptance of the sum appropriated page 208 his rejection of the acts to abolish his fees on tavern and marriage licences

5.   The Governor exercised usurped power and violated his constitutional authority wantonly in assenting to the late law of the territory which was almost unanimously rejected by Congress. On examination of the ordinance of Congress for the government of the territory it will appear that no such power is given him. He communicated the plan of this law to Mr Pickering late Secretary of State by letter dated in Jany or Feby 1800. It was urged by the Governor that the population of the Territory ought to be divided in order to prevent any part from governing itself for a great length of time because at such period as its self government commenced it would commence its opposition to the views of the then administration. It is hoped this letter is to be found in the office of state if not the substance thereof can be proved. The paper marked No 3 contains the governors letter to the then delegate in congress from the Territory pointing out the same plan and is expressive of the governors and local attachments

6.   This fact is too notorious to be denied

7.   The revocation of the commissions of Nathaniel Massie and others justices of the[1] court of common pleas for Adams County and the late case of Colo Finly stated at length in the paper marked No. 4 it is hoped[2] fully proves this charge

8.   John J Wills Esqr of Cincinnati in Hamilton County was appointed 1st prothonotary of Adams County afterwards recorder of deeds and register of lands in Ross County Mr George Gordon of Cincinnati succeeded Mr Wills in the clerkship of Adams County. The case stated by Judge Meigs is another in point where the same person is appointed to two different offices in different counties other cases could be stated if necessary

9.   For what cause the commissions were withheld from the militia

officers of Ross county is best known to the Governor An advertisement appeared in the sioto gazette (I think in October last) signed by the commanding officers of the militia for that county stateing that in consequence of the Govr. not haveing issued the necessary commissions the militia could not be diciplined. The paper marked No 5 exhibits further proof on this subject

10.   The paper marked No 6 exhibits positive proof of this avowal haveing been made in one instance in the house of Mr Joseph Tiffin in the Town of Chilicothe on the 19th of December 1801

MS (DLC); in Worthington's hand; endorsed by TJ: "Worthington's charges. references to documents." Dft (OChHi: Territorial and Early Statehood Manuscript Collection); undated; in Worthington's hand; incomplete, consisting of explanation and references only. Tr (Linda Elise Kalette, ed., *The Papers of Arthur St. Clair,* microfilm edition, 8 reels [Columbus, 1977], 7:204-9); in unidentified hands. Enclosures: (1) Proclamations by Arthur St. Clair creating the counties of Clermont, Fairfield, and Belmont, dated 6 and 9 Dec. 1800 and 7 Sep. 1801, respectively (printed in *Terr. Papers,* 3:526-8). (2) Address by St. Clair to the General Assembly of the Northwest Territory, 19 Dec. 1799 (see note to Document i). (3) Address by St. Clair to the General Assembly of the Northwest Territory, 23 Jan. 1802, in *Journal of the House of Representatives of the Territory of the United States, North-west of the Ohio, at the First Session of the Second General Assembly, A.D. 1801* (Chillicothe, 1801), 176-8. (4) St. Clair to William Henry Harrison, 17 Feb. 1800 (see Enclosure No. 3 at Document i). (5) Probably a copy of the *Scioto Gazette,* 2 Jan. 1802 (see Enclosure No. 2 at Document i). (6) Statement of Francis Dunlavy and Jacob White, dated 26 Dec. 1801 and attested by Joseph Darlinton, recording declarations made by St. Clair at the house of Joseph Tiffin on 19 Dec., in which the deponents state that St. Clair uttered "many words and Sentences in contempt and reproach of the Government of the United States" and declared that it would soon "settle down into an Aristocracy, and from thence into a Monarchy," which was the only government that could be sanctioned by God; St. Clair then added "several ludicrous

and sarcastic observations," stating that the militia was "all damned nonsense" and denouncing the "experiments" put forth by TJ in his 8 Dec. address to Congress as things "not to be admitted in government" (Tr in OChHi: Territorial and Early Statehood Manuscript Collection). Other enclosure not identified.

At the close of the assembly on 23 Jan. 1802, St. Clair justified his second veto of an ACT REGULATING MARRIAGES on the grounds that it allowed persons to wed "at too early a time of life" and that the power to grant marriage licenses properly resided with the governor and not with the prothonotaries of county courts (*Journal of the House of Representatives of the Territory . . . 1801,* 176-8).

The LAW IN THE TERRITORIAL STATUTE BOOK giving the governor four dollars for every tavern license granted was enacted by St. Clair and the territorial judges on 17 June 1795. The title of the law noted that it was ADOPTED FROM THE PENNSYLVANIA CODE (*Laws of the Territory of the United States North-West of the Ohio: Adopted and Made by the Governour and Judges, in their Legislative Capacity, at a Session begun on Friday, the XXIX day of May, One Thousand, Seven Hundred, and Ninety-five, and Ending on Tuesday the Twenty-fifth Day of August Following* [Cincinnati, 1796], 96-101).

DELEGATE IN CONGRESS FROM THE TERRITORY: William Henry Harrison.

NATHANIEL MASSIE was a leading figure in the settlement of the Scioto River Valley and a prominent ally of Worthington. In 1798, he clashed with St. Clair in a dispute over the location of the seat of ADAMS COUNTY. Massie wanted it at Manchester, a town he had founded and that was already well established. St. Clair named an alternate site and vehemently defended the authority of the governor to fix the location of county seats. When Massie and another justice, Benjamin Goodin, defied the governor and attempted to hold court at Manchester, St. Clair revoked the commissions of Massie and Goodin for having "Misdemened themselves in the execution of their office by attempting to disturb the regular administration of justice" (Cayton, *Frontier Republic*, 53-5, 60-1; Beverley W. Bond, Jr., *The Foundations of Ohio* [Columbus, 1941], 428-9; *Terr. Papers*, 3:515-16).

A territorial judge and former Federalist from Marietta, Return Jonathan MEIGS, Jr., had recently joined the Republicans in Ohio. He had traveled to Washington in January 1802, where he cooperated with Worthington and met with TJ several times before returning home in mid-February (ANB; Brown, "Frontier Politics," 249-50, 438).

On 10 Oct. 1801, ROSS COUNTY militia commanders James Dunlap and Elias Langham placed an ADVERTISEMENT in the *Scioto Gazette* calling for a militia muster at Chillicothe on the 20th. An announcement in the same newspaper on 24 Oct., however, stated that the muster was canceled because St. Clair had not returned from Marietta in time to issue the necessary officers' commissions.

JOSEPH TIFFIN operated a tavern in Chillicothe that was a popular gathering place for territorial legislators (Sears, *Thomas Worthington*, 56).

[1] Canceled: "peace."
[2] Preceding three words interlined.

From Delamotte

MONSIEUR   Havre le 30. Janvier 1802.

J'ai recû avec bien de la reconnoissance ma Commission de Vice-agent commercial dans ce port. C'est à vous, à tous égards, que j'en dois mes remerciements et je vous prier de vouloir bien les recevoir et les agréer avec autant de Complaisance, que je mets de prix au bienfait. Vous avés en même tems nommé m. Dobell, agent; vous avés surement eû de bonnes raisons pour le faire & cela ne m'a pas empêché, soit par vanité, ou par confiance dans votre bonté, de voir, dans votre Condescendence à ma priere, l'envie de me montrer que vous m'honorés de votre estime, chose que je prise à l'égal de tout.

J'ai fait présenter ma Commission au ministre des relations extérieures par un ami. J'ai été repoussé, comme mr. Cathalan & je le serai, je crois, constamment, parceque je suis françois. Je vois par tout ce qui se passe à ce sujet, que notre gouvernement n'a pas encore de sistême bien arreté sur cette matiere et je prends le parti de differer de faire aucune démarche, pour ensuitte faire celles que les circonstances me permettront

On dit en ce moment que la paix finale avec l'angleterre est signée & qu'elle sera annoncée officiellement au retour à Paris de notre premier consul qui est à Lyon. tout le monde le repête, personne n'y apporte de contradiction & je crois qu'on peut y avoir confiance. dès ce moment là, notre acte de navigation sera en activité sans restriction, c'est une perte considerable pour le Commerce des E.U. mais il est bien vrai aussi, que si la france devoit continuer à payer à l'étranger ce qu'elle lui vendoit autrefois, nous finirions par n'avoir plus le sol et nous sommes, en vérité deja beaucoup trop près de cette situation. Jamais pays, je crois, n'a eû autant besoin d'un peû de prospérité, que nous l'avons.

Je suis avec respect Monsieur Votre très humble & très obéïssant serviteur. DELAMOTTE

EDITORS' TRANSLATION

SIR   Le Havre, 30 Jan. 1802
I received with much gratitude my commission as commercial vice-agent in this port. It is to you, in all respects, that I owe my thanks for it, and I beg you to receive them and to accept them with as much indulgence as I place value on the kindness. At the same time you named Mr. Dobell, agent; you assuredly had good reasons to do so, and that has not prevented me— whether out of vanity or confidence in your kindness—from seeing in your affably acceding to my request, the desire to show me that you honor me with your esteem, something that I prize as equal to everything.

I had my commission presented by a friend to the minister of foreign relations. I was rebuffed, like Mr. Cathalan, as I believe I shall always be, because I am French. I see from everything that has happened on this subject that our government does not yet have a firmly fixed system on this topic, and I have decided to defer taking any step, so as later to take those that circumstances may allow me.

It is said at this time that the final peace with England has been signed and that it will be announced officially upon the return to Paris of our first consul, who is in Lyons. Everyone repeats it, no one contradicts it, and I think one may be confident of it. From that moment, our navigation act will be in effect without restriction; that is a considerable loss for U.S. trade, but it is also true that if France were to continue to pay to foreign countries what it formerly sold to them, we would end up not having a penny, and we are in truth already much too close to that situation. No country, I think, has had as great a need of a little prosperity as we have.

I am with respect, Sir, your very humble and obedient servant.

DELAMOTTE

RC (DLC); at foot of first page: "Monsieur Jefferson President des Etats unis d'Amerique"; endorsed by TJ as received 5 Apr. Recorded in SJL as received 4 Apr.

Delamotte's COMMISSION as vice commercial agent at Le Havre, dated 1 June 1801, was an interim appointment. After the Senate approved the nomination, TJ signed a new commission for Delamotte on 26 Jan. 1802 (both in Lb in DNA: RG 59, PTCC; JEP, 1:403, 405).

MINISTRE DES RELATIONS EXTÉRIEURES: Talleyrand.

PAIX FINALE: France and Great Britain did not sign the definitive treaty of peace until 27 Mch. (Parry, Consolidated Treaty Series, 56:298).

From Denniston & Cheetham

Your favour is received: but on account of making the use of it which you required, and which You will perhaps recollect, we are not able to mention the date. We are Sorry to give you So much trouble; we are in Some degree Sensible of the arduousness of the high function you fill and of the multiplicity of business You have to attend to. And yet it may be necessary for us sometimes to Commerce with you. We shall always feel a high Satisfaction in receiving answers from you to our Communications; but whenever you Shall find it inconvenient we will readily and Cheerfully dispense with them—

We propose to give you a true and Correct narative of the Suppression of Wood's History of the administration of Mr. John Adams. It Shall be as Concise as possible. Perhaps it may not be without its use, to impart to you, previously, Some information of Wood himself.

Wood is by birth a Scotchman. It appears from Credible information as well as from the title page of his "history of Switzerland" which was published at Edinburgh, that he was "Master of the Academy established at Edinburgh by the honorable the board of trustees for the improvement of Arts in Scotland." He is a Good Mathematician: an ellegant drawer and a Complete master of the Greek, latin and french languages.—But he has *no fixed principles in politics* and in every respect he is a man of Great indecision and versatility. He was one of the Edinburgh reviewers: but he can write with as much pleasure and with as great facility in defence of monarchy as in that of Representative government like our own. His history of Switzerland (which from the Scarcity of the work here you have probably not Seen) abounds with Sentiments as monarchical and despotic as any Contained in Burke's letters on the French revolution, or any other Anti-republican production. It was written in 1799. He has been in America about eighteen months. By profession he is a republican; in action *any thing*. We Confine this word, however, to his political acts; we know nothing of his *private dealings* that is dishonorable to him. He was originally introduced to Mr. Burr as a teacher of languages and the Mathematics. He taught his daughter the greek and latin languages and we believe Something of Drawing. Since then Mr. Burr has been his freind. This freindship was no doubt Commencd on honorable Grounds. What will be its termination we will not pretend to predict.

Mr. Wood was hired to write the history of the administration. He Contracted with Messrs Barlas & Ward, Booksellers in this City to write an octavo volume of 500 pages for 200 Dollars. The work was written according to agreement, printed by Messrs Barlas and Ward and according to Contract became their exclusive property. When the volume was ready for publication an overture was made by Mr. Wood to Messrs Barlas & Ward to purchase the Whole edition for the purpose of entire Suppression. The basis of the negociation was an offer to refund the net expences *only* of the edition. The poverty of Mr. Wood was however known to Messrs Barlas and Ward and of Course they refused to enter into a pecuniary agreement with him the fullfillment of which were to rest on him alone. Mr. Wood was therefore under the necessity of unfolding the name of his employer and to gratify whom the proposition for Suppression was made. Mr. Burr authorised Mr. Wood to Say in writing, if required that he would be responsible for the fulfilment of any agreement which Mr. Wood might enter into for the Suppression of the work. This was accordingly done by a letter written by Mr. Wood which we have Seen by permission of Mr. Barlas. Various letters Were exchanged Concerning the price of Suppression. 2000 Dollars were demanded by Messrs Barlas and Ward; 1100 were ultimately agreed upon; and Mr. Wood specially authorised by Mr. Burr consented to give it. In this transaction Wood was considered as the representative of Mr. Burr—

Secrecy was enjoined upon Messrs. Barlas & Ward. It was Stated at the Commencement of the negociation that the proposition for Suppressing the work was not to be made known unless Mr. Burr Should eventually recede from a mutual and final agreement—

It was found difficult however to procure the 1100 Dollars which was agreed upon to be paid for the Suppression of the Edition. A Second overture was therefore made, to wit, that the Sum Should be paid partly in Specie and partly in promisory notes with good indorsers. This was accepted, and a day appointed for a final Settlement. When the day arrived however even this mode of payment was found inconvenient. Procrastination ensued, and Messrs Barlas and Ward became alarmed. Thus Situated Mr. Barlass applied to Several persons for advice, and amongst others, to ourselves. At first he Spoke of the Subject with a degree of reserve incompatible with the objects of his enquiry. After two or three interviews, however, he opened his mind frankly, and disclosed the whole Scene. He related what we have here Stated—and what we Shall hereafter State. He was advised to obtain the Stipulated Sum if possible; but if in the end he Should find it impossible, then to publish the work as the only mean left to indemnify himself for the expence of printing the edition.

This was advised in contradistinction to a proposition of his own, namely to Sue Mr. Burr for the Sum agreed upon. This we thought the best plan he Could pursue to Secure the expence he had incurred in printing the edition. For owing to the Garrullity of Mr. Wood and Several other Circumstances, the Suppression had become a matter of Such notoriety as to form a Subject of Tavern Conversation. Of course it was Considered, and very Justly too, by Mr. Barlas, that the Sale of the work was already materially injured. Wood was willing to declare on oath that he was the agent for Mr. Burr and that he ratified the agreement made by Wood with Barlas & Ward. Many hindrances, however were found in the way of prosecution, and eventually Mr. Barlas Consented to wave it. In this Suspence Barlas & Ward were kept Six weeks, during which time this matter became more known to the public. At length Mr. Barlas applied to Mr. William Van Ness on the Subject, who has acted as a Sort of *private Secretary* to Mr. Burr during the negociation. He requested W. Van Ness to write to Mr. Burr who was then at Philadelphia on his way to Washington, to know positively whether he intended to pay the money or not! Accordingly a letter was written by him and an answer received which Simply Stated that "If Mr. Barlas looked to him for the money he might look." This was accepted as a Categorical refusal to fulfil the agreement.   This Answer delivered to them by Mr. Van Ness confounded Barlas & Ward. They became irresolute as Mr. Burr became imperious in refusing to Comply with the terms of the Contract. They at length half decided to prosecute him for the recovery of the 1100 Dollars. Accordingly accompanied by Mr. Wood they applied to Mr. Wortman* Counsellor at Law for advice. Mr. Wood made a declaration in writing of his agency to accomplish the Suppression of the edition. this we have read[1] The purport of the Declaration is briefly this "That he was the agent of and employed by Mr. Burr to negociate with Mr. Barlas and Mr. Ward Concerning the Suppression of the History.—That it was agreed to be Suppressed for 1100 Dollars according to instructions which he had received from Mr. Burr, and that Mr. Burr Consented to pay the money according to agreement." This declaration which is now in the hands of Mr. Wortman was not attested by Mr. Wood, but he explicitly declared that if called as an evidence into a Court of Justice he would there attest it.

* Mr. Wortman is the author of the pamphlet we Sent you a few days ago Signed "Lysander" of an octavo volume entitled "A treatise Concerning political enquiry and the liberty of the press." and of Several other tracts. He is personally acquainted with Mr. Gallatin and with the transactions here Stated.

They, nevertheless, at length determined again to make application to Mr. Burr by letter before they had recourse to law. Accordingly Mr. Barlas wrote himself to Mr. Burr at Washington about a fortnight ago. He Stated in his letter that if Mr. Burr would not comply with the agreement by paying the money within a *given day* he would publish the History and expose; in an appendix to it, *the whole negociation*. He was of opinion that rather than Mr. Burr would Suffer the part he had acted in the Scheme of Suppression to be exposed to the public, he would Instantly pay the money. No answer has been received to this letter. Nor Can we tell whether any will be. Such has been the negociation, and Such the train in which it now stands.

You may be Solictous to know Something of the Contents of this History which has been accompanied with So many Singular incidents. We have been favoured by Mr. Barlas with the reading of it. We will give You as accurate a description of the Contents as memory will permit; it must however be very Summary.

It Consists of 508 pages divided in 15 Chapters. The first treats of the Cause of the election of Mr. Adams and of the political Sentiments advanced in his defence, as he *Sportingly* terms it, of the American Constitutions. Mr. Wood occupies about *half a page* in delineating the *Cause* of his election. Respecting the Sentiments Contained in his Defence he says that they are those of Hume and Robertson on the Feudal Systems, and therefore by Confuting those two historians, on whose Sentiments those of Mr. Adams are founded, he Shall Confute him also. In his observations on this part he exhibits great want of reading as well as of intellect. His observations are exceedingly loose & puerile and Such as a man well read, and possessed of claims to Sound argumentation, would really be ashamed of. He has at least Sixty pages of extracts from Callender's History of the United States, his Prospect before us &c. &c. relative to Captures and adjudications of vessels. He has also many pages from the same author, Giving descriptions of various political Characters in the Union. The *whole* Sixteen letters of Mr. Jonathan Dayton to Mr. Childs Concerning land Speculations together with a bill in Chancery filed in this City by Childs against Dayton. These occupy about 30 pages. He treats of Logan's *embassy* to France, and inserts all the newspaper publications that appeared on that Subject. The *whole* of the Speeches of Mr. Adams delivered while he was President. These occupy at least 40 pages of the History. He has also a few Childish Comments upon them—Your Speech to the Senate on your inaugeration as Vice president. The titles of all the acts passed during Mr. Adams's administration. Biography of Mr. Adams taken from Morse's Geography—Biography of yourself taken principally from an European work Intitled "Public Characters," and from a pamphlet which appeared in Vindication of Your Character before your election. Extracts from these two works take up about 10 or 20 pages—A Short Character of Charles C. Pinckney of his own. A Biography of Mr. Burr taken principally from himself and from Governor Livingston's Character of his father which Mr. Wood says is exactly applicable to that of his Son! Character of Hamilton a view of his writings in and out of office. An account of our negociation with the Barbary powers, Consisting of all the official documents published on that Subject, together with about *half a page* of his own. A Confused and indistinct account of ministration of Mr Monroe at Paris with a long narative of an essay made by Mr. Adams while president to Convert *tin into silver*! Character of Pickering, Wollcot, McHenry &c. &c. Revelations of Pickering taken from Newspapers. In short it is a *mere compilation* totally uninterresting, and Cannot possibly be of any Service to our Cause. It is Composed as a man would compose a work merely for pay: mindful only of the bulk, but regardless of the Contents of the volume. It is however in tone *decidedly* republican and exceedingly Severe on the federal members of Congress from new England as well as other conspicuous Federalists throughout the Union.

Such then being the Character of the work, it may probably be asked, what were the motives of Mr. Burr for attempting to purchase its Suppression? Here the business is wrapped in profound Mystery and we are left entirely to Conjecture. It has been Intimated by Mr. Wood and Supposed by Mr. Barlas, that Mr. Burr intends by degrees to form a Coalition with the federalists and feels a Correspondent desire to Crush publications that reflect upon the heads of that party. This however, is Certain that many of those persons whom Mr. Cheetham described to You in the paper which he wrote at Washington have been most cordially engaged in the attempt to Suppress the History. It is generally Supposed here, but particularly by those who are acquainted with *interior* measures, and the General views of *the party* in this City, that he intends to avail himself of the anticipated and perhaps proffered aid of the federalists to elevate him at the next election to the presidential Chair. If this be not his Sole object in essaying to Suppress the history, we Confess our ignorance of it

It is impossible to obtain a Copy of the history, except for a few hours, and even this by Special favour. The Whole edition is in the hands of Messrs Barlas & Ward. Could we Get one for a fortnight, it

Should be obtained and Sent to you with great pleasure; but this is unpracticable. Whether the History will yet be published or not, we know not. At any rate we have relinquished the Idea of writing one ourselves. Mr. Wortman Intends to write the History of the Union, to Commence where Dr. Ramsay Concluded his history [of the] revolution and to Continue it to the end of Your Administration. [It] will embrace every thing that we had in View, and will Supercede the necessity of neglecting our paper to write the history of the Administration of Mr. Adams.

One thing, however, is indispensably prerequisite to the Completion of the work contemplated by Mr. Wortman, or of any other Political History of the union, and of which we beg leave to Say to You a few words—

You will remember that Dr. Ramsay in his preface to his history of the revolution States that he was four years in Collecting [material] for it, notwithstanding he had access to the Official documents [con]tained in the departments of State. It is a Serious misfortune to the country that the *State papers* of the General Government have never been published in regular volumes. These form the basis of the History of the United States. Of their Importance in this and other respect it would be Superfluous for us to Say any thing to you. You are fully Sensible of their Value. Nor are You less Sensible that Such of them as have appeared before the public, have been published in such a manner as to render it almost impossible for any man to Collect them. But if it were possible to Collect them few of the State papers have been published even in newspapers. In Consequence of repeated applications that have been made to us on this Subject, we have it in Contemplation [to c]ommence [a publica]tion of the State papers beginning with the first Congress in 1774 and to Continue them until the termination of Your administration. To this end we have already issued proposals, Stating that as Soon as 600 Subscribers Shall have been obtained, one octavo volume Consisting of 500 pages Shall be delivered to Subscribers every three months at two Dollars in Boards. It is our Intention to publish a regular and uninterrupted Chain of the State papers. Many of them we can obtain from a variety of publications. Others we presume can be had only from the Department of State. For this purpose we beg you to Grant us access to Such public documents as You may think proper for publication. Should you be so kind as to comply with this request, which may tend to the mutual benefit of the Country and ourselves, either of us will visit Washington for the purpose of transcribing them in Such a manner as you may be pleased to prescribe.—

To this part of our letter we Shall feel ourselves extremely oblidge by an answer as Soon as may be Convenient—

We are with the greatest respect and Sincerity your fellow Citizens

DENNISTON & CHEETHAM

RC (DLC); in David Denniston's hand and signed by him; torn; addressed: "To his Excellency Thos. Jefferson City of Washington"; franked; postmarked 1 Feb.; endorsed by TJ as received 4 Feb. and so recorded in SJL.

YOUR FAVOUR: TJ to James Cheetham, 17 Jan.

In late May 1802, David Denniston and James Cheetham published in New York a pamphlet on the SUPPRESSION of John Wood's *History of the Administration of John Adams*. The pamphlet was written by "A CITIZEN of New-York" and entitled *A Narrative of the Suppression by Col. Burr, of the History of the Administration of John Adams, Late President of the United States, Written by John Wood, Author of the History of Switzerland and of the Swiss Revolution* (see Shaw-Shoemaker, No. 2021). Cheetham was recognized as the author of the pamphlet, which elaborated on the information provided in the letter above. William P. Van Ness, Burr's representative, had completed the purchase of all 1,250 copies of the *History of the Administration* from publishers William Barlass and Matthias Ward for $1,000 about 12 May. After the publication of Cheetham's *Narrative*, Burr's supporters believed the suppression of the volume was only hurting the vice president. Van Ness, therefore, sent the copies he had recently purchased to a New York bookseller. They were advertised for sale on 3 June. The controversy continued with the publication at the end of July of Wood's *A Correct Statement of the Various Sources from which The History of the Administration of John Adams was Compiled*. Wood defended the suppression of his *History of the Administration*, noting that Burr and others had found numerous errors in the text. According to Wood, Brockholst Livingston gave a "decided opinion, that it was a libellous publication, and if published would be injurious to the community."

Wood charged that the followers of De-Witt Clinton were responsible for the suppression controversy, because they wished to see Clinton replace Burr as the party's candidate for vice president in the next election (Kline, *Burr*, 2:697-8n, 724-7, 732n; Cheetham, *Narrative of the Suppression*, 33-5; Wood, *A Correct Statement of the Various Sources from which The History of the Administration of John Adams was Compiled, and the Motives for Its Suppression by Col. Burr: With some Observation on A Narrative, by a Citizen of New-York*, 2d ed. [New York, 1802], 7, 15, 33-4). For William Duane's comments supporting the suppression of Wood's *History*, see Kline, *Burr*, 2:713-16.

ELLEGANT DRAWER: in 1799, the same year John Wood wrote *A General View of the History of Switzerland; with a Particular Account of the Origin and Accomplishment of the Late Swiss Revolution*, he also compiled *Elements of Perspective; Containing the Nature of Light and Colours, and the Theory and Practice of Perspective, in Regard to Lines, Surfaces, and Solids, with Its Application to Architecture*, which was published in London. Having settled in New York in 1801, Wood agreed to teach at an academy in Pine Street that prepared young gentlemen for Columbia College. He also planned to deliver lectures on navigation at his room in Fair Street and to establish a class for drawing and painting (*New-York Gazette and General Advertiser*, 20 Oct. 1801).

GARRULLITY OF MR. WOOD: Wood charged that the business became public "owing to the folly of Barlas, who ran among his friends," particularly George Clinton and Cheetham, seeking advice on "how he should proceed against the Vice President" (Wood, *Correct Statement*, 26).

The role of Republican lawyer Tunis WORTMAN in the suppression of Wood's *History of the Administration* is described in Kline, *Burr*, 2:647, 696-7. The pamphlet SIGNED "Lysander" published in New York in early 1802 previously has been attributed to Cheetham (see Sowerby, No. 3325). Entitled *Annals of the Corporation, Relative to the Last Contested Elections: with Strictures upon the Conduct of the Majority,* the work criticized the New York City Common Council. Wortman's earlier pamphlet, *A Treatise Concerning Political Enquiry, and the Liberty of the Press,* published in New York in 1800, has been described as a "full-length treatise on freedom of the press, the only American work of its kind." His other TRACTS included an oration before the Tammany Society in 1796, a response to criticism of TJ in the election of 1800, and an address before the Republican citizens of New York celebrating TJ's inauguration in 1801 (see Evans, Nos. 31665, 39149, 39150; Shaw-Shoemaker, No. 1691; Alfred F. Young, *The Democratic Republicans of New York: The Origins, 1763-1797* [Chapel Hill, 1967], 394).

The SIXTEEN LETTERS written by Jonathan Dayton to Francis Childs in 1796, along with other documents filed at the New York court of CHANCERY and reproduced by Wood in his history, had been printed in 1800 by Denniston as a pamphlet entitled *Public Speculation Unfolded; in Sixteen Letters, Addressed to F. Childs & J. H. Lawrence, of New-York: By Jonathan Dayton, of New-Jersey: While Speaker of the House of Representatives of the Congress of the United States* (see Evans, No. 37297). In the pamphlet the documents were introduced with a notice "To the Public," explaining that the letters related "to projects of a vast landed speculation; the profits of which, would be eventually realized by a Congressional law about that time to be passed." They also corroborated the charges which had been brought against Dayton in the *Aurora* "Concerning his holding the public money, and the non settlement of his accounts" with the Treasury Department. According to Wood, Burr disapproved of including these personal transactions in a "history of important events" because the letters "proved nothing more than a commercial transaction" similar to that practiced by many others (Wood, *History*

of the Administration, 194-220; *Public Speculation Unfolded,* 3-4; Wood, *Correct Statement,* 18-19; Syrett, *Hamilton,* 26:88). Burr had been friends with Dayton since his childhood years in New Jersey (Nancy Isenberg, *Fallen Founder: The Life of Aaron Burr* [New York, 2007], 8-9, 399).

BIOGRAPHY OF YOURSELF: Wood took long extracts from two sources in compiling his sketch of TJ. The first, *Public Characters of 1800-1801,* a British publication, included the life of "Mr. Jefferson, Vice-President of the United States of America." In later recommending the sketch in *Public Characters,* TJ observed, "I never knew, nor could conjecture by whom this was written; but certainly by some one pretty intimately acquainted with myself and my connections. there were a few inconsiderable errors in it, but in general it was correct" (*Public Characters of 1800-1801* [London, 1801; Sowerby, No. 402], 200-225; Wood, *History of the Administration,* 426-56; TJ to Horatio Gates Spafford, 11 May 1819, in DLC). Wood's second major source was John Beckley's *Address to the People of the United States; with an Epitome and Vindication of the Public Life and Character of Thomas Jefferson,* published in Philadelphia and other cities in 1800 (Gerard W. Gawalt, *Justifying Jefferson: The Political Writings of John James Beckley* [Washington, D.C., 1995], 166-89). For TJ's reaction to the biography that appeared at the close of Beckley's pamphlet, see Vol. 32:122-5. For Wood's other sources, see *Correct Statement,* 14.

BIOGRAPHY OF MR. BURR: Wood used James Hardie's biographical dictionary, which included a sketch of Aaron Burr, Sr., president of the College of New Jersey, as one of his sources on the vice president. Hardie included passages from William LIVINGSTON's eulogy at the funeral of Aaron Burr, Sr. Wood concluded his sketch of Burr with a quote from the Livingston eulogy, which he noted was APPLICABLE TO THAT OF HIS SON, by changing it from the past to the present tense (James Hardie, *The New Universal Biographical Dictionary, and American Remembrancer of Departed Merit,* 4 vols. [New York, 1801-04], 1:401-9; Wood,

History of the Administration, 456-63; Cheetham, *Narrative of the Suppression*, 12-15; Wood, *Correct Statement*, 12-13).

For the account of the person who came to the U.S. Mint and convinced Elias Boudinot and President Adams that he had discovered a chemical process to CONVERT TIN INTO SILVER, see Wood, *History of the Administration*, 503-5. For

Robert Leslie's account of the event, see Vol. 34:238.

PERSONS WHOM MR. CHEETHAM DESCRIBED TO YOU: see enclosure printed at Cheetham to TJ, 10 Dec.

Cheetham sent TJ A COPY OF THE HISTORY by Wood as soon as it went on sale in June 1802 (see Sowerby, No. 506).

[1] Preceding four words interlined.

From Lafayette

MY DEAR FRIEND   La Grange—10h pluviose jy the 30h 1802

I Have not this Long While Had the pleasure of a Letter from You—Yet I Hope You Have Received the Heartfelt Expressions of my old, Constant friendship, and the Affectionate, patriotic Wishes Which Accompagny You in a Station Where the Welfare of the United States, and the Cause of liberty are So Highly Interested—So Confused Have Been the Ideas of Europe that Never She Could be So Much Benefited, as in the present times, By the Example of a free Government—However Unpopular Liberal principles Now are in the old World, I am Convinced they Cannot fail Coming Again Into public favour—the More Sacred Names Have Been So Much Sullied, the peaceful Citizens Have Been So Cruelly trampled Upon in dirt and Blood that there is More to Be Lamented, than Wondered At, in the present Almost Universal disgust—You Will know By the papers, and Still Better by Mr Livingston's Correspondance that, in the Mean While, the Interior tranquility of france is perfectly Insured, and her External Influence [strenously] Supported—Bonaparte is just Returning from His Brillant Journey to Lyons Where He Has Accepted the presidency of our Young Cisalpine Sister—peace With Great Britain is Concluded—I am More and More Attached to My Rural Retirements—My family Agree in Opinion With me—they Request to Be Affectionately and Respectfully Remembered to You— My Son Has Returned to His Regiment in Italy—I Expect Him in the Spring, and probably to Marry a Very Amiable daughter to the Senator *tracy* Whom You Have known as a patriot Member of the Constituent Assembly—There Would Be an Affectation, My dear friend, in Seeming to be Ignorant of the Concern and Intentions You Have Expressed Respecting My private Affairs—I shall only Say that I am duly Sensible of these New testimonies of Your Affection to Me—And altho' it does Not Behove me Either to promote or to Anticipate, particularly in Matters of this Nature, Yet I Could Not forbear dropping a Grateful Word Upon it—It is probable You Will, by the present Opportunity, Receive official dispatches as I Have Been Asked for my Letters By a Note from the Commissary for Commercial Relations, Lequinio, Whom I Had Seen in the Beggining of the Revolution—I Hear He Has Gone far into the Jacobine party, Altho' I am Not Acquainted With particulars But from Some Late Circumstances I think He Will Behave Well in His New Capacity—Be pleased, My dear Sir, to present My Best Compliment to our friend Madisson, to Your family, to Mr dawson, and to Such other friends as are pleased to Enquire After their fellow Soldier and fellow Citizen— I am With High and Affectionate Respect

Yours   LAFAYETTE

RC (DLC); endorsed by TJ as a letter of 11 Pluviose received 2 July and so recorded in SJL. Enclosed in Joseph Marie Lequinio de Kerblay to TJ, 20 June 1802.

PLEASURE OF A LETTER FROM YOU: TJ had last written to Lafayette on 13 Mch. 1801. Lafayette's most recent letter to TJ was dated 21 June, received in September (Vol. 33:270; Vol. 34:403-4).

BONAPARTE had arranged for the meeting of the constituent council of the CISALPINE Republic in Lyons. He wanted to firm up French influence in northern Italy, and went to Lyons himself in January to make sure the council agreed to the new constitution, which was the work of Pierre Louis Roederer. The constitution provided for a president, a legislative council, and a council of state. Electoral colleges of landowners, businessmen, and intellectuals selected some council members. Bonaparte accepted the presidency himself after his brother Joseph and two Italians declined the office. He named an Italian, Count Francesco Melzi d'Eril, as his deputy and assigned the more routine duties of the presidency to Melzi. As a concession to the Italians, Bonaparte called the state under its new frame of government the Italian Republic (Desmond Gregory, *Napoleon's Italy* [Madison, N.J., 2001], 54-9).

In June 1802, Lafayette's SON, George Washington Louis Gilbert du Motier de Lafayette, married Françoise Émilie Destutt de TRACY. Her parents were Émilie Louise de Durfort-Civrac and Antoine Louis Claude Destutt de Tracy. Lafayette and Destutt de Tracy became friends when they were both army officers from aristocratic families, and both supported the French Revolution until the execution of Louis XVI. Destutt de Tracy was one of the intellectuals who came to call themselves *idéologistes*, taking the name from his work *Éléments d'idéologie*. They are better known by the label Bonaparte gave them, the *idéologues*. TJ was familiar with members of the group, including Volney and Cabanis, when they liked to gather at Auteuil under the patronage of Madame Helvétius. In the 1790s they became prominent in the class of moral and political sciences of the National Institute. Bonaparte was initially supportive of the group, and Destutt de Tracy was one of the original members of the Conservative Senate of France created by the 1799 constitution (Arnaud Chaffanjon, *La Fayette et sa descendance* [Paris, 1976], 165-6; *Biographie universelle, ancienne et moderne*, new ed., 45 vols. [Paris, 1843-65], 42:77-9; Tulard, *Dictionnaire Napoléon*, 600-1, 902-4, 1565; RS, 1:260-3; Vol. 31:405; Vol. 34:442n).

To William Wardlaw

DEAR SIR   Washington Jan. 30. [1802]

Your's of the 23d. is recieved, and the sum you desire £47.9.10=
158.30 D shall be paid for you to Dr. Jackson's representative. the remittance I made to Richmond was occasioned by mr Lilley's having
informed me he was to pay money to a mr Bonduron, which I now
find was a mistake for Burnley. however I can apply that remittance
to some future purpose. the variolous after the vaccine inoculation
has been tried here in several instances. a small inflammation at the
puncture always appeared, but nothing more. the inoculation here is
from our matter: that in Philadelphia from here. multiplied proofs
have been exhibited there that the Cowpox is an effectual preventa-
tive of the small pox. by a paragraph from a London paper I find a
physician there declaring that the safest rule is never to take matter
after the 8th. or 9th. day from the inoculation. our neighbor therefore
who did not take matter after the 8. times 24. hours, may rest perfectly secure. Accept my respect & best wishes.

PrC (MHi); partially dated; at foot of
text: "Dr. Wardlaw"; endorsed by TJ in
ink on verso with the date 1802.

YOUR'S OF THE 23D.: recorded in SJL
as received 27 Jan. from Charlottesville
but not found. REMITTANCE I MADE: see
TJ to George Jefferson, 7 Jan.

From Joseph Yznardi, Sr.

EXMO. SEÑOR   Philada. 30 de Enero 802
Muy Señor mio, y de mi Respecto
En 15 del Corriente tuvo el gusto de presentar á V.E mi gratitud
como permanente despues de la qual, comunico Aver llegado los
Vinos de Xerez á Baltimore, y boy á Mandarcelos desde ally con-
sistiendo en 1 Bota de 10 Años Seco, Igual al que enbarcan para el
Mercado de Londres y Media Bota de Calidad distinta Semejante á
Madera
1 Bota de Paxarete Seco y media Bota del Vino sin Color, ni Con-
posicion alguna que recomendaria á V.E para su gusto privado, y des-
pues podrá Elejir el que le Convenga Mejor para Reenplasar
    tengo Cartas de Cadiz de 29 de Nobienbre Comunicando qe en
Medina Cidonia Avia la Fiebre Amarilla que Morian 20 personas
diarias Siendo una Poblacion de 6 mil Almas, y Cituado en lo Mas
Saludable de Andalucía sin duda un grado de Altura mas qe los

Pueblos de la Costa, y como 30 Millas de Cadiz parage tan Ventilado, qe era el Ospital de Convalecientes

el 12 de dicho mes Suspendió el Bloqueo la Esquadra Inglesa á Cadiz y Sanlucar por Resultas de la Publicasion de la Paz el 11 del Mismo

Mr. Preble qe fue Nonbrado por Mr. Adams Consul de Cadiz Salio de España para esta con el fin de Reclamar dicho Oficio del Senado segun el Mismo dijo, en Madrid

tengo el Honor de Repetir a V.E los deveres de mi Obligacion, y de cer Exmo Señor Su mas Obediente Servr   JOSEF YZNARDY

E D I T O R S ' T R A N S L A T I O N

MOST EXCELLENT SIR   Philadelphia 30 Jan. 1802
   Dear Sir, and with my respect
   On the 15th of this month I had the pleasure of presenting to Your Excellency my gratitude for granting me a permanent post, after which you communicated that the wines from Jerez had arrived at Baltimore, and I am going to order to be sent from there:
   one cask of a ten-year-old dry wine, equal to the ones they ship to the London market, and a half cask of a different kind similar to Madeira;
   one cask of dry pajarete and a half cask of a wine without color or any additives, which I would recommend for Your Excellency's private use, after which you can choose what is best suited for you as a replacement.
   I have letters from Cadiz from 29 Nov. saying that in Medina-Sidonia there was yellow fever and that 20 people died each day in a population of six thousand souls, and situated in the healthiest part of Andalucía no doubt at a higher altitude than coastal towns, and about 30 miles from Cadiz, a spot that is so well ventilated that it is where the convalescent hospital was located.
   On the 12th of the said month the blockade of Cadiz and Sanlúcar de Barrameda by the British squadron was lifted as a result of the announcement of peace on the 11th of the same month.
   Mr. Preble, who was named by Mr. Adams consul of Cadiz, left Spain for this country with the objective of reclaiming the said post from the Senate, according to what he said in Madrid.
   I have the honor to repeat to Your Excellency the duties of my obligation, and to be, excellent sir, your most obedient servant,   JOSEF YZNARDY

RC (DLC); at foot of text: "Exmo. Sor. Dn Thomas Jefferson"; endorsed by TJ as received 3 Feb. and so recorded in SJL.

LOS VINOS DE XEREZ: according to TJ's financial memoranda, the wine mentioned in this letter arrived in Washington on 24 Feb. (MB, 2:1115). See also Yznardi to TJ, 12 Feb.

Some American newspapers, picking up a story printed in London during October, reported the outbreak of yellow fever at MEDINA-Sidonia in southern Spain. According to the London source, the Spanish government had ringed Medina-Sidonia with troops to enforce a quarantine, and authorities were implementing disinfectant procedures that had been developed in Britain and France (*Middlebury Mercury*, 6 Jan.; *Poulson's American Daily Advertiser*, 16 Jan.).

Henry PREBLE had written to TJ on 23 Oct. 1801 concerning his continuing wish to receive a consular appointment.

To Matthew Anderson

SIR   Washington Jan. 31. 1802.

I have recieved through the channel of mr Eppes a piece of silk which mrs Anderson has been so good as to present me, raised and manufactured in your own family. this sample of domestic skills is evidence that you possess the most pleasing of all human spectacles, a well ordered houshold, usefully employed. if my principles have pointed me out as worthy of this attention from mrs Anderson, it will add to their value in my own eyes; since next to an approving conscience, our best consolation is the esteem of that portion of[1] our fellow citizens who retired from the contentious bustle of the world, judge us in calm tranquility from our works alone. I pray you to make my particular thanks acceptable to mrs Anderson, and to recieve yourself assurances of my respect and consideration

TH: JEFFERSON

PrC (DLC); in ink at foot of text: "Mr. Matthew Anderson Gloucester."

Matthew Anderson (1743-1806), served in the Virginia General Assembly as a senator representing Gloucester, Middlesex, and Mathews from 1783 to 1794 and as a delegate representing Gloucester from 1801 to 1803 and from 1804 to 1805. He and his wife Mary Dabney Anderson were sericulturists at Exchange on the North River in Gloucester County, where they kept silkworms in the attic of their home and, in 1794, presented to George Washington enough silk for two suits (Leonard, *General Assembly*, 151, 198, 223, 227, 235; Association for the Preservation of Virginia Antiquities, *Epitaphs of Gloucester and Mathews Counties in Tidewater Virginia Through 1865* [Richmond, 1959], 88-9; Lyon G. Tyler, "Old Tombstones in Gloucester County," WMQ, 1st ser., 3 [1895], 184-5; W. P. Anderson, *Anderson Family Records* [Cincinnati, Ohio, 1936], 38-9; Mary Anderson to George Washington,

17 May 1794, in DLC: Washington Papers; Vol. 30:303-4).

A PIECE OF SILK: Samuel Latham Mitchill described to his wife a dinner party at the President's House in early February 1802 when "Mr Jefferson shewed us a peice of home-made Silken Cloth. The trees grow & the worms were bred in Virginia. And there too the Silk was wound, wove and dyed. The Peice is large enough to make a Surtout; and he talks of sending it to Europe to be made water-proof, before it is made into a garment." TJ extolled the virtues of water-proof cloth and demonstrated with his "Surtout of British Broad Cloth. . . . He took hold of one part of the Skirt, and myself of the other end, so as by skilful folding to make a hollow or Cavity. Into this some water was poured. We stirred and moved it about. I put my hand to the under-side and agitated it there. But not a drop came thro. The President said he had hung up such a woolen-bag of Water for several weeks & it did not leak at all, during the whole time.—Paper prepared in this Manner resists the Action of Water to a remarkable Degree. It will not receive the full charge of the liquid but repels it.—The Process is said to be cheap in England; and the introduction of such Clothing would guard a man as effectual-ly against a Shower of rain as the Coat of Feathers of a Water fowl" (Samuel L. Mitchill to Catharine Mitchill, 10 Feb. 1802, in NNMus).

[1] Preceding three words interlined.

From Andrew Ellicott

DEAR SIR   Lancaster Jany. 31st. 1802.

I have lately received some valuable astronomical observations, made at several places on the Mississippi, by my ingenious friend Jose Joahin de Ferrer: by these observations I shall be enabled to make some small corrections in the Map sent on some weeks ago by Mr. Duane; and which I presume has been safely delivered.—

Owing to a great press of business in the land office, and an uncommon portion of cloudy weather, I have made but few observations since I wrote to you last, and those have generally been equal altitudes of the sun, (to determine the error, and rate of going of the Regulator,) and the eclipses of Jupiter's satellites.—

Our legislature has been in session great part of the winter, but the republican interest has such a decided ascendency, that party violence appears to have wholy subsided in that body.—Govr. Mc.Kean's firmness, like the club of Hercules, has crushed the opposition, and in all probability secured his reelection.—

With the highest consideration and esteem I am your Hbe. Servt.

ANDW; ELLICOTT

RC (DLC); at foot of text: "Thos. Jefferson President U.S. and of the A.P.S."; endorsed by TJ as received 4 Feb. and so recorded in SJL.

Ellicott had also used the word INGENIOUS to describe José Joaquín FERRER y Cafranga in a letter to TJ in May 1801. Ferrer, who was originally from Spain but spent a good deal of time in North America, traveled down the Ohio and Mississippi rivers from Pittsburgh to New Orleans in the spring of that year. He had two chronometers and made astronomical observations along the journey to determine latitude and longitude of several locations. In 1809, the *Transactions* of the American Philosophical Society printed his data from that trip along with other sets of his observations. In Europe, Franz Xavier von Zach of Gotha, who regularly published contemporary astronomical data, also printed Ferrer's observations from the trip down the Ohio and Mississippi (APS, *Transactions*, 6 [1809], 159; John C. Greene, *American Science in the Age of Jefferson* [Ames, Iowa, 1984], 142; Vol. 30:161-2n; Vol. 34:120-1).

For Ellicott's description of the MAP he had prepared of the Mississippi River, see Vol. 35:106-7, 423-4, 548.

It was difficult to regulate a timepiece by observing the exact instant at which the sun reached its zenith at noon. The method of EQUAL ALTITUDES eased this problem by allowing the observer to calculate the moment when noon occurred by measuring the sun's altitude above the horizon once in the morning and once in the afternoon. Using a telescope, published astronomical tables, and a clock adjusted to local time, one could observe JUPITER'S SATELLITES to find the time difference from Greenwich, and therefore the longitude of the point of observation (Richard S. Preston, "The Accuracy of the Astronomical Observations of Lewis and Clark," APS, *Proceedings*, 144 [2000], 171-3).

In June 1800, when Thomas McKean was replacing numerous officeholders in Pennsylvania, he declared to John Dickinson that he was no HERCULES but had "to cleanse the Augean Stables with little or no aid." When Ellicott wrote the letter above, some OPPOSITION had arisen in the legislature over the fact that Alexander J. Dallas, the U.S. district attorney, was also recorder of the city of Philadelphia. In February 1802, McKean vetoed a bill that would bar Dallas and Michael Leib from dual officeholding. The legislature overrode the veto, but neither Federalists nor disenchanted Republicans could mount much of a challenge to McKean, who faced reelection in the fall of 1802 (Rowe, *McKean*, 320, 326-31).

To Dwight Foster

Th: Jefferson requests the favour of *The Honble Mr. Dwight Foster* to dine with him *the day after tomorrow*—at half after three, or at whatever later hour the house may rise.

Monday Feb 1st. 1802.

The favour of an answer is asked.

RC (PPAmP); printed form, with blanks filled by Meriwether Lewis reproduced in italics; addressed by Lewis: "The Honble Mr. Dwight Foster"; endorsed by Foster. See illustration.

Dwight Foster (1757-1823) was elected as a Federalist to the U.S. Senate from Massachusetts in June 1800, after serving in the U.S. House of Representatives since 1793. He was the younger brother of Senator Theodore Foster of Rhode Island (*Biog. Dir. Cong.*).

From Benjamin Hawkins

Tookau,bat,chee in the Creek agency 1st Feby. 1802.

I do myself the pleasure to send you a specimen of my tours through this agency in my journal down the Tennassee with the map of the river. I have made it a rule to travel with a pocket compass and time piece and have in likemanner noted every journey through this country; several of which, are ploted and the whole will be sent to the War office as soon as I have paper and leisure to copy them. I intended them in the first instance as military routes only, as I had no rule to reduce the curves of paths taken by time to the same exactness as those of a river: but they will be useful in the delineation of this part of the United States. I could not get a portable instrument to take the Latitude or I would have made it more complete. I shall at the first moment of leisure go down every river in this agency and deliniate them as I have done the Tennassee.

I have the honour to be with all possible respect my dear sir, Your most obedient servant BENJAMIN HAWKINS

RC (DLC); at foot of text: "Mr. Jefferson President of the United states"; endorsed by TJ as received 5 Mch. and so recorded in SJL. Enclosures not found.

NOTED EVERY JOURNEY: as he visited

various locations as Indian agent, Hawkins kept records of the courses he traveled and distances between landmarks. In some cases he made more detailed journals (Foster, *Hawkins,* 1j-89j, 105-13, 117-20, 143-51, 165-7; Vol. 33:110n).

To the Senate

GENTLEMEN OF THE SENATE

I nominate the following persons to office, as respectively stated.

David Latimore of the Missisipi territory to be a member of the legislative council thereof, in the place of Adam Bingaman who declined qualifying; the said David Latimer being one of two persons nominated by the House of Representatives of the sd territory for appointment in the place of the said Adam Bingaman.

John Taylor of New York to be a Commissioner to hold a treaty between the state of New York and the Saint Regis Indians, on matters concerning the state of New York, as explained in a letter from the Governor of New York, an abstract[1] of which is inclosed. also to be a Commissioner to hold a Convention between the Seneca Indians and the Agent of the Holland land company, for the purpose of reconveying to the Senecas certain parcels of their former lands as explained in a letter from the said agent, a copy of which is inclosed.

James Leander Cathcart, heretofore Consul at Tripoli, to be Consul at Algiers instead of Richard Obrian who desires to return.

William Jarvis of Massachusets to be Consul at Lisbon instead of John Bulkeley.

George Washington Mcelroy to be Consul at Teneriffe, instead of John Culnan who has abandoned the place.

Henry Molier of Maryland, to be Consul of Corunna.

William Riggin of Maryland to be Consul of Trieste in the place of John Lamson

Joseph Barnes a citizen of the US. now in Messina, to be Consul for the island of Sicily.

John M. Forbes of Massachusets to be Consul at Hamburg in the place of Joseph Pitcairn.

John Appleton of Massachusets to be Consul at Calais.

Bartholomew Dandridge of Virginia to be Commercial agent at Port Republicain in St. Domingo.[2]

Robert Young of Columbia to be Commercial agent at the Havanna in the place of John Morton resigned.

Timothy Bloodworth of N. Carolina, to be Collector for the district of Wilmington in that state in place of Griffith John Mcrea, dead.

John Slocum of Rhode island to be Surveyor of the port of Newport in that state in place of Daniel Lyman.

John Cross Jnr. of Rhode island to be Surveyor of the port of Pawcatuck, in that state, in place of George Stillman.

William Rogers of Maryland
Alexander Williams of Columbia
John A. Smith of Columbia.
Joseph W. New of Virginia.

} to be Surgeon's mates in the navy of the US.

TH: JEFFERSON
Feb. 1. 1802.

RC (DNA: RG 46, EPEN, 7th Cong., 1st sess.); endorsed by a Senate clerk; notations in margin by a Senate clerk on the disposition of nominations not reproduced here. PrC (DLC); with one entry interlined in ink (see note 2 below). Recorded in SJL with notation "nominations." Enclosures: (1) Abstract of George Clinton to Henry Dearborn, 26 Nov. 1801. (2) Paul Busti, agent of the Holland Land Company, to James Madison, 27 Dec. 1801 (Trs both in DNA: RG 46, EPIR, 7th Cong., 1st sess.; see Dearborn to TJ, 8 Jan.).

David Lattimore (LATIMORE, Latimer) was a Norfolk physician who moved to Natchez around 1801. William C. C. Claiborne described him as uniting "pure Republicanism, handsome Talents & an Honest Heart" (Madison, *Papers, Sec. of State Ser.*, 2:482; 3:159). John Adams had nominated ADAM BINGAMAN to the legislative council of the Mississippi Territory on 23 Dec. 1800 (JEP, 1:363).

JOHN BULKELEY: that is, Thomas Bulkeley, who was appointed consul general for Portugal in 1797 (JEP, 1:248).

In his lists of appointments and removals, TJ included DANIEL LYMAN and GEORGE STILLMAN among the Federalists to be removed for "using the weight of their official influence to oppose the order of things established" (Vol. 33:672).

ALEXANDER WILLIAMS: that is, Alexander McWilliams. See Robert Smith to TJ, 19 Jan.

Meriwether Lewis delivered this communication to the Senate on 2 Feb. Two days later, the Senate confirmed the nominations of Lattimore, Molier, Forbes, Dandridge, Young, Slocum, and the four navy appointees. The Senate referred the nomination of John Tayler to a committee (see Henry Dearborn to TJ, 8 Jan. 1802) and ordered the remainder of the nominations to lie for consideration. They were confirmed on 9 and 10 Feb. (JEP, 1:405-7).

[1] TJ first wrote "a copy" before altering the phrase to read as above.
[2] Entry interlined. Entry interlined in ink in PrC.

From Joseph Wheaton

EXCELLENT SIR   Washington Feby 1st. 1802

There being an office in your gift connected with the Legislature where I am placed, the compensation to which, aded to the small pittance I receive from the government, would enable me to support my little family in this city, and thereby prevent a painful seperation which necessity enforces.

I therefore beg leave to offer myself to your consideration for the appointment of librarian to Congress.

If twenty five years of faithful services and perseverance through the vicisitudes of the past; If the circumstances of Seven times elected to the office in which I Stand; If growing into advanced life in the service of my Country without the means of giving to a Small family a decent support, from the Savings of my earnings, are recommendations sufficient for the occasion, and your Excellency has not fully determined on the person to fill the office, permit me to hope for some claim to your notice.

If I should be successful in this; which hope inspires, it will be received with thankfulness, and gratitude.

I am Excellent Sir with the homage of my heart your faithful and obedient Servant   JOSEPH WHEATON

RC (DNA: RG 59, LAR); at head of text: "To the President of the United States"; endorsed by TJ as received 1 Feb. and "to be librarian" and so recorded in SJL.

A veteran of the Revolutionary War, Joseph Wheaton (d. 1828) of Rhode Island served as sergeant at arms of the U.S. House of Representatives from 1789 to 1807. He wrote TJ and James Madison on several occasions during their respective administrations, requesting appointments and seeking to vindicate his character. Detractors accused Wheaton of secretly harboring British and Federalist sympathies and of being an admirer of Aaron Burr. In 1806, he received a contract to cut a post road and carry mail from Athens, Georgia, to Fort Stoddert. His failure to do either earned him the enmity of the postmaster general, which resulted in a lawsuit and repeated petitions by Wheaton to Congress for compensation. He returned to the military during the War of 1812, serving as a deputy assistant quartermaster general in the army. Madison nominated him to be a deputy quartermaster general in 1814, but the Senate rejected the appointment (*Biog. Dir. Cong.*; Heitman, *Register*, 583; Madison, *Papers, Pres. Ser.*, 2:258-9; 3:502-4; Henry DeLeon Southerland, Jr., and Jerry Elijah Brown, *The Federal Road through Georgia, the Creek Nation, and Alabama, 1806-1836* [Tuscaloosa, 1989], 24-32; JEP, 2:543, 606; "Noname Iota" to TJ, 12 Apr. 1802; Gideon Granger to TJ, 23 Feb. 1807; Wheaton to TJ, 17 Oct. 1807; Abraham Bradley, Jr., to TJ, 6 Sep. 1808; RS, 1:350-2).

SMALL PITTANCE: by an act of Congress of 2 May 1800, the sergeants at arms of the House and Senate each received a salary of $500 per annum, plus $2 per day during a session of Congress. On 29 Apr. 1802, Congress altered the compensation to a salary of $800 per annum and no per diem payments (U.S. Statutes at Large, 2:58, 170-1).

Rather than reply by letter, TJ instructed Meriwether Lewis to inform Wheaton that the APPOINTMENT OF LIBRARIAN had already been given to John Beckley. Following Beckley's death in 1807, Wheaton made another unsuccessful bid for the position (Wheaton to TJ, 16 May 1807).

From John Wayles Eppes

DEAR SIR,   Feb. 2. 1802.

I forwarded to you a few days since a letter from Maria—My Father who is now in Town left her well yesterday.

You will find enclosed the journal of the house of Delegates containing the amendments proposed to the Constitution of the U States—They are postponed by the Senate until the next session—

Early in the present session of assembly a Resolution was submitted to the House of Delegates for inspecting the appropriations of money drawn from the contingent fund by the Executive—A measure at first originating with the Republicans in the House & intended merely as the basis of future regulations on this subject, has been artfully held up by the foes of Monroe as a censure on his conduct—I enclose you a copy of the report of the committee appointed to examine into the expenditure of public money by the Executive & of the Resolutions entered into on this subject by the House of Delegates yesterday—This stroke to weaken the confidence of the public in the Executive has been followed by an attempt to dismember the State and form a seperate government West of the Blue Ridge—Several meetings have been held by the members from that country on this subject—I attended their last meeting & to my great satisfaction found that of 56 members from the West of the ridge only 29 attended—That of these 14 were in favour of the Resolutions 14 against them & Mr. Brackenridge their chairman gave the casting vote in favour of establishing corresponding committees beyond the ridge to asscertain the sense of the people on the subject of a seperate Government—of these 14 a large Majority refused to sign the resolutions, so that it ends in smoke. The whole proceeding may be considered as an attempt on the part of the Federalists to lessen the weight of Virginia in the Federal scale. You have heard of the division of the high court of chancery—Genl. John Brown is elected chancellor for the upper District & Mr. Wirt our Clerk for the lower—

The Legislature will probably adjourn today or tomorrow—I will forward by tomorrows post Govr. Monroes letter on the subject of the public expenditure (not yet printed). It may be considered as one among the many proofs of his talents given during the present session of assembly—

We have heard by private letters from Washington of a derelection from principle *serious* tho' not *unexpected*.

Adieu accep for your health & happiness the warm wishes of affection Yours   JNO: W: EPPES

RC (MHi); addressed: "Thomas Jefferson President of the United States Washington"; franked; postmarked Richmond, 1 Feb.; endorsed by TJ as received 5 Feb. and so recorded in SJL. Enclosures: (1) Eight amendments to the Constitution of the United States proposed by the Virginia General Assembly, as considered in the House of Delegates on 26 Jan.: to prohibit the president from serving two consecutive four-year terms; to cut the term of U.S. senators to three years to be classed so that one-third go out of office every year; to give the House of Representatives concurrent power with the Senate in approving or ratifying all treaties "where their agency shall be necessary to carry the same into effect"; to designate specifically presidential and vice presidential candidates in future elections; to consider the common law of England as separate from the law of the United States, "except so far as it may be adopted by special statute, where its principles and objects are expressly sanctioned by the words of the Constitution of the United States"; to hold as sacred and inviolable the freedom of conscience, speech, and press; to declare federal judges ineligible for any other government appointment during their continuance in office and 12 months thereafter; to choose hereafter judges of the courts of the United States by joint ballot of the Senate and House of Representatives (JHD, Dec. 1801-Feb. 1802, 81-83). (2) For the report of the committee and the resolutions passed by the House of Delegates on 30 Jan., see below.

Although Eppes dated this letter 2 Feb., internal evidence and the postmark indicate that he wrote the letter a day or two earlier. Eppes was in Richmond representing Chesterfield County in the Virginia Assembly (Leonard, *General*

Assembly, 223). According to SJL, on 5 Feb. TJ also received a letter from Eppes dated 1 Feb., which has not been found.

LETTER FROM MARIA: Mary Jefferson Eppes to TJ, 24 Jan. 1802.

On 28 Jan., the Senate received and read the AMENDMENTS PROPOSED to the U.S. Constitution by the House of Delegates (see Enclosure No. 1 above). The next day the Senate resolved that it was "too late in the session to devote as much time as a full consideration of a subject so highly interesting will require" and POSTPONED the resolutions until the next General Assembly (*Journal of the Senate of the Commonwealth of Virginia. Begun and Held at the Capitol in the City of Richmond, on Monday the Seventh Day of December, One Thousand Eight Hundred and One* [Richmond, 1802], 65-7).

On 29 Dec., the House of Delegates appointed a committee to join with one from the Senate to examine the expenditures from the CONTINGENT FUND BY THE EXECUTIVE over the last year. The committee reported to the House on 23 Jan. that the executive had spent over $51,000 for contingent expenses and sundry appropriation laws and the House moved to submit a copy of the report to Governor Monroe. The report to the Senate on 1 Feb. itemized some of these expenses, noting that Monroe had spent $20.45 for the celebration of the 4th of July in 1801 and an additional $24.45 "for illuminating the Capitol and guarding it on that occasion." According to the *Virginia Argus*, the committee criticized Monroe for spending more than $100 for illuminating the capitol "in consequence of Mr. Jefferson's election" (JHD, Dec. 1801-Feb. 1802, 49, 51, 78-9; *Journal of the Senate*, 71-2; Richmond *Virginia Argus*, 9 Feb. 1802). For Monroe's analysis of the politics of the committee and the reports, see Madison, *Papers, Sec. of State Ser.*, 2:453-6.

HOUSE OF DELEGATES YESTERDAY: on Saturday, 30 Jan., the House resolved that after a fair and accurate investigation they were of the opinion that the expenditures were made in conformance with law and precedent; they expressed their approbation of the conduct of the Executive. The resolution passed with 94 yeas and 18 nays, Eppes voting with the majority. By an even larger margin the House resolved "That the General Assembly entertains a high sense of the distinguished ability, attention and integrity with which JAMES MONROE, Esquire Governor of Virginia, has heretofore discharged the duty of his office" (JHD, Dec. 1801-Feb. 1802, 88-90).

ATTEMPT TO DISMEMBER THE STATE: sectional tensions increased in Virginia after 1800 as the House of Delegates maintained representation based on existing counties rather than on actual population and thereby perpetuated a bias in tidewater over transmontane political power. Many residents of Virginia's western counties, especially state senator Thomas Wilson and delegate Daniel Sheffey, wanted more democratic representation in both legislative branches of government. Property qualifications denied the vote to many western Virginians who did not own the land on which they lived (James C. McGregor, *The Disruption of Virginia* [New York, 1922], 28-9; L. Scott Philyaw, *Virginia's Western Visions: Political and Cultural Expansion on an Early American Frontier* [Knoxville, Tenn., 2004], 142; Charles Henry Ambler, *Sectionalism in Virginia from 1776 to 1861* [Chicago, 1910], 78-80, 84-85; JHD, Dec. 1801-Feb. 1802, 37; Madison, *Papers, Sec. of State Ser.*, 2:453-6).

The meeting chairman was James Breckinridge (BRACKENRIDGE), a land speculator and delegate from Botetourt County from 1796 to 1802, who became a leading Federalist in the Virginia Assembly (DVB, 2:208-10).

In January 1802, the General Assembly divided the HIGH COURT OF CHANCERY into three districts: Williamsburg, Richmond, and Staunton. By joint ballot of both houses, John Brown was elected as judge of the upper district chancery court held at Staunton and William Wirt as judge for the lower district court held at Williamsburg (Shepherd, *Statutes*, 2:321; *Journal of the Senate*, 62, 64, 66).

I WILL FORWARD . . . MONROES LETTER: perhaps Eppes sent TJ *A Report of the Committee Appointed to Examine into the Executive Expenditures; Also the Governor's Letter of the 28th January, to the Speaker of the House of Delegates, Respecting Said Expenditures, and the Resolutions of the House on the Same*, printed on 1 Feb. 1802 by Meriwether Jones in Richmond (see Sowerby, No. 3336). In his letter to Larkin Smith of 28 Jan., printed in the pamphlet, Monroe defended the public expenditures, including $33.75, the "cost of powder which was used on the anniversary of our independence" and $25.48, the "expense attending the public joy" at TJ's election as president. Monroe explained that it was "the practice of all governments to dedicate certain days to public festivity. They give relaxation from labour, promote friendly intercourse among the people, and harmonize the society." In this country, Monroe maintained, it was "the practice to celebrate the birth day of principle" (*Report of the Committee*, 12-14; Monroe, *Writings*, 3:332-4).

From George Jefferson

DEAR SIR,   Richmond 2d. Febr. 1802

I paid Doctor Currie agreeably to your direction 50$:—which however, he returned some days ago, as he said the referees for whom it was intended, refused to receive any compensation: he has lodged with me some papers respecting that business, of which I suppose he has informed you.

I paid Mr. Eppes some weeks ago on your account £16.4. with which I imagine he has acquainted you.

I am Dear Sir Your Very humble servt.   GEO. JEFFERSON

RC (MHi); at foot of text: "Thos. Jefferson esqr."; endorsed by TJ as received 6 Feb. and so recorded in SJL.

YOUR DIRECTION: see TJ to George Jefferson, 14 Jan. For the PAPERS RESPECTING the arbitration with David Ross, see James Currie to TJ, 27 Jan.

At the sale of his tobacco crop to McMurdo & Fisher in January 1801, TJ noted that 902 pounds of tobacco belonged to John Wayles EPPES, and he deducted £16.4.9 from the total sale price of £813.19.9 as Eppes's share of the payment (MB, 2:1033).

From Levi Lincoln

SIR   Washington Feby 2d. 1802.

After the utmost attention which I have been able to pay to the questions, respecting the northwestern territory, which you did me the honor of submitting to my consideration there is a difficulty in giving a decisive answer. I can find no grounds, or principles for a very confident decision in, or out of the ordinance for the establishment of that Government. Nothing can be collected to aid the enquiry, from the acts by which similar Governments in other territories have been established, or from the journals of the proceedings of the assembly and the Governor of this territory, altho some of these very questions have been the subjects of zealous debate—

The territory is, as yet, considered to be under what is called its temporary Government by the ordinance. That expressly provides that all majestrates and other civil officers, shall during the continuance of the temporary Government, be appointed by the *Governor*, unless otherwise therein directed. It also ordained that there should be a court appointed, to consist of three judges, who should have a common law jurisdiction and reside in the district, and, expressly, that Congress should appoint the Governor, the Secretary, and all military general officers. In the 12th paragraph of the ordinance, it is said the Governor, judges, legislative council secretary and such other officers as Congress shall appoint, in the district, shall take an oath &c—In the direction for taking the oath of office there is a strong implication of the right of Congress or, rather, of the President to appoint these three judges, and I am informed, this has been the practice. Independent of this practice,[1] upon the mere construction of the ordinance, I should have hesitated in deciding against the right of the Governor to have made even these appointments. The authority of making appointments is, expressly, given to the Governor in all cases, in which it is not otherwise directed, and express positive provisions are not usually abridged by implications. As this implication does not necessarily extend beyond the three judges before named, I am inclined to think the Governor is justified by the ordinance in his appointment of all other judges & officers—

It is provided, by the 7th paragraph of the ordinance that the Governor, previous to the organization of the General assembly, shall appoint such majestrates, and other civil officers in each County and township as he shall *find necessary* for the preservation of the peace, and good order in the same; and that after the general assembly shall be organized, the powers and duties of majestrates, and other civil officers, shall be regulated and defined by the assembly. After the formation of the general assembly, they, are to determine what powers & duties are necessary to be exercised in existing counties & townships, & to define & regulate the same, for the preservation of peace & good order, This seems to involve the necessity of their determining what description of[2] majestrates & officers should possess these powers & discharge those duties. They having done this, the Governor is to make the appointments. The Provision in this paragraph appears to me to amount to this, that before the general assembly was organized the Govr. was to appoint such officers as he might judge *to be necessary*, afterwards, *such as* the legislature should judge to be necessary.—

The 8th paragraph of the ordinance provides, that for the prevention of crimes, the laws to be adopted or *made* shall have force in all parts of the district. And for the execution of processes civil and criminal, that the Governor shall make proper divisions, and from time to time, as circumstances should require, lay out such parts of the district, in which the indian title shall have been extinguished, into Counties and townships, subject however to such alterations as may, thereafter, be made by the legislature. The Authority which the ordinance gives to the legislature is, in general terms, to make laws in all cases for the good government of the district, not repugnant to the principles and articles of the ordinance.

The laying out of Counties and towns are usually considered as legislative acts, and in the present instances must be considered as appertaining to the legislature, unless, by a proper construction of the ordinance, it is secured to the Governor—It being once confessedly vested in him, & by general terms implying no limitation in point of time, the authority must be considered as still remaining with him, unless it is taken away, expressly, or by some strong implication, or by some unforeseen change of the subject matter, upon which, or of the circumstances under which the power is exercised— The civil and criminal processes, the *Execution* of which, were to be the means of preventing crimes and injuries, and which were to be effectuated by a division of the described parts of the district into counties & townships, are, recognized by the 9th paragraph of the ordinance to be such as should originate under *made*, as well as, under adopted laws, and if so it implys a power in the Governor to lay out counties & towns after the Genl assembly were sufficiently organized for the making of laws. This construction of the 8th paragraph is in some degree confirmed by the express limitations of the Governor's power contained in the 5th & 7th—as there was the same reason for being explicit in the first, as in the two last, if the same thing was intended—It, to my mind, appears to be further confirmed by an express power being given to the legislature to alter such townships and counties as shall have been laid out. On the idea, of the authority to lay out Counties, being vested in the Governor, after the formation of a legislature, this was necessary, otherwise not.

The ordinance provides, that, in case of the death or *removal* from office of a representative, the Governor shall issue a writ to the County or township for which he was a member, to elect another in his stead. I perceive no question on the Governor's transactions respecting the election of representatives, as returned by the secretary, excepting in reference to Meigs, who is said to have left the territory—If he had not resigned, previous to the issuing of the writ for the election of a representative in his stead, I conceive the writ must be considered as issuing illegally. Knowing that some very respectable Gentlemen are decidedly of the opinion, that the Governor has no right to lay out Counties under the ordinance, I have slept many nights, on my first impressions on the subject, and am still inclined to the opinion I have above expressed, notwithstanding any thing I have been able to learn respecting the matter,—I have the honor to be Sir with the highest respect & Consideration your Hum. Sevt   LEVI LINCOLN

RC (DNA: RG 59, LOAG); at head of text: "The President of the U States"; endorsed by Jacob Wagner. Printed in the first volume of the *Official Opinions of the Attorneys General of the United States* (Washington, D.C., 1852), 102-6.

QUESTIONS: TJ to Lincoln, 28 Jan. Congress had passed the ORDINANCE FOR THE ESTABLISHMENT of a government for the Northwest Territory on 13 July 1787. In Lincoln's references to sections of the law, he counted the title, "An Ordinance for the government of the territory of the United States North west of the river Ohio," as the first paragraph (*Terr. Papers*, 2:39-50).

The ordinance, which was adopted under the Articles of Confederation, specified that the territory's governor should take the OATH OF OFFICE "before the President of Congress" and that the judges, legislative council, and secretary should take the oath before the governor (same, 45).

The eleventh paragraph of the ordinance granted the legislature its general authority to MAKE LAWS. Counties and townships were RECOGNIZED in the ninth paragraph as the basis for representation in the assembly. 5TH & 7TH: the fifth paragraph of the ordinance enabled the governor and judges to adopt laws that would "be in force in the district until the organization of the general assembly therein, unless disapproved of by Congress; but

afterwards the legislature shall have authority to alter them as they shall think fit." The seventh paragraph said that the governor could appoint magistrates and county or township officials until the legislature was organized, but after that "the powers and duties of magistrates and other civil officers shall be regulated and defined by the said Assembly." The eighth paragraph said nothing about any change in the governor's power to make counties and townships with the advent of the legislature (same, 42-5).

Provision for writs of election following the DEATH OR REMOVAL of assemblymen was in the tenth paragraph of the ordinance. The transcript of the territory's executive proceedings that TJ sent to Lincoln on 28 Jan. evidently included a record of the writ of election that Arthur St. Clair issued to fill the assembly seat vacated by Return Jonathan MEIGS. In 1801, Meigs became U.S. agent for the Cherokee Indians and the War Department agent for Tennessee (same, 44; *Terr. Papers*, 3:531; Vol. 34:86n).

[1] MS: "pratice."
[2] Preceding two words interlined.

To Thomas Newton, Jr.

Feb. 2. 1802.

Th: Jefferson asks the favor of mr Newton to order, for him, 4. barrels of the Hughes's crab cyder which was the subject of their yesterday's conversation, to be forwarded to Richmond to the address of messrs. Gibson & Jefferson of that place. the risk of being adulterated by the batteau-men, in going up from Richmond renders it worth while to put each barrel into an outer one, which he will pray mr Newton to direct. not knowing the exact cost of the whole he incloses mr Newton an order for 28. Doll. on mr Barnes of George town who transacts all money matters for Th:J. and who will deliver the money to any of the messengers of the house or other person whom mr Newton will direct to call for it. he prays him to accept his salutations & respect.

RC (NjP: Andre De Coppet Collection); addressed: "The honble Thomas Newton of the H. of Representatives"; endorsed by Newton: "private." PrC (MHi); endorsed by TJ in ink on verso. Enclosure: Order on John Barnes for payment of $28 to Newton, Washington, 2 Feb. 1802 (MS in ViU; in TJ's hand and signed by him; endorsed by Barnes 31 Mch.; signed by Newton acknowledging payment in full on 1 Apr.).

Thomas Newton, Jr. (1768-1847), of Norfolk, Virginia, was a lawyer, merchant, congressman, and son of Thomas Newton, a correspondent of TJ's. After attending the College of William and Mary and studying law, Newton served in the Virginia House of Delegates and was a presidential elector in 1800. A Republican, he served in the U.S. House of Representatives from 1801 until 1829 and again from 1831 to 1833. After his retirement from Congress, Newton practiced law and held a court position in Norfolk (*Biog. Dir. Cong.*; DAB; CVSP, 9:190; RS, 3:611n).

In his financial memoranda, TJ recorded at 2 Feb. the order on Barnes to pay Newton $28 "for 4. barrels Hughes's crab cyder to be sent to Monticello" (MB, 2:1065).

From Samuel Quarrier

SIR/   City of Washington, Febuary 2d, 1802—

Excuse this inovation on you by me, as it arises not from any thing voluntary on my part, but in every respect the revers—
From your known philantrophy ime induce to request of you, A favour—My situation is truely disagreeable, and unhappy. Without friends, Without pecuniary resources, and without any prospect at present of bettering myselfe—The prospects I had in view, have vanished from the resent chang in the army department, an appointment I hoped for, is from that chang frustrated, since that ive left nothing undon I could do, to get into business in some of the department, it has proved fruitless—Under those circumstances its my wish to return to my Father, unfortunately the meanes is not in my power or gladly would I do it—From those considerations pardon me for the Liberty ime about to take, in that of the favour I aske, which causes sensations of the most unpleasant natur, When ime induced from necesety to request what delicasy does not sanction—The favour is the Loan of as much Money as will permit me to leave this place, and return to Richmond—Before I came to A resolution of addressing you on A subject of this kind, I left nothing undon, that Necesety could invent, or my imagination devise, to, not trouble you—for this eight days the subject of this Letter ive contemplated[1]—I was in hopes some fortuouse circumstance would intervene to spare me the Necesety of addressing you in the maner I have, that circumstance has not offered—Therefore I submit myself to your consideration, benevolence, and Philantrophy—The Obligation I will return with gratitude a sence[2] of the favour you may please to confer can never be erased from my memory—The Knowledge you have of me is but small, small as it is, with that information, and my present forlorn

situation, I hope will in part appologize for this Liberty—I shall wait your answer, personally, or any othe way you may please to communicate it—

With sentiment that breaths the strongest wishes for your prosperity and Wellfare, I am Very Respectfully   SAML. QUARRIER

RC (DLC); addressed: "Thomas Jefferson Esquire—President of the United States"; endorsed by TJ as received 2 Feb. and so recorded in SJL.

Quarrier had written TJ in August 1801 seeking AN APPOINTMENT, supported by recommendations from George Wythe and James Monroe. The following October, however, he was in debtor's prison and TJ deemed him to be "on questionable ground with me" (Vol. 35:83-4, 119, 478-9, 496).

MY FATHER: Richmond coachmaker Alexander Quarrier.

Following the receipt of the above letter, TJ sent Quarrier $25 in charity (MB, 2:1065).

[1] Quarrier here canceled "only."
[2] Quarrier first wrote "and a deep sence" before altering it to read as above.

From Samuel Quarrier

SIR/   City of Washington, Febuary 2d, 1802—

I received your kind favour and for it receive my best thankes—Unfortunately I did not state the amount of the sum In the Letter I wrote you this mourning, from that ime forced again to intrude myselfe on you, (indeed) greately against my wishes, or inclination—The application I made to you did not specify the amount of the Loane I requested—in that letter I desired as much as would permit me to leave this place for Ricd.—the sum I received is fully sufficient for that, tho not competent to relieve me from the imbarasment I as yet unhappily labour under, from that consideration I have to request the further extention of your philantropic aid—60 Dolls. with what you'v so friendly tendered me with will enable me to leave this place—Believe me Sir, I would not trouble you in this manner, if I could avoid it; the many unpleasant sensations I've experienced, and felt in the contemplation, and execution of this unpleasant business are ample testimony in my mind that nothing but real Necessity ever could induce me to take the Liberty I have—

Immediately on my return to Richd. I will remit[1] the favour, with thanks, never to be erased from me, while memory holds her seat, or gratitude claims acknowledgement, for obligations confered—

Receive all I have to give my greatest, and best wishes for your happiness, and Prosperity—I am with the most profound Respect—

                                      SAML. QUARRIER

RC (DLC); at head of text: "Thomas Jefferson Esqr. President of the United States"; endorsed by TJ as received 3 Feb. and so recorded in SJL.

[1] Word interlined in place of "return."

To the Senate and the House of Representatives

GENTLEMEN OF THE SENATE AND
OF THE HOUSE OF REPRESENTATIVES

I now lay before you

1. a return of Ordnance, arms, & military stores the property of the US.
2. returns of muskets & bayonets fabricated at the armouries of the US. at Springfield & Harper's ferry, and of the expenditures at those places: and
3. an estimate of expenditures which may be necessary for fortifications and barracks for the present year.

Besides the permanent magazines established at Springfield, Westpoint & Harper's ferry, it is thought one should be established in some point convenient for the states of North Carolina, South Carolina, and Georgia. such a point will probably be found near the border of the Carolinas, and some small provision by the legislature, preparatory to the establishment, will be necessary for the present year.

We find the United States in possession of certain iron mines & works in the county of Berkeley and state of Virginia, purchased, as is presumeable, on the idea of establishing works for the fabrication of cannon and other military articles by the public. whether this method of supplying what may be wanted will be most adviseable, or that of purchasing at market, where competition brings every thing to it's proper level of price and quality, is for the legislature to decide: and if the latter alternative be preferred, it will rest for their further consideration in what way the subjects of this purchase may be best employed or disposed of. the Attorney General's opinion on the subject of the title accompanies this.

There are, in various parts of the US. small parcels of land which have been purchased at different times for cantonments & other military purposes. several of them are in situations not likely to be accomodated to future purposes. the loss of the records prevents a detailed statement of these, until they can be supplied by enquiry. in the mean time one of them, containing 88. acres, in the county of Essex in New Jersey, purchased in 1799. and sold the following year to Cornelius Vermule and Andrew Codmas, though it's price has been¹ recieved, cannot be conveyed without authority from the legislature.

I inclose herewith a letter from the Secretary at War on the subject of the islands in the lakes and rivers of our Northern boundary, and of certain lands in the neighborhood of some of our military posts, on which it may be expedient for the legislature to make some provisions.

TH: JEFFERSON
Feb. 2. 1802.

RC (DNA: RG 233, PM, 7th Cong., 1st sess.); entirely in TJ's hand; endorsed by a clerk. PrC (DLC). RC (DNA: RG 46, LPPM, 7th Cong., 1st sess.); in Meriwether Lewis's hand, signed and dated by TJ; endorsed by a clerk. Recorded in SJL with notation "arms, mines, lands, islands." Enclosures: (1) "Return of Ordnance, Arms &ca. the property of the United States," listing quantities of brass and iron artillery pieces, gun carriages, artillery shot and shells, gunpowder, cartridge paper, rifles, muskets, pistols, swords, cutlasses, and other items (MS in DNA: RG 233, PM, undated, in a clerk's hand, signed by Henry Dearborn, at foot of text: "The Arms in possession of the Army are not included in the foregoing return," endorsed by a clerk; MS in DNA: RG 46, LPPM, in the same clerk's hand, signed by Dearborn, endorsed by a clerk). (2) Return of muskets and bayonets fabricated at the armory at Springfield, Massachusetts, from 1795 to 28 Nov. 1801, dated War Department, 8 Dec. 1801, giving figures for each year for a total of 16,120 muskets and 12,968 bayonets (MS in DNA: RG 233, PM, in a clerk's hand, endorsed by a clerk; MS in DNA: RG 46, LPPM, in a clerk's hand, endorsed by a clerk). (3) Return of muskets and bayonets fabricated at the armory at Harpers Ferry, Virginia, 1 Jan. to 30 Sep. 1801, dated War Department, 8 Dec. 1801, showing 260 muskets and the same number of bayonets (MS in DNA: RG 233, PM, in a clerk's hand, endorsed by a clerk; MS in DNA: RG 46, LPPM, in a clerk's hand, endorsed by a clerk). (4) Statement of expenditures at the armories, 8 Dec. 1801, reporting $192,847.01 expended at Springfield from 10 July 1793 to 31 Dec. 1800, $37,404.22 expended there from 1 Jan. to 30 Sept. 1801, $61,725.12 expended at Harpers Ferry from 1 Oct. 1798 to 31 Dec. 1800, and $13,489.86 expended there from 1 Jan. to 30 June 1801 (MS in DLC, in a clerk's hand, signed by William Simmons as accountant for the War Department, endorsed by TJ; MS in DNA: RG 233, PM, in a clerk's hand, attested as a true copy by John Newman as chief clerk of the department, endorsed by a clerk; MS in DNA: RG 46, LPPM, in a clerk's hand, attested by Newman, endorsed by a clerk). (5) "Estimate of Expenditures necessary for erecting and completing Fortifications and Barracks" in 1802; listing, for work at Portsmouth, New Hampshire, $1,000; Boston, $38,000; Newport, Rhode Island, $1,500; Philadelphia, $1,000; Norfolk, $12,000; Wilmington, North Carolina, $4,000; works in Georgia, $6,000; at Niagara, $3,000; and at Detroit, Michilimackinac, Chickasaw Bluffs, and Fort Massac, $4,000, making a total of $70,500 (MS in DNA: RG 233, PM, undated, in a clerk's hand, endorsed by a clerk; MS in DNA: RG 46, LPPM, undated, in a clerk's hand, endorsed by a clerk). (6) Levi Lincoln to Henry Dearborn, 25 Jan. 1802 (Tr in DNA: RG 233, PM, in a clerk's hand, at head of text: "Copy," endorsed by a clerk). (7) Dearborn to TJ, 5 Dec. 1801. Message and enclosures printed in ASP, *Military Affairs*, 1:156-9.

At some unidentified time, TJ received another RETURN OF ORDNANCE from the War Department. Although similar in format to the return submitted to Congress with the message above, the undated one was briefer, lacked some categories of materials, and reported quantities of saltpeter, "Brimstone" (sulfur), lead, and metal for casting brass cannons. With the exception of cutlasses, which numbered 454 in both statements, the quantities of items differed between the two returns, although some of that discrepancy could have been the result of different classifications of similar items (MS in DLC: TJ Papers, 119:20624; undated and unsigned; in the same clerk's hand as both versions of Enclosure No. 1).

In his annual message TJ had anticipated sending information about MILITARY STORES. The House of Representatives formed a committee in January to consider whether any addition to the stores was necessary, and on 2 Feb., after Meriwether Lewis delivered the message printed above and the accompanying documents, the House referred the portion of the message that related to military stores to that committee. The "residue" of the message was ordered to lie on the table. On 15 Mch. the committee submitted a report, which was tabled. Lewis also delivered the message and documents to the Senate on 2 Feb., where the message was read and it and the papers ordered to lie for consideration (JHR, 4:23-4, 35, 80-1, 137; JS, 3:176).

In an act of 1 May 1802 for military appropriations, Congress approved $70,500 for the erection and completion of FORTIFICATIONS AND BARRACKS (U.S. Statutes at Large, 2:183).

Concerning the IRON MINES in Virginia, see War Department to TJ, with reply, 10 Dec. 1801.

In March 1802, Congress passed an act allowing title to the land in Essex County, New Jersey, to be conveyed to CORNELIUS VERMULE and ANDREW CODMAS. The United States had bought the property for a military cantonment in 1799 and sold it to Vermule and Codmas in 1800 (U.S. Statutes at Large, 6:46).

An act approved on 3 Apr. 1802 appropriated up to $10,000 for expenses of negotiating and ascertaining the BOUNDARY between the United States and the British province of Upper Canada (same, 2:148).

¹ TJ here canceled "paid."

From Robert Smith

SIR: Nav Dep 2 Feb 1802

Doct S. Robinson has been highly recommended to me for a Surgs. Mate in the Navy—& I think he would make a good appointment— His services are wanted—

I have the honor to be with the greatest respect Sir your Mo: ob: sr: RT SMITH

RC (DLC); in a clerk's hand, signed by Smith; at foot of text: "Prest. United States"; endorsed by TJ as received from the Navy Department on 2 Feb. and so recorded in SJL with notation "nominn"; also endorsed by TJ: "nominn Doctr. J. Roberson." FC (Lb in DNA: RG 45, LSP).

On 3 Feb., TJ nominated Samuel ROBINSON of Pennsylvania to be a surgeon's mate in the navy (RC in DNA: RG 46, EPEN, 7th Cong., 1st sess.; PrC in DLC; recorded in SJL with notation "nomination Robinson surgeon's mate"). The Senate received the nomination the following day and consented to Robinson's appointment on 9 Feb. (JEP, 1:406-7).

Memorandum from Tench Coxe

Regulations of Navigation by the Government of the United States.

It has been suggested, that the United States would form a more principled, stable and safe commercial system, by taking measures for a perfect freedom and equality of commerce between them and any considerable foreign nation, which would be willing to reciprocate the same—

This reciprocity to extend to all the dominions of the two countries in order to render it just & equal.

But as France may, according to her arretè of 1784, confine our intercourse with her Sugar Colonies to one or two ports on an island & to particular commodities, contemplating our going to Bourdeaux for her colonial Sugars, and as England may exclude us from her Sugar colonies agreably to her ancient navigation System, & as Spain may continue to exclude us, it is necessary for us to consider ourselves, by anticipation, in such a *restricted* or *excluded* situation, and to determine what means of relief to our trade & agriculture we may be able to pursue.

To impose a duty upon foreign ships beyond our begets foreign countervailing duties, and burdens by the two Duties the foreign and american carriers of our produce, and bringers of our supplies. These Tonnages fall on the producer and upon the consumer, and give no preference, in the End, to our ships.

To impose duties upon all foreign goods from those places, much of which we must consume, and much of wch. are of kinds we do not raise imposes a duty upon the american consumer, but does not gain the prohibited advantage to our Ships—

To acquire *the lights* necessary to take one safe and equitable step from the ground of freedom and reciprocity, some reflections on our political œconomy, as connected with this subject, are thrown out in the Aurora of this day under the signature of Franklin. They were begun by a recurrence to first principles and passing to facts. From these suggestions of a line of conduct arose never before in the mind of the writer.

Since they were committed to paper, reflexion has shewn that we have unconsciously taken some steps connected with these principles; and if the internal revenue system shall be repealed, they will be sufficiently acted upon to enable us to form some Judgment of their soundness and present practicability. The common spirits of the British Windward Islands are dutied at 25 Cents. Our rival grain

spirits on the repeal will be at nought in the Scale. If the growth of new American productions, not eatable, or the increase of manufacturers do not keep up the prices of our grain, domestic spirits, undutied, will occasion the shipment to Europe, often in our vessels, of much of the British Windward Island Rum. So of their other rums. Perhaps it may be found expedient to advance the duty upon the principles contemplated in this note and in Franklin.
Feby. 3. 1802.

MS (DNA: RG 59, LAR); endorsed by TJ as received 6 Feb. and so recorded in SJL.

The Philadelphia *Aurora* of 3 Feb. included "Sketches of Political Economy for the United States of America" UNDER THE SIGNATURE OF FRANKLIN. The author advocated the encouragement of U.S. agriculture and commerce and the development of timber and other natural resources through a system of duties and drawbacks. Duties equal to those of Great Britain on "foreign malt liquors and distilled spirits, and on foreign materials for spirits" would ensure that American farmers would receive $1 per bushel for their rye and $1.25 for their wheat. "Franklin" sought to set impediments to "the *exclusive* carrying trade of foreigners in spirits, molasses, and cotton," and promote "our own beers, cider, spirits and cotton" without injury to the import carrying trade of the United States.

Invoice from William Duane

President of the United States 1802	To Wm. Duane.	Dr.
Jany. 4th. To 1 Glass Inkstand		1.
Feby 3 To 1 Bottle Red Ink		.31
" To 1 Ream of Printed Letters		22.
To 2 Wedgwood Inkstands		2.
		$25.31

MS (CSmH); in a clerk's hand; with order in TJ's hand at foot of text: "Mr. Barnes is pleased to pay this Th: Jefferson Feb. 17. 1802"; signed by Duane acknowledging payment; endorsed by John Barnes as paid in full on 22 Feb. 1802.

In a statement of TJ's account from 4 Jan. 1802 to 7 July 1803, Duane recorded the purchase date of the PRINTED LETTERS and WEDGWOOD INKSTANDS as 13 Feb. 1802. He also described the letters as "1 Ream Invitations 2 on a sheet 4to. post" with a price of $20 (CSmH).

To George Jefferson

DEAR SIR   Washington Feb. 3. 1802.

Doctor Currie informs me he put into your hands all the papers in David Ross's case which had been confided to him. I will pray you to send them on to me by [post?].—the money which was lodged with you for Borduron, will not be called for he having been paid through another channel. it will stand therefore to my general credit, and what you recieved for mr Short I shall exchange with mr Barnes for money here, except a fee out of it for mr Wickam whom I employ in a suit for mr Short and shall immediately desire him to call on you for his fee. Mr. Newton of Norfolk has undertaken to order 4. barrels of Hughes's crab cyder, double cased, to be forwarded to you, to be sent on to Monticello. be so good as to send them by the first boats, with 6. gross of the best corks, and 2. gross of bottles, as we have some bottles there.—the season for buying hams is now approaching. I must sollicit you to buy me an hundred & fifty of the best, that is to say small, fat & well cured. mr Macon's proved so good that I shall be very glad to have all his included in the number. no shoulders to be among them, but hams alone. be so good as to forward them here to mr Barnes as you receive them.   accept assurances of my affectionate attachment   TH: JEFFERSON

PrC (MHi); blurred; at foot of text: "Mr. George Jefferson"; endorsed by TJ in ink on verso. Recorded in SJL with notation "Bonduron. Ross. Short. cyder. hams."

CURRIE INFORMS ME: see James Currie to TJ, 27 Jan.

To James Monroe

TH: JEFFERSON TO GOVR. MONROE.   Feb. 3. 02.

Will you be so good as to deliver the inclosed letters to Prince Ruspoli, to whom I should have sent them before he left this place, but was prevented by indispensable occupations. as I know he is to call on you, the omission can be supplied; the object of the letters being to have him attended to at Monticello. should he be gone, or not go that rout, let them be sent to Monticello, as they respect some other matters.

The Senate recieved a recruit (mr Bradly) the day before yesterday. they yesterday discharged their committee on the Judiciary bill, and will this day read it a 3d. time & pass it. health & happiness.

TH: JEFFERSON

PrC (DLC); date added by TJ in ink; at foot of text: "Govr. Monroe." Enclosures were perhaps: (1) TJ to Thomas Mann Randolph, 3 Feb. (2) TJ to James

Dinsmore, recorded in SJL under 3 Feb., but not found.

Bartolomeo RUSPOLI, a member of a

noble family of Rome, had arrived in the United States during 1801. He first visited New York and Boston. Continuing his tour of the United States, Ruspoli traveled at least as far south as Charleston. After leaving the United States in 1802, he traveled in Ireland, Scotland, and England. He was a knight commander of the Order of St. John of Jerusalem (the Knights of Malta; his title was called *bailli* in French, *balì* in Italian, and sometimes "bailiff" in English). Late in the summer of 1802, Pope Pius VII offered him the position of grand master of the order. Control of Malta was still a source of international tension, however, and Ruspoli declined the appointment. Although sometimes called "prince," Bartolomeo Ruspoli was commonly referred to as "bailli" or "chevalier" to distinguish him from his brother, who held the hereditary title of prince (Norwich, Conn., *Courier*, 12 Aug. 1801; Charleston *City Gazette and Daily Advertiser*, 22 Mch. 1802; *Gazette of the United States*, 11 Dec. 1802; Hudson, N.Y., *Bee*, 22 Feb. 1803; Syrett, *Hamilton*, 25:432; 26:2; Madison, *Papers, Sec. of State Ser.*, 2:319; Francis Beretti, ed., *Pascal Paoli à Maria Cosway: Lettres et documents, 1782-1803* [Oxford, 2003], 148-9, 159-60; Michel de Pierredon, *Histoire politique de l'Ordre souverain de Saint-Jean de Jérusalem (Ordre de Malte) de 1789 à 1955*, 2d ed., 3 vols. [Paris, 1956-1990], 2:38-44; William Hardman, *A History of Malta: During the Period of the French and British Occupations, 1798-1815* [London, 1909], 449, 461-2; Claudio Rendina, ed., *La grande enciclopedia di Roma: Personaggi, curiosità, monumenti, storia, arte e folclore della Città Eterna dalle origini al Duemila* [Rome, 2000], 1050; Vol. 34:600).

To Thomas Mann Randolph

DEAR SIR   Washington Feb. 3. 1802.

Prince Ruspoli, a Roman Noble proposing in a tour which he is taking to Rockbridge, to pass by Monticello, I take the liberty of addressing him to your attentions. he will probably pass one evening only at Milton or Charlottesville; and, if you could ride with him to Monticello, he would probably be gratified by it, and have his enquiries more satisfactorily answered, than by mr Dinsmore, to whom I have given him a letter, desiring his attendance on him. as he will be with you about the time of the arrival of this weeks post, I prefer this opportunity of saying all is well.   a recruit having come in to the Senate the day before yesterday, they yesterday discharged the committee to whom they had referred the judiciary bill, and will this day read it the 3d time and pass it by 16. against 15. members, one member only being now absent. my love to my dear Martha & the family and affectionate attachment to yourself.

TH: JEFFERSON

P.S. Maria was well on the 24th. Ult. her little one beginning to cut teeth.

RC (DLC); at foot of text: "T M Randolph." PrC (CSmH); endorsed by TJ in ink on verso. Perhaps enclosed in TJ to Monroe, 3 Feb.

From Albert Gallatin

DEAR SIR   Feby. 4th 1802

I enclose E. Burroughs's proposals for two of the Chesapeak light houses. From every information, it is not probable that any other person will offer, and it is very desirable that we should, by availing ourselves of his proposals, secure the work being done next summer.

The only objection in the way is want of cession on the part of Virginia, but there is no doubt of its having been, or being hereafter obtained; and as Mr Burroughs leaves town on next Saturday, I would propose to agree to the terms proposed with only one additional condition that the execution of the contract shall depend upon the cession being obtained.

Your official approbation is by law necessary.

Respectfully Your obt. Servt.   ALBERT GALLATIN

RC (DLC); at foot of text: "The President of the U.S."; endorsed by TJ as received from the Treasury Department on 4 Feb. and "lighthouses" and so recorded in SJL. Enclosures: (1) "Proposals for building a Light House &ca. on Smith's point," by Elzy Burroughs, Washington, D.C., 3 Feb., with specifications for the construction of an "octagonal pyramid" lighthouse of stone to be completed by 1 Nov. 1802, for the sum of $8,750. (2) "Proposals for building a Light house &ca. on old point comfort," by Burroughs, Washington, D.C., 3 Feb., with specifications for the construction of an "octagonal pyramid" lighthouse of hard brick to be completed by 1 Nov. 1802, for the sum of $4,850 (FCs in Lb in DNA: RG 26, LDC). With the submitted documents, Gallatin noted: "The enclosed proposals of E. Burroughs for building Light houses at Point Smith, and old point comfort respectively are submitted to the President of the United States for his consideration and decision." TJ dated and signed his response on 4 Feb.: "Mr. Burroughs' propositions as to both light houses are approved" (FC in same).

William Miller, commissioner of the revenue, sent Elzy BURROUGHS'S PROPOSALS to Gallatin on 3 Feb., stating that although he had contacted others "who had turned their attention to business of this kind," Burroughs was the only one to offer proposals to construct the lighthouses for the "sum limited by the appropriation of congress." Benjamin H. Latrobe was one of those contacted by Miller, but he declined, noting that the sum appropriated was insufficient to procure his services. In 1798, Congress appropriated less than $3,500 for the Old Point Comfort lighthouse. The sum was raised to $5,000. In 1801, Congress set aside $9,000 for the erection of the lighthouse at Smith's Point (FC in Lb in DNA: RG 26, LDC; U.S. Statutes at Large, 1:553; 2:125; John C. Van Horne, ed., The Correspondence and Miscellaneous Papers of Benjamin Henry Latrobe, 3 vols. [New Haven, 1984-88], 1:197-9).

CESSION ON THE PART OF VIRGINIA: Miller informed Gallatin on 3 Feb. that he had instructed Edward Carrington to apply to the Virginia legislature for the cession of land for the construction of the lighthouse at Smith's Point. The act ceding the land was passed on 15 Jan. 1802 (FC in Lb in DNA: RG 26, LDC; Shepherd, Statutes, 2:316).

On SATURDAY, 6 Feb., Miller signed agreements with Burroughs for the construction of the two lighthouses. A paragraph was added to the agreement for the lighthouse at Point Smith, making it contingent upon the cession of land by Virginia (FCs in Lb in DNA: RG 26, LDC).

From Samuel Morse

Sir,   Washington, Feby. 4th. 1802.

The person who now has the honor of addressing you is the same who was lately the editor of a paper in Connecticut—his name Samuel Morse. One who seeks to be known to you, and presumes on this as a preliminary.

To leave the state of Connecticut, where the cant of hypocritical piety forms a principal part of the character of its inhabitants and hostility to free enquiry is constantly maintained, was pleasing to me. But to seperate from the wife of my bosom and the children of our love was painful and distressing, more especially as no settled prospect was open to my view.

When I determined to visit the seat of government, the urbanity of him who reigns in the hearts of Freedom's children, excited in me a strong wish to see him and seek his protection. I was not without a reflection that his exalted station would be thronged with the dependent, but I added another, that if I was not among those who deserved the esteem of a Jefferson; if my claims to notice are unworthy his attention; there are few, equally aspiring, who can better content themselves in a humble, but not *mean* state, than myself. Few who wish a favor can with less anxiety suffer a refusal.

The sentiments of a freeman are predominant in my breast—the love of liberty is my ruling passion. No favor can enslave or purchase my conscience, nor lessen the duties I owe to my country, to truth and honor. Favors granted with purposes hostile to these, I do not wish, nor would I knowingly receive. They would certainly fail of their object. The force of gratitude and the ties of personal affection are insufficient to make me a villain.

When with such sentiments I ask attention, I acknowledge I ought to have something more interesting to say than the limited theatre of my action is likely to afford. Will my tale compensate the president of the United States for its perusal? Will Thomas Jefferson think his moments not ill employed or will his gratification repay his trouble? Shall the hope be indulged that it may gain his esteem?

At the early age of 12 and a half years, I was deprived of my father by death. Possessing a fondness for knowledge, though the benefit of a school had not been afforded me for more than four months in the year, I had obtained for my age and situation, a considerable degree of information. From that period to the present, on general subjects, the aid of a preceptor has but casually been obtained. So great was my passion for learning, I chose to combat every opposing obstacle and strive to compass the possession of so much as might furnish me with the means of subsistence. Compelled by my circumstances to labor with my hands: (a destiny which I never thought disgraceful or unkind, except that my slender constitution was not equal to continual application) I was obliged to improve every opportunity for reading, and though not deficient in a taste for those diversions in which youths employ their leisure, I have spent many of the hours which my companions assigned for recreation, in the dearer society of books. My reading has not been systematic; I have perused all which opportunity has permitted, in my circumscribed course. As I have lost the fetters with the advantages of system, I may have profited as much by the absence of classical prejudice as I should have gained by its selection of studies.

The pursuit most consonant to my wishes would have been the law; but in addition to the difficulties which my pecuniary deficiences presented, my only parent was averse to that profession: as she conceived it one which extended the evils of human frailty and widened those breaches of social harmony which every good member should endeavor to heal.

It was in September, 1795, I first entered on the study of physic, under the care of a neighbouring practitioner. His inattention to me rendered me less diligent than what had been usual with me. I afterwards spent some time with a better preceptor. I was examined and received a Diploma according to the rules of the Connecticut Medical Society, on the 21st of May, 1799, three weeks after I had attained the age of 21 years. Candor however, bids me say, that had my means been greater, and my circumstances different I should have been more accomplished in the art.

A few months previous to compleating my 18th year, I became betrothed to a young woman who had engaged my affections, and from whom they have never swerved. This certainly had influence over conduct and fortune. It stimulated my exertions in the pursuit of knowledge, and caused me, in my pecuniary transactions at least, to be guided by the strictest prudence. In September 1797 we were married. She was the daughter of a respectable farmer, with whom she continued some time after our union and under whose protection she again resides.

It will readily be conceived that my situation was not so independent in a worldly view as to render me the possession of as much happiness as connubial bliss promised; that a wife and a growing family would excite a desire if not impose a necessity for a speedy settlement.

In November 1799, I visited the town of Danbury with intention to make it the place of my residence as a physician. The usual fate of young physicians, want of patients, attending me; I accepted an offer to teach a school for the winter. In the spring one of the partners of the printing office in that town, contemplated some other pursuit. The political agitation he chose not to take an active part in, and he was dissatisfied with the other proprietor. He wished to dispose of the property and by flattering representations, induced me to purchase. Unacquainted myself with the value of this property or the business, my estimates were necessarily made from the data given me. Considerable reliance was placed on the character of the man, and as in a business so little connected with the general pursuits of Society, few possess information sufficient to give advice with correctness; one other source of enquiry only, which could be deemed satisfactory remained within the limits of my researches. This was the other partner. His words were corroborative of the other's statement, but I have from him since learnt that his mouth was sealed by agreement.

The field of information thus closed to my view; it was impossible for me to learn, what I ought to have known, the real state of the establishment; I was therefore left open to deception and fraud. The time for which I had engaged in the school having expired; and a *cheaper* school for the summer being contemplated; I feared, and with justice that pecuniary difficulties would involve me and those I loved. Circumstances of greater delicacy rendered this prospect peculiarly distressing. In my talents as an editor my friends expressed a confidence and as it was a fact too notorious that the press had been basely prostituted to the support of unprincipled men and the propagation of opinions hostile to the cause of our revolution; they hoped my integrity and zeal would be such as to contribute in the execution of my duty, to the restoration of its purity and yeild some service to the community. I confess my own vanity and patriotism pointed to the accomplishment of their wishes.

Embarked in this business and finding that the supporters of the paper were determined I should not give currency to a single sentiment not in accord with their politics; finding too that I had been deceived in the value of the establisment. and that my partner was about to lay on me a considerable additional burthen or embarrass the business; believing too that this conduct gave me the greatest reason to suspect his moral honesty; I preferred to risque all in support of integrity and freedom to a continual opposition to my conscience, my own and my country's happiness. I chose the path I thought it my duty to tread, and serious as have been the consequences I cannot reproach myself for prizing the dictates of principle and honor above the rewards of servility and hypocrisy.

My success in this pursuit may be readily gathered from my present situation: the particulars have been detailed in letters I addressed the Secretary of State last Summer. I have only to add, I continued the paper until every principle of honor, friendship and private faith imperiously demanded of me to lay down a burden under which I was fainting and exonerate those whose confidence in me had subjected them to the danger of pecuniary loss. Enough had been sacrificed to my country—surely the smiling countenance of freedom's brighter orb justified me in remembering my friends, my family and myself.

I resigned the paper, purposing to proceed to Georgia and seek a livelihood in the practise of physic. My first object was to discharge all demands against me which the nature of the contract or the situation of the party imposed a special obligation on me to satisfy. This I was so far enabled to do that no one will be a material sufferer should I never be able to pay the remainder. On my arrival at New York, I found myself possessed of nineteen dollars only—the passage to Savannah was 25 dollars. What could I do? My friends in New Haven had but slight acquaintance in Georgia—I could not assure myself of any adequate protection when I arrived there. I could not, would not proceed without being able to pay my passage: nor would put myself in a character which must cast me into the back ground forever.

I resolved to visit this city, where I hoped I might find friends to advise me, and who would introduce me to those who would be of service to me.

Though not destitute of honorable ambition, my pretensions do exceed the bounds of reason. Any situation which should call into action what talents I possess, in such manner as to be beneficial to the community where I may reside, would be more gratifying to me than mere pecuniary considerations. I am ambitious to deserve the approbation of the good; to serve my country and prove myself an honest man. I am vain that I possess a heart devoted to my fellow beings; a moral conduct which cannot be impeached; an independent spirit; an integrity unshaken and an honor unstained. I am ambitious to preserve these inviolate.

What is your object, what are your wishes? may be asked me. I scarce know a reply. My country wants not my services, her necessities are supplied by abler children: and curse on the man who would create an unnecessary office for me to fill. The practice of physic is perhaps the most eligible pursuit, should a proper place of settlement be found. But here an immediate profit can hardly be expected, and from my attention to political and other objects for the last two years, my application to medical studies has been interrupted. I trust, however, that in this branch, care attention and industry would render me of use to my fellow Citizens.

Much as I wish to be in a situation in which my family can return to my protection; I should accept with pleasure one where an immediate income would soon to enable me to repay the debts I owe. But for this wish, I would look out an asylum in some of the rising states. Here however exists one fear—that the state of knowledge in new founded states would not furnish all the means of improvement I might wish. It is notwithstanding a rational hope that industry and perseverance would not be without their reward. The liberal laws of Virginia invite the sense of principle to her standard; but less populous states open a greater prospect to futurity.

In Connecticut, my circumstances at this time, and my uniform principles, oppose an effectual barrier against my success in any pursuit: more especially as every profession is already overstocked. Having, too, expended near two hundred dollars of the property bestowed on my wife; I shall expend no more without a well grounded hope of profit. If misfortunes attend me, I would if possible prevent them from discovering the abode of those who are dear to me or uniting others in my distress.

In selecting an object of pursuit; the state of my finances impose the necessity of deciding soon: yet my indecision is not lessened. Perhaps Georgia would be a place as eligible for the art of physic as would present: but if I am correctly informed, the state of Society would preclude the probability of success to a person in my circumstances, without patronage. Kentucky, Tennessee, or the Missisippi Territory probably afford as promising openings for any pursuit as can be found.

I have aspired to be known to you as a man and a fellow citizen: I hope in both I may be found not unworthy your knowledge and that an affectionate heart may deserve the esteem of a man elevated by the confidence which his priciples and virtues have gained, to the highest place in this nation and the most important in the universe.

With the highest respect and esteem, Yours   SAML MORSE

RC (DLC); at foot of text: "Ths. Jefferson, President"; endorsed by TJ as received 5 Feb. and so recorded in SJL.

SAMUEL MORSE: see Vol. 32:34. Morse wrote the SECRETARY OF STATE in May and June 1801 requesting employment in a government post and lamented the continuation of his newspaper, the *Sun of Liberty*, without relief from debt (Madison, *Papers, Sec. of State Ser.*, 1:220, 260-1).

To Anna Young

MADAM   Washington Feb. 4. 1802.

Immediately on reciept of your letter of Jan. 21. I referred it to the Secretary at war, who was best acquainted with the subject of it, desiring him to investigate the nature of your claim, to see whether it could be effected, and to point out the course to be pursued. he accordingly has made a thorough enquiry into it, and assures me that yours is one of a class of cases which have been barred by two or three different laws of the United States, which would render vain any attempt to bring it forward. it would have been more pleasing to me to have been able to assure you that your wishes could be fulfilled. but the laws being opposed to this, I can only relieve you from further useless pursuits, and assure you that my attentions have been duly bestowed on your case.

Accept my best wishes and respects.   TH: JEFFERSON

PrC (DLC); in ink at foot of text: "Mrs. Anna Young Norwich Connecticut."

TWO OR THREE DIFFERENT LAWS: resolutions of the Confederation Congress, dated 2 Nov. 1785 and 23 July 1787, limited the time for submitting any outstanding claims against the United States. An act of Congress, dated 23 Mch. 1792, declared that those resolutions, as far as they had barred claims by widows and orphans of Revolutionary War officers to seven years of half-pay, were to be suspended for a term of two years from the passage of said act (JCC, 29:866, 33:392; U.S. Statutes at Large, 1:243-5).

To Joseph Yznardi, Sr.

SIR   Washington Feb. 4. 1802.

I recieved yesterday your favor of Jan. 30. as I had before done that of the 15th. I had some days ago desired mr Barnes to remit you 403. Dollars for the wines formerly furnished, which he engaged to do this present week. if you will inform me also of the amount of those mentioned in your letter of the 30th. it shall be also remitted.

I have mentioned to mr Smith your desire to have a passage in the frigate going from Philadelphia, which he thinks can be admitted, and will write to you thereon. the Senate have confirmed your appointment as Consul, and you will recieve the commission as soon as it is made out. Accept assurances of my esteem & respect.

TH: JEFFERSON

PrC (DLC); at foot of text: "Joseph Yznardi esq."; endorsed by TJ in ink on verso.

PASSAGE IN THE FRIGATE: on 1 Feb., Robert Smith wrote Alexander Murray, the captain of the *Constellation*, which was at Philadelphia preparing for sea, to say that he had "no objection" to giving Yznardi passage to Gibraltar as he desired. Smith sent a countermanding instruction four days later, stating that "it has been determined not to admit the

practice of allowing our public ships to take passengers." Yznardi traveled to Cadiz aboard a Spanish vessel that left Philadelphia in June (in Lb in DNA: RG 45, LSO; NDBW, 2:19, 208).

TJ had issued a COMMISSION in October for Yznardi to be the U.S. consul at Cadiz. The new commission, which followed the Senate's approval of Yznardi among the interim appointments submitted on 6 Jan., was dated 26 Jan. (FC in Lb in DNA: RG 59, PTCC; Vol. 35:585).

Conference with Black Hoof

I. ADDRESS OF BLACK HOOF, [5 FEB. 1802]

II. JEFFERSON'S REPLY, 10 FEB. 1802

III. HENRY DEARBORN'S REPLY, 10 FEB. 1802

IV. HENRY DEARBORN TO CHIEFS OF THE DELAWARES
AND SHAWNEES, 10 FEB. 1802

EDITORIAL NOTE

Early in January, during the visit to Washington by the delegation of Miami, Potawatomi, and Wea Indians led by Little Turtle, the secretary of war received word from the quartermaster general, John Wilkins, Jr., at Pittsburgh, that another deputation of Native Americans was on its way to Washington. Dearborn asked Wilkins to help the group, which consisted of "Chiefs of the Delaware and Shawanees Nations of Indians," plus "eight young men" and two interpreters, in their travel arrangements. The secretary also sent a "passport" for the Indians. "The Citizens of the Country through which they pass," the safe-conduct certificate stated, "are desired to treat them in a decent and Friendly manner, and not suffer them to be insulted or molested on their way." On 14 Jan., Dearborn made the passport system general policy. In a circular to Indian agents, he stated that the president had "consulted several of the Chiefs of different Nations"—presumably Little Turtle, Five Medals, and others of their party, although perhaps also reaching back to Dearborn's meeting with the Cherokee delegation in July—and believed that issuing passes would defray some of the "many inconveniences" experienced by parties of Indians traveling to Washington. Applying

[513]

for passes in advance would also prevent delegations from arriving in the capital when the president was absent (passport, 5 Jan., Dearborn to Wilkins, 5 Jan., Dearborn to William Henry Harrison and others, 14 Jan., Lb in DNA: RG 75, LSIA; Wilkins to Dearborn, 29 Dec. 1801, 19 Jan. 1802, recorded in DNA: RG 107, RLRMS).

The principal member of the group on its way to Washington was Black Hoof, a Shawnee chief. Like Little Turtle, Black Hoof had fought against the United States until 1794, then signed the Greenville treaty and committed himself to acculturation and peaceful, cooperative relations with the U.S. He encouraged the Shawnees to learn to raise livestock, use plows and fences, and take up spinning and weaving. That policy put him into rivalry with Little Turtle. The areas occupied by their tribes in 1802 were in the same general region of the Northwest, Black Hoof's Shawnees in what is now northwestern Ohio and Little Turtle's Miamis along the Wabash River in what became the state of Indiana. They vied for influence with the U.S. government, each trying to obtain the most favorable annuities and concessions for his own people and affiliated tribes. That competition provides a context for the comments about William Wells, Little Turtle's interpreter and son-in-law, in Black Hoof's address at Washington (Document 1). Black Hoof implied that Wells failed to assist, and perhaps tried to impede, the eastward journey of the Shawnee and Delaware delegation. Unfortunately for Black Hoof, in a contest for the U.S. government's favor, Little Turtle had more experience calling on presidents. Black Hoof's visit to Washington in 1802 was his first journey of the kind. He also, like Little Turtle, had to contend with the fact that not all members of his tribe accepted change and the assimilation of new ways of life, which Black Hoof hoped would allow them to keep their land (ANB; Dowd, "Thinking and Believing," 315-17; Colin G. Calloway, *The Shawnees and the War for America* [New York, 2007], 109-25).

Seven Shawnees and five Delawares accompanied Black Hoof on the trip to Washington. Two of the Delawares were Tetepachsit, the primary chief of the Delawares on the White River in Indiana Territory, and Buckongahelas. During the American Revolution and until Anthony Wayne's victory at Fallen Timbers in 1794, Buckongahelas was a great war leader of the Delawares, allied with the Shawnees in fighting the expansion of the American settlement frontier. In addition to Black Hoof, the deputation's Shawnee members were Big Snake (Shemenatoo), a chief known as Lewis (Quitewepea), Paumthe, and Captain Reed (Hahgooseekaw). Tetepachsit, Buckongahelas, and Captain Reed were signers of the Greenville treaty. There had been a close association between Delawares and Shawnees for more than a century. Major groups of the two tribes had lived in proximity to one another in what had become a progressively westward migration through the eighteenth century. By the time Black Hoof's party made the journey to Washington, many Delawares lived on the upper West Fork of the White River in Indiana and a number of Shawnees, like Black Hoof, were in northwestern Ohio (*Philadelphia Gazette*, 29 Jan. 1802; Alexandria *Times; and District of Columbia Daily Advertiser*, 29 Jan. 1802; safe-conduct passes for "Buckingillis," 14 Feb., and Captain Reed, 16 Feb., in Lb in DNA: RG 75, LSIA; ANB, s.v. "Buckongahelas"; C. A. Weslager, *The Delaware Indians: A History* [New Brunswick, N.J., 1972], 308, 329, 335, 338-9; John Sugden,

*Blue Jacket: Warrior of the Shawnee*s [Lincoln, Neb., 2000], 206, 209, 229, 237, 238, 285-6n; R. David Edmunds, *The Shawnee Prophet* [Lincoln, Neb., 1983], 169; Sturtevant, *Handbook*, 15:222-4, 622-3; U.S. Statutes at Large, 7:53).

Two interpreters accompanied the group. One was George Ash, who translated the address that Black Hoof gave on 5 Feb. The other person mentioned as an interpreter was probably François Duchouquet, a trader who sometimes acted as an intermediary between Indians and whites. Black Hoof commended Ash and Duchouquet in his address, and both of them petitioned Congress while the delegation was in Washington—Duchouquet for monetary compensation, Ash for confirmation of a land grant. Isaac Zane, whom Black Hoof also mentioned in his address, had been one of the official interpreters at the Greenville treaty talks in 1795. He translated there for the Wyandots, however, not the Shawnees or the Delawares, and he does not seem to have been traveling with Black Hoof's group on the visit to Washington. He did petition Congress during that session, as Ash and Duchouquet did, but Zane's petition, which asked for confirmation of a tract given him by the Wyandots, came to Congress in December, well before the Shawnee and Delaware delegation arrived in the capital. One newspaper said that a government paymaster was traveling with Black Hoof's group. That official was probably the Mr. Darah who accompanied the party from the time it left Pittsburgh, and who was probably an employee of Wilkins's department (notes to Document I, below; *Philadelphia Gazette*, 29 Jan. 1802; ASP, *Indian Affairs*, 1:582; JS, 3:164-5).

The delegation reached Washington on the evening of 27 Jan. (Alexandria *Times; and District of Columbia Daily Advertiser*, 29 Jan. 1802). Sometime between their arrival and the first meeting with Jefferson and Dearborn on 5 Feb., Jefferson arranged for Edward Gantt to vaccinate younger members of the group, as Black Hoof mentioned in his address. The meetings with Jefferson and Dearborn beginning on the 5th followed the model of the conference with Little Turtle's delegation in January and Dearborn's conference with The Glass and other Cherokees in late June and early July 1801. On 5 Feb., speaking on behalf of "the Nation of our people," Black Hoof made an oration that enumerated the issues of concern to the Shawnees and Delawares he represented (Document I). Everyone reconvened five days later, at which time Jefferson and Dearborn responded to Black Hoof's address (Documents II and III). As he did with Little Turtle, Jefferson made his reply to Black Hoof a general statement of intention and policy that introduced Dearborn's reply, which referred more directly to the Indians' concerns. There is no direct evidence that Jefferson was present during the meetings with Black Hoof—the "Brother" to whom Black Hoof directed his address could have been Jefferson or Dearborn. However, the fact that the president scripted a response to Black Hoof's address, as he had with Little Turtle, speaking directly to the visitors with "I," "you," "we," and "our," using his comments to introduce and authorize Dearborn's, is a strong indication that he was present and not simply conveying his sentiments through Dearborn. Dearborn's reply, which repeatedly addressed the hearers as "Brothers," was certainly meant to be delivered orally, and almost surely Jefferson also read his address aloud at the meeting.

The War Department's record of the conference does not contain any closing remarks from Black Hoof similar to those that Little Turtle made on 7 Jan. (see Document IV of the Conference with Little Turtle at 4 Jan.). Black Hoof and his colleagues did receive an additional document from Dearborn. In his reply, Dearborn referred to "a written Instrument" that would contain the president's pledge "to protect you . . . against all wicked people, so long as you shall continue to act honestly and peacably with each other" (Document III below). Jefferson and Dearborn probably intended the "Instrument," which the secretary of war addressed to the leaders of the Shawnees and Delawares on the president's authority, to influence the members of the tribes who still had doubts about their relationship with the United States (Document IV). The document affirmed the president's "sacred regard" for treaties with the Indians and his intent to protect their lands, introduce "useful arts," and bring white offenders to justice. In return, the government expected an acceptance of the relationship by the Indians; the president, Dearborn advised, "trusts you will not force him to recede from this determination by an improper & unjust change of conduct." Dearborn also sent a gold chain home with the delegation as a symbol of the connection between the tribes and the United States.

The group may have split up for their homeward journey. On 14 Feb. Dearborn signed a passport for Buckongahelas that included an unspecified number of "Interpreters and associates," and on the 16th a passport was issued for Captain Reed alone. Black Hoof and others left Washington for Philadelphia on the morning of the 16th, Dearborn having furnished Darah with means to assist them in their travel. Like Little Turtle, Black Hoof made connections to the Society of Friends as he developed his relationship with the U.S. government. On his way home in 1802, he stopped for a time in Philadelphia to confer with Friends there. He later—again, much as Little Turtle had done—tried the experiment of allowing Quakers to set up a demonstration farm for the Shawnees (Dearborn to William Irvine, 10 Feb., passports, 14, 16 Feb., Dearborn to John Wilkins, Jr., 16 Feb., Dearborn to Israel Whelen, 4 Mch. 1802, Lb in DNA: RG 75, LSIA; Henry Harvey, *History of the Shawnee Indians, From the Year 1681 to 1854, Inclusive* [Cincinnati, 1855; repr. New York, 1971], 118-19, 129; Dowd, "Thinking and Believing," 317).

Members of the Shawnee and Delaware deputation addressed a communication to TJ from Philadelphia on 27 Feb. He received it on 3 Mch. and recorded it in SJL as a letter from a Delaware named Pawkanjelus (likely a variant spelling of Buckongahelas's name) "& others." That letter has not been found, but it may have prompted a brief order from Dearborn to Israel Whelen, the purveyor of public supplies. On 4 Mch., Dearborn authorized Whelen "to purchase six hats for the Indian Chiefs now at Philadelphia" at a cost of no more than four dollars per hat (DNA, RG 75, LSIA).

At least some of the travelers were still in Philadelphia on 17 Mch., when one of the Shawnees died. Published reports called him a chief, but did not name him or state the cause of his death. He was buried with military honors from the Philadelphia Volunteer Company, with the city's Tammany Society also in attendance. One of the chiefs made an address at the graveside, reassuring the dead man's spirit and bidding him farewell (Baltimore *Republican or, Anti-Democrat*, 22 Mch. 1802; *Gazette of the United States*, 22 Mch.).

I. Address of Black Hoof

BROTHER, [5 Feb. 1802]

According to the agreement of the Nation of our people, we shall address you on the important business of our affairs which is the cause of our long Journey to see you at this time.

Brother

You know the same God who made you made us and all things, why cannot we enjoy the good of this Land as well as our Brothers— our hearts are always sorry to think they do not know better.

Brother,

Consider our sad situation in the country we come from we live in a very bad place for farming, the water is very bad in the summer; if you will turn your head back, you will hear the lamentations of our women and cheldren distressed for want of clothing and by hunger, we hope you will pitty them and relieve them—

Brother,

We will offer our prayers to the great spirit above for your health, happiness and prosperity, and that he will direct you to have mercy on your brothers the poor Indians.

Brother,

We have many requests to make, and we hope you will comply with them while we are here, for we shall not be abl to come such a distance from our Country again—

Brother,

Our first request to you is that you will give us a good piece of land, where we may raise good Grain and cut Hay for our Cattle the place which will suit our nation is on the head of the Mad-River, joining our great friend Isaac Zean, down the river, eight miles & then across—streight to Stoney-Creek, or Big-Miamis down to the dividing line as drawn to Lorimein—the back line is from the said place down to a Creek of the name of Blanchard's Creek, and down to the grand Glaize or Fort Defiance and from thense to Fort Wayne and streight to the Wabash-river runing into the Ohio, excepting what belongs to our Brothers according to the Treaty of Greenville. It is our desire to live like good Brothers & good neighbors, as long as the Grass grows, & the water runs in the rivers.

Brother,

We wish no Indian should disturb us, and that you would give us under your hand a Deed that nobody shall take any advantage of us, likewise a salt Leak below the mouth of the Wabash where the Shawnees formerly lived—

[517]

Brother,

The second request we make is that you will stop your people from killing our Game, at present they kill more than we do they would be angry if we were to kill a Cow or a Hog of theirs, the little game that remains is very dear to us—

Brother,

We hope every request will be granted and we beg your assistance in geting all necessary Farming tools & those for building houses that we may go to work as quick as possible, it is the wish of all our Brothers and likewise to furnish us with some domestick Animals—

Brother,

We were told at the Treaty we never should want for provisions and that we should have better than our Fathers had, we have had only dry bread where we come from—we hope we shall have better provisions when we begin to work & till we have finished, for we shall not be able to provide for ourselves—

Brother,

Since we are here we shall inform you what took place between Mr Wells and us, last summer when we saw him at Fort Wayne he told us we were desired to come to this place, to see our Brothers, and he would provide every thing for our journey, and we should meet at St. Mary's. On our arrival there he made many difficulties to our coming here but told us to go to Chilicothe and there he would settle every necessary for our journey withe Governor St. Clair but to our great surprise he did not go that way. we were in great distress and the Governor would give us no lodging, so we had to lay out without a house and with much difficulty with him we got only Twenty dollars, which is only enough for one man. So Brother you see we cannot get justice for any offence at the place we come from; we therefore inform you that we will not have any thing to do with them & Mr. Wells in particular, we expect you will get a man who will pay more attention to his employment.

Brother,

Your Brothers the Delawares suppose you have heard what had past between them and Colonel Gibson at Port Vincenes, in regard to fourteen Horses stolen from our Towns at different times by the white people, we wish to know if we shall have any satisfaction here, we were told no settlement would be made but here—

Brother,

Two of the Horses were taken soon after they were paid for by the Shawnees, one the owner persued and took it the other was raised by the Nation and stole by the white people at Fort Hamilton—

Brother,

We hope you will give us power from under your hand that we may get back a little Girl stole from us and carried to Kentuckey, the Child was born and bred in our Town, we think it very hard that our children should be taken by force from us—

Brother,

We shall mention once more what bad People you have under you, last year we sent a memorandom for some Farming tools which were sent accordingly; but to our great surprize when we went to Detroit, they were all exchanged for old Blankets and damaged Goods so that we were very much disappointed and is the principal reason of our coming here—

Brother,

We shall mention to you our way of thinking, in regard to a Trade which was promised to us at Greenville, but we never yet have seen any, we would be very happy to have one of our Brothers he may depend upon being well treated and as well as a person appointed to stay at Fort Hamilton, to receive our things at, it is the nearest Post from both Towns the Delaware at White river and the Ottawa town.

Brother,

Our wishes towards our great Friend Francis Duchouquet we hope will meet yours, the man has lived & traded along time in our towns and we never knew any bad things of him. Our intention is to give him one mile square of land where he now has a House in our Country & as it is the will of the Nation, we hope you will sign a Deed that no one may ever disturb him and if you think him of service to us we would rather have him than any other person—

Brother,

The other Interpreter is a man we raised from a Child and look on him as one of ourselves, we therefore wish to give him Four miles down the river and one mile up the land, his name[1] is George Ash and the place we meane for him is at the mouth of Kentuckey on the Indian boundary line.

Brother,

We return you our thanks for sending the Doctor to inoculate some of our young men, in a few Days we hope they will be ready to travel. Your brothers the Indians hope you will continue taking care of them during the Journey back and let the same Person conduct us who came from Pittsburgh, his name is Darah.

FC (Lb in DNA: RG 75, LSIA); in a clerk's hand; at head of text: "To our Brother the President of the United States"; in margin at head of text: "Conference held with the Delaware and Shawanoe Deputation"; at foot of text:

"The above is a faithfull interpretation of a speech delvered to the President of the United States on the 5th: day of February 1802. by Black Hoof a Shawnoe Chief, in behalf of himself and the deputation from the Delaware & Shawnoe Nations then present," with facsimile signature of George Ash by a mark, attested by Joshua Wingate, Jr.

Black Hoof (Catecahassa, Cuttheweka-saw), a principal civil chief of the Shaw-nees, was known for his eloquence and or-atorical skill. The year of his birth is unknown, but he was thought to have been at least in his nineties when he died in 1831. He fought against the Virginians in the battle of Point Pleasant in 1774 and resisted the United States until 1794. He signed the treaty of Greenville and urged the Shawnees to adapt their way of life in order to coexist peacefully with the United States. He lived at Wapakoneta, on the Auglaize River in the northwestern part of what became the state of Ohio, where many Shawnees moved after the Greenville treaty. Beginning in 1805, Black Hoof's authority came under chal-lenge from Tenskwatawa, the Shawnee Prophet, who led a reform movement based on a rejection of accommodation with whites and their "civilization." The Prophet attempted to turn the Shawnees against Black Hoof by accusing the chief of witchcraft. Black Hoof journeyed to Washington again in 1807 and 1808 and emulated Little Turtle by arranging for the establishment of a demonstration farm on the Shawnees' lands under the auspices of the Society of Friends. The Prophet's threat to Black Hoof's leader-ship lessened in 1808, when the Prophet and his brother, Tecumseh, moved to the Wabash Valley. Later, Black Hoof resist-ed pressures to relocate west of the Mis-sissippi. He remained at Wapakoneta, where in the 1820s he was a source of in-formation for whites seeking to document the Shawnees' cosmology and culture. Al-though he relied on interpreters during his 1802 visit to Washington, later in his life Black Hoof could communicate in the English language (ANB; Dowd, "Thinking and Believing," 317-20; Ed-munds, *Shawnee Prophet*, 170-4; Cal-

loway, *Shawnees*, 54, 72-3; *American An-thropologist*, new ser., 42 [1940], 145-7; 46 [1944], 370, 372-5).

OUR GREAT FRIEND ISAAC ZEAN: in 1753, when Isaac Zane was nine years old, he was captured on the Virginia fronter by Wyandot warriors. He remained with the Indians as an adult. A merchant who met him in 1789 noted that Zane "still re-tains the English Language and behaves verry well." Zane was the older brother of Ebenezer Zane, the founder of the town of Wheeling, whose recollection of events from the 1770s TJ used in *An Appendix to the Notes on Virginia Relative to the Murder of Logan's Family*, published in 1800. This Isaac Zane was not TJ's ac-quaintance of that name who lived in the Shenandoah Valley and died in 1795 (Dwight L. Smith, ed., *The Western Jour-nals of John May, Ohio Company Agent and Business Adventurer* [Cincinnati, 1961], 131; John Gerald Patterson, "Ebenezer Zane, Frontiersman," *West Virginia History*, 12 [1950], 7; Roger W. Moss, Jr., "Isaac Zane, Jr., A 'Quaker for the Times,'" VMHB, 77 [1969], 302, 304; JS, 3:164-5; Vol. 28:350; Vol. 29:5; Vol. 31:479-80n).

For the DIVIDING LINE established by the Treaty of Greenville, see Conference with Little Turtle, 4 Jan., Document I. LORIMEIN: a place called Loromie's store on the Great Miami River was one of the landmarks used in the treaty to define the boundary and for other purposes (U.S. Statutes at Large, 7:49-50).

WE WISH NO INDIAN SHOULD DIS-TURB US: Dearborn may have had discus-sions with Black Hoof's associates that were not recorded as part of the formal conference. "They are extremely anxious to have a division of lands," Dearborn wrote William Henry Harrison on 23 Feb., "and to have a line agreed on and marked between the Delawares and their neighbors." TJ had assured them "that whenever they can agree with their neighbors on a boundary line in your presence, and the parties interested shall enter into explicit stipulations on the sub-ject to your satisfaction, that you will be requested to have the line so agreed on, run and marked at the expence of the United States" (*Terr. Papers*, 7:49).

KILLING OUR GAME: the treaty gave the Indian tribes the right, "so long as they demean themselves peaceably," to hunt both on their own lands and in the territory they ceded to the United States (same, 52).

Under Article 4 of the treaty, a tribe could request payment of part of its annuity in FARMING TOOLS, domestic ANIMALS, or subsidies to "usefull artificers" (same, 51).

John GIBSON was the secretary of Indiana Territory. Gibson in 1774 translated Logan's address to Lord Dunmore, which TJ published in *Notes on the State of Virginia.* Beginning in 1797, TJ consulted Gibson as he compiled the *Appendix* to the *Notes* in response to Luther Martin's newspaper attacks (DAB; Vol. 29:408-10).

LITTLE GIRL: the Greenville treaty required all parties to give up any prisoners they held. In the latter part of 1800 and into 1801, a report circulated in the United States alleging that the Indians of the Northwest still had white captives, particularly ones who had been so young when they were taken that they had forgotten their original names and identities. In a letter of 23 Feb. 1802 to Harrison that discussed the visit by Black Hoof's delegation, Henry Dearborn said that "a complaint was made by them relating to a white child taken from one of their people which case we understand is now pending in the District Court at Kentuckey, and of course no measures could be taken relative thereto." The person in question was probably Nancy Mason, in whose behalf Harry Innes, the U.S. district judge for Kentucky, had published a notice dated 6 Nov. 1801. Innes's announcement, which was intended to help locate members of Nancy's extended family, did not state her age, but indicated that she had recently been "returned from captivity." Shawnees had killed several members of her family and taken Nancy and her brother prisoner on the Ohio River about 12 years earlier (*Terr. Papers*, 7:49; *Gazette of the United States*, 1 Dec. 1801; *Stewart's Kentucky Herald*, 24 Feb. 1801; U.S. Statutes at Large, 7:49).

An article of the Treaty of Greenville stated that TRADE "shall be opened" with the tribes that were parties to the treaty. The United States was to license all traders and monitor their conduct. Built in 1791, Fort Hamilton was on the Great Miami River about 35 miles north of Cincinnati (same, 7:52; Washington, *Papers, Pres. Ser.*, 11:309n).

François or Francis DUCHOUQUET, a French Canadian by birth, traded in the Indian country and had commercial ties to Detroit. He probably accompanied Black Hoof's delegation to Washington as the second person referred to as an interpreter, and on 15 Feb. the House of Representatives received a petition from him seeking compensation for funds he had expended to ransom white captives in 1790. By an act of 16 Mch. 1802, Congress granted him $291.84. Dearborn asked Harrison to consider the question of the land grant Black Hoof requested for Duchouquet (John Sugden, *Blue Jacket: Warrior of the Shawnees* [Lincoln, Neb., 2000], 308n; *Terr. Papers*, 7:49; JHR, 4:97; U.S. Statutes at Large, 6:46).

GEORGE ASH had been captured as a boy and adopted by the Shawnees. He was with the Indians who routed Arthur St. Clair's army in 1791, and the next year he accompanied a Shawnee delegation that traveled to meet with the Cherokees and the Creeks (Sugden, *Blue Jacket*, 18, 121-2, 138-9). Ash, like Duchouquet, petitioned Congress during the stay of Black Hoof's delegation in Washington. Ash's petition, presented to the House of Representatives on 29 Jan., said the Shawnees had given him land "for various services rendered" and asked for confirmation of title to the tract. A House committee interviewed Black Hoof's party and recommended that Ash receive a tract limited to one square mile. No further action was taken at that time, and Ash petitioned again late in 1804. Reluctant to permit Indian tribes to make land grants, Congress, in a March 1807 act relating to public lands, gave Ash a preemption right allowing him to purchase 640 acres (JHR, 4:76; 5:53-4; ASP, *Public Lands*, 1:111, 238, 533; U.S. Statutes at Large, 2:449). According to the Greenville treaty, the BOUNDARY LINE of the Indians' territory ended at the Ohio River across from the mouth of the Kentucky River (same, 7:49).

SENDING THE DOCTOR: according to a story in newspapers in the spring of 1802, before Little Turtle's group left Washington, TJ convinced the "sagacious chief" and the members of his party to be vaccinated with kine pox. TJ also, the report stated, gave the delegation's interpreter some of the vaccine to take with him, along with instructions for how to begin vaccinating the Indians in the Northwest. The report may relate to Black Hoof's party rather than Little Turtle's, or perhaps some members of both groups received vaccination and the account that appeared in the newspapers conflated the events. The report, which gave Edward Gantt's name as "Ganet," stated that he vaccinated Little Turtle and 14 "other warriors." That figure comes much closer to matching the size of Black Hoof's group than Little Turtle's much smaller traveling party, although according to Black Hoof it was only some of the younger members of his group who received the vaccine anyway—presumably those not yet exposed to smallpox—and not the entire party. According to the published report, Little Turtle received the vaccine first, leading the way for the others. However, Benjamin Rush had inoculated Little Turtle against smallpox on one of the Miami's visits to Philadelphia in the 1790s. (John Adams probably saw the effects of the inoculation when he noted in February 1798 that Little Turtle seemed to be recovering from the disease.) Little Turtle might have undergone vaccination in 1802 to inspire other members of his party, except the published account portrayed him as ignorant of the concept of inoculation until TJ explained it to him on that occasion. Almost certain-

ly the newspaper story, which may have originated in New England, garbled and embellished whatever did occur, and Black Hoof's reference above appears to be the most reliable evidence of the vaccination of Native American visitors in Washington in the early part of 1802. In a letter to Edward Jenner in April of that year, Benjamin Waterhouse gave an account that was very similar to the one that appeared in the newspapers and likely originated with the same unidentified source, except Waterhouse had "nine or ten more warriors" being vaccinated in addition to Little Turtle (Boston *Independent Chronicle*, 20 May 1802; Keene *New-Hampshire Sentinel*, 29 May; Philadelphia *Poulson's American Daily Advertiser*, 1 June; George W. Corner, ed., *The Autobiography of Benjamin Rush: His "Travels Through Life" together with his* Commonplace Book *for 1789-1813* [Princeton, 1948], 240; Volney, *View*, 357-8, 370; Carter, *Little Turtle*, 4-5; Robert H. Halsey, *How the President, Thomas Jefferson, and Doctor Benjamin Waterhouse Established Vaccination as a Public Health Procedure* [New York, 1936], 54-5).

John Wilkins had advanced funds to Mr. DARAH (or Darrah) at Pittsburgh as Black Hoof's deputation journeyed to Washington. Dearborn provided Darah with $255 in Washington and authorized more money for him in Philadelphia and Pittsburgh as necessary to cover the travelers' costs (Dearborn to William Irvine, 10 Feb., and to Wilkins, 16 Feb., Lb in DNA: RG 75, LSIA; Irvine to Dearborn, 9 Mch., recorded in DNA: RG 107, RLRMS).

[1] MS: "nane."

II. Jefferson's Reply

BROTHERS OF THE DELAWARE AND
SHAWANEE NATIONS.

I thank the great Spirit that he has conducted you hither in health & safety, and that we have an opportunity, of renewing our amity, and of holding friendly conference together. it is a circumstance of great satisfaction to us that we are in peace and good understanding with all our red brethren, and that we discover in them the same disposition to continue so which we feel ourselves. it is our earnest desire to merit, and to possess their affections, by rendering them strict justice, prohibiting injury from others, aiding their endeavors to learn the culture of the earth and to raise useful animals, and befriending them, as good neighbors, in every other way in our power. by mutual endeavors to do good to each other the happiness of both will be better promoted than by efforts of mutual destruction. we are all created by the same great spirit; children of the same family. why should we not live then as brothers ought to do?

I am peculiarly gratified by recieving the visit of some of your most antient and greatest warriors, of whom I have heard much good. it is a long journey which they have taken at their age, and in this season: and I consider it as a proof that their affections for us are sincere and strong. I hope that the young men, who have come with them, to make acquaintance with us, judging our dispositions towards them by what they see themselves, & not what they may hear from others, will go hand in hand with us, through life, in the cultivation of mutual peace, friendship and good offices.

The speech which the Black hoof delivered us, on behalf of your nation, has been duly considered: the answer to all it's particulars will now be delivered you by the Secretary at war. whatever he shall say, you may consider as if said by myself, and that what he promises our nation will perform. Th: JEFFERSON
Feb. 10. 1802

PrC (DLC); date added in ink in an unidentified hand. FC (Lb in DNA: RG 75, LSIA). Recorded in SJL.

III. Henry Dearborn's Reply

Brothers,

Your Father the President of the United States having fully considered all that you communicated to him the other day respecting the objects of your long journey to this place, has authorized me to give you the following answer

Brothers,

In answer to your request respecting grants of land to your Nations and to your Interpretors, I must inform you that your Father the

President does not consider himself authorized to divide the Lands of his red children or to make any particular grants to any part of them. He considers the great Chiefs and Sachems, of your several Nations when met at your great council fires as the proper persons to make such divisions and grants; and he has no doubt but they will do what is just and equitable, and make such divisions, as will be satisfactory to all respectively concerned.—

Brothers,

The heart of your Father the President, is pained to hear that any disputes or misunderstandings have happened between you and some of your red brethren and Mr. Wells in relation to your journey to this place—he hopes that no more disputes will happen. If you do not like Mr. Wells you can apply to your good friend General Lyman at Detroit, whose ears will ever be open to your complaints, and whose heart will ever be disposed to afford you relief and comfort—

Brothers,

The Goods to which you are annually entitled by the Treaty of Greenville, will in future be delivered in good order in the month of July or the first of August, at places where it will be convenient for you to receive them, and better provisions will be furnished for you when you are in want at any of our Posts; but you ought not to expect supplies of provisions unless you are industrious and use all the means[1] in your power to provide for yourselves—

Brothers,

The great Council of the sixteen States now sitting at this place have under consideration the subject of establishing Trading houses in the country of our red brethren, North West of the Ohio, and what ever shall be agreed on by the great Council, will be strictly attended to by your Father the President—

Brothers,

Your Father the President will take care to have ploughs and other useful tools provided for such of his red children, as may be disposed to make a good use of them, and he will likewise furnish you with some Cattle, and other articles equally beneficial—

Brothers

Your Father the President is not acquainted with the situation and circumstances of the Salt Lick, you mention; but he will desire your friend Governor Harrison to attend to your request, he will know more about it. Governor Harrison, Governor St. Clair, and General Lyman will likewise be requested to punish all white people who take any of your horses, and to see that you have justice done you in all cases. And they will likewise be requested to punish every white man who shall be detected in killing your Game, or in hunting on your land without your permission, or who does any mischief to the red people. The case mentioned by you of the Child, is in a course of legal proceedings, and the interference of the President at this time would be improper—

Brothers,

Your Father the President will take good care of you while you stay here, and make provision for your comfortable return home. The man who came with you from Pittsburgh will return with you to that place and take care of you on the journey—

Brothers,

You will by the orders of the President of the United States, receive from me a written Instrument, in which your father the President promises to protect you, and all his red children of your Nations, against all wicked people, so long as you shall continue to act honestly and peacably with each other, and your white brethren—

Brothers,

When you are prepared to set out on your journey home, I hope that the Great Spirit will take care of you, and enable you to return in safety to your friends and families, and that you will find them all alive and in good health—

Given under my hand and the Seal of the War Office this tenth Day of Feby. One thousand eight hundred & two.   H. DEARBORN

S.W.

FC (Lb in DNA: RG 75, LSIA); in a clerk's hand; "L.S." within facsimile seal alongside dateline.

Since July 1801, former Massachusetts congressman William LYMAN had been a temporary agent for Indian affairs in the Northwest Territory and Indiana Territory. He hoped to obtain a different position in the government, and in March 1802, Dearborn accepted his resignation from the Indian affairs post (Dearborn to Lyman, 8 Mch. 1802, DNA: RG 75, LSIA; *Terr. Papers*, 7:26-9; Vol. 34:661-2; Vol. 35:511).

SALT LICK: as Dearborn expressed it to William Henry Harrison on 23 Feb., the delegation requested "that measures may be taken by the Government to aid them in leasing a salt spring on their lands near the mouth of the Wabash." Harrison could lease the spring, Dearborn advised, if he could find a reliable person willing to take the lease "on such terms as will be satisfactory and useful to the Indians" (*Terr. Papers*, 7:49).

[1] MS: "mans."

IV. Henry Dearborn to Chiefs of the Delawares and Shawnees

Friends and Brothers,

The deputation appointed by you to visit the Seat of Government have arrived and been welcomed by your father the President of the United States with cordiality; they have spoken and he has heard all the representations that they were instructed by you on behalf of their Nations to make to him, in his name I have answered them in sincerity and truth, and when they shall have reported to you what I have said, I trust that you will feel all uneasiness removed from your minds, and that you and your Nations will experience that satisfaction which must result from a conviction of the certainty with which you may continue to rely on the protection and friendship of the United States—

These can never be forfieted but by the misconduct of the red people themselves. Your father the President instructs me to assure you, in behalf of your nations, that he will pay the most sacred regard to the existing Treaties between your respective nations and ours and protect your whole Territory against all intrusions that may be attempted by white people; that all encouragement shall be given to you in your just persuits and laudable progress towards comfort and happiness by the introduction of useful arts; that all persons who shall offend against our treaties, or against the laws made for your protection shall be brought to justice, or if this should be impracticable, that a faithful remuneration shall be made to you, and that he never will abandon his beloved Delaware or Shawanoes nor their children, so long as they shall act justly and peacably towards the white people and their red brethren.

This is all that he requires from you in return for his friendship and protection; he trusts you will not force him to recede from this determination by an improper & unjust change of conduct; but that you will give him abundant reason to encrease if possible his desire to see you happy & contented[1] under the fostering care of the United States.

I send you by your beloved Chiefs a Chain: it is made of Gold, which will never rust, and I pray the Great Spirit, to assist us in keeping the chain of our friendship of which this golden chain is meant as an emblem bright for a long succession of ages—

Given under my hand and the seal of the War Office of the United States this 10th: Day of February 1802.　　　　H. DEARBORN
S.W.

FC (Lb in DNA: RG 75, LSIA); in a clerk's hand; at head of text: "To the Chiefs of the Delaware and Shawanoe Nations, the Secretary of War of the United States, sends Greeting"; in margin at head of text: "Protection for the Delaware & Shawanoe Nations of Indians"; "L.S." within facsimile seal alongside dateline.

[1] MS: "conteted."

To Aaron Burr

Feb. 6. 1802.

Th: Jefferson with his salutations to the Vice President returns him the letter he put into his hands for perusal. the Secretary at war *had* a high opinion of mr Barron: but on the informations he has recieved, that opinion is suspended. the matter being sub judice no more ought to be said, than that no prejudices will be in the way of justice.

RC (CtY); addressed: "The Vice President of the US."; endorsed by Burr. Enclosure not found (see Kline, *Burr*, 2:674).

SUB JUDICE: that is, "under judicial consideration." For George Baron's appearance before a court of inquiry at West Point, see Baron to TJ, 21 Dec. 1801.

Philippe Jacques Dahler to Jefferson and Congress

Strasbourg ce 17 Pluviôse an 10.
6 fevrier 1802.

MESSIEURS!

C'est pour procurer à ma famille des renseignemens sur l'existence où la mort de nôtre Oncle et depuis longtems vôtre compatriote Jean Daniel Hammerer que j'ose Messieurs m'adresser jusqu'à Vous respectables Président & Membres du Congrès.

Depuis 1774 époque de la derniere de ses nouvelles, nous lui avons écrit à reïtérées fois, sans avoir pu recevoir reponse, ni de lui ni des Siens.

Comme des arrangemens de famille exigent une nouvelle authentique, sur son existence où sur celle de ses rejettons ou héritiers, nous avons recours à vôtre bienveuillance, pour nous procurer, ce que nous avons sans succès taché à nous procurer par des autres canaux.

L'extrait de sa derniere lettre dont copie cy jointe vous fournira les details nécessaires à sa recherche. Nous désirons que lui en cas de son existence où ses rejettons nous fassent passer des témoignages légitimes de leures existences, et à tout événement oserions nous vous demander des certificats de vie ou de mort de son dernier rejetton.

Pardonnés ma franchise; attribués-la au denuement d'autres ressources; et au besoin urgent de ces pièces pour porter l'ordre, dans les affaires d'une famille.

pour nôtre gratitude de ce service nous offrons à l'Elite d'une Nation amie et Alliée de la Nôtre tout ce qui est de nôtre ressort

avec le plus profond respect J'ay l'honneur d'être Messieurs! Vôtre devoué PHILIPPE JACQUES DAHLER

EDITORS' TRANSLATION

Strasbourg 17 Pluviôse Year 10

GENTLEMEN! 6 Feb. 1802

It is in order to obtain for my family information about the existence or the death of our uncle, and your longtime compatriot, John Daniel Hammerer, that I dare, gentlemen, address myself even to you, respectable president and members of Congress.

Since 1774, the date of the last of his news, we have written to him repeatedly, without having been able to receive an answer, neither from him nor from his relatives.

Since family arrangements demand authentic information concerning his existence or that of his offspring or heirs, we have recourse to your kindness to obtain for us, what we have unsuccessfully tried to obtain through other channels.

The extract of his last letter, a copy of which is enclosed, will furnish you with the details necessary for seeking him. We desire that he, in case of his existence, or his offspring, send us legitimate proofs of their existence, and in any case we would dare to ask of you certificates of the life or death of his last offspring.

Forgive my frankness; attribute it to the total absence of other resources; and to the urgent need of those documents to bring order into the affairs of a family.

In our gratitude for this service, we offer to the elite of a nation that is friendly and an ally of ours all that is in our power.

With the deepest respect I have the honor of being, gentlemen, your devoted PHILIPPE JACQUES DAHLER

RC (DLC); at head of text: "A Mrs Mrs Le President & Membres du Congrès Gal des Etats Unis d'amerique" (to gentlemen the president and members of the General Congress of the United States); below signature: "Neveu de Jn Dl hamerer" (nephew of John Daniel Hammerer) and "ruë du corbeau No 5 à Strasbourg Departmt du Bas Rhin en france" (No. 5 Corbeau Street, Strasbourg, Department of Bas-Rhin, France); endorsed by TJ as received 8 Aug. and so recorded in SJL. Enclosure: John Daniel Hammerer to unidentified ("Messieurs chers amis & Cousins"), 1 Mch. 1774, from Augusta, Georgia, discussing family matters and relating that he came to Augusta on an offer of employment, but his plans have been disrupted by conflicts between the Georgians and the Creek Indians that could result in war; he may go to Savannah, where he has sent his wife and infant daughter for safety (Tr in DLC; in French, in Dahler's hand).

In 1765, when three Cherokees returned to America from a visit to Great

Britain, John Daniel HAMMERER, a Lutheran originally from Strasbourg, accompanied them. In Britain, Hammerer had issued a prospectus in which he proposed to go to Georgia, live among the Creek Indians, and recruit artisans and a farmer to help him instruct the Native Americans in the ways of civilization. After a stop in Williamsburg, Hammerer took up residence with the Cherokees. By 1767, he was teaching some children of that tribe to read and write, and the South Carolina legislature authorized the expenditure of up to £100 sterling in support of his work. By January 1779, Hammerer was in Savannah, where he established the *Royal Georgia Gazette*. He

appeared on the newspaper's masthead for less than a year. He was also a schoolmaster in the Savannah area (Hammerer, *Account of a Plan for Civilizing the North-American Indians* [London?, 1765]; Samuel Cole Williams, ed., *Lieut. Henry Timberlake's Memoirs, 1756-1765* [Johnson City, Tenn., 1927], 165-75; Rowena McClinton, ed., *The Moravian Springplace Mission to the Cherokees*, 2 vols. [Lincoln, Neb., 2007], 1:17, 588n; *Georgia Gazette*, 14 Jan. 1767; *New-York Gazette or the Weekly Post-Boy*, 23 Apr. 1767; *Royal Georgia Gazette*, 22 Feb. 1781; Brigham, *American Newspapers*, 1:131).

From James B. Heard

[on or before 6 Feb. 1802]

The Petition of James Brooke Heard, respectfully sheweth,

That he hath been presented by the Grand Jury of Washington County, in the District of Columbia, for retailing Spirituous Liquors without Licence, and upon a submission to the Court of the said District was fined according to Law, but hopes upon a representation of facts to your Excellency, that you will remit the said fine.

Your Petitioner had soon after the organisation of the Government of the District, applied to the Clerk of the County of Washington for a permit to retail Spirituous Liquors untill the meeting of the Court, and then applied for a Licence to the said Court which was granted!—

That when your Petitioner applied for the same, it was with a view to Keep an Ordinary; your petitioner not being advised that it was necessary to speak to the Court upon the Occasion, confined his application To the Clerk, as had been heretofore customary, who gave him a Licence to retail spirituous Liquors, which Licence intended to restrict the Sale of any quantity below a pint

Your Petitioner at the period of his application was prepared to pay the customary price of an Ordinary Licence, and was surprised at its not being demanded, but expected that under the new regulation it would be collected by a proper Officer—

Altho' ignorant of his restriction, Your petitioner had in one solitary instance only, disposed of a less quantity than a pint, Knowing that he had done so, he submitted his Case to the Court, who were bound to fine your petitioner as the Law directs and leave the remittance thereof to the proper Authority—

Your petitioner therefore prays your Excellency will remit the fine so innocently and unintentionally incurred,

And your petitioner as in duty bound shall ever pray

JAMES B HEARD

RC (DLC); undated; in an unidentified hand, signed by Heard; at head of text: "To the President of the United States"; endorsed by TJ as received 6 Feb. and so recorded in SJL with notation "petn. for remission of fine."

On 6 Feb., TJ received another undated petition almost identical to the one printed above and in the same hand, which was signed by James Thompson (RC in DLC, at head of text: "To the President of the United States," endorsed by TJ as received 6 Feb. and so recorded in SJL with notation "petn. for remission of fine"). TJ received a number of documents relating to the case of Heard and Thompson, which may have been forwarded to the president by the defendants, or perhaps by John T. Mason, the U.S. attorney for the District of Columbia. These include a copy of a license granted to Heard, dated 30 Apr. 1801, authorizing him to sell spirituous liquors in Washington County until the June meeting of the federal circuit court (Tr in same); a license granted to Heard, dated 23 June, authorizing him to sell spiritu-ous liquors in Washington County until the fourth Monday in June 1802 (MS in same); a copy of the circuit court proceedings against Heard and Thompson, which included a September 1801 presentment against them for retailing liquor in quantities less than a pint without a license and a December 1801 judgment that fined each defendant $16 plus costs, the execution of which was returnable to the March 1802 session of the court (Tr in same; TJ Papers, 116:20087); and an 8 Jan. 1802 affidavit of Robert Brent, a justice of the peace for Washington County, testifying that Heard and Thompson had sworn before him that each came to the June 1801 term of court with the intention of acquiring a tavern license, and that each believed that the license he received authorized the retailing of liquor in quantities of less than a pint; "they did so sell," Brent testified, "and have therefore Inocently incurred a presentment and fine" (RC in DLC; JEP, 1:404).

No evidence has been found that TJ ordered a remission of the fines against Heard and Thompson. See John T. Mason to TJ, 9 Feb.

From Thomas Mann Randolph

Dear SIR,   Edgehill Feb. 6. 1802

Mr Lillie has called since last post to request I would explain to you a blunder of John Perrie who wrote the letter for him informing you of the purchases of supplies he had made to be met by remittance from you. The pork was bought of Reuben Burnley alone to am't. of £:35.6.10 which sum Dr. Wardlaw has paid and written to you to request you would replace it in Philada. for him. Perries mispelling Burnleys name made you suppose purchases had been made from two persons which was not the case: the 112.$.50. lie in Richmond unapplied and 1.£.6 more than due to H. Allen remains in Lillies hands. The money inclosed to me came in good time and no inconvenience arose to any one from Marthas waiting for me to deliver it to Lillie, which she did because she expected me hourly and did not advert to the propriety of immediately dispatching such a thing.— Every thing goes so smoothly in your affairs here under Lillie and your chief[1] interest in Cravens (the peace of the negroes) is on such good ground I have nothing to communicate respecting them. I am satisfied since the return of my messenger from Bedford who accompanied Griffins foreman home that his conduct there has not been far from what his character promised and that the discontent with him arose from some delinquency in the neighbourhood by them which was about to be discovered & punished. The children, Martha & Virginia are all in the most perfect health. The good temper and promising qualities of the children, their steady health, fine growth & progress in their education which she directs & labors with all her powers make her feel and declare herself frequently to be as happy as any person on earth.

with sincerest attachment & affection   TH: M. RANDOLPH

RC (ViU: Edgehill-Randolph Papers); endorsed by TJ as received 10 Feb. and so recorded in SJL.

LETTER FOR HIM: according to SJL on 6 Jan. 1802, TJ received two letters from Gabriel Lilly at Monticello, dated 1 and 2 Jan., both of which are missing. WARDLAW HAS PAID: see TJ to William Wardlaw, 30 Jan.
MONEY INCLOSED TO ME: see TJ to Thomas Mann Randolph, 9 Jan. An undated letter from Martha Jefferson Randolph to TJ, recorded in SJL as received from Edgehill on 20 Jan., has not been found.

YOUR CHIEF INTEREST IN CRAVENS: John H. Craven leased fields from TJ at Monticello and Tufton and assumed responsibility for 45 slaves at those two places (Vol. 32:108-10). TJ hired Burgess Griffin to manage his Poplar Forest estate in BEDFORD county (Vol. 35:21-2).

[1] Word interlined.

From Jacob Wagner

6 Feby. 1802

J: Wagner presents his best respects to the President of the U. States and has the honor to enclose a list of the Justices for Washington County. Mr. Moore's name being inserted on an erasure of the original commission, it is probable, that he was substituted for Mr. Law, and J:W. thinks he remembers that Mr. Stoddert was substituted for Mr. Laird

RC (DNA: RG 59, LAR, 8:0412). Enclosure not found.

For a printed copy of the ORIGINAL COMMISSION, dated 16 Mch. 1801, in which the 15 justices of the peace for Washington County were named, including Benjamin More and Benjamin Stoddert, see RCHS, 5 [1902], 266.

On this date Wagner also wrote Meriwether Lewis. He had recently alerted the president's secretary about a discrepancy he had found in the "transcript of the Minutes of the Senate" of 6 Jan. regarding the appointments for Washington County, observing "that the name of *Benjamin Moore*, appointed a justice of the peace for this county, in the recess, was omitted in the nominations." After a further examination, Wagner found that John Laird, who was not appointed during the recess, was on TJ's 6 Jan. list of interim appointments. He also noted that "*Jonah* Thompson" appeared on the 6 Jan. list as "*Josiah* Thompson" (DNA: RG 59, LAR, 8:0413-14). See TJ to the Senate: Interim Appointments, 6 Jan., especially Documents II and III.

From Joseph Barnes

Messina Feb. 7—1802

Early in Octr. Last I did myself the pleasure of addressing Mr. Jefferson from Malta, purporting, from some fatality the unexpect'd & complete Success of the English in expelling the French from Egypt; the advice of preliminary Articles of Peace having been Signed on the first of Octr. disadvantageously for the English; the remissness as I conceived of Commodore Dale in not having immediately on his Arrival in the Mediteranean Sent circulars to all the consuls, Vice consuls or agents in the Several ports, to advise any Americans then in their respective ports of his Arrival, how to Act &c &c—To my knowledge Capt. Bowers of Charleston having Lain near three months in this port after the Arrival of Dale at Malta, Sail'd from necessity without any advice or protection from him! nor has any circular even yet appear'd to my knowledge in this place; nor, have I Learn'd of any overtures having been made on part of the Tripolians; nor any Atchievements of the American Frigates as yet against them—Promptitude is a desirable object. For, Should the hostilities of these Barbarians continue but a Short time under the present Circumstances of Peace between France, England &c the American commerce, which had So rapidly increased in the ports of Italy, the two Sicilies &c will be ruin'd—

There are four Frigates in the Mediteranean, and 'tis Said, which I hope is true as they have nothing to do at home, that Several others are coming—hope they will not only make a formidable appearance, but desperate efforts to effect, by a *Coup de Main*, if possible the *desired object—peace*.

Not doubting, from the Knowledge Mr Jefferson has of my abilities, principles & disposition; knowledge of the world, Languages, and the Solicitations, recommendations, & representations of my Countrymen, of the necessity of proper commercial agents, especially in the Ports of the two Sicilies, I flatter myself; tho' I have not as yet, of daily receiving advice from the department of State of the appointment Solicited of *Charge de faires* or Commercial Agent of the United States to the two Sicilies—or Marsielles in France—which would be more agreeable—as heretofore Suggest'd, my Solicitude arises; not from motives of interest. indeed Little is attach'd to the consulates in the ports of thes Countries, but from a desire to be useful & the pleasure I Should receive in promoting the interest & happiness of my countrymen—Thus waiting, I have Some time Since dispatch'd a Vessel Laden with 3500 Salmas, equal 75000 Gallons of Wine to order for the English forces in Egypt—having the confidence of the British Government—

Tis Said however on the final Articles of Peace being Sign'd the English are [to] give up Egypt to the Turks, Malta [to] the Maltese &c &c—

Some time Since I recd. a Letter from Mr Bingham of Philada. & Senator of the U.S. purporting that if I would only name the place, as of course Some are much be more disirable to reside in than others, that he would engage me Success—

In haste believe me Mr Jefferson yours most respectfully

J: BARNES

RC (DLC); torn; addressed: "His Excellency Thomas Jefferson President of the Unit'd States City of Washington pr the Brig. Fox Cap. Locke"; franked; postmarked Boston, 16 Apr.; endorsed by TJ as received 24 Apr. and so recorded in SJL.

FROM MALTA: no letter written by Barnes in October has been found or is recorded in SJL. The last one from him that TJ had received was that of 18 May 1801, from Messina.

SALMAS were a unit of measure in Sicily (Frederic C. Lane, "Tonnages, Medieval and Modern," *Economic History Review*, 2d ser., 17 [1964], 224).

William BINGHAM, no longer a United States senator, had relocated to England (ANB; Vol. 34:632, 670).

From Lewis DuPré

SIR: Washington 7th Feby. 1802—

My apology for troubling you a *sixth* time on an unpleasant subject, is recorded in the 21 & 22 verses of the 18 Chapter of St. Matthews Gospel—

I agree with you that I am a *Madman*, but not in supposing that I am the Instrument in the hands of Providence to produce important blessings to my fellow men—but in sacrificing so much to *common fame*. from an early period of my life I evinced an unshaken attachment to the cause of liberty—& love of my country—her interest has been ever dear to me, in supporting which I deem'd in necessary to advocate your interest—& in the struggle of politic's in *Charleston* was induced to sacrifice valuable connexions to my political sentiments—the joy resulting from the important discovery which was reveald to me wou'd, in itself have produced but half the satisfaction I experienced, when I considered that the important discovery had been reserv'd for an *American*, for a *genuine republican* & that at a time when a *Jefferson* fill'd the presidential Chair—this, Sir, is the sum of my *madness*—but I have done with these fine spun theories. I have already paid dearly for them—had I gone directly to Europe, I should have been not only noticed there, but *cherish'd*—the discovery wou'd then have reflected honor on my country—or had I depended on a *british consul* after I arrived in this City, rather than on the president & congress of the United States, my laurels wou'd not have been eclipsed by a Canadian *woodman* (who I am told is now on his way to Europe) whose Success, I hope, will not be blasted by his reliance on his own government—

All that remains, *now*, in your power to undo the very unfavorable impression that this business is likely to make on the minds of the American people—is, to recommend to the legislature to extend the usual term of patents on this occasion—I do not feel disposed to receive a patent for *only fourteen years*, as America will then be very far short of its ultimate population—

I remain, Sir, Your friend (notwithstanding)   L. DuPré
87 day

I have not shewn this to any person, neither do I keep a copy—LD

RC (DLC); endorsed by TJ as received 7 Feb. and so recorded in SJL.

Lewis DuPré (1762-1813) was an inventor, gardener, and writer from Charleston, South Carolina. He received patents in 1802 for a scientific steelyard and in 1807 for a pendulum screen used for sifting rice. Later in his life, he published a number of writings on religion and the abolition of slavery (*List of Patents*, 28, 59; *South Carolina Historical Magazine*, 71 [1970], 50; John Drayton, *A View of South-Carolina as Respects her Natural and Civil Concerns* [Charleston, 1802], 122; Charleston *City Gazette and Daily Advertiser*, 14 Nov. 1801; *Charleston Courier*, 14 Jan. 1813). In November 1801, DuPré publicly announced that he had "happily succeeded in the discovery of PERPETUAL MOTION." Presenting a petition to the House of Representatives on 5 Jan. 1802, he declared that it had pleased God "to discover to me the principles of the *perfect motion* (vulgarly called PERPETUAL motion)" and requested legislative support in his efforts to secure the "customarily exclusive pecuniary advantages" of his discovery. At the foot of his petition, DuPré gave the date of 1 Jan. 1802 and "50th day of Perfect Motion." On 11 Jan., however, Congress received a petition from Thomas Bruff, who in early 1801 had presented his ideas on perpetual motion to TJ. Bruff asserted to Congress that he had discovered the principles of perpetual motion in 1790, but, fearing to confide in others, had attempted to perfect the work on his own. Unsuccessful in his efforts, Bruff sought the support of Congress and to prevent DuPré's claim from supplanting his own. Both claims were referred to a House committee, which granted DuPré and Bruff permission to withdraw their respective petitions (Charleston *City Gazette and Daily Advertiser,* 14 Nov. 1801; JHR, 4:32, 44, 76, 86-7; New York *American Citizen and General Advertiser,* 15 Jan. 1802; *New-York Evening Post,* 18 Jan. 1802; Vol. 32:512-13; Bruff to TJ, 16 Dec. 1801).

TROUBLING YOU A SIXTH TIME: SJL records no previous or subsequent correspondence between DuPré and TJ.

87 DAY: presumably, the 87th day of perfect motion.

From Andrew Ellicott

DEAR SIR   Lancaster Feby. 7th. 1802

Your favour of the 29th. Ultimo has been duly received, and the proposition which it contains, I consider as one of the most honourable, and flattering incidents of my life; and was my own feelings, and inclination, alone concerned, I should not hesitate one moment in accepting the place you offer: but as there are some other considerations to be brought into view, and duly weighed, before I can give a definitive answer, I wish the subject to be suspended for a few days.—I should have replied to your favour immediately, but the multiplicity of business before the Board of Property, which is now sitting, and of which, (as Secretary of the Land office,) I have to do the duty of President, has prevented my paying immediate attention to other objects.

I have enclosed an extract from M. Depuis's Memoire on the origin of the constellations &c. which I suspect you must have seen before this, but if not, I presume it will be considered as a curiosity,—Your understanding the language in which it is written, so much better than myself, has rendered an attempt to translating it unnecessary.—

I am sir with the greatest respect, and esteem, your sincere friend, and Hbl. Servt.   ANDW; ELLICOTT

RC (DLC); at foot of text: "Thos. Jefferson President U.S."; endorsed by TJ as received 11 Feb. and so recorded in SJL. Enclosure: Extract from Charles

François Dupuis's *Mémoire sur l'origine des constellations,* stating that according to Charles Marie de La Condamine, the name given to the constellation Taurus by the people of the Amazon is "Ox Jaw," and according to Joseph François Lafitau, the Iroquois Indians call the constellation Ursa Major the female bear; Dupuis arguing that since the two groups of stars do not actually resemble the animals they are named for, the similarities in the names of those constellations is evidence of communication between the hemispheres in ancient times (MS in DLC: TJ Papers, 120:20781; in Ellicott's hand; in French).

Dupuis's *Mémoire sur l'origine des constellations et sur l'explication de la fable, par le moyen de l'astronomie* appeared in the fourth volume of Joseph Jérôme Le Français de Lalande's *Astronomie*, a book that TJ owned and recommended to others. The volume appeared in 1781, and the *Mémoire* was also published separately that year (Sowerby, No. 3796; Vol. 25:490; Vol. 32:180).

From John Guerrant

SIR   Richmond February 7th. 1802

Sensible of the honor which you have done me by my appointment of Post-Master at this place, I have as deliberately as I could weighed the advantages and disadvantages which wou'd probably result from my acceptance of it.

Being entirely unacquainted with the compensation, or the duties, annexed to this office, it became necessary that I should devote a short time to the obtaining the best possible Information on those points, and that I should, ascertain the probable amount of expences Incidental to its execution, including the charges of necessary house rents for the office and the accomodation of my family.

Upon Inquiry I find that the amount of compensation has not exceeded the sum of $1700. ℔ annum, and that a very great proportion of that sum must necessarily be expended in rewarding a faithful assistant, and in providing an house in an eligible situation for the office, and use of my family, added to which, the steady and unremited attention with which I shou'd certainly endeavour to discharge the duties of the office wou'd exclude the possibility of my attending with any advantages to the future management and Improvement of my farm.

I have the honor at present to hold an office under the Government of this state, which enables me to render some small services to my country, and affords a moderate salary, with some leisure time to attend to my farm on which my family resides.

Thus upon a comparison of my present situation, with that in which I should be placed by accepting the office which you have been pleased to offer me, having due regard to that Oeconomy which my circumstances and the cares of a large family at my time of life impose upon me, I feel myself constrained to decline accepting the office of Post-Master at this place, but while I do so, I Beg you to be assured of the grateful remembrance with which I shall ever recollect this Instance of the friendly attention with which you have been pleased to Honor me, and of my perfect disposition at all times to render my feeble aid in support of an administration which like yours has the constitution for its guide and the real happiness and wellfare of our Country for its end.

With perfect regard and esteem I am Sir Yr. Mo. Ob. Servant

JOHN GUERRANT

RC (DLC); addressed: "Thomas Jefferson Esquire President of the United States City of Washington"; endorsed by TJ as received 12 Feb. and so recorded in SJL.

A small planter in Goochland County, John Guerrant (1760-1813), of French Huguenot descent, was a Revolutionary War veteran. At first as an Antifederalist and later a Republican, he served in the House of Delegates between 1789 and 1796 and then was elected to the state council, the position he held in 1802. As president of the council, he served as lieutenant governor of the commonwealth in 1803 and 1805 (Heitman, *Register*, 264; Richard R. Beeman, *The Old Dominion and the New Nation, 1788-1801* [Lexington, Ky., 1972], 143, 250, 257-8, 268-9; Leonard, *General Assembly*, 175, 179, 184, 187, 191, 195, 199, 203; CVSP, 9:451; *The Articles of Confederation; the Declaration of Rights; the Constitution of this Commonwealth, and the Articles of the Definitive Treaty Between Great-Britain and the United States of America* [Richmond, 1784], 18; WMQ, 1st ser., 9 [1901], 274-5; *Virginia Argus*, 18 May 1803; *Alexandria Expositor, and the Columbian Advertiser,* 13 June 1803).

Announcing the APPOINTMENT of Guerrant as postmaster at Richmond in place of Augustine Davis on 9 Feb., the Richmond *Examiner* acknowledged that it was not known whether he would accept the position (Madison, *Papers, Sec. of State Ser.,* 2:450-1; *Gazette of the United States,* 19 Feb. 1802).

From Stephen Sayre

SIR   Philadelphia 7th. Feb. 1802

When I was at Burlington, some few weeks since, the Governor communicated to me the subject of a letter, which he had the honor of writing to the President, & the answer you were pleased to make.

It would look like ingratitude to deny him thanks for his good intention—and tho' I am always yet, in expectations of being usefully employ'd, under the Government, I wish to be so employ'd, because my services, my sufferings, & capacity give me a prescriptive right—not because a Governor, a Senator, or any other character may lend his name for that end.

If I desire your patronage, you will *not* with-hold it—if I do not, my friends may forever be silent—presuming when I say this, that my enemies have not succeeded in making any unfavourable impressions on your mind—and, that your own opinion always prevails,

I have a letter from your secretary of state, in which he says "In bestowing the advantages of employment, the only resource within the branch of the executive, the just rules of proceeding, must be founded on a consideration, of the fitness of particular qualifications, for the duties attach'd to particular offices, & *a comparison of the qualifications*, & *merits* of those, who are disposed to accept them."

It would not become me to make any remarks on the past observance of this virtuous maxim—I wish it may be adhered to, with firmness & manly resistance, against every local consideration, or pressing influence of the day—then the labourer, in the heat of the day, may hope to receive the same compensation, as he who came in at the eleventh hour—this has not yet been done—

Forgive me, if here I sport an opinion as to this passage in sacred Writ—I always thought it somewhat arbitrary & a little out of the ordinary rules of equity, to pay the idle scoundrel who work'd but one hour, the same wages, as to him, who work'd twelve. But hitherto we have, in our government, done worse—we have forgot those who toild in the heat of the day, & have paid them nothing.

It would be indecent in me to offer my advice to Mr Jefferson, but I know you have too much good sense, & good nature, to feel resentment, when I express my ardent wishes: that you would adopt, one great, & sublime principle, & pursue it, as far as it can be done, in wisdom—I mean; to find out, & employ those characters, who have done the most, & who are drove into the shades of retirement, by the loss of fortune, & the injuries suffer'd, in resistance, to the tyrant of Great Britain—when there are no more of this character, who have capacity to execute the duties of office, you may, with more safety, attend to the views of your cabinet ministers—you have express'd your embarrassment to Govr. Bloomfield, on this subject—is it because your heads of departments, cannot find the old & faithful friends & sufferers of the revolution, or is it because contending interests distract their councils?

you recommend industry, & the pursuit of independence, to those who are not in that situation—if this was meant to be apply'd to me; let me take the liberty of giving a plain answer, why that is unfortunately, too true—I am indeed so far from independance, or the means by which I can hope to acquire it, as to be, at this instant, at the mercy of a creditor; and for a debt, positivly, contracted, by & in the service of the public—and there are others of the same kind, which, hetherto, I have not been able to discharge—I might, it is true, pay some of them, but can never pay the whole, & while they hang over my head, how can I, in honor, expect or wish for aid, or credit, from my friends, who would, in any other case, probably, lend it

I appeal to your judgement, & feelings. Is it not a dishonor to my country, so long to leave me exposed to the duns of creditors, not mine, but theirs—have I not some claim on the executive, when it is known, that I was cruelly persecuted by our common enemies, not on personal account, but from attachment, & zeal, for my country—by the secret villainy of the british government I lost a fortune of £40000—by the intrigues of one family, I lost my rank, & just expectations of public employment—by the injustice & contracted principles of a party in our own, I am yet unpaid, a sum which would make me more than independent—& here let me observe: that the Legislature in 1799, voted payment 48. against 21 members—this must convince you, that my claims were on a solid basis.

I have now a fresh memorial before Congress—could I at this hour fortunately, come under the patronage of the Executive, my claims would not be disputed—to be neglected by both, is too hard, even for a mind more subdued by adversity than mine

I have often thought that I could render my country solid services were I placed at the head of a new State in the west. Perhaps you will deem it utopean, but, are there any solid objections against a system of Government, founded in the laws of honor,—integrity, & good faith—in which, all disputes shall be settled by conciliation, if possible, & by our neibours, in the last resort?—

are Lawyers, & expensive, endless, & irritating quarrels, necessary to society?

Is imprisonment necessary to pay debts? are there no criminals, where there are laws against crimes, lawyers to plead, Judges to condemn, & hangmen to execute.

I contend, that the policy of the Quaker is excellent, & may be impos'd; and, that if, one state in the union, could be brought under a system somewhat like theirs, all the rest would either follow the example, or do so partially

It was my design, in the begining of this letter, only to have reminded the President, that I am still in the land of the living & that from appearances, I may probably live, yet 65. years longer—*but, that I must have somthing to support life*

I am, with great respect   STEPHEN SAYRE

[539]

RC (DNA: RG 59, LAR); at foot of text: "To the President of the United States"; endorsed by TJ as received 10 Feb. and so recorded in SJL.

GOVERNOR Joseph Bloomfield wrote to TJ on 10 Nov. 1801; TJ's ANSWER to Bloomfield was dated 5 Dec. 1801.

LETTER FROM YOUR SECRETARY OF STATE: probably Madison to Sayre, 23 May 1801, not found, but acknowledged in Sayre to Madison, 9 June 1801. Madison reminded Sayre that the president was not bound to see to the compensation of every victim of injustice (Madison, *Papers, Sec. of State Ser.*, 1:226, 284-7).

PASSAGE IN SACRED WRIT: Matthew 20:1-16.

LEGISLATURE IN 1799: on 9 Feb. 1799, the Committee of Claims in the House of Representatives reported unfavorably on Sayre's petition for compensation as secretary of the American legation at Berlin in 1777. The House concurred with the committee's report. In April 1800, the House granted Sayre permission to withdraw his petition (JHR, 3:481; *Annals*, 8:2857, 10:667).

On 1 Mch. 1802, Sayre's MEMORIAL BEFORE CONGRESS requesting compensation of his services as secretary to the American commissioners at the Court of Versailles was referred to the Committee of Claims. The committee later recommended that Sayre have leave to withdraw his petition (JHR, 4:110; *Annals*, 11:854, 1076).

From Burgess Allison

HOND. SIR/   Bordenton Feb. 8th. 1802

The bearer Mr. John Jenkins, being possessed of very extraordinary talents for teaching the art of penmanship; many proofs of which he has given in the rapid progress of his Pupils, of which he has the most respectable testimony with him; and being desirous of exercising his wit in the condition of some of the Youth in Virginia: [I] have taken the liberty of giving him an introductory line, knowing your disposition to promote the useful arts & sciences. All he desires, in going to a place, is an oppertunity of proving by actual demonstration, in one or two Pupils, that he is capable of making a youth, from an awkward scribler, an elegant writer, in three or four weeks at farthest.

After having seen his Certificates, any mention you may make of him in the Circle of your Friends will have a tendancy to promote so laudable a design, and be of advantage to Society—With every Sentiment of Esteem,

I remain Your very Hbl. Svt.   B ALLISON

RC (MHi); torn; at foot of text: "Thos. Jefferson Esqr."; endorsed by TJ as received 24 Feb. and so recorded in SJL.

For JOHN JENKINS, see Vol. 19:120-1n.

From Daniel Carroll

Sir/   Washington Feby 8th 1802

In consiquence of an application to the Comrs of Washington by Mr Barry in the year 1800 for the removeal of the houses of Mrs Fenwick, situated in south Capitol street, and a valuation being had to that effect, & Mrs Fenwick haveing gone to a considerable expence in building a new house, under the expectation of receiving that valuation, which has since been refused her by the Commrs, as will appear by the inclosed letters. In the mean time her enclosures were removed, her garden broke up, & much incommoded in other respects—I beg leave to submit the letters and valuation to you, & beg if you see proper, you will direct payment to be made—I have the honor to be

    Sir Your Mo Obt. Sert.   DANL CARROLL OF DUDN

RC (DLC); at head of text: "The President of the United States"; endorsed by TJ as received 8 Feb. and so recorded in SJL. Enclosures not identified, but according to the minutes of the 9 Feb. meeting of the District of Columbia commissioners, they included "several letters which have passed between the Commissioners Mr Carroll and Mrs. Fenwick on the subject of removing her houses, also the valuation of those houses by Harbaugh & Duncanson" (DNA: RG 42, PC); see below. Enclosed in TJ to District of Columbia commissioners, 9 Feb.

Daniel Carroll of Duddington (1764-1849), a planter and merchant, owned over 1,400 acres of land in the federal district when its boundaries were established in 1791, more than any other single proprietor. His property included the site of the Capitol and a large part of the area to the south and east of it bounded by the Eastern Branch of the Potomac. In 1791, TJ as secretary of state advised President George Washington on a dispute between Carroll and Pierre Charles L'Enfant, during which L'Enfant tore down a house under construction by Carroll (Allen C. Clark, "Daniel Carroll of Duddington," RCHS, 39 [1938], 1-48; Washington, *Papers, Pres. Ser,* 9:220-5; Vol. 20:44-53; 22:390-2).

In an APPLICATION to the District of Columbia commissioners dated 26 June 1800, James BARRY, a Washington real estate developer, asked the board to remove Mary Fenwick's "Houses and Enclosures" on SOUTH CAPITOL STREET. The commissioners informed Fenwick that the two buildings and the fences impeded "free passage" for carriages traveling between public streets and otherwise hampered development of the area. The board threatened to remove the structures if Fenwick did not do so. On 21 Aug., the commissioners requested that Fenwick appoint a person to give a valuation for the property. A few days later, Carroll became involved in the case, with the commissioners informing him of the board's appointment of an assessor. On 20 Oct., the commissioners complained to Carroll of delays in obtaining a valuation and requested that he permit access to the buildings for an immediate valuation. The commissioners informed Carroll in the spring of 1801 that though the board favored the removal of "all obstructions in the Streets" of the city as a general rule, they lacked the funds to pay for Fenwick's houses. Because Fenwick's house predated the 1791 deeds of trust between the commissioners and the original proprietors of land in the federal district, its removal had to be considered necessary for the "public Interest" in order for the owner to be compensated. The commissioners considered the value of Fenwick's houses too high to justify the expense (commissioners to Fenwick, 31 July, 8, 21 Aug., 30 Oct. 1800; to Carroll, 26 Aug., 20 Oct. 1800, 31 Mch., 8 Apr., 22 June 1801, in DNA: RG 42, DCLB).

From the District of Columbia Commissioners

SIR,   Commissioners Office 8th. February 1802
We received by last post a Letter from the Governor of Maryland, and not having it in our power to pay the interest due to the State we have agreeably to the Governors request transmitted his letter with the inclosures to the President of the United States—
We are with sentiments of the highest respect Sir Yr. mo. Obt. Servts
                                                    ALEXR. WHITE
                                                    TRISTRAM DALTON

RC (DLC); in Dalton's hand, signed by Dalton and White; at foot of text: "President of the United States"; endorsed by TJ as received 8 Feb. and so recorded in SJL with notation "loan of Maryland." FC (DNA: RG 42, DCLB). Enclosure: John F. Mercer to the District of Columbia commissioners, Annapolis, 2 Feb., enclosing a letter from the treasurer of the western shore of Maryland, 2 Feb. (not found), and a copy of the 23 Dec. 1799 resolution of the Maryland General Assembly, authorizing the loan of $50,000 to the commissioners with the stipulation that if the interest were not paid on time, a suit would be instituted to recover the principal; the governor urges the commissioners to pay the overdue interest promptly; Mercer and the Maryland executive council request that if the commissioners cannot make the payment, they "submit this with its inclosures without delay" to the president in order "that competent measures may be adopted to forward such satisfactory payments" and thus avoid a suit (FC in Lb in MdAA, at foot of text: "The Commissioners of the Federal Buildings"; *Votes and Proceedings of the Senate of the State of Maryland. November Session, 1799* [Annapolis, 1800], 23; DNA: RG 42, PC, 9 Feb. 1802).

TJ returned the LETTER FROM THE GOVERNOR OF MARYLAND and the enclosures to the commissioners in person on 9 Feb. He recommended that they communicate the papers to the congressional committee, chaired by Joseph H. Nicholson, that was considering TJ's message of 11 Jan. to the Senate and the House of Representatives. The commissioners immediately did as TJ had advised, "without any formal message from him," and White and Dalton offered to come to the Capitol the next day to discuss the documents. On 10 Feb., the commissioners informed Mercer that they had met with the congressional committee, which was to report shortly, and from the "tendency of the conversation" they believed the report would be "favourable" (FCs in DNA: RG 42, DCLB; DNA: RG 42, PC, 9 Feb. 1802). The committee's report, submitted to the House of Representatives on 12 Feb., recommended that the sums required to pay the Maryland loans be advanced from the Treasury, if necessary, by the direction of the president, to be reimbursed to the Treasury as soon as other city debts were paid. The resolutions on the Maryland debt were incorporated as Sections 5, 6, and 7 of "An Act to abolish the Board of Commissioners in the City of Washington; and for other purposes" of 1 May 1802 (ASP, *Miscellaneous*, 1:260; U.S. Statutes at Large, 2:175-6).

To the House of Representatives

GENTLEMEN OF THE
HOUSE OF REPRESENTATIVES.

In compliance with your resolution of the 2d. inst. I have to inform you that, early in the preceding summer, I took measures for carrying into effect the act passed on the 19th. of Feb. 1799. chapter 115. and that of the 13th. of May 1800. mentioned in your resolution. the objects of these acts were understood to be, to purchase, from the Indians south of the Ohio, some portions of land peculiarly[1] interesting to the Union, or to particular states; and the establishment of certain roads to facilitate communication with our distant settlements. Commissioners were accordingly appointed to treat with the Cherokees, Chickasaws, Choctaws & Creeks. as these nations are known to be very jealous on the subject of their lands, the Commissioners were instructed, as will be seen by the inclosed extract, to enlarge, restrain, or even to suppress propositions, as appearances should indicate to be expedient. their first meeting was with the Cherokees. the extract from the speech of our Commissioners, and the answers of the Cherokee chiefs, will shew the caution of the former, and the temper of the latter: and that though our overtures to them were moderate, and respectful of their rights, their determination was to yield no accomodation.

The Commissioners proceeded then to the Chickasaws, who discovered, at first, considerable alarm and anxiety, lest land should be asked of them. a just regard for this very friendly nation, whose attachment to us has been invariable, forbade the pressure of anything disagreeable on them: and they yielded with alacrity the road through their country, which was asked, & was essential to our communication with the Missisipi territory.

The conferences with the Choctaws are probably ended, but as yet we are not informed of their result. those with the Creeks are not expected to be held till the ensuing spring. TH: JEFFERSON
Feb. 8. 1802.

RC (DNA: RG 233, PM, 7th Cong., 1st sess.); endorsed by a House clerk as "Confidential" and as referred on 9 Feb. to a committee, consisting of John Stanly, John Rutledge, John Dawson, William Dickson, and John Fowler, on the petition of Memucan Hunt and others. PrC (DLC). Enclosures: (1) "Extract from Instructions given to Wm. R. Davie, James Wilkinson and Benjamin Hawkins Commissioners on the part of the UStates for holding conferences and signing a treaty or treaties with several Indian nations," consisting of three paragraphs from Henry Dearborn's instructions of 24 June 1801 emphasizing that the commissioners are to "pay the strictest attention to the disposition manifested by the

Indians," since the government's proposals might excite the "ill humour which
propositions for further cessions sometimes awaken in them"; it is necessary for
the commissioners "to introduce the desires of the Government, in such a manner as will permit you to drop them, as
you may find them illy received, without
giving the Indians an opportunity to
reply, with a decided negative, or raising
in them unfriendly and inimical dispositions"; the commissioners are not to present proposals "in the tone of demands,"
but as propositions, "assent to which the
Government would consider as new testimonials" of the Indians' friendship (Tr in
DNA: RG 233, PM; in Meriwether
Lewis's hand). (2) "Extract from the
speech of the Commissioners of the US. to
the chiefs of the Cherokees assembled at
South West point Sep. 4th. 1801," an extensive extract of the record of a council
held on 4-5 Sep., in which the commissioners, on behalf of "your father, the
President," ask the Cherokees' permission
for the development of roads to connect
the Natchez settlements, Nashville, and
South Carolina, and for "houses of enter-
tainment" and ferries along the roads, for
which the Cherokees will be paid rent;
the commissioners stating also that the
Indians' "white brethren" want to purchase land, but the issue will not be
pressed if the Cherokees do not wish to
sell; Doublehead, answering for the
Cherokees, replying that they do not want
to sell any land and do not want the roads
developed; the Cherokees also expressing
dissatisfaction over encroachments by
settlements on their land (Tr in same, in a
clerk's hand except the title, which is in
TJ's hand; FC in DLC, in a clerk's hand
except title in TJ's hand, endorsed by TJ:
"Cherokee conference"). Enclosures endorsed by a House clerk as "Confidential"
and as referred to the committee on 9 Feb.
Message and enclosures printed in ASP,
Indian Affairs, 1:656-7. Enclosed in TJ to
Nathaniel Macon, 8 Feb.

By the RESOLUTION passed by the
House of Representatives on 2 Feb., the
president was "requested to inform this
House whether any, and what, measures

have been taken for treating with the Indians South of the Ohio, in consequence
of an act of Congress, passed the thir-
teenth of May, one thousand eight hundred, entitled 'An act to appropriate a certain sum of money to defray the expense
of holding a treaty or treaties with the Indians.'" John Stanly, a Federalist congressman from North Carolina, and John
Dawson were appointed to present the
resolution to TJ (JHR, 4:80; *Biog. Dir.
Cong.*). For the acts of 19 Feb. 1799 and
13 May 1800, see TJ to the Senate, 22
Dec. 1801.

In accordance with TJ's request for secrecy (see his cover letter to the speaker of
the House, Macon, at 8 Feb. below), the
journals of the House for 8-9 Feb. 1802
contain no mention of this message. The
endorsements on the message and enclosures indicate that the House dealt with
the papers off the record by nominally referring them on 9 Feb. to a committee established for another purpose three weeks
earlier. On 19 Jan., Stanly had presented
to the House a petition that Memucan
Hunt and two others had made to the
North Carolina General Assembly, along
with some resolutions by the assembly,
concerning lands in Tennessee granted in
an earlier period under North Carolina
authority. The House appointed Stanly,
Rutledge, Dawson, Dickson, and Fowler,
who were from North Carolina, South
Carolina, Virginia, Tennessee, and Kentucky, respectively, as a select committee
and referred the matter to them. Stanly
reported for the committee on 24 Mch.
According to the House journal, that report dealt only with the matter of the land
claims. On 30 Apr., as the session drew to
an end, the House postponed consideration of the land claims until Congress reconvened in the fall (JHR, 4:55, 157, 229,
252).

In an act for military appropriations approved 1 May 1802, Congress allowed up
to $40,000 for expenses of treaties held
with INDIANS SOUTH OF THE OHIO. The
sum was to include any of the $15,000
appropriated by the act of 13 May 1800
that had not already been spent. The new
act, as the one of two years earlier had
done, put a limit of $8 per day, exclusive

of travel expenses, on the compensation of individual treaty commissioners (U.S. Statutes at Large, 2:82, 183-4).

Hawkins, Wilkinson, and Andrew Pickens enclosed the minutes of their MEETING with the Cherokees in a letter to Dearborn on 6 Sep. 1801 (Foster, *Hawkins*, 383).

[1] Word interlined.

From George Jefferson

DEAR SIR,   Richmond 8th. Febr. 1802

I received two or three weeks ago of Mr. Creed Taylor 60$. on account of Littlebury Mosby's bond to Mr. Short. I should before now have given you this information, but Mr. T. informed me that he should make a further payment in the course of a few days—he however left Town (having been on the assembly) without again calling.

I inclose you under two seperate covers the papers left with me by Doctor Currie. by tomorrows post I will send you the bonds lodged here by Mr. Hanson.

I am Dear Sir Your Very humble servt.   GEO. JEFFERSON

RC (MHi); at foot of text: "Thos. Jefferson esqr."; endorsed by TJ as received 12 Feb. and so recorded in SJL.

HAVING BEEN ON THE ASSEMBLY: Creed Taylor represented Amelia, Chesterfield, Cumberland, Nottoway, and Powhatan counties in the state senate (Leonard, *General Assembly*, 225).

On 17 Apr. 1801, TJ authorized George Jefferson to receive discharged BONDS from Richard HANSON (see Vol. 33:548, 603).

To Nathaniel Macon

SIR   Feb. 8. 1802.

I now inclose the information desired by the resolution of the House of representatives of the 2d. instant. considering that it will yet be some time before the conferences will be held with the Creeks, and that the disclosure of the views explained in this message might have an unfavorable influence on the result of those conferences, I refer to the consideration of the house whether these communications should not be deemed confidential. Accept assurances of my high consideration & respect.   TH: JEFFERSON

RC (DNA: RG 233, PM, 7th Cong., 1st sess.); at foot of text: "The Speaker of the House of Representatives." PrC (DLC). Enclosures: TJ to the House of Representatives, 8 Feb., and enclosures.

To Samuel A. Otis

Feb. 8. 1802.

Th: Jefferson presents his salutations & respects to mr Otis. he observes on examining his press copy of the nominations of Jan. 6. in the 4th. page & 4th. line from the bottom, he miscopied *Jonah* Thompson, & wrote it *Josiah* which he prays mr Otis to suffer Capt. Lewis to correct with his pen.

in the same list of justices, John Laird is named instead of Benjamin Moore, the latter having been commissioned, and not the former. perhaps this last error cannot be corrected but by a message, and may therefore stand until he sends one on the subject of these nominations: for he has, within these two days recieved information from the clerk's office of the county that one of the gentlemen has resigned & three others have never qualified, in whose places therefore it will be necessary to substitute others, so soon as proper persons can be found. he understands the Senate are disposed to let these nominations lie a while.

RC (DNA: RG 46, EPEN, 7th Cong., 1st sess.); addressed: "Mr. Otis"; endorsed by Otis, in part: "Note from The President of the United States correcting a mistake in Message 6th Jany."

MISCOPIED JONAH THOMPSON: see Document VI, note 13, in TJ to the Senate: Interim Appointments, printed at 6 Jan. The change from "Josiah" to "Jonah" was not made in a Senate copy of TJ's 6 Jan. nominations or in the smooth journal of executive proceedings of the Senate, which was sent to the printer for publication (FC in DNA: RG 46, EPEN, 7th Cong., 1st sess., endorsed: "(Copy) Message—Jan 6. 1802 nom. Albert Gallatin et al."; smooth jour-

nal in DNA: RG 46; JEP, 1:404). A merchant, Jonah Thompson served as mayor of Alexandria from 1805 to 1808. His father-in-law, Francis Peyton, also received an appointment as justice of the peace for the County of Alexandria (JEP, 1:404; Miller, *Alexandria Artisans,* 2:184-5; Vol. 33:271, 674).

TJ sent a message to the Senate on the SUBJECT OF THESE NOMINATIONS on 5 Apr. 1802. TJ learned that Thomas Sim Lee had RESIGNED and Benjamin Stoddert and William H. Dorsey had NEVER QUALIFIED for justice of the peace for Washington County. William Fitzhugh, Richard Conway, and Thomas Darne declined qualifying in Alexandria County (JEP, 1:417-18).

From Robert Smith

SIR: Nav Dep 8th Feb 1802

I have the honor to request your signature to the enclosed Commissions & Warrants—they are wanted for the Surgeon's mate[1] recently appointed—& for other Commd & Warrant[2] long since appointed, who have lost their Commissions & Warrants—

I have the honor to be, with great respect, Sir, Your mo. ob. st.

RT SMITH

RC (DLC); in a clerk's hand, signed by Smith; at foot of text: "President United States"; endorsed by TJ as received from the Navy Department on 8 Feb. and "commissions" and so recorded in SJL. FC (Lb in DNA: RG 45, LSP).

[1] FC: "Surgeon's mates."
[2] FC: "commd. & warrant officers."

From Worsley & Murray

SIR,   Richmond, Feby. 8th. 1802.

We have taken the liberty to inclose you one of our Proposals for publishing a Richmond Edition of Doctor Ramsay's History of the American Revolution, and beg leave respectfully to solicit your patronage. It is really to be regretted that the art of Printing is not more encouraged in the State of Virginia; but, from the very flattering patronage we have received since we issued our proposals for publishing the above Work, we are induced to believe that it has been owing, rather to a deficiency of perseverance in Publishers, than a want of Public Spirit and liberality in the People.

We are, Sir, with the highest respect and esteem, Your Obedient Servants,   WORSLEY & MURRAY.

RC (CSmH); in Worsley's hand and signed by him; at foot of text: "Thomas Jefferson, Esqr."; endorsed by TJ as received 12 Feb. and so recorded in SJL. Enclosure not found.

William W. Worsley, printer of the Norfolk *Commercial Register* from August 1802 to January 1803, later entered printing partnerships in Richmond, Virginia, and Lexington, Kentucky (Brigham, *American Newspapers*, 1:163, 166; 2:1124, 1138, 1139). Worsley's partner in the proposed Ramsay edition may have been the Petersburg almanac printer William T. Murray (*Bannaker's Virginia and North Carolina Almanack and Ephemeris, For the Year of our Lord 1797* [Petersburg, 1796]; Evans, No. 47711).

TJ owned a two-volume Philadelphia edition of David RAMSAY's HISTORY OF THE AMERICAN REVOLUTION published in 1789 by Robert Aitken & Son (Sowerby, No. 490). While Ramsay's work was widely reprinted, no Richmond edition is known to have been published.

From Benjamin Smith Barton

DEAR SIR,   Philadelphia, February 9th, 1802.

I do myself the honour to introduce to your knowledge, one of our countrymen, Dr. John Watkins, a gentleman of much information, and of great merit. Dr. Watkins has just returned from Spain, and is on his way to the Missisipi, where he proposes to settle. In that part of North-America, he will have ample opportunities of collecting important materials for the natural history of the new world; and he is eminently calculated, by his talents and zeal, to accomplish this desirable end.

Dr. Watkins brought with him, from Spain, the original memoir (with plates) concerning the great animal (*Megatherium*) of South-America. From a careful inspection of the plates, it appears, that there must have been great affinities between this animal and that whose bones were found in Virginia, and of which you have given an account, in the *Transactions* of the American P. Society.

I have the honour to subscribe myself, Dear Sir, Your very humble and obedient servant, and affectionate friend, &c.

B. S. BARTON.

RC (DLC). Recorded in SJL as received 15 Feb.

Dr. John WATKINS, previously from Kentucky, had been in France and Spain attempting to secure a large land grant west of the Mississippi. In 1802 and 1803, he sent Barton letters and specimens relating to the NATURAL HISTORY of the Mississippi Valley. Watkins settled in New Orleans and became involved in politics (Madison, *Papers, Sec. of State Ser.*, 4:447; APS, *Proceedings*, 22, pt. 3 [1884], 328, 330, 334, 341; William C. C. Claiborne to TJ, 15 Apr., 29 May 1804, TJ to Claiborne, 30 Aug. 1804, in DLC).

What Barton called the ORIGINAL MEMOIR on the MEGATHERIUM—a large, extinct ground sloth—was Joseph Garriga's *Descripción del esqueleto de un quadrúpedo muy corpolento y raro, que se conserva en el Real Gabinete de Historia Natural de Madrid*, published in Madrid in 1796. An almost complete skeleton of the animal was found in South America in the 1780s and taken to Spain, where Juan Bautista Bru prepared and mounted the bones for the royal "cabinet" of natural history. Garriga, who was not a natural scientist, did not undertake to analyze the bones himself. Instead he printed, with an introduction, Bru's previously unpublished description of the fossils as well as five illustrative plates that had been prepared under Bru's supervision. The megatherium shared some characteristics with the megalonyx of VIRGINIA that TJ named and described in his 1797 paper for the American Philosophical Society (published two years later in the society's *Transactions*). In 1789, TJ had received from Madrid a handwritten description and partial sketch of the specimen from South America, which had not been named yet. TJ got those materials when he was about to leave France for the United States and could not give them much attention. In addition, that drawing and description did not emphasize the animal's claws, which for TJ, in 1796-97, were the distinctive feature of the megalonyx, and TJ did not make any connection between the megalonyx and the bones in the 1789 sketch. Just before he presented his paper to the APS, however, he saw in the *Monthly Magazine* of London an abridged, translated version of a report on the megatherium by Georges Cuvier. Although the *Magazine* did not say so, the notice was a condensation of a report by Cuvier to the National Institute of France, and a version also appeared in the *Magasin Encyclopédique* in 1796. The single illustrative plate that accompanied the précis in the *Monthly Magazine* did show all the claws, and TJ recognized that the megatherium and the megalonyx had anatomical similarities. Cuvier's account was the first published description of the megatherium fossils from South America and gave the animal its name, but Cuvier had seen only illustrations, not the bones themselves. Evidently he was unaware of Bru's manuscript describing the fossils. Garriga included a translation of the notice of Cuvier's report in his work, but sought to give primacy in the study of the megatherium back to Bru and to Spain (Robert Hoffstetter, "Les rôles respectifs de Brú, Cuvier et Garriga dans les premières études concernant Megatherium," *Bulletin du Muséum National d'Histoire Naturelle*, 2d ser., 31 [1959], 536-45; "Notice concerning the Skeleton of a very large Species of Quadruped, hitherto unknown, found at Paraguay, and deposited in the Cabinet of Natural History at Madrid. Drawn up by G. Cuvier," *Monthly Magazine*, 2 [1796], 637-8; Vol. 14:xxv-xxxiv, 40 [illus.], 501-2, 504-5; Vol. 29:291-304).

On 15 Aug. 1797, writing his first letter to John Stuart since the delivery of his paper on the megalonyx to the APS, TJ referred to the notice about the megatherium he had seen in the *Monthly Magazine*. Unfortunately, TJ did not name Cuvier or the publication, and mistakenly said that the report had been "published in Spain," which led Julian P. Boyd to conclude that TJ saw Garriga's publication in 1797. However, apart from TJ's error about the place of publication, all the facts he related to Stuart in that letter referred to the *Monthly Magazine* account. Moreover, as Barton's letter above makes clear, Bru's report and plates, as published in Garriga's *Descripción*, were unknown in Philadelphia until 1802. If TJ had known of Garriga's work in 1797, Caspar Wistar would have known of it also, yet in his detailed description of the megalonyx bones in the 1799 volume of the APS *Transactions*, Wistar said that he had seen only one illustration of the megatherium skeleton, the one in the *Monthly Magazine*. Barton's copy of Garriga's work—presumably the one that Watkins brought from Spain—was among Barton's books when his library was acquired by the Pennsylvania Hospital in 1829 (Julian P. Boyd, "The Megalonyx, the Megatherium, and Thomas Jefferson's Lapse of Memory," APS, *Proceedings*, 102 [1958], 431-2; APS, *Transactions*, 4 [1799], 531; Bedini, *Statesman of Science*, 272; Vol. 14:xxx-xxxi).

From Catherine Church

N. York Febry. 9th—

Your acquaintance my dear Sir with the amiable family Dupont & the very polite attentions of which they retain so lively an impression precludes all necessity of an introduction to Mde. Dupont whose individual merit is such as not to require a relative claim to admiration—I am however too proud in owning her as my friend & in the possibility of introducing her to *you* to neglect this opportunity of availing myself of these advantages; conciliating both my affection & my vanity, they are fraught with claims ever welcomed by a female heart & mind; the candor of this confession denotes how much I am gratified by the subjects which occasion it. In addition to the advantage of your society my dear Sir I very much wish that our charming friend may unite that of your Daughter's first as to her own gratification & secondly, as to that I shall receive in conversing of them with her—

Mama has been very ill. she is now much recovered & desires I would present you her compts. & assure you that she shall recieve a peculiar gratification in the attention she sollicits for our friend—As you no doubt retain some agreeable impressions of her country, you will not be displeased, in its being thus recalled to you by an *échantillon* of that grace of mind & elegance of manners which constitutes the superior distinctive[1] merit of her Country women—they could not choose a representative so well calculated to do them honor—

It is so long since I have heard from my friend Maria that I fear she has lost sight of me. Pray my dear Sir assure her, Mrs. Randolph & yourself, that I preserve with care every remembrance which composes my sincere & grateful regard to the friends of my infancy & unite to them every motive, which renders me desirous & proud to retain some portion of their friendship, & which so effectually conciliates my consideration & esteem—   CATHARINE CHURCH

RC (MHi); endorsed by TJ as received 15 Feb. and so recorded in SJL with notation "by Made. Dupont."

MDE. DUPONT: Françoise Robin Poivre Du Pont de Nemours.
ÉCHANTILLON: sample.

Although a year earlier she had signed her name as "Catherine" (Vol. 33:49), Church signed this letter and her next one to TJ, dated 29 Apr. 1802, as "Catharine."

[1] Word interlined.

From George Clinton

DEAR SIR   Albany 9th. February 1802.

My Nephew Mr. DeWitt Clinton will have the honor of delivering you this Letter. permit me to recommend him to your friendly Notice—He was this Day appointed a Senator from this State in the Congress of the United States (in the Room of Mr. Armstrong—who had recently resigned his Seat in that Body) and will immediately set out for the Seat of Government—It is reasonable to conclude that I feel a partiality for him as well from the consanguinity that exists between us as from his having at a very early period of Life been of my Family in the confidential Capacity of my private Secretary; But I can with great Truth assure you that these Considerations have no influence upon me in giving you his Character—His present Appointment (which was by a very large majority) as well as the different elective Offices which he had previously filled afford good Evidence of his possessing the Confidence of his Fellow Citizens—His political Principles are pure, and he has too much Integrity ever to deviate from them: nor will you find him destitute of Talents & Information

I am with great Esteem & Respect Yours sincerely

GEO CLINTON

RC (DLC); at foot of text: "Thomas Jefferson Esqr"; endorsed by TJ as received 23 Feb. and so recorded in SJL.

DeWitt Clinton delivered THIS LETTER to TJ on 23 Feb., the same day he produced his credentials and took his seat in the Senate (JS, 3:184).

VERY LARGE MAJORITY: by a 68 to 25 vote on 9 Feb., the members of the New York assembly chose DeWitt Clinton as their candidate to replace John Armstrong in the U.S. Senate. The state senate chose Matthew Clarkson, but Clinton won the joint vote of the two houses. Clinton was serving as a state senator from Queens County and as a member of the state's Council of Appointment at the time of his election (ANB; *Journal of the Senate of the State of New-York: At Their Twenty-Fifth Session, Begun and Held at the City of Albany, the Twenty-Sixth Day of January, 1802* [Albany, 1802], 3, 22; *Journal of the Assembly of the State of New-York: At Their Twenty-Fifth Session, Begun and Held at the City of Albany, the Twenty-Sixth Day of January, 1802* [Albany, 1802], 64-6).

To the District of Columbia Commissioners

Feb. 9. 1802.

Th: Jefferson presents his respects to the Commissioners and refers to them the inclosed letter from Mr. Carrol for their determination. if they will inform him when they are in session he will call on them in order to have a conference on the subject of the letter from the Governor of Maryland.

RC (ViU). Not recorded in SJL. Enclosure: Daniel Carroll to TJ, 8 Feb.

On the letter from the GOVERNOR OF MARYLAND, see the commissioners' letter to TJ, 8 Feb.

From the District of Columbia Commissioners

SIR   Commissioners Office 9th. February 1802

We have just received your Note with Mr. Carrolls letter to you, and several letters which had passed between the Commissioners, Mr. Carroll and Mrs. Fenwick respecting the removal of Mrs. Fenwicks houses—Our Sentiments of that measure are fully expressed in those letters, and we have not changed them; they would remain the same, if we had the sole authority in the case, which we do not conceive we have—By the Deed of Trust the Original Proprietors are entitled to retain the buildings, when the arrangements of the Streets &c will conveniently admit of it; but if the arrangements of the Streets will not admit of retention *and it shall become necessary* to remove such

buildings; then the Proprietor shall be paid the just valuation thereof; It is not said who shall have the power to judge of that necessity; but it seems from implication to result to the President who alone had the right to lay out the City; there is no act which even by implication vests the Commissioners with power over the subject—The facts in Mr. Carrolls case fully appear from the communications he has made to you, which you will receive inclosed. We are &c   A. White
                                                        T. Dalton

FC (DNA: RG 42, DCLB); in a clerk's hand; at foot of text: "President of the United States." Recorded in SJL as received 9 Feb. with notation "mrs Fen- wick." Enclosed in TJ to Daniel Carroll, 11 Feb.

YOUR NOTE: the preceding document.

From Pierre Samuel Du Pont de Nemours

Monsieur le Président   New York 9 Fevrier 1802.

Mon Fils et ma Fille vont vous voir un moment, car ils ne pourront pas s'arrêter beaucoup.—Celle ci accompagne son mari après une absence de treize mois.

Je me serais chargé du voyage avec un grand plaisir. Mon cœur a besoin de vous voir. Vous m'avez écrit une Lettre charmante. Et si je pouvais me remuer, je ne laisserais à personne une course qui pourrait m'approcher de vous même quelques minutes.—mais depuis quinze jours j'ai la goutte et sur la poitrine encore. Il faut bien me tenir coi.

Madame Du Pont, mon excellente Garde Malade et qui rend tant de justice à vos vertus, me charge de vous dire mille choses.

Agreez toujours mon respectueux attachement

                                        Du Pont (de Nemours)

EDITORS' TRANSLATION

Mister President   New York, 9 Feb. 1802

My son and my daughter are going to see you for a moment, for they cannot stay long. The latter is accompanying her husband after an absence of thirteen months.

I would have undertaken the trip with great pleasure. My heart needs to see you. You wrote me a charming letter. And if I could move, I would not leave to anyone else an errand that would bring me near to you even for a few minutes. But for the last two weeks I have had the gout, and even on the chest. I have to remain quiet.

Madame Du Pont, my excellent home nurse, and who acknowledges so justly your virtues, engages me to wish you all good things.

Accept forever my respectful affection. DU PONT (DE NEMOURS)

RC (DLC); at head of text: "A son Excellence Thomas Jefferson Président des Etats unis"; endorsed by TJ as received 15 Feb. and so recorded in SJL.

MON FILS ET MA FILLE: probably Du Pont de Nemours's son, Victor, and Victor's wife, Joséphine (Gabrielle Joséphine de la Fite de Pelleport du Pont). In January 1801, Victor had gone to Europe with his brother, Éleuthère Irénée du Pont de

Nemours, to promote the family's plans for a gunpowder manufacturing company in the United States. Victor departed from Bordeaux in December 1801. E. I. du Pont de Nemours had returned to the U.S. several months earlier to begin work on the project (Victor Marie du Pont, *Journey to France and Spain, 1801*, ed. Charles W. David [Ithaca, N.Y., 1961], xv; Saricks, *Du Pont*, 220-1; Vol. 32:315n; Vol. 34:620n).

From Thomas Eddy

RESPECTED FRIEND   New york, 2nd mo. 9th. 1802—

The Sanguinary Penal Laws of Europe, wch. were continued in their full extent in the United States, very soon claimed the attention of a people attached to principles of Freedom, Moderation & Justice—The Province of Pennsylvania under the Administration of the virtuous Penn early, but in vain, attempted the Establishment of a Code of Laws by which each crime received a punishment in proportion to its degree of enormity—Soon after the Revolution, encouraged by the spirit of Freedom to investigate a subject which they held of the first importance to Civil society, they framed a System of Penal Laws which reflects lasting credit on that State—

This State became enamoured with the alteration & Establishment made in Pennsylvania, and in 1796 adopted similar Laws—The Prison in New York serves to receive the Convicts of the whole State, and having bestowed several Years in the management of its concerns as one of the Inspectors, and believing it my duty to spread principles tending to promote the general good of Mankind, wch. perhaps when more known may be the means of bringing forward similar establishments. I was induced to publish a Pamphlet giving an account of this benevolent institution, with some occasional remarks—Perfectly satisfied that thou are attached to a reform, founded on the pure principles of Christianity, I am induced, without the pleasure of being personally known, to take the liberty of presenting thee with the account I have just published, and of wch. I crave thy kind acceptance—

I am with great respect & Esteem Thy Assured Friend

THOMAS EDDY

RC (DLC); endorsed by TJ as received 13 Feb. and so recorded in SJL. Enclosure: Thomas Eddy, *An Account of the State Prison or Penitentiary House, in the City of New-York* (New York, 1801; Sowerby, No. 2365).

Quaker merchant and reformer Thomas Eddy (1758-1827) of New York engaged in a variety of philanthropic and civic activities during his lifetime, most notably in the area of prison reform. In 1796, he helped to secure passage of an act by the New York legislature to create two state penitentiaries, one in New York City and the other at Albany. Eddy served as inspector and agent (warden) of New-

gate prison in New York City, where he emphasized a humane program of reformation rather than punishment. Although his tenure at Newgate began well, Eddy resigned in 1804 over disputes with new inspectors, and the reputation and effectiveness of the prison declined sharply in subsequent years. In his only other letter to TJ, dated 16 May 1817, he sought TJ's advice regarding the appointment of an engineer to oversee construction of the Erie Canal (ANB; W. David Lewis, *From Newgate to Dannemora: The Rise of the Penitentiary in New York, 1796-1848* [Ithaca, N.Y., 1965], 4-5, 29-53).

From Albert Gallatin

DEAR SIR   Feby. 9th. 1802

From the present situation of Mr Duane's account, as stated in the enclosed, and considering that the stamp act will most probably be repealed, leaving on our hands a large quantity of Surplus useless paper; it seems that it would be unjustifiable to extend the contract beyond the 400 thd. sheets already engaged, and that the advance which he may claim in relation to his existing contract does not amount to 500 dollars. He has delivered to the amount of 2,275 dollars & has received 3,545; so that we are still 1,270 dollars in advance to him.

How he can be relieved I know not; but you will see that the mode suggested, and which, under an impression that he had yet 2000 dollars to receive and had delivered paper to the amount heretofore advanced, had appeared eligible, is impracticable—

Respectfully Your obedt Servt.   ALBERT GALLATIN

RC (DLC); endorsed by TJ as received from the Treasury Department on 9 Feb. and "Duane" and so recorded in SJL. Enclosure: William Miller to Gallatin, Treasury Department, 8 Feb., noting that William Duane's contract was for the delivery of 400,000 sheets of paper by 15 Nov. 1801, for which Peter Muhlenberg, according to Gallatin's instructions, advanced him $3,000 in October; Duane still owes 172,500 sheets from that con-

tract; Duane also gave an order in favor of William Young for payment of 54,500 sheets, making a total of $3,545 advanced to his account, leaving a balance in Duane's favor of $455, upon delivery of all of the paper; Miller also noting that there is no need to extend Duane's contract for there was "no immediate pressure for Supplies: the demand for paper" having "considerably abated" (RC in DLC).

From John Thomson Mason

Feby 9th 1802

At a Circuit Court held for the District of Columbia in the County of Washington at December Term 1801, James B. Heard and James Thompson were each indicted for retailing spirituous liquors contrary to law

By the laws of Maryland no man is permitted to keep tavern without license first obtained from the Court of the County. The Court in granting or refusing such license have a discretionary power. They are directed to see that the public convenience requires that a tavern should be kept where it is proposed to be. That the man who asks for the license is of sufficient substance to keep a tavern, that he has a house stables &c fitted for the accomodation of travellers & others, and, that he has furnished his house with beds &c. He is called on to give Security for keeping a proper house, and is required to pay $16 as well as I remember, to St Johns College

A man must not retail spirituous liquors even as a Merchant or otherwise without a license for that purpose first obtained from the same Court. Here I presume the Court have no discretion. The person obtaining such a license is restrained from selling liquor in less quantities than by the quart, as well as I remember, and He is punishable if he suffers any spirituous liquors by him so sold to be drank in or about the house where it is so sold. For this License the person must pay $8 to St Johns College.

Our Court determined that these taxes by the act of assumption like all other state taxes were abolished. So that in Washington neither a tavern keeper or retailer pays any tax for his licence, save only certain fees of Office, which are the same in both cases

In the cases above stated of Heard & Thompson they were indicted for selling spirituous liquors to be drank at their respective houses. They admitted the fact, and produced each of them a licence to retail liquors under the law last stated. They also exhibitted the affidavits of each other, that they came together with a view to obtain tavern licence, and thought the Clerk had given such to them. But their Counsel being satisfied that these circumstances afforded them no excuse or protection at law, to save the expence of a Jury trial, confessed Judgment.

It is impossible for me to say whether the Court if they had been applied to grant tavern licence to these men, or either of them, would have done so. I know not the situation circumstances, character, pursuits in life or exact place of residence of either of them. I have heard

[555]

that Heard had previously to the assumption kept tavern. I have no knowledge of the fact, and I have also heard that Thompson since his residence in the City has kept a grocery Store and is in no wise provided for keeping a tavern, but of this I have no knowledge myself.

JOHN T. MASON Atty for the
District of Columbia

RC (DLC); endorsed by TJ as received 10 Feb. and "Heard Thompson case" and so recorded in SJL.

ST JOHNS COLLEGE: located in Annapolis, St. John's College was chartered by the Maryland legislature during its November 1784 session. To help support the institution, the legislature ordered that money collected from tavern licenses in the western shore of the state, except Annapolis and its precincts, be given to the visitors and governors of the college (William Kilty, *Laws of Maryland*, 2 vols. [Annapolis, 1799-1800], 1: chap. 37, sec. 22).

To Hore Browse Trist

DEAR SIR   Washington Feb. 9. 1802.

My information of the death of mr Steele was premature, altho' recieved from mr Hunter the member from Missisipi. the facts are these. early in autumn I was informed that mr Steele's state of health was desperate, and that he would send me his resignation & leave the territory, to try the only chance for his recovery. soon after this he grew so much worse as to be unable to leave his room, & has been going down hill ever since, his recovery being impossible. from this state of things arose a report of his actual death, which was sent on to mr Hunter. but it is now known that he was not dead on the [8]th. of December, which was subsequent to the date of the report. still we expect by every post to recieve information of his actual death. in the mean time many considerations enjoin that we say nothing about the eventual arrangement I had proposed to you. be so good as to present my respectful salutations to the ladies, & to accept assurances yourself of my esteem & best wishes.   TH: JEFFERSON

PrC (MHi); blurred; at foot of text: "H. B. Trist."; endorsed by TJ in ink on verso.

INFORMATION OF THE DEATH OF MR STEELE: see TJ to Trist, 17 Jan. 1802.

Narsworthy HUNTER was the congressional delegate from the Mississippi Territory (see Resolution of the Mississippi Territory General Assembly, 21 Dec. 1801).

To Abraham Baldwin

TH:J. TO MR BALDWIN   Feb. 10. 1802.

I recieved a message from you the other day on the subject of Cath-cart. he is the person who was appointed by mr Adams & confirmed by the Senate as Consul at Tripoli. he is personally known to me, & pretty well known. he is the honestest & ablest consul we have with the Barbary powers: a man of very sound judgment & fearless. he married the daughter of some respectable family in Phi[ladel]phia. his public correspondence is published & shews his understanding. [a vessel being] on her departure for the Mediterranean (the Enter-prize, Sterrett) it presses on [us] to send his commission by her: and makes it desireable the Senate should act on it immediately.

RC (DNA: RG 45, MLR); blotted; ad-dressed: "The honble Mr. Baldwin."

Baldwin's MESSAGE to TJ has not been found and is not recorded in SJL. James Leander CATHCART received the appoint-ment as consul at Tripoli in July 1797, al-though he did not take up his duties there until 1799. By late August 1801, TJ de-termined to appoint Cathcart in place of Richard O'Brien, the consul at Algiers, who had requested permission to resign. Probably to avoid any step that could be construed as provocation, TJ waited to make the change until some act of "hostil-ity" by Tripoli should allow him to re-move Cathcart as consul there. TJ's notes of the cabinet meeting on 18 Jan. 1802 show that by that time he and his advisers considered the United States to be at war with Tripoli, and an act of Congress approved on 6 Feb. authorized naval ac-tion and privateering against the North African state (see Circular to Naval Com-manders, 18 Feb.). The same day the statute became law, Madison had a copy of it prepared for Cathcart. Later, in April 1802, Madison informed Cathcart that the United States intended to make a show of force by sending its full Mediter-ranean squadron to Tripoli. Madison in-structed the consul to accompany the ships and negotiate a new treaty with the Tripolitans if that display of American strength had the desired effect (Madison, *Papers, Sec. of State Ser.*, 2:448; 3:135-8, 432, 540; DAB, 3:572; TJ to Madison, 28 Aug. 1801).

OF VERY SOUND JUDGMENT & FEAR-LESS: writing to Madison on 28 Aug. 1801, TJ said that he knew both Cathcart and O'Brien from "a pretty full acquain-tance" in Philadelphia. In 1798, Cathcart had married Jane Bancker Woodside of that city. She was the daughter of John Woodside, a longtime Treasury clerk (DAB; Vol. 34:272; Vol. 35:477n).

ACT ON IT IMMEDIATELY: the Senate approved Cathcart's nomination on 10 Feb. TJ signed a commission of that date, naming Cathcart consul general "for the City and Kingdom of Algiers" (Lb in DNA: RG 59, PTCC; JEP, 1:407).

From Samuel Quarrier

SIR   City of Washington Gail—Febuary 10th, 1802—

I hope my unfortunate situation will pardon, & excuse my intrud on you the contents of this letter, after the reception my last one meet with—from that transaction you must think me void of delicacy, of feeling, for to importune on A like subject, or extreemly implicated in distress. The latter sory am I to say is but too much the case—Distress I now feele which experience never yet taught me—in theory only I Knew what I Know too well in practise, from the short residence i've already had—permit me to informe you of my melancholy situation—Yesterday I was arested, & conducted to Prison, for the sum of 41 Dollars, I was ushered into the debtors appartment (A room about twelve feet square) where I found A parcel of Creatues in the form of men, thay where in the full tide of disipation—Drinking, swearing, gaming, with every other vice that Depravity could invent—Nature was at lenth exausted in the Vortext of intoxication, thay then strewed themselves on the floor, where sleep temporarily relieved them from theire misery, if such thay felt—The chance offered for me to address you, I embraced it—I took up the pen to solicit your friendly benevolence—thinking when you where acquainted with it, you might be indused to relieve me from What I suffer—I declare Sir, you'r the last one I should presume to think of troubleing upon an occasion like this, if I'd any one else to apply to, Its but too melancholy A truth I have not—heere I am close confined, in *Prison*, without one single cent, without cloths except those on my back, & whats worse the Loss of which is dearer to me than existance *Liberty*, as Cato says A day, an hour, of Virtuouse liberty is worth A hole eternity of Bondage—Language is poor to express to you my feelings on this unhappy business—I feele the most heart felt anguish, it is indeed A revers of fortune I but little expected—Never did I think my Father would have deserted me in this maner, to Leave me to perish to starve in A Comon *Prison*—Oh God exstend thy mercie to me thy unfortunate creature—

Pardon those exspressions which are the affects of A heart that feeles—You'r high, & respectable station in life ought to prevent my intrudeing myselfe, again on you—(exclusive of the reception I meet with by letter) Your Knowledg of me does not sanction my taking A Liberty of A pecuniary nature in any respect—except what your Kindness may dictate, was there any other sourse that I could apply I never would to you—On the perusal of this I hope, & trust you'll relieve, & help the unfortunate son of Alexander Quarrier—if ime so fortunate as to feele again your benevolent aid I shall immediately return to my Father where I shall apply to business, as soone as possible never again to leave it for meere speculative fansies, what I now suffer can never be erased from my memory, nor ever thought of without A Sight—

Be pleased to informe me by the Bearer of this the result of this my humble Letter—I beg, & request if theres any thing in this Letter that may not be proper, it will be overloocked by you as it must arise from ignorance, & inability, & not from A wish or Voluntary inovation from me—

May god grant you every blessing that this life can give, is the most fervent Prayre of the Miserable SAML. QUARRIER

RC (DLC); addressed: "Thomas Jefferson President of the Unites states of America City of Washington"; endorsed by TJ as received 13 Feb. and so recorded in SJL.

MY LAST ONE: Quarrier to TJ, 2 Feb. 1802 (second letter).

The quotation attributed to CATO the Younger is from act 2, scene 1 of Joseph Addison's play, Cato. A Tragedy (London, 1713).

To Daniel Carroll

SIR   Washington Feb. 11. 1802.

Immediately on the reciept of your letter on the subject of mrs Fenwick's case, I referred it, with the papers accompanying it, to the Commissioners. their answer, with the same papers, is now inclosed. you will observe they do not consider a question on the demolition or removal of a house, as decided by their first proceedings on the subject; nor until they give the final order for it: and that the house having never in fact been demolished or removed, it's demolition or removal is not to be paid for. my course of proceeding with the board of Commissioners has been as if we were two houses of legislation. where both concur affirmatively the thing is to be done. where either disagrees, nothing can be done. the board having negatived this proposition, it would have been useless for me to enter into the consideration of it, or to make up any opinion on the subject. Accept assurances of my esteem & respect.   TH: JEFFERSON

PrC (DLC); at foot of text: "Daniel Carrol esq."; endorsed by TJ in ink on verso. Enclosure: District of Columbia commissioners to TJ, 9 Feb.

YOUR LETTER: Daniel Carroll to TJ, 8 Feb. TJ sent it to the district commissioners the following day.

From Stephen Cathalan, Jr.

SIR   Toulon the 11th. February 1802

James Madison Esqr. Secretary of State, will I hope have been my kind Interpretor near you with my Letter to him of the 29th. Septber. last to Present you my respectfull thanks and deep sense of ever lasting Gratitude, as well as these of my whole family for the favor you have been so Good as to Confer on me in having Confirmed me in the honorable office I held since the year 1790, under the new Denomination of Commercial Agent of the united States at Marseilles & other Parts of it's Dependencies;—my heart was so much moved, by the honorable Expressions the Secy. of State here employed in his Letter, Inclosing my Commission, by your Direction in my behalf and my Good old Father, that I was then unable to express you, Sir, what I was feeling on Receipt of this emminent favor from you, Confered on me.

but I would now become guilty, of neglect, even ungratitude, if I should not embrace the favorable opportunity of Commodore Richd. Dale Esqr. chief Commander of the United States Naval Forces in the Mediteranean, ready to Sail from this Road for the U.S. on Board the Frigate President, to renew you direct by this Letter, not only the assurances of my everlasting Gratitude and acknowledgments, but the Promise that I will Continue to the utmost of my Power, to deserve the Confidence you have been So Good as to favor me with, Since, I had the honor of being Personally acquainted with you, Sir, to deffend, Protect, in this District, the Interests of the united States & their Citizens & Property, & to do every thing for the best of the service in my office, begging you to be persuaded, that if in any instance I should act in anything behond or short my Duties, it would be owing to my short habilities or ignorance; but not by any Private motives of Interests or any bad Intention on my Part, asking in such Instance (which I hope however never will be the case) your Indulgence as far as Justice on your Part will admit it.

Tho' Commodore Dale does not want my Testimony near you, neither Capn. Js. Barron Commander the President, to Justify the good choice, you have made of them, when appointed by you, Sir, it is however my Duty, to mention you that not only the Diciplin & Good order they kept on Board the President while in this Road or in this arcenal, was admired as well as the Frigate President, by all the chief officers of the French Navy of this Department, (who all did everything in their Power to assist and facilitate the Repairs of this Ship) but also the Constant assiduity of Commodore Dale & Capn. Barron in following the Dayly French Workmen on that Ship, in one of the most severe winter we had experienced in this Climate; attending from the Morning till night, without any interuption, & (this I have been a Witness, in Two voyages to this Place where I have spent 18 days,) without ever Indullging themselves nor any of ther officers being so near Marseilles which none of them have ever been at, to visit it by Land for one or 2 days during an Stay in this sad Place of 60 days; Tho' I must Confess, I have used all ways and means in my Power to tempt them to Go there, or at Least now to put at an Anchor in that Road, in order I might Receive them there in the manner their Public & private Caracter deserves it from me; there is but few officers of any Nation, but Americans who Constantly & without any such Relaxation, would have so well Performed their Duty; and Commodore Dale has ended by a severe sickness, whereof fortunately he is Just now Recovering.

I Part then with Sorrow & Regret from them, happy if I have obtained their esteem & Friendship, but they may be assured I will ever Remember of the agreable time I have spent in their Company while my Duty has required to be here near them.

Till now the Minister of Forreing Relations has not delivered my exequatur or my New Commission, t'is True that being Informed of some difficulties which I was far from expecting, since what I had the honor of mentioning you and to the Secry. of State, I have not asked it directly, but I am now employing some powerfull Friends or Relations near him & the First Consul, (this is the advice also of our Minister Plenipy. at Paris, who Can but employ friendly & verbal wishes for me near the Minister of Foreign Relations, but not act officialy in this peculiar affair in my behalf) and I am making a memorial in my behalf in which I state motives worth their Consideration, for an exception in my favor, since I observe, such exceptions in these about similar cases have very lately taken Place; & I hope at Length to succeed soon;—but in the mean time I continue to be still acknowledged, such, without any Difficulty nor Mollestation, and Commodore Dale is a Witness of it;—I hope, Sir, if you have been informed that such an unexpected Encroachment was then existing, you will have been so Good as to wait till all hopes of Success in my would be lost, before you think to appoint any of the Competitors I may have to fulfill this office, or as long as you observe that the Service of the United States will not suffer for my holding it.—it will be a new obligon. to which I will be indebted to you, and a convincing Proof of your kind Protection and of the Friendship I have been so long time honored with by you, & which is so precious to me & to my Family!

I have the honor to be with Great Respect Sir Your most obedient humble & Devoted Servant   STEPHEN CATHALAN JUNR.

RC (DLC); at foot of text: "Thos. Jefferson Esqr. President of the united States Washington"; endorsed by TJ as received 19 Apr. and so recorded in SJL.

Cathalan's letter of 29 Sep. 1801 to JAMES MADISON acknowledged one from Madison dated 7 July that enclosed Cathalan's COMMISSION as U.S. commercial agent at Marseilles. TJ signed another commission for Cathalan dated 26 Jan. 1802, following the Senate's confirmation of the appointment (DNA: RG 59, PTCC; Madison, *Papers, Sec. of State Ser.*, 1:386; 2:151; Vol. 34:334n).

Richard DALE brought the *President* to Toulon in December to repair damage done to the keel when the frigate struck a rock at Minorca (Madison, *Papers, Sec. of State Ser.*, 2:372n, 423; NDBW, 2:12, 13).

OUR MINISTER PLENIPY. AT PARIS: Robert R. Livingston had offered to see Talleyrand and urge that the French government recognize Cathalan as a U.S. commercial agent. Cathalan prepared memorials to Bonaparte and Talleyrand. In July 1802, they refused to grant him an exequatur, although Cathalan, who had an ally in Joseph Bonaparte, continued to represent U.S. interests at Marseilles (Cathalan to Livingston, 18 Jan. 1802, in DNA: RG 59, LAR; Madison, *Papers, Sec. of State Ser.*, 3:360, 381, 447, 573; 4:57, 186, 192).

Tench Coxe's Reflections on Cotton

Cotton of the U.S.

Every fact and reflexion upon the subject of cotton, enhances its importance to our Country. The whole Sugar colonies of Europe in the west Indies probably will make less in the Season of 1802, than the United States. Their sugar and coffee employing their laborers, and the first of those articles employing their *unbroken* lands, our cotton cultivation *with the plough* & the cheapness of our soil must enable us to take the business of supplying the world with cotton out of their hands. Were the Slave trade right, safe and constitutional, a single year would give us the cotton business, which they now do. But as labor is and is likely to be in America, we shall make a progress a little slower, but not less certain in transfering to our hands much of the business of raising those supplies, which they used to furnish. The western parts of Pennsa. *will be excited* to import, by the ohio &ca. the cottons of West Virginia, Kentucky, Tennessee & the Missa. territory. The capital stocks of Philada., Baltimore, New yk, Connecticut, *particularly Rhode Island*, Masstts. & New Hampshire will be tempted into bulky coarse Manufactures of cotton by Machinery and foreign Artists—*The Union* of the Provisions, coal, and cottons of the states on the waters emptying into Chesapeak bay seem to point that scene out as the one which will rise into *earliest* and *greatest* importance, on the atlantic side. But on the Western waters all these things uniting with the expense of procuring foreign goods & of getting their produce to market seem to ensure the early and great importance of the cotton manufacture. Their supplies of coal are vast and extracted from the earth at an expense unusually small. The extent of country however, over which this production spreads, promises the general establishment of the Cotton Manufacture, especially in the precious

Household line. The Southern Militia, (which for various reasons, exceeding in the aggregate the weight of those, which ever in any country were combined) the Southern militia, it is conceived would acquire the spirit of a corps, if the state Governments were to make a blue cotton cloth with white or yellow cotton under clothes their spring, summer and autumn peace uniform. It would certainly take at this moment, if introduced under impressive Auspices, and would have effects equally important in the good to the Militia, national manufactures, and this grand & novel cultivation.

Authentic information is recd. here, that France bars in future the importation of cotton Manufactures and establishes them in the Belgic Departments.

There can be no doubt, that the cotton production of America will deeply and rapidly affect the British & other European *woolen* Manufactures by the spring our cotton will give to the manufacture of cotton substitutes for woolen manufactures—

The return of the precise importation of foreign, and exportation of foreign & domestic cotton (distinguished) for each *port*, from 1789 to this time is respectfully, but most earnestly recommended to be prepared, and impressively reported & published with all possible dispatch, as a mattter which will give the last necessary spring to a *general* Cultivation. To a *great* cultivation, exportation & manufactures are the obvious and proper springs—

Feb. 11. 1802.

MS (NHi: Gallatin Papers); addressed: "The President of the United States"; endorsed by TJ as received from Coxe on 15 Feb. and so recorded in SJL with notation "Anon."

SUBJECT OF COTTON: for Coxe's long-term and unswerving advocacy of the cultivation, exportation, and manufacture of cotton, see Cooke, *Coxe*, 106-8, 402-3, 424-5.

On 16 Feb., TJ used the verso of Coxe's address sheet to forward Coxe's thoughts on cotton to Gallatin, with the note: "The inclosed is sent to you on account of the last paragraph. if you think with the writer (Tenche Coxe) perhaps someone in your office could make out the statement he recommends" (RC in same; addressed: "The Secretary of the Treasury," written below Coxe's original address, which TJ canceled).

From Manasseh Cutler

[11 Feb. 1802]

Mr. Cutler returns his most respectful compliments to the President of the United States, and begs him to accept his most grateful acknowledgements for the favour of a perusal of Dr. Lettsom's Observations on the Cow-pock. This work, with its plates, has afforded him great pleasure. The philanthropy of the Doctr., in the exertions he is making, & in adding the weight of his character, to render Dr. Jenner's invaluable discovery universally beneficial, does him much honour. Highly, indeed, must we estimate a discovery, which, by a process so easy & safe, bids fair to eradicate a disease which has been one of the greatest evils destined to man. So far as experiment is gone, the hope is encouraged that, in time, this most desirable object will be attained.

RC (MHi); undated; endorsed by TJ as received 11 Feb. and so recorded in SJL.

Manasseh Cutler (1742-1823), a minister, schoolteacher, congressman, and a native of Connecticut, lived in Ipswich Hamlet (now Hamilton), Massachusetts, since 1770. During the Revolutionary War, Cutler studied medicine and treated smallpox victims. He pursued other scientific interests after the war, particularly in botany, and was a member of several American learned societies, including the American Philosophical Society. Cutler, a

Federalist, served two terms in the U.S. House of Representatives, from 1801 to 1805. His journals and letters describe his life in Washington, including visits to the President's House (ANB; DAB; *Biog. Dir. Cong.*; William P. Cutler and Julia P. Cutler, *Life, Journals, and Correspondence of Rev. Manasseh Cutler, LL.D.*, 2 vols. [Cincinnati, 1888; repr. Athens, Ohio, 1987]).

Cutler recorded in a journal that on 8 Feb. he received from TJ, "with a very polite note," a copy of John Coakley LETTSOM's *Observations on the Cow-Pock* (Cutler and Cutler, *Life*, 2:72).

From the District of Columbia Commissioners

SIR,   Commissioners Office 11th February 1802

In compliance with your wishes as intimated to us, we transmit to you copies of the Acts of the late Presidents Washington and Adams directing the conveyance of the streets, and public appropriations in the City of Washington to the Commissioners agreeably to the Act of Congress entitled An act for establishing the temporary and permanent seat of the Government of the United States.

We are with sentiments of the highest respect, Sir, Yr mo Ob Servts   ALEXR WHITE

TRISTRAM DALTON

RC (DLC); in Thomas Munroe's hand, signed by White and Dalton; at foot of text: "President of the United States"; endorsed by TJ as received 11 Feb. FC (DNA: RG 42, DCLB).

For references to ACTS to reserve land in the federal district for public use, see Vol. 33:204-5; Vol. 34:334-6, 647-8.

To James Oldham

SIR   Washington Feb. 11. 1802.

Your favor of the 6th. is recieved, and in answer thereto I observe that there is to be a semicircular window in the pediment of the S.E. piazza. if I understand your drawing, the tympanum is 18. f $9\frac{1}{2}$ I wide at bottom, and 10. f $3\frac{1}{4}$ I on each side, clear, within the cornice. making the window then 4. f. wide (that is, on a radius of 2. f.) within the architrave, the architrave 8. I. sill 4. I. and leaving a margin 8 I. round the architrave and 4. I. under the sill, exactly fills the tympanum. should it be found however on trial, not to leave a margin equal to the architrave round it, and equal to the sill under the sill, the radius must be contracted till it will do that: for I take that to be the best way of proportioning the window to the pediment.

The bells of the raking cornice are to be put in square[1] to the soffite as those of the level soffite are. the other method would be too troublesome, & not have any better effect. I take for granted you have taken care to have a metop over the center of each arch so as to preserve openings for the windows. I had desired mr Dinsmore to order all the plank &c to be sawed which we should want. John Perry is to do the sawing, and if you want any particular stuff will saw it for you. Accept my best wishes.   TH: JEFFERSON

RC (MH); addressed: "Mr. James Oldham at Monticello near Milton"; franked and postmarked.

YOUR FAVOR: Oldham's letter to TJ of 6 Feb., recorded in SJL as received 10 Feb., has not been found.

[1] Word interlined in place of "perpendicular."

From Henry Voigt

SIR   Philada. Febr. 11th 1802

I found the watch exactly as you described it in the few lines laid in the watch. There is one thing however which I suppose has been done since you delivered the watch to the Gentleman; because if it had been done before, you would certainly have mentioned it;—The Stoper which silences the striking part was broke, and the Enamel of the Dial Plate chipt off in two places. This I thought proper to mention, that you may not blame me for that Accident. I have repaired the defects, and have no doubt but you will find her go well.

I have according to order sent you the four Medallions from Mr Reich. The price he puts on them is four Dol. each. I have likewise forwarded a quantity to Mr Duane for Sale, both of Silver and white metal, so that if any more be wanting, Mr. Duane will furnish them.

As there is a rumour of the Mint being abolished, in that case, I shall be obliged to go more extensively into the watch business, to procure a living for a large Family—Your Custom, & what you can recommend, will be esteemed a favour by Sir

Your most Obed Humle Sevt   HENRY VOIGT

RC (MHi); at foot of text: "To His Excellency T. Jefferson Pres. US."; endorsed by TJ as received 21 Feb. and so recorded in SJL.

ACCORDING TO ORDER: see TJ to Voigt, 16 Jan. 1802. On 18 Feb. 1802 in the Philadelphia *Aurora*, William DUANE advertised the sale of the medals by John Reich at the Aurora bookstore. Featuring "a striking likeness of Thomas Jefferson," the medals commemorated "American Independence, and the auspicious day, which raised Mr. Jefferson, to the dignity of President over a free people." Duane offered the medals in silver and in white metal, at the price of $4.25 and $1.25 each, respectively.

RUMOUR OF THE MINT BEING ABOLISHED: on 3 Mch. 1801, Congress had authorized a continuation of the Mint at

Philadelphia for two years, but calls for its abolishment continued from those critical of the high cost of its operation. On 29 Jan. 1802, Congressman William Branch Giles submitted a resolution calling for its discontinuation, arguing that "this establishment cost more than the benefits derived from it." The resolution generated considerable debate in the House, culminating in a bill passed on 26 Apr. that called for the Mint's abolishment. The bill failed, however, to receive the consent of the Senate. On 3 Mch. 1803, Congress allowed the Mint to continue at Philadelphia for another five years (Frank H. Stewart, *History of the First United States Mint, Its People and Its Operations* [Camden, N.J., 1924], 62-9; *Annals*, 11:291-2, 471-2, 473, 484-92, 1128, 1237-42, 1246-7; U.S. Statutes at Large, 2:111, 242).

From David Campbell

Campbella State of Tennessee Feby. 12th. 1802

I discover that in the Disposition of the Federal Troops, who are to be continued in service, a certain number are alloted for the Garrison at South West point.

Doctor Thomas I. Vandyke acts as physician to the Troops that are now stationed there; permit me to recommend him as a proper person to be continued in that appointment. He is a Gentleman of very amiable manners, well versed in the differrent branches of Science & Literature, and a skilful physician.

I am peculiarly happy to find that your administration meets with the highest approbation of the great bulk of the Citizens of this State. My sincere & fervent desire is, that you may live long to steer the Vessel of these great confederated Republics safe, through the Stormy Ocean of mens passions and Interests.

My Son Jefferson is yet my only male child; he is now twelve years old; a fine genius, and in truth a beautiful boy. To what Accademy would it be most proper to send him, or ought I to continue him longer at a private School in this State. If you can find as much leisure from your Official Duties, I pray you inform me on this Subject.

My attachment to your person and interest, inspires me with a confidence that you will receive this private correspondence with Complacency.

I am with the most sincere Sentiments of invariable Friendship Your Obt. Servt.   DAVID CAMPBELL

RC (DLC); addressed: "His Excellency Thomas Jefferson President of the United States of America City of Washington"; endorsed by TJ as a letter of 7 Feb. received 8 Mch. and so recorded in SJL.

In an undated letter that TJ received late in March, Tennessee's congressional delegation—Senators Joseph Anderson and William Cocke, along with William Dickson, the state's at-large member of the House of Representatives—also recommended Thomas J. VANDYKE to be surgeon and physician to the garrison at Southwest Point, a function he was already performing in an acting capacity. Vandyke's "Character as a man is unexceptionably fair," the legislators wrote, and "he is Justly held in Very high estimation" as a physician and surgeon (RC in DNA: RG 59, LAR; in Anderson's hand, also signed by Cocke and Dickson; endorsed by TJ as received 30

Mch. 1802 and "Thos. Vandyke to be Surgeon at S.W. point" and so recorded in SJL). Vandyke, who had been originally from Delaware, had been a garrison surgeon's mate with the army, 1794-95, and received an appointment as surgeon's mate in March 1802. In December 1800, Campbell had recommended Vandyke to be the U.S. agent to the Cherokees (Heitman, *Dictionary*, 1:982; Vol. 33:665, 667n).

Campbell informed TJ in the fall of 1791 that he had named his son JEFFERSON "that I might have the pleasure of hearing your name daily pronounced in my family" (Vol. 27:805; for TJ's reply, see Vol. 22:290). Thomas Jefferson Campbell attended public schools in Tennessee, read law, and became an attorney and politician (Robert M. McBride and Dan M. Robison, *Biographical Directory of the Tennessee General Assembly*, 2 vols. [Nashville, 1975-79], 1:113, 116-17; *Biog. Dir. Cong.*).

From James Dinsmore

SIR   Monticello Feb 12th 1802

nothing Material has occured Since My last of the 23d Ult. I am Still engaged in the dining room. & have got one of the arches up I Send you Inclosed two designs of a Sash for the arch leading to the bow, & will be glad of your determination or for any other design you may prefer. that I may get them Made, to further the work I will Make them at night as they must be put in before the architrave is put up. I find there has been a Mistake in the large patrias for the spaces between the Mutules in the cornice of the bow they are 11 incs.

& the projection of the plenceer is only 9 incs so that they are 2 incs two large the dimensions given for them was 9 ins by 11 in. you will have to get 22 (the number wanted) Made of 9 inchis diameter. the sooner they arrive here the better as they ought to be put on before the paistirers scaffold is Struck. I Shall want some Isinglass to put in the glue, a peice of Spunge, and two or three painters brushes of different sizes which Might Come along with them. Prince Ruspoli Called here yesterday. he was attend by Mr Randolph—Mr Wanschare will be obliged if you will send him ten Dollars.

I am Sir with Respect   JAS. DINSMORE

nails made from the 18th. Jan to the 6th Feb.

d	lbs	
XX.	165.6.	
XVI.	109.8	
X.	218.7.	amnt of nails Sold from 23d Jan. to the 12th Feb
VIII.	81.7.	
VI.	84.7.	£21–15– 7
IV.	32.	
	692.5	Cash rcd—£ 0 0 00

FC (ViU: Monticello); in Dinsmore's hand; on same sheet as letters of 12 Dec. 1801, 1 Jan., and 23 Jan. 1802. Recorded in SJL as received 17 Feb. Enclosures not found.

For a view of the entablature that Dinsmore was installing in the DINING ROOM at Monticello, see Stein, *Worlds*, 80.

PLENCEER: that is, plancere (see Asher Benjamin, *The Country Builder's Assistant* [Greenfield, Mass., 1797], plate 8; Evans, No. 31797).

From Albert Gallatin

SIR,   Treasury department February 12th: 1802

I have the honor to enclose the list of the several officers of Government with their salaries or emoluments as compiled in this or received from the other Departments, and arranged in the following manner.

They may be considered as forming two general classes: One consists of all those who are employed in the collection of the public revenue and receive their compensations by deducting the amount thereof from the monies collected by them. The other embraces all the other officers who receive their compensations from monies drawn out of the Treasury.

The first class is arranged under four general heads—Viz: 1st.

officers employed in the collection of the external revenues, 2d: Officers employed in the collection of the internal revenues, 3d. Receivers and Registers of the Land offices—4th. Deputy Post Masters.

1st. The officers employed in the collection of the external revenue are the Collectors, Naval officers, Surveyors, masters and mates of Revenue Cutters appointed by the President, and the port Inspectors, measurers, weighers and Gaugers who are appointed by the Collectors with the approbation of the Secretary of the Treasury, to which may be added the Bargemen employed by Collectors.

A few of the Collectors, Naval Officers and Surveyors, all the officers of the Revenue Cutters and the Port Inspectors receive a yearly, monthly or daily allowance. The greater part of the compensations received by the Collectors, naval officers and Surveyors arises, however, from commissions paid out of the revenue, and fees paid by the individuals. The measurers, weighers and Gaugers receive certain fees or allowances, determined by the specific services rendered, and paid out of the Revenue.

2d:—Officers employed in the Collection of the internal revenues, consist of Supervisors and two inspectors whose office still subsist, appointed by the President, collectors & auxiliary officers appointed by the Supervisors. The pay of all those officers, which consists partly of Salaries, partly of fees, and partly of commissions is paid out of the revenue. The emoluments in the enclosed List are (for both those classes), those received during the year 1800, although the names of those officers appointed by the President who were in office on the 31:st day of December 1801 have been inserted.

3dly. Receivers and Registers of the Land Offices, are appointed by the President. The Receivers receive one per cent, and the Registers one half ℔er cent on all monies collected; besides which the Registers receive certain fees from individuals.

4th: Deputy Post Masters are appointed by the Post Master General and paid by Commissions out of the monies collected. It must be observed that the amount of emoluments returned is the gross sum received by them, and includes the expenses of Store rent and Clerks.

The second class is arranged under the four heads of Civil, Foreign, Military and Naval Departments.

1st. Civil Establishment includes the President & Vice President, the Legislature and Officers atttached to the same, the Judiciary, the Departments at the Seat of Government, the territorial officers, and the several general establishments of Commissioners of Loans, Purveyor of public supplies, Mint, Surveying and Light Houses.

2d: The Foreign intercourse Establishment includes the Diplomatic establishment, Commissioners and Agents under or in relation to the British Treaty, and Consuls.

3d: The Military establishment includes the officers of the Army, the Agents of the Quarter Masters Department, the Superinten- dants and other officers of the Armories, the Superintendant and Store Keepers of the Military Stores, the Superintendants and other Agents of the Indian Department, and the Agents for Fortifications.

4th: The naval Establishment includes the Officers of the Navy and of the Marine Corps, the Navy Agents and the Superintendants of the Navy Yards.—

I have the honor to be Very respectfully Sir, Your mo. Obedt: Servt: ALBERT GALLATIN

RC (DNA: RG 46, LPPM, 7th Cong., 1st sess.); in a clerk's hand, signed by Gallatin; at foot of text: "The President of the United States"; endorsed by TJ as received from the Treasury Department on 13 Feb. and so recorded in SJL with notation "officers"; endorsed by a Senate clerk. Enclosure: "Report from the Secy. of the Treasury shewing, the names, salaries &c, of the Officers of Government" (MS in same; in various clerks' hands; divided into eight sections by cover sheets with titles in Gallatin's hand, beginning with No. 3, "External Revenues," Nos. 4 and 5, "Internal Revenue & [Land] Offices," No. 6, "Deputy Postmasters," No. 7, "Civil establishment," No. 8, "Foreign," No. 9, "Military establishment," and No. 10, "Naval establishment"; with an emendation in Gallatin's hand in the list of external revenue officers, noting at the entry for the collector at Savannah that Thomas de Mattos Johnson was "appointed in Decer. 1801" and, after "no return" in a clerk's hand, adding "has been furnished by his predecessor Mr Powell"; with the section on postmasters introduced by Granger, see below). Transmitted to Congress with TJ's message of 16 Feb. and printed in ASP, *Miscellaneous*, 1:260-319.

POST MASTER GENERAL: a letter from Gideon Granger at the General Post Office to an unnamed recipient, dated 5 Jan., appears at the head of the list of deputy postmasters in the roll of government officers submitted to Congress. Granger noted that he had compiled the list "in obedience to instructions received from the President through the Secretary of State." He reported that the people listed were "Deputy Postmasters at the places written against their names and that they received as a compensation for their services for the year 1800 the sums set against their names respectively." In cases where accounts had not been returned for 1800, Granger noted that "the best light has been given which the state of the Office admits of" (RC in DNA: RG 46, LPPM, 7th Cong., 1st sess.; in a clerk's hand, signed and dated by Granger; list of postmasters subjoined in a clerk's hand). Before Granger's letter and the list of postmasters were submitted to Congress on 16 Feb., TJ had Meriwether Lewis transcribe Granger's letter and the entire list (Tr in DLC; entirely in Lewis's hand). While Granger had arranged the information in alphabetical order according to the city or site of the post office, beginning with Aaronsburg,

Pennsylvania, Lewis arranged them according to states, beginning with Vermont. The list submitted by Granger concluded with post offices established in 1801. Lewis integrated the newly established post offices at the end of the appropriate states and noted that they were "established in 1801." While Granger's clerk used a separate column for remarks (often the last date when delinquent accounts had been received or the phrase "no accounts rendered"), Lewis interlined the information under the name of the postmaster. For the instructions Granger received for compiling the list, see TJ to Madison, 29 Dec. 1801.

From James Monroe

DEAR SIR   Richmond Feby 12. 1802

I have been requested by Colo. Goodall who is an honest republican character, I presume well known to you, to add his name to the list of candidates for the post office in this city. You will get correct information of every one not known to you from our members in Congress.

In a late letter to Mr. Madison I gave the details of some federal intrigues here during the Session of our assembly. He will I doubt not communicate these to you. Every days experience proves more clearly the difficulty of conciliating the federal party. It is wonderful to see how irreconcileable many of its members are. Altho' none of these people had cause of complaint agnst me yet it was manifest that many of them wod. have hewn me to pieces had they had it in their power—

    yr. friend & servt   JAS. MONROE

RC (DLC); endorsed by TJ as received 17 Feb. and so recorded in SJL.

COLO. GOODALL: Parke Goodall of Hanover County was a member of the House of Delegates in the 1780s and a delegate to the 1788 Virginia ratifying convention. Early in the Revolutionary War, he commanded a detachment of the Hanover military company under Patrick Henry. A letter from Goodall to TJ, dated 12 Feb. 1802 and received from Richmond on the 17th, is recorded in SJL but has not been found (Leonard, *General Assembly*, 138, 146, 157, 161, 165, 173; Robert Douthat Meade, *Patrick Henry: Practical Revolutionary* [Philadelphia, 1969], 48, 50-1; Madison, *Papers, Sec. of State Ser.*, 2:451n).

In a letter to Madison of 10 Feb., Monroe gave a detailed account of the FEDERAL INTRIGUES carried out during the meeting of the Virginia assembly (Madison, *Papers, Sec. of State Ser.*, 2:453-6). For a description of the conflicts, see John Wayles Eppes to TJ, 2 Feb.

From Thomas Newton

D Sir   Norfolk. Feby. 12. 1802

By my freind Mr Myers, at the request of Mr. Campo, a spanish
Gentn I send you two boxes of best Segars, which be pleased to accept off. they are such as cannot be purchased & if you do not smoke
our freinds Mr Burr & Mr. Galatin &c. who doeth will enjoy them
when you meet—I am most respectfully Yr. obt. Servt

Thos Newton

RC (DLC); endorsed by TJ as received 23 Feb. and so recorded in SJL. Enclosed in
Moses Myers to TJ, 23 Feb.

From Joseph Yznardi, Sr.

Exmo. Señor   Baltimore 12 de Febo. 1802

Muy Señor mio, y de mi Mayor Respecto

Repito á V.E Infinitas Gracias por su apresiable de 6 del Corriente
llena de pruebas de los favores con qe me Honrra

Inclusa allará V.E copia de la quenta qe Mr. Gordon de Xerez
mandó con los Vinos qe se han enbarcado en esta por el Paquete qe
Salio de aqui ayer para essa qe Celebraré lleguen bien acondisiona-
dos, y á gusto de V.E

tengo el Honor de Continuar con el favor de V.E, y pido á Dios gue
su Inportante Vida muchos Años

Exmo. Señor BLM de V.E su obte Servr   Josef Yznardy

No. 1	Pipe Sherry 10 Years equal to the London Marquet	188
2	a pipe Paxarete	202
3	half Pipe Natural Sherry	84
4	half Do Sherry with Color	94
		568
	Inshurans 6000 $ at 4 ℔ Ct	22.72
	Dollars	590.72

EDITORS' TRANSLATION

Most Excellent Sir   Baltimore 12 Feb. 1802

My most illustrious sir, and with my greatest respect
I thank you again for your esteemed letter of the 6th of this month full of
proofs of the favors with which you honor me.

Enclosed you will find a copy of the receipt that Mr. Gordon of Jerez sent with the wines that have been shipped in this city via the packet ship that left from here for that city (Washington) yesterday that I hope will arrive in good condition and to Your Excellency's taste.

I have the honor to continue in Your Excellency's favor, and I ask God that He preserve your important life for many years.

Most excellent sir your obedient servant kisses Your Excellency's hand.

JOSEF YZNARDY

RC (DLC); endorsed by TJ as received 13 Feb. and so recorded in SJL.

SU APRESIABLE DE 6: that is, TJ's letter of 4 Feb.

EQUAL TO THE LONDON MARQUET: TJ recorded the wines and their prices under the date 24 Feb. 1802 in his listing of "Wines provided at Washington" in his financial memoranda. He recorded the first item in Yznardi's bill as "Sherry of London quality 10 y. old." The second item TJ recorded as "dry Pacharetti." The wine that Yznardi listed as NATURAL SHERRY above, and which in his letter of 30 Jan. he called a wine without color or "composition," TJ called "white Sherry."

The SHERRY WITH COLOR, which Yznardi on 30 Jan. likened to Madeira, TJ recorded as "Sherry of a different quality." TJ sent 278 bottles of that sherry to Monticello, according to a note he added to his record of the wines in February 1803. TJ included the $22.72 for insurance in his financial record, and on 10 Mch. he sent Yznardi a check on the Bank of the United States, obtained through John Barnes, for the total of $590.72. In the wine list in his financial memoranda, under the date 6 May 1802, TJ added $156 that Yznardi had paid in duties on wines imported for him (MB, 2:1068, 1115; TJ to Yznardi, 10 Mch. 1802; Yznardi to TJ, 22 Apr. 1802).

From Horatio Gates

DEAR SIR   New York 13th: Feb: 1802

I take the Liberty this way to introduce to your Notice General Ebenezer Stevens, my Friend, and Companion, in the War; He Commanded my Artillery at Ticonderoga in 76, & again at Saratoga in 77, and assisted in the Capture of Lord Cornwallis Army at York. His many Emminent Services, will I am [sure] merit your Notice. Throughout the war, & [for] Years after The Peace, he was a most decided Whigg; Dr: Eustace of Massachusetts, now in Congress, served with General Stevens in the war; & is intimate with Him; and if The Generals political principles, received any Shock from the insiduous Acts of the Torys here; I trust his old Friends Ustace, and Myself, will yet set him right; it is not every good Sailor that can Calculate the Longitude, but an Honest man, like a good Seaman, is steady to his trust; so I believe my Friend will always be; —

I wrote yesterday to Mr: Maddison, he will shew you my Letter; I expect D'Wit Clinton will be sent immediately to The Senate, in the room of General Armstrong; whose extream bad Health, obliged him to Sacrafice his seat to his Republican principles; This truly Patriotic Conduct, will I am confident have its weight with you;—Persevere & your Adminis[tration] will exalt the U States to be the best of all possible Governments.—You have The people on your Side; go on, & prosper; That you may continue to enjoy the applause of a Gratefull People is the sincere wish of your Faithfull Friend; & Obedient Servant. HORATIO GATES.

P.S. Mrs: G. presents to You her Compts:, & requests when you Journey to the North, you will remember Rose Hill is ready to receive You—

RC (DLC); torn; endorsed by TJ as received 23 Feb. and so recorded in SJL.

For criticism of the political principles of EBENEZER STEVENS, who was serving as U.S. agent for erecting fortifications at New York, see Marinus Willett to TJ, 7 Sep. 1801.

I WROTE YESTERDAY: in a letter to Madison of 11 Feb., Gates noted that Armstrong had resigned because he was "afflicted with an inveterate Rheumatism, that has Tormented him all the Winter" (Madison, *Papers, Sec. of State Ser.*, 2:457).

From George Jefferson

DEAR SIR   Richmond 13th. Febr. 1802

Having received a letter from Mr. Barnes last night in which he desires us to remit him the 198.$: mentioned in your last, we conclude that you find you will not have occasion for it here, and therefore forward it to him agreeably to his direction.

I am Dear Sir, Your Very humble servt.   GEO. JEFFERSON

RC (MHi); at foot of text: "Thomas Jefferson esqr."; endorsed by TJ as received 18 Feb. and so recorded in SJL.

YOUR LAST: TJ to George Jefferson, 3 Feb.

From Levi Lincoln

SIR   Washington Feby 13. 1802

By the chronicle, received yesterday, we have learnt the fate of Mr Morton's motion in the legislature of Massachusetts. If the only object was, to obtain an address, the measure was certainly ill-concerted, they ought first to have known their numbers. It is apparent that the friends to the motion[1] did not expect to carry it, but meant it, as a measure to effect future elections. The inclosed letter from Coll. Hitchborn explains the matter, and his preposed motion, for the Senate, is on the same idea. It is evident from the republicans endeavouring to subject the federalists to the imputation of being opposed to particular measures of the administration, they consider these measures as popular in the country, and from the federalists evading a direct vote, by refering the matter to the next session, that they are of the same opinion. I forward, the communications from Mr Hitchborn, to prevent any uneasiness, on the idea, that, republicans had failed of their object.

The letter of Coll. Hay, the republican leader in the Vermont legislature respecting the appointment of Willard, which originally gave you much uneasiness, will I think give you complete satisfaction on that subject, and shew what attention ought to be paid to federal clamor—

If you are not too much engaged permit me to ask you to throw your eye over the letter, I have received from Mr. Waldo. I know these applications are regularly made through the secretary of State, to whom I have mentioned Mr. Waldo's name. My particular situation with respect to him, he being a family connection is an inducement, for my stating his wishes also directly to yourself. I should have waited on you in person, was it not for an ague in my face, which has afflicted me for several days, and which renders it inconvenient for me to be abroad—

I have the honor to be Sir with highest respect your most obedient Sert   LEVI LINCOLN

RC (DLC); addressed: "The President of the United States Washington"; endorsed by TJ as received 13 Feb. and so recorded in SJL. Enclosures not found.

For Perez MORTON'S MOTION in the Massachusetts legislature followed up by Benjamin Hichborn, see Hichborn to TJ, 25 Jan.

Udney HAY of Underhill, Vermont, was a member of the state legislature. In the 1790s, he opposed the Washington and Adams administrations and was a leader of the Vermont Democratic Society (John J. Duffy and others, eds., *Ethan Allen and His Kin: Correspondence, 1772-1819*, 2 vols. [Hanover, N.H., 1998], 2:403n; *Journals of the General Assembly of the State of Vermont, At Their Session, Begun . . . The Eighth Day of October, A.D. One Thousand Eight Hundred and One* [Windsor, Vt., 1802], [5]).

In the expectation that Stephen Cathalan, Jr., would not be recognized by the French government as U.S. commercial agent at Marseilles, John Jones WALDO, who was originally of Massachusetts, had begun to seek the position, enlisting the support of Americans in France such as Fulwar Skipwith and Thomas Sumter, Jr., and asking Robert R. Livingston to bring up the subject in a letter to Madison. In February 1801, John Adams had named Waldo to be commercial agent at Nantes and the Senate confirmed the nomination, but TJ considered it a midnight appointment and declined to send a commission to Waldo (Madison, *Papers, Sec. of State Ser.*, 2:360, 361n; 3:441, 447; JEP, 381, 385; Vol. 33:173n, 672, 677).

[1] MS: "mortion."

From James Monroe

Sir,   Richmond February 13. 1802

I enclose you some resolutions of the General Assembly of this Commonwealth, passed at its last session explanatory of a resolution of the preceding session authorizing a correspondence with you relative to the purchase of lands without the limits of the state, to which persons obnoxious to its laws or dangerous to the peace of society might be removed. You will recollect that as the precise import of the first resolution was not clearly understood, it was thought proper to submit our communication on it to the General Assembly, that its object and policy might be more accurately defined. The resolutions which I have now the pleasure to communicate to you have removed all doubt on that subject, by confining the attention in procuring the asylum sought to the accommodation of negroes only, and by specifying for what causes, under what circumstances, and (in the case of felons) to what countries it is wished to send them. You will be pleased to observe that there are two descriptions of negroes embraced by these resolutions, the first comprizes those who being slaves may commit certain enumerated Crimes. For such an asylum is preferred on the Continent of Africa or the Spanish or portuguese settlements in South America. The second respects free negroes and mulattoes, including those who may hereafter be emancipated and sent, or chuse to remove to such place as may be acquired. For these a preference is not expressed in favor of any particular region or Country, nor is the right of Sovereignty over such place desired. In removing these people without our limits no restraint is imposed to preclude the attainment of an asylum any where, whereby the object of the State might be defeated, or to prevent that attention to their interests in case an alternative of places is presented, by inhibiting a preference for that which may be deemed best adapted to their Constitution, genius and character. I have therefore to request that you will be so good as to endeavor to promote the views of the State in these important respects; being satisfied that they are founded in a policy equally wise and humane, with respect to ourselves, and the people who are the object of it. I am dear Sir with great respect and esteem yr. very obt. servant   JAS. MONROE

RC (DLC); in a clerk's hand; closing and signature in Monroe's hand; endorsed by TJ as received 19 Feb. and so recorded in SJL. FC (Vi: Executive Letterbook); in the same clerk's hand; at head of text: "The President of the United States"; lacks complimentary closing. Enclosure: Resolutions of the Virginia General Assembly, passed by the House of Delegates on 16 Jan. 1802 and agreed to by the Senate on the 23d, to resolve "a difference of construction" in the intent of the legislature's resolution of 31 Dec. 1800; resolving first "that as the resolution was not intended to embrace offenders for ordinary crimes, to which the laws have been found equal, but only those for conspiracy, insurgency, Treason, and rebellion, among those particular persons who produced the alarm in this State in the fall of 1800, that the Governor be requested in carrying the said resolution into effect upon the construction here given, to request of the president of the United States in procuring the lands, to prefer the Continent of Africa, or any of the Spanish or Portugal settlements in South America"; resolving also "that the Governor be requested to correspond with the president of the United States for the purpose of obtaining a place without the limits of the same, to which free negroes or mulattoes, and such negroes or mulattoes as may be emancipated may be sent or choose to remove as a place of asylum; and that it is not the wish of the Leg-islature to obtain on behalf of those who may remove or be sent thither, the Sovereignty of such place"; and resolving finally that the governor present the next General Assembly with "the result of his communications to be subject to their controul" (Tr in DLC: TJ Papers, 120:20682; in the hand of and signed in attestation by James Pleasants, who was elected clerk of the House of Delegates on 1 Feb. 1802 [JHD, Dec. 1801-Feb. 1802, 91]; with a footnote indicating that in the preface to the resolutions a reference to "December last" meant December 1800; TJ later received another Tr of the resolutions, also in DLC, from John Page; see Page to TJ, 29 Oct. 1804, 2 Feb. 1805, and TJ to Page, 27 Dec. 1804; printed in ASP, *Miscellaneous*, 1:466, and in *Annals*, 16:998-9 [appendix]).

RESOLUTION OF THE PRECEDING SESSION: the legislature's resolution of 31 Dec. 1800 (see TJ to Monroe, 24 Nov. 1801, second letter, and Monroe to TJ, 21 Dec. 1801).

From Samuel Quarrier

SIR   Saturday mourning Febuary 13th 1802

Pardon, & excuse an unhappy young man for importuning & intruding himself on you I could adress you more in the stile of adulation, & flattery, that you despise—I tell you my unfortunate situation without exageration, or without Varnish—No one wishes more for your, prosperity than the unfortunate writer of this—The tempestuous Ocean I could brave, the battles front I would not shrink from—Nay any danger that's respectable to man I could meet, with fortitude, & resolution—But this ignominious imprisonment unmans the heart, & depresses the Soul, as low as that of the unfortunate wretch, that toils in the mines[1] of Peru—In the extention of your philantropic humanity to the misfortunate solicitor hereof—Words are poor to exspress to you the gratitude that will be felt by the unfortunate & Wretched—   SAML QUARRIER

RC (DLC); addressed: "The President of the United States"; endorsed by TJ as received 13 Feb. and so recorded in SJL.

[1] MS: "minds."

From Arthur St. Clair

S<small>IR</small>,   Cincinnati 13h. feby. 1802

It is most probable that the violent exertions made last Winter, when my term of Office expired to prevent a renewal of it did not escape your notice, but it may not have come to your knowledge that, to accomplish that Object, the basest means—the vilest falsehoods, and the foulest Calumnies were resorted to; nor that, at the very moment, the authors of them were guilty of the blackest ingratitude. They succeded, however, so far as to produce doubts in the mind of the late President, nor was it till after much hesitation, and considerable delay and reluctance, that he made the nomination. By Letters received from Washington by the last Mail, I am informed that the same persons, or some of them are now, Sir, endeavouring to ruin me with You, and boast that my removal is decided on. I hope, and trust the case is not so. If they have, Sir, found their way to you, I entreat you not to give implicit credit to their Suggestions.—For ten years of the twelve I had held this Government, the confidence, the approbation, and the good wishes of the people attended me constantly, nor would they have been lessned but for the insidious practices of those Vipers I had imprudently taken to my Bosom. I dare to challenge all the World to produce one instance, in the whole of my Administration, where a single individual has met with oppression, or an Act to which the interest and welfare of the people was not the leading, if not the only motive—It is certainly true that I have, all along, used my best endeavours to keep the people steady in their attachment to the General Government—and, so long as this Country remains in a colonial state, and the administration is in my hands, so long will these endeavours be continued, by whomsoever that Government may be conducted. Placed at a distance from, and unconnected with any of the Parties in the united States, I have devoutly wished the general happiness and faithfully laboured for that of this particular Quarter, and thrown my mite into the general treasury towards it, by forming the people to habits of Industry—to obedience to the Laws—to moderation in opinions, civil & religious, and to virtuous Lives and Practices.

The loss of my Office would, I acknowledge Sir, be very inconvenient,—for, tho' the duties of it have occupied, constantly and exclusively, more than twelve Years, the expenses necessarily incident to it, and the maintenance of my family, on a very narrow scale, have swallowed up nearly the whole of what remains of my private Funds after the inroads made upon them by the tender Laws, and from the Salary I have not been able to save a single Cent. That is nothing. I may have been sacrificing to Vanity, tho' I have not been sensible of it—But, a removal cannot take place without deeply affecting my Reputation, and that, I own it, would be most severely felt—Health and Fortune which are already gone are nothing in comparison—I beg of you, Sir, if, from the representations that may have been made, it should seem to appear that such a measure would be proper, to postpone until I can have it in my power to wait upon you in person, or that you will be pleased to order an Enquiry into my Conduct.

With sentiments of the highest Respect, I have the honor to be, Sir,

Your obedient Servant   Ar. St. Clair

RC (DLC); endorsed by TJ as received 8 Mch. and so recorded in SJL with notation "S." Dft (O: St. Clair Papers), torn; endorsed by St. Clair as "private" and "to Mr. Jefferson President of the united States."

VIOLENT EXERTIONS MADE LAST WINTER: John Adams nominated St. Clair for reappointment to another three-year term as governor of the Northwest Territory on 22 Dec. 1800, but added the unusual step of accompanying the nomination with petitions he had received both for and against the governor. The Senate appointed a committee to consider St. Clair's nomination on 30 Dec., to which Adams sent two more petitions on 8 Jan. 1801. Presenting its findings to the full Senate on 3 Feb., the committee reported that the petitioners made several charges against St. Clair, "but have offered to the Senate no testimony in sup-

port of them." The committee added that the laws opposed by the petitioners that entitled the governor to certain fees "have been permitted to continue in force" by Congress, and further noted that the territorial legislature had addressed the governor the previous November "in terms highly honorable" to St. Clair. The committee recommended that the Senate consent to St. Clair's nomination, which it did the same day (JEP, 1:362, 364, 366, 376; Smith, St. Clair Papers, 2:526, 529, 530, 531; Sears, Thomas Worthington, 60-2).

LETTERS RECEIVED FROM WASHINGTON: on 18 Jan. 1802, Paul Fearing, the Northwest Territory's representative to Congress, informed St. Clair that the "Chillicothe agents" Thomas Worthington and Michael Baldwin had arrived in Washington (Smith, St. Clair Papers, 2:549-51, 557, 559).

From Andrew Ellicott

DEAR SIR   Lancaster Feby. 14th. 1802.

If the following proposed arrangement, for executing the Office of Surveyor General of the United States, should coincide with your ideas upon that subject, and come within the meaning of the *law*, I shall have no objection to the appointment.

First, The Surveyor General shall determine every geographical position necessary for forming a chart, or map, by which the vacant lands belonging to the United States, may be divided into districts, and the surveying executed with accuracy.

Secondly, subject to your approbation, the Surveyor General shall appoint a sufficient number of capable deputies to do the work in each district, agreeably to the mode prescribed by law.

Thirdly, when the Surveyor General is not engaged in the determination of the necessary geographical points to limit the several districts, he shall reside at the seat of government of the United States; and take charge of, arrange, and correct, (if necessary,) the publick charts, surveys, and drafts, not only of different parts of the country, but also of our extensive sea coast, and furnish correct copies of any of them, (when required,) to either of the principal secretaries, or any other person entitled to receive them.

Fourthly, The Surveyor General shall receive and examine the returns from the deputies, and arrange them, with all other documents belonging to the land department, for the use of the Secretary of the Treasury, or other proper Officer when required.—

I do not see that either of the foregoing articles clash in any manner with the law establishing the land office: The third embraces objects of considerable importance not otherwise provided for, and I am confident would be found of great publick utility if adopted.

I have lately received from Paris a splendid copy of De la Land's Astronomy in four volumes quarto: and last evening a letter from the celebrated[1] astronomer Delambre of the National Institute, and who was directed by that body, to notify me of the reception of my printed observations made on our southern boundary, and at other places. The work is not only spoken well of, but complimented far beyond its real merit, and a correspondence is requested.

You will find enclosed the occultations of three stars (of that cluster called the Pleiades,) by the moon,—these observations are of the greatest importance in settling, and correcting, the theory of the lunar motions.

I have the honour to be with great respect, and sincere esteem, your friend, and Hbl. Servt.   ANDW; ELLICOTT.

RC (DLC); at foot of text: "Thos. Jefferson President of the United States"; endorsed by TJ as received 18 Feb. and so recorded in SJL. Enclosure not found, but see below.

TJ referred Ellicott's requirements for the OFFICE OF SURVEYOR GENERAL to the secretary of the Treasury; see TJ's query and Gallatin's response at 24 Feb., below.

Ellicott and the French astronomer Jean Baptiste DELAMBRE had begun a correspondence in which they exchanged information about celestial observations (John C. Greene, *American Science in the Age of Jefferson* [Ames, Iowa, 1984], 139-40, 143, 156).

On 9 Feb., Ellicott observed the times at which three stars of the PLEIADES disappeared behind the moon. TJ apparently passed Ellicott's report along to the American Philosophical Society, which received it at a meeting in Phildadelphia on 19 Mch. and referred it to Robert Patterson. At a meeting on 2 Apr., the society agreed to publish the paper. When those observations did appear in the society's *Transactions*, they were incorporated into a report of December 1802 that Ellicott addressed to Patterson. It included the results of a series of varied astronomical observations, mostly of the satellites of Jupiter, that Ellicott made over a course of months at Lancaster, Pennsylvania (APS, *Proceedings*, 22, pt. 3 [1884], 321, 322; APS, *Transactions*, 6 [1809], 63).

[1] MS: "clebrated."

From "A Federalist Democrat"

SIR   New York [Feb.] 14th 1802

Having seen some Jacobins who under the name Federalists in a party together I thought I wou'd go & see who was there. When I saw a few fellow's together a drinking knowing them to be of the Jacn party I made them bleave that I was of their party when Shoking to relate they wished me to go to Washington & then assasanate you the first Opurtunity which I highly remonstrated against & when they saw that they made me take an Oath that I wou'd not let any body know which if it was not for that I wou'd inform you—I as a friend to you & in duty bound to Inform you being the father of us All—have done this to save your life

A FEDERALIST DEMOCRAT

RC (DLC); endorsed by TJ as received from "Anonymous" on 27 Feb. and "assassination" and so recorded in SJL.

To George Hay

DEAR SIR   Washington Feb. 14. 1802.

My absence from Virginia for many years back, with small intervals of residence only in it, has rendered me very much unpossessed of the state of things there. I did not recollect that you were a practitioner in Richmond until an answer from mr Wickham to the inclosed letter set me to looking about to whom I should address myself on his declining the business therein proposed. nor am I now certain whether you do practise in the courts there. but believing I have understood so, I ask the favor of you to undertake the matter proposed to mr Wickham in the letter of which I send you a copy because it contains a statement of facts supplementary to what appears in the documents. I enclose you an order on messrs. Gibson & Jefferson for your fee, and pray your attention to mr Short's interest in this suit, considering that he rendered a year's laborious & expensive service to the US. it would be hard indeed to say that he, and not the US. should lose the amount of his salary for the year. he has never re-cieved it, nor have the US. ever paid it, for as long as it is in the hands of their officer, it is in their hands, & unpaid. Accept assurances of my esteem & high consideration.   Th: Jefferson

PrC (DLC: William Short Papers); at foot of text: "George Hay esq."; endorsed by TJ in ink on verso. Enclosures: (1) TJ to John Wickham, 29 Jan. 1802, with en-closures. (2) Order on Gibson & Jeffer-son, not found.

ANSWER FROM MR WICKHAM: a letter of 9 Feb. from John Wickham, recorded in SJL as received from Richmond on the 13th, has not been found.

TJ apparently asked Albert Gallatin to

collect some documents pertaining to William SHORT's salary claim. On 3 Feb., Gallatin wrote TJ: "I enclose the attested copies required. The original of one of the papers is not in this office & appears to have been returned to you: the copy is en-closed" (RC in DLC; at foot of text: "The President"; endorsed by TJ as received from the Treasury Department on 3 Feb. and "mr Short's papers" and so recorded in SJL; enclosures not found).

From David Lummis

Sir   Philadelphia, February 15th. 1802.

Believing, as I do, that every individual in society has a right to communicate his ideas on subjects involving national concerns, in a proper manner, to the first magistrate of the people; I have taken the liberty to offer for your Excellency's consideration, a few thoughts on a subject of the greatest importance.

Doubtless it must be granted that the existence of Slavery in the United States is a great national misfortune; could therefore Slavery be abolished. consistently with the interest of individuals and the constitution of our country, it would be a great national advantage. These things being premised, I will give it as my opinion that we may find a suitable asylum for our Slaves in the french West India is-lands. Let me now suppose that the existing friendship between the United States and France will warrant the negociating anything mu-tually interesting to the parties. Then in the first place permit me to say (which I know from my own knowledge) That the *Blacks* in those Islands enjoy a *limited state* of *freedom*; That they are subjected to, and protected by, the operation of the civil laws; That by those laws each negro is obliged to reside on his respective plantation; That they are allowed for their daily labor one fourth of their earnings. Secondly, one Hundred negroes thus situated will make more sugar and coffee, than five hundred would formerly when slaves. Thirdly, It is impossible these negroes should ever again be reduced to Slavery, They may be extirpated, but they never can be brought to unconditional submission.

Fourthly, There is not one third, I believe I may say one fourth a sufficiency of hands at present to work that plantations to advantage. Now I trust it will be allowed that it is the interest of France to have negroes sufficient to keep the whole of her Colonies in high cultivation. But how is France to acquire this additional supply of hands? Not by a trade to Africa, for the expence attending this would not admit of the freedom of such imported negroes. and the retention of them in Slavery amongst free Blacks would be the cause of continual revolutions. I will here venture to assert that if France reflects deliberately on the best way to retrieve the lost revenue of those colonies without expence or bloodshed and in consistency with her Constitution (the boasted merit of which is the freedom of man) she will find it conducive to her interest to redeem our Slaves and become accountable to the United States for the amount thereof. The Government of the United States becoming responsible to the individual Slave holders. Now let us suppose for a moment that both Governments should consider this as an interesting subject for negociation. What will the Slave holder say, who is to have his plantation stripped of the means of raising produce? Many, no doubt, will at first object, but the greater number will gladly relinquish every Black in their possession when they find they are to have a compensation for their Slaves, and will be relieved from the fear of those terrible calamities which ever attend the insurrections of the negroes. Where is the American who adores the virtue of Our Constitution, and does not blush at the idea of holding Slaves? How inconsistent it is for *Us* to assert our own rights with such intrepid firmness while we hold fast the chains of Slavery upon our fellow men? But independent of the cruelty and impropriety of *Republicans holding slaves*, there are many other inconveniencies attending it. If the planter who lives in affluence on the labor of his negroes will but look around he may observe multitudes of poor White inhabitants in his neighborhood who are in want of the daily necessaries of life, and who have no means in their power to provide for the sustenance of their families. What is the cause of this distress? The planter must acknowledge that[1] he is at least the occasion of all these calamities. He has put all labor into the hands of

Slaves and thereby deprived the indigent whites of the power of supporting their families.

Hence it happens that in the Southern States it is reckoned degrading for a man to labor for the support of his family. It is esteemed humiliating for him to accustom his children to labor or to give them in their youth habits of industry. How many usefull Citizens are thus lost to the public? How many thro' idleness and want become a trouble to themselves and a nuisance to society? But could we suitably dispose of our slaves, this custom would be reversed, immedeate encouragement would be given to the white laborer, and the planter would in a few years find his plantation to produce as much, yes more, than when it was covered with negroes. If a planter who has, say, one hundred negroes, calculates the interest of his money in those negroes with what it costs him for their maintenace, their loss of time in sickness, or when absconded, Their total loss by death or otherwise, together with what they steal or waste, the advertising and rewards for runaways; He will find it amount to a sufficiency for the purchase of mules or Horses and the pay of laborers to produce him equally as much Crop as his Hundred negroes would have done. The emigrants from the Eastern states would press rapidly in to fill up the vacuum made by the absence of the Slaves. The price of labor would become low; Industry would be encouraged; and *Happiness* and *plenty* would smile on the *indegent*. How much more satisfactory would this be to a benevolent man than to hold his fellow Creatures in *bondage* contrary to the *true spirit of Republicanism*, and inconsistent with the genius of our government. How much preferable this to the keeping amongst us an enemy, which may one day not only destroy the lives and property of thousands, but prove the ruin of the whole republic? Thus far I wrote previous to the news of peace in Europe; but as that peace has made considerable alteration in the Opinions of political and commercial men concerning the french colonies in the West Indies and the disposition of the mother Country towards them, I have omitted the forwarding this for a few weeks in order to have the opportunity to make a few additional remarks. It has appeared in the antirepublican prints to be the intention of France in conjunction with the English to dispossess Tousaint, overthrow the present government of St. Domingo, and reduce again the negroes to slavery. This, no doubt is ardently desired by the English; But I cannot conceive that France will be so impolitic, so ignorant of the situation of her Colonies, of the expence attending such an undertaking, of the destruction it would be to the Colonies and the revenue arising therefrom, and of the impracticability of accomplishing it, as to undertake that object. Bonaparte, it is said, is sending to Hispaniola forty thousand troops, These, if it be the case, are barely sufficient to garrison the posts on the sea coasts, which probably may be the object of France that the Blacks at present occupying those posts may retire to the plantations, to work; but not as Slaves, for if that be attempted, there wanting at least One hundred thousand troops more, and even then nothing more could be done than to drive the blacks to the mountains, where they can neither be followed nor distressed, as long as they can procure ammunition, which they will undoubtedly take care to secure as soon as they perceive the shadow of white troops amongst them. The mountains produce provisions in abundance well calculated for the sustenance of the negroes; This is sufficiently proved if we consider the great body of Brigands which refused to agree to the Government of Tousaint in the spring of 1794. and continued there in plenty untill the spring of 1797. in defiance of Tousaint's army and till the white troops then on the Island, which was about ten times their number. It is said that the French have already blockaded Guadaloupe; They may also declare Hispaniola to be in the same situation; But I again repeat it, they can do nothing more than get possession of the sea ports, and forts on the coast, which the negroes will immedeately relinquish, and remove their arms and amunition to different parts of the interior, where they will part with their lives, rather than their liberties. And such a warfare if carried on for one year will prove the total destruction of every plantation, annihilate the revenue arising from the island, and must finally end in restoring the negroes to their present situation, or in totally destroying them, to effect which will be required six or seven years of continual war at an enormous expence. And is it not a well known fact that the French Republic is indebted to those very people for the preservation of the Colonies during the last seven years of the war? During which period they have been stripped of all the specie and property possible, under the idea that those colonies might fall into the hands of the British. Then can we believe that France will wish for the total destruction of those colonies for so many years, and in violation of humanity and their own Constitution, wantonly destroy or reduce to slavery, a people to whom they are so much indebted? No. I conceive not. But I mention these circumstances, knowing that this would ultimately be the issue, should the reduction of the Colonies be attempted. I should rather suppose it would not only be to the credit, but also the interest of France to let them remain as they are under the influence of good and wholesome laws which will diffuse amongst them the spirit of civilization and industry, and receive from the United States from time to time such a proportion of our negroes as can be most conveniently spared, or such as may be most ready and willing to go. Willing they undoubtedly will be when they know that they are purchasing on a credit their *Freedom* which is the thing they most desire yet little expect. By these means I conceive we might in a few years be happily relieved from this increasing evil, which is not only a dishonor to us as republicans, but menaces us with destruction. From my manner of writing it may possibly be thought that I am a member of the Abolition Society. That is not the case. For tho' I believe that the majority of that body are actuated by the best motives; Yet many of them if they can get a man's Slave to run away and can secrete him, or free him under any pretext whatever, They conceive they have done that negro justice, without once considering the injustice they have done the owner by depriving him of his property.

I have always been opposed to this mode of liberating negroes, and the more I see of it, the more I am convinced of its impropriety. Although I am an advocate for the abolition of Slavery, yet I think it a matter of great moment that it be effected in a manner which will not injure individuals nor the Community at large. Having given what has principally occurred to me on this subject, I have done. Should these hints contribute in any degree to so desireable an end, as the removing out of the way this reproach of republicanism, it would ever after be to me a source of the most refined pleasure and genuine happiness.

I have the honor to be, with sentiments of the most profound respect and sincere attachment Your Excellency's devoted friend and Fellow Citizen   DAVID LUMMIS

RC (DLC); month in dateline interlined; at foot of text: "His Excellency Thomas Jefferson President of the United States." Recorded in SJL as received from "Dummis" on 19 Feb.

[1] MS: "that that."

From Philadelphia Merchants and Traders

[before 16 Feb. 1802]

The Subscribers, Merchants and Traders of the City of Philadelphia
Respectfully Represent
That feeling themselves deeply interested in the decision of the

question now depending before the House of Representatives on the repeal of the Law for the organisation of the Courts of the United States, they beg leave to submit to the Consideration of the Government, that comparative view of the operation of the former and present judiciary establishment upon the parties to suits prosecuted in those courts; which their experience and observation have enabled them to form—

Under the former organisation of the Courts the parties who prosecuted or defended suits, were exposed to many inconveniences—   The great distance which the Judges were obliged to travel in their attendance upon the Courts, and the degree of duty imposed on them rendered their Sessions too short for the transaction of the business brought before them—   The delay to which the parties were, by this and other causes, unavoidably subjected, was continued and repeated; and in many cases to such a degree, as almost to defeat the object of their suit—Witnesses, whose Testimony was essentail to the just decision of a cause, frequently died, or left the Country, before it could be brought to a hearing—the parties themselves became insolvent and the consequence was, that justice was often defeated, and the public confidence in the administration of justice weakened—

These inconveniences were increased by the constant change of the Judges who presided in the Courts.   Those Gentlemen, though eminent for their abilities, their learning and probity, yet educated in states whose practice and principles of jurisprudence were greatly varient from each other, uniformity of opinion could not be expected.   Thus inconsistent and contrary decisions in different courts, and in the same court by different Judges were not unfrequent; and the citizens were left without a certain rule by which to direct their conduct—

By the new organisation of the judiciary,—these inconveniences have been removed—The Judges not obliged to travel over a great extent of Country and not limited to time in the Sessions, are enabled to remain as long as the business of the Court may require—Notwithstanding the accumulation of business which the old system had produced in the Court for the Eastern district of Pennsylvania, and the more than ordinary number of suits which the obvious benefits of the new one drew to that Court every cause in which the parties have been prepared for trial has been heard and decided—   And it is a tribute justly due to those who hold the administration of justice in the third Circuit, to declare, that those causes, though many of them of great importance, and requiring much time and fatigue in the investigation, and discussion, have been heard with exemplary patience—and attention; commented on with candour, elucidated with ability, and decided to the general satisfaction—

The nature of the questions usually agitated in the Courts of the United States, and the uniformity of decision which their present organisation will necessarily introduce, seem calculated to establish a system of general and commercial law, which will be of great benefit to the community in general, and particularly so to the commercial interest—This prospect is heightened in the Third Circuit by the consideration of the great talents, integrity and legal erudition of the gentlemen who at present occupy the seats of the Judges—

With proper deference and respect, therefore, the subscribers submit their opinion, that the present organisation of the courts of the United States, is highly beneficial in the administration of justice, and that its abolition will be of much public detriment—

If however the Government should deem it expedient to repeal the Law in relation to the general establishment, the Subscribers submit as their prayer, that it may be preserved as far as it respects the courts of the Third Circuit—Extensively connected as they are by foreign as well as domestic commercial relations, it is of high importance that a Court should some where subsist, the organisation and jurisdiction of which should be competent to the speedy and uniform decision of questions which those relations produce—   That object could not be attained under the former establishment of the Courts of the United States, and is rendered equally impracticable in the State Courts of Pennsylvania, from the great press of business already in those Courts—Besides occupied as the attention of the Circuit Court of the United States in this District principally is, by subjects of a Commercial nature, much greater opportunity is afforded them of digesting and maturing a system of general commercial Law than can possibly occur to the State Courts—A Court established upon these principles, the Subscribers conceive to be essentially necessary to secure the confidence of the Commercial interest abroad, and the want of such a Court will be of great injury to the trading part of the Community—

It may not be improper further to remark, that the extensive jurisdiction of the District Court, must in a great commercial city, draw before it such a degree of business, as to require almost the whole time and attention of the Judge who presides in it, and would allow him but little opportunity for attendance upon the Circuit Court, of which under the former establishment, he was a component part—Such is the fact in the District of Pennsylvania; and as the business of that

Court has become important, and is increasing, it is requisite that the Court of higher jurisdiction which is to review its decisions should possess sufficient insight to settle in ordinary cases, the principle which is litigated—But as appeals from the District Court, if reviewed in the Circuit Court under the former establishment, must have been heard and decided by a single Judge, the object contemplated by the appeal could not be obtained, and it became necessary to carry the cause to the Supreme Court of the United States, to the great delay of justice and expence of the parties— THOS. FITZSIMONS
and 224 other signatures

RC (DNA: RG 233, PMRSL, 7th Cong., 1st sess.); undated; at head of text: "To the President, the Senate & House of Representatives of the United States"; endorsed in a clerk's hand: "Representation of sundry Merchants and traders of the City of Philadelphia. 16 February 1802 referred to the committee of the whole House, to whom committed, on the 4th instant, the bill sent from the Senate, intituled 'An Act to repeal certain acts respecting the organization of the courts of the United States; and for other purposes.'" RC (DNA: RG 46, LPPMRSL); endorsed by a clerk. Recorded in SJL as received 17 Feb. with notation "Memorial on Judiciary Law."

Copies of the above memorial from the MERCHANTS AND TRADERS OF THE CITY OF PHILADELPHIA were sent to the Senate, the House of Representatives, and TJ. Both the Senate and the House received it on 16 Feb. The Senate tabled the memorial, while the House referred it to the committee appointed to consider the repeal of the Judiciary Act (JS, 3:182; JHR, 4:100).

REPEAL OF THE LAW: on 4 Feb., the House of Representatives took up the bill to abolish the Judiciary Act of 1801 that the Senate had passed the previous day. Federalists attempted to delay its consideration as long as possible, but the whole House began debating the bill on 15 Feb. On 3 Mch., after more than two weeks of extensive debates and further efforts to delay the vote, the House passed the bill by a 59 to 32 vote (*Annals*, 11:476-81, 510-22, 981-2; JHR, 4:84, 98-100, 118-20; JS, 3:177).

From Albert Gallatin

SIR   Treasury Department Feby. 16th. 1802

I have the Honor to enclose two Statements in relation to the marine Hospitals.—

The Statement A exhibits the balances remaining unexpended[1] in the hands of the several Collectors and Agents on the 30th. September last, or on the last day to which Returns have been receiv'd.—

The Statement B exhibits the total Amount receiv'd in each State, and expended by each Hospital from the Commencement of the Institution to the same day.—

The only ports where Hospitals have been establish'd or temporary relief afforded to the Seamen, are,—

1st. Boston, Newport, Norfolk and Charleston-South Carolina, where marine Hospitals have been, altogether established under the Laws of Congress, exclusively appropriated to the use of Seamen, and solely supported out of the funds, rais'd under the Authority of the United States.—The Hospital at Newport has lately been discontinued.—

2d. Baltimore, where the Hospital is in the same Situation as to it's funds, but is plac'd under the Controul of the board of Health.—

3d. New-York & Philadelphia, where sick Seamen are receiv'd in the City Hospital, at a fixed rate per week, paid out of the marine Hospital fund.—

4th. Portland, New London, Wilmington-North Carolina, Newbern, Edenton, and lately Newport and Alexandria, where temporary relief is afforded in private boarding Houses.—

5th. Savannah, from which no returns have been receiv'd.—

By the Statement B it appears that the whole sum receiv'd from Seamen, either in private or in public Service, amounts to 147,875. dollars and 58 cents, of which 6,185 $\frac{33}{100}$, have been applied to the purchase of the Hospital at Gosport near Norfolk, and 74,636 $\frac{51}{100}$, have been expended for the relief of sick Seamen; that 73,761 $\frac{61}{100}$, remain unexpended, in the hands of sundry Collectors, and Agents, and that 6,707 $\frac{87}{100}$, are due to certain Agents, who have expended more than has been receiv'd by them.—

This last circumstance has taken place in Newport Norfolk and Charleston, namely in three of the four marine Hospitals, which have been established: and it will be perceiv'd by a recurrence to the same statement, that to those three places, the Navy fund has been exclusively applied.—but this last fund being nearly exhausted, it is impracticable to continue any longer, the established Hospitals at Norfolk & Charleston, unless Congress shall think proper to grant them some aid, or to make such Alterations in the Law, as will permit a more general application of the fund.—

Under existing Circumstances, if no alteration shall be made, it will be necessary to write to the Collectors of both places, to discontinue *in toto*, the Hospitals, after the 31st. March next. For the advances made by them, must, by this time, exceed twelve Thousand dollars; these have been paid out of the proceeds of the duties on Import and Tonnage, and cannot be admitted to their credit; in their accounts as Collectors.—It will be necessary for them to continue to collect the Seaman-money, until they shall have been fully reimbursed for their advances.—

If it be asked why the funds have proven insufficient in those two places, the following reasons, it is believ'd, may be assign'd—1st. the Establishment of an Hospital; instead of having had recourse to City or State Institutions, as in Philadelphia and New York; which has drawn with it all the Expences of Superintendence attending Physicians &a. For what reason the Gosport Hospital was purchas'd from the State of Virginia, I am at a loss to know, but if it was intended for the Navy it shou'd be supported out of the funds appropriated for that Department and plac'd under its Controul.—The Building is much too large and in an unfinished State; and wants immediate and expensive Repairs.—2dly. Those two Seaports are more expensive and generally so far especially, as relates to non Residents more sickly than the more northern ports.—3dly. The provision of the Law which makes Seamen on board coasting vessels pay only in the port to which they belong is unjust in its operation and bears more particularly on the Southern Ports.—

It is necessary to state that Complaints are frequently receiv'd from those ports, where no relief has yet been granted; the Seamen complaining that they pay without deriving any benefit from it.—This may be true in some instances; but it is doubtful, whether the application of the funds, in such manner that they might find relief in all the important ports of the Union in case of Sickness,[2] may not be more beneficial to them, than a provision in the ports where they reside, and where they want it least.—

Whilst the Expenditure of the money, is restricted to the port or State, where it is collected, it cannot be consider'd in any other light, than as a Muncipal Establishment, and wou'd, more conveniently be plac'd, under the Controul of the State itself.—

I have the Honor to be very respectfully, Sir! Your Obt Servant.

ALBERT GALLATIN

RC (DNA: RG 233, PM, 7th Cong., 1st sess.); in a clerk's hand, signed and dated by Gallatin; addressed in Gallatin's hand: "The President of the United States"; endorsed by a House clerk. RC (DNA: RG 46, LPPM, 7th Cong., 1st sess.); in a clerk's hand, signed by Gallatin; addressed in Gallatin's hand: "The President of the United States"; endorsed by a Senate clerk. Enclosures: (1) Statement A, entitled "A Statement of Monies remaining in the Hands of Collector's & Agents, received by them for support of the Marine Hospitals established in the United States for the Relief of sick and disabled Seamen, up to the 30th. of September 1801, or so far as Returns have been received" (MS in DNA: RG 233, PM, arranged in tabular form by states, except for Palmyra and Detroit, the last two ports on the list, in a clerk's hand, endorsed by a House clerk; MS in DNA: RG 46, LPPM, in a clerk's hand, endorsed by a Senate clerk). (2) Statement B, entitled "Statement of the Marine Hospital Fund, from its Establishment to 30th. Septemr. 1801: taken from the Agents Accounts," with a total for the Hospital Fund of $141,690.25, plus $6,185.33 advanced by the Navy Department for the purchase of Gosport hospital and $6,707.87 due to agents, for a grand total of $154,583.45 (MS in DNA: RG 233, PM, arranged in tabular form by states, the final entry being "Tennessee & Detroit," in a clerk's hand, with the emendation "no hospital" in Gallatin's hand under the "Expenditures" column for New Hampshire, New Jersey, Delaware, and "Tennessee & Detroit," endorsed by a House clerk; MS in DNA: RG 46, LPPM, in a clerk's hand, incorporating the emendations from the MS in RG 233, endorsed by a Senate clerk). Transmitted to Congress with TJ's message of 24 Feb. and printed in ASP, *Commerce and Navigation*, 1:490-4.

For Gallatin's earlier assessment and statement on the MARINE HOSPITALS and an account of their establishment under the LAWS OF CONGRESS, see Vol. 34:678-81.

GOSPORT HOSPITAL: for a description of the repairs needed at the Norfolk facility, see Vol. 34:681-2.

According to Section 2 of "An Act for the relief of sick and disabled Seamen" of 16 July 1798, masters of COASTING VESSELS were to pay 20 cents per month per seaman to the collector at the port where the ship was licensed or enrolled (U.S. Statutes at Large, 1:605-6).

[1] RC in RG 46: "unexpected."
[2] RC in RG 46 lacks preceding four words.

To the Senate and the House of Representatives

GENTLEMEN OF THE SENATE, AND
OF THE HOUSE OF REPRESENTATIVES

I now transmit a statement of the expences incurred by the US. in their transactions with the the Barbary powers, and a Roll of the persons having office or employment under the US. as was proposed in my messages of December the 7th. and 22d.   neither is as perfect as could have been wished; and the latter not so much so as further time & enquiry may enable us to make it.

The great volume of these communications, and the delay it would produce to make out a second copy, will I trust be deemed a sufficient reason for sending one of them to the one house, and the other to the other, with a request that they may be interchanged for mutual information, rather than to subject both to further delay.

TH: JEFFERSON
Feb. 16. 1802.

PrC (DLC); presumably pressed from RC to the Senate (not found). RC (DNA: RG 233, PM, 7th Cong., 1st sess.); in Meriwether Lewis's hand, signed and dated by TJ. Recorded in SJL with notation "exp. with Barbary." Enclosures: Gallatin to TJ, 12 Feb., and enclosure. For other enclosures, see below.

Meriwether Lewis delivered TJ's message and accompanying documents to Congress on 17 Feb. The House of Representatives read the communication on that date and the Senate on 18 Feb. (JHR, 4:102; JS, 3:182). The documents relating to U.S. expenditures for the BARBARY POWERS remained with the House of

Representatives and the ROLL OF THE PERSONS HAVING OFFICE OR EMPLOYMENT in the U.S. government remained with the Senate. All of the documents relating to the Barbary expenditures were printed by order of the House as a *Message from the President of the United States, Transmitting Sundry Documents Relative to the Transactions of the United States with the Barbary Powers* (see Shaw-Shoemaker, No. 3363). Instead of arranging the enclosures as directed by Gallatin (see Enclosure No. 2, printed below), the printer placed Statement AA, the sketch of expenditures, first, followed by the general statement of appropriations and the other statements in alphabetical order, A through Z. William Duane, by order of the Senate, published *Message from the President of United States, Transmitting a Roll of the Persons having Office or Employment under the United States*, a pamphlet of over 150 pages (see Sowerby, No. 4166; Shaw-Shoemaker, No. 3360).

ENCLOSURES

I

From James Madison

Department of State:—
16 Feby. 1802.

SIR

I have the honor to enclose a letter from the Secretary of the Treasury to me, together with the documents accompanying it, containing an account of the monies drawn out of the Treasury under the several appropriations made for defraying the expenses incident to the intercourse with the Mediterranean powers, and statements of the credits obtained or claimed at the Treasury by the persons to whom they were advanced.

It would have been very desireable to separate the whole amount expended into the several subordinate heads of expense, intimated in the close of the Secretary's letter: but apprized of your wish to communicate, as soon as possible, such information as that letter affords, I forbear to detain it, especially as an opinion of the present[1] scantiness of materials to effect the separation referred to, does not encourage the hope of its being rendered perfect.

with the highest respect, I have the honor to be, Sir, your most obed. servt.

JAMES MADISON

RC (DNA: RG 233, PM); in Jacob Wagner's hand, signed by Madison; at foot of text: "The President of the United States"; endorsed by a House clerk.

[1] Word interlined, probably by Madison.

II

Albert Gallatin to James Madison

Treasury Department
Jany. 30th. 1802.

SIR,

In compliance with your request, I have the Honor to enclose an account of the monies drawn out of the Treasury under the several Appropriations made for defraying the expences incident to the Intercourse with the Mediterranean Powers; transcripts of the accounts of persons to whom the said monies were respectively advanc'd so far as the same have been settled at the Treasury, and statements of the Credits not yet ultimately admitted, but claim'd on account of such expences, so far as the same can be ascertain'd from the accounts render'd though not yet definitively settled by the accounting Officers of this Department.

The greater part of the Accounts being yet unsettled, and several of the most important not having yet been render'd, it is not practicable to state with precision, in what manner the whole of the sums drawn out of the Treasury has been ultimately applied.

It is however believ'd that the annexed Sketch (AA) will prove sufficiently correct to show, without material error, the gross amount actually expended.

The sums drawn out of the Treasury amount, including Dollars 5,083.30, reimburs'd to C. Colville & others for their Ransom

to   2,011,998.65.

Mr. I. Whelen Purveyor of Supplies has expended beyond the sum for which he is already debited in the Treausury Books, being principally for Timber and supplies receiv'd from the Navy Department 47,330.46.

making an aggregate amount of   2,059,329.11[1]

On the other hand it appears that two Items, making part of the sums drawn out of the Treasury, ought to be deducted from that gross Amount, the same not having been applied to the Object, for which they had thus been drawn.

1st. The amount advanc'd to Mr Francis late purveyor of Supplies on account of Mediterranean Powers, is   Dollars   288,782.12

The amount of credits claimd by him, on that account, is only   274,262.83

leaving a Surplus, not applied to that Object, of   14,519.29

2dly. The account render'd by Mr Pickering, late Secretary of State, is general and denotes only the persons to whom the public monies, drawn by him were advanc'd, without particularizing the Objects for which said Monies were advanc'd; which renders it impossible until those persons shall have settled their Accounts, to ascertain with precision, the credits to which He may be entitled under each distinct Object of Expenditure, respectively.

Mr. Kimbal, late Clerk in your Department has however at the request of the Comptroller drawn the Sketch of a particular Account showing the purpose for which the monies were respectively advanc'd.

The amount which he states to have been advanc'd by Mr Pickering to sundry persons in relation to Algiers and other mediterranean Powers is

310,466.17

To which shou'd be added, not being included in that Statemt.—

Amount of an Account now before the Comptroller 5,342.15.

and paid by Mr. Humphreys to J. Burnham for his Ransom being part of the monies charg'd to Mr Pickering 2,000.

making altogether   317,808.32

The Amount for which Mr. Pickering remains charg'd in the Treasury Books under that head is   Dollars   352,736.74

leaving a difference, if Mr. Kimbel's Statement shall prove
correct, applied to other Objects of 34,928.42
which sum added to the preceding Item of 14,519.29
makes the sum drawn out of the Treasury under the
appropriations for mediterranean powers but not applied
to that object 49,447.71
which sum deducted from the above shared gross amount of 2,059,329.11
leaves for the apparent sum, actually applied to that Object
as per Statement (AA) 2,009,881.40.
If to this sum shall be added the Expenditures on
account of the Voyage of the Ship George Washington
to Algiers in 1800, which have been defray'd by the
Navy Department and are stated at 36,255.82
The total Amount of real Expenditures will be Drs. 2,046,137.22
exclusively of sundry Expences incurr'd but not yet paid during the course of
last year.

It must be repeated, that altho this is probably an accurate Account of the
gross sums disbursed by the United States, the Documents in the Treasury
Department by no means, show the ultimate Application of the money but
only the names of the Individuals, who remain accountable

The account render'd by Mr Donaldson of which an Abstract (Z) is en-
closd is as far as has been ascertain'd the only one in the Department not alluded to in the Sketch (AA) which can throw any additional Light on the
Subject.

The Accounts when ultimately render'd and settled shou'd exhibit the
amount paid, in order to obtain Treaties, to each of the Barbary Powers;
the Amount lost by the various Remittances in Stock or bills of Exchange;
the Amount paid for the Annuity due to Algiers; and the Amount paid to
those several States as Presents or extorted at different times under various
Pretences.—It is presumable that there may be in the Department of State,
Information which, combind with the Accounts now enclos'd, wou'd assist,
even at present, in drawing a sketch of that kind.—

I have the Honor, to be very respectfully Sir, your Obt Servant,
ALBERT GALLATIN

List of Accounts &a. enclos'd.

General Statement of Appropriations
Particular Accounts of monies advanc'd to Individuals,
including the Amounts respectively accounted for and
settled at the Treasury A to P
Summary general Statement of Monies advanc'd
Explanatory Observations on the preceding Accounts
Accounts of monies re-imburs'd to sundry persons for
 their Ransoms R
Abstract of a particular Account render'd not yet passed T.
The above furnished by the Register.

Statements of credits claimd by sundry persons as furnish'd
by the Auditor S.V.W

Abstract of credits claimd by Mr Pickering furnishd
by Mr Kimbel   U

General Sketch of monies and Expenditures including
all the preceding Accounts prepar'd by the Secretary   AA

Abstracts of Expenditures of Ship George Washington
furnishd by Navy Department   Y

Abstract of Mr Donaldsons account furnished by the Auditor   Z

RC (DNA: RG 233, PM); in a clerk's hand, signed by Gallatin; at foot of text: "The Secretary of State"; list of enclosed accounts written on separate sheet; endorsed by a House clerk. Enclosures: (1) "Statement of all the sums Appropriated by law for carrying into effect Negotiations between the Mediterranean Powers and the United States, from the commencement of the present Government," with appropriations totaling $2,205,917.03, and expenditures to 30 Sep. 1801, totaling $2,006,315.35, followed by Statements A to P, particular accounts of monies advanced to individuals, beginning with an expenditure of $13,000 by TJ, as secretary of state in May 1791, "for effecting a recognition of the treaty with the Emperor of Morocco" (A) and followed by the accounts of Edmund Randolph (B), Timothy Pickering (D), John Marshall (N), and James Madison (O) as secretaries of state; Tench Francis (C) and Israel Whelen (M) as purveyor of public supplies; Samuel Meredith (G), Willing & Francis (I), and George Simpson (P), agents for the purchase of bills of exchange; James Hackett (E), Elisha and James Hill (F), Samuel Meeker for Matthew Irwin (H), and Jacob Sheaffe (K), contractors for building frigates; and William Eaton (L), consul at Tunis; and concluding with a summary table of Statements A to P, "showing that application of said moneys" totaled $13,000 for the emperor of Morocco, $258,846.58 for the dey of Algiers, and $1,734,468.77 for Mediterranean powers, for an overall amount of $2,006,315.35 (MS in same; in various clerks' hands; with several notations, perhaps in pencil, in an unidentified hand at unsettled accounts, including the phrase "before the auditor"; endorsed by Gallatin: "Register's accounts A to P"; endorsed by a House clerk). (2) Register's "Schedule of Appropriations by Law, and of Expenditures by Warrants in relation to the Mediterranean Powers," 22 Nov. 1801, summarizing the appropriations and expenditures stated in the previous enclosure, noting a balance of appropriations available as of 30 Sep. 1801 of $199,601.68, including $37,400.05 for the treaty with Algiers and $162,201.63 for Mediterranean powers (MS in same; in a clerk's hand, signed by Joseph Nourse; endorsed by Gallatin: "Register's Summary observations"). (3) "Statement of Reimbursements of certain sums advanced by the following Individuals for their Ransom from Captivity in Algiers," including $2,269.53 for Charles Colvill; $2,270.64 for John Robertson; $2,269.53 for John Burnham (Bwinham); and $873.60 for George Smith, for a total of $7,683.30 (MS in same; dated 26 Jan. 1802; in a clerk's hand, signed by Nourse; endorsed as "R"; endorsed by a House clerk). (4) Abstract of Timothy Pickering's account "in relation to Treaties with Mediterranean Powers," with the balance stated by the register to be $352,736.74 and the balance stated by the auditor to be $347,394.59, with an explanation for the discrepancy of $5,342.15 (MS in same; dated 26 Jan. 1802; in a clerk's hand, signed by Nourse; endorsed as "T"; endorsed by a House clerk). (5) In two parts, No. 1 consisting of two sketches of accounts with John and Francis Baring, the first from 13 Nov. 1795 to 1 Aug. 1797, the second from 12 Dec. 1797 to 22 Feb. 1799; No. 2 consisting of an "Abstract of certain Bills purchased by the Treasurer for remittances to Europe, on account of negotiations with the Mediterranean Powers, and charged to General account of remittances," totaling $99,911.80, and a second table citing Timothy Pickering's claim for bills remitted by him to John & Francis Baring, totaling $118,459.96 (MS in same; in several hands; endorsed "S" and "No 1 & 2"; with separate endorsements on No. 1 and No. 2, the first: "Jno. & Fras. Baring—Acct. Currt.," the second: "Bills remitted by the Treasurer and by T. Pickering" and, in another hand, "This statement is connected with the Acct. Curt. of J. & F. Baring"; endorsed by a House clerk). (6) "Abstract of Credits claimed by Tench Francis late Purveyor of Public Supplies under the Head of Treaties with the Mediterranean Powers Extracted from a General Account Current rendered to the Treasury by his Representatives," 2 Sep. 1797 to 26 Nov. 1800, for credits totaling $274,262.83 (MS in same; in a clerk's hand; endorsed by a clerk, in part, "V" and "No. 3" ; endorsed by a House clerk). (7) "Abstract of Credits claimed by Israel Whelen Purveyor of Public Supplies under the Head of the Barbary Powers extracted from Accounts rendered to the Treasury," in 1800, with 10 entries, for a total of $199,796.69 (MS in same; in a clerk's hand; endorsed "W" and "No 4"; endorsed by a House clerk). (8) "Credits claimed by Mr. Pickering, as pr. account of Kimball, exclusively of Sums paid to the Barings," for a total of $192,006.21, the largest sum being to Richard O'Brien for $180,000 (MS in same; with a note on verso in Gallatin's hand: "Amount pr preceding statement Drs. 192 006.21 Dr. advanced to & acknowledged by J. & F. Baring—118,459.96 Total amount of credits claimed, under this head, by acct. rendered by   Kimbal} 310,466.17"; endorsed as "U"; also endorsed by Gallatin: "Abstract of credits claimed by Timothy Pickering late Secretary of State under the Head of 'Mediterranean powers' as pr account stated by   Kimball late clerk in the Departmt. of State"; endorsed by a House clerk). (9) "Sketch of the Expenditures incident to the in-

tercourse with Mediterranean Powers," being a summary of the enclosures above, with the total withdrawn "per Register's account" of $2,006,315.35, to which was added the ransoms and recent expenses of Israel Whelen for a total of $2,059,329.11; in the credit column Gallatin notes that the total sum includes $49,447.71 in monies "Drawn out of the Treasury, but applied to other purposes, vizt.," $34,928.42 by Pickering and $14,519.29 by Francis, and when those sums were subtracted the total actually expended amounted to $2,009,881.40 (MS in same; in a clerk's hand; endorsed: "General sketch [AA]"; endorsed by a House clerk). (10) "Abstract of Expenditures for and on account of the George Washington, for the Voyage to algiers, in 1800," Navy Department, Accountant's Office, 14 Dec. 1801, noting expenditures totaling $36,255.82 (MS in same; in a clerk's hand, signed by Thomas Turner, accountant; endorsed as "Y"; endorsed by a House clerk). (11) "Joseph Donaldson Jr. Sketch of his accot. Current" from 14 June 1795 to 6 Apr. 1796 and from 6 Apr. to 31 Dec. 1796, noting connections to the accounts of John and Francis Baring, Timothy Pickering, and Thomas Pinckney, for a total expenditure of $415,975.44, including $7,717.41, the balance due Donaldson (MS in same, in a clerk's hand; endorsed as "Z"; also endorsed, in Gallatin's hand: "Donaldson's account"; endorsed by a House clerk). All printed in ASP, *Foreign Relations*, 2:368-81.

ANNEXED SKETCH (AA): see Enclosure No. 9, listed above.

C. COLVILLE & OTHERS: see Enclosure No. 3, listed above. Charles Logie, the British consul at Algiers, secured the freedom of Charles Colvill and John Robertson in 1790 and 1791, respectively, with private funds. In 1794, private donations were used to free George Smith, captured in 1785. The relatives of Captain John Burnham (Bwinham), captured in 1793, raised funds for his ransom the following year (Gary E. Wilson, "American Hostages in Moslem Nations, 1784-1796: The Public Response," *Journal of the*

Early Republic, 2 [1982], 128, 133; Vol. 18:399-400).

On 14 Nov. 1801, Hazen Kimball (KIM-BAL), the clerk who kept the accounts at the State Department, resigned (Vol. 33:512-3).

[1] MS: "2,059,320.11."

From Louis Thomas Villaret de Joyeuse

MONSIEUR LE PRÉSIDENT.   [16 Feb. 1802]

Votre excellence doit avoir été prevenu par le chargé d'affaires de la République française, que son Armée Navale était entrée dans les ports de St. Domingue. Le Gouvernement a voulu mettre un terme aux troubles civils et aux longues Calamités qui désolaient cette Colonie. Des forces considérables, un Capitaine général précédé par une réputation méritée de justice et d'humanité, Beau frere du premier Consul et longtemps distingué à la tète de nos armées; une administration entière, dont tous les membres sont connus par leurs lumieres et leur intégrité, tels étaient les bienfaits que la france envoyait à St. Domingue. Des Rebelles les ont accueillis par le feu et l'incendie; et la ville du Cap, à peine rebatie, a été de nouveau réduite en cendres par des Negres révoltés, qui n'ont pu fermer aux Vaisseaux de la république une rade qui lui appartient.

En annonçant ces évenemens à votre excellence, je crois [juste] de réclamer d'elle et du gouvernement Américain, les services [que] tous les peuples civilisés [se] doivent en pareille occasion. Je suis profondément convaincu que le premier et le plus fidele Allié des Etats unis, trouvera toujours leurs ports ouverts à ses flottes et à ses besoins. Je crois aussi fermement que l'interêt aveugle de quelques particuliers, se taira devant l'interét général des nations, et qu'aucun navire Américain n'apportera désormais des Armes, des vivres ou des munitions dans les ports occupés par les rebelles de St. Domingue, [cette] Colonie étant déclarée en état de siege.

De mon côté, Monsieur le Président, j'apporterai [les] soins les plus empressés à faire respecter le commerce li[bre] de vos Concitoyens, dans toutes les rades soumises à l'[armée] Navale de la République. Je me plais à vous en [donner] l'assurance en vous prians d'agréer mon respect.   VILLARET

MISTER PRESIDENT.   [16 Feb. 1802]

Your excellency must have been informed by the chargé d'affaires of the French Republic that its navy had entered the ports of Saint-Domingue. The government wanted to put an end to the civil unrest and continual catastrophes which have afflicted this colony. Sizable forces, a general with a deserved reputation for justice and humaneness—the first consul's brother-in-law, who has long distinguished himself at the head of our armed forces—and an administrative corps whose members are all known for their enlightenment and integrity: such were the blessings that France sent to Saint-Domingue. Rebels welcomed them with fire and conflagration; and the hardly rebuilt town of Cap-Français was again reduced to ashes by rebelling negroes who were unable to close off to the republic's vessels a harbor that belongs to her.

By informing your excellency of these events, I feel justified in requesting from you and the American government the services that all civilized people must render to one another in such circumstances. I am deeply convinced that the first and most faithful ally of the United States will always find its ports open to her ships and other needs. I also firmly believe that the blind interests of a few individuals will cede to the general interest of nations, and that from now on no American ship will bring arms, supplies, or ammunition to ports occupied by the Saint-Domingue rebels, this colony being acknowledged as under siege.

For my part, Mister President, I shall be most assiduous in insuring that the free trade of your fellow citizens is respected in all harbors that are controlled by the republic's navy. I am pleased to give you this assurance, and beg you to accept my respect.   VILLARET

RC (DNA: RG 59, NL); in a clerk's hand, signed by Villaret; text obscured by binding; at head of text, on printed letterhead with blanks filled by clerk: "En rade du Cap français A bord du vaisseau amiral l'Océan, le 27 Pluviose an 10 de la République. L'Amiral Villaret-Joyeuse. Au President des Etats Unis" ("in the harbor of Cap-Français aboard the flagship *l'Ocean*, 27 Pluviôse Year 10 of the Republic. Admiral Villaret Joyeuse to the president of the United States"); English date supplied. Recorded in SJL as received 16 Mch. 1802 with notation "S."

Louis Thomas Villaret de Joyeuse (1748-1812) joined the French navy as a volunteer in 1765. He became a rear admiral in 1793 and a vice admiral the following year. He commanded the flotilla for the expeditionary force sent to Saint-Domingue in 1801 and was captain general of Martinique and St. Lucia from April 1802 until 1809. He served as governor general of Venice, 1811-12 (Tulard, *Dictionnaire Napoléon*, 1725).

ARMÉE NAVALE ÉTAIT ENTRÉE DANS LES PORTS DE ST. DOMINGUE: the French expeditionary force under General Victoire Emmanuel Leclerc arrived at Saint-Domingue in late January and soon after commenced landing troops at the island's major port towns. Arriving off Cap-Français on 2 Feb., Leclerc sent a message from Bonaparte to the port's commander, Henri Christophe, which assured the island's inhabitants that they were Frenchmen and "all free and equal before God and the Republic." Bonaparte urged them to rally around Leclerc, but warned that those who did not would be destroyed "as the fire destroys your withered canes." Leclerc likewise promised that the liberty of the island's black inhabitants would be protected and declared that doubting such assurances would be deemed "criminal." Christophe, however, refused to surrender, and on 4 Feb. set fire to the town, which was largely destroyed by the ensuing conflagration. The port suffered a similar fate in 1793 near the start of the Haitian revolution (Laurent Dubois, *Avengers of the New World: The Story of the Haitian Revolution* [Cambridge, Mass., 2004], 157-9, 262-5; Madison, *Papers, Sec. of State Ser.*, 2:462-4, 499-504; *National Intelligencer*, 10 Mch. 1802).

LE PREMIER ET LE PLUS FIDELE ALLIÉ DES ETATS UNIS: Louis André Pichon had previously informed Bonaparte and Talleyrand that the United States favored the suppression of Toussaint's regime and would supply a French expedition to Saint-Domingue with provisions and other necessary supplies (Vol. 35:398n).

ÉTAT DE SIEGE: on 17 Feb. (28 Pluviôse), Leclerc declared a blockade of Saint-Domingue that allowed foreign vessels to enter only the ports of Cap-Français and Port-au-Prince. Vessels caught violating the blockade would be taken to these ports, where their cargo would be examined. Any arms or munitions found were to be confiscated. On 18 Mch., Pichon issued a proclamation reiterating the terms of the French blockade, adding that American trade with Cap-Français and Port-au-Prince remained open. Pichon advised, however, that merchants trading with the colony obtain certificates from French commissaries and commercial agents in America to ensure that their commerce met with "no interruption by incurring suspicion of improper conduct" (*National Intelligencer*, 19, 26 Mch. 1802).

From Tench Coxe

SIR   Phila. Feb. 17. 1802.

When your message to the legislature announced the idea of the abolition of the internal revenues, I presumed that it was after such examination of the subject as would give rise to the same idea among the members of Congress. I expected therefore the abolition of the little office on which all my income depends. I find from communications from several of the members, and the debates of the Representatives, that the measure is understood to have the support of a Majority of each house. I do myself the honor therefore to represent to you my situation.

When I was removed from my office, I found myself without any business or other means of commanding an income. My family was large and has been since increased to ten children. My property was not inconsiderable, but I had some pecuniary engagements. My expences were unavoidably not small, and since the office I held was at 2400 & then at 3000 Drs. ℔ annum, it may be supposed, I certainly became drained of money after Decr. 1797, by expences which that salary used to pay. From a confidence in my country and a desire to avoid business that would have abstracted me from my public duties & pursuits, I had turned all my property into new Lands, from which I could draw no income, and which I have been unable to sell at any price. They engaged none of my time in office, and promised a foundation for my large family. To procure a subsistence for my wife & children I have been forced to resort to the sales of my library, my most valuable, and by degrees very convenient furniture. Deducting the sacrifices of my removals to & from Lancaster, I drew about 1500 Dollars in 17 months from my Pennsa. office. With the sacrifice of the time & education of one of my sons, I could make that office produce £600. But that I have no chance or right to expect again. If I lose my present office, I must encounter real and deep distress, unless I should succeed in sales of property, and live upon my principal. My economy is and has been rigid. I do not hesitate to say confidentially that used as I have been to a liberal plain table, I have not a decanter of wine in my house. I could not think of luxuries, while I was unable to provide comforts for a tender family. I will not touch upon my claims, I only beg leave, in the most sacred confidence, to explain to you my reasons for the applications with which I have heretofore troubled you. In point of income I have been a straightened and often a distressed man in the hours which called for my utmost firmness from 1797 to 1801. If I am to lose my present lowly office, I must sustain deep distress till I can sell property for bread. I have never advised against the repeal. I have on the contrary explained & justified it, as I neither wish nor expect a continuance of an office for me, which ought otherwise to be abolished.

I know well that infinite devices have been used in procuring offices from you and from the Governor of Pennsa.—I have rested in both cases upon the knowledge of me that existed. Refraining from recommendations and interpositions with you and with him, I know that I have sustained indirect operations upon my pretentions of the most unkind, and antirepublican cast. The two persons who have done vast mischief to the Republican interest particularly one of them, is, I believe, better understood and happy is it for our cause that little injury to it can arise for a year or two from that quarter. I have however refrained from quarrels or complaints upon the Subject, and shall continue to do so, rejoicing[1] however that events, in relation to this matter, have occured to render any future abuse of your confidence, in the quarter, I allude to, less probable than heretofore—

Considering, as I most solemnly do, that the success of your administration has become, to appearance, necessary to the safety of our country & form of Government, you will not doubt my most ardent prayers for the protection of divine providence in the arduous duties of your station—

I have the honor to be yr. most respectful Servant

TENCH COXE

RC (DNA: RG 59, LAR); below signature: "private"; endorsed by TJ as received 20 Feb. and so recorded in SJL.

The DEBATES OF THE REPRESENTATIVES on the abolition of internal taxes began on 31 Dec. On 25 Jan., the House defeated by a 37 to 57 vote James A. Bayard's resolution to delay drawing a bill until the Treasury secretary gave a detailed account "of the expenses incurred in the collection of the internal revenues" and advised on how expenses could be reduced. On 15 Mch., the House began debating the bill brought in by the Committee of Ways and Means a week earlier. The legislation passed the House on 22 Mch. by a 61 to 24 vote and the Senate, with amendments, on 31 Mch. by 15 to 11. On 2 Apr. the House agreed to the Senate amendments. TJ signed "An Act to repeal the Internal Taxes" on 6 Apr. (*Annals*, 11:354-61, 447-58; JHR, 4:123-4, 138, 153-4, 175; JS, 3:196-8, 200-1; U.S. Statutes at Large, 2:148-50).

REMOVED FROM MY OFFICE: President Adams authorized the removal of Coxe as commissioner of the revenue in December 1797 (Cooke, *Coxe*, 307). ONE OF MY SONS: Tench Coxe, Jr., served as a clerk in the Pennsylvania Land Office (same, 364).

¹ MS: "rejoicing."

From Nicholas Reib

Philada. Feby 17th 1802

The subscriber wishes you profound health and that you may live long to the Service and as an Ornament to your Country—Your Administration being vested in Wisdom Justice & Philantropy and knowing that you are no Respecter of Person, and that truth & Justice is your Motto, he therefore trusts you will favour him in perusing and paying due Attention to these few lines.—On the 11th of Febuary 1778, An act was Passed in & by the Congress of the US. allowing each and every Artificer or Mechanic 20 Dollars pr Month besides bounty Clothing & Backration of which you will find a Copy thereof—My Account will show Clearly & Evident what my Claims to the US. are, and what I have Received in part. My Demand where $474.67. and that of my Sons $314.67.—In the Year 1782 I obtained a Certificate from the war office for $135.—In which the time of Payment was not Mentioned this Certificate the Assembly of Pennsylvania took up and Returned another in lieu thereof. after some time they annulled the same said Certificate. that the Brokers where advised to pay no more than 2/6 in a pound. as I could not Expect more than others I was under the necessity of taking $\frac{70}{100}$ pr Month Instead of 20 Dollars.—I Received a Certificate in the year 1794 for my son of which you have also a Copy by that I was Entitled to $9.30. pr month upon which I lost $30. I also employed a man during the war in my stead who I paid 20 Dollars bounty in the presence of Cap Sholten for which I have never Received a cent State Bounty.— In Consequence of which I have frequently presented Petitions until

March in the year 1794, when my whole Demand was approved & Recognised by Congress that I should Receive all that is Remaining unpaid, that is to say Months pay Bounty & Board. the Backration was Struck out which the Pennsylvania Legislature is to make good. the Approbation of my Demands you will find in the Journals of 1794. I pray you to forward me a Copy of the above aforesaid act. I could write a whole Volume of the Impropriety of Detaining the money so long. My son and myself have often been Requested to work at the Shoe making business in the Manufactory and that that was promised us, you can also observe in the Journals when we Left the Business.—I hope & pray you will gratify me with an Answer to this Address.—I am

Sir, Your Very Humble Servt.   Nicholas Reib

RC (DLC); in an unknown hand, signed by Reib; addressed: "His Excellency Thomas Jefferson President of the United States Washington Virginia"; endorsed by TJ as received 22 Feb. and so recorded in SJL. Enclosures not found, but see below.

Philadelphia cordwainer Nicholas Reib enlisted in Colonel Benjamin Flower's corps of artillery artificers in May 1780. Despite his advanced age and infirmities, he served until March 1782, when he employed another to serve in his place. Reib presented his first claim for back pay to Congress in May 1782, and petitioned repeatedly for the settlement or resettlement of his account until 1800 (Reib to Congress, 3 and 15 May 1782, in DNA: RG 360, PCC; JHR, 1:464-5, 658; 2:26, 447-8; 3:662, 698).

AN ACT WAS PASSED IN & BY THE CON-GRESS: a resolution by Congress of 11 Feb. 1778 allowed artificers in Flower's regiment to receive $20 per month, plus the same bounty, clothing, and benefits granted to the Continental artillery. On 19 Dec. 1782, however, this payment was reduced to $12 per month and Congress ordered that all unsettled accounts up to 31 Dec. 1781 be settled for pay and depreciation from 1 Aug. 1780 to 31 Dec. 1781 at a rate of $12 per month, with payments to be made in funded certificates (JCC, 10:149; 23:819-20).

Reib's SON, Peter Reib, served in Flower's regiment from May 1780 until August 1781, when he joined the crew of a ship of war. On 7 June 1794, Congress authorized the settlement of Peter Reib's account "on the same principles on which the accounts of those who served in the same corps were adjusted and settled" (U.S. Statutes at Large, 6:17).

To the Senate and the House of Representatives

Gentlemen of the Senate and
of the House of Representatives.

I lay before both houses of Congress, for their information, the report from the Director of the Mint now inclosed.

Th: Jefferson
Feb. 17. 1802.

RC (DNA: RG 46, LPPM, 7th Cong., 1st sess.); entirely in TJ's hand; date reworked by TJ from 16 to 17 Feb.; endorsed by a Senate clerk. PrC (DLC). RC (DNA: RG 233, PM, 7th Cong., 1st sess.); in Meriwether Lewis's hand, signed and dated by TJ; endorsed by a House clerk. Enclosure: Report of Elias Boudinot, 1 Jan. 1802, on the amount of coin issued by the Mint from 31 Dec. 1800 to 31 Dec. 1801, totaling $422,570 in gold coins, $74,758 in silver coins, and $13,628.37 in copper coins, for a total of $510,956.37; Boudinot also reports that most of the gold received by the Mint in ingots and lumps came from foreign ports, which, "had it not been for the Mint," would have been reexported to Europe rather than becoming an addition to the coinage of the United States; Boudinot adds that the Mint has thus far issued $93,019.19 in cents; by law, at the expiration of six months from the time when the Mint has paid $50,000 in cents and half cents into the Treasury, the treasurer of the United States was to announce the fact in at least two newspapers in Washington and state that no copper coins except those issued by the Mint were to pass as legal currency; to the best of Boudinot's knowledge, such an announcement has not yet been made (RC in DNA: RG 46, LPPM, in a clerk's hand, endorsed by a Senate clerk; PrC in DNA: RG 233, PM, in a clerk's hand, endorsed by a House clerk). Report enclosed in Boudinot to TJ, 1 Jan. 1802, which reads: "I have the honor of enclosing the annual Report upon the present state of the Mint, for the information of Government" (RC in DNA: RG 46, LPPM, at foot of text: "The President of the United States," report subjoined below inside address; PrC in DNA: RG 233, PM; recorded in SJL as received 9 Jan.). Printed in ASP, *Finance*, 1:731.

From Robert Smith

SIR!   Nav Dep 17 Feb 1802

Mr. Wm. S Butler, the son of Genl Butler, is desirous of entering the Navy as Midpn.—There are now vacancies, & I think his appointment would be a good one.

If you concur, your Signature will be necessary to the enclosed warrant.

I have the honor to be with the greatest respect Sir, your most obt. Servt.

                                                RT SMITH

RC (DLC); in a clerk's hand, signed by Smith; at foot of text: "Prest. U States"; endorsed by TJ as received from the Navy Department on 17 Feb. and "Butler Midshipman" and so recorded in SJL. FC (Lb in DNA: RG 45, LSP). Enclosure not found.

William S. BUTLER was the son of General Richard Butler of Pennsylvania, who was killed at the defeat of Arthur St. Clair's army by western Indians in 1791. He was promoted to lieutenant in the navy in 1808 and died in West Florida the following year (NDBW, *Register*, 8; Edward W. Callahan, ed., *List of Officers of the Navy of the United States and of the Marine Corps from 1775 to 1900* [New York, 1901], 94; PMHB, 7 [1883], 3; New York *Evening Post*, 15 Sep. 1809; Vol. 22:304n).

Circular to Naval Commanders

INSTRUCTIONS

To the Commanders of armed vessels belonging to the United States:
Given at the city of Washington, in the district of Columbia, this
18th day of February, in the year of our Lord, one thousand eight
hundred and two, and in the 26th year of our Independence.

WHEREAS it is declared by the act entitled "An act for the protection of the commerce and seamen of the United States, against the Tripolitan cruisers", That it shall be lawful fully to equip, officer, man, and employ such of the armed vessels of the United States, as may be judged requisite by the President of the United States, for protecting effectually the commerce and seamen thereof, on the Atlantic ocean, the Mediterranean and adjoining seas: and also, that it shall be lawful for the President of the United States to instruct the commanders of the respective public vessels, to subdue, seize, and make prize, of all vessels, goods, and effects, belonging to the Bey of Tripoli, or to his subjects.

THEREFORE, And in pursuance of the said statute, you are hereby authorized and directed to subdue, seize, and make prize, of all vessels, goods, and effects, belonging to the Bey of Tripoli, or to his subjects, and to bring or send the same into port, to be proceeded against and distributed according to law.

By command of the President
of the United States of America.   TH: JEFFERSON
President of the
United States of America.

RT SMITH
Secretary of the Navy.
To the Commander of the United States Frigate
called the John Adams

Printed form (CU-BANC); at head of text: "THOMAS JEFFERSON, President of the United States of America"; signed by TJ and countersigned by Robert Smith; "Frigate" and "John Adams" inserted in a clerk's hand in blanks at inside address. Printed form (NHi: Gilder Lehrman Collection at the Gilder Lehrman Institute of American History); signed by TJ, with "frigate" and "Congress" inserted by him. Printed form (DLC); unsigned. Tr (CSmH); addressed to the commander of the frigate *Constellation*.

Congress passed the ACT FOR THE PROTECTION OF THE COMMERCE AND SEAMEN OF THE UNITED STATES on 6 Feb. 1802 (U.S. Statutes at Large, 2:129-30).

From Thomas Newton

Dr Sir Norfolk. Feby. 18. 1802

I have not the pleasure of knowing whether the Cyder sent you proved to your liking, what was delivered here from the same person proved good, & I hope yours did also—if not please inform me & more particular care shall be taken if you should want more of having it put up by some of my friends. & be assured whatever we have this way shall be on notice sent of the best that can be procured, as it gives me pleasure to supply you with any thing from this quarter. Peace makes us a little dull at present tho I hope in a little time we shall get over the difficulties attending it. Brittish vessels I have heard are taken up at low freights, but I expect the active Americans, will be a match for them, as soon as a regular system of Trade commences. be assured that I shall take great pleasure in giving my little aid to render all in my power to assist you with any thing you wish from this place, & I hope you will command me without reserve. with the greatest respect & best wishes for yr health & happiness I am yr obt

T Newton

RC (DLC); endorsed by TJ as received 26 Feb. and so recorded in SJL.

To the Senate

Gentlemen of the Senate

I nominate the reverend Alexander McFarlan of Virginia to be a chaplain in the Navy. Th: Jefferson

Feb. 18. 1802.

RC (DNA: RG 46, EPEN, 7th Cong., 1st sess.); addressed: "The honourable The President of the Senate"; endorsed by a Senate clerk. PrC (DLC).

Alexander mcfarlan of Virginia was recommended to Robert Smith by former Virginia congressman John Nicholas, whose letter to Smith of 7 Feb. 1802 stated that McFarlan's "manners and temper" were well suited "to the station which he solicits" (RC in DNA: RG 59, LAR, endorsed by TJ with notation "McFarlan to be chaplain Navy"; Biog. Dir. Cong.). The nomination was presented to the Senate on 19 Feb. and approved 1 Mch. On 2 Mch., Smith sent TJ a brief letter requesting the president's signature on McFarlan's commission (RC in DLC, in a clerk's hand, signed by Smith, at foot of text: "The President," endorsed by TJ as received from the Navy Department on 2 Mch. and "McFarlan chaplain" and so recorded in SJL; FC in Lb in DNA: RG 45, LSP; jep, 1:407-8).

To the Senate and
the House of Representatives

GENTLEMEN OF THE SENATE AND
OF THE HOUSE OF REPRESENTATIVES

In a message of the 2d. instant, I inclosed a letter from the Secretary at War on the subject of certain lands in the neighborhood of our military posts, on which it might be expedient for the legislature to make some provisions. a letter recently recieved from the Governor of Indiana presents some further views of the extent to which such provision may be needed. I therefore now transmit it for the information of Congress.

TH: JEFFERSON
Feb. 18. 1802.

RC (DNA: RG 233, PM, 7th Cong., 1st sess.); endorsed by a clerk. PrC (DLC). RC (DNA: RG 46, LPPM, 7th Cong., 1st sess.); endorsed by a clerk. Enclosure: William Henry Harrison to James Madison, Vincennes, 19 Jan. 1802, wishing the president to be informed that in a "ridiculous transaction," which has only recently come to Harrison's attention, a court established at Vincennes under authority of the state of Virginia in 1780 granted to its own members a large tract of land extending 24 leagues along the Wabash River, 40 leagues west of the river and 30 leagues east, except for 20,000 or 30,000 acres surrounding Vincennes; that "some of those speculators who infest our country" purchased part of the claim, and through them "many ignorant persons have been induced to part with their little all to obtain this ideal property"; that Harrison expects hundreds of families to come to the territory in the spring to attempt to settle on the tract, and he has prohibited the county's

recorder of deeds and prothonotary from recording or authenticating any deeds there, "being determined that the official seals of the Territory shall not be prostituted to a purpose so base as that of assisting an infamous fraud" (Tr in DNA: RG 46, LPPM, 7th Cong., 1st sess.; in Meriwether Lewis's hand; endorsed by a House clerk). Message and enclosure printed in ASP, *Public Lands*, 1:111-12.

Meriwether Lewis delivered this communication to the Senate on 19 Feb. The Senate referred it to a committee consisting of Uriah Tracy, Stephen R. Bradley, and John Brown that had been formed on 15 Feb. to deal with that portion of TJ's MESSAGE of 2 Feb. pertaining to the subject matter of Henry Dearborn's letter to TJ of 5 Dec. 1801. The House of Representatives received the above message from Lewis on 18 Feb. and ordered it to lie on the table (JS, 3:181-2, 183; JHR, 4:103-4).

To Nicolas Gouin Dufief

SIR   Washington Feb. 19. 1802.

On the reciept of the Parliamentary debates I had desired mr Barnes to remit you the price, and thought it done, till the reciept of your last letter. but my note to him had got misplaced, and escaped his memory. He now tells me he has ordered paiment.

I have an edition of Homer's Iliad, Gr. & Lat. 12mo. printed by the Foulis in Glasgow, and should be very glad to get their corresponding edition of the Odyssey. if you have it, or can procure it in Philadelphia, I shall be obliged to you for it: as also for Chaptal's chemistry in French. accept my best wishes.   TH: JEFFERSON

PrC (DLC); at foot of text: "M. Dufief"; endorsed by TJ in ink on verso.

PARLIAMENTARY DEBATES: Dufief had shipped to TJ from Philadelphia in November the 24-volume second edition of the *Parliamentary or Constitutional History of England* from Benjamin Franklin's library. The price of the set was $30 (Vol. 35:482-4, 542).

According to SJL, the LAST LETTER from Dufief was one of 13 Nov. received on the 16th of that month (see note to TJ to Dufief, 1 Nov.); the more recent communication from Dufief referred to in the letter above has not been found and was not recorded in SJL.

ORDERED PAIMENT: under 16 Feb. 1802 in a statement of account with TJ dated 3 Mch. 1802, John Barnes recorded the remittance of $30 to Dufief in Philadelphia (CSmH).

From John Murray Forbes

SIR,   Philadelphia 19th. Feby. 1802.

Some pressing objects of business having Called me from the Seat of Government immediately after your nomination of me to the Consulate of Hamburg I Called to tender you an imperfect expression of the Sense I have of the honor you have Conferred on me in thus placing me in a Situation of the highest Commercial importance and responsibility and to pledge to you, Sir, my warmest wishes that I may render myself worthy of your Confidence by a faithful discharge of the duties assigned to me by law and by extending, on every occasion, to the protection of our Country men and Commerce the fullest exertion of my feeble talents and influence—I regret that I was not so fortunate as to procure the honor of a personal interview and beg you to accept this expression of my sentiments and to receive the assurances of my most perfect Respect & Consideration

JOHN. M. FORBES

RC (DNA: RG 59, LAR); at foot of text: "Thomas Jefferson President of the United States"; endorsed by TJ as received 22 Feb. and so recorded in SJL.

John Murray Forbes (1771-1831) was born in East Florida but educated in Massachusetts, where he became a friend and Harvard College classmate of John Quincy Adams. Forbes began a law prac-tice in Boston, but then entered into a business partnership with his brother, Ralph Bennet Forbes, and went to France as the firm's representative. When James Monroe was recalled as minister to France in 1796, both Forbes brothers signed a memorial in his behalf from Americans in Paris. In February 1801, John Adams named John M. Forbes as commercial agent at Le Havre and the

Senate confirmed the appointment. However, Forbes's commission was not sent to him before Adams left office, and TJ appointed another person to the post. Senator Theodore Foster and others urged TJ to appoint Forbes to another position. TJ hesitated after learning of a supposition by Samuel Smith, who did not know Forbes, that Forbes "Cannot be otherwise than Federal," but TJ in July 1801 made Forbes the consul at Hamburg. He issued a new commission in February 1802 following the Senate's confirmation of the appointment. In the 1820s, Forbes held a series of U.S. diplomatic posts in South America (DAB; commission, 4 Feb. 1802, Lb in DNA: RG 59, PTCC; Vol. 33:173n, 411-13, 671, 676, 677, 678; Vol. 34:415, 433; Vol. 35:498).

From George Hay

SIR   Richmond. February 19. 1802—

Your letter, covering several papers, relating to Mr Short's interest, in the question, depending, between the US and E. Randolph, was received last evening. An answer, would have been, immediately forwarded, if I had been able, at once, to determine, whether it would be proper for me to appear as counsel, against Mr. Randolph, in a cause which involves all that remains, both of his fortune and his reputation. My determination, reluctantly formed, is, not to engage in this Suit. I lived with Mr. Randolph several years, as a member of his family: and tho his mind is completely alienated from me, I cannot resolve to appear against him in the hour of his humiliation and distress. I could hardly bear, at the late trial, to be a witness of his agitation, his tears and his shame: it would be still more painful to be instrumental in producing them.—I speak this language with regret; but I owe to you an apology, for not accepting the trust which you have been pleased to propose; and I know not how to make it except by telling you the plain truth.

Mr. Call having appeared with Mr. Wickham on the part of Mr. Randolph, states to me, that he cannot advocate the claim of Mr. Short.

As you have but little knowledge of the members of the fœderal-Court-bar, I beg leave to mention, that in addition to the practitioners who reside in Richmond, the sessions are generally attended by Mr. Creed Taylor, Mr. Brooke, and Mr. Minor: to either of whom, or to any other person, the papers now in my hands, shall be transmitted, unless it is your pleasure that they shall be returned—

I am, with sentiments, of sincere respect, yr. mo. obt

GEORGE HAY.

RC (MHi); endorsed by TJ as received 24 Feb. and so recorded in SJL.

Daniel CALL was a prominent Richmond attorney. CREED TAYLOR lived in

Cumberland County. Francis Taliaferro BROOKE and John MINOR were from Fredericksburg (Madison, *Papers*, *Sec. of* *State Ser.*, 1:65; 2:455n; Vol. 31:166n; Vol. 34:109n).

From William Barton

SIR,   Lancaster, Feby 20th. 1802.

Amos Slaymaker, Esqr. (a respectable inhabitant of this neighbourhood) will have the honor of delivering this to You; together with a copy of my book, which I request You will do me the favor to accept, as a small token of my high respect for Your character.—I have accompanied this copy with a small engraved portrait of myself,—executed in a peculiar style, by Mons. St. Memin of Philadelphia, as a good specimen of the talents of that ingenious artist—The outline of the original drawing (which is as large as life, and finished in chalks,) is made by a mechanical apparatus, called the Physiognotrace; and from this he executes the print, in the reduced size. Mr. St. Memin's profiles are, generally, striking likenesses; and, considering the excellence of the workmanship, his price is very moderate.—I have taken the liberty of sending to You, Sir, this specimen of his art (which I procured for the purpose of gratifying my children), presuming that You may not have had an opportunity of seeing one of the kind, before; knowing that, in this case, it will be acceptable to You—*This* likeness, my friends say, is an excellent one.—

I feel very anxious for the fate of my book. Some of my friends— and among these, our worthy Governor,—persuade me it has some merit—Of one thing, however, I am sure;—it is *well-intended*. The work is now before the world; and I hope, for the sake of the *Bookseller* (who is a very worthy man), as well as on my own account, it will meet with a favorable reception among my Countrymen—Mr. Conrad has, I expect, sent 80 or 100 copies to Washington.—

Mr. Slaymaker informs me, that his journey to the seat of government is made in the hope of being able to succeed in procuring a contract for carrying a Mail from Philada. to Washington, by the route of Lancaster. In point of capacity and resources, he is, I believe, quite adequate to the undertaking. Though he professes to be a Federalist, he is a very decent and moderate man of that party; and many of his connections are most respectable Republicans.—

I have the Honor to be, With sentiments of the highest Respect And sincerest Attachment, Sir, Your most obedt. Servt.

W. BARTON

RC (DLC); at foot of text: "The President."; endorsed by TJ as received 2 Mch. and so recorded in SJL.

AMOS SLAYMAKER of Lancaster County, Pennsylvania, owned a stagecoach line in 1802 (*Biog. Dir. Cong.*; Philadelphia *Poulson's American Daily Advertiser*, 12 Feb.).

COPY OF MY BOOK: *A Dissertation on the Freedom of Navigation and Maritime Commerce* (see TJ to Barton, 12 Nov. 1801).

For the 1802 ENGRAVED PORTRAIT of Barton by Charles Balthazar Julien Févret de Saint-Mémin, see Ellen G. Miles, *Saint-Mémin and the Neoclassical Profile Portrait in America* (Washington, D.C., 1994), 244.

Philadelphia BOOKSELLER John CONRAD, whose name appears on the frontispiece of Barton's *Dissertation*, advertised the publication and sale of the book in the 12 Feb. issue of the *Philadelphia Gazette*. Rapine & Conrad in Washington followed, with an advertisement in the 24 Mch. issue of the *National Intelligencer*.

From Pierre Samuel Du Pont de Nemours

MONSIEUR LE PRÉSIDENT,   New York 20 Fevrier 1802

Il y a environ un mois que j'ai reçu des Lettres de L'Institut où l'on me disait: *Nous procederons incessamment à la nomination de vingt quatre membres étrangers. Indiquez nous les savans que vous croyez dans les Etats unis devoir être proposés.*—J'ai répondu sur le champ: "Vous trouveriez peu d'hommes en Europe, même pour les autres sciences, et aucun dans le monde pour notre Classe de morale et de politique qui puisse être comparé au Président Jefferson."

Voila que les gazettes m'apprennent que sans attendre mon avis l'Institut a pensé comme moi, et que c'est précisément à notre Classe des Sciences morales et politiques qu'il vous a attaché.

Permettez moi de me féliciter et de m'enorgueillir de ce nouveau rapport avec vous.

Salut et respect.   DU PONT (DE NEMOURS)

Puisque le Président des Etats unis se trouve Membre de l'Institut national de France, il faut qu'il contribue de son influence à rendre un service à un de ses confreres l'excellent Sculpteur Houdon—Celui ci a laissé en Amérique un très beau buste de Benjamin Franklin, lequel est actuellement chez moi.—Ce buste en marbre vaut cent louis de notre monnaie, environ 480 dollars

Rien n'est plus convenable à la Nation que de le placer dans votre Capitole, soit au dépens des Etats unis, soit à ceux de la corporation de Washington-City,[1] soit à ceux d'une Souscription de vingt quatre personnes à vingt dollars chacun.—Et Houdon à qui la

Virginie doit encore mille ecus sur la Statue de Washington, est dans un veritable besoin d'argent.

Je recommande cela à votre bonté, à votre dignité, à votre sagesse.

EDITORS' TRANSLATION

MISTER PRESIDENT,   New York 20 Feb. 1802

About a month ago, I received letters from the Institute in which they said: *We shall immediately proceed to the nomination of twenty-four foreign members. Point out to us the learned men in the United States whom you think should be proposed.* I immediately replied: "You would find few men in Europe, even for the other sciences, and no one in the world for our category of moral philosophy and politics, who could be compared to President Jefferson."

Now the gazettes apprise me that without awaiting my advice the Institute thought as I did, and it is precisely to our category of moral and political sciences that it has appointed you.

Allow me to congratulate myself and to take pride in this new relationship with you.

Greetings and respect.   DU PONT (DE NEMOURS)

Since the President of the United States happens to be a member of the National Institute of France, he must contribute his influence to render a service to one of his colleagues, the excellent sculptor Houdon. This man left in America a very fine bust of Benjamin Franklin, which is at present at my house. This marble bust is worth a hundred *louis* of our money, around 480 dollars.

Nothing is more appropriate for the nation than to place it in your Capitol, whether at the expense of the United States, or at the expense of the government of the city of Washington, or from the funds of a subscription of twenty-four individuals at twenty dollars each. And Houdon, to whom Virginia still owes a thousand crowns on the statue of Washington, is truly in need of money.

I recommend this to your kindness, to your dignity, to your wisdom.

RC (DLC); at head of text: "A son Excellence Thomas Jefferson Président de la Société Philosophique américaine, Membre de l'Institut national de France President des Etats Unis"; endorsed by TJ as received 27 Feb. and so recorded in SJL.

Du Pont had undertaken to sell some pieces by Jean Antoine HOUDON that the painter Robert Edge Pine had attempted to market in Philadelphia in the 1780s. Among those works was a marble bust of BENJAMIN FRANKLIN made by Houdon in France in 1778. Du Pont's effort to generate a subscription to purchase the bust failed, and in the 1870s it was acquired by the Metropolitan Museum of Art (Wayne Craven, "The Origins of Sculpture in America: Philadelphia, 1785-1830," *American Art Journal*, 9 [1977], 6, 7, 8; Joseph Breck, "Three Busts by Houdon," *Metropolitan Museum of Art Bulletin*, 7 [1912], 224; Charles Coleman Sellers, *Benjamin Franklin in Portraiture* [New Haven, 1962], 309-10; Vol. 15:xxxvii-xxxviii, 457 [illus.]).

[1] Preceding ten words interlined in place of "unis."

To John Page

My dear friend   Washington Feb. 20. 1802.

I pray you, in the first place, that the contents of this letter may be inviolably secret, until promulgated by some public act. in my letter of March 2d. I mentioned to you that the Mint had been left at Philadelphia merely because taken up by the legislature too late to decide on it. the subject is now resumed, and there is no doubt the institution will be suppressed. this of course prevents the prospect of employing your talents worthily in that department. another difficulty had occurred, of which at that time I was not apprised Virginia is greatly over her due proportion of appointments in the general government; & tho' this has not been done by me, it would be imputed as blame to me to add to her proportion. so that for all general offices persons to fill them must for some time be sought from other states, and only offices[1] which are to be exercised within the state can be given to it's own citizens. this leaves but little scope for placing talents in offices to which they are analogous, and must apologize for what I am about to propose to you. Colo. Heath, the Collector of the customs at Petersburg must be removed on account of the irritability of his temper, and the fury of his federalism. his office will probably be worth in future from 2. to 3000. D. a year as you will see by the inclosed paper. in proposing it to you, I am governed only by a desire to be useful to you, and at the same time to place the office in hands equal to it's duties & acceptable to the public. what it's labours are, I know not. it's responsibility is very great; as prodigious sums pass through it, which, where there is no bank to deposit them in for safe keeping, lie at considerable risk. it requires too the utmost vigilance of the principal over his clerks, as we have seen the Collectors of South Carolina, Pensylva & N. York and some others, not only ruined themselves, but their securities also, and still great loss falling on the public; and this from the sole frauds of the clerks. I should suppose indeed that nothing could secure the principal, but a rigorous[2] refusal to let his clerks ever touch a dollar, and an inflexible reservation of the care & custody of the iron chest to himself. with this precaution, these offices are the best in the US. although I know your character to be much inclined to indulgence, and confidence in others, yet I know also that when you are apprised that the safety of yourself & family, of your securities & of the public, and your own reputation also would require you not to trust any body but yourself, your sense of duty is too strong to leave any hesitation. I mention these circumstances, because I wish you to be apprised of the dangers as well as the benefits of the office, and to make up your judgment on a view of the whole subject. it would require your removal to Petersburg where the office is kept. taking convenient time to consider of it, you will be so good as to inform me as soon as you can decide whether you will accept the office or not. there was for some time an expectation that Colo. Davies's health would have produced a vacancy in that office, which is a better one than that of Petersburgh, but I believe that expectation is over. present me respectfully to mrs Page, & accept yourself assurances of my constant & affectionate esteem.

TH: JEFFERSON

P.S. Mar. 9. I have witheld this letter some days on an expectation that mr Gallatin would be able to say some thing further on the subject of the emoluments of the office. he says that a committee are about to propose reductions of the emoluments of all the collectors. he is of opinion this will be reduced so as to stand somewhere between two & three thousand dollars. I thought it best to apprise you of every thing. Gallatin mentions a very necessary caution against trusting the merchants beyond the time of their bonds so as to make yourself responsible. mr Gallatin says the office at Norfolk is not near so profitable as that of Petersburg.

RC (NjP: Andre De Coppet Collection); at foot of first page: "John Page esq." Address sheet (Lyne M. Shackelford, Orange, Virginia, 1976); addressed: "John Page esquire at Rosewell near Yorktown Virginia"; franked; postmarked 10 Mch.; endorsed by Page as a letter of the 9th received the 19th. PrC (DLC); endorsed by TJ in ink on verso. Enclosure not found.

MY LETTER OF MARCH 2D: no letter dated 2 Mch. 1801 or 1802 from TJ to Page has been found or is recorded in SJL. TJ probably meant his letter to Page of 23 Mch. 1801 (Vol. 33:422-3).

COLO. DAVIES'S HEALTH: William Davies was the collector at Norfolk (Vol. 34:681, 682n).

COMMITTEE ARE ABOUT TO PROPOSE REDUCTIONS: on 17 Apr., the House Committee of Commerce and Manufactures presented a bill to amend the existing act regarding compensations for external revenue officers. Passed into law on 30 Apr., the new act limited the annual emoluments received by collectors to $5,000, those by naval officers to $3,500, and those by surveyors to $3,000. The act also granted the collector for the district of Richmond an annual salary of $250, in addition to fees and emoluments, and discontinued an identical salary previously allowed to the collector at Petersburg (JHR, 4:207, 209-211, 228; U.S. Statutes at Large, 2:172-3; ASP, *Miscellaneous*, 1:274).

[1] Word interlined in place of "places."
[2] TJ here canceled "attention."

From Robert Smith

Sir   Nav: Dep: 20. Feb. 1802

I do myself the honor to enclose Warrants for

Charles Benson—of Fredericksburg

William Holmes. of Columbia

To be Midshipmen in the Navy.

Mr Benson is the Gentleman recommended to you by Mr. Mercer—Mr Page & others—Mr. Holmes is a smart young man of this place—There are Vacancies enough to admit their appt.—& if you concur, the enclosed warrants will require your Signature.

I have the honor to be, with great respect & esteem, Sir, your mo: ob: Servt: Rt Smith

RC (DLC); in a clerk's hand, signed by Smith; at foot of text: "President of the United States"; endorsed by TJ as received from the Navy Department on 20 Feb. and "Midshipmen" and so recorded in SJL. FC (Lb in DNA, RG 45, LSP).

TJ received letters recommending CHARLES BENSON from John Mercer, dated 23 Oct. from Fredericksburg; Mann Page, dated 24 Oct. from Mannsfield; and John Minor, dated 25 Oct. from Fredericksburg. All three letters were recorded in SJL as received 28 Oct. and joined by a brace and the notations "Chas.

Benson to be Midshipmn." and "N," which indicates that TJ forwarded them to the Navy Department. None of these letters has been found. A letter from Benson to TJ, dated 19 Nov. 1801 from Fredericksburg, was recorded in SJL as received 22 Nov., but also has not been found.

Both Benson and William HOLMES were assigned to the frigate *Adams*. Holmes died near Gibraltar in September 1802, while Benson was cashiered from the navy in June 1803 (NDBW, *Register*, 4, 26).

From John Dawson

Dear Sir,   City of Washington February 21st. 1802

I herewith hand to you some observations which have been transmited to me, and which appear to merit consideration—if the good of our country can be promoted by the plan, it will be the source of much pleasure to me.

With real esteem, Yr Most Obt   J Dawson

RC (MHi); at foot of text: "Mr. Jefferson"; endorsed by TJ as received 23 Feb. and so recorded in SJL. Enclosure not found.

From Pierre Samuel Du Pont
de Nemours

MONSIEUR LE PRÉSIDENT,　　　　　　　New York 21 Fevrier 1802.

J'ai l'honneur de vous prier de faire passer au Général Davies, dernierement l'un des Ministres Plénipotentiaires des Etats unis en France les Lettres ci incluses.

Je ne sais pas où demeure le Général; et Mr. Barbé Marbois en m'envoyant sa Lettre n'y a mis ni enveloppe, ni adresse.

Vous me ferez plaisir, avant de les acheminer, de lire les deux Lettres.—Il s'agit de rendre à notre Ami La Fayette un service honorable pour votre Nation, important pour lui dans l'Etat auquel sa fortune est réduite.—Il ignore entierement les projets de ses amis à cet égard.

Mais il est très bon et très convenable que vous soyiez prévenu de ce qu'on imagine et de ce que votre coeur favorisera.

Je vous en aurais parlé ou écrit dans tous les cas. Et, graces à l'impossibilité où je suis de trouver le Général Davies sans votre secours, voila ma confidence faite.

Salut et tendre Respect　　　　　　DU PONT (DE NEMOURS)

E D I T O R S' T R A N S L A T I O N

MISTER PRESIDENT,　　　　　　　New York 21 Fevrier 1802.

I have the honor to request that you send to General Davie, recently one of the ministers plenipotentiary of the United States to France, the letters herein enclosed.

I do not know where the general lives, and Mr. Barbé de Marbois did not include an envelope or an address when he sent me his letter.

You will do me a favor, before sending them on, to read both letters. It is a question of rendering to our friend Lafayette a service, both honorable for your nation and important for him in the state to which his fortune is reduced. He is completely unaware of his friends' plans in that respect.

But it is very good and very appropriate that you be advised of what is being devised and of which your heart will be in favor.

I would have spoken to you or written to you about it in any case. And, thanks to the impossibility of my finding General Davie without your help, my confidence is accomplished.

Greetings and affectionate respect.　　　　DU PONT (DE NEMOURS)

RC (DLC); at head of text: "a son Excellence Thomas Jefferson Président des Etats Unis"; endorsed by TJ as received 27 Feb. and so recorded in SJL. Enclosures: letters, not found, of Du Pont and François Barbé de Marbois to William R. Davie; see TJ to Davie, 28 Feb., and Davie to TJ, 20 Mch. 1802.

From Lewis Mayer

Frederick, Maryland, 21 Feb. 1802. Addressing the president in "the plain style of a simple unpollished youth," Mayer begs pardon for his rustic manners and assures TJ of the deep esteem he holds for his public and private character, in particular TJ's "disregard of personal distinctions" and disdain of pompous and hereditary titles. He hopes his humble petition will meet with a gracious reception. He is a native of Lancaster, Pennsylvania, the son of George Lewis Mayer, a mechanic and German immigrant who was versed in several languages. His father died "when the morning of my days scarce had dawned," and his mother apprenticed him for a "mechanical profession." Mayer dislikes manual labor, however, and spends his leisure hours in intellectual pursuits. Despite his lack of formal education, he is as optimistic about his prospects for "future excellence" as he is about the prospects of America, where liberty has its first asylum since the fall of the ancient republics and which will soon rival the glories of Greece and Rome. He wishes "to cast my mite into the trans-atlantic scale of literature," but poverty prevents his doing so. He seeks TJ's assistance, encouraged by the virtues of the president's "social character," and considers him to be the most eligible patron to provide a "school of wisdom and virtue." The Greek sages were famous for their generosity, "and may not the patronage of Jefferson become as famous for a school of Wisdom, as was the house of Aristides, or the school of Plato?" Mayer sees in TJ's soul a principle concordant with the Greeks for instructing young men "in the duties of a man and a public servant," and believes that liberty provides the best grounds to cultivate the arts and sciences. In America, merit is rewarded and "the most obscure citizen may asscend the grand stage of human concerns." In free governments, equality would quickly appear "if Fortune were as impartial as our Creator." Wealth is not aways a divine blessing, and many virtuous men toil in poverty. All humans are given a talent to excel in some manner, but liable to corruption by bad habits and depravity. As such, Mayer believes he must abandon his mechanic's trade and "apply my time to the study of the muses only," which he could do if led on the proper path. Mayer is now almost 19 years old, a time when the intellect is most susceptible to improvement, and such a favorable moment should not be neglected. His opportunity for study thus far has been erratic and confined only to subjects that interest him. His deficiency in books is another obstacle, possessing only an abridged version of Jedidiah Morse's geography, the second part of Noah Webster's *Grammatical Institute of the English Language*, and a handful of lesser titles. These works guide him "through the outlines only of those sciences, and then leave me in an abys of darkness." His ardor remains unabated, however, and he trusts that TJ, "the soul of the american people," will not betray the service of a fellow citizen to his private interests. "By a kind attention and a liberal donation," TJ will promote his future prosperity and happiness, and raise him from obscurity to become a useful servant in his beloved country. Mayer's soul, imagination, and happiness are at the precipice, and he urges TJ to "pause! illustrious sir! pause a moment befor you decide their fate!" A small sacrifice of TJ's wealth will be rewarded with "the gratefull remembrance of so noble an act." A postscript adds that Mayer cannot defray the postage on his letter and that he resides at the house of Jacob Steiner, Jr., a saddler.

RC (DLC); 8 p.; above postscript: "Thomas Jefferson L.L.D. President of the A.P.S. and President of the United States of America"; endorsed by TJ as received 5 Mch. and so recorded in SJL.

A native of Lancaster, Pennsylvania, Lewis Mayer (1783-1849) was the son of a German-born mechanic, who died when Mayer was ten. He subsequently moved to Frederick, Maryland, where he apprenticed as a saddler. Leaving the saddling business, he attended a local academy and was converted to the German Reformed faith. Ordained in 1808, he served as pastor to several congregations in Virginia and Pennsylvania, later receiving a doctor of divinity degree from Rutgers College in 1829. Emerging as a respected church leader, in 1825 he became the first professor at the German Reformed seminary in Carlisle, Pennsylvania. The institution struggled for a number of years, moving to York and finally settling at Mercersburg in 1837. Mayer left teaching in 1839 and retired to York. He published a number of works on theology and church history, including *History of the German Reformed Church*, which was printed posthumously in 1851 (DAB; Frederick, Maryland, *Republican Advocate*, 18 Oct. 1805; *Baltimore Patriot*, 1 Aug. 1829).

To Thomas Mann Randolph

DEAR SIR   Washington Feb. 21. 1802.

I am made happy by the regular accounts of the health of the inhabitants of Edgehill. here there has been an uncommon degree of sickness; ascribed of course to the mild winter, tho' we cannot see why. The H. of R. have now been a week debating the judiciary law, and scarcely seem to be yet on the threshold of it. I begin to apprehend a long session: however I believe all material matters recommended in the first day's message will prevail. the majority begins to draw better together than at first. still there are some wayward freaks which now & then disturb the operations.

I know nothing of the person from Loudon who went to take Shadwell, having never heard of him till your letter. in a letter to mr Craven, which he recieved on the day of the date of yours I expressed a wish that he could bring some good tenant to it; and as the man happened to be with him that very day, he made an agreement with him to take all except the yard on Peyton's terms: but as to the yard that remains to be arranged. I have written to him on the subject.   I forward you two newspapers presenting two versions of Hamilton's speeches. the language of insurgency is that of the party at present, even in Congress. mr Bayard in a speech of 7. hours talked with confidence of the possibility of resistance by arms. they expect to frighten us: but are met with perfect sang froid.   present my warmest affections to my ever dear Martha & the little ones, and be assured of my constant & sincere attachment.

TH: JEFFERSON

RC (DLC); at foot of text: "T M Randolph"; address clipped: "Thomas Man[. . .]"; franked and postmarked; endorsed by Randolph as received 1 Mch. PrC (MHi); endorsed by TJ in ink on verso.

YOUR LETTER: perhaps Randolph to TJ, 23 Jan., recorded in SJL as received from Edgehill on 27 Jan., but not found. LETTER TO MR CRAVEN: according to SJL, TJ wrote Craven on 6 and 19 Feb. TJ received letters dated 30 Jan. and 11 Feb. from Craven on 3 and 17 Feb., respectively. All of the correspondence is missing. Craven came from Loudoun County to lease Tufton and part of Monticello in 1800 (MB, 2:1030; Vol. 32:108-10). For Craven PEYTON's arrangement to have William Davenport take over his lease of Shadwell, see TJ to Peyton, 3 Dec. 1800.

HAMILTON'S SPEECHES: on 11 Feb., Alexander Hamilton spoke before a meeting of the New York City bar held to consider a memorial to Congress against the repeal of the Judiciary Act of 1801, as their colleagues in Philadelphia had done. On 13 Feb., the *New-York Gazette & General Advertiser* printed an account of Hamilton's statements at the meeting, in which he noted that repeal of the Judiciary Act would be an "unequivocal violation" of the Constitution. He spoke against a memorial to Congress, however, because it would have no impact. Hamilton stated that the repeal of the 1801 Act would destroy the independence of the judiciary "and we should, e'er long, be divided into separate confederacies, turning our arms against each other." On 15 Feb., Denniston & Cheetham's *American Citizen and General Advertiser* gave another account of Hamilton's remarks, reporting that near the close of the meeting he predicted that if the judiciary law were repealed "we should soon see State 'arrayed against State to embrue their

hands in each other's blood.' In which case, some daring usurper (he did not mention himself) would arise, seize the reins of government, and like Bonaparte, establish a despotism" (see Syrett, *Hamilton*, 25:520-7).

At the close of his speech on 20 Feb., James A. Bayard raised the POSSIBILITY OF RESISTANCE BY ARMS, if the Judiciary Act of 1801 were abolished. He argued: "You have a right to abolish by a law, the offices of the judges of the circuit courts.—They have a right to declare your law void. It unavoidably follows in the exercise of these rights, either that you destroy their rights, or that they destroy yours. This doctrine is not an harmless absurdity," he warned, "it is a most dangerous heresy. It is a doctrine which cannot be practised without producing not discord only, but bloodshed." Bayard warned again: "There are many, very many who believe, if you strike this blow, you inflict a mortal wound on the constitution. There are many now willing to spill their blood to defend that constitution. Are gentlemen disposed to risk the consequences?" Comparing the U.S. with France, Bayard concluded: "We are standing on the brink of that revolutionary torrent, which deluged in blood one of the fairest countries of Europe" (*Speech of the Honorable James A. Bayard, of Delaware. February 19, 20, 1802. On the Bill Received from the Senate, Entitled "An Act to Repeal Certain Acts Respecting the Organization of the Courts of the United States"* [Hartford, 1802], 27, 46-8; *Annals*, 11:648, 650). Bayard's speech was published in pamphlet form—sometimes along with that of William B. Giles, who defended the proposed legislation—in several cities, including Hanover, New Hampshire; Wilmington, Delaware; Boston, Worcester, Hartford, and Washington, D.C. (Shaw-Shoemaker, Nos. 1848-52, 2323-4, 3443).

From John Coburn

Sir.   Mason County. Kentucky—Feby. 22d. 1802.

Fame has taught me to believe, that to have access to you the voice of Justice & humanity requires not the aid of pageantry or numbers.

Permit a fellow man, who has been long and deeply impressed on the subject of slavery in the United States to address you, with the respect justly due to your character and office. Having reflected for many years with extreme regret, on the situation of the Blacks in the United States, I cannot but beleive that sound policy independent of every virtuous motive requires that some early and decisive steps should be taken, to avert the evils to which one day we shall be exposed, by retaining those unhappy people in bondage.

Painful and perplexing as this subject may be it claims an importance not inferior to many of the arduous duties about which you are occupied. It is greatly to be desired that some practicable mode could be adopted to soften the rigors to which those people are subject and at the same time produce the least violence to the feelings or interest of their holders.

Unable to discover any impropriety in this mode of application to the Chief Magistrate of our Country and uninfluenced either by religious zeal or a desire to attract towards myself the attention of those high in office, I venture an attempt to awaken in our rulers a desire to establish some plan, by which the unhappy condition of a large portion of human beings, may in time become more consonant to humanity and the eternal principles of Justice.

Amidst the various means of meliorating the condition of the Blacks amongst us, no plan appears to be so proper or practicable as Colonization; and I have been rejoiced to find this mode approved and confirmed in a re-perusal of your notes on Virginia.

It would be both unecessary and presuming in me on this occasion to discuss the right or policy of retaining our fellow men in slavery—the evil exists, & the only remaining enquiry is—In what manner can its abolition be most properly accomplished, with the least convulsion?—It would appear that an immediate emancipation of a large number of slaves would be productive of more injury than benefit, if they are suffered to remain among us. To permit those people to be let loose in their present debased state amongst the whites would eventually be to destroy the blacks and produce the most distressing scenes.

The means most likely to benefit both parties must be gradual and insensible in their operation, public opinion is tending irresistably to the abolition of Slavery—If then a full and fair opportunity was once offered for the exercise of the zeal and humanity of the whites, we have reason to hope, that an important change in the condition of the blacks would be accomplished without tumult or disorder.

Very many of our Citizens are disposed to comply with the dictates of their minds, and to restore the blacks to their rights, but finding it impracticable to accomplish it within ourselves, they are deterred from any attempt, and the great evil remains stationary, or rather increasing—It would perhaps be found adviseable for the more Southern states to have some distant spot to which they might send, the more restless, bold and daring slaves, to prevent the influence which they must ever have whilst surrounded by the less enterprizing—

It appears as if the period had arrived when the foundation of the gradual abolition of Slavery may be accomplished—The United States being in possession of a large unappropriated tract of Country could not perhaps dispose of a part of it, more advantageously than by establishing the seat of a Colony, to which all free and emancipated blacks should be sent.

Slavery being excluded from the Territory N.W of the Ohio, fewer obstacles would be found and less prejudice to encounter in the execution of this plan, than in any part of the United States.

Permit me Sir respectfully to intreat your attention to this interesting subject and submit to your consideration the propriety of laying it, before Congress at this session—If an attempt of this nature should meet with your approbation, great exertion would be made by a very numerous & respectable part of your Fellow Citizens to carry it into effect by every means within their power—

If Congress would appropriate a part of the most Southern and unappropriated territory NW of the Ohio, as soon as the Indian title could be extinguished, the Citizens of the United States would perhaps accomplish a real saving, and Government would justly merit the approbation of mankind.

It would appear that the Eastern & middle States could not reasonably object to a plan calculated to abolish slavery, as they have discovered their aversion to this evil—And the Southern States would not be affected only by the insensible operation of public opinion and the voluntary exercise of humanity—

It may not be considered improper in me, to suggest a few thoughts on the out-lines of a plan which appears to me practicable.

Suppose the tract designed for a Colony should be divided into Lotts of 25 acres of arable land—Let the fee simple of each donation be vested in the donee; either free or emancipated black person—It would for some time be necessary to have a garrison within the Colony, which might be composed of volunteer mechanics & husbandmen, whose duty it should be to defend and instruct the blacks— No transfer of land from the black to the white man should be permitted, and perhaps any traffic between them would be improper unless under special licences.

Resident superintendants might be appointed, with whose aid the Colony might regulate its own police under the guidance of Congress—As an inducement to industry and good behavior a bounty in Land might be given to those who merited it. Such regulations as an infant Colony and an unenlightned people might require, with proper schools would be necessary—

It is to be expected that the expense to the United States would be greatly lessned by the voluntary contributions of individuals, and it would perhaps be esteemed as meritorious a dying bequest, to give to the Colony, as formerly to the Church, or the establishment of high sounding alms—The zealous of every description and the humane might find a noble employment for their philanthrophy—

The wisdom and justice of adopting some mode to accomplish an object so desireable, as the liberation of oppressed man, must be too evident to a mind long inured to just reflection, to admit of additional motives being offered by me. I must however be permitted to call upon you in the sacred names of Justice and Humanity, to employ for this important purpose, that influence and those talents which have justly placed you the Chief among Americans—If this application proves abortive; feeble as the effort may be, it will stand on the records of time, as a warning to my Fellow Citizens of the impending dangers to which they are & will be[1] exposed by inattention to this subject. The convulsive struggles of violated justice and humanity to which we have recently been witness in Virginia and elsewhere, ought to be an awful and solemn memento, that to slumber on this occasion, is to be awakned 'ere long by the avenging hand of the long suffering and greatly oppressed—

I am Sir With the highest consideration and respect—Yr Fellow Citizen
JNO. COBURN

RC (DLC); at foot of text: "To Thomas Jefferson Esquire"; endorsed by TJ as received 8 Mch. and so recorded in SJL.

A native of Philadelphia, John Coburn (ca. 1763-1823) trained as a lawyer before moving to Lexington, Kentucky, in 1784, where he engaged in mercantile pursuits. He later relocated to Mason County, where he received a state judgeship. A Republican, Coburn served as a presidential elector in 1796, 1800, and 1804 and received several appointment offers during TJ's administration before finally accepting a position as a judge of the Louisiana Territory in 1807. Reappointed to the same office in 1811, he subsequently was made a collector of internal revenues for Kentucky in 1814 (Lewis Collins, *Collins' Historical Sketches of Kentucky. History of Kentucky*, rev. and enlarged by Richard H. Collins, 2 vols. [Covington, Ky., 1878], 1:367-8, 509; 2:578-9; JEP, 2:50, 57, 191, 457; *Terr. Papers*, 9:457, 537; 13:91-2, 569-70; 14:147, 342, 437-8).

[1] Preceding two words and ampersand interlined.

From Tench Coxe

SIR   Philadelphia Feb. 22. 1802

It is manifest to every person, who reflects on the affairs of the United States, that the present season rather offers a new, than a defective mass of commercial advantages. The acquisition of a large monied capital, and of a universal credit, public & private, have relieved us from the British monopoly, or at least afforded the sure means and this is *a revolution in trade*. To give activity to this power should be the object of the merchant & will be a pleasure and a credit to the Government.

The mass of importations, from the British European dominions are well ascertained to have been 18 millions of dollars before the abolition of the Fr. Monarchy, & 28 to 32 millions since, according to the years & valuations. This affords a vast range for inspection and consideration. Some of those things were not manufactures— Some were manufactures foreign to Britain. The rest were the manufactures of England, Wales, Scotland & Ireland. Every country in Europe affords some substitutes for a part of those goods, to be procured from them either by our newly acquired monied capital, or by the greater extent in which the American Merchant is known and confided in—Even the British Merchant imports directly from Germany, Russia &ca. commodities which rival, *here*, the manufactures of Britain and Ireland.

But, Sir, there is one other source of supply which has not yet struck the American mind in the best form—from which the British capitalist dares not draw supplies for us or for his fellow subjects— which the American Merchant cannot perhaps avail himself of without governmental countenance—and which may, it is believed, happily receive the attention of the Executive power—I mean, China.

The cheapness of living and of labor, and the imitative talents of that Country & people are well understood and ascertained. It has been the interest of the European manufacturing nations to avoid and discourage the importation of China manufactures, because they interfered with their own. But we who do not manufacture piece goods, and shall not for some time, are at present situated differently, for example, from the English. Lord Mc.Cartney went from England to China to extend the knowledge & sale of British manufactures. He was illy received. Were an American minister to go to China, to extend and improve the Chinese manufactures, and encrease the exportation, and consumption, it is believed, that a sincere well arranged mission of that nature would be differently received. It is not meant to be suggested or recommended that an embassy from America should be sent to China, but I have the honor to submit to your consideration, Sir, a special communication to that Government upon the subject of the Commercial intercourse between the two Countries.

America might be justly represented to them as having no manufactures of silk. The fact stated on page 45 Coxe's view of U.S. on silk, was received from Doctor Franklin. It has been corroborated by information from many others. The chinese manufactures of cotton are considerable, but not very various. They have other manufactures. Their talent at imitation is considered as very nice and almost perfect. The idea intended to be suggested and recommended is that of a direct communication in writing from the President of the United States to the Emperor of China, accompanied by a body of useful information upon the nature of our demand & consumption, the numbers of our people and consequent extent of our demand, our increase evidenced by copies of our two Census, our disposition to buy of them for money, or upon respondentia according to their usages, and according to the contracts which have & shall be made among the merchants from time to time. Such a communication, *to be accompanied by a very copious and nice collection of specimens of the various goods most in demand at all times in our markets, and these to be made up in the most perspicuous & impressive manner and to include the manufactures of all the European nations.* It would require some money but not a great deal, and as it would be desireable not to awaken the Jealousies of the European Merchants before the communication was recd. and considered, it would be desirable that it should be found that some existing provision of money would admit the expenditure. I do not know the exact details of the provisions for foreign intercourse, nor of the 10.000 Dollar fund but I do not recollect any other source so probable as one of those.

It might be sufficient to have these things carefully prepared, without any public notice of the thing—to have a confidential shipment of them, to the care of some respectable passenger or supercargo, to be delivered with the Dispatch, to the American Consul, and by him passed to the Emperor thro the Hands of the chief magistrate of Canton—I will not dwell longer upon a hint, which is sufficiently explained to facilitate its adoption, or rejection, as it may seem [best. It is] not at all improbable that such a communication might secure to the American trade both Justice and Favor, as feelings govern much in that half civilized nation. It is well understood that acts of injury & benefit are no where so highly rated—

I have the honor to be, Sir, yr. respectful hble Servant

TENCH COXE

RC (DNA: RG 59, LAR); torn; addressed: "The President" and "Private"; endorsed by TJ as received 26 Feb. and so recorded in SJL.

Coxe had advocated direct trade with CHINA in the 1780s, being one of the major investors in the successful voyage of the *Canton*, commanded by Thomas Truxtun in 1786. Seeking to improve trade relations with China, King George III appointed LORD Macartney (MC.CARTNEY) "Ambassador Extraordinary and Plenipotentiary" to Beijing in 1792. The mission was also supported by the British East India Company (Cooke, *Coxe*, 74-7; D. E. Mungello, *The Great Encounter of China and the West, 1500-1800* [Lanham, Md., 1999], 94-7; DNB; Vol. 32:35-7).

VIEW OF U.S.: in his 1794 publication, Coxe remarked, "Silk has long been a profitable production of Georgia, and other parts of the United States; and may be increased, it is presumed, as fast as the demand will rise. This is the strongest of all raw materials, and the great empire of China, though abounding with cotton, finds it the cheapest clothing for her people." In an author's note, Coxe reported that in 1789 a "large nursery of the white italian mulberry" was established in the United States, awaiting "an emigration from a silk country," being a part of the "plan to *foster and encourage,* but *not to force* manufactures" (Coxe, *A View of the United States of America, in a Series of Papers, Written at Various Times, between the Years 1787 and 1794* [Philadelphia, 1794], 45; see Vol. 28:309-10).

From John Drayton

South Carolina
Charleston Feby 22d: 1802

SIR

I have the honor to inform you, that Edward Croft Eqr., residing in this City, a young Gentleman of the bar, of respectability, is this day appointed and Commissioned, first Commissioner in this State; under the law, for the valuation of lands, houses, &c.: and in pursuance of the confidence, which you thought fit to repose in me.

I have made many fruitless endeavors before this service, could be performed: And Mr. Croft, has taken upon him the duties of the office, from a desire of aiding (as far as he can) the Administration of his Country: the emoluments of the office being too inconsiderable to be a sufficient inducement.

With Sentiments of high consideration I have the honor to be Sir, Yr. Most obt. Sert.

JOHN DRAYTON

RC (DNA: RG 59, LAR); at foot of text: "Thomas Jefferson Eqr President of the United States"; endorsed by TJ as received 5 Mch. and so recorded in SJL.; also endorsed by TJ: "Crofts Commr. of Direct tax."

On 10 Mch., TJ sent the Senate his nomination of EDWARD CROFT as FIRST COMMISSIONER of valuations for the Direct Tax in South Carolina, which was approved the following day. Croft was appointed in place of Edward Darrell, who died the previous November. A 16 Nov.

1801 letter from Drayton to TJ informing him of Darrell's death has not been found, but was recorded in SJL as received 27 Nov. with the notations "Darrel's death" and "T" (JEP, 1:409; Vol. 33:332n; Vol. 35:756).

THE CONFIDENCE, WHICH YOU THOUGHT FIT TO REPOSE IN ME: on 15 July 1801, TJ asked Drayton to locate a suitable person willing to accept the commissioner's appointment in South Carolina, an unremunerative office which TJ had great difficulty in filling (Vol. 34:136, 543).

From Lyman Spalding

MR. JEFFERSON, Portsmouth 22nd. Febry 1802.

Will you please to accept the humble offering of a faithful citizen in the Republic of science. If you deem it worthy the attention of the American Philosophical Society, I should think myself highly honoured by their acceptance of a copy.

With great esteem, Sir, I have the honour, to be yours.

L SPALDING.

RC (DLC); endorsed by TJ as received 5 Mch. and so recorded in SJL. Enclosure: Lyman Spalding, "Bill of Mortality, For Portsmouth, Newhampshire, for A.D. 1801," a printed table recording the number and causes of death, as well as the ages of the victims (MoSHi: Jefferson Papers).

Lyman Spalding (1775-1821) of New Hampshire earned his medical degree from Harvard in 1797, then went on to enjoy a distinguished career as a physician, educator, author, and inventor. He moved to Portsmouth in 1800, where he founded a medical society, established an anatomical museum, introduced smallpox vaccinations, and served on the town's board of health. From 1801 to 1811, he published a yearly bill of mortality for

Portsmouth, a compilation of vital statistics that detailed the number and causes of death of its residents, which he distributed to a variety of recipients. TJ received a number of these annual broadsides from Spalding, as well as a copy of his 1819 publication, *A History of the Introduction and Use of Scutellaria Lateriflora, (Scullcap,) As a Remedy for Preventing and Curing Hydrophobia, Occasioned by the Bite of Rabid Animals.* Spalding also played a leading role in the 1820 publication of *The Pharmacopoeia of the United States of America* (ANB; J. Worth Estes and David M. Goodman, *The Changing Humors of Portsmouth: The Medical Biography of an American Town, 1623-1983* [Boston, 1986], 1-41; TJ to Spalding, 11 Dec. 1819).

To Albert Gallatin

SIR   Washington Feb. 23. 1802.

I observe that a fund for the contingent expences of government subject to the President and to be accounted for by him personally, was created by the following appropriations:

1790. Vol. 1. pa. 88.   10,000. D
1794.   3.   118.   20,000.
1796.   3.   667.   20,000

of which sums accounts were rendered as follows
by Genl. Washington 1797. Feb. 15
    Mr. Adams   1798. Feb. 12
                         1799. Jan. 8 when an unexpended balance of 14,938.20 being carried by the act of Mar. 3. 1795. to the credit of the Surplus fund, a new Contingent fund of 20,000. D. was erected by the act of Mar. 2. 99. of which the following accounts have been rendered
by mr Adams   Jan. 20. 1800.
                         Jan. 16. 1801. when there remained an unexpended balance of 19,950. D. of which I presume it is incumbent on me to render an account for the year 1801. tho' no part of it has been expended, yet form requires that it should be so stated in an account certified by the Register. I have to ask the favor of you to direct such an account to be prepared and sent to me in duplicates for communication to the two houses. Accept assurances of my high consideration.

TH: JEFFERSON

PrC (DLC); at foot of text: "The Secretary of the Treasury."

The Appropriations Act of 26 Mch. 1790 established a $10,000 fund for the use of the president for CONTINGENT expenses, and called for "a regular statement and account of such expenditures to be laid before Congress at the end of the year." On 17 Jan. 1791, George Washington submitted his first statement exhibiting expenditures of $1,184.91, with the account certified by Joseph Nourse, register of the Treasury. In the statement of 15 Feb. 1797, Washington accounted for $11,998.84 in charges in 1796. John Adams accounted for expenditures of $403.18 in his report of 12 Feb. 1798 and $552.33 in his report of 8 Jan. 1799 (U.S. Statutes at Large, 1:105; Washing-

ton, Papers, Pres. Ser., 7:238; Eileen D. Carzo, ed., National State Papers of the United States, 1789-1817. Part II: Texts of Documents. Administration of George Washington, 1789-1797, 35 vols. [Wilmington, Del., 1985], 7:41-3; 34:293-7; Martin P. Claussen, ed., National State Papers of the United States, 1787-1817. Part II: Texts of Documents. Administration of John Adams, 1797-1801, 24 vols. [Wilmington, Del., 1980], 5:239-42; 11:8-13).

The Appropriations Act of 3 Mch. 1795 called for certain sums, unexpended over a designated period of time, to be "deemed to have ceased" and subsequently transferred to a Treasury account called the SURPLUS FUND. Under the Appropriations Act of 1799, $20,000 was set aside for "defraying the contingent expenses of the government," as the unexpended amount of the previous appropriations had been "carried to the credit of the surplus fund." Adams's annual account of 20 Jan. 1800 indicated that no expenses had been charged to the account during the year, leaving the full $20,000. According to the 16 Jan. 1801 report, Adams had spent $50, the cost of "a mission from Philadelphia to Mount Vernon, on public business," leaving an unexpended balance of $19,950 (U.S. Statutes at Large, 1:437-8, 720; *National State Papers: Adams*, 16:122-3; 23:20-1).

To Albert Gallatin, with Gallatin's Reply

TH:J. TO MR GALLATIN   [23 Feb. 1802]
the inclosed case is entirely unintelligible to me. can you make any thing of it?

[Reply by Gallatin:]
Nicholas Reib is an old German who has tormented Congress & more particularly the Pennsylvania delegation for several years with his claim. It has been repeatedly rejected. If an answer is thought necessary, it will be sufficient to tell him that the Executive has no power in that case & that his application must be to Congress—
    Respectfully your obt. Servt.   ALBERT GALLATIN

RC (DLC); undated; written on verso of address sheet, with Gallatin's reply written immediately below TJ's query; addressed by TJ: "The Secretary of the Treasury" in place of "The President of the United States," in an unidentified hand; readdressed by Gallatin: "The President of the United States"; endorsed by TJ as received from the Treasury Department on 23 Feb. and "Reib's case" and so recorded in SJL. Enclosure: Nicholas Reib to TJ, 17 Feb.

The following day, 24 Feb., TJ returned Reib's papers and explained that he had inquired into his case. "I find that it is not within the powers of the Executive," he informed Reib, "and that no authority short of that of the legislature can give effect to your claim" (PrC in DLC; at foot of text: "Mr. Nicholas Rieb"; endorsed by TJ in ink on verso).

From Moses Myers

Union Tavern Geo. Town Feby. 23d. 1802
M. Myers has the honor to Inclose a Letter from his friend Col. Newton with Two boxes of Segars—

RC (MHi); endorsed by TJ as received 23 Feb. Enclosure: Thomas Newton to TJ, 12 Feb.

Moses Myers (ca. 1752-1835), a mer-

chant, was born in New York City. Myers moved to Norfolk in 1787, a year after a trading company based in New York and Amsterdam in which he was a partner dissolved. In July 1802, he declined a commission from TJ to be a bankruptcy commissioner of Norfolk. An obituary described Myers as "at one time the most extensive merchant South of the Potomac" (Joseph R. Rosenbloom, *A Biographical Dictionary of Early American Jews, Colonial Times through 1800* [Lexington, Ky., 1960], 128; Madison, *Papers, Sec. of State Ser.*, 3:430; *Richmond Enquirer*, 14 July 1835; Thomas Newton to TJ, 10 July 1801).

To Andrew Ellicott

DEAR SIR   Washington Feb. 24. 1802.

On reciept of your favor of Feb. 14. 1802. I immediately referred it to the Secretary of the treasury to know whether the conditions you proposed were practicable? I now inclose you his answer, stating that all are, except that of residence at the seat of the national government. you will see that his reasons are derived from the express injunctions of the law, with which we[1] have not authority to dispense. I am in hopes that this can be yielded on your part. be so good as to let me know; and still to consider the injunction of secrecy as remaining.

I think while you were employed here, you made an Almanac for this latitude, in which I presume were inserted the rising & setting of the sun calculated for the latitude. having no meridian to set our instruments, I have usually observed the rising & setting of the sun by the clock, and taken the mean for the true noon, which would do pretty well were the sensible Horizon to East & West equally raised above the true. but this operation requiring two observations, I am often disappointed by clouds, by company at sunset, & sometimes by forgetting. for common purposes the true moment of sunrising or setting would answer. can your almanac be now got any where? did you make & preserve any observations on the elevation of the sensible horizon here, & particularly as seen from the President's house? Accept my salutations & best wishes.   TH: JEFFERSON

PrC (DLC); at foot of text: "Mr. Andrew Ellicott"; endorsed by TJ in ink on verso. Enclosure: see the following document.

ALMANAC FOR THIS LATITUDE: in November 1792, Ellicott sent copies of *Ellicott's New-Jersey, Pennsylvania, Delaware, Maryland and Virginia Almanac, and Ephemeris, for the Year of our Lord 1793* to TJ and George Washington. "The Astronomical part" of the compilation, Ellicott informed TJ at the time, was "adapted to the meridian, and latitude of the City of Washington." Referring to the subject in a 13 Apr. 1801 letter to TJ, Ellicott said that his intention to continue the calculation of that astronomical data in the Federal District "fell thro when I left the City." Ellicott ceased working as surveyor of the district in the spring of 1793 (Washington, *Papers, Pres. Ser.*, 11:443; ANB; Vol. 24:664; Vol. 33:581, 582n).

[1] TJ here canceled "cannot."

To Albert Gallatin, with Gallatin's Reply

TH:J. TO MR GALLATIN   [on or before 24 Feb. 1801]
   Are the within terms admissible?

[Reply by Gallatin:]

The 1st, 2d & 4th are either in pursuance of, or, not inconsistent with the law, excepting only the words "all other documents belonging to the land department;" the Surveyor general superintends the *surveying* department, & has nothing to do with the *sales* of the lands, these being under the superintendence of the several registers, who make their reports immediately to the Treasury.

The 3d, vizt residing at the seat of Government is inconsistent with the present laws which contemplate the office of the Surveyor general as permanently fixed in the N.W. Territory, & do not enjoin any duties or give any authority in relation to charts, & surveys of the other parts of the U. States.—A copy of the plat of public lands is to be kept open at the Surv. gen. office for public information—He is to transmit plats to the registers of the several land offices & to the Secy. of the Treasury—The Registers shall transmit accounts of sales to the Surv. gen. & to the Secy. of the Treasury—The Surv. gen. receives applications from Registers who want to purchase—On the whole throughout the Acts, the Surv. gen. office is considered as the general land office in the Western country & that of the Secy. of the Treasy. as its counterpart at the seat of Government. The Surv. gen. is also authorized to let upon leases the reserved sections which can only be done by an officer on the spot. But, in fact, his most important duty is the immediate superintendence of the surveyors & surveys which cannot be done at a distance from the scene of action.   A.G.

RC (DLC: TJ Papers, 121:20853); undated; written on a cover sheet alongside the address "President of the United States" in an unidentified hand; addressed on verso in TJ's hand: "The Secretary of the Treasury"; with Gallatin's reply written immediately below TJ's question; endorsed by Gallatin: "Remarks on Ellicot's propositions"; endorsed by TJ as received from the Treasury Department on 24 Feb. and "Ellicot" and so recorded in SJL.

WITHIN TERMS: see Andrew Ellicott to TJ, 14 Feb.

To George Hay

DEAR SIR   Washington Feb. 24. 1802.

I recieved yesterday your favor of the 19th. and am sorry you cannot undertake mr Short's defence against mr Randolph. but I am sensible it is a case of feeling, which no body can estimate but the party himself. I will trouble you therefore to return me the papers and I will write a line to one of the gentlemen of Fredericksburg with whom my communication by post will be so much readier than with the gentleman of Cumberland. I pray you to accept assurances of my esteem & high respect.   TH: JEFFERSON

PrC (DLC: William Short Papers); at foot of text in ink: "George Hay esq."; endorsed by TJ in ink on verso.

To the Senate and the House of Representatives

GENTLEMEN OF THE SENATE AND
OF THE HOUSE OF REPRESENTATIVES.

I communicate to both houses of Congress a Report of the Secretary of the Treasury on the subject of our Marine hospitals, which appear to require legislative attention.

As connected with the same subject, I also inclose information respecting the situation of our seamen and boatmen frequenting the port of New Orleans, and suffering there from sickness & the want of accomodation. there is good reason to believe their numbers greater than stated in these papers. when we consider how great a proportion of the territory of the US. must communicate with that port singly; & how rapidly that territory is increasing it's population & productions, it may perhaps be thought reasonable to make hospital provisions there of a different order from those at foreign ports generally.

TH: JEFFERSON
Feb. 24. 1802.

RC (DNA: RG 233, PM, 7th Cong., 1st sess.); endorsed by a House clerk. PrC (DLC). RC (DNA: RG 46, LPPM, 7th Cong., 1st sess.); in Meriwether Lewis's hand, signed and dated by TJ; endorsed by a Senate clerk. Recorded in SJL with notation "Marine Hospitals." Enclosures: (1) Gallatin to TJ, 16 Feb., and enclosures. (2) Extract of Evan Jones to the secretary of state, 10 Aug. 1801, noting the great number of "American citizens, especially Seamen and Boatmen from the Ohio" who die miserably in New Orleans every year "for want of a Hospital into which they might be put and taken care of" and calling for the establishment of a fund "for the preservation of those poor people by imposing a light tax upon every vessel and boat that comes in, as well as upon every seaman and boatman," estimating that about 200 vessels, with eight men each, and 350 to 400 boats, with four men each, "have come down from the Ohio" during the preceding 12 months (Tr in DNA: RG 233, PM, endorsed by a House clerk, together with Enclosure No. 3, as No. 5; Tr in DNA: RG 46, LPPM, endorsed by a Senate clerk). (3) Extract of E.M. [i.e. Elihu H. Bay] to the secretary of state, 4 Nov. 1802 [i.e. 1801], noting the absence of proper accommodations "for poor and infirm Seamen and Boatmen" at New Orleans, and observing that "Something like an Hospital establishment, to be superintended by American Physicians, would go a great way to alleviate the distresses of these useful men" (Tr in DNA: RG 233, PM, endorsed by a House clerk, together with Enclosure No. 2, as No. 5; PrC in DNA: RG 46, LPPM, endorsed by a Senate clerk; printed with full name and correct date in Madison, *Papers, Sec. of State Ser.*, 2:221-2).

Meriwether Lewis delivered the message and enclosures on MARINE HOSPITALS to Congress on 24 Feb. Both houses immediately read the documents. The House referred them to the Committee of Commerce and Manufactures the same day and they were printed. The Senate ordered them to "lie for consideration" (JHR, 4:106-7; JS, 3:184-5; *Message from the President of the United States, Accompanying a Report of the Secretary of the Treasury to Him, and Two Statements Marked A and B, on the Subject of Marine Hospitals; Also, Sundry Documents Respecting the Situation of Seamen and Boatmen of the United States, Frequenting the Port of New-Orleans, 24th February, 1802* [Washington, D.C., 1802; Shaw-Shoemaker, Nos. 3339, 3340]).

LEGISLATIVE ATTENTION: on 3 May 1802, TJ signed the law which set up a general fund to receive monies collected for the relief of sick and disabled seamen. It gave the president the power to distribute the monies "as circumstances shall require" for the seamen's benefit. To obtain consent for this new arrangement, which took control from the particular ports where the monies were collected, $15,000 was set aside for the erection of a marine hospital in Massachusetts. The "Act to amend an act intituled 'An act for the relief of sick and disabled Seamen'" also gave the president power to provide for U.S. seamen at New Orleans and to appoint a director for a marine hospital there. To cover the costs, the act required that the master of every "boat, raft, or flat" proceeding on the Mississippi to New Orleans pay the collector or naval officer at Fort Adams 20 cents per month for every person they employed, the amount to be deducted from the seamen's wages. The director of the marine hospital at New Orleans was also allowed to admit "sick foreign seamen" at the charge of 75 cents per day (*Annals*, 11:1163-4; U.S. Statutes at Large, 2:192-3). For the previous limitations on the distribution of marine hospital funds, see Vol. 34:678-82.

To Seneca, Onondaga, Cayuga, and Munsee Indians, with Henry Dearborn

BROTHERS,

Your friend Captain Chapin, has laid before your father the President of the United States, your talk made at Genisee-river, on the 12th: of November last, and the President has authorised me to give you the following answer.

Brothers,

Your Father the President of the United States is in his heart a friend to all his red children, and will at all times listen to their complaints, and do all that is in his power for their comfort. He considers you as a part of his great family; and as the Great Spirit, formed us all, it should teach us to live together like brothers.

Brothers,

Your friend Captain Chapin will be directed to procure for your use such kind of goods as will be most agreeable to you , with a due proportion of powder and lead for your huntsmen.

Brothers,

Your father the President will give Capt. Chapin instructions to furnish such of your people as in his judgement will make a good use of them, with a few ploughs, Oxen, Cows and Sheep, and also with some Wheels and Cards for spinning, and if those who may receive such articles this year, do actually use them to the best advantage, more will be furnished the next year; but if you expect your father the President to continue such supplies, you who are Chiefs, must take care that the friendship and benevolence of the President be not abused, by an improper use of the articles provided for you by his directions.

Brothers,

The heart of your father the President is rejoiced to learn that his red children are sensible of the bad effects of that Poison, which has done them so much harm, he hopes that you will not hereafter suffer any of it to be used in your Nations, he will then with more pleasure and better hopes, contribute all in his power for your advancements in comfort and happiness.

Brothers,

The President has spoken to Governor Clinton about purchasing your strip of land on Niagara-river, and he will willingly appoint Comissioners to assist Governor Clinton and your Nations in making the bargain for the land. And if the Cayugas and Onondago's wish to sell any of their lands, the President will assist them in disposing of it; but it is to be understood that Governor Clinton must be consulted before any sale can be made in the State of New York.

Brothers,

You may rest assured, that so long as your Nation shall conduct themselves peacably, honestly, and soberly among themselves and towards their white brethren, and shall make the best use in their power of such means for increasing their happiness, as may be furnished from time to time by their father the President, he will continue to be their friend, and to treat them as his Children.

Given at the War Office of the United Sates at the City of Washington, the 24th: day of February 1802.   H. DEARBORN

S.W.

FC (Lb in DNA: RG 75, LSIA); in a clerk's hand; at head of text: "To the principal Chiefs of the Seneca, Onondago, Cayuga and Delaware Nations"; in margin at head of text: "A Talk to the Seneca Onondago Cayuga & Delaware Nations."

Several years earlier Israel CHAPIN, Jr., succeeded his father as the U.S. agent to the Iroquois (Alan Taylor, "The Divided Ground: Upper Canada, New York, and the Iroquois Six Nations, 1783-1815," *Journal of the Early Republic*, 22 [2002], 65).

YOUR TALK: in November 1801, chiefs of the Senecas and some neighboring tribes gathered at Geneseo, New York, for the distribution of annuities in the form of goods. On 12 Nov., Red Jacket, the principal speaker of the Senecas, made an address to Chapin and asked him to "make known to the President the whole of our speech." The address was translated by an interpreter, Jasper Parrish, and written down, apparently with the expectation that Chapin would take it to Washington for transmittal to the president—"bring us his answer on your return," Red Jacket advised. Henry Dearborn framed the above response as if it would be delivered to its recipients orally. The repeated salutation of the listeners as "brothers" was typical of addresses made during face-to-face encounters, and mirrored Red Jacket's addressing of Chapin as "Brother" in the 12 Nov. address (Granville Ganter, ed., *The Collected Speeches of Sagoyewatha, or Red Jacket* [Syracuse, N.Y., 2006], 115-17; Conference with Little Turtle, at 4 Jan., and Conference with Black Hoof, at 5 Feb.).

In his address, Red Jacket made practical requests concerning the annuities that were paid in the form of goods. He asked that the government give the Senecas only very warm cloth—coarse, heavy wool or cotton flannel, rather than "fine broadcloths"—and that POWDER AND LEAD be provided for hunting. The tribe also wanted payments due to them from a land sale in the 1780s to be deposited in the Bank of the United States so that cash annuities from different sources could be paid at the same time each year. Most significantly, although on some previous occasions Red Jacket had rejected acculturation and change, he now declared that the Senecas were ready to follow George Washington's advice "to quit the mode of Indian living and learn the manner of White people." The Senecas "finde ourselves in a situation which we believe our fore Fathers never thought of," said Red Jacket: now the "White people are seated so thick over the Country that the dear have almost fled from us, and we finde ourselves obliged to pursue some other mode of geting our living." The Indians would accept OXEN, COWS, plows, farming utensils, and spinning wheels from the government and would learn to use them. The Senecas "must make use of Cattle instead of Moose Elk etc" and "sheep in place of dear" (Ganter, *Collected Speeches of Sagoyewatha*, 115-16).

THAT POISON: Red Jacket declared that the tribe had determined to "quit the use of liquor" (same).

In the address on 12 Nov., the Seneca orator also indicated that the tribe wanted to make a land swap with the Holland Land Company and were ready to sell a STRIP OF LAND along the Niagara River—property that Timothy Pickering had tried to interest them in selling as early as 1794. The ribbon of land at Black Rock was a traditional Seneca fishing site, but also a desirable travel corridor for white settlements. The Senecas had come to "fear incroachments," Red Jacket said, "a party of men having made a beginning there last summer." Selling that piece of land had become a point of sharp contention between political rivals in a Seneca council meeting in June 1801. Red Jacket favored selling the property, but his uncle, Handsome Lake, strongly opposed the idea. Handsome Lake later tried to have the sale overturned (same, 115, 117; Anthony F. C. Wallace, *The Death and Rebirth of the Seneca* [New York, 1969], 259-60, 265, 285).

CAYUGAS AND ONONDAGO'S: present at the annuities meeting on 12 Nov. when Red Jacket addressed Chapin were "Principal chiefs of the Senecas, Onondagas, Cayugas, and Delawares." The Onondagas and Cayugas were, like the Senecas, Iroquois tribes of the Six Nations. Red Jacket said that he spoke for the three tribes with regard to land sales: "our voices are one." The term "Delaware" was applied to various groups, none of which were Iroquoian. In this case it meant a band of Munsee-speaking Indians who lived near the Senecas in western New York but retained their own identity and were referred to alternately as Munsees or Delawares. They had some alliance with Red Jacket, for in the spring of 1801, Handsome Lake accused the Munsees and Red Jacket of witchcraft. Soon after, the Munsees moved from Cattaraugus Creek to Buffalo Creek, where they could be closer to Red Jacket. In March 1802, Handsome Lake met with TJ and Dearborn in Washington, declared that he spoke for the Senecas, and indirectly denounced Red Jacket (Ganter, *Collected Speeches of Sagoyewatha*, 115, 117; Wallace, *Death and Rebirth*, 255-61; Sturtevant, *Handbook*, 15:213, 223; ANB, s.v. "Red Jacket"; Conference with Handsome Lake, 10 Mch. 1802).

CONTINUE TO BE THEIR FRIEND: one of the Senecas' annuities derived from the sale of land rights to Robert Morris in 1797 and drew on dividends from shares of the Bank of the United States (see Memorandum on the Seneca Annuity, 19 Nov. 1801). The proceeds of the stock had been held in the Treasury, but in December 1801, Henry Dearborn opened an account in the B.U.S. for that Seneca fund. On 2 Mch. 1802, TJ wrote a brief instruction to George Simpson, the cashier of the bank: "Sir, You will place to the credit, and hold at the disposal of the Secretary of War, the avails of two hundred & five shares in the bank of the United States belonging to the Seneca Nations of Indians, and by them placed under my immediate superintendence and direction" (RC, facsimile in Kenneth W. Rendell, Inc., Somerville, Massachusetts, catalogue, 1972, in hand of Joshua Wingate, Jr., signed and dated by TJ, at foot of text: "George Simpson Esquire Cashier of the bank, U States," not recorded in SJL; Dearborn to Simpson, 18 Dec. 1801, in Lb in DNA: RG 75, LSIA). Also on 2 Mch., Dearborn drew on the Senecas' account for $6,250. Noting that the government's records on the Senecas' dividends had been lost in the War Department fire of November 1800, Dearborn asked Simpson for a statement of the dividends, the amounts drawn from that source, and any balance remaining. The money that Dearborn drew from the bank early in March was for Chapin; on 1 Mch., Dearborn instructed the agent to distribute, among "three or four of the best disposed chiefs" of the Senecas, a dozen sheep, some wool cards and spinning wheels, three or four milk cows, and two or three plows, each plow to have a yoke and a pair of oxen. Chapin was also to give plows, oxen, wool cards, and spinning wheels to the Tuscarora Indians to introduce "a spirit and knowledge" of agriculture and domestic arts to that tribe. In addition, Dearborn authorized the construction of "a cheap saw-mill" at the Tuscaroras' reservation. A century earlier the Tuscaroras lived in North Carolina, but in the eighteenth century a segment of the tribe, which spoke an Iroquoian language, moved north and became affiliated with the Iroquois confederacy. Although it was not written into the contract with Morris in 1797, the Senecas wanted the Tuscaroras to have a small tract in western New York, and by arrangements with the Holland Land Company the Tuscaroras occupied, in 1802, a reservation two square miles in size near the Niagara River. On 4 Feb. 1802, Dearborn had met with a group of Tuscaroras who were returning from a trip to North Carolina, where the tribe hoped to sell some land and use the proceeds to augment the reservation in New York. Dearborn had also seen that delegation in the fall of 1801 as they traveled through Washington to North Carolina (Dearborn to Tuscaroras, 2 Nov. 1801, 4 Feb. 1802, to Chapin, 1 Mch. 1802, to Simpson, 2 Mch., in Lb in DNA: RG 75, LSIA; Sturtevant, *Handbook*, 15:282, 518-21; Vol. 32:435-6n).

From Maria Cosway

DEAR SIR   Paris 25 Feb. 1802

I have had the pleasure of writting to you several times, but not that of hearing from you for a long time. Surely you have not forgotten such an old friend! I am now in the place which brings me to mind every day our first interview, the pleasing days we pass'd together. I send you the prospectus of a work which is the most interesting ever published as every body will have in their possession the exact distribution of this wonderfull gallery. The history of every picture will also be very curious as we have collected in one spot the finest works of art which were spread all over Italy.—I hope you will make it known among your friends who may like to know of such a work. This will keep me here two years at least & every body seem very Much delighted with this interprise.

Have we hopes of ever seeing you in Paris? would it not be a rest for you after your laborious situation? I often see the only freind remaining of our set, Madme: de Corney, the same in her own amiable qualities but very different in her Situation, but she supports it very well.—

I am come to this place in its best time for the profusion of fine things is beyond description & not possible to Conceive. It is so changed in every respect, that you would not think it the same Country or people.—shall this letter be fortunate enough to get to your hands! will it be still More fortunate to procure me an answer! I leave you to reflect on the happiness you will afford your ever afct: & sincere   M COSWAY.

RC (MHi); addressed: "Thomas Jefferson Esqre"; endorsed by TJ as received 2 June and so recorded in SJL.

Since her last letter to TJ, dated 20 July 1801 from London, Cosway had moved to Paris to execute a series of etchings of paintings at the Louvre. The etchings offer rare documentation of contemporary painting arrangements in the Grand GALLERY, where recently confiscated art from Belgium and Italy was publicly displayed in addition to France's royal art collections. A total of eight plates were published in 1802 through a business partnership with Julius Griffiths. Cosway left Paris in 1803 before completing the project (Andrew McClellan, *Inventing the Louvre: Art, Politics, and the Origins of the Modern Museum in Eighteenth-Century Paris* [Cambridge, 1994], 1, 114-23, 138-45, 256n; Stephen Lloyd, *Richard & Maria Cosway: Regency Artists of Taste and Fashion* [Edinburgh, 1995], 89-90, 135; Charles Pinckney to TJ, October 1801).

Proposal to Publish Etchings
of Pictures in the Louvre

GALLERY OF THE LOUVRE,
AT PARIS.

It is proposed to publish by subscription highly finished ETCHINGS, done by Mrs. MARIA COSWAY, of all the PICTURES which compose the superb collection in the gallery of the Louvre, comprising the most celebrated CHEFS-D'OEUVRE of the ITALIAN, FLEMISH, and FRENCH schools; with an historical account of each picture, and such authentic anecdotes of the artists, as may be new and interesting by

J. GRIFFITHS, ESQRE.

The above work will be published by numbers, each containing TWO etchings and the text, printed on superfine paper, with beautiful types; the first number will be ready for delivery on the 31st March next, and if possible, TWO will be given in each future month.

Each place will represent the pictures which compose ONE of the compartments of the gallery, which is at present divided into fifty seven, and the work will be continued until the whole of the collection may be compleated.

The size of the plates is twenty one inches in height by seventeen in breadth, and the TWO first will contain copies of the works of the following masters:

Raffaello	7	Procaccino	1
Giulio Romano	5	Domenico Feti	1
Tizziano	4	Sebastiano del Piombo	1
Leonardo da Vinci	2	Guercino	1
Paolo Veronese	2	Baldassar Peruzzi	1
Guido	1	Alessandro Veronese	1

The numbers will be delivered in strict conformity with the dates of the subscriptions, which it is requested may be paid on receipt of each number.

The impressions will be of two kinds, colored and plain.

PRICE TO SUBSCRIBERS,

For each number with two colored etchings,   L 1— 5—
Do.   with two plain   15—

PRICE TO NON-SUBSCRIBERS,

For each number with two colored etchings,   L 1—11—6—
Do.   with two plain   1— 1—

Subscribers, a list of whom will be given with the work, are sollicited to signify their intentions to M. COLNAGHI, Cockspur street, LONDON, who will carefully direct the numbers according to order, grant receipts for the amount of subscriptions paid (if required), and with whom may be seen a specimen of the etchings.

1st February 1802.

Printed broadside (DLC: TJ Papers, 120:20754).

From Albert Gallatin

SIR   Treasury Department Feby. 25th 1802

I have the honor to transmit the official statement of the contingent fund in the usual form. In order that it may be fully understood, I will add that the sums appropriated to discharge the contingent expences of Government amounted on the 1st of January 1801 to Drs. 19,950; that the fund received an accession during the course of the year 1801 of Drs. 961 & 80 cents, being monies formerly advanced out of the same, but which having been applied to other objects, have been charged in account to their proper appropriations, and credit given for the amount, to this fund; and that, no monies having been expended, during 1801, out of this fund, the whole unexpended balance, thus amounting to Drs. 20,911 & 80 cents has been carried to the credit of the surplus fund on the 31st Decer. 1801. The account is thus closed, the appropriation has ceased & determined; and there are not, at present, any monies appropriated to defray the contigent expences of Government.

I have the honor to be very respectfully Sir Your most obedt. Servt.

ALBERT GALLATIN

RC (DLC); at foot of text: "The President of the United States"; endorsed by TJ as received from the Treasury Department on 25 Feb. and "Contingent fund" and so recorded in SJL. Enclosure: see enclosure described at TJ to the Senate and the House of Representatives, 25 Feb.

On this date, Gallatin forwarded to TJ from the Treasury Department the register's statement on the contingency fund: "The Secretary of the Treasury has the Honor to transmit to the President of the United States, Triplicates of a Statement of Expenditures upon the Funds heretofore appropriated for discharging the contingent Expences of Government up to the 31st. of December last.—All which is respectfully submitted by Albert Gallatin" (RC in DLC, in a clerk's hand, signed by Gallatin; at foot of text: "The President of the United States").

From James Madison

2[5] Feby. 1802

The Secretary of State has the honor to lay before the President of the United States, copies of the following documents, viz.

A schedule containing a statement of the suits, in the Circuit Court for Maryland, ending with November term last.

A similar statement of suits in the District Court for Kentucky, ending with March term last.

A certificate of the Clerk of the Circuit Court for West Tennessee (and who was the Clerk of the late District Court for Tennessee) respecting the suits in the Courts of the United States within that State.

The two last mentioned papers are intended as corrections of the document referred to in your message to Congress at the opening of the present session, as containing a statement of the suits in the Courts of the United States: and the first mentioned Schedule to supply an omission in it.

This occasion being adapted to the purpose, the Secretary takes leave to mention some other imperfections of the document referred to in the message.

In Massachusetts 14 common Law suits being omitted at October term 1797, the whole number of common law suits should be 244 instead of 230; the aggregate of all the suits 323 instead of 320; and the number of suits decided, discontinued, dismissed and not prosecuted 282 instead of 283.

In Virginia, the aggregate should be 2162 instead of 2048; and the number decided, discontinued, dismissed and not prosecuted 1831 instead of 1717.

In North Carolina the aggregate should be 629 instead of 495, and the number decided, discontinued, dismissed and not prosecuted 495 instead of 361. And

In South Carolina the aggregate should be 882 instead of 1143 and the number decided, discontinued, dismissed and not prosecuted 621 instead of 571.

None of the above variations affect the whole number of causes stated to be depending in either of the Districts except that of Kentucky, to which an addition of 21 is made by the second statement received: but Maryland adds to the whole 60 of such causes. That the aggregate is not materially varied is also apparent from the annexed recapitulation.

It would be unnecessary to explain with minuteness how these errors originated: it is sufficient to observe that they arose partly from inexact statements returned to this Office by the Clerks of the Courts, and partly in analyzing and adding the numbers contained in the returns and transcribing the result.

All which is respectfully submitted.   JAMES MADISON

RC (DNA: RG 233, PM, 7th Cong., 1st sess.); in a clerk's hand, with date, complimentary close, and signature by Madison. PrC (DNA: RG 46, LPPM, 7th Cong., 1st sess.; endorsed by a Senate clerk). Enclosures: (1) Statement concerning suits in the circuit court for Maryland from May 1790 to November

1801, compiled by Philip Moore, clerk of the court (Tr in DNA: RG 233, PM; PrC in DNA: RG 46, LPPM). (2) Statement concerning suits in the district court for Kentucky from March 1790 to March 1801, and a certificate by Thomas Tunstall, clerk of the court, dated 13 Jan. 1802, stating that 294 suits "were in the name and for the benefit of the United States" and that 45 were "only depending" on 1 June 1801 (Tr in DNA: RG 233, PM; Tr in DNA: RG 46, LPPM, with certificate subjoined to statement). (3) Certificate signed by Randall McGavock, dated 1 Jan. 1802, recording 77 cases pending and undecided in the district court for West Tennessee of which 14 were decided at the April 1801 term, with 36 of the undecided cases adjourned into the circuit court for West Tennessee and 27 into the circuit court for East Tennessee (MS in RG 233, PM; PrC in DNA: RG 46, LPPM). (4) "Recapitulation of the suits in the Circuit Courts of the U. States, and the District Courts for Maine, Kentucky & Tennessee," indicating that 8,358 suits were instituted and 1,629 pending as compared with 8,276 suits, of which 1,539 were pending, in the former recapitulation (MS in DNA: RG 233, PM, in several clerks' hands, endorsed by a House clerk; PrC in RG 46, LPPM). Enclosed in TJ to the Senate and the House of Representatives, 26 Feb. 1802.

DOCUMENTS REFERRED TO IN YOUR MESSAGE: see No. 8 of the papers that supplemented the annual message in note to Document II of the Annual Message to Congress, printed at 8 Dec. 1801; ASP, *Miscellaneous*, 1:319-25.

To the Senate and the House of Representatives

GENTLEMEN OF THE SENATE & OF THE HOUSE OF REPRESENTATIVES.

No occasion having arisen, since the last account rendered by my predecessor, of making use of any part of the monies heretofore granted to defray the contingent charges of the government, I now transmit to Congress an official statement thereof to the 31st. day of December last, when the whole unexpended balance, amounting to 20,911. D 80 c was carried to the credit of the Surplus fund, as provided by law; and this account consequently becomes finally closed.

TH: JEFFERSON
Feb. 25. 1802.

RC (DNA: RG 46, LPPM, 7th Cong., 1st sess.); endorsed by a Senate clerk. PrC (DLC). RC (DNA: RG 233, PM, 7th Cong., 1st sess.); in Meriwether Lewis's hand, signed and dated by TJ. Recorded in SJL with notation "Contingent fund." Enclosure: "Account of the Application of Grants made by Congress for the Contingent Charges of Government," Register's Office, Treasury Department, 23 Feb., covering 31 Dec. 1800 to 31 Dec. 1801; showing a beginning balance of $19,950, no expenditures, and credits of $261.80 and $700, paid to Winthrop Sargent and John Steele, as governor and secretary, respectively, of Mississippi Territory, from the contingency fund but subsequently charged to Timothy Pickering's account as secretary of state, for a closing balance of $20,911.80, which was carried to the surplus fund on 31 Dec. 1801 (MS in DNA: RG 46, LPPM, in a clerk's hand, signed by Joseph Nourse, endorsed by a Senate clerk; MS in DNA: RG 233, PM, in a clerk's hand, signed by Nourse; MS in DLC, in a clerk's hand, signed by Nourse).

Meriwether Lewis delivered this message and statement to Congress on 26 Feb. In both houses the documents were read and ordered to lie on the table (JHR, 4:108; JS, 3:186). They were printed as *Message from the President of the United States, Accompanying an Official Statement of the Monies Heretofore Appropriated to Defray the Contingent Charges of Government, to the 31st of December, 1801, Inclusive. 26th February, 1802* (Washington, D.C., 1802). See Shaw-Shoemaker, No. 3342.

From "A—X"

[26 Feb. 1802]

"Read this
"And then to dinner
"With what appetite
      you may"
You are in danger a dreadful plot is forming against you— p—n. the method
—Julius Cæsar was cautioned for the Ides of March—I caution you for the last of April   A—X

NB. a curly headed
    one legged
    man head

RC (DLC); undated; addressed: "Thomas Jefferson President of Ud. Ss. Aa. City of Washington"; franked; postmarked New York, 26 Feb.; endorsed by TJ as received 3 Mch. and "assassination" and so recorded in SJL.

WITH WHAT APPETITE YOU MAY: a quotation popularized by the English poet Alexander Pope: "from thence (as *Shakespear* has it) *To dinner with what*

appetite they may" (*Letters of Mr. Pope, and Several Eminent Persons, From the Year 1705, to 1711,* 2 vols. [Dublin, 1735], 1:176). Pope's source, and possibly that of the author above, was William Shakespeare's *Henry VIII*, act 3, scene 2, in which an angry King Henry presents incriminating papers to Cardinal Wolsey with the command to "Read o'er this; And after this: and then to breakfast with what appetite you have."

From Anthony Campbell

SIR,   Washington City February 26 1802
    The chief magistrate of a free and enlightened people should not be addressed on light or trivial affairs; his mind must necessarily be employed on affairs of the greatest importance, and unrealized must be

the expectations that communications which have not for their object moral or political improvement should claim his attention. The want of these considerations indicate either ignorance or arrogance, or both. In addressing you in this instance I beg leave to plead exemption from each. It is not my disposition or inclination to be troublesome, but imperious necessity compels me to it. The subject at present is delicate, and it is with extreme timidity as well as reluctance, that it is again introduced to your notice. By having rendered "the State some service," I feel myself despised, neglected, and injured. That neglect, contempt, and injury has been to me the cause of the greatest discontent, as well a considerable degree of enquiry, and some surprize among a considerable portion of respectable republicans. It is a duty due to Society and myself to make the cause fully known to the only person on earth in whose power it is to have every murmer hushed and every anxiety removed. In the relation I will endeavor to be as concise as the nature of the case, my feelings, and a faithful detail of facts will permit.

The sacred regard every man owes to truth and his own reputation is paramount to all other consideration. Insensibility to these all important considerations indicate a total alienation of every other moral virtue. The individual devoid of spirit to defend his character when attacked by the poisonous breath of calumny is a reproach to himself—a disgrace to Society.

As a republican, such I have been from my earliest days, as such has Suffered, and as such has been the unceasing object of persecution, by british royalists on this side as well as on the opposite shores of the atlantic, I am prepared and will defend my character at every hazard. Descended from humble but honest parents, I am proud to say many of my nearest relations fought, bled, and died contending for the rights of humanity and America. Myself abhorring despotism and ardently attached to republican institutions, I have therefore the strongest attachments to bind me to the United States; and if I know my own heart, my latest breath will waft a prayer to Heaven for a perpetuation of their liberties.

This much for my practical political sentiments, and my opinions of part of the duties a man owes to Society and himself.—

Besides being supported by the strongest hereditary claims on national gratitude, perhaps few surviving individuals have stronger claims to the patronage of a republican administration. The mature part of my life and a competency has been devoted and sacrificed on the alters of Liberty. Numerous testimonials of the truth of these assertions are in my possession. One, and the most recent, is the certificate of three virtuous, respectable and influential american Republicans testifies that I have "rendered the United States an essential Service," and in the execution that I was actuated by a pure regard for the public good. As if to sink me deeper in the abyss of misfortune, this very national service, has been to me a cause of the most Serious injuries, and indeed the future evils it may produce are almost incalculable. It has deprived me of the means of procuring subsistance, it has totally exhausted my finances; it has subjected me to the greatest personal dangers, it has brought on me the vengeance of a wicked party infuriated by disgrace and disappointed ambition; with those who cannot and others who will not consider the springs of action, my fidelity has been brought in question to the utter rejection of my personal services in any way in which my usefulness could be employed; it has made life dreary and indeed in many instances a precarious tenure; with the most painful feelings, after having exhausted the generosity of my personal friends, my watch and even that part of my small wardrobe not in actual service were sacrificed to satisfy the importunate demands of nature; and Strange! but true, and what grieves me most, is the unworthy attempt, by either insiduous friends or avowed enemies to cast an odium on my moral character. These are not all, though the most conspicuous injuries the fruits of that national service.

To avert the dreadful calamities of poverty, I wrote eight letters to Mr Gallatin, on this subject and requesting him to restore, or use his influence to procure me a situation in some department of government where my usefulness and industry could procure a subsistence. Profound Silence were his answers! In conversation with a friend of mine he said I was "impeached with a breach of trust, 'till that was cleared up nothing could be done." Impartially, I will endeavor to examine the ground of this allegation. The presumption is, that this said "breach of trust," can only relate to the exposition of the irregularity of certain officers in the civil department of government. Granted Mr. Gardner and myself did communicate to the people of the United States those petty little Federal Faux paux. And this is the amount of that "breach of trust" that received the indirect applause of every honest man from New Hampshire to Georgia; this was the "breach of trust," that accelerated that happy reformation in political sentiments, which at present pervades all ranks of honest citizens; this was the "breach of trust" that roused deluded and deceived Americans from a dangerous lethargy; this was the "breach of trust" that materially assisted to derange the wicked plans of the sanguinary myrmidons of reviving toryism. on what Just ground can it be called

a "breach of trust"! It is an axiom in law, and in morals, that acces-
sories are as culpable as the principals. If we are guilty of a breach of
trust, Mr. Gallatin is equally criminal. He spent several days at his
lodgings in Philadelphia writing comments on these very exposi-
tions; particularly on Jonathan Dayton's accounts. Mr. Gallatin, Mr.
Beckly, Mr. Isreal, Mr. Smith, and many other respectable republicans highly applauded the action. Mr. Beckly and Mr. Isreal certify it
produced an essential national Service, and Mr. Gallatin calls it a
"breach of trust"! And are the virtues and disinterestedness of 1800
to be turned into a "breach of trust" in 1802! Strange inconsistancy!
great perversion! dangerous degeneracy! The applause of the virtuous is the strongest stimulus to generous Actions; even the Silent
approbation of the good, is a great, tho' not solid reward. But the
doctrine of admiring the treason and despiseing the traitor, is in this
instance too thinly disguised. In the present case it is inapplicable.
For let it be remembered that the action was committed at a time
when there was no hopes of gain, and a certainty to lose; let it be remembered, it was done when stern power, and dread poverty stared
us in the face; let it be remembered that bribes, intrigues, delusion,
nor personal influence of no description had no agency in the decisions that produced that action; let it be remembered, that we are
men, and had to contend with the internal Struggles of self love and
principle. Facts have demonstrated which was victorious, and which
was sacrificed. Let it be remembered to their eternal disgrace that
bribes were offered and menaces uttered to divert me from what I
conceived to be principle and to avert the impending torrents of conscious guilt that have since fallen on them: Let it be remembered,
that bribes were rejected; public and anonymous threats despised;
and let it also be remembered, that it was the dictates of cool and
unbiassed reason that led to that action, and in every instance and
in every Stage of the bussiness, private intrest was sacrificed in the
conscientiousness of performing a public duty.

Treasury rituals should not be wrapped up in eternal mystery; they
should not be inveloped in the inexplicable mysteries of Egyptian
priest-craft. The public should be made acquainted with the true
state of the national accounts. The accounts of public agents Should
be settled at the regular periods prescribed by law; no monies should
be advanced from the treasury unless under Specific and lawful appropriations; and public delinquents ought to be proceeded against
as the law directs. Simple adherence to these constitutional and lawful propositions would keep faithful and correct officers beyond the
powers of calumny. Adherence to Just principles will always render

secresy in the financial arrangement of a republic almost unnecessary. If profound secresy was absolutely necessary, no such sacred duty was imposed on us; or if the imposition of secresy was a practice, that part of the initiation ceremony was unfortunately omitted, the extent of my oath on entering the Treasury Department as a Clerk was simply thus: "I Anthony Campbell, do swear to support the constitution of the United States, and faithfully perform the duties of office, so help me God." Sworn before Richard Peters, Federal Judge for the district of Pennsylvania, and will be found on fyle in his office or in the office of the auditor of the treasury. My most rancourous enemies will not dare to appear in a Court of Justice to substantiate that I had in any instance violated the stipulations of the above obligation. Slander that injures a man in the ordinary avocations of life is a proper object of Judicial decision. If I have been a slanderer most certainly I deserve punishment. Less transgressions have been severely punished: If I in my turn have been injured, I have a right to satisfaction, my standing in society does not raise me above the reach of detraction, and it is more than probable a public opportunity will never occur in which my actions would recoil the slander

Unless the radical part of the installation into office was omitted it is probable my equals, inferiors and superiors in office were bound by the principles of the same obligation: If so let candor, and Justice point out who were violators of the constitution and the laws, and who unfaithfully performed the duties of office and who were really guilty of a "breach of trust." "No money shall be drawn from the treasury but in consequence of appropriations made by law: and a regular statement and account of the receipts and expenditures of all public money shall be published from time to time." Had the Treasury obligation not been imposed on us, then it might have been Said with ome degree of plausibility that we were guilty of a breach of confidence. To impose obligations, and when the principles of that obligation clashes with some favorite scheme to call the support of the obligation a breach of trust, is such a flagrant violation of every moral principle as must excite the indignation of even the most abandoned of the profligate. The supporters of such doctrine ought to be made known. The people want only correct information to be just. Are my enemies prepared to say no money has been advanced from the treasury but in consequence of specific appropriations made by law! Are they prepared to say, that true and regular statements and accounts of the receipts and expenditures of all public money was published at all times! Are they prepared to say, that the accounts of all public agents were settled at the regular periods stated by law! or are they prepared to say that the accounts of all public agents were settled by the rule prescribed by law, and that they have faithfully discharged the duties of office! If they answer in the affirmative at this time, I can only admire the wonderful elasticity of their consciences!!

But surely the constitution of the United States does not impose silence on clerks, it does not require that the conduct, and particularly the irregularities of public officers should be concealed; nor does the faithful performance of the duties of office consist in passive silence, obsequious obedience, or a concealment of the uses or abuses of public officers. Public vice and public virtue are equally interesting to the community. Each should be an object of the greatest attention to people in the habit of self government. corrupt practices, or lurking frauds sanctioned by the lapse of time, or the example of popular men are truly dangerous to Republics. A concealment of the weakness or wickedness of two or three individuals to the injury of the community is certainly criminal. If these premises are granted, it will require no great logical penetration to discover who were the transgressors of the most sacred moral and political duties.

All laws, however grievous constitutionally made by the legal representatives of the people should be implicitly obeyed, 'till a constitutional repeal could be effected. National treaties, constitutionally made by the constituted authorities, become the supreme law of the land, and their stipulations Should be faithfully and punctually fulfilled. If these axioms are founded in political morality, by extending the enquiry and going further into detail it will be more clearly seen who were truly guilty of a "breach of trust"—

Would it, or would it not have been a violation of the constitution and the laws and an unfaithful performance of the duties of office to have remained silent at a time I knew Jonathan Dayton, unconstitutionally, unlawfully, and under no pretext whatever, held in his hands large sums of the public money for long periods unaccounted for![1] He had the effrontery to apply to Mr. Nourse the register of the treasury for a receipt antedated, to shew he had paid the money into the public treasury, at a time[2] he really did not thus to decieve the American people.—

It would have been a violation of the Treasury obligation, to have remained silent, when I knew Timothy Pickering, could not under the appropriation laws account for large sums of public monies remaining in hand for long periods

It would have been a violation of that instrument, I swore to Support, to have remained Silent, when I knew Congress had made appropriations to maintain the national stipula[tions] and that under cover of those appropriations large sums were drawn from the public treasury which were not applied to the specific purposes for which they were intended, and were either retained in the hands of an individual, or directed into unlawful or improper channels!

Knowing these facts, it would have been a flagrant violation of political morality to have remained Silent, when the Out-Centinels of the republic, were sounding the tocsin of war, and the savage hordes of Tripoly, Tunis, and Algiers, were about to be let loose on the unprotected commerce, on the lives, and on the liberties of industrious unoffending and unsuspecting Americans!

I would have been consistant with the Eyes of humanity in this case to have remained Silent, when perhaps American freemen were dragging the galling chain of Slavery or Smarting under the lash of Barbarian taskmasters!

It would have been a violation of every moral and political duty to have remained Silent, when I knew the efficient cause of the dangers that then, and does still threaten the peace of the United States!

It would have been a violation of the constitution, and an unfaithful performance of the duties of office, to have remained silent, when inaccurate and irregular statements of the accounts of public money were published, when public agents were not compelled to settle their accounts at the periods prescribed by law; when the accounts of certain Collectors of the public money were not settled by the principles marked out by law; and when monies were advanced out of the public treasury to certain favorites, and at the expiration of a long period to protract payment bonds were taken payable at remote periods with an interest at 2 ℞ cent less than the republic paid at the same time!

It would not have been common honesty to have remain Silent when the finances of the Republic were rapaciously seized, profusely squandered and in many instances made subservient to the aggrandizement of the enemies of Republicanism!

It would not have evinced a Spirit of republicanism to have remained Silent at a time, when I knew the best qualification for office was avowed enmity to equal rights; when Virtue and patriotism were considered crimes; when all who did not shout hossannas to Federalism were considered as traitors; when british royalists, Old tories, or their children unequivocally preferred to native whiggs—or republican foriegners!

It would not have evinced a love of order or equal rights to have remained Silent when I wittnessed officers composed of british stage dancers, british tavern lagwags unnaturalized foreign mercenaries of every description, and a few giddy young men, carrying their insolence to an extent perhaps proportionately unparralled in the hystory of any nation!

Would it have been patriotic to have wrapped myself up in the mantle of hypocritic silence, when I knew (or even thought I knew) there was a party in power, whose grand object it was to annihilate every vestige of republicanism; to trample on equal rights;—to Subvert the dearest rights of man!!

It would not have been consistant with the feelings of a republican to have calmly viewed the Goddess of liberty almost frightened from her chosen seat, when monarchy was eulogized as the exclusive attribute of heaven; patriotism denounced as the Spirit of hell, and the votaries of liberty almost denied the comforts of social life!

Would it have been consistant with the principles of human nature, when an opportunity offerred, to not have retaliated on the persecutors of myself, and my unfortunate fellow exiles!!! Such were the reasons, the feelings and motives that produced the exposition of Federal irregularities; many more and Strong ones might be exhibited, but these are sufficient to demonstrate That it was not a "breach of trust." Can it be called so? Tryed by the constitution, by the laws, by the treasury obligation, by Justice, by honor, by humanity, by patriotism, or by the common feelings of animated nature it will be found I have not been guilty of a breach of trust. If it can be demonstrated, that I am guilty, or that it was an immoral action, then I will confess I am acquainted with no moral rectitude, and that I owe no duty to the Deity, to society, or to myself. Is it because mere chance cast me into the situation of a Knight of the quill, in the Treasury Department, that I am to violate the most binding and sacred obligations I owe to society; or view with passive Silence the dilapidation of a public treasury! Must I in dread of power, or the love of money sacrifice every tie of the Sacred principles of morality; or must I because a poor unfortunate exile calmly wait the bursting of the gathering storm, and peaceably Wittness the immolation of Liberty's last hope in every quarter of the globe! No. Forbid it Heaven! Nor do I suppose a single republican would expect such a prediliction of principle.   In many countries of Europe, where the heads of Departments are in the habits of tyranizeing over the minds as well as the purses of the people, Such a prostitution of principle would be in some degree excusable. But I hope in this country where the people are politically virtuous, enlightened, and uncorrupted in their manners both accessaries and principals would be called down right robbers. It is astonishing that republicans should be so blindly attached to Men as to endeavor to varnish their faults at the expense of truth and Justice! Astonishment is further excited to wittness the attempt to stigmatize those whose only crime was to expose public defaulters at the bar of public indignation.—Good God! is it possible that these disclosures are to be looked on as a breach of trust! Is it possible that silence in these cases is to be looked on as the test of honor & integrity! Is it possible that it is considered consistant with the fair and immutable truths of Republicanism to view with Silent indifference the dilapidation of a public treasury, and the demolition of every principle of equal rights!! If my person and reputation is to be sacrificed by cowardly insinuation or entire neglect, I hope an opportunity will be granted to defend myself. My crime and disgrace should be made known: Society should be guarded against all arch violators of morality. The assassins poniard is not more dreadful than the insiduous calumniator. Open candid and manly declarations are the characteristic marks of Republicans. In vindication of my reputation, to the bar of public opinion, I have no objection to make the appeal, and by its decision cheerfully abide. They will Judge impartially; they have decided on the infamy of Pickering and Dayton. They will pronounce the Just, the awful, but the henious sentence you are guilty of a "breach of trust." Republicans cannot be unjust. The letters that passed between Mr. Gardner, myself and others relating to this bussiness will be published in my defence if necessary,[3] They contain much useful information on the plans and system of ex–Federal measures, and not a word which I would desire to suppress. As every thing has terminated favorably, for the sake of Republicanism, I hope such a measure will be unnecessary.

The most dreary prospects were in view, when I made these disclosures to the people, I had no mercy to expect from an incensed party. Forced to fly from the despotism of my native country I dare not return. Moneyless I had not the means to convey me to another Country. Every impartial observer of the state of parties in this country must acknowledge that if the elections had not fortunately terminated in favor of Republicanism, I ought to consider myself fortunate to escape assassination.—ever Since I have been frequently and violently assaulted!

Timothy Pickering, Jonathan Dayton and others, have or have not been public defaulters. If they were, I contend it was meritorious to have them arraigned at the bar of public opinion. If they were not, I contend, that speedy, ample and examplerary Justice should be done to their characters. If it can be proved that they were, very unwillingly should I believe that the people of the United States, or any member of the present administration would look upon it as dishonorable to expose public defaulters.

The editors of Federal newspapers, their associates and supporters have been industrious in fabricating, propagateing and publishing the most malignant calumnies to blacken my character. Their Slanderous assertions have been indirectly Substantiated by the manifest cold neglect I have experienced. Hence it is a natural association of ideas, that he who has committed a public action, which his friends do not even indirectly countenance, must be a bad private character and unworthy confidence. The injuries are too manifest to be urged at this time. I have felt them. But to efface any received false impressions relateing to my moral character, I can only say, many respectable characters in Pennsylvania have known me from infancy; and to many virtuous republican natives of america Since the period of my arrival in this country. Doctor Reynolds and Joseph Scott the Geographer, have known my parents, and myself from my infancy. Four months after my arrival I had the happiness to form an acquaintance with Wm P Gardner a citizen long and conspicuously known for urbanity of manners, as he is for correct moral and political principles, and for every virtue which can dignify human nature. The private citizens, the select and common councils of Philadelphia, his native place, and the present Legislature of Pennsylvania have given satisfactory, ample, and honorable testimony in favor of his morality, talents and patriotism. Often with pleasure have I heard his liberal Sentiments, and Wittnessed his laudable exertions in the cause of civil liberty humanity and his Country. Known by him on a long and intimate acquaintance, to him I refer for a knowledge of my most private conduct. To Mr. Isreal Isreal present Sherriff of the City & County of Philadelphia, I have been privately and publickly known, to his letter addressed to Mr. Gallatin in my behalf I refer for my moral character. Soon after of my arrival it was my good fortune to form an acquaintance with Mahlon Dickerson Councellor at law in Philadelphia, a citizen who if life permits will one day, become a bright Star in the Galaxy of Republican virtue; to his letter of introduction to Doctor Logan, and to our own correspondence, I refer, for a knowledge of my moral conduct. Mr. Jones & Doctor Leib knows my character in Philadelphia. Generals Jackson, Sumpter & Dearborn, can give testimony of the favorable letters of introduction given to me by their friends at that place. Also the vice President. Enclosed is the original and unsolicited Sentiments of many respectable citizens and influential republicans of Philadelphia. In fact I defy my most rancorous enemies to substantiate a single gesture of mine incompatible with the demeanor of a moral citizen, much less the execution of an immoral action.

My situation at present is truly unhappy! tho' not of a misanthropic habit, in consequence of a disconted state of mind, my health is evidently declining. Ingratitude is the most detestible of human vices. It is distressing to wittness, but superlatively so to feel it. Fondly would I hope that my case may not be cited as the last sad example of the ingratitude of Republics.

It is honorable to be persecuted by the enslavers of the human race, to be neglected in my present situation and under the present circumstances, by those to whom I am attached is the extreme of cruelty. The abandonment of those from whom succour is expected excites the most painful feelings. The excrutiating torments created by the ingratitude of friends cannot without experience be even conceived by individuals of the greatest sensibility. The contemplation presents a dreary picture of human life. But I can hardly believe that the present administration will abandon one who made great voluntary Sacrifices on account of their principles. If they do it will furnish poor encouragement for future disinterestedness. Who that ever hears of my fate, will attempt to expose the avarice of some future corrupt officers! If at some distant day the public property should be embezzled, or the rights or liberties of the people Jeopardized by the cupidity of public officers, what obscure Clerk will rise superior to self interest and warn the people to avert the impending danger! Who will burst the trammels of power, reject corrupt bribes, despise the assassins threat, assist an injured people to assert their rights, and [hural] those from power who were inimical to the public good. Alas! none will dare to Storm the muddy torrent of corrupted power, if they are sure of disgrace, contempt and poverty as the reward of principle! I am a living example. By such examples the independance of the Just will be disheartened—corrupt chiefs will be encouraged—the wicked will be indefatigable in promoting and profuse in rewarding their minions. Timid virtue will be frightened, her seat will be usurped, the hearts of her votaries, and the blood of freedoms bravest champions will be frozen with terror. This is not an imaginary picture. What observer of events during a late period that has not seen it realized! Power and poverty are formidable enemies to virtue. I am as insensible to the glare of the one as to the gloomy darkness of the other. Poverty with all its concomitant horrors has no terrors for me, as virtuous death is preferable to a corrupt or inglorious life. If my cause had not got the ascendancy I should never have murmured at the hardest fate. It is the sarcasms of my enemies and the ingratitude of my friends that preys on my mind and wounds me to the Soul.

Written communications to Mr. Gallatin were not answered. Answers to personal applications to him, were evasive and unsatisfactory! Supported by respectable letters of recommendation, I applied to General Dearborn for a place in the army. His answer was prompt, explicit and truly republican; tho' a rejection to me reasonable and Satisfactory. He learned my finances were in a reduced situation, with a generosity, and I will say humanity peculiar to himself, he lent me the sum of one hundred and forty[4] dollars. My gratitude cannot be expressed, and he shall be punctually repaid with the first fruits of my labors. Advised by Mr. Beckly and Doctor Logan, I applied to Mr. Smith, for a pursership on board some of the Ships of War destined for the mediterenean, which was rejected. He having made arrangements, which gave a preferance to the former officers of that description. Since then I have travelled upwards of two hundred miles into the state of Virginia looking for the situation of a Schoolmaster in which I have been also disappointed. Thus disappointed, rejected and neglected, like a tennis ball I am cast from hand to hand. Pitied by some, despised by others, relieved by none and as a poisonous viper dreaded by even those who ought to be my friends. In these circumstances, and the most painful suspence I feel the most agonizeing tortures of the mind. My enemies are only truly consistant, industrious and unceasing, in their sarcasms and calumnious persecutions. Strong suspicions of my guilt rest on the minds of even those of similar sentiments. Some of them are of opinion that there must be something very objectionable in me, or I would not be abandoned by those for whom I made such Sacrifices. Thus inveloped in embarrassments, sunk in misfortunes, and overwhelmed in anxiety I am lost in the vortex of perplexity.

I solemnly declare if only possessed of one acre of land, on which to build a cot I could call my own, or possessed of five hundred dollars, I never would have thought of troubleing the present Administration for any favor whatever. In this happiest of countries, I see an ample field for industry; and there is little doubt but the Spring of industry will be rewarded with the harvest of independance. But without shelter, or fence, I am exposed to the inclement blasts of party malevolence, which destroys the germ, and indeed often the full grown tree of industry.

Under these circumstances, and thus unprotected my hope is fixed on you—to you I submit my case—confident you will not permit one who may be useful to Sink in despondency, if not into the dark pit of despair. Pardon the liberty of this appeal—it was the last alternative dictated by necessity.

If the exposition of Federal irregularities has produced a national benefit, I claim very little merit from the execution of the act. It is a duty I trust every honest man would have performed under similar circumstances, and accidentally[5] thrown into the same situation. It is my present situation the result of that action, I conceive entitled to consideration.

Independant of the intimation of Mr. Beckly, and the most favorable expectations founded on your Justice and professions, I am convinced any favor granted to me would meet the approbation of Republicans. Five respectable and influential Senators, and twelve members of the house of Representatives have promised to support and interest themselves in any reasonable favor granted to me. Unfortunate would I consider myself if my requests should appear unreasonable; if they are considered so I am a mortal.—whose situation does not command the most accurate information.

Having learned that it was in contemplation to erect a number of new Indian agencies, if it was not incompatible with previous arrangements, or in other respects considered unreasonable I would be desirous of serving the United States in such a capacity, and takes the liberty to solicit your patronage. Upon investigation if I should be found deserving no exertion of mine will be spared to discharge the duties with honor to myself, and profit to the Republic. Sufficient, satisfactory and respectable sureties will be given for responsibility and the faithful discharge of the duties.

If that should be rejected as unreasonable, I would next prefer the situation of a Clerk in the Custom–House of some Commercial Town. There is an objection to this request, Collectors employ their own Clerks. True. But the slightest insinuation from the superior Departments would ensure a situation. Other securities can be given for the faithful performance of duties.—

A situation in any of the public offices at this place, however lucrative could not give me satisfaction. There are here too many of my inveterate enemies, who attribute to me the demolition of their air built castles, and any situation that I could reasonaby expect would not put me beyond their resentment. I dread them, and not without dear bought experience. They wait only for a public or private opportunity to satiate their Revenge.

If you have read this far, I must solicit your pardon for [thus intruding on your time], by this tedious hasty and imperfect scetch, but I Judged it expedient to be this circumstantial in relating my situation and desires, for the purpose of a full and unequivocal explanation. To me suspense is dreadful. Indispensible necessity goads me beyond the bounds of moderation. As it is probable you are too often troubled with idle visitors and useless dialogues, I do not wish to intrude on time so precious and usefully employed. I will wait on you in the course of a couple of days, when if you are busy Mr. Lewis may be requested to give me a categorical answer.

[Sir] [. . .] accept sentiments of respect inspired by a contemplation of Superior Virtue. ANTHONY CAMPBELL

RC (DNA: RG 59, LAR); damaged; at foot of text: "Thomas Jefferson President of the United States"; endorsed by TJ as received 26 Feb. and so recorded in SJL. Enclosure not identified, but for recommendations from Philadelphia on Campbell's behalf, see Vol. 35:440-1n.

AGAIN INTRODUCED TO YOUR NOTICE: for Campbell's first letter to TJ, dated 12 Oct. 1801, see Vol. 35:437-41.

The CERTIFICATE dated 10 Aug. signed by John Beckley, Israel Israel, and Samuel Israel, portraying Campbell as rendering an ESSENTIAL SERVICE to the country, is described in Vol. 35:441n. I WROTE EIGHT LETTERS: for a description of Campbell's correspondence with the Treasury secretary, see same, 440n.

NO MONEY SHALL BE DRAWN FROM THE TREASURY: see Article 1, Section 9 of the U.S. Constitution. For the charge that Timothy Pickering as secretary of state had withdrawn $374,000 FROM THE PUBLIC TREASURY but had expended only $27,000 to fulfill the treaties with the Barbary powers and had not sent promised supplies to them, see William P. Gardner to TJ, 20 Nov. 1801, especially Enclosure No. 4. The first two enclosures described at this letter provided TESTIMONY IN FAVOR of Gardner.

MY FINANCES WERE IN A REDUCED SITUATION: on 15 Jan. 1802, TJ gave Henry Dearborn an order on Barnes for $50 "for Campbell in charity" (MB, 2:1063). MY HOPE IS FIXED ON YOU: in the summer and fall of 1801, before Campbell's first appeal to the president, Gallatin and TJ considered employment options in the government for the former Treasury Department clerk (see Vol. 35:55, 57n, 86, 108, 158, 284-5, 314). In March 1802, Dearborn recommended Campbell for a position in the army (Vol. 35:440n).

[1] Remainder of paragraph written at foot of page with marks for insertion at this point.
[2] MS: "at he a time."
[3] MS: "necessay."
[4] Preceding two words interlined.
[5] MS: "accidenttalally."

To James Madison, with Madison's Reply

TH:J. TO J.M.

Will you see if the inclosed is right, and make any alterations in it you think for the better? particularly is the expression *lately recieved* true? or should the word *lately* be left out?
Feb. 26. 1802.

[Reply by Madison:]

The word *lately* is true as it refers to the returns of Maryland & Kentucky—that from the former being an *original* statement—that from the latter a corrective one. The message seems to unexceptionably proper.

RC (DLC); addressed by TJ: "Mr. Madison"; with reply in Madison's hand written below the date; readdressed by Madison: "The President"; endorsed by TJ: "Departmt of State Message with corrected returns of causes in the courts of the US." Not recorded in SJL. Enclosure: TJ to the Senate and the House of Representatives, 26 Feb.

From Samuel Morse

SIR,   Aurora Bookstore Feby 26, 1802.

Having been sometime confined with the measles, I have failed in paying my respects to you as I intended; but being so far recovered as to be able to go out, I should be happy if my wish to see you might be gratified.

I had purposed to be introduced to you by my highly beloved friend Mr. Granger, but I fear that the brilliance of his worth would throw the faint glimmering mine into the shade, or that I might arrogate to myself that attention which his countenance alone could give me. Humble as are my claims to notice, much less to distinction, I feel an irresistible repugnance to assume the merits of another as a cover to my own weakness. Originating from these feelings, I possess a strong desire to wait on you unaccompanied. I beg however that you would consult your own feelings and convenience. If you should think proper to gratify me, you will take the trouble to leave a note for me at this place, and inform me when I shall attend you. All hours are to me equal.

Had I not the most exalted opinion of you as a man, I should not be thus free. If I am too much so, you will place it to the right account and pardon me, while you will believe me in the greatest sincerity, an admirer of your character and a lover of your patriotism

                                                                    S. MORSE

RC (DLC); at foot of text: "Th: Jefferson President U.S."; endorsed by TJ as a letter by "L." Morse, received from Washington on 26 Feb. and so recorded in SJL; TJ later changed the "L." to "S." in the endorsement.

From Anne Cary Randolph

DEAR GRAND PAPA   Edgehill Feb: 26. 1802

I am very glad that I can write to you I hope you are well we are all perfectly recovered from our whooping cough I thank you for the book you sent me I am translating Justin's ancient history I want to see you very much believe me Cornelia sends her love to you and has been trying to write to you adieu my Dear Grand Papa believe me your affectionate Grand Daughter   ANNE CARY RANDOLPH

RC (ViU: Edgehill-Randolph Papers); endorsed by TJ as received 3 Mch. and so recorded in SJL.

Anne Cary Randolph (1791-1826), eldest child of Martha Jefferson Randolph and Thomas Mann Randolph, was born at Monticello. At the parents' request, TJ selected the name of his first grandchild. She became his "chief assistant" in looking after the flowers and garden and other out-door activities. On 19 Sep. 1808, she married Charles Lewis Bankhead of Caroline County, son of TJ's close friend, Dr. John Bankhead, and Mary Warner Lewis Bankhead. He read law under TJ for several years, but then decided to become a farmer, purchasing Carlton, a farm of 800 acres adjacent to Monticello. He became an abusive alcoholic who could not take care of the property. In an effort to aid the couple financially, in 1815, TJ added 130 acres to the farm as a gift to his granddaughter. At about the same time, trustees were appointed to manage the estate. The couple had three sons and a daughter who reached adulthood. Anne died shortly after the birth of her son, William Stuart Bankhead. She was buried in the graveyard at Monticello (Monticello Association, *Collected Papers*, ed. George G. Shackelford, 2 vols. [Princeton and Charlottesville, 1965-84], 1:67-75; 2:39, 44; Betts, *Garden Book*, 341, 349, 352-3, 363, 367, 369, 380-2, 403; MB, 2:1269-70; RS, 1:245; 2:104n; Vol. 19:582, 644-5).

JUSTIN'S ANCIENT HISTORY: for TJ's editions of Marcus Junianus Justinus's *Historia Philippicae*, see Sowerby, Nos. 35 and 36.

From Ellen Wayles Randolph

MY DEAR GRAND PAPA   [ca. 26 Feb. 1802]

You do not know what I can do. I am reading the little books you brought me. I hope that I will be able to read very well before you come here. I am very well. I want to see you very much. Cornelia can say a great many of her letters. Virginia is very sprightly and very fat. adieu my Dear Grand papa believe your affections Grand daughter   ELEONORA WAYLES RANDOLPH

taken verbatim from the lips of Miss E.W.R.

M.R.

RC (ViU: Coolidge Deposit); undated, but TJ received this letter and that of Anne Cary Randolph printed directly above it on the same day; entirely in

Martha Jefferson Randolph's hand; addressed: "To Grand Papa"; endorsed by TJ as received 3 Mch. and so recorded in SJL.

From Thomas Jefferson Randolph

MY DEAR GRAND PAPA   [ca. 26 Feb. 1802]

I hope you are well, it gives me great pleasure to be able to write to you I have been through my latin grammar twice and mamma thinks that I improved in my reading. I am not going to school now but cousin Beverly and my self are going to a latin school in the spring adieu my dear Grand Papa I want[1] to see you very much indeed believe me your affectionate Grandson   THOMAS J R

RC (ViU); undated, but TJ received this letter and the two preceding documents on the same day; endorsed by TJ as received 3 Mch. and so recorded in SJL.

Thomas Jefferson Randolph (1792-1875), eldest son of Martha Jefferson Randolph and Thomas Mann Randolph, was born at Monticello. He was taught at home and at local schools until 1808, when he attended lectures on botany, natural history, anatomy, and surgery in Philadelphia, his grandfather arranging for his stay with the family of Charles Willson Peale. In 1809 and 1810, Randolph completed his formal education with courses in mathematics and natural philosophy at Louis H. Girardin's academy in Richmond, where John Wood was his teacher. In 1815, he married Jane Hollins Nicholas, daughter of Margaret Smith and Wilson Cary Nicholas, who was then serving as governor of Virginia. The couple at first resided at Monticello and Randolph took over the management of TJ's affairs. Between 1816 and 1839, they had 13 children. In 1817, they moved to TJ's Tufton farm. As executor of TJ's estate, Randolph worked tirelessly and, in the end successfully, to settle his grandfather's debts, which were intertwined with those of his father and father-in-law. He moved his family permanently to Edgehill in 1828. He became known as a good farmer and careful manager. Randolph served six terms in the Virginia House of Delegates between 1831 and 1843. His 1832 speech in the assembly on gradual emancipation and deportation of slaves was published as a pamphlet. Randolph served as a delegate to the Virginia constitutional convention of 1851-52 and at the Virginia convention of 1861, where he voted for secession. He participated in the Democratic National Conventions at Baltimore in 1844, 1852, and 1872. Randolph published *Memoir, Correspondence, and Miscellanies from the Papers of Thomas Jefferson*, the first collection of TJ's writings, four volumes in all, in 1829. That year he also became a member of the Board of Visitors of the University of Virginia, a position he held until 1857. He then served as rector of the university until 1864 (DAB; Monticello Association, *Collected Papers*, ed. George G. Shackelford, 2 vols. [Princeton and Charlottesville, 1965-84], 1:76-88; 2:34; *The Speech of Thomas J. Randolph, (of Albemarle), in the House of Delegates of Virginia, on the Abolition of Slavery* [Richmond, 1832]; MB, 2:1248; Leonard, *General Assembly*, 359, 363, 371, 379, 384, 404, 441, 474; RS, 1:190-1n, 520, 633-4; 2:95, 171-2).

[1] MS: "wat," with an "n" superscripted above the word for insertion, in an unidentified hand.

To the Senate and the House of Representatives

GENTLEMEN OF THE SENATE AND
OF THE HOUSE OF REPRESENTATIVES.

Some statements have been lately recieved of the causes decided or depending in the courts of the Union, in certain states, supplementary, or corrective of those, from which was formed the general statement accompanying my message at the opening of the session. I, therefore, communicate them to Congress, with a report of the Secretary of State, noting their effect on the former statement, and correcting certain errors in it, which arose partly from inexactitude in some of the returns, and partly in analysing, adding, & transcribing them, while hurried in preparing the other voluminous papers accompanying that message.   TH: JEFFERSON
Feb. 26. 1802.

RC (DNA: RG 233, PM, 7th Cong., 1st sess.); endorsed by a House clerk. PrC (DLC). RC (DNA: RG 46, LPPM, 7th Cong., 1st sess.); in Meriwether Lewis's hand, signed by TJ; endorsed by a Senate clerk. Enclosure: James Madison to TJ, 25 Feb. 1802, and enclosures.

Meriwether Lewis delivered this message and the accompanying documents to the House of Representatives on 26 Feb. The papers were read and referred to the Committee of the Whole House, which was considering the bill to repeal the Judiciary Act of 1801. The Senate also received the message and documents from Lewis on 26 Feb. They were read and ordered to lie for consideration (JHR, 4:109; JS, 3:186).

From Charles Peale Polk

SIR,   George Town Feby 28th. 1801 [i.e. ca. 27 Feb. 1802]

Conceiving in some measure of your many and important engagements, It is with extreme reluctance that, I intrude for one moment on your valueable time. But the *extreme distress* of a Dear family has Occasioned, and I trust will plead my Apology for writing this Letter.

You will recollect Sir, that in the course of last summer, I had the honor of waiting on you with a view of Obtaining some subordinate Appointment. Your Attention encouraged the hope of success; and supported by Mr. Madison's repeated Assurances of the friendship of the Administration and a sincere desire of doing something for me, I rested perfectly secure that the event would be brought about; and in consequence removed my family to this Town.

There is a vacancy, as a Clerk, at this time in the Office of the Accountant of the War Department. But I find that my want of an *extensive Knowledge* of Accounts, entirely disqualifies me for the Station. my expectation was that, I might be placed in one of the Public Offices, where Copying would be the principle business; but at present I can hear of no such situation.

It has not been in my power to Obtain any business in the line of my Profession for the greater part of the last Year, and I can Assure you Sir, that in Consequence, have been compelled to dispose of the principal part of my Household furniture for the support of my family.   After stating these facts Sir, I wish to address you as a Gentleman of fortune and *humanity* in behalf of a Dear suffering family who, at this time want the necessaries of Life; and hope that it may suit you to Afford some pecuniary aid, at present,

I have only to add the Assurances of the profound respect with which I ever have been, and am, Your Obd Servt.

CHARLES PEALE POLK

RC (DLC); misdated (see below); addressed: "The President of the United States"; endorsed by TJ as a letter of 28 Feb. 1802 received 27 Feb. and so recorded in SJL.

The nephew and adopted son of artist Charles Willson Peale, Charles Peale Polk (1767-1822) was born in Annapolis and worked in Baltimore as a portrait painter, drawing school master, and owner of a dry goods store. His work as an itinerant artist often took him to Hagerstown, Frederick, and Richmond. After James Madison gave him a letter of introduction to TJ on 2 Nov. 1799, Polk took TJ's likeness at Monticello and became a strong supporter of Jeffersonian Republicanism. In 1800, he was secretary of the county Republican committee in Frederick and reported on the likely electoral votes for Maryland. Upon TJ's election, he created a transparent painting for the Frederick illumination and celebration of the inauguration. Never as successful an artist as his uncle, Polk planned to start a Republican newspaper in 1800 and, in April 1802, considered opening a museum in

Washington. Neither venture materialized. Financial difficulties and the demands of a large family prompted him to seek a salaried government position and by late 1801 he and his family moved from Frederick to Georgetown. In a letter to Madison of 14 May 1801, he expressed gratitude for Madison's "friendly assurances" that he would try to aid Polk's family. Polk later wrote the secretary of state requesting his influence to secure a position under the postmaster general or a clerkship in the Treasury Department. He finally obtained the latter position (Madison, *Papers, Sec. of State Ser.*, 1:65-6, 175; 2:234, 372; 3:399; Linda Crocker Simmons, *Charles Peale Polk, 1767-1822: A Limner and His Likenesses* [Washington, D.C., 1981], 12-19; Peale, *Papers*, v. 2, pt. 1:423-4; MB, 2:1066; Vol. 31:xliii, 231-2).

PECUNIARY AID: on 27 Feb. 1802, TJ wrote an order on John Barnes to pay Polk $25 "in charity" (MB, 2:1066). Barnes also recorded the order at 27 Feb. in his statement of TJ's account for cash and orders, 3 Mch. (see Appendix IV).

From Thomas Ballendine

MOST VENERABLE, JUSTLY   George-Town

ESTEEM'D AND ELEVATED SIR,   February 28th. 1802.

Pity the sorrows of a poor—of a distressed—of an afflicted youth, whose dire Circumstances compel him to intrude upon you, the chief magistrate of this free and indepent Nation, for the purpose of imploring a melioration of my distresses, which unfortunately, have been occasioned by the too early gratification of my nefarious propensities; at this Confession Sir, let not your ire increase, as I am sensible that Truth, notwithstanding the vain and futile efforts of some to conceal it, must prevail and impressed with this Idea I candidly declare the cause of my misfortune.—

Indulge me I pray you in the relation of a brief account of my Life and actions.—My Relations are but few and they are natives of the British shore—My beloved Mother during the early days of my Infancy expired, and I was left to the Care of a tenderly affectionate Father, whose fond hope I by my imprudence baffled—he desighned to have educated me tolerably liberal in the Town in which he resided—but before I completed my Education I was put under the Tuition of a passionate Frenchman, and the shameful exercise of his prerogative over me, caused me to resolve to seek for an asylum of happiness, by crossing the procellous alantic ocean.—I, actuated by the foolish motive of being seen and known in the World—stimulated by a disire to get rid of my Praeceptor ventur'd to engage with a Captain of a merchant vessel to take me to America, without the previous consent of my ever memorable Father—but, alas, before we had half crossed the tempestuous Sea, I had cause to regret my departure from Liverpool, the place of my Fathers residence, but regret was useless—and after a tedious voyage we arrived at New-York.—at that place I accidentally had a fall which ruined the vision of my right Eye—I was here destitute of all the necessaries of Life and I led but a miserable existence a few months—I could not get in business; for I had no reccommendations and in fact I could do but little and I write a bad, uninteligible hand; here I resolved to remain no longer; and influenced by the delusive hope, that I might get with an Employer in this dreary looking place, I came here—but at the end of a long and painful Journey on foot I found no prospect of success—and have lived for these 8 or 10 months in a country retreat near this; working hard for my Bread—I would sooner abandon myself to the Beasts of the Forrest, then go from Door to Door begging Charity and in fact to see a young man aged but 18, walking through the Streets thus employed, would be disgusting to the warmest Friend of human nature; therefore seeing my great inability to procure money to enable me to return to my Father I apply to you, dignified Sir, honor'd by the smiles of greatness, and who have been so charactaristically distinguish'd for a charitable disposition—praying with all the fervor of a penitent supplicating Christian, that you may be disposed to annihilate my insufferable condition—which can be done by enabling me once more to embrace my belov'd Parent; fifty or sixty Dollars can do it; by economising that Sum—I can go to Baltimore and there sale to Europe.

This money cannot possibly injure you and it will be a charitable act—And I declare by the most holy—if ever I reach my native Land I will refund the Money.

Oh Sir I entreat you by all that is dear between a Father and Son, by all that is sacred in the eyes of a bountiful God—to relent towards me—Grattitude Sir shall ever praedominate on my frail mind and my Prayrs to the celestial Disposer of the Universe (although they may avail nothing) shall ever be for your protection—

I now wait with all the anxiety immaginable, for the return of the Bearer and Good Sir, send me I beseech you once more the charitable Gift or as little as you are pleased to bestow upon me a miserable outcast.

That you may continue to enjoy your elevation in this sublunary World and when consistent with your desire, meet with the happiest Eternity is the fervent prayr of your humble, unworthy, imprudent and obsequious Serveant   THOMAS BALLENDINE

N.B. The Bearer is an honest old man and the writer earnestly solicits a line from Mr. Jefferson mentioning what he sends. Oh that Mr. Jefferson could but concieve my anxious wish to see my Father. My deplorable emaciated state of Heath, my miserable existence, his noble heart (for so I can speak) could certainly not be so callous as to return the Bearer without some small consideration oh! ever so little.

T. BALLENDINE
Sunday night. 28th. Feb:

RC (MHi); addressed: "To the honorable Mr. Jefferson President of the United States of America City of Washington"; endorsed by TJ as received 2 Mch. and so recorded in SJL.

The BEARER of Ballendine's letter is identified on the address sheet by the name "Forrester." After delivering the above letter, he returned to inform Ballen-

dine that there was no reply. Undeterred, Ballendine wrote TJ again, inspired by "the faint glimmering of hope" that perhaps the president had not seen his first letter or that something had prevented him from answering it. "Oh good Sir excuse my once more troubling you," he wrote, "and hear the voice of Distress. Compassion, Compassion—I pray thee to have—Oh for God's sake, send me a little money by the Bearer" (RC in MHi; undated; at foot of text: "To the inestimable Mr. Jefferson"; endorsed by TJ as received 4 Mch. and so recorded in SJL).

To William R. Davie

DEAR SIR   Washington Feb. 28. 1802.

M. Dupont de Nemours, now settled at New York, sent me the inclosed letter, without any superscription, desiring me to address it, as he knew not your residence. he mentioned to me generally that it was on the subject of procuring some aid to La Fayette. on this I would make a single observation, in order that, if any thing is attempted, it may be on a practicable & admissible principle: that is that it should be proposed in the form of reimbursement of monies expended for the US. or indemnification for losses sustained in their service. while it is admitted that the Constitution gives the federal government a power to pay all just debts, it is insisted by most persons, that none of the purposes for which that instrument allows money to be raised on the people, comprehend pensions, gifts, or bounties. it is probable also that the idea of reimbursement or indemnification would be the most satisfactory to La Fayette. I beg your pardon for hazarding this suggestion; but being on the ground and more familiar with the ideas prevailing here than gentlemen at a distance are, & thinking it important that any proposition meditated should come forward at once in a correct shape, I thought the suggestion would not be unacceptable. I avail myself of this occasion of assuring you of my high respect & consideration   TH: JEFFERSON

PrC (DLC); at foot of text: "General Davie." Enclosure: François Barbé de Marbois to Davie, date unknown, not found; see Pierre Samuel Du Pont de Nemours to TJ, 21 Feb. 1801.

From Thomas T. Davis

SIR   City Feby. 28th 1802

The inclosed Petition was sent to me with directions to lay it before you—I know the Statement made by the Petitioners to be true—But dont know whether their case is within executive power or not. To you sir their Petition is submited by

Your obt. sert.   THS T DAVIS

RC (DLC); endorsed by TJ as received 1 Mch. and so recorded in SJL. Enclosure not found.

To James Monroe

DEAR SIR   Washington Feb. 28. 1802.

In a letter from Dupont de Nemours to me is the following passage. 'Houdon a laissé en Amerique un trés beau buste de Benjamin Franklin, lequel est actuellement chez moi. ce buste en marbre vaut cent louis de notre monnaie, environ 480. D. rien n'est plus convenable a la nation que de la placer dans votre Capitole &c. et Houdon, *a qui la Virginie doit encore mille ecus sur la statue de Washington*, est dans un veritable besoin d'argent?'   if the bust could be placed in our capitol as the 'pendant' to La Fayette, it would be well. in the latter branch of the quotation I feel a personal interest, as having been the instrument of the contract of the state. but I imagine this matter must hang on some difficulty of which I am uninformed. I thought it not amiss to quote to you both parts of the paragraph as the only person who could act on both subjects. the first question on the judiciary bill in the H. of R. and which will decide it's fate, it is thought will not be taken till the day after tomorrow. Accept assurances of my affectionate esteem & respect.   TH: JEFFERSON

RC (PHi); at foot of text: "Govr. Monroe"; endorsed by Monroe. PrC (DLC).

The LETTER from Du Pont de Nemours was that of 20 Feb.

AS THE 'PENDANT' TO LA FAYETTE: under resolutions of the Virginia General Assembly, Jean Antoine Houdon made two busts of Lafayette, one of which was presented to the city of Paris and the other placed in the Virginia Capitol in Richmond (Vol. 8:214-15; Vol. 9:213, 544, 613; Vol. 10:407-10, 414-16; Vol. 15:xxxviii).

HAVING BEEN THE INSTRUMENT: when TJ was in France, he and Franklin handled the arrangements for Houdon's marble statue of Washington for the state of Virginia, in response to a June 1784 resolution of the legislature (Vol. 7:378-9, 599-601; Vol. 29:37-8).

To Thomas Mann Randolph

TH:J. TO TMR.   Feb. 28. 1802. Washington.

All is well here, as I hope with you also, & I have not time to say more except that the question decisive of the bill repealing the late judiciary law in the H. of R. will not be taken till tomorrow or next day. my love to my dear Martha & the young ones.

RC (DLC); address clipped: "Thomas Mann R[andolph] at [. . .]"; franked and postmarked; endorsed by Randolph.

From Tench Coxe

Sir   Philada. March 1. 1802

The idea I lately took the liberty to suggest may have appeared visionary and strange, but on much reflexion I am convinced that it is the interest of the United States that such a measure should be adopted either by the Government, or by the mercantile interest varying the form of course so as to render it proper for them. I beg leave to submit the reasons.

We are now dependent upon one foreign nation in too great a degree for our supplies, our law notions, the stock of many of our monied institutions, our dresses, furniture & fashions, our didactic books and our credit business. I do not know the *new* source from which we can probably draw supplies so extensive as that I have pointed out. To teach that distant Nation to turn its industry to every species of manufacture would tend to a proper estimation of our consumption, by Europeans, and particularly by our present great supplier. She dares not interrupt our trade with the distant Nation, because it is their rule to banish, at once, all foreigners who impede the coming & going of other foreigners. Were she to give offence to that distant nation, it would affect her standing in all that geographical quarter of the world—To increase our independence on that country is to my mind an endeavour, which we are *solemnly* admonished to pursue.

Cheapness of supplies is the most important object to the farmer and the merchant.

The silk branch will be long maturing here, for we are above or beyond the little business of raising the worm. It may have risen to its height in France and Italy in monastries & convents, and among a numerous poor. It cannot injure us to fill our stores with cheap instead of dear foreign silks for use at home or sale to our West Indian, & South American neighbours.

It is confessed that the cotton branch is very differently circumstanced, but as the goods they make are generally fine, it will not interfere with our infant & bulky manufactures to import them from thence. A vast object would be to teach the distant nation to produce and procure from their neighbours, who may shut us out, the various groceries, which France and England may again prohibit. Coffee, cocoa, ginger, sugar, would all be procurable from China if they would attend to and improve the cultivation & preparation. These things would diminish the cultivation of cotton there, for they would make tropical productions for Europe & us. We shall be in a bad situation, if we depend upon European avidity for our supplies of Sugar, coffee, & cocoa particularly. The spices are not yet raised with sufficient generality, but the soil and climate of that country might do much for that branch, and their intercourse with better situated Asiatics might do more. China would be impatient and probably successful against European restrictions in Asia, and it might tend to give us at least an indirect participation in Asiatic productions, if her free port of Canton were made an Emporeum for that Quarter of the world. All its magazines would be open to us.—

It is through so great and numerous a nation that we can most easily hope for the emancipation of East Indian commerce—a great desideratum.

There are other considerations which might be detailed to prove the expediency of the attempt suggested; but the multiplication of all manufactures of which they have the raw materials, fine cottons excepted, the multiplication of Sugar, coffee, cocoa, pimento & ginger, the independency of our commerces, the independence of India commerce, & the probable friendship of China will be relied on for the present—This will be a lowpriced *cash* trade, for which we are now prepared—It will not diminish Revenue—

I have the honor to be, Sir, your respectful & obedt. Servt.

TENCH COXE

It will be remembered, that China extends from 20 to 41, and has 333,000 people. There is no such magazine of human industry and agricultural production under one Government any where upon Earth. It is a power with proper management capable of many beneficial applications. The present Executive power of the United States, and our kind of Government may derive much credit in the world by a private thorough survey of the different parts of the world, and by measures calculated to them to pursuits conducive to their own interests and ours—China is a vast object, and without one preventing bar, as it is humbly conceived. This matter hitherto unobserved on except in these two letters might be brought into commercial notice, if approved, and when more matured. If made public now it will[1] excite opposition and intrigue to defeat it *here* and *in Europe.* Institutions, filled with Englishmen and wth. importers from England would keep back specie, refuse discounts, embarrass insurances and play off the whole power of commercial devices. In case of a shock to G.B. or if a war with her, such a source of supply would be deeply important to this country as it regards mere supply and commercial revenue, on which we are about to rest—

RC (DNA: RG 59, LAR); at head of text: "private"; addressed in an unidentified hand: "The President" and "Private"; endorsed by TJ as received 5 Mch. and so recorded in SJL.

IDEA I LATELY TOOK THE LIBERTY TO SUGGEST: for Coxe's earlier promotion of commercial relations with China, see his letter to TJ of 22 Feb.

CHINA EXTENDS FROM 20 TO 41 degrees north latitude. 333,000 PEOPLE: that is, 333 million (H. Yuan Tien, *China's Strategic Demographic Initiative* [New York, 1991], 7).

[1] Word supplied by Editors.

From Edward Savage

SIR New York March 1 1802

I have just Return'd from Boston and found your Esteem'd favour of Janury 10 the Picture Fraimes Shall be Done as Soone as time will admit of. if you have the Prints, with you and Could have them Rold in a Small Role and then Put into a Small Box which would just Admit of the Role, and Send them to me by Some Person Comming on in the Stage or Some Vessel Bound to this City: I will have them put up in the Best manner I Possably Can. any Person will find it very Difficult to put those Large Prints into the Fraimes to keep a flat Surface, they are very apt to be pucker'd at the Corners.

I am Sir with Great Esteem your Humble Sert

EDWARD SAVAGE

N.B. if you Send the Prints Please to Direct them to E. Savage No 80 Greenwich Street N. York.

RC (DLC); endorsed by TJ as received 6 Mch. and so recorded in SJL.

To the Senate and the House of Representatives

GENTLEMEN OF THE SENATE AND OF THE HOUSE OF REPRESENTATIVES:

I transmit for the information of Congress letters recently recieved from our Consuls at Gibraltar and Algiers, presenting the latest view of the state of our affairs with the Barbary powers. The sums due to the government of Algiers are now fully paid up: and, of the gratuity which had been promised to that of Tunis, and was in course of preparation, a small portion only remains still to be finished and delivered

TH: JEFFERSON

March 1. 1802.

RC (DNA: RG 46, LPPM, 7th Cong., 1st sess.); endorsed by Senate clerks, noting referral to a committee and the results of the committee's report (see below). PrC (DLC). RC (DNA: RG 233, PM, 7th Cong., 1st sess.); in Meriwether Lewis's hand, signed by TJ. Enclosures: (1) Extract of John Gavino to the secretary of state, 29 Dec. 1801; Gavino, the U.S. consul at Gibraltar, reporting that the *Boston* under Daniel McNeill's command arrived there on the 22d and left the next day in expectation of joining Richard Dale in the Mediterranean; reporting also that four Swedish frigates commanded by Admiral Olaf Rudolf Cederström arrived at Malaga to cruise against Tripolitan ships, with orders to cooperate with Dale (Tr in DNA: RG 46, LPPM; in a clerk's hand; endorsed by a Senate clerk). (2) Extract of Gavino to the secretary of state, 11 Jan. 1802, reporting among other things that a British frigate arrived at Gibraltar on 7 Jan. with a British consul and an Algerian ambassador who had been in England; the British consul had a box of jewels from Rufus King for delivery to William Eaton, the U.S. consul at Tunis, as a present to the bey of Tunis; Gavino reporting also on the movements of an ambassador from Tripoli and noting in a postscript that Cederström had left Malaga to join Dale (Tr in same; in a clerk's hand; endorsed by a Senate clerk). (3) Richard O'Brien, Algiers, to Gavino, 28 Nov. 1801, reporting that Dale in the *President* arrived at Algiers in November and landed money; O'Brien has made a payment of one year's annuity, and reports that the U.S. is paid up in annuities to Algiers for the six years from 5 Sep. 1795 to 5 Sep. 1801; there are some other payments due, which O'Brien is attempting to resolve; O'Brien reporting also that the *George Washington*, convoying the supply ship *Peace and Plenty* to Tunis, was forced by bad weather to put in at Algiers for a time before proceeding, but O'Brien supposes they finally reached Tunis; Algiers has been fitting out six "of the largest Corsairs"; on its return trip from Tunis, the *George Washington* will convoy any vessels desiring its protection (PrC of Tr in same; misdated 28 Nov. 1802, corrected in ink by an unidentified hand). Printed in ASP, *Foreign Relations*, 2:381-2.

FOR THE INFORMATION OF CONGRESS: Meriwether Lewis delivered the above message and the accompanying documents to the House and the Senate on 2 Mch. The House referred the matter to the committee established on 15 Dec. to deal with protection of commerce against the Barbary states (see note to TJ to the Senate and the House of Representatives, 22 Dec. 1801). On 3 Mch., the Senate gave the message and documents to a committee consisting of Uriah Tracy, Jonathan Dayton, and DeWitt Clinton. They reported on 5 Mch. that publication of the papers was "unnecessary" (JHR, 4:110; JS, 3:187, 189).

Previously, the United States had paid annuities to ALGIERS in the form of naval supplies. In May 1801, TJ and the cabinet decided to offer a cash payment in lieu of stores for one year's annuity. When Richard Dale sailed for the Mediterranean he had $30,000 on board the *President* for the purpose, but with instructions that he was not to put the money ashore until the dey, Mustafa Baba, agreed to the arrangement. Dale stopped at Algiers in July and also sent a message to Richard O'Brien, the consul, in September, but not until November did Dale get O'Brien to resolve the matter with the dey. Mustafa consented to the deal, and Dale transferred the cash to O'Brien to make the payment (NDBW, 1:466, 506, 577, 620-1, 633; Madison, *Papers, Sec. of State Ser.*, 2:51, 432-3; Vol. 34:115).

The GRATUITY to TUNIS involved gifts that the United States had agreed to give Hammuda Pasha, the bey, for his consent to the treaty that was negotiated in 1797 and ratified, with some modifications, by the Senate in 1799. Some of the luxury items required for the gift, including jewelry, silks, fine cloth, an enameled poniard dagger with diamonds, and gold- and diamond-mounted guns and pistols, were impossible to obtain in the United States. In 1800, the State Department asked Rufus King to handle the matter in London. King commissioned the jeweled articles, which included a diamond ring, gold watches with diamonds for the bey and his son, and a gold snuff box with diamonds, from the firm that supplied jewelry to the British crown. In December 1801, when those items were ready and encased in a fitted box, King had them insured and placed them in the care of Lewis Hargreaves, a British citizen who was returning to Tunis. King, who had already shipped the cloth and silk, was still waiting for the firearms to be finished. According to Madison, TJ considered the demand for the luxury goods "extortionate," but believed that if they were "essential to the preservation of peace and the benefits of the Treaty with the Bey, they must be yielded to him." In 1801, the United States chartered the ship *Peace and Plenty* and sent it to the Mediterranean with cannons, gunpowder, naval stores, and lumber that were also part of the obligation to Tunis (Madison, *Papers, Sec. of State Ser.*, 1:200, 221, 347-8, 401, 414, 423; 2:316-17; King, *Life*, 3:246-7, 355, 438-9; 4:31; Vol. 33:591-2; Vol. 35:12-14, 31-3, 148-9, 162-4, 188-90).

From Robert Smith

SIR,   Navy Dept. Mar. 1. 1802

For some weeks I have been much importuned by Mr Brown respecting the Marine Barracks. I have invariably referred him to the propositions prescribed by you, which were some months since sent to him as your ultimate determination. I have, however, in consequence of his pressing solicitation this day taken the liberty of sending the enclosed to you.

It is proper, Sir, to inform you, that under the contemplated arrangements respecting the Marine Corps I shall have no kind of occasion for the Barracks.

I am, Sir, Respectfully Your Ob. Servt.   RT SMITH

RC (DLC); at foot of text: "The President"; endorsed by TJ as received from the Navy Department on 1 Mch. and "Brown's case" and so recorded in SJL. Enclosure not found.

For the involvement of contractor Robert BROWN with the construction of the MARINE BARRACKS in Washington, see Smith to TJ, 26 Oct. 1801. For the proposed reduction of the MARINE CORPS, see Vol. 34:373, 384, 398.

Also on 1 Mch., Smith sent TJ a brief letter requesting his signature on a warrant for George Bills, a boatswain on the frigate *Adams*, who "has been some time since appointed" (RC in DLC, in a clerk's hand, signed by Smith, at foot of text: "Prest U:States," endorsed by TJ as received from the Navy Department on 1 Mch. and so recorded in SJL with notation "Bill's," also endorsed by TJ: "George Bills warrt."; FC in Lb in DNA: RG 45, LSP; NDBW, 2:63, 70).

From Robert Eastburn

OH MAN   3mo 2d 1802 N: Brunswick New Jersey

Vested with mighty power honer & Great worldly Glory—may thou
be favoured duly to Remember: that the Great king Eternal that Governs all worlds—& that doth According to his holy will & pleasure in
the Glorious Regions of Immortal day: where we are Informed or pro-
fessedly Believe: that more than tenn Thousand times tenn Thousand
of Bright Serafic hosts Cast there crowns before him & with Adoring
wonder Stand Ready with Infinite Delight to perform his divine
will—he it is we are Informed that Raiseth up in this our State of Existance to mighty honer & pulleth down or when faithfully Revered &
humbly Served gently by the kind hand of mercy & Love Removes
from this probationary Estate: from this State of Tryal to dwell for
Ever in the Injoyment of his Spitial presence & it is the desire of thy
unknown freind that thou may be one of those highly favoured by the
maker of our frames whose Air it is we Breath & who only Need to
withdraw his Supporting hand of power & we Return to our prima-
tive dust butt Should A Conseption Arise that we would fly from his
presence & as the King of Iserail Expressed it—if I Could Take the
wings of the morning & fly to the uttermost parts of the Earth Even
there thou art & it is thy Right hand Alone that Cann Support the
flight & as Saith A Great poit Amazeing knowledge deep & high
where Cann A Creature hide within thy Surkling Armes & Ly Besett
on Every Side: then by way of humble petition Expresses Saying So
Lett thy Grace Saround me Still & Like A Bulwark prove to Gard my
Soul from Every Ill Secured by Soverain Love may thy Government
be In Righteousness in Support of the poor & the Needy & that thy
utmost Influence may be used to Brake Every undue Burden & that as
the holy Scriptures Express that the oppressed may become free: possessing no undue fear of man witch causeth a Snare butt may A due
fear of the Great I Am: the Great Jehova possess thy mind then Shall
thy Light Brake forth as the morning & Gradually Become Bright as
the Sunn in its maredian Glory—

then Shall thou nott have Cause to fear all the Injust Callumnies that
the Sons of Earth or powers of darkness cann Raise up Against thee:
butt may thou & me & our whole Land & all the habitations of Sorrow throughout our Globe become the habitations of humble Joy &
holy Rejoiseing that Sorrow & Sighing may flee away & that all the
kingdoms of the Earth may Become the kingdoms of our Lord & of
his Christ witch is I trust in the Sinseer desire of thy Aliterate

FREIND ROBERT EASTBURN

[669]

I hearby Inclose desireing thy Serious parusal one of the Correctors
of the happy man & true Gentleman with Some Remarkes thereon &
Should Any part thereof Nott Intirely unite with thy Sentiments may
A desposition prevail with us to Bare with what may nott Intirely be
So—butt as is Expressed in that piece that we may be favoured with
A willingness to come to the Clear Light.—
I have Vewed thy Speech on Entering thy higly Important office with
A degree of pleasure & my desire for thee is that wisdom from on
high may marke thy prosedure & that thou may be Blessd with faith-
full & Just Counsellers wise & Vertuous A Blessing to the presant &
Succeeding Generations
pleas to Excuse any Expressions that may Appear unpleasing as I
think I Cann with truth & In Sinserity Express that my Vews & desires are Simple & Sinseerly desireing thine & the Best Good of all &
that thy Government may be Honerable & praise worthy & that in the
End of thy dayes A Crown of unfaiding Glory may be thy portion
Thou will No doubt observe that I Rite in A Similer Stile to that of
the people Called quakers butt I am Nott Intirely united with any
Sosiety of people butt think duty calls me to be Simple & plain in my
Expressions & the primary cause of this present Adress is if I knows
my Self to putt in my mite in union to help to Support one of Great
pillers on witch the mighty fabrick Rests: or as thou wisely Expresses
that we may be Inabled to Steer the vessule witch we are all Im-
barked in Amidst the Coflicting Elements of A Troubled world &
how Truly desireable that we may all Arive Safe in the wished for
haven of Eternal Rest & felicity

RC (MHi); endorsed by TJ as received
6 Mch. and so recorded in SJL. Enclosure not found, but see below.

A merchant, Robert Eastburn (1742-
1815) lived in New Brunswick, New Jersey, and in addition to selling sundries,
groceries, dry goods, textiles, and stationery, also traded in land and buildings.
Eastburn's death was registered in the
records of the Rahway and Plainfield
Monthly Meeting of Friends and his
bequests included contributions to the
Humane Society of New Brunswick,
the New Jersey Bible Society, and the
building of a Friends Meeting House in
New Brunswick (Burlington *New-Jersey
Gazette*, 15 Jan. 1783; Trenton *True*

American, 21 Dec. 1807; New York
Weekly Museum, 9 Sep. 1815; William A.
Whitehead and others, eds., *Documents
Relating to the Colonial, Revolutionary
and Post-Revolutionary History of the
State of New Jersey*, 1st ser., 42 vols.
[1880-1949], 42:142; *Genealogical Magazine of New Jersey*, 27 [1952], 1, 78). In
a letter to TJ of 10 Feb. 1803, Robert
Eastburn claimed that his former occupation was as a ship carpenter (RC in MHi).
HAPPY MAN & TRUE GENTLEMAN:
a popularly reprinted late-eighteenth-
century broadside and essay on happiness
and Christian living. For a version of it
Eastburn had printed in 1807 by William
Elliott, see Shaw-Shoemaker, No. 13327.

Statement of Medical Services by Edward Gantt

Attendance on the President's Family commenced on the 28th. of May 1801 with a visit to Mrs. Murphy whom I continued to attend almost daily to the 2nd. of July—
Ursula inoculated 29th May. & board—
Mr. Julian Medicine & attendance for swelled Testicles—
Mr. Rapin visit & Venesection—
Mr. Julian   Attendance, dressing & Ointments, & medicine for a burnt Arm & Hands
Ursula   medicines & attendance from July 4th. to the 14th.—
Edwd.   A visit & medicines from Augt. 19. to 24
Christopher   Ointment
Knowles.   Septr. 28th. a visit & Venesection—attendance & medicine until October 11th—
Cramer.   Emetic
Ursula.   Ointment Jany. 3d. 1802—Since which there is no Charge on my Book—
The Charges for the above amount, at the usual mode of charging by the Doctors of George Town, to $76:57 which I received of Mr. John Barnes on the 2nd. of March—   Edwd Gantt

MS (DLC); entirely in Gantt's hand; frayed and clipped at bottom of sheet; with undated note by Gantt to John Barnes, at foot of document: "Sir The Statement above is as short a Mode as I can adopt to satisfy the President; If he desires it as soon as I can spare as much T[ime] [. . .] draw it off as it stands on my Books—I am [. . .]"; endorsed by TJ on verso.

Ursula, a 14-year-old slave from Monticello, was in Washington from 1801 to 1802 as an apprentice cook (Stanton, *Free Some Day*, 135).

Edward Maher, Christopher Süverman, and John Kramer were footmen (Vol. 34:489n).

Knowles: Noël De Clary, "garçon de cuisine" (Vol. 34:685n).

From James Hardy

Right Honble. Sire/   Johnstown in the County of Montgomery and State of New York 2d. March 1802.

I beg you will please to pardon my freedom? while I Inform you I left Old England on the 2 June 1795 and arrived at New York in 40 Days after—The causes of my Migration were my Civil and Religious Liberties. In this County I Purchased 112½ Acres of Land And about

2 years ago I Married a Citizen. I am qualified to vote in her Right, also in my own—At our last Election I was prohibited from voting in this Town for being an Alien, caused me go to Springfield in Otsego County where I voted for Our Govr., Lieut Govr. and the three Senators—Most of my Neighbours finding we had one Majestrate in this Village who was latly tried Cast and Fined 100 Dollars for Extortion! and our last Grand Jury (I was one of them) found another Bill against him for the like Crime! And another Justice, and an assistant Judge!!! who is a noted Tavern Haunter—they (i.e. my most respectable Neighbours) Petitioned our Honble Committee of Appointment who have Appointed me a justice of the Peace without my knowledge or Consent! however I have agreed to their solicitations— But Rt. Honble Sire Can I Legally act while I am an Alien? Causes me most humbly Petition you for my Naturalization?—And So Soon as I am acquainted with all the expences I will remit them as you may give orders.

In this County above Fifty espouse your Cause to one against you—may God bless you with Health and Long Life to Preside over us. I am with all Deference Right Honble Sir ever yours at Command while   JA'S HARDY

aged 56 years.

P.S. I was appointed a Majestrate in Old England in the County of Middlesex and Suburbs of London but I never Qualified owing to their Diabolical Test Act   JH—

N.B. this is our County Town in it are abt. 200 Houses in the Space of a $\frac{1}{4}$ of a Mile and the only two Majestrates are A. Rust convicted for Extortion; and Jno. McArthur a Judge and a Noted Tavern Haunter!!![1]

RC (DLC); endorsed by TJ as received 12 Mch. and so recorded in SJL.

COMMITTEE OF APPOINTMENT: that is, the Council of Appointment, which consisted of the governor and four state senators and controlled most state and local appointments in New York (Vol. 32:304n).

[1] Paragraph written on first page in left margin, perpendicular to text.

To the Mississippi Territory
General Assembly

SIR   Washington Mar. 2. 1802.

I recieve with great respect the approbation which the legislature of the Missisipi territory, in their resolutions of the 21st. of December last, have been pleased to express, on my declining to renew the commission of their late governor. the task of judging those, whose conduct in office calls for it, is always painful: but the grounds of judgment in that case were such as to leave no room to doubt the line of duty which I had to pursue. the testimony of the legislature, founded in what themselves have seen and felt, confirms the justice of that judgment.

I concur with them in entire confidence that our expectations from his successor will not be disappointed; and I avail myself of this opportunity of assuring them that on every occasion interesting to the prosperity, safety or happiness of the Missisipi territory, they may rely on a faithful & zealous discharge of my duties.

I pray you to accept for yourself & the Council[1] of the Missisipi territory, the homage of my high respect and consideration.

TH: JEFFERSON

RC (MsJS); at head of text: "To the honourable the President of the Council of the Missisipi territory." PrC (DLC). PrC (DLC); at head of text: "To the honourable the Speaker of the House of Representatives of the Missisipi territory."

Enclosed in TJ to William C. C. Claiborne, 7 Mch. 1802.

[1] Preceding word replaced with "House of Representatives" in PrC to speaker of the House.

From Samuel Morse

March 2, 1802.

S. Morse presents his affectionate regards to Mr. Jefferson. A young man, with whom he has become acquainted since his residence in this city, is about to begin a publication in Connecticut, under the title of the "Connecticut Republican Magazine," he is very desirous to wait on the president and ask his patronage as a subscriber. Mr Jefferson will feel the delicate situation of the writer between a wish to promote the interest of a publication which by becoming the depository of many valuable essays will, he hopes prove of use where it is very much wanted, and the anxiety he must feel, to preserve such an attention to etiquette as might screen him from the imputation of forwardness and assumption. Believing that in a republic, the citizens should as far as practicable be acquainted with those selected to conduct the public affairs; *feeling*, too, that a personal knowledge of the present chief magistrate must increase the sentiments generally felt in his favor by those who agree with him in politics; the writer has suffered a wish to oblige one who has expressed a high degree of confidence in him, to prevail over other considerations, and ventures to request permission of Mr. Jefferson to wait on him on Sunday morning with the young man in question.

RC (DLC); endorsed by TJ as received 3 Mch. and so recorded in SJL.

YOUNG MAN: Luther Pratt was a printing partner and then solo editor of the *Farmer's Oracle*, a weekly New York newspaper based first in Lansingburgh and later Troy from 1796 to 1798. After relocating to Connecticut, he solicited public support in October 1801 for the *Connecticut Republican Magazine*, a proposed 40-page octavo monthly publication "on subjects moral, political and literary." Pratt printed only one volume of four issues from his shop in Suffield, Connecticut, and included a biographical character sketch of TJ in his first issue of July 1802. He also printed David Austin's sermons; see Evans, No. 35125 (Brigham, *American Newspapers*, 1:597, 742; Kline, *Burr*, 2:684-5; Hartford *American Mercury*, 22 Oct. 1801; *Connecticut Republican Magazine* [July 1802], 1:25-31).

To Thomas Newton

DEAR SIR   Washington Mar. 2. 1802.

Your favor of the 18th. Ult. came to hand a few days ago. the reciept of the cyder had been acknoleged by mr Barnes to mr Taylor when he remitted him the cost of it (60.50) we have as yet tried only one cask of it, which is very fine indeed. not but that it has a little taste not belonging to it, & which I imagine is from the cask; but it is so slight as not to be percieved scarcely, nor to hinder it's being much admired. the other casks will probably be above all exception. I am sincerely thankful for the kind services you render me, and still offer. I will certainly avail myself of your goodness whenever occasion arises; and indeed I have proved this by the free use I have already made of it. I shall every year, at the proper season have occasion for an equal supply of Hughes's crab cyder; and should any more of the Brazil wine come to your market, I shall probably be again glad to purchase.

The H. of Repr. determined yesterday they would not rise till the question, so long debated, on striking out the 1st. section of the bill repealing the late judiciary law, should be taken. they accordingly sat till about 11 aclock in the night, when it was determined 60. against 31. that the clause should not be struck out, & the committee rose &

reported the bill to the house, so that I suppose it will this day be put to the question whether it shall be read a third time. whither those opposed to it will endeavor to spin out time still by proposing amendments, is not known; but it is probable that after so full a discussion they will suffer neither of the remaining questions to pass over the day on which they are proposed. they will now I presume proceed to the other important business.

Accept assurances of my constant & sincere esteem & respect.

TH: JEFFERSON

PrC (DLC); at foot of text: "Colo. Thomas Newton"; endorsed by TJ in ink on verso.

In his financial memoranda at an entry dated 24 Jan., TJ recorded that he gave an order on John BARNES to pay $60.50

to James TAYLOR, Jr., for 10 barrels of crab apple cider (MB, 2:1064).

The first SECTION of the judiciary bill contained the explicit repeal of the Judiciary Act of 13 Feb. 1801 (U.S. Statutes at Large, 2:132).

To John Wayles Eppes

DEAR SIR   Washington Mar. 3. 1802.

My last to you was of the 31st. of Jan. I now inclose you one for Maria. the H. of R. decided the great question on the repeal of the late judiciary bill, the night before last, by 60. against 31. it was yesterday past to the 3d. reading, and I expect it will be finally passed this day. this done, I am in hopes they will press forward the other important matters, as the season is now advancing which will fill them with impatience to get away. I formerly mentioned to you that I should want another fine horse, a match for Castor. I would not however wish the purchase to be absolutely made till next month, & then if 60. or 90. days paiment be allowed, I shall meet it more conveniently. but I must pray you to look out for a fine one. I need not say here of what sort, as you know my ideas fully on that subject as well [. . .] respecting price. where the animal is superfine, we must not stand [. . .] giving something more than he may be worth; because in buying one not superfine the whole money is thrown away. I should be glad to learn from you immediately what the prospect is: and if you should not be sending to Albemarle while I am there, I will send for him. or perhaps, should you make the purchase sooner, I might send from hence; as it would be a convenience to have him for my spring journey. I shall send this letter to City point, supposing that your most convenient post office. should there be a more convenient one, let me know it for my future government. all were well at Edgehill on the 13th. Ult. mr and mrs Trist are here. she expects to be in the straw every hour. accept assurances of my sincere & affectionate attachment.

RC (ViU); torn; addressed: "John W. Eppes at Bermuda Hundred near City point"; franked and postmarked. Enclosure: TJ to Mary Jefferson Eppes, 3 Mch. 1802.

For Eppes's involvement in the purchase of a FINE HORSE for TJ, see especially Vol. 33:37, 460; Vol. 34:374-5. As of September 1807, TJ still had not found a MATCH FOR CASTOR, a horse he replaced in 1808 (MB, 2:1221; Betts, *Farm Book*, 102-3; Eppes to TJ, 24 Sep. 1807, in ViU: Coolidge Deposit).

SHE EXPECTS TO BE IN THE STRAW EVERY HOUR: Mary Louise Brown Trist's second son, Hore Browse Trist, Jr., known as "Browse," was born on 19 Mch. 1802 (*Généalogie et Histoire de la Caraïbe*, 84 [1996], 1687).

To Mary Jefferson Eppes

MY VERY DEAR MARIA   Washington Mar. 3. 1802.

I observed to you some time ago that during the session of Congress I should be able to write to you but seldom; and so it has turned out. your's of Jan. 24. I recieved in due time, after which mr Eppes's letters of Feb. 1. & 2. confirmed to me the news, always welcome, of your's & Francis's health. since this I have no news of you. I see with great concern[1] that I am not to have the pleasure of meeting you in Albemarle in the spring. I had entertained the hope mr Eppes & yourself would have past the summer there. and being there, that the two families could have come together on a visit here. I observe your reluctance at the idea of that visit, but for your own happiness must advise you to get the better of it. I think I discover in you a willingness to withdraw from society more than is prudent. I am convinced our own happiness requires that we should continue to mix with the world, & to keep pace with it as it goes; and that every person who retires from free communication with it is severely punished afterwards by the state of mind into which they get, and which can only be prevented by feeding our sociable principles. I can speak from experience on this subject. from 1793. to 1797. I remained closely at home, saw none but those who came there, and at length became very sensible of the ill effect it had upon my own mind, and of it's direct & irresistible tendency to render me unfit for society, & uneasy when necessarily engaged in it. I felt enough of the effect of withdrawing from the world then, to see that it led to an antisocial & misanthropic state of mind, which severely punishes him who gives into it: and it will be a lesson I shall never forget as to myself. I am certain you would be pleased with the state of society here, & that after the first moments you would feel happy in having made the experiment. I take for granted your sister will come immediately after my spring visit to Monticello, and I should have thought it agreeable to both that your first visit should be made together. in that case your best way would be to come direct from the Hundred by Newcastle, & Todd's bridge to Portroyal where I could send a light Coachee to meet you, and crossing Patowmac at Boyd's hole you would come up by Sam Carr's to this place. I suppose it 60. miles from Portroyal to this place by that route, whereas it would be 86. to come from Portroyal up the other side of the river by Fredericksburg & Alexandria. however if the spring visit cannot be effected, then I shall not relinquish your promise to come in the fall. of course, at our meeting at Monticello in that season we can arrange it.   in the mean time should the settlement take place which I expect between mr Wayles's & mr Skelton's executors, and Eppington be the place, I shall rely on passing some time with you there. but in what month I know not. probably towards midsummer. I hardly think Congress will rise till late in April. my trip to Monticello will be about a fortnight after they rise, and I shall not be able to stay there more than a fortnight.   I am anxious to hear from you, as[2] during the period of your being a nurse, I am always afraid of your continuing in health. I hope mr Eppes & yourself will so make your calculations as to leave the Hundred by the beginning of July at least. you should never trust yourselves in the lower country later than that. I shall pass the months of August & September at Monticello where I hope we shall all be reunited. continue to love me, my dear, as I do you, and be assured that my happiness depends on[3] your affections and happiness. I embrace you with all my love.   TH: JEFFERSON

RC (DLC); at foot of first page: "Mrs Maria Eppes." Enclosed in TJ to John Wayles Eppes, 3 Mch.

MR EPPES'S LETTERS: John Wayles Eppes's letter to TJ of 1 Feb., recorded in SJL as received 5 Feb. 1802 from Richmond, has not been found.

[1] TJ here canceled "your reluctance."
[2] TJ here canceled "I cannot."
[3] TJ here canceled "seeing."

From George Hay

SIR,   Richmond. Mar 3. 1802

Your letter of the 24th of February, reached me this evening, and in conformity with your request, I now transmit to you, the papers relating to the question, between Mr Short and Mr. Randolph.

You will permit me to add, that I am much gratified by your ready admission of the apology, which my situation made it necessary for me to offer, and that I am, with real respect Yr. mo. ob. Sert.

GEORGE HAY.

RC (DLC: William Short Papers); addressed: "The President of the United States"; endorsed by TJ as received 7 Mch. and so recorded in SJL. Enclosures: see TJ to Hay, 14 Feb.

From "Thomas Khronyngler"

HONBLE SIR   Savannah 3d March 1802.

[. . .] [doubt] [. . .] much surprised at Receiving [. . .] letter of [. . .] this & much more when you [. . .] entire Stran[. . .]f the present is simply th[. . .] Father is involved, has [. . .] Do not think there is a worthy [. . .] deserving Compassion under the Canopy of Heaven, but the Principle thing Sir that lays deep to my Heart is this he has a large family consisting of several small children—and he has not wherewithall to give them an Education sufficent for them to maintain that place in the Community as it is my wish they should— You receive twenty five thousand Dollars ℔er Annum and I am confident you do not Labour half as hard as my Poor Sire but I hope you will not so construe what I have here inserted as to think that my meaning was so aimed that you did not do a sufficency—No Sir I candidly do not believe there is a man that is more capable or that would fr[. . .] or that does half as much for the Nation—

But to the Point how could you relish it Sir to transmit ℔er Mail only th[. . .] fifth Part of yr. Yearly Salary Oh what transport would y[. . .] give [. . .] true Republican oh [. . .]ould I Praise your Na[. . .] and Exorbitant if [. . .] [distre]ssed family your hear[. . .]

You will Excuse this[1] assumed Name I take as likewise the manner I have altered my Writing you may easily guess the Reason—

If you Sir should think worth your while to deign to answer a distressed fellow Citizen you will direct your Letter to the underwritten Name at Savannah

Permit me to Remain with due Respect Yr. Exys much obliged humble Servt   THOMAS KHRONYNGLER

RC (DLC); mutilated; endorsed by TJ as received 24 Mch. and "money" and so recorded in SJL.

[1] Author here canceled "feigned."

Appendix I

Letters Not Printed in Full

E D I T O R I A L   N O T E

In keeping with the editorial method established for this edition, the chronological series includes "in one form or another every available letter known to have been written by or to Thomas Jefferson" (Vol. 1:xv). Most letters are printed in full. In some cases, the letter is not printed but a detailed summary appears at the document's date (for an example, see Lewis Mayer to TJ, 21 Feb. 1802). Other letters have been described in annotation, which, for the period covered by this volume, are listed in this appendix. Arranged in chronological order, this list includes for each letter the correspondent, date, and location in the volumes where it is described. Among the letters included here are brief letters of transmittal, multiple testimonials recommending a particular candidate for office, repetitive letters from a candidate seeking a post, and official correspondence that the president saw in only a cursory way. In other instances, documents are described in annotation due to the near illegibility of the surviving text. Using the list in this appendix, the table of contents, and Appendix II (correspondence not found but recorded in Jefferson's Summary Journal of Letters), readers will be able to reconstruct Jefferson's chronological epistolary record from 1 Dec. 1801 to 3 Mch. 1802.

From Albert Gallatin, 2 Dec. 1801. Noted at Gallatin to TJ, 29 Nov. 1801.

To John Thomson, 2 Dec. Noted at Thomson to TJ, 10 Aug. 1801.

From District of Columbia Commissioners, 4 Dec. Noted at Memorial from the District of Columbia Commissioners, 4 Dec. 1801.

To James Workman, 4 Dec. Noted at Workman to TJ, 15 Nov. 1801.

From Joseph Nourse, 8 Dec. Noted at Albert Gallatin to TJ, 7 Dec. 1801.

From the Senate, 14 Dec. Noted at TJ to the Senate, 11 Dec. 1801.

From John Thomson Mason, 26 Dec. Noted at William Cranch to TJ, 19 Dec. 1801.

From Albert Gallatin, received 28 Dec. Noted at TJ to James Madison, 29 Dec. 1801 (second letter).

From Elias Boudinot, 1 Jan. 1802. Noted at TJ to the Senate and the House of Representatives, 17 Feb. 1802.

From John Vaughan and Charles Willson Peale, 1 Jan. Noted at TJ to Vaughan and Peale, 13 Jan. 1802.

From Thomas Jones, 7 Jan. Noted at Elijah Griffiths to TJ, 7 June 1801.

From George Jefferson, 12 Jan. Noted at Jefferson to TJ, 13 Jan. 1802.

From Albert Gallatin, 25 Jan. Noted at TJ to the Senate and the House of Representatives, 27 Jan. 1802.

From Albert Gallatin, 3 Feb. Noted at TJ to George Hay, 14 Feb. 1802.

To the Senate, 3 Feb. Noted at Robert Smith to TJ, 2 Feb. 1802.

From James Thompson, received 6 Feb. Noted at James B. Heard to TJ, [on or before 6 Feb. 1802].

From Archibald McClean, 22 Feb. Noted at David Jones to TJ, 3 Mch. 1801.

To Nicholas Reib, 24 Feb. Noted at TJ to Albert Gallatin, with Gallatin's Reply, [23 Feb. 1802].

From Hugh White, 24 Feb. Noted at TJ to the Aliens of Beaver County, Pennsylvania, 2 May 1801.

From Albert Gallatin, 25 Feb. Noted at Gallatin to TJ, 25 Feb. 1802.

From Robert Smith, 1 Mch. Noted at Smith to TJ, 1 Mch. 1802.

From Robert Smith, 2 Mch. Noted at TJ to the Senate, 18 Feb. 1802.

From Thomas Bailey, undated. Noted at James Madison to TJ, 8 Dec. 1801.

Appendix II

Letters Not Found

EDITORIAL NOTE

This appendix lists chronologically letters written by and to Jefferson during the period covered by this volume for which no text is known to survive. Jefferson's Summary Journal of Letters provides a record of the missing documents. For incoming letters, Jefferson typically recorded in SJL the date that the letter was sent and the date on which he received it. He sometimes included the location from which it was dispatched and an abbreviated notation indicating the government department to which it pertained: "N" for Navy, "P" for Postmaster, "S" for State, "T" for Treasury, and "W" for War. "Off." designated a person seeking office.

From John Tyler, 1 Dec. 1801; received 10 Dec. from Greenway.

From James Lyon, 2 Dec.; received 4 Dec. from Washington.

To David Higginbotham, 4 Dec.

From Gabriel Lilly, 4 Dec.; received 15 Dec.

From John Perry, 4 Dec.; received 9 Dec. from Shadwell.

From Martin Dawson, 5 Dec.; received 15 Dec. from Milton; notation: "for Brown Rives & co."

From Thomas Mann Randolph, 6 Dec.; received 9 Dec. from Edgehill.

From the Treasury Department, 8 Dec.; received 8 Dec.; notation: "Collector Louisville."

From the Treasury Department, 8 Dec.; received 8 Dec.; notation: "Collector Louisville & Collector Eggharbor."

From William Wingate, 8 Dec.; received 18 Dec. from Haverhill.

From Francis Eppes, 10 Dec.; received 17 Dec. from Eppington.

From Arthur Fenner, 10 Dec.; received 22 Dec. from Providence (first of two letters).

From Arthur Fenner, 10 Dec.; received 22 Dec. from Providence (second of two letters).

From Peter Lyons, 10 Dec.; received 17 Dec. from Studley.

From John Cross; received 12 Dec. from Rhode Island; notation: "to be Surveyor of Pawcatuck."

To Gabriel Lilly, 12 Dec.

To Reuben Perry, 12 Dec.

From Robert G. Sands; received 12 Dec.; notation: "to be Surveyor of North Kingston R.I."

From Arthur Fenner, 14 Dec.; received 5 Jan. 1802 from Providence; notation: "Cross vice Stillman."

From Philip Landais, 14 Dec.; received 21 Dec. from Albany; notation: "W."

From William Stewart, 16 Dec.; received 23 Dec. from Monticello.

To Martin Dawson, 17 Dec.

To Justin Pierre Plumard Derieux, 17 Dec.

To James Dinsmore, 17 Dec.

To Francis Eppes, 18 Dec.

From Arthur Fenner, 18 Dec.; received 30 Dec. from Providence.

To Gabriel Lilly, 18 Dec.

To John Perry, 18 Dec.

From Nicholas Rousselet, 21 Dec.; received 5 Mch. 1802 from Demerara.

From José García Armenteros, 22 Dec.; received 22 Nov. 1802 from Manila.

To Andrew Gregg, 22 Dec.

To Gabriel Lilly, 24 Dec.

From Thomas Newton, December 1801; received 24 Dec. from Norfolk; notation: "Starke vice Cornwell. W."

To William Stewart, 24 Dec.

From Samuel Llewellin, 25 Dec.; received 30 Dec. from Lancaster; notation: "N."

From James Oldham, 26 Dec.; received 29 Dec. from Monticello.

From Georgia Commissioners, 30 Dec.; received 30 Dec. from Washington.

From Joseph Stanton, Jr., 30 Dec.; received 30 Dec. from Washington.

From Gabriel Lilly, 1 Jan. 1802; received 6 Jan. from Monticello.

From Gabriel Lilly, 2 Jan.; received 6 Jan. from Monticello.

From William Wardlaw, 2 Jan.; received 6 Jan. from Charlottesville.

Petition from Allen Wiley; received 2 Jan.; notation: "referrd. to Commrs. Washn."

From Justin Pierre Plumard Derieux, 3 Jan.; received 13 Jan. from Sweet Springs.

From Andrew Gregg, 4 Jan.; received 5 Jan.

From John Wayles Eppes, 6 Jan.; received 12 Jan. from Richmond.

To Francis Eppes, 8 Jan.; notation: "by Dr. Robinson."

To Gabriel Lilly, 9 Jan.; notation: "940."

From the War Department, 9 Jan.; received 9 Jan.; notation: "Wells assistt. agent for Indians."

From Thomas McKean, 11 Jan.; received 27 Jan. from Lancaster; notation: "G. W. Mcelroy to be Consul Teneriffe."

From Gabriel Lilly, 14 Jan.; received 20 Jan. from Monticello.

From Dr. John Vaughan, 14 Jan.; received 17 Jan. from Wilmington, Del.

To Justin Pierre Plumard Derieux, 15 Jan.

From James Monroe, 15 Jan.; received 20 Jan. from Richmond; notation: "Moseley. Coleman."

From Jesse Simms, 15 Jan.; received 20 Jan. from Alexandria.

From James Oldham, 16 Jan.; received 20 Jan. from Monticello.

From James Taylor, Jr., 16 Jan.; received 23 Jan. from Norfolk.

From Thomas Paul, 18 Jan.; received 18 Jan. from Washington.

From Alexander J. Dallas, 20 Jan.; received 25 Jan. from Philadelphia; notation: "Macpherson to be contd."

From John Wayles Eppes, 20 Jan.; received 25 Jan. from Richmond.

From William McPherson, 20 Jan.; received 25 Jan. from Philadelphia.

From Martha Jefferson Randolph; received 20 Jan. from Edgehill.

From Jonathan Snowden, 21 Jan.; received 22 Jan. from Washington; notation: "W."

From Thomas Mann Randolph, 23 Jan.; received 27 Jan. from Edgehill.

From William Wardlaw, 23 Jan.; received 27 Jan. from Charlottesville.

From Aaron Burr, 25 Jan.; received 25 Jan.; notation: "Austin to be librarian."

From Hugh Chisholm, 25 Jan.; received 29 Jan. from Richmond.

From Joseph H. Nicholson, 26 Jan.; received 27 Jan. from Washington; notation: "Richd. Wilson to be librarian."

From Robert Wright, 27 Jan.; received 28 Jan. from Washington.

From Samuel L. Mitchill, 28 Jan.; received 28 Jan. from Washington.

From John H. Craven, 30 Jan.; received 3 Feb. from Monticello.

To John Wayles Eppes, 31 Jan.

From William Barry, 1 Feb.; received 4 Feb. from Philadelphia.

From John Wayles Eppes, 1 Feb.; received 5 Feb. from Richmond.

To William Barnwell, 3 Feb.

To James Dinsmore, 3 Feb.

From William Findley, 5 Feb.; received 18 Feb. from Lancaster; notation: "W."

From Kemp Catlett, 6 Feb.; received 10 Feb. from Colle.

To John H. Craven, 6 Feb.

To Gabriel Lilly, 6 Feb.

From James Oldham, 6 Feb.; received 10 Feb.

Petition from John Callier and others; received 8 Feb.; notation: "inhab. Tumbeckbe & Alibama. Missipi. S."

From John Moody, 8 Feb.; received 15 Feb. from Richmond.

From John Harvie, 9 Feb.; received 13 Feb. from Belvidere; notation: "Radnor."

From James Monroe, 9 Feb.; received 13 Feb. from Richmond; notation: "Davis [&ca]."

From John Wickham, 9 Feb.; received 13 Feb. from Richmond.

To Kemp Catlett, 11 Feb.

From John H. Craven, 11 Feb.; received 17 Feb. from Monticello.

From Parke Goodall, 12 Feb.; received 17 Feb. from Richmond.

From Thomas Mann Randolph, 13 Feb.; received 17 Feb. from Edgehill.

From Lewis Littlepage, 17 Feb.; received 18 Feb. from Fredericksburg.

From William Young; received 17 Feb. from Philadelphia.

From Joseph Boyer and Susanna Boyer, 18 Feb.; received 20 Mch.; notation: "petn for discharge of souldier. W."

From Narsworthy Hunter, 18 Feb.; received 19 Feb. from Washington; notation: "Feb. 8. [for 18.]."

From Nathaniel Macon, 18 Feb.; received 19 Feb. from Washington.

To John H. Craven, 19 Feb.

To James Dinsmore, 19 Feb.

From Laurence Hooff, 19 Feb.; received 20 Feb. from Alexandria.

From Samuel C. Landais, 19 Feb.; received 27 Feb. from New York.

From James Oldham, 20 Feb.; received 24 Feb. from Monticello.

To Gabriel Lilly, 21 Feb.

From Mann Page, 21 Feb.; received 25 Feb. from Mannsfield; notation: "Benson to be P.M."

From Charles Drew, 24 Feb.; received 2 Apr. from "Havanna prison"; notation: "S."

To James Oldham, 24 Feb.

From Philip Ludwell Grymes, 25 Feb.; received 5 Mch. from Brandon.

From Laurence Hooff; received 25 Feb. from Alexandria.

From George Andrews, 27 Feb.; received 3 Mch. from New York.

From "Pawkanjelus. a Delaware & others" [i.e. Buckongahelas], 27 Feb.; received 3 Mch. from Philadelphia.

From William Crooke, 28 Feb.; received 11 Mch. from Newport; notation: "to be navl. officer port Newport distr. R.I."

From Peter Legaux, 1 Mch.; received 19 Mch. from Spring Mill, Md.

From William Mazaree and John F. Frellent, 1 Mch.; received 6 Mch. from Baltimore; notation: "N."

From Lemuel Morton, 1 Mch.; received 14 Mch. from Plymouth; notation: "to be Post.M. Plymouth. S."

From Isaac Stephens, 1 Mch.; received 1 June from Boston.

Appendix III

Financial Documents

EDITORIAL NOTE

This appendix briefly describes, in chronological order, the orders and invoices pertaining to Jefferson's finances during the period covered by this volume that are not printed in full or accounted for elsewhere in this volume. The orders for payments to Étienne Lemaire and Joseph Dougherty pertain, for the most part, to expenses associated with running the President's House. The *Memorandum Books* are cited when they are relevant to a specific document and provide additional information.

Order on John Barnes for payment of $50 to Joseph Dougherty, Washington, 3 Dec. 1801 (MS in MHi; in TJ's hand and signed by him; signed by Dougherty acknowledging payment; endorsed by Barnes as paid on 3 Dec.). See MB, 2:1059.

Order on John Barnes for payment of $21.40 to Joseph Dougherty, 4 Dec. (MS in Sotheby's, 19 May 1997, Lot 116; in TJ's hand and signed by him; signed by Dougherty acknowledging payment; endorsed by Barnes as paid on 4 Dec.). See MB, 2:1060.

Order on John Barnes for payment of $295.91 to Étienne Lemaire, Washington, 7 Dec. (MS in MHi; in TJ's hand and signed by him; signed by Joseph Dougherty acknowledging payment; endorsed by Barnes as paid on 8 Dec.). See MB, 2:1060.

Order on John Barnes for payment of 11.67\frac{1}{2}$ to Joseph Dougherty, 12 Dec. (MS in MHi; in TJ's hand and signed by him; signed by Dougherty acknowledging payment; endorsed by Barnes as paid on 12 Dec.). See MB, 2:1060.

Order on John Barnes for payment of $92.25 to Étienne Lemaire, Washington, 14 Dec. (MS in ViU; in TJ's hand and signed by him; signed by Lemaire acknowledging payment; endorsed by Barnes as paid on 14 Dec.). See MB, 2:1060.

Order on John Barnes for payment of $77.47 to John H. Craven, Washington, 15 Dec. (MS in FMU; in TJ's hand and signed by him; signed by Craven acknowledging payment; endorsed by Barnes as paid on 15 Dec.). See MB, 2:1060.

Invoice by Jeremiah Williams for the sale of a half yard and $\frac{5}{8}$ of "India Dimity," at £0.10.6 per yard, totaling £0.11.9$\frac{1}{2}$, Georgetown, 16 Dec. (MS in MHi; in Williams's hand and signed by him acknowledging payment; with notation in TJ's hand: "making 21. stocks" at £0.2.6 each for a sum of $7, plus £0.11.9$\frac{1}{2}$ or $1.58, totaling $8.58, alongside which TJ wrote "1802 Jan. 28 paid cash"; endorsed by TJ: "Sempstress"). See MB, 2:1064.

Order on John Barnes for payment of $50 to Joseph Dougherty, 18 Dec. (MS in ViU; in TJ's hand and signed by him; signed by Dougherty acknowledging payment; endorsed by Barnes as paid on 18 Dec.). See MB, 2:1060.

Order on John Barnes for payment of $85.28 to Étienne Lemaire, Washington, 21 Dec. (MS in MHi; signed by Lemaire acknowledging payment; endorsed by Barnes as paid on 22 Dec.). See MB, 2:1060.

Order on John Barnes for payment of $100.33 to Étienne Lemaire, 28 Dec. (MS in MHi; in TJ's hand and signed by him; signed by Joseph Dougherty acknowledging payment on 29 Dec.; endorsed by Barnes as paid on 29 Dec.). See MB, 2:1061.

Voucher for a "verbal order" on John Barnes for payment to Joseph Dougherty of $16.56 for corn and $2.12 for "expenses on cyder," 4 Jan. 1802 (MS in MHi; in TJ's hand and signed by him; signed by Dougherty acknowledging payment; endorsed by Barnes as paid on 4 Jan.). See MB, 2:1062.

Order on John Barnes for payment of $257.44 to Étienne Lemaire, 4 Jan. (MS in MHi; in TJ's hand and signed by him; signed by Lemaire acknowledging payment; endorsed by Barnes as paid on 9 Jan.). See MB, 2:1061.

Order on John Barnes for payment of $150.82 to Étienne Lemaire, 11 Jan. (MS in MHi; in TJ's hand and signed by him; signed by Lemaire acknowledging payment; endorsed by Barnes as paid on 14 Jan.). See MB, 2:1063.

Order on John Barnes for payment of $50 to Mrs. Newman "or bearer," 15 Jan. (MS in MHi; in TJ's hand and signed by him; signed by Meriwether Lewis acknowledging payment; endorsed by Barnes as paid on 15 Jan.). See MB, 2:1063.

Order on John Barnes for payment of $84.60 to Étienne Lemaire, Washington, 18 Jan. (MS in MHi; in TJ's hand and signed by him; acknowledgement of payment marked by a cross, alongside which Barnes wrote "[Chris.] Julian his mark"; endorsed by Barnes as paid on 18 Jan.). See MB, 2:1063.

Order on John Barnes for payment of $42.37 to Joseph Dougherty, Washington, 19 Jan. (MS in MHi; in TJ's hand and signed by him; signed by Dougherty acknowledging payment; endorsed by Barnes as paid on 19 Jan.). See MB, 2:1063.

Order on John Barnes for payment of $18 to Joseph Dougherty, Washington, 25 Jan. (MS in CSmH; in TJ's hand and signed by him; signed by Dougherty acknowledging payment; endorsed by Barnes as paid on 25 Jan.). See MB, 2:1064.

Order on John Barnes for payment of $126.91 to Étienne Lemaire, Washington, 25 Jan. (MS in MHi; in TJ's hand and signed by him; signed by Lemaire acknowledging payment; endorsed by Barnes as paid on 29 Jan.). See MB, 2:1064.

Order on John Barnes for payment of $22.50 to William Duane, Washington, 26 Jan. (MS in ViU; in TJ's hand and signed by him; signed by Duane acknowledging payment, Georgetown, 27 Jan.; endorsed by Barnes). See MB, 2:1064.

Order on John Barnes for payment of $11 to John Minchin, Washington, 30 Jan. (MS in MHi; in TJ's hand and signed by him; signed by Michael Grimes acknowledging payment; endorsed by Minchin acknowledging receipt of payment, New Jersey Ave., 13 Feb.; endorsed by Barnes as paid on 13 Feb.). See MB, 2:1064.

Order on John Barnes for payment of $38.02 to Joseph Dougherty, Washington, 1 Feb. (MS in MHi; in TJ's hand and signed by him; signed by Dougherty acknowledging payment; endorsed by Barnes as paid on 1 Feb.). See MB, 2:1064.

Order on John Barnes for payment of $425.13 to Étienne Lemaire, Washington, 1 Feb. (MS in MHi; in TJ's hand and signed by him; signed by Joseph Dougherty acknowledging payment; endorsed by Barnes as paid on 1 Feb.). See MB, 2:1064.

Order on John Barnes for payment of $9.25 to Joseph Dougherty, 8 Feb. (MS in ViU; in TJ's hand and signed by him; signed by Dougherty acknowledging payment; endorsed by Barnes as paid on 8 Feb.). See MB, 2:1065.

Order on John Barnes for payment of $89.27 to Étienne Lemaire, Washington, 8 Feb. (MS in ViU; in TJ's hand and signed by him; signed by Lemaire acknowledging payment on 14 Feb.; endorsed by Barnes). See MB, 2:1065.

Order on John Barnes for payment of $14.04 to Joseph Dougherty, Washington, 15 Feb. (MS in MHi; in TJ's hand and signed by him; signed by Dougherty acknowledging payment; endorsed by Barnes as paid on 15 Feb.). See MB, 2:1065.

Order on John Barnes for payment of $76.42 to Étienne Lemaire, Washington, 15 Feb. (MS in ViU; in TJ's hand and signed by him; signed by Lemaire acknowledging payment; endorsed by Barnes as paid on 15 Feb.). See MB, 2:1065.

Order on John Barnes for payment of $35.48 to Joseph Dougherty, 22 Feb. (MS in MHi; in TJ's hand and signed by him; signed by Dougherty acknowledging payment for Étienne Lemaire; endorsed by Barnes as paid on 22 Feb.). See MB, 2:1066.

Order on John Barnes for payment of $111.80 to Étienne Lemaire, Washington, 22 Feb. (MS in MHi; in TJ's hand and signed by him; signed by Joseph Dougherty acknowledging payment; endorsed by Barnes as paid on 22 Feb.). See MB, 2:1065.

Order on John Barnes for payment of $60.02 to Joseph Dougherty "for the costs & labourers employed in filling the ice house," Washington, 24 Feb. (MS in MHi; in TJ's hand and signed by him; signed by Dougherty acknowledging payment on 25 Feb.; endorsed by Barnes). See MB, 2:1066.

Order on John Barnes for payment of $5.35 to Joseph Dougherty, Washington, 2 Mch. (MS in MHi; in TJ's hand and signed by him; signed by Dougherty acknowledging payment; endorsed by Barnes as paid on 2 Mch.). See MB, 2:1066.

Order on John Barnes, Georgetown, for payment of $250.30 to Étienne Lemaire, Washington, 2 Mch. (MS in MHi; in TJ's hand and signed by him; signed by Lemaire acknowledging payment; endorsed by Barnes; endorsed by TJ: "Lemaire Etienne François"). See MB, 2:1066.

Appendix IV

Statements of Accounts with John Barnes

E D I T O R I A L   N O T E

This appendix summarizes John Barnes's regular statements of accounts with Jefferson from 24 Mch. 1801 to 3 Mch. 1802, the end of Jefferson's first year as president. As Jefferson's financial transactions in Washington became more complex, Barnes began separating the statements into a private account, itemizing the president's calls for cash and his private expenses, and a household account, itemizing the expenses incurred in running the President's House, including purchases from Barnes's store. In late 1801, Barnes combined the private account and household account into two parts of one statement. By 1802, he no longer differentiated between the private and household expenditures and instead had a statement for cash and orders and another for purchases at Barnes's store. Periodically, Barnes brought the totals from the separate account statements into a general statement of accounts, where he also recorded Jefferson's income (if any), primarily his salary as president, and balanced the account. Check marks and other emendations on several of the itemized accounts indicate that the president carefully perused the statements submitted by Barnes.

Statement of TJ's account, Georgetown, 24 Mch. 1801, with entries from 30 Jan. to that date, recording cash payments to TJ of $20, $15 (in small silver by Mr. Pickford, Barnes's assistant), $35, $100 (ten eagles), and $30 at 30 Jan., 11, 27 Feb., and 10, 19 Mch., respectively; $2.40 for four muslin handkerchiefs at 30 Jan. and $7.50 for six cambric handkerchiefs at 2 Mch.; $20 in cash to John Hoomes's servant James at 3 Feb.; $259.50 and $250.67 to Conrad & McMunn at 5 Feb. and 2 Mch., respectively; $30 to Reverend John Debois at 17 Feb.; $0.13 for a "Spung" at 20 Feb.; payments of $7.47 for two pairs of black silk hose, $2.80 for two pairs of fine cotton hose, $46.89 for $37\frac{1}{2}$ yards of fine Holland cloth at $1.25 a yard, and $175 to Simon Chaudron for a gold watch, all at 21 Feb.; $9.25 to John Minchin on order by TJ and $1.50 for portage and box for a saddle at 10 Mch.; $51.50 to Polkinhorn & Andrews and $32.67 to John March at 17 Mch.; Barnes also recorded at 17 Mch. payments in Philadelphia by John Richards of $19.33 or five guineas to John James Barralet (at this entry, TJ wrote "23.31"), $5.50 to Nicholas Gouin Dufief for books, $8 to Andrew Brown, and $35 to Stephen Burrowes for a "patent saddle"; and at 24 Mch., a payment of $7.81 to J. M. Jackson for cambric tape and thread; with the total sum of the debits being $1,172.92 entered by Barnes at 24 Mch.; against credits of 234.66\frac{1}{2}$ carried forward from 15 Jan., plus 856.70\frac{1}{2}$ by a Treasury warrant for TJ's salary at 12 Mch.; Barnes closed the statement with a net balance in his favor of $81.55; beneath which TJ added, in pencil, two debits, $4 by an "error" of 17 Mch. at the Barralet entry and $60 for cash on 1 Mch., for a new net balance, added by TJ in ink below Barnes's balance in the debits column, of $145.55 in Barnes's favor (MS in ViU; 2 p.; in Barnes's hand and signed by him; with emendations by TJ; at head of statement: "Thomas Jefferson Esqr: In a/c, with John Barnes"; endorsed by TJ:

"Barnes John. his accounts from 1800. Mar. 17. to 1801. Mar. 24.") See MB, 2:1034-5; Vol. 32:497, 501, 560-1; Vol. 33:182, 251-4, 479n.

Statement of TJ's private account, 25 Apr. 1801, with entries from 28 Mch. to that date, starting with a balance of $246.45 in Barnes's favor carried forward from a previous statement, followed by a list of debits, that is, $250 (25 eagles) at 28 Mch.; $3.72 for an "[african] Cob—gold" on 30 Mch.; a remittance of $950 to Gibson & Jefferson at 28 Mch.; payments of $144.26 to Thomas Carpenter at 2 Apr.; $21.02 to Rapine, Conrad & Co. at 9 Apr.; $180.48 to Conrad & McMunn at 10 Apr.; and payments at 25 Apr. of $22 to Polkinhorn & Andrews, $4.87½ to John March for bookbinding, and $64 to Samuel Harrison Smith; for debits totaling $1,640.80½ and a new balance brought forward of $1,886.80½ in Barnes's favor (MS in ViU; 2 p.; in Barnes's hand and signed by him; at head of statement: "Thomas Jefferson Esqr. (Private a/c) dt. To John Barnes"; endorsed by Barnes). See MB, 2:1036; Vol. 33:478-9, 639-40.

Statement of TJ's household account, 25 Apr. 1801, with entries from 2 Mch. to 22 Apr. for Joseph Rapin's expenses, including a payment on 2 Mch. of $30.14½ in cash to Mr. Briesler for "sundry Articles left in the Store room"; a debit of $23.48 for unspecified expenditures by Thomas Claxton between 4 and 19 Mch.; a list of unitemized charges between 19 and 30 Mch. of $63.79½, $27.52, $8.66, $22.16, and $3.07 for "sundries & Cash paid" at Barnes's store; and between 8 and 16 Apr., payments of $7.25 for "cheese &c." and $8.63 for oil from Edgar Patterson's store and $6.36 for soap from John Laird; to which Barnes added two cash payments of $50 each to Rapin on 8 and 22 Apr., giving a subtotal of $309.88 for Rapin's expenses; below which Barnes recorded a payment of $2.33 to Michael Roberts for stationery for TJ's secretary, Meriwether Lewis, at 8 Apr.; followed by a list of Joseph Dougherty's expenses for "Stable use," including payments of $5.33 to David Ferguson for rye straw at 2 Mch., $14.37 to James Dunlap for hay at 13 Apr., and $14.28, $21.16, and $22.53 to Dougherty for "sundry" accounts, hay, and oats at 29 Mch., 2 and 15 Apr., respectively, for a subtotal of $77.67; with a total for the statement of $389.88 (MS in ViU; 2 p.; in Barnes's hand and signed by him; endorsed by Barnes: "State of the Presidents Household a/c to 25 April 1801"; endorsed by TJ: "Barnes John. series of accts."). See MB, 2:1040-1.

"Sketch or rough statement" of TJ's account, 14 May 1801, beginning with the balances of TJ's household and private accounts carried over from 25 Apr., for the sum $2,276.68½, followed by a list of subsequent charges on both accounts. For the household account, Barnes recorded payments of $27.50 to James Dunlap at 27 Apr.; cash payments to Joseph Rapin of $60 each at 27, 30 Apr., and 3 May and for $200 and $85.85 at 6 and 11 May, respectively; purchases at Barnes's store for $43.08 at 28 Apr., $6 at 2-4 May, and $13.08 at 7 May; $23.33 for hay and oats at 1 May; $1.37½ for the stationery account of TJ's secretary, Meriwether Lewis, at 9 May; $150.50 for payment on an invoice from the sloop *Hiland* at 12 May; and $127.13 for payment on an invoice from the schooner *Tryal* at 14 May; for a subtotal of $902.44½, which included a sum of $20.99, interlined by TJ at "2d. & 4th. May" for his store account with Barnes. For the private account,

Barnes recorded cash payments to TJ of $20, $30, and $50 ("3 US. Notes") at 3, 5, and 12 May; $350.12½ to Thomas Newton at 6 May; $51.25 to James Stuart at 11 May; $12 to Colin C. Wills at 12 May; a remittance of $300 to John Hoomes, a payment of $120.29 credited to John Richards per invoice, and a payment of $8 to Brown & Relf of Philadelphia, at 14 May; for a subtotal of $941.66½; giving a new balance of $4,120.79½ in Barnes's favor. At the foot of the statement Barnes entered a credit, dated 7 May, a Treasury warrant of $4,000, TJ's salary. In a postscript Barnes noted TJ's order to pay $30 to Rembrandt Peale (MS in ViU; 2 p.; in Barnes's hand and signed by him; with an emendation by TJ noted above, probably added when TJ viewed the account at 5 May, and three emendations by TJ, then canceled, being revised figures at the household account subtotal and totals brought forward; at head of statement: "Sketch, or rough Statement of the Presidents a/c with J. Barnes"; endorsed by Barnes). Enclosed in Barnes to TJ, 15 May. See MB, 2:1040-1; Vol. 33:595, 602; Vol. 34:37-8, 102-3, 113, 705.

Statement of TJ's private account, Georgetown, 23 May 1801, beginning with a list of debits from 3 to 14 May and a subtotal of $941.66½, identical to that in Barnes's sketch of the private account of 14 May; followed by a record of payments, including an order of $189.66 in favor of Valentine Fantrees and of $81.37 to Joseph Rapin, at 19 May; and at 22 May, a cash payment of $10 in silver to TJ conveyed by Joseph Dougherty; for a sum of $1,222.69½ in Barnes's favor (MS in ViU; 2 p.; in Barnes's hand and signed by him; at head of statement: "Thomas Jefferson Esqr: To John Barnes (Private a/c) from & after former a/c to 25 Aprl. viz"; endorsed by Barnes). TJ's order on Barnes for the $10 in silver is also in ViU (in TJ's hand and signed by him; endorsed by Barnes acknowledging payment of $10 to Joseph Dougherty). See MB, 2:1040-1.

Statement of TJ's household account, Georgetown, 23 May 1801, with entries from 27 Apr. to 21 May, beginning with the same debits that Barnes recorded in his "Sketch" of 14 May and the subtotal of that date of $902.44½; followed by a charge of $11.12 for transporting goods, "including Mr. Yznardy's wines," from the schooner *Tryal* to Barnes's store on an unspecified date; debits of $17.02 and $17 for purchases at Barnes's store on 14-15 and 18 May; $4 for a "London Castor Hat" for "John" (probably John Freeman) at 20 May; $4 for the same type of hat for Joseph Dougherty and $2 for "1 dozen red tape" for Meriwether Lewis's use at 21 May; for a total sum of $957.58½ (MS in ViU; 2 p.; in Barnes's hand and signed by him; at head of statement: "The Presidents Household To John Barnes from & after the former a/c to 25 April—viz"; endorsed by Barnes). See MB, 2:1040-2; Vol. 33:549-50; Vol. 34:38.

Statement of TJ's private account, Georgetown, 4 June 1801, with entries from 27 May to that date, including remittances of $184.07 to Daniel Trump and $30 to Rembrandt Peale at 27 May; a charge for $15 in cash to TJ at 31 May; and an order in favor of Dr. William Bache for $20 at 4 June; for a total sum of $249.07 (MS in ViU; 1 p.; in Barnes's hand and signed by him; at head of statement: "Thomas Jefferson Espr. (Private a/c)—3d. To John Barnes"). See MB, 2:1042-3; Vol. 34:38, 42, 47-8.

Statement of TJ's household account, Georgetown, 4 June 1801, with entries from 23 May to that date, charging TJ $9 for three dozen bottles of cider at 23 May; orders in favor of Joseph Rapin for $93.23 and $295.50 at 25 May and 4 June, respectively; a charge of $26.21½ for coffee, sugar, a tin funnel, and two pepper boxes at 26 May; $16.62 for "2 ice potts for Cream" by stage and $13.50 for hay from James Dunlap at 27 May; a charge of $12.50 for clothing for John Kramer, including a castor hat for $4, doeskin pantaloons for $7.50, and neck handkerchiefs for $1 at 27 and 29 May; followed by a charge of $1.04½ for clothes and shoe brushes; a payment of $1.56½ for five yards of "Coarse Catgut" at 30 May; and purchases of English porter, sugar, and olives on 1 and 4 June for the sum of $19.70; for a total sum of $488.86½, which Barnes summarized as "Household" items for $74.13½, "servant clothing" for $12.50, $13.50 for "stable use," and $388.73 in cash to the steward (MS in ViU; 2 p.; in Barnes's hand and signed by him; at head of statement: "The Presidents Household (3d. a/c) dr. To John Barnes"; endorsed by TJ: "J. Barnes's acct from May 22.–June 4. 1801"). See MB, 2:1041-2.

Statement of TJ's general account, Georgetown, 4 June 1801, bringing forward a balance of $456.96½ in Barnes's favor from 22 May, to which Barnes added the total debits on TJ's household and private accounts since that date, which were $488.86½ and $249.07, respectively, for a net balance of $1,194.90 in Barnes's favor (MS in ViU; 1 p.; in Barnes's hand and signed by him; at head of statement: "dr: Thomas Jefferson Esqr. In a/c with John Barnes Cr").

Statement of TJ's household account, Georgetown, 30 June 1801, with entries on the stable account dated 28 Feb. and 3 Mch. that were omitted from previous statements "for want of Vouchers," documenting cash payments to Joseph Dougherty for hay purchased from William Warfield for $19 and oats purchased from John Turnbull for $15.87; followed by a list of June expenses on the stable account, including $30.33 to James Dunlap for two loads of hay, $19.37½ to Polkinhorn & Co. for "saddlery," $10 to Mr. Smith, a stage driver, and $40.28 to Dougherty for "sundries," for a total charge on the stable account of $134.85½; beneath which Barnes recorded a payment of $9 to Michael Roberts for stationery for TJ's secretary, Meriwether Lewis, at 4 June; followed by "sundry extra" on the household account, specifically, $18.89 for "Canvas-making, thread & Cord" for 72 bags for hams on 12 and 18 June, $3 for freight on nine dozen hams from Norfolk at 13 June, and $2.62½ for freight on six boxes of liquor from Philadelphia at 17 June, for a subtotal of $24.51½; Barnes next lists payments in June to Joseph Rapin of $73.96, $81.74, $84.95, and $111.44, for a subtotal of $352.09; followed by a record of Rapin's purchases at Barnes's store between 5 and 30 June of cognac, English porter, brandy, port wine, coffee for servants' use, sugar, spermaceti candles, and "sundries," for a sum of $99.80, including a payment of $18 to Captain John Hand for two barrels of cider at 30 June; closing the statement with a total sum of $620.26 (MS in ViU; 2 p.; in Barnes's hand and signed by him; at head of statement: "President of the U States. His Household (4th Acct.) To John Barnes"; endorsed by Barnes as an account of 4 to 30 June 1801). See MB, 2:1043-5; Vol. 34:102.

Statement of TJ's private account, Georgetown, 30 June 1801, with entries from 5 to 28 June, recording remittances of $5, $10, $50 (by Joseph Dougherty), $100 (in two notes of the Bank of the United States), and $60 ($10 being in silver) in cash to TJ at 5, 7, 9, 17, and 28 June; $20 to "Revd Mr Lora" and $25 to David Austin at 9 and 25 June, respectively; $679.84 to Gibson & Jefferson "for the Amt passed by J Barnes to the Credit of" William Short and $400 to Andrew Dinsmore by way of John Richards of Philadelphia, both at 9 June; an order of $13 in favor of Valentine Fantrees at 16 June; and an order of $52 in favor of Samuel Carr at 27 June; for a sum of $1,414.84, to which Barnes added at the bottom of the statement a charge of $27 dated 6 June for six pairs of white silk hose at $4.50 each, for a revised total of $1,441.84 (MS in ViU; 2 p.; in Barnes's hand and signed by him; at head of statement: "President of the U States his Private a/c for the Mo. June with John Barnes"; endorsed by Barnes). See MB, 2:1042-5; Vol. 34:235-6, 295, 369, 705.

Statement of TJ's general account, Georgetown, 30 June and 6 July 1801, carrying forward the balance of the general account at 4 June of $1,194.90 in Barnes's favor, to which Barnes added the debits on TJ's private and household accounts of $620.26 and $1,441.84 from the statements of 30 June and a Treasury draft of $1,500 at 6 July, for a total debit of $4,757; Barnes credited TJ's account with $2,000 by a Treasury warrant at 8 June and two Treasury warrants of $1,500 and $500 at 6 July, closing the statement with a net balance of $757 in Barnes's favor (MS in ViU; 2 p.; in Barnes's hand and signed by him; at head of statement: "President of The U States In a/c with John Barnes"; endorsed by Barnes; endorsed by TJ: "Barnes John. Account June 4–July 6. 1801"). See MB, 2:1045-6; Vol. 34:521.

Statement of TJ's household account, 22 July 1801, with seven entries from 1 to 22 July for purchases at Barnes's store by Joseph Rapin of dumbfish (cured fish) from New York and other items for a sum of $91.45; followed by orders in favor of Rapin for $261.87, $40, $85.23, and $53.60 on 6, 13, 18, and 22 July, respectively, for a sum of $440.70; and lastly, the month's charges on the stable account in favor of Joseph Dougherty for $13.75, $72.64, and $16.95 on 6, 13, and 20 July, respectively, for the sum of 103.34; closing with a total sum of $635.49 (MS in ViU; 2 p.; in Barnes's hand; Barnes's date and signature clipped; at head of statement: "The President U States. Household a/c To John Barnes"; endorsed by Barnes as TJ's household account for 1 to 22 July 1801). See MB, 2:1045-7.

Statement of TJ's private account, Georgetown, 25 July 1801, with entries from 8 to 25 July, recording cash payments to TJ of $150 (in bank notes), $630 ($500 on Norfolk branch of the Bank of the United States and $130 in gold), and $20 at 8, 14, and 20 July, respectively; orders in favor of Samuel Harrison Smith for $10.17, Henry Ingle for $32.40, and Mary Turnbull for $5, at 8 July; orders in favor of Lloyd Gray for $10, Rapine, Conrad & Co. for $76, Thomas Walker for $8, and Thomas Claxton for $272.98, at 14 July; followed by debits on 16 July of $3 for a riding whip, $120.74 for groceries to Richmond, and $12.40 for dumbfish from New York; an order in favor of Edward Eno for $50 at 24 July; and lastly, at 25 July, payments of

$112.20 to Dr. David Jackson in Philadelphia and $150 to Meriwether Lewis for three months salary (from 1 Apr. to 30 June) at $50 a month; closing with a total charge of $1,662.89 (MS in ViU; 2 p.; in Barnes's hand and signed by him; at head of statement: "The President, U States, (Private a/c) to John Barnes"; interlined by TJ above Barnes's first entry: "July 6. To balance. 757 D."; endorsed by Barnes; endorsed by TJ: "Barnes John. accounts"). See MB, 2:1046-8; Vol. 34:332-3, 529, 567-8, 581-2, 706-7.

Statement of TJ's private account, Georgetown, 30 Sep. 1801, with entries from 27 July to 22 Sep., including cash payments to TJ of $300 (in gold), $10, and $20 at 27, 28, and 29 July, respectively; $250 for an order on the Bank of the United States in favor of Gibson & Jefferson and $67 to Jones & Kain at 27 July; orders in favor of Henry Ingle for $5.61 and Edward Gantt for $13, for "innoculating and Boarding" Meriwether Lewis's servant, both at 28 July; payment of $5 to Edward Frethy, barber, at 29 July; $0.84 for the "storage & cooperage" of plaster of paris at 1 Aug.; order in favor of Rapine, Conrad & Co. for $13.08 at 6 Aug.; payments of $50.75 and $100 to Thomas Carpenter, tailor, at 12 Aug. and 15 Sep.; $30 advanced to Martin Wanscher, plasterer, and $47.93 credited to John Richards of Philadelphia for "sundries" shipped to Richmond and related charges, both at 15 Aug.; $22.52 for groceries shipped from Alexandria to Richmond at 17 Aug.; $50 to Joseph Anthony for a book subscription at 4 Sep.; $2 to Captain John Hand for freight on a chariot harness at 10 Sep.; $700 remitted to James Taylor, Jr., of Norfolk at 8 Sep.; $268.12 to Roberts & Jones of Philadelphia at 16 Sep.; $1,000 to Conrad Hanse of Philadelphia for TJ's chariot at 18 Sep.; and $4.62 for freight on two cases from Baltimore at 22 Sep.; for a total of $2,960.47 in Barnes's favor (MS in ViU; 2 p.; in Barnes's hand and signed by him; at head of statement: "President of the U States (his Private a/c.) sundry disbursemts. By John Barnes. Commencing 27th July & Ending 22d Sept. 1801"; with a small check mark by the sum at each entry, probably added by TJ). See MB, 2:1048, 1050; Vol. 34:489n, 684-5, 707-8; Vol. 35:11-12, 95-6, 165, 224-6, 282-3, 328-9, 489.

Statement of TJ's household account, Georgetown, 30 Sep. 1801, with entries from 28 July to that date, beginning with charges on the stable account with payments to Joseph Dougherty of $41.22, 30.62\frac{1}{2}$, and $9.25 on 3 Aug. and 1 and 7 Sep., respectively, for oats, corn, rye straw, and blacksmithing, for a subtotal 81.09\frac{1}{2}$; followed by a list of cash disbursements to Joseph Rapin from 10 Aug. to 11 Sep. totalling $416.71, including $50 at 20 Aug. for 2 months wages; payment on 8 Sep. of $21.75 to Michael Roberts on the stationery account for TJ's secretary from March and April "not before charged or rendered"; followed by an enumeration of purchases at Barnes's store from 28 July to 30 Sep., including porter, cognac, souchong tea, brandy, whiskey, coffee, sweet oil, soap, candles, cheese, and "sundries" to the amount of $120.23; followed by a list of "Extra" disbursements, including payments of $60 to John Richards of Philadelphia for six boxes of "sirup of punch" and $2 for "extra freight" and storage in Alexandria on nine dozen hams at 29 July; $14.36 to Roberts's account "not before charged—or rendered" at 8 Sep.; $7.50 for a pair of buckskin breeches for Joseph

Dougherty at 17 Sep.; $25.18 for Dougherty's traveling expenses to and from Philadelphia, $2.50 to Dougherty for a whip and $1.25 for two brushes for the chariot, and $30 for Mr. Cromwell's pair of horses for the chariot, all at 26 Sep.; $1.25 for wharfage and hauling of two pipes of wine to Washington and $1.25 for the transport of the wine from Alexandria to Georgetown, on 26 and 29 Sep., respectively; for a subtotal of $145.29; with a total sum of charges for the statement of $785.07½ (MS in ViU; 4 p.; in Barnes's hand and signed by him; at head of statement: "To The President of the U States for Househd: disbursemts:—By John Barnes. Commencing 28th July & Ending 30th Sepr. 1801"; with a small check mark at several of the sums, including that for Barnes's store, at the two sums paid to Roberts, and at the other "Extra disbursemts.," 14 in all, probably in TJ's hand; endorsed by Barnes). See Vol. 35:11-12, 283n, 328-9.

Statement of TJ's general account, Georgetown, 30 Sep. 1801, carrying forward the 25 July balance of $2,065.88 in Barnes's favor, to which Barnes added debits at 13 Sep. of $1,000 for a note payable at the Bank of Columbia and the sums of $785.07½ and $2,960.47 from the statements of TJ's household and private accounts of 30 Sep., for a sum of $6,811.42½ in Barnes's favor; Barnes credited TJ's account with $4,000 by a Treasury warrant at 7 Sep. and $1,000 by a draft on Gibson & Jefferson at 10 days sight on Philadelphia at 17 Sep. for a net balance of $1,811.42½ in Barnes's favor; to which sum Barnes added a charge of $2.57½ for postage between Philadelphia, Richmond, and New York, "including a Stamp," bringing the balance to $1,814 in Barnes's favor (MS in ViU; 2 p.; in Barnes's hand and signed by him; at head of statement: "The President U States In general. a/c wth John Barnes"; endorsed by TJ: "Barnes John. series of accts. for 1801"). See MB, 2:1050; Vol. 35: 225-6, 270, 275-6, 282-3.

Statement of TJ's household account, 4 Nov. 1801, with entries from 1 Oct. to that date, enumerating purchases by Étienne Lemaire at Barnes's store for port, porter, cognac, cider, hyson and souchong tea, Jamaica spirits, coffee, a tin coffee pot, rice, sugar, vinegar, sweet oil, spermaceti candles, hair powder, starch, shoe blacking, "English fools Cap" paper, "1 Ream large Hott press" paper, plus a payment of $8.20 to Michael Roberts for stationery, for a sum of $135.23; followed by a list of TJ's orders on Barnes, specifically, $14 to John Christoph Süverman for wages at 2 Oct.; payments to Joseph Dougherty of $21.42, $17, $46.87, and $60 on the stable account at 5, 11 Oct., 2 and 4 Nov., respectively, and $21.80 at 23 Oct. for hauling coal; $39 to Edward Maher and $99 to Abraham Golden for wages and clothes on 8 Oct.; payments to Lemaire of $376.17, $51.66, $216.27, and $240.94 at 9, 11, 30 Oct. and 2 Nov.; $286.98 to Joseph Rapin at Philadelphia at 19 Oct.; $250 to John Davidson for 1,000 bushels of coal at 29 Oct.; the subtotal of TJ's orders being $1,741.11, for a total of $1,876.34; which Barnes summarized as $10.20 for secretary's use, $123.87 for stable use, and $1,737.27 for household use for a subtotal of $1,871.34, followed by a charge of $5 for "Chessmen," for a total of $1,876.34 (MS in ViU; 2 p.; in Barnes's hand and signed by him; at head of statement: "President US. (on Househd. a/c) To John Barnes"; with an emendation in TJ's hand at the 4 Nov. entry for payment to Dougherty, "for Baker," indicating that the money was to pay William Baker for hay; TJ also probably added the small check mark that appears at each entry alongside the sum at the payment orders). See MB, 2:1053-7; Vol. 35: 394-5, 436-7, 470, 757-8.

Statement of TJ's private account in Philadelphia, dated Georgetown, 4 Nov. 1801, with entries from 17 to 26 Oct., beginning with $2 to William Duane for books on 17 Oct.; $17.25 to Nicholas Gouin Dufief for books and $3 to Henry Voigt for repairing a watch on 21 Oct.; $15.67 to McAllister & Co. for spectacles and $45.50 to Ann Powell for cambric on 22 Oct.; $4.50 to David Kennedy for picture frames on 24 Oct.; $15 to M. Fisher for three thermometers on 26 Oct., for a subtotal of $102.92; below which Barnes recorded payments of $553.80 on Henry Sheaff's account for wine on 17 Oct.; $206 to Conrad Hanse for TJ's chariot and $204 to Thomas Claxton per order on 19 Oct.; and $30 to Daniel Trump for James Oldham on 22 Oct., for a subtotal of $993.80; followed by five entries dated 19, 21, and 22 Oct. for items delivered to William Stewart to take to Monticello, including $13.62 to Mr. Paxton for "sundries," $12 to Mr. Park for sash lines, $9.63 to Josiah Donath for glass, $ 0.30 to Mr. Brown for spelter, and $ 0.45 for boxes, for a total value of $36.50; Barnes ending the statement with a record of payment of $30 in cash to Mrs. Stewart for her use and for children's clothing at 20 Oct., plus $27 to her husband at 24 Oct. "as ℔ statement," for a final total of $1,190.22 (MS in ViU; 2 p.; in Barnes's hand and signed by him; at head of statement: "President U States. To John Barnes for sundry a/c (Private) via Philadelphia"; endorsed by Barnes). See MB, 2:1055, 1060-1; Vol. 35: 23-4, 181-2, 224-6, 328-9, 482-4, 676.

Statement of TJ's private account, Georgetown, 5 Nov. 1801, with entries from 7 Oct. to that date, showing charges of $1,884 ("5 Bank post Notes") for TJ at 7 Oct., $15 and $29.50 in cash to TJ at 11 and 29 Oct., respectively; $150 to Meriwether Lewis, his salary for three months ending 30 Sep. and $21 for a bank discount at 63 days on $2,000, both entered at 9 Oct.; $24 to Conrad & McMunn for "pr Glasses" at 27 Oct.; $22.40 for 12 pairs of fine cotton stockings at 30 Oct.; and $25 to David Austin at 5 Nov.; for a subtotal of $2,170.90, to which Barnes added $1,190.22, the sum of his disbursements in Philadelphia between 17 and 26 October brought forward from the 4 Nov. statement., for a total of $3,361.12 in Barnes's favor (MS in ViU; 2 p.; in Barnes's hand and signed by him; at head of statement: "President U States. To John Barnes (Private a/c)"; endorsed by Barnes). See MB, 2:1055-7; Vol. 35: 11-12, 412-14, 418.

Statement of TJ's general account, Georgetown, 5 Nov. 1801, bringing forward the debits of $1,876.34 on TJ's household account of 4 Nov. and $3,361.12 on TJ's private account of 5 Nov. for the sum $5,237.46; against a balance of $186 in TJ's favor carried forward from 7 Oct. and an additional credit of $2,000 by Meriwether Lewis's note of 9 Oct. payable at 60 days; for a net balance of $3,051.46 in Barnes's favor (MS in ViU; 2 p.; in Barnes's hand and signed by him; at head of statement: "President U States In a/c with John Barnes"; endorsed by Barnes).

Statement of TJ's household and private accounts, Georgetown, 4 Dec. 1801, with entries from 6 Nov. to that date, beginning with a list of purchases at Barnes's store from 6 Nov. to 2 Dec. for cognac, porter, coffee, souchong and hyson tea, a black teapot, blue broad cloth, "fine thickset" cloth, sugar, sweet oil, cheese, Barcelona nuts, a dozen red herring, "Stone pot oysters," prunes, muscatel raisins, vinegar, 12 bottles of Spanish olives, mustard, capers, cinnamon, cloves, soap, spermaceti candles, and writing paper, for the sum of £93.11.9 or $249.56; followed by 5 orders for cash to Étienne Lemaire for $24, $202.64, $187.12, $65.17, and $108.75 at 7, 9, 18, 25, and 30 Nov., respectively, for a sum of $587.68; three orders for cash to Joseph Dougherty for $31.23, $29.46, and $21.40 at 9, 30 Nov. and 4 Dec. for a sum of $82.09; plus additional payments on the stable account, including an order in favor of Dr. William Baker for $56 for hay on 25 Nov.; an order in favor of Dougherty for $50 for wages on 3 Dec.; and a charge of $6.50 for freight and expenses on "Boxes wine," for a subtotal of $782.27, which with the sum from Barnes's store, gives a total of $1,031.83 on the household and stable accounts; after which Barnes recorded debits to TJ's private account, including two payments of $5 to Edward Frethy, barber, at 6 Nov. and 4 Dec.; $20 to Thomas Newton of Norfolk at 6 Nov.; $176.62 to John March, bookbinder, and $22.99 to George Andrews for ornaments at 7 Nov.; $218.82 to Roberts & Jones of Philadelphia at 9 Nov.; $14 and $50 in cash to TJ at 27 Nov. and 4 Dec., respectively; $30 in cash to Martin Wanscher at 27 Nov.; $16 to William Brent for an assembly subscription at 30 Nov.; $8 for a beaver hat, band, and buckle at 4 Dec.; and lastly an entry dated 3 Dec. for $7, the discount paid at the Bank of Columbia for Meriwether Lewis's note of $1,000 dated 9 Nov.; for a sum on TJ's private account of $573.43; Barnes closing the statement with a balance of $1,605.26 in his favor (MS in ViU; in Barnes's hand and signed by him; at head of statement: "Thomas Jefferson Esqr. To John Barnes"; with emendations in TJ's hand, the first indicating that the 7 Nov. payment to Andrews was divided into two payments of $2.49 and $20.50 each, the second, appearing below Barnes's endorsement, being a calculation of the amount spent on groceries, with the sum of £68.12.4½ obtained by subtracting £24.19.4½ for clothes from Barnes's figure of £93.11.9 for total store purchases; TJ probably added the small check mark that appears at each entry alongside the sum for the orders of payment; endorsed by Barnes; endorsed by TJ: "Barnes John. series of accts. for 1801"). See MB, 2:1057-60; Vol. 35: 95-6, 226n, 355-6, 418, 588-9, 758-9.

Statements of TJ's accounts, Georgetown, 31 Dec. 1801, the first being TJ's orders on Barnes for private and household accounts, with entries from 7 to 31 Dec., including a payment $15 to Charles McLaughlin for an assembly subscription at 7 Dec.; payments to Étienne Lemaire for $295.91, $92.25, $85.28, and $100.33 at 7, 13, 22, and 29 Dec., respectively; cash to TJ for $95 ($75 being in Philadelphia bank notes) and $40 at 9 and 20 Dec., respectively; payments to Joseph Dougherty for $11.67½ and $50, at 12 and 18 Dec., respectively; $77.49 to John H. Craven at 15 Dec.; $22.29 to Samuel Smith and $80 in bank notes for Gabriel Lilly at 21 Dec.; and $10 to Daniel Trump for James Oldham at 31 Dec.; for a subtotal of $975.22½; followed by a list of purchases at Barnes's store, with entries from 5 to 30 Dec. for coffee, hyson tea, Jamaica spirits, cognac, cider, sweet oil, mustard, capers, olives, Jersey cheese, nuts (including almonds and Barcelona nuts), sugar, rice, starch, and boxes, with several items purchased from Benjamin W. Morris & Co., for a subtotal of £92.9.0½ or $247.53½, which, with the $975.22½ from the cash orders on Barnes, gives a total of $1,222.76, to which Barnes added $3.52 for postage on letters to and from Philadelphia, Norfolk and Richmond and stamps, for a total of $1,226.28 (MS in CSmH; 3 p.; in Barnes's hand and signed by him; at the head of each statement: "The President of the U States. To John Barnes"). See also MB, 2:1059-61.

Statement of TJ's general account, 31 Dec. 1801, carrying forward the 9 Dec. balance of $1,656.72 in Barnes's favor, to which Barnes debited TJ's account for $1,226.28 from the December statements above, giving a sum of $2,883 in Barnes's favor; Barnes crediting TJ with $1,800 by William Short's account, for a balance of $1,083 in Barnes's favor (MS in CSmH; 1 p.; in Barnes's hand and signed by him; at head of statement: "The President of the U States In a/c with John Barnes").

Statement of TJ's account of cash and orders, with entries from 1 to 29 Jan. 1802, including a payment of $150 to Meriwether Lewis on 1 Jan., for his salary for three months ending 31 Dec.; $5.35 for a bank discount paid on "E. P. note" at 63 days, with stamp at 1 Jan.; payment of $1,000 for Meriwether Lewis's note payable at the Bank of Columbia and $10.76 for "Bank disct paid on my own Note in lieu of the former" at 63 days, with stamp, at 6-7 Jan.; cash payments to TJ for $700, $2,670, $350, and $40, recorded at 2, 4, 8, 21 Jan., respectively; payments to Joseph Dougherty for $18.68, $42.37, and $18, at 4, 19, and 25 Jan., respectively; $5.25 to Edward Frethy at 4 Jan.; payments to Étienne Lemaire for $257.44, $150.82, $84.60, and $126.91 at 9, 13, 18, and 29 Jan., respectively; payment of orders in favor of Mrs. Newman for $50, Henry Dearborn for $50, and Thomas Carpenter for $148.87 at 15 Jan.; $10 to William Dunnington and $9 on Michael Roberts's account at 19 Jan.; $60 to James Taylor, Jr., of Norfolk at 26 Jan.; and $22.50 to William Duane at 27 Jan.; for a total sum of $5,980.49, to which was added $1,083 brought forward from Barnes's 31 Dec. statement, for a total of $7,063.49 (MS in CSmH; 1 p.; in John Barnes's hand; with a small check mark at each entry, except for Lewis's note of $1,000, probably added by TJ during a review of the account; at head of statement: "Thomas Jefferson Esqr. President US. In a/c with John Barnes"; at foot of statement: "This Amt. Card. to General a/c"). See MB, 2:1062-4. For TJ's use of the bank bills he received in his large cash payments from Barnes, see TJ's letters to George Jefferson and James Taylor, Jr., on 7 Jan., and to Thomas Mann Randolph, 9 Jan. 1802.

Statement of TJ's household account, with entries from 1 to 28 Jan. 1802, all purchases at Barnes's store, including six bottles of "preserved fruit in Brandy," cognac, Jamaica spirits, claret, cider, coffee, souchong and imperial tea, "2 Black tea potts" and a tea caddy, muscatel raisins, sugar, preserves, spermaceti candles, walnuts, Barcelona nuts, almonds, cloves, nutmeg, vinegar, "East India preserves" of lemon and another of ginger, with two "stone pots or Jars" for the same, two kegs of tongues and sounds, smoked herring, pickled oysters, bed cord, oil, a wagon whip, boxes, and writing paper, for a total of £110.17.11½ or $295.73 (MS in CSmH; 2 p.; in John Barnes's hand; at head of statement: "The Presidents Household a/c with John Barnes— Store a/c"; at foot of statement: "Card to general a/c").

Statement of TJ's general account, Georgetown, 30 Jan. 1802, carrying forward the 31 Dec. balance of $1,083 in Barnes's favor, to which Barnes debited TJ's account for $5,980.49 from the 29 Jan. statement for cash and orders on Barnes, and $295.73 for the January purchases at Barnes's store, for a sum of $7,359.22 in Barnes's favor; Barnes crediting TJ's account with $2,000 by Treasury warrant at 4 Jan. and a reimbursement of $12.67 by Thomas Carpenter for broad cloth at 9 Jan., for a total of $2,012.67, bringing forward a balance of $5,346.55 in Barnes's favor (MS in CSmH; 1 p.; in Barnes's hand and signed by him; at head of statement: "*General a/c* Thomas Jefferson Esqr. In a/c with John Barnes").

Statement of TJ's account for cash and orders, Georgetown, 3 Mch. 1802, with entries from 1 Feb. to 2 Mch., including cash payments to TJ of $8, $10, $10 (by Meriwether Lewis), and $20 (by Joseph Dougherty) at 1, 8, 18, and 27 Feb., respectively; orders in favor of Dougherty for $38.20, $9.25, $14.04, $35.48, $60.02, and $5.35 at 1, 8, 15, 22, 24 Feb. and 2 Mch., respectively; two orders in favor of Edward Frethy, each for $5.25, dated 2 Feb. and 2 Mch.; orders in favor of Étienne Lemaire for $425.13, $89.27, $76.42, $111.80, and $250.30 at 2, 13, 16, 22 Feb., and 2 Mch., respectively; orders in favor of Samuel Quarrier for $25 at 2 Feb. and Joseph Yznardi for $403 at 11 Feb.; payment of $50 to the "Revd Mr Eden" at 12 Feb.; order in favor of John Minchin for $11 at 14 Feb.; a remittance of $30 to Nicolas Dufief of Philadelphia at 16 Feb.; payment of $7.76 at 25 Feb. for freight on wines from Baltimore; order in favor of Charles Peale Polk for $25 on 27 Feb.; payment of $76.56 on 2 Mch. to Edward Gantt for the amount of his account for "Medicine & attendance to this day"; for the sum of $1,811.90, to which was added an order in favor of William Duane for $25.31 at 22 Feb., giving a total sum of $1,837.21 (MS in CSmH; 2 p.; in Barnes's hand and signed by him; with a small check mark at each entry probably added by TJ during a review of the account; at head of statement: "The President US. To John Barnes, Cash & Order, a/c"; with notation by Barnes: "Card. to a/c"). See MB, 2:1064-6.

Statement of TJ's account for purchases at Barnes's store, Georgetown, 3 Mch. 1802, with entries from 1 Feb. to that date, including coffee, souchong and imperial tea, cognac, sherry, porter, white wine vinegar, Barcelona nuts, sugar, preserves, oysters, smoked herring, six kegs of tongues and sounds, capers, a bottle each of "green Currants" and gooseberries, butter, spermaceti candles, soap, starch, foolscap paper, and a pair of shoe brushes, for a total sum of £94.15.2½, or $252.69 (MS in CSmH; 2 p.; in Barnes's hand and signed by him; at head of statement: "The President US: To John Barnes. Store a/c")

Statement of TJ's general account, 3 Mch. 1802, carrying forward the 30 Jan. balance of $5,346.55 in Barnes's favor, to which Barnes added debits of $252.69 and $1,837.21, the sums from the store account and the account for cash and orders at 3 Mch., for a sum of $7,436.45; Barnes crediting TJ's account with two Treasury warrants, one of 8 Feb. for $2,000, the other in Mch. for $3,000, for a total of $5,000, bringing forward a balance of $2,436.45 in Barnes's favor (MS in CSmH; 1 p.; in Barnes's hand and signed by him; at head of statement: "The President, U States In a/c with John Barnes").

INDEX

"A. B." (pseudonym): letter from, 266-8; criticizes Charleston custom house, 266-8, 384

abolition, 534n, 586

Aborn, Thomas, 320, 327, 332

Academia Botanica (Florence), 237n

Academia Sevillana de Buenas Letras (Sevilla), 236, 237-8n

Académie des sciences, 294, 295

Académie Royale des Sciences (Turin), 236, 237n

Académie Royale des Sciences, Belles-Lettres, et Arts (Lyons), 236, 237n

Académie Royale des Sciences, Belles-Lettres, et Arts (Rouen), 236, 237n

Accademia del Cimento (Florence), 237n

Accademia delle Scienze dell'Istituto (Bologna), 236, 237n

accountants, 92, 118, 133, 175n, 345n, 659

Account of the State Prison or Penitentiary House, in the City of New-York (Thomas Eddy), 553-4

Adams, Abigail, 165n

Adams, John: levees held by, xlvi; portraits of, xlvii; and District of Columbia, 13, 17n, 32, 564; and Tripoli, 65n; sends correspondence, papers to Congress, 67, 68n; and Friend's Orebank lease, 91n; instructions to American warships, 122n; and election of 1800, 128-9, 131; makes appointments, 185n, 244n, 434n, 483, 488n, 557, 608-9n; and Convention of 1800, 189n; and Ga. land claims, 202n; history of administration of, 228-9, 387, 472-80; and Little Turtle, 275, 522n; late-term appointments, 309, 311-13, 315n, 316, 321, 327n, 328, 333-4, 400n, 575n; removals by, 328, 602n; and France, 349; and St. Clair's reappointment, 578, 579n; contingent expenses, 627-8

Adams, John Quincy, xlix, 608n

Adams, Fort, 42, 45, 93-4, 420n, 632n

Adams (U.S. frigate), 615n, 668n

Adamson, William: letter from, 220-4; seeks assistance for Irish refugees, 220-4

Addison, Joseph: *Cato,* 558, 559n

Addison, Thomas: appointed justice of the peace, 314, 316, 318, 326, 335

Address to the People of the United States (John Beckley), 476, 479n

Africa, 576, 577n

Age of Reason. Part the Second (Thomas Paine), 31

Agricultural Museum (Georgetown, D.C.), 435n

agriculture: one of four pillars of prosperity, 63; fertilizer, 168; principal source of American wealth, 199; plows, 282, 288; viticulture, 373-6, 383n; wisdom of rural citizens, 390; agricultural societies, 423; publications on, 435n, 458n; promotion of, 503n. *See also* cotton; Indians: Economy; tobacco

Aikin, Charles Rochemont: *Jennerian Discovery,* 80, 189, 203, 341, 359, 370, 436, 454-5

Aitken, Robert, 235, 236n, 547n

Akin, James, 366n

Albany Register, 86, 87-8n

Albemarle Co., Va.: inns, 269n; Birdwood plantation, 420n; Carlton plantation, 656n

alcoholism: among Indians, 276, 278-9, 282-3, 288, 441, 443n, 633, 634n; removals from office due to, 329; among TJ's family, 656n; among candidates for office, 672

Alembert, Jean Le Rond d': *Mélange de Littérature, d'Historie, et de Philosophie,* x, 20, 21n

Alessandro Veronese. *See* Turchi, Alessandro (Alessandro Veronese, l'Orbetto)

Alexander, Archibald, 27n

Alexander, Charles: appointed justice of the peace, 314-17, 326, 335

Alexandria, D.C.: militia, 33; opposes bill for D.C. government, 72; newspapers in, 72; merchants, 133, 546n; Presbyterians in, 272n; Orphans Court, 318, 325, 333; mayors, 546n; care of sick and disabled seamen in, 590. *See also* District of Columbia

Alexandria Expositor, 352n

Alfred the Great, 149

Alger, James: appointed commissioner of loans, 319, 325, 328, 331

Algiers: tribute for, 59, 65n, 394, 594-5, 597n, 666-7; dey of, 65n, 667n; mediator between U.S. and Tripoli, 394n;

ommended by Monroe, 186; declines appointment, 536-7; identified, 537n
Guido di Pietro (Fra Angelico), 637
gunpowder: manufacture of, 129, 132, 553n; for Indians, 281, 633, 634n

Habersham, Joseph, 319, 322, 331, 379n
Hackett, James, 596n
Hadfield, George: letter from, 197-8; forwards letter, papers on dockyards, 197-8
Hadrian (Roman emperor), 9n
Hall, Charles, 434n
Hall, David, 218, 219n
Hall, Dominick A., 319, 325, 331
Hall, James (author): *History of the Indian Tribes of North America,* xlviii-xlix
Hall, James (N.C.): letter from, 27-9; *Brief History of the Mississippi Territory,* 27-8, 29n; sends book, seeks patronage, 27-9; identified, 28-9n; letter from cited, 29n
Hall, John: removal of, 317, 324, 329, 330n, 334
Hall, John (boatswain), 380n
Hamburg, Germany, 488, 608-9
Hamilton, Alexander: portraits of, xlvii; *Examination of the President's Message,* 55-6; as opposition leader, 81-2, 215, 216n; bullies Adams, 128-9, 131; financial system of, 391; TJ criticizes "half-lettered ideas" of, 391; biography of, 476; defends Judiciary Act, 618, 619n
Hamilton, James, 317, 324, 333
Hamilton, Robert, 319, 324, 328, 332
Hamilton, Fort, 518-19, 521n
Hammerer, John Daniel, 527-9
hams, 202, 504, 691, 693
Hand, John, 691, 693
Handsome Lake (Seneca Indian), 634-5n
Hanna, John A., 429n, 435n
Hanse, Conrad, 693, 695
Hanson, Richard, 545
Hanson, Samuel, 314
"Happy Man, and True Gentleman," 670
Harbaugh, Leonard, 541n
Hardie, James: *New Universal Biographical Dictionary,* 479n
Hardy, James: letter from, 671-2; seeks to become U.S. citizen, 671-2
Hargreaves, Lewis, 668n

Harison, Richard: removal of, 318, 323, 329, 330n, 335
Harmar, Josiah, 283n
Harmar, Fort, 284n
Harper, William, 313-15
Harpers Ferry, Va., 91n, 125, 499, 500n
Harris, Edwin L., 184n, 401n
Harris, John (military storekeeper), 442n
Harris, Simon: letter from, 378-9; names son after TJ, xi, 378; seeks postal contract, 378-9
Harris, Thomas Jefferson, xi, 378
Harrison, Richard, 442n
Harrison, William Henry: letter from, 242-4; and Indian affairs, 242-4, 275, 288, 289n, 520-1n, 524, 525n; identified, 244n; as secretary of Northwest Terr., 302n; as delegate to Congress, 463, 464n, 468, 469n; and land speculation, 607
Hartshorne, William, 417n
Harvard College: graduates, 100n, 118, 120n, 165n, 242n, 437n, 608n, 626n
Harvie, John: letter from cited, 683
Harwich, England, 198n
Hastings, Seth, 357n
Haswell, Anthony, 72
Havana, Cuba, 488, 683
Hawkins, Benjamin: letters from, 93-4, 486-7; as Creek agent, 65n, 93n, 154n; and treaty negotiations, 93-4, 190-2, 543-5n; and map of Tenn. River, 94, 486-7; criticized by DeLacy, 138-40, 149, 153; owns slaves, 155n; appointed Indian commissioner, 319, 326, 332, 543
hay, 689, 691, 694, 696
Hay, George: letters to, 581-2, 631; letters from, 609-10, 677-8; and Short's salary claim, 581-2, 609-10, 631, 677-8
Hay, Udney, 575
Haydn, Franz Joseph, 209n
Hays, Robert, 193n
Heard, James B.: letter from, 529-30; seeks remission of fine, 529-30, 555-6
Heard, John, 319, 324, 335
Helvétius, Anne Catherine de Ligneville, 481n
Hemings, Critta (1769-1850), 422
Hemings, James: suicide of, 20, 21n
Henderson, Bennett (d. 1793), 11n
Henderson, Bennett Hillsborough, 11
Henderson, Elizabeth Lewis (Mrs. Bennett Henderson), 11n

INDEX

INDIANS (*cont.*)
282, 284-5n, 338; regulation of liquor sales, 276, 278-9, 282-3, 285n, 288, 441, 442-3n, 633, 634n; form and style of Indian conferences, 276-8, 515; encroachment on Indian lands, 280-1, 288, 289n, 518, 521n, 525-6, 544n, 634n; Indian representation in Congress suggested, 337-8; jurisdiction of U.S. courts over, 442-3n; passports, 513-14, 516; salt licks, 517, 524, 525n. *See also* Greenville, Treaty of; Indiana Territory

Informant (Danville, Ky.), 305n
Ingle, Henry, 692-3
Inglis, James, 27n
Innes, Harry, 521n
insurance, 56
Interpreter (John Cowell), 40n
Ireland: British restrictions on, 26, 27n, 222; immigrants from, 26n, 219n, 220-4, 226, 234, 432n; rebellion of 1798, 26n, 220-1, 224n, 234; Catholics in, 27n, 452; manufacturing in, 222-3; dissenters in, 452
iron: ore deposits, 89-91, 137, 141, 168, 499, 501n; manufacture of, 91n, 224n
Irujo, Carlos Martínez de: and Yznardi, 4-6, 350-1, 381, 382; recalled by Spain, 6n; and Foronda's arrival, 235, 236n; recommends McElroy, 371, 372n
Irvine (Irving, Irwin), Gen. William, 69-70n, 441n
Irwin, Matthew, 596n
Isabella (brig), 383n
Israel, Israel: and W. P. Gardner and A. Campbell, 79, 643-4, 650, 654n
Israel, Joseph (master of *Trial*), 4, 5, 6n
Israel, Joseph (midshipman), 235n
Israel, Samuel, 643, 654n
Italy: learned societies in, 235-8; art, 245; relations with France, 481n; trade with U.S., 532. *See also* Cisalpine Republic; Sicily

Jackson, Agnes: letter from, 418; seeks TJ's assistance, 418
Jackson, David, 215-16, 482, 692
Jackson, Henry, 650
Jackson, Henry (Irish patriot), 220-1, 224n
Jackson, J. M., 688

Jackson, James: letter from, 224-5; as committee member, 52, 95n; and absence of S. R. Bradley, 224-5; as boundary commissioner, 682; letter from cited, 682
Jackson, Jonathan (carpenter), 418
Jackson, Susanna Kemper, 215-16, 231
Jackson, William, 182, 183n
Jacob (Bible), 300, 303n
Jamaica, 110, 189
James (John Hoomes's servant), 688
James River: transport on, 496
James River Company, 159, 371
Jarvis, Benjamin, 198n
Jarvis, William, 487
Jasper, Samuel, 311, 325, 331
Jay, John, 228-9, 387
Jay, Fort, 43
Jay Treaty: and import duties, 67, 68n, 89n; and debt claims, 103, 434n; commissioners appointed under, 213, 214n; secret instructions, 228-9, 387; compensation for commissioners, 232n; and withdrawal of British troops, 284-5n
Jefferson, George: letters to, 10, 338, 342-3, 344, 370, 503-4; letters from, 18-19, 51, 70, 268, 368-9, 371, 399, 492-3, 545, 574; handles shipments for TJ, 10, 51, 344, 504; tobacco for D. Ross settlement, 18-19, 70, 343, 369, 370, 399, 436-7; forwards TJ's account, 268; handles TJ's business affairs in Richmond, 338, 342-3, 368-9, 457, 492-3, 503-4, 545, 574; letter from cited, 368-9n, 679; collects payments, handles transactions for Short, 371, 504, 545
Jefferson, Jane Randolph (Mrs. Peter Jefferson, TJ's mother), 108

JEFFERSON, THOMAS

Agriculture
views on, 63; exchanges seeds, plants with friends, 275. *See also* Poplar Forest (TJ's estate); tobacco

Business and Financial Affairs
account with D. Ross arbitrated, 9, 18-19, 70, 97, 340-1, 343, 369-70, 399, 436-7, 492-3, 503-4; newspaper subscriptions, 88n; and Wayles estate, 157-8, 677; orders ducks, 216-17; orders cider, 270, 308, 343, 496-7, 504, 606, 674-5, 686, 691, 694, 696-7; sends halves of

JEFFERSON, THOMAS (*cont.*)

Personal Affairs

sends dinner invitations, ix, xii, xlvi-xvlii, 406 (illus.), 220, 242, 254, 427, 432, 435, 437, 486; invites family to Washington, xii, 426, 676-7; describes daily routine, xiii, 99, 261; expense of outfit in Washington, 19; receives sculpture, statuary, 19; suicide of James Hemings, 20, 21n; makes recommendations, 27, 29-30, 75; private secretary, 52-3, 312-13n; health of, 106-7, 178, 242n, 368, 426; employs dentist, 125n; orders wine, 163, 269, 339, 343, 351, 381-3, 482, 483, 512, 572-3, 674, 690, 693-8; clothing for servants, 181, 690, 691, 693-4; tailoring, 181, 689, 693, 697; receives invitations, 190; and L. Littlepage, 194; receives gifts, 202n, 572, 628; buys watches, has watches repaired, 240n, 565, 688, 695; strangers ask for money, 290-1, 396, 497-8, 498-9, 617-18, 660-2, 678; gives money in charity, 396n, 498n, 654n, 659n, 686, 692, 695, 697-8; sends gifts to grandchildren, 656; medical care for household staff, 671, 698; provides travel directions, 677; grooming, 693, 696; subscribes to dancing assemblies, 696. *See also* Kosciuszko, Tadeusz; President's House

Political Theories

economy in public expense, vii, 22-3, 60, 65, 129-30, 132; return government to republican principles, 23, 30, 165-6, 176; militia preferable to standing army, 62; Constitutional powers and limits, 252, 385; strength of republican government, 252, 384; freedom of the press, 258-9; and local government, 261; states' rights, 377; both parties are republican, 390-1; Hamilton's financial system entailed on country, 391; republicanism can be accommodated to French habits, 391; function of D.C. commissioners, 559

Politics

supports rights of aliens, x, 64, 129, 132, 220-4, 432; fears divisions among Republicans, x-xi, 81-2, 416, 618; Federalist leaders incurable, isolated, xiii, 106, 165, 176, 178, 390, 391, 618; expects cooperation from Congress, 19-20; suppression of Wood's *History,* 387; criticizes Hamilton's "half-lettered ideas," 391

Portraits

by Sharples, xlvii; on medals, 239-40, 386, 565-6; by Polk, 659n

President

communicates to Congress by message, vii, 52, 57, 178, 261-2, 270; and peace in Europe, vii-viii, 10, 19, 23, 58, 68; repeal of internal taxes, vii-viii, 10, 19, 23, 60, 111, 166, 178, 186, 231, 388, 416, 430n, 600, 602n; and Barbary affairs, viii, 3, 58-9, 192-3, 394, 557, 592-3, 605, 666-8; and Indian affairs, viii, 58, 190-2, 243-4, 543-5, 632-5; military reductions, viii, 47-8n, 60-3, 378, 388, 416; conference with Black Hoof, viii-ix, xlix, 277, 513-27; conference with Little Turtle, viii-ix, xlviii, 274-90, 513, 515; receives Mammoth Cheese, ix, xlix-l, 246-52, 261-2; rearrangement of judiciary system, x-xi, 63-4, 66n, 127, 130, 178, 417, 430n, 618, 638-40, 658, 663, 674-5; and Yznardi's conduct as consul, 6n; discharge of public debt, 10, 19, 60-1, 107, 129-30, 132, 166; and Gérard de Rayneval's claim, 10-11; and naval prizes, 12; and D.C., 32-41, 356-7, 361-2, 416n, 542n, 551-2, 559; removal of discriminating duties, 56-7, 67-8, 89; orders navy vessels to Mediterranean, 58-9, 62, 234-5, 394, 395; reduces diplomatic establishment, 60, 212n; and misapplication of public funds, 61; calls for reconciliation and harmony, 64-5, 176, 390; salary, 77-8, 107n, 678, 688, 690, 692, 694, 697-8; and Friend's Orebank lease, 90-1; and warrants drawn on Treasury, 107-8n, 182n; and conduct of McLane, 182-3; cabinet meetings, 192n; and census, 195; roll of government officers, 231-2, 592-3; preservation of president's records, 232-3; relief for Sedition Act victims, 258-60; issues

Marshall, Thomas (Indian trader), 138, 155n
Martin, Luther, 521n
Martin, Thomas, 319, 323, 334
Martinique, W.I., 110, 599n
Maryland: Frederick, l, 617-18, 659n; Williamsport, l; loans to D.C. commissioners, 14-16, 17n, 167, 346-8, 356-7, 361-2, 367-8, 542; census in, 73, 74n, 195; marshal for, 74n, 195, 318, 324, 329, 335; coal mining in, 168, 169n; Harford Co., 195n; Eastern Shore, 225-6; legislature, 225-6, 293, 347-8n, 542; Somerset Co., 225-6; courts, 226n; Governor's Council, 293; roads in, 417n; attorneys, 431n; Prince George's Co., 431n; Brookeville, 458n; Society of Friends in, 458n; sale of liquor in, 555-6; St. John's College, 555-6; circuit court cases in, 638-40; inaugural celebrations in, 659n. *See also* Baltimore, Md.; Republicans
Maryland, University of, 26n
Maryland Society for Promoting Useful Knowledge, 377n
Mason, Hezekiah: letter to, 252; letter from, 249-51; and presentation of Mammoth Cheese, 249-51; thanked by TJ, 252
Mason, John (Georgetown merchant): appointed justice of the peace, 314, 316, 318, 326, 335; as reference, 352, 435n; and Allegany Turnpike, 417n
Mason, John Thomson: letters from, 40-1, 555-6; and bill for D.C. government, 32-3, 40-1; health of, 40; and case of schooner *Peggy,* 122-3; and Houseman's case, 165n; letter from cited, 165n, 679; appointed U.S. attorney, 318, 325, 333; and D.C. building regulations, 337; and case of Heard and Thompson, 530n, 555-6
Mason, Nancy, 521n
Mason, Stevens Thomson, 197n, 444, 445n
masons. *See* Freemasons
Massac: customs district, 204, 321, 325, 332
Massac, Fort (Illinois), 42, 47n, 500n
Massachusetts: Baptists in, ix, 247; naval prizes carried to, 12; Springfield armory, 43, 378, 499, 500n; U.S. attorney for, 116, 120n, 319, 323, 333; Salem and Beverly collectorship, 116-20; newspapers, 119, 120n; Salem

naval officer, 119, 120n; trade with E. Indies, 119, 120n; elections, 120n; Gloucester collectorship, 120n; Newburyport, 175; Marblehead collectorship, 195-6, 205; legislature, 200n, 241-2, 429-31, 437n, 574-5; and election of 1800, 241; militia in, 241-2; governor, 242n; fast and thanksgiving days in, 255n; Haverhill, 379; postal service in, 379; roads in, 417; proposed address to TJ from, 429-31, 574-5; marine hospitals in, 632n; circuit court cases in, 639; Plymouth postmastership, 684. *See also* Boston; Cheshire, Mass.; Federalists; Maine; Republicans
Massena, André, 206
Massie, Nathaniel: and charges against St. Clair, 458-60; commission revoked, 468, 469-70n
mastodon: remains discovered in Hudson Valley, 22, 266n; C. W. Peale displays skeleton of, 264-6, 365-6, 386, 404-5; description of, 265
Mathematical Correspondent, 180n
mathematics: education, 174, 175n, 178-80; TJ's familiarity with, reduced over time, 176; books on, 305n
Mathews, John (surveyor), 114, 115n
Matthew, St., 533, 538, 540n
Maxwell, George, 318, 324, 333
Mayer, George Lewis, 617, 618n
Mayer, Lewis: letter from, 617-18; asks TJ for money, 617-18; *History of the German Reformed Church,* 618n; identified, 618n
Mazaree, William: letter from cited, 684
Mazzei, Philip, 237n
Meade, George: letter from, 109-11; sends news of peace in Europe, 109-11
Meade, Henrietta Worsam, 109-10
Meade, Richard Worsam, 110
medals, 235, 239-40, 386, 565-6
Medical Repository (New York), 360, 361n
medicine: dentists, 124, 125n; low standing of medical profession, 127-8, 130; physicians, 127-8, 130, 242n, 263-4, 373n, 405n, 428n, 432n, 435, 488n, 508-11, 566-7, 626n; diarrhea, 178n, 242n; contracts to supply, 215-16; gout, 270, 308, 553; invalids, 273, 405-6; medical schools, education, 352, 428n, 508, 657n; syringes, 377n; gravel, 394; surgeons, 395n, 397, 488, 501, 546, 566-7; teething,

INDEX

pewter, 377n

Peyton, Craven: letter to, 11; and lease of Shadwell fields, 11, 618, 619n; purchases land for TJ, 11; reports on division of Henderson lands, 11

Peyton, Francis: advises on appointments, 313; appointed justice of the peace, 314, 316-17, 326, 335, 546n

Pharmacopoeia of the United States of America, 626n

Phelps, Oliver, 81-2

Philadelphia: roads to, from, xlv; collector at, 19, 71, 110, 182n; observatory at, 22; banks, 71n, 696; mayors, 71n; merchants, 71n, 133, 307n, 371, 372n, 586-9; Republicans in, 71n, 182; and Revolutionary War, 71n, 307n; smallpox vaccination in, 80, 177-8, 235, 388, 454, 482; custom house, 111, 182; brokers, 114, 115n; surveyor at, 182, 183n; naval officer at, 183n; commerce of, 206; navy agent at, 211n; navy storekeeper at, 211n; printers, 236n; watchmakers, 240n; wine merchants, 269; French consul at, 297n; museums, 350n, 365-7; Common Council, 405n; State House, 405n; recorder, 486n; fortifications, 500n; militia, 516; Society of Friends in, 516; Tammany Society, 516; memorial from merchants and traders of, 586-9; hospitals, 590; care of sick and disabled seamen in, 590-1; shoe manufacturing, 603; cordwainers, 603n; booksellers, 610, 611n; postal service, 610; sheriff of, 650

Philadelphia Bank, 71n

Philadelphia Medical Society, 428n

Philadelphia Volunteer Company, 516

"Philanthrophos" (pseudonym): letter from, 31; sends publications, defends Christianity, 31

Philidor. *See* Danican, François André

Philippines, 152, 200-1

Philosophical Transactions (Royal Society of London), 265, 266n

Physical Investigations & Deductions, From Medical and Surgical Facts (William Barnwell), 432n

physics, 376

physiognotrace, xlvi, 610

Pichon, Louis André: and Gérard de Rayneval's claim, 11n; and naval prizes in U.S. ports, 12; and Saint-Domingue, 598, 599, 600n

Pickens, Andrew: and Indian treaty negotiations, 93, 94n, 190-1, 545n; appointed Indian commissioner, 319, 326, 332, 543

Pickering, Timothy: defeated for seat in Congress, 120n; and Short's salary, 163n, 456, 457n; as Ga. claims commissioner, 201-2; and Northwest Terr., 463; biographical sketch of, 476; and Barbary affairs, 594, 596-7n; and Indian affairs, 634n; and contingent expenses, 640n; accused of misusing public funds, 646, 649-50, 654n

Pickford, Mr. (Georgetown), 688

Pickman, William, 119, 120n

Pictet, Marc Auguste, 353, 354, 355n, 384

Pierce, John, 318, 323, 334

Pierce, John (paymaster general), 406

Piercy, James, 105, 106n

Pinckney, Charles: resigns from Congress, 262n; appointed minister to Spain, 310, 321, 323, 335

Pinckney, Charles Cotesworth, 476

Pinckney, Thomas, 597n

Pine, Robert Edge, 612n

Pippi de' Gianuzzi, Giulio (Giulio Romano), 637

Pitcairn, Joseph, 488

Pitt, William, 26, 27n

Pius VII, Pope, 451, 453n, 505n

Plain and Concise Projection for Clearing the Lunar Distances from the Effects of Parallax and Refraction (John Garnett), 50, 176

Plan With Proposals for Forming a Company to Work Mines in the United States (Benjamin Henfrey), 168, 169n

plaster of paris, 693

Pleasants, James, 577n

Pleiades, 580-1

plows, 282, 288

Plutarch, 152, 392n

Plymouth, England, 198n

Poems by Thomas Kennedy, 1

Point Pleasant, Battle of, 520n

Poland, 99-100

Political Writings of John Dickinson, Esquire (John Dickinson), 238-9

Polk, Charles Peale: letter from, 658-9; seeks appointment, charity, 658-9, 698; identified, 659n

Polk, William (Md.), 225-6

Polkinhorn & Andrews, 688-9

Polkinhorn & Co., 691

INDEX

Washington, D.C. (*cont.*)
13-16; Massachusetts Ave., 14;
wharves, 14; enumeration of houses
in, 16; council, 33, 217n; mayor, 33;
militia, 33; voting requirements in,
33; incorporation of, 33-4; Washington Navy Yard, 62-3, 197, 211n; newspapers in, 72, 73n; Republicans in,
72; hotels, boardinghouses, 83, 381n,
392; sugar manufacturing in, 106n;
stationers, 122n; market for fish, 175;
tailors, 181n; navy storekeeper at,
211n; bridges, 217n; Commercial
Company, 217n; manufacturing in,
222; prospects for, 222; Christ
Church, 225n; Episcopalians in,
225n; register of wills, 318, 325, 333;
printers, 352n, 417n, 446-7; smallpox
vaccination at, 361n, 387-8, 482;
quarries in, 381n; building regulations
in, 415-16; fires in, 418; carpenters,
418n; sale of liquor in, 529-30, 555-6;
jail, 557-8; packet service to, from,
572, 573; postal service, 610; reputation as unhealthy, 618; meridian line
at, 629; dancing assemblies, 696.
See also Anacostia River; District
of Columbia
Washington Federalist, xlix-l, 196-7n,
205n
Washington Printing and Bookselling
Company, 446-7
watches: repair of, 240n, 565, 695;
watchmakers, 240n; seized at customs, 353-5, 384; gold, 668n, 688;
purchased by TJ, 688
Waterhouse, Benjamin: letters to, 203-4,
373; letters from, 359-61, 454-5; publication of TJ's letters, 80, 454-5; supplies vaccine matter to TJ, 203-4;
letter to, misdirected, 341, 359, 370,
373; successful spread of vaccination,
359-61; and methods of vaccination,
454; reports vaccination of Indians,
522n
Waterman, John: letter to, 252; letter
from, 249-51; and presentation of
Mammoth Cheese, 249-51; thanked
by TJ, 252
waterproofing: clothing, 20, 181, 262,
484-5n; publications on, 20, 21n, 233,
262; paper, 233, 338-9, 485n
Watkins, Dr. John, 547-8
Watson, Richard (Bishop of Llandaff):
Apology for the Bible, 31n

Watson, William, 681
Way, Andrew, 73n
Way, George, 73n
Way & Groff, 27, 29-30, 72, 73n
Wayles, John (TJ's father-in-law), 157-
8, 677
Wayles estate, 157-8, 677
Wayne, Anthony, 275, 284n, 514
Wayne, Caleb P., 393
weather: hail, 28, 29n; floods, 207
Webb, Mr. (Charleston), 267
Webster, Noah: *Grammatical Institute,*
617
weights and measures: salmas, 533
Wells, John, Jr.: letter to, 252; letter
from, 249-51; and presentation of
Mammoth Cheese, 249-51; thanked
by TJ, 252
Wells, William: as Miami interpreter,
viii, 274-6, 278-80, 283n, 284n; identified, 284n; appointed Indian agent,
285n, 682; criticized by Black Hoof,
514, 518, 524
Wendell, Hermanus H., 318, 324, 333
West, Cato, 401n
West Indies: packet service in, 110;
trade with U.S., 502-3, 664-5; cotton
production in, 562; as asylum for
emancipated slaves, 582-6. *See also*
Saint-Domingue, W.I.
Weston, Nathan: letter to, 384-5; letter
from, 198-200; congratulates TJ, 198-
200; identified, 200n; thanked by TJ,
384-5
West Point, N.Y., 43-5, 180n, 499
wheat, 124, 268, 503n
Wheaton, Joseph: letter from, 489-90;
seeks appointment, 489-90
Whelen, Israel: resignation of, 307,
308n; purveyor of public supplies,
516, 594, 596n, 597n
Whipple, Joseph, 319, 323, 328, 334
whips, 692-3, 697
Whiskey Insurrection, 128, 131, 132n,
229n
White, Alexander: as D.C. commissioner, 13-17, 88, 166-7, 305-7, 337,
346-8, 356-7, 361-2, 415-16, 542, 551-
2, 564; letter from cited, 17n; and
L'Enfant's claim, 88; and repayment
of Md. loans, 346-8, 356-7, 361-2,
542; and removal of Fenwick's houses,
551-2
White, Hugh: letter from cited, 680
White, Jacob, 469n

A comprehensive index of Volumes 1-20 of the
First Series has been issued as Volume 21.
Each subsequent volume has its own index,
as does each volume or set of volumes
in the Second Series.

THE PAPERS OF THOMAS JEFFERSON are composed in Monticello, a font based on the "Pica No. 1" created in the early 1800s by Binny & Ronaldson, the first successful typefounding company in America. The face is considered historically appropriate for The Papers of Thomas Jefferson because it was used extensively in American printing during the last quarter-century of Jefferson's life, and because Jefferson himself expressed cordial approval of Binny & Ronaldson types. It was revived and rechristened Monticello in the late 1940s by the Mergenthaler Linotype Company, under the direction of C. H. Griffith and in close consultation with P. J. Conkwright, specifically for the publication of the Jefferson Papers. The font suffered some losses in its first translation to digital format in the 1980s to accommodate computerized typesetting. Matthew Carter's reinterpretation in 2002 restores the spirit and style of Binny & Ronaldson's original design of two centuries earlier.

✧